BY FAITH

BY FAITH

Sermons on Hebrews 11

❧

Thomas Manton

THE BANNER OF TRUTH TRUST

THE BANNER OF TRUTH TRUST
3 Murrayfield Road, Edinburgh EH12 6EL, UK
P. O. Box 621, Carlisle, Pennsylvania 17013, USA

*

Reprinted from *The Works of Thomas Manton*
published by James Nisbet & Co. in 1873

First Banner of Truth edition 2000
ISBN 0 85151 782 X

*

Printed and bound
in Great Britain by
The Bath Press

CONTENTS

vi

THE EPISTLE DEDICATORY.

To the High and Mighty Prince WILLIAM, By the Grace of God, King of England, France and Ireland, &c.

MAY IT PLEASE YOUR MAJESTY,—

THIS relict of the worthy deceased author was long since intended, when you were at a greater distance, to be sent abroad under the patronage of your great name. His own name indeed hath long been, and still continues, so bright and fragrant in England that your Majesty's condescending goodness will count it no indignity to yours to impart some of its more diffused beams and odours to it. However, if what there was of presumption in that first intention can be pardoned, no reason can be apprehended of altering it upon your nearer and most happy approach unto us.

The kind design and blessed effect whereof, compared with the scope and design of this excellent work, do much the more urgently invite to it; for as you come to us with the compassionate design of a deliverer, and the wonderful blessing of heaven hath rendered you also a victor and a successful deliverer, the design of this book is to represent that faith which is the peculiar and most appropriate principle of what is (like your own) the most glorious of all victories. You have overcome, not by the power of your arms, but by the sound of your name, and by your goodness and kindness, which so effectually first conquered minds as to leave you no opportunity of using the other more harsh and rugged means of conquest. Yea, and your success is owing to a greater name than yours; our case, and the truth of the thing, allow and oblige us in a low and humble subordination to apply those sacred words, 'Blessed is he that cometh to us in the name of the Lord,' the power of which glorious name is wont to be exerted according as a trust is placed in it. We acknowledge and adore a most conspicuous divine presence with you in this undertaking of yours, which is not otherwise to be engaged than by that faith of which the apostle and this author do here treat. This faith, we are elsewhere told, overcomes this world; and are told here in what way—by representing another, with the invisible Lord of both worlds, being the substance of what we hope for, and the evidence of what we see not, and whereby we see him who is invisible. This world is not otherwise to be conquered than as it is an enemy; it is an enemy by the vanities, lusts, and impurities of it. That faith which foresees the end of this world, which beholds it as a vanishing thing, passing away with all the lusts of it,—which looks through all time, and contemplates all the affairs and events of this temporary state as under the conduct and management of an all-wise and almighty invisible Ruler,—which penetrates into eternity, and discovers another world and state of things which shall be unchangeable and of everlasting permanency, and therein beholds the same invisible glorious Lord, as a most gracious and bountiful rewarder of such as serve and obey him with sincere fidelity in this state of trial and temptation here on earth,—such a faith cannot but be victorious over all the lusts, vanities, impurities, and sensualities of this present evil world. Such a faith, working by love to God and good men, and all mankind, and being thereupon fruitful in the good works of piety, sobriety, righteousness and charity, will be the great reformer of the world, conquer its malignity, reduce its disorders, and infer a universal harmony and peace.

Even among us the noblest part of your Majesty's conquest is yet behind. It cannot but have been observed, that for many years by-past a design hath been industriously driven that we might be made papists, to make us slaves; and for the enslaving us, to debauch us, and plunge us into all manner of sensuality, from a true apprehension, that brute and slave are nearest akin, and that there is a sort of men so vile and abject (as the ingenious expression of a great man among the Romans once was) *quos non decet esse nisi servos*—to whom liberty were an indecency, and who should be treated unbecomingly if they were not made slaves, that we should be fit to serve the lusts and humours of any other man, when once we were become servile to our own. And next, that the religion might easily be wrested away from us which was become so weak and impotent as not to be able to govern us; and that if humanity were eradicated, the principles and privileges that belong to our nature torn from us, easy work would be made with our christianity and religion. What hath been effected among us by so laboured a design, through a long tract of time, is before you as the matter of your remaining victory, which, as on our part, will be the more difficult, where the pernicious humour is inveterate. So your majesty's part herein will be most easy, your great example being, under the supreme power, the mover, the potent engine which is to effect the hoped redress, and your more principal contribution hereunto consisting but in being yourself, in expressing the virtue, prudence, goodness, and piety, which God hath wrought into your temper. The design of saying this is not flattery, but excitation. Give me leave to lay before your Majesty somewhat that occurs in a book written twenty-seven years ago, not by way of prophecy, but probable conjecture of the way wherein a blessed state of things in these parts of the world is likely to be brought about :—

'God will stir up some happy king or governor, in some country of Christendom, endued with wisdom and consideration, who shall discern the true nature of godliness and christianity, and the necessity and excellency of serious religion, and shall place his honour and felicity in pleasing God and doing good, and attaining everlasting happiness, and shall subject all worldly respects unto these high and glorious ends; shall know that godliness and justice have the most precious name on earth, and prepare for the most glorious reward in heaven,' &c.

With how great hopes and joy must it fill every upright heart daily (as they do) to behold in your Majesty and in your Royal Consort, (whom a divine hand hath so happily placed with you on the same throne) the same lively characters of this exemplified idea ! It cannot but inspire us with such pleasant thoughts that winter is well-nigh

gone, and the time of singing of birds approaches; the night is far
spent and the day is at hand,—a bright and glorious morning triumphs
over the darkness of a foul, tempestuous night.   The sober, serious
age now commences, when sensuality, falsehood, cruelty, oppression,
the contempt of God and religion are going out of fashion; to be a
noted debauchee of a vicious life and dishonest mind, capable of being
swayed to serve ill purposes without hesitation, will no longer be
thought a man's praise, or a qualification for trusts.   It shall be no
disreputable thing to profess the fear of God and the belief of a life
to come.   A scenical, unserious religion, a spurious, adulterated christianity, made up of doctrines repugnant to the sacred oracles, to sound
reason, and even to common sense, with idolatrous and ludicrous formalities, and which hates the light, shall vanish before it.   There shall
be no more strife about unnecessary circumstances; grave decencies in
the worship of God that shall be self-recommending, and command a
veneration in every conscience, shall take place.   There shall be no contention amongst christians; but who shall most honour God and our
Redeemer, do most good in the world, and most entirely love and
effectually befriend and serve one another, which are all things most
connatural to that vivid realising, victorious faith here treated of.

Nor are other victories alien to it, over the armed powers of God's
visible enemies in the world, such as he may yet call your Majesty
with glorious success to encounter in his name, and for the sake of it.
In some following verses of this chapter (wherein the line of the
apostle's discourse went beyond that of this worthy author's life) this
is represented as the powerful instrument which those great heroes
employed in their high achievements of subduing kingdoms, working
righteousness, or executing God's just revenges upon his unyielding
enemies, obtaining promises, stopping the mouths of lions, quenching
the violence of fire, escaping the edge of the sword, whereby out of
weakness they were made strong, waxed valiant in fight, turned to
flight the armies of the aliens.   By this faith they (in the prophet's
lofty style, Isa. xxxiv. 5), as it were, bathed their sword in heaven,
gave it a celestial tincture, made it resistless and penetrating.   This
is the true way, wherein, according to the divinest philosophy, the
spirit of a man may draw into consent with itself the universal
almighty Spirit.   And if the glorious Lord of Hosts shall assign to
your Majesty a further part in the employments of this noble kind,
may he gird you with might unto the battle; may your bow abide in
strength, and the arms of your hands be made strong by the hands of
the mighty God of Jacob, even by the God of your fathers, who shall
help you, and by the Almighty who shall bless you; and may he most
abundantly bless you with blessings of heaven above, blessings of the
deep that lieth under, blessings of the breasts and of the womb.   May
he cover your head in fight, and crown it with victory and glory, and
grant you to know, by use and trial, the power of that faith, in all its
operations, which unites God with man, and can render, in a true and
sober sense, and to all his own purposes, an human arm omnipotent.
Which is the serious prayer of

Your Majesty's most devoted and most humble servant and subject,

JOHN HOWE.

TO THE READER.

Thou art here presented with a third volume of the works of the late reverend and learned Dr Thomas Manton, whose great name is sufficient to recommend it to thy perusal, when thou art assured it is his own. These sermons and treatises were either written from his own notes, or carefully compared *verbatim* with them, and amended by them; and whosoever were acquainted with the spirit and preaching of the author will find he hath no cause to suspect being imposed on herein. His copious invention, clear and succinct opening of gospel mysteries, close application to the conscience, with that admirable variety of handling the same subject which sometimes occurs, are scarce imitable by any. It were needless to add anything to the testimonies that have been given him by those who have published his former works.

What the author's opinion about publishing posthumous works was may justify what of this kind hath been already done and is now tendered to thee, which I shall give you in his own words in his epistle before Dr Sibb's 'Comment on the 1st. Chapter of the 2d Epistle to the Corinthians:'—'Let it not stumble thee that the work is posthume, and cometh out so long after the author's death; it were to be wished that those that excel in public gifts would during life publish their own labours, to prevent spurious obtrusions upon the world, and give them their last hand and polishment; as the apostle Peter was careful to write before his decease, 2 Peter i. 12–14; but usually the church's treasure is most increased by legacies. As Elijah let fall his mantle when he was taken up into heaven; so God's eminent servants, when their persons could no longer remain in the world, have left behind them some worthy pieces as a monument of their graces and zeal for the public welfare, whether it be out of a modest sense of their own endeavours, as being loath upon choice, or of their own accord, to venture abroad into the world, or whether it be that being occupied and taken up with other labours, or whether it be in a conformity to Christ, who would not leave his Spirit till his departure, or whether it be out of a hope that their works would find a more kindly reception after their death, the living being more liable to envy and reproach; but when the author is in heaven, the work is more esteemed upon earth. Whether for this or that cause, usually it is that not only the life, but the death, of God's servants hath been profitable to his church, by that means many useful treatises being freed from that privacy and obscureness to which by the modesty of the author they were formerly confined.'

To all this may be added that not many days before the author departed this life he declared his intentions of publishing something himself but his sudden death prevented him.

And let none wonder that in the author's so constant course of preaching the same matter may sometimes recur. In some places thou wilt find notes of reference; in others the same matter is handled with such variety as to prevent tediousness, in which the author had a singular excellency. However, repetitions of the same truths have their use. 'To write the same things to you,' saith the apostle, 'to me is not grievous, for you it is safe,' Phil. iii. 1. Our knowledge is imperfect, and needs a continual increase; our memories are slippery and frail, and need to be refreshed; our attention is dull, and many truths slip by us at the first hearing without regard; our hearts are backward to our duty, and we need frequently to be excited. We more blame a dull horse than the rider, who frequently quickens him with a spur. It savours too much of pride of knowledge, and a curious itch of novelty, when we cannot endure to hear more than once of the same truths; and such a humour is not to be gratified, but mortified.[1] But though some may quarrel, I doubt not but the serious christian will receive benefit by what is here offered, which, that it may be thy lot, is the earnest prayer of

Thy affectionate servant in the work of the gospel,

WILLIAM TAYLOR.

[1] See the Author's Twenty-fifth Sermon on John xvii.

SERMONS UPON HEBREWS XI.

SERMON I.

Now faith is the substance of things hoped for, the evidence of things not seen. HEB. xi. 1.

IN the close of the former chapter the apostle had spoken of living by faith, and thereupon taketh occasion to show what faith is. He that would live by faith had need search out the nature of it; an unknown instrument is of little use. It is true, a man may act faith that cannot describe it artificially, as an infant may live, that doth not know what life is; but however, it is more comfortable when our thoughts are distinct, explicit, and clear, concerning the nature of those graces that are so necessary for us, and the christian life is much more orderly, and less at random and peradventure. And therefore the apostle, to teach them this holy art of exercising faith, and living by faith to more advantage, he gives them here an excellent description of it, ' Now faith is the substance,' &c.

In the words there is the thing described, and the description itself. The thing described is Faith; the description is this, ' It is the substance of things hoped for,' &c. The description is proper, according to the rules of art, *Habitus distinguuntur per actus, et actus per propria objecta*, habits are described by their formal acts, and acts restrained to their proper objects; so faith is here described by its primary and formal acts, which are referred to their distinct objects. The acts of faith are two; it is the substance, it is the evidence. Think it not strange that I call them acts, for that is it the apostle intends, therefore Beza says, in rendering this place, he had rather paraphrase the text, than obscure the scope; and he interpreteth it thus—Faith substantiates or gives a subsistence to our hopes, and demonstrates things not seen. There is a great deal of difference between the acts of faith, and the effects of faith. The effects of faith are reckoned up throughout this chapter; the formal acts of faith are in this verse. These acts are suited with their objects. As the matters of belief are yet to come, faith gives them a substance, a being, as they are hidden from the eyes of sense and carnal reason; so faith gives them an evidence, and doth convince men of the worth of them; so that one of these acts belongs to the understanding, the other to the will. By the one faith is a convincing demonstration, and by the other a practical application. By the one act it turns hope into some kind of present fruition and by the other things altogether invisible are represented to the soul with clearness and certainty. In short, by faith things hoped for have a being; things not seen have an evidence.

I shall discuss the parts of the text as they lie in order.

First, I begin with the first act and object, 'Faith is the substance of things hoped for.'

1. Let me open the phrases. *Faith* is sometimes taken for the doctrine of faith, and sometimes for the grace of faith. Some take liberty to expound it of the former, the doctrine of faith, that is, the substance of things hoped for. I confess the words agree well, but not the scope; the doctrine of faith, *Fides quæ creditur*, is the substance of things hoped for; the word and faith do come under one description. But the apostle's drift here is to show, not what we do believe, but how we live by faith; therefore the grace is here understood, not the doctrine. Now the grace of faith is considered here, not as it justifies but rather as it sanctifies, as it is an instrument in the spiritual life. He speaketh of those acts which faith discovereth most in its use and exercise to baffle temptations, and to make us stand our ground under sore assaults, troubles, and persecutions.

Now this faith is the 'substance,' ὑπόστασις; that is, the word. Some difference there is about the rendering of it; the most usual significations of it are confidence and substance. Sometimes it is put for confidence, and for a firm and resolved expectation; as Heb. iii. 14, 'We are made partakers of Christ, if we hold the beginning of our confidence firm, or steadfast unto the end,' ἀρχὴν τῆς ὑποστάσεως, it is the same word; but there we render it confidence; and it seems to be parallel with ver. 6, 'If we hold fast the confidence, and the rejoicing of the hope, firm unto the end.' So 2 Cor. ix. 4, 'In this confident boasting,' ὑποστάσει ταύτῃ τῆς καυχήσεως, it is the same word. And thus the Septuagint translates the Hebrew word, which they render sometimes by *spes*, sometimes by *hypostasis;* and so in profane authors, Plutarch calls those that stand out after the field is won, ὑφισταμένους, because of their great confidence. Polybius calleth the valorous resistance of Horatius Cocles, ὑπόστασιν, which use of the word is proper to the original of it, ὑφίστασθαι, *firmiter stare.*

2. The second explication is the *substance.* The word signifies substance or subsistence; because confident expectation gives our hopes a kind of present or actual being, and apprehends things to come as present and subsisting, and causes them to work, as if they were already enjoyed; therefore our translators, fitly I conceive, render it here substance, saith the Greek scholist, τὰ ἐν ἔλπισιν, &c. Though things in hope are absent and to come, yet in the certain firm expectation and persuasion of the believer, they are present and real; so that the meaning is, faith doth not only look out with cold thoughts about things to come, but causes them to work as if they had already a being, and the believer were in the possession and enjoyment of them. And in this sense it is the substance of things hoped for; it gives them a being, while it beholds them in their original fountain, which is the word of promise; and while it unites and joins the soul to them by earnest hope, which is as it were an anticipation of our blessedness, and a pre-occupation of the joys of the world to come, faith causeth

such a subsistence and fiducial presence of the things hoped for in the mind of a believer, as that he concludes not only that they may be, or shall be, but that they already are. Faith is the substance, and that ' of things hoped for ; ' so he calls all the blessings of the covenant which are not yet enjoyed. Many things indeed were hoped for by the patriarchs, and believers of the old testament, which are now past, which are matters of mere belief, and not of hope to us, and so come under the latter description of faith, the evidence of things not seen, as the incarnation of Christ: yet their faith made those things present to them : John viii. 56, ' Your father Abraham rejoiced to see my day.' Abraham saw that day, and had a distinct view of it, though they were to them things hoped for ; yet we believe them, though we do not see them. But there are other things which are only promised by God, and not yet enjoyed, that are simple matters of hope—as the general resurrection, the happiness of the glorified estate. Now faith doth as it were give a real being to them as if they were present. But then there are other things that may be enjoyed in this world, though not for the present, yet in some season ; as the gracious presence of God, and his favourable returns after absence, and some estrangement, and deep affliction ; these things may also be comprised in this expression, being things we hope for according to promise, and though they be absent, faith gives them a being and presence. You will find faith to be a kind of prophetic grace ; for to faith, when God is absent, yet then he is present ; when he hides his face, faith can look behind the veil, and there see fatherly love, and a God of mercy. And in scripture upon this account the children of God answer themselves, and antedate their praises. When they ask anything of God in prayer, faith asks and answers itself ; it makes the help and mercy present which we ask according to God's will : Ps. vi. 4, ' Return, O Lord, deliver my soul ; ' then he answers himself, ver. 8, 9, ' The Lord hath heard the voice of my weeping ; the Lord hath heard my supplication.' But chiefly the expression reflects upon and is meant of those blessings which are only in expectation, and never in actual and complete enjoyment in this world, as heaven and the glory of the everlasting state ; faith gives a being and real subsistence in the soul to the glory that is yet to be revealed.

Obj. I have done with the exposition, only here is a doubt ; does not this confound faith and hope, to make things hoped for to be the object of faith, for graces differ in their objects ?

Sol. I answer, There is a link between the graces, but no confusion ; they are akin, but not confounded one with another. Blessedness to come is an object of faith, and an object of hope ; it is an object of faith as it is present in the promises, or present in our hearts ; and an object of hope in regard of its futurity, as it is yet to come. Faith is the ground of hope. Faith believeth, and hope expecteth. Faith first closeth with *verbum Dei*, the word of God, that assures us of such a blessedness ; then hope is carried out towards *rem verbi*, the thing promised. Faith makes all things certain, and in a sort already present ; but hope looks out for a full accomplishment. Faith gives us a right, and persuades us of the truth of things promised, and hope looks after the manifestation of them in possession. Faith is the hand, and hope is the eye of the soul. Faith lays hold upon the promise, and hope looks out after the things promised. Faith awakens hope, and hope cherishes faith, bringing in constant support to it.

Out of this first clause let me observe—

Doct. That a lively faith doth give such a reality, certainty, and present being to things hoped for and yet to come, as if they were already actually enjoyed.

And thus it is said of Abraham, John viii. 56, that 'he saw Christ's day.' Though there were many successions of ages between Christ and Abraham, yet faith made it present, represented it as if it were before his eyes; 'he saw my day,' not by a naked supposition but by real prospect, such as wrought upon his heart, and 'he was glad,' and leaped for joy. And so in this sense a believer is said to have eternal life, John iii. 36. He is not only sure of it when he dies, but hath it here in some sense: Heb. xi. 13, 'These all died in faith, not having received the promises, but having seen them afar off.' Without faith we cannot see things at a distance. Here I shall show—

1. How faith doth this.

2. The benefit and advantage of this property of faith in the whole business of the spiritual life, how this is the great ground of our living by faith.

First. How does faith give a subsistence or present being to things hoped for? How can we be said to have that happiness which we do but expect?

I answer: Faith takes possession four ways—(1.) *Spe*, by hope. (2.) *Promissis*, in the promises. (3.) *Capite*, in our head. (4.) *Primitiis*, in the first-fruits.

1. *Spe*. By a lively hope it doth as it were sip of the cup of blessing, and preoccupy and foretaste those eternal and excellent delights which God hath prepared for us, and affects the heart with the certain expectation of them, as if they were enjoyed. It appears by the effect of this hope, which is rejoicing with joy unspeakable and full of glory, 1 Peter i. 8. Joy is proper to fruition and enjoyment. We delight in a thing when we have it, and we delight in a thing when we hope for it; for a christian's hope being built upon certain and unerring grounds, it causeth the same effect also. Natural hope is the flower of pleasure and foretaste of happiness; so spiritual hope is the harbinger and forerunner of those eternal and unmixed delights which the Lord hath prepared for us. Hope must needs make things present; for mark, it is more than supposition and conceit. Heaven in the thoughts differs very much from heaven in our hope, as much as taste doth from sight, or longing from looking. Hope causeth rejoicing—an affection proper to present possession. Where it is anything strong, it diverts the mind from present wants and miseries and comforts us, and doth us good with the evidence of a future blessed estate reserved for us in the heavens. Hope is not a presumptuous conceit, like the supposition of a beggar imagining himself to be a king, and how much power and glory it will bring to him when he is arrived to it; but like the expectation of a prince who is the undoubted heir of a crown, and knows that one day he shall possess it. There is not only a naked supposal, but a real certainty and expectation; therefore it must needs cause

some present joy.   Bare contemplation works a kind of union.   There is a union between the thoughts and the object, as there is between the star and the eye ; it is present in my eye, though the star be a thousand miles distant : so there is a kind of union between the thought and the thing thought of ; but much more a union between hope and the thing hoped for : for the soul doth as it were sally out by desire, and the effect of hope is far more real than the effects of naked and fond imagination.   It filleth the soul with lively comfort : ' Rejoice in hope,' saith the apostle, Rom. xii. 12.   Joy or delight is the effect of fruition or present enjoyment, yet delight is given to hope ; for delighting is the complacency of the soul in a thing obtained ; now hope, where it is strong, gives us a sweet contentment and joy from the evidence of a future blessed estate : Heb. iii. 6, ' Whose house are we, if we hold fast the confidence and rejoicing of hope firm unto the end ; ' and Rom. v. 2, ' We rejoice in hope of the glory of God.'   Hope, by a mystery, and spiritual kind of magic, fetcheth heaven from heaven, and makes it exist in the heart of a believer.   It doth not only, like the spies, bring us tidings, and a glorious report of that heaven, but makes heaven to stoop and earth to ascend, and brings the believer into the company of the blessed, and brings down the joys of the Spirit into the heart of a believer.   We cannot hope for anything, but we must in part possess the thing hoped for ; much more in spiritual things.   Faith doth not only unite you to Christ, but puts Christ and heaven into the soul by hope.   There is the Lamb, the white throne, the glorified spirits, the upper paradise, and the tree of life in the soul, made really present to us by faith through a lively and watchful hope.

2. Faith takes possession, and gives a being to the things hoped for—*promissis*, in the promises.   There is not only the union of hope, but a clear right and title ; God hath passed over all those things to us in the covenant of grace.   When we take hold of the promises, we take hold of the blessing promised by the root of it, until it flows up to full satisfaction.   Hence those expressions, believers are said ' to lay hold of eternal life,' 1 Tim. vi. 12–19, by which their right is secured to them ; ' And he that heareth my words, and believeth in me, hath eternal life,' John v. 24.   Christ doth not only say, He shall have eternal life, but, *jus habet*, he hath a clear right and title to it, which is as sure as sense, though not as sweet.   Faith gives us heaven, because in the promise it gives us a title to heaven ; we are sure to have that to which we have a title ; a right is enough, though there be not always an actual feeling ; he hath a grant, God's word to assure him of it.   He is said to have an estate that hath the conveyance of it, but it is not necessary he should carry his land upon his back.   The fee of heaven is made over to us in law though not in deed ; it is ours before we possess it, because God hath passed his word that we shall have it.   And we hold it by covenant right, though we have it not by actual possession.   It is not only prepared for us in the designment of God, but given in respect of the indefeasableness of our right and property : Luke xxii. 29, ' I appoint unto you a kingdom.'   Now faith receives the kingdom.   We take hold of the thing promised by the root of it, and then we are sure of it ; the promise is not a dry root, and the hand of faith is not a barren soil ; but when once the hand of

faith takes hold of the promise, your interest will grow up into stalk and bud, and flower, and bring forth the fruit of full contentment. Now this contents a believer for the present, because faith considers what the promises are, and whose they are.

[1.] What are the promises?

(1.) Partly thus: They are the eruptions and overflows of God's grace and love. God's heart is so big with love to the saints that he cannot stay till the accomplishment of things, but he must acquaint us beforehand what he means to do for us: 'Before they spring forth,' saith God, 'I tell you of them,' Isa. xlii. 9. God's purposes of grace are like a sealed fountain, but his promises like a fountain broken open; before his purposes be brought to pass, he will tell us of them. The Lord might have done us good, and given us never a promise; but love concealed would not have been so much for our comfort. Now faith, seeing the testimony of God's love, counts itself bound to rest on the promise, and doth in effect say to the soul, as Naomi to Ruth, 'Sit still, my daughter, until thou know how the matter will fall; for the man will not be in rest, until he have finished the thing,' Ruth iii. 18. So faith saith to the soul, Sit still, until thou know how the matter will be; for God will not be at rest till he hath accomplished all that he hath spoken to thee. God accounts our purposes to be obedience, because they are the first issues of our love: Ps. xxxii. 5, 'I said I will confess my sin unto the Lord, and thou forgavest mine iniquity;' and Heb. xi. 17, 'By faith Abraham offered Isaac,' because he did it in vow and purpose; much more should we accept promises which are the declarations of God's purposes as performances: it will in time come to pass.

(2.) Faith looks upon them as the rule and warrant of our certainty. They show how far God is to be trusted, even so far as he is engaged; *promittendo se facit debitorem*, God hath entered into bonds, and made himself a debtor to his creatures by his promises. The purposes of God are unchangeable; but now when his purposes are declared in his promises, you have a further holdfast upon him. God will try our faith, and see what credit he hath with men, whether they will depend upon him when there is security put into our hands. Well then, faith takes hold of the blessing, the promise; why? God hath passed his word, the word is gone out of his lips, and he cannot in honour recall it,' Ps. lxxxix. 34; we may challenge him by his promise. Saith Austin of his mother, 'Lord, she was wont to throw thee in thy hand-writing;' 'she was wont to plead promises. God hath entered into bonds, and you may come and plead, and put those bonds in suit: Ps. cxix. 49, 'Remember the word unto thy servant, upon which thou hast caused me to hope.' An usurer thinks himself rich, though he hath little money in the house, because he hath bonds and good security. He that hath a thousand pounds in good security is in a better case than he that hath only a hundred pounds in ready money. A christian accounts God's promises to be his estate and patrimony, to be his substance and inheritance.

(3.) The promise is a pawn of the thing promised, and must be kept till performance comes. God's truth and holiness are left at pledge with the creature, and he will set them free; his honour lies at stake, and you may tell him of it: 'Lord, for thy mercy and truth's sake,' Ps. cxv. 1. God is interested to vindicate his name from calumny and reproach. Well then, faith, looking upon the promises as the eruptions of God's love, flowing from God's eternal love, as so many bonds and holdfasts upon God, and looking upon them as a pawn left us till the blessing come, upon all these advantages it serves instead of fruition; it entertains things to come with like certainty as if they were accomplished.

[2.] Faith considers whose the promises are; they are God's, who is faithful and able. The faithful and almighty God, he cannot say and unsay. We have it under assurance enough if we have it under his word. There is both Sarah's and Abraham's faith commended to us in scripture; Sarah's, 'because she judged him faithful who had promised,' Heb. xi. 11. That God who cannot lie, that God who hath been ever tender of his word, that God who will destroy heaven and earth rather than one iota of his word shall pass away, he hath left us promises, and is not this as good as payment? Then faith looks upon God's almightiness. This was Abraham's faith: Rom. iv. 21, 'Being fully persuaded that what he had promised he was also able to perform.' It is a difficult thing to see how we shall be secured from so many temporal dangers, and brought safe to eternal happiness. Aye, but God is able, and we have his word; his saying is doing; 'God spake the word, and it was done,' Ps. xxxiii. 9. What can let the all-sufficient God? His promises are performances.

3. We have it *in capite*, in our head. That is a christian's tenure; he holds all in his head by Christ. Though he be not glorified in his own person, he is glorified in his head, in Jesus Christ. When Christ was glorified, we were glorified; he seized upon heaven in our right: John xiv. 2, 'I go to prepare a place for you.' Christ is gone to heaven in our name, to possess it in our stead; therefore a believer is assured he shall share therein. Therefore as Christ's glorification is past, so in a sense a believer's glorification is past; the head cannot rise, and ascend, and be glorified without the members: Eph. ii. 6, 'And hath raised us up together, and made us sit together in heavenly places in Christ Jesus.' The apostle speaks of it as a thing past. He doth not say, We shall rise, shall sit down with him; but we are risen, and are ascended, and are sat down with him in heavenly places. In the right, and by virtue of the head, all of us are already glorified—an expression which implies greater certainty than a single prediction and promise; and all this that our comfort might be more abounding, and our courage more strong against dangers, death, difficulties, and all that may befal us in the way to heaven. Look, as we say of an old decrepit man, such an one hath one foot in the grave, a believer hath more than one foot in heaven; his head is there; we have taken possession of it in Christ, or rather he hath taken possession of it in our name; and as soon as we are united to Christ we are interested in this comfort, even whilst we lie groaning under pressures and miseries. Nothing but faith can unriddle this mystery, that a believer should be on earth, and yet in heaven; converse with sinners, and yet be in the company of glorified saints; or humbled with the pressures and inconveniences of the present state, yet be ascended and sit down with Christ in heavenly places. Faith gives you an actual

right and investiture in regard of your head.   As soon as we are sanctified we are in a manner glorified also, and have not only a title and right in ourselves, but an actual possession in our head.   As the head is crowned to reflect a glory and honour upon the whole body, so Jesus Christ is crowned, and we are glorified with him ; and this makes the right more strong ; for nothing on earth can take that happiness from me which Christ keeps for me in heaven.

4. Faith gives being *in primitiis*, in the first-fruits.   The Israelites had not only a right to Canaan given them by God, but had livery and seizin of Canaan, where the spies did not only make report of the goodness of the land, but brought the clusters of grapes with them, not only to encourage them to conquer, but actually to instate them in the possession of the land ; so doth God deal with a believing soul, not only give it a right, but give it some first-fruits ; there is not only a report and promise, but God hath as it were given us livery and seizin of heaven.   A believing soul hath the beginnings of that estate which it hopes for ; some clusters of Eschol by way of foretaste in the midst of present miseries and difficulties.   This is the great love of God to us, that he would give us something of heaven here upon earth, that he will make us enter upon our happiness by degrees.   Saith the apostle, 1 Cor. xiii. 13, 'Now abideth faith, hope, charity.'   Belief in this life is instead of intuition : by faith we begin our glory, and hereafter it is perfected, and made up in sight and vision.   We have something by way of advance and foretaste, in our wants and present dangers.   In nature things do not arrive at once to their last perfection ; so it is in grace, God carrieth us on by degrees to heaven's glory and happiness.   We have something by way of essay and prelibation, before we possess and enjoy the sovereign good, and those riches and treasures, and that fulness of eternal glory which God hath provided for us.   But what are these first-fruits ?   They are three—union with Christ, the joys of the Spirit, and grace.

[1.] Union with Christ.   There is some enjoyment of God in Christ here, this is the chiefest part of eternal life.   What is heaven but the eternal enjoyment of God in Christ ?   And it is in a sort begun here. Union makes way for presence ; though we are not present with Christ, yet we are united to Christ ; and faith makes way for fruition.   Then it will be 'God all in all,' 1 Cor. xv. 28 ; now it is 'Christ in us the hope of glory,' Col. i. 27.   Now he comes to dwell in our hearts by way of pledge, that once the soul shall come to be filled up with God ; this is an earnest and beginning of our full enjoyment of him.   And when once this is done, then we may be certain of glory.   I say, eternal life is begun when we are united to Christ.   It is the same in substance, though not in degree, with the life of heaven.   When once we are united to Christ, we can never be separated.   Christ is still a head, he can never leave his old mansion and dwelling-place.   Saith Luther, 'You can as soon separate the leaven from the dough, when one is wrought into the other, as you may separate Christ and a soul that is once united to him :' 1 John v. 12, 'He that hath the Son hath life.'   You have the fairest part of eternal life already when you have Christ in you.

[2.] The joys of the Holy Ghost.   When a man hath received the consolations of the Spirit, he is in the skirts and suburbs of heaven, he begins to enter upon his country and inheritance. Heaven begins in us, when the Holy Ghost comes with peace, confidence, and joy, and doth leave a sweet sense and relish upon the soul. Fulness of joy, that is the portion of the life to come, and is reserved for God's right hand; but here is the beginning of heaven; and peace of conscience and joy in the Holy Ghost is but the pledge of that joy which the blessed spirits have. And therefore the comforts of the Holy Ghost which we have here in this world are called ' joy unspeakable and full of glory,' 1 Peter i. 8, because it tends and works that way towards our glorious and happy estate in heaven. As the odours and sweet smells of Arabia are carried by the winds and air into the neighbouring provinces, so that before travellers come thither they have the scent of that aromatic country; so the joys of heaven are by the sweet breathings and gales of the Holy Ghost blown into the hearts of believers, and the sweet smells of the upper paradise are conveyed into the gardens of the churches; those joys which are stirred up in us by the Spirit before we get to heaven are a pledge of what we may expect hereafter. God would not weary our hopes by expecting too much, therefore he hath not only given us his word, but he gives a taste and earnest here as part of the sum which shall be paid us in heaven; by these sweet refreshments of the Spirit we may conceive of the glory of the ever-lasting state. Look, as before the sun ariseth, there are some forerun-ning beams and streaks of light that usher it in; so the joys of the Holy Ghost are but the morning glances of the daylight of glory, and of the sun of happiness that shall arise upon us in another world.

[3.] There is grace also which is the earnest of glory; it is the livery and seizin, the turf that puts us into possession of the whole field. Grace is the beginning of glory, and glory is but grace perfected. Grace is glory in the bud, and moulding, and making; for when the apostle would express our whole conformity to Christ, he only expresseth it thus, ' We are changed into his image from glory to glory,' 2 Cor iii. 18, that is, from one degree of grace to another. It is called glory, because the progress of holiness never ceaseth till it comes to the perfection of glory and life eternal. The first degree of grace is glory begun, and the final consummation is glory perfected. All the degrees of our conformity to Christ are so called. It is a bud of that sinless, pure, immaculate estate which shall be without spot and wrinkle; the seed of that perfect holiness which shall be bestowed upon us hereafter. Thus the spiritual life is described in its whole flux; it begins in grace, and ends in glory. See the golden chain: Rom. viii. 30, ' Whom he hath called, them he also justified; and whom he justified, them he also glorified.' There is no mention of sanctification, for that is included in glory. Grace is but young glory, and differs from glory as an infant doth from a man; therefore by degrees the Lord will have you enter upon your everlasting inheritance. As the heir receives his estate by parcels, so do we; first God gives us a seed, and an initial fruition, then we are drawn on further and further to a full enjoyment. The new creature, like metal in the forge, it is heaven in the moulding and framing; and God gives us the draught here below, which glory will at length finish above. Upon all these grounds faith works as if the thing were enjoyed; while we hope and have a certain expectation, it doth as it were taste the bless-ing; and whilst it looks upon them in the sure promises of God, and in our head; or that which Christ hath done for us in the first-fruits; so our hopes are made to work upon us as if they were already accom-plished and enjoyed.

SERMON II.

Now faith is the substance of things hoped for.—HEB. xi. 1.

Secondly, The benefit and advantage of this act, and the use of faith in the spiritual life.

1. It is very necessary we should have such a faith as should substan-tiate our hopes, to check sensuality, for we find the corrupt heart of man is all for present satisfaction. And though the pleasures of sin be short and inconsiderable, yet because they are near at hand, they take more with us than the joys of heaven, which are future and absent. A man would wonder at the folly of men that should with Esau sell his birthright for a morsel of meat, Heb. xii. 16, that they should be so profane as to sell their Christ and glory, and those excellent things which the christian religion discovers, to part with the joys of chris-tianity for the vilest price. When lust is up and set agog, all consider-ations of eternal glory and blessedness are laid aside to give it satisfac-tion. A little pleasure, a little gain, a little conveniency in the world will make men part with all that is honest and sacred. A man would wonder at their folly, but the great reason is, they live by sense: 'Demas hath forsaken me, having loved this present world,' 2 Tim. iv. 10; there lies the bait, these things are present with us; we can taste the delights of the creatures, and feel the pleasures of the flesh; but the happiness of the world to come is a thing unseen and unknown. 'Let us eat and drink, for to-morrow we shall die,' 1 Cor. xv. 32. This is the language of every carnal heart, let us take up with present things. Who will venture upon the practice of a duty difficult and distasteful to his affections, and forego what we see and enjoy upon the uncertain hopes of things to come? Present advan-tages, nay vanities, though they be small and very trifles, yet have more power to pervert us than good things at a distance, nay, than all the promises of God to allure and draw in our hearts to God. And here lies the root and strength of all temptations; the inconveniences of strictness in religion are present, there is a present distaste and present trouble to the flesh; and the rewards are future; here is the great snare: therefore how should we do to check this living by sense that is so natural to us? Why, faith substantiating our hopes pro-vides a remedy; for that makes things to come to work as if they were already enjoyed; the day of judgment to work upon us, as if we did see Christ upon his white throne, and the books opened and heaven as if we were ready now to enter into it. Where faith is lively and strong, and is the evidence of things not seen, it baffles and defeats all

temptations.   The war and conflict in men's hearts is carried on under
these two captains, faith and sense.   All the forces of the spiritual and
regenerate part are drawn and led up by faith ; sense on the other side
marshals all the temptations of the world and the flesh ; sense is all
for enjoyment and actual possession.   Now faith, to vanquish it, gives
a substance, and makes things to come present to us, and makes us
sensible of other satisfactions and contentments, which are far better ;
and there lies the strength of the renewed part ; and the great success
of the spiritual battle is in the liveliness of hope and in the certainty of
faith, that it may make those things work as present which sense
judgeth absent and afar off.   That is the reason why faith and sense
are so often opposed in scripture ; faith forestalls the joys of heaven, and
makes them to be in the mind and judgment, and upon the heart of a
believer, that the restraint from present delights may seem less irksome ; if it be laborious and difficult to serve God, yet it is for heaven.
All that the devil can plead, who works by sense, is the enjoyment of a
little present profit and pleasure ; he cannot promise heaven and glory,
or anything hereafter ; now therein he thinks he hath the start of God—
heaven is to come, but the delights and advantages of sin are at hand.
Faith, to baffle the temptation, strongly fixeth the heart of a believer
upon things to come, that in some sort it doth preunite their souls and
their happiness together, and by giving them heaven upon earth confirms the soul in a belief of better things than the devil or the world
can propose.   Thus you see that to defeat the temptation there needs
faith, that it may strongly fix the heart of a believer upon things to
come and put him within the company of the blessed ; that in some
sort he may have heaven upon earth, and such a certain persuasion of better things, that he may look upon all that the devil,
the world and the flesh do oppose to him as a weak and paltry
thing.

2. It gives strength and support to all the graces of the spiritual
life.   The great design of religion is to bring us to a neglect of present
happiness, and to make the soul to look after a felicity yet to come ;
and the great instrument of religion, by which it promoteth this
design, is faith, which is as the scaffold and ladder to the spiritual
building.   It is useful to all the other graces, whether they be doing
or suffering graces.   We are assaulted on every side, both ' on the right
hand and on the left,' as the apostle saith, 2 Cor. vi. 7 ; on the one
side by the pleasures of the flesh, on the other side by the frowns of
the world ; and therefore the armour of righteousness must be fitted
on both sides, that we may be strengthened on the right hand against
the pleasures, profits, and honours of the world, and on the left hand
against troubles, disgraces, and bitter persecutions.   If we would stand
our ground, and be faithful in the business of our heavenly calling, we
must look for these two things, to do for God, and to suffer for
God ; for these two ways a christian approves himself to God ;
by suffering we declare our loyalty, by doing we perform our
homage.

Ques. Indeed it is a pretty question, In which of these we manifest
most love to God, either mortifying our lusts, or renouncing our
interests—to which the chiefest crown of honour is due ? whether to

be set upon the head of the suffering faith, or the active or doing faith?

Sol. It may be pleaded on the one side, that in holiness, or the active part of duty, we only give away our ill-being for Christ by crucifying our lusts, which are enemies to our peace as well as to the crown of heaven; but by suffering, we lose being and well-being, our lives and livelihood, and all for Christ; therefore it seems there should be more love in that. But on the other side, it may be pleaded thus, that there are many that suffer for Christ, who sacrifice a stout body to a stubborn mind; and because they are engaged they will suffer, yet are not able to quit a lust for him. And it may be pleaded, the victory is less over outward inconveniences, than inward lusts which are rooted in our nature, and so more hard to be overcome; and the enduring trouble and hardship is more easy than subduing of sin, and that it is the sharpest martyrdom a man can endure to tame his flesh, *majus in castitate vivere, quam pro castitate mori*—it is a harder thing to be a holy person than to be a martyr. Thus you see each part indeed hath its difficulties, which I have mentioned; partly to satisfy them that are not called to suffer, yet thou hast employment enough by faith to mortify thy lusts, and indeed there is the harder work; it is more easy to withstand an enemy than a temptation. When we conflict with an enemy, we do but conflict with an arm of flesh and blood; but when the apostle speaks of the inward warfare, he saith, Ephes. vi. 12, 'We fight not with flesh and blood, but with principalities and powers.' And partly to show, that there are inconveniences on both hands, and a great deal of difficulty, and there is need of all the strength that possibly we can have, both for doing and suffering. We need faith on either side, that we might be holy and willing to do for God; and that we may be courageous and willing to die for God.

But why should I debate this difference? Let me compound it rather; holiness and suffering must both go together, for no one can suffer for Christ, but they whose hearts are drawn forth to love him above all things. The priests under the law were to search the burnt-offering, and if it were scabby, or had any blemish upon it, it was to be laid aside and not offered. The Lord doth not desire a scabbed carnal man should suffer for him. He that keeps the commandments is best able to suffer for them. In Mat. v., first Christ saith, 'Blessed are the pure in heart,' ver. 8, then, 'Blessed are they that suffer for righteousness' sake,' ver. 10. The blessing of martyrdom is put in the last place, implying that a martyr must have all the precedent graces of meekness, humility, poverty of spirit, &c. Therefore we must look for doing the will of God, and suffering the will of God, before these promises be accomplished, and the things we hope for brought about.

[1.] To suffer for God. It is oftentimes a crime to be faithful to Christ's interests, and a matter of danger to be a thorough christian; when men are exposed to affronts, and troubles, and disgraces, they need all the wisdom and grace that possibly they can get together. Now faith is 'the substance of things hoped for;' there will be our best furniture; why? for this will teach us to counterbalance our temptations with our hopes. It puts your hopes in one balance, when the devil puts the world with all terrors, disgraces and losses in the other ; and then the soul triumphs, and says, that our losses are no more to be compared with our gains, than a feather is to be set against a talent of lead. 'I reckon,' saith the apostle, Rom. viii. 18, 'that the sufferings of this present time are not worthy to be compared with the glory that shall be revealed in us;' and the bitterness of the cross is allayed and sweetened by comparing our hopes with it. Thus Moses sets the recompense of reward against the loss of the pleasures, treasures, and honours of Egypt, Heb. xi. 24, 25. And those forty martyrs Basil speaks of that were kept naked in the open air in a cold frosty night, and to be burnt the next day, they cried out, 'Sharp is the cold, but sweet is paradise; troublesome is the way, pleasant is the end of the journey ; let us endure the cold for the present, and the patriarch's bosom shall soon warm us,' &c. These passages will truly open the meaning of the apostle, that 'faith is the substance of things hoped for,' &c., when we can really set one against the other, and bear the hardest lot that can befal us upon expectation of our blessed hopes. And that of the apostle doth notably open it, 2 Cor. iv. 16, ' For this cause we faint not,' &c., why? ver. 18. 'While we look not at the things which are seen, but at the things which are not seen ; for the things which are seen are temporal, but the things which are not seen are eternal;' that is, when we are supported and fortified by a remembrance and certain expectation of our blessed hopes. When the Jews were full of fury against Stephen, Act. vii. 56, 'he saw the heavens opened;' and so he fortified himself against the anger, and shower of stones from the people. There was somewhat of miracle and ecstasy in that vision, the glory of heaven being represented not only to his soul, but possibly to his senses by some external representation. But as to the substance of the comfort itself, it is that which falls out ordinarily in a way of believing ; faith opens heaven to a believer, and brings him to the company of the blessed ; and when the soul is taken up with the thoughts of another world, it can better digest trouble here. Faith is the perspective of his soul, he seeth heaven opened and glory prepared for him, and then the temptation vanisheth. This is the reason believers can endure plundering 'and spoiling of goods,' Heb. x. 34. ' Faith is the substance of things hoped for.' Let goods go, saith a believer, so he may keep his interest in the better and more enduring substance. The christians in the primitive times were first exposed to the rapine and malice of the rude people, before actions at law or any legal process was formed against them by the persecuting edicts of the Roman emperors for their profession. And the Jews were most fierce against christians in that kind ; they would spoil them, and they could have no advantage against them. Now 'they took joyfully,' they were willing to part with them as Joseph with his coat to keep his conscience ; and to quit all worldly possessions, because they had an assurance of a better and a more enduring substance. So that it is of great use to support suffering graces, as fortitude and self-denial.

[2.] To do for God. As to the doing part, those graces serve for doing the will of God, which is our constant trial. Look to the several parts of our duty.

(1.) For the destructive part, or the work of mortification. When heaven is in the eye and heart of a believer, when it is preoccupied by his faith, sin hath less power upon the heart. When faith gives substance and being to your hopes, it will appear in your lives ; you will mortify corruption, and study holiness, while you can set the pleasures on God's right hand against the pleasures of sin ; and you can reason thus, Rom. viii. 13, 'If I live after the flesh, I shall die ; but if I, through the Spirit, mortify the deeds of the body, I shall live.' You will be more able to bear with the difficulties of religion, when you see you do not act upon an uncertain futurity ; you do not fight as those that are uncertain ; as the apostle speaks, Heb. x. 36, ' That after ye have done the will of God ye might receive the promise.' Nay, before we have done the whole will of God, faith receives the promise ; we have the root, though not the blossom. It is true, Christ calls to suffer unpleasing austerities ; aye, but heaven makes amends for them all. Therefore whenever sensitive desires insinuate themselves, faith can see carnal pleasures are base, and but the happiness of beasts; and they are short, 'pleasures of sin for a season,' Heb. xi. 25, and they issue themselves into unspeakable torments ; ' they shall mourn at last,' Prov. v. 11. When the devil would make you faint and lazy in the work of the Lord, faith can represent the short continuance of the present difficulty ; so when the devil would beget irksome thoughts of duty, faith can represent endless delights that will follow ; and then the believer determines, it is better to go to heaven with labour, than to hell with pleasure. This is that which made Moses, who had an eagle eye, so victorious : Heb. xi. 26, 'He had respect to the recompense of the reward,' which made him despise the pleasures, and treasures, and honours of Egypt. The looking upon the recompenses makes hope to have such an influence on the life; for those views and foretastes of heaven will beget such a strong persuasion in the heart of a believer, that all the reasons in the world shall not alter, or break the force of his spiritual purpose. When the devil tempts to filthiness, uncleanness, wantonness, faith presents hopes of being consorts and followers of the unspotted and immaculate Lamb. When we are tempted to neglect duty for worldly advantages, faith doth oppose the glory of our inheritance, the riches of the new Jerusalem, and what is the hope of our high calling, and the good treasure God hath opened to us in the new covenant. If we are tempted to hunt after worldly honour, faith proposeth a crown of righteousness which the just and righteous God will give us at that day. If the fear of disgrace make us loosen and slacken our duty, faith proposeth the confusion of face wherewith the wicked shall appear before the throne of the Lamb, and the disgrace that shall fall upon the wicked at the great day. So when we are tempted to murmuring and repining under the cross, faith will assure that though the way be rough, the end of the journey will be sweet. So that the promises are like cordials next the heart, and keep the poison from seizing upon the vital spirits, and preserve the soul in a holy generousness and bravery for God ; they tell us of rivers of pleasure that stream out of the heart of Jesus Christ, and the sweet content we shall enjoy with God for evermore.

(2.) For diligence and seriousness in a holy life. The nearer things are, the greater and the more they work upon us, and the further off the less. Those never thought of repentance that put far away the evil day, Amos vi. 3. A star at a distance, though of great magnitude, seems like a spark or spangle. We are sensible of things more, the nearer they are; distance doth much alter our apprehensions of things; we have not the same notions of eternity, living as we shall have when we come to die. Oh! when time begins to draw to an end, and we are going into the other world, what would we give to live over our lives again? Oh, how diligent, watchful, serious should we be if we had the sense of eternity upon our hearts! Now how shall we do to make things at a distance to be near to us? Thus, faith is the perspective of the soul. As by a perspective glass we see things at a distance as if they were present and near at hand; so faith apprehends things at a distance, and makes them work upon us. Certain expectation produceth industrious prosecution: Phil. iii. 14, 'I press on to the mark,' saith Paul, 'for the prize of the high calling of God in Christ Jesus.' We make the world believe that heaven and hell are things spoken in jest, whilst we are so careless about them; but when we apprehend them in good earnest, and have a true sense of them, then we fall a-working out our salvation with fear and trembling; we see that all the diligence and holy care we can use is little enough to carry away this great prize of the eternal enjoyment of God. By faith you look within the veil, and lift up the heart to the heavenly joys, and this keeps the heart watchful over the blessed hope. It is the description of a believer: Jude ver. 21, 'Looking for the mercy of our Lord Jesus Christ unto eternal life.' Now we have no other eye but faith, and faith stands you in stead, as it confirms you in the certainty of your hopes. Heaven is in the heart by faith, and therefore the heart is in heaven by spiritual meditation; all their thoughts are about their country: Phil. iii. 20, 'For our conversation is in heaven;' and all the business of their lives is to approach nearer to their hopes. Paul was taken up into the third heaven. Faith giveth you a temperate and deliberate view, though not by such a rapid motion, yet by serious and solemn thoughts, and so keeps the soul in a heavenly frame and expectation. It puts your head above the clouds, and in the midst of the world to come. The apostle biddeth us to lay up in store for ourselves a good foundation against the time to come, 'that we may lay hold of eternal life,' 1 Tim. vi. 19. Now faith doth not only lay the first stone, but the whole heap is increased, the work of holiness is carried on by the help and assistance of faith, which keepeth heaven and eternal life in the view of the soul, and so encourageth heavenly motions and endeavours.

(3.) For contentation, that is a necessary part of the holy life. This contentation is two-fold; under the difficulties and inconveniences of the present life, and under the want and distance of our future comfort.

(1st.) Under the difficulties and inconveniences of the present life. Faith sweetens all the afflictions of this life by presenting the advantages of the future, and balanceth what we feel with what we do expect. The shortest life is long enough to be sensible of inconveniences and many calamities. But though the way is rough, faith 'seeth heaven at the end of the journey, and so it conveyeth real support and comfort into the soul and heart of a believer. A christian may live in the sweetness of tranquillity in the midst of all outward disturbances, because the presence of his hopes makes amends for all, and giveth him a happy dedolency that he feels nothing; whereas when faith is weak we soon faint: Ps. cxix. 92, 'Unless thy law had been my delight, I had perished in my affliction.' There is such a sweetness in the word, that when faith takes hold of it, the sense of worldly misery is overwhelmed and quenched. Faith is like a cordial that keeps off the poison of affliction from the vital spirits, and the poison of the encumbrances of the present life from the soul: Ps. xxvii. 13, 'I had fainted, unless I had believed to see the goodness of God in the land of the living,' that is, without the sense of eternal happiness I had been utterly lost. Heaven is properly the land of the living, and that he respecteth. To see God in the land of the living is as much as to enjoy God in heaven; and so the Chaldee explaineth it, in the land of life eternal.

(2dly.) It helps us to contentation under the want and distance of our future comforts. Let it not seem a paradox, that here the conflict is hardest. It is easier to bear the evil than wait for the promised good, for sorrows are better and sooner allayed than desires. Desires are the vigorous bent of the soul, and they are impatient of check, chiefly when they are drawn forth upon reasons of religion, and usually after much mortification. It is very hard to tarry the Lord's leisure for the enjoyment of their hopes, when their hearts are weaned from the world; their pulse then beats strongly towards Christ, and it is a hard matter to cool and restrain the vehemency of their desires, especially towards our latter end. The nearer we are to the enjoyment of any good, the more impatient we are of the want of it; as a stone moveth faster, when nearest the centre. All natural motion is swifter in the close; so a christian's motions, though slow in the beginning, are swift in the close; therefore their hearts beat with longing desires, ready to break within them for the enjoyment of Christ. And this burden is the greater, because faith gives a partial enjoyment; but the same faith, which stirs up those desires, also yields the remedy against the vehemency of them. Desire is not only the fruit of hope, but patience: 2 Peter iii, 12, 'Looking for,' or waiting for, and yet 'hastening to the coming of the Lord.' The word in the original, 'looking for,' notes a patient bearing: now these two words seem contrary, waiting, yet hastening. This is the disposition of the people of God, they look for, and they hasten to the Lord's coming. They covet the everlasting state, and yet wait God's leisure. There is a vehemency and yet a regularity in their expectations, and both are promoted by this act of faith: for faith gives certainty, and that quiets the soul, though there be not present enjoyment. The first effect of faith is a present interest and title, and 'He that believeth maketh not haste,' Isa. xxviii. 16. Those prelibations of heaven we have in the world, the scripture gives us under a double notion; the first-fruits, and earnest; the first-fruits or tastes how good; and an earnest or pledge, how sure. Under the quality of the first-fruits, so they do awaken desires and vehement longings: Rom. viii. 23, 'We that have the first-fruits of the Spirit, even we ourselves groan within ourselves, waiting for the adoption, to wit, the redemption of our bodies.' A christian hath tasted how sweet God is in Christ, therefore he groans after the full enjoyment of him. As they are an earnest, 2 Cor. i. 22, ' Who hath sealed us, and given us the earnest of the Spirit in our hearts;' so it is a ground of waiting. We may trust God if he hath given us an earnest. It is not for the comfort of a man to carry his inheritance at his back, it is enough that he hath a right and title. Faith is every way as sure, though not as sweet as sense; and therefore a believer waits as long as God hath anything for him to do in this world upon this security of faith. It is true, he is in a strait, his desires press him, yet he will wait. Thus St. Paul, Phil. i. 23, 24, ' I am in a strait between two, having a desire to be dissolved, and be with Christ; but to abide in the flesh is more needful for you.' A christian is thus divided between his own profit and God's will, and God's glory; but at length faith casts the scales, and brings him to a holy contentation with the pleasure of God. The first-fruits beget longings; and the earnest keeps us from murmuring and discontent; so the sureness sweetens the pain which the remoteness occasions.

Use 1. To examine whether you have this kind of faith or no, which is the substance of things hoped for. To discover how little of this faith there is in the world, consider—

1. Many men say they believe, but alas, what influence have their hopes upon them? Do they affect them? Do they engage them as things present and sensible do? Alas, in the general, things temporal work more upon us than things eternal, and things visible than things invisible. A small matter will prove a temptation; a little pleasure and profit, how doth it set you a-work? We have not half that seriousness in spiritual business that we have in earthly. Surely men do not believe heaven, because they are so little affected with it; because they mind and care for it and labour for it so little. Alas! they live as if they never heard of any such thing, or believe not what they hear; every toy and trifle is preferred before it. If a poor man understood that some great inheritance was bequeathed to him, would not he often think of it, and rejoice in it, and long to go and see it, and take possession of it? There is a promise of eternal life left with us in the gospel, but who puts in for a share? Who longs for it? Who takes hold of it? Who gives all diligence to make it sure? Who desires to go and see it? Oh, that I might be dissolved, and be with Christ! Because these hopes have so little influence on us, it is a sign we do not make them exist in our hearts.

2. You may discern it by your carriage in any trial and temptation. When heaven and the world come in competition, can you deny present carnal advantages upon the hopes of eternity? do you forsake all as knowing you shall have a thousand times better in another world? So did Moses, Heb. xi. 24, 25 ; the reason is rendered—' For he had respect to the recompense of reward; 'then is the best time to judge of your spirit; then God puts you to it; therefore they are called temptations and trials. Certainly it is of much profit to observe the issue and result of these deliberate debates and conflicts that are in the conscience. Now where faith is the substance of things hoped for, there will be a denial of present carnal advantages; heaven will be as present as the temptation,

and you will see Jesus Christ outbidding the world ; nay, that momentary sufferings are not meet to be named the same day with your hopes. If the world should come in competition with glory, to violate conscience for a present satisfaction, faith comes away from the contest with an holy disdain and indignation at such a comparison. In vain is the snare laid before the bird that is of so high and so noble a flight. The servants of the Lord were tortured, Heb. xi. 35 ; in the original it is ἐτυμφανίσθησαν, they were stretched out as a drum, yet they would not accept of deliverance, that they might obtain a better resurrection. Will you be taken off the rack ? No. The world offered them a release, but faith offered them a resurrection, the raising of the body out of the grave to the glory of God. The world suggests earthly enjoyments, present advantages, You may have such and such preferments for the violating of conscience ; then faith comes with the treasures of the covenant. We are put to our choice many times either to wrong conscience, or accept of the world's profits ; outward conveniences are put into one scale, faith puts your hopes into the other ; one is present, the other is absent. Now observe the workings of your spirits in such cases. I confess there may be a resistance sometimes out of stubbornness, but if there be faith, it will work thus, by presenting your hopes, and casting the balance by an exceeding weight of glory. We can lose nothing, saith faith, but we shall have better in heaven ; we can gain nothing, but Christ will be more advantage to us. Upon this a believer sells all to purchase the pearl of price.

3. If faith do substantiate your hopes, though you do not receive present satisfaction, you may discern it by this, you will entertain the promises with much respect and delight. Are they dear and precious to you ? You would embrace the promises if you looked upon them as the root of the blessing. It is said of the patriarchs, Heb. xi. 13, that 'they saw the promises afar off, and were persuaded of them, and embraced them.' When they were to go out of the world, they took their leave of the promises with embraces ; though they came not to possession, they were persuaded of the possession ; though they lived many years before the promises concerning the Messiah took effect, yet they embraced them. Such ceremonies and compliments pass between friends ; we hug them and commend them to the Lord ; so faith hugs the promises, and commends them to God's power. Oh ! these are sweet promises ; these one day will bring a Messiah, and yield a saviour to the world. Old Jacob, when he took leave of his sons, he blessed them ; he saith to one—' His bow shall abide in strength,' Gen. xlix. 24 ; this shall be a victorious warrior ; to another, so and so. Or, as we do, when we part with children of great hopes, just so did these holy patriarchs deal with the promises when God had given them but an obscure signification of heaven and a Christ ; they were embracing these sayings as the comfort and strength of their souls ; when they went down to the grave ; they could not with Simeon hold Christ in their arms, yet they held the promises in the arms of their faith. So it will be with you ; you will rejoice in God because of his word, Ps. lvi. 4. When you take hold of the promise, you have the blessing by the root, and this should fill you with holy joy, oh, these are great and precious promises ! 2 Peter i. 4. Here is a promise that will yield me heaven ; this complete holiness,

this the fruition of God. By this promise I can expect to meet the
faithful of God in heaven; by this promise I can expect to sit down
with Abraham, Isaac and Jacob; by this promise I can look for the
abolition of sin; by this for the bruising of Satan under my feet; by
this for a freedom from all temptations, desertion and trouble. And
they will cherish a little spark of grace; here is a bud of glory; here
are some morning glances, some forerunning beams of the light that
shall shine upon us in heaven.

4. You may discern it by this, the mind will often run upon your
hopes. Where the thing is strongly expected, the end and aim of your
expectation will still be present with you. Thoughts are the spies and
messengers of the soul. Hope sends them out after the thing expected,
and love after the thing beloved; therefore it stands upon you to see
how your thoughts and principal desires are fixed. Where the thing
is strongly expected thoughts are wont to spend themselves, and to be
set a-work in creating images and suppositions of the happiness we shall
have in the enjoyment; and so the future condition will often run in
your mind, and be present with you. For instance, if a poor man were
adopted into the succession of a crown, he would please himself in the
supposition of the honour and splendour of the royal and kingly state
that is set up in his own thoughts. And did we believe we are heirs
of the kingdom of heaven, co-heirs with Christ, we would often think
of the happy time when we shall come to heaven, and see Christ in
the midst of his blessed ones; when we shall see Abraham, Isaac, and
Jacob in the kingdom of heaven, that are sat down at the feast of God,
and see Paul with his crown of righteousness upon his head. But alas!
it may be said of many, heaven is not in their thoughts, their hearts
dwell in this world, because they do not expect a better: therefore they
are always transported with admiring thoughts of worldly greatness;
always thinking what it is to enjoy thousands, and to have no complaining in their families; thinking of pulling down barns, and raising
greater, and advancing their posterity. We are thinking of our pleasures, lusts, profits. These are the pleasing thoughts wherewith we
feast our souls. We should still observe what it is we meditate upon
most, which way the contrivances and deliberations of your souls do
tend. Are your thoughts taken up with these carnal projects? with
those whose character it is, Phil. iii. 19, 'That they are enemies of
the cross of Christ, who mind earthly things?' or 2 Peter ii. 14, 'A
heart exercised with covetous practices,' always running upon some
worldly designs, plotting how to get the world into their net? Christ
describes the worldly person: Luke xii. 17, 18, 'He thought within
himself,' &c. He created images and suppositions in his soul of barns,
possessions, and heritages; for that is the Holy Ghost's word of the
carnal man, διελογίζετο, he dialogised and discoursed with himself.
But on the other side heaven will be more in the eye and mind of a
christian; and these provisional thoughts are the spies sent out to welcome our hopes. I will tell you what such an one is doing; he is framing
suppositions of the welcome he shall receive of Jesus Christ at his first
coming to glory; he is thinking of the joy between him and his fellow-
saints, when they shall meet in heaven; there is a stage set up, and a
sweet representation and acting over of heaven in their thoughts.

5. You may discern it, by your weanedness from the world. They that know heaven to be their home, reckon the world a strange country. There is a more excellent glory sealed up to them in Christ, and they do the less care for worldly advantages; certainly they do not lay out their strength and their care upon them. . Who would purchase a rattle with the same price that would buy a jewel? or dig for iron with mattocks of gold? They will not wear out their affections on carnal things; faith aquainteth them with nobler objects. The woman, when she knew Christ, left her pitcher, John iv. 28, 29. When Christ told Zaccheus that ‘salvation was come to his house,’ then ‘Lord, half of my goods I give to the poor,’ &c. Luke xix. 8, 9. But now when men only relish and favour earthly things, and live as if their hopes were only in this world, they either have no right to heaven, or believe they have none.

6. There will not be such a floating and instability in their expectation. You have already blessedness in the root, in the promises; and though there be not assurance, there will be an affiance, and repose of the mind upon God: if there be not rest in your souls, yet there will be a resting upon God, and a quiet expectation of the things hoped for. Faith is satisfied with the promise, and quietly hopes for the performance of it in God’s due time: Lam. iii. 26, ‘It is good that a man should both hope, and quietly wait for the salvation of the Lord.’ Belief is often intermixed with doubtings, yet there will be the patience of hope, that is the least; we should not entertain jealousies and suspicions of God. There is a free promise, though not a certain evidence, and there will be longing, where there is not comfort.

Use 2. To exhort you to work up faith to such an effect, that it may be the substance of things hoped for.

1. Work it up in a way of meditation. Let your minds be exercised in the contemplation of your hopes: Mat. vi. 21, ‘Where your treasure is, there will your heart be.’ There is nothing that you prize but your minds will run upon it. How, freely and frequently can we think of other things, our lusts, our pleasures, our ordinary occasions! and shall we have never a thought of that place where our treasure is? Our God, our Christ, our happiness is there; should not our hearts be there too? Oh! take a turn now and then in the land of promise; see what is made over to you in Christ, think of the beauty and glory of that happiness; surely if we did believe and esteem it, we would have freer thoughts of that heaven, and that happiness God hath made over to us.

2. Work it up in a way of argumentation. Faith is a reasoning grace: Heb. xi. 19, λογισάμενος, ‘Accounting that God was able to raise him even from the dead.’ Reason with yourselves thus: Is there not a blessed estate reserved in heaven for all that come to God in Christ? and so for me if come to Christ? Others have the possession, and thou hast the grant; the deed is sealed, and thou hast the conveyances to show; hast thou it not under God’s hand and seal? hast thou not a promise made to all that believe and repent of their sins, and are willing to walk with God, and are fruitful in good works? Is not heaven made over to such? and God’s promises were ever made good: 2 Cor. i. 20, ‘All the promises of God in him are yea, and in him amen.’ Nay, hath not Christ seized upon heaven in the name of all such as

come to God by him ? And hast thou not had some first-fruits, O my soul, some foretastes, some earnests of the Spirit ? Hath not God given thee a little comfort, a little grace, as an earnest to assure thee of the greater sum ?

3. Work it up in a way of expectation. Look for it, long for it, wait for it: Tit. ii. 13, ' Looking for the blessed hope: ' and Jude, ver. 21, ' Looking for the mercy of God unto eternal life.' I have a gracious God, and a tender-hearted Saviour in heaven ; I am therefore looking and longing till I am called up to the enjoyment of them.

4. Work it up in a way of supplication. Put in thy claim—Lord ! I take hold of the grace offered in the gospel ; and desire the Lord to secure thy claim : Ps. lxxiii. 24, ' Thou shalt guide me with thy counsel, and afterwards receive me to glory ; ' and Ps. xliii. 3, ' O send out thy light, and thy truth ; let them lead me, let them bring me unto thy holy hill, and to thy tabernacle.'

5. Work it up in a way of close and solemn application. In the Lord's supper, there thou comest by some solemn rites to take possession of the privileges of the covenant, and by these rites and ceremonies which God hath appointed, to enter ourselves heirs to all the benefits purchased by Christ, and conveyed in the covenant, especially to the glory of heaven ; there you come to take the cup of blessing as a pledge of the ' New wine in your Father's kingdom,' Mat. xxvi. 29. God here reacheth out to us by deed, or instrument, what was by promise due to every believing sinner before.

6. Work it up in your conversations by constant spiritual diligence. Is heaven sure, so sure as if we had it already, and shall I be idle ? Oh what contriving, carking, striving, fighting, warring is there to get a step higher in the world ! How insatiable are men in the prosecution of their lusts ! and shall I do nothing for heaven, and show no diligence in pursuing my great happiness ? Oh, let me ' work out my salvation with fear and trembling,' Phil. ii. 12. Shall men rise early, and go to bed late, and all for a little maintenance to support a frail tabernacle that is ever dropping into the grave, and crumbling to dust ? and shall I do nothing for my God and everlasting hopes ? Certainly if we did believe these things, we should be more industrious.

Use 3. To press you to get this faith. There are some means and duties that have a tendency hereunto.

1. There must be a serious consideration of God's truth, as it is backed with his absolute power : ' I change not, therefore you are not consumed,' Mal. iii. 6. If either the counsel or the being of God change, it must be out of forgetfulness or weakness. It cannot be out of forgetfulness, for all things past and to come are present to God ; it cannot be out of weakness, for his truth is backed with an absolute power ; therefore a hope founded upon his promise is not liable to distrust. Truth cannot deceive, nor be deceived. Princes and potentates may often break their word out of weakness, lightness, or imprudence, they cannot foresee inconveniences ; their light is bounded as well as their power ; but in God there is no error or mistake ; no weakness and therefore no change: 2 Tim. i. 12, ' I know whom I have believed, and I am persuaded that he is able to keep that which I have committed unto him against that day.' I know I have given up my soul to an

able God; and I have waited for the accomplishment of the will of an able God; and Jude, ver. 24, 'To him that is able to keep you.' Faith stands upon these two supports, God's truth and power; his mercy is engaged by his truth, and dispensed by his power; therefore take this truth and power of God, and cast it into the lap of the soul by faith; and then you may be as certain of the event as if it were already exhibited.

2. You must relieve faith by experiences: by considering what is past we may more easily believe that which is to come.

[1.] Cast in experiences of what is past. The patriarchs believed Christ's coming in the flesh, as we believe and own: John viii. 56, 'Your father Abraham saw my day;' and one miracle doth facilitate and prepare belief for another. The belief of our future greatness is facilitated by the example of his own abasement. When Christ was apparelled with flesh, we may easily believe we shall be clothed with glory. Our misery cannot hinder us from being glorified with God, since Christ's glory did not hinder him from being abased with men. If Christ could die, then a sinner might live. If he can suffer upon a cross, then we may reign in glory. If the greatness of promises raise any doubt, let us look to Christ; for, lest high promises should find no credit with our understanding, God clears up faith by this wonderful instance.

[2.] God hath taken you into an estate of grace and marvellous light; it is a wonderful thing that God should call poor sinners. God hath given us not only promises, but assurances; an earnest as well as his word. All that is past is but a foundation; he that spared you will much more save you; glory and pardon issue out of the womb of the same grace. Nay, glory is a lesser thing than reconcilation, or the first act of pardon. The apostle puts a much more upon it: Rom. v. 10, 'For if when we were enemies, we were reconciled to God by the death of his Son: much more being reconciled, we shall be saved by his life.' When a sinner comes to be accepted into grace, there is the greatest conflict, for there is a great conflict between justice and mercy: therefore it is harder to get the guilty sinner to be absolved, than a pardoned sinner to be blessed. If he has called me, will he not glorify me? As among men it is easier to keep a pardoned man from execution, than to get a guilty man to be pardoned; so the apostle makes it an easier thing to give glory, than it is to give grace and pardon.

[3.] Compare your hopes with carnal hopes. When you look upon your own hopes, you may say with David, Ps. xxxi. 19, 'Oh, how great is thy goodness which thou hast laid up for them that fear thee!' We may say we have a great deal laid up, and a great deal laid out; somewhat in hand, and more in hope. In spiritual matters our expectation comes far short of enjoyment, but in carnal matters the hope is far above the comfort; therefore they are called vanity and vexation of spirit; we expect more, and therefore are vexed with disappointment. Carnal hopes are but like dreams of waking men, that make way for fear and for sorrow. If you live in the hope of much from the world you will be but like dreamers, that have an imaginary content in their sleep, but they meet with real disappointment when they awake; so when we expect much from the creature, we meet with nothing but burden, vanity, and vexation.

[4.] Make it the work of your lives to get your own title confirmed, and assured to the conscience. Christians are to blame for continuing so long in uncertainties, because they do not get their own title confirmed: 1 Tim. vi. 20, 'Laying up in store for yourselves a good foundation against the time to come, that you may lay hold of eternal life.' If you would make eternal life present to the soul, then lay up solid evidences. And mark, he speaks 'laying up' to note this work is always a doing; always we must be laying this foundation.

SERMON III.

And the evidence of things not seen.—Heb. xi. 1.

I come now to the second part of the description—'And the evidence of things not seen.' In which you have—

1. The act—*it is the evidence.*
2. The object—*of things not seen.*

[1.] The act, which belongs chiefly to the understanding, as the other doth to the will. By the first act, faith is the hand of the soul to lay hold of eternal life; by this act, faith is the eye of the soul to look towards it, and represent it to us.

[2.] The object—'Things not seen:' it is of a larger extent than the former. All matters of faith are not future, and the objects of hope, 'things not seen,' is a term more capacious and comprehensive than 'things hoped for.' We believe past and present things as well as future, but we cannot be said to hope for them; as the creation of the world, the deluge, the deliverance of the church out of Egypt and Babylon; Christ's incarnation and passion, his glorious ascension, the effusion of the Holy Ghost upon the apostles; all these things are past, and cannot be called things hoped for; but are here in a more comprehensive expression said to be 'things not seen.' Many present things we believe, as God's providence, the intercession of Christ, the influences of his grace upon the hearts of believers, pardoning mercy; these, because they could not be comprehended in the former 'things hoped for,' are delivered to us in this latter expression, 'things not seen.'

My business mainly is to discourse of the object, 'Things not seen.' But in my way,—

First, Concerning the act. Faith is said to be ἔλεγχος, 'the evidence.' The word is by some rendered the argument of things not seen; by others the demonstration; by us the evidence, and that not altogether unfitly. For though the original word hath a special emphasis, which I shall open by and by; yet this word 'evidence' is of great significancy. Evidence is most proper to objects of sight, and notes clear, distinct, and full apprehension of objects present; therefore the testimony of eye-witnesses in matters of fact, we call it the evidence; and hence it is translated to signify the clear sight of the mind; the clear and satisfactory apprehension is called an evidence, when the object is represented so as the desire of knowledge is fully satisfied concerning the truth and worth of it; for this end doth faith serve in the soul, to give us a satisfactory knowledge of truths delivered in the word. This doth somewhat clear the text.

But we must a little examine the original word: ἔλεγχος is a term of art, and implies a conviction by way of argument and disputation. Aristotle saith, it is συλλόγισμος τῆς ἀντιφάσεως, a convincing argument or dispute, which infers conclusions contradictory to those which we held before. And in this sense it is said in scripture: John xvi. 8, 'The Spirit ἐλέγξει shall convince,' or reprove; so that ἔλεγχος is a confutation of an opinion which men were possessed of before. So it is used Titus i. 9, where, speaking of the office of a minister, ἐλέγχειντούς ἀντιλέγοντας, to convince gainsayers, that is, confute their cavils and prejudices against the truth. Again, the philosopher describes this conviction to be such an arguing by which we prove τὸ μὴ δύνατον ἄλλως ἔχειν ἀγγ᾽ οὕτως ὡς ἡμεῖς λέγομεν—the thing is impossible to be otherwise than we represent. Therefore this was a fit and chosen word by the apostle, to show it was a clear or infallible demonstration of eternal verities delivered in scripture, that the man to whom it is made cannot think otherwise than as it is represented to him. Out of all which we may gather that there is in conviction—

1. A representation of clear grounds.
2. These drawn forth in argument and discourse.
2. A confutation of prejudices.
4. A sweet constraint of the mind to assent and subscribe to the truths delivered. All these are in faith—

[1.] A clearness and perspicuity of light.
[2.] A seriousness of arguing and dispute.
[3.] Confuting of prejudices.
[4.] A sweet consent, or rational enforcement of the mind, a compulsion of the soul by reasons, an answerable assent to the truth of religion as certain and worthy; as I shall declare in this following discourse.

I shall wind up all in this doctrine,

Doct. That true faith is an evidence or convincing light concerning eternal verities. Or take it thus:—It is a grace that representeth the things of religion with such clearness and perspicuity of argument, that a believer is compelled to subscribe to the truth and worth of them; as a man yieldeth, when he seeth clear evidence to the contrary.

There are in faith four things:—

1. A clear light and apprehension. As soon as God converteth the soul, he puts light into it. In the old world you know the first thing that God made was light; so in the new creation, when he comes to convert sinners he infuseth light, brings in a stock and frame of knowledge into the soul; therefore it is said, Heb. viii. 10, 'I will put my laws into their minds, and write them in their hearts'—the first

and great privilege of the covenant.   There is a double allusion.   ' I
will put my law into their minds;' that alludes to the ark, as the
tables were kept in the ark; 'I will write it upon their hearts;' as
the law was written upon the tables, so God writes it upon their
hearts; so doth God do at first conversion; and therefore wherever
there is faith, there must be light.   It is true, this change is not so
sensible; light enters, like a sunbeam, gently and without violence;
God opens the window, and draws the curtain.   This is a most necessary act.   Yet there is a sensible difference afterwards: Eph. v. 8,
' Ye were sometimes darkness, but now are ye light in the Lord.'   The
devil carrieth on his kingdom by blindness and darkness, and Christ
governs by light.   The devil keeps men in bondage and captivity by
blinding their eyes, by casting a veil of prejudices before their eyes:
2 Cor. iv. 4, ' The God of this world hath blinded the minds of them
which believe not.'   And God recovers them out of this captivity by
opening their eyes: Acts xxvi. 18, ' To open their eyes, to turn them
from darkness to light, and from the power of Satan to God.'   There
cannot be any act of a rational soul about an object without knowledge
or light.   And therefore when God would draw our consent to his
covenant, he begins with the understanding, and the light of the
glorious gospel shines in upon us.   That which is unknown is neither
believed, nor hoped for, nor desired, nor laboured after.   When Christ
saith to the blind man, John ix. 35, 36, ' Dost thou believe in the Son
of God ? ' he answered, ' Who is he, Lord, that I might believe on him ?'
Certainly that which we believe we must have a thorough sight of.
I say, a man must understand things before he will close with them,
and receive them.   And therefore the first thing that God doth is to
give us a mind to know him : 1 John v. 20, ' And we know that the
Son of God is come, and hath given us an understanding that we may
know him that is true:' and the new creature is created in knowledge,
Col. iii. 10, that so it may be able to act with reason and judgment
towards objects proper for it: for, according as things are known, so
they powerfully draw and attract the heart.   The understanding is the
great wheel of the soul, and guide of the whole man; therefore there
must be something done to satisfy that; grace will begin there, and
there the Lord sets up the light of faith.   As sense is the light of
beasts, and reason the light of men, so faith is the light of christians.
And as there is a distinct light, so there is much argument and discourse.   God lays up principles, and faith lays them out; it is a
prudent steward and dispenser of the knowledge which God hath
treasured up in the heart; therefore when unbelief makes opposition,
and when the heart is careless, then faith fetcheth the law out of the
ark, and pleadeth and argueth with the soul.   As upon the approach
of an enemy against a country they draw out their forces; so doth
faith bring forth the force of the soul, use reason and discourse, and
draw conclusions out of the principles of the word, that it may beat
its enemy.   Reason is the great enemy of faith; and when it is sanctified it is the great servant of faith; by discourse and disputing it doth
convince the soul: Rom. vi. 11, ' Reckoning yourselves,' or reason
yourselves by argument, 'that you are dead to sin, and alive to God;'
Rom. viii. 18, ' I reckon that the sufferings of this present time are

not worthy to be compared with the glory that shall be revealed in us;'
that is, I reason thus. And it is said of Abraham, Heb. xi. 19, ' He
accounted that God was able to raise him;' he reasoned the case thus
within himself, There is nothing impossible to God. This is the great
advantage of a believer when he can draw out particular discourses
and arguments, and fortify himself by such conclusions as are opposite
to his particular distrust and trouble, when he can reason from his
happiness to come, his interest in Christ. By this means faith doth
set on either the promise or the threatening ; as suppose, if the heart
be backward, and loath to come to the work of mortification. If
it be given to carnal pleasure, faith comes and reasons thus, Rom.
viii. 13, ' If you live after the flesh, you shall die,' but you do live
after the flesh, therefore you shall die; but if you through the Spirit
mortify the deeds of the body, ye shall live—if you will take pains in
the exercise of religion, though severe for the present, yet it shall be
sweet for the time to come, you shall live. That is the reason why
the word is full of syllogisms and discourses ; they are but copies of
what faith doth in the heart.

2. Faith is a convictive light, that findeth us corrupt and ill-princi-
pled, and full of prejudices against the doctrine of the gospel ; and it
is the work of faith to root out of the soul those carnal prejudices,
carnal counsels, carnal reasonings, and carnal excuses which rise up,
and exclude and shut out that doctrine which the gospel offereth to
us.

[1.] Against the truth of the gospel. The heart of man is naturally
full of malice and atheism. Man is not white paper, he is prepossessed
with thoughts ' that exalt themselves against the knowledge of God in
Christ Jesus,' 2 Cor. x. 6. The truths of religion are opposite to corrupt
desires, and these desires have leavened the soul with carnal prejudices,
and this begets jealousies and suspicious reluctations. Now it is the work
of faith to captivate and subdue those thoughts, to batter down those
prejudices that lift up themselves against the knowledge of God and
obedience of Christ. And therefore one great work of the Spirit is,
to reprove and convince the world not only of sin, but of righteousness and judgment, John xvi. 8 ; the Spirit doth it as the author, and
faith as the instrument. We are leavened with these evil maxims,
that sin is not so dangerous as it is represented to be ; that holiness is
not so necessary ; that the doctrines of Christ are but fables ; and
therefore the apostle saith, 2 Peter i. 16. ' We have not followed
cunningly devised fables, when we made known unto you the power
and coming of our Lord Jesus Christ ;' implying that there is such a
thought in the heart of man. Man hath a great many sottish conceits
of all these things, but especially of the gospel ; for conscience will
sooner yield to moral truths than truths evangelical, and the doctrine
which concerns the happiness of another world. We are by nature
sooner convinced of sin than of righteousness, our thoughts being more
presagious of evil than of good, because of the guilt ; conscience seeing
nothing but sin, can infer nothing but punishment ; but we had need
be convinced of all three, sin, righteousness, and judgment. It is notable that there is no figure so common in scripture as a *prolepsis*, or

anticipation of objections. Divine doctrine findeth us full of prejudices, and there is an aversion, or bearing off in the intellective faculty, as well as a dissent. Now faith never leaveth till it bringeth in other principles.

[2.] Great prejudices there are against the worth of the gospel: 1 Cor. ii. 14, 'The natural man receiveth not the things of the Spirit of God: for they are foolishness unto him; neither can he know them, because they are spiritually discerned.' If we be convinced that there are such things as the scripture sets forth, we are not convinced of their worth, when we do acknowledge their being; we think it a folly to be troubled about things that are to come; that a man may be saved without so much ado; and why should he venture himself upon the displeasure of the world, and the consequences of it on things that will fall out we know not when? These conceits we are leavened with: but faith is a convincing light that will disprove those corrupt and carnal principles we drink in.

3. It is an overpowering and certain conviction, that is, such as dispossesseth us of our corrupt principles and grounds, and argueth us into a contrary opinion and contrary belief. Men may have some knowledge of the gospel, and yet not have faith; they may have some smitings of heart, and disapprove of the principles wherewith they are led, and practices wherein they walk, and yet have not faith, but only a loose and wavering opinion of the things of God. Then is the soul convinced, when it is rationally, and above all cavil and contradiction, constrained to consent to the truth and worth of the things propounded in the covenant; when there is a subduing and silencing of all those carnal principles and reasonings which were wont to prevail against the truth. What the apostle saith of the great truth of the gospel, the grand article of the christian faith, Christ's dying for sinners, is true of the whole frame: 1 Tim. i. 15, 'This is a faithful saying, and worthy of all acceptation, that Jesus Christ came into the world to save sinners.' These things are propounded by faith, so as to beget a firm assent to them as true, and a consent to embrace and pursue them as good. In these two expressions, 'faithful and worthy of all acceptation,' the apostle showeth what faith aims at; it represents the whole frame of religion as true; and it representeth religion as worthy of all acceptation, and then the sanctified will doth embrace it. So that the first part of the conviction of faith is a subscription to the truth. The conviction of faith bringeth the soul to a certain assent, how contrary soever it seem to sense or reason; though it seeth nothing in sense, yet it seeth a clear certainty in the word. For though there can no reason be given of the things believed, yet faith seeth reason enough why we should believe them, and so close with them upon the authority of God speaking in the word. Faith, as the substance of things hoped for, resteth upon the power of God: but as it is the evidence of things not seen, so it resteth upon the truth of God. By this firm assent the soul doth so close with truth, that it can never be divorced: 1 Thes. i. 5, 'Ye received the word with much assurance, and with much affliction,' ver. 6. Though it be contrary to inward dispositions, and though it expose to outward troubles, yet they had much assurance and evidence within themselves. Alas! men may talk of Christ and

heaven, and have some cold opinions about things to come ; they may deliver this to others, but still their evil scent remaineth with them, and their evil principles taint their hearts, and sway their practices all this while ; ' and they do not know the grace of God in truth,' Col. i. 6, and have not any sense of that they seem to know. No, a natural man cannot be brought to look upon the things of religion as every way certain, and above all contradiction, and to say with the apostle : Phil. i, 9, 'That their love abounds yet more and more in knowledge and in all judgment.' As cooks may dress meat for the master of the family, and his friends and children, but themselves taste not of it ; so carnal men may learn things in a disciplinary way ; they may know the literal meaning and sense of the promises, but are not convinced of the truth, and of the spiritual real worth of them ; that is, they have not a thorough sound persuasion and solid apprehension of the sinfulness of sin, of the beauty of holiness, of the excellency of Christ, of the preciousness of the covenant, of the rich treasures of grace ; *Hæc audiunt quasi somniantes.* Carnal men hear them as if they were in a dream ; they look upon and entertain these things as fancies, or dreams of golden mountains, or showers of pearl falling out of the clouds in a night dream.

4. It is a practical conviction. He that believeth is so convinced of the truth and worth of these things, that he is resolved to pursue after them, to make preparation for his eternal condition. Answerable to the discovery of good and evil in the understanding, there is a prosecution or an aversation in the will ; for the will necessarily follows the ultimate resolution of the judgment. Now many men have a partial conviction, but they are not thoroughly possessed of the truth and worth of heavenly things ; there is a simple approbation, but not a comparative approbation, so as to draw off the heart from other things, and ultimately to incline and bend the heart to look after them ; that is, by a simple approbation they may apprehend that it is good to be in covenant with God, but they do not like the terms. But now the last and practical conviction is, when it draweth the soul to an actual choice, when it begets not only a simple approbation, but a practical decree, when the soul saith, 'It is good for me to draw nigh to God,' Ps. lxxiii. 28 ; when, all things considered, a man is convinced that he ought to look after heaven upon God's terms. It is one thing to desire a commodity simply, another thing to accept of it at such a rate and price. Many men like pardon of sin, and eternal life, and come and cheapen the great things of the gospel, but they do not go through with the bargain. This is the conviction of faith when it makes us sell all to buy the pearl of great price, and sways the whole man to pursue and look after those things God hath propounded. Thus faith brings the soul to a consent ; it convinceth not only of the truth, but the worth of religion, and proposeth it as fit for choice. This is the end of all knowledge and understanding : Ps. cxi. 10, 'A good understanding have all they that keep his commandments.' Those that know God aright, they love him also ; they know him as they are known of him. Now God knows us to love us, and to choose us, and to assume us to himself in Christ ; so we know him, when we love him, and choose him for our portion. There cannot be a greater

despite done to God, than to know God and choose the world; saith Christ, John xv. 24, 'You have both seen, and hated both me and my Father.' This is a hatred of God, when we have known God and yet turned aside to the world. Faith draweth altogether unto choice; doth not merely fill the head, but enters into the heart; it is a prudent and full consent. And that is the reason why faith is not only opposed to ignorance but to folly: Luke xxiv. 25, 'O fools, and slow of heart to believe,' &c, for there may be folly where there is not ignorance. Every wicked man in Solomon's sense is a fool. Then do we believe matters of salvation indeed, when we consent to them as good and worthy to be embraced: Rom. vii. 16, 'I consent to the law, that it is good.' They see the ways of God are best and most satisfactory, then the practical judgment is gained.

Use. To put us upon examination and trial, whether we have such a faith or no, as is an evidence or convincing light; you may try it by the parts of it. There is the assent of faith and the consent of faith; a clear light and firm assent, and a free consent to the worth of the things of God.

1. There is a clearness and perspicuity in the light of faith, which doth not only exclude the grossly ignorant, but those that have no saving knowledge. All wicked men, though never so knowing, and never so learned, and never so well accomplished with the furniture of gifts, they are under the power of darkness. There is 'a form of knowledge,' Rom. ii. 20, as well as 'a form of godliness;' there is but a model of truth in their brains, a naked speculation; they may be able to discourse of the things of God, yet they cannot be said to have the life of God. A wild plant and a garden plant have the same name and common nature, yet differ much in their operations and virtues; so do common knowledge and the light of faith. There are two differences.

[1.] The light of faith is full of efficacy, the other not. Common water and strong water are alike in colour, but much differ in their efficacy, virtue and taste; so the common knowledge of men, though for the object it may reach as far as the light of faith, a carnal man may know all that a believer knows, yet there is not such an efficacy. This light doth not discharge its office to encourage to confidence, to quicken to obedience, to fill the heart with gladness; this light never enters upon the affections—'Wisdom entereth not upon his heart,' Prov. ii. 10. Though they have knowledge, yet they are 'barren and unfruitful in the knowledge of Christ,' 2 Peter i. 8. It is light, but it doth little good, it is idle and ineffectual, it doth not ascend to the affections or practice.

[2.] The light of faith is full of practical discourses, always reasoning and improving the truth. The devil diverteth wicked men; though they have eyes, yet there are no holy arguings. The heathens are described to have 'a vain mind, and a dark heart,' Eph. iv. 17, 18. The apostle means they are full of vain principles, dark in their understandings, corrupt in their inferences. Their heart was blind which should have directed them in the ordering their conversations. A wicked man doth not discourse of things in the time and season of them. The mind of a christian is stirred up by faith to holy reasonings: This will be your portion, and the fruit of such doings. It is said of Mary,

Luke ii. 19, 'She kept these sayings, and pondered them in her heart;' she traversed them in her mind by reason and discourse.

2. We may know whether faith be an evidence by the firmness of our consent. Most flatter themselves in this, they think they do not doubt of the principles of religion, but surely close with the truth of the word, yet this evidence is wanting; for if men were more convinced, there would be a greater conformity in their practices to the rules of religion. Our consent is very weak; how does it appear? Partly, because sense is more believed than the word. We build more upon assurances of our own devising, than upon that which God hath given us. Our Saviour impersonates all our thoughts in that speech, Luke xvi. 31, 'If one went unto them from the dead, they will not repent;' we think the prophets have not spoken so feelingly and mournfully, as one from the dead would, if they should come from the flames. When we will indent with God, as the Jews, Mat. xxvii. 40, 'If he be the Son of God, let him come down from the cross, and we will believe in him;' or, as the devil himself, who proposed such terms to Christ, Mat. iv. 3, 'If thou be the Son of God, command these stones to be made bread.' Partly, because temporal things do work far more with us than spiritual; we fear temporal death more than spiritual, and will lose spiritual contentments for fleshly. And partly, because we are not affected with the things of religion as we would be, if they were before our eyes; if we had with Stephen a sight of heaven, or if we could behold Christ in his glory, or coming in his majesty, these things would make us more careful.

But we may know whether the light of the gospel doth shine into our minds with such a convincing overpowering light; and our hearts are possessed of the truth and worth of what God propounds in his covenant, by three effects of faith; the mind, the heart, and the life will be altered.

[1.] The judgment will be altered. Thou wilt have other apprehensions of God, Christ, and eternity; heaven and hell will seem to you other things than they did. Before they were looked upon but as fancies, and as things talked of in jest; but now they will be apprehended as high and important realities, about which the soul is deeply concerned: Eph. i. 18, 'The eyes of your understandings being enlightened, that ye may know what is the hope of his calling, and what the riches of the glory of his inheritance in the saints.' When our natural blindness is removed, there is another manner of discerning things, and a sounder, belief of them than before; then a man was in darkness, now he sees by another light, now he hath eyes indeed. As they say in nature, *non dantur puræ tenebræ*, there is no such thing as pure darkness; so it is true in moral things also. In a state of nature there is not pure darkness; there are some glimmerings of an everlasting state, and some superficial apprehensions more or less in men according to the advantages of their education. But now their eyes are opened; they have another judgment about these things; they are clearly discerned, so as to shake and move the heart, and pierce the soul to the quick.

[2.] The heart will be altered. When faith gives us a sight of things, the heart is warmed with love to things so seen; 'Being persuaded, they embraced,' Heb. xi. 13. Affection follows persuasion. When we are soundly persuaded, then the heart embraceth, closeth with them, and entertaineth them with the tenderest welcome of our souls; whereas before we talked of heaven and hell in jest, now we mind them in downright earnestness. The light and knowledge of heaven and hell that we had by education, tradition, customary talking, reading and hearing, it never pierceth the soul to the quick, never warmeth the affections; but when we have this evidence concerning things to come and things unseen, then the heart is affected.

[3.] The life will be altered. Art thou taken off from earthly things and wordly vanities, and seriously set a-work to make provision for eternity? I tell you, the most visible and sensible effect of a sound conviction is a diligent pursuit, when a man is set a-work by the notions he hath of God, Christ, and eternity; 1 Cor. ix. 26, ' Therefore I so run, not as uncertainly: I so fight, not as one that beats the air.' Oh then, there is running, striving, fighting. The man is certainly persuaded of things to come, and he will be taken off from those trifles and childish toys which did engross the former part of his life; and then all thy thoughts, and serious cares, and fears will be diverted into another channel, and taken up about those better things which thou art convinced of by faith. Faith hath light in it, such a light as finds us corrupted, but dispossesseth us of those evil affections, and sways our practice. Therefore, are your judgments, your hearts, and your lives altered? by this you may know whether you have been acquainted with this work of faith namely, as it is ' an evidence of things not seen.'

SERMON IV.

And the evidence of things not seen.—HEB. xi. 1.

Secondly, I come to the object, ' Things not seen.' Faith is an evidence, but what kind of evidence? of things that cannot be otherwise seen, which doth not disparage the evidence, but declare the excellency of faith. ' Not seen,' that is, not liable to the judgment of sense and reason.

What are those ' things not seen'? Things may either be invisible in regard of their nature, or of their distance and absence from us. Some things are invisible in their own nature—as God, angels, and spirits; and all the way and work of the Holy Ghost in and about the spiritual life. Other things are invisible in regard of their distance and absence; and so things past and to come are invisible; we cannot see them with our bodily eyes, but they are discovered to us by faith. In short, these ' things not seen,' are either matters of constant practical experience, which are not liable to outward sense, or principles of knowledge, which are not suitable to natural reason.

1. Matters of practical experience. The blessings of religion as the enduring substance, Heb. x. 34, the benefit of affliction, the rewards and supplies of the spiritual life, answers of prayer, they are things

not seen in regard of the bodily eye and carnal feeling; but faith expects them with as much assurance as if they were corporeally present, and could be felt and handled, and is assuredly persuaded of them, as if they were before our eyes.

2. Principles of knowledge. There are many mysteries in religion above reason; until nature put on the spectacles of faith, it cannot see them; as the incarnation of Christ, the doctrine of the trinity, natural parts cannot discern the truth or worth of them; they find no sap, or savour in the truths of the gospel. They are unseen to reason, but faith makes them clear to the soul.

Doct. That the evidence of faith is conversant about things unseen by sense or natural reason.

The point admits of much speculative debate, but I shall handle it only in a practical way.

That faith is conversant about things unseen I shall prove by three reasons taken from the differences of time.

1. Because much of religion is past, and we have bare testimony and revelation to warrant it; as the creation of the world out of nothing, the incarnation, life, and death of Christ; these are truths not liable to sense, and unlikely to reason—that the vine should grow upon one of its own branches, that God should become a man, and die. Now upon the revelation of the word, the Spirit of God makes all evident to faith. As the centurion, when he saw the miracles of Christ's death said, ' Truly this was the Son of God,' Mat. xxvii. 54; so by the Spirit in the hearts of believers, they are convinced, surely this is no other than the word of God. Faith can see God veiled under a curtain of flesh, and Christ the Son of God hanging and dying on a cross. Yea the more impossible the thing is to nature, the fitter object of faith, when it is accompanied with divine testimony. If carnal reason object against these things, we must renounce and give it the lie when it contradicts divine truth; for though the truths of the gospel are hidden and strange to reason, they are open and evident to faith. There are several lights God hath set up in the world, and they must keep their place; there is sense, which is the light of beasts; reason, which is the light of men; faith, which is the light of saints; and vision, which is the light of glory: now all these lights are not contrary, but subordinate. If we should examine all things by sense, we should lay aside many things evident to reason; as to sense a star is no bigger than a spangle, or spark; but reason knows, because of the distance, we must much otherwise conceive of them. So if we should lift up reason against faith we should discard many principles and articles of religion which are of greatest concernment. It is an old error to oppose the course of nature to God's word. Those mockers in Peter erred, because they examined things by sense: 2 Peter iii. 4, ' All things continue as they were from the beginning of the creation.' When men will believe nothing above their reason, and above their sense, it is a sign they want the light which God hath set up in the church, the light of faith, Jude 19, ' Sensual, not having the Spirit.' Men that go according to reason only, go most against reason; nothing can be more irrational than to consult with nature about supernatural things, and to fetch the judgment of spiritual things from sense; it is all one

as if we should bring down all rational affairs to the judgment of sense, and seek a law for man among beasts ; reason must not be captivated to fancy, but to faith.   Much of religion is past, and consists of articles unknown.

2. Much of religion is yet to come, and therefore can only be discerned by faith.   Fancy and nature cannot outsee time, and look beyond death : 2 Peter i. 9, ' He that lacketh these things,' that is, that lacketh faith, and other graces that do accompany it, 'is blind, and cannot see afar off ; ' unless faith hold the candle to hope, we cannot see heaven at so great a distance.   Heaven and the glorious rewards of religion are yet to come ; faith only can see heaven in the promises and look upon the gospel as travailing in birth with a great salvation.   Faith must supply the room of sense, and believe heaven though it see it not, and look for it though we enjoy it not.   As reason must not jostle out faith, so faith must not be uncertain, though it cannot aspire to the light of glory.   The apostle saith, ' We walk by faith, not by sight,' 2 Cor. v. 7 ; that is our light here.   Graceless souls may be sharp-sighted in all things that concern their temporal interest, and talk of the affairs of the present world ; but as for the things of the other world they are stark blind.

3. That of religion which is of actual and present enjoyment, sense or reason cannot discern the truth or worth of it ; therefore faith is still the evidence of things unseen.

[1.] It cannot discern the truth of it.   There are few things in religion but the truth of them is contradicted by carnal sense.   Eternal life is promised to us, but first we must be dead ; the resurrection of the body, but first we must moulder to dust in the grave.   Blessedness is promised to us at last, but in the meantime we are of all men most miserable ; a comfortable supply of all things, but in the meantime we hunger and suffer thirst.   God saith he will be a present help in a time of trouble, but he seems to be deaf to our prayers ; therefore faith is conversant about things present.   The carrying on the work of grace is a thing invisible : Col. iii. 3, 'Our life is hid with Christ in God.' I say, the secret power and influence, by which grace is fed and maintained, is carried on from step to step in despite of devils or men. Therefore the apostle begs, Eph. i. 18, 'That their eyes might be opened ; ' why ? what should they discern ?—'that they might know the hope of their calling, and the riches of the glory of his inheritance in the saints.'   The power that goes to the maintaining of grace, till we come to the possession of the rich and glorious inheritance which God hath provided for us, it is a matter of faith not of sense.   What would become of us, if faith did not supply the place of sense, and the promise did not make amends for enjoyment ?   That phrase of ' living by faith,' is always used in opposition to present feeling.   It is mentioned in four places of scripture, twice in the case of justification, Rom. i. 17, Gal. iii. 11, when we are dead in law, lost in the sense of our own consciences ; then when we can cast ourselves upon the mercies of God in Christ, this is living by faith.   And it is used twice in the case of great troubles and anxiety ; when we have nothing else to live upon but our own sorrows and tears, when the destroyer in the land wasted and devoured all they had, then ' the just shall live by faith,'

Hab. ii. 4. So when their goods were plundered, Heb. x. 34, then 'the just shall live by faith,' ver. 38, so that the whole life of a christian is made up of riddles ; and faith is still opposite to sense. This indeed is living by faith, to see that in God which is wanting in the creature. The whole business of christianity is nothing else, but a contradicting of sense ; God's dealing seemeth often to make against his promise, and his way is contrary to the judgment of the carnal mind. Where would religion be were it not for faith ?

[2.] As the truth of religion is not always visible to sense, so the worth of religion is checked by carnal reason : 1 Cor. ii. 14, 'The natural man receiveth not the things of the Spirit, neither can he receive them, because they are spiritually discerned.' Carnal reason judgeth it to be a foolish thing to renounce present delights and present advantages. Suffering zeal seemeth peevishness and frowardness to a carnal judgment and active zeal a fond niceness. Look, as astronomers have invented names of bears, lions, dragons, for those things which are glorious stars in the heavens; so doth carnal reason miscall all the graces of the Holy Spirit. When a men makes conscience of his ways, carnal reason says that which carnal men do, We shall have you turn fool now! So that he that will be wise to salvation, must become one of the world's fools, that he may be wise, 1 Cor. iii. 18. Therefore that we may be sincere and strict in religion, and faithful with God, willing to do and willing to suffer, there is need of faith, that we may quit visible conveniences for invisible rewards, and despise things that are seen for things that are not seen : 2 Cor. iv. 18. 'While we look not at the things which are seen, but at the things which are not seen ; for the things which are seen are temporal, but the things which are not seen are eternal.' That made the apostles renounce worldly interests, and mortify carnal affections. Faith discovered a worth and beauty in things not seen to reason and sense.

Having showed that faith is an evidence, and such an evidence as falls upon things that are not seen, I shall show now what is the advantage of this in the spiritual life ; for to that end doth the apostle bring this description, that they may live by faith. The use of it is exceeding great.

(1.) To embolden us against the difficulties and inconveniences of our pilgrimage. When we look to things seen, we may descry as many enemies as creatures, and are ready to cry out, as the prophet's man, 'Alas, Master, what shall we do ?' 1 Kings vi. 15. Now faith presents invisible supplies in visible dangers. If Satan be at our left hand ready to resist us, God is at our right hand ready to strengthen us. If men pursue us with their hatred and displeasure, faith represents God following us with his love and kindness. It is said of Moses : Heb. xi. 27, 'By faith he forsook Egypt, not fearing the wrath of the king ; for he endured, as seeing him who is invisible.' Moses would run the hazard of Pharaoh's wrath ,would turn his back upon such a fertile land as Egypt was, to go with the people of God into the wilderness, and all because he saw invisible things. Faith sees God assisting in a spiritual manner, and then all difficulties are reconciled and all terrors that arise from visible things are mitigated and made more comportable by invisible supplies.

(2.) To help us to bear afflictions, out of a hope of a comfortable issue. Faith can see fruit budding out of the dry rod of affliction. Ask sense, and it will tell you of nothing but aches and smart: Heb. xii. 11, 'No affliction for the present seemeth joyous, but grievous.' For the present it is a grievous thing to lie under the strokes of God's providence. If we should consult with present feeling, we should be like children, nothing but howl; but now faith can prophesy glad tidings at midnight, and see quietness and pleasantness in the midst of smart, and rich incomes of grace and purposes of love, when God seems to deal roughly with us.

(3.) It is of use to unfold the riddles of providence. The dispensations of God are full of mysteries; the way is shame when the end is glory. There is a handwriting of providence which is like Belshazzar's, we cannot read it; usually like the Hebrew tongue, it must be read quite backwards. Christ brews the water of life out of gall, wormwood, and blood. Joseph must be sold, then honoured; first a slave, then a favourite; cast into the dungeon, that he may be preferred at court. When God meant to bless Jacob, he makes him halt and lame, for he breaketh his thigh. The empty bucket goes down into the pit that it may come up full. Now nothing is out of order to providence, therefore nothing is out of order to faith. In the saddest providences, faith expects a good issue: Ps. lxxiii. 1, 'Truly God is good to Israel.' At the end of the six days God saw all that he had made, and behold it was very good; so for these six thousand years all his works of providence are good, very good. Faith, ploughing with God's heifer, comes to learn his designs: Job xi. 6, 'And that he would show thee the secrets of wisdom, that it is double to that which is; know therefore that God exacteth of thee less than thine iniquity deserveth.' Divine providence hath two faces; that which is visible and outward is full of rigour, and God seems to be against us. Ay, but there is that which is not seen, and there is love, and sweetness, and clemency; like a picture, here the face of a virgin, there the form of a serpent. That which is not seen to sense is a thousand times more comely than the surface. Common light can discern nothing of this mixture: Eccles. viii. 14, 'In the day of adversity consider.' Some lessons are easy to sense, but others are hard enough to faith. Sense judges only of the outside, and bark, and rind of God's dispensations, and therefore we are perplexed and at a stand; but faith goes into the sanctuary, Ps. lxxiii. 17, and consults with God's word, and looks within the veil, and engageth us to wait, and teacheth us how to solve the dark riddles of providence. There are secret and invisible things which God maketh known to waiting souls.

(4.) To help us in duties of charity, that we may be rich in good works. The loss and detriment that cometh to our estates by large distributions, in doing worthily for God in our generation, by helping the poor, relieving the needy, promoting the ordinances of God; the loss is visible; ay, but faith sees it made up again, and that there is no such usury as lending to God. This is a duty where faith is most sensibly acted; here God proveth faith, and here we prove God. 1. We prove God—'Prove me, saith the Lord, by riches and offerings;' Mal. iii. 10. 'If I will not open you the window of heaven, and pour you out a blessing.' Here faith maketh sensible experiments, and adventureth upon God's word. God giveth us a bill of exchange; we have nothing but a promise for what we lay out upon a work of religion: Prov. xix. 17, 'He that hath pity upon the poor lendeth unto the Lord; and that which he hath given will he pay him again.' Charity and alms is a kind of traffic, and there is a great deal of faith and trust exercised in it, if he lay out a sum upon his word and bond. A carnal mind thinks all lost and gone because he will not take God's word; but now he that believes can see profit temporal and spiritual to arise out of this. 2. Here also God trieth us—'Faith is the evidence of things not seen.' You see no profit, but can you believe it? Eccles. xi. 1, 'Cast thy bread upon the waters; for thou shalt find it after many days.' When a man goes about doing good, such liberal distributions to a carnal mind are but like sowing the seed in a moorish ground, or like ploughing the sea; as foolish and as vain a course as if a man should cast his bread, that is, his bread corn, upon the waters. The vulgar read it *super transeuntes aquas*, cast it upon the running stream. We cannot look for a crop out of the water; it is carried down the stream, and a man shall never see it again. Ay, but faith, which is an evidence of things not seen, will help us in this case even to distribute our substance, for God will make it up again. When you can wait upon God contrary to sense and experience, then you have the true kind of faith.

(5.) In desertion, when God hides himself, faith only can find him out. When all comforts are lost to sense, they are present to faith. Faith can see God under his mask and veil: Isa. xlv. 15, 'Verily thou art a God that hidest thyself, O God of Israel, the Saviour.' When God means to be a saviour, he may hide himself, but faith waiteth upon him in the deepest and blackest desertion. John ii. 4, Christ rebukes the Virgin Mary—'Woman, what have I to do with thee? mine hour is not yet come;' yet ver. 5, 'His mother saith unto the servants, Whatsoever he saith unto you, do it.' She had received a sharp rebuke from Christ, yet she knew he would do something, and therefore saith, 'Fill the waterpots.' True faith can pick love out of God's angry speeches, and draw gracious conclusions from the blackest and hardest premises. Saith Job, if he shall kill me, and lay more terrors upon me, 'Though he slay me, yet will I trust in him,' Job xiii. 15; and saith David, Ps. xlii. 11, 'Hope in God, for I shall yet praise him.' When there are no apparent evidences, all comforts and graces are spent, there is not a drop of oil in the cruse, nor a dust of meal in the barrel; yet hope can hang upon a small thread. They will wait, trust, and look for something of favour from God.

(6.) This faith is necessary to believe the spiritual mysteries of religion. So faith sees a virtue in Christ's death: Gal. ii. 20, 'Nevertheless I live; yet not I, but Christ liveth in me; and the life which I live in the flesh I live by the faith of the Son of God, who loved me, and gave himself for me.' This is a mere riddle to sense, so to believe the salutary and gracious fruits and effects of christian ordinances, which are to appearance mean and poor, but the worth and fruit of them is unseen. Saith Tertullian, *Nihil adeo ac offendit hominum mentes, quam simplicitas divinorum operum*, there is nothing offends men's minds so much as the simplicity of his ordinances. Plain preaching seems a poor, useless thing; a vain artifice to catch souls, it is as much despised by carnal reason in the heart, as it is by vain men in the world, yet this is God's way to convert the soul: 1 Cor. i. 21, 'It pleased God by the foolishness of preaching to save them that believe.' The waters of baptism heathens were offended at, when christians talked of such glorious things as to be born again, united to Christ, possessed of the Spirit, and they could see nothing but going down into the water. To find spiritual comfort and ravishing joy in the Lord's supper, when we see nothing but a piece of bread and a draught of wine; for ordinances that have no pomp and splendid appearance in them, yet to be sanctified to the most high and mysterious uses of our religion, this is that which is matter of faith.

(7.) That we may look for life in the hour of death. When sense and understanding is departing, oh! then to comfort ourselves with the love of God that shall never depart; to look for life and resurrection among dry bones, and to look on the grave as a place not of destruction, but of delivery—these are all things unseen, and require faith to believe them. Who would think such a pale horse as death should be sent from Christ to carry us to glory? and that the funerals of the body shall not be the funerals of the christian, but only of his sin and of his frailty? *Miseria moritur, homo non moritur;* it is but a shed taken down, that it may be raised in a better structure; that the way to live for ever is to die first, that we may be killed and not hurt; to believe that the morsels for the worms should be parcels of the resurrection: Job xix. 26. 'Though after my skin worms destroy this body, yet in my flesh shall I see God;' and then to send our flesh in hope to the grave: Ps. xvi. 9, 'My flesh also shall rest in hope;' to go to the grave as a bed of ease and chamber of rest, of which Christ keeps the keys; all this is matter of faith. Our Saviour saith, John xi. 25, 'He that believeth in me, though he were dead, yet he shall live;' he puts the question, 'Believest thou this?' ver. 26; nothing else will assure it you. But have you faith? David puts the supposition: Ps. xxiii. 4, 'Though I walk in the valley of the shadow of death, I will fear no evil, for thou art with me;' though I walk side by side with death; though my bones be cast into a common charnel, and I converse with skulls, yet Christ will look after this dust, and those rotten relics of mortality. Faith must assure and persuade us of all this.

(8.) To believe a change of the greatest flourish and outward prosperity. When men have such a high mountain as seems to stand strong, who would think that it can ever be removed? Wickedness regnant and triumphant is ruinous and tottering in the eye of faith: Micah iv. 11, 12, 'Many nations are gathered together against Zion, that say, let her be defiled, and let our eye look upon Zion; yet they know not the thoughts of the Lord, nor understand his counsel.' In private cases, to look upon unjust gain that comes in plentifully upon us as a certain loss, and to see God's curse upon great and ill-gotten revenues; to determine, that 'better is a little with righteousness, than great revenues without right,' Prov. xvi. 8. How better? If we consult with sense, there is no such thing; but faith assures us. Would men make haste to be rich if they had this rich faith? it would tell them, This is the way to bring ruin upon themselves and their posterity: to see ruin in the midst of abundance, and loss in the midst of gain; that righteousness is the only way of gain, and scattering the **ready**

way to increase, is the work of faith: Prov. xi. 24, 'There is that
scattereth, and yet increaseth ; and there is that withholdeth more than
is meet, and it tendeth to poverty.' Thus you see this faith runs through
all religion, and hath an influence upon every practical thing almost.

Use 1. Information. I shall draw from hence four practical corollaries.
If the object of faith be things unseen, then,

1. Christians should not murmur if God keep them low and bare,
and they have nothing they can see to live upon. As long as they do
their duty, they are in the hands of God's providence. If God exercise them with troubles, humble them with wants, and delay their
hopes, they have a faith which should be instead of vision and enjoyment ; and when they want all things, they should be as ' possessing all
things,' 2 Cor. vi. 10. They have an all-sufficient God to trust to, a
God that bears the purse for them. If you are reduced to hard short
allowance, live upon the promise—a believer has all things in the
promise, though nothing in possession. This is the happiness of heaven,
that God is all in all without the intervention of means. This life of
faith is heaven antedated and begun, to see all in God in the midst of
greatest wants.

2. In the greatest extremity that can befall us there is work for faith,
but no place for discouragement ; your faith is never tried till then.
The church could bring one contrary out of another : Micah vii. 9.
'Though I fall, I shall arise ;' and, saith Jonah, chap. ii. 7, 'When my
soul fainted in me, then I remembered God.' In a spiritual death, when
our comforts are spent, and all fail, then is a time for faith. Faith
can traffic with Christ in the dark, and take his word for that of
which we have no appearance at all. As Rom. iv. 18, 'Abraham
believed in hope against hope ;' that is, in hope according to promise,
though against hope contrary to the course of nature, when all natural
arguments, appearances, and grounds of hope are cut off.

3. That a christian is not to be valued by his enjoyments, but by
his hopes. 'He hath meat and drink which the world knows not of,'
John iv. 32, and can go to the rock when creatures have spent their
allowance. To appearance his life is worse than other men ; ay, but
his better life is hidden with God, he hath invisible things to live upon,
his main portion lieth in things not seen. The whole christian life is
nothing else but a spiritual riddle full of mysteries and wonders ; he
can see things not seen, fulness in want, special love in common mercies,
grace in a piece of bread. A wicked man's enjoyments are sweet to
sense, ay, but they are salted with a curse : but now in the deepest
expressions of hatred, a child of God by faith can see God's love.

4. Christ may be out of sight, yet you not out of mind. He consults
not with sense, for that makes lies of God—'I said in my haste, I am
cut off from before thine eyes ; nevertheless thou heardest the voice of
my supplications when I cried unto thee.' If God will not look to me,
I will look to him. The dam leaves her nest, but she leaves her heart
behind, and she will return. The sun at midnight seemeth low, but it
will rise again : Ps. xcvii. 11, 'Light is sown for the righteous, and
joy for the upright in heart.'

Use 2. Reproof to those that are all for sense and for present appearance.

1. Such as do not believe without present feeling.

2. Such as cannot wait upon God without present satisfaction.

[1.] There are some gross sensualists that examine all things by experience, and will not take God's word for truth, unless they feel it; whereas feeling is left for the life to come; here God will try us by faith. There are atheists in the church, but none in hell. The devils and damned spirits tremble at that which you doubt of. Here we have the light of conscience, reason and faith; but there men are left to feeling and experience; and therefore those that measure all things by present sense, and so disbelieve the world to come, they are hence to be reproved. Foolish men may go to school and learn of the ant. Since they will not learn of God, they may learn of the creature: Prov. vi. 6–8, ' Go to the ant, thou sluggard; consider her ways, and be wise : which having no guide, overseer, or ruler, provideth her meat in the summer, and gathereth her food in the harvest.' There is a natural providence and instinct in these creatures to provide for their future state. Oh then, what a sot is he that will not think of his state to come, nor of any condition beyond that which he now enjoys? they are worse than the ant—than the meanest and the lowest creature, that because they see not God or Christ, or heaven or hell, therefore question whether there be indeed any such thing, yea or no : I say many such there are in the world that say, as Thomas did out of weakness, John xx. 25, ' Unless I see in his hand the print of the nails,' &c., ' I will not believe;' they will not believe that God hath provided such a deplorable and miserable estate, where the wicked shall be tormented for ever and ever, and cast out from the presence of the Lord to the devil and his angels, because they see not these things.

[2.] It reproves those that cannot wait upon God without present satisfaction, that faint if the appearance of things suit not with their mind and expectation. We are all apt to be led by sense, and to plead natural improbabilities; and when any difficulty ariseth that checketh our hopes, we question the promises of God, and say with Mary, Luke i. 34, ' How can these things be ? '

(1.) This is a great dishonour to God, to trust him no further than we see him. You trust the ground with your corn, and can expect a crop out of the dry clods, though you do not see how it grows, nor which way it thrives in order to the harvest. It is a great folly to distrust the Lord, because the mercies we expect do not presently grow up and flower in our sight and apprehension. Abraham gave glory to God ' by believing in hope against hope,' Rom. iv. 18. That is an honour to God indeed, when in defiance of sense, and all outward probabilities, we can depend upon him for the accomplishment of his promise; whereas otherwise, when we confine God to present likelihoods, and must have satisfaction to our senses, or else we will not believe nor take things upon God's bare word; nor stay ourselves upon the name of God—' Except we see signs and wonders we will not believe,' John iv. 48. It is a great dishonour to God ; ' we limit the holy one of Israel,' Ps. lxxviii. 41, confining him to our circle of means.

(2.) It is contrary to all the dispensations of God's providence. Before he gives in any mercy there are usually some trials. Abraham had the promise of a numerous issue, but first Sarah's womb was long barren. Nay, after that God tried him again when he hath a child, he must sacrifice Isaac, the child of the promise. It was a hard thing for faith to interpret how he should offer Isaac, and yet believe that 'in Isaac all nations should be blessed.' Their obedience was to conflict not only with reason but with faith, and to find out an expedient to reconcile the precept with the promise; but yet he had a faith to believe it: Gen. xxii. 5, 'He said to his young men, abide you here with the ass; and I and the lad will go yonder and worship, and come again to you.' It was neither a lie nor equivocation, but words proceeding from the assurance of faith; for though Abraham knew not how, yet he tells Isaac, ver. 8, 'God will provide himself a lamb for a burnt-offering.' And as he used Abraham the father of the faithful, so he doth all his children. Christ's kingdom is described thus: first he comes as a root out of a dry ground, Isa. liii. 2. When the tree of Jesse was withered and dried up, when it was worn down to its root and stumps, God makes it to scent and bud again; then comes Jehovah the branch; then afterwards, Luke xvii. 20, 'The kingdom of God comes not with observation.' When the kingdom of Christ was to be set up, what appearance was there? a crucified man, and a few fishermen to begin this glorious empire! What should we have done if we had lived in Christ's time, and seen the despicable beginnings of his kingdom—we that are so amazed at every difficulty and cross providence? David was first hunted like a partridge upon the mountains, that he might be settled upon a throne. Thus God is still wont to try our faith before he satisfy our sense, and to leave some weakness upon the means that the mercy may be more glorious. Consult the whole course of God's providence, and all the experiences of the saints, and you will find it to be so: Isa. xlviii. 7, 'They are created now, and not from the beginning, even before the day, when thou heardest them not, lest thou shouldst say, Behold I knew them.' Things raised out of the earth, a man could not have thought there had been any such means and instruments in the whole creation. 'He hath chosen'—τὰ μὴ ὄντα—'things that are not,' 1 Cor. i. 27; that is, things that seemed to have no such use and efficacy, 'to confound things that are.' Micah v. 7, 'And they shall be as the dew from the Lord, as showers upon the grass, that tarrieth not for man, nor waiteth for the sons of men.' The herbs of the garden have visible means of supply, they are watered by hand, they tarry for man, and depend upon man's industry and providence; but they shall be as the grass in the wilderness, which thriveth by dews and showers from heaven, that come without man's thinking and care. Those that are acquainted with the usual traverses and ways of providence cannot but trust God. Usually we look on God's works by halves and pieces, and so distrust. There is a great deadness upon the means, when God will employ them to the highest uses and purposes. A painter draweth half a man, and then there is no beauty. When we look into the fiery furnace, and see nothing but devouring flames, who would think God could bring forth a vessel of honour from thence? God's dispensations have not left their wonted course, he tries us with such unlikelihoods.

(3.) It is contrary to the nature of faith—'Hope that is seen is not hope; for what a man seeth, why doth he yet hope for?' Rom. viii. 24. Faith gives over work when we come to fruition; the trial of it is in difficulties. Faith is faith indeed, when it can expect in the midst of dissatisfactions, and hath no relief from sense, nor help from outward things : John xx. 29, ' Blessed are they that have not seen, and yet believe.' That is true faith, when we can expect blessings upon God's warrant ; though we cannot discern the way, manner, nor means, yet we hold fast the conclusion, all will work for good. Instruments miscarry ; but faith looketh not to instruments, but to the promise : Esther iv. 14, ' If thou altogether hold thy peace at this time, then shall there enlargement and deliverance arise to the Jews from another place.' Her petitioning was the only visible likely way ; but if God would not use it, he was satisfied with his word. Nay, sometimes the word of God seems to be tried as well as we : Ps. xii. 6, ' The words of the Lord are pure words, as silver tried in a furnace of earth, purified seven times.' He speaks not only of the purity and excellency of the word, but of the stability and certainty of it ; when the promise is cast into the fire, and seems to lie a-burning, it is not consumed, but comes out with greater brightness and lustre. There are many, if God give them health, peace, plenty, and all manner of prosperity, then they believe him to be their God ; but if they see no external evidences of his favour, they will not believe in him ; this is to live by sense, not by faith ; for faith is the evidence of things not seen, it can raise us above sight, and support us against sense.

(4.) It will weaken our hands in duty when we look to every present discouragement. Solomon saith, Eccles. xi. 4, ' He that observeth the winds shall not sow ; and he that regardeth the clouds shall not reap.' He that is deterred from sowing his seed by every wind, and reaping his corn by every cloud, will never do his business ; so he that looketh to every discouragement can never act worthily for God, but is marred by every difficulty ; he is off and on, as outward things succeed or miscarry : James i. 8, ' A double-minded man is unstable in all his ways,' full of distractions and faintings, up and down with hopes and fears, as worldly things ebb and flow.

SERMON V.

And the evidence of things not seen.—HEB. xi. 1.

Use. 3. If faith be such an evidence of things not seen, then let us examine—have we this faith that can believe things not seen ? This is the nature of true faith. Hope built upon outward probability is but carnal hope ; but here is the faith and hope we live by, that which is carried out to things not seen with the bodily eye. Take these directions to discover it.

1. How doth it work as to Christ now he is out of sight ? His visible presence is long since removed, and he is withdrawn within the veil and curtain of the heavens, there to perform his ministration before the Lord. Can you love Christ, and enjoy Christ, and converse with him in heaven at the right hand of the Father, as if you did see him, and converse with him bodily in the days of his flesh ? It was the

commendation of their faith : 1 Peter i. 8, ' Whom having not seen,
ye love ; in whom, though now ye see him not, yet believing, ye rejoice
with joy unspeakable and full of glory.' Though you never saw him,
yet can you repair to him to solve your doubts and answer your scruples,
depend upon the merit of his death, and embolden yourselves in your
addresses to God upon the account of his satisfaction ? Though he
died sixteen hundred years ago, yet can you conceive hope by his blood
as if it were shed afresh, and running before your eyes ? for so should
believers do : Eph. iii. 12, ' In whom we have boldness, and access
with confidence, by the faith of him.' Alas ! to most christians Christ
is but a name, a fancy, or an empty conceit, such as the heathens had
of their topical gods, or we of tutelar saints, some for this country and
some for that. Do you pray as seeing him at God's right hand in
heaven pleading your cause, and negotiating with God for you ?

2. How doth it work as to his coming to judgment ? Is the awe of
that day upon your hearts ? and do you live as those that must give
an account even for every idle word, when the great God of recompenses shall descend from heaven with a shout ? Rev. xx. 12, ' I saw
the dead small and great stand before God,' &c. Have you such a
sight as St John had ? Indeed he saw it by vision, or by the light of
prophecy ; but the light of faith differs but little from the light of
prophecy. They agree in many things, as in the common ground.
What is the ground of the light of prophecy ? the foundation of it is
divine revelation, and the same ground hath faith. And they agree
in the evidence. What is prophecy ? a certain foreknowledge of
things to come ; and what is faith ? an evidence of things to come.
Thus they agree. They differ in these things : the light of prophecy
depends upon special grounds, which is extraordinary revelation ; but
the light of faith hath but that common ground, the ordinary revelation God hath made of his mind in scripture ; and they differ somewhat
in the degree. Indeed there is more of ecstasy and rapture of mind
that accompanieth the light of prophecy ; but in the light of faith
there is some answerable affection, some impression left upon us.
They differ something too in the duration and continuance with us ;
the light of prophecy is but at times, when God will show such a
sight or vision ; but the light of faith is a constant, steady view. Well
then, what John saw once by the light of prophecy we see constantly,
and are persuaded of it as certainly as if the trumpet were now sounding ; as if the throne were set, and the books were already opened, and
the trembling sinners were all summoned before the Lord, expecting
their doom and sentence. Have you a sight of judgment to come ?
It is a thing unseen, but as faith gives you an evidence of it, doth it
quicken your desires and your longings after this day ? doth it awaken
your diligence ? doth it make you awful and serious in the whole
course of your conversation, both in your outward carriage and secret
practices, as if all were seen ? for you have seen the day of the Lord.

3. How can you comfort yourselves in the midst of all your straits
and sorrows with the unseen glory of another world ? Do not you
faint in your duty, but bear up with that courage and constancy which
becomes christians : 2 Cor. iv. 16, ' We faint not,' why ? He gives
you the reason of it, ver. 18, ' While we look not at the things that

are seen, but at the things that are not seen.' This is an evidence of our looking to things not seen, when we faint not, but go on with courage and constancy, as it becomes the heirs of the grace of life, upon sight of the invisible world. So 1 John iii. 2, 'It doth not yet appear what we shall be; but this we know, that when he shall appear, we shall be like him.' And so you are no more affected with the disgraces and scorns of the world than a prince in disguise, who travels abroad unknown, if he meets not with respect and reverence answerable to his quality; he knows he is his father's heir, and this comforts him; and the unseen glory in the world to come puts comfort and strength into your hearts.

4. How doth it work as to the threatenings of the word? Can you mourn for a judgment in its causes, and foresee a storm when the clouds are but a-gathering? As Josiah had a tender heart, and trembled when the curses of the law were read: 2 Chron. xxxiv. 19, 'When the king heard the words of the law, then he rent his clothes.' It is not said when he heard news of Pharaoh Necho's invasion: no, all was quiet and composed, no trouble then had a foot in his kingdom; 'but when he heard the words of the law, he rent his clothes,' then he is solicitous to get things redressed. This general description that faith is the evidence of things not seen, the apostle exemplifies in the instance of Noah: Heb. xi. 7, 'By faith Noah, being warned of God of things not seen as yet, moved with fear, prepared an ark,' when there was no visible preparation towards the deluge; when the world was eating, drinking, marrying, giving in marriage, building, planting, and all things went on as they were wont to do. Are you humbling your souls and fighting in secret when anything is done to bring you or your nation in danger of a threatening? God describes a gracious heart thus—'He trembles at my word,' Isa. lxvi. 2; he not only trembles at my judgment, but at my word, before the smoke or the flame of judgment breaketh out. Alas! most men are not moved with these things till the curse of God seize upon them. They know not that they which do such things as they do are in danger of the curse of God. There are threatenings against their practices everywhere, yet who lays it to heart? Ps. xc. 11, 'Who knows the power of thine anger? even according to thy fear, so is thy wrath.' The word of God moveth us not till we smart in our flesh. This faith, which is the evidence of things not seen, it is to be referred to the threatenings as well as to the promises. And all our diligence and caution, our watchfulness, our humiliation, that we may avert God's judgments, ariseth from this faith.

5. How doth your heart work upon the promises in difficult cases? Thereby God tries you, and thereby you may try yourselves: John vi. 5, 6, 'When Jesus lifted up his eyes, and saw a great company come unto him, he said unto Philip, Whence shall we buy bread that these may eat? and this he said to prove him.' God often useth the like kind of dispensation to his people. There are many mouths, and no bread; great troubles, and no means of escape; this he doth to prove you, but God knows how to order this for your comfort. When we judge by sense, and reason, and outward probabilities, in such kind of extremities we are driven to our wits' end. Now faith, which lives above sense,

will be a support and strength to your souls. In such cases reason and faith, and sense and faith, come in competition. How, which way do the workings of your spirits incline—to reason, or faith? Faith can take God's word in the midst of all difficulties; and when sense seeth nothing but hazards, wants, sorrows, then faith holds with the promise against these appearances, and rests on God whatever we feel to the contrary: Hab. iii. 17, 18, 'Though the fig-tree shall not blossom,' &c., 'yet I will rejoice in the Lord, I will joy in the God of my salvation.' Those hopes which hang upon the life and presence of the creature, when the creatures fail, they fail; when bread and outward supplies are gone, they are lost and undone; but the children of God have built upon a promise, and when creatures have spent their allowance, when they can no longer live upon bread, they can live upon the promise and word of God. Therefore God will prove him, and exercise him with straits and troubles; but then can he depend upon the Lord. A believer can say yea with a promise, when all the world saith no to him. The apostle saith: 2 Cor. i. 20, 'All the promises of God are in him yea, and in him amen.' The promises say yea to our hopes, and amen to our desires; and in all difficult changes still the promises keep their note, they are yea and amen. You desire such a thing according to the will of God—Amen, saith the promise, so it shall be. May I hope for such a mercy or comfort?—Yea, saith the promise. Now in straits you will find the comfort of such a truth. You ask of creatures and present appearances, May I look for good? and they answer no, but the promise still saith yea: now a believer is contented with the promises, yea, though all the world say no. Christians! there needeth nothing to your comfort but this, first to establish a regular hope, and then to trust the affirmation of the promise. Now hereby may you discern your spirits. Can you with certainty depend upon the promise, and with a quiet and calm expectation wait for the blessing of the promises in the midst of all pressures whatsoever? Carnal men limit God, and give laws to providence: Ps. lxxviii. 41, 'Yea they turned back, and tempted God, and limited the Holy One of Israel.' They bind the counsels of God by their outward appearances: 1 Peter iv. 19, 'Wherefore let them that suffer according to the will of God commit the keeping of their souls to him in well-doing, as unto a faithful creator.' They give up their souls to God, and all their affairs to his disposal. He is faithful, and will be mindful of them, and he is a creator and hath power to help them, and this quiets and calms their souls under all providences.

6. You may try your assent to the promises by the adventures you make upon God's word. The promises are so many bills and bonds which God hath taken upon himself. Now what will you venture upon the warrant and encouragement the word gives? Certainly he that will venture nothing thereupon doth not believe what God hath said, 'Whoso shall confess me before men, him shall the Son of man confess before the angels of God; but, he that denieth me before men, I will deny him before my Father, and before his holy angels,' Luke xii. 8, 9. Can you adventure upon Christ's word to confess him, though you should deny your present interest? so Luke ix. 24, 'Whosoever shall save his life shall lose it; but whosoever will lose his

life for my sake, the same shall find it.' Now urge the soul with this promise, Can I be willing to fall a sacrifice upon the interest of religion upon such a hope, or quit temporal conveniences for the enduring substance? Now lest your heart should deceive you, because every one is not called to suffer, and resolution in cold blood may faint when they come to trial, therefore look to such things as are of present use and experience. Practise upon that promise: Luke xii. 33, 'Sell all that you have, and give alms: provide yourselves bags that wax not old, a treasure in the heavens which faileth not.' Now say, What have I ventured upon this promise? can I look upon no estate so sure as that which is trusted in Christ's hands? Do I indeed count this the best way to entail a blessing upon me and my children and family afterwards, not to purchase house to house, and field to field, but to found a covenant interest, and lay up a treasure for them in Christ's hands, by a large, liberal, and free distribution to the poor? But if this seems hard though it be a clear precept in the gospel, and everywhere we are called upon to lend unto the Lord, what lusts can you renounce upon the security of eternal life? Practise upon that promise: Rom. viii. 13, 'If we live after the flesh, we shall die; but if we through the Spirit mortify the deeds of the body, we shall live.' Now am I willing to undergo the severities and tedious hardships of a christian life? to be much in mortifying and subduing my flesh? Can I yield to this upon these hopes? do I look upon it as better to take pains than suffer pains, to be held with cords of duty than chains of darkness, and run the hazard of being separated for ever from the presence of the Lord? Certainly, when you can neither renounce lusts nor quit interest, nor make any spiritual adventures, you do but look upon the gospel as a fable. What have we ventured upon those bonds God hath given us, and those obligations he hath taken upon himself, that he will bless us if we will yield to these and these conditions? All promises imply some duty; it is improbable we should believe them if we will undergo no hazard for them.

7. You may know whether you have this faith, which evidenceth things to come, and find out the weakness or strength of it by observing the great disproportion that is in your affections to things of sense, and things of faith. It is true, a christian is not all spirit, and therefore sensible things work more with the present state of men than things spiritual. But yet certainly in a child of God, one that believes, that hath the evidence of things not seen, there will be some suitableness. We are diverted from looking after things to come as long as we have carnal comforts to stop the mouth of conscience. But did we soundly believe the truth and worth of the great mysteries of salvation, surely we would learn more to despise temporal things in comparison of eternal. Therefore examine a little the affections and dispositions of your souls as to things present and things to come, temporal things and eternal. Examine a carnal man by his esteem; he is sensible of the sweetness of outward comforts, but hath no taste and savour of things that are to come. The former insinuate themselves into his heart with a great deal of satisfaction; he is moved and affected with them— 'Who will show us any good?' Ps. iv. 6. Carnal pleasures tickle him with a great deal of delight, but he hath no taste of communion with

God. Carnal riches, with him they are the only substance, whereas spiritual and heavenly things are but as a notion. Whereas the scripture is quite otherwise; it speaks of outward things as but a fancy: Prov. xxiii. 5, 'Wilt thou set thine eyes upon that which is not?' and of spiritual things, as those which only may be called substance: Prov. viii. 21, 'That I may cause those that love me to inherit substance, and I will fill their treasures.' Now which dost thou esteem, thy treasure and thy substance, the world or heaven? things present, or the great things God hath promised? which are the things most take with thy heart, and draw forth thy esteem? So examine his care and industry. We toil for matters of the world, and are never weary; rise up early, go to bed late, eat the bread of sorrow, and all for a little pelf; we make nothing of the hardest labours to accomplish our worldly delights. But now, to pray, read, meditate, perform acts of worship to God, how difficult are these? and how soon do we cry out, what a weariness is it? A little time spent in duty is with a great deal of murmuring; doth not this bewray too much unbelief? 'So is he that layeth up treasures for himself, and is not rich towards God,' Luke xii. 21; that is, so earnest and diligent to grow great in the world, but cares not to furnish himself with grace. When there is such a disproportion in his care, is he persuaded of these things? There is a wide and sensible difference between things temporal and eternal, so should there be in our pursuit after them. Now when it is not only a nice debate that prevails most with men, but a plain clear case, it shows we are not fully persuaded of them. So examine a man by his hopes, and see whether he hath this evidence of things not seen. Compare your hopes in God's promises with your hopes in a temporal case; it is good to put things in a temporal case and instance: Mal. i. 8, 'Offer it to thy governor, will he accept of it?' If a prince or potentate of the world should make you a promise of a temporal inheritance, or pass over the reversion of an earthly estate for thee and thy heirs, how wouldst thou rest contented, and be satisfied with such a conveyance? so hath God done in the covenant; by a formal compact he hath demised and made over to us the great blessings of the gospel; and yet how little are our hearts satisfied with it, how full of doubtings! what unstable thoughts have we about these things! If I had such great promises from an able and faithful man, would I not be more cheerful, and bear up upon these hopes? I have these promises from God, that cannot lie. So examine his fears: when a man threatens a little danger, we are careful to abstain from what may displease him, yet we can swallow lust without remorse. Adultery is punished with death in some countries; but God says: Mat. v. 28, 'That whosoever looketh on a woman to lust after her hath committed adultery with her already in his heart.' And God threatens again and again, not only with temporal but eternal death, torments that shall be without end and ease; yet these things do not work upon us. God saith, Rom. viii. 13, 'If you live after the flesh, you shall die;' that the delicacies of the fleshly life, if indulged, will be mortal to us. Alas! who fears this death? it is a thing to come and unseen; God doth not presently execute his sentence upon evildoers, therefore we are

not moved with it. It argues either unbelief or very great incogitancy about things of such great concernment.

8. You may know whether you have this faith by your thoughts of
the ways of God, when they are despised or opposed. Faith, which is
the evidence of things not seen, can see a great deal of beauty in a despised way of God, and glory in a crucified Christ; as the good thief
upon the cross could see Christ as a king, when he hung dying on the
cross in disgrace: Luke xxiii. 42, 'Lord, remember me when thou comest
into thy kingdom.' Religion is often veiled under obscurity, slightings,
disgraces, and contradictions of the world. God trieth us, as it were
in a disguise. Now if we can spy out this inward beauty and inward
glory in his ways when they are divested of all outward glory, here is
an act of faith—'Christ came to his own, and his own received him
not.' A carnal heart sees no worth in anything but what is full of
pomp and outward splendour, it knows all things after the flesh; but
a gracious heart sees a great deal of worth and beauty in the despised
ways of Christ. It is said of Moses, that by faith he 'esteemed the
reproaches of Christ greater riches than the treasures of Egypt,' Heb.
xi. 26; that is, when it was a reproachful thing for him, who was so
great and high in favour, to own an afflicted people, who were
so burdened as they were in Egypt. Thus you have seen how
you may find out whether this faith be wrought in your
souls.

Use 4. To press you to get this faith, which is the evidence of
things not seen, that you may believe that which God hath revealed
in his word, and that solely upon God's authority and the account of
his word; to quicken you to get this faith, which is of such great use
to you.

1. Consider that all the difficulty in assenting to doctrines of scripture
was not only in the first age. You are ready to think this faith was
of use when christianity was first set up in the world, and when it was
new and despised, and the powers of the world were against it; but
now it is owned by all, there is no such difficulty; yes, very much still.
I confess, when it was a novel doctrine, hated, oppressed, persecuted,
and the generality of its professors were the poor of this world, there
were mighty prejudices against the ways of God; but there were then
helps; there was the sensible evidence of miracles to confirm this faith,
and there was an extraordinary zeal and holiness in those that
promoted it, which was a special means to strike a reverence into the
consciences of men, which sensible evidence now we have not. Ay,
but the articles of religion are still the same, and men are the same,
and every age hath its own prejudices; so that it is still hard to
believe. (1.) Because the same articles of religion that were propounded to them are propounded to us also. A man that only
hearkens to his own reason, it is hard for him to believe that there is
one God, and yet three that are God; that by faith a man is united to
Christ, yet he on earth, and Christ in heaven; that God requires faith
and conviction of all, and binds men to use the means, and yet in his
secret good pleasure determines to give it to a few. These things are
expressly revealed in the word, which are hard to be understood by
carnal reason; and we cannot see how they can be. There are many

doctrines which must not be chewed, but swallowed ; *de re constat, quamvis de modo non constat.* (2.) Men are the same that they were before ; still natural men favour not the things that are of the Spirit, therefore are not apt to believe them that they are true. Still we are wedded to sense, and therefore not easily persuaded of things to come ; still men love not holiness, but walk after their own lusts ; therefore they will not believe God is so unmerciful as to damn all those that are not holy, and that none shall be saved but those that are born again, and walk in such a strict way of communion with God, and in the ways of godliness. (3.) Every age hath its own prejudices. Christianity was a novel doctrine. Ay, but then they had miracles ; but now there is less holiness, but no miracles ; now men are subject to atheism, because of scandals : 2 Peter ii. 2, ' Many shall follow their pernicious ways, by reason of whom the way of truth shall be evil spoken of.' And now there are many divisions, and variety of thoughts and opinions about matters of religion, which makes men suspect all. Therefore Christ prays : John xvii. 21, ' Father, let them be one, as we are one, that the world may believe that thou hast sent me.' So that if it were a difficult thing to believe then, so it is now. Therefore it concerns us to be soundly rooted in this faith.

2. Consider the benefit of a sound conviction. A clear evidence of the mysteries of salvation is a great ground of all reformation of life. What is the reason that men are so backward to practise, that they experience so little of what they believe and have received of the christian faith ? because the evidence is not clear. I do not say their interest, but the evidence and certain belief of these things. Usually christians think it is their only work to clear up their particular interest ; that is a great work—'We must give all diligence to make our calling and election sure,' 2 Peter i. 10. But that is not the only work ; there is a former work, which is the foundation of all, and that is, to settle the soul in a sound belief of the things to come, and have the hopes of christianity evidenced to us ; if our belief of this were more steady, there would not be such a deformity in our practice. Our affections are glued to earthly things, because we are not persuaded of heavenly things ; there is a privy atheism, which, like a worm at the root, eats out the strength and vigour of our graces, and causeth them to languish. When the mind is satisfied, and brought to a full assent, there will be a greater awe upon the practice : Heb. xi. 6, ' He that cometh to God must believe that he is, and that he is a rewarder of them that diligently seek him.' This is the first thing that we should be persuaded of, that certainly there is a God ; and this God will be good to all that seek after him in Christ. If we had such a persuasion of this, we could not be so cold and careless in duty, and so bold in sin ; but we have a wavering trembling assent, and some imperfect opinions about the things of God, and not a full persuasion : 1 Cor. xv. 58, ' Therefore be ye steadfast, unmovable, always abounding in the work of the Lord ; forasmuch as you know that your labour is not in vain in the Lord.' If we did once know and were persuaded of this, if we had an evidence of things to come, and things unseen, we would be more steadfast and unmovable in the work of the Lord. If our expectations were greater, our observation of God would be

greater, the business of eternal life would not be so neglected; conscience would not be so sleepy, nor should we venture upon sin so often as we do; this would put life into every exhortation you hear and read. Alas! we press and exhort day after day; it works not, why? because it is not 'mingled with faith in them that hear it,' Heb. iv. 2. What earnest affections of soul would there be towards God and heavenly things if we did truly believe these things.

3. The more faith depends upon the warrant of God's word, the better; and the fewer sensible helps it hath, the more it is prized; As Christ saith, John xx. 29, 'Blessed are they who have not seen, and yet have believed.' It is the weakness of men, they will not believe unless the object of faith some way or other come under their sense. The word of God is enough.

4. Sensible things will not work, if we do not believe the word; those that think Moses and the prophets are but a cold dispensation in comparison of this, if one should come from the dead, for then they would repent and turn to God, let them read Luke xvi. 29–31. There were miracles heretofore; faith was confirmed to sense; God condescended to the weakness of the first age; but yet it is said of the people of Israel, Ps. lxxviii. 22, 23, 'They believed not in God, and trusted not in his salvation: though he had commanded the clouds from above, and opened the door of heaven,' &c. There were ever unbelievers, and carnal wretches, let God use what dispensation he will, and there will be so still. There is more in the harmony and correspondency of scripture to work men to a sense of believing than if one should come from the dead.

5. We have need now to look after this faith, which is the evidence of things not seen, because the great reigning and prevailing sin is infidelity and unbelief; which is seen by our cavilling at every strict truth, by our carelessness in the things of God, by the looseness and profaneness of those that would be accounted christians. Certainly, generally men take the great truths of religion for fabulous delusions, and look upon Christ as an impostor, and the doctrine of the resurrection from the dead, and eternal life, as so many idle dreams; else they could not cavil so at every strict truth and be so careless and profane as they are; for these things are irreconcilable.

6. We ought to look to this faith, because none are so resolved in the great matters of faith but they may be more resolved; no man doth so believe but he may believe more: 1 John v. 13, 'These things have I written to you that believe on the name of the Son of God.' Our assent to divine truth is not a thing that is *in puncto*, that consists in one indivisible point, so as it cannot be more or less; but it is a thing that is ever growing and never so perfect as it should be, till we come to fruition. There is something 'lacking to your faith,' 1 Thes. iii. 10; 'therefore labour after this faith which is the evidence of things not seen.'

Obj. While we establish a faith which is the evidence of things not seen, doth not this make way for every fancy and fond credulity? This was the objection that Celsus brought against Origen, that faith introduced all kind of error into the world, and cast out science. I answer!

Ans. 1. There is a reason why we believe, though we cannot always see a reason of what we do believe. Though there can be no reason given of many things that are to be believed ; yet faith sees reason enough why they should be believed, and that is the authority and veracity of God speaking in the scriptures.

2. There is an aptitude or objective evidence in what is revealed in scripture, to beget faith in those that diligently exercise themselves, and had eyes to see it. The main truths which are delivered there are delivered with such reasonableness that they assure us of the rest.

Use 5. Direction to get and increase this faith.

1. Beg the illumination of the Spirit of God to show you the truth of the word, and the good things offered therein. This evidence is from the Spirit; therefore Paul prays for the Ephesians: chap. i. 17, 18, ' That the God of our Lord Jesus Christ, the Father of glory, may give unto you the spirit of wisdom and revelation in the knowledge of him: the eyes of your understandings being enlightened, that ye may know what is the hope of his calling, and what the riches of the glory of his inheritance in the saints.' You may have literal knowledge from men, but that is weak and washy, like a golden dream of rubies ; saving knowledge is only from the Spirit. They differ as strong water and running water, which have the same colour, but they differ in their taste and virtues.

2. Employ your reason, serious consideration, and discourse. The devil throws the golden ball in our way, of honour, pleasure, and profit, to divert us from heavenly things ; and the intention of the mind being diverted, the impressions of religion are weak and faint ; as when the bird often leaves her nest the eggs are chilled. Inconstancy is as great an enemy to faith as ignorance. The scattering and vanity of the thoughts make our assent but weak and trembling: Deut. xxxii. 29, ' Oh that they were wise, that they understood this, that they would consider their latter end,' not only to know, but to consider it. Men have not such a deep apprehension of the beauty of holiness, and the excellency of Christ, because they do not exercise their thoughts more upon these things. By consideration truths are kept near the heart, and in the view of the understanding.

3. Labour to get a heart purged from carnal affections. Where there is more purity there will be more clearness: Mat. v. 8, ' Blessed are the pure in heart, for they shall see God.' Sin doth weaken our faith. We shall always stagger and waver in an uncertain doubtfulness concerning supernatural verities while we indulge our lusts. Sin blinds our eyes: 2 Cor. iv 3, 4, ' If our gospel be hid, it is hid to them that are lost: in whom the God of this world hath blinded the minds of them which believe not, lest the light of the glorious gospel of Christ, who is the image of God, should shine unto them.' We had need keep that eye clear that shall discern things unseen, and the comforts and blessedness of another world. By sin you grieve the Spirit, which should help you in believing: Eph. iv. 30, ' And grieve not the Holy Spirit of God, whereby you are sealed unto the day of redemption.' And hereby you provoke God to give you up to natural prejudices: 2 Thes. ii. 11, ' For this cause God shall send them strong delusions that they shall believe a lie.' Men sin away their faith, wound their

consciences, put out that light that should guide them. And therefore get your hearts purged from sin ; for as faith makes way for holiness, so doth holiness again for faith.

SERMON VI.

For by it the elders obtained a good report.—Heb. xi. 2.

The whole chapter is mainly spent in the praise of sanctifying faith— a necessary grace, and of a universal influence into all the parts of the spiritual life.

Divers things are attributed to faith, and that several ways : either as acts or as effects, or as fruits and consequences of faith.

1. As acts, which decipher the essence and formal nature of it, ver. 1. These are the *elicite*, or formal acts of faith, which substantiates things hoped for, and convinceth of things that are not seen.

2. Then there are the effects of faith, or, as the schoolmen call them, *imperate* acts, which flow from the primary acts, as hope, valour, patience, christian self-denial ; all which are the progeny of faith, as in opening the following verse will appear.

3. Then there are the fruits and consequences of faith, which follow faith though they do not flow from it ; as the recompenses and rewards of religion, temporal or eternal, which a believer receives not from the power and worth of his faith, but from the free grace of God. Faith is a condition by the ordination and appointment of God, but not a cause ; that distinction is necessary for the clearing many parts of the chapter. Such a fruit of faith you have in the text, the approbation or testimony which the ancient fathers received from God in the word, 'For by it the elders received a good report.'

To commend that faith which he had before described, the apostle brings the experience of the elders, or of the Old Testament saints. Here you have—(1.) The persons—*The elders :* (2.) The means— *By it ;* (3.) The blessing—*They obtained a good report.* Or else— (1.) The condition—Faith ; (2.) The consequent—ἐμαρτυρήθησαν. they were witnessed to or spoken of with respect in the world ; and (3.) The subject in which both these do meet and concur.

' The elders ; ' by faith ' the elders obtained a good report.'

' The elders,' πρεσβύτεροι, the patriarchs, fathers ; the word is rather proper to the life of man than to the age of the world. The ancients are called οἱ παλαιοὶ, *homines prisci sœculi*, but the words are confounded. And they might well be called elders, not only for their antiquity, and living in the first ages of the world, but because most of them were μακρόβιοι, of wonderful long life.

' By it,' ἐν ταύτῃ. It is not *for* faith, but *by* faith, for faith is as improper as for works ; but having faith, not by the worth and influence of it as a cause, but through faith as a condition appointed and ordained by God.

'They obtained a good report,' ἐμαρτυρήθησαν; the word signifies they received a testimony; they were attested to, or witnessed of. Now this testimony which the faithful receive is double : inward, or the testimony of conscience ; outward, or the testimony of God in his word.   (1.) Inward, or the testimony of conscience : 1 John. v. 10, 'He that believeth on the Son of God hath the witness in himself.' (2.) Outward, from God in the word; they received a testimony.   What is that ? they were chronicled and set out in the scriptures as a pattern for all future ages.   This is most proper, and therefore it is elsewhere rendered 'of good report:' Acts vi. 3, 'Look you out among you seven men'—μαρτυρουμένους—'of honest report.'   And it suiteth with the context, for what is spoken here in the general is in particular applied to Abel and Enoch.   To Abel, ver. 4, 'He obtained witness that he was righteous;' it is meant in the scriptures, where his usual title and appellation is, 'righteous Abel,' as I shall show in that verse.   So to Enoch, ver. 5, 'He had this testimony, that he pleased God'—a testimony from God in his conscience, and it is now recorded in the word.

After the apostle had laid down the description of faith, he applies it to the patriarch fathers, or ancient servants of God under the dispensation of the Old Testament.   Hence observe—

Obs. 1. That the fathers under the law had the same kind of faith that we have.   They had the same promises, not of Canaan, but of heaven : Heb. xi. 13, 'And confessed that they were strangers and pilgrims on the earth;' they sojourned here as in a strange country, and counted the world a strange place, and looked for heaven as their home, as we do. And the promises were made to them upon the same terms of grace. The same reason or inducement that moves God to covenant with us moved God to covenant with the fathers of the Old Testament: Deut. vii. 8, 'Because the Lord loved you,' &c.   The merit upon account of which he might receive them into favour was the same, the blood of Jesus Christ: Heb. xiii. 8, 'Jesus Christ the same yesterday, to-day, and for ever.'   It is not meant of his eternal divinity, and the unchangeableness of his godhead, but of the manifestation of his grace.   The ages past and the ages to come, they are all one in Christ.   Though we lived not in Christ's time, yet we have salvation by him, 'for he is the same for ever;' and though they lived not in our time, yet they had salvation by him, 'for he was the same yesterday,' &c.   He is called the 'Lamb slain from the foundation of the world,' Rev. xiii. 8, that is, in God's decree ; and he was slain in the figures and types of his death.   Though Christ's blood was not as yet shed, yet it was decreed to be shed in the purpose of God, and so it was as effectual to them as to us.

Use. Free grace is no novel doctrine, it is the old course which God hath always taken for saving of souls.   The curiosity of man is altogether for new ways ; but however the new may seem more plausible, yet the old is more certain and true : Jer. vi. 16, 'Ask for the old paths, where is the good way,'—the ancient way of God's grace,—'and walk therein, and ye shall find rest for your souls.'   Novelty maketh things liable to suspicion.   *Verum quod primum,* that is true which is the first.   Though error be very ancient, error may be mouldy, as well as truth greyhaired ; yet that which is oldest is best, and truth is first. Now this is God's old way, to bring in sinners to Christ by free grace. When we shall come to heaven, and sit down with Abraham, Isaac, and Jacob, we shall hear the elders of old reading lectures of free grace, and singing praises to the Lamb, by whose blood they were redeemed, and by whose merit they were brought to glory. There will be Abraham, and Moses, and all the worthies of God; God hath used several dispensations, but the end of the journey is the same.

Secondly, 'By it the elders obtained a good report.' I observe again—

Obs. 2. That the apostle ascribes their renown in the church to their faith. By it they obtained. They were famous for other graces,—Abel for righteousness and innocence; Enoch and Noah for walking with God; Moses for meekness, and wise conduct; Abraham for obedience; others for their valour and resolution; but mark, the crown is set upon the head of faith; 'by it the elders obtained a good report.' Nay, throughout the whole chapter many effects here spoken of do more directly and formally belong to other graces, as to self-denial, and christian fortitude, rather than to faith; yet still the apostle saith, by faith they did this, by faith they did that. Though the private soldiers do worthily in the high places of the field, yet the general bears away the honour, he gets the battle and wins the day ; so here, all graces have their use in the holy life, all do worthily in their order and place ; love worketh, hope waiteth, patience endureth, zeal sparkleth, and obedience urgeth to duty ; but faith bears away the prize, this is the chiefest pin and wheel in the whole frame of salvation. Partly because it is the grace of reception on our part, by which we receive all the influences of heaven. On Christ's part it is all ascribed to the Spirit, on our part to faith ; Christ lives in us by his Spirit, and we live in him by faith. There is no more intrinsic worth in faith than in any other grace, but Christ hath appointed it to this office. And partly because it directs and quickens all other graces—'Faith worketh by love,' Gal. v. 6. It feeds hope, it teaches patience to wait, it makes zeal to sparkle, it gives relief to self-denial, and encourageth obedience. Faith is like a silken string, which runs through the chain of pearl ; or like the spirits that run with the blood throughout all the veins. Other graces without faith are but the moral elevations of nature ; this gives a man acceptance with God ; this conserves his other graces, and preserves him against assaults. It is called 'the shield of faith,' Eph. vi. 11, as the shield covereth the whole armour. God hath assigned this office to faith to quicken and preserve graces, and conquer difficulties : 1 John v. 4, 'This is the victory that overcometh the world, even our faith.'

Use. It shows what should be our principal care—to get faith and to maintain faith.

1. To get faith, in some sense there is as great a necessity of faith as of Christ. What good would a deep well do us without a bucket? John iv. 11, 'The woman saith unto him, Sir, thou hast nothing to draw with, and the well is deep;' so for us to have a deep well and a fountain of salvation, when we have nothing to fetch water out of these wells of salvation, what will it stead us ? Faith is the life of our lives, the soul of our souls; the *primum mobile*, that moves all the wheels of

obedience. He that hath a mind to work would not be without his tools. We can do nothing in religion without faith. Oh! beg faith; it is necessary—*necessitate medii:* you may as well want Christ as faith; God will not violate his own order. All other graces follow the proportion of faith.

2. Maintain and keep it lively. Of all graces it is the most excellent, and of all graces it is most assaulted. The malice and spite of Satan is at your faith. Saith Christ to Peter: Luke xxii. 31, 32, 'Satan hath desired to have thee, that he may sift thee as wheat; but I have prayed for thee, that thy faith fail not,' he would undermine thy faith. Usually there are no defects in the life, but first there is some decay of faith. You had need keep that grace lively by which you live. The scripture speaks not only of a living faith, but of a lively faith and a lively hope, 1 Peter i. 3. The means to keep it lively are—

[1.] Meditation; that is the great fuel of faith, it keeps in the fire in the soul; it is both wood and bellows. Now meditation must look forward and backward; backward with thankfulness, and forward with hope. (1.) Backward with thankfulness upon the love of Christ, often considering the greatness and willingness of his passion. There is not a greater incentive to obedience than to consider the sufferings of Christ. A soldier, when his request was denied, showed the emperor his wounds. Oh! feed your faith with such a sight, show it the wounds, and the sufferings and bruises of Christ, then the soul will not be so sluggish and averse from duty: 2 Cor. v. 14, 'The love of Christ constrains us.' Meditation helps faith, and faith awakens love, and then love presseth and urgeth the soul to obedience, and will not let us be quiet. I have observed that we are more affected with what men suffer for us than what men do for us, because there is more self-denial in suffering, but only courtesy in doing. Oh, what hath Jesus Christ suffered for us? He came from heaven, and when he was to go up to Golgotha, there was no reluctation in his spirit; he did not plead, It will cost me dear, it is a hard work! but, Lo, I come to do thy will, Ps. xl. 7, 8; here are cheeks for the nippers, a back for the smiters, here is a body for the cross; and when faith urgeth this, the soul will be ashamed to go less cheerfully to the throne of grace than Jesus Christ went to the cross. (2.) Look forward upon Christ's purchase. Heaven is a fair field for meditation, and faith hath a pleasant walk when it can walk through the land of promise; as God bade Abraham: Gen. xiii. 17, 'Arise, walk through the land in the length of it, and in the breadth of it, for I will give it thee.' Meditation should awaken faith, and encourage it to walk through the land of promise, All this will the Lord give thee. Moses' faith was the more resolved because heaven was still in his eye: Heb. xi. 26, 'For he had respect to the recompense of the reward.' Keep the eye steady in the view of glory. The transfiguration of Jesus Christ fitted him for his suffering. The messengers of the cross, they came to him in shining garments, 'to talk of his decease that he should accomplish at Jerusalem,' Luke ix. 31. It will not be mercenary for us to use the same art. Let faith climb up into the high mount by meditation, and in our thought foretaste the glory of the everlasting state, that we may be fitted to do and suffer for God.

[2.] Frequent act and exercise : James ii. 22, 'By works faith was made perfect.' How could this be ? rather faith makes works perfect. It is not meant in that sense, as if work did communicate any merit and value to faith, but only that hereby it is more increased, more drawn up to the height and perfection. All graces are perfected by much use and exercise ; so is faith. Look, as the exercise of the members of the body increaseth their vigour and strength, and therefore the right arm is biggest, because of much exercise ; so inwardly the soul is bettered, and faith is much improved by frequent operation. Neglect of grace is the ground of its decrease and decay. Wells are the sweeter for the draining ; so graces are the better for this exercise.

3. A careful use of ordinances ; there faith is begotten, and there it is increased. Look, as the strength of the body increaseth by degrees, so doth the soul. We grow up to our complete stature and strength in religion by the constant supplies and ministration of the word ; the soul must be fed as well as the body. There is no stop in grace, still we must be growing : ' They that are planted in the house of the Lord, shall flourish in the courts of our God,' Ps. xcii. 13 ; Luke viii. 18, ' Take heed how you hear, for whosoever hath, to him shall be given.' How comes this to be the reason of the precept ? Our Saviour hereby implies, that the more we hear, the more we increase. None want ordinances so much as those that think they do not want them. Painted fire wants no fuel, and counterfeit graces need not constant support from ordinances ; but true grace languishes in the neglect of them, for the use of ordinances is God's way and method.

Obs. 3. That the faith of the elders was an active faith, that discovered itself by good fruits and gracious actions ; otherwise it could not have brought them into credit with the church. God only knows the heart. It is actions that discover their faith, and the strength of their assent. It is but a necessary postulation, James ii. 14, ' Show me thy faith by thy works ; ' men have no other discovery. A bare profession or fruitless observation of the ceremonies and rites of religion would never have continued their memory in the scripture, nor made them famous. A hidden faith is of no account ; it must be discovered in the life. The apostles speaks of the Romans : chap. i. 8, ' Your faith is spoken of throughout the whole world ; ' compare it with chap. xvi. 19, ' Your obedience is come abroad unto all men.' The faith that brings in a good report must be showed by some visible public actions.

Use. Do not content yourselves with an idle naked faith. There is more necessary to endear you to the churches of God, than a barren profession ; there are many qualifications necessary in order to a good report.

1. Mortification. Men naturally reverence strictness. It is said, ' Herod feared John, knowing that he was a just and an holy man,' Mark vi. 20. This will beget a fear and an awe upon worldly men, the strictness and severity of your lives. Mortified christians are the world's wonders : 1 Peter iv. 4, ' Wherein they think it strange that you run not with them to the same excess of riot, speaking evil of you.' They wonder how they are able to withstand desires so pleasing and so satisfactory. Wicked men will be always speaking evil of the children of God ; yet they dread those whom they slander ; when they see them

mortified and heavenly, their hearts are convinced when their tongues revile. There is a majesty and beauty in a mortified life ; some strictures and beams of the divine power that darts reverence into man.

2. Self-denial, nothing being a greater reproach unto religion than self-seeking. The world will be apt to suspect religion, as if it were but a device to gratify interests ; and where professors are altogether for worldly greatness, the suspicion is fed. There is no such way to stop the clamour, as by renouncing interests ; then the world will be convinced, that you think a good conscience worth something. We must overlook concernments, as well as renounce lusts. Trace all the instances, and you will find, that by this the elders live in the records of the world. A coward and an epicure are the stains of mankind. Faith is tried by its fortitude and valour, as well as by its heavenly progeny. The memory of the martyrs lives now, because of their spiritual fortitude and valour. When men can for a good conscience sacrifice their interests, it discovers the glory of religion. This will put to silence the clamours of the world, and right religion when it is suspected.

3. Duties of charity. These are visible fruits, and very much endearing to men in the world. Jesus Christ would have religion honoured this way, therefore this was the great rule our Lord taught, ' It is more blessed to give than to receive,' Acts xx. 35. It is the great principle of our religion to be giving ; nothing is more taking with the world than bounty. See what the apostle saith : Rom. v. 7, ' For scarcely for a righteous man will one die,' that is, for men of rigid innocence a man would hardly be brought to suffer ; ' but for a good man,' that is, one that is bountiful and communicative, ' a man would even dare to die.' This doth exceedingly melt and win upon the hearts of the men of the world.

4. A holy strict life and conversation : 2 Cor. viii. 21, ' Providing for honest things, not only in the sight of the Lord, but also in the sight of men.' Men must not have wherewith to blemish our walking. The world would fain blemish religion and religious persons, therefore they pitch upon the least failing. We read of Naaman, 2 Kings v. 1, ' He was a great man with his master, and honourable, but he was a leper ; ' and that stains all his glory. This is usually the form of men's commendations, they are thus and thus ; but they will pitch upon the least failing. Usually the world's commendation is like Joab's salute to Abner,—compliment, and smite him under the fifth rib ; they commend with many words, but they stab with a but. As an archer draws back his hand, that the arrow may pierce the deeper ; therefore we had need be strict. The world is quite contrary to God, who, in the midst of many failings, takes notice of a little good : 1 Peter iii. 6, ' Even as Sarah obeyed Abraham, and called him lord.' The whole history is full of unbelief, nothing savoury but that word, and the Spirit of God takes notice of it. So James v. 11, ' You have heard of the patience of Job ; ' though a great many murmurings are recorded, yet the Holy Ghost pitcheth upon this, not the other. But the world passeth over the good, and pitcheth upon what is evil ; as vultures flee over many gardens, but pitch upon a dead carcase. You may

observe how differently the world deals with astrologers and physicians; if astrologers fail often, and hit but once, the world cries them up for cunning men, but in a physician one gross miscarriage stains all his worthy cures. See the proneness of nature to unworthy arts; so they deal with the children of God, observe their failings and sore places, but overlook their worthy acts.

5. The duties of civil righteousness, these things are precious in men's eyes, and by these the world is preserved and kept up. The apostle speaks to subjects, that they should obey their governors, 'That they might put to silence the ignorance of foolish men,' 1 Peter ii. 15; these mastiffs will be opening their throats. Now we cannot muzzle them better but by duties of righteousness to men, which very much recommend our religion to God. These things draw men to the truth, and approve of the faith of the gospel. This is that which men praise most, and therefore hereby we shall remove all occasions of . offence.

Obs. 4. One of the rewards of an active faith is a good report. Here I shall show—

1. The reasons of God's ordination.

2. In what manner the Lord bestows this blessing upon believers.

3. Whether in the exercise of faith we may have an eye to this recompense, and respect the blessing of a good report.

First, For the reasons of God's ordination and appointment. I shall touch upon those that are of a chief regard and consideration.

1. That every necessary blessing may be adopted and taken into the covenant, and provision made against all inconveniences that may befal us in the way of religion. As the psalmist saith of Zion, Ps. xlviii. 12, 13, 'Walk about Zion, and go round about her; tell the towers thereof: mark ye well her bulwarks; consider her palaces;' that is, see if any thing be wanting that is necessary for use or ornament; so walk through the land of promise, and survey the riches of the covenant, see if any necessary defence or privilege be wanting to believers. The world is apt to clamour, and wicked men are ready to cast reproach upon the servants of the Lord, therefore among other blessings God hath provided for their repute and honour. Look, as against outward wants, God hath raised up a bulwark of promises to assure us of outward sustentation, and a supply of necessary provisions; so against reproaches there are frequent promises of providing for our renown and esteem in the world: 'That he will bring forth thy righteousness as the light, and thy judgment as the noonday,' Ps. xxxvii. 6. A believer is secured against all the assaults of the world. There is balm in the covenant against the wounds that are made by the fist of wickedness, or the breach that is made by the tongue of reproach. This is the usual trial of God's people, when they are exempted from other sufferings: Ps. lxiv. 3, 4, 'The wicked whet their tongue like a sword, and bend their bow, to shoot their arrows, even bitter words; that they may shoot in secret at the perfect: suddenly do they shoot at him and fear not.' Perfection meets with envy; men malign what they will not imitate. Religious eminency usually is blasted with slander; men scorn to see any above them. They that are at the bottom of the hill curse those that are atop. The world would have all equal; therefore when they cannot reach the eminency

of religious persons, they blast it till their repute be stained, and they are rendered criminal; they cannot make them like themselves, which is the revenge that wicked men take. Godly men's lives are a reproach to their conscience; so 'Noah by preparing an ark condemned the world,' Heb. xi. 7; and therefore by censure, and reproaches they stain their credit, that their own sin may be less odious, and avenge the wounds of their consciences by their reproaches of godly men. Now God has provided not only against their open assaults of violence, but against their privy detractions; as he hath secured our persons against their injuries, so our names against their reproaches. Every blessing is adopted and taken into the covenant.

2. Because of the great inconveniences of reproach and infamy, either to God and religion itself, or to good men. (1.) The great inconveniencies which redound to God and religion itself. The credit of religion depends much upon the credit of the persons that profess it. When godly men are evil spoken of, the way of truth suffers: Ezek. xxxvi. 20, 'They have profaned my holy name, when they said to them, These are the people of the Lord, and are gone forth out of his land,' that is, by their scandals. The offences charged upon the worshippers of God redound to God himself, and prove in effect the disgrace of Jesus Christ. They are called christians to the disgrace of Christ. When David fell, 'he gave the enemies of the Lord occasion to blaspheme,' 2 Sam. xii. 14. Men are apt to fly from the person to the profession. Hatred, saith the philosopher, is πρὸς τὰ γένη, to the whole kind; therefore wicked men that hate religion do not seek to blast the repute of particular persons, but even of religion itself: as Haman thought scorn to lay hold upon Mordecai alone, therefore he sought to destroy all the nation of the Jews, Esther iii. 6. Now God will provide for his own honour in the honour of his servants. It was a credit for David to have so many famous worthies under him, therefore they are called David's worthies; believers are Christ's worthies, he will be honoured in their renown. It is an honour to Christ, when believers are unspotted. It was the brag of the King of Assyria: Isa. x. 8, 'Are not my princes altogether kings?' When Christ adopts a people to himself, it is, 'that they may be to him for a name,' Isa. lv. 13. What is the reason Christ forms such excellent vessels of mercy out of thorns and briars, out of crabbed and sour trees, but that they may be to him for a name? And at the day of judgment, the Lord will be 'glorified in his saints, and admired in all them that believe,' 2 Thes. i. 10, not only in his own personal glory, and the brightness of his presence, but in the social glory that results from the dignities and privileges of his people: then Christ will be admired in his saints, now he will be honoured in his saints. Believers had need to be careful of their lives, for the credit of Christ lies at stake. (2.) The inconvenience that redounds to good men. Observe all the passages of providence, and you will see, that infamy is but the forerunner of greater trouble; showers of slander are but the presages and beginnings of grievous storms; first it rains down in slander, then comes a storm of persecution. The devil is first a liar, and then a murderer; wicked men take the more liberty to vex the children of God, when they are represented as criminal. It was a fashion in the primitive times to invest christians with bear-

skins, and then to bait them as bears; and it is an usual practice of
Satan to put the skin and livery of shame upon christians, and then
bait them.   He first blasts the repute of religious persons, then perse-
cutes them as offenders.   This is the meaning of that expression, Ps.
v. 9, 'Their throat is an open sepulchre;' that is, the slanders of the
wicked are but preparatives to death, an alarm to persecution; as when
the sepulchre is opened, it is prepared and ready to swallow the dead
carcase.   The same expression is used elsewhere of the force of the
Babylonians: Jer. v. 16, 'Their quiver is an open sepulchre;' that is,
you can expect nothing but death from the force and puissance of their
assaults; so here, the throat of the wicked is not only a burying-place
for your names, but your persons; first, men slander, and then molest
the children of God.   Certainly we had need look about us; you do
not know the issue and result of the present reproaches, which we cast
one upon another.   Eusebius, lib. viii. chap. 1, showeth that the persecutions of the heathens took their rise from the mutual provocations,
and reproaches of the christians.   The devil is afraid to meddle with
unstained innocency.   When Valens the Arian emperor raged like a
fierce beast against the orthodox, and the pastors of the churches were
suppressed, he durst not meddle with Paulinus, out of a reverence to
the unspottedness of his life and fame.   And Ignatius in his epistle to
the Traltians, speaketh of Polybius their bishop, that he was of such
a clear reputation, that the atheists stood in fear of him.   Wicked men
cannot with any advantage to their designs meddle with such.   A good
report is a great security and protection against violence.

3. That God may retaliate with faith.   Believers honour him, therefore he will honour them: 1 Sam. ii. 30, 'Those that honour me I
will honour.'   Never did any lose by a care to honour God.   Now
believers do not only honour God, by ascribing to him the glory of his
excellency by internal acts of faith, but by their outward conversation:
Mat. v. 16, 'Let your light so shine before men, that they may see your
good works and glorify your Father which is in heaven;' 1 Peter ii. 12,
'Having your conversation honest among the gentiles; that, whereas
they speak against you as evil-doers, they may, by your good works,
which they behold, glorify God in the day of visitation.'   God's returns
of blessings do often carry a proportion and suitableness to our acts of
duty.   None ever lose by honouring God; besides the recompenses of
the world to come, he casts honour upon them in this life.   The life
of a believer is a real honouring of God; for nothing honoureth
God so much as the active faith.   Formal professors serve Christ just
as the devil did; the devil carried him up into an high mountain, but
it was to tempt him to throw himself down again; so they seem to set
him upon the highest point of eminency in their professions and expressions, but they throw him down again, and deny him in their lives
and conversations.   Formal christians are like an ungracious son, he
will be apt to quarrel for the honour and repute of his father, yet his
courses are far more grievous to his father than other men's reproaches;
so those that seem to plead for the repute of their religion are a more
real dishonour to Christ than the blasphemer, or Turk, or pagans.   The
Lord is not pleased with empty prattle: Ps. l. 23, 'Whoso offereth
praise glorifieth me; and to him that ordereth his conversation aright

will I show the salvation of God.' No such glory as that which results to God from the christian conversation.

4. That this may be a bait to draw in others to a liking of his ways. The virgins are allured by the smell of his fragrant ointment, Cant. i. 3. When Christ's name, and the name of religion is fragrant, and yields sweet perfume in the nostrils of the world, this draws them in. It is a usual prejudice against the strictness of religion, men think it will be a debasing to them, and take off from their honours and esteem. *Coguntur esse mali, ne viles habeantur.* It is much against the hair and bent of nature to own the despised ways of God, that which brings nothing but infamy and reproach ; therefore men stand off and are prejudiced. I confess this is their great sin. They should take up David's resolution : 2 Sam. vi. 22, ' I will be yet more vile.' But now God condescends to their infirmities, and casteth honour upon his servants to invite the world, because the temptation of honour is very taking with ingenuous spirits. Of all possessions, fame comes nearest to grace ; some providences seem to be like Haman's proclamation before Mordecai, ' Thus shall it be done to the man whom God delighteth to honour : ' or to speak in the language of the psalmist, Ps. cxlix. 9, ' This honour have all his saints.'

Secondly, In what manner doth the Lord dispense this privilege ? And it is grounded upon an objection, that may be framed thus ; the servants of God are often clouded with black reproaches, ' They took away the spouse's veil,' Cant. v. 7 ; that is, her honour and name. David complains, Ps. xxii. 6, ' He was a reproach of men, and despised of the people ;' so the apostle, 1 Cor. iv. 13, ' We are made as the filth of the world, and are the offscouring of all things to this day.' God's jewels are often counted the world's filth. Therefore how doth God give in this recompense to the active faith ? I answer, in several propositions.

1. The blessing is not absolutely complete in this life. As long as there is sin we are liable to shame. A good name is an outward pledge of eternal glory. When sin is abolished then may we expect perfect glory. In a mixed estate we must look for mixed dispensations. Here we pass through honour and dishonour, evil report and good report, 2 Cor. vi. 8. Thus it will be ; there are changes and imperfections in our outward condition, as well as in the inward frame of our souls. Here God doth but begin to glorify, and begin to honour us, therefore it is not absolutely complete.

2. The wicked are not competent judges when they judge of the faithful : Luke vi. 26, ' Wo unto you when all men shall speak well of you.' General applause can seldom be had without compliance, and without some sin ; therefore it is spoken as a cursed thing to gratify all, and seek to draw respect from all. There is one rare instance in the third Epistle of John, ver. 12, ' Demetrius hath a good report of all men, and of the truth itself ;' that is, he is generally well-famed, but usually the world is froward, and will blast those that differ from them ; John xv. 19, ' If you were of the world, the world would love its own ; but because you are not of the world, but I have called you out of the world, therefore the world hates you.' It is suspicious to be dandled upon the world's knees. These elders obtained a good report ;

but when ? in the scriptures, in the churches. It is a favour to be the
object of wicked men's reproaches. That of an heathen was notable,
Quid mali feci? what evil have I done? when he was entertained
with general applauses. The respects of an enemy makes a man
suspected.

3. We have the approbation of their consciences, though not the
commendation of their lips; and their hearts approve when their
mouths slander; and we have their reverence, though not their praise.
Wicked men dread the heavenliness and strictness of the children of
God, though they do not actually honour them ; their malice and
hatred is more against the party, than against their personal failings,
which is sometimes acknowledged ; *Caius Sejus vir bonus, nisi quod
christianus.* They had nothing against Daniel but only in the matter
of his God, Dan. vi. 5. And Trajan's testimony in Tertullian is full,
' That he could find no fault in them worthy of death or of bonds, only
they were wont to hear sermons, to sing psalms to God and Christ.
Otherwise for their conversation, they were very honest, conformable
to the laws of their princes, and forbade murder, theft, adultery, and
other sins, which were destructive to human societies.'—*Tertul. Apolog.
adversus gentes.* Oh ! if we did not let fall the majesty of our conversations, we should approve ourselves to the consciences of wicked
men, and our only crime would be our profession.

4. There are some special seasons when God will vindicate his people from contempt. There is a resurrection of names as well as of
persons. When they seem to be buried in the throat of the wicked,
which is an open sepulchre in obloquy and reproach, God raiseth them
up in honour. The Lord saith, ' that he will establish Zion, and
make Jerusalem a praise upon the earth,' Isa. lxii. 7; so Zeph. iii. 18–20,
' I will gather them that are sorrowful for the solemn assembly,
who are of thee, to whom the reproach of it was a burden. Behold, at
that time I will undo all that afflict thee, and I will save her that
halteth, and gather her that was driven out ; and I will get them praise
and fame in every land, where they have been put to shame. At that
time will I bring you again, even in the time that I gather you : for
I will make you a name and a praise among all people of the earth,
when I turn your captivity before your eye, saith the Lord.' The prejudices of the world vanish, and the renown of the people of God is
cleared up. Strong prejudices have a strong antidote. ' Christ was
declared to be the son of God with power by the resurrection from the
dead,' Rom. i. 4. There are strong providences which roll away the
reproaches of God's children, Zech. iii. 4, ' Take away the filthy garments from him.'

5. Those that do observe the usual course of God's providence shall
find strange traverses in reference to the good report of the saints.
God is ever ready to confute the reproaches of the wicked, and to clear
up the innocency of his particular servants. It is good to observe
providence herein, how God brandeth the wicked, and discovers the
hypocrite, and vindicates and rolls away contempt from the godly. He
brands the wicked; that of Solomon is a positive rule : Prov. x. 7, ' The
name of the wicked shall rot.' God leaves them to rottenness and
stench, and pours infamy upon them, that their names have an ill

savour to them that are of their own party.   So observe how providence doth discover an hypocrite, God giveth them up to folly and sin,
whereby they contract a blot and blemish to themselves: Prov. xxvi.
26, ' His wickedness shall be showed before the whole congregation.'
God will put off his vizard, and expose him to shame and contempt.
There is seldom a hypocrite upon the stage of the world, but his disguise falls off one time or the other.   Yea, sometimes the very secret
sins of God's children are made manifest: 2 Sam. xii. 12, ' Thou didst
it secretly, but I will do this thing before all Israel, and before the sun.'
God would shame David for his secret sin and wickedness.   Observe
again how providence at other times doth vindicate the godly, and cast
shame upon those that do accuse them : 1 Peter iii. 16, ' Having a
good conversation, that whereas they speak evil of you as of evil-doers,
they may be ashamed that falsely accuse your good conversation in
Christ.'   All the reproaches of the wicked are but like the dashing of
the waves against the rock ; the foam returns upon themselves ; but
God's people have the glory; or as they that spit against the wind, the
drivel is cast upon their own faces.   Patience and a good conversation
will soon dispel all those mists and clouds.   Hair will grow again
though shaven, as long as the roots remain ; so though the razor of
censure bring on baldness and reproach upon the head of religion and
ways of God, yet while the root doth remain, while there is a good
conversation, it will spring up again.   Trust God with your repute,
and good names as well as your estate ; the hearts and tongues of men
are in his hands, and he can overrule them ; nay, you have given some
occasion because of your folly, yet be more circumspect, and so trust
God.

Thirdly, Whether in the exercise of faith we may eye a good report ?
is not this vain-glory ?   I answer in four things.

1. Our chief care must be to do the duty, and trust God with the
blessing ; this is the temper of a christian.   Men usually do quite otherwise ; they would enjoy the blessing, and neglect the duty : ' yet honour
me before the people,' said that sly hypocrite, 1 Sam. xv. 30.   We are
careless of service, and yet hunt for praise.   *Laus humana non appeti
debet, sed sequi ;* outward praise must not be the aim of the action, but
the event.   And again, Aquinas ; *Gloria bene contemnitur, nihil male
agendo propter ipsam, et bene acquiritur, nihil malo agendo contra
ipsam.*   We must do well, that we may not miss of a good report ;
and we must not do ill, that we may obtain it.   We must do things
that are praiseworthy, though not to that end.   Do what may be seen,
though not to that end that it may be seen : Mat. v. 16, ' Let your light
so shine before men, that they may see your good works, and glorify
your Father which is in heaven.'   It doth not show what is the aim
and chief end of a christian, but what will follow upon such an innocent,
pure, and holy conversation : Luke xiv. 10, ' Sit at the lowest room,
that when he that bade thee cometh, he may say unto thee,' &c. (*that* is
taken for *then*) ; that is, when you are so modestly humble, then the
master of the house will bid you sit higher.   When the heart runs out
upon praise more than duty, it is naught.   Therefore take heed of such
secret whispers of vanity, and suppositions of applause, hearkening after
the echo, the running out of the spirit or soul by unworthy low aims,

and carnal reflections. We are commanded to do things that are 'of good report,' Phil. iv. 8. though not with that aim.

2. If we expect it as a blessing of the covenant, we must rather look for it from God than from men, expect it as the gift of his grace for our encouragement in the ways of religion. Usually we do quite otherwise, and therefore are more careful of credit than of conscience, and are not careful of pleasing God so much as compliance with men. A man that expects a good name differs as much from him that hunts after vain glory, as he that looks after an estate differs from him that would only please himself in the repute of it, or being accounted rich. You must prefer the testimony of a good conscience before the applause of men: 2 Cor. i. 12, 'This is our rejoicing, the testimony of our conscience;' found all your hopes in the inward witness of the Holy Ghost, and take more care to be good, than to seem to be good. The people of God may be described thus; they perform inward duties cheerfully, that they may approve their hearts to God; and outward duties watchfully, that they may not taint their actions with any unworthy aim. Others are altogether for pleasing of men, and careless of grieving the Spirit of God.

3. All the respect that we have to men, is by a greater care of duty, to prevent undue surmises and suspicion: 2. Cor. viii. 21, 'Providing for honest things, not only in the sight of God, but in the sight of men.' To clear up their hearts to God, and clear up their religion to men: 1 Peter iii. 16, 'Having a good conscience, that whereas they speak evil of you, as of evil-doers; they may be ashamed, who falsely accuse your good conversation in Christ.' Thus are you to cut off occasion from them that desire occasion to reproach you. This is but a necessary aim to undeceive the world.

4. The glory of God and the credit of religion must be at the utmost end of all: Mat. v. 16, 'Let your light so shine before men, that they may see your good works'—he doth not stop there, 'and glorify your Father which is in heaven;' and 1 Pet. ii. 12, 'That whereas they speak against you as evil-doers, they may by your good works, which they shall behold, glorify God in the day of visitation.' Still the utmost end must be the glory of God and credit of religion. Usually men desire a name and repute in the world, on design to promote carnal and secular advantages, but our main end should be God's glory, and adorning the gospel. All a christian's actions and aims terminate in reasons and ends of religion, and they eye self only in subordination to those great ends.

Use 1. Prize this blessing; it is a sweet encouragement to you in the work of God. I observe that usually men first make shipwreck of a good name, then of a good conscience. He that is tender of his conscience will not be over lavish of his credit. The old testament, which speaketh sparingly of heaven, speaketh often of the advantage of a good name: Eccles. vii. 1, 'A good name is better than precious ointment.' Religion preserves the name from rottenness and putrefaction; this will embalm, perpetuate, and preserve your memories in the churches. Religion with a good name is like a comely body in a handsome garment; a jewel set in iron hath not the lustre as when set in gold. Grace hath its lustre, though clouded with reproaches, but a good name will make you more cheerful; 'For a good report maketh the bones fat,' Prov. xv. 30. And it will make you more useful; a blemished instrument is of little use. The priests under the law were to have no outward blemish or deformity. It is a qualification of a bishop, 1 Tim. iii. 7, 'That he must have a good report of them that are without;' not only be known in the churches, but of unstained life in the world. Who would drink of a suspected fountain? or take meat out of a leprous hand? Men are prejudiced with the offering of the Lord when the priests are scandalous: 1 Sam. ii. 17, compared with ver. 25.

Use 2. Be careful how you prejudice the good name of a believer; you cross God's ordination. How ought you to tremble, when you go about to take off the crown which God hath put on their heads! Num. xii. 8, 'Wherefore then were ye not afraid to speak against my servant Moses?' What! against Moses! Did not your knees smite one against another for very fear? 'Thus shall it be done with the man whom the king delighteth to honour,' Esther vi. 9. A man should be afraid to dishonour those whom God will honour. You are the worst thieves, you rob them of the most precious jewel; no treasure like a good name: Prov. xxii. 1, 'A good name is rather to be chosen than great riches.' This is the very devil's sin; it is his proper work to be the accuser of the brethren, Rev. xii. 10; to frame mischievous insinuations against the children of God. The devil doth not commit adultery, break the sabbath, dishonour parents, but he doth accuse the brethren. You are but acting the devil's part, while you are scandalising those that are eminent for grace: Ps. lxiv. 3, 'They whet their tongue like a sword, and bend their bows, to shoot their arrows, even bitter words.' It is meant of those that speak against religious eminency; and see their judgment, ver. 7, 8, 'But God shall shoot at them with an arrow, suddenly shall they be wounded; so they shall make their own tongue to fall upon themselves.' Better a mountain fall upon you, than when he shall come to visit this sin, the mischief of your evil tongue should fall upon you. Most odious it is in those that pretend to be christians, to do it to one another; as for one soldier to defame another, or for a scholar to despise learning. We should rejoice in the repute of others, that they have a worthy name, and not blemish it; as the apostle, Rom. i. 8, 'I thank my God through Jesus Christ for you all, that your faith is spoken of throughout the whole world,' that you are eminent believers; so Col. i 3, 4, 'We give thanks to God, since we heard of your faith in Christ Jesus, and of the love which ye have unto all the saints.' That Christ hath worthies abroad, this should be our joy. We should preserve the repute of others, because it is a good means to keep our own. Rash censures meet with a retaliation: Mat. vii. 1, 'Judge not, that ye be not judged.' But you will say, If the man do but profess religion, must we not speak evil of him? no, unless it be done with grief; that one which belongs to Christ should dishonour himself and his profession. There may be malice where there is truth, if we are glad of their failing; 'Of whom I have told you often, and now tell you even weeping, that they are enemies of the cross of Christ,' Phil. iii. 18; he speaks of licentious persons under a form of godliness, which drive on a secular design. Take heed what thou sayest of those who in outward profession are more zealous than thou. John Baptist's head in a charger is an ordinary dish at our meals. When men's hearts are warm with wine and good cheer, then the children of God are brought in like Samson, to make sport for the Philistines. When they are full, then they call for a holy person, upon whom they may vent their malice, as the Babylonians called for an holy song: Ps. cxxxvii. 3, 'Sing us one of the songs of Zion.'

Use 3. To press you to this active faith. There is great reason for it upon these grounds.

1. Because there are so many censures abroad. In times of division men take a liberty to blast opposite parties. Now shine forth in the lustre of an holy conversation, that envy may find nothing in you: Neh. v. 9, 'Ought ye not to walk in the fear of our God, because of the reproach of the heathen our enemies?' Should not we be of more strict and holy conversations, that we may silence censures and re-proachers? Well-doing is the best confutation of slanders: 1 Peter ii. 12, 'Having your conversation honest among the gentiles; that whereas they speak against you as evil-doers, they may, by your good works, which they shall behold, glorify God in the day of visitation.' The apology is soon diffused, though not by your own mouth; wicked men become our compurgators. Words are apt to beget strife, and are more liable to suspicion: by a good life you approve yourselves to their consciences. Revengeful replies lose their majesty. When John's disciples came to Christ to know whether he were the Messiah or no, saith our Saviour, Mat. xi. 4, 'Go tell John the things you see and hear.' Christ doth not plead for himself, but shows his works. So this will be the best confutation, those real apologies are best; let the world see what is in us by the strictness and holiness of our lives and conversations.

2. Because there are so few good works abroad. Man is no further esteemed than he is useful. Many of the heathens were canonised for their usefulness. There is no such way to keep your memory savoury in the church as by public usefulness. For hereby a christian doth not only provide for present esteem, but for future. These elders in the text live in the world to this day. Every age should yield some honourable instances of the efficacy of faith: how few hath Christ in this age whose memory will be fresh and savoury in the church of God? God hath still his worthies. Transmit a good example to posterity; you may live and do good hereby after you are dead, 'Who being dead, yet speaketh,' Heb xi. 4; as Elias lived again in John Baptist, 'who came in the spirit and power of Elias,' Luke i. 17. Look, as a wicked man lives after he is dead in his evil example, and his sin is perpetuated, as Jeroboam did in the lives of the wicked kings, who walked in his way; so do you live in some pious monument of your faithfulness to God. I have observed why most good works have been done by superstitious men, who had been men of infamous life, that they may retrieve the wickedness of their life by some acts of charity. But good men do few public works, partly because usually God's people are humbled with wants and poverty, and so have not such advantage in regard of worldly concernments. Or else they do it in a more secret way, and retail their charity out in secret by several parcels; as good housekeepers are not prodigal in feasting. Or else, that they may abhor the way of doing good only at their death, when they can keep their

wealth no longer.   Worldly men are like the mice, which, they say,
feed inthe golden mines; they eat the ore, but do not deliver it up again
till they die, and are cut asunder.   It is said of wicked men, 'their
bellies are filled with hid treasure,' and when they die they leave their
substance to their children, Ps. xvii. 14; but the children of God do
good in their lives.

SERMON VII.

*Through faith we understand that the worlds were framed by the
word of God, so that things which are seen were not made of
things which do appear.*—HEB. xi. 3.

IN these words the apostle beginneth the history of faith, and therefore
goeth so high as God's ancient work of creation.   His drift is to prove
that faith satisfieth itself in the word of God, though nothing be seen ;
and he proveth it in the first instance and exercise of faith that ever
was in the world—the creation.

In the words you may observe—(1.) The doctrine of the creation laid
down ; (2.) The means whereby we come to the understanding of it.

1. The doctrine of the creation is delivered in all the necessary circumstances of it.

[1.] The matter framed—τοὺς αἰῶνας, the ages, that is, the world
which hath endured so many ages ; the essence and duration of a thing
being so near akin, they are often taken for one another: Eph. ii. 2,
'Wherein in time past ye walked, κατ' αἰῶνα, according to the course
of this world :' which is necessary to note against the Socinians, who
to evade that testimony for the Godhead of Christ:' Heb. i. 2, 'By whom
also he made the worlds,' understand it of the ages, and the collection
of the church in all times.

[2.] The manner—κατηρτίσθαι, he curiously jointed and made it,
and digested it into an exquisite rank and frame.

[3.] The instrument—ῥήματι Θεοῦ—*By the word of God.*   It
may be taken either for his substantial word, or his word of power, by
which all things were produced out of nothing ; ' He spake, and it was
done,' Ps. xxxiii. 9.

[4.] The term from whence God's action took its rise—ἐκ μὴ
φαινομένων—*Of things which do not appear.* ἐκ doth not properly note
the matter ; and when we say, God made the world out of nothing, our
meaning is not, that nothing is the matter whereof the world is made,
as if God should bestow a new fashion and shape upon nothing ; but
only that it is the *terminus a quo*, not *materia ex qua*, as much
as to say, God made the world when nothing was before ; God had not
any matter to work upon.   There are some difficulties attending the
Greek phrase, but I shall consider them hereafter.

2. The means whereby we come to understand this great mystery
—πίστει νοῦμεν—*By faith we understand.*   Reason will give us a

glimpse, but by faith alone we can unfold the riddle and mystery of the world's creation.

I begin with the means of knowledge as being first in the words, ' By faith we understand.' Whence observe—

1. That it is of great profit and comfort to believers to consider the creation.

2. That we can only understand the truth and wonders of the creation by faith.

The first point is a preparative to the whole discourse; it is this—

Doct. 1. It is a necessary exercise for the children of God to turn their minds to the creation.

Reasons :—

1. It discovereth much of God. God hath engraven his name upon his works; as those that make watches or any curious pieces write their names upon them ; or, as he that carved a buckler for Minerva had so curiously inlaid his own name, that it could not be razed out without defacing the whole work ; so hath God. The creatures are but a draft and portraiture of the divine glory. In the creatures we may discern—(1.) His essence ; (2.) His attributes.

[1.] His essence. Creation is the true note of the true God ; the first cause is the supreme being ; therefore creation always is avouched on the behalf of the divine majesty of God: Jer. x. 11, 12, 'Thus shall ye say unto them, The gods that have not made the heavens and the earth, even they shall perish from the earth, and from under these heavens. He hath made the earth by his power, he hath established the world by his wisdom, and hath stretched forth the heavens by his discretion.' Jonah i. 9, 'I am an Hebrew, and I fear the Lord, the God of heaven, which hath made the sea and the dry land.' Isa. xlv. 6, 7, ' I am the Lord, and there is none else; I form the light, and create darkness,' &c. and ver. 8, 'I the Lord have created it.' So the apostles: Acts xiv. 15, ' That ye should turn from these vanities unto the living God, which made heaven and earth, and the sea, and all things that are therein.' Acts xvii. 24, ' God that made the world, and all things therein.' Rom. i. 20, ' For the invisible things of him from the creation of the world are clearly seen, being understood by the things that are made, even his eternal power and godhead.' This was the heathens' bible, and out of this will they be arraigned at the day of Christ: the creatures will witness against them—they discovered an eternal essence, but the world discovered it not. God at first spake to the world not by words but things, and taught them by hieroglyphics. The scriptures are but a comment upon this book of the creatures.

[2.] His attributes. They are all engraven upon the creatures, but he that runneth may read these three attributes, goodness, power, and wisdom, which call for love, reverence, and trust. Ἐποίησεν ὡς ἀγαθὸς τὸ χρήσιμον, ὡς σοφος τὸκάλλιστον, ὡς δύνατος τὸ μέγιστον—Basil. The goodness of God is seen in the usefulness of the creatures to man ; the power of God in the stupendousness and wonderfulness of the works ; and the wisdom of God in the apt structure, constitution, and order of all things. First he createth, then distinguisheth, then adorneth. The first work was to create heaven and earth out of nothing ; there is his power. God's next work is a wise distribution and ordination, he distinguisheth night from day, darkness from light, waters above the firmament from waters beneath the firmament; the sea from the dry land; there is his wisdom. Then he decked the earth with plants and beasts, the sea with fishes, the air with birds, the firmament with stars; there is his goodness. Let us explain these a little more particularly.

(1.) His goodness. The creation is nothing else but an effusion of the goodness of God: Ps. cxv. 3, 'Our God is in heaven, he hath done whatsoever he pleased.' He acteth at liberty; he might have made it sooner or later; the only reason is the counsel of his own will: Rev. iv. 11, 'Thou hast created all things, and for thy pleasure they are and were created.' Creatures work out of a servile necessity. The trinity was not solitary. God was happy enough without us, and had a fulness and sufficiency of happiness within himself, only he would have us to participate of his goodness. God's great aim was to communicate his goodness to creatures; and therefore in making the world, he did not only aim at his own glory, but the benefit of man, that man might have a place for his exercise and a dwelling for his eternal rest. A place for his exercise: Isa. xlv. 18, 'He created it not in vain, he formed it to be inhabited;' so Ps. cxv. 16, 'The heaven, even the heavens are the Lord's, but the earth hath he given to the children of men.' In heaven God sitteth in his palace, in the midst of his best creatures; but the earth, the round world is ours. And heaven was prepared before the beginning of the world for their place of rest: Mat. xxv. 34, 'Come, ye blessed of my Father, inherit the kingdom prepared for you from the foundation of the world.' His love was towards us before the world was, and we shall reap the fruits of it, when the world shall be no more.

(2.) His power. God brought all things out of the womb of nothing; his *fiat* was enough: Isa. xl. 26, 'Lift up your eyes on high, and behold who hath created these things, that bringeth out their host by number; he calleth them all by names, by the greatness of his might, for that he is strong in power, not one faileth.' The force of the cause appeareth in the effects, and God's power in the creatures. This is the most visible attribute: Rom. i. 20, 'For the invisible things of him from the creation of the world are clearly seen, being understood by the things that are made, even his eternal power and godhead.' Men touched with no sense or reverence of religion, yet will have this in their mouths, God Almighty.

(3.) His wisdom. The admirableness and comely variety of God's works doth easily offer it to our thoughts. In the work you may discern a wise workman: Ps. cxxxvi. 5, 'To him that by wisdom made the heavens: for his mercy endureth for ever.' So Prov. iii. 19. 'The Lord by wisdom hath founded the earth; by understanding hath he established the heavens.' The wisdom of God appeareth—(1.) In the order of making; (2.) In the order of placing all creatures.

(1*st.*) In making of them. In simple things, God began with those which are most perfect, and came nearest to his own essence. His first creature is light, which of all qualities is most pure and defecate, and is not stained by passing through places most impure. The first garment God put on in the creatures' eyes was light; Ps. civ. 2, 'Who coverest thyself with light as with a garment.' Then all the elements in mixt bodies; God took another method, from imperfect to perfect: first, things that have a being, as the firmament; then life, as plants; then sense, as beasts; then reason, as man.   First, God would provide the places of heaven and earth, and then the creatures to dwell in them; first the food, then the beasts.   Provision was made for the inhabitants of the earth, as grass for beasts, and light for all living and moving creatures.   God provided for the necessities of beasts, ere he would bring them into the world.   God made first plants, that have but a growing life; then beasts, fishes, fowls, that have a feeling life; then man that hath a rational life.   God would teach us to go from good to better.   Man was made last, as most excellent; his palace is furnished with all things necessary, and then like a prince he is sent into the world to rule and reign.

(*2dly.*) In disposing all things into their apt cells for the beauty and service of the whole.   There are not such great beasts in the earth as in the sea, to avoid a waste of food, which would be consumed by the beasts of the land, to the prejudice of man.   All things are wonderfully made.

2. It is a wonderful advantage to faith to give us hope and consolation in the greatest distresses.   The whole creation is a standing monument of God's power; we see what he can do: Ps. cxxiv. 8, 'Our help is in the name of the Lord, who made heaven and earth.'   As long as heaven and earth is standing, we need not distrust God's power: Jer. xxxii. 17, 'Ah Lord God, behold, thou hast made the heaven and the earth by thy great power, and stretched out arm; and there is nothing too hard for thee.'   So Ps. cxlvi. 5, 6, 'Happy is he that hath the God of Jacob for his help; whose hope is in the Lord his God, which made heaven, and earth, and sea, and all that therein is, which keepeth truth for ever.'   The works of creation are but pawns and pledges of the possibility and certainty of every thing promised.   Every promise is as powerful as God's first creating word, 'let there be light,' let there be day.

3. It putteth us in mind of our duty.

[1.] To stir up in us a reverence and dread of God above the creatures.   We are used to things of sense, they work with us.   Make much of the creator, and the creatures shall do thee no harm: Acts iv. 24, 'Lord, thou art God, which hast made heaven and earth, and the sea, and all that in them is.'

[2.] To stir up humility to God: Rom. ix. 20, 'Nay, but O man, who art thou that repliest against God?   Shall the thing formed say to him that formed it, Why hast thou made me thus?'   Isa. xlv. 9, 'Wo unto him that striveth with his maker; let the potsherd strive with the potsherds of the earth.   Shall the clay say to him that fashioneth it, What makest thou; or thy work, He hath no hands?'   Gen. xviii. 27, 'Behold, now I have taken upon me to speak unto the Lord, who am but dust and ashes.'

[3.] To make us humble and kind to men: Acts xvii. 26, 'And hath made of one blood all nations of men, to dwell on all the face of the earth.'   *Omnis sanguis concelor*, Isa. lviii. 7, 'That thou hide not thyself from thy own flesh.'

Use. It serveth to quicken us to think of the creation.   But oh, how backward, cold and sluggish are we in this work! either we use the creatures as beasts, without thankfulness, and looking up to the creator; or else, as philosophers, there is more curiosity than profit in our researches: but I observe christians are coldly affected with such an argument. The causes are these—

1. We have an higher light. Sense in beasts is more acute, so reason in heathens, because it is their only light. But this should not be, we should not slight the works of God, because of a higher revelation. When a man is able to read, he should not lay aside the use of letters. The creation is a good primer for us to spell in, though not so good as the grammar of the scriptures. When we have a free use of reason, we find a good help in books; in youth, because we have no experience, we are more prone to thoughts of atheism; therefore, says Solomon, Eccles. xii. 1, ' Remember thy creator in the days of thy youth.' But excellent arguments for conviction may be drawn hence, when we have higher knowledge.

2. Because these objects are familiar and frequent. *Homini ingenitum est magis nova, quam magna mirari.* This is the wretched disposition of man, to admire things that are new, rather than things that are great. We give money to see strange beasts; you may think with yourselves, when you see people pressing to see a new sight, there is a greater miracle every day; we are injurious to God, when we do not glorify him in his creatures, when we do carelessly pass by such goodly works.

3. This proceeds from laziness. It is easier to read a chapter in the word, than the book of the creatures, the act is more outward and corporeal, the other putteth us to the pains and trouble of discourse: there is no duty so spiritual as meditation, therefore we withdraw the shoulder. Though this was pleasant to David, Ps. civ. 34, 'My meditation of him shall be sweet; I will be glad in the Lord.'

4. From worldliness. Our heads and hearts are so taken up about our own work, that we have little leisure to mind God's; like a company of ants, we crawl up and down, and do not regard the great things about us.

Here I shall— (1.) Lay down motives to quicken us to this necessary work of reflecting upon the creation of the world, that was made by the power of God out of nothing. (2.) Offer directions how to reflect upon the creature with comfort and profit.

First, for the motives.

1. The creatures are apt to teach us. All the creatures of God, they have a voice, and read a lecture to us of the glory of the divinity. The first bible was the book of nature; God spake to the world, not by words, but by things, and taught men by what he had written of his glory upon the creation. As many creatures as there are, so many letters there are, out of which we may spell God; the book is written within with glorious angels, and without with corporeal substances that discover the glory of God; it may teach us unspeakable wisdom, unmeasurable goodness, infinite power. The world is a book, God's power was the hand with which it was written, and his wisdom was the pen, and the letters are the creatures; some are lesser letters, some greater, but out of the whole there is a volume of praise to the creator. Nay, the world is not only a book, but a teacher; not only a dead letter, but a living voice: Ps. xix. 1, ' The heavens declare the glory

of God, and the firmament showeth his handy work.' Lesser creatures have a voice to proclaim the excellency of their creator. An ant and a gnat may take the pulpit, and preach a God to us. 'Their line is gone out into all the earth, and their words to the end of the world,' saith the psalmist, ver. 4. We should so hearken to the creature, as if we did hear God himself speak to us; 'and day unto day uttereth speech, and night unto night showeth knowledge,' ver. 2. Other preachers are soon spent and tired, but the creatures are constant preachers, always calling upon us night and day to mind God; and, ver. 3, 'There is no speech nor language, where their voice is not heard.' Though the languages of all nations scattered over the world be very different, yet there is one book may be read in every country; the heavens speak Greek to the Grecians; they speak English to us; so many creatures, so many preachers there are of God's wisdom, power, and goodness. Nay, the creature that seems most gross, the dull earth, the heaviest and grossest element, and the mute fishes, proclaim God: Job xii, 8, 'Speak to the earth, and it shall teach thee, and the fishes of the sea shall declare unto thee.' Though the fishes have no sound, cannot make so much as a rude noise, though they have no voice, yet they are able to preach God unto us, and teach us, that there is a sovereign providence by which all things are guided and governed.

2. God hath made man fit to learn, he hath given us faculties to this purpose, that we may understand the creatures: Eccles. iii. 11, 'He hath set the world in their heart.' The great work of God's Spirit is to pluck the world out of our hearts; what is the meaning then of it? He hath not only given us the creature to contemplate, but an ability, an earnest desire, to search into the secrets of nature, that we may understand the voice of the creation. Men are the most considerable, and the most considering part of the world. The creatures praise God, that is, they offer matter of praise: Ps. cxlv. 10, 'All thy works shall praise thee, O Lord, and thy saints shall bless thee;' they are as a well-tuned harp, but man maketh the music. We should not be silent, when the creatures proclaim their creator. Man is made to consider all the rest of the creatures, therefore is placed in the middle of the world, that he may look round about him. Man hath reason given him; and shall man that hath reason make no more use of the stars than the creatures do, only to see by them? Man is to discourse of them. He hath given us a body bored through with five senses to let out thoughts, and to take in objects; to taste the goodness of God in the creatures, and see divinity in them, and hear the voice by which they proclaim the glory of God. A philosopher, being asked, why he had eyes? answered, *Ut miracula Dei contempler.* Creatures are mutes, when neglected, and vowels, when we consider them.

3. God himself delights in the view of his own works. God observed every day's work, and said, it was good; he took a complacency in it: Prov. viii. 30, 'Rejoicing in the habitable parts of the earth.' Ps. civ. 31, The Lord rejoiceth in his works:' God rejoiceth in the view of his own works; therefore there is great reason for us to study and contemplate them.

4. This was God's great aim and end in making man, that he

might have a witness and publisher of his own glory. That this was the aim of God, to have his works viewed distinctly, may be discovered by many things; that he did prolong his work for six days, when he might have made all things in one day. And this was the reason why he made man last, that when he was made he might contemplate all the rest of the creatures. *Deus te quasi testem, laudatoremque tanti operis sui in hunc mundum induxit*, Lactantius. When God had made the whole world, there wanted one to be a witness of the work, one to admire the greatness and goodness of it, therefore man is brought into the world for this purpose; when God's feast was prepared, then man was invited to come and taste. The first sabbath was appointed for contemplation; it is the sweetest rest that we can enjoy, to view the works of God. Now consider what an injury and unthankfulness will this be to God, to cross the aim of the creation, and to pass by such a goodly frame with a careless eye. If a father should build a great house or palace for his son, and he should not so much as deign to look upon it, what an ingratitude would this be! So when God hath furnished his palace with such variety of all creatures, then not to consider and regard the operation of his hands, what an unkind return would this be! If you should make a sumptuous feast, and your guests will not so much as look upon your table, you would count this a great affront; so this is a great affront to the divine majesty, not to look upon his works, since the beauty and order of the creation is a feast for the mind. The world is not only the house of man, but the temple of God. Many came to see Solomon's temple from afar, and many go to Jerusalem to see the temple of the sepulchre; you need not go so far. When the ethnics slandered the primitive christians, that they had no temple, they answered, *Dei templum esse universum hoc quod cernitur*—this world that we behold is God's temple.

5. The creatures signify nothing to us, if we do not consider them; without meditation we receive no good: Ps. cxlv. 10, 'All thy works praise thee.' The creatures are as a well-tuned instrument, but it is man that must make the music. The creatures, if they be not regarded, are but mutes, they make no sound. There we read the beauty, wisdom, and majesty of God: Job xii. 7, 'Ask now of the beasts, and they shall teach thee; and the fowls of the air, and they shall tell thee.' Ask the creatures questions. Though the creatures have neither voice nor ears, yet we may consult and confer with them; when we think of them, they answer and resolve the questions put to them, though not to the ear, yet to the conscience. Ask the creatures, Is there a God? they answer, Yea. What kind of God is he? they will answer, A wise, powerful, and good God. By meditation we may easily make out these collections. It is great unthankfulness, that the creatures should proclaim the glory of God to no purpose; that we should be silent when the creatures speak. Christ said, the stones would cry if these should hold their peace. Shall the heavens declare the works of God, and shall man regard them not? Shall we be deaf, when the creatures don't cease to cry to us.

6. It is a duty that lies upon all reasonable creatures. (1.) The angels delight in this work; Job xxxviii. 7, it is said, when the earth was

founded, 'the morning stars sang together, and all the sons of God shouted for joy;' that is, when God first laid the foundations of the heavens, the angels, like birds at the break of day, welcome the dawning of the creation and the first appearances of the love of God to the creature, and still they are praising God for his essence and works. It cannot literally and properly be understood. There is but one morning star, not many; the stars were not created when the foundations of the earth were laid, not till the fourth day, Gen. i. 16. The angels are as it were spiritual stars. God is the sun and angels the stars. God is the Father of lights, and those angels are the stars derived from God. (2.) The saints of God, they make it their work. Much of the scripture is spent in this purpose. The whole book of Job is interspersed with several passages, chap. xxxvii. xxxviii. xxxix. David is a professed student in the works of God; many psalms are composed to give God the glory of the creation—Ps. viii. and xix., civ., cvi., and cxlvii. Meditation is the most spiritual part of worship, therefore to the children of God it is wondrous sweet. It is true Christ crucified is a chief object, Ephes. iii. 10, but the world created must have a room and place. (3.) The heathens by the light of nature acknowledge it to be their duty. I might produce many instances; Tully saith, *Animarum, ingeniorumque naturale quoddam pabulum est contemplatio, consideratioque naturæ :* consideration of nature is the food of the soul, the solace and refreshment of the rational soul. Another saith, Θεατὴς ἐγένετο τῶν ἐργῶν Θεοῦ ὁ ἄνθρωπος ; the world is a great theatre wherein the creation is acted and drawn forth; God is the author, and man is made to be the spectator. Another said, *Os hominum sublime dedit, cœlumque tueri jussit*—God has given man an erect countenance, that he might look up to heaven. Anaxagoras being asked, why he was born? answered, Εἰς θεωρίαν ἡλίου καὶ σελήνης καὶ οὐρανοῦ—For contemplation of sun, moon and heavens. The sun, moon, and stars are the natural apostles ; though they cannot preach Christ, yet they preach God. Heathens must be called to account at the last day for not reading the book of nature: 'He left not himself without a witness,' Acts xiv. 17; and the apostle tells heathens, when justice shall make a solemn triumph, Acts xvii. 31, 'He hath appointed a day, in the which he will judge the world in righteousness by that man whom he hath ordained.' What will become of us, that have not only the book of nature, but the comment of scripture ? God hath unfolded the meaning of the creature in the word. We shall have many witnesses against us at the day of the Lord.

7. It is a work that is of great profit; partly to heighten fancy, and make it fit for meditation. Many find meditation a burden because of the barrenness and leanness that is in their understandings. Oh! practise upon the creation, and you will find fancy to be much elevated and raised. Anthony the devout hermit, that is so much spoken of in ecclesiastical story, being asked, how he could profit in knowledge, and spend his days in the desert without men and books? answered, I have one book I am always studying, and turning over day and night; and so I find my hours to be both pleasant and profitable ; and it consists of three leaves and three letters ; the three leaves of it are the heavens, the earth, and the waters. The letters are the inhabitants of these houses. If you look into the heavens, there are stars, and angels, and.

fowls; if you walk on the earth, there are living creatures, and chiefly man, if you look into the seas, there are fishes. Partly because you will hereby have an excellent advantage to know God, and keep God present in your thoughts. Man is much led by sense; in the benefit of fruitful seasons, and temperament of the heavens, and plenty of fruits of the earth, you may be reading the goodness of God; in thunders, lightnings, tempests, earthquakes, hail, snow, pestilence, comets, you may read the majesty and the terrors of the Lord; in the guidance of the world, and measure of the stars, and all created beings, you may observe the wisdom of God; so that religion is as it were made sensible. And partly, you will have this profit, a sweet opportunity to compare the old and the new creation together. Eph. ii. 10, We are said to be 'the workmanship of God, created in Christ Jesus to good works.' The old world and the new heart, they are both God's work: Eph. iv. 24, 'That ye put on the new man, which after God is created in righteousness and true holiness.' There you may see beauty and order brought out of nothing. Every man is a lesser world, a model of the universe; the globe in the head, the sun and moon in the eyes; there is the liver like the ocean, which receiveth all the lesser streams, conveyed by the channels of the veins. But now a new man is a new creature, a new world; instead of the sun that shines in the firmament, there is the sun of righteousness, the ebbings and flowings of the influences of grace, the air which we receive by the inspiration of the Holy Ghost, and blow out again in prayers; there is the fire, by which the Holy Ghost warmeth and inflameth the heart. Many such sweet resemblances might be made.

8. If there were no profit, yet it is a matter of much spiritual delight to reflect upon the creature. Man is a creature taken with variety and beauty. Now what prospect is more various and beautiful than the works of God? when we are weary of one object we may go to another. Unclasp the book of nature, turn over a few leaves of that large volume, see what delight and contentment reason will find; when we walk abroad, these meditations will be best company for us. Look upon the spangled firmament, bestudded everywhere with stars, like so many golden nails fixed and struck into it, or like so many little holes in a thick covering, disclosing the beauty and glory that is within. There you may see the sun like a giant rejoicing to run his course, or like a bridegroom coming out of his chamber. There are the influences of the Pleiades, and the bands of Orion; there is Mazzaroth in his season, and Arcturus with his sons. There the moon like a rich diamond shines out with a foil of darkness and blackness, to set forth the lustre of it; and the constellations are as so many several families of stars; all which may ravish us with delight and wonder. If you come lower, consider the fire that burns not, the treasures of snow and hail, meteors as much feared as wondered at. There are the clouds, which Job calls the bottles of God, which, like so many tankard-bearers, convey their influences to all the houses of the earth, or like water-pots, refresh the garden of the world. Come we lower, and there is the earth interlaid with water, enamelled and decked with flowers and grass, variety of beasts in the field, and plentiful fruits of the land. And in the sea, as the papists say of Aquinas, *quot articulos, tot miracula;* so many fishes, so many

wonders ! the number, vastness, motion, perfection of all these do loudly proclaim the praise of God. Look upon yourselves, what delight is it to contemplate our own nature ! Our generation is wonderful ; we are poured out as milk into the womb, curdled like cheese, fenced with skin and bones. In the body there is an admirable structure, all the members conspiring to the beauty, decency, and use of the whole : Ps. cxxxix. 14, ' I am fearfully and wonderfully made.' Then if we look upon the soul, there is a sparkle of the divinity, and beam of God. Who can trace the flights and workings of reason, and the several traverses of the spirit of a man ? Look on the lesser, the most inconsiderable creatures. Pauses in music serve to make harmony, as well as the more perfect notes. Austin in some respects preferred a gnat before the sun, to see a little animated dust move up and down in such regular motions, with such handsomeness of body, eyes, feet, and wings ; it mightily delights and sets out the glory of God.

SERMON VIII.

Through faith we understand that the worlds were framed by the word of God, so that things which are seen were not made of things which do appear.—HEB. xi. 3.

Secondly, I come to give you some directions how to reflect upon the creatures with comfort and profit.

1. Be much in occasional meditation. There is nothing within the whole circumference of nature but will give matter to you. The creatures that are all round about you, are as the phylacteries that were worn under the law ; the Jews were to have ' fringes on the borders of their garments, that they may look upon them, and remember all the commandments of the Lord to do them,' Numb. xv. 38, 39. The creatures are as it were those fringes and borders, that wherever we turn our eyes, we may read God in the creature. Therefore when you are walking in the fields, or going to your country-houses, consider the works of the Lord ; look round about upon the beautiful frame before your eyes ; do but consider what a rich canopy God hath stretched out over your heads ; you should be full of good highway thoughts, Luke xxiv. 17; Christ inquires after their highway speeches ; ' What manner of communications are these that ye have one to another as ye walk ? ' So the Lord looks after your highway thoughts. When you see the sun glittering and shining forth in his beams like a bridegroom newly dressed, you should be then forming of some thoughts of the excellency and glory of God, who is the maker of it. When you pass by the sea, consider the immensity and dreadfulness of God by the horror of the waves and his wonderful works : Ps. cvii. 23, 24, ' They that go down into the sea, see the works of the Lord, and his wonders in the deep.' When you are cast upon storms and tempests, remember by whose breath all these are blown. When you hear the thunder, this is the

voice of the Lord ; look upon it as a trumpet the Lord hath sounded
to call the world together to a dread and reverence of his majesty.
There are day thoughts, and there are night thoughts ; David had his
day meditation, and his night meditation ; the 19th psalm seems to be
penned in the day, for there he speaks only of the sun ; when David
in the morning saw the sun breaking out, and enlightening the world,
then he thinks of the glory of God.   And the 8th psalm was a night
meditation : ' Lord, when I consider thy heavens, the work of thy
fingers, the moon and the stars that thou hast ordained, what is man ! '
It is probable that meditation was in the night, because he doth not
mention the sun, but the moon and stars.

2. There must be also set and solemn meditation upon special
occasions.   Set meditation brings in profit to the soul.   Passant and
transient thoughts are more pleasant, but not so profitable.   Meditation
that is deliberate, is of most use.   Usually sudden thoughts pass away
from us, and do not return with such advantage ; as children shoot
away their arrows at rovers, and do not look after them ; or as a ball
stricken in the open field goes out from us but a ball stricken
against a wall doth return to our hand again ; so those passant
thoughts go away from us ; but when there is a fixed mark, some
bound set, those thoughts return to our hand again with much comfort
and spiritual advantage ; when we aim at some particular thing and
fix our mark, our thoughts return with advantage.   Scattered rays
heat, but burn not.   When the beams of the sun are contracted in a
burning-glass, a narrow place, then they fire ; so when our thoughts
are more particular and set, then they warm the heart, and return to
us with advantage.   There are several special occasions when we should
propose to ourselves the thoughts of the creation.

[1.] When we are not affected with the majesty and glory of God.
Usually we are moved more with God's benefits than with his glorious
essence.   This is our infirmity ; we should rise up to such a height as
this, to love God as he is, *diligibilis naturâ*, lovely in himself, all self-
respects secluded and laid aside.   This is pure love without self-love,
when we can love God, and respect God for the greatness and glory of
his essence, though there were no influences and comfort going out from
him to the creature ; for then he is honoured as the chiefest good, and
the utmost end.   But how should we get our hearts affected with
God's glorious essence ?   Study the perfections of God in the creation,
that you may not only love him for his influences of mercy, but reverence
him for his majesty and glory : Ps. civ. 1, ' Bless the Lord, O my soul :
O Lord my God, thou art very great.'   David would praise and bless
God for his greatness ; how doth he do it ? he spends his thoughts upon
the creation throughout the psalm.

[2.] When you are haunted with thoughts of atheism.   The best of
God's children are sometimes tried and exercised in the sorest way,
and we are apt to doubt sometimes of the supreme truth, whether there
be a God or no ?   Now if your hearts make any question of it, go ask
of the creature, as Job saith, ' Ask now the beasts, and they shall teach
thee, and the fowls of the air, and they shall tell thee : or speak to the
earth, and it shall teach thee ;' nay he sends them to the fishes, that are
mute and make no noise,—' And the fishes of the sea shall declare unto

thee. Who knoweth not in all these, that the hand of the Lord hath wrought this?' Job xii. 7–9. The world could not make itself; that which is supported by another must needs be framed by another. Now the creatures hanging upon God as a garment upon a nail; take away the nail, the garment falls down; they all proclaim they have an excellent, powerful, and a wise creator. If you see a great house, and nothing in it but mice and vermin, you conclude, surely the mice could not frame such a glorious palace, neither could the pieces come together by chance. As the letters of Homer's poem could not come together by chance; so survey the creation, all these things could not come together by chance, they must be made by something; the very heathens could argue thus.

[3.] When you doubt of the promises of God, because there are appearances to the contrary. When you look for trouble think of the creation, that you may trust in the power of God when you see no means. Tully brings an Epicurean disputing thus against the creation: If the world were created, where are the tools and instruments? where are the workmen employed in so great a work as this is? and because these could not be assigned, he concludes such a thing could never be, but all things came together by chance. So we say, If the Lord means to bless us and do us good, where are the instruments? and where is the appearance of any probability in the course of second causes? 'Lift up your eyes to the heavens, and look upon the earth beneath,' saith the prophet, Isa. li. 6; from whence came all this excellent harmony that is in the parts of the creation? So Isa. xl. 1, 2, 'Comfort ye, comfort ye, my people, saith your God; speak ye comfortably to Jerusalem.' God sends his prophet with glad tidings to afflicted Israel; ay, but where is the comforter? we are under sorrows and bondage. Consider who made the heavens, ver. 12, 'Who hath measured the waters in the hollow of his hand, and meted out heaven with a span, and comprehended the dust of the earth in a measure, and weighed the mountains in scales, and the hills in a balance?' See he produceth the works of the creation for their encouragement. So David, Ps. cxxiv. 8, 'Our help is in the name of the Lord, who made heaven and earth;' that is, as long as I see such a glorious fabric before mine eyes, heaven and earth made out of nothing, I will never doubt and distrust God.

[4.] When your hearts faint in regard of outward supplies and temporal provision, survey the creatures. Who is it that feeds the beasts of the earth, and makes some of the fowl fattest in winter when provisions are scarcest? At whose charge are all the fish of the sea and the beasts of the forest maintained? Who spreads a table for all creatures? The world is but God's great common; he is landlord, he looks after all his creatures, that they be all supplied: Mat. vi. 25, 'Take no thought what you shall eat, or what you shall drink, nor yet for your body what you shall put on; is not the life more than meat, and the body than raiment?' As if he had said, God that gave you life out of nothing, certainly he will give you food; and he that gave you a body, he will provide for you raiment. And Christ sends us to the creation, ver. 26, 'Behold the fowls of the air, for they sow not, neither do they reap, nor gather into barns, yet your heavenly Father feedeth them; are ye not much better than they?' So David, Ps. cxlv. 16, 'Thou openest thine hand, and satisfiest the desire of every living thing.'

[5.] Greaten the privileges of your covenant interest. Now if you would know what it is to have God for your God in covenant, consider the creation, the work of his hand ; the mighty power of that God that made the world is made over to you in the covenant of grace. See Jonah i. 9, ' I am an Hebrew, and I fear the Lord, the God of heaven, which made the sea, and the dry land.' You have the creator to provide for you : 1 Cor. iii. 22, 23, ' All things are yours, for you are Christ's, and Christ is God's.' Thou hast God himself, and he hath all creatures at his command and beck, and by possessing God, who is all in all, we possess all things. This will help us to enlarge our thoughts according to the extent of the covenant.

3. There are proper objects for God's several and special excellences. Because one creature could not represent the infinite perfection of God, therefore he hath multiplied them, and given to every one some special property, whereby he may be known and discovered. For instance, if you would meditate of God's purity and holiness among the creatures you must single out the light, which of all qualities is most pure ; though it pass through the most impure places, it is not tainted ; it is some resemblance of the holiness of God : 1 John i. 5, ' God is light, and in him is no darkness at all.' Look upon the sun, by that means you may the better consider the purity and holiness of God ; the sun is but as the black and sutty bottom of a caldron in regard of God. So for God's immensity and greatness, pitch upon the vastness of the firmament, or the sea, or upon any other immense or great body. Of the vast magnitude and huge extension of the firmament, how many millions of miles do the stars take up in their tract and course ? Astronomers reckon two hundred thirty-nine thousand miles ; what is this to God ? 1 Kings viii. 27, ' The heaven of heavens cannot contain him.' Isa. xl. 12, ' He hath measured the waters in the hollow of his hand, and meted out heaven with a span,' &c. The sun is reckoned to be a hundred and sixty-six times bigger than the earth ; what is this to God ? The psalmist speaks of the ' great and wide sea,' Ps. civ. 25. Man cannot think of such a vast body as the sea without some religious horror and dread of God : it represents to us the infiniteness of God. So for the power of God, think of his upholding the earth ; there is the great instance of God's power, that so vast a weight as the body of the earth and waters is together should hang in the thin air, which of itself will not so much as sustain a tennis ball or feather, yet this is the only supporter of the earth and the waters ; the immovable dwelling-place of all the living creatures is hung upon nothing but upon the air. Sometimes it is said that the earth is founded upon the waters, as Ps. xxiv. 2, ' He hath founded it upon the seas, and established it upon the floods ;' at other times, as Job xxvi. 7, ' He hangeth the earth upon nothing.' This great weight, it hangs merely upon the power of God, and therefore this discovers the greatness of the creator. So in bridling the sea, Job xxxvii. 10, ' The breadth of the waters is straitened.' God handles it as a nurse her babe, who turns and sways the child by the fire ; so doth God with the sea : Job xxxviii. 8, 9, ' Who shut up the sea with doors, when it brake forth as if it had issued out of the womb ? When I made the cloud the garment thereof, and thick darkness a swaddling band for it.'

If you would meditate upon the faithfulness of God, you cannot have a better object than the constant course of the heavens and recourse of the seasons; they still remain as they were from the beginning of the world, and so they will continue: Ps. cxix. 90, 91, 'Thy faithfulness is unto all generations : thou hast established the earth, and it abideth. They continue this day according to thine ordinances; for all are thy servants.' Ps. lxxxii. 9, 'Thy faithfulness wilt thou establish in the very heavens;' that is, in the constant motions and courses of the stars in the heavens, God hath given the world a document of his truth and faithfulness. How many thousand years hath the sun kept his course without errors and alterations? So constant are the courses of the heavens, that astronomers are able for a great while before to tell when an eclipse shall be to an hour and minute. Jer. xxxi. 35, 36. 'Thus saith the Lord, which giveth the sun to be a light by day, and the ordinances of the moon, and of the stars, for a light by night; which divideth the sea, when the waves thereof roar; the Lord of hosts is his name : If these ordinances depart from before me, saith the Lord, then the seed of Israel also shall cease from being a nation before me for ever.' If you would think of the wisdom of God, then think upon the multitude of creatures that are in the world, yet they are all marshalled and guided in their order and course; such an innumerable company of creatures kept like a well-ordered army without any rout or confusion. Ps. cxlviii. 6, 'He hath established them for ever, he hath made a decree which shall not pass.' All the creatures, though so many, they keep their path and their course, and God wisely orders all for the service of the whole; and that discovers the wisdom of God. So for the unweariedness of his mercy and bounty; the stars go long journeys, yet are never tired, but continue their beneficent influences : Job xxxviii. 31, 'Canst thou bind the sweet influences of the Pleiades?' The sun riseth fresh every morning to communicate its influences; so the compassions of God come in fresh every morning : Lam. iii. 22, 23, 'It is of the Lord's mercy that we are not consumed, because his compassions fail not : they are new every morning; great is thy faithfulness.'

4. Above all things meditate much upon the heavens, and upon man. Upon the heavens, that you may know God; upon man, that you may know yourselves. The smallest things are of use and profit. Christ takes notice of the lilies of the field in Mat. vi. 28, 29, the beauty nature hath bestowed upon the lilies; 'so that Solomon in all his glory is not arrayed like one of them;' but now the heavens and man are the chiefest objects. The heavens are God's dwelling-place, and man is God's image; therefore here are the chiefest representations of the deity and godhead.

[1.] Look up to the heavens; there is God's royal house and pavilion, and a lively character of the divine perfections. Job and David were great students in the heavens: Ps. xix. 1, 'The heavens declare the glory of God, and the firmament showeth his handywork.' Some of the heathens made gods of the sun and stars for their glory and beauty. And indeed the Lord speaks to his own people, as if they were in danger, being such glorious bodies, and lively representations of the divine glory : Deut. iv. 19, 'Take heed, saith God, lest thou lift up thine eyes to heaven, and when thou seest the sun, and the moon, and the stars, even all the host of heaven, shouldst be driven to worship them, and serve them.' The sun is a representative of God, so the psalmist sets him out, Ps. xix. There is the omnipresence of the sun, ver. 6, 'His going out is from the end of the heaven, and his circuit unto the ends of it.' The omnisciency and omni-efficiency of it, 'nothing is hid from the heat thereof;' the sun is *totus Oculus,* one broad eye that looks over all the world. So is God, 'all things are naked and open to him,' Heb. iv. 13; and his virtue reacheth to the smallest creatures. I have heard of a philosopher that would lie upon his back all the day, to look upon the beauty of the sun. Certainly we may stand gazing and admiring the heavens, and, oh, how many sweet thoughts might it occasion of the majesty of God, and the glory of the everlasting state! This is but the canopy, but the outward veil, and the covering of the beauty and glory that is within; it is but the outside of the heavenly palace where we shall reign with Christ for ever. There are some have gathered all divinity out of the heavens. There is but one heaven and one sun, to teach us there is but one God. The properties of heaven, motion, light and heat, are some kind of resemblance of the mysterious trinity. The vast extension of the heavens shows the infiniteness of God; the thinness of the air shows the spiritual essence of God; the incorruptibility of the heavens shows the immortality and immutability of God; the influences of the heavens discover the sweet emanations of the divine goodness; the order of heaven, God's wisdom; the brightness of heaven, the majesty of God; the purity of heaven, the holiness of God; the subtility and thinness of heaven, the simplicity of God; and the spheric form of the heaven discovers to us the eternity of God, without beginning and without end. The heavens are the natural catechism out of which you may read all points that are not mysterious, and do not depend merely upon revelation.

[2.] Think upon man. Man is not only the creature of God, but the image of God. One calls man the masterpiece of nature; it is good to consider ourselves; there is nothing nearer to ourselves than ourselves. Man, as he is the image of God, so he is the image of the world, the short draft and model of all the rest of the world. Look upon soul and body, all is full of wonders. In the body to consider the excellent symmetry and proportion of all the parts, how the joints and muscles are ordered for the service and beauty of the whole frame, the outward shape and the inward motion full of wonder. Oh, how excellent a painter is the creator, that can draw such an image out of the dust, and scarce two men alike in face! to see so many millions in the world, and everyone known from the other by some notable mark of difference in the face; yet the outward part is nothing to the inward parts. It is reported of Galen, that great physician, when he was cutting up a man, and saw the wise disposing of all the entrails, certainly, says he, He that made man doth not require the sacrifice of beasts, but only to admire his wisdom, goodness, and power. The psalmist saith: Ps. cxxxix. 14, 'I am fearfully and wonderfully made.' There is much of God in our very bodies. You will say, our bodies we have them from our parents; no, you shall see all we had from our parents was but a title to the first Adam's guilt and sin, and a pledge of misery and of our everlasting unhappiness; we have nothing else. Our parents of themselves could not form such an excellent body; therefore not only the soul but the body is of God; they are but lower servants, God himself was the architect, the wise builder. If thy parents could form thy body, then they could tell how many muscles there are, and how they are placed in the body, how many veins and sinews, how many bones greater and lesser; but they know not, it is a thing of chance to their work, therefore it is the exact composure of God. Besides, if thy parents could make thy body, then they could repair it when it is wounded, and restore it when sick. He that makes a watch can mend it when it is broken and discomposed. It is God alone that made it. Then for the soul, there is the chief part of man. There is nothing nearer to God than the soul but only the angels, therefore we can hardly know him by the creature without considering our own souls. This leaves man without excuse; he had a rational soul to know his creator. Thy soul is a spirit as God is, in the same rank of being. The sun is not a spirit. Those glorious bodies that shine in the heavens, they are not advanced to the nobleness with thy soul. Then thy soul is invisible as God is; you may as well deny your own soul as deny God is because he cannot be seen. Thy soul is immortal and incorruptible, as God is. In the very essence of thy soul there is much of God to be seen, in the operations of the soul, it is in every part of the body; *tota in toto, et tota in qualibet parte;* all in all parts, and all in the whole; so God fills all the world, for he is everywhere, and yet nowhere in a sense. When a member is withered or cut off, the soul suffers no loss: so the Lord in all the changes of the world suffers nothing; sometimes he lets out his goodness in the creature, and sometimes the creature is destroyed, yet there is no alteration in God. And then who can trace the several traverses and flights of reason? The soul cannot only hear, see, smell, and taste, but it can discourse also of things invisible, the essence of God and angels. If there were nothing to discover God in your souls, and the impressions of God upon your souls, yet the several arts and crafts that are abroad in the world, (these inventions are common, therefore less observed), how could these things be found out? they display the wisdom of God. For to instance in common things: in the craft of husbandry, who doth not admire to see the various inventions in husbandry and gardening, in ordering the corn and fruits of the earth, Isa. xxviii. from ver. 24 to the end? He concludes all, ver. 29, ' This also cometh forth from the Lord of hosts.' And so for the smith's craft: Isa. liv. 16, ' I have created the smith that bloweth the coals,' &c. It is God that teacheth to cast iron into various shapes and figures. The inventors of arts among the heathens they counted gods. It is God teacheth men curious inventions. It is true, other creatures have their arts, but nothing like man. The birds curiously build their nests, the foxes dig their holes, and the little spider can make a curious web to catch flies, but they do these things by instinct of nature, and therefore do them always in one and the same manner; but the arts of man are various and innumerable. Nothing can escape that which the wit of man cannot take, neither birds by their flight, nor beasts with their greatness, nor fishes in the depth of the water: James iii. **7,**

'For every kind of beasts, and of birds, and of serpents, and things in the sea, is tamed, and hath been tamed of mankind.' Man is able to tame all beasts, to bring them to his own use and purpose; but God made them. In the art of navigation consider the wonders of the Lord; that such great vast burdens should dance upon the tops of the water, that ships should as it were fly with sails as with wings, and run with oars as with feet. And then in painting and architecture much of the wisdom of God is seen. Oh, consider and use this as an argument to set out the glory of God. Man can build houses, but God built heaven and earth. The painter is able to paint with colours; but admire him that could paint so fairly that had no other pencil but his hand, and no other paint but a little dirt.

5. You must not only consider what is made, but to what end. In the works themselves we may consider God's power and wisdom; but in the end we may consider God's goodness, and our own duty. Now the ends of the creation were many, chiefly these three; man's good, the creator's praise, the glory of Jesus Christ.

[1.] When thou art thinking of the creation, consider, all this was made for man's good. The whole world is but the great house and palace of little man. Oh, how great is the goodness of God to sorry man! whole nature is but his servant. The angels were made for man: Heb. i. 14, 'Are they not all ministering spirits, sent forth to minister for them who shall be heirs of salvation?' Those courtiers of heaven, those masterpieces of the creation are man's servants. The stars were made to give us light and heat, to cherish man and to cherish the earth; and the waters were made for man's good. The whole earth is but man's garden; the plants of it for our use for meat and medicine; the beasts for our food and clothing; nay in the bowels of the earth there are laid up veins of treasure to maintain commerce between nation and nation; though men be scattered in the several climates of the world, yet God will bring them together by traffic. Nay, all sublunary things were not only created for man's use, but most of them subjected to man's dominion. See the charter, all is made over to us: Gen. i. 28, 29, 'Have dominion over the fish of the sea, and over the fowl of the air, and over every living thing that moveth on the earth. And God said, Behold, I have given you every herb bearing seed, which is upon the face of all the earth, and every tree, in which is the fruit of a tree yielding seed; to you it shall be for meat.' They all serve for the uses of man, and are made over to him. It is true, the heavens are for the use of man, but they are not under the dominion of man; that is reserved to God alone; therefore it is said: Ps. cxv. 16, 'The heaven even the heavens are the Lord's, but the earth he hath given to the children of men.' But though the heavens be the Lord's, that is, reserved in his power, yet they serve for the use of man. The air serves to give man breath; the firmament serves to give man light and heat; and the heaven of heavens serves for his eternal and blessed habitation. Oh, the goodness of God to man! 'Lord, what is man, that thou art mindful of him!' How may we break out into such a holy wonder and admiration!

[2.] They were made for God's glory: Rom. xi. 36, 'All things,' saith the apostle, 'are of him, and through him, and to him:' 'of him' in creation; 'through him' in the sustentation of his providence; and 'to him,' that is, for the uses and purposes of his glory; all things return to the womb of their original, out of which they once came. The Lord deals with us just as Potiphar dealt with Joseph, he gave him power over all things, but only his wife, that he kept to himself; therefore by way of meditation we may reason as Joseph, Gen. xxxix. 8, 9, 'Behold, my master wotteth not what is with me in the house: and he hath committed all that he hath to my hand. There is none greater in this house than I, neither hath he kept any thing back from me but thee, because thou art his wife: how then can I do this great wickedness, and sin against God?' So do you reason with yourself; Oh, I have a bounteous creator, God hath given me all things, for my use and comfort, and all the articles of the lease and grant are only that I should serve his glory! Oh, let me not rob him of that; let me enjoy the creature, but give God the glory; let me not pervert the end of my creation; all should be to his praise. All the creatures do as it were proclaim to us, Man! glorify thy creator; God hath given us to thee to serve thee, that thou mightest serve him; we die for thy good and support, that thou mayest live; we are ready to fall down and perish for thy food. Oh, therefore be thou contented to suffer any inconvenience, if it be the loss of life, that the glory of God may live. We will give thee food, meat, nourishment, all that thou requirest, if thou wouldest love him, and praise him, and live to the glory of God. Saith the sun, I will give thee light and continued influences and rays every morning, if thou wilt but glorify thy creator. It is said: Prov. xvi. 4, 'The Lord hath made all things for himself.' In a sort we may say, God made all things for man, and man for himself; it follows, 'and the wicked for the day of evil.'

[3.] Therefore doth he create the world to make a fair way for Jesus Christ, Col. i. 15. The apostle proves the godhead of Christ by this argument: 'He is the firstborn of every creature; for by him all things were created, that are in heaven and in earth, visible and invisible, whether they be thrones, or dominions, or principalities, or powers; all things were created by him and for him.' Creation is but one step to the execution and advancement of God's decrees. We were first made that we might afterwards be redeemed. Christ gave us our lives at first, and afterwards he saved our lives. First he created us, and then prevented our execution. The world was but one step to heaven. First he gives thee thyself, then all things in the world, then he would give thee himself. The angels were made ministering spirits, and the Son of God was made a servant for thy sake. Oh, the wonderful love of God! When he founded the world, then he prepared heaven for thee that art a member of Christ. All was in a subordination to his wise decrees.

6. We should specially meditate upon the goodness and beneficence of God. When we taste the sweetness of the creatures, then is a special time of devising arguments of praise and studying thanks. It is said, Acts xiv. 17, 'Nevertheless he left not himself without a witness, in that he did good, and gave us rain from heaven, and fruitful seasons, filling our hearts with food and gladness.' Mark, this was God's testimony to the gentiles; this preached God to them. Oh, therefore lift

up a solemn thought on these occasions. In the spring-time, when nature is in its pride, think who it is that milketh out the fruits of the earth, that ripeneth the apples on the tree, that seasons the grass, and makes it fit for food for the beasts. Or else when you have had any liberal or comfortable use of the creature, then the heart should be raised up to God. Usually when God remembers us most, and we abound in creature comforts, we forget God and slight the creator. Oh ! remember this is to despise God in the day of his magnificence. Look, as when Vashti refused to come, when the king was minded to show himself to his nobles, it is said, Esther i. 12, ' The king was very wroth, and his anger burned in him ;' so here, the lord sends to invite thy soul to come to him in the spring-time, in the time of gladness of heart; when you abound in comforts, he sends these messengers that thou mightest come and solace thyself with him. Should we not come then, his anger would be raised ; especially when we abuse the creatures to riot, and our abundance to vanity and excess ; consider what an injury this is to God, to abuse that which he hath made. If we have made any thing, and another come and scorn and abuse it, it enrageth us : consider what it is to abuse the workmanship of God.

SERMON IX.

Through faith we understand that the worlds were framed by the word
of God, so that things which are seen were not made of things
which do appear—HEB. xi. 3.

7. COME not off from any meditation, till you have found some sensible profit. I will show you what are the usual fruits of solemn and serious thoughts of the creation. If your thoughts be serious, thus it will be :—

[1.] There will be a greater disposition and aptness to praise the Lord. If you have meditated aright the heart will be more affected with the lustre of his glory shining forth in the creature : Rev. iv. 11, ' Thou art worthy, O Lord, to receive glory, and honour, and power ; for thou hast created all things, and for thy pleasure they are and were created.' Cold and dead thoughts vanish without use and profit. When you think of the creation aright, there will be found in you dispositions to praise God that he should devise all this for man. Who can touch the harp of the creatures without being ravished with the music ? who can read that book that is framed with such excellent art, and not commend the author ? who can hear the creatures preach a sermon, and not say, Blessed be the God that made them ?

[2.] The soul will be raised into some wonder and admiration at the goodness and wisdom of God. Pythagoras boasted he had gotten this advantage by philosophy, *Nihil admirari*, to wonder at nothing ; but certainly when we survey the works of God, we cannot choose but wonder at all things. This is the least respect you owe God to wonder at his works; and till your hearts be thus heightened, your thoughts have not been ponderous and serious, nor sufficiently exercised. It is very observable the children of God never come off from the meditation of his works without admiration: Ps. viii. 3, 4, 'When I consider the heavens, the work of thy fingers, the moon, and the stars which thou hast ordained; what is man, that thou art mindful of him! and the son of man that thou visitest him!' So Ps. civ. 24, there is another meditation of the creation, and see how he concludes: 'O Lord, how manifold are thy works! in wisdom hast thou made them all: the earth is full of thy riches.' We are apt to wonder at the workmanship of man; at a curious picture, or at a building fairly contrived, we wonder at the skill and art of the workman. Certainly you set God much below a painter and a carver, when you can look upon this goodly frame of the world, and never wonder at it. Consider, you never rightly glorify and praise him till there be admiration. Admiration is that operation of the understanding by which it is carried out to objects above its reach and perception. Wonder seizeth upon you either by new things, or by miraculous things. You cannot tell how to comprehend strange things, they do for a while suspend the act; but things that are wonderful indeed, and which after contemplation and search we cannot apprehend and find out to their perfection, they wholly astonish and overwhelm the faculty. Now such are the works of the Lord; upon an intimate contemplation of them we shall find them above the reach of our understanding, and we can only say, 'O Lord how wonderful are thy works!' Till there be this admiration, the affections are not proportionably lifted up to the object. There is no object within the whole circumference of nature but, so far as we discern God in it, will raise our wonder.

[3.] If you meditate aright, the heart will be more drawn off from the creature to God. This is the main end either of making the creature, or of meditating upon the creature. Of making the creature: Acts xvii. 26, 27, 'He hath made of one blood all nations of men for to dwell on all the face of the earth, and hath determined the times before appointed, and the bounds of their habitation, that they should seek after the Lord, if haply they might feel after him and find him.' We are apt to stay in the creature, and forget the creator; this is quite contrary to the end of God, they are to show us how good and how sweet the Lord is. This was the reason why God made the world, and filled it with inhabitants, that the world might wonder at him; but we doat upon shadows, and leave the substance. This is as if a mighty emperor should gather all his nobles together, that they might come and admire his royalty; and when they come, they turn their back and admire his picture and shadow. Consider, all the creatures are but rude adumbrations or shadows of the glory of God, to help the memory; but they must not intercept the affection, and forestall the heart. Should we be so foolish as go to the shadows, those obscure resemblances, and leave the creature that is so full of majesty and glory? Would we be contented with a painted horse for our use, or painted bread for our food? Why are we then contented with those shadows of God? Meditation is nothing but a parley and discourse with the creature about the chiefest good. Job makes hue and cry after wisdom, Where is the chiefest good?   Is it in the earth? no, that is too gross.   Is it in heaven? no, the heaven of heavens cannot contain him.   Is it in the depth? no, he is a greater depth than can be fathomed.   What is the husk of the creature to the bread of eternal life? what are the drossy shadows and obscure resemblances to God, who is the substance himself?

[4.] If you have rightly meditated upon the works of creation, there will be more fear and dread of God, that will arise from the consideration of his majesty and power impressed upon the creature.   When we look upon God in his works we see him in his royalty, therefore there must needs be a great deal of fear upon the heart: Jer. v. 22, 'Fear ye not me, saith the Lord? will ye not tremble at my presence, which have placed the sand for the bound of the sea by a perpetual decree, that it cannot pass it; and though the waves thereof toss themselves, yet can they not prevail; though they roar, yet can they not pass over it?'   Mark, he calls for fear, because he hath made the creature, and hath ordered all things with such exact wisdom.   Who can think of the dreadful waves that are bound up by God, and not have some horror upon his heart?   They that do not thus discourse upon his works, God saith, they are brutish: ver. 24, 'And say not in their hearts, Let us now fear the Lord our God that giveth rain, both the former and latter in its season.'   Oh, when we come to take abroad God's greatness and excellency, how can we but dread and reverence him?

[5.] If you meditate rightly upon the workmanship of God, there will be more love to God for all his kindness, and for all those effusions and communications of his goodness to the creature.   Here we come to see how much we are bound to God.   Usually we are far more affected with what man doth for us, than with what God doth for us; as, for instance, we love him that helps us and delivers us out of straits; but we do not love him that made us out of nothing; this seems nothing to us.   Every petty courtesy obligeth us to men, and we do not consider we owe all to God, life, breath, and being, and all.   If man should do half so much for us, how are we obliged to him?   God hath done incomparably more, and we do not esteem it.   What is the reason? is it this, man's courtesy seems more, because his abilities are less? or is it because he gives from himself? how poor is this!   Doth water lose its nature, because it is in the sea, and not in the bucket and cistern?   Are God's benefits the worse because he is the author, whose nature it is to do good?   Consider, waters are sweeter in the fountain than in the rivers.   There is more condescension in God than in man.   When man loves us, he does but love his equal, and draws out his bowels to his own flesh, Isa. lviii. 7.   Consider, the earth is full of the riches of his goodness, therefore love the creator.

Another fruit of meditating upon the works of God will be obedience.   Oh, what an interest hath God in you by making you out of nothing! what a title hath he to your heart!   If the husbandman counts that tree his own which he hath planted; or the carver that image his own which he has made; certainly thou art God's, and he may call thee his own, who hath made thee out of nothing.   There is a difference between making out of nothing, and making out of something.   Men cannot make any piece of workmanship, but they must have matter to work upon; but the Lord made thee out of nothing, therefore certainly thou art his; and therefore the right and dominion of God must be infinitely greater than that of man ; and what a right hath God by his providence!   Thou hast a right in thy servant, who hath his well-being from thee, and therefore surely God hath a right to thee, who by his providence supplies thee with all things thou wantest.

[7.] Meditation on the creature will beget trust and dependence on God; this is the main thing that God aimeth at, that we be drawn to trust in God, when we think of the creature.   The heathens knew much of God in the general, they were able to discourse of his eternal power and godhead; but when they came to draw practical inferences, how they should trust in him, then 'they became vain in their imagiations, and their foolish hearts were darkened,' Rom. i. 20, 21.   When we consider the great effect of his mighty power, and yet do not trust in the Lord, these are but vain imaginations.   The chief thing in meditation on the creation is, that you should come away with the greater trust, for in the creation there are all arguments of trust.   There you learn the freeness of God's grace, when God made all things out of nothing, certainly the creature could merit nothing ; and there you learn the exactness of his care, because in his wise decrees he had a care of thee when thou wert not, therefore he will have a care of thee when thou art : Ps. cxlv. 15, ' The eyes of all wait upon thee, and thou givest them their meat in due season ; ' therefore he will supply man. And so then you learn the greatness of his power ; and that is the reason of the apostle's expression : 1 Peter iv. 19, 'Commit your souls unto God as unto a faithful creator.'   Thence doth the quiet rest and establishment of spirit arise; he is able to raise means, to create deliverances, to supply all your wants, and relieve you in all your distresses.

Doct. 2. We understand the truth and wonders of the creation by faith, and not by reason.

Take these propositions to clear the point—

1. There are three sorts of lights which God hath bestowed upon men ; the light of nature, the light of grace, and the light of glory.   These are like the three several lights God hath set up in the firmament, the sun, the moon, and the lesser stars.   There is the daylight of glory, which is the sun when it arises in its strength and brightness; and there is the light of faith, which is like the moon, a light which shines in a dark place ; then there is the weak and feeble ray of reason, which is like the light of the lesser stars.   By the first light, we see God as he is in himself; by the second, God as he hath discovered himself in the word; by the third, God as he is seen in the creature.   By the light of glory we behold God in himself, ' we see him face to face,' 1 Cor. xiii. 12.   The expression is used in opposition to the veil of the shadows of the law : here we can only behold God as he is veiled under words of corporeal and sensible significations; but there ' we shall see him as he is,' 1 John iii. 2.   By the second light we see God as he is pleased to reveal himself in his word : and by the light of reason we see God in his works, as he hath displayed his glory in the whole frame of the

world: so that there is vision, faith and reason. The one is the fruit of our glorification, and the other of our redemption, and the last of our creation.

2. In this world reason had been enough, if man had continued in his innocency. His mind then was his only bible, and his heart his only law and rule; but he tasted of the tree of knowledge and hereby he and we got nothing but ignorance. It is true, there are some relics of reason left for human uses, and to leave us without excuse; therefore it is said, John i. 9, 'That Christ is the true light, which enlighteneth every one that cometh into the world.' It is by his grant that a little reason is continued to us. But now in matters of religion, we had need of external and foreign helps. Man left to himself would only grope after God. In many things reason is altogether blind; in other things the light of it is very faint, weak and ineffectual. This is the sad state of man since the fall, his reason is blind; and that not only out of weakness, but out of prejudice; there is not only darkness in our mind, but there is pride and malice too, by which we are set against the truths of the word.

3. The only remedy and cure for this is faith, and external revelation from God. The blindness of reason is cured by the word; the pride of reason is cured by the grace of faith. Revelation supplies the defect of it; and faith takes down the pride of it, and captivates the thoughts into the obedience of the truths represented in the word; so that reason now cannot be a judge; at best it is but a handmaid to faith. And though the mysteries of religion transcend reason, yet that is not an argument of the falsity of the word, but of the imbecility and weakness of our own reason: and those mysteries, which we cannot comprehend, do but put us in mind of the sad consequences of the fall of man.

4. The doctrine of the creation is a mixed principle; much of it is liable to reason, but most of it can only be discovered by faith. We must consider the creation two ways, either *ex parte rei*, or *ex parte modi*; either the thing itself, or the necessary circumstances. For the thing itself, that was known to the heathens, that there was a creation; but the manner how was wholly hidden from reason, and can only be supplied by revelation of the word. Nature doth confess a creation, but faith must teach us what it is.

More distinctly I shall lay down my sense in these further propositions—

[1.] By the light of nature it may be known that there was a creation. It may be proved by evident reason that there was a first cause, from whence all propagation begins; otherwise we shall be left to a perpetual wandering, and shall not know out of what womb all things that are in the world issued forth. Plutarch propounds the question; whether the hen were before the egg, or the egg before the hen? Look upon all creatures; is the acorn before the oak, or the oak before the acorn? the spawn before the fish or the fish before the spawn? therefore at first there must be fishes created, and there must be oaks created. To this purpose the apostle quoteth Aratus, Acts xvii. 28, τοῦ γὰρ καὶ γένοι ἔσμεν, for we are his offering.

[2.] The heathens discovered that there was also a first mover, a first cause of all things in the world.   Aristotle, though he held the eternity of the world, confesseth there was πρῶταν αἰτίαν κόσμου καὶ τῆς τάξεως πάσης ; and he saith that Homotimus and Anaxagoras were necessitated by the appearance of the truth to acknowledge it ; and that all perfections which are in other things by participation, are in the first cause essentially ; and that this first cause was of such infinite power and wisdom, as appeared, because all things are ordered to such good uses and purposes.   The apostle saith, Rom. i. 19, 20, ' That which may be known of God is manifest in them ; for God hath showed it unto them.   For the invisible things of him from the creation of the world are clearly seen, being understood by the things that are made, even his eternal power and godhead.'   And he disputes upon it as a granted principle, that there was a first cause : Acts xvii. 28, ' For in him we live, and move, and have our being ;' and Acts xiv. 15, ' He is the living God, which made heaven, and earth, and the sea, and all things that are therein.'

[3.] This knowledge in the heathens was but faint, and full of hesitancy and confusion, of very little profit and comfort.   Though they did acknowledge a God and first cause, yet they multiplied feigned deities and set up many gods ; they had not any full and saving light, which might be a comfort and profit to their souls ; they could not see this first cause, so as to fear him, and trust in him for his power, love him for his goodness, and honour him and adore him for his wisdom : Rom. i. 21, 22, ' They become vain in their imaginations, and their foolish heart was darkened ; professing themselves to be wise, they became fools.'   They could not draw out the necessary consequences of these truths, to love, trust, fear, worship, and honour this first cause ; there they were vain in their imaginations.   Therefore our Lord proposeth the gentiles as a pattern of unbelievers : Mat. vi. 32, ' After all these things do the gentiles seek,' when he spoke how we should trust God.   They had but rude and imperfect notions of the power and care of God, and could not apply them for their profit and benefit, therefore they are carking and caring, and cannot trust God.

[4.] The manner and the necessary circumstances of the creation were wholly unknown to the heathens.   Effects discover the cause, but they cannot discover the circumstances of action, because those depend wholly upon the will of the agent.   So because the circumstances of the creation were not necessary, but did wholly depend upon the will of God, reason and nature cannot know them, unless God make them known in the word ; as, for instance, they knew not perfectly who made the world ; not when, nor how it was made, nor whence it was made.   Not who made the world : though they had some rude and gross conceits of the first cause, yet they looked upon him as a servile agent, working out of mere necessity, communicating his influences, because he could not choose to do otherwise.   So when the world was made, the beginning and duration of it, this was wholly hidden from the heathens.   The scripture can only show it to us.   Therefore many of the heathens complained of the great defect that was in their chronicles, that they had not an ancienter monument than the destruction of Troy ; *Cur supra bellum Trojanum, et funera Trojæ* ; so Lucretius, Macrobius.   The writings of Moses are much more ancient than all the gods of the heathens. The wars of Troy were about the time of the judges. The youngest prophets of the old testament were before the oldest philosophers and historians of the gentiles. Then they knew not whence, from what term, God should begin his work. This is a maxim of nature, *ex nihilo nihil fit*—that nothing can be made, out of nothing ; therefore this puzzled them how the creature should be first made, since it was contrary to that natural maxim, that the whole world should be framed out of nothing, and that by the mere word of God; this never sunk into the heads of the wisest heathens. Hence proceeded such difference of opinions among them ; some held the world to be a work of mere chance, as Epicurus and Leucippus ; others, that it was eternal and coeval with the first cause, as Aristotle ; and the Platonists, that it was made out of some eternal pre-existent matter. Then they could not tell how it was made in six days ; nature, reason, and discourse could never have found out that, which Moses hath written concerning the distinct originals of all propagation, and the framing of every creature in its rank and place ; they could see such things, but not the original of the fowls, of fishes, of man, and of all the beasts of the field. Nature could propound questions, how were these made? but nature could never assoil them. Then they could not tell the end why the world was made. Aristotle saith, We are not at all bound to the first cause, whether he did good or evil, because he did work out of servile necessity, and could do no otherwise. Moses tells us, God made all things for his glory, that he may be worshipped, and honoured, and served by the creature ; that the highest heaven was a place for man ; that the soul might enjoy bliss and eternal communion with God. All these circumstances were hidden from them ; they were not matters of sense, they were not before our eyes ; but faith makes us to apprehend the six days' works, as if we had seen and stood by, as the angels did, applauding every day's work. They were not matters of reason, because transcending those principles that are agreeable to the rules of nature ; and they depend merely on the unlimitedness of God's will, and the exuberancy of his power.

Use 1. For information. If by faith only we can understand the truth and wonders of the creation, then,

1. It informs us, that reason is not the judge of controversies in religion, and the doubts that do arise about the matters of God are not to be determined by the dictates of nature. If then we leave the written word and follow the guidance of our own reason, we shall but puzzle ourselves with impertinent scruples, and leave ourselves under a dissatisfaction. Usually men of parts and ingenuous education are liable to this snare ; for having the highest claim to the exercise of reason, they are apt to set up reason above the word. Celsus said to his fellow heathens, that we should follow reason, and that all error was brought into the world by faith. And Galen, when he read some passages of Moses, said, *Multa dicit, nihil probat*—he saith much, but he proves nothing. In many things we have only the saying of scripture, and it is enough the scripture saith it. If we should believe no more than the strength of reason and discourse will assure us, we should soon deny the doctrine of the trinity, the deity of Christ, and the creation ; reason can never trace these things. This is the inlet of all

atheism and profaneness, when men set up reason as the highest tribunal. Indeed there are many uses of reason ; partly to prepare and induce us to hearken to the word of God ; this is the mind God hath given us to know him, the stock left in nature, upon which he would implant faith. And partly, it is of great use, that after we have believed, we may receive an additional confirmation ; when we believe a thing, reason may judge, if it be not equal and fit we should believe it. Faith makes advantage of the confessions and acknowledgments of nature : there is no truth we believe, but afterwards we may find excellent advantages to confirm us in it by rational searches. These confirmations of reason are of great use for the quenching those fiery darts which Satan flings into the soul, by which he would bear down all principles of religion. And partly, to prevent absurd intrusions upon our belief and fanatical opinions. Ignorance and error have many times been veiled under a pretence of mystery, and things hidden from reason. Though reason must be captivated to faith, yet not to fancy. Reason is made a judge many times where the word is silent; but for the truths revealed in the word, though they are above reason, yet they are not against reason ; though reason cannot comprehend them, yet they are not repugnant to reason. And partly reason is of great use, that we may search the scripture, and draw out necessary consequences from the truths revealed in the word ; this we may do by the warrant of Christ. The mysteries of salvation must be believed first, that we may understand them ; we must receive them from God's bare testimony, afterwards search them out, that our belief may be the more distinct and explicit. Thus reason serveth faith. There is a great use of reason in religion, so it keeps its place, being subordinate to faith.

2. It informs us that the heathens had never light enough for salvation. Their charity is too large who think that the heathens may be taught enough by those natural apostles, sun, moon, and stars. Certainly they are blind in the work of redemption, since they are so blind in the work of creation. Though God hath not left himself without witness, Act xiv. 17, that is, such as may lead them to God the creator, yet not to lead them to God the Redeemer, there is enough given to the heathens for conviction, but not for conversion. Therefore all those that God would call to himself, he gave them a higher light, even the revelation of the word. Though nature tells us, there is a God, yet what he is, and how to be worshipped, and how he came to be displeased with the world, and how he came to be reconciled, of all this it telleth us nothing. Nature finds itself depraved, but it knows not the remedy and cure.

3. It shows us the great advantage that we have by faith, and by the written word. If we had been left to the puzzle and distraction of our own reason, how should we have known whence the world came, and how it was made by God ? Reason, as it exerciseth itself in several ways since the ruin of it in Adam's fall, is of several dimensions, according to men's natural constitution, moral education, and industry. But he hath given us the blessed rules of his word. What a puzzle and distraction were the philosophers left in ? A poor child learneth more by a catechism, than all the philosophers by their profound

researches; those that have the smallest abilities of reason may here learn. The philosophers, though they spent all their days in painful studies, and were endowed with rare abilities of learning, yet what novices were they in spiritual things! they cannot tell what the happiness of the soul is, nor where it shall be enjoyed, nor the means to attain it; they know not how the world was made, nor how it shall end.

4. It informs us, that religion is not illiterate. Grace doth not make men simple, but rather perfects human learning. None discern truths with more comfort and satisfaction than a believer; it solves all doubts and riddles of reason. *Quod ratio non capit, fides intelligit.* Simple men despise learning, and carnal men despise grace, both on the same grounds. Faith and reason must go together, though reason must be subordinate. We should not despise the help of human learning, neither should we despise grace, as if it did make men dull, and blunt the edge of their parts. Reason and faith, when kept in their proper place, are of excellent advantage. Join faith with your study, and all will be more clear, otherwise we shall stumble at truths. When these three lights are in conjunction, the light of parts, the light of refined reason and the light of grace, they bring forth admirable and happy effects. But on the other side, the decay of learning hath been the sensible abatement of religion. Religion hath never lost more than when outward helps have been despised, which men do to hide their own ignorance. When the apostle speaks against the vain abuse of learning, he gives God thanks: 1 Cor. xiv. 18, 'I thank God, I speak with tongues more than you all,' implying that it is the usual course of men to speak against that which they want. A heated iron pierceth into a board though blunt, more than edged tools when cold. Holiness and outward advantages must go together.

5. We learn hence the properties of faith to have knowledge, assent, and obedience in it; therefore it is not a blind reliance, but a clear, distinct persuasion of such truths, concerning which human discourse can give us no satisfaction. Faith is opposite to three things. The knowledge of it is opposite to ignorance; faith brings the soul to the understanding of the things of salvation. And it is opposite to folly; it makes us improve the mysteries of salvation to our spiritual comfort: Luke xxiv. 25, 'O ye fools, and slow of heart to believe;' and Eph. i. 18, 'That the eyes of your understanding being enlightened,' &c. There is the wisdom of believers to apply truths to their spiritual advantage. And it is opposite to incogitancy and carelessness of spirit, it makes us turn our minds upon the things of religion.

6. It is the nature of faith to subscribe to a revelation in the word, though reason give little assistance and aid. The word is enough to faith, though the thing seem unlikely to reason; it stands not upon appearance or probabilities. When we have a doctrine laid down in the word, we must not mind whether it be probable, otherwise we should never believe a creation, which is the making of all things out of nothing.

Use 2. It serves to stir you up to act faith. What is the use of faith upon the creation? To answer all the objections of reason, and settle the truth in the soul, and to improve it for spiritual uses and advantages, and to facilitate the belief of other truths upon this ground; did he make the world out of nothing? Many truths are less wonderful than this.

SERMON X.

Through faith we understand that the worlds were framed by the word of God, so that things which are seen were not made of things which do appear—HEB. xi. 3.

Now I come to consider the circumstances of the creation; and the first is, 'that the worlds were made,' or framed. In the original, it is, κατηρτίσθαι, 'set in joint,' a metaphor taken from the perfect frame of man's body, where every member, vein and artery is aptly disposed, and in its proper place; so are all creatures settled in their due proportion and order; there is nothing wanting either for use, or for ornament; it is all fitly framed and made up into a complete mass and body. The note is this, viz.

Doct. That the world was framed in an accurate, orderly, and perfect manner.

1. I shall illustrate the point by some similitudes out of scripture.

2. I shall show wherein the harmony and perfect order of the creation did consist.

3. I shall answer a doubt that may be commenced against the doctrine.

First, To illustrate the note by some similitudes out of scripture. The perfection and order of the world is compared to man's body, to a host or army, and to a house or excellently contrived building.

1. It is compared to the body of a man. The world is set in joint, and there is a great deal of likeness and similitude: 1 Cor. xii. 12, 'As the body is one, and hath many members; and all the members of that one body being many, are one body;' that is, though they be of different shape and different uses, yet they all make up but one body. So the several ingredients into this great mass and lump are for the matter, worth, and influence of a diverse nature; yet all these members and pieces of the creation are tied to one another by secret bands and ligaments, as the members of the body are; such a confederacy and compliance is there between all the parts of the world, they fall into one common frame as several joints, by a mutual agreement and proportion.

2. It is compared to an host or army: Gen. ii. 1, 'Thus the heavens and the earth were finished, and all the host of them;' Ps. xxxiii. 6, 'By the word of the Lord were the heavens made, and all the host of them, by the breath of his mouth; he gathereth the waters of the sea together as an heap, and he layeth up the depth in storehouses.' Therefore God is called the Lord of hosts upon this reason, because the creatures were not huddled together in confusion, but stand like soldiers in their orderly rank, as a well-marshalled host under the

conduct of God. This word host doth not only imply their services and operations under God's command and conduct, but their order and government. The Septuagint render it by κόσμος, to signify the beauty of it. All the parts of the creation are like a well-ordered army standing in rank and file, the places of their abode as so many tents. And God hath his magazine and treasury out of which he doth supply them : Job xxxviii. 22, 23, 'Hast thou entered into the treasures of the snow? or hast thou seen the treasures of the hail, which I have reserved against the time of trouble, against the day of battle and war?'

3. It is compared to a curious house. The universe hath an excellent resemblance to a frame of building, Job xxxviii. 4–6. There you have this notion, where we are told of laying the foundation, and the corner-stone, and of a line, and measure, and the like; all figurative terms which are taken from an outward building. The whole world is but one great house; the earth is the floor, the sea is the watercourse for it ; heaven is the arch and roof of it ; God is the architect of this house, but man is the inhabitant and tenant. And lest he should want comfort, the sun and stars are like so many windows to let in light, all to set forth the glory and magnificence of God. There are several rooms and chambers in this house ; therefore the prophet speaks, Amos ix. 6, 'He buildeth his stories in the heaven.' The earth by its own proper weight remains unmovable in the centre of the world, and the spheres one above another are as so many stories in a house.

Secondly, Wherein this order and beauty of the world doth consist. It stands in six things.

1. In the wonderful multitude and variety of creatures, distributed into so many several excellent natures and forms, they all do proclaim the beauty and order of the whole world. It is no difficult thing with one seal to make many impressions of the same stamp, or to print many sheets with the same letters when once set; but that God should diversify forms, and that in such an infinite manner, that he should leave such different impressions from the seal of his power, according to the platform of his own counsel, this can never sufficiently enough be admired ; herbs, plants, flowers, fruits, birds, beasts ; and among living creatures there is a great deal of difference in figure, taste, colour, and smell ; then such variety of living creatures ; among men, men's faces though they were all drawn by the same pencil, yet what difference is there ! Scarce two men alike among so many millions. The stars the apostle saith, 'one differs from another in glory,' 1 Cor. xv. 41. The angels are above them, and there is a great deal of difference among angels ; some are thrones, some dominions, some powers, some principalities, as the apostle reckons them up, Col. i. 16. So that when we consider this, the wonderful diversity of forms, we may cry out, Ps. civ. 24, 'Lord, how manifold are thy works! in wisdom hast thou made them all.' The world would not have been so beautiful, if all had been great, none small ; if all hot, no creature cold ; all moist, no dry; or all dry, and no moist; as the frame of men's bodies would not have been half so beautiful, if all were eye, or all head, or all heart, or all brain ; or, as in outward things, are all not rulers and captains,

but there is a difference. This speaks the beauty and excellency of the world, the variety of God's works.

2. The beauty and artificial composition of all things. Human wit cannot reach it; whether we respect the outward shape or inward frame, look upon man; 'He is fearfully and wonderfully made,' saith the psalmist, Ps. cxxxix. 14. The beauty of women overcomes, besots, and takes away the heart of wise men, it is so great; nothing can be added or taken away from any creature, but there will be deformity and ugliness. Do but take away an eye from a man; or add a mouth to him; how deformed would it be, to see a man with one eye, or two mouths! Nay, look upon the baser creatures, those that seem to be the most uncomely parts of the creation, yet there is a beauty in their make and frame. A man would look upon a swine as a filthy creature, yet to see a swine without ears, how uncomely! Nay, go to lower things; God hath showed his power in great things, but his wisdom in small. In a gnat, in a grain of mustard seed, how much of God may be seen! What virtue is there in that small seed to grow up into a tree! Certainly, nature is nowhere seen so much as in the least things. Christ sendeth us to the lilies of the field, Mat. vi. 29. What curious drafts are there in the flowers of the field! Solomon sends us to the ant. So we may go to a gnat; to see such a little creature to have feet, head, and heart, all the inward senses, and all the outward senses, all necessary sagacity for its own preservation; how wonderfully are these little creatures made! But now look to man's inward frame, there is more, all full of riddle. Galen, when he was dissecting the hand of man, he fell into a great admiration of that God that made man. It is wonderful to consider the continual motion that is in man's body, and that without alteration. Men have laboured much to make a clock that should run by the force of a weight for four and twenty hours. Oh, how great is the wisdom of God, and the power of God that made man! So that there is a clock that still strikes within him from his birth till he comes to die, and be no more in the world—that the nutritive power should be working perpetually without intermission, that there should be a continual beating of the pulses, that the lungs and arteries should move without ceasing to seventy or ninety years, nay, before the flood, nine hundred years. All the creatures are curiously and wonderfully made and framed.

3. The order and beauty of the world consists as in their composition, so in their disposition, and in the apt placing of all things. When we look upon every creature, we shall see it could not have a better place than God hath bestowed upon it; the superior and inferior bodies are all exactly ordered. The earth, of all bodies the most heavy and ponderous, is lowest, and the foundation of all the rest. The elements as they are more pure and simple, so they have an upper place—the waters above the earth, and the air above the waters. Then the stars, which are most pure and simple, they have the uppermost places of the world; and the sun, as king and prince, placed in the middle of the stars. So that the air and water, which are of a middle purity, are like so many couples and loops which tie heaven and earth together, and they are between them both. The air conveys the influences of the stars to the earth, and preventeth emptiness and vacuity.

The water that is more impure, though not altogether so gross a body as the earth, insinuates itself with the earth, and makes it fruitful. Living creatures, because they are made up of elements, they are placed in them, some in the air, some upon the earth, some in the water, that so from above and beneath they may receive comfort and profit; heat and comfort from above, and food from beneath. Then they are exquisitely and accurately placed: creatures that are hugest and of the greatest multitude are put into the sea, Leviathan is to sport there, lest if they should be upon earth, they might be an annoyance to man, and cause too great a waste of food. And therefore the reasonable creatures, they are in the highest and lowest parts of the world; the angels in the highest heavens, and man upon earth; because in both ends of the world God would have some to behold his glory, and to contemplate the whole frame. In short, the earth, the dwelling-place of man, standeth fixed and unmoved. The sea rolls up and down to keep it pure and fresh; the heavens move to convey their influences; the clouds are carried hither and thither, God rides up and down upon them, as princes in their chariots: Isa. xix. 1, 'The Lord rideth upon a swift cloud, and shall come into Egypt;' Ps. xviii. 10, 'And he rode upon a cherub and did fly, yea he did fly upon the wings of the wind;' that so the earth might receive due moisture for the use of man. Then the distribution of the waters into all the parts of the earth, as it were by pipes, conveyances, and channels, prepared on purpose, that all the creatures may have drink and refreshment. The psalmist takes notice of that, Ps. civ. 10, 11, 'He sendeth the springs into the valleys, which run among the hills. They give drink to every beast of the field, the wild asses quench their thirst; he watereth the hills from his chambers.'

4. This accurate frame is seen in the wonderful consent of all the parts of the world, and the proportion they bear one to another. There are several steps and degrees in the creature, by which we may go higher and higher, and climb up till we come to God himself. The proportion of the creatures leads us up to God. As to instance, in the general rank and kind of all things in the world, the lowest creatures have only being; others have not only being, but life, as plants; others have not only life, but feeling and sense, as beasts; others have not only life and sense, but reason and understanding, as men. But now man is in a lower sphere of understanding, he receives objects by his senses, and he needs his fancy, therefore there is a higher sphere of understanding creatures, even angels, and they have a higher manner of reason and understanding than man. So above the angels, there is a God. Nature climbs step by step, and leads us to God. A stone hath being, but not life. A plant grows, but feels not as a beast. A beast hath sense, but cannot discourse and reason as a man; and sense is more imperfect, than reason, because it must have a corporeal organ or instrument. Man's reason is lower than angels, because man, in all the discourses and traverses of his mind, needs the help and ministry of imagination and fancy, which angels need not. But now an angel is lower than God, but yet higher than man, he doth not need the outward species and shapes of things to be received by the senses, but the understanding of an angel requires either some revelation, or the presence of the object: but now

God hath a higher manner of understanding—he is a pure act ; above all these, he needs nothing without himself ; needs not the presence of the object, as angels do ; nor an instrument, as the beasts do ; nor imagination, as man doth ; for he knows all things that may be by his own all-sufficiency, and all things that shall be by his wise decree. Nature grows from worse to better, from lower to greater, till it brings us up to the being of beings and chiefest perfection. In metals there is the same proportion ; some baser, others more noble ; first iron, then lead, then tin, then brass, then silver, then gold. In plants some have only leaves, others flowers, others fruits, others aromatical gums and sweet spices. So in sensible creatures there is a wonderful difference in their ranks, from a gnat till you come to a man : there is a progress in nature, that still man may go further and further, till he find out the first cause. The whole world is a poem of praise, in which some verses have long feet and some short ; there are some small and inconsiderable creatures, and others higher, and nearer to the great perfection of God, that we may climb up from the creature until we come to converse with God.

5. In the mutual ministry and help of the creatures one to another. They are disposed in such a comely order, that they yield a mutual supply one to another, such as may best conserve the universe, cherish man, and glorify God. For instance, the earth is cherished by the heat of the stars, moistened by water, and by the temperament of heat and moisture it is made fruitful, and sends forth innumerable plants for the comfort and use of living creatures, that living creatures may be for the use of man ; it is wonderful to consider the subordination of all causes, and the proportion they bear one to another : the heavens work upon the elements, the elements work upon the earth, the earth yieldeth fruits and plants for the use and comfort of man and other living creatures. The prophet takes notice of this admirable climax and gradation that is in nature : Hosea ii. 21, 22, ' Saith the Lord, I will bear the heavens, and they shall bear the earth, and the earth shall bear the corn, and the wine, and the oil ; and they shall bear Jezreel.' We are always looking to the next hand ; we call upon the corn, wine, and oil, and they can do nothing, except the earth send forth sap and influence. The earth can do nothing without the clouds, unless God unstop the bottles of heaven, and let out the rain ; the clouds can do nothing without the stars, and the stars can do nothing without God ; the creatures are all beholden one to another, and all to God. There is an excellent knot and chain of causes in the creation. Look, as the joints of the body are hollow to take in one another, so there is an established order in the course of nature, all the causes hang together.

6. In the wise government and conservation of all things according to the rules and laws of the creation. Divine providence is mightily seen in this, in the guiding of all things by the laws of nature, as in the constant course of the stars, by which we have the seasons of day and night. That man may go forth to labour, the sun gives him light ; and that man may go to his rest, the sun travels to the other hemisphere ; and God draws a curtain of darkness round about us, that we may sleep without disturbance ; so also that we may have winter and summer, spring and harvest in their seasons, according to God's promise, Gen.

viii. 22. The sun hath its period and point in the heaven, according to which it doth rise and set. David takes notice of the sun's setting: Ps. civ. 19, 'He appointeth the moon for seasons; the sun knoweth his going down;' the meaning is, he hath appointed the moon for seasons,' the months being distinguished by the course of the moon. 'The sun knows his going down,' the days being measured by the motion of the sun. The length and shortness of days are all measured by God, and the sun knows when to set at an hour and minute according as God appointed him. Though there be every day some variety according to the degrees of the zodiac, yet the sun observes the just points of the compass: Job xxxviii. 12, 'He causeth the day-spring to know his place.' The sun knows when to rise at such and such an hour, and such a point of the heavens, he knows his place. So it is very notable for the other stars, though they move most swiftly, and though they never cease; though some go round in a slower, and some in a swifter space, yet they always keep their measures and proportions, and their motions are equally distant. The stars go round in four and twenty hours, and the planets in various motions, and though there be so many ten thousand millions of stars, yet they do not interfere and jostle one another. It is notable when God would express the numerousness of Abraham's posterity, he useth three expressions to him: Gen. xxii. 17, 'They shall be as the dust of the earth, as the sand of the sea-shore, and as the stars of heaven.' From this expression, wherein he promiseth him a multitude of children that should come of his loins, we may conclude that there must needs be a great company of stars. Now that in such a crowd and throng of stars that are always moving, there should be no clashing, no confusion, no interfering with one another, but still they keep their path, and go on according to the law and decree which God hath set unto them; who can admire this sufficiently? So in upholding all ranks of all other creatures, and guiding them for the great purposes and uses of providence. His gathering together the drops of the air: Job xxvi. 8, 'He binds up the waters in his thick clouds, and the cloud is not rent under them;' that he should keep up such a quantity of water in the thin clouds, as in so many bottles or barrels, till they be condensed into rain and then pour them out in drops for the good and use of man. So the power of God is mightily seen in bridling the sea. Though it be above the earth, yet it is said: Ps. civ. 9, 'He hath set bounds to the waters, that they may not pass over, that they turn not again to cover the earth.' Though above the earth, yet the Lord keeps them up in a heap together, and keeps them back that they shall not return to drown the world.

Thirdly, I come to answer an objection that might be commenced.

Obj. If God made the world in such harmony and order, whence came all those disorders that are in the world? We see some creatures are ravenous; other creatures are poisonous; all are frail, and still decaying and hasting to their own ruin. Whence come murrains, sicknesses, and diseases? whence come such destructive enmities and antipathies between beast and beast, yea and beasts of the same kind? whence come such dislocations, and unjointings of nature by tempests and earthquakes? All elements have been one time or other routed into confusion; the air hath been imprisoned in the bowels of the earth, from whence come earthquakes; the sea swelleth above its banks, from whence come inundations; the earth rolled hither and thither in the sea, which maketh dangerous shoals and quicksands; and the fire reserved for the vastation of that great day, 'When the heavens shall pass away with a great noise, and the elements shall melt with fervent heat; the earth also, and all the works that are therein shall be burnt up,' 2 Peter iii. 10. Whence do these come?

Ans. I answer. All these confusions and disorders of nature are the effects of sin. Our sins are as a secret fire that hath melted and burnt asunder the secret ties and confederations of nature. Thence are there so many destructions and degenerations, such enmities, cruelties, and antipathies among the creatures. Man, being the Lord of all things, was not only punished in his own person, but in the creatures, which are his servants and retinue. The Lord had given to us the free use of these things, and dominion over them; but upon our rebellion, the frame of nature is much altered and changed: Gen. iii. 17, 'Cursed is the earth for thy sake; in sorrow shalt thou eat of it all the days of thy life.' The word there used is אֲדָמָה, to show that it is cursed in that regard as it belonged to Adam, and was part of man's possession; and by earth he doth not only mean the lower element, but the whole visible world; it was made for man, and it was all cursed for man's sake. So it is taken elsewhere: Ps. cxv. 16, 'The heavens, even the heavens, are the Lord's; but the earth hath he given to the children of men;' and where it is said, 2 Peter iii. 7, 'The heavens and the earth that are now,' &c.—that is, the world. Wherever thou seest thorns and thistles to grow, remember that sin is the root of them. Whenever thou seest the seas toss, and the confederation of the creature to be disturbed, this is the fruit of man's disorder and rebellion against God. Whenever thou seest a fruitful land grow barren, that is the actual curse, a fruit of the original curse that is passed upon the earth for man's sin. So Rom. viii. 28, the apostle saith, 'The creature was made subject to vanity, not willingly, but by reason of him who hath subjected the same in hope.' Mark, the creature groans under the burden of vanity and corruption; what is the reason? It is not the fault of the creature, not willingly, for by the bent and poise of nature they all seek their own preservation; they have a constant inclination to their own good; but we, that had freewill and abused it, brought misery upon ourselves and the whole creation; therefore the apostle saith, 'It was by reason of him who hath subjected the same in hope.' It noteth both the efficient and meritorious cause; by reason of man as a sinner and by reason of God as a judge; so the creature is subjected and brought under the burden of vanity. God, to show how much he was offended with man, would discover it by the confusions and disorders of nature. As Moses in a holy anger broke the tables when he saw the people turn aside to idolatry; so when man turned unthankful and rebellious to God the king, it dissolved much of the order and beauty which otherwise would have been in the creation.

Obj. But because the objection speaks of many things, Whence come venemous things, &c. therefore take another question, what that is we may properly look upon to be a fruit and issue of the fall?

I answer, all corruptive and destructive alterations; for in entire nature all alterations should have been perfect. So also the dying of the creature to feed and clothe man is a fruit of the fall, the issue of sin. It was sin that took away the usefulness of the creature to man; for in innocency they were all obedient to man; the creatures were ready to fall at his foot, and were at his beck. So all the enmities of creatures among themselves are the fruit of the curse. All monstrosities and deformities came in by the fall. Therefore the prophet when he speaks of our restoration by Christ, it doth imply the restoration of the creature. The sun, by reason of sin, hath lost much of his light. When man is fully restored in glory, 'The light of the moon shall be as the light of the sun; and the light of the sun shall be sevenfold, as the light of seven days,' Isa. xxx. 26, 'then the lamb and the lion shall lie down together,' Isa. xi. 6, 7, for thus it was in innocency. Those places decipher the happiness of the creature upon man's full restoration; and imply how it was before man's fall, God made all things good,' Gen. i. 31. But now before the fall I suppose there were some things poisonous, and some things corruptible; and my reason is, because God would have the world to be furnished with all kinds of natures; therefore there ought to be corruptible natures as well as incorruptible, and poisonous creatures as well as those that are wholesome, though they could do man no harm. If a man comes into an artificer's shop, and seeth many instruments, he thinks them superfluous; at length he takes up a sharp-edged tool which wounds him; this is no blame to the artificer but to himself; it is his own fault, because he did not know the use of it: so these things were to set forth the glory of God; but when man by sin lost his knowledge, they proved obnoxious and hurtful to him. Now for toads and venomous plants, I believe most of them were the fruits of the curse of the earth, they being not so much parts of the world, as plagues of the world; therefore they came in by the fall, and so should put us in mind of the degeneration of the creature.

Use 1. It discovers the glory of God.

1. The whole world is but God's shop, where are the masterpieces of his wisdom and majesty; these are seen very much in the order of causes, and admirable contrivance of the world.

[1.] The wisdom of God and his counsel is mightily seen. The world is not a work of chance, but of counsel and rare contrivance. All that the Lord did here, he did it by art, and according to the inward idea and frame that was in his own mind; therefore the prophet saith, Isa. xl. 12, ' He hath weighed the mountains in scales and the hills in a balance.' God did as it were take a balance into his hands and weigh out all the creatures; he hath disposed all things by number, weight, and measure; he hath done it in exact proportion. Oh, let us admire the wisdom of God! it is above our search: Eccles. iii. 11, 'No man can find out the work of the Lord from the beginning to the end;' we may admire it in the general, and say it is all good, but we cannot find it out. Some little glimpses of his wisdom we have, that we may cry out, He is a great God, wonderful in counsel, mighty in working. But oh, the rare and wonderful contrivance! we cannot discern all the beauty and all the order of it. Did we but consider the various disposition of light and darkness, of heat and cold, of moisture and dryness, the artifice that is seen in all things that he hath made, we should say, certainly he that made these things is a wise God, and wonderful in counsel. We know the power of God by making all things out of nothing; but we know the wisdom of God by making all things in such an exquisite frame and order. Do but compare it with yourselves; we are soon tired, it is much to us to promote a petty interest in the world, to spread our small nets, and extend and reach out our heart to the cares of our private families; but how wise is that God that had the model of all things within himself, from the elephant to the ant, that disposed of all things in such a manner, that hath made and formed them with such apt proportions, that guideth the courses of the heavens, and keepeth the stars in their paths and order!

[2.] The majesty and greatness of God. Look up to him, that is at the upper end of all these causes, that are so sweetly subordinate to one another in the world; and he can turn them as he pleaseth: Job, speaking of the bright cloud, saith, chap. xxxvii. 12, 'It is turned round about by his counsels; that they may do whatsoever he commands.' Look up to him that is the head of angels. We are dazzled at the splendour and magnificence of an earthly king or prince; when we see him surrounded with dukes, earls and lords, these seem great things to us. How should we wonder at the majesty of God, that is encompassed with cherubim and seraphim, principalities, powers, thrones and dominions! How do we wonder at the majesty of kings riding in triumph in their chariots! Oh, how should we wonder at him that rides upon the wings of the wind! It was the brag of the king of Assyria, Isa. xix. 8, 'Are not my princes altogether kings?' But he hath angels for his courtiers, and clouds for his chariots, Ps. xviii. 10, 11, and a golden garment of light for his covering, Ps. civ. 2, whose throne is in heaven, and footstool is upon earth; and in heaven he sits in great majesty, commanding all things; and hath all creatures ready pressed for his service; he can but beckon to them, and they engage in his quarrel: Judges. v. 20, 'They fought from heaven; the stars in their courses fought against Sisera.' He hath the stars in order, and all causes in order to fight his battles against a wicked man. The fighting of the stars I believe might be explained out of Josephus, lib. v. cap. 6, who thus relates it: 'When Israel was to engage against the Canaanites, there arose a great storm of hail, which the wind drove violently in the faces of the Canaanites, and did so benumb their hands with cold, that carried the targets, darts, and slings, that they could not use them; and did so batter their eyes, that it took away their sight, that they could not look up: but it came on the backs of the Israelites, which encouraged them to fall upon them, so that they made an utter slaughter of them.' Certainly the force of the stars is very great upon storms of hail, thunder, and winds: Job xxxvii. 6, 'He saith to the snow, Be thou on the earth: likewise to the small rain, and to the great rain of his strength.' So, ver. 12, 'He turned it about by his counsels, that they may do whatsoever he commandeth them upon the face of the world in the earth.' He can call the winds, and they will make a ready answer to God: Job. xxxviii. 35, 'Canst thou send lightnings, that they may go, and say unto thee, Here are we?' All creatures are ready; he doth but beckon to the creatures, and they presently go

upon his errand; Lord, here are we, send us : whether shall I go?
saith the lightning ; where shall I go? saith the thunder; where shall
I go? saith the hail. They are ready to be despatched in an errand
for the punishment of sinners.

SERMON XI.

*Through faith we understand that the worlds were framed by the word
of God, so that things which are seen were not made of things
which do appear.*—HEB. xi. 3.

Use. 2. It showeth us the excellency of order ; how pleasing order and
method is to God : God hath always delighted in it. All his works
are managed and carried on in an accurate order. So in all artificial
works ; God speaks like a wise architect about the ark of Noah ; God
gave directions how it should be framed : Gen. vi. 15, 'The length of
it shall be three hundred cubits, the breadth fifty cubits, the height
thirty cubits.' So for the tabernacle, it was according to the pattern
in the mount, Exod. xxv. ; so for the table of show-bread, the knobs,
bowls, and shafts of the candlestick, God gave special directions about
them. Certainly God is a God of order, and not of confusion, 1 Cor.
xiv. 33. All order is from God ; but all discord and confusion is from
the devil. Order is pleasing to him in the state and civil administrations, in the church, and in the course of your private conversations.
    1. In civil administrations in the commonwealth, there are several
orders and constitutions that God hath made. The beauty of the
world lieth in hills and valleys ; so in the state, some advanced to high
places, others are low and poor. To bring all to one size, pitch and
level, would soon introduce confusion into the world. There is order
in heaven, order in hell, and there should have been order in innocency.
There is order in heaven among the good angels. The scripture speaks
of an archangel, 1 Thes. iv. 16 ; though he be not a monarch, there
are others of the same rank and order : Dan. x. 13, 'Michael, one of
the chief princes, came to help me.' And we read in Job of the morning stars,' Job xxxviii. 7 ; that is, the archangels that excel the rest in
glory. There are many of them, and God himself presides among
them. Then there are inferior ministering angels, thrones, principalities, powers, dominions. Though we cannot define the difference, yet
the scripture plainly intimates one, and lays down an order and subordination among the angels. Nay, there is some kind of order in hell
itself. There is a prince among the infernal spirits ; whence comes
that expression, 'The devil and his angels,' Mat. xxv. 41 ; and Rev.
xii. 7, 'The dragon and his angels,' who is 'called the devil and Satan,'
ver. 9. Jesus Christ, though he doth not positively lay it down, yet he
doth not deny the common opinion of the Jews, that Beelzebub was the
prince of evil spirits. The devils are not without their head and prince.
And in innocency there should have been order too, if we had continued

in that state. There would have been government and some inequality;
there would have been difference of sex, women and men; the relation
of fathers and children; the disparity of age, young men and old; now
much more is there need of it since the fall. There can be no peace
without it. *Pax est tranquillitas ordinis*—peace is the quiet of everything in its proper place: it is a great blessing when all keep their due
subordination, when magistrates keep their place, ministers and trades-
men keep their place; otherwise things will be shamefully brought
into confusion. Thus civil peace is the fruit of order, when every one
keeps their place. When the elements are out of their places, then
there are confusions in nature.

2. The Lord loves order in the church. I have observed the church
is set forth in scripture by the same similitudes and resemblances by
which the frame of the world is; by an army, and by a house, and by
the body of man. By an army or host: the church is ' terrible as an
army with banners,' Cant. vi. 4; when all administrations are regularly
carried according to the mind of God. It is compared to a house:
Eph. ii. 22, 'In whom you also are builded together for an habitation
of God through the Spirit.' And the prophet speaks of the order of
the church: Isa. liv. 12, 'I will make thy windows of agates, and thy
gates of carbuncles.' It is compared to the body of man, which receives
supplies and nourishment from the head: Col. ii. 19, 'And not holding
the head, from which all the body by joints and bands having nourishment ministered, and knit together, increaseth with the increase of
God.' Usually we are very loose and arbitrary in point of order. That
is the great security, the fence and hedge of religion, when some
instruct in the word, some are for inspection of manners, some minister
to the poor; when there are some to govern, and others to be governed;
when all keep their place, the church is beautiful, and terrible as an
army with banners. This was the rejoicing of the apostle, Col. ii. 5,
' To behold their order and steadfastness.' The order of the church
doth not consist in idle foppish ceremonies, but in decent administrations. But when men set the feet where the head should be, make
every one to be guides to the church, then the beauty of the church is
defaced, and all error and confusion is let into the church. The apostle
complains of ' Some that did walk disorderly,' 2 Thes. iii. 11, ἀτάκτως
the word signifies out of rank; this provokes the just suspension of
the influences of his grace.

3. The excellency of order in private conversation. We must be
more orderly in disposing our actions for the conveniency of the spiritual
life. Nothing so fit for a man as order and method in his private conversation but more especially in the spiritual life. We should not
walk at random and at large. Till there be a settled frame in the
course of our lives, it will never do well; that we may not live at adventure in religion, and do good by flashes. God complains of them
that are only good by fits, Hosea vi. 4. If we do not task ourselves,
and propose a settled course, we shall be fickle and inconstant, off and
on with God: Ps. l. 23, ' To him that ordereth his conversation aright,
will I show the salvation of God.' We should state all the courses
and exercises of religion in the holy life; that so our duty may not be
a hindrance, but a help to another. We act loosely when we act

arbitrarily, and at random; and shall be soon taken off by every alle-
gation and plea of the flesh, if we do not lay a necessity upon ourselves,
and settle a stated course of religious duties in our lives.   You may
do this lawfully: to this end God hath given us spiritual prudence
and christian discretion.   There are precepts in general for giving and
doing, but for measure, number, and order, God would leave that to
christian discretion.   It is said, Ps. cxii. 5, 'A good man guides all
his affairs with discretion.'   Do not think such a stated course will be
a snare to you, but it will prove a great advantage, and be a hedge to
duty.   All the experiences of the saints seal to it ; they could not else
secure themselves against neglects and omissions, if they did not lay
an engagement upon themselves by their own purposes and constitutions.   Duties of ordinary recourse may be easily thus disposed.   I
confess it requires some wisdom to state it aright, lest we lie bound in
chains of our own making, and watchfulness and resolution that we
may keep it.   When the proportions are rational, every idle objection
should not take us off, for it is in the nature of paying a vow.   Time
dedicated to God is not in our power, nor revocable upon every slight
occasion, only in case of inviolable necessity, to which duties of a divine
institution do give place.

Use. 3. It discovers the odiousness of sin that disjointed the frame
of nature.   When God made the world, 'he saw everything he had
made, and behold it was very good,' Gen. i. 31 ; but Solomon when
he looked upon it, he saw all was 'vanity of vanities,' Eccles. i. 2.
What is the reason? sin intervened and so the course of nature was
altered.   It had been otherwise but for sin ; the creature had continued
in their order, had we continued in our innocence.   Let me spread
a few considerations before you.

1. Do but consider what cause God hath to be angry with us.   We
are angry with those that break down a curious frame or contrivement
we have made, as if any break curious glasses, pictures, or images, or
a handsome structure.   But consider, we have cracked the frame of the
universe.   The ties which hold the world are loosened by our sins, and
much of the accurate order of the universe is inverted.   There is a
vanity among the creatures themselves, and sin and rebellion to us.
Therefore when thy thoughts are cold and barren in acknowledging sin,
especially in conceiving the evil that is in original sin, consider of this
circumstance ; it turned a paradise into a wilderness and rude common ;
it broke the frame of nature.   As Moses, when he was angry with the
Israelites, broke the tables ; so God hath broken the great frame of
nature.   Let that break your hearts which hath broken the world ; and
that which hath wrought so much mischief in nature, let it trouble
your souls.

2. Consider what a fit circumstance and consideration this is to
represent the odiousness of sin ; here we have a sensible and constant
memorial of the fruits of our rebellion.   Man, being in a lower sphere
of understanding, knows causes by their effects.   Oh, see what a cause
sin is; look upon the effects of it in the disorders that are in the
world: Jer. ii. 19, 'Know therefore, and see that it is an evil thing
and bitter, that thou hast forsaken the Lord thy God.'   What would
you think of that gall, a drop of which is enough to embitter an ocean

of sweetness ? Such is sin. One sin poisoned all mankind at once, and cracked and dissolved the frame of nature. There were indeed presently upon the fall two dreadful effects of sin's influence, the misery Adam brought upon his own posterity, and the vanity he brought upon the creature; both are sad and continual resemblances. The first I confess is a very great representation of the evil of sin; every child that is born is a new memorial of the fall. God as it were said to Adam, as the prophet to Gehazi, 2 Kings v. 27, 'The leprosy of Naaman shall cleave unto thee, and to thy seed for ever;' now thou hast sinned, every child born shall be a leper. So all the children of Adam are as so many pledges and memorials of the folly and disobedience he had committed against God. But look without, and the creatures are made unhappy by man's fall. When we have drawn company with us into misery, their sight and presence doth but increase our sorrow; as if a prodigal should look upon the lean faces of his family, he cannot but with the more regret own the shame of his own excesses. We may all go to God, and say with David, 2 Sam. xxiv. 17, 'Lord, I have sinned, and I have done wickedly; but as for these sheep, what have they done?' so, Lord, we and our fore-fathers have all sinned against thee; but what have the creatures done, that they are destroyed and devoured? These memorials are constantly represented; not a bit we eat, not a cloth we put on, but may return these thoughts into our minds, these are the fruits of our sin. In innocency Adam was not ashamed of his nakedness, and the creatures might not be slain for our food.

3. We have no cause to exempt ourselves from this duty of mourning by laying the guilt upon Adam; as if he only were unthankful and rebellious against God. Consider, by sin we do as it were consent to Adam's act, and so we are accessory *post factum* to his guilt. Imitation is an approbation, and an implicit and interpretative consent. Saith Christ to the Jews, Mat. xxiii. 37, 'O Jerusalem, Jerusalem, thou that killest the prophets;' and ver. 36, 'Whom ye slew between the temple and the altar.' How did they slay them? Because they continued still vexing the servants of God, therefore they are said to slay Zacharias. They that go on in any sin, do subscribe to the acts of those that went before them; we have continued in Adam's course of rebelling against God, therefore we are justly chargeable with his act. The father is fore-faulted for rebellion, and the child, continuing in the same course, doth approve his act, and besides his own personal guilt, is chargeable with the crimes of his forefathers. So that we may say, we have unsettled the universe. Jude 11, it is said 'these perished in the gainsaying of Korah.' How could that be, when there was such a huge distance and space of time between these and Korah? The meaning is, by practising the same sins, they came into a fellowship of the guilt; and imitating the fault, they became liable to the same judgment. Adam's first act brought on the original curse upon the creature, but our actual sins bring in an actual curse. As there is original and actual sin, so there is an original and an actual curse. It is true, Adam alone brought on the original curse: Gen. iii. 17, 'Cursed be the ground for thy sake:' but we bring on an actual curse: Ps. cvii. 33, 34, 'He turns rivers into a wilderness, and water-springs into dry ground; a fruitful land into barrenness, for the wickedness of them

that dwell therein.' Our actual sinning spoils the earth, and makes it barren and disorders the elements, and makes the rain from heaven unseasonable. Yea, we are guilty every day of doing that which Adam did once—laying a greater burden upon the creatures by abusing them to pomp, pride, excess, and carnal trust ; so you need not complain of Adam, but of your ownselves. The creatures do not say, Lord, avenge our quarrel upon Adam, but upon these who have abused us : Hab. ii. 11, ' The stone out of the wall shall cry out, and the beam out of the timber shall answer it.' The stone and timber shall cry, Lord, avenge us against this oppressor ; the house that is builded by extortion is crying to God against the unjust possessor. So James v. 3, 4, ' The rust of the gold and silver shall be a witness against them. Behold, the hire of the labourers, which have reaped down your fields, which is of you kept back by fraud, crieth.' The rusty coin out of the coffer crieth, and requireth vengeance at God's hands ; the creatures that have been abused to disorder and excess do cry out of the glutton's belly and drunkard's throat, O Lord, avenge us ! The clothes upon our backs do as it were cry, Lord, we are abused to pride and vanity ; take notice of our quarrel and plea against man !

4. If we do not bemoan this disorder of nature, the very creatures will shame us. They groan under this burden of vanity that is brought upon them ; but we are senseless, slight and careless. It is even true what Christ said in another case, Luke xix. 40, ' If these should hold their peace, the stones would immediately cry out.' So, if we hold our peace, the creatures will speak to our shame. Whither is man fallen ? The senseless and inanimate creatures are more moved with the evil of the present state than we are. That is the reason the prophet doth turn so often to the creatures, and address himself and speak to them : Jer. xii. 4, ' How long shall the land mourn, and the herbs of every field wither for the wickedness of them that dwell therein ? ' And Lam. ii. 18, ' O wall of the daughter of Sion, let tears run down like a river day and night.' The prophet calls upon the wall because the people were senseless. We go dancing like madmen to our misery and execution ; and the creatures mourn and groan under the burden of our sins: Hosea iv. 3, ' The land mourneth,' viz. for oaths, but where is the swearer that mourns ? The prophets often turn from men, and speak to the creatures: Deut. xxxii. 1, ' Give ear, O ye heavens, and I will speak ; and hear, O earth, the words of my mouth.' And Micah vi. 2, ' Hear, O mountains, the Lord's controversy.' And, Jer. xxii. 29, ' O earth, earth, earth, hear the word of the Lord;' because men will take no notice. The prophets may fret out their hearts, and spend their lungs in vain, before men will be sensible ; therefore he speaks to them. You hear the ox lowing, and the creatures groaning under the present vanity, and you do not lay it to heart. When you see unseasonable weather and barrenness, consider all these are the fruits of the original curse.

5. We of all the other parts of the creation have most cause to lay it to heart, because there is none so disordered and shattered by the fall as man is. There was none so excellent as man, being at first framed by the counsel and contrivance of God. When the world was made, it was said, ' Let it be ; ' but man was made by counsel, ' Let

us make man after our own image,' Gen. i. 26. Man was made at first after the image of God, now he is scarce the image of himself; like a defaced picture, that hath some obscure lineaments of a fair draft. Man was a comely, beautiful, orderly creature at first; but now there are but some obscure relics of this left. The soul was to be a good guide to the body, and the body a dexterous instrument of the soul; but now both are out of frame; we have spoiled the temper of our bodies, and the order of our souls. The rabbis say, when Adam tasted the forbidden fruit, his head ached; certainly it is true in a spiritual sense, then began aches and pains; how is all shattered and discomposed! We read in ecclesiastical story of a famous captain who triumphed in many battles, but afterward he fell into disgrace with the emperor, and first his lady was deflowered before his face, then his eyes bored out, and he was turned out like a blind beggar begging, *Date obolum Belizario*, give one halfpenny for poor Belizarius. Before the fall, man was the favourite of heaven, but after the fall he was presently made a slave of hell, his will was deflowered, then his eyes were pulled out, so that now having little knowledge and little wisdom even to guide ourselves in a moral course, the passions rebel against reason, and many times man is not only tempted, but drawn aside by his own lusts, and enticed, James i. 14. Nay, many times the body riseth up in arms against the soul. Paul groans because of a law in his members, Rom. vii. 23. Oh what a poor disordered routed creature man is! body and soul all discomposed and out of order.

6. There is a loss to us by the disorder of nature, and by the distempering of the creature. Man by the fall lost *imperium sui*, the command of himself, and *imperium suum*, his command over the creatures; they are enemies to man because he hath rebelled against God. If ever we find them hurtful and rebellious, we may thank ourselves, they do but revenge their maker's quarrel. They think it is their duty to turn off their allegiance from him that hath proved a traitor to God, therefore they sometimes oppress us with their power and greatness. It is usual with God to execute his judgments by the creature: Pharoah and the Egyptians were drowned in the sea; the earth opened to swallow up Korah and his company; the stars fought against Sisera; Herod was eaten up with lice; Egypt devoured with frogs. Therefore the vanity of the creature is a loss to us; there is not only an enmity between them one among another, but they have lost their allegiance to man. Nay, they are ready to go if the Lord do but hiss for them. Job xxxviii. 35, ' Canst thou send lightnings, that they may go, and say unto thee, Here we are?' The lightnings say unto God, Here we are; the winds say, Shall we go and blast their fruits and trees? here we are, Lord, send us. The clouds say, Shall we pour out in abundance, and overwhelm the earth? Isa. vii. 18, ' The Lord shall hiss for the fly that is in the uttermost part of the rivers of Egypt, and for the bee that is in the land of Assyria.' It is an expression that sets forth the power of God over the creatures. If God do but signify his pleasure, they are very ready to avenge their creator's quarrel against man.

The second circumstance in the creation is the instrument or means by which all things were created, and that is, ' By the word of God.'

Here a question ariseth, what is meant by the word of God? whether that which they call God's external imperial word, or whether God's essential and substantial word? The reason of the doubt is, because God made all things by Christ, and Christ is often called the word. It is his solemn title, and that in reference to the creation: John i. 1, 'In the beginning was the word, and the word was with God, and the word was God;' and ver. 3, 'By him were all things created.' And Heb. i. 2, 'He hath in these last days spoken unto us by his Son, whom he hath appointed heir of all things, by whom also he made the worlds.' So that Jesus Christ is the eternal word. I shall answer this doubt in these propositions.

1. It is very true that the second person, the Lord Jesus Christ, had a great stroke in the creation: Ps. xxxiii. 6, 'By the word of the Lord were the heavens made, and all the host of them by the breath of his mouth.' There is the whole trinity; there is the Lord, and the word of the Lord, and there is the breath of his mouth; that is, Father, Son, and Holy Ghost. Prov. viii. 22, 'The Lord possessed me in the beginning of his way, before his works of old.' There is Christ's eternity, and his hand and power in the creation: ver. 23, 'I was set up from everlasting, from the beginning, or ever the earth was;' that is, in the first emanation of his power, Christ was then discovered: John i. 3, 'By him were all things made that were made.' Col. i. 16, 'By him were all things created that are in heaven, and that are in earth.' Probably this may be held forth in that speech ten times repeated: 'The Lord said, the Lord spake.' Nay some of the Jews acknowledge an uncreated word in all those expressions. Philo saith, ὁ λόγος τὸν κόσμον ἐποίησεν. And it is not to be disregarded, that the Chaldee paraphrase makes the word to be God himself.

2. Yet, besides this essential word, it is clear that we must understand also his imperial word, or the word of his command; so it is interpreted, Ps. xxxiii. 9, 'He spake, and it was done; he commanded, and it stood fast.' Here was God's imperial word. So Ps. cxlviii. 5, 'He commanded, and they were created.' God did create the world by his call and imperial word. So Rom. iv. 17, 'He believed in God, who quickened the dead, and called things that be not, as though they were,' that is, by a call he maketh them be. Moses bringeth in God speaking imperially, 'Let it be.'

3. This imperial word must not be understood properly as if God spake; as if there were an audible voice, 'Let there be light;' but it must be understood ἀνθρωποπαθῶς, after the manner of men. It is an allusion to princes, if they would have anything done, they do but say, Let it be done, that is enough; as the centurion in the Gospel, Mark viii. 9, 'I say to this man, Go, and he goeth; and to another, Come, and he cometh; and to my servant, Do this, and he doeth it.' When God said, 'Let it be,' he did but signify his will, and the effect presently did follow. So that by the word of God you must understand the effectual decree of his will concerning the making of all the creatures, and the present execution of it. And this manner of speaking is used to show with what swiftness and easiness all things were brought to pass which God willeth, and that it is infinitely more easy with God to do

what he pleaseth, than for man to speak a word, or think a thought of what he would have to be done.

Quest. Here is another question. If nothing is to be understood but God's will, and willing the creation of all things? then whether the making of the world in six days be only for our understanding, or whether it be so really and indeed; whether all things were not created in the twinkling of an eye by God's will and pleasure; or whether it were done by distinct days, as the history in Genesis seems to intimate? The doubt hath been moved by divines of the greatest note. Austin expressly was of this opinion; so Cajetan, and some among the reformed; their reason is, because God is omnipotent, and could make all things in a moment, therefore why should he make such a slow progress, and go from day to day? And the author of Ecclesiasticus saith, ' He that liveth for ever, made all things at once.' They quote scripture for it: Gen. ii. 4, 5, 'In the day that God made the earth and the heavens, and every plant of the field before it was in earth, and every herb of the field before it grew.'—in that very day say they, when God created the heaven and the earth, he created all the other creatures. And they say that the mentioning of the six days was only inserted by Moses, because by so many distinctions and representations God showed his creatures to the angels, and to declare the natural dependence of all things upon one another, and also for our incapacity to conceive distinctly of things at once.

Ans. But all this is but a figment and gross supposition without the scripture. Though God could make all things in a moment, yet we must not reason from God's power to God's will, nor instruct him how to bring forth his work: Rom. xi. 34, ' For who hath known the mind of the Lord? or who hath been his counsellor?' And for that place, Gen. ii. 4, 5, 'In the day that the Lord made the earth and the heavens,' &c., some answer thus: It is true they were all made, *potentia*, in power, though not *actu*, actually in one day. Or rather the word day must be twice repeated: in the day that God made the heavens and the earth; and in the day that God made the plants, &c, for day there is taken more largely for time. But to confirm you in the history of Moses, it is plain that God made the world in that order; there are these apparent reasons for it—

[1.] If God made the world all at once, how could Moses with truth put down such a distinct commendation of every day's work?

[2.] Moses wrote historically, therefore his words must be properly understood.

[3.] Why should he say, God made light before the firmament and stars, if we go to natural dependence and order? It should be first the firmament, then the stars, then light. Therefore it is certain Moses followed that order in his history, that God observed in the production of all things.

[4.] If all creatures were thus created together, how could there be darkness upon the face of the deep? And how could the earth be said to be without form and void? Then it would have plants and beasts, if all were made together.

[5.] The reason of the sabbath would be to no purpose; how could Moses say with truth, Therefore the sabbath must be sanctified, because

God rested the seventh day? Therefore we may conclude, that though the effect followed as soon as God willed it, yet God willed the creation of all things in order; such a creature this day, and such a creature the next day.

Use 1. It helpeth us to conceive of the creation, all things were done by his word according to his will. The Gnostics feigned the aspectable world was made by the angels; but the scripture is plain: 2 Peter iii. 5, 'By the word of the Lord the heavens were of old, and the earth standing out of the water, and in the water.' He made them all without help and without labour; no creature, no instrument was serviceable to him in it; all was infinitely more easy to God than the conceiving of a thought can be to yourselves.

Use 2. Here is much comfort and profit to you.

1. Much comfort to poor souls that are smitten with remorse, and touched with a deep sense of their misery and wretched and sinful condition by nature. Usually, at first conversion, you may observe men have such a strong sense of the present evils and distempers of their spirits, that they are apt to sink under the burden of their discouragements, and to say, surely this hard heart will never be softened! this blind mind will never be enlightened! these stubborn affections will never be subdued and mortified! Consider the first creation when you expect the new creation. Think of the power of him that can call the things that are not, as though they were; one creating word is enough. Compare the benefit of the first creation and the second together: 2 Cor. iv. 6, 'God, who commanded the light to shine out of darkness, hath shined into your hearts,' &c. In the original it is ὁ εἰπὼν—he that spoke light out of darkness, by his word he could bring it forth presently; he can speak light to our souls, though there were nothing but darkness, confusion and disorder. You may go to God as the centurion, Mat. viii. 8, 'Speak the word only, and my servant shall be healed.' So do you say, Lord, speak but the word, then my soul shall be clean. It is observable that Jesus Christ, when he would discover any notable effects, he speaketh creating words; as 'Be thou clean;' 'Be thou made whole;' 'Follow me;' 'Lazarus, come forth.' How may a poor soul go to God when he is thus discouraged, and say, Speak light out of darkness, speak grace, O Lord, one word is enough, thou canst easily reach the bottom of the electing faculty.

2. It is of great use to encourage believers to wait for the accomplishment of the promises. Every promise rightly understood is a creating word. When God saith that he will make them perfect to every good work, it is as much as if he said, Be thou perfect, be thou justified, be thou sanctified, be thou enabled to every work of holiness, be thou glorified. When he saith, 'It is your Father's pleasure to give you a kingdom,' to make you able to every good work, to keep you by his power to salvation, he hath signified his pleasure, and that is enough to assure us it shall be effected. Look upon the word of God in creation as a pledge of the accomplishment of the promises. We doubt, because we are ignorant of the power of God's word. Your unbelief would be much abated if you would consider his creating the world,—how God could bring all things out of nothing. All the creatures are looking-glasses, that we may read what God can do by his word; in them his

sufficiency and efficacy are proposed to us to behold. When we have nothing left us but a promise, we may see all things in it. If God hath made heaven by his word, he can give thee heaven, and make good his promises by his word. God's word is the foundation of the creature's being, and the foundation of your faith. If heaven could be made and prepared by the word of his power, certainly the promises will be accomplished and made good to your souls, and you shall be brought to heaven by the word of his truth.

The third and last circumstance is the matter, or rather term, from which God's work began; there was no prejacent or pre-existent matter. It is a note of form and order; *ex nihilo*, that is, *post nihilum*—'So that things that are seen were not made of things that do appear.' The words have undergone variety of constructions. Calvin, leaving out the preposition, rendereth it, *Ut non apparentium spectacula fierent*, making it parallel with Rom. i. 20, 'For the invisible things of him from the creation of the world are clearly seen, being understood by the things that are made, even his eternal power and godhead.' But this is to force the grammatical construction. Some understand by 'things not seen,' the idea or module of all things in the divine mind; but this is to bring down the apostle's language to the doctrine of the school of Plato. Some understand the chaos, and that the apostle alludeth to the translation of the Septuagint of what is in the original, 'And the earth was without form, and void,' Gen. i. 2, the Septuagint renders ἡ δὲ γῆ ἦν ἀόρατος καὶ ἀπαρασκεύαστος—The earth was invisible and unprepared. This may be in part respected here, for ' darkness was upon the face of the deep ;' and so it may well be called, 'things not appearing.' Rather by τὰ μὴ φαινόμενα you may understand τὰ μὴ ὄντα—out of nothing. And the word was suited with the apostle's scope, which is to prove that faith contents itself with the word of God, though nothing be seen; that which was not at all could not be seen. Though these two latter expositions may be compounded, all things were made either immediately by God out of nothing, or immediately out of the chaos.

Quest. But here may be a doubt: How did God make all things out of nothing, since man was made of the dust of the earth? and all things were made out of the chaos, the first mass and lump that was without form? I answer, There is a double creation : out of nothing, and out of that which is as good as nothing.

1. There is a creation out of mere nothing; so the Lord framed many things, as the heaven of heavens, the dwelling-place of God and angels, and the spirits of blessed men. He could not make that from the earth and water, for that was not. So the chaos, or the earth that was void and without form, God made that out of nothing. And God made light out of nothing—' He commanded light to shine out of darkness,' 2 Cor. iv. 6. So the angels, and the souls of men, which were breathed into them by the breath of God: Gen. ii. 7, 'God breathed into his nostrils the breath of life, and man became a living soul.' God made all these out of mere nothing.

2. God made some things out of foregoing matter, which is yet called a creation, because the matter was altogether indisposed and unfit for such a use. There was no disposition in the matter to receive

such a shape as God bestowed upon it; the form was merely from the power of God, as the firmament was made out of the water: Ps. civ. 3, ' He layeth the beams of his chambers in the waters ;' that is, the firmament, which was made by the rarefaction and expansion of the waters. So the sun, moon, and stars were made out of the first light; for either it was annihilated or it yet remaineth. Annihilated it could not be, for the wise God made nothing but for some end, and we do not read that he abolished anything he had made; therefore it remaineth dispersed in the sun, moon, and stars, otherwise what is the use of it ? Fishes were made out of the waters: Gen. i. 20, ' Let the waters bring forth abundantly the moving creature that hath life.' Birds were made out of the earth, and so beasts: Gen. ii. 19, ' And out of the ground the Lord formed every beast of the field, and every fowl of the air.' The body of man was made out of the dust of the ground; Gen. ii. 7, ' And the Lord God formed man out of the dust of the ground ;' and the woman was taken out of the man : Gen. ii. 22, ' And the rib, which the Lord God had taken from man, made he a woman.'

Use. God by this would teach the world what to think of him. He created the world out of mere nothing, or out of matter not prepared; he created them wholly by his word, having no partaker with him. The great thing that we should learn hence is God's power. That you may consider it with profit, I shall lay down a few propositions.

1. Power is one of God's greatest perfections; that serves most for the comfort of the creature. It is love to make a promise; truth to regard his promise; and it is his power that makes good his promise. The warrant of our faith is the truth of God; but the proper ground of our faith is the power and sufficiency of God. When the apostle speaks of Abraham that was the father of the faithful, his faith is bottomed and founded on God's power; he believed that God was able to do it: Rom. iv. 21, ' Being fully persuaded that what he had promised he was able also to perform.' This is the proper ground of our faith, that God is every way sufficient to make good his promise. It is the prime perfection of God; for it is the power of God that maketh all other the perfections of God valid and effectual for the comfort of poor creatures. Therefore may we receive comfort from his mercy, because he is able to show mercy ; therefore may we depend upon his goodness and truth, because it is seconded with the power and all-sufficiency of God: Eph. iii. 20, ' He is able to do exceeding abundantly above all that we ask or think, according to the power that worketh in us.'

2. In the creation there is no attribute so eminent as God's power. There was wisdom and goodness shown in the creation, but the main attribute is power. God's wisdom and his goodness appear in the creation, as they exist in created things; but God's infinite power is in himself. Therefore, when the apostle speaks of the knowledge of heathens, Rom. i. 20, he saith in the creation was manifested ' his eternal power and godhead.' That was the principal thing discovered in the work of creation : Rev. v. 12, ' Worthy is the lamb that was slain to receive power and riches,' &c.

3. We must not only with a naked, idle speculation reflect upon

God's power but improve it to the uses of religion, as to fear and to trust.

[1.] To fear: Ps. xxxiii. 8, 'Let all the earth fear the Lord; let all the inhabitants of the world stand in awe of him;' Job xxxvii. 23, 24, 'Touching the Almighty, we cannot find him out; he is excellent in power . . . men do therefore fear him.' We should have a dread of God because of such power. Who would not fear to enter into the lists with him? By sins committed against God you draw omnipotency about your ears. Would you engage the mighty God against you? There are two causes of carnal com liance: we presume of God's mercy, and fear man's power. To check it, consider God is able by the rebuke of his countenance to turn us to nothing, that made us out of nothing.

[2.] Improve it to trust. In all your straits and exigencies, when nothing appears, then wait upon the Lord; he can create means when he finds none; he can produce all possible things into act, or leave them still in the womb of nothing. He can do you good by contrary means; as Christ cured the blind man's eyes by clay and spittle, by that which seemed to put them out.

SERMON XII.

By faith Abel offered unto God a more excellent sacrifice than Cain, by which he obtained witness that he was righteous, God testifying of his gifts : and by it he, being dead, yet speaketh.—
HEB. xi. 4.

THE apostle cometh to illustrate the properties of faith by the special experiences of the saints. He begins with Abel.

But you will say, Why doth he pass by Adam, the first man, and the first believer in the world? For four reasons.

1. Because Abel was the first persecuted man for righteousness, by Cain professing the same worship: whereas Adam lived a quiet life, without assault and molestation. And so it suits with the apostle's scope, which is to embolden believers against troubles and persecutions for Christ's sake. Here was the first instance of the distinction of men, Cain and Abel, brothers born of the same womb; nay, which is more, supposed to be twins of the same birth; yet one the seed of the woman, and the other the seed of the serpent. Therefore Abel is fitly propounded as the first pattern of faith; as Cain was the patriarch of unbelievers, as Tertullian calls him. And the apostle says, Jude 11, 'They have gone in the way of Cain.' This was an early instance of the enmity between the seeds, and the first pledge of the spite and malice which carnal men do now manifest against the children of God because of the old hatred. Adam was the first sinner, but Cain the first murderer. Therefore the apostle doth well begin with Abel, who was the first-fruits of the faithful; in him the envy and malignity of

the world began to taste the blood of martyrs, and ever since it is glutted with it.

2. Because Abel was the first person that was never in a possibility to be saved by any other way than that of faith. Adam had other means propounded to him at first in the covenant of works, and therefore he is passed by, and Abel is fitly represented as the first evangelical believer.

3. After the fall, Moses speaks nothing notable of Adam. Though he was received to grace, yet God did not put that honour upon him which he did upon some of his posterity. And because of his great unthankfulness, he having received so much, therefore he is passed by, and not propounded to the church as one of the glorious witnesses and examples of faith. Observe from hence the scandalous falls of God's children are of dangerous consequence. Though the wound be cured, yet there are some scars remain ; and though free grace makes them vessels of mercy, yet it doth not use and employ them as vessels of honour. There are more than probabilities of Adam's faith, yet it is not famous in the church. The apostle beginneth with Abel.

4. Because Abel was a special type of Jesus Christ. He was a type of him in his temporal calling : Gen. iv. 2, 'Abel was a keeper of sheep.' πρωτοποίμην—the first shepherd ; so Jesus Christ is ἀρχιποίμην— the chief shepherd of our souls ; Heb. xiii: 10, 'The great shepherd of the sheep.' And so also he was a type of him in his righteousness and innocency. It is notable that Abel is seldom spoken of in scripture, but he is honoured with this appellation, 'righteous Abel.' Moses is spoken of for meekness, Phinehas for zeal, but Abel for righteousness : Mat. xxiii. 35, 'From the blood of righteous Abel,' &c. And this the apostle might intend in part when he saith in the text, 'By which he obtained witness that he was righteous ;' that is, he is spoken of in the scriptures and in the church of God as righteous ; and herein he was a type of Christ : 1 John ii. 1, 'Jesus Christ the righteous.' Then again, in his death, Abel came to sacrifice, and solemnly to remember Christ, and that provoked Cain's envy. The offering of the lamb did not only signify the shedding of Christ's blood, but Abel himself is made a type of the death of Jesus Christ. Abel is slain by the envy of Cain ; so was Jesus Christ by the envy of the priests and his maglignant Jewish brethren : Mat. xxvii. 18, 'He knew that for envy they had delivered him.' Envy slew Abel and betrayed Christ. There was only this difference between the blood of Christ and the blood of Abel : the blood of Abel called to God for vengeance upon the murderer, and the blood of Christ for mercy even upon his persecutors—mercy for unthankful men. Therefore the apostle saith, Heb. xii. 24, the blood of Christ 'speaketh better things than the blood of Abel.' Abel's blood crieth thus to the Lord, Vengeance ! vengeance ! vengeance upon murderous Cain ! Christ's blood cries, Pardon ! pardon ! Father, be appeased, be merciful to these poor sinners ! Thus you see from the very cradle of the world there were presignifications of Christ, not only in things, but in persons. The sacrifice and sacrificer both represented Christ, who was both priest and offering : Abel's lamb signified Christ, the 'Lamb of God, that taketh away the sins of the world.' Now to show that God would not be appeased with any irrational offering, Abel himself was to be sacrificed, as well as his sacrifice ; Jesus Christ the priest himself

is to be slain. God did teach the old church by persons as well as things, to signify not only the satisfaction of Christ, but the person of Christ, ' Who by the eternal Spirit offered himself without spot to God,' Heb. ix. 14.

We have seen the reasons why the apostle beginneth with Abel; let us hear what is said of him—' By faith Abel offered unto God a more excellent sacrifice than Cain.'

In which words these things are considerable—(1.) Abel's action; (2.) The consequents, or fruits of it.

1. Abel's action—*He offered a more acceptable sacrifice than Cain.* In that you have three circumstances—

[1.] The principle or root of it—*By faith.*

[2.] The nature of it—*He offered sacrifice.*

[3.] The comparative excellency—πλείονα θυσίαν παρὰ Κάϊν; that is, *He offered a better sacrifice than that which Cain offeerd.*

2. You have the consequents of the whole work; they are two—

[1.] There is a testimony.

[2.] A special privilege.

(1.) A testimony, the inward testimony of his person—*By it he obtained witness that he was righteous.* The outward testimony of this performance—*God testifying of his gift.*

(2.) The special privilege by it—*He, being dead, yet speaketh.*

I shall begin with the explication of the necessary circumstances of Abel's action, and inquire—(1.) What was the occasion of this sacrifice? (2.) What was the warrant of this sacrifice? (3.) Wherein lies the excellency of it above that of Cain? (4.) What kind of faith this is that the apostle intends, when he saith, ' By faith he offered,' &c.

First. What was the special occasion of this sacrifice? That may be gathered out of the phrase used: Gen. iv. 3, ' And in process of time it came to pass, that Cain brought of the fruit of the ground an offering unto the Lord.' In process of time, or as it is in the margin, at the end of days; in the original it is, מקץ ומים—at the end 'of the year, or revolution of days. The Hebrews are wont to reckon their time by days, as being the more natural distinction. Years are more artificial, and depend upon the institution of man; and therefore is the term day so often used for time in scripture. Now God hath taught Adam by revelation, and he his son by instruction, that men should at the year's end, in a solemn manner, sacrifice with thanks to God, when they had gathered in the fruits of the earth. This tradition was afterwards made a written law: Exod. xxii. 29, ' Thou shalt not delay to offer the first of thy ripe fruits, and of thy liquors; the first-born of thy sons shalt thou give unto me.' It was an order then newly inforced, though it had been observed from the beginning of the world; so Exod. xxiii. 16, ' And the feast of harvest, the first-fruits of thy labours, which thou hast sown in the field: and the feast of ingathering, which is in the end of the year, when thou hast gathered in thy labours out of the field.' The very heathens themselves did by tradition derive and propagate this custom one to another, for among other things they retained it, even in their darkest ignorance. I remember, Aristotle in his ' Ethnics ' (lib. viii., chap. 8.) hath such a passage as this, Αἱ γὰρ ἀρχαῖαι θυσίαι καὶ σύνοδαι φαίνονται γένεσθαι μετὰ τὰς τῶν καρπῶν συγκομιδας—That all the ancient meetings and sacrifices were wont to be after the gathering in of the first-fruits, that they might distribute the due portion of the increase of their fields to the gods; so that at the end of days, when the year was run round, and the vintage and harvest-time was past, they were to come in token of thankfulness, and present the first-fruits unto the Lord. In short, these solemn sacrifices at the end of days had a double end and use.

1. To be a figure of the expiation promised to Adam in Christ.

2. To be a solemn acknowledgment of their homage and thankfulness to God.

[1.] The general use of these sacrifices was to remember the seed of the woman, or Messiah to come, as the solemn propitiatory sacrifice of the church. And indeed there was a notable resemblance between those offerings and Jesus Christ: Abel offered a lamb; and Christ is ' the Lamb of God, that takes away the sins of the world,' John i. 29. And because of these early sacrifices, therefore is that expression used, Rev. xiii. 8, 'The Lamb of God, slain from the foundation of the world;' that is, slain in types, sacrifices, and presignifications. And he also is the first-fruits: Ps. lxxxix. 27, 'I will make him to be my first-born, higher than the kings of the earth,' saith God, speaking of Christ. Col. i. 15, 'He is the first-born of every creature;' and the first-begotten: Heb. i. 6, 'Again, when he bringeth in the first-begotten into the world.' Christ is called the first-born and the first-begotten, partly in regard of the eternity of his person—it was without beginning, before the world was—and partly because of the excellency of his person, he being more glorious than angels or men. Though God had other children by creation besides Christ, yet he is the first-born. What shall we gather from hence?

Doct. That in all our addresses to God we must solemnly remember and honour Christ.

In the feast of the first-fruits they were to have an eye to the Messiah that was to come, though he were but darkly revealed. God will have men to ' honour the Son as they honour the Father,' John v. 23. We must do duties to God, so as we may honour Christ in them. It may be you will ask, How do we honour Christ in doing of duties?

(1.) When you look for your acceptance in Christ, as Abel comes with a lamb in faith. Adam hid himself, and durst not come into the presence of God till he had received the first promise and intimation of Christ. And truly guilt cannot approach majesty armed with wrath and power without a mediator. The patriarchs were to profess homage, but by sacrifices typing Christ: Ephes. iii. 12, ' In him we have boldness and access with confidence, by the faith of him.' Oh, you cannot come with confidence unless you come with a mediator in the arms of faith! Thus must all do that would be accepted of God. When shall we honour Christ in our addresses to God, and lift up a confidence proportionable to his merit? at least come not in your own names.

(2.) This is to honour Christ in duties, when you look for your assistance from the Spirit of Christ. The Lord hath promised to shed abroad his Spirit upon his ascension. You honour God in Christ when you worship God through Christ: Phil. iv. 13, 'I can do all things through Christ which strengtheneth me.' You draw nigh to God with more encouragement by expecting the supplies of the Spirit.

(3.) When the aim of the worship is to set up and advance the mediator. This was the solemn drift of the patriarchs, and the general intention of all their sacrifices—to look to the promised seed; and therefore the parts of their worship did exactly resemble the mediatory actions of Christ. In all the worship of the gospel, in your thoughts you must not only advance God, but lift up the mediator. When the apostle compares the worship of the christian with that of the Gentiles, he saith, 1 Cor. viii. 5, 6, 'There are gods many, and lords many, (many mediators) but to us there is but one God, the Father, of whom are all things, and we in him; and one Lord Jesus Christ,' &c. This is the right frame of a christian's heart in all his addresses: he looks up to one Lord as the fountain of mercy, and the ultimate object of worship, and one mediator. We must look to him as the conveyance and golden-pipe of mercy, by whom all blessings descend to us, and through him all our prayers ascend to God. This is to honour the mediator; to make Christ the means, and God the object and last end.

[2.] The special use of this worship was to profess their homage and their thankfulness to God. They were to come as God's tenants, and pay him their rent. Therefore God puts words into the Israelites' mouths: Deut. xxvi, 10, 'I have brought the first-fruits of the land, which thou, O Lord, hast given me.' The note from hence is,

Doct. That in the times of our increase and plenty we must solemnly acknowledge God.

The best way to secure the farm, and keep it in our possession, is to acknowledge the great landlord of the whole world—Lord, I have been a poor creature, and thou hast blest me wonderfully. There is a rent of praise and a thank-offering due to God. As Jacob acknowledgeth God thus, Gen. xxxii. 10, 'I am not worthy of the least of all thy mercies, and of all the truth which thou hast showed unto thy servant; for with my staff I passed over this Jordan, and now am I become two bands.' Thus we should come with a rent of praise, and with a thanksgiving to the Lord. But alas! how few think of this? We offer to him our lusts, but do not come with our thanksgiving to God. *Qui majores terras possident, minores census solvunt*—Those that have received most blessings from God forget the great landlord of the world. We are *Canistæ*, as Luther calls such of Cain's sect, because we do grudge God a little when he hath given us abundance: 1 Cor. xvi. 2, 'Upon the first day of the week let every man lay by him in store as God hath prospered him.' These offer according to their calling; Cain comes as a husbandman, and Abel as a keeper of the sheep. Consider, the first fruits sanctified and blessed the whole lump: Rom. xi. 16, 'For if the first fruits be holy, the lump is also holy.' When you give God his portion, you can the better take comfort in what is left.

Secondly, The second question is, What was the warrant of this worship? Was it devised according to their own will, or was it commanded by God? The reason of the inquiry is because the papists say that before the law the patriarchs did, without any command, out of their private good intention, offer sacrifice to God; and they prove it, because the gentiles that were not acquainted with the institutions of the church used the same way of worship. But this opinion seemeth little probable,—

1. Because this is above the light of corrupt nature to prescribe an acceptable worship to God. Corrupt nature will tell us indeed that God is to be worshipped; but for the manner, God himself must prescribe it; for the gentiles might take up the way of sacrifice by tradition, or by perverse imitation, through the instigation of the devil, who would be worshipped the same way God was.

2. It was by some appointment; for no worship is acceptable to him but that which is of his appointment. You know the solemn profession of God against will-worship in scripture—'Who hath required this at your hands?' Isa. i. 12. God will always be his own carver, and not leave his worship to the allotment of corrupt nature. He appointeth what he will accept.

3. There could have been else no faith nor obedience in it, if the institution had been wholly humane; there is no faith without some promise of divine grace, no obedience without some command. And Cain would not have been culpable for any defect in the worship, if it had been left to his own will; for where there is no law there is no transgression.

4. The wonderful agreement that is between this first act of solemn worship and the solemn constitutions of the Jewish church, doth wonderfully evince it (as we shall prove by and by), that there was some rule and divine institution according to which this worship was to be regulated, which, probably, God revealed to Adam, and he taught it, as he did other parts of religion, to his children: therefore it was done by virtue of an institution. Abel looked to the command of God, and promise of God, that so he might do it in faith and obedience.

The note from this—

Doct. That whatever is done in worship must be done out of conscience, and with respect to the institution.

Quest. But you will say, What is it to do a thing by virtue of an institution? For answer—

[1.] I shall show you what an institution is. Every word of institution consists of two parts—the word of command, and the word of promise. To instance in any duty of worship: in hearing the word, Isa. lv. 3, 'Hear, and your souls shall live;' in the sacrament—'Do this;' there is the word of command; then 'This is my body and blood;' there is the word of promise. In baptism: Acts ii. 38, 'Be baptized, every one of you;' there is the word of command; 'For the remission of sins;' there is the word of promise. God doth not require duty merely out of sovereignty, but in mercy. In the law it is sometimes a motive—Do thus and thus, for I am the Lord; God's sovereignty is pleaded. In other places—Do thus, and this shall be your life; there is the promise; and this will do you good. It is the condescension of God to require no duty but for your profit—'You shall not seek my face in vain.' Duty is not a task, but a means; he encourageth, when he might transact all things by way of charge and imperial command. God that requireth worship, doth also reward it; precepts and promises go hand in hand. Christianity is famous for pure precepts and excellent rewards. God's services will not be uncomfortable; for all his institutions are made up of a word of command and a word of promise.

[2.] What is it to do a duty in respect to the institution? I answer, it is to do it in faith and obedience: faith respects the word of promise, obedience the word of command. Customary approaches bring God no honour and glory; therefore first the command must be the reason of the duty. Then the promise must be the encouragement, the *ratio formalis*—the formal reason of all duty and obedience, is God's command; and the *ratiomotiva*, the moving and persuasive reason, is our own profit and God's promise. Obedience to the command is my homage, and faith one of the purest respects I can yield to God.

Ques. But now how shall I know when I do duty in faith and obedience? I answer—

(1.) You come in obedience when the command is the main motive and reason upon your spirit to put you upon the duty. It is enough to a christian to say, 'This is the will of God,' 1 Thes. v. 18. The bare sight of God's will is enough. It is custom to do as others do, but religion to do what God commands, because God hath commanded: Exod. xii. 26, 27, 'It shall come to pass, when your children shall say unto you, What mean you by this service? that ye shall say, It is the sacrifice of the Lord's passover.' Ask your heart, Why do I pray and hear? The Lord our God hath commanded it. Now this will be evident to you by your continuing in duties, though the success be not presently visible. The soul is of Peter's temper: Luke v. 4, 5, saith Christ, 'Let down your net for a draught.' Alas! 'Master (saith Peter) we have toiled all night, and have taken nothing; howbeit at thy word I will let down the net.' So the soul encourageth itself, I have had no sensible communion with God, yet I must perform my duty; I will do what God hath commanded, let God do what he will; success is God's act, duty mine. Then you come in obedience to the performance of any holy service.

(2.) Would you know when you come in faith? when you look to the word of promise? You may know that by the earnest expectation and considerateness of the soul. Those that come customarily do not look to the end of the service, nor why God hath appointed it. It is said, Ps. xxxii. 9, 'Be ye not as the horse and mule, which have no understanding;' that is, to go on without consideration. Man is to work for an end, to design somewhat, especially in duties of worship, which are the most serious and important affairs of our whole lives. Therefore what do you look for in your worship? Many look to the work wrought, but not to the end. God's institutions are under a blessing; and there must be an actual waiting, or you do not come in faith. And you will know this by the importunateness of your souls in pressing God with his word. Ah, Lord! thou hast made a promise to those that wait upon thee that thou wilt bless them; now 'remember thy word unto thy servant, upon which thou hast caused me to hope,' Ps. cxix. 49. By this you may try your hearts.

Thirdly, The third question is, Wherein lies the difference between the two sacrifices? Some place it only in the acceptation of God as if the sense were, Abel offered *gratiorem*, a more acceptable sacrifice, better in God's esteem; but in the original it is πλειονα, more sacrifice; *uberiorem*, saith Erasmus, a larger, a more plenteous, *majoris pretii*, a more excellent and a more beseeming sacrifice. It was better, not only in God's esteem, but in its own worth and value.

Briefly, there is a threefold difference between Abel's and Cain's sacrifice.

1. In the faith of Abel. Abel's principle was faith, Cain's distrust. The one came in faith, looking to the promised seed, and so the duty was effectual for his comfort and encouragement, he was accepted with God; the other came to it as to a dead ceremony and task against his will, a superficial rite of no use and comfort. That which is done in faith pleaseth God, otherwise it is but an idle rite and naked ceremony. God looks for habitual faith; but in all that proceed to a justified state he looks for actual faith, without which our sacrifices are but an abomination to him; Prov. xxi. 27. 'The sacrifice of the wicked is abomination,' how much more when he bringeth it with a wicked mind. Though a wicked man bring it with the most advantage, with good intentions, yet it is an abomination; much more if he bring it with a carnal aim and a grudging spirit and evil mind, as Cain did. But of this hereafter.

2. The second difference lay in the willing mind of Abel. Abel came with all his heart, and in a free manner, to perform worship to God; and he brought the best, the fattest, and costliest sacrifice he could, as far as the bounds of God's institution would give him leave. But Cain came with a sullen, covetous, unthankful, and fleshly spirit; he thought whatever he brought was good enough for God. Cain was envious to God before he was envious to his brother; he offered with a grudging mind whatever came first to hand, but kept the firstfruits to himself. Cain looked upon his sacrifice as a task rather than a duty; his fruits were brought to God as a mulct and fine rather than an offering, as if an act of worship had been an act of penance, and religion was his punishment. Note from hence—the worth of duties lies much in the willing mind of those that perform them.

[1.] There must be the mind. God doth not require ours, but us. Abel brought his lamb, and himself too; but Cain offered not himself, he brought only his offering. God would have us, when we come to him, to bring ourselves; though he need us not, yet we have need of him. The Lord complains that they did not bring themselves: Jer. xxix. 13, 'Ye shall seek me, and find me, when you shall search for me with all your heart.' This is right Cain's trick, to bring God our gift, and not ourselves.

[2.] The mind must be willing and free. Probably that which did put Cain upon duty was the awe of his parents, or the rack of his own conscience; therefore he would do something to satisfy the custom. He would bring of the fruits, and there was all, but was unmindful of what God had done for him, and distrustful how God would reward him. Many are of Cain's spirit; we think all is loss that is laid out upon God, and therefore do not come readily: Ps. cxix. 108, 'Accept,

I beseech thee, the free-will offering of my mouth, O Lord.' All your duties should be free-will offerings. A christian should have no other constraint upon him but love : 2 Cor. v. 14, ' The love of Christ constraineth us.' The devil rules the world by enforcement and a servile awe, and so captivates the blind nations ; but God will rule by the sceptre of love. God would have his people a willing people. Their heart shall be their own law. In all our addresses to God we should come to him upon the wings of joy and holy delight.

3. The third difference is in the matter offered. It is said of Cain's offering, Gen. iv. 3, ' That he brought of the fruit of the ground an offering unto the Lord.' The Holy Ghost purposely omits the description of the offering. Being hastily taken, and unthankfully brought, it is mentioned without any additional expression to set off the worth of them ; it should have been the first and the fairest. But for Abel, see how distinct the Spirit of God is in setting forth his offering : ver. 4, ' And Abel, he also brought of the firstlings of his flock, and of the fat thereof ;' not only the firstlings, that the rest might be sanctified, but he brought the best, the chiefest, the fattest. All these were afterwards appropriated to God : Lev. iii. 16, 17, ' All the fat is the Lord's.' Now observe from hence—

Doct. That when we serve God, we must serve him faithfully, with our best.

It is a high dishonour and contempt to God when we bring him a contemptible offering, and think anything is good enough for God : Mal. i. 14, ' Cursed is the deceiver, that hath a male in his flock, and voweth and sacrificeth to the Lord a corrupt thing ; for I am a great king,' &c. When we do not offer God the flower and spirit of our souls, we reflect a dishonour upon God. Our duties are so to be ordered that they may argue a proportionable reverence and dread of God. Alexander would be painted by none but Apelles, and carved by none but Lysippus. Domitian would not have his statue made but in gold or silver. God, the great king, will be served with the best of our affections. When we care not what we offer to God, how will he accept us ? How shall he esteem that which we do not esteem ourselves ? Cain's offering was not so much an oblation as a refusal, a casting off ; a rejection of that which was not fit to be reserved for himself, he gives it to God. It must needs displease God, since it could not please himself : in short, God must have the best of our time, and the best of our parts.

[1.] God must have the best of our time. Consider, we can afford many sacrilegious hours to our lusts, and can scarce afford God a little time without grudging. Is not there too much of Cain's spirit in this ? We adjourn and put off the work of religion to the aches of old age : when we have scarce any vigour, any strength of affections left, oh ! then we will worship God. We devote to Satan the flower of our lively youth, and fresh age, and adjourn to God the rottenness and dregs of our old age : Eccles. xii. 1, ' Remember thy Creator in the days of thy youth.' Why ?—because the prints of God's creating power are then more fresh in our natures, and we have a fairer experience of God's creating goodness than in age. Then is the fittest season to estimate the benefits of our creation. Old age are the days in which we have no pleasure ; these are our fresh, choicest days, full of contentment.

[2.] With your best parts. You come to worship God not only with your bodies, but your souls, with the refined strength of your reason and thoughts : Ps cviii. 1, 'I will sing and give praise even with my glory.' If David had anything he called his glory, God should have it.

Application to the sacrament. You have heard of Cain and Abel, in what they agreed, and in what they differed. They agreed in the general action—both drew near to God, and worshipped ; in the general nature of that action—they both brought an offering ; in the general kind of that offering, which was of that which belonged to each of them ; Cain, a tiller of the ground, brought of the fruit of the ground ; Abel, a keeper of sheep, brought of his flock, Gen. iv. 3, 4. They differed thus—one offered in faith, the other not : they differed in the matter of sacrifice—Abel brought the first and fattest ; of Cain it is only said he brought an offering : they differed in acceptance. Now this showeth you—

1. What you are to do in the Lord's supper.

2. What to expect.

1. What you are to do. Offer to God in the most beseeming manner what will become the majesty of God, the love of Christ, your faith in him and love to him. If you have anything better than another, let God have it. But you will say, What is this to the Lord's supper, where we do not come to offer, but to receive ; not to offer sacrifice but to receive a sacrament ; not to feast God, but to be feasted by him ?

Ans. [1.] There is a difference between sacraments and sacrifice, but they have a mutual relation one to the other. A sacrament implieth a sacrifice. The only sacrifice to please God was that of Christ, who offered up himself through the eternal Spirit to God. Christ offered the sacrifice to please God ; and being appeased by Christ, he offereth his gifts to us ; as Esau, when reconciled to Jacob, offered him gifts, Gen. xxxiii. 15.

[2.] Though we do not offer a sacrifice, yet we remember a sacrifice offered for us ; and therefore it teacheth us how to be rightly conversant about such a duty. The use of the sacrifices was—(1.) To exercise brokenness of heart : Ps. li. 17, 'The sacrifices of God are a broken heart.' I deserved to die, tormented by the wrath of God. (2.) To testify faith in the satisfaction and sacrifice of the messiah that was to come, and to seek reconciliation with God by him, Lev. i. 3. (3.) To express their hearty thankfulness to God, and desire to please him and walk with him in a course of true obedience : Ps. l. 5, 'Gather my saints together unto me ; those which have made a covenant with me by sacrifice.' Now, if we would come as Abel, and not as Cain, thus must we do : broken-hearted sinners must remember Christ, and apply him to the comfort of their souls, and make use of this duty to that end.

[3.] Though it be no sin-offering, yet it is a thank-offering. This in the text was in part so. There are eucharistical as well as ilastical sacrifices, as most of the sacrifices under the law : Heb. xiii. 15,

' By him therefore let us offer the sacrifice of praise to God continually, even the fruit of our lips, giving thanks to his name.' Hereby you bind yourselves to obedience and thankfulness : Rom. xii. 1, ' I beseech you therefore, brethren, by the mercies of God, that you present your bodies a living sacrifice, holy, acceptable to God, which is your reasonable service.'

2. What we are to expect—a testimony that we are righteous—some witness from God of the acceptance of our persons and gifts, not extraordinary by fire from heaven, but by the Holy Ghost : Mat, iii. 11, ' He shall baptize you with the Holy Ghost, and with fire.' When the Holy Ghost came down on the apostles, ' there appeared unto them cloven tongues, like as of fire, and it sat upon each of them,' Acts ii. 3. This spirit we expect : Rom. viii. 16, ' The Spirit itself beareth witness with our spirit, that we are the children of God.' And in token that he is pleased with us in Christ, he feedeth us from his own table.

SERMON XIII.

By faith Abel offered unto God a more excellent sacrifice than Cain, by which he obtained witness that he was righteous, God testifying of his gifts : and by it he, being dead, yet speaketh.—HEB. xi. 4.

In order to the further opening this text, I shall handle three points—

1. That carnal men may join with the people of God in external duties of worship.

2. Though they do join, yet in the performance of them there is a sensible and manifest difference.

3. This different performance ariseth from the influence and efficacy of faith.

Doct. 1. That carnal men may join with the people of God in external duties of worship.

We see in the first worship upon record there is a Cain and an Abel ; so in Christ's parable : Luke xviii. 10, ' Two men went up into the temple to pray ; the one a pharisee, and the other a publican.' And our Lord saith, Mat. xxvi. 41, ' Two women shall be grinding at the mill ; the one shall be taken, and the other left ;' meaning, the one shall be taken by Christ into heaven, and the other left for devils to be carried into hell. It is wonderfully strange that God should make such a distinction ; but much more strange that two persons shall be praying at the throne of grace, the one taken, and the other left. The reasons of this point, why carnal men do join in external duties of worship, may be reduced to three heads—

1. Natural conscience will put men upon worship.

2. Custom will direct to the worship then in use and fashion.

3. Carnal impulses will add force and vigour to the performances. Take all together, and then you have full account of a natural man's devotion.

First, Natural conscience will put men upon worship.   There are some few principles that are escaped out of the ruins of the fall ; as Job's messengers, ' I only am escaped alone to tell thee,' Job i. 16.   There is a little common light left to tell us that there is a God, and, by conse-quence, that this God must be worshipped by the creature.   Therefore mere natural conscience may suggest worship, and check for the omis-sion of it ; especially when we are serious, and natural light is clear and undisturbed, and men give their consciences leave to speak out.   The very heathens were sensible of the necessity of worship, and often speak of beginning all enterprises with God, and say men must be praying to God if they would have a blessing upon their affairs.   The apostle saith, Rom. ii. 14, the heathens had ' the work of the law written upon their hearts ; ' that is, the external part of obedience, the outward part of worship, and avoiding gross sins.   And the conscience of every natural man is like that of the heathens, only somewhat more enlightened by living in the church.   But until they are regenerate they have nothing but the light of nature to guide them, though improved by custom, edu-cation and literal instruction ; and whatever they do, they do it out of the dictate of natural conscience.   Natural men are loth to be wholly without worship.   Conscience, like the stomach, must be filled, and have something to pacify it, lest it should bark at us, and reproach us all the day long.   Men must put on the garb of religion, or their own conscience will not let them be quiet.   Thoughts will excuse or accuse, though blindly, and with much imperfection ; and though carnal men are slight in their duties, yet duty there must be.

Secondly, Custom will put us upon the worship then in use and practice.   Natural conscience will tell us that God is to be wor-shipped ; but how, it learneth from custom and education : so Ezek. xxxiii. 31, ' They come unto thee as the people come ;' that is accord-ing to the manner of religion then in fashion, according to the devotion of the times.   And therefore carnal men go on coldly in the run and tract of accustomed and practised duties.   *Non exploratis rationibus traditionis,* saith Cyprian : they take up duties upon trust, and they look not so much to the reason and nature of worship, as to the custom and practice of it.   Cain went up with Abel ' in process of time,' or at the year's end, the stated time of worship ; so do men pray, hear, keep the sabbath according to their light, and when the laws of their country and the awe of their education challenge these duties at their hands :   Ephes. ii. 2, ' Ye walked according to the course of this world (κατ᾽ αἰῶνα, according to the time ; the apostle means in gentile worship, as well as in the vanity of their conversations—'according to the doings, or trade, of Israel,' 2 Chron. xvii. 4.   So the Geneva trans-lation and the Hebrew word signifieth.)   Men do according to the common trade and rate of duty.   All a natural man's religion is but cold conformity to what others practise ; and their worship riseth higher and higher according to the rate of their company and education.   That custom hath a main influnce upon their acts of devotion and religion is clear, because they do not so much look to the nature of ordinances as to what hath been practised in and about them, and do not regard the reason and occasion of duties so much as use and custom.   This is clear by the instance of that case so solemnly propounded : Zech. i. 3,

'Should I weep in the fifth month, separating myself, as I have done these so many years?' Mark the reason and impulse; for the understanding of which you must know that the Jews in the fifth month kept a day for the temple; for you shall see, 2 Kings xxv. 8, 9, the destruction of the temple happened at that time, therefore every seventh day in the fifth month they kept an anniversary fast in remembrance of the temple; but now they were returned from their captivity, and the temple re-edified, and God's service restored, and yet they make it a solemn case whether they should do it, because they had done it these many years. Men are loth to quit a custom in religion, though the reason of it be gone; for they look more to the practice of men than the nature of the ordinance. As some of our ceremonies were first practised upon special occasion in the primitive church, though others came in afterwards by superstition and corruption, yet when the reason is gone, men would continue the rite, and are loth to quit their old custom, and think worship is suppressed with a vain rite because this is the main principle which puts them upon work, practice, and custom.

Thirdly, Carnal impulses will add force and vigour to the performance. The ordinances of God may conduce to some end that suiteth with corrupt nature, and upon that account and reason men will be earnest and busy.

There are two carnal ends upon which men act in duties of religion—vainglory and secular advantage.

1. Vainglory. Men join with the people of God in actions of worship that they may have occasion to discover their parts with the more applause. The apostle speaks of some that 'preached the gospel out of envy,' Phil. i. 15 ; to rival the apostle in his esteem, that they might set up their own worth. And that is the reason why the apostle would not have novices or young men called to the office of public teaching : 1 Tim. iii. 6, 'Not a novice, lest, being lifted up with pride, he fall into the condemnation of the devil,' that is, lest, being unmortified, they should debauch the ordinances of God to the service of their own pride and ambitious affectation. That vainglory is a main principle to put men upon praying, preaching, conference, or any duty wherein there is some exercise of gifts, is clear, because in public duties that are open, and liable to the observance of others, men put forth themselves with the greatest vigour, quickness, and strength; whereas in private addresses to God they are more slight and careless. A christian is best tried and exercised in private and secret intercourses between God and his soul; where they spread their own case before God, there they enjoy most communion with God, therefore there they find most quickening and enlargement. A man cannot so well taste his spirit, and discern the working of it in public addresses, because other men's concernments and necessities are taken up in prayer, and he cannot be so affected as in his own case. Besides when the address is directly to God, he should have our best, for certainly he bids most for our affections. What is the applause of men to the inward approbation of God, sealed up to us by the testimony of the Spirit? What is vainglory to eternal glory?

2. Another carnal principle is secular aims and advantages. It is the great wisdom of God to mingle our concernments with his own ; else few would mind religion, and exercise their gifts for the benefit of

the church. Carnal fuel keeps in the fire of most men's devotions. I say God hath so coupled our interest with his own, that in duties most are swayed with a carnal bias and secular respect, and they go of their own errand, out of a mere carnal respect, to gratify their private interest, when they pretend most to do God's business; as those that 'followed Christ for the loaves,' John vi. 26. *Quandoquidem panis Christi jam pinguis factus est,* &c.—because Christ's bread is buttered with worldly conveniences, religion hath many to follow it; there are esteem, honour, countenance, maintenance that follow duties of religion, therefore they are merely done with respect to those low and base ends. Duties of the first table are not costly, and most apt to be counterfeited. Christ speaks of some 'that made long prayers to devour widows' houses,' Mat. xxiii. 14. The meaning is, that they might be thought godly and conscientious, and so be intrusted with the estates of widows and orphans, or draw contributions. Many times in holy duties invocation of the name of God is made to serve the concernment of the shop, and religion is pretended to countenance base aims. This is the great difference between a carnal and godly man: the one performs all his civil duties with religious aims; the other performs all his religious duties with secular aims. Self is the main motive of their respects to God; and as they act in their own strength, so to their own ends.

Use 1. It serves to inform us that the bare performance of the duties of religion is no gracious evidence. Cain may sacrifice as well as Abel. A christian is rather tried by his graces than by his duties; and yet this is the usual fallacy, the paralogism and false reason that we put upon our own consciences. We secure ourselves upon no other grounds but this, because we are conversant in holy duties. All the claim and title most men have to heaven is only some external acts of duty; they pray, and hear, and keep the sabbath, as the people used to do: James i. 21, 'Be ye doers of the word and not hearers only, deceiving your own souls.' The word is—παραλογιζόμενοι, 'putting a false reasoning upon yourselves. We reason thus, He that hears the word shall be everlastingly happy: but I am a hearer of the word. Oh! saith the apostle, ' be not hearers only.' And though the premises come last in sight, yet we hold fast the conclusion, and think ourselves to be in a sure estate; and this is all the ground of our confidence, an act of duty. Mat. vii. 24, the foolish builder represents those that lay the ground of their confidence in bare attendance on religious duties. Foolish men will raise a high Babel of confidence upon the weakest foundation that may be; they are apt to rest upon unwarrantable evidences; they think they must needs be saved because they hear the word and pray in the name of Christ Do but search what are your evidences and foundations upon which you build. Some live only by guess, and devout aims and conjectures, and never consider upon what terms they stand with God; others content themselves with very slight evidences, and think their hearts are good merely because they practise some external duties. Thou prayest, so many a pharisee; thou worshippest God in the time of the solemn returns of duty, so did Cain; and therefore build not upon these things. But because this is a conceit deeply rooted in our nature, I shall lay down a few convictive propositions.

1. The bare performance of any outward duty is not enough to endear

you to God. God doth not look to the outward acts, but to the frame
of the spirit. You may cheat conscience and deceive man by these outward acts of duty, but God is not mocked. When he comes to weigh
the action, he doth not consider the fair pretence, but the disposition
of the heart : Prov. xvi. 2, 'The Lord weigheth the spirits;' he looks
that the aim should be as good as the action, and the principle every
way as good as the performance. If we did but go to the balance of
the sanctuary and weigh our spirits, we should not be so carnally confident as usually we are. Heathens did regard ἔργον νόμου, Rom. ii.
15, 'Which show the work of the law written in their hearts.'

2. A man may miscarry though he be employed in the highest ministries and duties of religion. You shall see among other things that
are pleaded in the day of judgment this is one: Mat. vii. 23, 'We have
prophesied in thy name, and in thy name cast out devils;' consider, a man
may do great service in the church, and yet come short of heaven ; cast
out devils, and yet be cast out among devils ; a man may not only be
a hearer, but a preacher of the word ; they may prophesy in Christ's
name, and yet he will not own them. O the sad case of such ! Like
the way-marks set up in high-ways, that direct others to travel, but do
not stir themselves ; after they have taught others, they themselves are
cast-aways : or like those that made Noah's ark to save others, and
were drowned themselves in the water : or like the moon which gives
light to others, but it hath none rooted in its own body ; they may
do much service for Christ, yet be in a bad condition.

3. The heart may be somewhat exercised in duty, and yet it is no
gracious evidence. There may be an exercise of memory, wit, and invention in and about the service of God, yet all this while the heart not right.
Christians are not measured by their gifts, but by their graces. Gifts
are for the body, the church ; therefore they may be bestowed sometimes upon carnal men, and poured out in a large measure on them :
1 Cor. xiii. 1, 'Though I speak with the tongue of men and angels, and
have not charity, I am become as sounding brass, or a tinkling cymbal.'
Parts make but an empty sound. That is not the more excellent
way.

4. There may be some exercise of affection, and yet men may miscarry ; as there may be an exercise of joy in duties, and grief in the
defect of duties.

[1.] There may be some kind of joy in duties. The stony ground
'received the word with joy,' Mat. xiii. 20. Men, out of a carnal respect,
may delight in the ordinances of God. A judicious man may delight
in judicious preaching, and take pleasure in the gifts of the minister
and the gracefulness of his utterance, when there is no grace in the
heart: Ezek. xxxiii. 32, 'Thou art unto them as a very lovely song of
one that hath a pleasant voice, and can play well on an instrument.
They take delight in the tunable cadency of expressions, but yet ' they
hear thy words, and do them not.' Men may delight in the carnal part
of ordinances when there is no true, real, and spiritual delight in the
soul. There is a higher delight than all this, which seems spiritual,
but is not, when a man delights and finds contentment in the exercise
of his own gifts rather than in communion with God. There is a secret
complacency, a tickling of the heart at the conceit of our own worth, in

the carriage of a duty, when we come off roundly, when parts have their free course and career; and this not only in public, where we have an advantage to discover our parts with applause, but many times in private intercourses between God and our souls, to which no eye is conscious. When a man is conceited of his gifts and abilities, he may delight in the exercise of them. Whatever we have, the worth of it is known in the exercise; especially gifts, for they are of the nature of those things that are πρὸς ἄλλο, not for enjoyment, but use. Therefore a man that hath a high conceit of his gifts for praying, preaching, and conference may take a carnal delight in the exercise of them. Nature takes delight in the exercise of its own gifts; as when parts are vigorous, the tongue can speak much and well, invention is quick and fresh. A man feedeth his own pride by the excellency of speech.

[2.] There may be some grief for the defects of duty which yet is not right: as when the heart is troubled for outward defects rather than inward, for weakness and brokenness of expression rather than deadness of spirit, and we look more to the liveliness and freshness of parts than of graces. It is true God should be served with all we have, with the vigour of parts as well as the exercise of grace; and therefore it is just matter of grief to a child of God when he cannot have his senses exercised, and nature is not ready to serve grace. But I say when we are only troubled for outward defects, for deficiency or lameness of parts and do not look at the exercise of grace, the heart is not right with God. There may be a great deal of hardness of heart and flatness of affections when parts are quick and fresh, but then the heart is not troubled; as a man may be copious in confession, and declaim against sin with much ornament and passionateness of speech, and yet he is not touched, though he findeth no acts of spiritual shame and remorse. Should we but confess half so much to man against ourselves as we do against God, and should we implead ourselves at the bar of men as we do at the bar of God, there would be greater exercise of remorse. But we are not ashamed when we represent our case before God. And if a man should be ashamed of the filthiness of his life, it should be rather in confession before God than man; for man is but his guilty fellow-creature. On the contrary, the heart may be truly affected when the language is troubled and broken, and there may be much vehemency of spirit when we cannot find words to give it vent to God. We read Moses cried to God, and yet of no words he spake, Exod. viii. 12. And the Spirit's assistance is not to give us words, but he helps our infirmities with sighs and groans, Rom. viii. 26. There is a language in sighs and groans; they make the best melody in the ears of God, even when the speech is troubled and broken.

5. It is not enough to make conscience of the duties that we perform. Natural men may engage in the acts of worship upon the mere enforcement of natural conscience; as the mariners in their distress 'called every one upon his God,' Jonah i. 5: it is but a carnal principle and impulse. Now because it is a hard matter to distinguish the workings of natural conscience from the workings of grace, I shall give you some notes. When we work out of natural conscience, it may be discerned several ways.

[1.] It usually smites for total omissions, not for spiritual neglects and perfunctory performances. There will be restless accusations in the heart if a man totally omit duty; but the conscience doth not smite for customariness of spirit in praying and hearing.

[2.] Natural conscience works chiefly by the means of slavish fear, by the terror and awe that it impresseth upon the spirit. Faith works by love, but natural conscience works by fear; and so the working of it may be known, because it is altogether from the threatenings in the word, as faith doth from the promises and mercies of God: Rom. xii. 1, 'I beseech you, brethren, by the mercies of God,' &c. Natural conscience works from hell, and from our own disquiet. Faith carrieth a man out of himself, and casts all his actions and affections into the mould of the word; but carnal men are forced to it by the rack of their own thoughts, and considerations taken from hell and torment. It is true we must believe the threatenings of the word as well as the promises; but love hath the greatest stroke in all their duties: 2 Cor. v. 11, 'Knowing therefore the terrors of the Lord, we persuade men.' That was one reason which did engage him to faithfulness in preaching the word; compare it with ver. 14, 'The love of Christ constraineth us.'

[3.] Natural conscience doth not do duties out of gratitude or thankfulness, but the great gospel-principle is gratitude. If there were no law to bind a regenerate man, yet he would not be ungrateful to God; but nature is rather prone to a sin-offering than a thank-offering. When our consciences are troubled, that we may lick ourselves whole again, then carnal men would perform duties, but not out of thankfulness to God. Under the law, when they came with their burnt-offerings, they were to offer to God a thank-offering, Lev. vi. 12. God will have thankfulness attend all our obedience; but nature only performs duties when we are troubled.

[4.] Natural conscience convinceth us of the duty, but not of the goodness of the duty; it shows us the need, but not the worth of worship; therefore there is a rising of heart, and a great deal of prejudice against that we perform. It makes a man to do duties, because he dares not do otherwise. Still the service of God is a burden and a weariness: they look upon God as an austere and hard master, Mat. xxv. 24. They think God is too strict, too exact, and deals with them upon justice; but where love and grace is the principle, there 'the commandments are not grievous,' 1 John v. 3; but we act with a great deal of delight and complacency in them.

[5.] Natural conscience works but at times, when convictions are strongest; it makes us mind duty in a sick qualm. When terror flashes in the face of a natural man, then he will apply himself to God. Usually a natural conscience doth use duties just as we take strong waters, not for a constant drink,—then they would mar the stomach, —but only to help us at a pang; so when we are in trouble, then nature chiefly puts us upon duty, then we are most enlarged and quickened: Hos. v. 15, 'In their affliction they will seek me early;' when distress is laid upon them: Jer. ii. 27, 'In the time of their trouble they will cry, Lord! save us.' All the duties of natural men are forced out of them, like water out of a still, by a sense of wrath; they come not so freely as from a sense of love.

Use 2. If it be so, that carnal men may join with the people of God in duties of worship, here is direction ; in all your duties put your hearts to this question, Wherein do I excel a hypocrite? So far a natural man may go. As Christ said, Mat. v. 47, 'Do not even the publicans the same?' When thou art praying and hearing, and thy heart doth not go out with such delight and complacency to God, say, May not a carnal man do this? A christian should do duties in a distinguishing manner, that there should be a sensible difference between them and others.

Ques. But you will say, wherein lies the essential difference between the performances of carnal men and the children of God? This must be the work of the next doctrine.

SERMON XIV.

By faith Abel offered unto God a more excellent sacrifice than Cain, by which he obtained witness that he was righteous, God testifying of his gifts ; and by it he, being dead, yet speaketh—HEB. xi. 4.

Doct. 2. That there is a sensible difference between the godly and the wicked in their several duties and performances.

1. Why it is so?
2. What is the difference?

First, Why the children of God act in a different manner than the wicked?

Ans. They have another nature, and other assistance.

1. They have another nature than wicked men. Water can rise no higher than its fountain; acts are according to their causes; nature can but produce a natural act. The children of God have the spirit of grace bestowed upon them : Zech. xii. 10, 'I will pour upon them the spirit of grace and of supplication.' First of grace, then of supplication ; therefore their addresses come out of a principle of grace. A new work requires a new nature. As Christ spake in the matter of fasting : Mat. ix. 12, 'New wine must not be put into old bottles ;' new wine and old bottles will never suit. Duties well done will make natural men either weary of their natural estate, or their natural estate will make them quite weary of their duty.

2. They have other assistance. The children of God have a mighty Spirit to help them : Jude 20, 'Praying in the Holy Ghost.' They pray not merely by the strength of parts, but by the Spirit. Natural men have only the rigour of natural parts, and some general assistance, whereby their gifts are heightened for the use of the church and good of the body, but they have not the special operation of the Holy Ghost ; therefore, let them do what they can, they can never get up their worship to that height and latitude unto which godly men are raised. Look as in Elijah's time, 1 Kings xviii. 38, there was a contest between him and Baal's priests, the fire came down and devoured Elijah's

sacrifice. But Baal's priests might fetch blood from themselves, but not fire from heaven; so carnal men may force nature, beat themselves, cut their flesh, but their sacrifice will not burn; there is no holy flame by which their hearts are heightened and carried out as christians; they act in their own strength, and to their own ends, therefore there must need be a difference.

Secondly, Wherein lies the difference between the worship of the godly and the worship of carnal men that live in the church? I answer, In three things mainly—in the principle, in the manner, and in the end.

1. In the principle. Natural men do nothing out of the constraints of love, but out of the enforcement of conscience; duty is not their delight, but burden. Cain's sacrifice was tendered rather like a fine, than an offering; so are all their services. There are several sorts of principles of worship: some are altogether false and rotten, some tolerable, some good, and some are excellent.

[1.] Some are altogether false and rotten; as custom, and the statutes of men. Thus it is with wicked men, there is more of conformity than devotion; their worship is not so much an act of religion as of man observance. Men do as they learn of their fathers, or as authority commands, or as others expect from them.

[2.] Some principles are more tolerable; as enforcement of conscience, fear of eternal torment, natural desire of welfare and salvation. Men must pray, and keep up some worship, else they are afraid they shall be damned. Alas! this is but a natural act of self-love. Our salvation is never regularly desired but with subordination to God's glory. Or else they do it out of hope of temporal mercies. Men pray that God may bless them in their calling; constant observation of worship brings in a blessing, therefore they pray out of such a low end: Hosea vii. 14, ' They howl upon their beds,' saith the prophet, ' for corn, wine, and oil.' This is but a brutish cry : beasts will howl for things they stand in need of ; so men may pray for outward conveniences without any grace. Consider, God's worship must not have an end beneath itself. We act preposterously, and not according to the laws of reason, when the means are more noble than the end, and worship is prostituted to such a base end as merely to serve our outward conveniences; when self is the end of prayer, it is not worship, but self-seeking. All gracious actions are to have a reference and ordination to God, therefore the spiritual life is called 'a living to God,' Gal. ii. 10 ; much more acts of worship, which are more raised operations of the spiritual life; there the addresses are more directly to God, and therefore must not be prostituted to a common use.

[3.] There are some good and sound principles, though in the lower form of good things; that is, when duties are done out of an enlightened conscience, and with respect to the command, and the general rewards and compensations of religion. It is true, acts thus done, upon these principles, are rightly done, because they are done in faith and obedience, which is that which constitutes and makes up the essence of a religious act; and usually these are the first dispositions of the soul after grace is first received. Therefore the apostle saith, ' He that cometh '— προσερχόμενος, or is coming on—' to God,' his main work is to ' believe

that God is, and that God is a rewarder of them that diligently seek him,'
Heb. xi. 6. He is to act his faith upon the reward God hath promised,
and obedience upon the duty he hath required.

[4.] There are more excellent and raised principles of worship; and
that is when duties are done out of a grateful remembrance of God's
mercy to us in Christ, to testify our thankfulness to God : Luke i. 74,
'That we, being delivered out of the hands of our enemies, might serve
him without fear ;' or else when they are done out of a pure love to
God, because we delight in his presence. Job xxvii. 10 makes that
the note of a hypocrite, 'Will he delight himself in the Almighty?
will he always call upon God?' A vile carnal man, natural conscience
will make him call upon God in his straits ; but doth he this out of
delight? or else from the excellency and sweetness of the work of
obedience? as, Ps. cxix. 140, 'Thy law is very pure, therefore thy
servant loveth it,' when a man can love pure and holy duties because
they are pure and holy, and for that very reason. Though there were
no heaven nor hell, yet a child of God finds such a privilege in worship,
and such a sweetness in communion with God, that he cannot omit it.
What delight can be more sweet and ravishing to their souls than
communion with God? God usually carrieth men on from one
sort of principles to another : first from those that are sinful
to those that are tolerable ; then to those that are good ; then to
those that are rare and excellent. First he brings them on from custom
to conscience ; then from conscience to obedience ; then from obedience
to delight, to see the beauty of his ordinances and sweetness of his
ways.

2. There is a difference in the manner how these duties are to be
performed ; this is to be regarded as well as the matter. A man may sin
in doing good, but he can never sin in doing well. A man may sin
though the matter be lawful, for the manner is all: Luke viii. 18. 'Take
heed how you hear,' saith Christ ; not only *that* you hear, but *how* you
hear. A man must not only make conscience of the very act of worship,
but of the manner how he performs it. There are several differences between the children of God and others in the manner
of worship ; it must be done humbly, reverently, affectionately.

[1.] It must be done humbly. It is not worship without it ; they
have a deep sense of their own vileness. In scripture the saints of the
Most High in all their addresses to God, have always low thoughts of
themselves ; as the centurion : Mat. viii. 8, 'Lord, I am not worthy that
thou shouldst come under my roof ;' and the great example of faith,
Abraham—'O Lord, I am but dust and ashes,' Gen. xviii. 27. When
we come to converse with God, it will put us in remembrance of our
distance. Rev. v. 8, 'The elders fell down before the Lamb.' There
will be a comparing of ourselves with God. Alas! what is our drop to
his ocean? What is a candle before the sun? The children of God
shrink into nothing, whether you respect the benefit they receive, or the
glory of God's presence in worship. Gen. xvii. 3, when God came to
tender his covenant to Abraham, 'he fell upon his face,' in humble
adoration of God, because of the richness of his bounty. So when you
consider the glory and majesty of God, you must humbly adore in the
presence of God.

[2.] You must come with reverence: Eccles. v. 1, 'Keep thy foot when thou goest to the house of God.' When you go to worship, consider what you are about to do. We had need to awaken our drowsy and careless spirits, that we may have fresh and aweful thoughts of God in worship. Exod. iii. 5, 'Put off thy shoes from thy feet;' lay aside the commonness of your spirit, and the ordinary frame of your heart. God complains of some that were careless, and brought the sick and the lame! Mal. i. 14, 'Cursed be the deceiver, that hath a male in his flock, and voweth, and sacrificeth to the Lord a corrupt thing; for I am a great king, saith the Lord of Hosts.' Wicked men's approaches are rude and unhallowed, because they do not consider what a great king God is; therefore they will bring less to their great king than to an ordinary governor. We are more slight in our addresses to God than to an ordinary king. Wicked men, that are given up to vain superstition, may seem to be reverent in their gestures, and have more of the garb of religion; but the main thing they have not,—fresh and aweful thoughts of God; they do not come as into the presence of a great king.

[3.] It must be with affection; God must be served with the heart. There are two things notable in the affections, —vehemency and complacency.

[1.] Vehemency: Ps. lxiii. 8, 'My soul follows hard after thee.' A man should not faint when he comes to seek God; our motion should not be weak, but an earnest travail of the spirit to find God. Wicked men's prayers are but paper-and-ink devotions; they do not lay out their hearts and affections before God. At best, their prayers are but a little spiritless talk and prattle, and tongue-babbling. The Lord looks after the reaching forth of the soul: James v. 16, 'The effectual fervent prayer of a righteous man availeth much;' δέησις ἐνεργουμένη—we translate it 'effectual fervent;' the word signifies prayer possessed of the Spirit. Prayer must be full of life and vigour. And ver. 17, it is said, 'Elijah prayed earnestly.' In the original it is, προσευχῇ προσηύξατο, he prayed in prayer. It was not only tongue, but heart prayer; the spirit prayed while the mouth was praying. The Spirit assists in groans rather than words, those inward reachings forth of the soul after God.

(2.) Your duties must be managed with complacency and delight: Ps. lxxxiv. 10, 'One day in thy courts is better than a thousand' elsewhere.' The Lord will have the exercise of your joy. Now, that a man may delight in the worship of God, there seems to be two things necessary: spiritual esteem, that we may look upon it as a privilege that there is more delight in it than in the house of mirth; and a childlike confidence, that we may have some hopes towards God, otherwise duty will be a sad burden. Carnal affections beget weariness; and carnal doubts beget fear and trouble. We have to do with God the fountain of blessing, and with our God. None complain of duties so much as they that have least cause. Men that are most perfunctory in God's service find it most irksome; as those that brought the sick and the lame came puffing and blowing to the temple as if they were tired, and cried, 'What a weariness is it!' Mal. i. 13. Partly because they have no spiritual esteem, and do not know how to value communion with God, what it is for a creature to have such near approach to him. Partly because they have no child-like confidence. Worship returns their fears upon them, and puts them to a new penance, and brings their sorrow to their remembrance; therefore they cannot act with any complacency. Isa. lviii. 13, the prophet bids us 'call the sabbath a delight.' When we rest in the bosom of God all day, there are actual emanations of grace and comfort.

3. There is a difference in regard of the end. Now there is a general and a particular end of worship.

[1.] A general end, and that is twofold; to glorify God and to enjoy God; the one is the work of duty, and the other is the reward of duty. (1.) The great end of duty is to glorify God. Grace heightens all our natural actions to a supernatural intention: 1 Cor. x. 31, 'Whether therefore ye eat or drink, or whatsoever ye do, do all to the glory of God.' Eating and drinking; therefore especially must duties of worship, and those solemn operations of the new nature. Duties of worship and exercises of grace must be to the glory of God. God is said 'to inhabit the praises of Israel,' Ps. xxii. 3; meaning the temple, the place of worship where God was chiefly honoured and praised. Duties of worship are chiefly for the honour of God. Now carnal men have other ends; either they use duty in design as hypocrites; or with a natural end, as to satisfy natural conscience. With a design, which is hypocrisy. Religion is one of the best commodities in his way of trade and commerce; therefore carnal men make ordinances to lacquey upon their private ends; they pray and preach for esteem and gain to set off themselves; they use the holy things of God for some base ends of their own: 2 Cor. ii. 7, 'We are not of those that corrupt the word of God, καπηλεύοντες.' This is the true Simony, to huck out the gospel, and sell our holy things. Hypocrites look upon religion as a device fitted for their turns—*Quantas nobis comparavit divitias*, or else carnal men use worship for a natural end, which is the worship of a natural conscience, and is prostituted to self-respect. A natural conscience is hearty and real in its worship, but not spiritual, because it merely aims at self, some temporal commodity, or eternal salvation, as a mere hire. O Christians! look to your ends. Many look that the matter be good, that they can raise themselves into any quickness and smartness of affection; but the end is all: Col. iii. 23, ' Whatsoever ye do, do it heartily, as to the Lord, and not unto men.' Let God's glory be at the end. (2.) The second end of worship is to enjoy God. Many mind duties as a task, and as the mere homage of the creature, and look not upon it as a means of communion, by which God will let out himself to us. This must be your aim, to use duty to further your joy in the Lord. Duty is expressed by 'drawing nigh to God,' Heb. x. 22. You must renew in every exercise your access to God by him. Now carnal men are content with the duty instead of God and satisfy themselves with the work wrought, though there be no intercourse between God and their souls. Therefore a godly man looks at this, what of God he hath found; how he hath come to Christ as to a living stone. You must not be content with the duty instead of God.

[2.] There is a particular aim, and that is always suited to the particular part of worship, and that is a right intention. It is a sign you do not come customarily when you come to seek that for which God hath instituted that special worship. As in the word, the end of that is to submit ourselves to Christ as our teacher or to promote our life or the liveliness of our souls; therefore when you come to be taught by Christ, you come aright to hear the word. And in prayer the particular end is that we may make use of Jesus Christ as our advocate to God the Father, and may solemnly act our graces in opening our case to God. So in the sacrament, when you come to Christ as the master of the feast, to refresh your souls with the renewed sense of his bounty; as Christ said to those that went to hear John, Mat. xi. 8, ' What went you out into the wilderness to see?' so, for what reason did you put yourselves upon such worship? Well then, see that you offer a sacrifice more excellent than carnal men; look to your principle, manner, and end.

Use. To press you to see that you offer a sacrifice more excellent than common men. Here I shall speak to three cases, concerning the principle, the manner, and the end of duty.

1. For the principle, Whether or no it be not a mere natural act to eye the reward, and in what manner it is lawful?

2. For the manner, Whether the children of God may not be surprised sometimes with perfunctory deadness, and wicked men may not by some high impulses be raised to some extraordinary quickness and zeal in duties of worship?

3. For the end, Whether the children of God may not reflect sometimes upon a carnal end in the duties of worship, and how far this is a note of insincerity?

Case 1. For the principle, Whether or no it be not a mere natural act to perform duty with an eye to punishments and rewards? The reason of the inquiry is because I pressed before, that duties, for the principle of them, should be acts of faith, love, and obedience, and not merely done out of the enforcement of conscience; and many press men to acts of religion upon conceits abstracted from all respects to rewards or punishments.

I shall answer this case— (1.) By laying down several spiritual observations; (2.) By stating the question.

The spiritual observations are these—

1. To act in holy duties with respect to terrors and punishments is a far lower principle than to act with an eye to the recompense of reward. Why? because it comes nearer to the rack and enforcement of natural conscience. Hope is a better principle than fear. Bare reason will show that fallen man is liable to judgment, and natural credulity doth more easily suit with the threatenings than the promise; for guilt sitting heavy upon the conscience makes the soul to be more presagious of that which is evil than of that which is good; and the punishment of sin is far more credible than the reward of grace. The heathens that had committed sin knew themselves to be worthy of death; so the apostle, Rom. i. 32. And we see by common experience those doctrines that concern the conviction of sin, make a greater impression upon the soul than gospel promises.

2. I observe, that the consideration of threatenings and punishments are more proper for the avoiding of sin than for the practising of duty; for as nature doth more hearken to threatenings, so nature is more sensible of sins of commission than of omission. Duty is an act of life, and tendeth to life; and therefore the proper respect that draws on the

soul to duty is the reward, and the proper dissuasive from sin is the threatening and punishment: Rom. viii. 13, 'If you live after the flesh, you shall die ; but if ye, through the Spirit, mortify the deeds of the body, ye shall live.' When the apostle would dissuade them from sin, he lays death before them ; when he would draw them to the practice of holiness, then he propounds encouragements of life and peace.

3. That fear which is culpable is rather an impression than a voluntary act of the creature. It is not a fear begotten by the exercise of our faith or thoughts upon the threatening of the word ; but a slavish terror is enforced upon the soul by the spirit of bondage and the evidence of a guilty conscience. When the children of God do make use of terrors, they act their own thoughts upon them ; as Paul : 2 Cor. v. 11, 'Knowing the terror of the Lord, we persuade men.' The apostle in his own thoughts graciously considered the severity of the process Jesus Christ would use at the day of judgment. But now the thoughts of the curse in wicked men are but involuntary impressions ; they care not for duty, and they would not willingly fear the threatening. *Non peccare metuunt, sed ardere*, saith Austin, they are not afraid to sin and offend God, but they are afraid to be damned. There is impressed upon them, against their will, a fear of damnation, so that they act out of a mere constraint of terror ; when they dare not do otherwise, then 'they come with their flocks and with their herds to seek the Lord,' Hos. v. 6. That they do not willingly fear the threatening is plain, because they are so apt to take all advantages to enlarge themselves, and to get free of this awe ; for their desire is not so much to please God as to dissolve the bonds of conscience, and allay their own private fears.

4 When natural men look after the rewards and recompenses of religion, they have wrong notions and apprehensions both of heaven and duty: of heaven as the end, and of duty as the means. (1.) Of heaven ; they have nothing but loose, sudden, indistinct desires of happiness. Nature poiseth us to an eternal good, for our own ease and pleasure ; therefore natural men may have loose desires of happiness : Num. xxiii. 10, 'Let me die the death of the righteous, and let my last end be like his,' and John vi. 34, 'Lord, evermore give us of this bread.' They look upon heaven as a place of ease and pleasure, and therefore conceive some loose sudden wishes. There needs some grace to desire that which is truly the heaven of christians, which is to enjoy God in an eternal and gracious communion ; this will require some exercise of faith, and some spiritual esteem. (2.) They have wrong thoughts of duty ; they look upon it as a work by which they must earn the wages of heaven. A natural spirit can never be evangelical. Therefore the sure notes of undue reflections upon the recompenses and punishments which God hath propounded are these two—merit and slavish fear. When natural men look upon terror, the spirit is altogether servile, and vexed with such scruples as do not become the liberty of the gospel, or haunted with such thoughts as do not become the tenour of the gospel. Saith Christ, Luke xvii. 10, 'When ye have done all, say, We are unprofitable servants.' Though we look to the reward, yet we should not look for it as a salary from a master, but as a gift from a father. It is mercenary to act for hire and wages, and establish merit in our private thoughts.

(5) The acts of the creature are never gracious but when they are ultimately terminated on God. When natural men act in the duties of religion, self is always both in the beginning, and end, and middle of the work; they act from self-love, in self-strength, and with self-respects. But in a godly man all his acts terminate on God; he makes God the fountain, the object, and the end of all his duties, and so his acts come to be gracious. But now for the applying of promises: there is a great deal of difference between seeking self in God and seeking self in the creature. A hypocrite always looks to self, but it is in the world; he looks more to credit or profit than to heaven or hell. Self-love, which is an innocent disposition in nature, is improved by grace, for when we seek our welfare in God, that is right; for this is one of the ends of religion—to enjoy God, as well as to glorify God.

(6.) The children of God are sometimes stirred and cheerfully drawn out in duties of religion, by the lower rewards and conveniences of the present life, and that without sin. Obedience is their principle, but the concurrence of outward encouragements may carry them on with more facility and alacrity; as, for instance, a diligent servant goes about his master's business readily, but with more gladness when he meets with fair weather and good speed. So we must primarily look at the will of our master, and discharge our work, whatever our entertainment be; but if God give us the advantage of profit and credit, and a good name, we must be more cheerful in his service. A wicked man looks altogether to those outward respects; he is forward when his own interest and God's are twisted together; he may be then carried out with zealous earnestness, but the unsoundness of his heart is herein seen, in that he prefers self before God. When self is severed from the commandments of God, he lets them alone; but the children of God have learned to pass 'through honour and dishonour,' 2 Cor. vi. 8; they still keep on in the way of duty, whatever entertainment they find in the world. Outward conveniences are very useful to encourage us in our way, and to make our duties more dear and sweet to us. Look, as ciphers added to figures increase the sum, so these things that are as ciphers in comparison of graces, yet if they are found in the way of obedience, they increase the sum: Eccles. xi. 7, 'Wisdom is good with an inheritance.' It is good without, but then there are more obligations. The main principle is obedience, and this is but their accidental encouragement.

Quest. These observations premised, I come to state the question, How far it may be excused from a mere act of self-love for a christian to reflect upon the rewards and punishments of religion? Here I shall show—

1. You may make use of them.
2. In what manner.

[1.] You may make use of them. There may be a religious use of punishments and rewards in the matter of duty by natural reason. Punishments are the objects of fear, and rewards the objects of desire and hope, and the faculties may be exercised about their proper object without sin. But there is an exercise, not only of nature, but of grace. It was an argument of Paul's faith when he reflected upon the day of judgment, 2 Cor. v.11, 'Knowing therefore the terror of the Lord, we

persuade men.' It was an argument of Moses's faith 'to have an eye
to the recompense of reward,' Heb. xi. 26. It is some glory to God
when we can believe his word, when we trust in him as one wise to
observe, and able and willing to recompense, whatever we do for him.
Besides, as there is an act of faith in it, so there is an act of spiritual
esteem : it is a sign there is grace, when we can prefer the recompenses
of God before present advantages and the allurements of men. And
it is an act of spiritual fear to value the threatenings of God before the
terrors of men. And it is an act of faith to expect and wait for the
accomplishment of these things. It is a prime article to believe 'that
God is a rewarder,' Heb. i. 6; and it needs a spiritual eye to see the
riches of our high-calling ; therefore the apostle desires that God would
open their eyes, that 'ye may know what is the hope of his calling, and
what the riches of the glory of his inheritance in the saints,' Eph. i.
17; that they might be acquainted with the mysteries of the gospel
and the rewards of obedience, to keep them still in sight, that upon
the encouragement of them we may discharge our duty.

[2.] How, and in what manner you may use them right ; for rewards
are but encouragements of obedience, not the formal reasons of it.
Gratitude, love of God and his honour, these must be the chief incentives,
and have the preferment above all self-respect in our obedience. The
formal reason of every duty must be obedience to God; but the encouragements are the promises and recompenses.

(1.) You may use them to encourage and quicken a backward heart.
We look upon duty through carnal prejudices, and count it a sore exaction, and so draw back ; in such a case we may safely use God's arguments
as encouragements. God propoundeth them to us in the word, and
pleads with us upon this advantage, and seeks to whip us into obedience
by the spur of threatenings and hopes. God pleads with his people,
Jer. ii. 31, 'Have I been a land of darkness to you? have I been a
wilderness?' Is there no blessing grows there? no sun-shine? All
the argumentative part of the word is taken from the recompenses and
threatenings. Surely it is not good to be wise above the scriptures ;
we may use that which the scripture useth. Thus the apostle shows
he presseth onward upon this advantage : Phil. iii. 14, 'I press toward
the mark for the prize of the high calling of God in Jesus Christ;'
the glorious recompenses and high prizes God had set before him at
the end of the journey, this made him make progress in the way of
religion.

(2.) In the spiritual conflict, to baffle and defeat a temptation. So
you may use these rewards and punishments ; for herein you do but
declare the high esteem you have of your hopes, more than the bait
that is presented in the temptation. Let us cast our hopes in another
scale : 2 Cor. iv. 18, 'We look not to the things that are seen, but to
the things which are not seen,' &c. When things seen come to stand in
competition with our high hopes, it is not only lawful but necessary to
reflect upon the recompenses. We expect great things from God ; he
hath promised things unseen. So the apostle, when likely to be discouraged by the inconveniences of this life : Rom. viii. 18, 'I reckon
that the sufferings of this present time are not worthy to be compared
with the glory that shall be revealed in us.' Moses counterbalanceth

' the pleasures of Egypt, with the recompense of reward,' Heb. xi. 2-6 ; and Jesus Christ counterbalanceth the shame of the cross with the glory of his exaltation : Heb. xii. 2, 'Who, for the glory that was set before him, endured the cross, and despised the shame.' What is carnal ease to heavenly pleasure? the fulfilling of a carnal desire to the filling up of the soul with God ? This is nothing but a holy design to outweigh a temptation by putting the glory of our hopes in the other scale ; by opposing the joys of heaven to the pleasures of sin; and the sweetness of eternal communion with God to the gratifications of the flesh.

(3.) To renew the solemn remembrance of your hopes with thankfulness that your heart may the more admire the riches of free grace. By this means the great gospel principle will be the better strengthened, which is gratitude and thankfulness. Now we may be the more thankful, and more drawn out in the admiration of grace. Oh, how should we esteem the Lord's service ! He might enforce duty upon us, but he is pleased to quicken us by the reward. Oh, that he should reward such worthless services, and honour our obedience with such recompenses and privileges ! This is a right reflection when our thoughts are carried out to the reward, as rather admiring God's bounty than respecting our own benefit. Gratitude is by this means strengthened, and hath the greater force upon the soul. Gratitude doth not only look to mercies in hand, but also look for mercies in hope. The bird of paradise can sing in winter ; faith can give thanks for our hopes before enjoyment. You may say, as Ps. xiii. 19, 'Oh, how great is thy goodness which thou hast laid up for them that fear thee ! which thou hast wrought for them that trust in thee before the sons of men.' There is not only goodness laid out, and thankfulness for that, but for goodness laid up in hope, those excellences and glorious rewards God hath provided for us ; this should put us upon admiring grace.

SERMON XV.

By faith Abel offered unto God a more excellent sacrifice than Cain, by which he obtained witness that he was righteous, God testifying of his gifts : and by it he, being dead, yet speaketh—HEB. xi. 4.

Case. 2. The second case respects the manner of duties : they must be done with vehemency and complacency. Now here arise two cases :—

1. Whether the children of God may not be surprised sometimes with perfunctory deadness? Can their souls go out to God always with holy fervour and holy ardencies ?

2. Whether wicked men may not by high impulses be raised into extraordinary quickness in duties of worship ? and whence this comes ?

First, Whether the children of God may not be surprised sometimes with perfunctory deadness? &c. I answer—

1. It may be so indeed. Sometimes their affections are like the

faint hands of Moses, that flag and hang down: Gal. v. 17, 'The flesh lusteth against the spirit, so that they cannot do the things they would.' So Paul complains, Rom. vii. 18, 'How to perform that which is good, I find not;' he could not κατεργάζειν, go through with his work; like a sick man, that cannot do what he would.

2. Though there may such deadness fall upon them, yet still there is a willing bent of the heart towards God. Graces that live may not always be lively: there is a living faith and a lively faith; and there may be deadness in the children of God, though there be not an utter death. Look, as our saviour found in his own experience when he was to suffer for us, just so it is with us when we come to perform duty. In Christ the manhood sank by a just aversation at the greatness of his sufferings; therefore, Mat. xxvi. 41, 'The spirit is willing but the flesh is weak;' the flesh—that is, the manhood—is not able to bear such a brunt, though the spirit had freely given it up. So the inward man goes out to God freely, though there be the outward reluctation of the carnal man: Rom. vii. 22, 'I delight in the law of God after the inward man.' Though there were strugglings, yet the bent of his heart was toward God. This will appear, because the children of God in such indispositions are not idle, but seek; they are seriously displeased with the distempers and uncomfortableness of their souls, as appears by their strugglings with God and striving with themselves. By their strugglings with God: Ps. cxix. 28, 'Strengthen thou me according to thy word;' and ver. 32, 'I will run the way of thy commandments, when thou shalt enlarge mine heart.' When they have felt their straits and deadness, they would fain be set free; and so, by their striving with themselves, weariness and deadness may seize upon the heart in prayer, but then a christian bestirs himself. Always you shall find when the children of God are calling upon God they are calling upon themselves; there are resuscitations and awakenings of their drowsy souls. Therefore it is said, Isa. lxiv. 7, 'There is none that calleth upon thy name, that stirreth up himself to take hold of thee.' There must not only be a calling upon God, but a stirring up ourselves: Ps. lvii. 8, saith David, 'Awake up, my glory; awake, psaltery and harp: I myself will awake early.' It is not a sign of no grace to be troubled with indispositions; but it is a sign of no grace to rest in them.

Secondly, May not wicked men by high impulses be raised into extraordinary quickness in duties of worship? and whence comes this?

Ans. This may be, and there are many causes of it in a hypocrite. It may come from the constraints of carnal ends: delight may carry us on freely in the outward part of worship; joy is the strength of the soul. We are more ready in that which we delight in. In superstitious men it comes sometimes from fanatic delusions and transportations. False experience may whet the wit, though the heart be not made the more humble or holy. And sometimes, in carnal men in distress, it may come from unsound fervour of carnal affections, and they may seek their earthly comforts with a great deal of earnestness. The motions of lust are always violent and rapid; and a carnal spring may send forth a high tide of affection. You know it is said, Hos. vii. 14, 'They howl upon their beds for their corn, wine, and oil;' their prayers may be sharpened to howling when they are pleading for the concernments of the belly. But most usually it doth arise from the quickness and vivacity of nature. In youth, where there hath not been a great waste of spirits, usually there is a kind of natural vehemency. And some men we see are of temper fierce and earnest; and they may seem very affectionate and loud in language, vehement in expression, and all this out of the eagerness of the bodily spirits, and mere heat and contention of nature; but all this while they have no spiritual affections. As I have read of Graccus, that was so earnest in speech that one was wont to come to him and sound a retreat to his spirit, *ut revocaret eum a nimia contentione dicendi*—that he might call him from too great a contention of speech. It is with many men now as with a bell, which is carried by its own sway. Now it is a dangerous folly to mistake everything for grace. I confess there is a great deal of use of this vivacity of nature, it serves to deliver and set off vehement affections; but lungs and sides must not be mistaken for grace, and the agitations of the bodily spirits for the impressions of the Holy Ghost. Men may work themselves into a great heat and vehemency by the mere stirring of their bodily humours; and it is easy for men of an affectionate temper to put on a passion, though their hearts be not affected; as corrupt lawyers can plead on either side with a like earnestness. We cheat ourselves with common operations. Parts can furnish the tongue with matter, and an eager spirit can supply the room of christian affections. As a man by overmuch contention of speech may seem to be mightily transported and raised in declaiming against sin, when in the meantime he hath no true indignation against it, and so is but ' like sounding brass or a tinkling cymbal,' 1 Cor. xiii. 1. There are men that cannot contain themselves in prayer when they are but a little heated and agitated, and yet have no raisedness of affection, no earnest pursuits and reachings-forth after God in their souls; it is the travail of the body only, and not the travail of the soul. David supposeth that there may be crying to God with the tongue when the heart regards iniquity; Ps. lxvi. 18, ' If I regard iniquity in my heart, the Lord will not hear me.' There may be a forcing of nature into expressions when no serious indignation is kindled in the heart against sin, and an aversion of heart to holiness. St Austin made zealous prayers that God would mortify his lusts; but his heart would always object, *Noli modo*, &c.—Lord, do not hear me just now; I am afraid lest God should hear me. At least their hearts do not pray in prayer, notwithstanding this outward vehemency of their tongue.

Ques. But you will say, How shall we discern this false vehemency from that which is true, and that which is holy fervour and going out of the spirit towards God? It may be tried by the irreverence of your souls in prayer, and carelessness of your souls after prayer.

1. By the irreverence of soul in prayer. When there is not a due consideration of the nature and presence of God, certainly it is a natural transportation; when men are drawn out to a great heat of affection yet no reverence of God. In a distempered heat in prayer or preaching men are apt to forget themselves; they do not consider to whom or before whom they speak, therefore they are ' rash to utter anything with their mouth,' Eccles. v. 1, 2. Men may be hasty to utter words,

though there be no due affection and reverence in the spirit. A true earnestness of spirit makes us remember God the more, because we are enjoying communion with God ; but a false earnestness is counted but babbling. Mat. vi. 7, our Saviour speaks of those 'that thought to be heard for their much speaking.' Carnal worshippers place much in this, in their vehement pronouncing ; as Baal's priests, Elijah bids them 'cry aloud,' 1 Kings xviii. 27 ; so they place much in the mere extension of their voice, and crying aloud.

2. It may be discerned by the carelessness of their souls after prayer ; when men are vehement in worship, and never look after the effects of worship. Usually men throw away their prayers, as children shoot away their arrows, and never look after them. True vehemency will stir up a like earnestness in the expectations and endeavours of the soul : Ps. lxxxv. 8, 'I will hear what God the Lord will speak.' There will be hearkening after the success of such earnest prayers that have been poured out with height of affection. Now to pray against sin and not strive against it, and not to look after the return of it, shows a false heart, and that it was but a feigned and personated heat, like acting of a part upon a stage, till the task of prayer was over. Desire is a vigorous bent of the soul ; it is an active affection, that will put men upon endeavours ; and you will be stirring, waiting, seeing how your prayers are accomplished ; otherwise it is but a passion put on for a time. When a man prays vehemently for grace, and then goes out and sins against his prayers, how can those prayers be right ? It is but an empty declamation, especially if men confute their own prayers with their lives ; like those that sacrificed to Esculapius, and prayed for health, but kept on their riotous feasts.

Case 3. The third case is concerning the end of duties, Whether or no the children of God may not reflect sometimes upon a carnal end in duties of worship ? And how far is it a note of insincerity ?

I answer in several propositions—

1. The best trial of a christian is in his duties of worship. If at any time, there he may discern the effects and operations of the new nature, and the actings of grace in his own soul ; for there sins are most checked, there he comes more solemnly to exercise his grace, there his addresses are immediately to God. It argues much of unmortifiedness to have carnal reflections when we are conversing with God. It is God's complaint, Jer. xxiii. 11, ' Both the prophet and priest are profane ; yea, in my house have I found their wickedness, saith the Lord.' To conceive those fleshly motions in God's house is a matter of high aggravation ; for here we come to set up grace in authority most solemnly, and act it in the highest way of operation towards God.

2. As a christian is tried in his duties, so our duties are tried by our designs and aims. It is not the excellency of the outward address, it is not the vehemency of the inward affection, but the integrity of the end and aim towards God. Practice may be overruled by custom ; excellency of speech may be drawn forth upon carnal impulsions ; affections may be made violent by lust : but the genuine birth of the spirit is the end and aim we propose to ourselves. And therefore a child of God can appeal to God's omniTanscience for his love to him. Human infirmities may make us fail in all other parts of duty, but

grace will set the end right, which is usually proportioned to the frame of the heart. As the heart is, so is the end. This is the great differencing circumstance: Prov. xvi. 2, ' The Lord weighs the spirits, *quo animo ;* with what end and aim an action is done. Christ saith, ' The light of the body is the eye,' Mat. vi. 22. A single aim and intent towards God is the best discovery of our sincerity in religious duties.

3. Yet notwithstanding the carnal part will be interposing and vexing the spirit with carnal aims, as the daughters of Heth vexed Rebecca, Gen. xxvii. 46. In the best duties we ever perform we plough with an ox and an ass. When we come to do good, evil will be present: Rom. vii. 21, ' I find then a law, that when I would do good, evil is present with me.' And as evil, so also evil aims; I know no difference. Corruption may cast in vain-glorious glances, or covetous thoughts and reflections upon external advantages, as well as blasphemies and sins of another nature.

4. Though the carnal nature may vex the new nature with those carnal reflections, yet there is a sensible difference still between them and others, because grace hath the strongest influence. And though there be carnal reflections, yet there are not carnal principles: these are but collateral and supervenient glances, not the main motives and chief reasons of their worship, which are obedience and love to God. It is hypocrisy to act in design, but this they do not; though carnal aims run in their minds too much, yet when they do, they are resisted there. As when Abraham had divided the sacrifices, ' the fowls came down; but Abraham drove them away,' Gen. xv. 11 ; so when we come to pour out our spirits in duties of religion, the fowls may come, carnal thoughts may rush into our minds; but they do not rest there, the soul drives them away. The constant bent and aim of the spirit is to serve God and enjoy communion with God, though these carnal reflections may encumber their souls. Therefore a christian is to try himself by the mainspring of his soul—what is the weight, the poise within to worship; for a christian hath a double principle, flesh and spirit, but not a double heart ; a hypocrite hath a double heart; he doth but put on a pretence of worship, and useth it in design. It is true, we cannot come into the presence of God without sin, yet a child of God will come without guile. He cannot bring a pure heart absolutely clean, but he brings a true heart, Heb. x. 22 ; the desire of his soul is towards God ; and the chief reason that puts him upon worship is to glorify and enjoy God.

Doct. 3. This sensible difference between the duties of the godly and the wicked is occasioned by the influence and efficacy of faith.

Here I shall state—(1.) What this faith of Abel was ; (2.) I shall handle the general case.

First, What this faith of Abel was.

1. There was a faith of his being accepted with God when his service was suited to the institution. He believed that God would by some visible testimony manifest his acceptation. Such a promise was intimated to them, as appears by God's expostulation with Cain : Gen. iv. 7, ' If thou doest well, shalt thou not be accepted ? ' As if God should have said, Did I promise to accept any other service but what was conformed to my appointments ? There was a belief of God's essence and attributes, and a consequent love to him, willing to give God the best.

2. It was a faith in the general rewards and recompenses of religion. Abel looked to the good things to come, and so his hopes had an influence upon his practice; Cain's heart was altogether chained to earthly things, therefore he looks upon that as lost which was spent in sacrifice. This may also be probably collected out of Gen. iv. 8, 'And Cain talked with (or said to) Abel his brother.' Here is mention of some speech of Cain to Abel, but it is not expressly set down what the discourse was. Indeed in the Hebrew text there is a pause extraordinary, implying some further matter to be added. The Septuagint adds, 'And he said to Abel, Let us go out together into the field.' The Targum of Jerusalem reads it thus, 'And Cain said to Abel his brother, Let us go out into the field. And it came to pass when they were in the field, Cain said to his brother, There is no judge, no judgment, no other world, no reward for the just, no vengeance for the wicked; neither did God make the world in mercy, nor in mercy was thy sacrifice accepted.' All which when Abel had denied, in the height of that discourse, Cain rose up and killed him. From whence we may collect that the faith that had an influence upon his sacrifice was faith in the general rewards and compensations of religion.

3. It was a faith in the Messiah to come. The first-born of God was typed out in those first-fruits, and therefore is Christ called 'the Lamb slain from the foundation of the world,' Rev. xiii. 8; that is, in those offerings and sacrifices. And this is the apostle's drift in this place; they had a promise, 'That the seed of the woman should break the serpent's head;' and in those darker times Abel had a faith in this promise, and this faith bettered his offerings. All the patriarchs obtained that renown they had in the churches of Christ by faith in the Messiah. Out of that expectation he brought a well-beseeming sacrifice to God. In these times of the gospel all is more clear and open, and therefore God requires more from us; the persuasions of faith are greater, therefore the operations of faith must be greater too.

Secondly, For the reasons of the point, Why faith makes this difference between worship and worship, that it makes the duties and worship of believers to be so different from that of carnal men?

1. I answer, because it discerneth by a clearer light and apprehension. Faith is the eye of the soul. A beast liveth by sense, a man by reason, and a christian by faith. By sense a beast discerneth what is convenient and inconvenient to their manner of life; reason guides ordinary men in their choice and course of affairs; but faith is the light of a christian in the whole business of this life, but chiefly in his worship. Now the discerning work of faith is conversant both about God as the object of worship, and about the work itself; in short, to represent the truth of God's being and the worth of God's service.

[1.] To represent to us the truth of God's being: faith 'seeth him that is invisible,' Heb. xi. 27. Every natural man is an inward atheist, because he wants the light of faith; he cannot see God, therefore he does but serve God as he would serve an idol; all their worship is customary, and done in obedience and conformity to the common practice. As the scoffer said of the worship of God, *Eamus ad communem errorem* —Let us go to the common error and mistake. Certainly their hearts are not touched with the sense of God's being; and therefore the first and general act of faith in and about duties of worship is wanting.

which is to keep the heart aweful by a clear sight and apprehension of God: Heb. xi. 6, 'He that cometh to God must believe that he is.' The great work of faith, and that which is the foundation of all, is to help us to proper thoughts and conceptions of God—a thing which wicked men can never attain to; for though they are able to discourse of God's attributes, though they have a naked model and idea of the truth of religion, yet in worship they know not how to raise their hearts into a due apprehension of God. But as the heathens abused their γνωστον Θεου, and their practical thoughts in worship were gross carnal imaginations, Rom. i. 22; so do these, they never have fresh and aweful thoughts of God. Now this troubles the children of God when faith is drowsy, and they are not able to form proper and becoming thoughts of God in their worship and invocation; so that this first thing is of great advantage and putteth a difference between worship and worship. Faith keeps God in the view of the soul.

[2.] Faith discerns the worth of his service. When we look upon duty with a carnal eye, the soul is prejudiced, and we consider it as a sour task and rigid exaction, and so the soul drives on very heavily. Now faith convinceth of the worth of divine service, and representeth more of privilege than of burden in it. In the eye of faith, service is an honour and duty a privilege: Ps. lxxiii. 28, 'It is good for me to draw near God.' Mark, it is not only meet or just, but good. Faith sees a great deal of excellency and sweetness and privilege in it: and so it makes reason and the sanctified judgment to issue forth a practical decree, 'It is good,' which sways and determines all the operations of the soul. The first inquiry of the creature is, What is lawful? then, What is possible? then, What is profitable? Do not leave these questions to the decision of human reason, then you will quickly be discouraged; but put the controversy into the hands of faith, and that will judge it is good, sweet, and easy: Ps. xix. 10, 'Thy testimonies are more to be desired than gold, yea, than much fine gold; sweeter also than the honey and honey-comb.' A carnal man may understand the nature and necessity of duty, but he is not convinced of the worth of it. Faith is an affective light; it determines all practical cases on religion's side, and leaves a spiritual esteem upon the soul: Ps. lxxxiv. 1, 'Oh! how amiable are thy tabernacles, O Lord!' Oh! when shall these be the workings of our spirits? Faith seeth that duty is a reward to itself, that here the noblest faculties are exercised in the noblest work; and therefore if there were no other reward, if there were no heaven, they find such pleasure in the duty that it were allurement enough of itself; as a martyr, when he came to die, said he was sorry that being to receive so much wages, he had done so little work. This makes the soul bend all its strength and all its power in seeking of God. The children of God do duties in another manner, because they look upon God and duty with other eyes.

2. Faith receives a mighty aid and supply from the Spirit of God. Faith plants the soul into Christ, and so receives influence from him; it is the great band of union between us and Christ, and the hand whereby we receive all the supplies of Jesus Christ. Christ lives in us by his Spirit, and we live in him by faith. Until faith come, there can be no vital influence. Wicked men's gifts may be elevated; God

may work as *author naturæ*, the author of nature, though not as *fons gratiæ*, the fountain of grace. Therefore it must needs make a difference. What is the vigour of parts to the efficacy of the spirit? Faith draws Christ into the duty, and his Spirit bears a part of the burden: Rom. viii. 26, 'The Spirit'— συναντιλαμβάνεται — 'helpeth our infirmities.' We tug, and the Spirit helpeth also. This then is the work of faith, to receive the supplies of grace. An actual faith hath the promise of an actual assistance ; and when God's power is glorified, then it is exercised : Ps. lxxxi. 10, 'Open thy mouth wide, and I will fill it.' Look, as little birds open their mouths, and then the great one feeds them ; faith is nothing but an opening of the soul upon God, then Jesus Christ gives in a supply of grace.

3. As it receives a mighty aid, so it works by a forcible principle, and that is by love ; for 'Faith works by love,' Gal. v. 6. We live by faith, and we work by love. Where faith is, there is love ; and where love is, there is work. Affection follows persuasion, and operation follows affection. First there is a persuasion of the love of God, then thankful returns of affection to God, and they are manifested by holy operations for the glory of God. Faith filleth the soul with the apprehensions of God's love, and then maketh use of the sweetness of it, to urge the soul to duty. There is a twofold advantage we have in love : it will be active and self-denying. (1.) Active : it puts the soul upon work ; it is a laborious grace, and the spring of all action ; therefore labour and love are often joined together in scripture : Heb. vi. 10, ' God is not unrighteous to forget your work and labour of love ;' 1 Thes. i. 3, 'Remembering your work of faith and labour of love.' Love will put us upon work for God. Jacob endured much toil for Rachel, because he loved her. Christ gageth Peter upon this point : John xxi. 15, ' Simon Peter, lovest thou me ? feed my sheep.' The church of Ephesus, when ' she lost her first love,' she 'left her first-fruits,' Rev. ii. 4. If love be not faint and languid, the soul will be kept open and liberal for God. Love will carry a man through, and poiseth the soul to those holy duties which are tedious and irksome to flesh and blood. (2.) It acteth with self-denial and complacency against carnal ease and present advantage, though it be tedious, and put us upon inconveniences in the world. Inward duties are against carnal affections, outward duties are against carnal interests ; yet love will carry them through with delight and complacency : 1 John v. 3, 'This is the love of God, that we keep his commandments, and his commandments are not grievous.' It takes off the natural irksomeness which is in the heart. Love makes a great change in the heart. While the heart is naturally corrupt, sin is a delight, and the commandment is a burden ; but when the love of God is let into the heart, corruption is counted the yoke, and duty is counted the delight and pleasure of the soul. The children of God, we hear them complaining, not of the law, but of their own corruption : Rom. vii. 14, 'The law is spiritual ; but I am carnal, sold under sin.' Natural men are always quarrelling with their convictions, their conflict is against the light that shines in their mind ; but spiritual men are always conflicting with their lusts ; and their groans arise from another principle—not because the law requires duty, but because they cannot perform it, by reason of those reluctations that

are in their evil natures. Love will carry them to duty that is against the hair and bent of nature. It went much against the heart of Hamor and Shechem to be circumcised, and that rite was odious among the gentiles; yet it is said, Gen. xxxiv. 19, 'That the young man deferred not to do it, because he had a delight in Jacob's daughter.' So though duty be never so much against the bent of nature and the course of worldly advantages, yet duty will be sweet to them, for love will carry them through for the delight they have in Christ: 2 Cor. v. 14, 'The love of Christ constraineth us.' Though he draws trouble upon himself, yet love carries the soul away against all reluctations.

4. It discourseth and pleads with the soul with strong reasons and enforcements. Faith is a notable orator to plead for God; it pleads partly from the mercies, and partly from the promises of God.

[1.] From the mercies of God, both special and common. (1.) God's special love in Jesus Christ. The arguments of faith are dipped in Christ's blood, therefore they have the greater strength and force in the soul: Gal. ii. 20, 'I live by the faith of the Son of God;' and the argument of faith is there intimated by the apostle, 'who loved me, and gave himself for me.' When the soul is backward, faith will say, He freely gave himself for me, shall I not do something for thee that hast left so much glory for me? That hast pardoned so many sins, conveyed so many blessed privileges, estated me in such large hopes, shall I think anything too dear for him? When Christ was to suffer upon the cross, he did not say, This is hard work, and it will cost me dear; I must endure contempt, bitter agonies, and foul ignominy, and be exercised with the wrath of God. No, but he said, 'I come to do thy will, O God;' Heb. x. 7; Father, I come to satisfy thy justice; sinners, I come to save your souls: Isa. liii. 11, 'He shall see of the travail of his soul, and be satisfied.' That word implies both the cost and the gain; it would cost him much agony of spirit, and the gain is implied. He shall see that which he hath travailed for; he shall see a company of children he hath gained to himself. When Christ saw all this, he said, It is enough; so I may rescue these poor souls, I am contented with the temptations of the wilderness, the sorrows of the garden, the ignominy of the cross, the wrath of my Father, the suspension of the comforts of my godhead. Faith comes and represents this to the soul; then the believer cannot say nay: he is overcome, and brought with cheerfulness into God's presence. There is no oratory like that of faith. (2.) Then it argues from common mercies. As Abel, God had blessed his increase, therefore at the year's end he comes to return the fat and fairest to God. Faith reasons with the soul, Wilt thou not honour the God of thy mercies? Thou livest in him, and movest in him, and hast thy being from him; what wilt thou do for God? Faith gives in a bill of blessings—Lo! thus God hath done for thee; he hath given thee life, estate, all kind of comforts; and what honour and service hath been done to God for all this? As that king said, Esther vi. 3, 'What honour and dignity hath been done to Mordecai for this?' The apostle urgeth their common enjoyments: 1 Tim. vi. 17, 'Charge them that are rich in this world that they be not high-minded, nor trust in uncertain riches, but in the living God, who giveth us richly all things to enjoy.' The Lord hath enlarged his hand of bounty; he hath clothed thee, fed thee, and opened the treasures of the sea and land to give thee provisions; what hast thou done for God? Nature abhors unthankfulness. Holy David, 2 Sam. vii. 2, his heart reasons within him, 'I dwell in a house of cedar, but the ark of God dwelleth within curtains;' as if he had said, Here the Lord hath built me a stately house, but what have I done for the ark of God? When you survey the great plenty and bounty of God, it is a wonder you have not such inward discourses in your souls. Carnal men are the more secure and careless of the worship of God for their outward enjoyments; as the sun moveth slowest when it is highest in the zodiac; but the zeal of God's children is heightened, and their thankfulness is quickened.

[2.] Faith reasons from the promises of God, which are the common-places and topics of faith from which it gathers arguments. Now the promises that faith urgeth are promises of assistance, acceptance, and reward. Faith seeth assistance in the power of God, acceptance in the grace of God, reward in the bounty and kindness of God.

(1.) It reasons from the promises of assistance. We hate that which we cannot perform. Men love an easy religion, and such as is within the compass of their own strength and power; therefore the apostle shows one of the reasons why carnal men are so prejudiced against the law of God, because they have no power to fulfil it: Rom. viii. 7, 'The carnal mind is enmity against God, for it is not subject to the law of God, neither indeed can be.' Wickedness takes the advantage of weakness, and so the soul is prejudiced. Help engageth to actions; when we know we have no strength, and the burden is heavy, we let it alone. The great excuse of the creature is for want of power. Now faith reasons from the promises of divine assistance, Alas! thou art a weak creature, it is true, but God will enable thee: 2 Cor. iii. 5, 'Our sufficiency is of God;' thou mayest be strong in God when thou art weak in thyself: 2 Cor. xii. 10, 'For when I am weak, then am I strong.' An empty bucket may be the sooner filled. To what end hath God laid help upon Christ? The soul saith, I can do nothing; but faith replies, 'In the strength of Christ I can do all things,' Phil. iv. 13. Did you ever know a command that requires grace without a promise that God would give grace? Do not entertain jealousies of God without cause. God doth not require work and deny assistance; he doth not desire brick and deny straw. Wait on God, and he will strengthen thee: Ps. xxvii. 14, 'Wait on the Lord; be of good courage, and he shall strengthen thy heart.' Faith encourageth the soul to wait upon God.

(2.) It reasons from the promises of acceptance. Doubts weaken the soul, and jealousy makes the heart faint and the hands feeble, and the soul is burdened in holy duties, and drives on heavily. Distrust will say, Will the Lord regard such a sinner as I am? accept such green figs? regard such weak and spiritless services of such an unworthy creature? Now faith argues, Do you endeavour, God will accept you: 2 Cor. viii. 12, 'If there be first a willing mind, it is accepted according to what a man hath, and not according to what he hath not.' Faith shows how willing Jesus Christ is to accept the service and pardon the defects of his people: Cant. v. 1, 'I have eaten my honeycomb with my honey.' Faith reasons, Thou art afraid to come to God, but to what end serves a mediator? Eph. iii. 12, 'In whom we have boldness and access with confidence by the faith of him.' Faith shows the mediator to the soul and thus argues—Upon whom do you pitch your hopes of success and acceptance? on the worthiness of your own work, or on the worthiness of Christ the mediator? Faith pointeth at Christ, Look, soul, there is an angel with a golden censer stands at the altar; he is ready to perfume the sacrifice. Though your prayers, as they come from you, are unsavoury breath in the nostrils of God, yet there is a mediator to perfume those services; they do not go immediately to God, but pass through a mediator into the hands of God: Rev. viii. 3, 4, 'And another angel came and stood at the altar, having a golden censer; and there was given unto him much incense, that he should offer it with the prayers of all saints upon the golden altar which was before the throne. And the smoke of the incense, which came up with the prayers of the saints, ascended up before God out of the angel's hand.'

(3.) Faith argues from the promises of reward. When the soul is backward, you do not work for nothing, or for that which is nothing worth; there is a reward: 2 Cor. vii. 1, 'Having these promises, dearly beloved, let us cleanse ourselves from all filthiness of the flesh and spirit, perfecting holiness in the fear of God.' And they are called, 2 Peter i. 4, 'Exceeding great and precious promises.' In the original it is, τὰ μέγιστα—the greatest things. Now faith saith, If the world can bid more than thy Saviour hath done, choose it. Look, here is the greatest things; if you suffer loss, if your carnal interest be endamaged, it will be abundantly made up in Christ. Faith brings all to the balance, and weighs every discouragement. As the apostle seems to stand with a pair of scales, and cast in present inconveniences and future recompenses: Rom. viii. 18, 'I reckon, that the sufferings of this present time are not worthy to be compared with the glory which shall be revealed in us.' I reckon and find this is too light to be compared to my joy. Faith shows there is no recompense to the joys of heaven, and no inconveniences to the torments of hell. Thus you see the reasonings of faith upon all these grounds, that it is impossible but there should be a difference between the service of believers and of carnal men.

Application.—To press you to exercise faith in all your duties of religion. James ii. 23, it is said, 'Abraham's faith wrought with his works.' Let us consider God and duty. Here arise some cases—

1. Concerning the discerning work of faith, How shall we do to see him that is invisible? or to conceive of God in prayer, so as to find an awe of him upon our spirits?

2. Concerning the receiving part of faith, How shall we do to interest ourselves in the assistance of Jesus Christ, and borrow help from heaven, when we are employed in duties of worship?

3. Concerning the reasoning work of faith, how far is assurance necessary? How shall we set faith on arguing when our evidences are dark?

Case 1. Concerning the discerning work of faith, How we shall do to see him that is invisible, and rightly to conceive of God in prayer

so far as to find an awe upon our spirits. It is a great trouble to
God's children, that they are not able to form proper apprehensions
and conceits of God in their approaches to him. Moses' curiosity did
in part arise from this ground : Exod. xxxiii. 18, 'Lord, show me thy
glory.' And the disciples were troubled that they were not able to
conceive distinctly of the Father : John xiv. 8, 'Show us the Father,
and it sufficeth us.' I know they intended a corporal sight ; however,
it argues a weakness in the soul that they know not how to conceive
of God as they ought to do.

I shall answer this case in several directions—

1. You must renew and revive the act of your faith in God's essence
and presence.

2. You must conceive of him aright, according as he hath revealed
himself.

3. There must be such a representation of God as to make the
spirit aweful, not servile.

4. You must in prayer form proper notions of God, according to
those requests that we put up to him.

5. Frame fit notions concerning the trinity.

See these heads fully handled, ver. 6.

SERMON XVI.

*By faith Abel offered unto God a more excellent sacrifice than Cain,
by which he obtained witness that he was righteous, God testifying
of his gifts : and by it he, being dead, yet speaketh*—HEB. xi. 4.

CASE. 2. For the receiving part of faith, How shall we do to interest
ourselves in the assistance of Jesus Christ ?

1. We must lie at God's feet in a sense of our own weakness ; as
Jehoshaphat said in another case, 2 Chron. xx. 12, 'Lord, we have no
might.' So, when you come to engage upon any duties, acknowledge
your weakness : 2 Cor. iii. 5, 'Not that we are sufficient of ourselves
to think anything as of ourselves ; but our sufficiency is of God,'—he
speaks of the management of the work of the ministry.

2. You must plead God's promises, wherein he hath engaged to help
you in holy duties. You must come and throw him his handwriting,
show him his promises ; as Tamar dealt with Judah, when she showed
him the ring and staff—' Whose are these ? ' Gen. xxxviii. 25. Urge
God with his promises in a humble plea of faith : Ps. cxix. 49,
'Remember thy word unto thy servant, upon which thou hast caused
me to hope ;' Lord, is not this thine own promise ? and didst thou not
by this draw out and invite my hope ? Not as if God needed the
mementoes of his creatures ; but it is the only rational way to make
our confidence arise. Look, as by wrestling we gain a heat to ourselves ;
so we, wrestling with God by prayer, revive the grounds of our hope,
—show him his own institution, that there may be greater confidence
in our own souls.

3. Cast yourselves upon the performance of duty in the expectation of his help. It is true God is not bound to give the arbitrary assistances of his Spirit; he doth all things according to his pleasure. But though God be not bound, you are bound; you must engage in duty whatsoever the success be. Say then, I will do what God hath commanded, let God do what he please. There is much of faith in this. The work of faith is to bring us to a cheerful engagement. By this means God's power is glorified, that he is able to help you; and God's mercy is glorified, you leave the business with him, and trust to his mercy. And his sovereignty is much glorified when you can lie at his foot, and leave him to the working of his own grace; as David: Ps. lxxi. 16, 'I will go in the strength of the Lord God;' that is, to the duty of praise; Eph. vi. 10, 'Be strong in the Lord, and in the power of his might.' The Lord chides his children for this, because they would neglect duty out of their own discouragement. Thus, Jer. i. 7, when God sent him in a message—'Say not, I am a child; for thou shalt go to all that I shall send thee, and whatever I command thee thou shalt speak;' and Exod. iv. 10–12, when Moses would excuse himself —'I am slow of speech, and of a slow tongue. The Lord said unto him, Who hath made man's mouth? . . . Have not I the Lord? Now therefore go, and I will be with thy mouth, and will teach thee what thou shalt say.' Weakness must never be urged to exclude duty; when there is a clear command, we should cast ourselves upon the duty, and refer the help to God's good pleasure.

Case 3. The third case respects the reasoning work of faith, How far is assurance necessary, that so faith may have some strength and encouragement, that we may be persuaded into acts of obedience by these arguments of faith? I answer—

1. We live by faith, and not by assurance. The first act of faith is vital, and unites and implants into Christ: Heb. iii. 14, 'For we are made partakers of Christ, if we hold the beginning of our confidence steadfast unto the end.' If you can but maintain the first act of faith, this is enough to make you partakers of Christ, when you can roll and cast the soul upon Christ.

2. Assurance is very comfortable, and we have a great loss, when we are upon terms of uncertainty. It is far better to say, Christ died for me, than barely to say, Christ died for sinners; then the arguments of faith are more sharpened, and fall with a more direct stroke upon the soul, when once you can plead, all this he hath done for me, and this is for my sake.

3. We may reason from the general acts of Christ's love, when we are not able particularly to apply them. And that gratitude is very pure when I can bless God for Christ without reflection upon my own private benefit, for putting salvation into so possible a way. This is enough to urge the soul to duties of obedience: Titus ii. 11, 12, 'For the grace of God that bringeth salvation, hath appeared to all men, teaching us, that denying ungodliness and worldly lusts we should live soberly, righteously, and godly in this present world.' That general salvation that the grace of God hath brought into the world ministers holy arguments and discourses to the soul, whereby we may resist lusts and overcome temptations—'He came into the world to

save sinners, whereof I am chief,' saith Paul, 1 Tim. i. 15. Here is some kind of application in this, when we take hold of the promises on the dark side; when we can reason as Paul—'It is a faithful saying, and worthy of all acceptation,' Christ died for sinners.

Now I come to handle the consequents of Abel's faith.

1. The first is a testimony—*By which he obtained witness that he was righteous, God testifying of his gifts.*

2. The second a special privilege—*By it he, being dead, yet speaketh.*

First, The testimony, and that is double—(1.) Of his person, 'That he was righteous;' (2.) Of his performance, 'God testifying of his gifts.' The one proves the other: he proves his person was accepted of God, because God gave testimony concerning the acceptance of his gifts. By which, by what? In the original it is δι ἧς. Some apply it to faith—by which faith he obtained witness; others apply it to sacrifice, by which sacrifice he obtained witness.

There are arguments on both sides. Most probably it must be referred to faith—' By faith he obtained witness that he was righteous.'

1. Because the apostle had laid down the general proposition; ver. 2, that 'by faith the elders obtained a good report;' and now he comes to make it good by special instances, for by it Abel 'obtained witness that he was righteous.'

2. If it be referred to offering sacrifice, the apostle would rather have said δι οὖ, by which act of his, in offering sacrifice. However, in a sound sense, it may be referred to either. His righteousness may be referred to his faith, and the testimony of his righteousness to his sacrifice, which was but the witness of his faith. It is one thing to be righteous, and another thing to obtain witness that we are righteous. By faith Abel was a righteous person *in foro cœli*, accepted in the Messiah in the court of God; but by his better sacrifice, as a fruit of faith, he obtained the testimony of his righteousness *in foro conscientiœ*, in his own feeling, and *in foro ecclesiœ*, in the solemn approbation of the church.

He obtained witness that he was righteous, ἐμαρτυρήθη εἶναι δίκαιος, he had a good report of his righteousness. It is the same word with ἐμαρτυρήθησαν, ver. 2. How did he obtain this witness? I answer, Either in the word of God: Gen. iv. 4, 'The Lord had respect to Abel, and to his offering' (and everywhere he is spoken of as a holy and righteous man; it is his solemn title, 'righteous Abel,' Mat. xxiii. 35); or else it may be meant of the respect God bore to his person and sacrifice, for so the apostle himself proveth it—'God testifying of his gifts,' viz., by some outward and visible demonstration of acceptance, to which now is equivalent the inward witness of the Holy Ghost; for when graces have their full work and exercise, God there gives in the light and comfort of them. For a more full clearing of this passage, you must know this sacrifice was an act for the election and consecration of one of the two brethren as the head of the blessed seed and race. I say, the trial now was which of them God would choose, in whose family the line of the church and the blessed generation was to be continued. As afterwards Moses puts Korah upon the like trial, when he had a contention with Aaron about the succession and line of the priesthood: Num. xvi. 6, 7, 'This do: Take you censers, Korah, and all his company; and put fire therein, and put incense in them before the Lord to-morrow: and it shall be, that the man whom the Lord doth choose, he shall be holy'—whom God will decide by special testimony and designation from heaven, he shall be holy and set apart. Upon such an occasion as this is were the two brothers before God at this time, as appeareth partly from God's answer to Cain, when Cain took it ill that his younger brother should be preferred before him: ver. 7, 'If thou doest well, shalt thou not be accepted? And unto thee shall be his desire, and thou shalt rule over him;' meaning thus, if he had rightly offered, he should have been accepted with God, and have had pre-eminence, and been head of the blessed line and race. As also it appears by what is said, Gen. iv. 25, when Eve had her third son born, and she calls his name Seth, 'For God,' saith she, 'hath appointed me another seed instead of Abel whom Cain slew;' not only another son, but another seed; Cain being, to their knowledge, rejected by God, she had greater joy from the birth of this son, because now there was one raised up to continue the holy seed. And it is not of small consideration that carnal hypocrites are said by the apostle, Jude 11, 'to walk in the way of Cain;' for he is the patriarch of unbelievers, as Abel was to be the head of the believing state. This was the occasion of this solemn sacrifice, whom God would accept as holy and righteous, and as head of the blessed line. Now this was the type and sign of the general acceptance of all believers in Jesus Christ; so that upon the whole we may pronounce that by faith he was righteous and accepted with God, and that by faith acting in his sacrifice he received witness that he was righteous, accepted, and chosen by God. By faith he was righteous, that is, by faith in the promised seed. He was not righteous by his own worth and merit; partly because it is the apostle's scope to show that the righteousness of all ages did reside in Christ, which was apprehended by the faith of the patriarchs which made them famous in the churches; and partly because his own personal merit and righteousness is actually disclaimed by his sacrifice; for it was a sacrifice of propitiation, disclaiming of his own righteousness, and a solemn protestation of his hopes of acceptance in the promised seed.

'God testifying of his gifts.' How so? The apostle points to what was said: Gen. iv. 4,.5, 'The Lord had respect to Abel, and to his offering; but unto Cain, and to his offering, he had not respect.' How was this known? It must be known by some visible token, for thereupon Cain was angry with Abel, and in his envy and wrath slew his brother; therefore there must be some token of the different acceptance of God. Now what was this visible token? Divers conceit divers things. One saith that the smoke of Cain's sacrifice was beaten downwards towards the earth, which was a testimony of God's detestation, and the smoke of Abel's sacrifice went up to heaven, as it were into the nostrils of God; but this is a groundless conceit, that cannot be established by the least probability of conjecture. Others think that it was by some apparition of an angel, or some different appearance of God to them; but this also is asserted without warrant or probable reason. Therefore it is most probable that this visible sign that God gave as a token of the accepting of his offering was this—viz., the consuming of Abel's sacrifice to ashes by fire coming down from heaven. What is in the Hebrew ‏וישע‎ God respected Abel, is rendered by others ἐνεπύρισεν, God regarded Abel, and set his sacrifice on fire. And indeed there is much ground for this opinion, for this is the usual sign in the word of God of favourable acceptance. Let me name a few places to you: there is a prayer, Ps. xx. 3, 'The Lord accept thy burnt-sacrifice.' In the margin it is, The Lord turn thy burnt-offering to ashes, because the devouring of the sacrifice was a sign from heaven of God's acceptance. So when God accepted Aaron's sacrifice, Lev. ix. 24, it is said, 'There came a fire out from the Lord, and consumed upon the altar the burnt-offering and the fat; which when all the people saw, they shouted, and fell on their faces.' When Solomon was accepted, 2 Chron. vii. 1, it is said, that 'fire came down from heaven and consumed the burnt-offering and the sacrifice;' this was a solemn token. When Elijah and Baal's priests would put it to trial who was the true God, 1 Kings xviii. 38, 'The fire of the Lord fell, and consumed the burnt-sacrifice.' This was a token God would give to Gideon, Judges vi. 21, 'There arose fire out of the rock, and consumed the flesh and the unleavened cakes.' Manaoh, when Samson was to be born as the deliverer of the church, Judges xiii. 20, 'The flame went up towards heaven from off the altar; and the angel of the Lord ascended in the flame of the altar.' And 1 Chron. xxi. 26, when David offered solemn sacrifice to God, it is said, 'God answered him from heaven by fire upon the altar of burnt-offering.' This was the usual sign of acceptance. Fire upon the sacrifice was a token of God's favour; but fire upon the sacrificers was a token of God's curse and wrath. When Aaron's two sons had displeased the Lord 'fire came down from the Lord, and devoured them,' Lev. x. 2. So that out of subsequent experiences we may gather what kind of testimony it was. And indeed herein also, as in the sacrifice, there was some type of Christ; for he who is our sacrifice of propitiation was to be offered upon the altar of the cross; as he was to be roasted in the flames of his own love, so in the fire of divine wrath. Out of the whole you see the privileges were then more sensible. The head of the elect family God would decide; and the testimony is sensible, for fire came and devoured the sacrifice, which is now supplied us by the suggestion of the Holy Ghost.

I draw three points from the words thus opened—

1. That by faith we are justified and made righteous. It is said, '*By which* he obtained witness.'

2. That upon the solemn operation of faith in holy duties we obtain witness that we are thus righteous, and are accepted with God.

3. That the works only of such righteous persons are accepted with God.

First Abel's person is accepted in Christ by faith, and the apostle infers that, because God accepted his gifts.

Doct. 1. By faith we are justified, made righteous, and accepted with God.

Justification by faith is one of the most cardinal articles of religion; and here it is confirmed by the instance of Abel, one of the ancientest experiences of the church.   Therefore I shall not pass it over without some regard.

Three things I shall inquire into—(1.) How we are justified by faith ; (2.) Why faith is deputed to this service of all other graces ; (3.) What kind of faith it is that justifieth.

First, How we are justified by faith ?

Ans. 1. Negatively : (1.) Not by faith as a joint cause with works ; (2.) Not by faith as an act and grace in us ; (3.) Not by faith as it receives the Spirit's witness.

1. Not by faith as a joint cause with works ; as the papists say that we are justified by faith, as it receives a merit and value by works. This were to part stakes between God and the creature, and to confound the covenants, which are altogether inconsistent, as the apostle reasoneth, Rom. xi. 6, ' If by grace, then it is no more of work ; otherwise grace is no more grace.   But if it be of works, then it is no more grace ; otherwise work is no more work.'

2. Faith doth not justify as it is an act of grace in us, but relatively and instrumentally ; not as it works by love, but as it apprehends Christ ; not as if the act of believing were instead of perfect obedience to the law, but only with reference to the object as it lays hold of Jesus Christ, because of its necessary concurrence as the instrument and condition of the covenant.   There are different expressions in scripture ; sometimes God is said to justify, and Christ is said to justify, and faith is said to justify, but with a different respect.

[1.] God is said to justify, and that two ways ; partly as the first moving cause.   The rise of all is God the Father's mercy in ordaining Christ : Rom. iii. 24, ' Being justified freely by his grace, through the redemption that is in Christ Jesus.'   By the antecedent and free electing love and mercy of the Father, as the first moving cause.   Partly, as the supreme judge : Rom. viii. 33, ' Who shall lay anything to the charge of God's elect ?   It is God that justifieth ; ' that is, how shall the executioner lay anything to my charge ?   God is there spoken of as the supreme judge.   So Rom. iii. 26, ' The Father is said to justify him which believeth in Jesus ; ' 1 John ii. 1, ' If any man sin, we have an advocate with the Father,' &c.   In the order of the persons he sustaineth the person of the highest judge, and all things are authoritatively ordered by him.

[2.] Christ is said to justify ; as Isa. liii. 11, ' By his knowledge shall righteous servant justify many ; ' that is, Jesus Christ, as God's righteous servant of his eternal decrees.   Now Christ justifies, partly by meriting that righteousness for us which will serve for justification. It is he that hath procured it by his obedience and death, and suffering in our stead ; and therefore he is said to introduce ' an everlasting righteousness,' Dan. ix. 24.   His obedience is the matter of our justification, being ' the the Lord our righteousness,' Jer. xxiii. 6.   And partly by interceding for us, that we may be interested in this righteousness, that the Spirit may work faith in us.

[3.] Faith is said to justify, because without it we cannot apprehend the righteousness of Christ ; as the hand may be said to feed and nourish the body, but the nutritive virtue is not in the hand, but in the meat.   And therefore when faith is said to justify, it is meant, as it receives the righteousness of Christ, and with reference to its object. There is nothing more usual than to apply that to the instrument that is proper to the object; and usually in the expressions of the word it is complicated and folded up together with its object. Faith in Christ, faith in his blood—it receives all its merit and value from thence. As also the righteousness of faith is spoken of as contradistinct from the righteousness which is in ourselves; therefore it cannot be understood of faith itself, but of the righteousness of Christ: Rom. x. 3, 'They being ignorant of God's righteousness, and going about to establish their own righteousness, have not submitted themselves to the righteousness of God;' and, Phil. iii. 9, 'And be found in him, not having mine own righteousness, which is of the law, but that which is through the faith of Christ, the righteousness which is of God by faith.' Yea, there are distinct places which call it 'God's righteousness,' in opposition to any act of man and make faith only to be the instrument to receive it: Rom. i. 17, 'The righteousness of God is revealed from faith to faith;' that is, in opposition to the act of man, procured and merited by a person, that is, God, and accepted by God: Rom. iii. 21, 22, 'The righteousness of God, which out of the law is manifested,' &c; 'even the righteousness of God, which is by faith of Jesus Christ unto all, and upon all them that believe.' We are not said to be justified *propter fidem* but *per fidem*.

3. Again, faith doth not justify in the sense of the Antinomians, as a receiving witness of the Spirit's testimony. They say there is the sealing and receiving witness, and make the sealing witness to be the Spirit of God, and the receiving witness to be faith. They take faith to be nothing else but assurance; but that is a thing that follows upon faith. We may be justified, though we have not received this solemn testimony and witness by the Holy Ghost. Assurance is spoken of as a thing consequent to faith: Eph. i. 13, 'After ye believed, ye were sealed with that Holy Spirit of promise;' first faith, then sealing. The Spirit's testimony is nothing but the certioration of grace already wrought, and is subsequent to the testimony of the renewed conscience: Rom. viii. 16, 'The Spirit itself beareth witness with our spirit that we are the children of God.' The Holy Ghost doth not seal to a blank. First there must be faith, then the Spirit of God puts on his seal.

Ans. 2. Positively, faith only justifies as an instrument which God hath deputed to the apprehension and application of Christ's righteousness. The whole order and process is this: by effectual calling God begets faith; by faith there is union wrought with Christ; by being united to Christ there is possession of all of Christ; upon this possession God looks upon us as righteous; God looking upon us as righteous, pronounceth the sentence of justification; which sentence is double, an acquitting us from our sins, and accepting of us in Christ—we are absolved from all sin and death by a free and full pardon, and that is done chiefly by the passive obedience of Christ— and we are accepted as righteous to eternal life, and that is the fruit of his active obedience, or of his fulfilling the law for us.

1. By effectual calling God begets faith. The immediate end of effectual calling is to work faith. We are called to holiness and called

to glory; these are expressions everywhere in the scriptures; but the immediate fruit of calling is faith : 2 Thes. ii. 14, ' Whereunto he called you by our gospel to the obtaining of the glory of our Lord Jesus Christ.' ' Whereunto,' meaning faith, mentioned in the words before; there is the first end of calling to close with Christ ; then the last end, that we may be glorified. The voice of all the calls and invitations of the word is, Come unto me, and come unto Christ.

2. By faith there is union wrought with Christ. Faith is the bond of the spiritual union. We are said to live in him by faith : Gal. ii. 20; ' The life which I live in the flesh I live by the faith of the Son of God.' And he is said to dwell in us by faith : Eph. iii. 17, ' That Christ may dwell in your hearts by faith.' Now union there must be, for Christ's garments do only cover the members of his own body.

3. Being united to Christ, we are possessed of all that is in Christ, so far as is consistent with our capacity of receiving, and God's ordination and appointment in giving. Union gives us interest in the personal merits and righteousness of Christ, and the benefit of his mediatory actions ; they are ours to all effects and purposes, as if we ourselves had satisfied and obeyed the law. Why ? because it is not in a person severed from us ; it is in our head, in one to whom we are united by a strait bond of union, and therefore they are reputed as ours. It is true, we are not mediators and redeemers as Christ, because that is not consistent with our estate, nor with the will of God ; but it consists with the will of God, that we shall be made righteous with his righteousness : 1 Cor. i. 30, it is the Father's pleasure, ' In him are ye in Christ Jesus ; ' that is, by virtue of our union, God hath willed this ; ' who of God is made to us wisdom, righteousness, sanctification, and redemption ; ' 2 Cor. v. 21, ' He was made sin for us, who knew no sin, that we might be made the righteousness of God in him.' There is as real a donation and as effectual an application of Christ's righteousness to us, as there was of our sins to Christ. And as by virtue of the latter it pleased the Father to deal with Christ as a sinner; so by virtue of the former it pleased the Father so to deal with us, and to accept of us as righteous. Look, as we may be by the ordination of God made guilty of Adam's sin, though we be not in his public capacity of being a public person and representer of all mankind ; so we may be made righteous with Christ's active obedience, though we are not mediators and redeemers, for that was his particular capacity and relation fixed in his person. In short, being united to Christ, we are interested in all his actions as if they were ours; for when we are one with him in the spirit, then we are considered by God as one with him in law. The judicial union always follows the mystical. As the payment of the debt surely is imputed and reckoned to the debtor; so Jesus Christ being our surety, Heb vii. 22, his righeousness is imputed to us. Therefore by union we are said, Gal. iii. 27, ' to put on Christ,' with all his personal merits and righteousness.

4. Upon this God looks upon us as righteous. For mark, though justification be a judicial act, yet it is not a naked sentence of pardon without any ground or reason ; it hath a real ground and foundation, —the donation and application of Christ's righteousness to believers. Therefore when God looks upon a sinner as a sinner, he will never

acquit him; but it is founded upon the donation of a true and perfect righteousness, proved by Christ, and communicated to believers upon God the Father's ordination and appointment; for the apostle saith, Rom. iii. 26, 'God will be just, and the justifier of them that believe in Jesus.' When a person is made thus righteous, then God is just in justifying him. God will pronounce none just but those that by faith are thus interested in the satisfaction of Christ. There is first a true donation and effectual application of Christ's righteousness, then is the sentence passed in the court of God.

5. The sentence of God is twofold—(1.) He absolves us from all sin and death, and he doth that by a free and full pardon; (2.) He accepts us as righteous to eternal life. The parts of our justification are privative and positive: John iii. 16, 'That whosoever believeth in him should not perish, but have everlasting life.' The one is done by Christ's passive obedience and the other by Christ's active obedience.

[1.] For the former part; the form of that is laid down, Job xxxiii. 24, there is the formal sentence of God the Father, 'Deliver him from going down to the pit, for I have found a ransom.' Let that soul live, and deliver him from hell and death. Look, as when Abraham found the ram, he let Isaac go; so God, receiving a ransom, a satisfaction to his justice by the sufferings of Christ, the sinner is absolved—'Deliver him.' And indeed this is that we may plead when our consciences return upon us and implead us, that we are one in law with Christ, his ransom is our ransom: Gal. ii. 20, 'I am crucified with Christ;' that is, I have satisfied the law in Christ. Faith must look to the surety, and see justice satisfied, and all for me: Col. ii. 14, 'Blotting out the handwriting of ordinances that was against us, which was contrary to us, and took it out of the way, nailing it to his cross.'

[2.] The second part of the sentence is accepting of us as righteous unto eternal life; for Christ hath not only satisfied the old covenant by his death, but ratified the new by his solemn obedience; not only taken away the reign of sin, but also established the reign of grace; therefore the apostle saith, Rom. v. 21, 'As sin hath reigned unto death, so might grace reign through righteousness unto eternal life, by Jesus Christ our Lord.' Now the form of acceptance to life we have in those words, Mat. xxv. 34, 'Come, ye blessed of my Father, inherit the kingdom prepared for you from the foundation of the world.' It will be most comfortable when we shall hear this out of Christ's own mouth at the last day.

Secondly, The reasons why faith is deputed to this service.

1. Because it is the most receptive grace. Other graces are more operative, but faith is most receptive, so fitly suiting the needy condition of the creature. It is the empty hand of the soul to take in the fulness of Christ. Since the fall man is needy and indigent, and lives by borrowing; therefore those graces are most serviceable that are most receptive. Love gives, but faith takes and borrows. We are beggars now rather than workers; therefore the honour is put upon faith rather than love.

2. Because it is most loyal and true to God. It looks for all from him, and ascribes all to him. This is the reason the apostle giveth why faith is made to be the condition of the new covenant: Rom. iii. 27, 'To

exclude boasting;' that the creature may look for all from God. God would humble proud creatures; whatever they have, it is but borrowed.

3. To make the way the more sure: Rom. iv. 16, 'Therefore it is of faith, that it might be by grace; to the end the promise might be sure to all the seed.' Things are not so floating and uncertain as when built upon works. We have a sure foundation in Jesus Christ, and a sure tenure by covenant: 2 Sam. xxiii. 5, 'He hath made with me an everlasting covenant, ordered in all things and sure.' And we have a sure holdfast by faith: Heb. vii. 19, 'Which hope we have, as an anchor of the soul, both sure and steadfast.'

Thirdly, The third question is, what this faith is that justifieth? It is not a general assent, or loose acknowledgment of the articles of religion. The apostle shows that the devils may assent to the truth of the word, and brings the primitive and fundamental truth of all for the confirmation of it, that there is one God. There is a faith which (to distinguish it from all others) is called justifying, described thus—It is a grace wrought in our hearts by the Spirit of God, by which the soul doth rest and cast itself upon Christ, tendered to us in the offer of God for pardon and acceptance. I shall not stand examining every part of this definition, but shall endeavour to discover the nature of faith in the acts of it. There are some things implied, and other things more express and formal in faith.

1. That which is implied in faith is knowledge and feeling.

[1.] There must be a distinct knowledge: Isa. liii. 11, 'By his knowledge shall my righteous servant justify many;' and therefore the faith that justified the sinner pre-supposeth knowledge. The first creature that God made was light; and so it is in the new creation, the first thing is light. God bringeth into the soul in conversion a stock of truth as well as a frame of grace. Heathens that are wholly ignorant of Christ cannot be justified by him, nor christians that only know him at random, and by a general tradition, for this begets but a loose hope. And though none so confident as ignorant men, which make a full account, that they shall go to heaven, yet when they are anything serious, we find all their confidence to amount to no more than a bare conjecture, or a blind and rash presumption. And usually, the more ignorant the more persuming; they cherish a blind hope. As Paul saith, Rom. vii. 9, 'I was alive without the law once;' that is, in his own persuasion and account. It is a long time ere men can get knowledge enough to be out of conceit with themselves, and to discern their own delusions. The blind world doth not look after justification by Christ, but only liveth by guess and devout aims; some loose hopes they have conceived, out of common tradition and good meanings, by which they secure themselves in their fond presumption. There must be some competent and distinct knowledge of the mysteries of salvation, that we may not foster a blind and mistaken hope.

[2.] There must be upon this knowledge some feeling and experience, which the apostle means when he calleth it, Heb. vi. 5, 'Taste of the good word of God, and the powers of the world to come;' some common efficacy and virtue of the spirit. There is a form of knowledge as well as a form of godliness: Rom. ii. 20, 'Which hast the form of knowledge, and of the truth in the law ; ' some unactive light and speculative contemplation, a naked model of truth, such as scholars have in the brain, or men may gain by parts and attendance on the word. But there must be some feeling and experience, which we usually call conviction ; and to consider it only as it concerns our present purpose, it respects two things—a sense of our misery, and our own inability to overcome it. Man is a secure creature, therefore there must be a sense of misery ; and man is a proud creature, therefore there must be a sense of our own insufficiency.

(1.) A sense of our misery by sin, and of God's curse due to us. This justifying faith supposeth ; for why should a man look to be justified till he be condemned ? Who would care for balm that is not wounded ? for a pardon that is not accused in his own conscience ? Man is a lazy creature, and will not apply himself to the work and care of religion, till he be spurred on and driven to it by his own need. Christ saith, Mat. ix. 12, 'They that be whole need not the physician, but they that are sick.' Men are at ease and heart-whole, and till they are possessed with a deep sense of their own misery they do not care for Christ. The stung Israelites looked up to the brazen serpent ; and those that were 'pricked in heart cried, What shall we do ?' Acts ii. 37. Men slight mercy till they need it, and are careless of the great salvation till God affect them with the sight of their own sins and his wrath. Israel in Egypt was not easily weaned from the flesh-pots till their burdens were doubled ; so till wrath presseth to anguish, till it sits heavy upon the conscience, we do not groan for a deliverer : Jer. xv. 17, ' I sat alone because of thy hand, for thou hast filled me with indignation.' This makes us to sit alone, and ponder seriously upon the matter. It is true, the degree is various and different : this sense of misery worketh in some as far as horror ; in all it worketh so far as to make them anxious and solicitous about a saviour, and about our everlasting condition. In short, Jesus Christ doth not seek us till we be lost, and we do not seek him till we be lost.

(2.) There must be a sense of our own inability to help ourselves. Man is not only apt to be secure, but self-confident ; and therefore till the soul seeth nothing within itself and nothing without itself but Christ, who is the only way, we shall never go to him. Man is a proud creature, loth to be beholden. A borrowed garment, though of silk, doth not suit with proud nature so well as a russet-coat of our own. So this full satisfaction of Christ, proud man regards it not ; we go about to establish our own righteousness. Legal dejection is always accompanied with pride and self-love. The sinner is cast down, but not humbled ; doth not come and lie at the feet of Christ, that he may be beholden to him for mercy ; therefore there must be somewhat more than a sight of misery. Look, as the Corinthians did not care for Paul because they thought they were full of gifts : 1 Cor. iv. 8, 'Now ye are full, now ye are rich, ye have reigned as kings without us ;' no more do men for Christ, as long as they have anything of their own. This is the reason why Paul accounts not only his pharisaical righteousness, but his best works loss, Phil. iii. 8, because it hindered him from looking after the righteousness of Christ. We would be sufficient to ourselves, happy within ourselves. Justifying faith implies that man hath given up all his own confidences; for why should we lean upon another when we have a sufficiency in ourselves? Flesh and blood would have its own righteousness; and as long as we can keep conscience quiet by external acts of duty, by any care and resolution of ours, we will never seek after the righteousness of Christ. It is never well till conscience be brought to say as Peter, ' Lord, to whom shall we go? thou hast the words of eternal life,' John vi. 68. We must confess that all our own works are nothing; Christ only it is that can cure and help us. This is that which is implied.

SERMON XVII.

By faith Abel offered unto God a more excellent sacrifice than Cain, by which he obtained witness that he was righteous, God testifying of his gifts : and by it he, being dead, yet speaketh.—Heb. xi. 4.

2. THAT which is the express and formal in justifying faith is a resting upon Christ, or a closing with Christ.

Now because here are many acts and degrees, I shall endeavour to open it to you, and that I cannot do better than in the terms of scripture. It is usual in scripture to express the tendency of the soul towards Christ by words that are proper to outward motion. There are four notions used in scripture—(1.) Coming to Christ; (2.) Running to Christ; (3.) Seeking of Christ; and (4.) Receiving of Christ. All these must be explained with analogy and proportion to external motions. Coming to Christ notes the purpose and resolution of the soul; running to Christ notes the earnest desire of the soul to enjoy him; seeking of Christ notes the diligence of the soul in the use of means; and receiving of Christ notes the welcoming of Christ into the soul with complacency, rest, and delight.

[1.] There is coming to Christ, which notes our first act of faith, our resolution and purpose to close with him. It implieth the lowest act and degree of saving faith. While the soul is in the way, it is said to be coming to Christ, resolved in his heart to be contented with nothing but Christ; therefore it is expressed always by such names as imply a present motion : Phil. iii. 12, ' Not as though I had already attained, or were already made perfect, but I follow after,' &c; John vi. 35, ' He that cometh to me shall never hunger,' &c.—ὁ ἐρχόμενος, he that is coming to me; it implies a motion in its tendency, when we are in the way. As the prodigal determined in himself, ' I will arise, and go to my father,' Luke xv. 18 ; when the soul, according to the offer of God, resolves to cast itself upon Christ for mercy and salvation. Now if this resolution be full and serious, it gives a just right and title to Christ; for, John. vi. 37, Christ saith, ' He that cometh to me,'—though he doth but do that,—' I will in nowise cast him out,' it gives you a title. So when the prodigal said, ' I will arise, and go to my father,' presently it is said ' The father ran, and fell on his neck, and kissed him,' ver. 20,

As soon as there was a purpose, he was entertained and embraced by God. So David, Ps. xxxii. 5, when he issued forth a practical decree, 'I said, I will confess my transgressions unto the Lord, and thou forgavest the iniquity of my sin.' This gives you safety and a right to Christ, though the other acts may yield you more comfort: Heb. iii. 14, 'We are made partakers of Christ,'—that is, we have a right to Christ and all his merits,—'if we hold the beginning of our confidence steadfast unto the end;' that is, the first act of faith; if we can but maintain that, it gives us a right to Christ, if we hold but our resolution to cleave to Christ, notwithstanding disadvantages. Coming implies a resolved adventure upon the invitation of God; the soul will cast itself upon Christ, and see what God will do for it, which yields you safety, though not comfort; when we resolve to cast ourselves upon his grace, whatever come on it; and though we cannot lay claim to his righteousness, yet we will wait and rest upon him, whatever comes of it.

[2.] Running to Christ; that notes not only the tendency of the motion, but the fervour and earnestness of desire. The soul cannot be quiet till it be with Christ: Cant. i. 4, 'Draw me, and we will run after thee.' When God had put forth the attractive force of his grace upon the soul, then the motions of the soul are fervent and earnest: Isa. lv. 5, 'The nations that know not thee shall'—not only come, but—'run to thee.' The soul that thirsteth after Christ with such a desire as will not be satisfied without an enjoyment—this is faith; therefore it is called 'a hungering and thirsting after righteousness,' Mat. v. 6. Hunger and thirst are those appetitions of nature which are most implacable, that cannot endure check. *Venter non habet aures*—the belly hath no ears; and hunger and thirst will not be allayed with words and counsel. So the soul will be satisfied with nothing but Christ. It edgeth the purpose with desire; our souls will not be quiet without him. It is resembled to the panting of the chased hart: Ps. xlii. 1, 'As the hart panteth after the waterbrooks, so panteth my soul after thee, O God.' The soul thirsteth after the righteousness of Christ, and the comforts and refreshments of his grace. The hart of itself is a thirsty creature, especially when it is chased. The Septuagint hath it ἡ ἔλαφος, the she-hart. Passions in females are most vehement. Therefore the earnest longing and desire of the soul for Christ is expressed by the panting and breathing of the chased she-hart after the waters. And Cant. ii. 5, it is expressed by being 'sick of love.' Vehement affections, when satisfaction is denied, cause languor and faintness in the body; so the soul vehemently longs and is sick for the love of Christ. Sometimes it is expressed by earnest expectation: Ps. cxxx. 6. 'My soul waiteth for the Lord, more than they that watch for the morning; and the psalmist redoubleth it—'I say, more than they that watch for the morning.' Look, as the weary sentinel that is wet and stiff with the dews of the night watcheth for the approach of the morning, so doth the poor soul wait for the dawning of grace and first appearances of God's love.

[3.] Seeking of Christ: Isa. lv. 6, 'Seek ye the Lord, while he may be found;' and Ps. xxvii. 8, 'Seek ye my face.' Seeking implies diligence in the use of means. Vigorous desires cannot be idle; where there hath been running, there will be also seeking: Cant. iii. 2, 'I will arise now, and go about the city, in the streets and broad ways I will seek him whom my soul loveth.' The spouse sought her beloved throughout the city. Jerusalem is a figure of the church; and in the ordinances of God christians go through the city from one ordinance to another, from meditation to prayer, from prayer to meditation, from both to the word, that still they may hear of their beloved. The earnest desire of the soul will bewray itself by the holy use of means to meet with Christ. Seeking doth not only imply a bare waiting, but a waiting in the use of means to find him whom their souls love. They are tracing his foot-steps by the shepherd's tents, and pursuing him throughout the whole city.

[4.] Receiving of Christ; this is when faith is grown, and full ripe: John i. 12, 'To as many as received him, to them gave he power'— ἐξουσίαν, the right and honour—'to become the sons of God.' Receiving is a considerate act of the soul by which we take Christ out of God's hand, and apply him to ourselves. And this suiteth with the formal nature of faith and the offer of God: in the covenant God offereth him, and we take him by the hand of faith; in the promises of the gospel God makes a deed of gift; and so in the Lord's supper, when we come to be infeoffed in the covenant 'Take, eat, this is my body,' 1 Cor. xi. 24. And here we come to take and receive him. Now this receiving implies an appropriation and more particular application of Christ to our use; and though it doth not go so high as assurance or an adjudging of Christ to be ours, yet there is a laying hold of Christ held out in the word of promise, and a desire to draw all things to application. Now concerning these acts of faith take these rules—

(1.) When you cannot comfort yourselves in one act of faith, you must make use of another; as, for instance, it is impossible the soul should be always running, always upon the bent of vigorous and strong desires; but do you come to him? That gives you a right to Christ, if there be a settled resolution and purpose of the soul to cleave and rest upon him and no other for acceptance with God. So you cannot take comfort in receiving of Christ; a secret suspicion draws back the hand of faith; ay, but do you seek him? You may take comfort in that. The terms are diversified in scripture lest any of them singly should trouble believers.

(2.) All the acts of justifying faith respect the person of Christ: it is coming to Christ, running to Christ, seeking of Christ, and receiving of Christ. Faith is not merely assent; in the scripture notion it is affiance. Usually men content themselves with a naked persuasion or inactive assent. The act of faith must be immediately terminated upon the person of Christ. Christ's righteousness is not obtained by an assent to the truth of any promise merely, or any proposition in the word, but by a union with Jesus Christ. We must be united before we can be possessed of his righteousness. We are not united to any promise, but to Christ. Look, as the imputation of Adam's sin is charged upon us by our union to him, so is the imputation of Christ's righteousness when we are united to him, when we take and receive him. It is not merely because you are of this opinion that Christ came to die for sinners, but there must be the hand of faith to take Christ out of the hand of God the Father, and receive him and embrace him. There must not only be an assent in the judgment, but a consent in the heart to cleave to Christ. Christ commended Peter for his confession in saying, ' He was the son of God,' Mat. xvi. 16. And the devil confessed as much—'Jesus, thou son of God, and thou holy one of God,' Mark i. 24. Saith Austin, *Hoc dicebat Petrus, ut Christum amplecteretur; hoc dicebant dæmones, ut Christus ab iis recederet*—Peter assented to that truth, that Jesus was the son of God, but how? that he might embrace Christ; the devils assented to this truth, that Christ might depart from them.

(3.) True faith will never rest in any lower act, it is always renewing its own acts, and perfecting and ripening itself, that from weak beginnings it may grow up into some confidence before God. It ripens purposes into desires, desires into waiting, waiting into seeking, seeking into receiving, and receiving into the fulness of assurance, always struggling with doubts and fears; as John wrote his epistle to this end, that those which had believed might grow up to greater steadfastness in faith: 1 John v. 13, ' These things have I written unto you that believe on the name of the son of God, that ye may know that ye have eternal life, and that we may believe on the name of the son of God.' As he that had faith in the Gospel is complaining of the relics of unbelief: Mark ix. 24, ' Lord, I believe; help thou mine unbelief.' False graces do not wrestle with that which is contrary, nor aim at growth; but living graces will be always drawing onward to perfection.

(4.) The less of comfort we receive in the exercise of faith, the more there should be of duty. Christians look too much on sensible consolation; but when by faith they can't sensibly apply the comfort of the gospel, they should be more exercised in the duties of it. Two things are always necessary in faith, and are undoubted evidences of your gracious estate: an esteem of Christ and diligence in duty.

(1*st*.) An esteem of Christ. When you cannot have sensible consolation, keep up your esteem. Though they cannot say Christ is theirs, yet they can say Christ is precious to them: 1 Peter ii. 7, ' To them that believe he is precious.' Therefore the apostle saith, Heb. iii. 6, ' Whose house are we, if we hold fast the confidence, and the rejoicing of the hope firm, unto the end.' In the original it is καύχημα τῆς ἐλπίδος, if we can glory in the hopes of christianity whatsoever they cost us. The apostle means, when men can make an open profession that they have a good bargain in Christ, and can glory in their hope, whatever it cost them in the world. Esteem is far more than sensible comfort, and a better evidence.

(2*dly*) Diligence in the use of means. It is said, Prov. viii. 34, ' Blessed is the man that heareth me, watching daily at my gates, waiting at the posts of my doors.' Though you are not able to apply Christ with comfort, yet you will watch at his gates for your dole of comfort. So, Isa. xxvi. 8, the church professeth this, ' In the way of thy judgments we have waited for thee; the desire of our soul is to thee, and to the remembrance of thy name.' There is more of resolution, though less of consolation. When there is nothing but angry frowns from God, no sensible tokens of his love, yet an obstinate faith will not be discouraged.

Use. If all the righteousness which saints expect reside in Christ, and we only receive it by faith, then it serves to press us to look after this righteousness. Take these arguments to quicken you—

1. What will you do without it? All our graces are imperfect and mixed with sin : your natures are full of sin, and your services are full of weakness. God can endure no imperfection, because of the holiness of his nature ; and God will not release his law, because of the severity of his justice : Ps. cxliii. 2, 'Enter not into judgment with thy servant.' He doth not say, Lord, enter not into judgment with unbelievers, but with thy servants,—those that study to approve their hearts to him. There is no obtaining of the blessing, but in the garments of our elder brother. The creature's fig-leaves will never cover a naked soul from the sight of God. We can scarce keep up a fair show before a discerning man, and what shall we do before the pure eyes of God's glory?

2. Consider, there is a full righteousness in Christ—'We are complete in him,' Col. ii. 10. Whatever there is in sin, there is more in Christ; for the sin of our nature there is the absolute intregrity of the human nature of Christ; and for the sin of our lives there is Christ's perfect obedience, who did what was required, and suffered what was deserved. Justice can make no further demands. The law is fulfilled both in the commination and precept; all is done in our surety. Here is an infinite treasure that will serve you all : 1 John ii. 28, 'And now, little children, abide in him, that when he shall appear, we may have confidence, and not be ashamed before him at his coming.' When Jesus Christ shall come in majesty and glory, if we have Christ's righteousness, we may endure Christ's judgment.

3. Consider the readiness of God to give you this righteousness. This was the very purpose and design of God the Father : Rom. iii. 25, 'Him hath God set forth to be a propitiation through faith in his blood ;' John vi. 27, 'Him hath God the Father sealed.' He hath appointed Christ for this very end. It is not a thing of our devising, but of God's appointment. We read of an emperor that had a great emerald made in the manner of a looking-glass, in which he was wont to look upon horrid aspects that by reflection upon the glass might be pleasing to him, that there he might see the bloody contest with delight. This God the Father hath done ; he hath set forth Jesus Christ, that so in him we might be acceptable and pleasing in his sight.

4. It is as really ours when it is given as if we had merited in our own persons. God's judicial acts are not grounded upon a fiction, but upon a truth. Look upon the relation as you are espoused and betrothed to him. *Uxor fulget radiis mariti*—a wife shares in all the honours of her husband ; so we are possessed of what is in Christ. The debtor is acquitted by the payment of the surety. The members share in the honour of the head. Look, as Christ satisfied for your sins as if he had committed them, so thou art accepted for his righteousness as if thou hadst satisfied : 2 Cor. v. 21, 'He was made sin for us that knew no sin, that we might be made the righteousness of God in him.' It is good to consider how really Christ was handled ; so real will our acceptance be with God. Christ lay under the wrath of the Father; his sufferings were not a fiction, no more are thy privileges.

5. Consider the excellency of this righteousness in two respects.

(1.) It is better than that we had in Adam in innocency; that would have been but the righteousness of man, but this is the righteousness of God; as Rom. iii. 22, it is called 'the righteousness of God which is by faith.' We are now in a nearer relation to the Lord than in Adam, being united to God by Christ. Adam was but God's servant, but we are made his sons and children; the union and relation is nearer. The prodigal after his return hath the best robes, Luke xv. 22. Nay, in some sense our case is better than that of angels: angels are confirmed by Christ, but it is in their own righteousness; but the righteousness of Christ is ours. (2.) You are as righteous as the most righteous saints are; as David that was a man after God's own heart, Abraham that was the friend of God, men that had such access and familiarity with God: Rom. iii. 23, 'The righteousness of God, which is by faith of Jesus Christ unto all and upon all them that believe; for there is no difference.' None of the saints have cleaner linen, nor are decked with a better vesture. In sanctification there are degrees, and a great deal of difference; but not in justification. As in the manna none had over, none under, all alike proportion and measure; so in the righteousness of Christ all have a like measure: 2 Peter i. 1, 'To them that have obtained like precious faith with us, through the righteousness of Christ.' It is a righteousness of the same nature and property; the foundation of it being in Christ, it is all one. It is said, Acts xi. 17, the gentiles had obtained 'a like gift with us;' that is, the same gift that the apostles had. Luther had an apt comparison to set out this: a giant holds a jewel in his hand, and a child may hold the same jewel; but the giant holds it with a stronger hand; so, though there be different degrees of faith, yet herein it is all alike precious; it is the same righteousness of Christ.

6. Consider the fruits and benefits of this righteousness.

[1.] Access to God. We may minister before the Lord in our priestly garments, we may worship in the holy place when Christ hath put his robes upon us. When Joshua the high priest was before the Lord, he was there in his filthy garments, Zech. iii. 5; but he was clothed with change of raiment to minister before the Lord. So we had filthy garments; therefore the Lord comes and takes them away, and clothes us with clean garments: Eph. iii. 2, 'In whom we have boldness and access with confidence by the faith of him.' Our imperfections need not encourage us; Christ's righteousness is not a covering that is too short. It is said, Rev. i. 13, Christ was clothed 'with a garment down to his feet.' Christ's righteousness is a long garment; all our defects are removed out of the light of God's countenance. When Joseph was brought out of prison before Pharaoh, his raiment was changed; so when we are to appear before God, the king of kings, certainly our raiment must be changed: Isa. lxiv. 6, 'Our righteousness is as filthy rags,' saith the church.' Now, that we might not appear before the great king with a bundle of rags, Christ hath dyed us a purple robe in his own blood, that our garments may be changed, and we may come with boldness.

[2.] We are freed from the guilt and punishment of sin, so that all afflictions have lost their curse and sting, and are become medicinal. We may have bitter dispensations many times, but they are not salted with a curse.   We may cry with Luther, Strike, Lord! strike! my sins are pardoned.   When God hath laid up comfort in the heart beforehand, all our corrections lose their property, and they are federal dispensations; as David: Ps. cxix. 75, 'I know, O Lord, that thy judgments are right, and that thou in faithfulness hast afflicted me.'   When God thresheth us, it is but that our husk may come off.   They are not acts of revenge to satisfy justice, but only to free us of a mischievous disease; and death is a friend, it is a remedy whereby we may be delivered into glory: 1 Cor. xv. 55, 'O death, where is thy sting? O grave, where is thy victory?'

[3.] This will give us comfort in the hour of death.   When the soul, smitten with the sense of sin, is drawn to the tribunal of God, oh then, the righteousness of Christ is a comfort.   Chemnitius observeth, *Aliter de justificatione sentire homines, quando in disputationibus cum hominibus sui simillimis rixantur; aliter in meditationibus, quando corum Deo sistunt conscientiam.*   Men dealing with men like themselves may cry up works; but when they plead their cause before God, then who can speak of his own righteousness?   Then they tremblingly fly to the horns of the altar and to mercy.   There is no screen to draw between us and wrath but Christ, no way to answer justice but in the satisfaction of Christ, no way to appear before holiness but by the obedience of Christ.   Let one of those audacious volume writers come and say, Lord, cast them out of heaven that cannot approve themselves to thee by their own graces.

[4.] Then we are made heirs of eternal glory; therefore it is called justification unto life.   A pardoned person is made a favourite: Rom. viii. 30, 'Whom he justified, them he also glorified.'   Christ doth not only prevent the execution, but we are also saved.   It is much to be delivered from wrath to come: Rom. v. 9, 'Much more then, being justified by his blood, we shall be saved from wrath through him;' as if it were a lesser thing to glorify a saint than to justify a sinner. When God can accept of us out of his free grace, certainly he will give us heaven.

Ques. You will say, What shall I do?   Here is nothing to do but to receive and take Christ out of the hands of God.   We are not exhorted to justify ourselves as we are to sanctify ourselves.   Justification is God's act; yet there must be something done to obtain it; not by way of causality, but by way of order.   God doth not justify stocks and stones, but men; neither doth he justify mules and horses, and those that will kick again, but those that will submit to his righteousness.   A sick man must yield to take physic, and a poor man must hold out his hand to receive an alms.

There are two general means—(1.) Disclaim your own righteousness; (2.) Apply yourselves to the righteousness of Christ.

First, Disclaim your own righteousness.   In the new covenant he cometh most worthy that cometh most unworthy; Christ speaks a 'parable against those that trusted in themselves that they were righteous,' Luke xviii. 9.   There one comes and pleads his works, as appealing to justice; the other comes and pleads his sins, as waiting for mercy. What is the issue of all?   It is said, ver. 14, 'This man went away justified to his house rather than the other.'   We must come sinners into his presence ; the sinner is justified rather than the worker. We must come naked, that he might give us raiment. Take notice of Paul's solemn renunciation, Phil. iii. 7–9, ' What things were gain to me, those I counted loss for Christ ; yea, doubtless, and I count all things but loss for the excellency of the knowledge of Christ Jesus my Lord, for whom I have suffered the loss of all things, and do count them but dung that I may win Christ.' He had more cause than any to have confidence in the flesh and glory in himself ; but all this was so far from being a gain, as they were a loss to him. He thought it was an advantage and a step to mercy, when it was a dangerous allurement to hypocrisy and self-confidence. He reckons up his moral excellences, his natural privileges, and his own righteousness ; but all this was so far a disadvantage to him as they kept him from being hungry and more earnest after the righteousness God offered to him in Christ.

Now because this is a hard matter, a man would fain maintain the dignity of works, and proud nature is loth to stoop and sue *in formâ pauperis ;* and men would rather oblige God than come as beggars and be beholden to him : Rom. x. 3, ' Going about to establish their own righteousness, have not submitted themselves unto the righteousness of God.' It is a matter of great difficulty to captivate the pride and prejudices of reason ; therefore I shall lay down the more effectual considerations that are likely to draw us off from our own righteousness, and bring us to submit and yield to God's terms. I shall lay down five considerations—The exact purity of the law, the holiness of God, our proneness to sin, the strictness of the last day's account, and the danger of resting upon anything in ourselves.

1. Consider the exact purity of the law. Usually men are alive in their own hopes and conceits, because they do not look as they should into the law of God : Rom. vii. 9, ' I was alive without the law once.' While Paul looked upon the law through pharisaical spectacles, he thought he was perfect and alive,—that is, in a good condition before God ; ' but when the commandment came,'—that is, with full light and conviction,—' sin revived, and I died ; ' Paul was struck dead, then it revived the sentence of death in himself. A short exposition of the law begets a large opinion of our own righteousness. We are all Pharisees by nature, and in the private glosses of our own thoughts, we regard no more of the law than external obedience, ἔργον νόμου, the mere work of the law, and therefore we are not driven to seek the righteousness of Christ. We see it plainly that common people hope to be saved by their good works and good meanings. The more ignorant men are, the greater confidence in themselves. That is the reason the apostle saith, Rom. x. 3, ' Being ignorant of the righteousness of God, and going about to establish a righteousness of their own.' Men do not consider what a righteousness becomes God's presence. Now when the law comes, it gives sin its due dimensions, and the sinner his due load and burden. Oh ! look then into the purity of the prohibition ; for the law condemns not only acts, but thoughts ; not only sins perfectly formed, but lusts ; it reacheth to the little foxes and Babylon's brats. And in duty it doth not only require the work wrought, but an exquisite frame of spirit, with the motions and opera-

tions of the soul ; all thy heart, all thy soul, all thy might.   It is no matter though our meaning be good ; the law would have us bring our duties and acts of obedience not only to the touchstone, but to the balance ; it must hold exact weight, as well as be of a good kind.

2. Consider the holiness of God.   The great business of justification is to give us a righteousness that will endure God's sight, that we may be able to stand before God ; hence those phrases, 'justified in his sight,' Ps. cxliii. 2, and Rom. iii. 20 ; and 'glorying before God,' Rom. iv. 2 ; and 'the answer of a good conscience towards God,' 1 Peter iii. 21. So that if we would look for a proper righteousness fit for justification, we are to draw the soul into God's sight, and to think of the pure eyes of his glory.   Now it is said, Job xv. 15, ' The heavens are not clean in his sight,' that is, the holy ones in heaven, the angels that are con-firmed in their own righteousness, they are not clean in the sight of God's holiness.   They not only cover their feet, that is, that which is the meanest and lowest of the angelical nature, but their faces, that which is most glorious in their nature ; they were ashamed of that which was best in their nature, as being abashed at the presence of God's holiness.   Oh ! what will become of us vile worms ?   'What is man, that he should be clean ?   And he which is born of a woman, that he should be righteous ?' Job xv. 14.   If the court of heaven be not clean in his presence, how shall we do for a righteousness that must endure the eyes of God's glory ?—' Who can stand before this holy God ?' 1 Sam. vi. 20.   Alas ! in the state you are, you can no more expect that God should delight in you than you can delight in a toad, because of the contrariety of nature ; yet this is but a finite com-parison.   Now in vain is it to think God should act contrary to his nature, that ever holiness itself should delight in a sinner.   Oh ! what shall I do to come before God's holiness ?

3. Consider our proneness to sin.   Men that have low thoughts of the degeneration and corruption of nature have as low thoughts of the righteousness of Christ ; therefore consider how corruption is apt to bewray itself in duty, business, recreation, in all conditions and actions of life ; all is tainted : ' Innumerable evils have compassed me about,' Ps. xl. 12.   And consider, whoever appears before God must be clothed with some righteousness.   Now go to our duties,—' Our righteousnesses are as filthy rags,' Isa. lxv. 5.   The better part of our lives are spotted and defiled.   Certainly those works that need pardon themselves can never justify us.   *Mala mea purè, mala sunt et mea ; bona autem mea, nec purè bona sunt, nec mea*—our evil works, they are merely evil, and they are ours ; but our good works are neither ours ; nor are they purely good.   Certainly a man cannot merit with that which doth not deserve acceptance.

4. Consider the strictness of the last day's account.   Justification is principally intended for that time.   Christ's righteousness was ap-pointed for Christ's judgment : 1 John ii. 28, ' And now, little children, abide in him, that when he shall appear, we may have confidence, and not be ashamed before him at his coming.'   This God aimed at, to establish such a righteousness that we might not be ashamed at Christ's coming : 1 John iii. 21, ' If our hearts condemn us not, then have we confidence towards God ; ' and Luke xxi. 36, you have the like expres-

sion, ' That ye may stand before the Son of man.' Now when every
idle word shall be weighed in God's balance, what will you do then?
Things will not be huddled up at that day, but conscience will be
extended to the recognition of all the sins you have committed; and
what will you do for a righteousness at that day, when the secret stores
of your thoughts and the hidden things of the heart shall be made
manifest: 1 Cor. iv. 5, ' Until the Lord come, who both will bring to
light the hidden things of darkness ; and will make manifest the
counsels of the hearts.' Light words will weigh heavy in God's balance.
The comfort of justification is never tried till the last judgment.

5. Consider the danger of resting upon anything in ourselves. Alas !
when you go to mix the covenants, you quite undo your hopes in Christ ;
it is plain you hold by the former covenant. If you do but set up
anything of self, it makes the promise of Christ of none effect. Here
you are put to your choice by what covenant you will be judged ; either
the covenant of works, in which there is judgment without mercy, or
by the law of liberty. If you set up yourself, you cast off the new
covenant. Carnal confidence rendereth you obnoxious to the whole
law: Gal. iii. 18. ' For if the inheritance be of the law, it is no
more of promise.' If you hold by the former covenant, you are
quite undone ; you shall not have a drop of grace : Rom. xi. 6, ' If
it be of works, it is no more grace.' You are bound to fulfil the
whole law; if in any case you set up self, 'Christ shall profit you nothing,'
Gal. v. 2. God will deal with you, either altogether by works, or
altogether by Christ; these things cannot be mixed. When you seek
to piece up the righteousness of Christ by any graces or duties of yours,
by resting in yourselves, you destroy the whole. It must not be a
patched righteousness ; the piece of new cloth maketh the rent the
worse.

SERMONS UPON HEBREWS XI.

SERMON XVIII.

*By faith Abel offered unto God a more excellent sacrifice than Cain,
by which he obtained witness that he was righteous, God testifying
of his gifts: and by it he, being dead, yet speaketh.*—HEB. xi. 4.

Secondly, The second general means is to apply yourselves to the
righteousness of Christ. There are many steps and progresses of the
soul in this work—desire it, seek it, wait for it, take Christ upon any
special offer, then upon the act of faith consider your privileges and
make your claim; and that your claim may be warranted, there must
be a care of holiness.

1. Desire it earnestly. Grace is wrought by knowledge, but it is
first known by desire and spiritual esteem. Appetite follows life; so
when God begins to infuse life in the soul, it is first discerned by
desire: Mat. v. 5, 'Blessed are they that hunger and thirst after
righteousness.' How passionately doth Paul speak, Phil. iii. 9, 'That
I might be found in him, not having mine own righteousness.' All
things else he accounted dung, dog's-meat, loss rather than gain.

2. You must seek it. Lazy wishes are only the fruits of conviction.
Men could wish they were interested in so great comfort. But now
serious desires will put you upon endeavours: Mat. vi. 33, 'Seek ye
first the kingdom of God, and the righteousness thereof.' The great
design and work of christians should be to get a part in Christ, in God's
kingdom, and God's righteousness, as the way to it; seek it first, above
all things, and above all pursuits. Men make it not their work, but
their by-work, and regard it now and then in some pang of conscience.
Oh, then for a garment to cover them, then for a righteousness to shelter
them from wrath! but this should be the first thing; it is a worthy
pursuit, and it will make amends for all the pains you are at in seeking
it.

3. Wait for it. Grace is not at the creature's beck. Before ever
God will show mercy, he will first declare his sovereignty: Isa. xxvi.
8, 'In the way of thy judgments have we waited for thee.' Though
they meet with nothing but rough answers—though God seems to hide
himself, yet in the midst of his judicial dispensations you should continue waiting. Nothing declares the creature's subjection to God so
much as tarrying of his leisure; alas! otherwise it is a sign we ascribe

to ourselves, when we prescribe to God, when we would have him come in at our time and pleasure. Remember the righteousness of Christ is a great blessing, and God doth not owe it you; God may give it to whom he will, and when he will. Impatience always shows there is some confidence in your own righteousness. You should say as the church doth: Lam. i. 16, 'My comforter that should relieve my soul is far from me;' 'but I have rebelled against him,' ver. 18. God suspends comfort, but it is not my due; but I have rather merited the contrary. Thoughts of merit beget murmuring. When the soul is possessed of its own guilt, it will tarry the Lord's leisure. Consider, God hath waited long ere you came to this, to look up to him for the righteousness of Christ; therefore you have good cause to wait upon him for his good pleasure.

4. When there is any special offer in the word, do not delay, but take Christ; do not draw back the hand of faith. I know a guilty creature will be full of suspicions; and the truth is, the grace of the gospel is so rich that we know not how to credit it. But when there is a fair offer, do not let suspicion take in the hand of faith, but receive Christ when he is tendered in the promises of the word. Sometimes God doth, as it were, call you by name: John x. 3, 'He calleth his own sheep by name;' he doth, as it were, point to you when he speaks to men in your case and condition. Oh! consider, these are fair seasons of grace, and you must not let them slip: 2 Cor. vi. 1, 2, 'We beseech you that you receive not the grace of God in vain;' 'for I have heard thee in an acceptable time. Now is the accepted time, now is the day of salvation.' There are certain beautiful seasons wherein God will be found, when you see yourselves to be as it were pointed at. Look, as wicked men neglect seasons of conviction, so do believers many times dispute away seasons of grace, those that are in the way of faith. Poor lost creatures are apt to be suspicious; but when the offer of grace is full and express to your case, do not neglect it; as Benhadad's servants watched for the word 'brother,' so should you be asking for these gospel seasons. Jesus Christ will sometimes give a glimpse of his countenance, and look through the lattice.

5. Upon the act of faith consider your privileges, and humbly make your claim. Whenever you have taken Christ upon those seasonable offers, consider what a great privilege you enjoy: John v. 24, 'He that believeth in me hath everlasting life, and shall not come into condemnation, but is passed from death to life.' Christians are wanting in their improving their spiritual interest; they are willing to prize Christ, but do not consider what they have in him. If you cannot feel sensible consolation, yet act spiritual reason and discourse. Consider, such an act gives interest in Christ; why then should I not have Christ, and in Christ righteousness? Isa. xlv. 24: The church is brought in, speaking, 'Surely shall one say, In the Lord have I righteousness and strength, even to him shall men come.' This is glorying, or rejoicing in hope, Heb. iii. 6; that is, a reckoning upon our privilege, what we shall have and enjoy in Christ. Whosoever takes Christ, he puts him on; then he is interested and invested with all that is Christ's: Gal. iii. 27, 'As many of you as have been baptized into Christ, have put on Christ.' By the internal baptism we have an interest not only in his person, but in his righteousness, life, spirit, dignities, and merits;

it is good to ampliate our thoughts according to the extent of our privileges.

6. That your claim may be warranted the more, there must be a care of holiness. Works are not the condition of justification, yet they are the evidence of it. Faith justifies, and works justify: James ii. 24, 'Ye see then how that by works a man is justified, and not by faith only.' By the righteousness of faith we are acquitted from sin, and by the righteousness of works we are acquitted from guile and hypocrisy; therefore this is the evidence that will make all sure: 1 John iii. 21, 22, 'If our hearts condemn us not, then we have confidence towards God. And whatsoever we ask we receive of him, because we keep his commandments,' &c. This will increase the confidence of faith, when there is a train of graces. Though works have nothing to do in the court of heaven in matter of justification, yet they have a voice and testimony in the court of conscience. Seldom do we receive any solemn assurance but upon the evidence of sanctification. Faith gives us a title to Christ's righteousness, but works give an evidence of it. Our comfort indeed is founded upon Christ's righteousness and his satisfaction, but it is found in Christ's way; therefore consider how the promises are diversified: Mat. xi. 28, 'Come unto me,' saith Christ, 'all ye that labour and are heavy laden, and I will give you rest'; but then, ver. 29, 'Take my yoke upon you, and learn of me; for I am meek and lowly in heart: and you shall find rest for your souls.' The act of faith gives us an interest; but that we may have the comfort of it, we must abide under his discipline. This is God's course; first he pours in the oil of grace, then the oil of gladness, when our sanctification is evidenced unto us. The apostle gathereth it out of the type of Melchisedec: Heb. vii. 2, 'First being, by interpretation, king of righteousness, and after that also king of Salem; that is, king of peace.' First he sanctifieth and disposeth the heart to righteousness, then gives peace of conscience and comfort; that is the order, he reconcileth us to God by his own righteousness, and then gives peace in our souls by working our hearts to a holy disposition.

Use 2. To condemn them that seek righteousness in themselves. Nature is prone to this, and none more apt than those that have least reason. Former duties do not discover weakness, and so are more apt to puff up. Give me leave a little to speak of this; partly because it is so natural to us, and partly because many decry resting in duties so far, that they decry the very performance of them, and instead of Papists turn Familists. This resting in our own righteousness is sometimes more gross and open, when men make it their plea; sometimes more secret and imperceptible; we may discover it by observing the disposition of the soul with reference to sins, mercies, duties, and comforts.

1. By observing the frame of the heart with reference to sin. Usually when men rest in duties, they make the performance of them to be the ground of an indulgence to sin, and take the more liberty to sin, out of a hope to make amends by their duties.

[1.] This indulgence is sometimes antedated before the performance, as when men allow themselves in present carnal practices by the purpose of an after-repentance. It is as if men should distemper the body by excess, and then think to mend all by giving themselves a vomit; or contract a sickness by drunkenness, hoping to cure all by physic.

Tunc demum a peccatis desistam, cum baptizatus ero. Conviction
would not let men sin so freely if they did not make fair promises of
reformation : this is making a Christ of your repentance and prayers.
So some men moil in the world, and dream of a devout retirement
hereafter ; thus rich they will be, and then they will live privately,
and mind religion.

[2.] Sometimes the indulgence is post-dated, which is most grossly
done by them that perform duties with an aim either to excuse or to
promote sin : Prov. xxi. 27, ' The sacrifice of the wicked is abomination : how much more when he bringeth it with a wicked mind ? ' as
Balaam's altars were built, and sacrifices made with this intent, that
he might curse Israel, Num. xxiii. ; or more closely, by others who
would redeem their negligence in one duty by the frequent performance of another, and please God by what doth not displease themselves ;
as the Jews hoped to repair their want of mercy by the multitude of
their sacrifices. The Pharisees tithed mint and cummin to excuse
themselves from the weighty things of the law, Mat. xxiii. 23. Conscience, like the stomach, will be craving ; and a man must do something
to keep it quiet, as by a moral course, or some formal acts of piety.
By others it is done yet more closely, that grow vain and wanton after
some solemn duty : Ezek. xxxiii. 13, ' If he trust to his own righteousness, and commit iniquity,' &c. Many times we find that the heart
groweth loose, licentious, vain, wanton, and proud after solemn duties,
which argueth a secret confidence in what we have done ; thus Josiah's
breach with God was ' after his preparing the temple,' 2 Chron. xxxv. 20.

2. With respect to mercies ; and so observe the frame of your hearts
in the want of mercies, or in the enjoyment of them.

[1.] In the want of mercies. Men expect blessings out of a conceit
of some worth that is in themselves, and ascribe too much to their own
duties. We all disclaim it ; but it may be known by this, if we
murmur when God doth not come in at our times and seasons. Those
that prescribe to God do ascribe to themselves : Isa. lviii. 3, ' Wherefore have we fasted, say they, and thou seest not ? wherefore have
we afflicted our soul, and thou takest no knowledge ? ' Luke
xviii. 11, 12, ' I am not as other men are, extortioners, unjust, adulterers,
or even as this publican : I fast twice in a week, I give tithes of all
that I possess.' Because we do not break out into such bold challenges,
we think ourselves innocent ; but murmuring argueth some thought of
desert. Where nothing is due, we cannot complain if nothing be given.
The plea of works may be plainly read in our discontents ; if God be
not a debtor, why do we then complain ?

[2.] In the enjoyment of mercies, men secretly ascribe to themselves,
as if God did see more in them than others : Deut. ix. 4, ' Speak not
in thy heart, after that the Lord thy God hath cast them out from
before thee, saying, For my righteousness the Lord hath brought me in
to possess this land.' It rather manifests itself in thoughts than words.
Now because these thoughts are not always impressed on conscience,
men evade it ; but here you will discern it again by some disdain at
providence. Spiritual pride, or conceit of our own worth, entertaineth
crosses with anger, and blessings with disdain ; discontent or disdain
will discover it to you : Mal. i. 2, ' I have loved you, saith the Lord :
yet ye say, Wherein hast thou loved us ? ' By a gracious, humble

heart all mercies are received with admiration. Where sin is great nothing can be little, nothing is theirs but sin; therefore they wonder that anything should be theirs but punishment: Luke. i. 43, 'And whence is this to me, that the mother of my Lord should come to me?' so 2 Sam. vii. 18, 'Who am I, O Lord God? and what is my house, that thou hast brought me hitherto?' Not, Wherefore have we fasted? but whence is it? and what am I that God should do thus and thus for me? Do but compare Mat. vii. 22, 'Many will say to me in that day, Lord, Lord, have we not prophesied in thy name? and in thy name have cast out devils? and in thy name done many wonderful works?'—they plead their gifts and employments in the church—with Mat. xxv. 38, 39, 'Lord, when saw we thee an hungered, and fed thee? or thirsty, and gave thee drink? when saw we thee a stranger, and took thee in? or naked, and clothed thee? or when saw we thee sick, or in prison, and came unto thee?' The one wonder God should reject them, who had done him so much service; the other wonder Christ should take notice of such worthless services, though none perform duties with more care, none overlook them with more self-denial.

3. With respect to duties. Here also are two notes.

[1.] When men are not actually sensible of their own weakness, unprofitableness, and defects in duties. Men set a high value on their actions, and therefore reckon of the merit of them. The elder brother pleaded: Luke xv. 29, 'Lo, these many years do I serve thee; neither at any time transgressed I thy commandment.' We rest upon that of which we are conceited. Formal men have least cause, and yet are most apt, to rest in duties, because they go on in a dead course, without feeling their defects, or being sensible of their needing the supplies of the Spirit; as painted fire needeth no fuel. But the children of God perform them with more feeling of their own weakness and wretchedness; and so their hearts are kept humble and thankful, both which check merit. Thankful: 1 Chron. xxix. 14, 'Of thine own have we given thee.' Humble, for there may be a show of thankfulness, and yet the heart may be conceited: Luke xviii. 11, 'God, I thank thee I am not as other men are;' but 'all our righteousnesses are as filthy rags,' Isa. lxiv. 6. Now we must have actual distinct thoughts of this, or else it is impossible that such a proud creature as man should go out of himself. Christ requireth it in every duty: Luke xvii. 10, 'When ye shall have done all those things that are commanded you, say, We are unprofitable servants;' therefore you do not discern this secret vein of guilt by gross thoughts of merit, but by high thoughts of duty. When a man is not always sensible of the imperfections of his services, he is apt to build upon them. How do you come off from duty? You have more cause to be humble than to be lifted up; for what is God's be thankful, for what is your own be humbled, and pray, God be merciful to me!

[2.] When men are more careful of the work wrought than of the interest of the person; when we would have the person accepted for the work's sake rather than for Christ's sake, they lay the foundation of their comfort within themselves. Now this is not only by common people, who hope to be accepted for their prayers and their good meanings, but in those that are careless to get an interest in Christ: James

v. 16, 'The effectual fervent prayer of a righteous man availeth much. Most men look to the qualification of the duty, not of the person; but the person must be righteous, as well as the prayer fervent. It is not duty that worketh out your atonement with God; our acceptation with God doth not depend upon the worth and merit of works. Do not think duties will serve the turn: 2 Cor. xiii. 5, 'Know ye not your own selves, how that Christ is in you, except ye be reprobates?' The word ἀδόκιμοι, reprobate, is there taken in a mollified sense for those that are not in Christ; and therefore, before duties, your great care should be not only to raise the heart, but to examine the state.

4. With respect to peace and comfort, take these notes.

[1.] If you were never driven to change your copy and tenure. All Adam's posterity is under a covenant of works, and seek to be saved by doing. Those that never saw they rested in works, and were never driven to settle their comfort upon gospel terms, are in a dangerous case. The voice of nature is, What shall we do? and till we are frighted out of ourselves we never look farther. When the Israelites heard the thunderings, they were affrighted. Nature is put to flight: Heb. vi. 18, 'Who have fled for refuge to lay hold upon the hope set before us;' Phil. iii. 9, 'And be found in him, not having mine own righteousness, which is of the law, but that which is through the faith of Christ, the righteousness which is of God by faith;' Gal. ii. 19, 'For I through the law am dead to the law, that I might live to God.' A man goes not to chancery till he is cast at common law.

[2.] When conscience is awakened, if men fetch their comfort from their duties. The law leaveth men wounded and raw, and they lick themselves whole again by some offers of obedience. Carnal men are careful of worship only upon some gripes; they use their duties as men do strong waters in a pang; duties should be a thank-offering, and they make them a sin-offering—a sleeping sop to allay conscience. As when men have offended their superiors for a while they become more pliant and obsequious. It is good in gripes of conscience to observe whence you fetch your comfort, and how it groweth upon you; the trial is most sensible: Ps. xciv. 19, 'In the multitude of my thoughts within me thy comforts delight my soul.' Though every child of God hath not peace of conscience, yet it would much undeceive our hearts if we did observe how we come to be satisfied with our estate, and from whence that peace which we have doth arise.

[3.] Upon what terms do you constantly maintain your life and peace with God; upon the foundation of works, or through the merits of Christ? I confess works are a good encouragement, by way of evidence and assurance; but still the foundation must be Christ: 1 Cor. iii. 11, 'For other foundation can no man lay than that which is laid, which is Jesus Christ.' The believing soul will never be diverted and taken off from Christ, but will still cry, What would become of me were it not for free grace? Neh. ix. 31, 'Nevertheless, for thy great mercies' sake thou didst not utterly consume them and forsake them, for thou art a gracious and merciful God;' 1 Cor. iv. 4, 'For I know nothing by myself, yet am I not thereby justified; but he that judgeth me is the Lord.' Christ must still lie as a bundle of myrrh with us: Cant. i.

13, 'A bundle of myrrh is my well-beloved unto me; he shall lie all night betwixt my breasts.'

Use 3. Information; to direct us how to understand this great truth. For your better information, and because I will not perplex these discourses with disputes, I shall lay down several propositions; take them all together—

1. That to justify is to account or accept as righteous.

2. None are accounted or accepted as righteous but those that indeed are so.

3. Every righteousness will not serve the turn, but such as will satisfy God's justice.

4. God's justice will never be satisfied till the law be satisfied.

5. The law will never be satisfied but by active and passive obedience.

6. This satisfaction is only to be had in Christ.

7. There is no having this righteousness in Christ but by imputation.

8. There is no imputation but by union.

9. There is no union but by faith.

[1.] To justify is not to make righteous, but to account or accept as righteous. This is the use and force of the word in scripture: Rom. ii. 13, 'Not the hearers of the law are just before God, but the doers of the law shall be justified.' It cannot be taken for the infusion of righteousness, because the doers of the law are therefore righteous in themselves because they do the law; but the meaning is, are accounted just. It is opposed to condemnation and accusation, therefore it must be taken for accounting righteous; as Rom. viii. 33, 'Who shall lay anything to the charge of God's elect? It is God that justifieth, who is he that condemneth?' That which is opposed to accusation is justification; and that it is meant of an accepting in court is clear by Ps. cxliii. 2, 'Enter not into judgment with thy servant, O Lord, for in thy sight no man living shall be justified;' that is, in thy righteous and strict judgment none can be accepted as righteous.

[2.] None is accounted righteous before God but he that indeed is so; for otherwise the rule standeth good: Exodus xxxiv. 7, 'He will by no means clear the guilty.' It is part of God's name that he proclaimed before Moses: it must be such a righteousness as will endure God's sight; so that when God casts his eye upon it, he cannot choose but account you righteous, which cannot be by a fiction or an imaginary righteousness—'For the judgment of God is according to truth,' Rom. ii. 2, be it in mercy or in judgment. And it is a thing God hates in man: Prov. xvii. 15, 'To condemn the just, and justify the wicked, are both an abomination to the Lord.' Therefore there must be such a righteousness as, God looking upon it, he must needs account you righteous.

[3.] Every righteousness will not serve the turn, but such only as will satisfy God's justice, because by the work of redemption the Lord is to suffer no loss; the repute of his justice is still to be kept up, otherwise the notions of the deity would be violated. In the work of redemption he is not unrighteous; therefore the apostle is very zealous: Rom. iii. 4, 'Yea, let God be true, and every man a liar; as it is written, That thou mightest be justified in thy sayings and mightest overcome when thou art judged,' &c; God is necessarily just as well as necessarily merciful. Now both attributes must shine with equal glory. If he did altogether spare, where were his justice? and if he did accept men upon ordinary terms, and did altogether save, where were his mercy? God's infinite wisdom hath determined the controversy, and the apostle gives us an account of it: Rom. iii. 24, 25, 'Him hath God set forth to be a propitiation through faith in his blood, to declare his righteousness for the remission of sins;' and it is again repeated—'To declare, I say, at this time, his righteousness, that he may be just, and the justifier of him that believeth in Jesus.' God would not only glorify grace, but he would be just in justification; therefore, 1 John i. 9, 'If we confess our sins, he is faithful and just to forgive us our sins, and to cleanse us from all unrighteousness;' and again, chap. ii. 1, 'We have an advocate with the Father, even Jesus Christ the righteous.' God would not forgive sins, but so as that it might stand with his justice; for mercy and justice are to shine with an equal glory.

[4.] God's justice can never be satisfied till the law be satisfied. Why? because it is the outward rule of his justice, and the visible measure of his dealing with man; and therefore the satisfaction of his justice must be carried on according to the tenor and terms of the law; therefore was Christ made under the law. Now this was the great controversy how to salve the authority, power, and worth of the law. Christ professeth he came to fulfil it: Mat. v. 17, 18, 'Think not that I am come to destroy the law or the prophets: I am not come to destroy, but to fulfil,' &c. And the apostle shows plainly the doctrine of justification doth not make void the law: Rom. iii. 31, 'Do we then make void the law through faith? God forbid: yea, we establish the law;' therefore legal and gospel righteousness differ, because the one is not inherent in us, the other is; and in the manner of receiving it.

[5.] The law can never be satisfied, as for fallen man, but by an active and passive obedience—that is, by suffering what is imposed, or by doing what is commanded by the law; for in the law there were two things, the precept and the sanction, the duty and the penalty. The law doth not only say, Do, and live; but, Sin, and die. To Adam it was proposed in the primitive form, Gen. ii. 17. Now the law must be fulfilled in the threatening and precept, that there may be a freedom from the curse, and a right to eternal life. And indeed Jesus Christ, by being made under the law, by sustaining the penalty and performing the obedience of it, hath done both: 1 Thes. i. 10, there is one part—'Even Jesus, who delivered us from the wrath to come;' and Ephes. i. 6, there is the other part—'We are accepted in the beloved.' God freeth none from hell but those Christ suffered for; and accepts none to life but those Christ hath performed obedience for.

[6.] This satisfaction can be performed by none but Jesus Christ; for, alas! we could neither bear the penalty nor discharge the duty; —not bear the penalty, for we should have always been satisfying, always paying, but never could be said to have satisfied; and we could never discharge the duty of it, for the law is 'become weak through the flesh,' Rom. viii. 3; that is, as the case stands now with man fallen. Those works that need pardon themselves can never satisfy': Acts iv. 12,

'Neither is there salvation in any other, for there is none other name under heaven given among men whereby we must be saved.'

[7.] There is no having of this righteousness from Christ but by imputation. I know here some boggle and say, Imputation is nowhere found in scripture. I answer, We do not stand upon words and syllables; but this is most proper, and it may be well gathered, for Christ is said 'to be made righteousness,' 1 Cor. i. 30; righteousness is said 'to be imputed without works,' Rom. iv. 6; and 'faith is imputed for righteousness,' Rom. iv. 22. To clear the proposition, it must needs be by imputation—(1.) Because this righteousness must be *in justificato*, in the justified person. This righteousness, one way or other, must belong to the person justified, otherwise the Lord cannot look upon us as righteous. The man was cast out 'that had not on him the wedding garment,' Mat. xxii. 11–13. Now by infusion it cannot be, all inherent righteousness being imperfect; therefore it must be by imputation. (2.) Consider what imputation is. To impute is to reckon a thing to our score and account; and those things are said to be imputed to us which are accounted ours to all intents and purposes, as if they were our own. Now in this sense our sins were imputed to Christ, and Christ's righteousness is imputed to us. The apostle makes the parallel: 2 Cor. v. 21, 'For he hath made him to be sin for us, who knew no sin; that we might be made the righteousness of God in him.' Look, as Christ was so dealt with as if he had been a sinner, so we are as if we were righteous. Our iniquities were not infused into Christ, but imputed and laid upon him: Isa. liii. 6, 'The Lord hath laid on him the iniquity of us all;' so is his righteousness upon all them that believe. And the apostle useth another comparison; as Adam's guilt is laid upon us, so is Christ's righteousness;—'As by one man's disobedience many were made sinners; so by the obedience of one shall many be made righteous,' Rom. v. 19. In short, the apostle saith, 1 Cor. i. 30, that Christ is 'made unto us of God righteousness;' and the whole righteousness is imputed to satisfy the obligation of the law, and to repair Adam's loss; for we were guilty of death, and we came short of glory: Gal. iv. 4–6. 'When the fulness of time was come, God sent forth his Son, made of a woman, made under the law,' &c.

[8.] There is no imputation but by union. All interest is founded in union: Gal. iii. 27, 'As many of you as have been baptized into Christ have put on Christ;' all his merits and satisfaction are theirs, as if performed in their own persons: 1 Cor. i. 30, 'Of him are ye in Christ Jesus, who of God is made unto us wisdom, and righteousness, and sanctification, and redemption.' We are interested in all, as we are in him; by being one with Christ we put him on.

[9.] There is no union but by faith; then God receives us into grace: Rom. x. 10, 'With the heart man believeth unto righteousness.' It is the ordination of God that this grace should unite us to Christ, and so give us a right to all that is in Christ; indeed it is the fittest grace to receive the fruits of union. I confess there is a moral union by love that gives comfort; but faith begins the mystical union, and so gives safety.

SERMON XIX.

By which he obtained witness that he was righteous, God testifying of his gifts—HEB. xi. 4.

Now I come to the second doctrine. *Δι' ἧς,* 'by which' may be referred to *θυσία* or *πίστις* ; and I referred the righteousness to faith, and the testimony to the sacrifice. For the clearing of which you may remember, I observed that in this duty of sacrifice the two brethren did appeal to God, and put it to trial, whom the Lord would choose and design to be head of the blessed seed and race ; and the Lord by fire from heaven, which was the then visible testimony of acceptance, determined the matter on Abel's side ; besides, the apostle proveth that the solemn testimony of his righteousness was first given to him by God's witnessing of his gifts. Whence I observe—

Doct. 2. That upon the raised operations of faith with other graces in solemn duties, we usually receive the testimony of righteousness in Christ, or acceptance with God.

Abel's testimony was extraordinary, by fire from heaven ; but still God is not wanting to witness concerning the services of his people: all is not left in the dark, and to the decision and revelation of the last day. Instead of those outward dispensations, we now receive an inward testimony of the Spirit, and upon the exercise of grace God giveth us this testimony. Now there are two special seasons of the exercise of grace on our part, and so of the manifestations of comfort on God's part ; there is the season of afflictions and the season of duties ; and in both God's people receive from him the solemn witness and seal of the Holy Ghost. In afflictions when we need comfort, and in duties when we seek comfort, we have the sweetest experiences of the testimony of the Spirit. Upon afflictions, you have it set down : Heb. xii. 11, ' Afterward it yieldeth the peaceable fruit of righteousness unto them that are exercised thereby.' The sweet and last fruit and issue of it is peace of conscience ; so Rom. v. 3–5, ' Tribulation worketh patience, and patience experience, and experience hope, and hope maketh not ashamed ;' upon what ground ? ' Because the love of God is shed abroad in our hearts by the Holy Ghost.' Affliction puts us upon the exercise of grace, and the exercise of grace occasioneth sweet experiences of God in our souls, by which hope is more and more kindled ; and this is ratified by the confirmation of the Spirit.

But we are to speak of experiences in solemn duties, wherein God is wont to open himself to his people, and all jealousies and misunderstandings between him and his servants are cleared up ; and there he breaks in upon them sensibly for the furtherance of their joy.

I shall prove this is God's wonted course—(1.) By the experiences of the saints ; (2.) By the promises of God ; (3.) By several arguments and reasons.

1. By the experiences of the saints. When the scriptures were written, God's ways were extraordinary, and therefore most of the instances are extraordinary ; but however, we do not urge the manner, but the thing itself. The leading instance shall be that of Joshua the

high priest. When he was ministering before the Lord, it is said, Zech. iii. 3, 4, ' Joshua was clothed with filthy garments, and stood before the angel ; and he answered, and spake unto those that stood before him, saying, Take away the filthy garments from him ;' and God gave this testimony to him, ' I have caused thine iniquity to pass from thee, and I will clothe thee with change of raiment.' I know that visional type doth mainly respect the restoration of the church of the Jews, the church of the Jews being represented in Joshua, who was the chief-officer of the church ; however, there is something moral in it. In the time of his ministration his filthy garments were taken away, which is the usual emblem of sin in scripture, and change of raiment is put on him, which is an emblem of the righteousness of Christ applied and put on by faith, as it is explained by the Spirit of God himself. So Cornelius, Acts x. 3, it is said an angel came about the ninth hour to assure him God had taken notice of his graces and duties : ver. 4, ' Thy prayers and thine alms are come up for a memorial before God.' Note the circumstance of ' the ninth hour,' which was one of the hours of prayer : Acts iii. 1, ' Peter and John went up together into the temple at the hour of prayer, being the ninth hour,' which this proselyte observes ; and therefore about the ninth hour, in the middle of his prayers and devotions, an angel comes to him and assures him what acceptance he had found. So the prophet Daniel : chap. ix. 20, 21, ' And while I was speaking, and praying, and confessing my sin,' &c.; ' yea, whilst I was speaking in prayer, the angel Gabriel, whom I had seen in the vision at the beginning, being caused to fly swiftly, touched me about the time of the evening-oblation.' The Spirit of God placeth a great deal of emphasis upon this circumstance. At the very instant of prayer, when he was earnestly pleading with God, God answers his request, and an angel is despatched to come and certify to him his acceptance ; God overtakes his duty by a speedy return of mercy. That way of assurance is extraordinary ; but God's wonted course is many times to give in a solemn assurance of his favour in the very time of our prayers; so Acts iv. 31, ' When they had prayed, the place was shaken where they were assembled together, and they were all filled with the Holy Ghost.' Mark, in the very time and act of their prayer there is a miraculous descent of the Holy Ghost upon them ; the instances are singular and extraordinary, yet there is some analogy and proportion between them and ordinary cases. Though God's dispensations be now more spiritual, yet they are very sensible still ; though we cannot expect voices, raptures, shakings, oracles, and angels, yet we may expect to hear the trumpet of the assemblies, which the psalmist expresses by the ' joyful sound,' Ps. lxxxix. 15 ; that is, the testimony of the Holy Ghost and spiritual experiences, as will appear more fully by the next head.

2. By the promises of God. God hath promised to meet his people with sensible comforts, to talk and confer with them in their duties ; the very aim of all duties is more immediate communion with God. See God's promises to his old church, while grace was more sparingly dispensed : Exod. xxix. 42, ' At the door of the tabernacle of the congregation, there will I meet with you, and speak there unto you.' It is meant of God's gracious and social presence with his people in duties

of worship; there he will meet, and speak, and confer with them for
their comfort and satisfaction : Isa. lviii. 9, ' Thou shalt call, and the
Lord shall answer ; thou shalt cry, and he shall say, Here am I.' Mark,
when complaints are heightened into cries, then God's answer will be
more sensible ; when we come in an affectionate manner, not only call,
but cry. Sometimes God plainly discovereth himself in the very time
of the duty ; he meets with them in such and such ordinances, as if he
should say, Poor soul, what would you have ? here am I to satisfy thee.
He communeth, talketh with them, and tells them their sins are pardoned, and they are accepted in Christ : Ps. xxxvi. 7–9, 'Thou shalt
abundantly satisfy them with the fatness of thine house, and make
them to drink of the rivers of thy pleasures ; ' there comforts are dispensed, there flow the rivers of spiritual pleasure and chaste delights
of the gospel.

Obj. But you will say, This is not always so ; there are many wait
upon God long, and feel no comfort. I answer, It is true. Such dispensations are free, they are not at the creature's beck : God will be
master of his own mercies ; we have deserved nothing, and we cannot
murmur if we receive nothing ; yet if ever they find spiritual consolation, it will be in God's house. This is the established means ; if ever
you taste the fatness and sweetness of grace, it will be by waiting upon
him there. Earnest and affectionate duties are seldom without comfort
and profit. And again I answer, that delight, which is a duty, makes
way for delight which is a dispensation : Cant. ii. 3, ' I sat down under
his shadow with great delight, and his fruit was sweet to my taste.'
When you delight in God, then the Lord will give in sensible consolation. Delights are mutual and sensible ; God delights in us, and we
in God. When we delight in him, in the word, in prayer, or in the
supper, by way of return God sends us secret consolation : Isa. lxiv. 5,
' Thou meetest him that rejoiceth, and worketh righteousness, those that
remember thee in thy ways.' Those that delight in God's company, that
do good with a willing heart, are bountifully entertained, sweetly
refreshed, and sent away with a feast of loves. In our affectionate and
spiritual duties, Christ will come and say, ' Well done, good and faithful
servant, enter into thy master's joy ! ' The present returns and recompenses, when we come before the throne of grace, carry some proportion
with the entertainment we shall find with God hereafter when we come
to be seated upon the throne of glory. I say, in earnest prayer, though
we can prescribe nothing, but this is his wonted course, his answer is
sensible in his ordinances. Saith Luther, *Utinam eodem ardore*, &c.—
Would to God that I could always pray with the like fervency and
earnestness ! Why ? for I sensibly receive this answer, Thy desires are
granted, *Fiat quod velis*—Be it unto thee as thou wilt. When we rejoice
to converse with God in the ways of righteousness, then his dispensations of grace are full of sweetness.

3. The reasons why God observeth this course ; to exhibit and give
out more sensible manifestations of his grace in the time of ordinances,
when our graces are raised and drawn out to the height. The question
consisteth of two parts.

[1.] Why grace or sanctification is necessary to the receiving of the
testimony of the Spirit ?

[2.] Why upon the raised operations of grace God is wont to give it into his people?

First, Why grace is necessary by way of evidence, though not by way of merit and cause?

Ans. 1. Because this is the most sensible effect of God's spiritual bounty, for it is a work of God within us, and so more apt to give us an evidence. Election, that is in heaven, a secret which lies hid in the bosom of the Father; redemption, that is without us, upon the cross; justification is God's judiciary act, a sentence of the judge without us; but sanctification is a work upon our heart, therefore it is called the 'earnest of the Spirit,' 2 Cor. i. 22, and 'the first-fruits of the Spirit,' Rom. viii. 23. Grace is an earnest to show how sure, and the first-fruits to show how good heaven is; by grace God gives us a taste to show how sweet, and a pledge to show how sure all the privileges of christianity are made over to our souls.

2. Because it is the best way to prevent delusion; immediate revelation would be more uncertain and liable to suspicion, and we may lie down in sorrow, notwithstanding flashes of comfort. There is no way to discern the operation of the Spirit from counterfeit ravishments, but by sanctification and grace. There is a great deal of deceit in flashy joys, but this is a solid witness and evidence: 1 John iii. 19, 'Hereby we know that we are of the truth, and shall assure our hearts before him;' that is, without fear of presumption and hypocrisy, we may come and plead our interest before God. Acts of comfort are sweet and delightful when felt, but yet are but transient acts; they soon pass away, they come and go, they are acts of God's royalty and magnificence, and you know every day is not a feast-day, God doth not always feast us with sensible consolation; but grace is a solid and abiding evidence: 1 John ii. 27, 'The anointing which ye have received of him abideth in you;' and 1 John iii. 8, 'His seed remaineth in him.' Lively acts of joy and comfort are but like those motions of the Spirit upon Samson; it is said the Spirit came upon him 'at times,' Judges xiii. 25, heightening of his strength and courage; so these come upon us but at times. Therefore standing evidences which are drawn from grace are far more certain than sensible consolation.

3. Because the Spirit's witness is seldom single, but given in conjunction with water and blood: 1 John v. 8, 'There are three that bear witness in earth, the Spirit, and the water, and the blood;' not only the blood of Christ, which witnesseth their redemption, but the water of sanctification, which witnesseth their interest in that redemption; and then the Spirit comes and seals it in the heart of a believer. The Spirit's testimony is made to be subsequent, and follows the testimony of our renewed conscience, Rom. viii. 16; for the Spirit's witness is nothing but his owning of grace in the heart, which is his own impress and seal, and assuring the soul. This is a stamp and fruit of mine; it is the ratifying of his own work to believers.

4. Because grace giveth most clearness, calmness, and serenity of mind, so that we are most able to judge of those experiences. Wherever there is purity, there is a witness, for it brings in light and comfort into the soul. Lusts are the clouds of the mind, which darken the judgment and distress the conscience; and therefore the apostle saith,

2 Peter i. 9, that when men neglect to grow in grace, 'they are blind, and cannot see afar off;' they have no spiritual discerning, and are not able to judge of spiritual matters. An impure soul is always in the dark, full of doubts and fears; certainly the more grace, the more confidence, for there is more clearness of discerning. Guilt begets a servile fear and awe. Shame and fear entered into the world with sin; it weakens confidence. Compare Gen. ii. 25, with Gen. iii. 10; in the former place it is said, 'The man and the woman were both naked, and were not ashamed;' why? because they were in a state of innocency; but in the other place, 'I was afraid, because I was naked.' As soon as sin came into the world there was fear upon the conscience of the guilty creature.

5. Because of the inseparable connection, that is, by the ordination and appointment of God, between grace and comfort: Eph. i 13, 'In whom, after that ye believed, ye were sealed with that Holy Spirit of promise.' In the original it is, τῷ πνεύματι τῆς ἐπαγγελίας τῷ ἁγίῳ —Ye were sealed by the Spirit, the Holy Spirit, the Spirit of promise. There are three articles; he seals as the Spirit of God, and as the Holy Spirit; he will not seal to a blank, but where there is holiness and grace wrought in the heart. The apostle proves this is the method of God out of the names of Melchisedec: Heb. vii. 2, 'First being by interpretation king of righteousness, and after that also king of Salem; that is, king of peace.' First he bestows grace, and then gladness; first he disposeth the heart to righteousness, then works peace in the soul: Ps. cxix. 165, 'Great peace have they that love thy law;' they maintain and keep their comfort without interruption. Acts ix. 31, there is such another connection—'The churches walked in the fear of the Lord, and in the comfort of the Holy Ghost:'—the more grace, the greater comfort and satisfaction. This is the way which God hath appointed.

Secondly, Why these graces must be exercised in holy duties.

1. Because thereby God would endear duty to the creature, by making it the means of comfort. This is the best course to maintain the traffic and commerce that is between God and the creature. Look, as there is commerce between two distant places by trading, so between us and heaven, by exchange of duties and comforts; our prayers come up before him, God's blessings come down to us. Who can expect gold from the Indies, but those that trade there in ships? Who can expect these rich dispensations of God, but those that trade with him in holy service? It is true, every time we bring our wares to God we do not make such a good market, because God rather gives than sells, and he gives at pleasure, though usually there is some defect in us, but this is God's established course. Or look, as the earth and the air maintain a commerce one with another: the sea and land send up vapours and exhalations into the air, and the air sends down sweet showers and sweet dews for the refreshing of the earth; unless the earth sendeth up vapours, the air sendeth down nothing; and so, unless we come and converse with God in holy duties, there are no dews and refreshments that come down from above for the watering of a parched heart; and without the religious ascent of prayers and graces we have no influences from heaven. This is God's established order.

2. Because when our graces are exercised, then there is most rational likelihood that we shall receive this testimony from God. Consider it with respect to either witness that must concur to the settling your peace : for look, as under the law everything was to be established in the mouth of two or three witnesses, so it is in the great matters of our peace likewise. There is the Spirit and the renewed conscience, by which our peace is established ; and if we consider either, we shall find we are most likely to receive this testimony when grace is exercised. Look upon it—

[1.] On the Spirit's part. Those raised operations of grace are the special fruits of the Holy Ghost ; he not only works grace at first, but he gives actual help for the exercising of it ; and therefore when he hath moved and stirred us most, he is most like to seal. It is the constant method of the Spirit first to work grace, and then to seal it ; the more conspicuous the work, the more of this sealing may we expect.

[2.] It is more rational upon our part ; for the more our graces are exercised, the more they are in view of conscience. Grace exercised and drawn out into action is more apparent and sensible to the soul ; acts are more liable to feeling than habits. Fire in a flint is neither seen nor felt, but when knocked against a steel, then you may discern it ; so when we draw out that which lies hid in the soul, then conscience can take the more notice of it. Roots under ground in winter are not observed till they shoot forth in the spring ; the stream is seen when the fountain is hid ; the apples, leaves, blossoms, and buds are visible when the life and the sap is not seen ; so acts are taken notice of by conscience when useless habits lie out of sight ; or if they be drawn out by imperfect operations, when our motions are faint and weak, they are like the waters of Siloah that run slowly—a man can hardly discern whether it be living water or a standing pool. No wonder our comfort is so weak, when sanctification runs so slow, and is scarce to be discerned. By experience we find that raised operations bring comfort and peace with them ; we feel a great calmness and serenity in our consciences after some solemn duty, because conscience can sweetly reflect upon the exercises of grace, and quiet itself with the discharge of its own duty ; then there is a peace and contentment within the soul.

3. I prove it by the rule of proportion. Look, as great sins destroy our comfort, so also the raised exercise of graces in duty increase our comfort. Scandalous sins, like a blot upon our evidences, do obscure them, waste conscience, and eclipse our comfort ; and when we return to folly, we smart for it : Ps. lxxxv. 8, ' The Lord will speak peace to his people ; but let them not return to folly,' implying they hazard all their comfort when they give way to great corruptions : so on the contrary side, when we exercise our graces, they administer comfort. All that can be objected against this is, that there is no merit in duties as there is in sins ; but though duty do not merit comfort, yet it is the measure of it, for hereby the heart is prepared for peace, and usually according to the preparation of the heart ; so God comes in with the supplies of comfort : Ps. x. 17, ' Thou wilt prepare their heart, thou wilt cause thine ear to hear.' When the heart is mightily drawn out in duty, answerable

are the returns of God's grace. Vessels thus prepared are of a larger size, and can receive more of the bounty of God: Jer. xxix. 13, 'Ye shall seek me and find me, when ye shall search for me with all your heart.' God's answers of grace are according to the excitations of grace.

4. Because it is the best way to bring us to improve comfort. That which cometh from God and in God's way leadeth us again to God. There is nothing which raiseth the soul to such a degree of reverence and to such a wonder of grace as the experiences of duty do; then the heart is full of joy and the mouth full of praise, and God hath all the honour: these are the lasting experiences that both endear God and endear the ways of God to us. (1.) They endear God: Ps. cxvi. 1, 2, 'I will love the Lord, because he hath heard my voice and my supplication; because he hath inclined his ear unto me, therefore will I call upon him as long as I live.' (2.) They endear the ways of God to us. Comforts received in the way of duty come double to us: Ps. cxix. 93, 'I will never forget thy precepts, for by them thou hast quickened me;' I will never forget such a sermon and such an ordinance wherein I have received such quickenings and such sweet enlargements from the Lord. The myrrh which Christ had left upon the handle of the lock made the spouse more earnest after Christ. What made David pant after God? the sweet experiences of duty: Ps. lxiii. 2, 'To see thy power and thy glory, so as I have seen thee in the sanctuary.' Look, as when the springs are low, a little water cast into a pump brings up a great deal more; so when God hath cast a few experiences into the soul, it breeds more affection, more love, and more joy. Now it is no wonder vain spirits question duties when God never ministered comfort to them that way; they are full of satanical illusions and fanatic joys and conceits of comfort in the neglect of ordinances, but they never received the solid comfort of ordinances.

Use 1. It serves to inform us what little reason they have to complain of the want of comfort that are not diligent in the exercise of grace. Usually we lie upon the bed of ease, and expect God should drop comfort into us out of the clouds: 2 Peter i. 5, compared with ver. 10; 'Giving all diligence, add to your faith virtue,' &c; then ver. 10, 'Give all diligence to make your calling and election sure.' We must be much in the exercise of grace before ever the Lord gives us comfort. Whatever he may do for some out of the prerogative of free grace we cannot tell; yet usually after much waiting and diligence, we receive this testimony from God. We find the Israelites in the wilderness were fed with manna from heaven, but the standing rule is—'In the sweat of thy brow thou shalt eat thy bread,' Gen. iii. 19; 'And he that will not work, let him not eat,' 2 Thes. iii. 10. Comfort is the recompense of industry and the encouragement of faith and obedience. If we should gain assurance by neglecting the means, we should soon lose it again; the Spirit would not speak so clearly as before. Comfort is a free dispensation, but always given in the use of means. The clock runs upon its own wheels; however, there must be weights hung on, and we must draw them up at the appointed times. So God's dispensations run upon their own wheels; they are free, but they have their proper weights; and unless we pull up the weights by faith and prayer, the clock of mercy will stand still; certainly it will speak no comfort nor sound peace to our souls. A fond expectation it is to look for comfort, and yet to live in sin, or else content ourselves with the low and faint operations of grace. Alas! they that look for a full joy and yet walk in darkness, John will tell them plainly they lie, 1 John i. 6; and so men, distracted with the din and hurry of worldly cares and businesses, choke conscience, and so can never hear the voice of the Spirit. The children of God are to blame also; their sanctification is low; and scarce to be discerned, therefore no wonder their comfort is but low. Grace, if any way exercised, is seldom without a witness. Never expect comfort either in the neglect or decay of holiness; there will always be a doubting of the truth and a jarring between your consciences and desires.

Use 2. To press you to three things—to be much in duties, to draw out your graces to a high degree, and to observe your experiences.

1. To be much in duty. There are sweet comforts to be dispensed, there is marrow and fatness, and all you can desire; comforts that differ only from the joys of heaven in the degree and in the manner of fruition; rivers of pleasure that flow from God's house; therefore be frequent in holy duties. Solomon saith, Prov. xxvii. 18, 'He that keeps the fig-tree [shall eat the fruit thereof.' Certainly God is not a hard master; if you keep close to Christ in duty, you shall taste of the fruit thereof; but alas! otherwise, if you neglect duties of religion, where will you have comfort? He that is a stranger to God is and must necessarily be a stranger to the joys of the Spirit: Job xxii. 21, 'Acquaint now thyself with him, and be at peace.' Usually we have peace and satisfaction after long acquaintance and familiarity with God, but those that are seldom or cold and customary in duties can never expect any solid joy.

2. To draw out your graces to some raised and high degree—'Then thou shalt call, and the Lord shall answer; thou shalt cry, and he shall say, Here am I,' Isa lviii. 9. It will be sweet to hear Christ say, 'Well done, good and faithful servant.' Look into the sphere of nature or sphere of grace, all excellent things are obtained with difficulty, and they will cost us much labour and sweat; so will all ravishing sweet comforts cost us much pains in the duties of religion: Acts xxvi. 7, it is said, 'The twelve tribes served God instantly day and night.' In the original it is ἐν ἐκτενείᾳ, with the utmost of their strength, with their extended abilities. You should seek God, and raise your graces to a vigorous degree and height; then the Lord will come in: Jer. xxix. 13, 'You shall seek me and find me, when you shall search for me with all your hearts.' Alas! many vainly accuse mercy when they themselves are idle, and do not seek God with all their hearts.

3. To observe experiences. It is good to listen to the softer whispers and suggestions of the Holy Ghost. Still be looking for God's answer and God's return; as the psalmist saith, Ps. lxxxv. 8, 'I will hear what God the Lord will speak, for he will speak peace to his people.' Ah! hearken and wait still, when God will drop out a word of peace and comfort, that you may be able to know the purposes of his grace. If the oracle be silent, beg the more: Ps. lxxxvi. 17, 'Show me a token for good.' So go to God for some comfortable experiences of his grace, especially after great sins, deep distress, and strong desire:

Ps. li. 8, 'Make me to hear joy and gladness, that the bones that thou hast broken may rejoice;' his conscience was troubled, and he begs peace in his conscience.

Use 3. To put us on the trial, how shall we discern the testimony God giveth us in duties? I answer, Two ways: by impressions and by expressions, for God writeth and speaketh.

1. By impressions, which are left to be managed by our reason, and discourse. By impressions I mean two things—

[1.] Those gracious experiences we have of quickening enlargement and actual excitation in the duty; these are tokens for good: Ps. x. 17, 'Lord, thou hast heard the desire of the humble, thou wilt prepare their heart, thou wilt cause thine ear to hear.' Fire from heaven was the visible testimony of old; that which answers it now is fire in the affections; there is a communion with God in grace, though not in comfort; the motions of your hearts towards God are discovered by the enlargement of your desires; unutterable groans are a fruit of the Spirit's presence as well as unutterable joys; he is not only called 'the Comforter,' John xiv. 26, but 'the spirit of grace and supplication,' Zech. xii. 10.

[2.] The frame of the spirit after duty. Peace, as well as joy, is a fruit of the Holy Ghost: Rom. xiv. 17, 'The kingdom of God is not meat and drink, but righteousness, and peace, and joy in the Holy Ghost.' God giveth you a rest from the accusations from conscience, though not sensible consolations; as when a man cometh from a prince cheerful because of his hopes, though he hath not received an actual answer to his request. Suavities and joys are mere dispensations: 2 Cor. iii. 17, 'Where the Spirit of the Lord is, there is liberty.' Many of his children God keepeth in the lower way, and usually, though they have less of comfort, they have more of grace; there is an impression of confidence and support is given, though not ravishment. By conversing with God christians learn to rejoice in their hopes, though they have not enjoyment: Heb. iii. 6, 'Whose house are we if we hold fast the confidence and the rejoicing of the hope firm unto the end.' It is a great matter to have impressions of confidence and encouragement in waiting.

2. By expressions; when God doth, as it were, speak to us, and we are comfortably persuaded by the Spirit of God that we are accepted with him. Heretofore God spake to the ear audibly and by oracle: Gen. xv. 1, 'The word of the Lord came unto Abram in a vision, saying, Fear not, Abram,' &c; but now he speaks by his Spirit, not by voices and oracles; such things are the dotages of distempered persons. A voice there is: Psa. li. 8, 'Make me to hear joy and gladness,' &c.; David prayeth for it: Ps. xxxv. 3, 'Say unto my soul, I am thy salvation;' but this voice is inward and secret, not to our ears, but to our hearts: 1 John v. 10, 'He that believeth in the Son of God hath the witness in himself;' Rom. v. 5, 'The love of God is shed abroad in our hearts by the Holy Ghost, which is given unto us.' God speaks to us by our own thoughts, which may be discerned to be the voice of the Spirit by the certainty and sweetness of it. The Spirit's voice can hardly be discerned from the voice of renewed conscience, because it insinuateth itself with our discourse and reason: Rom. ix. 1, 'I speak the truth

in Christ, I lie not, my conscience also bearing me witness in the Holy Ghost.' It can only be distinguished by its certainty and overpowering light: Lam. iii. 24, ' The Lord is my portion, saith my soul ;' and the Spirit assureth us it is true. Now the Spirit's witness is sometimes more sensible, and accompanied with sweetness; but at all times certain, and accompanied with peace. The Spirit's witness concerning us must be understood with analogy to his witness concerning the word ; sometimes it is more high and sensible ; we cry, as the centurion, Mat. xxvii. 54, ' Truly this was the Son of God ;' it is he, and it can be no other. At other times there is a more temperate confidence ; so here conscience witnesseth we can be no other but the sons of God, and then it leaveth a marvellous sweetness upon the soul, and a reverence of grace. At other times confidence is more deliberate and temperate ; and though there be not such a lively sweetness and strong consolation, that is, the effect of solemn duties, raised meditation, fervent prayer, and the like, yet there is serenity and calmness of mind, which is the same which I called peace of conscience before, but only that it is not built upon future hopes, but a present interest.

Use 4. To direct us how we should behave ourselves with reference to this matter.

1. If God giveth sustentation and support, we must be contented, though we feel no sweetness and sensible consolation. For—

[1.] God is not a debtor, and may do with his own what he pleaseth in dispensations of comfort, as well as dispensations of grace : Phil. ii. 13, ' For it is God that worketh in you, both to will and to do of his good pleasure.' And—

[2.] We may want it without sin ; it is a preferment, and we must tarry till the master of the feast do bid us sit higher. We sin if they be despised : Job xv. 11, ' Are the consolations of God small with thee ?' not if they be enjoyed ; it is not the want of comfort, but the contempt of it that is culpable. Such things as are mere dispensations and proposed as rewards are different from duties. To want grace, though it be God's gift, is a sin, because the creature is under an obligation ; but not to want comfort, because that is merely given, not required.

2. When God speaketh comfort, you must hear ; you grieve the Spirit by resisting his witness, as well as his work. It is the duty of the creature to listen : Ps. lxxxv. 8, ' I will hear what God the Lord will speak; for he will speak peace unto his people and to his saints ;' it is irreverence and contempt when God speaketh, and we will not hear. A friend would take himself to be affronted at such a carriage ; if we are to wait, certainly we are to hearken. Now because persons of much fancy and great affection are wont to be full of scruples, and to underrate their own spiritual estate, and to suspect all that maketh for their comfort, let me tell you when comfort ought not to be suspected.

[1.] If it come in God's way, in duty, and upon the raised operations of grace, which note will distinguish it from delusions. Comforts and ravishments in the neglect of ordinances, as in fanatical persons, are always deceitful. God hath promised to talk with his people at the sanctuary door, and to meet them that remember him in his ways : Isa. lxiv. 5, ' Thou meetest him that rejoiceth, and worketh righteousness, those

that remember thee in thy ways.   And so it is also distinguished from
that confidence that is in ignorant persons, which is nothing but a blind
presumption, which would vanish if it did come to the light: John iii.
20, 'For every one that doeth evil hateth the light, neither cometh he
to the light, lest his deeds should be reproved.'   If in prayer or deep
meditation God giveth in strong consolation, never suspect it.

[2.] If it lead us to God.   Carnal security and presumption never
urgeth to thankfulness, nor to a rejoicing in God ; they do not taste the
sweetness of grace, and therefore have no reverence, no wonder at it :
1 Peter ii. 9, 'But ye are a chosen generation, a royal priesthood, an holy
nation, a peculiar people, that ye should show forth the praises of him
who hath called you out of darkness into his marvellous light.'   Fanatical joys put men upon pride, and a contempt of ordinances ; but in
solid joys the soul is filled with reverence as well as sweetness : Ps.
cxvi. 12, 'What shall I render unto the Lord for all his benefits towards
me ?'

SERMON XX.

*By which he obtained witness that he was righteous, God testifying of
his gifts.*—Heb. xi. 4.

Doct. 3. That only the works of persons who are righteous are accepted
with God.

It is clear from the apostle's argument—*He obtained witness that he
was righteous.*   Why?   *God testified of his gifts.*   If God accept of his
gift, he was a righteous person ; for God accepts the services of none
but those that are righteous.   First God accepts the person, and then
the performance ; so Gen. iv. 4, 'God had respect to Abel, and to his
offering ;' first to Abel, and then to his offering.   The person pleased
him in Christ, and then his sacrifice.   It is said, Judges xiii. 23, by
Manoah's wife to him, 'If the Lord were pleased to kill us, he would
not have received a burnt-offering, nor a meat-offering at our hands.'
She builds the acceptance of the person upon the acceptance of the
service ; for God accepts the gifts and offerings of none but those whose
persons please him in Christ.   So the Lord himself says, Mal. i. 10, 'I
have no pleasure in you,' no delight in their persons ; then it follows
presently, 'I will not accept of an offering at your hand.'   Before the
person pleaseth God, the work cannot, for these reasons—

1. Because this is the method of the covenant of grace, not to accept
the person for the work's sake, but to accept of the work for the person's
sake.   God doth not accept us for our prayers and good duties ; that
was the tenor of the first covenant, whereby our justification depended
upon the worth and value of our works.   It is not now, Do and live,
but, Believe and live ; it is not according to the work that we are accepted,
but according to our interest in Christ, Eph. i. 6, 'He hath made us
accepted in the beloved.'   Alas ! when a man is out of Christ, it is not

enough for him to do his best; the law is not relaxed; it requires duty without abatement, or else it enforceth punishment without any mitigation. Do and live, sin and die. It doth not accept of our prayers, our tears, and our best, for the least failing renders us guilty of transgressing the whole law; so that, upon that supposition, 'if it were possible to keep the whole law, and offend in one point, he is guilty of all,' James ii. 10. That rule brooks no exception, until we change our copy; till we be in Christ, one failing is enough to provoke God's displeasure. If a natural man could be supposed to keep the whole law and break but in one point, he is undone.

2. Because otherwise our duties receive defilement from our persons; like precious liquor in a tainted and unsavoury vessel, or like that jewel put into a dead man's mouth, that loseth all its virtue: Prov. xxi. 27, 'The sacrifice of the wicked is an abomination to the Lord;' mark, 'how much more when he bringeth it with a wicked mind?' When it is represented to God with all the advantages imaginable, yet it is abominable because it is a wicked man's prayer; but usually there is some foul defect, that their very persons taint their services.

Obj. 1. Is not God then a respecter of persons? will not this infringe the justice of God? I might answer thus—If he should, he is under no rule; the moral law is a rule to us, but not to God; and he may do with his own creature as pleaseth him, and with his own grace as pleaseth him; Mat. xx. 15, 'Is it not lawful for me to do what I will with my own?'

But I answer rather, Respecting of persons, when it is sinful, is this, when in any cause we give more or less than is meet to any other person, because of something that hath no relation to the cause, as in judgment. When we wink at moral excesses, and acquit a man from the sentence of the law for his greatness, or when we deny right to a poor man because of his poverty. Now such a respect of persons cannot be imagined in God; for—

[1.] There is a cause why God should accept the services of justified persons, because he hath received a satisfaction in Jesus Christ. We are made comely in his comeliness; Christ hath paid down a valuable consideration why all your persons and services should be accepted, though accompanied with weakness: Heb. x. 19, 'Having therefore boldness to enter into the holiest by the blood of Jesus;' this acceptance is purchased for us by the blood of Jesus. It was God's bargain with Christ, that he would love, bless, and justify all his seed, if he would lay down his soul as an offering for sin, Isa. liii. 10. There is the solemn bargain, 'When thou shalt make his soul an offering for sin, he shall see his seed, he shall prolong his days, and the pleasure of the Lord shall prosper in his hand.'

[2.] There is great reason why God should refuse the services of wicked men, because besides the state of their persons, there are gross defects in their services; if he sacrifice, it is 'with an evil mind,' Prov. xxi. 27. For the principle, it is not out of obedience but custom; for the manner, it is not with the affection of a child but with bondage; for the end, it is not for God's glory but to promote secular interest. So that, *a posteriori*, these circumstances clear the justice of God; their most devotional aim is to please God, that they may the better quiet themselves in their vanity and excess; but the reason why they are not accepted is because they have no interest in Christ.

Obj. 2. Will it not open a gap to looseness? If wicked men be not accepted, why do they pray and hear? had they not as good do nothing? I answer, No.

[1.] Because this would be a way to increase their sin, wholly to neglect them. There is no reason why God should lose his right because we have lost our power. Inky water will never wash the hands clean, and our sinfulness doth not take off our obligation; God hath required it, and a wicked man is still under an obligation; a drunken servant is not exempted from obedience though he be disabled for work. The command of God is absolute and peremptory, that all the sons of men should worship and fear him; therefore to leave off duty would make the state more sinful. One sin cannot cure another; there is more sin in the total defect than in the bare performance of duty.

[2.] Because duties are the means God hath appointed to break off their sin, and come out of this miserable condition. If none of their works can please God, yet it is good to stand in the road of mercy, and to lie at the pool, John v. 7; though God doth not accept us for these things, yet these are the means God hath appointed for us to use. Simon Magus was bid 'to pray, if perhaps the thoughts of his heart might be forgiven him,' Acts viii. 22; but the man that neglects the means cuts off himself from all hope, he reprobates himself and becomes his own judge; he doth as it were say, I will never be saved. When men give over praying, and hearing, and reading, as the apostle saith, 'you judge yourselves unworthy of eternal life,' Acts xiii. 46.

Obj. 3. From experience God doth reward many wicked men, therefore how can it be said their duties are not accepted? 1 Kings xxi. 29, Ahab's humiliation kept off the judgment, and Nebuchadnezzar had the land of Egypt for his service against Tyre, Ezek. xxix. 18–20; that is nothing but a prophetical prediction. He did not think of accomplishing God's decrees, and the expression 'of giving him the land of Egypt for his labour' is taken from the manner of men; when a servant doth his work, he hath his reward. But for God's rewarding of wicked men, I answer—

[1.] This is *ex largitate donantis*, out of the overflow of his own love and mercy; they can claim and look for nothing: James i. 7, 'Let not that man think that he shall receive anything of the Lord.' Though something may be given him, yet there is nothing theirs by way of promise; all the promises being made and made good in Christ; that is to them that have an interest in him: 2 Cor. i. 20, 'For all the promises of God in him are yea, and in him, amen.'

[2.] These mercies are not given for their sakes, but to give the world a document of God's bounty. Saith Calvin, *Deus sæpe rependit mercedem umbris virtutum, ut ostendat sibi placere virtutes ipsas*—God doth often reward the shadow of virtue that he might show that grace itself is very pleasing and acceptable to him; when Ahab doth but counterfeitly humble himself, God will suspend the judgment to show how he prizeth true repentance.

[3.] All the blessings that wicked men have are but temporal, and salted with a curse; there is nothing of acceptance to life. Ahab's humiliation gained but a delay of wrath, and that increased his sin. Children have the bread of life, dogs have but the crumbs and offals of providence. Wicked men do not serve God with all their heart, therefore their mercies are defective as well as their duties.

Use 1. It serves for terror to wicked men. A natural man is in a wretched estate; his most glorious acts, his very prayers, that are dressed up with a fair pretence of devotion, are abominable before God: Prov. xv. 8, 'The sacrifice of the wicked is an abomination to the Lord' —not only his sins, but his duties. It is the greatest despite that can be done to a man, that when he hath set himself to please, yet he is still hated. So it is with wicked men; though they may preach, pray, and prophesy in Christ's name, yet nothing is well taken from them. Cain was punished for his murder, but was not accepted for his sacrifice. Ἐχθρῶν δῶρα ἄδωρα—the gifts of enemies are giftless gifts; wicked men are God's enemies, and so nothing is pleasing that comes from them. It is true, Jesus Christ saith, Isa. xlix. 4, 'I have laboured in vain, I have spent my strength for nought and in vain;' but this was his comfort, 'his judgment was with the Lord, and his work with his God.' But with wicked men it is otherwise; they labour and toil, but all in vain. It may be they may have their penny of profit in the world, and that their gifts may be useful in the church, and they may have temporal reward, but it is salted with a curse; their sacrifice is but carrion, their prayer but babbling, and their table of the Lord is but the table of devils: Titus i. 15, 'To the pure all things are pure; but unto them that are defiled and unbelieving is nothing pure; but even their mind and conscience is defiled.'

Use 2. To represent the privilege of persons justified: their persons please God, and so do all their works. You may improve it for comfort and thankfulness.

1. For comfort. When you are discouraged with your infirmities, your many failings in every duty, Christ will accept you: Ps. xxxiv. 15, 'The eyes of the Lord are upon the righteous, and his ears are open to their cry.' Consider, thou art troubled about the imperfection of thy works; they cannot be worse than thy person when God took thee into grace. God that pitied thee when thou wert in thy blood and perfectly evil, he will accept and love thee when thou art in thy person sanctified; though there be abundance of dross, he can see there is some gold; though abundance of wax, yet there is some honey: Cant. v. 1, 'I have eaten my honeycomb with my honey.'

2. For thankfulness. Oh! what a mercy is this, that God should testify concerning our gifts, such worthless duties so tainted and defiled by the adherency of corruption! There are many considerations to stir up our thankfulness.

[1.] That which is good is rather his own than ours, yet God will put it upon our account: 1 Chron. xxix. 14, 'Who am I, and what is my people, that we should be able to offer so willingly after this sort? for all things come of thee, and of thine own have we given thee.' When you come to God with the best enlargement and quickness of affection, it is the Lord that made us thus willing; yet God counts them as our duties, though they may be fruits of his own Spirit. Then—

[2.] They are mingled with a great deal of weakness and defilement

—*Partus sequitur ventrem ;* our duties have more of us than of the Spirit, therefore they are filthy and defiled. Observe the practice of the saints, their remarkable blemishes : Jacob seeks the blessing with a lie ; Rahab entertains the spies, but makes a lie about dismissing them ; Sarah calls her husband 'lord,' but her words are full of discontent and murmuring and distrust of God's promise. Moses smote the rock twice ; once in obedience and once in indignation. Who would think of such weak services, that God should accept of them ? nay, not only accept of them, but delight in them : Prov. xv. 8, 'The prayer of the upright is his delight ;' that the holy God should delight in such creatures as we are ! We have imperfect conceits of God's holiness, otherwise we would wonder that he should accept of our faulty performances ; that the holy and pure God should not only accept, but delight in the prayer of a worthless creature. Then—

[3.] There is no profit redounds to God for all this, the advantage is ours : Prov. ix. 12, 'If thou be wise, thou shalt be wise for thyself ;' Ps. xvi. 2, 'My goodness extendeth not to thee.' God is blessed for ever, sufficiently happy without the service of the creature. Job xxii. 2, there is a question propounded, 'Can a man be profitable to God, as he that is wise may be profitable to himself ?' God is eternally and everlastingly happy ; he is incapable of improvement ; all the comfort and profit is ours, yet that he should delight in them !

Use 3. Direction to teach us what to do in our preparation to duties and holy exercises. If God accept the person and then the performance, look to your state, as well as to the frame of your hearts. Many men heap up duties upon duties, go round in a circle of religious exercises, as if they would work out their salvation that way, but do not regard the interest of their persons. Consider, examination is one of the preparative duties, as well as purgation of sin and excitation of the affections : 2 Cor. xiii. 5, 'Examine yourselves whether you be in the faith.' We must prove our state still, otherwise we shall be disallowed. It is not necessary only to examine ourselves before the Lord's supper, but before other solemn ordinances. God would fain draw the creatures to a certainty, therefore he hath required often trial to look into their state. This is the method of God's acceptance ; first the Lord cleanseth, fits, and consecrates the person to be a spiritual priest, and then he is to offer : Mal. iii. 3, 4, 'He shall purify the sons of Levi, and purge them as gold and silver, that they may offer unto the Lord an offering in righteousness.' Where God speaks of worship in the times of the gospel, first we must be purified and set apart for the priesthood, then offer up our gift ; first there is a 'purging of the conscience from dead works,' then we are meet 'to serve the living God,' Heb. ix. 14 ; first we are 'washed from our sins in his blood ;' and then 'made kings and priests to God,' Rev. i. 5, 6. There must be an interest founded, and a ground of acceptance for our persons. God will accept nothing at the hands of an enemy ; duties are but varnished sins. This should stir you up to the trial of yourselves, whether you are justified and reconciled to God.

But you will say, What shall men do that have no assurance, that cannot discern the interest of their persons in Christ ?

I answer, by distinguishing—The case concerneth either persons that have lost assurance, or those that have never gained it.

1. To those that have lost assurance by turning to folly, or tasting of the forbidden fruit of sin. By scandalous falls conscience is weakened, and prayer is interrupted; as the apostle speaketh of family jars: 1 Peter iii. 7, 'Likewise ye husbands, dwell with them according to knowledge, giving honour unto the wife as unto the weaker vessel, and as being heirs together of the grace of life, that your prayers be not hindered.' By allowance of passion, and wrath, and domestical disorder, the heart is discomposed, and we cannot with such a holy boldness and confidence call God father. The like may be said of many foul falls, by which conscience is wounded, and men have lost the peace and calmness of their spirits. Now, in such a case, men are not to come reeking from their sins and rush upon duty; that would argue little reverence of God, and will find little acceptance with him: Isa. i. 15, 16, 'When ye spread forth your hands, I will hide mine eyes from you: yea, when ye make many prayers, I will not hear: your hands are full of blood. Wash ye, make you clean, put away the evil of your doings from before mine eyes,' &c. Neither are they wholly to decline worship and restrain prayer; that would increase the distemper, and add sin to sin. David got nothing by his silence: Ps. xxxii. 3, 'When I kept silence, my bones waxed old, through my roaring all the day long;' Ps. li. 3, 'I acknowledge my transgression, and my sin is ever before me.' However, the main care of the next duty must be to get the person reconciled by these solemn acts.

[1.] There must be serious acknowledgment of sin with shame and sorrow. This is God's established way for fallen saints: 1 John i. 9, 'If we confess our sins, he is faithful and just to forgive us our sins, and to cleanse us from all unrighteousness.' This is the saint's practice: Ps. li. 3, 'I acknowledge my transgression, and my sin is ever before me;' and this is the most rational course. It is impossible it should be otherwise, either on God's part or ours. We are under a sequestration till we make suit to God: Num. xii. 14, 'If her father had spit in her face, should she not be ashamed seven days?' Tender hearts will melt and mourn.

[2.] They must run to the old fountain opened for their uncleanness. There is no reconciling ourselves to God, but by Christ: Mat. iii. 17, 'This is my beloved Son, in whom I am well pleased.' We must come with Christ in our arms: 1 John ii. 1, 'If any man sin, we have an advocate with the father, Jesus Christ the righteous.' Duties are not our atonement, but Christ's intercession, which is the renewed application of his merit.

[3.] They must earnestly sue out their former estate, and the wonted effects of his favour: Ps. xxv. 6, 'Remember, O Lord, thy tender mercies, and thy loving-kindnesses, for they have been ever of old;' Ps. li. 12, 'Restore unto me the joy of thy salvation.' Christ doth not only intercede, but the believer must also, the earnest motions of the Spirit being the copy of his intercession.

2. It concerneth those that never got assurance. To those, I answer in several propositions:—

[1.] Assurance is very necessary and comfortable in our approaches to God; such addresses do most become his grace. Christ hath taught us to begin our prayers with 'Our Father;' Heb. x. 21, 22, 'Having an high priest over the house of God; let us draw near with a true heart, in full assurance of faith, having our heart sprinkled from an evil conscience, and our bodies washed with pure water.' Having such free offers, such an abundant merit, such sweet experiences, God looketh that we should draw nigh in the assurance of faith: 1 Tim. ii. 8, 'I will therefore that men pray everywhere, lifting up holy hands without wrath and doubting.'

[2.] Every suppliant cannot sail with such full sails into the haven of grace, nor all persons at all times; there is a weak faith as well as the faith of Abraham, and yet a weak faith is faith. David and Heman, two choice spirits, sometimes wanted comforts, and it is God's usual course still with many of his dear children; they have less peace, that they may have more grace; and God withholdeth comfort out of wise dispensation to engage them in the more duty: every one hath not an abundant entrance into heaven, 2 Peter i. 11.

[3.] When we cannot reflect upon our actual interest, the direct and dutiful acts of faith must be more solemnly exerted and put forth.

(1.) You must disclaim earnestly your own personal righteousness. This complieth with God's end; for therefore do his respects begin with the person, that the work may not be the ground of acceptance: Dan. ix. 18, 'We do not present our supplications before thee for our righteousnesses, but for thy great mercies.' Every one cannot go to the highway of comfort; there is safety in going the low way of humiliation, and in the sense of your own unworthiness for all acceptance with God in Christ.

(2.) You must adhere to God in Christ the more closely; faith giveth safety, though assurance giveth comfort. There may be a dependence and renewing of confidence, and a waiting with hope, in every duty; and a christian, though he be without comfort, yet he is not without encouragement; there are invitations to wait upon God, and they cast themselves upon God in this hope: Ps. xxii. 8, 'He trusted on the Lord, that he would deliver him.' It is good when you can refer yourselves to God's acceptance upon the hopes of the gospel.

(3.) There must be consecration when you cannot make application. It is sweet when we can say, mutually 'I am my beloved's, and my beloved is mine,' Cant. ii. 16; but it is safe to say, 'I am my beloved's,' and he is mine by choice, though I cannot say he is mine by gift. A christian resigneth up himself to God: Ps. cxix. 94, 'I am thine, save me.' David pleadeth his choice; he taketh Christ as a Lord, though he cannot apply him as a saviour.

(4.) These direct acts may be pleaded to God in prayer: Phil. iii. 9, 'And be found in him, not having my own righteousness,' &c., and so casting ourselves upon God: Ps. cxix. 49, 'Remember thy word unto thy servant, upon which thou hast caused me to hope.'

Secondly, 'By it he, being dead, yet speaketh.'

The words are enigmatical, a holy riddle; and they include a seeming contradiction, that a man should speak, and yet dead ; therefore the words, as all dark places, are liable to several constructions.

In the general, we are certain it must be some privilege and consequent of his faith ; for the apostle saith, 'By it.' Some take the word's *speaking*, συνεκδοχῶς, for *living*, as if it intimated the resurrection ; though slain by Cain, he yet speaketh, converseth with the glorious saints above, to the praise and glory of the Lamb for evermore, upon whom he had pitched his faith.   Certain it is that the Jewish doctors make it to be one of the great arguments of life after death, the crying of Abel's blood.   Again, some translate λαλεῖται, passively ; he is yet spoken of, as if it implied nothing but his name living ; yet in the church that is the usual recompense of faith.   God perpetuates the names of the godly when the names of the wicked shall rot ; but this the apostle had spoken of already, 'By which he obtained witness that he was righteous ;' he is famous for his righteousness through all ages.   Again, others take it as a metaphor, 'speaks ;' that is, doth as it were speak, and it may be by way of exhortation or clamour.

1. By way of exhortation : though he be dead, yet still by his example, he preacheth to the church.   Thus dead persons may be said to speak by their example ; and voice is often in scripture given to inanimate things ; the creature is said 'to groan,' Rom. viii. 22, and the heavens 'to declare the glory of God,' Ps. xix. 1, 2.   Abel, the first martyr that died for the service of God, is a speaking instance and example for all ages.   He speaks several lessons—(1.) That duty is not to be declined though we get hatred by it.   (2.) That we must be obedient even to the death ; and when we are called to it, we must seal our faith and profession with our blood.   (3.) That the rage of the wicked against the righteous is very great.   (4.) That God will call wicked men to an account for our blood, as he did Cain for Abel's blood. But this cannot be the meaning, because this is no peculiar privilege of faith.   All examples have a voice, the creation hath a voice ; but—

2. I suppose another speaking is intended ; the crying of his blood, a clamorous speaking for vengeance upon Cain.   Two reasons for this—

[1.] Because it suits best with the expression of Moses : Gen. iv. 10, 'The voice of thy brother's blood crieth unto me from the ground.' Now the apostle's design is to abridge the history in Genesis.

[2.] Because it suits with the other expression of the apostle.   Abel's speaking is mentioned : Heb. xii. 24, 'The blood of sprinkling speaketh better things than the blood of Abel ;' the blood of Abel speaketh after he was dead punishment, but the blood of Christ speaketh pardon.

Obj. An objection may be framed against this in the text—' He being dead, yet speaketh ;' ἔτι, yet, or to this day.

I may answer, The present tense is put for the preterperfect tense—change of tenses is usual in scripture ; or 'yet,' that is, after his death, though not till the apostle's days.   But I rather pitch upon another answer, because there is a special emphasis in the expression, Abel's blood is still crying.   There are Cains alive to this day : some that walk in the way of Cain, as Jude speaks, ver. 11; he was the patriarch of persecutors, therefore Abel's blood is not fully revenged to this day, but cries for vengeance still. Those that inherit the rage of former persecutors do always inherit their guilt; for imitation is a kind of consent, as if we had been by and consented to the fact: Mat. xxiii. 35, 'That upon you may come all the righteous blood shed upon the earth, from the blood of righteous Abel to the blood of Zecharias, the son of Barachias, whom ye slew between the temple and the altar.' The blood of Abel was revenged upon the Jews that killed Christ. These two are mentioned because of two remarkable circumstances at their death. Of Abel it is said, Gen. iv. 10, 'His blood cried from the ground.' Zecharias, when he died, said, 2 Chron. xxiv. 22, 'The Lord look upon it, and require it.' All the martyrs join in one common cry against the persecutors of all ages: Rev. vi. 9, 10, 'I saw under the altar the souls of them that were slain for the word of God, and for the testimony that they held. And they cried with a loud voice, saying, How long, O Lord, holy and true, dost thou not judge and avenge our blood on them that dwell on the earth?' That is to be understood metaphorically. Passions of revenge being not proper to the glorified saints, the meaning is, their blood is as it were newly shed, and cries to God afresh, requiring vengeance; so that Abel and all the saints still cry, though some succession of ages are passed since their blood was shed. Many things notable are implied in this clause. I shall despatch all in some brief hints.

First, Let us take notice of his dying—'He being dead.' The history is in Genesis. There were probably two causes of the murder; one plainly expressed in scripture, the envy of Cain; the other implied—that is, indignation against the reproof of Abel.

First, One cause is plainly expressed. God accepted Abel; he had a better offering, and therefore Cain slew him: 1 John iii. 12, 'Not as Cain, who was of that wicked one, and slew his brother; and wherefore slew he him? because his own works were evil, and his brother's righteous.' The note is this—

Doct. 1. Persecution usually ariseth from envy.

Men malign what they will not imitate; when others are holier than their interest and vile affections will give them leave, therefore they hate them. Our Lord himself was delivered for envy: Mat. xxvii. 18, 'Pilate knew that for envy they had delivered him;' his disciples sold him out of covetousness, and his enemies persecuted him out of envy.

To apply this let us hate this sin with the more indignation. Alas! we are apt to envy each other's gifts, esteem sancity, and grace; from thence arise contentions and quarrels, and they end in blood. The first man that ever died in the world was slain and murdered by envy. Pride gave us the first merit of death, and envy the first instance of it: Gen. xxxvii. 11, 'His brethren envied him;' they envied Joseph, and then conspired his death. Envy may be impeached as the cause of most of the blood that hath been spilt in the world; that is the reason why envying and murder are so often joined together, Gal. iv. 21.

Secondly, The second cause is implied—viz., indignation at reproof:

Gen. iv. 8, 'And Cain talked with Abel his brother;' what their talk was we find not. The hint is—

Doct. 2. Another cause of persecution is indignation at reproofs.

The world would fain sleep quietly in sin, and complain that these bawling preachers trouble their sinful rest. When a man holds out the testimony of Jesus, he torments and troubles them: Rev. xi. 10, 'The witnesses tormented the dwellers upon earth;' their testimony was the world's torment.

Use 1. It teacheth us to bear it the more patiently: James v. 10, 'Take, my brethren, the prophets, who have spoken in the name of the Lord, for an example of suffering affliction and of patience.' Did you ever hear of any that spake in the name of the Lord, and the world not hate them? The cross is very kindly to our rank and order; Abel, that is but now a priest, presently is made a martyr.

Use 2. Bear reproof patiently. Storming at reproof is the cause of that hatred that is against the ministry: Jer. vi. 10, 'The word of the Lord is unto them a reproach; when he came to reprove, they thought he had railed.'

From the murder itself—'He slew his brother.'

Doct. 1. Hatred of the power of godliness began betimes.

There is an old prediction: Gen. iii. 15, 'I will put enmity between thee and the woman, and between thy seed and her seed.' There are two parties that will never be reconciled. And here are two brothers, one of them the seed of the woman, and the other the seed of the serpent; though they were brothers, came of the same womb, and brothers of the same birth as is conceived. The apostle speaks of two other brothers of the same father, one persecuted the other: Gal. iv. 29, 'As then, he that was born after the flesh persecuted him that was born after the spirit, so it is now.' And in all ages of the world we may say, 'So it is now;' and so it will be for ever: this is the old hatred.

Then consider Abel's death, not only as the death of a saint, but as the death of a brother. The note will be—

Doct. 2. The strife of brethren usually ends in blood, or in sad and dreadful accidents.

Solomon saith, Prov. xviii. 19, 'A brother offended is harder to be won than a strong city; and their contentions are like the bars of a castle.' You may as soon surprise a strong city barred, as gain an offended brother. It is a hint useful to those families where discord ariseth by reason of difference in religion. Difference in brothers is like a rent made in the whole cloth; a seam may easily be sewn, but a rent in the whole cloth cannot; the nearer the union, usually the greater rent. A Spanish preacher that embraced the Reformation was slain by his own brother. Some may be restrained by the severity of laws; but in times of public tumult there have been many such sad instances among nearest relations.

It followeth, 'yet speaketh.' Consider it under a twofold regard, as the common murder of a man, or as the murder of a saint.

First, As the murder of a man; this was a murder done in secret, yet Abel's blood speaks to God, that is, God took notice of the fact though past human cognisance. The note is—

Doct. 3. That murder is a crying sin.

It will out one way or other, God cannot want witnesses. We have seen in providence strange ways for the discovering of murder. Remember that is God's office, to be inquisitive for blood: Ps. ix. 12, 'When he maketh inquisition for blood, he remembereth them.'

Use 1. It is terror to them that are secretly guilty of murder. Many times wicked men act at a distance, nobody can tell who hath done the harm, yet God will find them out. Or if men should occasion public changes or confusions merely to promote their private interest, to build up a name to themselves, 'the stone out of the wall shall cry, and the beam out of the timber shall answer it,' Hab. ii. 11. Or if a man hath plotted the death of any merely to enrich himself, the Lord takes notice of it.

Secondly, Or look upon it as holy blood that was shed, as the blood of a martyr. The note is—

Doct. 4. The blood of a martyr hath a loud voice in the ears of God.

It implies two things—God's love to his oppressed children, and a certainty of vengeance to the oppressors.

1. God's love to his oppressed children. Vengeance is quick-sighted on their behalf. Though the children of God are dumb, like sheep before their shearers, yet their blood cries. Christ spake no words of revenge, but rather prayed for his enemies; yet for shedding his blood, 'Wrath came to the uttermost upon the Jews,' 1 Thes. ii. 16; Gen. iv. 10, it is, 'The voice of thy brother's blood cries unto me.' Every drop was precious, and every wound hath a mouth open to God: Ps. cxvi. 15, 'Precious in the sight of the Lord is the death of his saints.' God hath a precious account of them after death. God's love lasteth after death. He is in covenant with their blood and with their dust when it is in their grave, therefore he will know what is become of them. Nay, he doth not only take notice of their blood but of their tears: Ps. lvi. 8, 'Thou tellest my wanderings; put thou my tears into thy bottle: are they not in thy book?' Men may burn their bodies, but they cannot blot their blood and tears out of God's register.

Use, This is comfort to the children of God. He doth not only take notice after their death of the cry of their blood, to avenge it on their enemies, but to recompense the innocent, to reward them; for that is one effect of its crying. God doth not only take notice of Cain, but vindicates innocent Abel; therefore is he slain, that he may live for ever; slain, that God may bestow upon him a happy life. When your blood is shed for the testimony of God, treasure up this comfort; God will not be wanting to reward it. The two first martyrs in the old testament and the new were Abel and Stephen. What doth Abel signify, but vanity and mourning? and Stephen signifies a crown. Your mourning in the world doth but make way for a crown of glory: James i. 12; 'Blessed is the man that endureth temptation, for when he is tried, he shall receive the crown of life.'

2. It implies certainty of vengeance to the oppressors; when the parents did not accuse, yet the blood cried. The children of God may not know who harms them, yet their wrongs cry loud in the ears of God. Abel's blood did not only cry in God's ears, Gen. iv. 10, but cried in Cain's conscience, ver. 13. How many cries are there? The affliction itself that cries; God hath an ear for affliction. He heard the affliction

of Hagar, Gen. xvi. 11. Then your tears have a voice: Lam. ii. 18, 'Their heart cried unto the Lord, Let tears run down like a river day and night : give thyself no rest ; let not the apple of thine eye cease.' Then the prayers of saints have a voice : Luke xviii. 7, 'Shall not God avenge his own elect, which cry day and night unto him ?' The martyrs under the altar cry : Rev. vi. 9, 'The souls under the altar cried with a loud voice, How long, O Lord, holy and true, dost thou not judge and avenge our blood on them that dwell on the earth ?' Persecutors' consciences, they cry, O thou bloody Julian! thou hast murdered the children of God, and hast been guilty of oppression ! As is storied of the king of France, that was author of that bloody massacre, he could never sleep afterward, but was haunted with terrors in his conscience, and at his death blood issued out at all the pores of his body.

Use. What terror and astonishment should this be to the enemies of the church, be they secret or open! Oppressed innocency will cry aloud ; they may forgive, but the Lord forgets not. The Lord will not only take notice of their blood, but bottle their tears: Ps. lvi. 8, 'Thou tellest my wanderings ; put thou my tears into thy bottle : are they not in thy book ?' God kept a register of David's sufferings ; every weary step was recorded in God's book ; it is but folly and madness to think to hide your practices, or to escape punishment.

SERMON XXI.

By faith Enoch was translated that he should not see death ; and was not found, because God had translated him : for before his translation he had this testimony, that he pleased God.—HEB. xi. 5.

THE apostle makes it his chief scope in this chapter to convince the Hebrews of the nature, and worth, and efficacy of saving faith. To that purpose he layeth down the acts of sanctifying faith, ver. 1, and throughout the chapter he treats of the effects, fruits, and consequences of faith. Here we meet with a consequent or fruit of faith in the instance and example of Enoch, who, among the rest of those glorious lights wherewith this chapter is adorned, shineth forth like a star of the first magnitude. Let me inquire why the apostle mentioned Enoch next to Abel, Seth and other holy patriarchs of the blessed line and race being passed by ? I answer, Though the Spirit of God is not bound to give an account of his method, and therefore is not to be vexed with the bold and daring inquiries of human reason, yet because all things in the scripture are ordered with good advice, a few humble inquiries are lawful and profitable.

1. Enoch was the next solemn type of Christ; Abel was a type of Christ's death, and Enoch next proposed as a type of his ascension. חנוך from חנך *dedicavit*, the dedicated, or the dedicator, (Christ), 'hath consecrated for us a new and living way through the veil, that is to say,

his flesh,' Heb. x. 20; therefore he is called ἀρχηγὸς ζωῆς, ' the prince of life,' Acts iii. 15, and he said, John xiv. 3, ' I go to prepare a place for you.' Tertullian calleth Enoch, *Candidatum æternitatis;* and others have called him *Obsidem et testem vitæ æternæ,* the pledge and witness of eternal life; so was Christ dedicated to this purpose, that he might be the captain of life and salvation to the church, and he is gone to heaven as a pledge of our eternal glory.

2. Because between these two instances there is a fit proportion: Abel was an instance of the efficacy of faith, and Enoch of the consequent and reward of faith; Abel, he suffered for righteousness, and the instance of Enoch shows what is the fruits of suffering faith—that faith which doth engage us in suffering doth interest us in the reward. In Abel's death the holy patriarchs saw what they might expect in the world; and in Enoch's translation they saw what they should receive from God. The Lord would give them this perfect document both of the present operation of faith and the future reward of faith.

3. Because he was an eminent saint, the next that is taken notice of in the history of Moses. The apostle mentions not all the saints in the blessed line, but only the choicest. Now Enoch is many ways eminent and notable; for his birth we find, Jude 14, ' He was the seventh from Adam;' usually that is the number of perfection. Some that would turn all things into an allegory descant thus: That as there were six from the creation that died, and the seventh was translated alive from earth into heaven; so for six thousand years death shall reign, but in the seventh millenary it shall cease, and eternal life shall succeed. But this is but a fond conjecture; they are more pious that observe that the seventh man was dedicated to God, and God takes him for his special servant, as he takes the seventh day for his special day; but, chiefly, he is notable for his life and conversation: Gen. v. 24, ' Enoch walked with God;' that is, wholly dedicated himself to the service of the Lord—a phrase given to those that by express profession were set apart for the Lord, either as prophets, priests, or kings, for special service by office and ministration. But usually it is applied to persons employed in the exercises of piety and holiness: walking with God in the old testament, and well pleasing to God in the new, are synonymous terms. Another thing is notable in his life, that he lived as many years just as there are days in the year—three hundred and sixty-five years, Gen. v. 21, 22. Enoch was translated next after Adam's death, as will easily appear by chronology; as soon as Adam died Enoch was translated. God in Adam would give the world a pledge of the fruit of sin, which was death; in Enoch, a pledge of the fruit of holiness, which is immortality and eternal life.

In the words there is a proposition, and the confirmation of it.

1. The proposition or assertion of the apostle is, that *by faith Enoch was translated that he should not see death.* The proposition implies two things—the blessing, and the means of obtaining it: the blessing —' He was translated;' the means—' By faith.'

2. The confirmation, which respecteth both the blessing and the means. He proves that Enoch was translated, out of that phrase of Moses; for saith he, *He was not found, because God had translated him.* And then he proves that it was by faith in the latter part of the text

—For before his translation he had this testimony, that he pleased God.
In which reasoning there is a perfect syllogism : whosoever is translated
on or after his pleasing God is translated by faith.   Enoch was translated on or after his pleasing God, therefore he was translated by faith.
The major is proved by the sixth verse—'Without faith it is impossible to please God ;' the minor by the history of Moses—'For before
his translation he had this testimony, that he pleased God.'

Let me illustrate the words.

' By faith ; ' that is, by faith in the being of God, and in the promise
of the Messiah and of the world to come.   Now the reason why his
translation is attributed to faith is given by the apostle—'For before
his translation he had this testimony, that he pleased God.'   His faith
was the fountain of his godliness, and his godliness was the pledge of
glory ; his faith respected his pleasing God, and his pleasing God was
an evidence of his interest in eternal life.

' Enoch.'   We read of two Enochs—one of the race of Cain,
another of the line of Seth ; the hypocritical church imitating the true
church, as in outward rites, so in having the same names : the Enoch
here meant was of the family of Seth.

' Was translated,' transplanted—$\mu\epsilon\tau\epsilon\tau\epsilon\theta\eta$: the apostle useth this
word to note his transportation to heaven.

There are many questions for the opening of this translation ; as
(1.) Whether he were translated in soul and body ? (2.) Whether he
died in the translation ? (3.) To what place he was translated, whether
to heaven or some earthly paradise ?

1. Whether he were translated in soul and body ?   Some think he
was translated in soul only, and not in body, as if there were nothing
extraordinary in the history of Enoch, and his body was left on the
earth.   This is altogether improbable.   The phrases imply something
more than ordinary : Gen. v. 24, 'And Enoch walked with God, and
was not ; for God took him.'   Why should there be such special
phrases, ' he was not,' and ' God took him,' if an ordinary thing were
intended ?   So the apostle here—'That he should not see death.'   It
might have been enough to have said he died, as of all the rest ;
therefore there was somewhat of miracle in it, for he was gathered by
God into glory, both in soul and body.

2. Whether he died in the translation or no ?   I answer, No, but
was only changed ; for the apostle saith 'that he should not see death.'
The Chaldee paraphrase renders it, and ' he was not,' *Quia non mori
eum fecit Deus*—Onkelos, *Non occidit eum Deus*.   Probably, as those
that live at the last day, the apostle saith, ' We shall not all die, but
we shall all be changed,' 1 Cor. xv. 51.   He was transported to heaven
in a moment, without the pains' and horrors of a natural death ; and
being purified in soul, and purged from corruption in his body, was
presently clothed with a glorified body.   As Elijah was carried alive
soul and body into heaven, 2 Kings ii. 11 ; so those that live at the
Lord's coming ' shall be caught up alive into the clouds, to meet the
Lord in the air,' 1 Thes. iv. 7.   And when the apostle himself would
express his own desires, that he might go to heaven in this manner (for
the first believers thought the day of judgment was at hand), he saith,
2 Cor. v. 2, ' In this we groan, earnestly desiring to be clothed upon

with our house which is from heaven;' and ver. 4, 'Not that we would be unclothed, but clothed upon, that mortality might be swallowed up of life;' that is, he desired that glory might come on him without dissolution, without the trouble and pain of sickness and diseases—'Not that I might be unclothed,' and put off the body, but 'clothed upon,' invested with the qualities of a glorified body.

3. Whither he was translated, to what place? Some say to the earthly paradise, others to the heavenly paradise.

[1.] Some say to the earthly paradise; so Haimo and others, there to stand in a happy condition until the last act of the world shall be brought on the stage, and then to fight with their imaginary antichrist. But that was defaced by the universal deluge and flood in Noah's time—'The highest hills that were under the whole heaven were covered,' Gen. vii. 19, and the custody of the seraphims and flaming-sword was removed when the beauty and pleasure of it was gone; and the most probable opinion is, that paradise was in Armenia. Now Armenia was covered, and Noah's ark rested on the mountains of Ararat, or Armenia, Gen. viii. 4.

[2.] Some say to a heavenly paradise, by which they understand not the heaven of heavens, but some third place, which is called in scripture paradise, and Abraham's bosom, in which the souls of some rest until the last day, not fully perfected and blessed. Tertullian, Austin, and many of the fathers, were of opinion that the souls of martyrs did straightways flit hence into the presence of God, but the souls of common christians went to paradise, by which they understood *secreta animarum receptacula, sedesque in quibus requiescunt*—some unknown place, where they did enjoy happiness, congruous and convenient to their condition: and in such a place they would place Enoch. But all these things being devised without warrant and leave from the scriptures, little heed is to be given to them. Briefly, an earthly paradise it cannot be, that is defaced; a third place it cannot be, that being devised without warrant from the scriptures. Heaven only remaineth, whither God translated him both in body and soul, there to enjoy the comforts of his presence; it would have been an infringement of his happiness to separate him from his God, with whom he had walked here in spiritual communion. So the Targums, or expositions of the Jews, Jonathan, *Translatus fuit, et uscendit in cœlum,* &c; Josephus calls it ἀναχώρησις πρὸς τὸν θεόν; the Arabic version, *Translatus est in paradisum.*

That 'he should not see death;' that is, that he might not die a natural death by a dissolution of the body, but undergo a sudden change of qualities.

But you will say, How can this stand with the general curse of God pronounced upon all mankind in Gen. ii. 17, 'In the day thou eatest thereof, thou shalt surely die,' thou and all thine? and Gen. iii. 19, 'Dust thou art, and to dust thou shalt return;' or that eternal decree, Heb. ix. 27, 'It is appointed for all men once to die.'

I answer, This was an extraordinary instance, that doth not cross the rule; it was a special dispensation that the Lord might give the patriarchs a document and instance of eternal life, and the sudden change of qualities was something analogical to death; and were it not for this special dispensation of God, he was under that obligation, but the Lord was pleased to privilege him for the great purposes of his glory.

'And he was not found.' The words relate to what is said, Gen. v. 24, ' And he was not.' The phrase is used, Jer. xxxi. 15, ' Rachel weeping for her children refused to be comforted for her children, because they were not.' This phrase is often put for those that are dead : Gen. xlii. 36,' Joseph is not, and Simeon is not ;' he supposed them dead, or knew not what was become of them, but it is taken for any disappearance.

'For before his translation he had this testimony, that he pleased God.' Some make it to be an inward testimony in his conscience ; others, some visible and public honour that was done to him before the world, the story of which is not now extant. Most probable, it is the testimony that is given him in scripture : Gen. v. 24, ' And Enoch walked with God,' which the Septuagint renders—$\epsilon \dot{\upsilon} \eta \rho \dot{\epsilon} \sigma \tau \eta \sigma \epsilon \ \tau \hat{\omega} \ \theta \epsilon \hat{\omega}$, in that and other places, which we shall hereafter explain.

But you will say, How can this be said to be before his translation, for the testimony of Moses was long after the translation of Enoch ?

I answer, The apostle is to be understood thus : Enoch had this testimony in scripture, so that before his translation the scripture witnessed he pleased God ; not before his translation he received this testimony ; and that is the order of Moses : Gen. v. 24, ' Enoch walked with God, and he was not, for God took him.'

A few hints from what hath been spoken before I begin the two main and principal points.

Obs. 1. There is a life everlasting prepared for God's children. The instance God would give the fathers was in the translation of Enoch ; the instance God would give believers in the times of the gospel was in the ascension of Christ. As soon as Adam died Enoch was translated. In Adam God would give the world a pledge of the fruit of sin, which is death ; and in Enoch God would give a pledge of the fruit of holiness ; and that is immortality and eternal life. Enoch was not merely translated for his own benefit and comfort, but for the comfort of other patriarchs against the fear of daily crosses in this life, and against the terrors of death ; they saw there was now like to be violence in the world. There was one martyr—Abel was slain. Now that they might have comfort against this, God translated Enoch. The great instance God gives in the times of the gospel was the ascension of Jesus Christ ; when the human nature was carried into heaven, that was a pledge of our glorification. He carried our flesh into heaven, and he left his Spirit with us ; he took our flesh into heaven that he might prepare a place for us, to receive heaven in our right, and he left his Spirit with us, that we might be prepared for heaven. Heaven is not only prepared for believers by Christ's ascension—'I go to prepare a place for you,' John xiv. 2, but believers are prepared for heaven—' vessels of mercy prepared unto glory,' Rom. ix. 23. Look, as in all contracts pledges are mutually taken and given, so Christ would take a pledge from us, even our nature, and give a pledge to us —his Spirit ; therefore we are as sure as ever Enoch was to be translated to bliss if we have an interest in Christ : John viii. 51, ' Verily, verily I say unto you, If any man keep my saying, he shall not see death.' Enoch was translated that he should not see death; and Christ, under a deep asseveration, makes the same privilege to every believer. Death, since the death of Christ, will not be deadly to them; in death itself they see life. It is true, Enoch was translated in body and soul; yet, however, we are presently with the Lord in soul as soon as we are dissolved.

Use 1. Is to reprove believers for minding the present life as much as they do. We busy ourselves too much in the world, and toil in gathering sticks to our nests, when to-morrow we must be gone and flit away. Here we 'dwell in houses of clay, whose foundation is in the dust, which are crushed before the moth,' Job iv. 19, and we are consumed by the blast of his nostrils. Man is but a little enlivened dust, and we are, like potsherds, soon broken. Hereafter we live, now we are dying every day, saith Austin, *Nescio an vita mortalis, an vitalis mors nominanda est ;* I do not know whether I should call this life a living death or a dying life.

Use 2. Is comfort to believers in the hour of death: John xi. 25, 'He that believeth in me, though he were dead, yet he shall live.' When you go down to the grave, you may go down with this assurance, that you shall live; though you look upon your flesh as morsels for the worms, yet you may look upon it also as parcels of the resurrection. God is in covenant with a believer's dust; the body, that seems most to suffer, shall be raised up again.

Obs. 2. That life everlasting cannot be obtained but by some change, by flitting and removing out of this present life. Enoch died not, yet, however, he was changed; God took him: 1 Cor. xv. 50, 51, 'We shall not all die, but we shall all be changed. Flesh and blood cannot inherit the kingdom of God ;' that is, as now invested with these qualities.

Use. This may comfort believers against the terrors of death. The only use of death is to put off the old earthly qualities, that we may put on the new and heavenly; death doth only pluck off the rotten garment. Christ will call the grave to an account: Rev. xx. 13, 'The grave gave up her dead ;' as Joseph left his coat in his mistress's hand and fled away, so we leave the upper garment of the flesh in death's hands, but we fly away; and Christ, at last, will say, Grave! where is my Abraham, my Isaac, and my Jacob's dust?

Obs. 3. That the body is a partaker with the soul in life eternal; Enoch was translated both body and soul. It is a comfort we can say with Job, 'With these eyes we shall see God,' Job xix. 26, though our body be eaten up with worms. This body, as if he did knock upon his breast, 'This corruptible must put on incorruption, and this mortal must put on immortality,' 1 Cor. xv. 53; so Phil. iii. 21, 'Who shall change our vile body,' &c. Look, as the world, when consumed with fire, it is the same world for substance, it shall be only a purging fire; so this corruptible body is the same body for substance, though God doth away the corruptible properties of it.

Use. This is a great comfort against the difficulties and inconveniences of the holy life. The same eyes that have been lifted up to God in prayer, those eyes shall see Christ upon his white throne, and those spirits that are now spent and wasted in holy exercises shall be recruited. A body wasted in sin is a sad prognostic of the devouring burning, but a body wasted in duty shall be restored and repaired again; so it is comfort against the inconveniences of the common life. Many indeed have a vile body, because subject to diseases, humbled with pains and aches, racked with the stone and the gout; this vile diseased body shall be a glorious body. Christ's body was first vile, then glorious; first scourged, mangled with whips, then crowned with honour and glory; and he sat down with God. Oh! let us bear all these; they will be full of nimbleness, vigour, beauty, and glory, like Christ's glorious body.

Obs. 4. Heaven is but a translation to a better place. When you die, you are but translated. Enoch walked with God here; but when he was translated, he lived with God in an uninterrupted glory. Many times Christ comes into his garden to gather lilies; and they are cropped here, that they may be transplanted from the winter to the summer gardens, from the church and lower dispensation of the ordinances to paradise, that we may read divinity in the face of the Lamb for evermore, as scholars that are sent from the grammar-school to the university.

Use. Let it not be irksome to us to be loosed from the body that we may be present with the Lord and joined to Jesus Christ; it is but a removal and preferment, therefore it teacheth christians to grow weary of the world. The world is the place of your pilgrimage, the place of sorrow and sin: certainly we have little reason to love the world. (1.) It is Satan's circuit; when God calls Satan to an account, Job i. 7, ' Whence comest thou? ' Satan answered, ' From walking to and fro in the earth.' (2.) It is sin's house of office, a place of defilement: Isa. xxiv. 5, ' The earth is defiled under the inhabitants thereof.' (3.) It is a common inn for all sorts of men, for bastards as well as sons: Ps. cxv. 16, ' The heaven, even the heavens, are the Lord's: but the earth hath he given to the children of men.' Wicked men have a creature-right, it is given to them, they have a right by providence; nay, here we are not only fellow-commoners with wicked men, but fellow-commoners with beasts; they have a creature-right too, as well as we. (4.) It is the shambles of the saints: Rev. xviii. 24, ' In her was found the blood of prophets and of saints, and of all that were slain upon earth; ' there they are grieved, vexed, and slain. Now, who would grieve to be transplanted to a higher and happier region, where nothing that defiles grows, nothing troubleth in those holy, blessed, and quiet mansions? Death is a preferment.

Obs. 5. That some are carried to heaven by a special and privileged dispensation. The entrance into glory is very different. God is not bound to the ordinary course of nature. Enoch and Elijah were both transported in soul and body; Elijah was sent to heaven in a fiery chariot. And so shall those that live at the last day ' be caught up in the clouds, to meet the Lord in the air,' 1 Thes. iv. 17. Look, as God took away Enoch without the pain of sickness and trouble, so he carries many more joyful and singing to heaven. And therefore, in giving grace and glory, God will use a liberty and the prerogative of free grace. Some seem to be rapt up into heaven by a fiery chariot, by strong elevation of comfort and joy in the Holy Ghost, but others are carried in the lower and darker way of sorrow, trouble, and soul-sickness.

Use. It is the duty of believers to be doing what is required, and to refer mere dispensations to God's good pleasure. Free grace is dispensed in a different way.

Obs. 6. That the persons which are honoured in this extraordinary way were Enoch and Elijah; and what were they? They were two that shined like stars in a corrupt age, those that contested with the corruptions of their own times. The note is this—viz., God's heart is especially set to honour them that are zealous for his glory in corrupt times. In the days of Enoch men were very corrupt, therefore the flood was threatened. Now Enoch kept a constant counter-motion to the times; he did not only walk with God, but reproved the vices of others: Gen. v. 24, 'He walked with God,' and he reproved the ungodly men of his age, Jude 14, 15. It is a standing rule, God will honour those that honour him. Public and zealous instruments are carried on by a mighty hand of providence, and sent to heaven in a glorious way.

Use. Oh then, learn first 'to have no fellowship with the unfruitful works of darkness,' and then 'to reprove them,' Eph. v. 11; contest zealously for God. God will put honour upon them in the eyes of the world; not only give them glory in heaven, but public and visible honour here, that all might take notice of them.

I come to the points, which are two—

1. The right and interest of believers in the happiness of the eternal state.

2. The necessity of pleasing God, or walking with God, before we come to the full enjoyment of him. Which two points afford two doctrines.

Dcct. 1. That the end and the great privilege of faith is to be translated out of the world into the happiness of the eternal state.

1. I shall prove the point by scripture: 1 Peter i. 9, 'Receiving the end of your faith, the salvation of your souls.' Heaven is there proposed as the chief end and reward of faith; all that we do, all that we suffer, all that we believe, it is with an aim at the hope of the salvation of our souls. The last article of our creed is everlasting life. We begin with belief in God, and we end with life everlasting; there is the sum and result of faith, eternal life and glory: John xx. 31, 'These things are written, that you might believe that Jesus is the Christ, the Son of God, and that believing, you might have life through his name.' The end of the word is faith, and the end of faith is eternal life; all the duty part of the word may be reduced to faith, and all the promissory part to life. It is also the great privilege of faith: Eph. ii. 8, 'By grace ye are saved, through faith.' The foundation of glory is laid in mercy on God's part, and it is received by faith on our part: it is given of grace, not sold for works; and received by faith, not purchased by desert.

2. I shall by a few reasons prove the interest of believers in eternal life, and why faith gives a title to glory.

[1.] Because by faith we are made sons; all our right and title is by adoption. Children may expect a child's portion, as in natural things : the title follows the birth, natural or legal.   We hold heaven as co-heirs with Christ: 1 John iii. 2, ' Now we are the sons of God, and it doth not yet appear what we shall be; ' that gives us a right. Now faith in a juridical sense makes us sons : John i. 12, ' To as many as received him, to them gave he power to become the sons of God; ' he gave them ἐξουσίαν, as a right to the inheritance and sonship.   So also in a real, though spiritual sense : 1 Peter i. 3, ' He hath begotten us again unto a lively hope, to an inheritance incorruptible, undefiled,' &c.   The new birth is by the infusion of faith ; all relations to God are built on that change : our hope depends upon our new birth.

[2.] These are the terms of the eternal covenant between God and Christ, that believers should have a right to heaven by Christ's death ; therefore, whenever the Father's love, and Christ's purchase are mentioned, faith is the solemn condition.   The Father hath meant to dispose of heaven to a sort of men, but upon what condition : John iii. 16, ' God so loved the world, that he gave his only-begotten son,'— what to do? and upon what terms ?—' that whosoever believeth in him should not perish, but have everlasting life;' so again, John vi. 40, ' This is the will of my Father that sent me, that every one which seeth the Son, and believeth on him, may have everlasting life ; and I will raise him up at the last day;' upon that condition Christ bargained with God, and God with Christ.   So for the purchase of Christ: Heb. ix. 15, ' He is the mediator of the new testament, that by means of death, for the redemption of transgressions that were under the first testament, they which are called might receive the promise of the eternal inheritance.'   When Christ died, as the mediator and testator, he made believers his heirs.   There is no other name expressed in his will and testament, but they that believe, and they that are called, which are all one ; therefore they are called, Heb. vi. 17, ' heirs of promise.'   Our inheritance was dearly purchased, Christ was to be a mediator by means of death, but it is made over to believers by will and testament.

[3.] Because faith is the mother of obedience, which is the way to eternal life ; faith gives a title, and works give an evidence.   This is the drift of the apostle here—Enoch pleased God before he was translated, therefore by faith he was translated ; for ' without faith it is impossible to please God.'   God hath no respect to works without faith ; the way to be made happy is first to be made holy, and all the influences of grace are received and improved by faith.   Faith is the mother of grace, and grace the pledge of glory.   All your works are not evidences of eternal life, but as they come from faith.   It is faith that kindles love and inflames zeal, and quickens obedience.

[4.] By faith that life is begun which shall only be consummated and perfected in glory.   The life of glory and the life of grace are the same in substance, but not in degree.   Here faith takes Christ, and then life is begun, though in glory it is perfected: 1 John v. 12, ' He that hath the Son, hath life;' it is begun in him already.   When the soul is changed by grace, there is a foundation laid for the changing of body and soul by glory: the Spirit will not leave his mansion and dwelling-place.   When Christ hath once taken up his residence in the heart, and begun life there, he will not depart.   Believers are said to be raised up at the last day by the spirit of holiness dwelling in them, Rom. viii. 11 ; and Rom. v. 2, ' By whom also we have access by faith into this grace wherein we stand, and rejoice in hope of the glory of God.' Faith anticipates heaven, and begins the life of glory by hope and the joys of the Holy Ghost.

Use 1. To press you to get faith upon this ground and motive, it will give you an interest in heaven. Heaven is the portion of believers. Dogs, and they that are without, cannot have the children's portion. Unbelievers are strangers to the comforts of religion for the present, therefore much more hereafter, when the definitive sentence is passed upon them. Oh, who would not labour for faith upon this ground? Faith must needs be an excellent grace, that bringeth such a salvation ; it giveth you an interest in Christ and heaven. Faith ennobles the blood ; no birth like it; it entitles us to the highest inheritance that is in the world. No dignity like that to be a son of the king of heaven, to be of kindred with all the saints, to be of the royal and noble blood. See how the apostle compares one birth with another : John i. 12, 13, ' Who are born, not of flesh, nor of blood, nor of the will of man, but of God ;' that is, not in that unclean lustful way that the children of the highest nobles and potentates of the earth are begotten. Faith can make the poorest beggar to be richer than the greatest monarch : James ii. 5, ' Hath not God chosen the poor of this world, rich in faith, and heirs of the kingdom?' the sons of the potentates of the world cannot show the like ; to be an heir-apparent of heaven is better than to be possessor of the whole world. Oh, do but consider the inheritance ! the birth is noble, but the estate exceeding large. If you would have me express it to you, I must tell you the best commendation of heaven is silence, when the great voice saith, Come up and see, then we shall know what heaven is ; but now our ear hath received a little thereof in the promises ; therefore I shall speak something of it.

[1.] Consider the evil we are delivered from. We are freed from hell—' They shall not perish,' John iii. 16, and ' shall not come into condemnation,' John v. 24. Consider wicked men, their change is terrible. Wicked men grow upon the bank of hell, and when they are cut down they slip in, and there is their portion. When the inhabitants of hell are described, those that hold hell by tenure, Rev. xxi. 8, ' The fearful and unbelievers,' are in the front. Hell is the portion of unbelievers that never would own the faith, and the portion of apostates that have renounced the faith, and the portion of hypocrites that do but counterfeit faith.

[2.] Consider the good that is prepared for us, the excellency of the reward that God hath prepared for believers ; it is life, and a crown of life ; there is more in the accomplishment than in the promise. The word doth but speak of it in part, prophecy is but in part ; the word is suited to our present estate ; we have not affections and apprehensions large enough for such an excellent glory ; God is ever better to his people than his word. The incomparable privileges a believer hath in this life, those pledges and first-fruits they here enjoy, do show the heavenly life must needs be glorious and excellent. The joy of the Holy Ghost is ' unspeakable and glorious,' 2 Peter i. 8 ; heaven therefore must needs be more excellent and glorious. Let me instance in two things. (1.) The perfection of your nature. In heaven there is no want and no weakness; the body remains in an eternal spring of youth, the blossoms of paradise are always green and the soul is filled up with God; every faculty finds a satisfaction. We see what we now believe, and possess what we now love. Alas! here, though we know indeed that God is, yet we do not know what he is completely. The knowledge of God and the love of God shall be our sole employment, and we shall have constant communion with God, without weakness, weariness, and diversion, and God will be always fresh to us; as the angels that have beheld his face for these thousand years, yet still delight in God; we shall never be cloyed, because satisfied. And the perfection of heaven shall be so great, that, besides the personal glory of Christ there shall be a great deal of happiness redound by the glory of his saints; Christ will so set forth the riches of his goodness that he will be 'admired in all them that believe,' 2 Thes. i. 10; that is, in the glory that he puts upon the saints. (2.) The communion and company you shall there have. As soon as the soul departs out of the body you shall be carried by angels in triumph to Christ. Believers have the same entertainment which Christ had. Christ was welcomed to heaven with acclamations: Dan. vii. 13, it is said, 'One like the Son of man came with the clouds of heaven, and came to the ancient of days, and they brought him near before him.' He was 'brought,' that is, by a train of angels, and there conducted and welcomed to heaven with a Well done, and well suffered for the souls of men! So shall your souls be carried by angels into Abraham's bosom, Luke xvi. 22. Why into Abraham's bosom? Christ himself was not ascended, therefore it is said into Abraham's bosom; but you shall be carried into Christ's bosom. Look, as God did as it were take Christ by the hand when he ascended, therefore it is said, Acts ii. 33, 'Being by the right hand of God exalted.' It principally notes the power of the divine majesty; but it is an allusion to the entertainment we give to a friend or guest we would welcome, we take them by the hand; so will Christ entertain you. How sweet will it be when Christ shall give us the right hand of fellowship? The eye that cannot now endure to look upon the sun shall see the clarity and brightness of the divine essence beaming forth in Christ; we shall see Christ himself upon his white throne, and see all the holy ones of God: Mat. viii. 11, 'We shall sit down with Abraham, Isaac, and Jacob, in the kingdom of heaven,' and remain ever in his presence. It is sweet now to meet with the servants of God in an ordinance to praise God; what will it then be when we shall praise God for ever in the great assemblies of the spirits of just men made perfect? Consider, all this is made over by faith; we have the right and title in this world, but the inheritance is in our Father's keeping, it is reserved in the heavens, therefore get and keep faith.

Use 2. It serves to direct you how to exercise and act faith in order to the everlasting state. Five duties believers must perform.

[1.] The first work and foundation of all is to accept of Christ in the offers of the gospel; there is the foundation of a glorious estate. God excludes none from heaven that receive Christ into their heart. The first gospel commission that Christ signed and sent into the world contained this article—'He that believeth shall be saved,' Mark xvi. 16. And when the jailer said in his trouble, 'What shall I do to be saved?' it is answered, 'Believe in the Lord Jesus, and thou shalt be saved,' Acts xvi. 31 ; receive Christ into your heart, and he will receive you into heaven. Let us bring our beloved into our beloved's house, into our hearts, and he will then bring you into those mansions that are in his father's house. The primary office of faith is to close with Christ. There the foundation is laid rightly to receive Christ; and when the union is begun there is a pledge of glory : Col. i. 21, 'Christ in you the hope of glory.' The great work of a christian should be to get Christ in him ; there is the beginning of heaven.

[2.] It directs you to exercise your faith, to believe the promise of heaven which God hath made. Certainly faith is very weak in this particular, else we should have more ravishment and enlargement of affection. And the reason of this weakness of faith is, partly because it is wholly future, and the promise seems to be checked and defeated by death, and partly, because of our great unworthiness compared with the largeness of the recompense. Guilty sinners have low thoughts of the grace of God ; therefore it is a mistake of christians to think they only doubt of their own interest, they doubt of the main promise : Heb. xi. 6, 'He that cometh to God must believe that he is, and that he is a rewarder,' &c ; it is one of the fundamental truths never closely and surely enough laid up in your souls. A guilty creature is apt to straiten the divine mercy ; and we cannot believe God will do all this. Consider the riches of God's mercy, and the sufficiency of Christ's merit. God's mercy is one relief ; it is rich enough and full enough to give us heaven and glory. When God gives, he will give like himself. The two great perfections of the godhead are immensity and eternity ; he will give, with reference to his immensity, 'an exceeding weight of glory ;' and, with reference to his eternity, 'an eternal weight of glory ;' the apostle mentions both in 2 Cor. iv. 17, &c. This is a benefit fit for God to give. Then ruminate in your thoughts upon the abundant merit of Christ Jesus ; it is a high dignity, but remember it is purchased with a great price. Consider the humiliation of Jesus Christ, that you may believe your own exaltation. Certainly if God can abase himself, we may expect that the creature may be advanced and glorified ; and if Christ is clothed with our flesh, we may the better wait to be appareled with his glory. Consider, if Christ's glory could not hinder him from dying for us, certainly our misery cannot hinder us from reigning with Christ ; the giving of Christ makes all more credible : Rom. viii. 32, 'He that spared not his own Son, but delivered him up for us all, how shall he not with him also freely give us all things?' These things will facilitate the belief of heaven.

[3.] Get your own title confirmed ; lay claim to your inheritance ; seize upon heaven as your right and your portion, so as not only to believe heaven is possible and credible, but that it is your right, and made over to you in the testament of Jesus Christ : 1 Tim. vi. 19, 'That you may lay hold of eternal life.' A christian should possess and enter upon it as his own inheritance—This is mine. It was sweet when God said to Abraham, Gen. xv. 1, 'I am thy shield, and thy exceeding great reward.' Consider the grace that is wrought in you ; it is the earnest and the pledge of glory, it is the bud of glory ; therefore let us 'rejoice in hope of the glory of God,' when we have 'access to his grace by faith,' Rom. v. 2. A christian should look upon his present standing as a pledge of glory. Heaven, the apostle calls it 'the prize of our high calling,' Phil. iii. 14 ; he that hath given me Christ, and called me, can glorify me. God hath called me to grace that I may wait upon him for glory ; therefore rest upon the promise till you come to enjoy it, and until God measures the performance into your bosoms.

[4.] Let us often renew our hopes by serious and distinct thoughts. This is the way to anticipate heaven, by musing upon it: Heb. xi. 1, 'Faith is the substance of things hoped for,' &c. Wherever there is faith it will send out some spies to look within the veil, and see the glory that is there. We should always be thinking and ruminating upon it. If a man were adopted to the succession of a crown, he would always be pleasing himself with the supposition of the glory ; so when poor creatures are called to such hopes, they should be creating suppositions and images. Worldly men feast their spirits with worldly hopes ; they are thinking of the increase of their trade and promoting their gain: James iv. 13, 'To-day or to-morrow we will go into such a city, and continue there a year, and buy and sell, and get gain ; ' so a believer will be sending out spies, and feasting himself with his glorious hopes. A child of God doth translate himself by degrees, and weans himself from the world more and more, and is putting his heart into* heaven before his person is there ; he is 'seeking things that are above,' Col. iii. 1, and seriously musing upon them ; his heart is in heaven before his body—'Our conversation is in heaven,' saith the apostle, Phil. iii. 20 : all the business of their lives is laid so that they may look heavenward. As a man beyond the seas, when he hath gotten an estate there, will be forming his business so that he may draw it home ; so a christian is compassing this in the whole course of his life, that he may get home, and return to his country. It is a hard matter to get the heart to the study of heavenly things ; the children of God should do so. The sabbath-day is the image of heaven, and the communion we have with God in the ordinances is the pledge of that communion we shall have with God in heaven : God hath appointed that day on purpose for our help.

[5.] Another work of faith is earnestly to desire and long after the full accomplishment of glory. Faith bewrayeth itself by desires, as well as thoughts. All things hasten to their centre. Heaven is our home, and we should be hastening thither, not only in thoughts but desires. The world to a christian is but *libera custodia*, a larger prison, where his soul is kept under a restraint, and from the full enjoyment of Christ ; therefore a christian's life is spent in desires and groans : Rom. viii. 23, 'We that have the first-fruits of the Spirit, even we ourselves groan within ourselves, waiting for the adoption, to wit, the redemption of our body.' Mark, 'we that have.' A man that once hath tasted of the clusters of Canaan, he is weary of the wilderness ; so a christian is groaning for home, and for heaven, and for the full enjoyment of Christ, as the apostle saith, 2 Tim. iv. 8, 'They love his appearing.' Their hearts are always drawing towards Christ ; if Christ doth but say, I come, he echoes again, 'Come, Lord Jesus Christ, come quickly,' Rev. xxii. 20.

Use 3. To exalt the mercy of God to believers; once sinners, and by grace made believers. Observe the wonderful love and grace of God in three steps—

[1.] That he hath provided such an estate for believers. What a miracle of mercy is this that God should think of taking poor despicable dust and ashes, and planting them in the upper paradise, that they should be carried into heaven and made companions of the angels. How would we wonder if God should take a clod of earth and place it among the stars, that it may shine there! And how much more may we wonder when the Lord is pleased to take us out of the grave, and out of the earth, and lift us up above all heavens! when a man that is made of the dust of the earth is ἰσάγγελος, equal to the angels.

[2.] That this state is provided freely, and upon such gracious terms. The terms are faith, and not merit; that is the tenor of the new covenant. Believe and live, not do and live; but works serve to evidence that interest. The Lord hath said, John iii. 36, 'He that believes in the Son of God hath everlasting life;' he hath it, as sure as if he were possessed of it. God will exclude none that will but accept of the offer; therefore if thou dost but rely upon Christ by a true and proper faith, thou art in a safe condition: John v. 24, 'Verily, verily, I say unto you, he that heareth my word, and believeth on him that sent me, hath everlasting life.' Amen, amen. Will you believe Christ upon a double oath, when he plighteth his truth? Let us not straiten the promises; all that believe shall partake of that marvellous glory—all the difficult work was done by Christ—'He was taken from prison and judgment,' Isa. liii. 10, that we might not come into condemnation.

[3.] That God should send up and down the world to offer this salvation to men. The prophet saith, 'The salvation of the Lord is gone forth,' Isa. li. 5; and 'Wisdom hath sent forth her maidens,' Prov. ix. 3. And God hath sent forth his ministers, given us commission to open the grace of the gospel; and yet how is it scorned by men as if heaven were not worth the taking. If we did believe that there were such a glory, and that our eyes should behold it, how would it raise our hearts in thankfulness to God.

Use 4. Comfort to God's children against wants, and against troubles and persecutions, and against death itself.

[1.] Against wants. Let us be content with any condition in the world, since we are so well provided for in a better. Alas! after a short time we shall have no need of these things: Luke xii. 32, 'Fear not, little flock, it is your father's good pleasure to give you a kingdom.' Oh, you need not distract yourselves with worldly cares, there is a kingdom provided! It is grievous, I confess, to see wicked men abound with ease and plenty, and the children of God humbled with wants; but consider, if you have not so much money and means as others have, yet you have a better portion in Christ. God hath given you faith, and you are rich enough in Christ: James ii. 5, 'Hearken, my beloved brethren, hath not God chosen the poor of this world, rich in faith, and heirs of the kingdom, which he hath promised to them that love him?' Alas! wicked men that have large possessions, yet they may perish, notwithstanding their outward enjoyments.

[2.] It is great comfort against troubles and persecutions. Let us

continue in the faith. There is comfort enough provided for us in the
reward of faith : 1 Thes. iv. 18, ' Comfort one another with these words.'
What words ? why, that Jesus Christ will come in the clouds and meet
believers, and they shall be for ever with the Lord. We pitch too
much upon a carnal hope, and we think that this way and that way
deliverance will come from something we fancy in the world, but we do
not look after the glory of the everlasting state. There is an eye of
flesh, when there is no arm of flesh—suppositions of worldly help. God
will whip us for this vain confidence. We should comfort ourselves
that there is an everlasting portion. When the Lord would comfort
the patriarchs concerning the murder of Abel, there was the translation
of Enoch ; so when the apostle St Peter writes to the distressed
Hebrews (he had much ado to wean those godly Hebrews from carnal
thoughts of a temporal salvation and a temporal Messiah, from the
pomp and splendour of an outward deliverer), he proposes this to keep
up their joy : 1 Peter i. 9, ' Receiving the end of your faith, the salvation of your souls.' The encouragements of the world run in another
strain, looking for supplies in this and that corner of the world.
St. Paul continued in steadfastness, not only under the difficulties but
dangers of christianity : 2 Tim. iv. 8, ' I have fought a good fight, I
have finished my course, I have kept the faith.' Why ?—' For henceforth there is laid up for me a crown of righteousness,' &c ; that is,
that he was thinking of what comfort it would be when he should sit
in heaven among the glorified saints with his crown of righteousness
upon his head. The christian's life is not only a race but a warfare.
We must not only run, but fight ; therefore the apostle saith, Heb. xii.
1, ' Run with patience the race that is set before you.' Now that which
should keep us up is a garland of immortality and glory which Christ
hath wreathed for us. The primitive christians, when they were under
deep and dreadful persecutions, how did they comfort themselves with
the kingdom that is above ? The heathens suspected them as if they
intended to change the government. When you hear us talking of a
kingdom, you vainly and without reason suppose it is a human and
earthly kingdom ; no, we profess to hope not for an earthly but heavenly
kingdom.

[3.] It is a comfort against death itself. There is a glorious state
provided for believers. It is the end and privilege of faith to be translated out of the animal and corruptible life into that which is heavenly
and immortal. Death to the godly is but a sleep, and the grave but
a chamber of rest. Indeed the grave to wicked men is a prison, where
their bodies are kept, that they may not infect and corrupt the church ;
but to the godly their life is not extinguished, but hidden, Col. iii. 3 ;
and when Christ, who is their life, appears, then the veil is taken off,
and they shall appear with him in glory. Death to them is a translation ; life is not taken away, but changed—changed from a miserable
and corruptible life to that which is blessed and eternal. It is true,
death takes away the life of the body, which consists in the union of the
body and the soul, and this it doth but for a while ; but it doth not
take away the life of the soul, for that is immortal : it feedeth on your
dust, but the soul is in paradise—in Abraham's bosom, and it hath
nothing to do with the spiritual life ; still it is united to Christ. Look,

as when Jesus Christ died (and Christ and a believer run parallel), the personal union did not cease ; so when we die, the union with Christ doth not cease ; we die as creatures, as members of the first Adam, but we are sure to live as members of Christ ; Jesus Christ is our head in the grave. The death of the wicked is an execution ; it is indeed an act of vengeance. God orders death to be a trap-door to let them into hell ; but death to a godly man is an act of your Redeemer to translate you, and bestow upon you the happiness of eternal glory.

SERMON XXII.

By faith Enoch was translated that he should not see death ; and was not found, because God had translated him : for before his transla-tion he had this testimony, that he pleased God.—Heb. xi. 5.

The second general point is the necessity of the holy life.

Doct. 2. Those that would live with God hereafter must learn to please God ere they depart hence.

In the prsuance of this point I shall examine—

1. What it is to please God.

2. The necessity of pleasing God ere we depart hence. Where (1.) The necessity of the thing itself ; and there I shall show what respect and ordination the holy life hath to eternal glory. (2.) The necessity of the time, or the necessity of pleasing God, ere we flit out of the pre-sent life.

First, What it is to please God—'He had this testimony, that he pleased God.' It is a phrase by which the apostle interprets that place in Genesis, chap. v. 24, 'And Enoch walked with God.' In the Sep-tuagint it is ἐυηρέστησε τῷ θεῷ, Enoch ' well pleased God ;' so that to please God is to walk with God. The only difference between them is that the one relates to God, the other to ourselves. Pleasing of God implies his gracious acceptation, and walking with God implies our duty. Elsewhere the phrases of pleasing God and walking with God are joined in scripture ; as Col. i. 10, 'That you may walk worthy of the Lord unto all well-pleasing.' Walking notes the fixing and the holding of a settled course in our lives, that our intention and main scope must be to please God ; so 1 Thes. iv. 1, ' We beseech you,' saith the apostle, ' as ye have received of us how you ought to walk, and to please God, so you would abound more and more.' Walking notes the course of life, and pleasing on our part notes the aim of the believer ; all his care is to approve himself to God. On our part, it notes our endeavours ; on God's part, the success of our endeavours, his gracious acceptation. By this collation of places, we find that pleasing of God is all one with walking with God ; but because I intend to handle the phrase in the full latitude of it, I must make it yet more comprehensive ; for by the context you will find that it not only implies ' walking with God,' but, which is another distinct phrase of scripture, ' coming to God,' as you may see, ver. 6, for after he had said, ' Enoch had this testimony, that he pleased God,' he adds, 'For he that cometh to God,' &c., as if pleasing God and coming to God were all one.   So that the whole duty of man in the present life is comprised in this phrase of 'pleasing God;' and it is explained by these two parts—by 'coming to God;' and when we are come, 'to walk with God.'   I shall inquire—

1. What it is to 'come to God?'
2. What it is to 'walk with God?'

First, What it is to 'come to God?'   It is a usual phrase by which faith is set out in scripture.   Coming and believing are all one : John vi. 35, 'He that cometh to me shall never hunger, and he that believeth in me shall never thirst,'—where coming and believing are put as terms of the same import and signification.   Now this coming to God implies several acts of the soul, which must be explained with analogy and respect to outward motion.   In every motion there are two bounds and stages from which we come, and to which—*Terminus a quo, et ad quem.*

1. That which we come from is the curse and misery of our natural condition, or else we can never please God; as the apostle proveth, Rom. viii. 8, 'They that are in the flesh cannot please God.'   Mark the distinctness of the phrase,' ἐν σαρκὶ ὄντες, they that 'are in the flesh;' they that grow upon the old root, and are in their unregenerate state and condition.   There is a great deal of difference between being in the flesh, and having the flesh in us.   The children of God, as long as they live in the world, have a mixed principle, they have flesh in them; but they are not so properly said to be in the flesh, for that notes an absolute immersion in the carnal state, as being in the faith notes a state of believing: 2 Cor. xiii. 5, 'Examine yourselves whether you be in the faith;' so being in the flesh notes a corrupt and carnal state.   Now they that are thus in the flesh can never please God, that is, can never be accepted with him; so that out of this state we must come if we would perform this great duty.   Now this coming out of the flesh is done by several acts, several progresses and tendencies, by which the soul comes from the curse and misery of the carnal state.

[1.] By a sensibleness of our distance from God in such a condition. There is no coming but presupposeth a sense of absence.   Guilty creatures are at a vast distance from God.   There is a great gulph between us and heaven, an unpassable gulph; therefore the natural state is expressed by the prodigal's 'going into a far country,' Luke xv. 13.   There is a distance and departure from God; therefore it is said, Eph. ii. 13, 'You were sometimes afar off, but now are made nigh by the blood of Christ;' afar off, not only out of the church, but out of the state of grace.   Naturally we are all at a great distance in our minds and affections from God, and God is at a great distance from us; heaven is closed up against the access of a guilty creature.   Among other things this is one of the fruits of Adam's fall and disobedience; Adam did not only lose the image of God, but the fellowship of God; therefore ever since, the soul and God are at great distance and elongation.   So the psalmist expresseth it: Ps. lviii. 3, 'The wicked are estranged from the womb, they go astray as soon as they be born, speaking lies.' There is a strangeness between us and God, and we cannot come mutually to converse together. Now actual sins make the breach wider and greater: Isa. lix. 2, 'Your iniquities ·have separated between you and your God;' they make us careless of communion with God, and they make God resolved against any fellowship, or having any communion with us. Fallen man, at length, is not only come to be like the beasts, but like the devils; he puts on not only the brutish disposition of the irrational creatures, but the disposition of Satan himself; for the devils cannot endure the thoughts of God—'The devils believe and tremble,' James ii. 19. They hate their own thoughts of God; therefore they cannot endure the presence of Christ, but cry out, Mat. viii. 29, 'Jesus, thou Son of God, art thou come to torment us before the time?' This was the language of the devils; the presence of God was a bondage and a torment to them. So it is with guilty sinners; they cannot endure the presence of God, they speak just like the devil, Job xxi. 14, 'Depart from us, for we desire not the knowledge of thy ways.' Carnal men hate the thoughts of God. Now the first work of the Holy Ghost is to make the soul to be sensible of this distance and alienation from God.

[2.] There must be also a sense of the misery of such a condition. Men care not for God till they are sore pinched and urged with their own wants. When the prodigal was in a far country (by which the state of nature is represented), there with riot he spent his substance; but 'when he began to be in want,' then he thinks of returning to his father, Luke xv. 14. Men do not desire to recover their communion with God till they are thoroughly bitten with a serious remorse; God sends his hornet and stings their consciences, then they think of running to God. All the addresses to Christ in the days of his flesh began in the want of the creatures; the blind and lame and deaf, some possessed with devils, their maladies and miseries brought them to Christ, else there would not have been so great resort to him. So it is here; men never come to Christ till they are displeased with their natural state. Look, as Joab neglected to give Absalom a visit till he burned his cornfield, 2 Sam. xiv. 30, 31. Joab had never come if he had not set his barleyfield on fire; so the Lord lets in some sensible displeasure into the soul, and they begin to see the misery of a state of distance and alienation from God; and then they think of returning to God, and cry out, Oh, that they might be united to God! Look, as it is with believers in point of heaven, where there is the nearest communion with God;—we are apt to neglect breathing and panting after heaven when it is well with us in the world; but when the world is crucified to us, a dead and useless thing, oh, then, woe is me that my pilgrimage is prolonged! as David, when he was driven from his own palace, and was forced to wander up and down, then he says, 'Woe is me that I sojourn in Mesech, that I dwell in the tents of Kedar!' Ps. cxx. 5;—so also it is with sinners in point of communion with God in grace; they do not think of returning to God and making up the breaches, and removing the distance between God and them, till God hath made them weary of their carnal state, by letting some sense of his displeasure light upon their consciences.

[3.] There must be a sense of our inability to return and come to him. Man is a proud creature, and loth to be beholden; he would be happy and sufficient to himself; we would eat our own bread, and wear our own apparel; and if we could heal our own wounds we would never return to God. Conviction usually endeth in hypocrisy, when the soul is not wrought off from its own strength. If men can heal conscience, and dress up a form of religion, there they rest; men stay in themselves till this be done. We are all by nature absent from God, and the scripture showeth us our inability to return. The state of fallen man is resembled by the wandering of sheep: Isa. liii. 6, 'All we like sheep have gone astray.' Of all creatures, sheep are most apt to stray, and most unable to return. Swine and dogs know the way home again, but sheep do not: so it is with the soul. Saith Austin, *Domine, errare per me potui, redire non potui;* Lord, I could go astray, and wander by myself, but I knew not how to return. It is Christ's office to bring us to God; God hath set up a mediator to make up our distance from God. It is Jesus Christ alone that must carry the strayed lamb home upon his own shoulder, as the Holy Ghost alludes to that similitude, Luke xv. 5. We can never go to God upon our own feet, but we must be carried home upon the shoulders of Christ; therefore conviction will never be successful till it brings the creature to come and lie down at God's feet as utterly undone, and to say, Jer. xxxi. 18, 'Turn us, Lord, and then we shall be turned.'

2. The next bound and stage in this motion is, to whom we do return, and that is to God; to God, through Jesus Christ, for otherwise he can never be well pleased with us. He hath proclaimed from heaven he will never be pleased with his creatures till they become one with Christ: Mat. iii. 17, 'This is my beloved Son, in whom I am well pleased.' And Christ himself, when he professeth the quality of his offices, saith, John xiv. 6, 'I am the way, the truth, and the life.' Now the several tendencies of the soul towards God are a serious purpose to come to God, an earnest desire, and a constant waiting.

[1.] A serious purpose and practical decree issued forth in the soul. As the prodigal, when he was humbled with want, resolves, Luke xv. 18, ' I will arise, and go to my father;' so there is a resolution, I will arise, and go to God. All grace is founded in this practical decree. So David professeth his own shyness, that for a long time he kept off from God, and there was a distance between him and God; but at length he took up a serious purpose and determination that he would go and humble himself to God: Ps. xxxii. 5, 'I said, I will confess my transgressions unto the Lord,' &c. The soul, being inclined by grace, resolves to come to God through Christ. The scripture ascribeth much to this πρόθεσις, and settled resolution, that 'with full purpose of heart they would cleave unto the Lord,' Acts xi. 23. Our own wants and needs will make us full of anxious traverses, but the resolution and decree of the soul comes from grace; for herein lies the formal essence of faith, a resolved casting of the soul upon Christ, which is the issue and result of all those anxious and serious debates that were wont to be in the soul, by which, in the prophet's language, Jer. xxx. 21, 'The heart is engaged to approach to God;' when there is a charge laid upon the soul, by which the soul is engaged to come into his presence.

[2.] There is an earnest desire of enjoying communion with God in Christ: Ps. lxiii. 8, 'My soul followeth hard'—or maketh hard pursuit—'after God;' and the pursuance of the soul is by desires; they are evidenced to be gracious, because they are not only after ease and comfort. Such desires may arise from self-love, but after a constant communion with God: Ps. xlii. 1, 'As the hart panteth after the water-brooks, so panteth my soul after thee, O God;' not only after the sweetness and refreshment of grace, but after intimate converse with God: Ps. xxvii. 4, 'One thing have I desired of the Lord, that will I seek after, that I may dwell in the house of the Lord,' &c. And they are after grace as well as after comfort: Ps. cxix. 5, 'Oh that my ways were directed to keep thy statutes!' All the endeavours of a natural man are to go away from God; but when a soul is touched with grace, it can never have enough holiness, and enough grace, and enough communion with God.

[3.] Constant and industrious waiting. Many times God makes the soul wait long; he hath waited long upon us, and therefore he makes us to wait long ere we receive the sensible effects of grace. Therefore this coming to God is described by an industrious and constant waiting; as Benhadad's servants watched the king of Israel for the word 'brother, 1 Kings xx. 33, so the soul waits upon God for one glimpse of his love.' David expresseth this earnest waiting by the waiting of a sentinel or watchman for the dawning of the day: Ps. cxxx. 6, 'My soul waiteth for the Lord more than they that watch for the morning; I say, more than they that watch for the morning.' Look, as the weary sentinel that is stiff and wet with the dews of the night waits for the dawning of the morning, when he may be taken off from his charge and duty; so doth the poor soul wait for the first dawning and breaking out of the rays of grace upon the soul. Now this is not only done by a christian at his first conversion, but after coming and renewing his accesses to God by Christ.

Secondly, What it is to 'walk with God?' That is the original expression, from whence this of pleasing God is taken, Gen. v. 22. Now, what is the meaning of that? Some read it, *Vacavit Deo*—he sequestered himself, to converse with God from the distraction of worldly affairs; others render it, *Ambulavit in timore Dei,*—he walked in the fear of God; the Targum of Jerusalem, He served, or laboured in the truth before the Lord. Others apply it to public office and service in the church, as if it were proper to those that were employed in the function of the priesthood: certainly in such a restrained sense it is taken, 2 Sam. xxx. 35. But this would be a sense too restrained, especially since it is here explained by the apostle by pleasing God. Therefore it notes any solemn profession of religion, or consecration and dedication to God's service; for I find this phrase applied to persons that were of eminent and great holiness, especially in an evil and corrupt age, as here to Enoch, when men degenerated, and a flood was threatened. So it is applied to Noah—'Noah was a just man, and perfect in his generation; and Noah walked with God,' Gen. vi. 9, contrary to the corruptions and manners of his age. So it is applied to Levi; when the Lord speaks of the privileges of the house of Levi, he saith, Mal. ii. 6, 'He walked with me in peace and equity, and did turn many from iniquity;' that is, he held on God's side against the revolt and rebellion of the other tribes that had gone away after the calves in Dan and Bethel. It noteth a consecration of our lives to God's service, and special communion with him. The metaphor seems to be taken from two friends that agree and resolve to go a long journey, that they will keep the same way and course, as the Lord himself explains his similitude, Amos iii. 3, 'Can two walk together except they be agreed?' In the context God threatens the alienation and estrangement of his presence from them; for, saith God, You and I have gone hand in hand together; but now, if you take different courses, we must needs part: as two travellers, whose journey is not the same, cannot long travel together; so saith God, If you will take that path, I must break off communion with you, and withdraw my presence. Thus you find that he that by solemn vow and agreement with God hath set up his resolution to sequester and consecrate himself to the service of the Lord, is said to walk with God.

Now there are many parallel expressions, that differ only in sound; as, walking before God; so saith God to Abraham, Gen. xvii. 1, 'Walk before me, and be thou perfect.' It notes the very same thing. Thus Hezekiah, Isa. xxxviii. 3, 'I have walked before thee with a perfect heart.' The parallel phrases in the new testament are 'walking in Christ,' Col. ii. 6; and 'walking in the truth,' 2 John 4. In the general it notes special strictness and communion with God in the course of our lives; more particularly, I shall show you negatively what it doth not imply; then positively, what it doth imply.

1. Negatively, what it doth not imply.

[1.] Not such a strictness as to abridge ourselves of the holy use of the necessary comforts of this life. I ground this upon that place, Gen. v. 22, 'Enoch walked with God, and begat sons and daughters.' The holy and pure use of the creatures may stand with the strictest rules of profession. There may be a walking with God without monkery, and a sequestration of ourselves from worldly affairs. Enoch had a body as others had, and he needed the refreshment and support of meat, drink, and sleep, and the modest use of conjugal society, and yet walked with God; that is, in all these comforts he enjoyed God.

[2.] It doth not imply such a strictness and exactness as is wholly exempt from infirmities; for we read in scripture that Noah was one that walked with God, yet Noah was overcome with drink, Gen. ix. 21. Alas! in our journey many times carnal affections creep upon us, and bewray themselves by some indecent and impure actions, yet the Lord pardons them out of grace; though he be displeased with our sins, yet he accepts of our company still, accepts of our persons with Christ. On God's part the society and fellowship is not broken off, because they are interested in Christ; and on the believer's part the godly do not break off communion with God, because they recover themselves by repentance; there is a vigilant custody over their ways, but treacherous nature will be tripping now and then, and draw us to inconveniences. Alas! what then? The people of God are restless till they rise again, and recover the sense of God's favour; and when they stumble, they do not lie in the mire of sin, but endeavour to rise and keep on their journey; their constant purpose is to walk in a constant communion with God.

2. Positively, what is walking with God? There are two terms in the scripture; there is 'walking;' and then walking 'with God.'

[1.] Walking, that doth imply a way, and some motion in that way.

(1.) There must be a way. If we walk with God, it must be in his own ways. Now there are several ways of God; there are ways in which God walks to us, as Ps. xxv. 10, 'All the ways of the Lord are mercy and truth.' It is meant of the ways of his providence and dispensations to us; they are all stamped with the character of mercy and truth. And then there are ways in which we walk to God, and with God, and those are spoken of: Isa. ii. 3, 'He will teach us his ways.' And what is that way? that is his revealed will in the word. All our steps are but acts of obedience, conformed to the will of God; our whole course is a declining of evil and doing of good. We walk alone when we go out of the broad path and road of duty: Ps. cxxv. 5, 'They that turn aside to crooked ways shall be led forth with the workers of iniquity.' When they are in any crooked deviations of spirit, which are constant and allowed, they are none of those that God will keep company with. God holds communion with us in all his ways. It is a mistake to think our communion with God is only when we are practising duties of the first table, in the exercises of religion; then we do more intimately converse with him in meditation, prayer, and hearing. This is indeed the heaven of a christian; but God holds communion with us also in the necessary duties of our calling—in the shop, as well as in the closet. A man walks with God, it is true, as travellers sometimes may sit down and refresh themselves, but all the day they keep company. That is somewhat like communion with God in ordinances; but all the day we should keep God company. It is the dotage of foolish men to think all the world must be turned into a cloister, or we can have no company with God. We are indeed to sequester ourselves from the distractions of the world, but not from the employment of the world. There must be an even hand, that we may converse with God in worship, and in the duties of our calling: piety must not make us lazy, nor yet frugal diligence profane.

(2.) Walking doth not only imply choice of a way, but motion. In this motion there are two things—diligence and progress. (1.) An active diligence. Speculation doth not make us christians; no, nor a naked profession. We have a race to run; God cannot endure idlers, and those that merely dress up a profession. Deeds speak louder than words in God's ear; therefore there must be much spiritual diligence to prevent what is displeasing to God, and to practise what is acceptable. Treacherous nature is always apt to draw back and fly out, therefore we had need make a solemn covenant with our mind, will, and senses; with our mind, that we may not think evil, and provoke God with our thoughts; and with our wills, that we do not consent to evil; with our senses, that they may not be inlets to a temptation—all must be under the coercion of a severe discipline: Prov. iv. 23, 'Keep thy heart with all diligence, for out of it are the issues of life.' Christianity was never made for idle ones and lazy persons; as a bird in the air must always be moving on the wing, so we must be always in our flight and motion. There must be a constant diligence to guard the heart, to bring it to a serious performance of the duties of religion, and to keep it upright in duty. (2.) A progress. He that walks makes more steps than one; so a christian is in a continual journey, and God is in his company. Now we must make a continual progress. ·It is said, Ps. lxxxiv. 7, ' They shall go from strength to strength, till they appear before God in Zion.' The original word is, they shall go on from troop to troop; for it is an allusion to the solemn journey to the temple thrice a year. This was their ambition, who should outreach one another. When they had overtaken one troop, they strove to overtake the other troop; so in their solemn journey to heaven they shall gather new strength and courage, till they come to the triumphant church, and appear before God in Zion. A christian in his journey is like a man going up a sandy hill, if he doth not go forward, he goes backward; so we go backward when we do not make effectual progress; or like a man rowing against the tide, if he do not ply the oar, he goes backward—if there be not an effectual progress, there will be a sensible decay.

[2.] I come to show what this term ' with God ' implies.

(1.) The company and presence of God. He must needs be present with us that walks with us. How can God be absent from any? The apostle saith, Acts xvii. 27, ' He is not far from every one of us.' We are not so near to ourselves as God is to us. Who can keep his breath in his body for a moment if God were not there? God is present with us; but the meaning is this, that we must be present with God. Usually, we are at too great a distance in our minds and affections; therefore walking with God implies actual thoughts of his presence; he must be represented as the beholder of all our thoughts, words, and actions. The world is a great theatre, and the spectators are God and angels. I confess we little think of it; there is a fond levity in our minds. As to us, the world is like a hill of ants; you stand by, and they run up and down, and do not think of your presence and being there; so the Lord stands by and observes all our motions, and we run up and down like busy ants, and do not think of God's presence; there is a great hurry and clutter of business, and few thoughts of God. It is a description of carnal men: Ps. lxxxvi. 14, ' They have not set thee before them.' There are some have never any thoughts of God; they have nothing before their eyes but the world and worldly business. As it is storied of the panther, when she is hunted she hides her head, and when she doth not see the hunters, she thinks she is not seen by them; so we do not think of God, and therefore vainly imagine that he doth not think of us. In heaven, indeed a man doth nothing else but think of God; the divine essence is impressed there upon our minds, it is a part of our glory: Ps. xvii. 15, ' When I awake, I shall be satisfied with thy likeness;' we shall endlessly lose ourselves in the contemplation of the divine perfections. Now for the present faith serves instead of vision. God must be acknowledged as present with us, as certainly present as those outward objects with which we do converse, or as a man is whom we see with our bodily eyes. The soul hath its object and its senses as well as the body. There is a commerce between spirits; they see and hear, and converse with one another; so must our souls with God and holy angels. A christian can never be alone; by thoughts his soul converseth with God; they see him whom the world cannot see. We see that according to the different ranks of beings they have different objects: the beasts have eyes and senses to see external objects, and they judge by sight according to the form and outward appearance of things. Men have reason; that is higher than sight. Reason corrects sense in many things; as a star to sense seems but like a spark or spangle, reason can judge it to be greater—as big as the world. Christians have a higher light; they have faith to see him that is altogether invisible. Now this is the great advantage of religion; to see God by us, with us, and in us; nothing makes a man more holy than this. It is said, 3 John 11, 'He that doth evil hath not seen God;' that is, he doth not think of God's presence; he is as if he had no God to see him. Now, because it is impossible in the present life to have perpetual actual thoughts and considerations of God's majesty and goodness, there must be set times to represent the truth and glory of his being to the soul, till at length it be habituated to us; and when it is habituated upon every temptation, there will be actual discourses about his presence, especially when you are tempted to secret sins; as Job speaks of his unclean glances, chap. xxxi. 4, 'Doth he not see my ways, and count all my steps?' When there is an inward impure thought arising in the heart, it will be checked by this, Is not this liable to God's eye? as Joseph, when he was tempted to sin by the advantage of privacy, Gen. xxxix. 9, 'How can I do this wickedness, and sin against God?' Is any place private to God? The majesty of God will always run upon the thoughts, upon every temptation.

(2.) Familiarity. A beggar may be in the presence of a prince, but cannot be said to walk with him, for that noteth a social communion; a servant may be in company with his master, but he waits upon him, doth not walk with him. But now God hath taken all his saints into the honour of his friends; he is ours in covenant; we do not walk with him as with a stranger, at a distance, and with wary reservation, as with another man's God, but with our friend—with our God, with our confederate in Christ, one that is in covenant with us. There is abundance of intimate converse and familiarity between God and believers: 1 John i. 3, 'Truly,' saith the apostle, 'our fellowship is with the Father, and with his Son Jesus Christ.' How? by walking in the light: ver. 7, 'If we walk in the light, as he is in the light, then have we fellowship one with another;' that is, we with God, and God with us, as two friends and companions would walk together. There is the familiarity of discourse. It is not a mute, silent walk, but such as is full of sweet and interchangeable discourses, many sweet dialogues between God and us. Sometimes God, and sometimes we begin the conference; sometimes God speaks to the soul, and the heart answers God. God speaks to us by the injection of holy thoughts, by the motions and actual excitations of his grace; and the soul again speaks to God by prayer, meditation, and pious addresses: Ps. xxvii. 8, 'When thou saidest, Seek ye my face; my heart said, Thy face, Lord, will I seek.' The heart, moved and inspired by the spirit, gives God an answer. Sometimes, again, we begin the conference; we ask counsel of God in doubtful matters, when the soul is engaged with many anxious traverses, and knows not what to do. Now God answers us by the whispers of his Spirit; as the Israelites, Judges i. 1, 'Who shall go up for us against the Canaanites?' In all difficult and uncertain matters they make God their counsellor; and then the Lord leads them by his Spirit, and gives them an answer by casting powerful and overswaying considerations into their minds; as David saith, Ps. xvi. 7, 'My reins instruct me in the night-season.' In the silence of the night, when we are free from the hurry of distractions, then God inwardly speaks to us by our own hearts and by our own consciences, and sometimes we crave his help as well as his counsel. There is not a day passeth but there is some occasion offered to confer with God for christians that mind their work and their souls. Carnal men feel no impulses to prayer; they are not only strangers to God, but to their own souls. God and they are unacquainted, and they and themselves are unacquainted; for if men did not converse[1] with themselves, and mind the state of their souls, they would find there are many doubts need to be assailed, many wants to be supplied, many corruptions to be weakened and mortified. But when they leave off conference with themselves, no wonder they are so careless of holding conference and communion with God; when they and themselves are brought together, they will not be quiet till they and God are brought together. David speaks of sevenfold addresses in one day: Ps. cxix. 164, 'Seven times a day do I praise thee.' Oh, what a spirit are they of that can pass whole days and whole weeks and never speak a word to God, never give God a visit! Can these be said to walk with him? Now all our communion and speaking with God does not lie in prayer only; for look, as wants put us upon prayer, so blessings upon praises. The vapours and showers do maintain a mutual commerce between the earth and the air; the earth sends up vapours, and the air sends down showers; so it is here—blessings and praises maintain a mutual communion between God and us; God sends down the shower of blessing, and then we send up the vapour of praise, so that the soul lives in a holy sweet way of communion with him.

(3.) The fear of God. There must be a humble reverence if we keep God company. We are in the presence of the 'great king,' as the prophet calls him, Mal. i. 14; it is his pleasure to hold familiarity with us, but we must never forget our distance; there must be a constant fear and a reverend respect to God. It is a profanation to think of him without reverence, as well as to speak of him without reverence. Our familiarity with God must not be rude and careless, but such as becomes the distance that is between God and us: Micah vi. 8, 'What doth the Lord require of thee, but to walk humbly with thy God?' When we converse with God, we must not forget ourselves; we must remember the distance between infinite purity and a poor spotted creature. The angels and blessed spirits that enjoy the highest way of communion with God, they stand in dread of his presence. Fear is a grace in heaven as well as love; the angels clap their wings and cover their faces, and cry, 'Holy, holy, holy,' &c., Isa. vi. 2, 3. Those immaculate spirits are abashed at the glory of his holiness, and do not only praise, but fear him; for fear is an essential respect that is due from the creature to the godhead. It is true, faith is a grace which suits with our present estate, therefore it vanisheth in heaven, where we have full enjoyment; but fear is a necessary respect of the creature to the supreme majesty; there is a reverent and aweful, but a delightful dread in the angels; they have higher apprehensions of his holiness than we have, therefore reverence him the more. We have but low thoughts of that which is his chiefest glory, his holiness, therefore we do not reverence him as the angels do. Now if the angels are

---

[1] Qu. 'Did converse?'—Ed.

abashed at his presence, despicable dust and ashes have more cause to fear. Why? because we have sin in us, and are not out of danger of punishment. But angels are out of danger of punishments; they do not fear God for his commutative justice, but only reverence him for his holiness; but here we have sin in us, and can never have an absolute assurance of God's favour, therefore we have more cause to stand in dread. We may sadly reflect upon this, because we are guilty of such a negligent security, and we converse with God rather as an idol of our own fancy than a king of glory; there is not a reverent respect upon the soul. Oh, consider, there is practical atheism in irreverence! It is hard to say which is worse, to deny God, or not to fear him; an atheist makes him nothing, and a careless person makes him an idol—*Malo de me dici nullum esse Plutarchum, quam malum esse Plutarchum ;* and in the issue it is all one to deny his being and not to acknowledge his perfection, and to behave ourselves suitably. It is worse to behave ourselves to God as if he were a weak God, than absolutely to deny his being; but, alas! we never tremble but when he thunders, and when God shows himself terrible in some instance of judgment and vengeance. Alas! it is much for us, in our prayers and supplications, to be aweful in our special addresses to God, and yet fear is a grace that is never out of season and exercise: Prov. xxviii. 14, 'Happy is the man that feareth always;' not that perplexeth himself with scruples and terrors—that is a torment, not a blessedness—but that bears a constant reverent respect to God's presence. So again, Prov. xxiii. 17, 'Be thou in the fear of God all the day long.' In secret and in company, in the shop and in the closet thou art still in God's company, and still God is to be feared. But you will say, This is very hard, to keep the soul under an actual awe and trembling, and in the fear of God; therefore there must at least be a habitual awe; that is, a reverent and serious constitution of spirit, so that a man would not do anything that is unseemly in God's sight.

(4.) A care of obedience, or a holy ambition to please God and approve ourselves to him. Now in this pleasing of God there must be—

1*st.* An avoiding of whatever is grievous and displeasing to him. He that seeth God to be always present certainly he will be afraid to displease him; he will be always reasoning and discoursing thus in his soul, How will God like this with whom I am present, and before whom I am? You know the question of Ahasuerus concerning Haman, when he threw himself upon the queen's bed, Esther vii. 8, 'Will he force the queen before my face?' so, should I go about to grieve God before his face? to betray his cause, and comply with his enemies when he looks on? It is impudence to sin before any looker-on,— before a man, or before a child; but this in the presence of the just, powerful, and avenging God. Would a man ease himself, or void his excrements, before a prince? The comparison is not too homely, for this is the type which God gave his ancient church. There was a law, that if they went aside to ease themselves, they should cover their filth with a paddle, 'for the Lord walketh in the midst of the camp,' Deut. xxiii. 12–14. God would teach them by this similitude to avoid whatever is unseemly in his presence. There must be constantly manifested a respect to his presence; so Joseph: Gen. xxxix.

9, 'How shall I do this wickedness, and sin against God?' Sin is, on our part, a departure and a going out of God's presence; and as to God, it makes him to break off the journey—'Can two walk together except they be agreed?' Amos iii. 3. He cannot walk with us, and draw nigh to us, if we turn aside to those crooked paths.

2dly. There must be a constant care of those things God likes of, not only a declining of evil, but a doing of good. Take one disposition that is very pleasing to God. When your hearts are carried out wholly to spiritual things, then God delights to hold company and communion with such. When Solomon desired wisdom, and passed by riches and honour, it is said, 'The thing exceedingly pleased God,' 1 Kings iii. 10; so when the bent and strength of your desires are carried after spiritual blessings, that you may be wise to salvation, the thing is very pleasing to God.

3dly. This pleasing of God implies the uprightness of our aim, that the man is as good as the action. The main intent of the soul must be to please God, as his will must be the rule of your life; so his glory must be the end of your lives: Gen. xvii. 1, 'Walk before me, and be thou perfect.' God can look into the bottom of the heart; he weighs the spirits, and knows what are the inward propensions, the inward inclinations, the proposal we make to ourselves; so Hezekiah: Isa. xxxviii. 3, 'I have walked before thee with a perfect heart.' The heart must be sincere and rightly set, the aim must be to please God; negatively, it must not be to please ourselves, or to gratify the flesh in the conveniences of the present life, in outward profits and delights: Rom. viii. 12, 'We are debtors, not to the flesh, to live after the flesh.' A man that walks with God must dissolve the natural contract and agreement that is between him and the flesh; we are come under the bond of the new contract to please God. Look, as Jesus Christ, when he came to purchase this communion and this society with God, it is said, Rom. xv. 3, 'He pleased not himself;' so when we come to enjoy this communion, we are not to please ourselves, and so also our aims must not be to please men. He is nothing in christianity that doth not count the judgment of man a small thing, 1 Cor. iv. 3. When we give up ourselves to walk with God, we must remember we are not to seek for the humour of men: 1 Peter iv. 3, 'That he no longer should live the rest of his time in the flesh, to the lusts of men, but to the will of God.' Men of sociable, sweet dispositions are loth to displease those with whom they do converse; and so they are mightily prone to carnal compliance. The apostle disclaims this, Gal. i. 10, 'If I yet pleased men, I should not be the servant of Jesus Christ.' The Pharisees were angry when Paul revolted from their confederacy, when he that was their prime instrument turned preacher of the gospel. Company and humouring of men many times is a mighty snare to sordid spirits, but if it be done out of worldliness, it is worse; many men would please God so as they may not infringe their secular interest. Oh, consider, God will never walk with us as long as mammon is in company, when the bent of the heart is set that way: the world is to be our servant, not our fellow. When we walk with God we must have no other companion but God alone. Walking with God is usually a counter-motion to the times. Enoch, and Noah, and Levi, walked contrary to the times; it is an owning of God when others forsake him. But then, affirmatively, the great aim must be pleasing God alone; he is our companion. This must be the aim and scope of our lives, to please God; we must study to please him, and give him content in all things.

Quest. But if you will ask, Whether an actual intention of pleasing God in every good action be always necessary?

Ans. It is very convenient, but not absolutely necessary. A son is careful to please his father, though he doth not always actually think of it; there is a general and habitual intention, though in every act of duty the thought be not continued. Many good actions may proceed from the force of the habitual intention, when the actual intention or thought ceaseth; as an arrow from the aim of the archer, when his eye is taken off from the mark; or rather, a man that journeys to such a place doth not always think of his journey's end; but we should retain it in our thoughts as much as we can, that the heart may be more upright, and for the prevention of evil and carnal reflections: Rom. vii. 21, 'When I would do good, evil is present with me.' In short, a purpose of humouring the world or displeasing God cannot stand with grace.

(5.) A continual dependence upon God and a confidence of his assistance: Gen. xvii. 1, 'Walk before me;' it is different from the phrase of Enoch walking with God; that is, maintain a courage and confidence becoming my presence. A man may trust himself in God's company and defence. They that are always in the king's presence are sure of his favour and defence if they be in distress; God is at hand, and they may cast themselves into the bosom of providence in all dangers and troubles, and wait for the divine help. Usually we torment ourselves with unnecessary cares and fears about the event and success of things: a man that is in God's presence may refer himself to his care and protection. That this is plainly intended in this exposition, is clear by what is said in Acts ii. 25, 'I foresaw the Lord always before my face, for here he is at my right hand, that I should not be moved.' When a man walks with God, whenever he enters into the combat and list, God will be his second, ready to fight for us, in us, and by us. To open that expression, 'He is at my right hand.' When a man is at the right hand of God, that notes honour and glory put upon the creature; but when God is at the right hand of man, that notes help and aid. If the world offers foul play in our christian course, it is in God's presence; our second will come to our rescue. He that walks with God walks safely; when the devil is at our right hand, God is there to check the devil. The way to heaven is a dangerous journey, it lies through a howling wilderness; we shall meet with wolves and bears in the shape of men, and therefore woe be to him that is alone; but now when we have such good company, we may adventure freely, when God himself is our guide and leader.

(6.) Contentation. You must give up yourselves to God's disposal to shorten or lengthen out the journey as he shall see cause; for you walk with God, and follow the Lamb wheresoever he goes; so as, wherever God leads you, you must follow. Heaven is the place of rest, but for the time of our translation we must not be our own carvers.

It is good to groan and long for home, but still we must wait God's leisure; it is he that appoints the way and the stages of the journey. It is said of David, Acts xiii. 36, 'After he had served his own generation by the will of God, he fell asleep.' The will of God doth determine how long David was to serve him. We have a wise companion, and he knows the way to glory better than we, and he knows by what methods to bring us to glory. When God hath no further work to do by us, then he will give us our wages: Job xiv. 14, 'All the days of my appointed time will I wait till my change come;' our time is appointed, therefore we must wait. The walk in paradise is more pleasant than in the garden of the church; but the time of change is appointed; if it comes sooner than we expect, it is no loss; if it comes later, we must be contented. They that walk with God in earth cannot be separated from him in heaven, therefore it is no loss; for if you change place, you shall not change your company; you shall be nearer to him, and have sweeter communion with him, and you shall walk with him in a more glorious way. The heavenly state is described thus, Rev. iii. 4, 'They shall walk with me in white;' that is, in perfect joy and innocency, without sin and without temptation. Our garments here are often defiled, black, and spotted; but there 'they shall walk with me in white.' When we walk with God in the upper garden of paradise, there we shall have the same company in a better way; or, suppose the Lord should leave you to be harassed and worn out with the troubles of the world, if it come later, yet we must wait. The wise God knows when we are fittest for glory, and when glory is fittest for us: Job xiv. 5, 'His days are determined, and the number of his months are with thee; thou hast appointed his bounds that he cannot pass;' days and months to a precise time, all are defined by God. We live not at our own pleasure, nor at the pleasure of any creature; therefore though your pilgrimage be prolonged, you must be contented. Consider the precedent, Gen. v. 22, 'Enoch walked with God three hundred years:' he spent three hundred years in communing with God—a long age, and, as matters then went, very degenerate. But consider, the way should not be very tedious when we are in God's company; therefore when in trouble, we must refer ourselves to our guide, and with meekness, quietness, and contentation, we must follow him.

Use, Let me exhort you to come to God, and to walk with him; you have all the encouragement in the world to do both.

1. Come to God. You may come, and you must come; you may come, you are invited—'Come to me,' saith Christ, Mat. xi. 28. Though you are poor, guilty sinners, harassed and worn-out with your own fears and dissatisfactions, you may come, and you must come; either you must come to Christ, or lose eternal life: and it is very sweet to come to Christ. All good is in the chiefest good; the nearer we are to God, the nearer to the centre of rest and happiness; therefore every day and in every duty make nearer accesses and approaches to God by Christ.

2. When you are come to God, walk with him. Consider what encouragement you have: God is our companion, the Son is our saviour, and heaven is our patrimony; the way is safe, and the end

is glorious. It is a great honour when a great man will take you into his company and walk with you. The Lord hath put this honour upon all his saints, that they shall walk with him in a way of federal communion.

SERMON XXIII.

For before his translation he had this testimony, that he pleased God.—
Heb. xi. 5.

Secondly, Now I come to the other branch, to confirm the point by showing—(1.) The necessity of pleasing God; (2.) The necessity of pleasing God in the present life.

First, The necessity of pleasing God; for whosoever will live happily with the Lord in glory must have a care to please him in the present life.

1. Because this is the means and condition without which we shall never come to enjoy God; it is the way to fit the sons of God for glory, though not the cause of glory: Heb. xii. 14, 'Follow peace with all men, and holiness, without which no man shall see the Lord.' The apostle presseth there peace and holiness; but mark what he saith of holiness—without which no man shall see the Lord. He presseth them to follow both; but observe the difference: we must follow peace, that we may walk with men; and holiness, that we may walk with God. They that prefer peace before holiness may gain favour with men, but they lose fellowship and communion with God. God's stipulation with mankind is not made up together of promises; he promiseth much, but he requireth something; as he giveth many blessings, so he requireth many duties; not for which, but without which we shall never be blessed; it implies not a condignity of merit, but an ordinability to the reward. It is required of all those that will be saved: holiness is appointed by God as the way, heaven as the end of the journey. Wherever the scripture speaks either of the decrees of God, or those ordinances of judgment and justice by which he will govern the world, or the covenant of God, there is a duty left upon man. Thus the apostle, Eph. ii. 10, 'We are created in Christ Jesus to good works, which God hath before ordained, that we should walk therein.' They are not the cause of our salvation, or the merit by which we acquire a right, but they are the way and path by which we get to it. There is a great deal of dispute about the necessity of walks;[1] there is *necessitas præsentiæ* though not *efficientiæ.* Observe the constitutions of heaven, this is the order: he will appoint first holiness, then happiness; there is no causality, but order. God's decrees have put salvation into this way and course—first faith, then works, then glory: Eph. i. 4, 'He hath chosen us, that we should be holy.' The eternal counsel of God respecteth both the end and the means. Holiness is a necessary effect of election, and it must have a room; it is necessary, not as a cause, but as a condition. We are not chosen because we were holy, but that we might be holy: Rom. viii. 29,

---

[1] Qu. 'Works?'—Ed.

'Whom he did foreknow he did also predestinate, to be conformed to the image of his Son.' This was the solemn appointment of God, that those whom he had marked out by his own choice and eternal counsel to be heirs of the grace of life should be conformed to his Son, first in holiness, then in glory. God hath bound himself by promise to deal this way with the creatures, that whosoever shall embrace the agreement of the new covenant shall be saved.

2. There is a necessity of it by way of sign, and as a pledge of our living with God hereafter—' Before his translation he had this testimony, that he pleased God.' This is that testimony which witnesseth to us our interest in the everlasting state. When holiness is our care, it is a token that heaven is our portion; God will not own us for his own, neither can we take this honour upon ourselves unless we have this mark. The merit of Christ, apprehended by faith, gives us our right and title; but holiness doth evidence and confirm our right and title; we can have no assurance till then. Good works are *eternæ felicitatis præsagia*, the necessary forerunners and presages of eternal happiness. Never can there be a sound hope towards God where there is not a religious and conscionable desire of walking before God in all well-pleasing; otherwise men do but confute their hopes, and live down their own expectations. In establishing assurance there is a double witness—the spirit and conscience: both have a voice; the Spirit hath a voice, but none can hear it but holy persons. The person must be qualified first to receive the testimony of the Spirit; for the Spirit when he comes to witness to us, doth not reveal to us so much the purposes of God as the gifts of God: 1 Cor. ii. 11, 'For what man knoweth the things of a man, save the spirit of man which is in him?' The Spirit's testimony is always subsequent to that of the renewed conscience; for the Spirit's testimony is nothing but the evidencing and owning of its own work; and the testimony that we have from the Holy Ghost is not intuitive, but discoursive; the Spirit doth not comport at first with such a report as this is, that mercy is prepared for thee from all eternity; but thou art holy, and therefore thou art in a state of grace and favour. Then conscience hath a voice. Now the testimony of conscience ariseth from comparing our actions with the rule, the conversation of men with the stipulation of God. By a single apprehension it looks up to what God requires, then by reflection how we answer it; and so gives sentence: Heb. xiii. 18, 'We trust we have a good conscience, in all things willing to live honestly;' 1 John ii. 3, 'Hereby we know that we know him, because we keep his commandments.' The soul is persuaded that it hath an interest in God because it keeps his commandments; there is some ground and warrant for the report of conscience. General hopes are but a deceit, and fond credulity without ground.'

3. It is necessary by way of preparation. Those that walk with God are meet to live with God; they change their place, but not their company; here they walk with God, and there they live with him for ever. The vessels of glory are first seasoned and prepared with grace; God's qualifying grace makes way for his rewarding grace: Col. i. 12, 'Who hath made us meet to be partakers of the inheritance of the saints in light.' Alas! what should carnal and sensual persons do in heaven?

those blessed mansions that are above would be to them as melancholy and obscure shades.   How can they endure the perpetual presence of God, that now cannot endure the thoughts of God ? or how can they delight in the communion of saints to whom now good company and holy conference is as a prison ? how can men leap from the lap of delight into the bosom of Abraham so suddenly ? what should swine and dogs do with such a holy place in the upper paradise ?   Heaven is an intimate familiarity with God, and therefore it is not for mere strangers ; heaven is said to be prepared for us, and we are said to be prepared for heaven.   Christ is gone in person to heaven to prepare a place for us, and hath left his Spirit upon earth to prepare us for heaven ; and this is the reason of those expressions so often used in scripture, of being ' worthy of eternal life,' and walking ' worthy of the high prize of our calling,' and ' worthy of God : ' the meaning is, beseeming and becoming.   We are put into a holy meetness and fitness for such holy rewards : Rev. iii. 4, ' They shall walk with me in white, for they are worthy ; ' that is, fittingly disposed and prepared ; as in another case, Mat. x. 11, ' Into whatsoever city or town ye shall enter, inquire who in it is worthy ; ' that is, prepared by the Holy Ghost to receive the doctrine of life, and to entertain God's messengers ; inquire who hath a good report and are lovers of religion, ready to entertain the word and the messengers of the word.   So here they are ' worthy ; ' that is, fittingly disposed, meet to receive such a portion in glory.   It is not any equality of worth that is implied there ; but that which is meet, convenient, and becoming.   God works in the hearts of believers an aptitude for blessing, then he bestows them upon them ; first, he gives the heavenly mind, then the heavenly state ; the new creature for the new heavens and the new earth. Wicked men have a portion suiting to them, and becoming their affections ; sensual pleasures for a sensual heart ; so God's children, before they have their portion, they are suited to it, that they may have a portion suited to their heart.   This is the great mercy of God, that he will never advance our condition till he hath changed our hearts.   A king may advance a slave to a high place of trust, but he cannot give him gifts and fitness ; he may change his state, but he cannot change his nature ; but God, before he gives heaven, he gives a heavenly inclination ; and before he gives communion with himself in glory, there is communion with himself in grace.

Secondly, The necessity of pleasing God in the present life—' For before his translation,' it is said, ' he had this testimony, that he pleased God.'   There is a time for all things, and the time of pleasing God is in the present life.

1. Because this is the time of grace.   Here we are invited to walk with God : now we have the means, then we have the recompenses ; here Christ saith, Mat. xi. 28, ' Come to me,' in a way of choice communion ; then, Mat. xxv. 34, ' Come, ye blessed of my Father, inherit the kingdom.'   Now we come to receive grace, then we come to him to receive glory ; here God makes an offer, and there he makes it good. Upon gospel terms he holds out the golden sceptre, therefore here is the time to please God.   When the angels came with a song to publish the tidings of salvation, mark the burden of their song : Luke ii. 14, ' Peace upon earth, and good-will towards men.'   Now the Lord offers

to be reconciled : the church is the seminary of heaven, and here we are trained up for glory. We shall never have such golden seasons again ; you shall hear of no gospel afterward ; there shall be no more tenders and offers of grace. Zanchy speaketh of some that had a fancy that the gospel should be preached in the other world to those that never heard of Christ in this world—to children, Turks and pagans, alleging that place, 1 Peter iii. 19, ' By which he went and preached to the spirits in prison ; ' but this is as a fancy and nothing to thy case. Now only doth Christ say, ' Come ! ' If you refuse him now, he will hereafter say, ' Depart ! ' This is the season of grace.

2. This is the time of our exercise and trial. As death leaves us, so judgment finds us ; our everlasting woe or weal hangs upon the present moment. Hereafter is not the time of labour, but of rewards and punishment. Then there will be no more room for repentance, though we should seek the blessing with tears, Heb. xii. 17 ; therefore here is, the time of our exercise and of our work ; we are now put to our choice. There is no triumph without warfare—' They are not crowned except they strive lawfully,' saith the apostle ; that is, according to the laws of the race, 2 Tim. ii. 5 ; so we cannot expect our crown till we have been exercised in the duties of holiness. They that live in the Lord die in the Lord, and they shall hereafter reign with the Lord. It is said of ungodly men, ' their iniquities shall find them out,' Num. xxxii. 23 ; and of the godly ' their works follow them,' Rev. xiv. 13 : they reap the fruit of their works in the other world. We may observe, many live as if they never thought to die ; therefore when they come to die they die as if they never thought to live. Oh consider, your works do not die when you die ; they are kept in a safe register, and they will find you out : Eccles. xi. 3, ' If the tree fall toward the south or toward the north, in the place where the tree falleth there it shall lie.' As we live, so we die, and so we shall arise and come to judgment. Here is the time of our trial and exercise. Look, as the Jews upon the sixth day were to provide for the sabbath, and therefore they were to gather two omers of manna then ; the present life is our sixth day, here we are to make provision ; they that did not provide on the sixth day had nothing on the sabbath ; so we shall have nothing to do with the everlasting sabbath unless we make provision in the present life. Here we are *in via*, then *in termino*. Death will at length cut us down and deprive us of further opportunity : Eccles. ix. 10, ' Whatsoever thy hand findeth to do, do it with thy might ; for there is no work, nor device, nor knowledge, nor wisdom in the grave whither thou goest.' When this life is ended, all opportunity of doing good ends with it. The next life is not *sæculum operis*, but *mercedis*. Therefore now we must be making out our qualification : Gal. vi. 10, ' As we have therefore opportunity, let us do good unto all men.' Opportunities are passing, and being passed will not return ; they are confined within the narrow precincts of the present life. Afterwards, the time of our trial and exercise is past : John ix. 4, ' I must work the works of him that sent me while it is day : the night cometh, when no man can work.'

3. The sooner we begin the better.

[1.] Because you make a necessary work sure, and put it out of

doubt and hazard.   The time of this life is uncertain : James iv. 14,
' Whereas ye know not what shall be on the morrow ; for what is your
life ? it is even a vapour, that appeareth for a little time, and then
vanisheth away.'   And a work of necessity should not be left on per-
adventures ; therefore we must bestir ourselves without delay.   We
know not how soon opportunity will be over ; it cannot be done too
soon, it may be too late, and therefore it is good to be of the surer side.
Ludovicus Capellus telleth us, out of Rabbi Jonah's book of the
mystery of repentance, that when a disciple came to his teacher to know
what was the fittest time to repent in, he answered, ' One day before
death,' meaning presently ; for we have not assurance of another day :
Prov. xxvii. 1, ' Thou knowest not what a day may bring forth.'   Our
greatest works, and of most absolute necessity should be done first, and
have the quickest despatch, lest it be too late before we go about them.
Oh, woe to us, if God should call us off before we have minded coming
to him, and walking with him !

[2.] In point of obedience, God presseth to ' now.'   God doth not
only command us to please him, but to do it presently : Heb. iii. 7, 8,
' To-day if ye will hear his voice, harden not your hearts.'   God standeth
on his authority, and will have a present answer.   If he say, ' To-day,'
it is flat disobedience for you to say, ' To-morrow : '   2 Cor. vi. 2, ' Now
is the accepted time, now is the day of salvation.'   At this instant you
are charged in his name, as you will answer the contrary.   You say,
no ; I will please the flesh a little longer.   It were just with God, if
you refuse him, never to call you more.

[3.] In point of ingenuity.   We receive a plenteous recompense for
a small service.   When a man thinketh what God hath provided for
them that love him and serve him, he should be ashamed that he should
receive so much and do so little ; and therefore he should redeem all
the time that he can, that he may answer his expectations from God.
Shall we adjourn and put off God to our decrepit time, when he hath
provided for us eternal happiness ?   Can a man, which hath any
ingenuity in his breast, be content to dishonour God longer, and grieve
his Spirit longer, provided that at length he may be saved ?   Those
that have any due sense of God's kindness, or their own duty, will think
God hath been too long kept out of his right, and that all the time that
remaineth is too little to express our love and thankfulness to him : 1
Peter iv. 3, ' For the time past of our life may suffice us to have
wrought the will of the gentiles.'   Men that delay, do in effect say,
Let me despise thy commands and abuse thy mercies a little longer ;
but then, when my lusts are satisfied and youthful heats are spent, I
will see what I can do to be saved.   What baseness of spirit is this !

[4.] It is our advantage to begin betimes, both here and hereafter.

(1.) Here.   The sooner you begin to please God, the sooner you have
an evidence of your interest in his favour, more experience of his love,
more hopes of being with him in heaven ; and these are not slight things.
When once you taste the comfort of them, you will be sorry that you
had begun no sooner ; as Paul complaineth, ' that he was born out of
due time,' 1 Cor. xv. 8.   He lost the advantage of seeing Christ in the
flesh, and personal conference with him, and so you will lose many sweet
visits of love and experiences of grace that otherwise might fall to your

share: Rom. xvi. 7, 'Who were in Christ before me.' An early acquaintance with Christ bringeth many benefits with it of peace, and comfort, and joy, and hope, which others that set forth later want. The consolations of God should not be vile and cheap with us; if you were acquainted with them, you would leave your husks for bread in your Father's house.

(2.) The sooner you begin with God, the greater will your glory be hereafter; for the more we improve our talents here, the greater will be our reward in heaven: Luke xix. 16–19, 'Then came the first, saying, Lord, thy pound hath gained ten pounds; and he said, Well, thou good servant; because thou hast been faithful in a very little, have thou authority over ten cities. And the second came, saying, Lord, thy pound hath gained five pounds; and he said likewise to him, Be thou over five cities.' See Christ's answer, Mat. xx. 23, ' To sit on my right hand and on my left, is not mine to give, but it shall be given to them for whom it is prepared of my Father.' There are degrees of glory set forth, by sitting on the right hand to some, and left hand to others; as in hell, there is a hotter and cooler judgment: certainly, they that have long pleased God and made it the whole business of their lives shall have larger measures of happiness.

Use 1. If there be such a necessity of pleasing God, and giving up ourselves to the severities of religion, then it serves for reproof of divers sorts of persons; as—

1. Those that, though they live as they list; as if they were sent into the world for no other purpose but to gratify their carnal desires, yet lay as bold a claim and title to heaven as the best; they doubt not but glory belongs to them, though they cannot make good their title. It is true, here in this world is the time of God's patience, and God keeps on open house; here the wicked, as well as the godly, have some taste and some experience of God's bounty. The world is a common inn for sons and bastards, but heaven is a pure place; no unclean thing enters there. There are no swine in the upper paradise. At the great assembly and congregation, God will make a separation: Ps. i. 5, ' The ungodly shall not stand in the judgment; nor sinners in the congregation of the righteous.' Wicked men shall not be able to look Christ in the face, they shall not mingle themselves with that glorious assembly of saints—' The place of dogs is without,' Rev. xx. 15. There is no point more pressed in religion than the separation God will then make, and no point less granted; for we all flatter ourselves with general and deceitful hopes of mercy: ' Know ye not,' says the apostle, 1 Cor. 6, 10, ' that the unrighteous shall not inherit the kingdom of heaven? Be not deceived,' &c. We are all apt to deceive ourselves with a general loose hope. Universal salvation is written in the heart by nature; that is the reason why we are so prone to hearken to the doctrine of universal grace. Men are apt to deceive themselves with such a lying hope. Our desires do by degrees settle into opinions. Careless people would fain have it so; they would have God guide and govern the world after another manner; they would have heaven, and they would not be at the pains of strictness to conquer lusts and subdue unruly affections; they would not be at the trouble to dedicate and give up themselves to the will of God; and by little and little their desires

grow into hopes.   Men will never be persuaded that God will ever damn his own creature; therefore, as ignorant people, they say, He that made me will save me, though there be express words to the contrary, Isa. xxvii. 11 ; and therefore they please themselves with a naked hope of mercy, without making good their own interest.   Consider, you have no liberty to sin by Christ's death.   Christ died to gain you to please the Lord, and walk before him in all holiness : 1 Peter i. 18, 'Forasmuch as you were redeemed not with corruptible things, from your vain conversation,' &c.

2. It reproves them that think that every slight profession of the name of God will serve the turn; no, you must walk with God and please God.   We are mistaken in the business of pleasing God ; it leaves a great burden of duty upon the creature ; it notes a universal constant care to please God at all times and in all things ; it is resignation and giving up yourselves to the will of God: Rom. xii. 1, 'I beseech you, brethren, that ye present your bodies a living sacrifice, holy, acceptable to God, which is your reasonable service.'   Now wordly men that have not God in all their thoughts, or else wholly devote themselves to humour their own lusts, to please themselves and to please the flesh, not to please the Lord, yet, because of some slight acts of duty, they will foster and cherish great hopes in their bosoms. Oh, consider, you that please the flesh and deny yourselves in no carnal delight, you must look for your reward from the flesh.   If you have lived as those that would gratify yourselves in all your carnal desires, you are not meet for heaven.   Or else men will rest in this ; they will please God where they do not displease themselves, or wrong or endanger their own interest.   Alas ! this is man-pleasing and walking with mammon, not with God ; they mind duty only, as it lies in mammon's road.   Consider, walking with God is not a step or two— practising duty now and then; but a 'walking worthy of the Lord,' as the apostle saith, 'unto all well-pleasing,' Col. i. 10.   It requires much severity of life and solemn sequestration from the distractions and pleasures of the world, a great deal of self-denial, and still waiting upon God in holy services.   Now, men that are only varnished over with the general name of christians are far from this. Oh, consider, what God is, and what you expect from him, and what in reason is suitable hereunto !   God will not be put off with anything ; you are 'to walk worthy of God, who hath called you unto his kingdom and glory,' 1 Thes. ii. 12.   Oh, but we cannot endure to hear of such strictness, and think it is rank puritanism.   But do you know that God is a great king, and will not be served with what costs you nought, you that wipe your mouths, and think sins are but petty slips and small escapes ; that God's patience will suffer all and his grace pardon all ; that no man can be perfect; that the purest saints have fallen into as great faults ; and that you shall do well enough, though you be not so strict and so nice ?   Oh no, it cannot be ; these are vain thoughts —spider's webs, sorry fig-leaves, sandy foundations ; all these notions the scripture useth in this case.   Our presumption of the end is upheld by our presumption of the means ; it is not presumption simply to think you shall be saved, but to make every slight act a ground of hope. Men have no solid grounds of assurance, but usually make up in the

strength of persuasion what is wanting in the grounds and warrant of it, as if bold-faced confidence would serve instead of duty.

3. It reproves those that would please God, but with a limitation and reservation so far as they may not displease men, or displease the flesh. Oh, if you please God, it requireth a solemn sequestration for his use, much self-denial, ' to be followers of them, who through faith and patience inherit the promises,' Heb. vi. 12. There is none went to heaven but one time or another they were sorely put to it; and God will try whose interest is greater in us; the fleshly interest or his interest, whether sensible things have a greater hand and power over us, or his promises : the best have need to look how they acquit themselves upon trial.

4. It reproves those that adjourn and put off the work of religion from time to time, till they have lost all time; that use to put off God to the troubles of sickness or the aches of old age. It is Satan's great artifice to cheat men of the present season by future promises. Oh, consider, the work is great, and life is short ! If we did live as many years as days, or as many years as there be days in the year, as Enoch did, yet there would be enough to take up our time. The journey to heaven is long, and we have but little time ; we can never outgrow our duty ; still there would be room for abounding in the work of the Lord. Consider again, no season can be fitter than the present time. But still we want something ; in youth we want wisdom ; and in age we want vigour and strength ; and, besides, it is very uncertain whether God will give us another opportunity. We have not a lease of to-morrow ; if we had, it is doubtful whether ever we shall have a heart to make use of it. We cannot presume of our own hearts, because grace is not in our own power ; we cannot presume on God's mercy, for he hath made no absolute promise ; we cannot presume of any singular efficacy that will be in old age or in death, because moral means do not work without special grace. Although we see we are declining every day, yet we are as the bad thief who had one foot in hell ; yet he mocks and scoffs at Jesus Christ, and dies blaspheming; nay, we have shrewd presumptions of the contrary, because there will be a greater disability either in respect of ourselves or grace—and use makes our hearts readier to sin ; and by long continuance the habit of displeasing God will be strengthened. Satan is never more busy than when life draweth to an end, and thou hast never less strength to resist him. Long use makes your hearts obdurate, and long resistance will grieve the Spirit of God, and sins of an unregenerate life will make death more terrible : and therefore do not adjourn and put off God. Certainly when a man is unfit for every common secular employment, he is much more for spiritual ; the trouble of pains and aches, and decay of spirit, and the diversion of business, and the importunity of Satan's temptations, these things should put us upon taking hold of the present season. It is to be suspected, when we will not leave our sins till we leave our lives, how shall we then distinguish nature from grace ? or that it is more than natural affrightment, arising from the sense of disease and pain, or natural desires of happiness ? And besides, the invitations of scripture call for a present obedience, a yielding up ourselves, not upon force, as when we come to die ; but they call for

willing and ready obedience : Heb. iii. 13, 'While it is called to-day;'
and Eccles. xii. 1, 'Remember thy Creator in the days of thy youth:'
in thy young and flowery age, when thou mayest more glorify God.
And then we do not know how long the day of grace will continue ;
the day of grace is not always as long as a man's life : the Lord
may pass the sentence of obduration and final hardness upon us.
Alas ! corruptions will grow upon us, and carnal desires grow up
with us, and our affections grow more stiff and hardened every
day, as letters in the bark of a tree. Consider, a man cannot
come soon enough into the arms of mercy, nor soon enough out
of Satan's power ; a man can never too soon begin his journey
towards heaven. If you did but mind your. salvation in earnest, you
would be more in haste. The heirs of promise are described to be
'those that fly for refuge, to lay hold upon the hope set before them,'
Heb. vi. 18 ; there is an avenger of blood at their heels, they see wrath
pursues after them ; therefore they fly for refuge. And consider again,
there is little love of God showed in this, that you repent only when
you can sin no longer ; when you can be content God should be dishonoured for a long time, provided that at length you should be saved.
Oh, do but consider what an ill requital you make to the Lord for his
purposes of grace towards you ! he thought of us before there was
hill or mountain. As long as God is God, he is the God of the elect:
Ps. ciii. 17, 'From everlasting to everlasting thy loving-kindness is to
them that fear thee.' If God hath loved us from one eternity to another,
what ingratitude is this to confine him to the odd corner of our lives,
to the aches and phlegm of old age ! Again, it is a great honour to seek
the Lord betimes. Mnason is famous for this in scripture, because he was
'an old disciple:' and the apostle speaks of Andronicus and Junia,
'who were in Christ before me,' Rom. xvi. 7—sooner than me in grace.
It is a mighty privilege to be in Christ before others.

Use 2. If there be no hope of living with God without pleasing
God, oh, then make it the aim and scope of your lives to please the
Lord ! You that have already given up yourselves to the will of God
had need to be quickened again and again to make good your resolution. See how earnestly the apostle speaks : 1 Thes. iv. 1, 'We beseech
and exhort you by the Lord Jesus, that as ye have received of us, how
you ought to walk, and to please God, so ye would abound more and
more.' This is the work and business of your lives, to keep company
with God, to enjoy him in a gracious communion. Take a direction
or two what you shall do ; take the commandment for your rule; take
the promises for your encouragement ; and make the glory of God your
great aim. Look to the commands that you do not err ; look to the
promises that you may not be disconsolate ; look to the glory of God
that you may be sincere, and keep on in an even course of holiness.

1. Look to the commandments as your rule : Micah vi. 8, 'He
hath showed thee, O man, what is good ; and what doth the Lord
require of thee, but to do justly, and to love mercy, and to walk humbly
with thy God?' God hath told you what will please him. Because
the characters that are engraven upon your hearts are blurred, and a
man can hardly read them ; therefore God hath given us his word, and
there are his decrees and ordinances of judgment and justice recorded

how he governs the world. A man is pleased when we do his will; God's will is in his word. God will accept of nothing but what he hath required, otherwise we walk at random. I shall not unravel the decalogue; a short summary is useful to us. It is good to have all christian obedience summed up into brief heads. Sometimes the will of God is summed up in one word, sometimes in two, sometimes in three; the apostle sums it up in one word: 1 Thes. iv. 3, 'This is the will of God, even your sanctification,' that you should grow more holy and holy every day; so Gal. v. 14, 'The law is fulfilled in one word, even in this, Thou shalt love thy neighbour as thyself.' Sometimes the scripture doth sum up all christian obedience into two heads, as all sins by the apostle are referred unto two heads: Rom. i. 18, there are the breaches of God's will, 'unrighteousness and ungodliness;' so the great things required are holiness, or godliness and righteousness, the exercise of religion, and a civil honest conversation: Luke i. 74, 75, 'That we should serve him without fear, in holiness and righteousness before him, all the days of our life.' Sometimes the Spirit of God abridgeth all duty into three heads. Titus ii. 12, would you please God and walk with God; there is the sum of all; to live 'soberly' with respect to ourselves, 'righteously' in respect of others, and 'godly' with respect to the Lord himself: 'soberly' in opposition to the lusts of the flesh. You should make straight steps to your feet; there is need of a great deal of severity; all your affections should be under a prudent coercion and restraint. There is too great a wantonness in professors. Men justify sensuality, and call it living to the height of the creature; the apostle taxeth such, Jude 19, 'Sensual, having not the Spirit.' They pretend to a special singularity of having the Spirit, yet walk to the utmost of christian liberty, yea, and many times exceed their bounds, burden their souls with excesses; therefore you should walk soberly, take all the creatures with thanksgiving, and use them as medicines to repair nature when it is tired with services, not as fuel to brutish lusts. Then the will of God is, that you should walk 'righteously.' Oh, the sadness of the fraud, oppression, and seeking to aspire and domineer by faction that is among professors! Now you are to walk righteously; that is, not only not to snatch from others, but to give of your own, to give and forgive. As you are not to take from others by hooking-in their estates by violent oppressions, so you should also lay out yourselves and part with your worldly comforts for the glory of God and necessities of the saints; you should walk with holy meekness and patience, not returning injury for injury. The next is 'godliness;' you should give God his portion, and bewail it that you have so often denied it him. If our bodies be but defrauded of a night's sleep, we are troubled and complain; if we feel the pain of hunger, we complain. Oh, do not neglect God and your precious souls! I remember St Bernard hath a pretty note of Martha's complaining of Mary, that she sat at Jesus' feet, while herself was employed in all the business of the family. Oh, saith St Bernard, 'That is a happy family where Martha complains of Mary!' Oh, how few families do thus complain! The world eats up our time, our care, and our thoughts, and God hath but little share, little worship, and little reverence.

2. Let the promises of God be your encouragement. All the sweet thoughts of a christian arise from the ample and gracious thoughts of God, expressed in the promises : Ps. xciv. 19, 'In the multitude of my thoughts within me (saith David) thy comforts delight my soul;' when his thoughts were interwoven and intricated like the boughs of a tree. It is good to see that you fetch all your comforts and encouragements from God's promises, and not from carnal hopes: 2 Cor. v. 7, 'We walk by faith, not by sight.' This is to live by faith, to have recourse to the promises of a better life, when we have any burden upon us. A christian's comforts all lie within the veil; they are not taken from visible enjoyments or carnal hopes; the promises of God are his enjoyment.

3. You should make the glory of God your chiefest end, or you will be very irregular, and cannot keep pace with God in a constant course of duty. Look, as a man that hath a nail in his foot may walk in soft ground, but when he comes to hard ground he is soon turned out of the way, so when a man hath a perverse aim, he will soon be discouraged with the inconveniences that will trouble him in religion. The spiritual life is called 'a living to God,' Gal. ii. 19. The end must be right, otherwise the conversation will be but a vain pretence, that will please men, but not God: Prov. xvi. 2, 'All the ways of a man are clean in his own eyes, but the Lord weighs the spirits.' The chiefest thing God puts into the balance is the temper of the mind, the bent of the heart; what you are moved by, and what sways you. Therefore your chiefest care must be to set the heart right in all actions, those that are of the most trivial concernment; in the use of our christian liberty, the necessary actions of our life; in our duties: 1 Cor. x. 31, 'Whether you eat or drink, or whatsoever you do, do all to the glory of God.' This must be the bias upon the christian spirit, that he may be led on with a constant respect to the Lord's glory; as we act from him, so we should act for him and more to him—a by-end will make you eccentrical in your motions.

SERMON XXIV.

But without faith it is impossible to please Him; for he that cometh to God must believe that he is, and that he is a rewarder of them that diligently seek him.—HEB. xi. 6.

THE Apostle had spoken of Enoch's translation as a consequent of his pleasing God, and upon the supposition of his pleasing God he proves his faith. The reason is rendered in this verse, because ' Without faith, it is impossible to please God ; for he that cometh to God,' &c. In the words there are two general parts—

1. A proposition—*Without faith it is impossible to please God.*

2. The reason of it—*For he that cometh to God must believe that God is, and that he is a rewarder of them that diligently seek him.*

To begin with the proposition—'Without faith it is impossible to please God,' which, being a formal doctrine of itself, I shall use this method—

1. Explain the words.

2. Give the necessary inferences and corollaries, both doctrinal and practical, that may be gathered hence.

First, For the explication, ' without faith ; ' that is, without saving and justifying faith, without faith in the Messiah. I prove it, because that is the faith spoken of in the context ; it is the drift of the apostle to prove that the elders, the fathers of the old testament, were saved by the same faith that we are. Again, this kind of faith is expressed in the following words—in 'coming' and 'seeking ;' he that 'cometh to God,' and that diligently ' seeks him.' Again, we cannot conceive God to be a rewarder out of Christ ; guilty nature presageth nothing but evil. The apostle speaks of the gentiles, Rom. i. 32, 'That they know the judgment of God, that they that commit such things are worthy of death.' You can look for nothing but death by God's justice without a Christ and a mediator ; but because this is a weighty matter, and the apostle seemeth to make the catechism or summary of necessary points very short ; for he mentions only two articles—God's being and God's bounty—his essence and his reward, without any mention of Christ, as if this were enough to please God, or enough for acceptance to salvation ; therefore I shall discuss and examine the matter. Many in these last times of the gospel are weary of the christian profession, and are ready to revolt into libertinism and atheism, as if nothing was necessary to please God but a general faith in his being ; and therefore I shall

1. Prove that this general faith is not enough.

2. Show what is the scope of the apostle, and why he mentions only God's being and bounty.

3. Show how the place is to be explained.

1. That this general faith is not enough ; for two reasons—

[1.] Partly because more is elsewhere required : John xvii. 3, ' This is life eternal, to know thee the only true God, and Jesus Christ whom thou hast sent.' This and nothing else is eternal life ; that is, the means or way to life eternal.

The knowledge of Christ is every way made as necessary to salvation as the knowledge of God, for indeed without Christ we can never come to enjoy God. There is a great gulf betwixt him and us ; all gracious commerce is broken off between God and the fallen creature, and therefore, John xiv. 6, 'No man can come to the Father but by me.' In the fallen estate of man there is need of a mediator. Man in innocency might immediately converse with God ; God loved his own image in Adam ; and what could a just and holy man fear from a just and holy God ? But now of God's creatures we are made his prisoners; we can expect nothing from his mercy, because he is just ; and therefore if the creature would have comfort, another principle must be taken in ; we must not only know God to be the true God, but Jesus Christ whom he hath sent. The great inquiry of the whole world is, wherewith shall I please God ? Micah vi. 8, ' Wherewith shall I come before the Lord, and bow myself before the high God ? ' How shall he give his justice content and satisfaction ? Solomon saith, that when man had lost his innocency, he was full of inventions : Eccl. vii. 29, ' God hath made man upright, but they have sought out many inventions.' Man at first had wisdom and light enough to guide him to happiness, but ever since we have been given to roving and fond counsels, and we seek here and there how to return to that happiness we had lost. But among all the inventions of man he never found out a sufficient ransom to expiate sin, to reconcile us to God, to sanctify human nature, that we may again hold commerce with heaven ; so that there is somewhat more required than a sight of a divine essence, and a general belief of his rewards ; even the knowledge of Christ, without whom there is no salvation.

[2.] Partly because many that never pleased God may go so far ; as the devils that are condemned to everlasting chains of darkness, and the heathens that are altogether ignorant of Christ, and carnal christians that never felt the saving efficacy of his grace. The devils believe God's essence and his everlasting recompenses. His essence : James ii. 19, ' Thou believest that there is one God, thou doest well ; the devils also believe and tremble.' The devils themselves are under the awe and dread of this truth. There may be atheists in the world, but there are none in hell ; the devils believe there is a God, and they could never exempt and free themselves from the horror and thought of it. So they believe his recompenses : Mat. viii. 29, ' What have we to do with thee, Jesus, thou son of God ? art thou come hither to torment us before the time ?' The devils have some sense of the day of judgment, though they cannot hope for any release, and can look for nothing but an increase of torment ; yet they know there is a time coming, and they tremble for the present at the thought of it. So for heathens ; they believe that God is, and that there are some rewards ; though their belief of these things be very weak and imperfect, and mingled with falsities and absurd conceits of their own, yet they had some knowledge of the reward of virtue. Epictetus requireth two things that are necessary to piety— ὄρθας ὑπολήψεις περὶ Θεῶν ἔχειν, ὡς ὄντων, καὶ δικοῦντων τὰ ὅλα καλῶς καὶ δικαίως—That we should conceive of the gods, first as being, then as guiding all things with goodness and justice. So Ælian saith, That the very barbarians did affirm that there was a God, and that he had a care of all human affairs, to reward what was good, and to punish what was evil. And Seneca—*Primus est deorum cultus deos credere, deinde reddere illis majestatem suam, et reddere bonitatem, sine qua nulla majestas.*—The first thing that we must do is to believe there are gods, then acknowledge their majesty and power, then their goodness, without which all religion would perish. And Plutarch—οὐ γὰρ ἀθάνατον καὶ μακάριον μόνον ἀλλὰ καὶ φιλάνθρωπον καὶ ὠφέλιμον ἀναγνώσκειν χρὴ τὸν Θεόν. It is necessary ,if we would begodly, that we should not only believe there is a God, immortal and happy, but that he is a lover of men, if we exercise ourselves in virtuous things. I might produce many instances in this kind ; but I forbear, lest it should seem to savour of affectation and blustering in an unknown language. So for carnal men, where the sound of the gospel hath come, those that have not a dram of grace, they have this general faith, that God is, and that God is a rewarder ; therefore this cannot be enough to please God, and to be accepted to salvation to have such apprehensions. A man is not saved by holding a right opinion of God. A man may be a christian in opinion, and a pagan in life and practice; we must make a particular application of those things, that so our own interest may be sure. When a man is ready to perish and drown, it is not enough to see land, but he must reach to it, and stand upon it, if he would be safe; so we must get an interest in God. The apostle requires ' coming and seeking' in this place; ' coming ' implies desire of communion with him, and ' seeking,' a diligent use of the means that we may enjoy him. There must be an application of those things to a practical end, else the general notion and opinion will do us no good.

2. The scope of the apostle is not to set down the whole object of faith, but the first foundation—namely, what faith is absolutely necessary, and previous either to the seeking of the favour of God or any act of obedience; for unless we do believe that there is a divine power, and that there are recompenses appointed to encourage the duty of the creature, all religion would be but a dead custom, and would be soon abolished. Therefore, I suppose, the apostle, to prove his argument with more advantage, proceedeth, *ex concessis*, from things that common reason will grant to be necessary to every good action. He instanceth in the principal radical truths, which are the foundation of all religion, that there is a God, and that this God will reward all virtue; there is a God all-sufficient, and he will be good to the creature.

3. These two articles must be enlarged and explained according to the analogy of faith and the declaration which God hath made of his will in the gospel; all breviates, wherein religion is reduced to a few heads, must still be explained according to the extent of the rule of faith. Look, as in the commandments, where all moral duties are reduced to ten words; so in the summaries of the gospel, those things must be explained by the extent of the rule of faith; for instance, in the first article, ' He that cometh to God must believe that he is;' that is, he is as he hath revealed himself, one in three persons; for otherwise we worship an idol, and not that which is God. We form an idol when we think of God out of the trinity; therefore we must believe that he is in that manner as he hath revealed himself in the scripture. So for the other article, ' That God is a rewarder;' that is in the way that God hath revealed himself according to the tenor of the covenant of grace; that he is a rewarder in and through Christ as mediator; that he will give us all the blessings of the covenant, justification and remission of sins, as the pawn of glory, and sanctification as the beginning of glory; and then glory itself as the perfection of all; and all these things in and through Christ. It is true, in innocency there were but two things to be believed; that God is, and that God is a rewarder. But now, after the fall, both before and after the law, the catechism was enlarged, and we have to look not only to our creator, but to our saviour, the mediator; but after Christ's coming the will of God is more explained, and our belief is required to be more explicit.

' It is impossible;' not in regard of the absolute dominion and sovereignty of God—he might have taken another course of salvation—but in regard to his will, and the course into which our salvation is stated and disposed. God can save a man without faith, as, saith Mr Perkins, he can enlighten the world without the sun; but this is the way which, in wisdom and justice, he hath found out. God's will is the supreme rule; and as God hath ordered the way by which he will bring creatures to happiness, so *ex hypothesi*, it is impossible ever to be accepted of God without Christ.

'To please God;' what is that? In the former verse I told you what is in Gen. v. 24, 'Enoch walked with God;' it is in the Septuagint, Enoch pleased God. Walking with God notes obedience, and pleasing of God the success of obedience. To please God here is to be accepted in any act of duty and obedience; to be accepted to life as conformable to God's will. Now it is impossible we should be thus accepted without faith in Jesus Christ. Thus I have opened the propositions.

Secondly, I come to the inferences that may be drawn from hence; some are doctrinal, some of practical consideration.

First, It is impossible to be saved without true faith in Jesus Christ; or, that there is no religion but that which teacheth rightly to believe in Christ, that can be looked upon as a way of salvation. Jews and Turks and infidels can never please God, nor be accepted to life, because they have no faith. There are many that say that every man shall be saved in his own religion—Turks, Jews, heathens—if they be true to their principles—and devout in their own religion. Symmachus, a wicked heathen pleading for paganism against the christians, and for the ancient worship of the gods, saith thus, *Æquum est quicquid omnes colunt, unum putetur, eadem spectamus astra, commune cœlum est, idem nos mundus involvat; quid interest quod quisque sua prudentia verum inquirat? Uno itinere non potest perveniri ad tam grande secretum.*— It is but equal, that though we take several ways, yet we should live together, as those that agree in the same worship. We behold the same stars, and we hope for the same heaven, and we live upon the same earth, what matter in what kind of way we seek out the truth. This opinion layeth a foundation for atheism and libertinism, and doth much take off from our thankfulness that we owe to God for that excellent treasure which he hath opened to the church in the scriptures; so that they which plead for the heathens had need look to themselves, lest they themselves are not found christians. Clear it is, if we will hearken to what is revealed, that there is no salvation in any other but in Christ, Acts iv. 12. God hath acquainted the creature with no other way how we may come to life. Now, the heathens had no knowledge of Christ; they had only some general knowledge of a divine power, they had τὸ γνωστὸν Θεοῦ—'That which may be known of God,' Rom. i. 19: some general notice of a divine being, which served to leave them without excuse, but not to save them. It is true, they might by the creation understand God's eternity and power—attributes that are obvious, but more terrible than comfortable to sinners—but for any knowledge of Christ, they could have none. Sun and moon could not preach Christ, though they might preach a God; but the way of salvation by Christ, the very angels come to know by the church: Eph. iii. 10, 'To the intent that now unto the principalities and powers in heavenly places, might be known by the church, the manifold wisdom of God.' Christ, then, they knew not; and without Christ there is no salvation.

Many objections are against this—

Obj. 1. Say they, it is true; they cannot be saved without Christ;

but they are saved by Christ, though they have no knowledge of him ; as Peter was delivered by the angel out of prison before he wist who it was, Acts xii. 9. 10 ; so they feel themselves to be saved before they know their saviour.

Ans. The apostle saith, ' Without faith it is impossible to please God.' He doth not only say without Christ, but without faith ; so that not only the benefit of Christ is established in this doctrine, but the necessity of faith : so John xvii. 3, ' This is life eternal to know thee the only true God, and Jesus Christ, whom thou hast sent. As none can be saved without Christ, so none can have benefit by Christ, but those that know him, and that believe in him.

Obj. 2. But say they, by some extraordinary ways God might reveal himself and discover Jesus Christ to them.

Ans. This we cannot judge ; we are to keep to the rule. Only let me hint that the ground of this conceit is naught ; that because the heathens had many moral virtues, therefore they think God was bound to reveal Christ to them, they having so far improved nature. This is again a falsehood, because those things which do not come from faith, and were not done for the glory of God, were not accepted with God ; they were but sins set off with the fairer lustre and varnish ; and the only privilege they could have by that was *ut mitius ardeant,* that they may have a cooler hell.

Obj. 3. It is said of divers, they were persons devout and feared God before ever they had any knowledge of Christ ; as Acts xvi. 14, ' A certain woman which worshipped God, heard us ; ' so it is said, Acts ii. 5, ' There were dwelling at Jerusalem devout men, out of every nation under heaven,' that were not as yet christians ; but they repented, and were converted by the sermon of Peter. So Acts x. 2, ' Cornelius was a devout man that feared God with all his house ; and ver. 34, 35, it is said, ' God is not a respecter of persons, but in every nation he that feareth God, and worketh righteousness, is accepted with him.'

Ans. These places do either speak of a natural devotion, which may arise merely from the instinct of conscience, therefore our translation useth the expression ' devout,' not ' religious ; ' or, they speak of proselytes that did actually profess the Jewish worship, or were acquainted with it, though they did not join with them, as many of the Romans did, though they were not actually circumcised. In Acts, chap. xvi., where Lydia is said ' to worship God,' it is meant only out of blind instinct of conscience ; in the second of the Acts, it is spoken there of Jewish proselytes that came up to Jerusalem to worship at the feast. Concerning Cornelius, though he were not a professed proselyte, yet he was acquainted with the doctrine of the Jews, and had some knowledge of God. Such an one was the eunuch, Acts viii. They knew and feared the true and living God, and had faith in the Messiah to come, though they had not faith concerning the person of Christ ; they expected the redemption of Israel, upon which faith, being drawn out into acts of obedience, they were accepted of God, as the patriarchs were that did believe in the Messiah to come. As to Cornelius, it is clear he was exactly religious ; he was already converted by being acquainted with the Jewish doctrine concerning God and the Messiah ; his prayers and alms came up before God. Now God heareth not sin-

ners ; and for that general conclusion in Acts x. 34, ' Whosoever feareth God, and worketh righteousness, is accepted of him.' I answer,
righteousness is there taken for any conformity to the will of God,
revealed either in the law or gospel. He that renounceth his own
righteousness, and casteth himself upon the merits of Christ in the
sense of the gospel, is a worker of righteousness, and God will accept
of him of whatever nation he be. The expression showeth that all
distinctions are taken away, and the pale of grace is enlarged.

Obj. 4. If God will not accept the gentiles without faith in Christ,
then he requires that which is impossible ; there being no revelation
of Christ made to them, and they having in Adam not so much as a
power to believe in Christ ; for if he had not sinned he had no need of
a mediator ; and, therefore, how can the Lord require faith of them
for their acceptation to life ?

Ans. 1. At the last day the gentiles shall not be responsible for
want of faith in Christ, but for not keeping the moral law which was
written upon their hearts, and for not obeying the dictates of their own
consciences, as the apostle proves at large : Rom. ii. 12.–14, ' As many
as have sinned without law, shall also perish without law,' &c ; for
God deals with men according to the measure of their light, and in
the process of the last day he will call the heathens to an account for
not living according to the dictates of reason and conscience : God
will exact no more than he gives. It is true, he doth not give them
further means ; but that is not their sin, but their infelicity and punishment for their sin, though they can never be accepted without Christ.

2. For what we received in Adam, I answer, Though Adam was not
bound to believe in Christ, yet he had a power of believing all that
was revealed of God, as he that is fallen blind had a power of seeing
the house afterward built.

Use. To apply this first inference. If there be no way of life, no
doctrine of salvation but only the christian religion, that which holds
forth God in Christ, then—

1. It presseth us to bless God for the knowledge of the gospel.
Oh, how many thousands in the world are there that are as sheep,
whom no man taketh up, but are spilt upon the great common of the
world, and left to the process of divine justice. Let us bless God for
our privileges, that we have such fair advantages ; certainly if we look
to the hole of the pit out of which we were digged, we were as bad as
others. The old Britons worshipped the most monstrous and mis-
shapen idols ; this was our original in the day that God looked upon
us. If we abuse our privileges, and be unthankful for the light of the
gospel, he may return us again to our old barbarism. The Lord
threatened Israel : Hosea ii. 3, ' I will strip her naked, and set her as
in the day that she was born.' The Lord may strip us naked, and
take away all our spiritual favours ; and while we run after new lights,
the Lord may remove the old light from us. We are afraid of popery ;
this is not altogether so bad as atheism ; therefore let us be thankful
and careful to improve those advantages God hath put into our hands.
We cannot be thankful enough for the knowledge of God in Jesus
Christ, it is a great mystery, not only pleasing to the thoughts, but
healing to the soul. The Lord is angry with the gentiles, and hath
brought many judgments on them for putting the finger in nature's

eye.   Oh, what will be our misery for quenching or slighting the light of the gospel, and the excellent revelation God hath made to us of Christ.   The heathens had some obscure knowledge of God, but we have the revelation of the knowledge of God in the face of Jesus Christ. By their own consciences they knew the moral law; God offered terms of duty to them, but he offers terms of salvation and grace to us.

2. It presseth us to prize orthodoxism, and, above all things, look to this, to be right in point of belief.   Every man shall not be saved in every persuasion, nay, though they do in general acknowledge Christ.   There are a sort of libertines risen up, that think the differences and controversies in Christendom with Socinians and Arminians are but vain and frivolous, and that a loose belief of God and Christ is enough.   If this general faith be enough, then why hath God revealed so many things to us, and given us a more ample rule, if with safety to salvation we may be ignorant of them?   Why hath he appointed us to contend for the faith of the saints, and for the truth that is revealed in the scripture? as whether you are redeemed with a satisfaction, or whether you are justified by his righteousness or works ? It is no matter, say they, for these lesser explications.   Such men seem to tax the scriptures, that they have redundancies and superfluous doctrines, and they seem to tax the holy apostles of rash zeal, when they disputed so earnestly for the faith of the saints; as Paul against justiciaries for the righteousness of faith, and James against antinomians and libertines for care of good works.   And they tax the holy martyrs of folly, that they would shed their blood for less concerning articles ; so all be resolved into Christ.   Men think this is enough.   Men need not inquire into the manner of the application of his righteousness, the efficacy of his price, the merit of his passion, as if it were enough to hold a few generals, and the more implicit our faith is the better ; whereas, the Lord would have us to abound in knowledge, and to have the word dwell in us richly.

What articles are absolutely necessary to salvation will be hard to define and determine, and what that measure of faith is without which we cannot please God.   And I know not by what rule to proceed; if we should make it too large, it would be a ground of ignorance and laziness; if we make it too strict, it would be a ground of uncharitableness to them that labour under invincible prejudices.   Only that you may not be loose in this matter, take a few rules.

[1.] The foundations of religion are God and Christ, and they must be held with great certainty : John xvii. 3, ' This is life eternal to know thee the only true God, and Jesus Christ whom thou hast sent.'   We cannot be saved unless we hold one God in three persons, and Jesus Christ as mediator.   These are the supreme truths that are clearly revealed and propounded to our faith.   But now for practical truths ; for the way of enjoying God and Christ, they are revealed in other texts : John xvi. 8, ' When the comforter shall come, he shall convince the world of sin, of righteousness, and of judgment.'   This is the doctrine the Spirit teacheth in the church, to convince of sin, and the curse that remains upon man while he is under the power of nature ; of ' righteousness,' of the sufficient satisfaction of the Lord Jesus Christ, of judgment and holiness.   It is very dangerous to hearken to those that lessen the misery of nature, or the merit and satisfaction of Christ, or the care of good works; all such opinions are irreconcileable to the covenant of grace, and overturn the main pillars upon which salvation stands. When men advance nature or depress Christ, or decry good works, as long as they live according to their principles, they can never be saved.

[2.] We must be earnest concerning the particular explication of those truths, as they are delivered in scripture. Every piece and parcel of truth is precious, and a little leaven of error is dangerous. The apostle, speaking of error, saith, Gal. v. 9, 'A little leaven leaveneth the whole lump.' He speaks there of errors in matters of justification, which of all matters of religion is most nice and delicate; error fretteth like a gangrene, till it eateth out the heart of religion. Men think it is enough to be careful of fundamentals and that all other knowledge is *scientia oblectans;* only a knowledge for delight, and not safety. Oh! consider it is very dangerous to err in the particular explication of those doctrines; to stain the understanding, though we do not wound it. I confess there are some truths of lesser importance; there are *maculæ et vulnera intellectus*—the spots of the understanding as well as the wounds of it. Now it is dangerous to be wanton in opinions that seem to be of a smaller concernment. Men that play with truth, they run themselves into a snare; and though they err but in a small matter, yet they are liable to more insinuations. Some say fundamentals are few; believe them and live well, and then you shall be saved. This is as if a man in a building should be only careful to lay a good foundation, no matter for the roof, windows, or walls. If a man should come and untile your house, and tell you—Friend, I have left the foundation standing, the main buttresses are safe; you would not take it well. Why should we be more careless in spiritual things?

[3.] No lesser error, be it never so small, is to be held and kept up out of interest, and against the conviction of conscience, because we can plead there is salvation in that way. This is some men's first inquiry, Is there salvation in such a way? therefore let us not stay in lesser errors. If they are held up against conscience, they are damnable; for then they come under the notion of allowed known sins. To hold up any lesser way merely out of interest, and not out of conscience, it is very dangerous; and it is an argument of an unsubdued will, or that the heart is wedded to secular interest; and it is a preferring the favour of men before the favour of God, as our Lord saith, John xii. 43, 'They loved the praise of men more than the praise of God;' for though there may be salvation in both those ways, yet you are to own God in all his truths. Phil. iii. 15, the apostle speaks in the case of circumcision and uncircumcision —'Let us therefore, as many as be perfect, be thus minded; and if in anything ye be otherwise minded, God shall reveal even this unto you.' Circumcision and uncircumcision are nothing in themselves, but much if they are held up for the preservation of our interest, and merely that we may cleave to such a party. And mark, it is all one whether there be a plenary conviction or a secret fear or suspicion; and we do not search, as many men are afraid to search, lest truth should make against their interest. These are those that Christ describes : John iii. 20. ' They will not come to the light, lest their deeds should be reproved ; ' and ' they are willingly ignorant,' 2 Peter iii. 5 ; when men labour for distinctions to daub over the matter, and to hide the truth from conscience ; or when they are unwilling to search, being afraid lest they should find it too soon.   As in practicals, a man is not willing to be informed what he should do for good uses, and how strict he should be in his conversation, that he may please himself in his carelessness ; this is a sign of an unsubdued heart ; so in these cases, a man is willing to be ignorant ; they are loath to be informed, and will not sift truth to the bottom, lest it may intrench on his worldly conveniences ; usually in truths of the present age, interests make the heart thus doubtful and suspensive.   This is the first instance which concerned heathens and aliens from the commonwealth of Israel.   You have seen there is no salvation in any way, but only in that way which holds forth faith in Jesus Christ.

SERMON XXV.

But without faith, it is impossible to please him ; for he that cometh to God must believe that he is, and that he is a rewarder of them that diligently seek him.—HEB. xi. 6.

SECONDLY.   The second inference concerneth the children of believing parents.   If without faith it be impossible to please God, then children must have some kind of faith, else they can never be accepted to life. I know that the apostle doth principally speak of adult or grown persons, men of age, such as come to God, and seek him ⁚ but though, however, the rule is general, there is no salvation but by Christ, and there is no way of salvation by Christ but by faith ; and by the analogy of faith it concerns all that are accepted to salvation ; so that infants come under the rule, therefore some kind of faith they must have.   It were uncharitable and contrary to the rich grace of the covenant to deny salvation and eternal glory to infants.   The scripture showeth, that ' they are holy,' and dedicated to God, 1 Cor. vii. 14 ; and Christ says, ' of such is the kingdom of God,' Mat. xix. 14.   Now this faith of infants is a matter very intricate and difficult.   Several opinions there have been about it.   Origen held that infants were saved by virtue of those good works, the faith and obedience which they yielded to God in the bodies of other men before they were born, when their souls animated other bodies.   The Pelagians, against whom Austin disputes hard, that infants were saved out of the foresight of those good works which they would have performed, if God had suffered them to continue in the world.   Against this Austin disputes, proving every man is to be judged, not according to what he would do, or might have done, but ' According to what he hath done in the body, whether good or bad,' 2 Cor. v. 10.   And if this pretence were allowable, and a ground of salvation, then the men of Tyre and Sidon would be in a capacity of life without repentance ; for if they had had the means, saith Christ, ‘ They would have repented long since,’ Mat. xi. 21. Ambrose saith, They are saved by the faith of the church : Mark ii. 5, when Jesus saw ‘ their faith,’ that is, the faith of the sick man that was healed of the palsy, and of those that brought him. But that seemeth improper by their being in the church ; they have a right to visible ordinances ; but grace is God's gift, and must be dispensed in his way. Beza saith, They are saved by the faith of their parents imputed to them. As they were infected by the sin of Adam by natural generation ; so by virtue of the covenant of grace they are saved by the faith of their parents, but the child is not concerned in the acts of the father.

It is true, the faith of the parents makes way for the interest of the children in the covenant ; but every one is saved by his own faith— ‘ The just shall live by his own faith,’ Rom. i. 17. It is not in the power of another to damn or save me ; for the immediate parents are not representatives and common persons, as Adam was. Though Adam be a means to transfuse and bring sin, yet the faith of the parents could not involve and put into a state of salvation and acceptance with God. The Lutherans, they say, that children have an actual faith, though, say they, the act be to us unconceivable. But this were to offer violence not only to our reason, but our very senses. Children are everywhere described to be those in scripture that ‘ Know not their right hand from their left,’ Jonah iv. ult. We see they have not the use of reason, therefore they have no knowledge of Christ and the mysteries of religion, and cannot have such an actual faith.

What faith, then, is left for infants, by virtue of which we may establish their acceptation with God ? Some think that this question is altogether unnecessary, and say, that the scriptures are so sparing in this matter, that grown persons may be more careful of their own faith rather than of the faith of infants, who must be left, say they, to the free grace and pleasure of God. For my part I should think so too, and should not start this controversy were it not already agitated ; and were not the comfort of parents very much concerned in it, I should leave them to the grace of God. But upon those reasons, I think it necessary to be determined ; and I doubt not but it will make much for the glory of God and your own consolation. What is then to be said in this matter ?

1. Let it be premised, that the question is concerning the infants of believing parents ; as for others, we leave them to the judgment of God. Some indeed think that all infants, as they perished in Adam, without knowledge of him, so they are redeemed by Christ without knowledge of Christ. As the Arminians say, that of infants there is neither election nor reprobation, and that no infant can be condemned for original sin ; both which assertions are false. For we find that the predestination of God hath plainly made a difference between infant and infant : Rom. ix. 11–13, ‘ The children being not yet born, and having done neither good nor evil, that the purpose of God according to election might stand, it was said, the elder shall serve the younger, as it is said, Jacob have I loved, and Esau have I hated.’ Jacob in his mother's womb was in a state of election ; and it is notable, that in many other places the scripture speaks as if God's decrees were

dated from the womb and from the conception; as Jer. i. 5, 'Before I formed thee in the belly I knew thee, and before thou camest forth out of the womb, I sanctified thee, and ordained thee a prophet to the nations;' partly, because to sense that was the first time of our exist- ence; and partly, because God's decrees do then begin to operate and to bring forth. God doth, as it were, then say, This is a birth I must look after; this is an instrument whom I have pre-ordained to make use of for special purpose. Man's ordination is at grown years, but God's from all eternity. And because of the special care of providence, it is said to begin then when the child is in the womb, Gal. i. 15, 16, 'When it pleased God who separated me from my mother's womb, and called me by his grace, to reveal his Son in me, that I might preach him among the heathen; immediately I conferred not with flesh and blood.' The apostle mentions three things as the ground of his min- istry: God's pleasure, or everlasting counsel, his separation from his mother's womb and actual calling. First, God determines from ever- lasting, and then the decree begins to break forth; and there is a special care of God about the birth, and afterward there is actual calling. All this is brought to prove that even children before they are born do not only fall under the care of providence, but under the special notice of God's decrees; and that other opinion, that none is condemned for original sin, is also groundless and contrary to the scripture; for we read, Eph. ii. 3, 'That we were by nature the children of wrath, even as others.' It is mercy, that God will say to any that are in their blood and filthiness, Live. Who can quarrel with his justice that he should damn any, though he see nothing but original pollution in them? Among men we crush the serpent's eggs before the serpents be grown; and might not God destroy us for our birth- sin? I confess some among the orthodox think, that all infants that die in infancy belong to God's election; so Junius, and so Mr Fox, upon Rev. vii. 9, where there is a distinction between the sealed and unsealed, which he applies to unbaptized infants both in or out of the church. But I answer, as for those that are born out of the church, we have no warrant to judge them, as the apostle saith, in somewhat a like case, 1 Cor. v. 12, 'What have I to do to judge them that are without?' So what have we to do with them that are without? God's judgments are to be adored rather than curiously searched into; yet this is manifest by the whole current and drift of scripture, that there is a great deal of difference between those that are born in and those that are born out of the covenant. It is said to believing parents, 'The promise is unto you, and unto your children,' Acts ii. 39. I cannot apply that comfort to infidels. And those that are born within the pale are called 'children of the covenant,' Acts iii. 25. Those that are born without the pale of grace, are counted unclean; but others, holy, dedicated to God: 1 Cor. vii. 14, 'Else were your children unclean, but now are they holy;' so that there is a difference between infant and infant. The children of unbelieving parents are plainly asserted by the apostle to be unclean; we cannot have such comfortable hopes of them, and cannot say they are saved; therefore we must leave them to God's judgment. The question at present is of the children of the cove- nant, and those that are born within the pale of grace. And therefore—

2. Of those children dying in infancy, I assert, that they have faith, not actual faith, but the seed of faith, by virtue of God's election and his grace issuing out to them through Christ in the covenant, which I shall confirm by showing—(1.) That it may be so ; (2.) That it must be so ; (3.) That it is even so ; (4.) How it is so, or what kind of faith they have : which things being cleared, the way to application will be easy.

[1.] That it may be so, because the only prejudice against this opinion seemeth to arise from the impossibility of the thing ; and the Socinians that bring down all things to the line and rule of corrupt reason, count the faith of infants a thing so impossible, that they say it is a greater dotage than the dream of a man in a fever ; therefore my first work is to prove that they are capable of faith. Certainly, totally incapable they are not, like stocks and stones, and things without life ; and yet out of these God can raise up children to Abraham. Nor altogether as incapable as the younglings of beasts, because the perfection of their life is only sense and natural instinct, whereas children have reason. Now reason is in a nearer propinquity to grace than sense, therefore utterly incapable they are not, as stones, or as brute creatures are.

But to come more closely. The only reason why they are said to be incapable of faith is, because they cannot exercise it. Now, that they are not incapable of faith, though they cannot exercise it, I shall prove by several instances. This supposition will seem to infer that it may be so. If infants had been born of Adam in innocency, they had been capable of original purity and of the principle and root of all faith, and assent to the word of God would naturally have been in them, which in time, and according to the degrees of age, would have put forth itself. Infants in their measure should have been as Christ was. As soon as he was born, he was filled with the Holy Ghost, yet he grew in wisdom and knowledge, Luke ii. 40–52, The graces of the Holy Ghost did exert and put forth themselves in Christ by degrees. Now this, according to their measure, would have been the condition of infants born of Adam, if he had stood in innocency ; therefore there is no repugnancy, but that by a supernatural work the seed and root of grace may be in them. I say, it is no more inconceivable than the original purity of infants, if they had stood in Adam. And I shall show you by another instance. Take nature as it is now corrupted ; if they are capable of sin by nature, why not of grace, by a work of the Spirit of God above nature ? Now we see that they are capable of the root of sin, which lies hid in infants, and bewrayeth itself in time ; and if they are capable of sin, which is one habit, why are they not capable of grace, if the Spirit of God will work it, which is another habit ? They are sinners not by any act of their own, but by an hereditary habit, or vicious nature received from Adam, though not exerting and putting forth itself by any act. So they may have grace, though not exerting and discovering itself by any acts yet lying hid and shut up in the habitual principle of grace. As they are defiled by the sin of Adam, though they be not capable to understand it, so they may be sanctified by the Spirit of Christ, though they be not sensible of the merit of Christ, nor capable of understanding the way and the work of redemption. To take off the prejudice of incapacity, take some resemblances of it in common things. We see that infants are capable of reason, though not of discourse; they are rational creatures. Infants have reason and understanding, though it lie hid for a while. The whelp of the wolf has a principle of rapacity, which discovers itself afterward. The vital and vegetative force in any plant lies hid in the seed and root, which to appearance is dead and dry, and afterwards plainly discovers and puts it forth ; so infants, though they have no actual sense and knowledge of the redemption of Christ, yet they may have some impressions of the divine image upon their souls, which in time shows itself by light in the understanding, by purity in the heart, and by conformity in the life to the law of God. Again, that it is not impossible appears by those expressions in scripture, where some are said to be sanctified from the womb; as of John Baptist, it is said, ' He shall be filled with the Holy Ghost, even from his mother's womb,' Luke i. 15. Grant it to be a peculiar privilege of John, but it is not so in all elect infants; yet it may be so. So those expressions of trusting God from the mother's womb, David speaks it of his own person, as a type of Christ: Ps. xxii. 9, 'Thou didst make me hope when I was upon my mother's breasts;' and Job saith, chap. xxxi. 18, 'From my youth he was brought up with me as with a father, and I have guided her from my mother's womb;' meaning, he had an *indoles*, or disposition of pity, put into him at his nativity. So also, why may not a principle of faith be put into us in the womb, if God will work it?

2. I shall prove that it must be so ; how else should infants be saved ? There is no salvation without the covenant, and in the covenant there is no salvation but by faith in Christ. By their natural birth, all children are children of wrath, enemies to God, guilty before God. As we read it, the word is ὑπόδικος, liable to the process of divine justice: Rom. iii. 19, ' All the world is become guilty before God,' and so are infants ; there is no reason to exempt them. They are all dead in sin ; and the scripture saith expressly, 'He that believeth not, is condemned already,' John iii. 18 ; that is, liable to the sentence of condemnation ; so that believers they must be, or else they must be damned ; and regenerate they must be, or else we know there is no way of entering into the kingdom of God. Let any one show us any way or pleasing God without faith, or of entering into heaven without regeneration. John iii. 3, Christ hath expressly said, ' Except a man be born again, he cannot see the kingdom of God.' In the first commission of the apostles, when they went forth to preach the word of life, this was the tenor of the gospel : Mark xvi. 16, ' He that believeth shall be saved ; and he that believeth not shall be damned.' Let men show any ground in scripture of a middle sort of men, between believers and unbelievers, or any other way of salvation but by Christ ; and in Christ, but by faith in Christ. If men say, All those places belong to grown persons, or those that are of age ; by this shift you may elude any scripture ; and where then shall we have a rule whereby to judge of infants ? which, how comfortless it will be to parents, and how derogatory to the grace of the covenant, anyone cannot choose but see.

[3.] That it is so I shall prove from the promise of God ; for God being faithful and true, his promise is as good as a positive assertion : God promiseth grace and glory to infants. Grace, Isa. xliv. 3, ' I will pour out my Spirit upon thy seed, and my blessing upon thy offspring.' In the original, upon thy ' buds;' where the Spirit is promised to be poured out upon infants, not only on their seed in general, as implying persons of age, but on their ' buds,' ere they come to grow up to stalk and flower. Then for glory, Christ saith, Mat. xix 14, ' Suffer little children to come to me, and forbid them not, for of such is the kingdom of heaven ;' heaven is theirs by grant and promise. Elect infants in general have *jus ad rem*, a right to heaven ; but there is no *jus in re*, no actual right or interest, but by faith. But what need we argue, when we have a plain assertion ? Luke xviii. 17, ' Whosoever shall not receive the kingdom of God as a little child, he shall in no wise enter therein ;' they have not only a right to the kingdom of God, but they receive the kingdom of God ' as a little child receiveth it.' The sense carrieth it so ; that is, receiveth it by faith, accompanied with humility. But more plainly yet : Mat. xviii. 6, ' Whosoever shall offend one of these little ones which believe in me,' &c ; there is the very word —' which believe in me ; these little ones.' Christ speaks not metaphorically, but literally ; ' these,' such as were then before him, and of them he saith, ' which believe in me.' Some make exception against this, and say, The child to which Christ alluded was then grown. I answer, that cannot be : for in Luke it is called βρέφος, an ' infant,' Luke xviii. 15 ; in Matthew παιδίον, a ' little child ;' and Mark ix. 36, it is said, ' Christ took him in his arms.' And besides, in children that are more grown, pride, fierceness, and other ill qualities are bewrayed ; therefore such an one would not have been so fit for Christ's purpose to be propounded to the apostles for a pattern of meekness and humility. As they are called rational before they had the use of reason, so we have found that infants may, must, and have a principle of faith, from whence they may be said to be believers.

[4.] How is it so. What is the faith which children have ? I proved before that actual faith they have not, which begins in knowledge and ends in affiance. It remains therefore that they have the seed of faith, or some principle of grace conveyed into their souls by the hidden operation of the Spirit of God, which gives them an interest in Christ, and so a right to his merit for their salvation. I confess among the orthodox there are different expressions about this matter, but they all agree in the thing. Some call it a habit of faith, some a principle, some an inclination, some the first-fruits of the Spirit, others the gift of the Spirit, which answers to actual faith. All agree in this, that it is some work of the Holy Ghost, which gives them a relation to Christ, and by virtue of this relation, they have an interest in his merit for the remission of sins and acceptance with God. The more usual terms are principle and habit. Some dislike the word habit, because the word is not scriptural, and because it seems more proper to faith that is grown and actually exercised, and because the habit of grace is not the condition of the covenant. More properly, it may be called the principle, or the seed of faith ; for so the work of the Holy Ghost is expressed, 1 John iii. 9, ' Whosoever is born of God doth not commit sin ; for his seed remaineth in him : and he cannot sin, because he is born of God ; ' where the grace of regeneration is called the seed of God, which is cast into their hearts by the Spirit of God in a way unknown to us. In short, it is the work of grace, whereby the heart is quickened with spiritual life, and made a sanctified vessel to receive Christ. By the sanctifying Spirit all outward means are supplied, and infants are enabled unto that, which Dr Ames calls 'a passive reception,' by which they are in Christ, and united to him. It is not altogether without act, though it be such an act as is proper to their age.

Obj. But you will say, Do all elect infants receive this sanctifying work of the Holy Ghost, or seed of faith? We see many infants of believers, whom in charity we judge to be elect, because the promise is made to them and their seed ; yet, when they are grown up we see they show themselves to be never regenerated in their infancy.

I answer, in this case we do not speak universally, but indefinitely ; we do not say that all infants do believe in Christ, but infants—and in the judgment of charity we presume it of all infants, that die in their infancy. We must leave God to the liberty of his counsels, lest the freedom of grace should seem to be prejudiced by the merit of any family. God will take one and leave another, take Jacob and leave Esau ; only we say this in the general, that we have more cause to hope well of all the children of believing parents. Why? because the grace of election runs and flows most kindly in the channel of the covenant, and therefore there is greater hope of such. Rom. xi. 24, the apostle calls them, ' The natural branches,' so as that they were more easily grafted in. The apostle puts a ' how much more,' upon them ; ' How much more shall the natural branches be grafted into their own olive tree ? ' God may suffer the branches of the covenant to grow wild, and may graft in a strange slip, but it is most kindly to the natural branches ; they have a greater sufficiency of means, an external right, as soon as born. Certainly it is a great advantage to be born of parents within the covenant ; they have an excellent inheritance, till they disinherit themselves by their own unthankfulness and rebellion. Look, as we judge of the graft by the stock from whence it is taken, until it bring forth other fruit, by which it may be discerned ; so for children, we judge of them by their parents until they come to years of discretion and choose their own way, and so do actually choose or refuse the grace of God.

Use. 1. To press parents to bless God for the rich grace of the covenant. Ah, consider not only your persons are accepted with God, but also your seed, by virtue of which the merit of Christ is applied, and the Spirit of Christ infused into them, leaving God to the liberty of his counsel. Oh, how greatly doth the Lord love those that fear him ! He cannot satisfy himself in doing good, only to other persons, but will do good to their children and posterity for their sakes. So that though they are broken off by their positive unbelief and apostasy, yet as the Jews were hated for their own sake, yet they are beloved for their fathers' sake, and therefore they shall be again grafted into the stock ; so they are under the care of providence until they are converted. Oh, how should we entertain the grace of the covenant with humility and reverence, and stand and wonder that God should not only accept our worthless persons, but also graft our seed into the stock of grace. When God came to tender the covenant to Abraham, Gen. xvii. 3, it is said, 'Abraham fell upon his face,' a posture of humble reverence, as wondering at the large and diffusive mercy of God; and David, 2 Sam. vii. 18, 19, when God had taken him into covenant and his children, 'O Lord God, what am I? and what is my father's house, that thou hast brought me hitherto?' that thou hast heaped so many privileges upon me. 'And yet this was a small matter in thy sight, O Lord God; for thou hast spoken also of thy servant's house for a great while to come, and is this the manner of man?' He stands wondering at grace. Natural love like a river is descending: it runs downward. All our care next to our souls is for our children; for in them our life is multiplied and continued in the world. Children are the parent multiplied; therefore one saith of children, They are 'a knotty eternity;' when the thread of life is run out, there is a knot knit, and it is continued in the child. Therefore what a mercy is it that God hath not only provided from eternity for our souls, but hath spoken a good word concerning our house for a great while yet to come, that he will continue his grace in our line.

Use 2. It should encourage parents to found a covenant interest in their own persons. Oh, lay the foundation of it in yourselves! Ps. ciii. 17, 'The mercy of God is from everlasting to everlasting upon them that fear him, and his righteousness unto children's children.' Oh, it is much that it is from everlasting to everlasting; that we may go from one eternity to another; that we may look backward and see purposes of eternal grace, and look forwards to see possessions of eternal glory. But this is not all his righteousness unto children's children! Learn to fear God; that is the best way of providing for your children. We all seek the welfare of our children. You may heap up riches and honour upon them, and leave a curse with it; you may entail them an estate, and wrath with it; but leave them a covenant interest, that is an excellent inheritance. Wicked parents do as it were stop the way of God's mercy from descending upon their posterity; at least, they do not open a passage and channel, that grace may run down freely and with an uninterrupted course. God often threatens, that 'The posterity of the wicked shall be cut off,' Ps. cix. 13. You may not only injure your own souls, but your posterity. Oh, for your poor babes' sake, learn to fear God, that you may not leave them to the wrath and displeasure of God! It is said to Cain, Gen. iv. 10, 'Thy brother's blood crieth to me from the ground.' Some commentators infer that Cain was accountable not only for the murder of Abel himself, but for the murder of all the holy seed that should come of his loins. God will require not only the neglect of your own souls at your hands, but visit you for neglecting your children; that you have not taken a course to open a passage, that grace may descend to them.

Use 3. Here is comfort to believing parents concerning their children dying in infancy. We should not doubt of their salvation, unless we should wrong the covenant of grace. To what end doth God say, I am your God, and the God of your seed? Consider, Jesus Christ himself was the advocate of children, and would plead their right against his own apostles, when they thought Christ would have nothing to do with children: Mat. xix. 14, 'Suffer little children to come unto me, and forbid them not, for of such is the kingdom of heaven'—suffer them to come ; I have provided heaven for them, as well as for others. And Christ that hath said, 'Of such is the kingdom of heaven,' certainly will find out a way how to settle the title upon them, and to enstate them into the kingdom of heaven.   David, when his child died, comforted himself in this : 2 Sam. xii. 23, 'But now he is dead, where-fore should I fast ?   Can I bring him back again ?   I shall go to him, but he shall not return to me.'   It is not only meant of the state of the dead, that were a brutish argument, but 'I shall go to him ;' the meaning is, to the glory of the everlasting state ; nay, though they die without the seal of the covenant.   The Hebrew children were murdered as soon as born, Exod. i. 22 ; and Mat. ii. 16.   The children of Beth-lehem shed their blood by martyrdom, before they shed their blood by circumcision, and therefore leave them in Christ's arms.

Use 4. To teach us confidence in the power of divine grace.   God can shine into the dark hearts of children, therefore certainly there is no heart so dark but God can enlighten it.   Our trouble at our first conversion doth not arise out of the doubting of God's love, so much as of his power.   This hard heart will never be softened ; these rebellious affections will never be subdued to the discipline of the Spirit ; this blind mind will never be enlightened.   If once they could glorify the power of his converting grace, comfort would sooner be settled in their heart.   Ayè, but the Lord can shine into the hearts of infants, therefore do not doubt of it.   You see what he can do in those that have not the use of reason.   God can give the principle of grace : Isa. lxv. 20, 'The child shall die an hundred years old, but a sinner, being an hundred years old, shall be accursed ;' speaking of the grace of the gospel.   There are many expositions of that place.   Some carry it this way, that a child in the christian state shall be as perfect and as ripe for heaven as if he were a hundred years old.   This is the power of divine grace, therefore wait upon God.

Use 5. Here is encouragement to the neglected duty of education. Many times we neglect our little children, think we can do no good upon them.   Oh, water the seed of grace, for aught you know they may be sanctified from the womb.   It is said of John the Baptist, Luke i. 15, 'He shall be filled with the Holy Ghost from his mother's womb.'   Oh, this will make them exert and put forth those hidden operations of grace which God worketh upon their souls ; therefore water the seed of grace with the dew of education.   God will call you to account for the education of your children : Ezek. xvi. 20, 'More-over, thou hast taken thy sons and thy daughters, whom thou hast born unto me, and these hast thou sacrificed unto them to be devoured : is this of thy whoredoms a small matter, that thou hast slain my children ?' that is, dedicated to me by circumcision.   Consider, they are God's children, and you are only entrusted with them that you may bring them up.   Let us, that have been instruments to convey an evil nature to them, assist them in the work of grace.   Many have been converted by private education before they have been called by the ministry of the gospel.   You cannot do your children worse hurt than to let them run wild.   Consider they are the natural branches of the covenant, and you should bestow culture upon them.   Dionysius, the tyrant, to be revenged of his adversary, brought up his child to riot and wantonness. You cannot do yourselves a worse injury, nor yourselves a greater revenge, than to let your children run wild.

SERMON XXVI.

But without faith it is impossible to please God.—HEB. xi. 6.

THIRDLY. The third inference is concerning carnal and unregenerate men. 'Without faith,' the apostle saith, 'it is impossible to please God;' therefore, certainly a man in his natural condition can do nothing that may be accepted with God. I shall confirm this with other places of scripture: Rom. viii. 8, 'They that are in the flesh cannot please God;' 'in the flesh,' that is, in a carnal state; it is opposed to 'them that are in Christ,' ver. 1. There is an utter impossibility that anything of theirs should be accepted with the Lord; which ariseth partly from the state of the person, and partly from the quality of the service which natural men perform.

1. From the state of the person. Unregenerate men are enemies to God, and therefore he will not accept of a gift at their hands. There is no reconciliation till an interest in Christ; for God will not be appeased with duties; the honour of appeasing and satisfying his justice is left alone for Jesus Christ. So it is proclaimed from heaven, Mat. iii. 17, 'This is my beloved son, in whom I am well pleased;' so Eph. i. 6, 'He hath made us accepted in the beloved.' Jesus Christ is the favourite of heaven; he must mediate for us. As, when 'Herod was displeased with the men of Tyre and Sidon, they made Blastus the king's chamberlain their friend, and desired peace,' Acts xii. 20; so if ever we would find acceptance with God, we must have a friend and favourite in heaven that must plead our cause. Now, till you have an interest in his merit and intercession, God will not accept an offering at your hands; and therefore you shall find it is God's method in the covenant of grace, to begin first with the interest of the person, and then to accept of the work. See with what scorn God rejects the offering and the best services of wicked men, however accommodated: Prov. xv. 8, 9, 'The sacrifice of the wicked is an abomination to the Lord, but the prayer of the upright is his delight. The way of the wicked is an abomination unto the Lord, but he loveth him that followeth after righteousness.' Many things are notable in these two verses. First, he saith, The sacrifice of the wicked is an abomination; God is so far from accepting their choicest duties that he hates them. It is grievous that God should not accept: ay, but he doth abominate them. And mark the antithesis—'The sacrifice of the wicked,' and the 'prayer of the upright.' Sacrifice was the more outward and costly part of worship. Wicked men may do more in the outward rite than the godly themselves, to recompense the defects of inward piety; but though they come with sacrifices, yet the single prayer of the upright

is more accepted with the Lord. And mark, he saith, ver. 6, ' The way of the wicked is an abomination,' not only their sacrifice or their exercises of religion, which may be counterfeited, but their way, their second-table duties, which, because of the benefit that men receive by them, are more pleasing and plausible ; yet their way, that is an abomination. They may do much ; they may build colleges, promote learning, relieve the poor ; yet all is an abomination, because the person is wicked. Solomon doth not say their adultery is an abomination, but their charity, their civility. But saith he, ' They that follow after right-eousness,' that is, that make it their sincere aim, though they cannot always be masters of their own desires and perform their intentions, yet God loves them that follow after righteousness, their hearts are set right. But the wicked, those that are in an unjustified estate, do what-ever they will, they are an abomination to the Lord ; they are punished for their sins, and are not accepted for their duties. Now, lest you should think that all this doth arise from some gross defect that is in the service itself, you shall see that it is from the hatred God bears to their persons, until they be reconciled to him in Christ. I shall prove that out of Prov. xxi. 27, ' The sacrifice of the wicked is an abomination ; how much more when he bringeth it with a wicked mind ? ' Suppose a wicked man should do his best, yet the person is not recon-ciled to God ; and so at best it is but a wicked man's offering ; therefore till we change our copy this will be our case ; it will be an abomination to the Lord. Thus you see, from the interest and quality of the person, they are in an unjustified and unreconciled estate, there-fore nothing of theirs can please God.

2. Consider the defect of the service. A natural man can never do or perform an act of pure obedience. It is true, his works are materially good : but it is not the matter which makes a work good. Velvet is good matter to make a garment of, yet it may be marred in the cutting ; pieces of timber are good matter for a house, but it must be judici-ously framed ; so these actions are for the matter good in themselves, yet they are not pleasing to God, because they are faulty in the most necessary circumstances. Whatsoever is well done must come from a principle of faith and love ; and it must be done to God's glory, other-wise it is not reckoned among duties, but sins. Now here a wicked man is always culpable ; he can neither act out of faith, which he hath not ; nor to God's glory, he cannot make that his aim, therefore still he sins. It is true, he sins more in things that are evil in themselves ; as in theft and in lying, than in sacrifice ; in adultery than in prayer, because the act itself is sinful ; but in those duties that he doth per-form, the matter of them is conducible to the good of human society. But it is all one as to their acceptance with God ; for it is not enough that a thing be good in itself, but it must be done to a good end ; that is a necessary circumstance, in which a wicked man is defective. Prov. xxi. 27, ' The sacrifice of the wicked is an abomination : how much more (saith the Spirit of God) when he bringeth it with an evil mind ? ' Usually wicked men have an evil mind in all that they do ; they have a carnal, or a natural, or, at best but a legal end.

[1.] A carnal end. Usually they make a market of religion, and their righteousness is set to sale. Whatever they do, they do it to please men rather than God ; and how can they expect their reward of God ?

So our Saviour, when he speaks of the hypocrisy of those that pray, fast, and give alms, he saith, Mat. vi. 2 –16, ' They have their reward;' they give God an acquittance and a discharge, for all that they do is to please men and not to please God; therefore they have their reward, that is, that they look after. By a vile submission, they make the service of God to stoop to their secular interests. Mat. xxiii. 14, the Pharisees ' made long prayers to devour widows' houses;' that is, to get a fame and a repute to themselves, that they might be entrusted with widow's estates. Thus the apostle speaks of some, Phil. i. 15, ' That preached Christ out of envy and strife, not of good will.' They may preach and pray to show their gifts; and the end is carnal, to provide for their secular interest. Now this is a vile scorn put upon God, when religion is made a cover for an unclean intent; it is as if you should take a cup of gold, made for the king to drink in, and make it a vessel to hold dung and excrements. Or else—

[2.] Their end in all they do is natural. It is grace that sublimates the intentions of the creature. A carnal man can go no higher than self, as water cannot ascend beyond its fountain. All that a carnal man do this for self-interest. If they eat and drink it is for self, to gratify appetite, not that they might be more cheerful in the service of God. If they pray, it is for self: Hosea vii. 14, ' They have not cried unto me with their heart (saith the Lord) when they howled upon their beds; they assemble themselves for corn and wine.' All their prayers do arise from a brutish instinct after their own ease and welfare; ' Not unto me,' saith the Lord; God is neither at the beginning nor at the end of the action. If they spend their strength in holy services, as a wicked man may do, it is but to feed their own bellies; it is still to make a god of themselves, and they lay aside the Lord, Phil. iii. 19. The apostle speaks there of false teachers, who spent their strength in the work of the gospel, out of a selfish principle, to flow in an abundance of wealth and worldly pleasures; therefore he saith, ' Their god is their belly.' Always observe, a man makes a god of that which he makes his utmost end, and accounts to be his chiefest good. Thus do all natural men set up self instead of God. Now, how can God accept an action, when his majesty is laid aside and self is set up in his stead ?

[3.] Take wicked men at the best, it is but a legal end. When wicked men are most devout, it is but to quiet conscience and to satisfy God for their sins by their duties. They would fain buy out their peace with heaven at any rate; as appears by the inquiry mentioned by the prophet: Micah vi. 6–8, ' Wherewith shall I come before the Lord, and bow myself before the high God? Shall I come before him with burnt-offerings, with calves of a year old; will the Lord be pleased with thousands of rams, or with ten thousands of rivers of oil? Shall I give my first-born for my transgression, the fruit of my body for the sin of my soul?' What shall I give for the sin of my soul? and wherewith will God be appeased? If peace of conscience were to be purchased with money, men would part with anything rather than their sins, for nothing is dearer to men than their sins; not their children, not their estate, not their first-born. Thus carnal men, by an excess of charity, seek to expiate the offences of a carnal life, and would be liberal, so they may be sinful. Now this is that which makes men hated and more abominable to God; while they think to purchase their own pardon, and hire God to be gracious; when they do things that carry a fair show in the world, they think God is bound to forgive them their sins; and so they cause the Lord to hate them so much the more, since they neglect Christ, 'In whom alone he is well pleased.'

Use 1. This serves to represent to us the misery of natural men. This should amaze them to think that all they do is abominable in God's sight. They are debtors to the whole law, and yet they can do nothing that can be pleasing to God. Their duties cannot quit old scores, if they perform them never so exactly; they can never come up to such a pitch of duty and such a pure act of obedience as God requires; there is a vast debt upon them, and they are not able to pay one farthing. To enforce the consideration, reflect upon your own misery and the opposite happiness of the children of God.

1. Your own misery. Of all men, you are in a miserable condition, and God will take nothing in good part from you. How will you do to please him? No condition, no duty of yours, no enjoyment of yours, can render you acceptable to God; no outward condition can endear you to God. Wealth and authority in the world will nothing avail you against the process of divine justice. Men are taken with pomp and high places. We are apt to favour the rich in their cause, but divine justice will not be bribed; all those things are but fuel to kindle the fire of hell. As a stone that falls from a high place is the more bruised and broken, so the greater your advantages are in the world of authority and place, the greater the judgment; the mighty shall be mightily tormented; no excellency of gifts, learning, wit, and such like things. God is not taken with parts; all those qualities and endowments are but like a jewel in a toad's head—the person is displeasing to God. What pity is it to see that old complaint verified—*Surgunt indocti et rapiunt cœlum, dum nos cum doctrinâ detrudimur in Gehennam:* the unlearned may arise and take heaven by violence, when you with all your learning are thrust down to hell. So for moral honesty; it is but sin dressed up more handsomely, and set off with a fairer varnish. Whatever doth not come from a pure fountain of faith and obedience, and is not done to God's glory, it is but like a spiced carcase—it is but sin and nature perfumed. To instance in things that are more commendable—liberality to learning, giving of alms, building of churches, civility of life; these are good in themselves, and glorious in men's eyes, but they are abomination before God. Mark the emphasis of our Saviour's words: Luke xvi. 15, 'That which is highly esteemed among men is an abomination in the sight of God;' not only that which 'pleaseth' men, but is 'highly esteemed;' and he saith it is not only 'not accepted,' but it is βδέλυγμα—an 'abomination to God;' that which is a rose to us, is a nettle to him. Carnal ends are as odious to God as gross sins are to men. Nay, go to religious duties; a wicked carnal man may pray, but his prayer is turned into sin, as a jewel in a dead man's mouth. Your prayers, because they come from dead men, 'men dead in trespasses and sins,' lose all their worth and efficacy, how good soever the action be in itself; so that when a man comes to please God, he grieveth him more. A carnal man may be employed in the offices of the church: Mat. vii. 22, 'We have prophesied in thy name, and in thy name have cast out devils, and in thy name done many

wonderful works;' and yet Christ saith, 'I know you not; depart from me, ye that work iniquity,' ver. 23. A man may spend his strength and his spirits in the ministry; yet after all this may be a castaway. Christ will not take acquaintance with them that are in such a nearness of office and ministration—'I know you not.' It is strange that Christ should not know them, when they can challenge acquaintance with him by such a good token; We had such gifts and such offices. Some men have only gifts for others; and after they have wasted themselves and swaled away like a candle in the work of the ministry, they may go out in a snuff. Gifts and employments are for the body. No doubt, in Noah's time, some that built an ark for others perished in the waters; so after we have built an ark for others, and represented Christ to them, if we do not get an interest in him ourselves, we are cast away; or like the clouds that moisten the earth, but are themselves scattered by the winds, we may moisten and convey the influences of heaven to others, but are scattered, as those that Christ refuseth, by the breath and fury of the Lord; or like the water of purification, under the law, that cleansed the leper, but was itself unclean, so men that are employed as instruments in the cleansing of others, may themselves be unclean and disallowed by God. They may deserve well of the church, and yet be unthankful to God and unfaithful to their own souls; nay, you may be orthodox, and side with the better part, and yet all this will not render you acceptable to God: Gal. v. 6, 'In Christ Jesus neither circumcision availeth anything, nor uncircumcision, but faith that works by love.' That was the controversy among the believers of that time, whether circumcision were to be kept up. Christ doth not love men for their opinion, but for their obedience. Some that are orthodox may go down to hell. The devils themselves have great skill in many points of faith; nay, which is more, men may suffer for religion for that which they call their conscience, yet all this in vain: 1 Cor. xiii. 2, 'If I give my body to be burnt, and have not charity, it profiteth me nothing;' without faith all this is nothing. The suffering of a wicked man, it is but like the cutting off a swine's head, or offering of a dog in sacrifice: as, under the law, the priest was to make inquiry if the sacrifice were sound, if it were not scabby or lame. God doth not love a scabby sacrifice; and when men are tainted with enormous lives and conversations, their sufferings will not endear them to God; nay, whatever you do in your lawful employment, in your calling, it is all sin. The whole trade and course of a wicked man's life is nothing but sin, because all those actions are not elevated by grace to a supernatural intention: Prov. xxi. 4, 'The ploughing of the wicked is sin;' whatever they do—their speaking, eating, drinking, trading—all is sin, because there is no grace. How should this take us off from our vain confidences! I have nothing but sin, I can do nothing but sin; and how should this bring the soul to lie at God's foot for mercy!

2. Consider the opposite happiness of the children of God, this will aggravate your misery. The smallest works of a man that is reconciled to God in Christ are rewarded. A cup of cold water shall not want its reward, Mat. x. 42. If a carnal man offers rivers of oil, ten thousands of sacrifices, yet they are nothing; whereas the weakest and poorest services on the other side are accepted. They that are in a state of grace have liberty of constant access to God, and God hath

promised to take notice of their persons and prayers : Ps. xxxiv. 15, ' The eyes of the Lord are upon the righteous, and his ears are open to their cry ; ' God is ready to receive and entertain them whenever they come to the throne of grace, but, as it follows in the next verse, ' The face of the Lord is against them that do evil ; ' as by a frown we discourage a supplicant. Certainly, it is a great mercy that we have an access to God, and the liberty to stand before him daily ; nay, the weakness of their duties shall be dispensed withal. A child of God is guilty of many failings, *Partus sequitur ventrem*, the birth hath more of the mother in it than of the father ; so, though the Spirit of God help them in their services, yet there is much of their own weaknesses mixed with it ; yet God will accept it : Cant. v. 1, ' I have eaten my honey-comb with my honey ; ' the honeycomb is bitter, but Christ will eat it for the honey's sake. We serve Christ in our duties as he was served on the cross, we offer him wine mingled with myrrh, but he will dispense with imperfections ; then their sins of life shall be pardoned. It is true, the children of God have not a dispensation to sin ; yet God will handle them with much indulgence when they are through the prevalency of corruption and infirmity drawn to sin. A hireling is soon dismissed when he doth not give content ; but a child is not cast out of doors for every offence : saith God, ' I will spare them, as a man spareth his own son that serveth him,' Mal. iii. 17.

Use 2. To represent to us the necessity of being in a state of faith, or else neither person nor work can please God ; there must be a change of our state, as well as doing our duties. It is in vain to persuade people to change their actions, while their state is unchanged. If the person be not in favour, the works are hated ; duties may further our delusion, but cannot further our happiness. Many heap up duty upon duty, as if they thought to please God that way. I do not blame men for using means, but for neglecting an interest in Christ. Who will look for grapes upon thorns ? No man can offer a sacrifice to God till he be first made a priest ; first, there must be a consecration of their persons : Mal. iii. 3, ' He shall purify the sons of Levi, then they shall offer unto the Lord an offering in righteousness ; ' Heb. ix. 14, ' How much more shall the blood of Christ purge your consciences from dead works, to serve the living God.' First, the christian must be consecrated before he can minister before the Lord in holy things : 1 Peter i. 2–5, ' Ye are a holy priesthood, to offer up spiritual sacrifices, acceptable to God by Jesus Christ.' Men must be kings and priests to God before they offer sacrifice to God. A natural man is a bad priest, and his own evil heart is an ill altar. Our persons must be reconciled to God, and under grace by Christ, and received into the number of those God approves, and whom he delights to be worshipped by. Under the law, the priests, when they went to sacrifice, were washed in the great laver of water, Exod. xxix. 4 ; so must a christian in the laver of regeneration, Tit. iii. 5, and then come and worship ; they must change their state, then the Lord will accept of their offering in Christ.

Use 3. We learn hence, that the opinion which makes God to bestow grace upon the preceding works and merit of man is false. We have not only to do with the Papists here, but Arminians, who establish an infallible attendance of grace on natural endeavours. They say, if a man do use well his natural strength and abilities; if he do as much as he can, God will certainly help him to supernatural grace. If they stir themselves in good earnest to seek the grace of conversion, they shall infallibly and without miscarrying find it made good to them ; so Arminius, *Faciunt quod in se est, dantnr a deo infallibiliter, et ex certâ lege auxilia prœvenientis gratiœ.* It is true, we hold that it is the ordinary practice of free grace. God is seldom wanting to them that are not wanting to themselves ; but to hold such an infallibility, and to lay an obligation upon God, this is a falsehood, contrary to the canon of the apostle—' Without faith it is impossible to please God ;' without faith all our actions are sins, therefore they cannot oblige God to give more grace. But say they, Without faith it is impossible to please him, so as their persons should be accepted to life and salvation ; but it is not impossible to please him, and so to be accepted as to receive more grace. But I answer, that the text excludes both ; it is impossible to please God in any sense. Besides, pleasing God is all one with walking with God ; for what is in the original ?—' Enoch walked with God '—is in the Septuagint, ' Enoch pleased God ;' and it signifies an established communion of comfort and grace between God and the creature ; it is meant of acceptation to grace as well as glory. But to handle the argument more fully, I shall show—

1. The inconveniency and falsehood of this doctrine.

2. Handle some objections.

First, The inconvenience of this doctrine, that if men would do their utmost, God will necessarily come in with grace.

1. That never a natural man did his utmost.

2. If they did so, God is not obliged to come in infallibly with supplies of grace.

[1.] Never a natural man did his utmost. See the character of such kind of men, that they do not act their abilities—' But what they know naturally, in those things they corrupt themselves,' Jude ver. 10. It is but a fancy to suppose that any do improve nature to the uttermost. The scripture generally sets out natural men as unfaithful. He that had but one talent hid it in the earth, Mat. xxv. 18 ; and God seems to plead against them upon this issue, that they are unfaithful in common gifts : Luke xvi. 11, ' If therefore ye have not been faithful in the unrighteous mammon, who will commit to your trust the true riches ?' Earnestness in the use of means is the first impression of the efficacy of the Holy Ghost, and proceeds from the seed of grace, which God hath cast into the heart.

[2.] If he did do his utmost, yet God is not bound ; for if God be obliged and bound, it must either be by the merit of the creature, or by some promise he hath made ; there is no other obligation upon God. Now, no man can engage the grace of Christ, and there is no promise on God's part.

(1.) No man can engage God to give him converting grace ; this would tie grace to works, and then man would make himself to differ ; and our debt to grace would be taken off, and the difference that is between us and others did arise from ourselves : this would make men sacrifice to their own net. Now this is contrary to scripture. No man can earn anything of God: Rom. ix. 16, 'It is not of him that willeth, nor of him that runneth, but of God that showeth mercy;' not upon the motion of our will, nor by virtue of our endeavours, but God merely acts out of the freedom of his own grace; not by our desires, which is implied in 'willing;' nor by virtue of our endeavours, which is implied in 'running;' so 2 Tim. i. 9, 'Who hath saved us, and called us with a holy calling, not according to our works, but according to his own purpose and grace, which was given us in Christ Jesus before the world began.' God's liberty is not abridged by any act of the creature, neither is he necessitated to have mercy upon us rather than upon others. Many inconveniences would follow according to this doctrine; as that the creature must bid and buy and engage Christ before they have an interest in Christ. It is against reason: all those foregoing endeavours cannot please God, being void of faith and mixed with sins; and that which deserves wrath cannot prepare for grace. It is against experience: many shall endeavour, but not obtain, because all works that are done in the state of nature cannot make us a whit more accepted with God. Therefore God, to show that his grace runs freely, and is not drawn out by our endeavours, saith—'Many shall seek to enter in, and shall not be able,' Luke xiii. 24. Then again, this would make the creature to come and to plead with God; whereas the Lord will have us to lie at the foot of his sovereignty; the Lord will be the disposer of his own mercy. It crosseth the order of God in the dispensation of his grace, which is to bring the creature upon his knees, to be willing to refer all to his sovereignty—'Lord, thou hast mercy on whom thou wilt have mercy, and whom thou wilt thou hardenest.' This would cross the work of humiliation, by which the Lord would bring the creature to absolute submission to his own sovereignty. When we have done all, God is not our debtor; he oweth us nothing but vengeance.

(2.) There is no shadow of any engagement, by promise on God's part, whereby he should undertake to any of us; there is no such promise as this—Do this by the strength of nature, and thou shalt have supernatural grace, but because they urge many things.

Secondly, I shall come to some objections.

SERMON XXVII.

But without faith, it is impossible to please him.—HEB. xi. 6.

Obj. 1. 'For unto every one that hath shall be given, and he shall have abundance; but from him that hath not, shall be taken away even that which he hath,' Mat. xiii. 13, and Mat. xxv. 29. They say, God is obliged by promise to him that hath many acts of nature, to give acts of grace; but I answer, that place speaks of those that have grace already. It is the reason Christ assigns, why it was given to them to know the mysteries of the kingdom of God, and the reason is taken from the course God keeps in dispensation of his grace; such as have found grace in God's eyes, they have the fountain gift, and they shall have others to perfect their salvation. *Deus donando se facit debitorem*—God, by giving them grace already, hath made himself a debtor to them for new influences and all outward means, whereby they shall increase in grace and strength. In Mark iv. 24, it is said, 'Take heed what you hear, for with what measure you mete it shall be measured to you again, and unto you that hear shall more be given.' I answer, this still implies not a bare use of means while we are in a state of nature, but faith in hearing, without which the word never profiteth: so Prov. viii. 34, 'Blessed is the man that heareth me, watching daily at my gates, waiting at the post of my doors;' that is, that waits in faith; those that have grace by waiting upon the means, grace in the same kind shall be increased in them. We must not invert the method of the covenant. Another place is, Acts x. 34, 35, 'Of a truth I perceive (saith Peter) that God is no respecter of persons; but in every nation he that feareth God, and worketh righteousness, is accepted of him:' from whence they argue, that if a man have a natural reverence of God, and do the works of righteousness, he shall be accepted of God to further grace.

But I answer, it is clear that the place speaks of God's consequent love to the work of his own grace; for it is impossible that ever a man can fear God and work righteousness until he hath some grace wrought in him; those things are not the effect of nature, but of grace. That place only shows that Peter was convinced of his error; he thought none could be saved, but either a Jew, or a proselyte—one converted to the Jewish religion. Now I see my mistake, that of a truth, wherever there is real grace in any, God will accept of him. Take the sentence either in a legal or evangelical sense. If you take it evangelically, the sense is—whoever worketh righteousness, that obeyeth the gospel, and renounceth his own righteousness, and seeks the favour of God in Christ, he shall be accepted with God; or if you take it in a legal sense, those things are not the fruits of mere nature, it is to be expounded by way of evidence—whoever thus worketh righteousness it is a sign he is accepted with God; and he that fears God, it is a visible sign and testimony by which the favour of God towards him may be cleared up.

Obj. 2. Again, Christ is said to love the young man that was of a civil life: Mark x. 21, 'Jesus, beholding him, loved him.' I answer, this was but a human affection, which our Lord manifested in all cases out of respect to human society; 'Christ loved him,' that is, showed some outward signs of favour and respect to him; as we pity a man that is in a dangerous course: it is pity such courteous persons should go to hell. Our Saviour 'loved him,' certainly he could not approve of his hypocrisy, vanity, and self-confidence; but pitied him as one that with so much care kept the law, which others did not, and yet deceived himself with a vain opinion of righteousness. Christ, as man, was to have all human affections; but as lord and judge of the creature, so he hated him, as will be manifested at the last day.

Again, they say, God rewards wicked men for their natural actions; as Ahab's humiliation was rewarded with a suspension from wrath, 1 Kings xxi. 29, and Jehu's obedience was rewarded with the reign of his posterity to the fourth generation, 2 Kings x. 30.

I answer, This God may do out of his own bounty. Wicked men can look for nothing; it is his grace to reward wicked men's actions; and he may do it to make them more culpable, and to encourage the godly, as many times a general will reward the valour of an enemy to encourage his own soldiers. It is a document of God's bounty to the world, to prize true grace the better; and it is notable, all those blessings were but temporal, and salted with a curse: dogs may have temporals, the offals of providence.

Obj. 3. Again, what ground have we to persuade men to the use of means, if all their endeavours be in vain, and if God will not accept them? I answer—

[1.] We have ground to press them to duty, that wicked men may be more sensible of their own weakness. Men think it is easy to believe till they put themselves upon the trial, action, and endeavour; as the lameness of the arm is found by exercise. Solomon saith, Prov. ii. 2, 3, ' Apply thine heart to understanding;' then saith he, ' If thou criest after knowledge, and liftest up thy voice for understanding;' &c., ' then shalt thou understand the fear of the Lord, and find the knowledge of God.' Certainly, he that seeks knowledge will be driven to cry for it to free grace; and they that attempt the duties and exercises of religion, will see the necessity of divine help, and will be forced to lie at God's feet. Were there no other end but this, that wicked men may be certainly convinced that all their sufficiency is in God, to bring them to cry to God, Lord, help me against my unbelief, this were enough. When we look to towns in a map, we think the way to them easy, as if our foot were as nimble as our thoughts, but we are soon discouraged and tired, when we meet with dangerous and craggy passages, and come to learn the difference between glancing and serious endeavours. So in matters of religion, he that endeavours to bring Christ and his soul together, before he hath done, will be forced to sit down and cry, Lord, help me! As in the matters of the world, young men have strong hopes, therefore think it is nothing to live in the world; but when they are engaged in the cares of a family, they are soon crushed. So in the spiritual life; nothing doth rebuke sudden and easy hopes so much as trial and experience; then men find their hearts are hardly brought to apply themselves to the means whereby they may draw nigh to God, and see that no man can come to God without an attractive force, and unless the Father draw him.

[2.] Another reason why we press wicked men to do duty, is that they may manifest their obedience to God by meeting him in his own way. This is the way of God's working, by antecedaneous acts to fit us for grace, therefore the act must be done; for though we have lost our power, God hath not lost his right. It is true, we can never do anything with acceptation, yet still we are bound to be doing; as a drunken servant is obliged to do his master's work, though he hath disabled himself for it. So our nature had a power, though our persons were never invested with it; our disability will not disoblige us; so, though there be no hope of succeeding, yet we are bound to do. So Peter, though there were no fish come to hand, yet howbeit at thy command we will cast out the net. Wait at the pool; impotency can be no excuse for neglect.

[3.] That they may manifest their desires, men say usually they have no power when they have no heart.   He that hath a mind to the pearl of price, he will be doing, though he can do nothing acceptable; his desires being the vigorous bent of the soul will put him upon endeavours.   It is a usual way to pretend impotency, as a cover of laziness; but now neglect of means shows that the impossibility is voluntary; when we do not what we are able, it is a sign that we love our bondage.   A carnal man cannot please God; why? because he minds earthly things; the heart is carried out that way, and will not be subject to God, Rom. viii. 7, 8.   Men prefer the world before God, and content themselves with some lazy wishes, and then think to cast the blame upon God.   A wicked man is to be doing to show his desires are real: Prov. xxi. 25, 'The desire of the slothful killeth him: for his hands refuse to labour;' he hath but some sluggish wishes, that serve only unprofitably to vex the soul.

[4.] We put wicked men upon doing, because our endeavours are the condition *sine qua non*; without this the Lord seldom meets with the creature: Rom. x. 14, 'How shall they believe in him of whom they have not heard?'   If ever I find Christ, I must find him in this way of hearing and praying.   Though the means have no effective influence, yet without these I cannot come to Christ: Acts xiii. 46, 'Since ye put away the word from you, and judge ourselves unworthy of eternal life;' it is meant there of a refusal and neglect of the means; they save God the labour, and pass sentence upon themselves.   There is no having of children but in a state of marriage.   Now men marry, though the rational soul be infused by God; and so there is no having of grace but in the use of means, therefore we should use them, though still grace be the gift of God.   We do not say it is in vain to marry, because man cannot beget the soul; so it is not in vain to hear and pray, though these things have no effectual influence: these are the means, without which God will not give it.

[5.] If men do not do something, they will grow worse and worse; standing pools are apt to putrify.   Man is of an active nature, never at a stay, but either growing better or worse; and when we do not improve nature, we deprave it—'They corrupt themselves in what they know,' Jude 10.   Voluntary neglects draw on penal hardness; and so our natural disability is increased.   Much sin and hardness would be prevented by the use of means—'Thou wicked and slothful servant,' Mat. xxv. 26.   A slothful servant soon becomes an evil servant, and barren trees will soon become rotten trees, Jude 12; where ordinances are neglected, we draw penal hardness upon ourselves.

[6.] It is good to make trial upon a common hope; it may be, you may meet with God.   The apostle puts Simon Magus upon prayer out of a bare probability: Acts viii. 22, 'Pray to God, if perhaps the thoughts of thy heart may be forgiven thee;' though it be great uncertainty, a peradventure, and a thousand to one; yet pray, it is the safest course.   As the lepers, 2 Kings vii. 3, 4, 'They said one to another, Why sit we here until we die?   If we say, We will enter into the city, then the famine is in the city, and we shall die there; and if we sit still here, we die also.   Now therefore come, and let us fall to the host of the Syrians; if they save us alive we shall live, and if they kill us we shall but die.'   Such reasoning there usually is when God brings sinners home; if we do nothing, we are sure to die; if we pray and read and meditate, we can but die ; but there is some common hope ; it may be we may live. All God's children are thus brought in ; the soul is willing to acts of obedience, though it knows not what will come of it ; as Abraham obeyed God, not knowing whither he went. I am to do what God commands, let God do what he will ; it may be there may be life; I cannot do worse, I may do better. All saints are at first carried on by such a common hope; the first essay of their faith is but dark resolution; but blind peradventure, Who knows what God may do ?

[7.] It is God's usual way to meet those that seek him, and to give the Spirit to them that ask him : we do not know what importunity will do. This is the usual practice of God's free grace ; sometimes he doth, sometimes he doth not; but it is good to wait at wisdom's gate. God is not bound, but it is his ordinary practice. Obey the Lord, and sue out the blessings upon common hope ; when there is no absolute assurance, those things will prosper. Why should we fall. a disputing ? we are in great danger, and this is God's usual way. We are to do what we can ; God is wont to meet his people in this way. Though he hath nowhere said, Do this by the power of nature, and thou shalt have grace ; yet it is good to wait upon God, for he usually meets with them that seek him in his way, and blesseth them that are followers in all christian endeavours.

[8.] The neglect of means out of a carnal principle, either out of an averseness to grace, or an ill-conceit of God, proves very pernicious. Nature is backward and shy, and then we would justify it by wrong thoughts and groundless jealousies of God : Mat. xxv. 24, 'I knew that thou wert a hard master, and therefore I hid my talent.' We think that God hath shut us up under a fatal impossibility, so we pretend we can do nothing ; as they that heard Christ say—'No man can come to me except the Father which hath sent him draw him,' John vi. 44— murmured and drew back at that saying ; so we have wrong thoughts of God, and are jealous without cause. We are loath to use the means, and then blame God for not giving the power. It is a jealous fancy of God without warrant ; you are under an obligation, and that must be regarded.

[9.] This is no small encouragement, that Jesus Christ, that hath the grant of the elect, is to see the promises to be made good to them. The new heart, and the infusion of converting grace is a thing promised to natural men that are elect before they are in Christ, and Christ will see to the accomplishment. Whatever Christ's intent is towards you, certainly his will will be no hindrance to our duty ; therefore upon all these grounds we might press men to wait upon God in the use of means, that so, if it be his gracious will, they might receive mercy for their souls.

Fourthly, We may infer hence the necessity and excellency of faith.

1. We may gather from hence the excellency of faith ; he nameth no other graces. Whatever glorious virtues are found in God's children, none of them can make them acceptable with God but faith ; how ? not for any excellency that is in faith itself, because of all graces it hath least of worth, but in regard of its object. Though faith in itself be a needy grace, yet it hath a worthy object ; it receiveth Christ and all the blessings of the covenant. Therefore the apostle calls it ' precious '

faith, 2 Peter i. 4, because it is conversant about a precious Christ, and precious promises, and precious righteousness.

Obj. But you will say, Charity or love is elsewhere preferred before faith, therefore how can faith be accounted the most excellent grace? 1 Cor. xiii. 13, 'Now abideth faith, hope, and charity, these three; but the greatest of these is charity.' It is true, before he compares gifts and graces, but here he compares grace and grace, and he judgeth the crown and pre-eminence to charity. When extraordinary gifts cease in the church, these shall be perpetually had in esteem; these three abide, and that which is greatest is charity.

Ans. It is true, in some kind of operations other graces may have the pre-eminence, but in the matter of pleasing of God the pre-eminence is put upon faith. Love seems to have an advantage of faith in this, that we give by love, and we receive by faith; now, it is more blessed to give than to receive. The chiefest answer is, when extraordinary gifts cease, these three abide, and the chiefest of these three is charity, which is most abiding; for when faith and hope are turned into fruition, love then abideth, it is the grace of heaven; but for matter of acceptance, it is faith that is the chief grace.

2. The necessity of faith. There is as much necessity of faith as of Christ. What good will a deep well do us without a bucket? and an able saviour, if we have not faith to take hold of him? Look, as on God's part, there is need of the intervention of Christ's merit to satisfy justice; so on man's part, that the sinner may have an actual interest herein, there is need of faith: you can neither work without it, nor please God without it.

Not work without it. There is as great a necessity of faith as of life—'I live by the faith of the Son of God,' Gal. ii. 20. And you cannot 'please God' without it; for always you shall see all the blessings of the covenant are granted us upon this condition, Rom. x. 9, 'If thou shalt confess with thy mouth the Lord Jesus, and shalt believe in thine heart, that God hath raised him from the dead, thou shalt be saved;' he puts it upon that issue. The gospel is not only a charter of grace and precious promises, but it is a law of faith; that is the condition upon which they are dispensed; so Acts xvi. 31, 'Believe in the Lord Jesus Christ, and thou shalt be saved:' it is the condition of the covenant. The Lord neither will nor can save you without faith; he cannot, because he will not, as his pleasure is now stated. God cannot lie, he hath stated the course and order of our salvation. Now, unless the Lord should reverse the great law and institution of heaven, by which he will govern the world, we may say he cannot save without faith. So the scripture speaks: Mark vi. 5, 'He could do no mighty works there because of their unbelief;' he could not, because of God's settled course, that he will not dispense blessings without faith. Therefore it is notable, that it is the great thing we must preach, and the great duty you must practise: 1 John iii. 23, 'This is his commandment that we should believe on the name of his Son Jesus Christ.' And when we receive our commission as ministers of the gospel, this is the sum of all:' Mark xvi. 16, 'He that believeth shall be saved, and he that believeth not shall be damned.' And this is the great work which you must practise: John vi. 28, 29, 'What shall we do that we might work the works of God?' What work shall we do ? say they, speaking according to the tenor of the covenant of works : saith Christ, 'This is the work of God that you should believe on him whom he hath sent :' all other things are but your by-works, but this is your main work, that you bring your hearts to close with me.

Now if you ask me the reasons why God hath put so much honour upon this grace, why it is impossible without faith to please him ? you may as well ask me, Why God will give light to the world by the sun or water by the fountain ? The Lord's own will and designation is the supreme reason, both in nature and grace ; but because God is a God of judgment, and doth all things with advice and wisdom, because there is a sweet conveniency and congruity in all divine appointments, therefore I shall give you some reasons why the Lord hath put so much honour upon the grace of faith. The great design of God is to humble the creature, but exalt Jesus Christ and promote holiness. Now there is nothing so serviceable for such uses and purposes as the grace of faith.

[1.] It is faith that humbles the creature, and sends us out of ourselves to look for all in Christ ; one of God's designs in the way of salvation is to humble the creature. Now of all graces, faith strips a man naked of his own worth, and sends him to God's mercy in a mediator, so the apostle argueth : Rom. iv. 16, 'It is of faith, that it might be of grace, that the promise might be sure to all the seed ;' therefore God hath stated the way of salvation in the way of faith, that it might be of grace. Faith is the only virtue that can stand with the free grace of God ; for it doth not work by procuring and meriting, but by expecting and receiving what God will bestow upon us ; it brings nothing to God of our own, and can offer nothing by way of exchange for the mercy we expect. It receiveth a gift, but it bringeth no price ; it deals not by way of exchange as with justice, but by way of supplication and reception as with grace. If we were to deal with justice, then certainly the honour of it would be put upon other graces ; as love that might give somewhat by way of exchange. All that faith doth is to send the creature as needy and destitute to the throne of grace : Eph. ii. 8, ' By grace ye are saved through faith ;' justice gives what is due, but mercy gives what is promised ; the original cause is grace, the means is faith, and the end is salvation. Faith doth not come to God, as claiming acceptance for what we have done, but comes with an empty hand to receive what grace and mercy is willing to bestow upon us in Christ.

[2.] God puts this crown of honour upon the head of faith, because it unites us to Christ, out of whom there is no pleasing of God. This reason stands upon two propositions—there is no pleasing God out of Christ and no interest in Christ, but by faith.

(1.) There is no pleasing of God out of Christ. We are all by nature children of wrath until we are reconciled to God by his Son. God is a holy and a just God, and so he cannot be at peace with sinners ; as God is a holy God, so he hates us, because of the contrariety that is between his nature and ours : as he is a just God, so he is obliged to punish us. God in himself is a consuming fire ; he cannot endure us, nor we him. God will never gratify the creature, so as to violate the notions by which his own essence is represented ; therefore naked mercy can do nothing for us till there be satisfaction to justice. Holiness awakens justice, and justice awakens wrath, and wrath consumes the creature; and therefore unless there be a screen drawn betwixt us and wrath, what shall we do? Saith the apostle, Eph. i. 6, ' He hath made us accepted in the Beloved.' In the original it is ἐχαρίστωσεν —he hath ingratiated us in Christ. As a favourite in court makes terms for the rebel, and endears him to the king, so we are returned by grace to Christ. This is that which the Lord hath proclaimed from heaven, that all creatures should take notice of it: Mat. iii. 17, 'This is my beloved son, in whom I am well pleased,' in him, and in no other. This voice came from God not only to show his love to Christ but to give satisfaction to the world—to reveal the pleasure of the Lord to the world, how he will be appeased and satisfied towards us. It is notable, in the Gospel of Luke, these words are spoken to Christ himself: Luke iii. 22, 'Thou art my beloved son, in thee I am well pleased.' But in Matthew they are directed to the world—In him you shall be accepted. God did as it were proclaim to the whole world, if ever you will return to grace and favour to me it must be by my Son. When God looks upon men as they are in themselves, he seeth nothing but a mere abomination: Ps. xiv. 2, 3, ' The Lord looked down from heaven upon the children of men, to see if there were any that did understand, and seek God. They are all gone aside, they are all together become filthy, there is none that doeth good, no, not one.' In the original it is, they are altogether become stinking: God can see nothing but objects that provoke his hatred and aversation. This is the condition of every natural man. So the Lord utters that sorrowful speech concerning man, Gen. vi. 6, ' It repented the Lord that he had made man, and it grieved him at his heart;' he cannot look upon man with any pleasure. But when he looks upon man in Christ, then he is well pleased; he doth as it were say, World, take notice, in him I will be appeased toward you. I have read of an emperor that had a great emerald, in which he would view the bloody fights of the gladiators with pleasure, though they were cruel and detestable in themselves; yet, as they were represented and reflected upon the emerald, so they yielded pleasure and delight. So it is here, God looks upon men in Christ; though we are detestable and abominable objects of his loathing and aversation in ourselves, yet in him he will accept us and do us good. It is notable, what is spoken of Christ, Isa. xlii. 1, ' Behold my servant whom I uphold, my elect in whom my soul delighteth,' is spoken of the church; Isa. lxii. 4, ' Thou shalt be called Hephzibah, and thy land Beulah, for the Lord delighteth in thee.' God delights in them, because he delights in Christ: in and through him he is well pleased with our persons, which otherwise are stinking and abominable.

(2.) There is no receiving of Christ but by faith, and therefore it is said, John i. 12, ' To as many as received him, to them gave he power to become the sons of God, even to them that believe on his name.' Faith is expressed by receiving; it is the hand of the soul by which we receive and take home Christ to our own souls: 2 Cor. xiii. 5, ' Examine yourselves whether you be in the faith; prove your ownselves, know ye not your ownselves, how that Jesus Christ is in you, except ye be reprobates?' Mark there, ' in the faith, and Christ in us,' are made parallel expressions. Our being in the faith is the only means of our union with Christ, that makes Christ to be in us; it is the bond that fastens the soul and Christ together: Eph. iii. 17, 'That Christ may dwell in your hearts by faith;' as a workman makes his house, and then dwells in it, so by faith the soul is fitted for the reception of Christ. Unbelief rejects Christ, and puts him away; Christ stands at the door and knocks, and men will not open to him; but faith is an opening to Christ, a consent of will to take him for ours.

[3.] Faith, it is the mother of obedience, therefore there is good reason to exalt it. Now holiness is effectually promoted by no grace so much as by faith; partly, because faith receives all supplies from heaven. Faith that receiveth Christ, receiveth all his benefits and graces: Gal. iii. 14, 'That the blessing of Abraham might come on the gentiles through Jesus Christ: that we might receive the promise of the Spirit through faith;' that is, the Spirit of God, by whose assistance the holy life is managed and carried on: Gal. ii. 20, 'I live by the faith of the Son of God.' Faith looks up to Christ as distributing grace; and so the strength and power of the inward man is much increased, and a man is enabled for all the offices of holiness. Partly by its own effective influence. There are two powerful affections by which the spiritual life is acted and improved: they are fear and love. Now faith is the mother of both: no faith, no love nor fear. Fear, by which we are fenced against the delights of the world; and love, by which we are steeled against the difficulties of the world; for fear puts on the spectacles of faith, and so seeth him that is invisible. We fear God because we believe that he is. A carnal man looks upon God as an idol and fancy, therefore doth not stand in any awe. So love is strengthened by faith. The apostle saith, 'We love him because he loved us first,' 1 John iv. 19. Our love to God riseth according to the proportion of the assurance we have of God's love to us; then our love is carried out with a greater height and fervour after him. Now there is nothing adds such constraint and force to love as faith: 2 Cor. v. 14, 15, 'The love of Christ constrains us; because we thus judge, that if one died for all, then were all dead: and that he died for all, that they which live should not henceforth live unto themselves, but unto him that died for them, and rose again.' When we have apprehended the love of God in Christ, and what great things God hath done for us, then it puts the soul upon answerable returns. The more certainty we have of the love of God, the stronger impulses of love shall we feel in our souls to God again. Shall not I love him much that hath done so much for me? that hath forgiven me much? that hath been so gracious to me in Christ, and provided such ample recompenses in heaven? We find it in outward matters: jealousy and suspicion is the bane of love. So in divine matters it is true, the more we doubt of God's love, the more faint, and cold, and weak will our love be to God. There are no such motives and incentives to duty as the apprehension of God's love to us in Christ.

SERMON XXVIII.

But without faith it is impossible to please him.—HEB. xi. 6.

LET us now inquire what this faith is. There are three acts of it: knowledge, assent, and affiance. The two former do respect the word, and the last respects Christ offered in the word. The former acts respect *id quod verum est*, that which is true; the last, *id quod bonum est*, that which is good. All are necessary; there is a receiving of the word, and a receiving of Christ in the word. Sometimes we read of receiving of the word: Acts ii. 41, 'They received the word gladly;' that notes only knowledge and assent. But at other times we read of receiving of Christ: John i. 12, 'To as many as received him,' the act of faith is directed to Christ's person.

1. There must be knowledge, for this is a necessary part of faith: we must see the stay and prop before we rest on it; there is an impression of truth upon the understanding. See the expression of the prophet, Isa. liii. 11, 'By his knowledge shall my righteous servant justify many.' The first and radical act of faith is there put for the essence of it; now without this we can neither please God nor be satisfied in ourselves. We cannot please God: Prov. xix. 2, 'Also that the soul be without knowledge, it is not good:' or, as in the original—'The heart without knowledge can never be good.' All that we do in an ignorant state is but superstitious formality, not an act of religion. Look, as the fruit that hath but little of the sun is never concocted, and comes not to full maturity and ripeness; so those acts that are done in a state of ignorance are outward formalities that God will not accept. Nor can we be satisfied in ourselves. How shall we be able to plead with Satan, and answer the doubts of our own consciences, unless we have a distinct knowledge of the mysteries of salvation, and of the contrivance of the gospel? He that is impleaded in a court, and doth not know the law, how shall he be able to stand in his own defence? So how shall we be able to answer Satan and our own fears without knowledge? Look, as we fear usually in the dark, so ignorant souls are always full of doubts and surmises; and it is a long time ere the Lord comes and settles the conscience.

Now every kind of knowledge will not serve the turn. There is a form of knowledge as well as a form of godliness: Rom. ii. 20, 'Which hast the form of knowledge, and of the truth in the law.' The apostle means a naked model of truth, to be able to teach others: but they want a new light put into their hearts by the Spirit of God. It must not only be a formal apprehension, but a serious and considerate knowledge. For faith is a spiritual prudence; it is opposed to folly as well as to ignorance: Luke xxiv. 25, 'O ye fools, and slow of heart to believe all that the prophets have spoken!'—ἀνόητοι, ye mindless men. When men never mind, they do not consider the use and fruit of knowledge; when they do not draw out the principle of knowledge for their private advantage, they are fools. Everything in faith draws to practice; it is not a speculative knowledge, but a knowledge with consideration, a wise light: Eph. i. 17, he calls it 'A spirit of wisdom and revelation in the knowledge of him.' It differs from a traditional and disciplinary knowledge, a literal instruction which we convey from one to another. By this men may be made knowing, but they are not prudent for the advantage of the spiritual life.

2. Next to knowledge there must be assent. Believing is somewhat more than knowledge; we may know more than we do believe, and therefore there must be an assent to the truth of the word: 1 Thes. i. 5, 'For our gospel came not unto you in word only, but also in power, and in the Holy Ghost, and in much assurance.' There is some assurance that doth not concern the state of a believer but the word of God, receiving it above the cavils and contradiction of the privy atheism that is in our own mind. Now, concerning this assent, I shall speak to two things: it must be to the whole word of God and with the whole heart.

[1.] It must be to the whole word; it must be a receiving of the word indefinitely, all that God hath revealed. God prescribeth the conditions which he requireth, and offereth promises; we must consent to the whole. In the word of God there are doctrines, promises, threatenings, precepts—all these must be entertained by faith before we come to the act of affiance. The doctrines of faith concerning God and Christ, the union of the two natures, the mystery of redemption, we must receive them as 'faithful sayings,' 1 Tim. i. 15. Usually there is some privy atheism: we look upon the gospel as a golden dream, and a well-devised fable. Saith Luther, 'Carnal men hear these things as if the mystery of the gospel were but like a dream or shower of rubies fallen out of the clouds;' therefore there must be a chief care to settle the heart in the belief of these things as faithful and true sayings. Christians would not find the work of their particular faith so irksome if they had but 'the assurance of understanding,' Col. ii. 2; if their hearts were rooted in the truths of the gospel. Then there are threatenings of the word, to show how abominable the creature is to God in a natural condition, and to what punishments we are subject and liable. Now these must be applied with reverence and fear, that we may be roused out of our carnal estate, and chased like the hart to the refreshing streams of grace. There must be a firm belief of all the threatenings and curses of God. Then the promises of the word, these are principally calculated for faith, and these must be applied to the soul: John iii. 33, 'He that hath received his testimony hath set to his seal that God is true.' We must come and set to our seal, and say, Lord, thou wilt never fail thy creatures, if they should venture their souls upon the warrant of such as these are. Then there is believing of the commands, not only that they come from the Lord, that they are laws established and enacted by the supreme ruler of heaven and earth; but we must believe they are just, good, holy and true. So David, Ps. cxix. 66, 'Teach me good judgment and knowledge, for I have believed thy commandments.' When we believe the commandments are of divine original, and that they are holy, and good, and fit to be obeyed, this is that which the apostle calls a 'consenting to the law, that it is good,' Rom. vii. 16. Such an assent must there be to the whole word.

[2.] It must be with the whole heart. For this the intellectual assent is not enough, unless it be accompanied with some motion of the heart; there is somewhat besides understanding, not only knowledge and acknowledgment, but there must be consent of the will.   We must not only reflect upon the things that are propounded as true, but as good and worthy of all acceptation : Acts viii. 37, 'If thou believest with all thy heart, thou mayest be baptized.' We must assent to the threatenings of the word with trembling and reverence, to the promises of the word with delight and esteem : Acts ii. 41, 'They received the word gladly,' to the commandments of the word with some anxious care of strictness and obedience, to the doctrines of the word with consideration.

3. There is affiance, which is an act which doth immediately respect the person of Jesus Christ.   For we are not saved by giving credence to any axiom or maxim of religion, but by casting the soul upon Christ. Faith is thus described by resting upon God, 2 Chron. xiv. 11 ; by staying upon God, Isa. xxvi. 3 ; by trusting in Christ, Mat. xii. 21, Ps. ii. 12.   There must be some carrying out of the soul to the person of Christ himself.   The devils may have knowledge—'I know thee who thou art, the holy one of God,' Luke iv. 34.   And the devil may have some assent too ; there are no atheists in hell.   Nay, they assent with some kind of affection—'They believe and tremble,' James. ii. 19.   Therefore there must be an act of faith that carrieth out the soul to Christ himself.   Believing in Christ noteth a recumbency—'Believe in the Lord Jesus Christ, and thou shalt be saved,' Acts xvi. 31 ; it is Paul's counsel to the gaoler.   It is an allusion to a man that is ready to fall, that stays himself by some prop and support ; so it is staying our souls upon Christ when we are ready to sink under the burden of divine displeasure, or are overwhelmed with terrors of conscience.   Now let us a little consider this act in its progress and growth.

[1.] This act of affiance must arise from a brokenness of spirit.   The soul must be broken and dejected with a sense of God's wrath, or else it can never come and lean upon Christ.   It is the work of God to comfort those that are cast down.   There is no dependence upon God for comfort till we are cast down and dejected with the sense of his wrath.   This casting our souls upon Christ doth suppose a being possessed with the fear of death ; then we take hold of the horns of the altar with Adonijah.   Till there be a due sense and conviction of conscience, it is not faith, but carnal security.   It is a great mistake to think God requires faith immediately of any.   He requires faith of none immediately but those that are broken and contrite, that are dejected with a sense of their own wretched condition out of Christ.   Therefore when Christ invites persons to grace, still he directs his speech to them that are thirsty, hungry, weary, because they are in the next capacity of believing : Mat. xi. 28, 'Come unto me, all ye that are weary and heavy laden, and ye shall find rest for your souls.'   Those are invited to Christ that groan under the heavy load upon their consciences : Isa. lv. 1, 'Ho, every one that thirsteth, come to the waters,' &c.   Christ speaks to those that are dejected with the sense of their natural condition.   It is in vain to boast of peace of conscience when we were never troubled.   Believing is a swimming to the rock.   Now he that stands upon the firm land cannot swim ; that is not a work for him, but for those that are in the midst of the waves, ready to perish in the tempestuous waters.   Men of an untroubled and unmoved conscience, their next duty is not to believe in Christ ; but those that are ready to despair, they are called to swim to the rock, and run to Christ, the rock of ages, that they may not be swallowed up of divine displeasure.

[2.] This act is put forth with much difficulty and struggling. It is a hard matter to bring Christ and the soul together. There is a great deal of struggle ere we can cast our souls upon Christ. We must reason with our own fears, plead and dispute with ourselves and with God, and cry long and loud many times at the throne of grace. As when the prodigal began to be in want, then he deliberates with himself—In my father's house there is bread enough and to spare. The case of a soul in coming to Christ is much like the case of Peter in coming to Christ upon the waves : Mat. xiv. 28–30, Peter, when he saw Christ, he acknowledged him for his lord and saviour ' Peter said unto him, Lord, if it be thou, bid me to come on the water. And he said, Come. And when Peter was come down out of the ship, he walked upon the water to go to Jesus ; but when he saw the wind boisterous, he was afraid, and beginning to sink, he cried, saying, Lord, save me.' Peter left his ship, and resolved to venture on Christ's call ; but he found difficulty. So it is in our coming to Christ, when by an undoubted assent to the truth of the word we are convinced in conscience that Christ is the alone saviour, that he is a rock for shelter in the midst of waves ; by the impulses of grace the soul begins to make out to Christ. Christ saith, Come, come, and the soul is even overwhelmed with the tempests of wrath and waves of divine displeasure ; therefore we had need encourage our hearts in God, and cry, Lord, arise and save us. After we have left the ship of our carnal confidence, after the soul is in its progress to Christ, there is a great deal of difficulty to bring God and the soul together. God doth not meet every soul as the father of the prodigal, half way ; but there is a long suspension of comfort that may cast us upon difficulties, that we may struggle with our own unbelieving thoughts.

[3.] Though there be no certainty, yet there is an obstinate purpose to follow after Christ. It is true, the aim and end of all faith is to draw the soul to certainty and particular application, to assurance of pardon, that we may say, My God and My rock. But though the soul meets with many difficulties, yet there is an obstinate purpose ; the soul will not let go his hold on Christ. When we can plead with our own objections and fears, and say, Lord I will not give over ; and with Jacob, ' I will not let thee go till thou bless me,' Gen. xxxii. 26, and with Job, ' Though he slay me, yet will I trust in him,' Job xiii. 15. Whatever displeasure the Lord seems to manifest against them, yet they will follow on in a way of trust : Phil. iii. 12, ' I follow after, if that I may apprehend that for which also I am apprehended of Christ Jesus,' &c. Christ hath touched my heart, and I cannot be quiet till I have got him. This is a right disposition of heart. When Christ hath apprehended us, the soul follows on with an obstinate resolution, until it can apprehend Christ and take hold of the skirt of his garment.

Use 1. To put us upon the trial, Have we true faith ? there is no acceptance with God without it. The great object of trial and search is faith : 2 Cor. xiii. 5, ' Examine yourselves, whether ye be in the faith,' or in a believing state. Conviction mainly respects faith : John xvi. 9, ' He shall convince the world of sin, because they believe not in me,' without it, we are liable to the power and curse of the law against sinners. Faith makes the difference among men before God : Gal. v. 6, 'For in Christ Jesus neither circumcision availeth anything, nor uncircumcision, but faith which worketh by love.' When God proceedeth to judgment against sinners, he doth not ask, Is he baptized ? is he civil ? but doth he believe ? there is the most important question in christianity.

Now there are different degrees of faith : Mark xvii. 20, 'If ye have faith as a grain of mustard seed ;' Mark viii. 26, 'Why are ye fearful, O ye of little faith ?' All the trees of God's garden are not of the same growth and stature, there are cedars and shrubs. The least degree of faith is faith, as a drop of dew is water as well as a flood ; and the lowest measure and grain of saving faith is grace ; the motion of a child newly formed in the belly is an act of life, as well as the walking of a man. Some, like John Baptist, can only 'spring in the womb ;' they have a seed of grace, though they be not grown up into a tree. In Christ's family there are 'little children,' as well as 'fathers,' 1 John ii. 12–14. Christ himself was once a little stone, though he grew a great mountain, that filled the whole earth. All plants in Christ's garden are growing when they are young and weak. We must not despise the day of small things ; we must look indeed chiefly after truth, not growth. It is well if we endure the touchstone, though not the balance : 2 Tim. i. 5, 'When I call to remembrance the unfeigned faith that is in thee ;' the question will be resolved into that at last. There is a counterfeit faith that is not profitable. Simon Magus believed, Acts viii. 13 ; and many believed in Christ's name, to whom he would not commit himself, John ii. 23, 24. When the devil destroyeth men, he doth not forbid them to believe ; he changeth himself into an angel of light. Presumption is rather of means than of end ; most deceive themselves with a false faith. There is nothing but the devil can counterfeit it—Felix trembled, Esau wept, Ahab humbled himself, Simon Magus believed, Judas repented, Pharaoh prayed, Saul confessed, Balaam desired, the Pharisee reformed — we had need to look to ourselves. But how shall we state the marks by which men may come to the knowledge of their state ? especially, how shall we discern what is true faith ? In the first times of the gospel the difficulty lay without ; the gospel was a novel doctrine, opposed by worldly powers ; bleak winds that blow in our backs blew in their faces. The gospel, as a novel doctrine, was represented with prejudices, opposed with scorn and extremity of violence ; there was more in assent than now in affiance. Now the gospel by long prescription and the veneration of ages hath gotten a just title to our belief ; there is nothing in a literal and uneffectual assent. Every man pretendeth to esteem Christ, and acknowledge Christ for saviour of the world ; how shall we disprove them ? The scriptures are rather a treasury of doctrines than a register of experiences. But yet we are not wholly left in the dark ; by the light of the Spirit the doctrines of the word may be suited to all cases. The scripture is not such a dark rule but that it will discover the thoughts of the heart ; and what is this faith unfeigned, the *minimum quod sic*, the least degree of faith, without which we are not accepted ?

I might answer generally, that the least degree of true faith beginneth in contrition, and endeth in a care of obedience. But because there may be in the wicked some occasional doubtings, such as arise by starts out of the trouble of an evil conscience and some smooth moralities, that may look like gospel reformation, we must go more particularly to work. I do again return the question, What is the lowest degree of true saving faith?' By way of answer—

1. I shall show that the question is necessary to be determined, partly for the comfort of troubled consciences. God's children are many times persuaded they have not faith, when indeed they have. It would be a great settlement if we could clear up the work of Christ: Mat. xvii. 20, ' If ye have faith as a grain of mustard seed,' &c. Though you have mountains of guilt, it is a great peevishness not to acknowledge the crumbs; we think we are dogs, but we have crumbs. To deny that you are Christ's is not self-denial, but grace-denial, to belie God's bounty: Cant. i. 5, 'I am black, but comely;' and ver. 2, 'I sleep, but my heart waketh;' Mark ix. 24, ' Lord, I believe, help thou my unbelief.' And it is a ground of unthankfulness: Zech. iv. 10, 'Who hath despised the day of small things?' God will be acknowledged in the low beginnings of grace. Partly as it is a ground of hope: Phil. i. 6, ' Being confident of this very thing, that he, which hath begun a good work in you, will also perform it until the day of Jesus Christ;' it is the bud of glory, a seed of everlasting life. The Spirit never forsaketh us, something is to be done till the day of judgment; the soul is exactly purified at death, and the body will be raised at the great day. It is an advantage to be able to urge deliverance from the lion and bear; the great Philistine shall also be overcome, only we must not rest in those beginnings. Initial grace is but counterfeit, unless it receive growth and access; things that are nipped in the bud show that the plant is not right.

2. It is possible to find out the least and lowest degree of faith. Scriptures show that there is a beginning, upon which we may conclude an interest in Christ: Heb. iii. 14, 'For we are made partakers of Christ, if we hold τὴν ἀρχὴν τῆς ὑποστάσεως, the beginning of our confidence, stedfast unto the end,' if we retain the first principles and encouragements to believe; if we can hold it out, we are safe. There are some grains and initials of faith; and the scripture discovereth what they are, for it layeth down the essentials of faith, we are not left in the dark.

Having premised these things, let me come now to show what it is, because faith is a capacious word, and involveth the whole progress of the soul to Christ. It is hard to state this matter in one word, unless it were as ambiguous as the question itself; therefore I shall take liberty to dilate and enlarge myself, by showing you what is most necessary, and what are the lowest and most infant workings of faith.

[1.] There must be out of a deep conviction a removing of our own righteousness. Affiance beginneth in self-diffidence. Faith implieth that we are touched in conscience, and that the heart is elevated above self, utterly abhorring our own merits: Ps. cxlvii. 3, 'He healeth the broken in heart, and bindeth up their wounds. Faith is a seed of heaven, not found in unploughed or fallow ground—a sound conviction of self-nothingness, especially if joined with addresses to grace, is a good evidence of it. The soul looketh upon all that it hath or can do, like a ship without a bottom, to be a hindrance, not a gain; and unless Christ help they are utterly and eternally lost: Phil. iii. 7–9; 'What things were gain to me, those I counted lost for Christ. Yea, doubtless, and I count all things but loss for the excellency of the knowledge of Christ Jesus my Lord, for whom I have suffered the loss of all things, and do count them but dung, that I may win Christ. And be found in him, not having my own righteousness, which is of the law, but that which is through the faith of Christ, the righteousness which is of God through faith.' The soul in this condition is between life and death; it is a twilight in the soul, neither perfect day nor perfect night, like a child in the place of breaking forth of children; if we be not still-born we are in a fair way of faith; if we run to mercy, there is hope. 'The publican, that smote his hand upon his breast, saying, God, be merciful to me a sinner, went down to his house justified rather than the other,' Luke xviii. 13, 14. The parable is spoken against those that trusted in themselves, that they were righteous. Discovering of an ill condition may be sometimes in the wicked, but the soul is not purged from carnal confidence and set to work upon the mere warrant of God's grace.

[2.] An esteem of Christ. In faith there is not only a conviction of the understanding, but some motion of the will; all motions of the will are founded in esteem. This is a low fruit of faith: 1 Peter ii. 7, 'To them that believe he is precious.' To an hungry conscience Christ is more precious than all the world besides; he seeth the truth and preciousness of the rich offers of grace in the Lord Jesus Christ, the sweetest happiest tidings that ever sounded in his ears, and entertaineth it with the best and dearest welcomes of his heart, it is better than life. This is the same with 'tasting the good word of God,' Heb. vi. 5, only it is more constant. Carnal men may have a vanishing and fleeting glance, but these are serious and spiritual motions and affections of the heart towards Christ. Wicked men soon lose their relish and taste, like those that cheapen things, and taste them, but do not like the price. This maketh us part with all: Mat. xiii. 44, 'The kingdom of heaven is like to a treasure hid in a field, the which, when a man hath found, he hideth, and for joy thereof goeth and selleth all that he hath and buyeth that field.' This esteem begetteth self-denial; estate, credit, friends, all shall go, so I may enjoy Christ. Wicked men have some relish; they prize Christ in pangs of conscience. All apostasy cometh from a low estimation of Christ after a taste; it is the highest profaneness: Heb. xii. 16, 'Profane Esau, for one morsel of meat, sold his birthright.' Well then, is Christ precious? Dost thou embrace the reconciliation that he hath purchased with all thy heart?

There is but one objection against this act and disposition of faith; this prizing of Christ seemeth but a natural act. Esteem is pure when it is drawn forth upon religious reasons; these acts are not gracious, because the ground is carnal—viz., offers of nature after ease. How will you do to comfort a troubled conscience that maketh this reply? It is but a natural motion after ease; we look on Christ for comfort?

I Answer, (1.) By setting before him the indulgence of God. We may make use of God's motives; he suffereth us to begin in the flesh, that we may end in the spirit: Mat. xi. 28, 'Come unto me, all ye that labour and are heavy laden, and I will give you rest.' There is faith when we trust Christ upon his own word. If a prince should offer a general pardon to rebels, with a promise that he would restore their blood, and now they lay down their arms and submit to mercy, it is counted an act of obedience. If Christ maketh proclamation, Come, and I will ease you, do you think it is a wrong faith to take him at his word, and to love him for his condescension?

(2.) To press him to perfect these acts. It is good to be doing rather than censuring. Idle complaints do but vex the soul. Those rebels that submit to a prince because of his pardon may afterwards enter into an entire friendship. Christ is lovely in himself; by acquaintance our affections grow more pure. We first esteem him out of hope, and then out of gratitude. Love to his person is the fruit of experience. In a treaty of marriage, the first proposals are estate and conveniences of life; conjugal affection groweth by society and commerce. It is a good advantage to love Christ upon any terms.

(3.) By discovering the mistake. There is some spirituality of esteem when we can prize a pardon and acceptance with God. Bastard motives are fame, and ease, and worldly honour, and the sunshine of worldly countenance. Besides, this esteem of Christ ariseth from a spiritual reason, because we are unsatisfied in our own righteousness: Phil. iii. 7, 8, 'What things were gain to me, those I counted loss for Christ. Yea, doubtless, and I count all things but loss for the excellency of the knowledge of Christ Jesus my Lord, for whom I have suffered the loss of all things, and do count them but dung that I may win Christ.' Because we have a low esteem of ourselves, therefore we have a high esteem of Christ. Now it is an effect of grace to prize Christ for his righteousness, which is the esteem that groweth out of sound conviction.

[3.] Another act which ariseth out of this is a resolution to cast ourselves upon Christ; then faith is budded and formed. Rolling upon Christ is the formal, vital act of faith; and a sound purpose of acknowledging him for a saviour is the lowest degree of that act. And therefore if, out of a sight of thy own lost condition and an esteem of Christ, thou resolvest to cast thyself upon him, thou dost truly believe. Partly because in this resolution there is a compliance with the decrees of heaven, of setting up Christ as the alone saviour of the world; this decree is ratified in the court of conscience. There is another decree passed and ratified with the consent of my will, that Christ shall be my saviour: Ps. lxxiii. 28, 'It is good for me to draw nigh to God; I have put my trust in the Lord God, that I may declare all thy works.' There is recumbency or sincere adherence, which is the formal nature of faith, expressed by a believing on him. This resolution is always accompanied with a great confidence of the ableness of Christ to do us good: Mat. ix. 21, 'If I may but touch his garment, I shall be whole.' Paul after experience had no more: 2 Tim. i. 12, 'I am persuaded that he is able to keep that which I have committed unto him against that day.' Partly because such an act findeth a sweeter welcome than it can expect. David received comfort upon it: Ps. xxxii. 5, 'I said,

I will confess my transgressions unto the Lord, and thou forgavest the iniquity of my sin.' 'I will arise and go to my father,' saith the prodigal, in Luke xv. 18; 'but when he was yet a great way off, his father saw him, and had compassion, and ran, and fell on his neck and kissed him,' ver. 20. Therefore, when a poor soul casts himself upon Christ with a purpose never to forsake him through God's grace, I do not doubt to pronounce him a believer, though there be much doubts and uncertainty about the success of such addresses. As a man falling into a river, espieth a bough of a tree, and catcheth at it with all his might, as soon as he hath fast hold of it, he is safe, though troubles and fears do not presently vanish out of his mind; so the soul, espying Christ as the only means to save him, and reaching out the hand to him, is safe, though it be not presently quieted and pacified.

Now this act discovereth itself by three things.

SERMON XXIX.

For he that cometh to God must believe that he is, and that he is a rewarder of those that diligently seek him.—HEB. xi. 6.

(1.) By desires, a constant and earnest desire to go to Christ: Mat. v. 6, 'Blessed are they that hunger and thirst after righteousness; for they shall be filled.' Now no work of nature hath God made a promise of grace to. There may be velleities; Balaam and others had wishes, but not real desires. In these constant serious desires the soul cannot be quiet without Christ: Ps. xlii. 1, 'As the hart panteth after the waterbrooks, so panteth my soul after thee, O God.' The soul earnestly desires to be a partaker of Christ and his merits. These desires are drawn out in prayer. In the want of an expected good we sally out after it by passionate desires, earnest sighs and groans.

(2.) By pursuits. Whosoever is moved to make after Christ as the only means of his acceptation with God, truly believeth; who make this their work, John vi. 27, 'Labour not for the meat that perisheth, but for that meat which endureth unto everlasting life, which the Son of man shall give unto you.'

(3.) By rejoicing in hope when we have nothing in fruition: Heb. iii. 6, 'If we hold fast the confidence and the rejoicing of the hope firm unto the end.'

To sum up all: the lowest act of faith we have found to be the resolution of a humbled sinner to cast himself on Christ. Recumbency is the formal vital act of faith, and a purpose of recumbency the lowest degree of that act. Well then, if, out of a sight of thy lost condition and a high esteem of Christ, thou resolvest to cast thy soul upon him, thou dost truly believe. Now this purpose is bewrayed to be serious and real by desire, by pursuit, and sometimes as faith receiveth strength and growth by rejoicing in our future hopes when we have nothing in actual feeling and fruition.

Though I suppose nothing of moment can be objected against the decision of this question, yet because some desire to clear this recumbency from that leaning on the Lord which is spoken of, Micah iii. 11, ' The heads thereof judge for reward, and the priests thereof teach for hire, and the prophets thereof divine for money; yet will they lean upon the Lord and say, Is not the Lord among us? none evil can come upon us.' Whence they infer there may be a leaning and recumbency where there is no grace.

I answer by a κατάχρησις. Leaning is put for a vain trust; the prophet speaketh according to their presumption; they thought it leaning or staying on the Lord when it was but a foolish confidence built upon an ill ground, the presence of God in the outward ordinances and services of the temple, as if this would secure them against all dangers, and God would be for them, though in their persons they were never so wicked and unreformed.

But to clear it more fully: in all recumbency we must not only regard the act and the object; it is not enough that there be confidence or strength of resolution, and that this confidence be in pretence placed on God and Christ; as carnal men will say, I pitch all my hopes on Christ for salvation. A wicked man may make a bold and daring adventure, and lean upon the Lord, though at length the Lord will jostle him off. But there are other circumstances which must be considered, as (1.) The necessary method and order of this recumbence; (2.) The warrant or ground of it; (3.) The fruits and effects of it.

1st. The method and order of it. It is the resolution of a humbled sinner to cast himself upon Christ. We still run to Christ out of a sense of our own misery. The heart must be touched by the word. When conscience is drowsy, it is but a presumptuous act; and the devil, to delude them in an imaginary faith, suffereth them to hold out Christ in a naked pretence. The end and use of faith is to lift up that which is cast down; therefore it is sometimes expressed by a catching or taking hold of Christ, as those that are ready to perish in the waters catch hold of a bough; as Adonijah, when guilty of death, took hold of the horns of the altar: Isa. lvi. 4, ' Thus saith the Lord unto the eunuchs that keep my sabbaths, and choose the things that please me, and take hold of my covenant.' So the heirs of promise are described to be those ' who have fled for refuge to lay hold upon the hope set before them,' Heb. vi. 18; it is an allusion to those that fly from the avenger of blood. Wrath maketh pursuit, and the believer runneth to the city of refuge. Whosoever sets his face to Christ when chased out of himself by his own fears, and tremblingly flieth to undeserved grace,—whosoever, I say, findeth himself in truth to be thus affected, need not doubt of his interest in Christ; he is driven from sin and wrath, and drawn to Christ to seek salvation alone in him. Certainly he is an heir of promise, and God hath sworn to him. So in the metaphor of leaning on Christ, it supposeth a falling unless Christ did bear us up. This is the sure method of grace; God comforteth those that are cast down, Christ hath a napkin for the wet face of sinners. This is not only true at first conversion, but every time we renew our access to him, it is either out of new troubles, or out of a constant tenderness of conscience. Therefore in heaven there is no faith, because there is no contrition, but a perfect oblivion of misery; the soul being full of joy, faith hath no place and use. Therefore it is in vain to boast of quiet of conscience and leaning on the Lord, as wicked men do, when the soul was never troubled. We must consider the method and order of grace. A wicked man is never reconciled to God, because he never saw there was need to seek reconciliation, his conscience is sleepy and drowsy. Here is the constant trial then; all acts of faith at first conversion and afterwards begin at conviction, and a sense of our vileness and nothingness. But you will say, Then a believer's life must be a bondage; are we always to put ourselves into scruples and fears? And if the terrors of the Lord do still chase us to Christ, this would prejudice the comfort and assurance of grace. I answer, There is a great deal of difference between a troubled stormy conscience and a tender awakened conscience; the one is a dispensation, the other a duty. Though there be not a fear that is contrary to faith, a legal dejection; yet there is a constant conviction and deep sense of our own vileness and nothingness. We have all cause to be continually humble and nothing in our own eyes, as Paul groaned sorely when yet he blesseth God for Christ: Rom. vii. 24, 25, 'O wretched man that I am! who shall deliver me from the body of this death? I thank God through Jesus Christ our Lord.' He had such a real confidence as produced thanksgiving. So that this is the necessary order of grace, without which we shall not prize Christ. This is wanting in carnal men; a bare supposition would destroy their peace.

2dly. The warrant or ground of it. He casteth himself upon Christ that goeth to work considerately, and understanding what he doth; as Paul saith, 2 Tim. i. 12, 'I know whom I have believed.' True confidence is an advised act, it is built on the offer of God and the ability of Christ. They go and show God his own handwriting, and modestly challenge him on his promise: Ps. cxix. 49, 'Remember thy word unto thy servant, upon which thou hast caused me to hope.' They know Christ is so able they may trust in him. Now this resolution in wicked men is but a blind adventure, like a leap in the dark, they do not weigh the danger. Look to the ground of your trust. The two builders, Mat. vii. the wise and the foolish builder, are not commended or discommended for the structure, but for the foundation—the one built on the rock, the other on the sand. Natural conscience is crafty, and pretendeth fair; they say they trust in Christ, as those that leaned on the Lord but upon an ill warrant, external privileges; they rest not on God, but on the temple. Therefore they are said to trust in lying words: Jer. vii. 4, 'Trust ye not in lying words, saying, The temple of the Lord, the temple of the Lord, the temple of the Lord, are these!' So carnal men have a few ignorant hopes, and trust in their baptism and good meanings, and Christ beareth the name; they are borne up with the bladders of their own confidence, a few windy, empty hopes.

3dly. The effects and fruits of it. Affiance cannot consist with a purpose of sinning, with the purpose of casting ourselves on Christ. There is an unfeigned purpose of obedience; he that trusteth in the Lord hateth sin. Can a man be an enemy to him that saveth him? Now, wicked men cast away their souls, and then trust Christ shall save them; it is, as if a man should plunge himself in the deep, upon presumption that he shall find a bough to take hold of. God in mercy hath provided faith for the fallen creature as a remedy ; it is an abuse of it to plunge ourselves again into sin. Look, as it is a vanity to cast ourselves into straits, and then to see how God will help us; so here, we tempt free grace to our loss. Wicked men embrace Christ with treacherous embraces, like Judas' kiss to betray him ; as Joab took Abner aside to smite him under the fifth rib: Heb. x. 22, 'Let us draw nigh ($\mu\epsilon\tau\grave{\alpha}$ $\dot{\alpha}\lambda\eta\theta\iota\nu\hat{\eta}s$ $\kappa\alpha\rho\delta\acute{\iota}\alpha s$) with a true heart, in full assurance of faith, having our hearts sprinkled from an evil conscience, and our bodies washed with pure water ;' if not without sin, yet without guile ; there must be an upright and unfeigned purpose to walk in new obedience. There is a notable place : Jer. vii. 9, 10, 'Will ye steal, murder, and commit adultery, and swear falsely, and burn incense unto Baal, and walk after other gods whom ye know not ; and come and stand before me in the house, which is called by my name, and say, We are delivered to do all these abominations ?'—we are delivered, all these are expiated by sacrifice ; Christ died for me as well as you, we shall do well enough. What ! will ye be worldly, sensual, neglect duty, be drunk, be careless in the course of your conversations, and say, We are delivered, Christ died for us ? And will he discharge you from the guilt of these sins when you turn again to the practice of them ? It is true, there is a bath for uncleanness, and there will be continual failings, but certainly they that continue in the constant practice of iniquity have no comfort and benefit by it : John xiii. 10, ' He that is washed needeth not save to wash his feet, but is clean every whit.' There will be some fleshly adherences and failings after we are washed in the laver of Christ's blood, as a man that goeth from the bath, when he hath washed his body, may defile his feet ; but when you make it your constant practice to commit iniquity, it is in vain to pretend to rest on Christ.

Use 2. Exhortation to press us to faith. It is the commandment which we must teach : 1 John iii. 23, 'This is his commandment, that we should believe on the name of his son Jesus Christ ;' and it is the work which you must practise : John vi. 29, 'This is the work of God, that ye believe on him whom he hath sent ;' this is your $\check{\epsilon}\rho\gamma o\nu$; it is but waste time that you spend on pleasures and worldly businesses. Men think they are only to follow their callings, they make their temporal and worldly business their work, and so do not apply their minds to believe in Christ. Oh, consider, when there was an invitation, business would not suffer them to regard it ! Mat. xxii. 5, ' They made light of it, and went their ways, one to his farm, another to his merchandise.' It is not whoredom, drunkenness, and extortion, but an immoderate following of their lawful profits and pleasures—a farm, a marriage, a yoke of oxen—things plausible in their kind, and one would think necessary : Luke x. 42, ' Mary hath chosen the better part, which shall not be taken away from her :' these things ought not to be undone. How can men sleep or work till they have cleared up their interest in Christ ? nay, in spiritual employments, closing with Christ ; the pre-eminent duty is not your work so much as your faith. The disciples in their converse with Christ bewrayed many weaknesses, but Christ was never angry with them so much as he was for their want of faith:

Luke xxiv. 25, ' O fools, and slow of heart to believe all that the prophets have spoken!' and Mat. viii. 26, 'Why are ye so fearful, O ye of little faith?' Oh, consider, to quicken you, it is the grace that bringeth God most glory, and doth you most good. Some cry up charity, because they mistake the nature of faith— they depress it, they omit what is chiefest in faith, and they speak of it as if it were nothing worth. And so others make faith a pendulous hope, and therefore cry up obedience and love.

1. It bringeth God most glory. It is notable that faith doth that to God in a way of duty, which God doth to the creature in a way of grace—it justifieth, sanctifieth, glorifieth. It justifieth, and that is a relative word, against the slanders and contempts of the world. So it is said, Luke vii. 29, 'And all the people heard him, and the publicans justified God, being baptized with the baptism of John;' it defendeth his honour and the truth of his grace. The pharisees said, It was a foolish doctrine. How a believer justifieth God against the contempt of the world and the suspicions of his own heart! Whatever conscience saith to the contrary, the Lord is just, gracious, merciful. Unbelief slighteth God and Christ, as if he were not worth the taking; the truth of the gospel, as if it were not worth credit; his worth, as if he did not deserve respect; his power, as if he were not able to save a sinking soul; it putteth a lie upon the whole contrivance of grace. Oh, how sweet were it if we could justify God against the prejudices of our own hearts! they make the blood of Christ a base thing, the Spirit of Christ a weak instrument. So it sanctifieth God: Num. xx. 12, 'Because ye believed me not, to sanctify me in the eyes of the children of Israel.' To sanctify, is to set apart for special uses and purposes; so we are said to sanctify God when we give him a separate and distinct excellency from all the powers in the world. He is not a common help and saviour, none so holy and gracious; it setteth the Lord with admiration above all created powers, for trust, fear, and dependence: Isa. viii. 13, 'Sanctify the Lord of hosts himself, and let him be your fear, and let him be your dread.' When we see man is not to be trusted nor feared, but God, we set him on the highest point of eminency, aloof from the creatures. Is there any like him for pardon, for power, for holiness? So it glorifieth God: Rom. iv. 20, ' He was strong in faith, giving glory to God.' God doth as it were receive a new being from faith; though he be infinitely glorious in himself, yet he counteth himself glorified by the faith of the creature; he hath a second heaven in the heart of a believer, there he dwelleth by faith, and displayeth the pomp of all his excellences. Now unbelief dethroneth God, it will not let him set up a new heaven or place of residence in the conscience.

2. It doth you most good; your life, your peace, your glory, all hangeth upon it. Your life: Gal. ii. 20, 'I live by the faith of the Son of God;' you may be as well without life as without faith. So for peace, would not a man be friends with God, and live at amity with heaven? Rom. v. 1, ' Being justified by faith we have peace with God through our Lord Jesus Christ;' and for glory, 1 Peter i. 9, ' Receiving the end of your faith, even the salvation of your souls.' Faith beginneth salvation, and heaven is but faith perfect and believing

turned into fruition.   You are in the suburbs of heaven as soon as you close with Christ ; it putteth you above the clouds, and in the midst of glory to come.   All the blessings of the covenant are made over to faith.   It is God's acquittance which he showeth to Christ ; as when men are obliged to pay great sums of money, they receive an acquittance, as an acknowledgment that the money is received : John iii. 33, ' He that hath received his testimony hath set to his seal, that God is true.'   We give it under our hand and seal, that God is as good as his word.

But how shall we do to get faith ?   I answer—

[1.] The habit of faith is freely given and wrought by God himself : Phil. i. 29, ' To you it is given on the behalf of Christ to believe on him ; ' Eph. ii. 8, ' By grace ye are saved through faith, and that not of yourselves, it is the gift of God ; ' Heb. xii. 2, ' Looking to Jesus the author and finisher of our faith.'   And therefore the general means are waiting upon the word and prayer ; commend thy case to God by prayer, and wait for an answer in the word.   Hearing there must be : Rom. x. 14, ' How shall they believe in him, of whom they have not heard ? '   God will not infuse faith when asleep ; you must lie under the authority of the word.   God's seasons are not at our beck ; if the first stroke of the flint doth not bring forth the fire, you must strike again ; it is good to be constant.   And then if God suspend the influences of his grace, pray remember the promise of giving the Holy Spirit : Luke xi. 13, ' If ye then, being evil, know how to give good gifts to your children, how much more shall your heavenly Father give the Holy Spirit to them that ask him ? '   Knock once more ; a holy importunity argueth some presence of the Spirit, though we are not sensible of it ; it is good to be earnest, and to follow God with renewed requests and expectations.

[2.] I answer, Because we are required to believe ; though it be his gift, God requireth it of the creature.   It is good to be doing ; let us use the means, and leave the blessing to God ; he may come ere we are aware, and though we can do nothing spiritually, yet it is good to be doing rationally.   It is true, faith is not a work of nature, but this is the way of God's working.   There are secret elapses of the Spirit of God, as Samuel thought Eli called, when it was the Lord ; there may be a spiritual work where we think it merely rational : besides, we are under a law ; God respecteth not what we can do, but what we ought to do.   Three things are to be done—(1.) Something to humble the soul and fit it for faith ; (2.) Something to further the immediate working and actings of faith towards Christ ; (3.) Something for the regulating of these actings.

First, To fit the soul for faith, it is good to offer humbling matter. God was angry with Pharaoh : Exod. x. 3, ' How long wilt thou refuse to humble thyself before me ? '   Certainly we might do something.

(1.) Reflect on your present condition, and think of changes.   It will not be ever with thee as it is now.   I must die, and must come to judgment.   Draw it to a short issue : Mark xvi. 16, ' He that believeth and is baptized shall be saved, but he that believeth not shall be damned.'   Do I believe ? upon what terms do I stand with God ? what

assurance have I of his love? Especially do it, when God giveth thee
a hint in his providence: 1 Kings viii. 47, 'If they shall bethink themselves in the land, whither they were carried captives, and repent and
make supplication unto thee in the land, of them that carried them
captives, saying, We have sinned, and have done perversely, we have
committed wickedness,' &c. Retirement gave them an opportunity to
converse with themselves. It is good for us and our consciences to be
together sometimes and enter parley, What am I? how do matters
stand between God and me? Man has a conscience—a power to talk
with himself: Ps. iv. 4, 'Commune with your own heart on your bed,
and be still;' he can look inwardly to ask himself what he hath done:
Prov. xx. 27, 'The spirit of man is the candle of the Lord, searching
all the inward parts of the belly:' it is God's deputy, it sets up a
tribunal within a man's self.

(2.) Examine yourselves by the law of God. A daily view of sins
doth much conduce to humbling. Conscience is blind in many cases,
therefore take the law along with you, and look into the purity of it:
Rom. iii. 20, 'By the law is the knowledge of sin;' not only *quoad
naturam peccati*, but *quoad inhærentiam in subjecto*. To man fallen,
that is the nature and office of it: Rom. vii. 9, 'For I was alive without the law once; but when the commandment came, sin revived, and
I died.' Paul was never troubled till the law was brought home to his
conscience.

(3.) Aggravate thy sins from the consideration of God's love. Two
things very much humble the soul, light and love. So it was in Saul's
case: 1 Sam. xxiv. 16, 17, 'And Saul lifted up his voice and wept.
And he said to David, Thou art more righteous than I; for thou hast
rewarded me good, whereas I have rewarded thee evil.' There is a
natural ingenuity in the sourest nature to make us relent, when we
have done wrong to a kind person. Take the same course with your
souls; all this is done against a merciful God, and against special offers
of love. Surely you have very hard hearts, if they will not be melted
with offers of grace.

(4.) Do not skin over the wounds of conscience: Jer. vi. 14, 'They
have healed also the hurt of the daughter of my people slightly, saying, Peace, peace, when there is no peace;' they put it off, rather
than put it away; stop the flux of humours, rather than cure the
distemper. Better keep conscience raw than let it fester into an
ulcerate sore: Ps. li. 3, 'I acknowledge my transgressions, and my sin
is ever before me.' This must be the disposition of your hearts,
otherwise, your iniquities will find you out; we must have a care
of quenching the Spirit, when a ray of conviction is darted into our
bosoms.

(5.) Propound the encouragements of a common faith. Observe
that mercy is made an argument to draw men to the highest pungent
afflictive sorrow: Joel ii. 13, 'Rend your hearts, and not your garments,
and turn unto the Lord your God: for he is gracious and merciful;' it
noteth a deep and heightened sorrow upon the motive of God's goodness. The apostle tells them of a promise, Acts ii. 39; after they
were pricked in hearts, ver. 37; Mat. iii. 2, 'Repent ye: for the kingdom of heaven is at hand;' that is, the whole gracious administration

of Christ. Partly because else there would be a despondency and despair, it is a dangerous temptation to say there is no hope : Jer. xviii. 12, 'And they said, There is no hope; but we will walk after our own devices, and we will every one do the imagination of his evil heart:' it is the nature of man to be led by hope, much more in a duty so distasteful to flesh and blood as humiliation is. Partly because greatness of sins should increase our repentance, but not diminish our faith. Rend your hearts, be deeply humble, but still remember God is merciful.

(6.) Compare thy own want with the blessed condition of those that enjoy grace. As the prodigal : Luke xv. 17, 'How many hired servants of my father's have bread enough, and to spare, and I perish with hunger !' Christ cannot want a people, but I may want a saviour: blessed are they that are at peace with God through Christ, but I am an alien and stranger to those joys. Emulation is a means to humble us; the meanest of God's family abound in spiritual comforts.

Secondly, Do something to further the immediate workings and actings of faith ; that is your work when the heart is humble and sensible.

1. Consider God's gracious invitation. God hath fully opened his mind concerning the receiving of sinners that come to Christ. He prays us to come, makes public proclamation : Isa. lv. 1, 'Ho, every one that thirsteth, come ye to the waters, and he that hath no money : come ye, buy and eat ; yea, come, buy wine and milk without money, and without price.' God by his ministers goes a begging to poor creatures: 2 Cor. v. 20, 'Now then we are ambassadors for Christ, as though God did beseech you by us ; we pray you in Christ's stead, be ye reconciled to God.' He pitieth those that do not come to him, Ps. lxxxi. 13, 'Oh that my people had hearkened unto me, and Israel had walked in my ways !' so Luke xix. 41, 42, 'When he was come near he beheld the city, and wept over it, saying, If thou hadst known, even thou, at least in this thy day, the things which belong unto thy peace !' He professeth his loathness that any should perish : Ezek. xxxiii. 11, 'As I live, saith the Lord God, I have no pleasure in the death of the wicked ; but that the wicked turn from his way and live : turn ye, turn ye, from your evil ways, for why will you die, O house of Israel ?' he reasoneth with them—'Why will you die ?' So Ezek. xviii. 31. He chideth them for not coming, John v. 40, 'Ye will not come to me, that ye might have life.' He promiseth and offereth to them all the favour that may be: John vi. 27, 'Labour not for the meat that perisheth, but for that which endureth unto everlasting life, which the Son of man shall give unto you ;' Mat. xi. 28, 'Come unto me, all ye that labour and are heavy laden, and I will give you rest.' Ye need not fear an entertainment. Now it is a great advantage to faith to consider these passionate forms. Show yourselves men by a literal revolution of the promises; though it be but an act of understanding and memory, yet God may bless it. Constant thoughts have a natural efficacy; when God is in them, and giveth his blessing, they work much.

2. Season the heart with gracious maxims and discourses, such as these. The more angry you conceive God to be, the more need you

have to fly to his mercy. Use a point of gospel logic, and make advantage of the temptation. Satan saith, Thou art a grievous sinner, and conscience can witness the accusation; though you take the principle, yet beware of the devil's inferences; the principle may be true, yet the inference a lie. I am a dog, yet there are crumbs for dogs: Mat. xv. 27, 'Truth, Lord, yet the dogs eat of the crumbs, which fall from their master's table.' It is an excellent wisdom to turn discouragements into motives of believing; to make that an argument to draw us to Christ which would seem to drive us from him. Therefore I ought to come to Christ. Again, God's mercy is as infinite as his wrath; I fear his wrath, why should I not hope in his mercy? Believing is a command as well as a privilege; God is worthy to be obeyed, though I be not worthy to be received to mercy. Sins should not hinder a man from duty, nor sickness from the remedy: look upon thyself as under an obligation. Again, presumers are seldom troubled about their estate; their peace is broken when it is but suspected; there is no fear of presumption when the heart is touched: Ps. lvi. 3, 'What time I am afraid I will trust in thee:' it is good to give duties their due time and season. Again, in this work Christ will help me; if there be anything of faith he will cherish it: Mat. xii. 20, 'A bruised reed shall he not break, and smoking flax shall he not quench.' He cherisheth not only the bright torches, but the smoking wick; he hates unbelief as much as you do, and will strengthen you against it, for it is the greatest enemy of his kingdom. God usually appeareth in the creature's humiliation: Ps. li. 17, 'The sacrifices of God are a broken spirit, a broken and a contrite heart, O God, thou wilt not despise;' if thou canst say he will not accept thee, he will not despise thee. Humiliation is a good beginning, a fruit of Christ's purchase; and Christ did not only purchase the beginnings of grace, but the perfection and increase: you have your souls at a good advantage. When Paul was fasting, God sendeth Ananias, Acts ix. 10; and when Cornelius was fasting, he sendeth him an angel, Acts x. 30, 31, Christ's wounds are like those of a surgeon, not of an executioner; when he wounds and opens the vein, he thinks of binding it up again. Many such reasonings and discourses may we have within ourselves.

3. Make adventures. Faith at first goeth after Christ with a weak and trembling foot, it is a mere trial and essay: Joel ii. 14, 'Who knoweth if he will return, and repent, and leave a blessing behind him?' It is a thousand to one but he doth: Amos v. 15, 'It may be that the Lord God of hosts will be gracious unto the remnant of Joseph;' Jonah iii. 9, 'Who can tell if God will turn; and repent, and turn away from the fierceness of his anger that we perish not?' It is pride and curiosity to pry into God's purposes; what have you to do with God's counsels? But you have a fair offer. Why should I ascend unto heaven? the word is near me: Rom. x. 6–8, 'Say not, Who shall ascend into heaven to know the mind of God?' he hath declared his will in his offer, why should I dispute it? When Ebedmelech cast a cord to Jeremiah in the dungeon, shall he fall disputing; It may be thou dost not intend to pull me up? It is a vanity to wrong ourselves by affected scruples; there is pride and curiosity in the jealousy, but obedience in the adventure.

4. If, after all, this brings no comfort, run to him, and acknowledge your misery and impotency. *Agnosco debitum, confiteor impotentiam.* 'Turn me, O Lord, and I shall be turned,' Jer. xxxi. 18. *Da quod jubes, et jube quod vis.* Lord, thou hast forbidden despair, and commanded calling for mercy; I cast myself at thy feet, give me grace. Our trials are but to show us our weakness, that we may fall down, and take all at the hands of mercy. If we be not thus affected, we have no cause to complain of God's rigour, but our own penury and sin: Rom. xi. 32, 'God hath concluded them all in unbelief, that he might have mercy upon all.'

5. Observe the seasons of God's gracious approaches: Ezek. xvi. 8, 'Thy time was a time of love.' Grace hath its seasons: Isa. lv. 6, 'Seek ye the Lord, while he may be found; call ye upon him, while he is near.' There are seasons of sweet and spiritual refreshings; as Benhadad's servant watched for the word, 'brother.' God will be observed; it is Satan's sport to see us slip our seasons. Observe the sweet motions in the heart when the Father draws you.

Thirdly, To regulate faith, that you may not deceive yourselves with a vain confidence. It is needful to deny ourselves, our interests, or our lusts. Something is to be forsaken. Put cases—Are you come up to God's terms?—What lusts or interests do you stick at? as Christ trieth the young man, Mat. xix. 20, 'If thou wilt be perfect, go and sell that thou hast, and give to the poor, and thou shalt have treasure in heaven, and come and follow me.'

SERMON XXX.

For he that cometh to God must believe that he is, and that he is a rewarder of those that diligently seek him.—HEB. xi. 6.

For he that cometh to God—I opened this in the former verse. Coming to God principally noteth an aim at communion and fellowship with him. It is the same with faith: John vi. 35, 'He that cometh to me shall never hunger, and he that believeth on me shall never thirst;' where coming and believing are all one; it is the lowest degree of faith; the next degree is seeking diligently—it is walking with God here, and living with him for ever. The note is this—

Doct. That it is the nature of faith to make a man come towards God, and to get communion with him through Christ.

I shall show—

(1.) What it is to come to God; (2.) That there is no coming to God but by Christ.

1. What it is to come to God. Coming to God notes three things, for it is a duty always in progress.

[1.] The first address of faith. To come to God is to desire to be in his favour and covenant—to be partakers of his blessings in this life and of salvation in the life to come: Heb. vii. 25, 'He is able to save them to the uttermost, that come unto God by him,' that is, those that in and through him desire to enjoy friendship and communion with God.

[2.] Our constant communion with him in holy duties—coming to him ' as to a living stone,' 1 Peter ii. 4.   In all exercises of religion we renew our access to Christ, and by Christ to God; in hearing, as a teacher; in prayer, as an advocate for necessary help and supply; in the Lord's supper, as the master of the feast: Prov. ix. 2, ' Wisdom hath killed her beasts, she hath mingled her wine, she hath also furnished her table;' Mat. xxii. 4, ' I have prepared my dinner, my oxen and my fatlings are killed, and all things are ready.'

[3.] Our entrance into glory : Mat. xxv. 34, ' Come, ye blessed of my Father, inherit the kingdom prepared for you from the foundation of the world.' We have not complete communion with Christ till we are raised from the dead, and by him presented to the Father ; then do we indeed come to God by him.

2. There is no coming to God but by Christ: John x. 9, ' I am the door ; ' there is no entrance but through him : John xiv. 6, ' I am the way, the truth, and the life ; no man cometh unto the Father but by me.' Now we are said to come to God by Christ in a twofold respect, —(1.) By his merit ; (2.) By his grace.

[1.] By his merit. As paradise was kept by a flaming sword, so all access to God is fenced and closed up by his justice and wrath; there was no pressing in till Christ opened the way, God became man, drawing near to us by the veil of his flesh: Heb. x. 19, 20, ' Having boldness to enter into the holiest by the blood of Jesus.   By a new and living way, which he hath consecrated for us through the veil, that is to say, his flesh ; ' so by his sufferings: 1 Peter iii. 18, ' For Christ also hath once suffered for sin, the just for the unjust, that he might bring us to God.'   Now, as in all acts of religion we are coming to God, so we must still hold on by Christ till we come to our journey's end, and use him as our continual mediator and advocate, carry our petitions in all our addresses, and make our moan to him.

[2.] By his grace. Christ carries us home on his shoulders rejoicing ; as a man when he had found his lost sheep, Luke xv. 5.   None can come to the Father but by him : John vi. 44, ' No man can come to me except the Father, which hath sent me, draw him '—none can come without a divine power.

Use. Admire the privilege, that we may come to God.   We of ourselves are inclined to stand off.   Peter speaketh what is the disposition of all sinners—' Depart from me ; ' we cannot endure God's company ; we lost his image and fellowship with him. If we worship, we would be like the Israelites, every man in his tent-door. But now we have free leave to come to the throne of grace : Heb. x. 19, ' Having boldness to enter into the holiest by the blood of Jesus.' Whilst on earth we have free trade unto heaven ; we need not change place, but affections. When thou art dealing with God in prayer, this liberty was purchased for thee by the blood of Jesus. None but the high priest might enter into the *sanctum sanctorum ;* but this privilege we have, and it will stand, for it was dearly bought: Heb. iv. 16, ' Let us therefore come boldly to the throne of grace, that we may obtain mercy, and find grace to help in time of need.' God hath now laid aside the terror and rigour of his justice, that we may open our case to God; oh, let us make use of our liberty!

Must believe that he is, &c. As if the apostle had said, At least, there must be this faith; he must be persuaded first of the truth of God's being; secondly, of the certainty of his bounty, and doing good unto those that come to him. Here are two articles mentioned—God's being, and God's bounty; 'He is,' and 'He is a rewarder,' &c. The apostle saith that this must be believed if we would please God; he doth not say, This is all that must be believed; but this certainly must be believed. For these are the general truths which are the foundation of all that which is called religion in the world—that there is a God, and that he takes notice of human affairs. None would seek the favour of God unless he did believe his being and bounty; and no man will be touched with any care of religion unless he doth assent to these supreme truths; yet there is a God, and that he hath such respect to human affairs, as that he will reward the obedient and revenge the disobedient. These are principles that are evident by the light of nature; and they are mentioned, because therein the faith of the patriarchs was most exercised, and because these are the foundations of all religion. The main work of religion is to bring our souls to God, and the main ground and reason is the truth of his being and recompenses. If there is a God, there are everlasting recompenses—rewards for the good, punishments for the wicked. Rewards are only mentioned as suiting more with God's goodness, and as being more proper objects for faith; the other, for fear. And therefore he that would come to God; that is, he that would maintain friendship and communion with him, and seek his favour (for he speaks of Enoch's pleasing God), must firmly believe these things; or, if you take coming to God for our address and approaches to God in holy duties, still these two principles are of use to us. Every time we come to God we must revive this thought upon our hearts,—Surely there is a God, and it will not be in vain to inquire after him; for this puts life and strength and quickening into our duties,

The point I shall now discuss is this—

Doct. That the first point of faith, if we would have anything to do with God, is to believe that there is a God.

This is the primitive and supreme truth, therefore let me discuss it a little; the argument is not needless.

1. Partly because the most universal and incurable disease of the world is atheism; it is disguised under several shapes, but atheism it is that lies at the root, and blasts and destroys all practice and good conscience; and therefore it is good to deal upon this argument, and to reflect the light of this truth upon our conscience, and to take all occasions to batter down that atheism that is in our hearts. I know to chop logic with a sturdy settled atheist will be to little purpose. General maxims can hardly be proved by truths more clear and evident than themselves, and it is not good to loosen foundation stones. We cannot guard them so much by argument, as they are guarded by their own light and the sense which nature hath of them; and therefore Aristotle said, That they are rather to be confuted with blows than arguments that will deny there is a God; as Gideon taught the men

of Succoth with briars and thorns. Protagoras was banished by the
Athenians for denying this truth. But it is not for their sakes. but
because such kind of surmises are wont to arise in the hearts of men,
where they do not grow into settled atheism, even in the hearts of all
unrenewed men, that there is no God ; therefore it is good to speak to
this argument : Ps. xiv. 1, ' The fool hath said in his heart, There is no
God,' &c ; and it is quoted by Paul, Rom. iii. 10, to prove the degeneration of all men. Every natural unrenewed man is a kind of atheist ;
though he dare not lisp out such conceptions, yet he hath it in his
heart ; there is something there that is ever rising up against the being
of God ; nay, such a thought may come by fits and glances into the
hearts of good men. Privy atheism is in the hearts of all men, and
therefore it is good sometimes to settle the belief of this supreme truth,
to stand upon our guard, and in defiance of such thoughts, that the
heart will ever and anon be casting up, to call to the help of reason.

2. Because supreme truths should be laid up with the greatest certainty and assurance. Christians are mistaken very much, if they think
all the difficulty of religion lies in affiance, and taking out their own
comfort, and in clearing up their own particular interest. Oh, no ; a
great deal of it lies in assent ; there is privy atheism at the root, and
therefore doth the work of God go on so untowardly with us—therefore
have we such doubtings and so many deformities of life and conversation. If the fire were once well kindled, it would of its own accord
burst out into a flame, and burn clear ; so if assent were firmly rooted,
if we were once settled under the power and dominion of this truth,
confidence would follow of its own accord, and the whole business of
religion, both as to comfort and practice, would be far more easy to us.
All our doubts come from want of a firm assent to the being of God,
and to the word of God. Indeed, at first, while we are learners of religion, it becomes us to drink in these principles and maxims of religion
without discussion ; we take them in as men do pills ; we do not chew
them, but swallow them ; and it is fit it should be so. *Oportet discen-
tem credere,* a learner must believe, but afterward we must inquire into
the reason of these things ; nay, when a man is first converted, and
begins to be serious in religion, when a man is touched in conscience,
his will is more exercised than his understanding ; he needs Christ,
and all the endeavours and resolutions of the soul are to get an interest
in him. And he doth not so much debate the mystery of religion as
his own particular case ; his heart is carried out after comfort, and he
seems mainly to desire some satisfaction ; but he doth not look into the
grounds from whence this doth arise. As men in a deep thirst swallow
their drink before they know the nature of it, or discern the taste of it ;
so when we are under a great thirst, or under great famishment as to
spiritual comfort, and have great troubles upon us, we take up with the
comfortable notions of Christ and salvation by him, and easily drink
in these and other truths ; we catch at them without looking into the
grounds or reasons of them, but afterwards we see this needs to be the
care and labour of the soul, to strengthen our assent and fortify ourselves against those doubts of mind which shake us, and to settle the
heart in those supreme truths which in our necessity we took in without discussion.

3. I would handle this argument—That there is a God, because it is good to detain the heart a little in the view of this truth, and to revive it in our souls. There is a double reading of that place: Ps. x. 4, 'God is not in all his thoughts;' or else, all his thoughts are that there is no God; the one makes way for the other. It is a great evil, when we cannot endure to think of God, and to fasten our meditations upon his being and the perfections of his nature, for by degrees his memory is defaced and blotted out of our minds; therefore a forgetfulness of God is a kind of denial of him: Ps. ix. 17, 'The wicked shall be turned into hell, and all the nations that forget God.' Mark, not only they that deny God, but forget God; that is the portion of them that do not mind nor regard him and his judgments; and therefore we should often meditate of God, and think of him, not by starts and sudden glances, but have deliberate thoughts of him. And therefore, that you may have some hints of meditation whereby to enlarge yourselves in the thoughts of God, and to give us some help to hold our minds in the view of it, it is of great use in the spiritual life to prosecute this argument.

Having premised these things concerning the usefulness of such a discourse, I shall speak to this point, to prove that there is a God.

Here we may appeal not only to scripture, but to nature. We say that principles can only be demonstrated *testimoniis, effectis et absurdis:* principles, when we would come to demonstrate them, must be proved by testimonies, by effects, and by showing the absurdities of the contrary; and such kind of arguments I shall produce.

[1.] That there is a God may be proved by conscience, which is as a thousand witnesses. The heathens, which never heard of scripture, yet had a conscience that did accuse and excuse—μεταξὺ ἀλλήλων—by turns, Rom. ii. 15. There is something within men that will chide them for sin; yea, for secret sins, to which none are privy but themselves. Wicked men seek to blot out these feelings of conscience, but can never wholly extinguish them—'The sinners in Sion are afraid,' Isa. xxxiii. 14. Wicked men are without faith, yet they are never without fear. There is a conscience in men that appals the stoutest sinner, after the commitment of any gross evil; though it be secret and beyond the cognisance and vengeance of man, yet conscience will be smiting him, his heart will reproach him for it, therefore surely there is a God. You shall see the Holy Ghost, when he lays down the atheism of men, yet he observes this order, Ps. liii. 1, 'The fool hath said in his heart, There is no God.' Now, how doth he prove, there is a God? It follows, ver. 5, 'There were they in great fear where no fear was;' that is, where there was no outward cause of fear, where none sought to hurt them, yet were they under a fear; he speaks of those that live most atheistically. This appears by the instance of Joseph's brethren, accusing themselves when none else could accuse them: Gen. xlii. 21, 'We are verily guilty concerning our brother's blood;' conscience began to accuse them. Though a man should hide himself from all the world, he cannot hide himself from himself; his heart will pursue him, and represent his guilt. Now that there is such a hidden fear in men's hearts after sinning, that the heart will smite us for evil when the crime is secret, this argues there is a

God; yea, there is a fear to be found in the most obstinate sinners, and those that are of greatest power and place in the world, that can carry on their wickedness without control, as the most powerful princes. Caligula, it is noted of him that he would sometimes counterfeit the thunder, yet when it thundered indeed, how was he terrified and afraid! Those that would study to cast away all conceit of God, yet they have this fear upon them. And it is not a fear that they may be found out by man, and punished by man; for sometimes this fear prevails so far, as they would have counted man's punishment a favour, and therefore have sought it, or else have laid violent hands upon themselves. What should be the reason of all this, but that they have a fear of an avenger and judge that will call them to an account; and therefore they cannot prevent or dissemble their gripes, so greatly have these fears of conscience been increased upon them—'They know the judgment of God,' as the apostle speaks of the heathens, Rom. i. 28; that is, they have a sense that there is a just avenger of sin, and that therefore they are liable to judgment; yea, those that have been professed atheists, yet have been smitten with these horrors of conscience. *Affirmant interdiu, noctu tamen dubitant,* saith Seneca—Though they will speak with confidence against God in the day, yet in the darkness of the night they are in doubt. Especially, in distress and trouble, then are these notions revived. As another heathen observes, When it thunders, then they wax pale and are affrighted. Diagoras, an atheist among the heathens, denied there was a God; yet when he was troubled with a strangury, he acknowledged a deity. Calvin, in his comment upon the 115th Psalm, gives us a story of a scoffing atheist, a merry fellow, whom he met with in an inn, that would talk very slightly and contemptuously of God and of religion, and dropping out his atheism upon all occasions, and jeering. When Calvin reproved him for it, he would put him off with this, *Cœlum cœli Domino*—'The heavens of heavens was the Lord's;' God must content himself with heaven, 'but he hath given the earth to the children of men:' here we may do what we please; God was shut up in the heavens, and he had no care nor sense of things below. But before they parted, this man was exceedingly gripped with the colic, and twinged with his pain; then he would be crying out—*O Deus, O Deus*—O God, O God! Now, saith Calvin, the heaven of heavens is the Lord's, and the earth belongeth to the children of men. When God doth awaken conscience by any sickness or trouble, they are arrested by conscience in the name of the great God whom they deny. Belshazzar seemed a jovial fellow, and a man of great confidence and bravery, but when he was besieged by a great army of Persians, and danger was at his doors, he falls a quaffing and carousing, as if he would out-laugh his danger; and not only so, but bids a defiance to the God of heaven, and he doth it in the vessels of the temple. But see how soon God takes off the edge of his spirit! Dan. v.; a trembling doth seize upon him, and a few letters upon the wall make his knees smite one against the other for fear. So how merrily soever these men do carry it for a while, and how much they may seem to smother their fears while they wallow in their sins; yet when the Lord stings them with his hornet, and puts them to pain; when he casts them into sickness, or when they are solitary, then there is a hidden fear in their heart, and they are haunted with these pangs of conscience, and are sensible of an avenger and a judge. And this proves plainly that there is a God; as they say things written with the juice of a lemon appear not till the paper be brought to the fire, then all is legible; so such characters of a God are there engraven upon the hearts of men, that when they are sick and ready to die, when they are upon the confines of eternity, as they begin to have a sense of the torments of hell for sin, their notions of a God revive, and fear seizeth upon them, and the most sturdy atheists then have been forced to acknowledge a God. Thus you have the testimony of conscience to prove it.

[2.] As conscience shows it, so the consent of all nations. There are none so barbarous, but they worship some God. Aristotle saith, in his book *de Cœlo*, 'That all men, how brutish soever they were, yet have a notion of a deity impressed upon them, which they cannot wear out.' All nations rather than they would have no God, will have a false god: some worship the stars, some the stones, some the beasts, or a piece of wood,—anything they met first in the morning. Though they differed concerning the number and nature of their gods, and the manner and rites of worship, yet they all agreed in this, that there was a God, who ought to be worshipped and respected by men. Certainly there is somewhat in this; for either this must come from some instinct of nature, or from tradition; both prove the truth we have in hand. If you refer it to the instinct of nature, that doth not carry us to falsehood, but truth; if to tradition, it must have a beginning, and therefore the very idolatry of the heathens is, saith Calvin, 'A pregnant instance and apparent evidence of this natural truth, that there is a God.' There were none so barbarous but they worshipped some god, as the pagan mariners: Jonah i. 5, 'They cried every one to his god;' yea, those that are most estranged from human society, that have lived in deserts without law or government, yet have been touched with the sense of a deity, which must needs arise from a natural instinct; they would rather worship anything, yea, the very devil, than have no god,—a piece of wood or stone; as the prophet takes notice of such brutishness in those that would burn one piece, and make an idol of the other, and worship it, Isa. xliv. 15–17. Now this general consent of nations cannot be any deceit or imposition of fancy, by virtue of long custom or tradition, because it is found in people most barbarous and free from all traffic and commerce, and because falsehood cannot be so universal and so long-lived as the conceit of a deity. Besides, though they do what they can to blot out these notions and instincts of conscience, yet still they remain with them; an invention so contrary to nature would long ere this have been worn out of the minds of men, therefore this general consent of nations proves that 'there is a God.'

[3.] It may be evident also by the book of the creatures. Surely there is a God, because these things are made in such exactness and order. There is a description of God, Zech. xii. 1, 'Thus saith the Lord, that stretcheth forth the heavens, and layeth the foundations of the earth, and formeth the spirit of a man within him.' Should we take this method, the heavens, the earth, the souls of men, which are the work of God, they all proclaim that there is a God! Man could never raise such a roof as heaven, nor lay such a floor as earth, nor form himself. The world and all those things that are made, must be from some cause; for nothing could make itself, nor can be its own cause; and these things, they could not come together by chance, because of the perfection that is in all things in themselves, and their mutual subserviency and relation to one another, and their inclination to certain ends. There is an order in everything for the beauty and conservation of the whole; all things are under a law and course—' He appointeth the moon for seasons, the sun knows his going down,' Ps. civ. 19. The sun and moon keep at a due distance for the use of the world, and still observe the just points of the compass, and set and rise at such an hour; therefore certainly this was not done by chance, and it could not be made by man. He could not make great things, for he cannot make the least; he cannot make a lily, or a pile of grass, and therefore certainly he cannot produce such a beautiful fabric as this is. And, as Tully makes the comparison, a man coming into a house where there are no living creatures but weasels, rats and mice, and seeth a fair structure, he could not conceive the house could make itself, or had no other maker but the creatures he finds there—' Every house is builded by some man,' as the apostle reasons, Heb. iii. 4; 'but he that built all things is God.' Now when a man considers all things are managed with wisdom, he must needs conclude there must be some cause of all these things—some wise creator of them. Man could not make the world; man cannot form himself; he doth not know the number of his muscles and bones; he cannot restore any one of his joints which are lost; and therefore it must be made by God.

This was that which puzzled the heathens to find out πρῶτον αἴτιον — the first cause of the world, and all the order that is therein. Plutarch disputes it, which could be first, the egg before the hen, or the hen before the egg; the acorn before the oak, or the oak before the acorn. Such an uncertainty will there be in an all debates till we come to this supreme truth, and to determine upon a first cause, which Anaxagoras and others were necessitated and driven to acknowledge at last; and therefore surely he that looks upon the world, and upon all the order therein, he will see that 'there is a God.'

The world is sometimes compared to a book, sometimes to a preacher. To a book; the book of the creature is a large volume wherein God would set forth himself; the diversity of creatures are as so many letters out of which we may spell his name; the most excellent creatures are capital letters, and the lower creatures lesser letters; so that a man may plainly see God in all those things that are before his eyes. If you cannot read yourselves, the very beasts will teach you; nay, go to the mute fishes, that can hardly make any sound, yet they have voice enough to proclaim their creator: Job. xii. 7–9, 'Ask of them and they will tell thee;' that is, go, look upon them; consider them in their number and in their variety and different kinds; their frame and make, and how they are wonderfully preserved; they all proclaim some wise creator which made them.

Look upon the glorious bodies that are above, the constancy of their motion, their admirable beauty, their variety, their regularity; as to the general ends of their creation, this cannot be from itself, but there must be some supreme and infinite cause. Look upon the sun, that representative of a God, the brightness of whose beams will speak out an infinite majesty that made it, and the extent of his influence— 'Nothing is hid from the heat thereof,' Ps. xix. 6. That will speak him omnipresent God, and the indefatigableness of his motion, an infinite God. The sun, moon, and stars in the heavens, they go abroad into all lands, and speak to every people in their own tongue—English to the English; to other nations, in their own tongue—that there is one infinite, eternal power, which made me and all things else. Nay, let man but look upon himself; let him but consider the flights and traverses of reason, the wonderful workings of his own soul, the admirable structure of his body, the symmetry of all the parts, the different faces that are in several sorts of men, though there be so many millions in the world, yet not one like another in the compass of the face—all which proclaims a wise creator, who made all things.

And again, look upon nature, and you will find an order, an ascending proportion still lifting you up to something that is more excellent; for there is always a gradation in the creatures.

In the general, there are elements, metals, plants, living creatures, and then living creatures of a higher and lower rank, still leading to something that is more perfect.

In metals, there are some more base, and others more noble, to lead you higher and higher; there is iron, lead, tin, brass, silver, gold.

In plants, some bear leaves, others flowers, others fruits, others aromatical gums and spices.

There is a progress in nature in all kinds of creatures, to lead up man still to something more excellent; especially in living creatures, there is an ascending proportion which leads them up to God, and more especially in man.

Some creatures have only being; others besides being, have life; others, besides life, have sense; others, besides sense, have reason and understanding; and man is in a lower sphere of understanding than the angels, and the angels than God. And so we may come up to the most perfect and the highest of all beings; for instance, a stone hath not life, that grows not as a plant; a plant hath life, but feels not as a beast who hath sense; a beast who hath sense, discourseth not as a man who hath reason; and man's reason is lower than that of the angels, because it needs the ministry of fancy and imagination; fancy needs outward sense, which an angel needeth not; and an angel he is lower than God, because angels, that they may know anything, need either the presence of the object, or some revelation (if it be to come) concerning it. Therefore they are said to know the wisdom of God by what he hath revealed to the church: Eph. iii. 10, ' To the intent that now, unto the principalities and powers in heavenly places, might be known by the church the manifold wisdom of God.' But now, God's understanding is a pure act, who knoweth all things past, present, and to come; who needs nothing without himself; neither organ, imagination, nor presence of the object; he knows all things that may be, or can be, by his own all-sufficiency, and all things that shall be by his wise purpose and decree. Thus the creatures discover a God.[1]

[4.] As creation, so also providence discovers a God. All natural

[1] See this head of the Creation more fully handled in the third verse.

things work for an end, and therefore they are governed by the counsel of some wise ruler ; for all things that work for an end, it must either be by their own choice or by the government of another.   Many things cannot do so by their own choice, because they have no knowledge, yet they have a clear and certain inclination to some end ; therefore this bespeaks the wise governor of the world, that sways all things.   The parts of the world being disposed into such an order, and the sweet harmony and agreement of things, which are of such different and destructive natures, show there is a wise God that guideth all things to a certain end ; all would run into disorder and confusion, if it were not poised with the art and care of providence.   Many times, when we are stupid, and do not mind these things, then God discovers the sway of his providence more sensibly.   God will awaken us by more notable effects : sometimes by miracles, exceeding the force of all natural causes ; sometimes by sudden and unexpected strokes in the rescue of the good and destruction of the wicked, especially of the atheists, few or none of which have escaped without some remarkable token of divine vengeance : Ps. ix. 16, ' The Lord is known by the judgment which he executeth ; the wicked is snared in the works of his own hands ; ' and Ps. lviii. 10, 11, ' The righteous shall rejoice when he seeth the vengeance ; he shall wash his feet in the blood of the wicked.   So that a man shall say, Verily, there is a reward for the righteous ; verily, he is a God that judgeth in the earth.'   God doth so sensibly interpose in the eyes of men to those that discern his dealings, that they are even forced to say, ' Verily, there is a reward for the righteous,' &c.

[5.] That there is a God, appeareth by several experiences.   By the power of his word breaking in upon the consciences of men : 1 Cor. xiv. 25, ' And thus are the secrets of his heart made manifest ; and so, falling down on his face, he will worship God, and report that God is in you of a truth.'   Surely there is some God guides these men.   I might instance, in the prediction of things to come, which could never be foreseen by any created mind hundreds of years before they came to pass.   Cyrus was named a hundred years before he was born, Isa. xlv. 1 ; and hundreds of years before Josiah was born, it was prophesied of him, 1 Kings xiii. 2, ' Behold a child shall be born unto the house of David, Josiah by name, and upon thee shall he offer the priests of the high places,' &c.   And the building of Jericho was foretold five hundred years before it was re-edified, Joshua vi. 26, compared with 1 Kings xvi. 34.   There were many prophecies of things long before ever they came to pass, and they had their certain and effectual accomplishment.   To instance, in those general prophecies of the rejection and casting off of the Jews and the calling of the gentiles, which were prophesied of long before they were brought about ; but all that was foretold was accomplished.   The devils may guess at things, but they cannot certainly and infallibly know them ; God avoucheth it as his own prerogative, and he puts his godhead upon the trial : Isa. xli. 21–23, ' Produce your cause, saith the Lord ; bring forth your strong reasons, saith the king of Jacob.   Let them bring them forth, and shew us what shall happen : let them show the former things, what they be, that we may consider them, and know the latter end of them ; or declare us things for to come.   Show the things that are to come hereafter, that we may know that ye are gods.' God puts it to the decision and trial. These predictions certainly were, and, as certainly, were accomplished, which shows there is a God. There are devils, and they would undo all things, were they not bound up by the chains of an irresistble providence. God suffers them now and then to discvoer their malice, that we may know by whose goodness we subsist. Plutarch speaketh of some that by seeing of ghosts believed there was a God. There are virtues and vices, therefore there is a God; there is a distinction between good and evil, therefore there is a God. For good is not by the appointment of man's will, for then every thing that man wills would be good; it cannot be out of any eternal reason which is in the things themselves. What should differ the conjugal act from adultery, or the process of a magistrate from that of an assassinate? No, it is from a proportion and conformity to some supreme being, that doth interpose by a law that makes those things good, and these evil. Thus you have the arguments to refresh your souls, with the reviving of the sense of his being upon your hearts.

SERMON XXXI.

For he that cometh to God must believe that he is, and that he is a rewarder of those that diligently seek him.—HEB. xi. 6.

I NOW come to the improvement of this great truth.

Use 1. If there be a God, let us charge this truth then upon our hearts, that we may check those private whispers and suspicions that do arise—too often, the Lord knows—against the being and glory of God. Many times we are apt to think that God is but a fancy, that religion is but a state-curb, and the gospel a cunningly devised fable—a quaint device to please fond and foolish men; and all is but invented to hold men in awe. Oh, but to check these whispers of vanity, consider, in such truths as these, we may appeal not only to scripture, but to nature. You will never be able to recover your consciences out of this dread of the Lord's being. The devils are under the fear of a deity; they believe there is a God, and they tremble at the thought of it—' Thou believest that there is one God, thou dost well; the devils also believe and tremble,' James ii. 19. The devil can never be a flat atheist in judgment; that will not stand with the state of a damned angel, because he hath a sense of the wrath of God tormenting him; he feels that there is a God, and believes there is a God: there may be atheists in the church, but there are none in hell. And therefore charge this truth upon your hearts, that you may more check and humble yourselves for such atheistical thoughts and suggestions as these are, for they should not be passed over without humiliation, they are of so foul a nature. It is irrational to think that there is no God, the creatures confute us. We cannot look abroad but something offers itself to our eye to mind us: surely there is an infinite and eternal power.   Oh, when thoughts rush into your minds, that have a tendency towards atheism, as denying of providence, let them be abhorred and rejected.   See how David takes up his heart when his thoughts arose, not against the being of God, but against his providence: Ps. lxxiii. 22, 'So foolish was I and ignorant; I was as a beast before thee;' when he had ill and unworthy thoughts of the providence of God.   So take up your hearts—Oh, how brutish and beastly is this!   When you go about to ungod God, and put him out of the throne, you do unman yourselves, you are as beasts; common sense and reason will teach you otherwise.   Thoughts which strike at the being of God are thoughts of a dangerous importance; therefore you should not smother them, or lightly digest them.

A little to aggravate the sin.   Wrath came upon the Jews to the uttermost for killing Christ in his human nature, but these atheistical thoughts strike at God and Christ, and all together.   And therefore look upon these suggestions, when they rush in upon your minds, as dangerous; and cry out, O what a foul heart have I, that will cast forth such mire and dirt!   Aggravate this sin, and make it odious to the soul, that we should think of him as nothing, who is so glorious in in himself, and so gracious to them that know him.   Other errors may in part darken the understanding of man, but this, if given way to, will prove a total eclipse of all spiritual light; others may trample on a precept, but this is to strike at God's very essence and being. Consider, too, that thoughts are liable to God's judgment; God hath provided for the safety and majesty of princes: Eccles. x. 20, 'Curse not the king, no, not in thy thought; and curse not the rich in thy bed-chamber; for a bird of the air shall carry the voice, and that which hath wings shall tell the matter.'   Not only seditious and rebellious practices, but disloyal thoughts against magistrates, are liable to judgment; how much more, then, are atheistical thoughts, which strike at the being of God?   There is a language in thoughts, and they are heard in heaven; and therefore whenever such thoughts arise in your minds, make them odious, seriously humble yourselves that your hearts should cast up dishonourable thoughts of God.

Use 2. It reproves those that either wish down, or live down, this supreme principle.

1. Some wish it down: Ps. xiv. 1, 'The fool hath said in his heart, There is no God:' the heart is the seat of desires; they are the fool's wishes and desires, rather than his formal and explicit thoughts.   'The fool'—that is the unrenewed man, so the apostle explains it—'hath said in his heart;' that is, it is a pleasing thing for him to imagine and suppose it; so that they are pleased with the supposition, if there were no God, none to call them to an account for their sins; what kind of lives would they live? then they might let loose the reins, and be freed from all those fetters and restraints, and those melancholy and sad thoughts which religion imposeth upon them.   Naturally desires and thoughts run that way.   This argueth enmity and hatred to God, when we wish that he were not.   Look, as it is with a malefactor that is guilty of treason, it would be pleasing to him to think the court rolls should be burnt where his crimes are recorded, and the judge destroyed; so it would be pleasing to carnal men, who are all become

guilty before the great God, that all the memorials of God should be defaced.

2. Some live it down. It is possible there may be some atheists for a while in opinion ; but they are but few, if any—that are directly and purely so; but there are more in affection, and most in conversation: Titus i. 16, ' They profess that they know God, but in works they deny him.' Your assent to this supreme principle will be judged of by your lives. There is a real language in your conversation ; that is the best image and the best copy of your thoughts. Works discover what is in the heart, what secret principles lurk there, though they be not explicitly owned. Well then, when a man doth that which manifestly infers this conclusion, there is no God, then he lives down this principle; when he cares not to seek peace with God, to humble himself by repentance, to sue out for grace by Christ, then he is a practical atheist: you that should bring God into respect with others, make others suspect whether there be a God or no. There is not a greater temptation to atheism than the lives of scandalous professors, those that talk much of religion, and do not live up to the power of it. When a heathen had surprised a christian in an act of filthiness, he came to him with this smart question — *Christiane, christiane ! ubi Deus tuus ?*—Christian, christian ! where is thy God? thy God that seeth all things ? When you profess to believe an omniscient God, and yet live in filthiness, and allow yourselves in cozenage, oppression, deceit, fraud, and privy sins, and give up yourselves to a course of sin and filthy excess; when you are not ashamed to do that before God which you would blush to do before men, then you live down this principle. ' The thief is ashamed when he is found,' saith the prophet, Jer. ii. 26. Why ? we are always found of God ; God's eye is upon us. Now, when you have no sense of this, and make no reckoning of his eye and presence, so far you live down this truth. The apostle saith in 3 John, ver. 11, ' He that doth evil hath not seen God.' He that goes on in a course of sin, certainly his heart was never touched with a true sight of God ; for if a man thought there were a God to call him to an account and punish him, how could he thus freely give up himself to what is contrary to the will of God?

Use 3. If there be a God, then beware of such opinions and practices as strike at the being of God.

First, Opinions. The devil is crafty, he assaults us by degrees, he takes his aim at a distance, he does not directly strike at this, that there is no God ; he dares not rise up against this truth, which is written upon the face of all things and upon the heart of man ; but he approacheth nearer and nearer towards it, and he seeks by degrees to undermine our assent thereunto. There are many opinions which do conduce towards atheism, and aim at the undermining this supreme truth in our hearts. As—

1. Libertinism—that men of all religions shall be saved. Religion is the actual acknowledgment of God, that which preserves and keeps up his respect in the world ; and therefore to make many doors to heaven, is to widen the gates of hell ; it is but a pretence to out-face conscience, when it presseth us to the choice and love of truth. They think if men can smooth their carriage a little, and live a good life—heathens, Turks,

and men of all religions may be saved. No; deceive not yourselves; there is but 'one faith,' but 'one Lord,' Eph. iv. 5. If you do not establish one faith, you will soon deny one Lord; for one doth preserve and establish the other: Micah iv. 5, 'For all people will walk, every-one in the name of his god; and we will walk in the name of the Lord our God for ever and ever.' In these latter times of the gospel, some grow weary of the christian religion, and by an excess of charity would betray their faith, and write and plead for the salvation of heathens, Turks, infidels, that, provided they go not against their consciences, they may be saved. The good-fellow gods of the heathens could brook company and partnership, but the true God will be acknowledged and owned alone, or else you can have no true happi-ness: Mat. iv. 10, 'Thou shalt worship the Lord thy God, and him only shalt thou serve.' As the sun drowneth the light of the lesser stars, and as there is but one God, so there is but one way to God. Then there are a sort of libertines that prevail among us, that say, It is true, there is some danger if a man be a Turk or an infidel; but among christians, it is no great matter whether a man be a papist or a protestant, of this or that profession, provided he doth act as his country doth. This is to strike at the being of God. It is no small matter of what party you cleave to in religion: Rev. xiv. 13, 'Blessed are the dead that die in the Lord, from henceforth.' The meaning is this, those that fell under pagan superstition, they all cried up them as happy; they were looked upon as saints and martyrs that died by that perse-cution—ay, but saith the Spirit—'From henceforth write it;' that is, those christians which stood up for the honour of God against anti-christian persecutions they are also happy. Such an indifferency in religion is not to be allowed.

2. The denying of particular providence, and exempting of human actions from God's predetermination and dominion. Many think that the world is but as a great clock, which is set right at first by God, afterwards it is left to its own motion. The heathens had such a sense of God that they counted them atheists that denied providence; and to deny providence is to exempt the creature from subjection and dependence upon God. Therefore take heed of those doctrines that would make God an idle spectator of the world, as if he were shut up within the heavens, and had nothing to do with the affairs of the world. But they fall out, as men will. The scriptures tell you there is not a sparrow that can fall to the ground without your heavenly Father, and that he looks after the young ravens, and feeds them. It was the wicked blasphemy of Vorstius to say, God was not at leisure to tell the gnats, and count the number of your hairs; to feed the ravens, and look after every creature, and so would exempt many things from God's providence; but exempt anything from providence, and you will soon run into all manner of libertinism. If Satan and wicked men may do what they will, and God be only a looker-on, then we may worship the devil lest he hurt us; and fear men, though God be propitious to us. Heathens, though they acknowledged a God, yet, because they exempted evil actions from the dominion of providence, they fell into many mistakes in worship—this was one. The heathens had a conceit there were evil powers, which were first to be pacified;

then good powers, that were afterwards to be invoked—first, they would appease evil powers, sacrifice to evil gods, and then invoke the good; therefore it is dangerous to exempt anything from God's providence, for it is God that orders all the evil that falls out in the world.

3. Denying the immortality of the soul. Besides that, it cuts off the hopes of the everlasting recompenses, and so destroys the chiefest part of God's providence, it is a stroke at God's being, who is the supreme of spirits. There is an order among spirits; first, the souls of men, then angels, then God. And look, as God under the law forbade cruelty to the beasts; as in that law, that birds were not to be killed in breeding time; that they should not seethe a kid in the mother's milk; that a good man should be merciful to his beast; now these laws, as divines well observe, are a rail and fence about the life of man. God would have us at such a distance from cruelty, that he would not have us cruel to our beasts. So say I; there are orders and degrees of spirits, which are as it were a fence about the sense we have of the being and majesty of God; so that to deny the immortality of the soul is a stroke at a distance at the eternity and being of God. For one great argument, to prove the being of God is the immortality of the soul. If the soul be not extinguished with the body, there must be some supreme infinite spirit to which it is gathered; and indeed the sleep of the soul is a step to this opinion. Hearken not to those opinions; it is good to take the little foxes: Cant. ii. 15, 'Take us the foxes, the little foxes that spoil the vines.' It is good to resist errors when they come with the most modest appearance.

4. Another thing that tends extremely to atheism, is popery; for though they have the principles of christian religion among them, yet there are so many superadditions, that it is a dangerous inducement to atheism; and for matter of experience, this is clear, that where popery has the most absolute command, there atheism most abounds. Now how doth popery tend to atheism? Upon several accounts; partly, because it is a pompous formal religion, consisting of many idle and ridiculous ceremonies, which cannot but beget a secret contempt and scorn of religion, in the eyes of wise and considering men; and partly, because though they have the fundamentals of christianity amongst them, yet take the superstructures of popery, and it is a doctrine calculated for the present world, and fitted for human policy and for temporal ends; and partly, as it is supported by forged miracles, and lying legends—all which are very apt to beget suspicions in the hearts of men, and make them to question all, when they see religion supported with so many lies and forgeries; and partly, because these opinions are so monstrous, as that of transubstantiation and others, which are contrary to the nature and being of God; and from thence have a mighty tendency to breed atheism in the hearts of men.

5. The expectation of new light beyond the scripture—a conceit that possesseth the hearts of many now-a-days. I do not speak of degrees of knowledge—for so certainly we are to expect new light every day; as long as we are in the world, we grow in knowledge—but I speak of a new revelation. It is possible that future light may disprove many of our present practices; but when we expect new revelations

beyond the word, it leads to atheism. Fundamental truths should be sure: Deut. xii. 30, 'We should not enquire after their gods.' The Wigelians, who are the same with our familists, expect *seculum Spiritus sancti*—the age of the Holy Ghost; for they imagine God the Father had his time, that was the law; God the Son had his time, that was the gospel; and the Holy Ghost shall have his time, when there shall be new revelations given to the world, and we shall be wiser than the apostles, and have a clearer light. Some expect a time before the resurrection, when we shall live here in the world without ordinances. Ay; but 'This gospel of the kingdom shall be preached in all the world, for a witness unto all nations; and then shall the end come,' Mat. xxiv. 14; 'And I am with you alway, even to the end of the world,' Mat. xxviii. 20. No other revelation is to be expected till the Lord come. These are but vain devices to cheat you of your religion, and to keep the soul from a settlement in the present truth, and that way of religion that God hath appointed and set up, to keep up his respects in the world. Thus you need to be skilled in the subtle enterprises of Satan, that lies in wait to deceive.

Secondly, There are practices, which are most contrary to the essence and glory of God; as—

1. Hypocrisy, which is an implicit blasphemy: Rev. ii. 9, 'I know the blasphemy of them that say they are Jews, and are not;' when a man makes it all his business to hold up a fair pretence in the world, and makes a fair show in the flesh; but he careth not how he be before God, and cherishes noisome lusts in his heart. Do they walk answerably to the belief of a God that have no regard to the eye of God? No, they disbelieve this truth, and it is hereby weakened more and more in their hearts. Hypocrites are the greatest practical atheists in the world; they do in effect say, So we can carry it plausibly and handsomely before men for worldly ends, we need not stand for the eye of God.

2. Epicurism and carnal living, whereby men contemn God. When men are full, and enjoy a great deal of plenty, they spend all their time in eating, drinking, hunting, hawking, sporting, carding, dicing, and wholly give up themselves to carnal pleasures and vain delights; they do not seek after God: Ps. xiv. 1, 'The fool hath said in his heart, There is no God. They are corrupt, they have done abominable works;' and ver. 2, 'The Lord looked down from heaven to see if there were any that did understand, and seek God.' A dissolute luxury rooted by custom will soon deface the impression and memory of a God. Who would sin if they thought there was a God who knew all, and would punish the sinner? 3 John 11, 'He that doth evil hath not seen God.' When men wallow in all manner of sensual delights and filthiness, this raiseth steams and vapours in the soul. The smoking of fleshly lusts mightily clouds the mind, so that the awe and feelings of conscience are by degrees worn out: Prov. xxx. 9, 'Lest I be full, and deny thee, and say, Who is the Lord?' When men live at ease, and have wholly given up themselves to vain pleasures, and are inordinately set upon liberty, they grow impatient of restraint and strong desires, as men in high places are impatient of contradiction; and because conscience is clamouring, and religion will be interposing and awakening their hearts,

therefore they question the truth and being of God, else they cannot keep all quiet in their souls. Men believe what they desire; none so apt to deny God as those that would be glad if there were no God. When men are willing to sin, and loath to seek quiet in repentance, they seek it in atheism and unbelief—first, they wish there could be no religion : and by little and little they wear out the feelings of it, and silence all the checks they have in their consciences.

3. Scoffers. Scoffing at matters of religion is both an effect and cause of atheism. Apostates are always great scoffers, because they seek to deface and blot out the reverence of those truths and that religion they have forsaken, which otherwise would put them to trouble and horror. Thus Julian the apostate, when he revolted from the christian faith, was a mighty scoffer. Men of a vicious life and frothy wit are of a fit temper for the devil to make atheists of. Every man is under the awe of some religion more or less; they have too much knowledge to be idolaters, and too little grace to be religious ; therefore they fall a mocking and scoffing at all things that are sacred ; and so they deface the knowledge of God in their souls: 2 Peter iii. 3, ' There shall come in the last days scoffers, walking after their own lusts.' And Calvin, in his comment, takes notice of such ; that there are certain men of Lucian's spirit, under colour of declaiming against superstition and the fond conceits of popery ; they abhor all religion, and cry down all that is holy and sacred. The rabbis have a conceit upon those words—*Diis non maledices,* ' Thou shalt not speak evil of the gods.' Though they are out in the exposition—for it is meant of magistrates —yet they expound it, they should not scoff at the gods of the gentiles, lest, say they, we provoke them to scoff at the true God, and so our reverence and respect to religion be weakened. Many men get a vein at jesting at sermons, and applying scripture to every profane and common matter ; they make it as sauce to their meals, and make the word of God and holy things to lackey to their sports and profane mirth; so that by a custom of scoffing at holy matters, and by venting the superfluities of their frothy wit, they blot out a reverence of God, and exceedingly weaken the awe of religion ; and this conduceth to eclipse the light that is in our minds concerning this supreme truth that there is a God.

Use 4. If he that cometh to God must believe that God is. It directs us what to do in fierce and boisterous temptations. It is not good to leave the dispute then, in a time of temptation, to the uncertain traverses and debates of reason: foundation-stones must not be loosened. When our hearts are under the cloud of a temptation, the devil will be too hard for us in matter of argument; we must believe that God is. It is a matter not only of science, but of faith ; it is revealed in scripture, and therefore say, Though I could not make it good against all those fiery darts the devil casts into my soul, yet I will believe it. Though it be good to see upon what firm footing we stand at other times, yet in a time of temptation it is confutation enough to say to Satan, Thou liest ; and hold fast that principle he would wrest from us. In principles, sometimes we must answer Satan with resolution ; the world shows, and the creature shows, there is a God ; but if the world did not, it is enough that the word of God saith it. And therefore, though the devil should puzzle reason and put the thoughts to a *non-plus*, yet whatever he should allege to the contrary, say, This is a maxim of God's word, and I will, and do, and must believe it. Doubts, which strike at first principles, are not to be scanned and examined; for when you think to conquer atheism by your own wit and reasoning, the devil will be too subtle for you. Satan is a better disputant than many a poor christian; therefore believe it, though you cannot dispute it out. I commend this, because it hath always been the practice of the saints, that when they have been sorely shaken and assaulted, yet they were resolved to stick to principles, and in the hour of temptation they fixed their resolutions and would not be removed from them. As David, Ps. lxxiii. 1, he was under an atheistical temptation, and had brutish thoughts that there was no providence, because the wicked were exalted, and it went ill with the righteous; yet he holds fast this principle—'Truly God is good to Israel;' I will never be brought off from this. So Jer. xii. 1, 'Righteous art thou, O Lord, when I plead with thee;' he would lay up this principle, this truth, with great assurance at that time, I take this for a principle that God is righteous, though I cannot answer all my thoughts about his administrations in the world.

Use 5. If this be the first point of faith, to believe that there is a God, then it shows with what care we should maintain this principle. There are certain seasons when it is most assaulted.

1. There is a general season, and that is in the latter times. Atheism will then more abound, though it be more disguised. *Mundus senescens patitur phantasias*—the world, when it grows old, begins to dote, as old men come to dotage. There are many dreams and delusions the old world is subject to; many errors then are set a-foot. Well then, there being a secret cognation and link between truth and truth, therefore all errors do more or less shake the primitive and supreme truth; and also, we had need to fortify ourselves because of the many divisions which are in the church. Divisions in the church breed atheism in the world, therefore Christ prays, John xvii. 21, 'That they all may be one in us: that the world may believe that thou hast sent me;' that is, that the carnal world may know that I am no impostor. When there are divisions in religion it makes men suspect all, and then they will not believe Christ is the true Messiah. I remember, one observes, that when there is but one main division, that adds zeal of both sides; but when we are crumbled into many divisions and fractions, then religion is exceedingly weakened; and men grow cold and indifferent, and begin to lose all awe of religion and all sense of God; therefore you had need to stand your ground, and be fortified against atheistical thoughts because of the scandals of religion. We are told, 2 Tim. iii. 1, 2, 'In the last days perilous times shall come. For men shall be lovers of their own selves, covetous, boasters,' &c. 'Having a form of godliness, but denying the power thereof,' ver. 5. Now when they see the professors of religion so scandalous, unrighteous, turbulent, and self-seeking, and wallowing in filthy delights, and yet pretend to strictness in religion, and all this is carried on under a form of godliness, men will think that religion itself is nothing else but an empty pretence, or a cover for unclean intents and evil practices, and so cast off all.

And they will be strengthened herein by the world's continuance ; so the apostle Peter : 2 Peter iii. 4, 'All things continue as they were from the beginning of the creation.' There are no preparations towards the accomplishment of the christian's great hopes and Christ's coming to judgment ; therefore it is the most needful point that can be pressed to fortify your hearts against atheism. These are the general seasons.

2. There are certain particular seasons when we are most in danger of atheism ; usually when the soul is under a passion and pet against providence, and we cavil at God and repine at his dispensations ; for all grievances breed passions, and passions exceedingly cloud the soul, and then we are in danger. There are several seasons when this is like to befall us.

[1.] When we see the holy and pure worshippers of God to be in the worst case, then we fall into a distrust of all religion ; and if there be a God, that he doth neglect his duty to the world. When mischief falls upon the good, it is a shrewd temptation to atheism ; indeed nothing should be out of order to faith, and providence should not work thus on us, but thus it doth. This hath been a wind that hath shaken not only shrubs and reeds, but the tallest cedars in Lebanon ; as David, Jeremiah, Habakkuk, and the holy men of God, they have been questioning, Why doth the way of the wicked prosper ? This hath been their great temptation. God's children must be put to sore trials that their graces may appear ; they will not understand that this is the place of exercise, nor of recompenses, and therefore they take offence against God.

[2.] When our own prayers are not heard, when we have been solicitous at the throne of grace with much earnestness and importunity, and yet speed not, we are apt to be so partial to our own desires, that we fall a questioning the being of God himself, as if we would take a kind of revenge upon him, because he hath not heard our prayers. Fond creatures would have grace at their own beck and command, and if we be disappointed, and God do not come in when we will, then we storm. And thus the devil hath a great advantage against many poor trembling souls that have lain under the terrors of the Lord ; they have been calling for mercy and quietness of conscience, and yet their fears increase. Now the devil abuseth their discontent, and seeks to draw them to atheism. Exod. xvii. 7, when Israel wanted water, then they said—'Is the Lord among us or not ?' and the prophet, Hab. i. 2, 'O Lord, how long shall I cry, and thou wilt not hear ! even cry out unto thee of violence, and thou wilt not save !' He had been calling upon God, and the Lord seemed not to answer. How did this work ? it brought him to this temptation, to question the being of God ; but see how he corrects himself : ver. 12, 'Art not thou from everlasting, O Lord my God, mine holy one ? O Lord, thou hast ordained them for judgment.' Thus he doth expostulate with himself, Why should I have these dreadful thoughts ? God is God still ; and then he begins to recover out of the temptation. Pettish desires, that are earnest and solicitious, and finally crossed, do always put us upon murmuring, and murmuring upon doubts and discontent ; and then the devil hath a great advantage, for he works exceedingly upon spleen and stomach.   Therefore when men are in a pet, angry with God, and have not their heart's desire, they are liable to this sin.

[3.] When oppression goes unrevenged, men pervert judgment, and others forswear themselves ; and our innocence doth not prevail, but we perish in it ; the devil works upon this, and takes advantage of our discontent.   Diagoras, a notable atheist among the heathens, became so upon this occasion ; he saw a man deeply forswearing himself, and because he was not smitten suddenly with a thunderbolt, he turned atheist, and falls a questioning whether there was a God or no.   When we see such oppression, it is a sore temptation, and we cry out, Is there a God ?   See how the Holy Ghost prevents such kind of thoughts as these are : Eccles. iii. 16, 17, ' I saw under the sun the place of judgment, that wickedness was there ; and the place of righteousness, that iniquity was there.'   What then ?   He interposeth timely, for fear lest a temptation should prevent him—'I said in my heart, God shall judge the righteous and the wicked : for there is a time there for every purpose, and for every work ;' ver. 18, ' I said in my heart concerning the estate of the sons of men, that God might manifest them, and that they might see that they themselves are beasts.'   God will have a time to judge this matter ; he doth recover this great principle out of the hands of the temptation.   So Eccles. v. 8, ' If thou seest the oppression of the poor, and violent perverting of judgment and justice in a province, marvel not at the matter.'   A man's heart is apt to rise upon such an occasion ; he stands trembling—What ! is there any divine power, any God that takes notice of human affairs ?   The Holy Ghost interposeth seasonably—' For he that is higher than the highest regardeth, and there be higher than they.'   There is a God.   A man is apt to unravel all religion in his thoughts, and to think that there is none to take cognisance of the matter ; therefore when it goes ill with the best, when your prayers are not answered, when oppression goes unrevenged, you should guard your heart with this consideration, There is a higher than the highest.

SERMON XXXII.

For he that cometh to God, must believe that he is, and that he is a rewarder of those that diligently seek him.—HEB. xi. 6.

Use 6. Here is a direction to us in our addresses to God.   Fix our thoughts on the consideration of his being—' He that cometh to God, must believe that God is '—say, I do not go now to speak to an idol, but to the living God.   Every one that comes to God should by actual thoughts revive this principle upon his memory and affections, for this will be of great advantage to him—Why ?

1. To avoid customariness ; for otherwise we shall be perfunctory and customary.   It was the saying of a wretch, speaking of public worship—*Eamus ad communem errorem*—Let us go to the common error.   If men do not say so, or think so in opinion, yet this is the

language of their practice; they do not act as unto a God. The God of a carnal customary worshipper is but an idol. In the duty of prayer, many a man comes and makes a large confession to God, but feels no grief and shame. Let him but speak half so much against himself to his guilty fellow-creature, one that is but despicable dust and ashes, the man would blush and be ashamed; yet he can speak it to God, and have no remorse. If they are put upon examination before a magistrate, and make such a confession, how would they tremble! yet they are not humbled at the remembrance of God. Alas! man hath but a drop of indignation against sin; the best are made up of mixed principles; man cannot be so severe as the holy God. Man hates evil, because it is against his interest; but God hates evil, because it is against his nature. And therefore what is the reason we have not this remorse, shame, and lively sorrow, when we are repeating the sad story of our lives to God? It cannot be from confidence of God's mercy; for when conscience is awakened and scourged for those sins, it is the most difficult thing in the world then to get comfort; but we are customary and careless, and do not weigh the matter; so for supplication, we do but tell a fair tale, and make it but a matter of talk, and do but fill up a little time with words, and consider not that we are speaking to the living God; if we did, we would be more reverent and serious when we make mention of him. Put it in a temporal case: Mal. i. 8, 'If ye offer the blind for sacrifice, is it not evil? and if ye offer the lame and sick, is it not evil? offer it now unto thy governor; will he be pleased with thee, or accept thy person?' If I were admitted into the presence of a great king, and were to make my requests in a matter of great concernment, would I not look after them, and observe how my requests are granted? But, alas! we throw away our prayers, as children shoot away their arrows, and never look after them. So for thanksgiving, we would have a more warm sense of the courtesies of men, if a man had but done half so much for us; but we give the Lord but cold and drowsy thanks.

2. To avoid irreverence. The angels are said to have six wings—'And with twain they covered their faces, and with twain they covered their feet,' &c. Isa. vi. 3. They fear not commutative justice, and are assured of the favour of God; yet they clap their wings, and cover their faces. Fear is a duty compatible with the blessed estate; we have more cause, but they have more grace; we do not see him that is invisible, and visible objects only work upon us.

3. To avoid deadness. I am speaking to the living God, Heb. ix. 14, 'To serve the living God.' Worship must be proportionable to the object of worship. The heathens offered a flying horse to the sun as most suitable, because of the swiftness of his motion. Dead service may become a dead idol, but not a living God. I should raise up myself and deal in good earnest with him.

4. To beget a confidence. God is not a vain help that cannot save us,—'We trust in the living God,' 1 Tim. vi. 18. Baal's priests may draw blood from themselves, but could not get a word of answer from their idol; but we speak to a God that is at the other end of causes, that hath influence upon all things, one that needs but speak the word, and we shall be whole.

But what thoughts are fittest to fix our hearts on the being of God when we are in prayer? or so to keep our hearts under a sense of God's being in that duty, as that we may conceive of him aright? I shall handle this case—

[1.] For the necessity of it; it is not a curious business, as those requests, Exod. xxxiii. 18, ' Lord, show me thy glory ;' and John xiv. 8, ' Show us the Father, and it sufficeth us ;' but it is necessary, for without it our services are profane, customary, irreligious. John iv. 22, ' Ye worship ye know not what ; we know what we worship.' Our cogitations do fleet and vanish without some determinate and comprehensible object, whereon to fix and fasten them. As a ball struck in the open air never comes to hand again, so are our thoughts lost and scattered, except we determine and settle them on some notions of God that may be expressive of his being.

[2.] Because it is difficult to determine it for two reasons :—

(1.) Because of the infiniteness and incomprehensibleness of God's essence. God is said sometimes to dwell in light, and sometimes to dwell in darkness. He is said to dwell in light, to show the greatness of his majesty : 1 Tim. vi. 16, ' Who only hath immortality, dwelling in the light, which no man can approach unto, whom no man hath seen, nor can see.' And he is said to dwell in darkness, to show our weakness and incapacity to apprehend him : Ps. xviii. 11, ' He made darkness his secret place, his pavilion round about him were dark waters, and thick clouds of the sky.' When we come to discourse of God, we are as a man that is born blind, who knows there is light in the world, though he cannot conceive what a kind of thing it is. So reason and conscience will tell us that there is a God ; but what God is, and how to form proper thoughts of him, that we cannot tell.

(2.) Because of the danger of erring, lest while we go about to establish a right notion of God, we make way for atheism. Prying too far into his majesty may prove a temptation. We cannot search out the Almighty to perfection : Judges xiii. 18, ' Why askest thou thus after my name, seeing it is secret ? ' It is impossible for man to comprehend God.

Now I shall answer the case in some propositions :—

First, That you may conceive aright of the nature of God, above all things, you must renew and revive the act of your faith in God's essence and presence ; that he is, and that he is present with us, when we pray to him.

1. That he is. So it is in the text—' He that cometh to God must believe that he is.' Though we cannot conceive what he is, yet we must be sure to fix our hearts in this, that he is. This is the great principle and ground-work of all, and it must be laid as a foundation of our worship and approaches to God. The work of faith is to give us a sight of him that is invisible. When Moses asked God's name, God answereth him—' I am,' Exod. iii. 14, ' I am hath sent me unto you.' God would give him no other name than this—' I am,' which deciphereth his essence. Certainly acts of worship would be managed with more awe and reverence, if this principle were firmly laid up in the heart, that God is. Reason shows that he is, though we know not what he is ; faith can only show what he is to us. Vision will show us what

he is in himself; that is, our happiness and glory in heaven: 1 John iii. 2, 'When he shall appear, we shall be like him, for we shall see him as he is.' Now we must actually revive this faith, that God is; we must see him that is invisible: Heb. xi. 27, 'By faith Moses forsook Egypt, not fearing the wrath of the king; for he endured, as seeing him that is invisible.' It is a great work of faith to believe that God is—that there is an invisible God, that so you may adore a spiritual majesty, which you know to be, though you cannot comprehend him, how he is, and what he is, nor search out the almighty to perfection.

2. That God is present with you in the worship that you are about to perform, that he is an all-seeing Spirit, and that he is intimately acquainted with all the workings of your hearts: John iv. 24, 'God is a Spirit, and they that worship him must worship him in spirit and in truth.' He sees how your spirits and hearts work in all your approaches to his majesty, and you should so regard him as if you did see him with your bodily eyes. All duties are expressed in scripture by drawing nigh to God, for they bring the soul into God's presence. Prayer is but our conference with God: Gen. xviii. 27, 'I have taken upon me to speak unto the Lord, who am but dust and ashes.' Now all speech is to them that are present, and hearken to us: if we speak to God, we must conceive him to be really present, hearkening to us. And hearing is God's conference with us: Acts x. 33, 'We are all here present before the Lord to hear all things that are commanded thee of God;' and therefore when you come to pray, say, I have not to do with men, but with God; when you come to hear, say, I have not to do with the preacher only, but with God: Heb. iv. 12, 'All things are naked and open unto the eyes of him with whom we have to deal.' Certainly, God is, whom I worship this day. I am going to confer with the true God, and to hear him speaking to me; he is present with me, and therefore to be thought of, as if I could see him with my bodily eyes: Acts xvii. 27, 'God is not far from every one of us.' When we come to worship God, he is not only near us, but within us, more intimately present with us than we are with ourselves. You could not keep your breath in your bodies, nor speak a word, if he were not there; as, if the sun should withdraw his light, all would be darkness. This is the first thing, if you would rightly conceive of God; when you come to him you must fix your heart in the apprehension of his essence and presence.

Secondly, You must conceive of him aright, and according as he hath revealed himself; lest in worshipping God you worship an idol. It is a high contempt of his majesty if we do not conceive of him according to his excellent glory. Now for the conceiving of him aright, which was the difficulty propounded, take these two rules—

1. There must be no carnal conceit and representation in your minds. Though we cannot conceive of him as he is, yet we must take heed that we do not conceive of him as he is not. We are all born idolators, and are naturally prone to fashion God according to some form of our own —to turn the glory of God into the fashion of a corruptible thing. Look, as some have an external idol, so we have a mental idol, when we are transforming the essence of God into fleshly conceits of our own. We must conceive of God, purely, simply, spiritually, as of a spiritual being, without form and without matter; and as of an infinite being,

without all limits and bounds. It was the saying of a heathen, Those
that made images and pictures of God, took away fear and established
error. Pictures to represent God do debase the nature of God, and
make him contemptible; and images of God are so natural to us, that
we can hardly dispossess our minds of them. Imaginations are as bad
as images; he that forbiddeth images in the church, doth also forbid
them in our mind. A picture or corporeal resemblance of the divine
essence is worse in the mind than in the glass windows. By pictures
and resemblances of the divine essence, heathen idolatry began: Rom.
i. 21, 'They were vain in their imaginations;' and then it follows, ver.
23, 'They changed the glory of the uncorruptible God into an image
made like to corruptible man, and to birds and fourfooted beasts, and
creeping things;' and ver. 25, 'Who changed the glory of God into a
lie, and worshipped the creature more than the creator, who is blessed
forever.' We that converse altogether with material and sensible beings,
are very prone to conceive of God according to those things about which
we are conversant. And that is the reason why there are so many
cautions in the word everywhere against it: Deut. iv. 15, 16, 'Take
good heed unto yourselves; for ye saw no manner of similitude in the
day that the Lord spake unto you in Horeb out of the midst of the fire;
lest you corrupt yourselves and make you a graven image, the similitude
of any figure, the likeness of male or female.' When God discovered
himself to his people, there was no image, no outward figure; there was
only a voice. Though common awe may restrain us from making an
outward image, yet we are very prone to frame inward images, and
draw representations of God in our minds. There are secret atheistical
thoughts within us, by which we are apt to debase the nature of God
to the common likeness, and fancy him according to the shape and fashion
of visible substances. Therefore the Lord saith, Isa. xl. 18, 'To whom
will you liken God? or what likeness will you compare unto him?'
We are apt to liken God to some outward and visible being; but in all
your addresses to God, you must conceive of him as a Spirit, without
figure and shape. It is true, the scripture doth often use words that
are of a corporeal sense and signification concerning God, but that is
for the infirmity and weakness of our apprehensions. God lispeth to
us in our own dialect; but whatsoever is spoken to us after the manner
of men must be understood after the manner of God. Serapion, dwelling too much on these carnal expressions, fell into the error of the
Anthropomorphites, who believed God to have a human shape. Sensible things indeed are of use to us in prayer, but then they should be
used by way of argument rather than representation. When we argue
a minori ad majus, from the lesser to the greater, it is good. As when
we would advance God, and exalt his love and care in our thoughts,
we may argue from sensible things, and reason from the wisdom of a
father, or from the bowels of a mother: Isa. xlix. 15, 'Can a woman
forget her sucking child that she should not have compassion on the son
of her womb? yea, they may forget, yet will not I forget thee;' and Mat.
vii. 11, 'If ye then being evil know how to give good gifts unto your
children, how much more will your father which is in heaven give good
things to them that ask him?' There is no father or mother like God;
no father so wise, no mother so tender as God is. Again, when we would

shame ourselves when we are but coldly affected with our approaches to God, we may reason—If I were to accuse myself as thus guilty before a common judge, would I not tremble ? If I should come in such a cold manner to man, would he regard me ? Mal. i. 8, 'Offer it to thy governor ; will he be pleased with thee, or accept thy person ? ' You must take heed that you conceive of God purely, simply, spiritually.

2. We must conceive of God according to his praises in the word. Hereafter we shall see him as he is, which is our happiness in heaven ; now we can only see him as he is pleased to reveal himself to us. This way is most easy and of greatest profit and safety ; for though these representations are imperfect notions and conceptions, that are not every way proportionable to the nature and infiniteness of God, yet they are enough to beget reverence. Therefore it is observable, when Moses desired to see God's glory, the Lord pardoned what was of curiosity in the request, and answered him in what was necessary ; and what doth God do ? He only proclaims his name : Exod. xxxiv. 6, ' The Lord, the Lord God, merciful and gracious,' &c. These are the conceptions we must have of God. And so, when we would form a proper notion of God in our addresses to him : 1 Tim. i. 17, ' Now unto the king eternal, immortal, invisible, the only wise God, be honour and glory for ever and ever. Amen.' Thus must we conceive of God as a spiritual essence, as the great governor of the world—most wise, most holy, infinitely and eternally good; I might heap up for this many places of scripture. These are names which are given to those things, which we would most magnify and commend ; and so, when they are conceived in a spiritual mind, they are most fit to stir up worship and religious affection to God; whereas we draw a snare upon ourselves when we would go higher and see his essence. Face to face is the dispensation of another world, when we shall have other eyes and other hearts ; now all we can do, and as much as we can aspire to, is to look upon his back parts, and to consider those praises which the scripture puts upon him. Œcolampadius, when he was preaching a sermon to young men, said, If you would know what God is, you must first know what goodness is, what justice, mercy, bounty, loving-kindness, and truth is; then you shall know God, for God is mercy, goodness, loving-kindness, and truth itself. And you must know that these attributes are in God in an infinite manner, of which finite creatures are no competent judges ; and then look upon all these perfections as shining forth, and discovering themselves in the human nature of Christ. He that cannot look upon the sunbeams in its strength at noon-day, may take view of it in the water, or when the moon is at full ; so we that cannot behold the glory of the divine majesty as he is in himself, may safely behold his perfections as they shone forth in the man Christ Jesus. This is the way of knowing God, by fixing our minds upon him as the first cause, the creator and governor of all things.

Thirdly, There must be such a representation of God as may make the spirit aweful, but not servile ; we must have such thoughts of God as may increase our reverence, not weaken our delight ; the spirit begets aweful, but yet ingenuous thoughts of God. This is a rule, that our affections in our services must be suited to the nature of God. Now, in all the scriptual descriptions of God, there is a mixture and com-

position of God's attributes, to show that there should be a like mixture
in our affections.   As in God, there is a mixture of justice and mercy,
and of power and love ; so in us, there should be a mixture of hope and
fear, of joy, delight, and reverence, that the excesses of one affection
may be corrected by the mixture and exercise of another.   That there
is such a mixture in God's attributes is clear : Deut. vii. 7–10, ' The
Lord thy God, he is God, the faithful God, keeping covenant and mercy
to them that love him, and to them that keep his commandments, and
repayeth them that hate him.' So Exod. xxxiv. 6, ' The Lord, the Lord
God, merciful and gracious,' &c. ; but then it is added, ver. 7, ' He will
by no means clear the guilty.'   So Jer. ix. 24, ' I am the Lord, which
exercise loving-kindness, judgment and righteousness in the earth ;'
and Daniel ix. 4, ' O Lord, the great and dreadful God, keeping covenant
and mercy to them that love him, and to them that keep his commandments '—a dreadful God, and yet full of mercy and sweetness.   The
like mixture should there be in our affections, when we come to address
ourselves to God : Ps. ii. 11, ' Serve the Lord with fear, and rejoice with
trembling.'   There must be joy, but mixed with a holy trembling : so
1 Peter i. 17, ' If ye call on the Father, who without respect of persons
judgeth according to every man's work, pass the time of your sojourning
here in fear.'   There is a mixture in God's appellations and our affections.   In God's appellations he is a father and yet a judge ; and there
must be the like mixture in our affections, and in the temper and
disposition of our spirits, ' to call him father,' and yet ' serve him
with fear ; ' there must be a child-like reverence and a child-like
confidence.   Now, because this is the exact temper of spirit that is fit
for duty, I shall a little examine what considerations are most proper
and likely to keep the spirit aweful, and what considerations are most
likely to keep the spirit cheerful in a way of hope and filial confidence.

1. The considerations that are like to keep the spirit aweful.

[1.] Consider his wonderful purity and holiness.   There is no
attribute that drives a creature to astonishment and self-abhorrency
so much as God's holiness.   We dread him for his wrath, power, and
justice ; but all these are rooted in his holiness : 1 Sam. vi. 20, ' Who
is able to stand before this holy Lord God ? '   This is that which makes
the guilty tremble, and the purest creatures are abashed at the presence
of God.   It is said of the cherubim : Isa. vi. 2, 3, ' they covered their
faces, and ' Cried one to another, and said, Holy, holy, holy is the Lord
of hosts.'   This awed the angels—God's holiness, his immaculate and
unspotted glory, and they covered their faces as if they were ashamed of
those seeds of folly that are in the angelical nature, the changeableness
of their nature.   Though the angels do not fear the strokes of God's
justice, yet they tremble at the purity of his presence.   And the children
of God dread him for his holiness ; so the prophet cries out : Isa. vi. 5,
' Wo is me ! for I am undone ; because I am a man of polluted lips,
and mine eyes have seen the King, the Lord of hosts.'   This is that
attribute in which the creatures are most defective, and in which God
doth most excel ; and therefore it renders God most awful, and affects
the creature with shame.   Joshua xxiv. 19, ' You cannot serve the
Lord, for he is an holy God.'   It is his holiness awakens his justice,
which makes him take notice of our failings.

[2.] Reflect upon the majesty of God and the glory of his attendants. Whenever we come to worship him, we worship him in the presence of angels and archangels. The children of God find by experience that not only the presence of God, but the presence of angels is a very moving consideration. We are more apt to conceive of finite essences than of that which is infinite, as coming nearest and bordering more upon our own manner of being, and because we can more securely and without danger form a representation of them. Therefore consider you are standing before God and all his holy angels: Ps. cxxxviii. 1, 'Before the gods will I sing praise unto thee.' The Septuagint reads it—'Before the angels.' The angels are present in the assemblies of the saints, which was deciphered by the pictures of the cherubim which were in the temple; and upon this account, the apostle urgeth reverence in the worship of God, that the women should cover their heads, 'because of the angels,' 1 Cor. xi. 10. They are conscious to all those impurities and indecencies in worship that we are guilty of; and therefore to greaten our reverence of God, it is good to consider that we worship him in the presence of his holy angels. The saints in the old testament trembled at the appearance of an angel. If we should come before an earthly prince sitting on his throne, environed with his nobles, how should we be afraid! Consider, thou standest before God, who is encompassed with cherubim, seraphim, thrones, dominions, angels, archangels: Dan. vii. 10, 'Thousand thousands ministered unto him, and ten thousand times ten thousand stood before him.'

[3.] Compare the divine glory and our own vileness: Gen. xviii. 27, 'I have taken upon me to speak unto the Lord, who am but dust and ashes.' We should think of the frailty of our constitution, and the impurity of our hearts: Eccles. v. 2, 'Be not rash with thy mouth, and let not thine heart be hasty to utter anything before God: for God is in heaven, and thou upon earth.' There is not so great a distance between heaven and earth as beween God and you. The prophet useth an expression, Isa. xl. 15, 'All nations before thee are but as a drop of a bucket, and are counted as the small dust of the balance.' If you should put a great weight in one scale, and nothing but dust in the other, this is a small resemblance of the disproportion between God and us. I confess our expressions are many times humble, but the tongue prescribes to the heart, rather than the heart to the tongue; and so they are but a vanity of speech, which the Lord abhors, vain compliments, that do not arise from a deep and inward sense of God's excellences.

2. The considerations that are likely to keep the heart cheerful. There is not only fear required, but such a fear as is consistent with a holy ingenuity and confidence, that is becoming the sweetness of religion. Worship is not the task of slaves, but the duty of children; and God would have you come with an ingenuous liberty and freedom into his presence. To this end—

[1.] Consider the sweet representations that are made of God's mercy in scripture. Luther said, It is the intent of the whole scripture to represent God to be merciful to sinners. This is the attribute he most delights in. See how God proclaimed his name, Exod. xxxiv. 6, 7, 'The Lord, the Lord God, merciful and gracious, long-suffering, and abundant in goodness and truth, keeping mercy for thousands, forgiving iniquity, and transgression and sin, and that will by no means clear the guilty; visiting the iniquity of the fathers upon the children, and the children's children, unto the third and to the fourth generations.' There is more of mercy; and God begins with mercy, because it is his chiefest attribute; so Micah vii. 18, ' Mercy pleaseth him.' It is the delightful act of God to exercise mercy; the expectation of it is not more pleasing to you than the exercise of it is to God; it is like live honey, that drops of its own accord. Justice and all punitive acts are said to be extorted from him. Though God is necessarily just, as well as necessarily merciful, and vindictive justice be part of his essence, yet that which God delighteth in is mercy, James ii. 13, ' Mercy rejoiceth against judgment.' When in the conflict of the attributes, mercy can be exercised and gets the upper hand, there is a triumph and rejoicing in heaven. Gracious dispensations come freely, but judicial and penal acts are expressed in scripture as if they were forced and drawn from God: Isa. xxviii. 21, ' That he may do his work, his strange work; and bring to pass his act, his strange act;' and Lam. iii. 33, ' He doth not afflict willingly, nor grieve the children of men.' When there is a rod in his hand, there are tears in his eyes. This is the whole design of the scriptures to represent God so, as that we may pitch upon God as merciful, gracious, and willing to do good to the creature.

[2.] Look upon God as he hath revealed himself in Jesus Christ. The gospel is the image of Christ, and Christ is the image of God. There is the likeness and picture of Christ in the gospel, but Jesus Christ is the lively image: 2 Cor. iv. 4, ' Lest the light of the glorious gospel of Christ, who is the image of God, should shine unto them;' that is, lest they know the mercifulness of God's heart in Jesus Christ: the gospel shows how full of mercy Christ is, and Christ shows how full of mercy God is; and ver. 6, ' To give the light of the knowledge of the glory of God in the face of Jesus Christ.' God hath stamped his image on the gospel, as Cæsar's image is on the coin; but Christ is the image of God, as Cæsar's image is on his son: Col. i. 15, ' Who is the image of the invisible God.' Look into the gospel, and there you read of the condescension of Christ, how he went about doing good, healing the sick and diseased; now, just as Christ was in the days of his flesh, so is God ready and willing to do us good. The whole life of Christ was nothing but mercy and love. Now, Christ is God's lively image and picture; he shows what God is: John i. 14, ' The word was made flesh, and dwelt among us, and we saw his glory, the glory as of the only begotten of the Father, full of grace and truth.' There were many emissions and beamings forth of the divine glory in the life of Christ, but that which chiefly shone out was the divine mercy: Acts x. 38, ' He went about doing good, and healing all that were oppressed of the devil.' You should study God in Christ. When Philip said to Christ—' Show us the Father, and it sufficeth us,' Christ chides him upon this account—' Have I been so long with thee, and hast thou not known me ? He that hath seen me hath seen the Father,' John xiv. 7–9; you need no other discovery than my person. God is best known in Christ, wherein, as in a glass, we may find his wisdom, power, goodness, and mercy ; wherein God displays his glory, without

overwhelming the creature. In Christ's transfiguration, the disciples
fell down like dead men, Mat. xvii.; they could not contain themselves.
But they that cannot look upon the sun may look upon his image in
the water; so they that cannot look upon God in himself, may look
upon God in Christ: the divine perfections working through the
human nature of Christ are more intelligible.

Fourthly, We must in prayer form proper thoughts of God, according to those requests that we put up to him. We cannot without
great distraction run through all the divine attributes at once; it is
impossible your thoughts can be fixed on so many subjects, and therefore you should single out such thoughts and considerations as will
suit with your particular requests to God. Holy men of God everywhere do this; as the apostle Paul, when he prays for peace, gives
God a suitable appellation: 2 Thes. iii. 16, 'The Lord of peace himself
give you peace always by all means.' So when he prays for patience
to bear with the infirmities and differences of others, he gives God a
suitable appellation: Rom. xv. 5, 'The God of patience and consolation
grant you to be like-minded one toward another;' God, that hath
abundance of patience, bestows it on you, that you may carry it thus.
So when he speaks of the comfort that he received in his affliction, he
styles God, 2 Cor. vii. 6, 'God that comforteth those that are cast
down.' It is a commendable policy, and a great help to our thoughts
in prayer, when we pitch upon an attribute that suiteth with our present
wants, or doth imply an ability and disposition in God to do us good.
When you come to be humbled in the presence of God, you must look
upon Christ as a judge; when you come to have your sins mortified,
you must look upon Christ as a physician. In your closet-addresses
to God, suit the descriptions of God according to your exigencies and
wants. When David begs defence, then God is his 'fortress' and
munition of rocks;' when he begs success against enemies, then God is
the ' horn of his salvation;' in a time of peace, God is his 'habitation;'
in a time of war, he is his 'refuge:' Ps. xci. 9, 'Because thou hast
made the Lord, which is thy refuge, even the most high thy habitation.'
alluding to the time of peace and the time of trouble.

Fifthly, Frame fit notions concerning the trinity, that there are three
persons in one godhead. Now to direct you, herein take these rules—

1. This mystery is to be believed, not disputed, and committed to
the anxious traverses of our own reason. Silence reason, by what is
revealed; anxious inquiries do but distract the mind. We shall never
know the full of this mystery till we come to heaven: John xiv. 20,
'At that day ye shall know that I am in my Father, and ye in me,
and I in you.' But though we know not how it is, it is enough for us
to know that it is so.

2. The real and practical honour of the trinity is best. Then do
we honour the trinity in unity, not when we conceive of the mystery,
but when we make a religious use of this high advantage—to come to
God, in the name of Christ, by the Spirit, and look for all from God
in Christ through the Holy Ghost. Direct your prayers to God the
Father; Christ prayed to the Father, Mat. xi. 25, 'I thank thee, O
Father, Lord of heaven and earth,' &c. So the saints in their addresses: Eph. iii. 14, 'For this cause I bow my knees unto the Father

of our Lord Jesus Christ.' In the name of Christ, John xiv. 13, 'Whatsoever ye shall ask in my name, that will I do.' By the Spirit, Jude 20, 'Praying in the Holy Ghost;' Rom. viii. 26, 27, 'Likewise the Spirit itself also helpeth our infirmities,' &c., 'because he maketh intercession for the saints according to the will of God.' Christians need not puzzle themselves about conceiving of three in one, and one in three; let them in this manner come to God, and it sufficeth; make God the object, and Christ the means of access, and look for help from the Spirit.

3. If the thoughts be coldly and frigidly affected to any of the persons, you must use a cure. Many times there are many secret thoughts of atheism, which arise in us about the divine essence and subsistences; and you must seek help against them, for when they are smothered they beget a rooted hypocrisy. Thus ignorant persons think altogether of God the Father; they worship God Almighty without distinct reflections on the personal operations of Father, Son, and Holy Ghost, or the contrivance of salvation. Fond persons honour the Son, but neglect the Father; they carry all their respects to the person of Jesus Christ. Most neglect to glorify the Spirit. In times of knowledge, God would have our thoughts more distinct and explicit. All persons are interested in the work of grace; the love of the Father maketh way for the glory of the Son, and the glory of the Son for the power of the Spirit. No man cometh to the Son but by the Father: John vi. 44, 'No man can come to me, except the Father which hath sent me draw him.' No man can come to the Father but by the Son: John xiv. 6, 'I am the way, the truth, and the life, no man cometh to the Father but by me.' And no man is united to the Son, but by the Holy Ghost: 2 Thes. ii. 13, 'God hath from the beginning chosen you to salvation, through the sanctification of the Spirit, and belief of the truth.' The inchoation is by the Father, the dispensation by the Son, and the consummation by the Holy Ghost; it is God's choice, Christ's purchase, and the Spirit's application. More particularly, if you are coldly affected towards God the Father, consider he spared not his own Son: John iii. 16, 'For God so loved the world, that h gave his only begotten Son, that whosoever believeth in him, should not perish, but have everlasting life.' His love brought Christ to you, and you to Christ, the Father's pure elective love: John xvii. 6, 'Thine they were, and thou gavest them me, and they have kept thy word.' His love keepeth you in Christ: John xvi. 27, 'For the Father himself loveth you, because ye have loved me, and have believed that I came out from God.' If you are coldly affected towards Christ, think that 'he loved you, and gave himself for you,' Gal. ii. 20; if towards the Spirit, consider that it is God the Spirit that exhibits, applies, and seals all to us: Eph. iv. 30, 'Grieve not the Holy Spirit of God, whereby ye are sealed unto the day of redemption.' The persons in the trinity glorify one another: John xvi. 14, 'He shall glorify me; for he shall take of mine, and shall show it unto you;' there is the Spirit's glorifying Christ. John xiv. 13, 'Whatsoever ye shall ask in my name, that I will do, that the Father may be glorified in the Son; there is Christ's glorifying the Father. Phil. ii. 9, 10, 'God hath exalted him, and given him a name above every name: that

at the name of Jesus every knee shall bow, of things in heaven, and things in earth, and things under the earth; and that every tongue should confess that Jesus Christ is the Lord, to the glory of God the Father;' there is the Father's glorifying Christ and an honour and and glory thence redounding to the Father.

SERMON XXXIII.

And that he is a rewarder of them that diligently seek him.—
HEB. xi. 6.

Two principles are necessary to be firmly believed of all that would entertain communion with God—God's being, and God's bounty; God's being 'That he is,' and God's bounty—'That he is a rewarder of them that diligently seek him.' Both these principles give life to all our duties and services; and therefore a man that would please God, and live in his favour and friendship, or that would come to God, that would have anything to do with him in prayer, praise, or any other service, he must be firmly persuaded of these two things.

1. Of the being of God—that God is; otherwise why should we be touched with any sense and care of religion, unless we believe that there were a God to whom this religion is tendered; that God is not a fancy, a nothing, but a true and real being, and that the God whom we serve is he. Without this all worship would be but a foolish custom and empty formality, and a compliance with a common error, for why should we go to him whom we conceive not to be? And therefore he that would have anything to do with God must fix his heart in a belief of this principle, that God whom I now serve is that infinite, that eternal power that made me and all things.

2. The bounty of God—'He is a rewarder of them that diligently seek him,' where observe—(1.) The notion by which his bounty is expressed—'He is a rewarder,' or a giver of rewards, μισθαπόδοτης. (2.) The objects or persons to whom—'Of those that diligently seek him.' Where again we may take notice of the act, 'they seek him,' and the manner 'diligently.' Both are folded up in one word in the original, τοῖς ἐκζητοῦσιν; the word ζητεῖν signifies to seek, and the compound ἐκζητεῖν, to seek out till one find. Now God must be sought out; we must do our uttermost to seek him till we find him; therefore our translators fitly render the word by two, 'that diligently seek him.' Now this qualification is to be understood both inclusively and exclusively. [1.] Inclusively: to involve all that would give up themselves in his holy word to inquire after God. The Lord takes a charge upon himself impartially to reward all that seek him: whether rich or poor, bond or free, he is a rewarder to them; indefinitely to all them that seek him. [2.] Exclusively: he rewardeth none but those; they and they only do find and enjoy him. The point of doctrine will be this—

Doct. That the fountain of all obedience, gratitude, and service to God is a firm belief of his being a rewarder of all them that diligently seek him.

I shall (1.) Explain the proposition that is to be believed, and give the sense of it—that God is a rewarder of such; (2.) Inquire into the nature of this faith, and show how this is to be believed; (3.) Tell you what influence it has upon our obedience and service to God.

First, Here is the proposition that is to be believed—'God is a rewarder of them that diligently seek him.' The proposition intimateth somewhat to be expected on God's part, and something to be done on our part.

First, on God's part. He is μισθαποδότης, a reward-giver, which implies these four propositions—(1.) That not only his essence, but his providence is to be believed by us. (2.) In his providence the gracious recompense is only mentioned; it is not said he is a revenger, which is a notable part of his providence, but he is a rewarder. (3.) To show how fitly this grace is expressed by the term 'reward.' (4.) This reward is principally in the next life.

1. We are bound to believe not only his essence, but his providence. For here are two principles—that God is, and that he is a rewarder; by which last his providence is intimated, namely, that he regardeth human affairs, and will judge accordingly, blessing the good and punishing the evil. It was the conceit of Epicurus and his followers that it would not stand with the happiness of God to trouble himself with the affairs of the world; and practical atheists, and sinful, secure persons are of his mind; they think that the heavens are drawn as a curtain between us and God, and that he is not at leisure to mind the affairs of this lower world; so they are brought in speaking, Job xxii. 12–14, 'Is not God in the height of heaven? and behold the height of the stars, how high are they? And thou sayest, How can God know? can he judge through the dark clouds? Thick clouds are a covering to him, that he seeth not, and he walketh in the circuit of heaven.' Our eyes and perspectives are too short for us to look above the clouds and mists of this lower world, and to understand the affairs of the world above us; and therefore we muse of God according to the manner of us finite creatures, as if God could not see us, and judge of the state of things here below, because of the great distance between him and us; or at least that he hath other things to do than to mind the affairs of mankind, or to trouble himself with our actions. Thus vainly do we deceive ourselves, like that foolish creature, the panther; when it is hunted, it hides its head, and then thinks itself safe, not seen, because it sees not. The clouds and darkness that are about God may hinder our sight of him, but they do not hinder his sight of us. Oh no; Prov. xv. 3, 'The eyes of the Lord are in every place, beholding the good and the evil.' Nothing can be done without his providential assistance, and therefore nothing can be done without his privity and knowledge. He is nearer to us than we are to ourselves, and knows our very thoughts, —not only our meaning before we speak, but our thoughts before they are conceived: Ps. cxxxix. 2, 'Thou understandest my thoughts afar off.' The mischief is, we do that which we would not have to be seen, and then would fain believe that God doth not see us. This conceit,

that God doth not mind the affairs of the world, will destroy all worship of God and respect to him. If there be no providence, then no worship, no prayer, no praise. The two first motives that ordinarily induce men to worship are fear and hope; fear that God will avenge their misdeeds, and hope of relief when they lie under straits and necessities. But now if God were mindless of the affairs of this lower world, and had left all things to their own way, we should have nothing to fear and nothing to hope for from his providence, and so God would not be regarded by us. The Epicureans indeed say that God is to be worshipped for the eminency of his dignity, and the excellency and greatness of his nature; but alas! that would breed a faint respect, for who regards those in whom they are not concerned? Here in the world we hear of mighty kings and potentates, but we regard them not unless they govern and protect us; then our peace and safety depends upon them. I say we hear of great emperors and kings abroad in India and China; what doth the interest of their courts, or the vastness of their armies move us? Every mean gentleman that is able to do us either a good or bad turn is more respected than those mighty monarchs. And so God would not be respected if he should only shut up himself within the heavens, and not regard the affairs here below. Well then, God sees. The accurateness of his providence, of his seeing all things, is described to us by many metaphors in scripture. The most solemn and notable is that of a record. He so sees and regards all things as to write them in books to keep them upon record: Mal. iii. 16, 'The Lord hearkened and heard, and a book of remembrance was written before him.' God hath his registers and books of record, the counterpart of which is our conscience, where all things are written that we do think and say; but this book is in our keeping, and therefore it is often blurred and defaced; but all is clear and legible in the book of God's remembrance. Certainly we would be more advised in our speeches and actions if we knew that there was a secret spy about us to write down all that we do: so Ps. lvi. 8, 'Thou tellest my wanderings: put thou my tears in thy bottle: are they not in thy book?' God hath a bottle for all the tears of his people,—they are not as water spilt upon the ground,—and he has a book wherein he records all their sorrows. Many times books are written in their defence, and the memorials of their innocency here in the world are destroyed; but all is entered in the records and rolls of heaven. Thus does God take notice of all the actions and affairs of the world. You must not think of him as of the Persian monarch living in ease and pleasure, and leaving the care of provinces to his *satrapœ*, his deputies and vicegerents. No, his eyes run to and fro through the whole earth; he observeth all, noteth all that is done here in the world. And— which is the other part of his providence—he judgeth accordingly. He is called: Jer. li. 56, 'The Lord God of recompenses,' because he does reward his friends, and punish his enemies. I say, God is not an idle spectator. Providence doth many times interpose notably now. We find sometimes obedience laden with blessings; and vengeance treadeth upon the heels of sin, especially for some notable excess and disorder: Ps. lviii. 11, 'So that a man may say, Verily there is a reward for the righteous; verily he is a God that judgeth in the earth.' Many that knew not what to think of God's providence before, that were at a loss, yet when it is all brought about, they may see there is a reward for the righteous. We often, like ignorant and impatient spectators, will not tarry till the last act of the tragedy, till the way of God hath its course; for if we did, we should soon find that all things are in the hands of a righteous judge. Now and then God will give the world a taste of his recompenses, as he did in the prosperity of Abraham and punishment of Cain, to show there is a providence. But at other times the wicked are prosperous, the godly are afflicted, to show that the last act of providence is yet behind, and that there is a judgment to come. As in the parable of Dives, he was happy till his death, and lived in luxury and pleasure, whilst Lazarus was humbled with poverty, and rough-cast with sores. But the great and solemn day is to come when God will call all the world to an account and general audit, and justice and mercy shall both have their solemn triumph; and as our work hath been, so shall our wages be; that which is good shall be found to praise and honour, and that which is evil lie under its own shame. Well then, he that cometh to God must believe that God is a rewarder, it implies his providence; the Lord takes notice of human actions, and that he will judge accordingly.

2. Among the recompenses of God, that which comes from grace is only mentioned. The great God in recompenses is not only a rewarder of them that seek him, but a revenger of them that hate him; but his vengeance and punishment is not propounded as so necessary to our first faith, to him that comes to God so much as his reward. Why does he instance in this part of providence? Partly, because God delights to manifest himself to the world in acts of grace rather than in acts of judgment—'Mercy pleaseth him,' Micah. vii. 18. Goodness and grace are natural to God. Anger, and wrath, and vindictive justice suppose our sin; they are extorted from him. And therefore if we would have a right notion of God, next to the being of God we must believe his goodness. From the beginning of time until now the usual acts of God's providence are the effluxes and emanations of his goodness. What hath the world been but a great theatre, upon which mercy hath been acting a part almost these six thousand years? His mercy is over all his works, and therefore God is called the 'Father of mercies,' 2 Cor. i. 3, not the Father of justice. When he proclaimeth his name, we hear first of his mercy, and still more of his mercy: Exod. xxxiv. 6, 7, 'The Lord, the Lord God, gracious and merciful, long-suffering, and abundant in goodness and truth,' and justice is brought in to prevent the abuse of mercy, and to invite men to take hold of it. And then, partly, because this is an encouragement to bring in them to God who else would run away from him because of his terrors and his own natural bondage, as Adam ran into the bushes. Though there be amiable excellences in the nature of God, yet the naked contemplation of these cannot allay our natural fears, nor quench our natural enmity against God, but rather increase them. As good qualities in a judge will never draw the prisoner's heart to affect him; to tell the prisoner that his judge is a grave, comely person, of profound knowledge, of excellent speech, a strict observer of the law; but he is a judge, and so his heart stands off from him. And so it is between us and God:

though we should tell men of the perfections of God's nature, yet as long as the guilty sinner reflects upon him as his judge, he stands aloof from God. The wrath of God is like a flaming sword ready drawn and brandished to keep us from him; his justice makes us stand at a distance: Rom. i. 32, 'Knowing the judgment of God, that they that do such things are worthy of death;' but his goodness, and readiness to reward, that is the motive to draw in our hearts to him. Christians, all this is spoken that we might have a right notion of God in himself. Œcolampadius, when he was preaching to children, first he tells them, There is a God, and then saith he, If you would know what God is, you must not conceive of him by pictures that you have seen. Do you know what mercy, lenity, patience, bountifulness, goodness is?—that is God. You must believe there is a God, and then you must see what he is; he is a God merciful, gracious, ready to reward and do good. This doth draw in the heart of a creature to him. As Luther saith, this is the whole design of the scripture, to represent God in such a manner, as bountiful and ready to do good to his creatures that come to him.

3. This grace is expressed by the word 'reward.' It is a metaphor taken from hired servants: Mat. xx. 8, 'Call the labourers, and give them—μισθὸν—their hire.' Now some go upon this word as if here they had a clear foundation for the merit of the creature from the two words μισθὸς and ἀποδόσις, of which the word in the text is compounded, but vainly; for work and reward are relatives indeed, but not merit and reward. God is a rewarder, but how? out of his own bounty, and the liberality of his grace, not out of our merit and desert. You shall see the word is taken in scripture sometimes for any fruit and issue of our pains, so it be grateful to us, though no way deserved by us, as that vainglory men seek for in the world: Mat. vi. 2, it is said, 'They have their reward.' No man can say they deserve it, but it was the reward aimed at and chosen by them. Anything we look at as the fruit of our pains is called the reward. And sometimes any fruit of the divine grace: as Ps. cxxvii. 3, 'Lo, children are an heritage from the Lord; and the fruit of the womb is his reward,' that is, his gracious gift; and so μισθὸς and χάρις, reward and grace, are all one, and promiscuously used; as Mat. v. 46, what is there, 'What reward have you?' in Luke vi. 32, it is χάρις, 'What grace, or what thank have you?' So God is said to reward those whom he remembers out of mere mercy and bounty; his reward is worth the seeking after; not that our work is meritorious and worthy of that reward. Well then, the reward of grace is understood; μισθὸς hath more relation to God's promise than the work. Indeed it stands upon two feet, upon God's promise and upon Christ's merit. We have a reward, which by virtue of Christ's merit, and God's promise we may expect; but as to us, it is freely bestowed upon us. The apostle plainly shows this distinction of a reward of debt and a reward of grace: Rom. iv. 4, 'To him that worketh,' that is, he that will establish his own righteousness or works for justification—to him 'is the reward reckoned, not of grace, but of debt.' He intimates plainly there is a reward κατὰ χάριν, according to grace. Once more it is called, Col. iii. 24, 'The reward of the inheritance; such as proceedeth not from the worth of the work, but from God's free grace. If the reward be a servile work, the inheritance

is for children. But briefly : the recompenses of God's justice and
mercy are called rewards, partly to note the persons to whom it is
given ; a reward is not given but to those that labour.   Heaven is not
for idlers and loiterers ; it is a reward, it is given after labour ; not as
if any did deserve it by their work, as a labourer is worthy of his hire.
Among men, he that hires has benefit by the labour of him that is
hired ; but ' we are unprofitable servants,' Luke xvii. 10 ; and ordinarily
there is a due proportion between the work and the wages ; but here
there can be none at all, for eternal life, which is that reward, consists
in the vision and fruition of God himself ; yea, it is God himself,
united and conjoined to us by this vision and fruition : Gen. xv. 1, ' I
am thy shield, and thy exceeding great reward.'   Now no works of
men can bear a proportion to such a reward.   This argument seems of
such weight that Vasquez denies this uncreated reward to fall *sub
condignis meritis Christi*, to be deserved even by Christ's obedience.
But that is false, for the obedience of Christ is of infinite value.   Well
then, a reward it is, because it is a consequent of labour—*Posito opere
recte colligimus certitudinem secuturæ mercedis ;* by the gracious constitution and ordination of God, who hath appointed that our good
works should have such an issue and event.   Again, a reward it is
called, because it is not given till our work be ended : 2 Tim. iv. 7, 8,
' I have fought a good fight, I have finished my course, I have kept
the faith. Henceforth there is laid up for me a crown of righteousness,
which the Lord, the righteous judge, shall give me at that day.'   When
we have done our work, then we shall receive our wages.   Again,
reward it is called to note the sureness of it.   God in condescension
calleth it a reward.   We may expect it as a labourer doth his hire at
night, for the Lord hath made himself a debtor by his own promise :
James i. 12, ' He shall receive the crown of life which the Lord hath
promised to them that love him.'

4. This reward is principally in the next life.   That suits with
Enoch's instance, his translation to heaven, to a place of blessedness ;
and that is called κατ' ἐξοχὴν, the reward in scripture : 1 Cor. iii. 14,
' If any man's work abide which he hath built thereupon, he shall
receive a reward ;' Rev. xi. 18, ' The time is come that thou shouldst
give reward unto thy servants the prophets.'   Now is the time of God's
patience, and hereafter of his recompenses.   Now is the time of our
exercise and service, hereafter of our enjoyment.   Alas ! all that we
have here, it is not our wages, it is but our vales, the overplus and
additional supply that God gives in upon the better portion that we
expect from him : as Mat. vi. 33, ' All other things shall be added
unto you.'   Other things are cast in over and above the bargain.   A
christian does not count this his reward ; he does not give God a discharge, though God should bless him with comfort and with increase in
this life, that is the spirit of an hypocrite to give God his acquittance
for other things. So it is said of the hypocrites, ἀπέχουσι μισθὸν—' They
have their reward,' Mat. vi. 2.   The word signifies they give God their
discharge.   A man loseth nothing by God in the world ; God may
cast in outward things to commend our portion, and to make it more
amiable to us, because we consist of body as well as soul, and have the
interest of both to mind ; he may add these ciphers to the figure, give

in those things as appurtenances to heaven, but it is heaven they take
for their portion.   He may increase worldly things upon them as he
thinks fit, but they that take up with this as their portion and reward,
the honours, pleasures, and treasures of this life, are bastards, not sons ;
as bastards have means to live upon, though they do not inherit.   The
scripture everywhere condemns us for fastening upon the world as our
portion : Ps. xvii. 14, ' Which have their portion in this life ; ' and
Luke xvi. 25, ' Son, remember that thou in thy lifetime receivedst thy
good things ; ' and Jer. xvii. 13, ' They that depart from me shall be
written in the earth.'   Oh, to be condemned to this happiness is the
greatest misery, to expect nothing else but this ; therefore we must
protest against this kind of reward ; as Luther tells us, *Valde protestatus sum, me nolle sic a Deo satiari*,—I earnestly protested to God
that he should not put me off with gold, riches, and the transitory things
of the present life.   We that are heirs according to the hope of eternal
life expect better things in a better state, or else God would not answer
the magnificent expressions wherein he hath spoken to us in his covenant.   He hath told us, I will be your God, and that he himself, and
all that is his, shall be ours.   Certainly the magnificence of this expression is not verified and made good unless he hath better things to
bestow upon us than what this world yields.   Therefore the apostle
tells us : Heb. xi. 16, ' He is not ashamed to be called our God, because
he hath provided for us a city.'   Now that God hath a city and a
heavenly inheritance to bestow upon us, he may with honour take that
title upon himself to be the God of his people.   Neither would it answer
the desires of his people, who look after a more perfect enjoyment of
God than this life will permit.   Therefore whatever here we have in
temporal things, and what we have in spiritual things, it is not our
reward.   These are magnificent, as remission of sins, adoption, righteousness, grace, peace of conscience, joy in the Holy Ghost ; these are
but the beginnings and presignifications of a more blessed estate, these
are but the suburbs of heaven ; our advance-money before our pay comes ;
but our great reward is hereafter.   Certainly it cannot be otherwise if
you consider the being of God as infinite and eternal ; God will give
like himself.   As it was said of Araunah, 2 Sam. xxiii. 24, ' All these
things did Araunah as a king give to the king '—he was of the blood-
royal of the Jebusites, and he carried it becoming his extraction ; so
there will be a time when God will give like himself.   It does not
become a mighty emperor to give pence and shillings, or brass farthings,
it is below his greatness ; so there will come a time when the Lord, as
he is an infinite and eternal being, will give us ' a far more exceeding
and eternal weight of glory,' 2 Cor. iv 17.   Now it is very little God
discovereth.   God doth communicate and discover himself to the
rational creature as he is able to bear ; Job xxvi. 14, ' Lo, these are
part of his ways ; but how little a portion is heard of him ! '   There
is a time coming when the Lord will communicate himself to reasonable creatures in a fuller latitude than now he doth ; therefore there
is a more exceeding weight of glory we expect from him.   Again, if
you consider the largeness of Christ's merit and condescension.   No
wise man will lay a broad foundation unless he means to build an
answerable structure thereupon.   Well then, when God hath laid such
a notable foundation as the blood of Christ, the death of the Son of

God, I say, certainly he hath some notable worthy blessing to bestow upon us. There was price enough laid down, the blood of God; God would not be at such expense for nothing. What will not that purchase for us? In short, godliness must have a better recompense than is to be had here in the world. Take away rewards and take away religion, these things we enjoy here are but the offals of providence, enjoyed by God's enemies; they have the greatest share of worldly things: Ps. xvii. 14, 'Whose belly thou fillest with thy good treasures.' The more wise any are, the more they contemn these things. And would God put a spirit into a man to contemn his rewards? Would he give us wisdom and grace that we might slight that which he hath appointed for our reward? Therefore certainly this is not the reward.

The afflictions of men good and upright show that 'if we had our hopes only in this life, we were of all men most miserable,' 1 Cor. xv. 19; for here many times the best go to the wall. And therefore out of all we may conclude that there is a reward for the children of God hereafter. Thus I have gone through the first thing that is implied in this proposition, that that is to be believed and embraced by us. If we would have life put into our services— if we would have zeal for God, and delight in communion with him, look upon God as one that takes notice of human affairs, that delights in acts of mercy, that hath by his promise established a sure course of recompenses, and that the full of what is provided for us is in the world to come.

Secondly, There is something to be done on our part. God is a rewarder, but to whom?—'To them that diligently seek him,' and to none but them. Here—(1.) What it is diligently to seek God? (2.) Why is this clause put here, that he is a rewarder of such?

1. What it is to seek God? Sometimes it is taken in a more particular and limited sense for prayer and invocation, for seeking his counsel, help, and blessing; as in Isa. lv. 6, 'Seek ye the Lord while he may be found; call ye upon him while he is near.' Seeking the Lord and calling upon him are made parallel expressions. So Exod. xxxiii. 7, 'Every one that sought the Lord,'—that is, that went to ask his counsel,—'went out unto the tabernacle of the congregation.' 'More largely, it is taken for the whole worship of God, and that duty and obedience we owe to him; as 2 Chron. xiv. 4, 'Asa commanded Judah to seek the Lord God of their fathers, and to do the law and the commandment;' that is, to worship and obey him; so in 2 Chron. xxxiv. 3, it is said of Josiah when yet young, that 'he began to seek after the Lord God of his father David.' Obedience is called a seeking of God, because it is a means to further our communion with him. But a little to open the formality of the expression.

[1.] Seeking implies some loss or some want, for that which we have we seek not for. Now God may be considered either as to his essence and omnipresence, or as to his favour. As to his essence, so God can never be lost nor found, for he is everywhere present, in heaven, in earth, in hell: Acts xvii. 27, 'He is not far from every one of us;' he is within us, without us, round about us, in the effects of his power and goodness. But with respect to his favour and grace, so we are said to seek after God: Ps. cv. 4, 'Seek the Lord and his strength, seek his face evermore;' that is, his powerful and favourable presence, comforting, quickening, and strengthening our hearts. This is that we want, and this is that we seek after.

[2.] Seeking implies that this must be our aim and scope, and the business of our lives and actions, to enjoy more of God till we come fully to enjoy him in heaven. The whole course of a christian must be a seeking after God, a getting more of God into his heart: Ps. lxiii. 8, 'My soul follows hard after thee.' It is not a slight motion or a cold wish, such as will easily be put off or blunted with discouragement, or satisfied with other things; but such as engages us to an earnest pursuit of him till we find him, and till we enjoy him in the completest way of fruition. Wicked men in a pang would have the favour of God, but they are soon put out of the humour, and take up with other things. Therefore this must be the scope of our whole lives, especially in the nobler actions of our lives. The noblest actions of our lives are our engaging in duties of worship in the ordinances of God ; now there we must not only serve God but seek him. What is it to seek God in ordinances ? In a word, it is this to make God not only the object, but the end of the worship ; not only to come to God, but to come to God for God, so as to resolve that we will not go from him without him, *abs te absque te non recedam.* As Jacob said: Gen. xxxii. 26, 'I will not let thee go, except thou bless me.' And therefore seeking God notes our scope ; when we make this the great aim of our lives, especially in the duties of religion, in acts of worship, we desire to meet with him.

[3.] It implies a seeking of him in Christ. For without a mediator guilty creatures cannot enjoy God. We cannot immediately converse with God, there must be a mediator between God and us : John xiv. 6, 'I am the way, the truth, and the life; no man cometh to the Father but by me.' There is no getting to God but by Christ. God in our nature is more familiar with us, and more especially found of us: Hos. iii. 5, 'They shall seek the Lord their God and David their king,' that is, Christ. There is no seeking or finding of God but in and by Christ. Saith Luther, *Horribile est de Deo extra Christum cogitare*—It is a terrible thing to think of God out of Christ. As Themistocles, when he sought the favour of Admetus, which had been formerly his enemy, the historian tells us he snatched up his child, and so begged entertainment of him. We are enemies to God ; if we go to him we must carry Christ with us. It is Christ's great work to bring us to God. He died for 'that end, that he might bring us to God,' 1 Peter iii. 18 ; and it is the great duty of a christian ; he ought to come to God by him—'He is able to save them to the uttermost that come unto God by him.' Heb. vii. 25. And therefore since we have lost the favour of God, we shall never find him but in Christ.

[4.] This seeking is stirred up in us by the secret impressions of God's grace, and the help of his Spirit. All the persons are concerned in it, 'For through him we have an access to the Father by one Spirit,' Eph. ii. 18. Natural men are well enough pleased without God or they have but faint desires after him. Take men as they are in themselves, and the psalmist tells us, Ps. xiv. 2, 'No man understandeth and seeketh after God;' they have no affection, no desire of communion with him. So Ps. x. 4, 'The wicked, through the pride of his counte-

nance, will not seek after God; God is not in all their thoughts.'
Wicked men cast God out of their minds, never care whether he be
pleased or displeased, whether he be enjoyed or hide himself from us.
Ay, but the Spirit of God works this work in us. How so? The
spirit of bondage brings us to God as a judge; God as a judge sends
us to Christ as mediator; and Christ as mediator, by the spirit of
adoption, brings us back to God again as a father; and so we come to
enjoy God. The divine persons make way for the operations of one another. Saith Bernard, *Nemo te quærere potest, nisi qui prius invenerit;
tu igitur invenire ut quæraris, quære ut inveniaris, potest quidem in-
veniri, non tamen præveniri*—None can be beforehand with God; we
cannot seek him till we find him; he will be found that he may be
sought, and he will be sought that he may be found; his preventing
grace makes us restless in the means, and puts us upon those first
motions and earnest addresses towards God.

SERMON XXXIV.

And that he is a rewarder of them that diligently seek him. —
HEB. xi. 6.

[5.] THIS seeking must be our ἔργον, our business, as well as our scope; a
thing that we would not mind by the by, but as the great work we are
to do in our lives here in the world: Deut. iv. 29, 'Thou shalt find
him if thou seek him with all thy heart and with all thy soul;' and
Jer. xxix. 13, 'Ye shall seek me and find me, when ye shall search for
me with all your heart;' and 2 Chron. xv. 15, 'They sought him with
all their hearts, and their whole desire, and he was found of them.
Many are convinced that they cannot be happy without the favour of
God; their consciences tell them they must seek after God, but their
affections carry them to the world. Oh, but when your whole hearts
are in this, when you make it your great business, then shall you find
him. If you content yourselves to look after God by the by only, and
as a recreation, and with a few slight endeavours, and do not make
this the great employment of your lives, you will never find him.
Certainly we were made for God, it was the end of our creation; therefore this must be the business of your lives. God made us for himself,
and we can never be happy without himself. And as it was the end
of our creation, so it is the end of his gracious forbearance and indulgence in the course of his providence. Wherefore doth God forbear with
sinning man, when he punished the apostate angels presently?—'That
they might seek the Lord, if haply they might feel after him and
find him,' Acts xvii. 27. We do not live to live, but we live to seek
God. When we had lost God by Adam's apostasy, God might have
cut off all hope that ever we should find him again; as the angels,
when they lost their chiefest good, could never recover their first estate.
But it is God's indulgence to deal with us upon more gracious terms,

that we might seek after him. God needed not seek the creatures, he had happiness enough in himself; but we needed such a creator. He that hides himself from the sun impairs not the light thereof. We derogate nothing from God, but it is a loss of benefit to us that we seek him not, for the present and for the future. If you seek him, you shall be happy for the present; for the God of Jacob hath pawned his word to you that none shall seek him in vain:' Isa. xlv. 19, ' I said not to the seed of Jacob, Seek ye me in vain; and Ps. xxii. 26, ' They shall praise the Lord that seek him.' You will have cause to bless God ere the search be over. And for the future: Amos v. 6, ' Seek the Lord, and ye shall live well then.' Here is the great work and business of your lives, diligently to seek after God. Though it may be at first you do not find him, yet comfort thyself that thou art in the seeking way, still in pursuit of him. Better be a seeker than a wanderer: Ps. xxiv. 6, ' This is the generation of them that seek him, that seek thy face, O Jacob.' Though thou dost not presently feel the love of God, and hast no assurance of thy pardon, nor sensible comfort from his Spirit, yet continue seeking; here is your business, here is your work.

2. Why is this put here, ' He that cometh to God must believe that he is a rewarder of them that diligently seek him '? (1.) It is put exclusively. Privileges in scripture are propounded with their necessary limitation ; we disjoint the frame of religion, if we would sever the reward from the duty. God is a rewarder, but to whom ? To the careless, to the negligent? Oh, no! he will be an avenger to them : Ps. ix. 17, ' The wicked shall be turned into hell, and all the nations that forget God ;' not only they that deny God, but they that forget God, that do not seek after him. As they cast God out of their mind and affections, so God will cast them out of his presence. (2.) It is put inclusively : God will impartially reward every one that seeks him, without any distinction. The door of grace stands open for all comers. Every one that seeketh God finds entertainment, not only in regard of the answers of grace for the present, but as to eternal recompenses hereafter.

[1.] For the present. Oh, do not conceive of God after a carnal manner! It was the corrupt theology of the gentiles, *Dii magna curant, parva negligunt,* that the gods did look after great things, but small and petty things they left to others, as if the great God did act according to the advice of Jethro to Moses: Exod. xviii. 21, 22, ' Thou shalt appoint rulers of thousands, hundreds, and fifties, and tens, and let them judge the people at all seasons : and it shall be, that every great matter they shall bring unto thee, but every small matter they shall judge.' But the Lord's providence here in the world extends to every one that seeketh him, and he hearkens to the prayers of the poorest beggar as well as the greatest monarch ; persons despicable in the world may find audience and acceptance with God: Ps. xxxiv. 6, ' This poor man cried, and the Lord heard him ;' David speaks it of himself, when he was a ruddy youth following the ewes great with young. There is none among the sons of men that hath cause to say as Isa. xl. 27, ' My way is hid from the Lord, and my judgment is passed over from my God ;' that is, God hath so much to do in the world that he forgets me, he doth not mind my case ; for the Lord hath a providence.

[2.] Hereafter they will find in him a rewarder. There is none so poor but he will find God makes good his promise. There is a notable expression, Eph. vi. 8, 'Knowing that whatsoever good thing any man doth, the same shall he receive of the Lord, whether he be bond or free.' He speaks to encourage servants (who at that time were slaves) in singleness of heart to go about their duty. Even the basest drudgery of servants is a doing good, and comes within the compass of those good works which God will take notice of. God does not look to the external splendour of the work but to the honesty and sincerity of it, though it be of a poor drudge and slave that is faithful in his calling. Nay, God will rather forget princes, lords, and mighty men of the earth, vain and sinful potentates, than pass by a poor servant that fears him. You find that God gave the angels charge over Lazarus' soul, Luke xvi. 22, 'The beggar died, and was carried by the angels into Abraham's bosom.' The beggar's soul is thus conducted in state to heaven. Whoever seeks him will be sure to find him a rewarder.

Secondly, I come to the nature of this faith. You have seen the thing that is to be believed; but how is it to be believed?

1. It must be a firm and certain persuasion. The reward is sure on God's part. Men may be ignorant, forgetful, unthankful, as Pharaoh's butler forgat Joseph, Gen. xl. 23; but the Lord is righteous, and will not forget your labour of love: Prov. xi. 18, 'To him that soweth righteousness shall be a sure reward.' It may be the work you do for God is like ploughing or sowing, difficult and hard work, but we are sure of an excellent crop. When we feel nothing but trouble and inconvenience, sense will make lies of God, and we are apt to say, 'I have cleansed my heart in vain,' Ps. lxxiii. 13. But the Lord will not forget this service you do for him. Under the law God would not have the hireling defrauded of his wages because he hath lifted up his soul to it. The man comforted himself with this thought: he should have his recompense at night. So when thou hast lifted up thy soul to look for those great things promised, God looks upon himself as bound; therefore this must be entertained with a strong faith, and without doubting. We read in scripture of a threefold assurance; an 'assurance of understanding,' Col. ii. 2; an 'assurance of faith,' Heb. x. 22; and an 'assurance of hope,' Heb. vi. 11. All this represents the firmness of that assent by which we should receive the promises.

2. It must not be a naked assent, but a lively and operative faith, urging and encouraging us to seek after God upon those hopes. There are many that are able to dispute for the truth of the rewards of religion, but yet do not feel the virtue of them. This is not enough, to have notions and opinions that God is a rewarder, but we must have a lively operative faith: Phil. iii. 14, 'I press toward the mark for the prize of the high calling of God in Jesus Christ.' That is a due apprehension of the reward, when we are engaged thereby to the duties which the reward calls for: Heb. xi. 13, 'They were persuaded of them, and embraced them;' when it ravishes the affections and engageth the heart; when it keeps us from fainting under the cross, 2 Cor. iv. 16; when it abates the eagerness of our pursuit after worldly things; when we are more contented with a little here, because we are persuaded we shall have enough with God. A rich man that

hath a vast inheritance of his own, to see him among the poor that glean up the ears of corn that were scattered, this were an uncomely thing. Oh! do we look for so great blessedness, and are we scraping so much in the world, — ' We that are begotten to a lively hope'? 1 Peter i. 3. Such a faith produceth sobriety and moderation to worldly things; 1 Peter i. 13, ' Be sober, and hope to the end for the grace that is to be brought unto you at the revelation of Jesus Christ.' In short, we that look for such things should give diligence to be found of him; and what manner of persons ought we to be? ' 2 Peter iii. 11. If it be not a dead and a naked opinion only, to dispute about the rewards of religion, but a well-grounded confidence, it will quicken our endeavours, moderate our desires, allay the bitterness of the cross, and help us on in the way to heaven.

3. It is an applicative faith. We must believe God is not only a rewarder, but say with Paul, This he will be to me; for so we have the expression, 2 Tim. iv. 8, ' Henceforth there is laid up for me a crown of righteousness,' &c.; this is proposed and made over to me for my comfort and my quickening. Salvation in general hath no such an efficacy: 1 Cor. ix. 26, ' I run, not as uncertain.' In the Isthmic games, to which the apostle alludes, held near Corinth, a man might run, but he was not certain whether he should have the goal or no; but I run not as uncertain, as one that hath the prize in view, and am comfortably assured I shall obtain it. This quickeneth us to a comfortable, willing industry.

Thirdly, The influence that it hath upon our obedience and service to God.

1. To keep the heart free and ingenuous. We are apt to look upon God as a Pharaoh, harsh and austere, as if he had required work where he will not give wages. But think of his mercy and kindness, and readiness to reward the services of his people, that you may come to him with an ingenuous confidence. Our obligations to God are absolute; we are bound to serve him, though nothing should come of it. Ay, but he is pleased to move us by rewards, ' to draw us with the cords of a man, and with the bands of love,' Hos. xi. 4. When he might rule us with a rod of iron, and require duty out of mere power and sovereignty, he will govern us rationally, by precepts and rewards. Men do not use to enter into covenant with a slave, yet God is pleased to indent with us; he would have us to look upon him as a rewarder. In all our services we are to remember that God is, that we may be aweful; and ' he is a rewarder,' that we may be ingenuous.

2. To keep the heart sincere and upright. Oh, there is nothing makes the heart so sincere as to make God our paymaster, and to look for our reward from him only. Carnal affections will draw us to seek praise and honour of men, some present profit, some reward here: Mat. vi. 2, ' They have their reward,' and give God a discharge; but a man's sincerity is to look for all his reward from God: Col. iii. 23, ' Knowing that of the Lord ye shall receive the reward of the inheritance.' You have a master good enough, and need not look for your pay elsewhere.

3. To quicken us in our duty, and make us vigorous and cheerful and diligent in our service: 1 Cor xv. 58, ' Therefore, my beloved brethren, be ye stedfast, unmovable, always abounding in the work of

the Lord, forasmuch as you know that your labour shall not be in vain in the Lord.' Idols can do nothing for their worshippers ; these will deceive you, but God will not be served for nought; your duty that you do to him will return into your bosoms, and will bring a blessing ; not like a ball struck into the air, that returns not again to you, but like a ball struck against a wall, that returns to your hand again. Let us who are bred up in the belief of this principle, bless God—

[1.] That there is a reward. He might have cut off all hopes and left us under the despair of the first covenant, and then our guilty fears would represent God under no other notion but that of an avenger ; and our punishment might have begun with our sin, as the fallen angels were held in chains of darkness, under an everlasting horrible despair of mending their condition. When once we had lost God, we might never have found him more; his language to the fallen creature might have been only thunder and wrath. Or if he would quit us from what is past, and release our punishment for the future, he might only have ruled us with a rod of iron, and imposed laws upon us out of mere sovereignity, and say, Thus and thus shall ye do, 'I am the Lord;' or, at least, have held us in bondage, and suspended the pub-lication of a new and better covenant, and kept it in his own breast, that we might wholly stand to his arbitrary will, whether he would reward—yea, or no. Thus the Lord might have done with us ; but he will rather draw us by the cords of a man, hold us to our duty by the sense of our own interest, and give us leave to encourage ourselves with the thoughts of his bounty. There are many in the world that think it unsafe to use God's motives, and destroy his grace, for which we have cause to bless God. They say, God is to be worshipped, though we had no benefit by him, merely for the excellency of his being; but this is but a fancy and an airy religion ; to abstract religion from re-wards is to frame a religion in conceit. The two first notions of God are his being and his bounty, and we must reflect upon both. It is a description of the people of God, Rom. ii. 7, 'That by patient con-tinuance in well doing, they seek for honour, and glory, and immor-tality.' We may seek honour from God ; and a great part of our sin-cerity lies in this, to make God our paymaster ; and therefore let us bless God that there is a reward.

[2.] That there is so great a reward : Mat. v. 12, 'Rejoice and be exceeding glad, for great is your reward in heaven'—such as we may admire rather than conceive ; and 2 Cor. iv. 17, 'Our light affliction, that is but for a moment, worketh for us—καθ' ὑπερβολὴν εἰς ὑπερβολὴν, —a far more exceeding and eternal weight of glory.' Heaven will not admit of a hyperbole. In other things, fancy may easily overreach, the garment may be too big for the body; but all our thoughts come short of heaven. God himself will be our reward : Gen. xv. 1, 'Fear not, Abraham ; I am thy shield, and thy exceeding great reward.' When he would encourage us to well-doing, he goes to the utmost; he hath no greater encouragement to propound to us. As the apostle said, Heb. vi. 13, 'When God made promise to Abraham, be-cause he could swear by no greater, he sware by himself.' God hath no greater thing to give us, and therefore saith, 'I will be your reward;' though he does not for the present make out himself in that latitude to us, that he will hereafter when God is all in all. There is enough to counterbalance all the inconveniences of religion ; when you sit down and count the charges, you will be no losers. The difficulties of obedience, the sorrows of the cross, shall all be made up to you in this reward ; and therefore let not your hearts be faint, nor your hands shake, but ' Press on toward the mark for the prize of the high calling of God in Christ Jesus,' Phil. iii. 14. If it be a painful race, remember what is the crown; we run for the everlasting enjoyment of the blessed God. As we christians' have the noblest work, so we have the highest motives ; there is a reward, and a great reward.

[3.] That this reward is so freely dispensed, and upon terms of grace—χάρισμα—' The grace of God is eternal life,' Rom. vi. 23. Such are the riches of his grace to lost sinners, that we can hardly believe, especially with application, what is told us of this readiness of God to do good to the creature, and to reward our slender services. But then how should this encourage us to draw nigh to the fountain of rich grace, for pardon, life, and glory, when so much is so freely prepared for such unworthy ones: Ps. xxxvi. 7, ' How excellent is thy loving-kindness, O God ! therefore the children of men put their trust under the shadow of thy wings.'

[4.] That all this is made known to us, and that we are not left to uncertain guesses and conjectures. The heathens were sensible of the recompenses of another world ; they had some dreams of elysian fields, and fancies about noisome rivers, and obscure grottoes, and dismal caverns in the earth, as places of punishment ; but they knew not whether this were a fable or a certain truth. As men that see a spire at a distance in travelling ; sometimes they have a sight of it, and sometimes they have lost it, and cannot tell whether they saw it or no. Thus it was with the heathens: saith Lactantius—*Virtutis vim non sentiunt, cujus præmium ignorant*—they were ignorant of the power of godliness, because they knew not the rewards of godliness. But all is clear and open to us, and established upon certain terms : 2 Tim. i. 10, ' Jesus Christ hath brought life and immortality to light by the gospel.' Well then, if these be the thoughts that enliven all our duties, how clearly may we take God under these notions—' That God is, and that he is a rewarder.'

[5.] That it is so surely made known unto us. God foresaw that in this lower world, where God is unseen, where our trials are so great, where our hopes are to come, where the flesh is so importunate to be pleased and gratified with present satisfactions, God foresaw, I say, that we would be liable to much doubting and unbelief ; and therefore he hath not only passed his word that there shall be a reward, but hath given us a pawn and earnest of it in our heart, to assure us of it: 2 Cor. i. 22, ' Who hath also sealed us, and given the earnest of the Spirit in our hearts.' The comforts that we have in well-doing in this world are not only *dona*, gifts of God, but *arrha*, an assurance that God will give us more ; they are a taste how good, and a pledge how sure our reward shall be.

[6.] That we have hopes and encouragements to put in for a share, and come and take hold of eternal life upon these terms ; that we cannot only say in general, 'God is a rewarder,' but he will be so 'to me,' 2 Tim. iv. 8, 'Henceforth is laid up for me a crown of glory.' This was not peculiar to Paul only, for he saith—'And not only for me, but for all that love his appearing.' All those that do believe the rewards of the christian religion, and act upon this encouragement, and serve God faithfully, all that prepare for it, may say, 'For me,' there is a crown of life ; this I expect from God's hand. Oh, then blessed be his name that hath given us 'so good hope through grace,' 2 Thes. ii. 16. That is cause of rejoicing and thanksgiving indeed : Luke x. 20, 'Rejoice that your names are written in heaven.' When we can see our names in Christ's testament, look upon ourselves as concerned in this reward, that we have a title to it ; or if we have not a title, the door is open, the promise is sure, the way is plain, the helps are many, and we may have a title if we will. And therefore let us bless God that there is a reward, a great reward, a reward so freely dispensed, and this made known and assured to us by the joys of the Spirit, and that we have hopes and encouragement to go on in well-doing upon this ground.

Use 2. If God be a rewarder of them that diligently seek him, then here is a reproof, because so few seek after God. Paul charges it upon all natural men : Rom. iii. 11, 'There is none that seeketh after the Lord ;' we all at first go wandering after our own fancies, and never think of returning to God, as our chief good, till we have tried ourselves with a thousand disappointments, and are scourged home to him ; yea, it were well if we would seek him at the last or were brought to God upon any terms. But, alas ! some seek him not at all ; others do not seek him diligently, but in a slight and overly fashion.

1. Some do not seek him at all. Alas ! there are many that run away from God, and are never better than when they can get out of his eye and presence—'God is not in all their thoughts,' Ps. x. 4. As the prodigal went from his father into a far country, so a carnal man is ever running from God. He runs from his own conscience, and cannot endure to commune and hold a little parley with his own heart, because he finds God there. He shuns the presence of holy men, because they have God's image—they put him in mind of God ; slights the ordinances of worship, lest they revive a sense of God in his heart, and he meet with God in them. The word brings God too near him, and awakens his fears. Prayer he slights, because it engageth him to speak to God. He shuns the thoughts of death, because then the spirit must return to God that gave it. If the Holy Ghost stirs up any thoughts of God in his heart, he will not cherish them ; he abhors his own thoughts of God, and is ready to say as Satan, Mat. viii. 29, 'What have we to do with thee, Jesus, thou Son of God? Art thou come hither to torment us before the time?' Thoughts of God and Christ and heavenly things are a torment to him.

2. There are others that do not seek him diligently, and with their whole hearts. Oh, to what a sorry use do the most of us put our lives ! We are hunting after the profits of the world and the pleasures of our senses, but we do not inquire after God. Most of us have cause to blush and to be ashamed,—How little is our delight in God? how

seldom do we think or speak of him? how cold is our affections to him? how dead and careless are our prayers that we make?—our thoughts are taken up with trifles, and God finds no room there. If any speak of God in our company, or mention his great love to sinners, we frown upon the motion, and think it unseasonable for those meetings and hours that we have consecrated to mirth and carnal sports, as if our thoughts of God were like gall and wormwood to embitter the pleasure we affect. We had rather have anything than God, his gifts than himself, yea, the worser sort of them, than his favour and grace; and then we offend him, we do not take such care to please him, and reconcile ourselves to him by the means he hath appointed. They that do indeed love God, and seek after God, they are with him morning, noon, and night; nay, they do carry God along with them in all their businesses and occasions: Ps. xvi. 8, 'I have set the Lord always before me;' and Ps. cxxxix. 18, 'When I awake, I am still with thee.' We that seldom think or speak of God, do we seek after God? surely no.

Use 3. To exhort us to seek God, and to seek him out till we find him.

1. To seek God. Motives—

[1.] To enjoy God, who is the centre of our rest, and the fountain of our blessedness, is the chief end for which we were made. Man was made to use the creatures, and to enjoy God. All things were made to glorify God, but some creatures to enjoy him, as men and angels. We sin against the law of our creation, and swerve from the great end of our lives and actions, if this be not all our hope and all our desire: Ps. lxxiii. 25, 'Whom have I in heaven but thee? and there is none on earth that I desire besides thee.' Nothing but God can make us happy.

[2.] It is our business to seek him, as well as our happiness to enjoy him. Since the fall, God is lost, and out of the indulgence of his grace offereth himself to be found again, and inviteth us to communion with himself, that we may have everlasting blessedness: Amos v. 5, 'Seek ye the Lord, and ye shall live.' Now, for us to despise this grace and turn our backs upon this offer, not to regard it in our thoughts, not to pursue it with earnest endeavours, it is a slighting of God's mercy: Ps. lxxxi, 11, 'But my people would not hearken to my voice; and Israel would none of me.' He offereth himself, and we make little reckoning of it.

[3.] Because we are sluggish and backward, all external providences tend to quicken us to this duty. Mercies: Acts xvii. 27, 'That they should seek the Lord, if haply they might feel after him, and find him.' God refresheth our sense and taste with his goodness—with new experiences every day, that set us a-work anew in seeking after him. Afflictions: Hos. v. 15, 'I will go, and return to my place, till they acknowledge their offence, and seek my face: in their affliction they will seek me early.' This is the right use of all our troubles to drive us home to God, to quicken us to look after communion with him, and to make up our former negligence with double diligence herein, to set an edge upon our affections. God knows want is a spur to a lazy soul.

[4.] All ordinances are appointed for this end and purpose, that we might seek after God and find him : Exod. xx. 24, 'In all places where I record my name I will come unto thee, and I will bless thee;' Mat. xviii. 20, ' Where two or three are gathered together in my name, there am I in the midst of them ; ' there he cometh most sensibly to manifest himself to us ; Rev. ii. 1, 'These things saith he that holdeth the seven stars in his right hand, that walketh in the midst of the seven golden candlesticks.' His special presence is in his church. If we find him not in the time we seek him, we shall soon after : 2 Sam. vii. 4, ' And it came to pass that night, that the word of the Lord came unto Nathan ; ' Cant. v. 5, ' I rose up to open to my beloved, and my hands dropped with myrrh, and my fingers with sweet-smelling myrrh upon the handles of the lock ; ' some impression was left that worketh afterward.

[5.] It is the end of the Spirit's motion : Ps. xxvii. 8, ' When thou saidst, Seek ye my face ; my heart said unto thee, Thy face, Lord, will I seek.' God speaks to us by the injection of holy thoughts and the inspiration of his grace, and we should, like a quick echo, take hold of this.

[6.] Let me press you, because all the pretences that keep you from seeking God are in vain ; as (1.) That there is no need of seeking God ; or (2.) That it is in vain to seek God.

(1.) That there is no need of seeking God. We should always be seeking of God, till our loss by the fall be fully made up in heaven ; we should still seek God, till we enjoy him among his holy ones. We seek God on earth, but we find him in heaven : Ps. cv. 4, ' Seek the Lord, and his strength, seek his face evermore.' We need him every hour for direction, protection, strength, and comfort ; we are in danger to lose him, if we do not continue the search : all the while we are in the world this work must be plied close.

(2.) As the devil saith to the secure, There is no need ; so to the fearful and troubled sinner, that it is in vain to seek God, especially when former endeavours succeed not—there is no hope for him. Oh, but seek him ! the God of Jacob hath not said, ' Seek ye me in vain,' Isa. xlv. 19. He hath engaged himself plainly, openly, and perspicuously, not in obscure and ambiguous terms, such as may bear contrary senses, that their fraud and ignorance may not be discerned ; and he performeth what he promised : Ps. xxii. 26, ' They shall praise the Lord that seek him : your heart shall live for ever.' *Neminem tristem dimisit,* He never sent any away sad, but will comfort them. Wisdom is light and knowledge to the soul : Prov. xxviii. 5, ' They that seek the Lord understand all things'—the meaning of all his providences. And it is comfort to the soul ; Ps. lxix. 32, ' Your heart shall live that seek God ;' and protection, Ezra viii. 22, ' The hand of our God is upon all them for good that seek him, but his power and his wrath is against all them that forsake him.' So that we shall have cause to praise God before the search be over : Mat. vi. 33, ' Seek ye first the kingdom of God and the righteousness thereof, and all these things shall be added to you.' But besides this, if there were nothing in hand, there is much in hope ; it bringeth an everlasting reward : Amos v. 6, ' Seek ye the Lord and ye shall live ; ' and in the text, ' He is a rewarder of them that diligently seek him.' They that do not seek his face shall never see his face ;

however, if we do not sensibly find him, yet we may comfort ourselves, that we are in a seeking way, and still in the pursuit: Ps. xxiv. 6, 'This is the generation of them that seek him, that seek thy face, O Jacob. Selah.' This is the mark of God's chosen people, and we should be still wrestling through disappointments. Better be a seeker than a wanderer. But the wicked are described by this— that 'They are all gone out of the way,' Ps. xiv. 3.

2. For the manner—seek him out.

[1.] Seek him early, whilst you have strength to serve him, and whilst you have means to find him. This is a work that must not be put off: Isa. lv. 6, 'Seek ye the Lord, while he may be found, call ye upon him while he is near.' God will not always put up with your frequent denials. There is a time when God will be gone, and seeking will be to no purpose: compare Prov. i. 28, 'Then shall they call upon me, but I will not answer; they shall seek me early, but they shall not find me;' with chap. viii. 17, 'I love them that love me; and they that seek me early shall find me.' There is a seeking out of self-love, and a seeking out of love to God. When death cometh and their day is past, many at last may seek God; and their straits may drive them to him, who were never put to it by any sense of sin. While hot and eager in sinning, they are not sensible of it; as Samson knew not that God was withdrawn while he slept in Delilah's bosom, till he knew the Philistines were upon him; and then it was too late. The greatest contemners and despisers of God do at last see that there is no happiness but in God; but then miss the blessing, as Esau did, though he sought it with tears. Therefore will you despise grace to the uttermost, and weary it out to the last gasp? It may be by thy lamentations on thy death-bed, God will learn others to take heed of trifling with him. Oh then, if they could but call time back again! What, Lord! not give me one hour, or one day more? There is no place without examples of this kind, of those that lament their time is out and opportunities lost, when God hath offered grace to them. Some instances there are, whom God sets forth to be terrors to the secure world, who are as good as men risen from the dead, to tell others of the vanity of their sinful courses; who, looking upon time past, see it is irrecoverably lost, and gone away as a dream and a shadow. Upon time present they feel their souls naked, their accounts not made up, an end come to all their hopes and comforts here; body sick, conscience trembling, heart hard, God departed, and the grave opened for their filthy carcases, and devils waiting for their secure souls, and for time to come think of nothing but hell and horror and judgment to come; and so they lie complaining, that they had not improved their time. But much time is lost, wishing others to take warning by them, and saying to them, Oh, do not cast away mercy, nor let the precious blood of Christ, which is worthy to be gathered up by angels, run a wasting; now I see the end of my joys, and the beginning of my torments! Oh, then, seek God out of love to God: 1 Peter iv. 3, 'For the time past of our lives may suffice us, to have wrought the will of the gentiles;' Hos. x. 12, 'For it is time to seek the Lord.' Misspent time in neglecting or refusing to seek the Lord ought to be redeemed, and will be so in all that are sensible of their own case. When God maketh an offer, we should be so far from delaying or putting off our

seeking after him, that we should look back upon the time already
spent out of communion with God as very long, too long for the good
of our souls.   It should be a grief of heart to us to think of pleasing
the flesh, or living in a state of estrangement any longer.   Otherwise,
we do in effect say, We have not taken time enough to dishonour God
and destroy our own souls : Luke xiii. 25, 'When once the master of
the house is risen up, and hath shut to the door and ye begin to stand
without, and to knock at the door, saying, Lord, Lord, open to us ;
he shall answer and say unto you, I know ye not, whence ye are ;'
John vii. 34, 'Ye shall seek me, and shall not find me.'   Most men
think Christ a thorn in their side, and that it will never be well till he
be gone ; but then they shall seek him, and shall not find him, though
they would have him.   Though they put away Christ and his truth,
yet in ensuing calamities they as earnestly beg for their Messias.   So
Hos. v. 6, 'They shall go with their flocks and with their herds to seek
the Lord ; but they shall not find him ; he hath withdrawn himself
from them.'   Men contemn the offered grace.   The foolish virgins
sought when it was too late : Mat. xxv. 11, 'Lord, Lord, open to us.'
Therefore early, while God stretcheth out his arms, let us not receive
his grace in vain.

[2.] Seek him with all the heart, not with a double heart, or a
divided heart : James i. 8, 'A double-minded man is unstable in all
his ways ;' their hearts hang between two objects—God and the world ;
the conscience is for God, and the heart for the world : Ps. cxix 10,
'With my whole heart have I sought thee :' when the prevalency
of our affections carrieth us to God, and we seek him for himself.

[3.] Seek him earnestly.   Carnal men will now and then throw away
a prayer.   Our affections are strong for earthly things, why not for
God ?   Ps. xxvii. 4, 'One thing have I desired of the Lord, that will
I seek after ; that I may dwell in the house of the Lord all the days
of my life, to behold the beauty of the Lord, and to inquire in his temple :' this is our great business.

[4.] Seek him constantly and unweariedly ; do not give over till you
enjoy God.   You must not be discouraged with every disappointment.
When God seemeth to put us off : Luke xi. 'Because of his importunity, 8, διὰ τὴν ἀναιδειαν, he will rise and give him as many as he
needeth.'   God hideth himself many times, that we may the more
earnestly seek after him ; as Cant. iii. 1, 3, 'By night on my bed I
sought him whom my soul loveth ; I sought him but I found him not.
I will rise now, and go about the city in the streets, and in the broad-
ways, I will seek him whom my soul loveth ; I sought him, but I found
him not,' &c.   The woman of Canaan that came to Christ would not be
put off ; the lord may be hidden to influence our desires ; the children
of God are never satisfied while they are in the world : 2 Cor. v. 6,
'Whilst we are at home in the body, we are absent from the Lord :'
we cannot have complete fruition till we be where God is.

SERMON XXXV.

By faith Noah, being warned of God of things not seen as yet, moved with fear, prepared an ark to the saving of his house ; by the which he condemned the world, and became heir of the righteousness which is by faith.—HEB. xi. 7.

IN the history of faith the apostle passeth from Enoch to Noah. He is fitly subjoined as being the next person of eminency in the line of the church. Enoch was famous for walking with God, and so was Noah : Gen. vi. 9, 'Noah was a just man, and perfect in his 'generation; and Noah walked with God.' Enoch received a testimony that he pleased God, and so did Noah ; he is said, ' to find grace in the eyes of the Lord,' Gen. vi. 8. And therefore Noah is the fittest instance that could be mentioned, next to Enoch, as being the inheritor and successor of his graces and privileges Besides, the former verse spoke of the respects of faith to the rewards of religion, ver. 6, ' He is a rewarder of them that diligently seek him.' Therefore now the apostle would bring an instance of the respects of faith to the threatening and commination of the word—' By faith Noah,' &c. The person then whose faith we are now to consider is Noah, the true Janus, with a double face, looking forward and backward ; the last of the patriarchs of the old world, and the first of the new. In the commendation of his faith we may take notice of many circumstances—

1. The ground of his faith—*Noah being warned of God.*

2. The strength of it, intimated in the object—*of things not seen as yet,* or of things that by no means could be seen.

3. The consequents and the fruits of his faith, and they are four—

(1.) *He was moved with fear*, or out of a religious respect to God (so the word signifies) ; (2.) *He prepared an ark ;* (3.) *He condemned the world ;* (4.) *He became an heir of the righteousness which is by faith.* I shall open each part in this order and method proposed.

But before I discuss the parts, let me premise somewhat. That we have not only to do with a private instance and example of faith, but such as is of public use and accommodation. God's dealing with Noah, and the world in his time, was a pledge and a type of his dealing with the world in all after ages. To amplify this—

[1.] It was a pledge, or a public evident testimony of future dispensations ; this was a document God would give to the world. In the destruction of the old world he would show his displeasure against sin, and in the preservation of Noah the privileges of the godly.

(1.) The destruction of the old world was a pledge of his vengeance and recompense upon sinners in all ages. It is notable that in the book of Job, those that denied providence, that God took notice of human affairs, they are called to look upon this instance, the example of the old world : Job xxii. 15, 16, ' Hast thou marked the old way which wicked men have trodden ? which were cut down out of time, whose foundation was overthrown with a flood.' God's first dispensations were visible pledges and testimonies : his dispensation to Sodom was a pledge of hell-fire; and his drowning of the world, it being a more universal instance of his displeasure, was a pledge of the general judgment. Here we may read several things: the severity of his justice, the verity of his threatenings, and the greatness of his power and majesty. The severity of his justice: oh, what a dreadful instance was this of God's displeasure against sin and sinners! Luther saith, *Moses vix sine lachrymis scripsit, et nos esse saxeos, si siccis oculis ista legere possumus* —Moses could not write it without tears, and we have stony hearts if we can read it with dry eyes. The whole world perished in the deluge of water which sin vomited out; men, women, infants, beasts, and all things in the world perished. For forty days together nothing but rain, rain, rain; and the great deep opened its mouth, and sent forth floods. It would have melted a heart of stone to hear the cries and shrieks of parents, women, and children. God now had rained 'a horrible tempest' upon sinners, Ps. xi. 6; the whole world was become now as one great river, and all things in the world were now afloat. Again, we have a pledge of the verity of the threatenings, what would come of their carnal course. The foolish world thought this was but a dream of the good old man, but see how the Lord made good Noah's word. It is said, Hos. vii. 12, 'I will chastise them as their congregation hath heard.' God would have us mark not only his justice, but his truth in all his dispensations; he will not only chastise them as they had deserved, but as their congregation had heard. There is a double conviction, and such as may keep the soul in more awe and obedience. And then it is an evidence of the power and majesty of God, that he cannot want instruments of vengeance; fire and water are at his beck and command. He that punished the old world with water to quench their heat of lusts, can punish the new world with fire because of the coldness of love that shall be in the latter days. Whenever the Lord will dissolve the confederacies of nature, what can poor creatures do? Oh, let us regard the power and majesty of God, and the rather because we are kept by a continual miracle: the water is above the earth, as may be proved by undoubted arguments, and the whole world would become but as one great pool were it not for the restraint of providence.

(2.) The preservation of Noah was a pledge of God's mercy in the preservation of his people. In general and common judgments God can make a distinction. In the primitive times the christians were troubled how God should punish those seducers by whom religion was scandalised and yet save the godly; and what doth the apostle say to this? 2 Peter ii. 9, 'The Lord knoweth how to deliver the godly out of temptation, and reserve the unjust to the day of judgment to be punished.' The Lord knows he is versed in the art, it hath been his practice for many thousands of years; and there he brings the instance of Lot, how he was delivered out of Sodom, ver. 7; how the good angels were preserved when the bad were tumbled down into the place of darkness, ver. 4; and he brings the instance of the old world, how God could rescue Noah, and avenge the disobedience of the old world, ver. 5. Especially this is a pledge of the different recompenses that shall be made at the last day, when all the ungodly world shall perish, but the elect shall be taken into glory. You shall see vengeance executed upon the ungodly. Christ will have it done not only in his own sight: Luke xix. 27, 'Those mine enemies that would not that I should reign over them, bring hither and slay them before me,'—Christ will see execution done himself in his own person; but it shall be done in the sight of the godly. The wicked are first punished in the sight of the godly, before the godly are taken into glory: Mat. xxv. 46, 'These shall go away into everlasting punishment,' and then 'the righteous into life eternal.' You shall first see the wicked have their doom, then you shall receive your privilege. Thus you see it was a pledge of God's general dispensations both to the godly and the wicked.

[2.] It was a type, too; for all things happened to the fathers by way of type and symbol, and so did this.

(1.) There is a great similitude between the day of judgment and the drowning of the world in several cases. It is good, I know, to be wary in allegories, yet we find in scripture the flood is mystically applied. There is a resemblance between the destruction of the old world, and the day of judgment when Christ shall come in glory. And that is the reason why the days of Noah and the day of the general judgment are often compared together; the flood was to them as the general judgment is to us: 2 Peter iii. 6, 'Whereby the world that then was, being overflowed with water, perished;' so Mat. xxiv. 37–39, 'As in the days of Noah they were eating and drinking, marrying and giving in marriage, and knew not until the flood came, and took them all away. So shall also the coming of the Son of man be;' and in Luke xvii. 26, 27, the like comparison is made. The comparison holds true in several cases. Those that lived in Noah's time a little before the flood, were extremely secure; their ears were sealed up with their bellies, they nourished their heart with pleasure; they ate and they drank, they married, they gave in marriage; as if they had said, Come let us eat, drink, and enjoy the pleasures of the flesh while we may; if this scrupulous fellow's words be true, we shall surely die; they looked upon him as an old doting man that dreamed of destruction. Just such kind of men shall there be at the last day, men of a secure luxury, that shall scoff at the ministers of the gospel when they press strictness and holiness, and propound the threatenings of God. It is said of the men in Noah's time: Mat. xxiv. 39, 'They knew not till the flood came, and took them all away.' They knew it well enough; Noah gave them warning; but they took no notice of any such threatenings; they behaved themselves as if they had known no such matter, though they knew there was such a thing threatened. The scripture measures our thoughts by our practice. So carnal men, the day of the Lord comes upon them, and they know not till the judgment takes them away; they do not believe in the great day of accounts, for they live as if there were no such day when they securely give themselves up to secular business, and neglect their poor souls. And look, as it was with sinners at the coming of the flood, so will it be with those carnal wretches at the judgment day; when the great deep had opened its mouth, and all the world was like a deep river swiftly flowing, the waters prevailed and increased greatly. They that did not fear before, how did they run to and fro—from the lower rooms to the higher, from the floors to the tops of the houses, from the houses to the trees, from the valleys to the hills, and yet still the waters increased upon them. Some possibly might swim towards the ark, and desire that refuge which before they despised; but still the waters prevailed over them, and so they were drowned. Such will be the consternation of the wicked in the great day. The hypocrites in Zion shall be afraid, and they shall cry, Who shall hide us? and, Where shall we go from the wrath of the Lamb: Rev. vi. 15–17, 'And the kings of the earth, and the great men, and the rich men, and the chief captains, and the mighty men, and every bondman, and every freeman, hid themselves in the dens and in the rocks of the mountains, and said to the mountains and rocks, Fall on us, and hide us from the face of him that sitteth on the throne, and from the wrath of the Lamb; for the great day of his wrath is come, and who shall be able to stand?' Then they shall cry out, Oh, that I had accepted Christ, and that I had gotten into the ark! All the wolves shall tremble then at the presence of the glorious Lamb, when he shall come in majesty and power.

(2.) In the preservation of Noah and his family there was a type. Noah and those that were of his household were under the oath and covenant that they should be safe: Gen. vi. 18, 'With thee will I establish my covenant; and thou shalt come into the ark, thou and thy sons, and thy wife, and thy sons' wives with thee.' God had passed his word. God made two covenants with Noah; one when he went into the ark, that he should be safe; and another, when he came out of the ark, that the waters should no more return: Gen. viii. 21, 'I will not again curse the ground any more for man's sake,' &c. This may be spiritually applied of God's oath to believers as soon as they close with Christ. See how the Spirit of the Lord applies it: Isa. liv. 9, 'As I have sworn that the waters of Noah should no more go over the earth; so have I sworn that I would not be wroth with thee, nor rebuke thee;' it is an allusion to the later covenant. God invites us by his promise and covenant to come to Christ, and we shall have security there; then he plighteth his oath that a deluge of wrath shall never return more; they shall be safe for the present, and happy hereafter. Again, as there was no safety but in the ark, the only means of salvation was the ark, and then the ark must not only be looked upon, but entered into; so there is no safety but in Jesus Christ; and it is not enough to know Christ, and to have a naked contemplation of his sufficiency to save sinners, but our safety by Christ is by virtue of our union with him: Rom. viii. 1, 'There is no condemnation to them that are in Christ Jesus.' As they that were in the ark were safe, so those that are in Christ, united to him, are secured. Again, look upon the ark as an instituted means, which preserved them in the midst of the deluge. God, by his absolute power, could have preserved Noah upon the waters or in the waters as well as in the ark, as he saved the fishes in the water; yet he is pleased to prescribe some probable and likely means of safety, and the means prescribed must be used. So if we would be saved, we must use the means of salvation, however derided, as baptism and the word. For the word: 1 Cor. i. 21, 'It pleased God by the foolishness of preaching to save them that believe.' Though the world opposeth and despiseth it, yet this is the way and means. So also for baptism, for so the apostle applies it, 1 Peter iii. 20, 21, 'Which sometimes were disobedient, when once the long-suffering of God waited in the days of Noah, while the ark was a-preparing.

wherein few, that is, eight souls, were saved by water. The like figure whereunto even baptism doth also now save us.' Look, as those eight souls that were in the ark were saved, the ark being borne up by the water; so God hath appointed the water of baptism, and other means, to be the means of our salvation. Again, the carpenters that made the ark had no entertainment in the ark; for they wrought as Noah's workmen for their hire, not as the servants of providence for the ends of God. And so there may be some men that are employed and minister in holy things, that may build up an ark wherein others may enter and be safe, but after preaching to others themselves may be cast away, as the apostle seems to imply, 1 Cor. ix. 27, 'Lest that by any means, when I have preached to others, I myself should be a castaway.'

Now I come to the words themselves—'By faith Noah, being warned of God of things not yet seen, moved with fear, prepared an ark,' &c.

First, I shall take notice of the ground of his faith—'He was warned of God.' In the original it is χρηματισθεὶς, warned by an oracle; the word is proper to those dispensations which God used in the primitive times in the planting of the church. It is said of the wise men χρηματισθέντες κατ' ὄναρ, Mat. ii. 12, 'Being warned of God in a dream;' so of St Paul, Acts x. 22, ἐχρηματίσθη ὑπ' ἀγγέλου ἁγίου, 'Being warned from God by a holy angel.' Now in this warning of God I shall observe several things.

First, I observe God's condescension, in that he would be pleased to give warning. He acquainted Noah with his purpose that he might acquaint the world. Oh, what a slow progress doth God make in his judgments! Though the pace of mercy be swift and earnest, yet judgment walketh with leaden feet. When God comes to refresh a sinner, he comes 'skipping over the mountains,' Cant. ii. 8, as if he never could be soon enough. And the father 'ran to meet his son,' Luke xv. 20. But yet now in the progress of his judgments God's motion is slow, and he comes on by degrees. The apostle takes notice of this, 2 Peter iii. 20, 'The long-suffering of God waited as in the days of Noah, while the ark was preparing,' God waited long, and Noah gives warning; there were one hundred and twenty years respite for repentance, and all the while Noah is building the ark, and he is preaching of righteousness to the ungodly, to see if he could move them to repentance. Nay, when the time was expired, God allows seven days more, Gen. vii. 4; and when those seven days were expired, the heavens did not pour out of a sudden, but the rain was increasing till it came to the height—forty days and forty nights. When God would discover his goodness and power, he did it in a small time; he perfectly made the world in six days: but now, to show his pity and patience when he would destroy the world, he allows forty days, to see if any of them would then repent; though they were drowned, yet they might be saved eternally hereafter. Thus still is God wont to give his people warning of their approaching dangers. Judgment seldom takes the world by surprise; but first there is notice given. It was the law of arms which God established among the Israelites; when they came before any city to assault it, they were first to offer terms of peace:

Deut. xx. 10, 'When thou comest nigh unto any city to fight against it, then proclaim peace unto it;' so still the Lord observes the same course. God first summons a parley, and would fain capitulate with sinners; gives warning of his purpose, that they might prevent their ruin by repentance: Jer. xviii. 11, 'Behold I frame evil against you, and devise a device against you; return ye now every one from his evil way, and make your ways and your doings good.' God would fain be prevented, Behold, I tell you what I am doing; if you be wise, repent. If God threatens, it is that he may not punish; and when he punisheth, it is that he may not punish for ever. God is still giving warning. But you will say, How doth he give warning now oracles are ceased? Why, by the threatenings of the word; and this should be as forcible a warning as if the Lord had given you a solemn prediction. Certainly, there is a great deal of keenness in Elisha's sword: 1 Kings xix. 17, 'Those that escape from the sword of Jehu shall Elisha slay.' The prophets, they have a sword: Hos vi. 5, 'I have hewed them by the prophets: I have slain them by the words of my mouth.' It is true, we do not speak by oracle, and so sensible an inspiration as the old prophets did; but when the practice is threatened in scripture, and condemned by the word, it is as much as if we had a particular oracle: the constitutions of heaven will not be violated.

To apply this hint.

Use 1. Take notice of the rich mercy and patience of God, and aggravate it by his great hatred of sin. Though God hates sin exceedingly, yet how long doth he bear with sinners? how long doth he protract his wrath? and how many courses doth he take to reclaim you from the evil of your ways? You may sooner reconcile fire and water than God and sin: Ps. l. 21, 'These things hast thou done, and I kept silence; thou thoughtest that I was altogether such an one as thyself: but I will reprove thee, and set them in order before thine eyes.' He is no favourer of your sins, but only gracious. Under the law, the mercy-seat was the cover of the ark; and there was the book of the law, where all God's curses were kept, that was put into the ark: Exod. xxv. 21, 'And thou shalt put the mercy-seat above upon the ark, and in the ark thou shalt put the testimony that I shall give thee,' —to show that mercy hath the moderation of all threatenings; and therefore is it that we are not consumed. Mercy suspends the execution of his just revenge: we wrest destruction out of God's hands, judgment is called his strange work.

Use 2. Again, whenever you are warned of the evil of your ways, lay it to heart. We cannot determine the actual events; God hath put times and seasons in his own hands. We may show you the merits of the fact, a storm in the black cloud, and then you should tremble; and therefore do not think slightly of reproof and threatening. When Lot told them of the wrath of God against Sodom, 'He seemed to his sons-in-law as one that mocked,' Gen. xix. 14; so men think we work ourselves into a passion and rage. But when warning is neglected, wrath is exasperated. This will be your great torment in hell, to think you were warned of the evil of your courses, and you would not regard it. Look, as Reuben said to his brethren, Gen. xlii. 22, 'Did not I warn you to do nothing against the child?' So will the Lord say when you are under torment, Did not I warn you? Your own heart will return upon you, as the heart of him that dreamt he was boiling in a kettle of scalding lead, and his heart cried to him, It is I that have been the cause of all this; so your hearts, when in torment, will upbraid you with the frequent warnings you have had.

Secondly, I observe again, that this warning was immediately made to Noah, who was a prophet and a righteous man, and by him it was delivered to the world at second-hand. God usually revealed himself to holy and righteous persons; they are his familiars, and you know it is a part of friendship to communicate secrets; and therefore the Lord will communicate his secret to them that fear him : Ps. xxv. 14, ' The secret of the Lord is with them that fear him, and he will show them his covenant;' Gen. xviii. 17, 'Shall I hide from Abraham the thing which I do?' God looks upon it as a violation of friendship to Abraham to conceal this matter from him ; and so to his prophets, as it is expressly said : Amos iii. 7, ' Surely the Lord God will do nothing, but he revealeth his secret to his servants the prophets,' God's messengers are as his heralds, to offer terms of peace, and to proclaim war to the world ; and he gives them commission to go of his errand. It is true there is no necessity laid upon God that he should do it always; but this is the course which he usually takes, and this was the way he often used in the old testament, oftener than in the new. What should be the reason of this? not because his grace is straitened : it is more enlarged in the gospel, for the defect of prophecy is recompensed by the clearness of saving truths. God opened his mind to them about particular events and successes, because evangelical truths were not so open and clear as they now are, and the eternal recompenses were more darkly delivered to the patriarchs. But now, God having opened his good treasure to us, we have higher arguments of piety, a larger measure of gifts, clearer discerning and understanding of the truths of the word, therefore prophecy ceaseth. Yet now, in the times of the gospel, he doth not altogether fail his people; for though they can have no certain knowledge of future contingencies, yet he begets some strong instinct in the mind of his children, puts it into their hearts to avoid this and avoid that : we have no infallibility of the event, yet we may discern much of the providence of God.

To apply this hint.

Use 1. When the generality of holy men are apprehensive of judgments, it is a sad omen ; when they have ill thoughts of the times, it is a sad presage. When the prophet was making up his stuff, it was a prognostic of ruin to Jerusalem, Ezek. xii. 3–7. When you see them ready to depart, it is a sad thing, for God is wont to communicate his secret to them that fear him. Then again—

Use 2. It presseth us, if we would know the secret of the Lord, be holy. Grace opens the eyes, and a man discerns things more clearly. A holy man hath a greater insight into truth than a carnal man, for lusts are the clouds of the mind. He that is encumbered with lusts is blind : 2 Peter i. 9, 'He that lacketh these things is blind, and cannot see afar off.' Grace will be an advantage to you in point of knowledge.

Thirdly, I observe, in Noah being warned by God that this warning was by oracle and special revelation; from whence I note that revelation is the ground of faith; for faith relates to some divine testimony. What we know by reason is knowledge or opinion, but not faith, which supposes a revelation and a testimony. Now divine revelations can only be the object of faith, because they are certain infallible truths, and cannot deceive us, and such whereunto men absolutely give credit. But you will say What revelations have we now oracles are ceased? I answer, It is true, these are God's ancient ways. Of old time, God spake—πολυμερῶς καὶ πολυτρόπως—'at sundry times and in divers manners' to his people, Heb. i. 1. Sometimes he spake to them by voice, sometimes by vision, sometimes by dream, sometimes by miraculous inspiration, or by urim and thummim, or by a sign from heaven, or by an angel; now God speaks to us by his Son. God's mind is fully revealed and disposed into a settled course. Enthusiasts may delude themselves with their own imaginations. Christians now have but two revelations; the one is ancient, and the other is new, and happens every day: there is the light of the word and the light of the Spirit.

1. The light of the word; this is our oracle, and therefore it is called, 'The oracles of God,' Rom. iii. 2. This is our urim and thummim, God tries us by that; the standing rule of justice is settled in the word, and this is more sure and less liable to deceit than an oracle, voice, or angel; for the devil may transform himself into an angel of light. Saith the apostle: 2 Peter i. 19, 'We have a more sure word of prophecy; whereunto ye do well to take heed, as unto a light shining in a dark place'—more sure than what? He speaks of the voice upon the holy mount, the voice that came from the excellent glory, that said, 'This is my well-beloved Son,' Mat. xvii. 5. Oracles and voices as to us are more liable to deceit. The apostle doth not say, We have a more *true* word, but a more *sure* word. The oracle was true, because it came from God; but a standing rule is not so liable to deceit and mistake as a transient voice.

2. We have the light of the Spirit in our hearts, by which our understandings are opened; we cannot be able to understand the word without this inward revelation of the Spirit. When we are reading and hearing the word, we cannot discern it with any favour, till the Spirit opens our eyes. As Christ, when he came to his disciples—first he opened the scripture, then he opened their understandings, Luke xxiv. 44, 45. And it is the Spirit that gives us a constant revelation, that reveals the secrets of God to us—all his purposes of grace concerning our souls: Rom. viii. 15, 'Ye have not received the spirit of adoption, whereby we cry, Abba, Father.' The Spirit of God, by inward suggestions, tells us God is our Father. By this voice God saith, I am thy salvation, as David prays, Ps. xxxv. 3, 'Say unto my soul, I am thy salvation.' It is the Spirit that comes and reveals to us when it is a fit season to come and call upon God; and when the arms of mercy are ready and open to receive us; and what are the answers of our prayers? 1 John v. 6, 'It is the Spirit that beareth witness, because the Spirit is truth.'

Use, Learn hence whereon to bottom faith—upon the word of God. Let us be contented with this dispensation. Foolish creatures would give laws to heaven, and we would indent with God upon our own terms and conditions. Look, as the devil comes and indents with Christ: Mat. iv. 3, ' If thou be the Son of God, command that these stones be made bread;' he would have him do a miracle, else he would not believe him. And the Jews would indent with Christ: Mat. xxvii. 40, ' If thou be Christ, come down from the cross and we will believe.' So carnal men indent with God. We think if God did speak by miraculous inspiration, then things would not be so doubtful. Oh, let us be contented with our light! the Lord hath stated our salvation in an excellent way. Chrysostom saith, The saints do never complain of the darkness of the word, but of the darkness of their own heart: Ps. cxix. 18, ' Open thou mine eyes that I may behold wondrous things out of thy law:' David doth not say, Lord make a plainer law; but, Lord, open mine eyes. If things be dark to you, do not accuse the scriptures, as if they were an uncertain rule, but desire the Lord to open your eyes that you may look into them. We would have Christ speak to us from heaven, as he did to Paul. Men that neglect ordinances require miracles; they would have all things decided by voice, oracles, and miracles, because they would save the pains of study, prayer, and discourse. If men were not drowned in lusts and pleasures, all would be clear. When the church was destitute of outward helps, God used the way of miracles and oracles; but that dispensation is not continued, because we have a better way: providence, the Spirit, and the word, take them all together, do exceedingly open the mind of God to us. We have the advantage of the revelations and miracles of former ages, and we have a supply by ordinary and standing means. Instead of new miracles, we have the testimony of the church, who hath had experience of the power and force of the word for many ages, and invites us to believe. Observe, every age of the church hath sufficient means so proportioned to the diversity of times that no age could have better than the present; but we affect the extraordinary signs and revelations of former generations. In this case, it is all as God will; and God's wisdom knows what is best for us. When miracles were most rife, they were not exercised at the will of man. The apostle saith: Heb. ii. 4, ' God bearing them witness with signs and wonders, and diverse miracles, and gifts of the Holy Ghost, according to his own will;' it was not as the apostles would. The Lord is a wise God, and he knows what dispensation is fit for every age. There are a great many reasons why God should use the way of miracle and oracle then; as that there might be some external motive to draw the world to hearken to the doctrine of the gospel. The apostles' work was to lay the canon and foundation, but we do but explain it. Saith St Paul, 1 Cor. iii. 10, ' As a wise master-builder, I have laid the foundation, and another buildeth thereupon.' We only explain what the apostles had laid down; our duty is only to build upon the apostles' foundation. Now we know explication and inference need the confirmation of reason and discourse rather than of miracle. It is true, for the apostles' part of their work was to explain the old testament; but that was somewhat obscure, and that was not acknowledged of all nations, only received among the Jews; therefore there was need of miracle to make their interpretation authentic, and that they might lay a clear foundation of faith for all nations; and besides, the church then was not armed with magistracy, and therefore much of the coercive discipline which God then used was by miracle. Ananias was struck dead with a miracle: Acts v. 5, 'And Ananias hearing these words fell down, and gave up the ghost.' But now, when magistrates should be nursing-fathers, the dispensation ceaseth. Besides, this should be a consideration to content us. Those that had miracles were not merely converted by the miracle, but by the hearing of the word; the miracle was only the occasion, not the cause of conversion. The bells may call the people together to hear the word, but the word converts. Miracles were as bells to draw the heart to hearken to the doctrine of Christ. The fowler's pipe may allure the birds, but they are caught by the net. Let it suffice, then, that you have the word of God confirmed by miracle, sealed by the blood of so many martyrs, manifested to your consciences by such divine force. All the miracles we have now are either inward and spiritual; they are miracles of grace in changing the heart. The children of God have testimony enough within themselves; they feel the force and power of the word upon their consciences: John viii. 32, 'You shall know the truth, and the truth shall make you free.' When the word doth help to disentangle us from lust, we cannot have a more clear revelation and warrant from God concerning the truth of it: John xvii. 17, 'Sanctify them by thy truth, thy word is truth.' When God sanctifies the heart by the word, then we know it is truth, or else outward miracles; God's wonderful providence in maintaining the church by suffering and martyrdom, not by the power of an outward sword. This is the finger of God: Neh. vi. 16, 'It came to pass, when all our enemies heard thereof, they were much cast down in their own eyes; for they perceived that the work was wrought by our God.' These are the miracles and oracles we are to expect.

Here is an objection. It is said: Acts ii. 17, 'It shall come to pass, that in the last days I will pour out of my Spirit upon all flesh: and your sons and daughters shall prophesy, and your young men shall see visions, and your old men shall dream dreams,' &c; so that it seems God would still continue the dispensation in the last days, that he will give us visions, dreams, and oracles again.

I answer, These are but figurative expressions, to signify the gifts of the Holy Ghost, which we receive by virtue of Christ's ascension, abundance of knowledge, faith, and holiness; for mark, the words are quoted out of a prophet. Now the prophet speaks according to the dispensation of his own age, or else how should he be understood by the men of his time. Dreams and visions were the ordinary means whereby God then revealed himself to his prophets, and therefore the prophet useth words calculated to the Jewish dispensation. In the prophetical writings, whenever they spake of the worship in the new testament, they used words suited to the then present worship; as altars, sacrifices, incense, and the like, which are words proper to the legal rites; so when they speak of the gifts of the new testament, then they use the words—prophecy, vision, and dreams. All the meaning is, God in the latter days would give them abundance of light and knowledge, for, take the words literally, they were not made good in the case to which he applyeth the prophecy. The apostle applies it to take off the reproach of the people that said they were filled with new wine. Now they could not be said then to see visions and dream dreams; but the words set out the excellent gifts of the Spirit in the new testament. But if you would more particularly know why the Spirit of God should use these words of prophecy, visions, and dreams; that sons and daughters should prophesy, &c., I answer then, By prophecy you may understand the gifts of illumination; by vision, gifts of consolation; and by dreams, the gifts of sanctification.

1. By prophecy, the gifts of illumination, or a clear understanding of God's will in Christ, which should be in the new testament above the old testament—'Your sons and daughters shall prophesy;' that is, the little boy and girl shall be able to understand the mysteries of salvation in scripture; they need not run to the prophet for the meaning of such a ceremony and rite.

2. Then by vision understand a more intimate apprehension of the truth, or a manifestation of things to the conscience, gifts of consolation. We have a kind of vision here, when we have a lively sense of divine grace: here we see as in a glass; hereafter we shall see face to face.

3. Then by dreams you may understand the more inward instincts and motions of the Holy Ghost, by which the soul, being severed from worldly desires and objects, is raised to the contemplation of heaven and spiritual things; as dreams are the thoughts and commotions of the soul, which are framed when the outward senses are shut up. When a man neither seeth, heareth, smelleth, toucheth, nor tasteth, then the soul worketh on things at the greatest distance; so, possibly, it signifies those spiritual instincts, those sanctifying motions, by which the soul is raised up to the contemplation of heavenly mysteries: then there is such a distribution of the persons to amplify the clause that went before —'I will pour my Spirit upon all flesh.' 'Old men,' to show that no condition is excluded from the communion of the Spirit, your 'sons and daughters,' that is, your children, they shall have their memory sanctified to retain prophecy; your 'young men' shall have visions, their consciences sanctified, to feel the force of what is in their heads; and your 'old men' shall dream dreams; they who are deadened to the world shall have their affections raised to heaven, and God will clearly manifest himself to them.

SERMON XXXVI.

By faith Noah, being warned of God of things not seen as yet.—
HEB. xi. 7.

FOURTHLY, I observe that this warning was of a judgment to come—'Being warned of things not seen as yet;' that is, of the horror of the flood. From whence I note that the threatening as well as the promise is the object of faith; not only the mercy of God in the promise, but the judgment of God in the threatening, is to be applied by faith. I shall confirm the doctrine in hand with some reasons.

1. Because every part of divine truth is worthy of belief and reverence, because it is the word of the same God; and that is the reason why we read of faith in the promises, faith in the command, faith in the threatening. There is faith in the promises: Ps. cxix. 49, 'Remember the word unto thy servant, upon which thou hast caused me to hope;' there is faith in the commandment: Ps. cxix. 66, 'Teach me good judgment and knowledge; for I have believed thy commandments;' that is, I have believed them to be of divine authority, and to be just, equal, and good; and there is faith in the threatening, 'By faith Noah, being warned of God,' &c. It is true, belief in the threatening is not so much pressed in scripture, because guilty nature of itself is presagious of evil: Rom. i. 31, 'Knowing the judgment of God, that they which commit such things are worthy of death.'

2. Because faith is but a loose presumption, if it be not carried out to the threatenings as well as the promises. In all right belief there is mixture. Men that look altogether to be honeyed and oiled with grace, to be fed with the promises and feasted with love, they mistake the nature of God and the state of his economy, and the manner of his dealing with the world; they mistake the nature of God, for God is just as well as merciful. And in such a mixed dispensation hath he revealed himself to the creature: Ps. cxvi. 5, 'Gracious is the Lord, and righteous; yea, our God is merciful;' gracious, and yet righteous. And they mistake the ordinances of God and the state of his dispensations; for he will be known in his judgments, as well as in his mercies. God hath always delighted to deal with men in the way of a covenant. Now the right covenant form is a precept invested with a promise and a threatening; therefore we are bound to believe that God will condemn the obstinate as well as save the penitent. In the covenant which God made with man in innocency, it is notable the only memorial we have is of the curse; nothing but that is mentioned: Gen. ii. 17, 'In the day thou eatest thereof thou shalt die the death.' The promise is but implied; if thou forbearest eating, thou shalt live; but the threatening is expressed, What was the reason? Partly because the effect of that covenant was only to oblige the guilty creature to death; and partly because God would show us that man's nature doth always need a bridle. In the state of innocency, when we were most holy, as there was use of a law for the exercise of obedience, so there was use of a threatening to keep him from sin, because of the changeableness of his nature; therefore it is much more needful now in our degenerate estate. Though the new nature needs no other argument but love and sweetness, yet the old nature needs a curb and restraint. Therefore men that would only hear of promises and arguments of grace, sin against God's ordination and the wisdom by which he will govern the world; they would have God yield to them and speak them fair, else they will be none of his; so that the faith they cry up is rather a fond delicacy, or carnal presumption, than a serious respect to God.

3. Because it is necessary and profitable. There is no part of scripture without use and profit. Man may write a book, but there may be a great deal of waste in it; but when God hath written a volume or book, there is nothing in it but what is of profit: Rom. xv.

4, 'Whatsoever things were written aforetime were written for our learning, that we through patience and comfort of the scriptures might have hope.' It is true, it is the aim of the whole scripture to beget hope; ay, but there are some things, in order to hope, that are first to work upon fear; something to bridle the flesh as well as to comfort the spirit, though all endeth in hope. There is nothing in the word of God superfluous, and the threatenings are a considerable part of the word. .

But more particularly I shall show you how the threatenings are necessary.

[1.] To beget humiliation for sins past. In the threatenings we see the desert of sin, therefore after grievous offences it is good to wound the heart this way with the more remorse. Josiah's heart was tender and made soft—by what? by the threatening: 2 Kings xxii. 19, 'Because thine heart was tender, and thou hast humbled thyself before the Lord, when thou heardest what I spake against this place, and against the inhabitants thereof, that they should become a desolation and a curse,' &c. Certainly there is great advantage by the commination. You will never understand how displeasing things are to God till you look upon the flying roll, and read the curses; then the soul will say, Oh, what have I done? I have done that which makes me guilty of all the curses of the law; and this will make you earnest after pardon, nay, it will make the pardon more welcome when it comes; We have deserved to be cast into hell, but grace hath saved us. Then will your hearts be enlarged in praises and thanksgivings to God, and you will exalt him to the highest heaven who hath delivered you from the lowest hell. Daniel, when he was in the den, had more cause to bless God than if he had been kept out of the den; to be in the midst of lions, and to see their mouths muzzled. So when we think of the evil of sin, and the terrible consequents of sin, and all this taken away by Christ, how will this commend our portion? how will we bless God for Jesus Christ? This is the fruit of sin, but 'there is no condemnation to them that are in Christ,' Rom. viii. 1.

[2.] The consideration of the threatening will be an advantage to us to make us vigilant and watchful; when we see the danger we shall not be so secure. This is the argument by which Christ himself would convert Paul: Acts ix. 5, 'It is hard for thee to kick against the pricks.' It is a metaphor taken from a husbandman's goad or prick; wanton oxen, when they run against the goad, they do not hurt the goad, but themselves. So it will be dangerous for you, God's wrath will gore the soul. We should have this goad and prick before our eyes; and this will make us watchful. Solomon saith, Prov. i. 17, 'Surely in vain the net is spread in the sight of any bird.' Birds, when they see the snare, will not venture upon the bait; and so, when we see the danger and consider the sad consequences of sin, it will make the soul to be the more careful; we will not dally with sin, and grow so bold with God and his cause.

[3.] It is an excellent means to strengthen us against carnal fear. The fear of man is apt to prove a snare, Prov. xxv. 24. Solomon spake it, and many of the servants of God have found it so. It was fear that made Abraham deny his wife, and it was fear that made

Peter deny his master.   Now there is no way to cure the fear of man but by presenting the fear of God.   Look, as Aaron's rod devoured the rods of the magicians, and as the stronger nail drives out the weaker, so doth the fear of God drive out the fear of man.   What is the ground of all carnal compliance?   We fear man's power, and presume of God's mercy ; a slight belief is given to the threatenings of God, and we think the wrath of man is more to be feared than the wrath of God.   The only cure will be to consider that there are no terrors to those which faith represents ; therefore holy persons always used this remedy to drive out the fear of man by the fear of God.   It is said ' The mid-wives feared God, and did not as the king of Egypt commanded them,' Exod. i. 17 ; and the Holy Ghost prescribeth this remedy, Isa. viii. 12. 13, ' Fear not their fear, nor be afraid, but sanctify the Lord God of hosts in your hearts, and make him your fear and your dread.'   The prophet speaks against those that would cry up a confederacy with them that cry up a confederacy ; that would yoke themselves in com-bination with the public enemies of God.   Oh, think of the terrors of the Lord, and that will quell and allay all the terrors of men.   So our Saviour : Luke xii. 4, ' Be not afraid of them that can but kill the body. But I will warn you whom you should fear : Fear him, which after he hath killed hath power to cast into hell.'   The terrors of the Lord, and the threatenings of the Lord, they are the cure against the terrors of men.   Better all the world your enemy than God.   We live longer with God than we do with men ; he can kill body and soul.

[4.] The threatenings of the word are necessary to be propounded to our faith, to check indulgence to carnal pleasure.   Pleasure and delight are dear bought if they cannot be compassed but with the danger of our souls ; and therefore there is no way to counterbalance delight but by fear, to consider the wrath of God that shall come upon every sinner : 2 Peter ii. 10, ' But chiefly them that walk after the flesh in the lust of uncleanness.'   Whoever escape they are sure to be punished ; there is bitter judgment for these sweet pleasures.

Use 1. Here is counsel to the children of God, not only to take a view of the land of promise, but it is good sometimes to take a view of the land of darkness ; they should not only reflect upon the promises, but the threatening ; it is profitable, though less pleasing.

Quest. Here ariseth a case, Whether or no the children of God, those especially that have received the first-fruits of the Spirit, and have a sense of the favour of God, whether they may make use of the threat-ening and terrors of the Lord or no ?   I answer to this affirmatively ; they may, and they must, and shall prove it by several reasons.

1. It is a part of the Spirit's discipline, necessary because of the remainders of corruption, and the Holy Ghost makes use of every advantage.   There are some corruptions that will bear down all milder arguments, that will not be restrained by any calm motives.   You had as good discourse with the rough wind as hope to charm the rage of lusts with the soft and comfortable words of the grace, mercy, and kindness of God ; therefore it is good to propound terrors.   The apostle Paul, though he were a sanctified and chosen vessel, yet he saw a need of making use of the terrors of the Lord.   It is true, he saith, 2 Cor. v. 14, the love of Christ constrained him.   The great motive of

obedience was the love of God. But he makes use of the other argument: ver. 10, ' Knowing the terrors of the Lord, we persuade men.' It was the terror of the Lord which made him so faithful in his work against all the disadvantages he met withal in the world. Sometimes it is necessary we should stand in the way of a furious lust with a flaming sword. The children of God find all methods little enough to break the force of a boisterous inclination.

2. Because the wrath of God is the proper object of fear, yea, the highest object. The wrath of man is the object of fear; therefore much more the wrath of God. The apostle saith, Rom. xiii. 3, ' That rulers are a terror to evil-doers;' much more should the wrath of God and destruction from the Almighty be a terror to them; Ps. xc. 11, ' Who knows the power of thine anger? according to thy fear, so is thy wrath.' Affections may lawfully be exercised about their proper objects without sin. Fear was planted in us for this very purpose; and grace doth not abolish nature, but regulate it; as Joshua made the Gibeonites to be hewers of wood and drawers of water, so grace serves our natural affections. Indignation and fear are good for the uses of the sanctuary, for the expulsion and extermination of sin; indignation against ourselves for sins committed, and fear for the prevention of sin.

3. We may make use of the Spirit's argument without sin. Usually men, instead of being over-spiritual, grow over-carnal. Terrors and threatenings are propounded to us to drive us from sin, even to men that are assured of God's love. Though we have an indefeasible right in the great inheritance, yet we must look upon the Lord ' as a consuming fire,' Heb. xii. 29. The Lord would help our infirmity this way. This argument is of most force, because the Spirit of God argues and discourseth in the heart of believers just as he argues in the scripture; now, thus the Spirit argues in the scripture, and therefore the word of God is called ' The sword of the Spirit,' Eph. vi. 17. In all your inward combats, or the civil wars of the soul, the renewed heart makes use of scripture arguments; and in scripture, as God encourageth with love, so he aweth with threatening.

4. The threatenings are a part of the object of faith, and therefore they may be used. They are propounded to be believed as well as the promises; and you should as surely consider God will condemn the wicked and impenitent as save them that believe and repent; and as there should be a closing with and loving the promise, so a trembling at the threatening; it is a note of God's children, Isa. lxvi. 2, ' They tremble at his word.'

5. I prove it from the example of the saints; and surely they were not under a lower dispensation than we are. Job bridled and curbed the excesses of his power and greatness hereby, for saith he, Job xxxi. 23, ' Destruction from God was a terror to me.' Men in great places have shrewd temptations to oppress: Oh, but, saith he, I dare not, because of God's terrors. So Noah was warned by God, and out of fear of the threatening prepared the ark. So Paul, he mortified and kept down his body, ' Lest,' saith he, ' I should be a cast-away,' 1 Cor. ix. 27. We cannot pretend to a higher dispensation than Job, Paul, and other holy persons, as if they were but novices in the school of Christ. Your undaunted courage is to be suspected. Sin is not less

rooted in us than it was in Paul, or less dangerous to us; neither are we more skilful than holy Paul: the devil is as subtle and our corruptions are as strong as ever.

6. The promises will be the better relished when we reflect upon the threatening; the bitterness of the threatening makes us to relish the sweetness of the promise. God is therefore the most desirable friend, because he is the most dreadful adversary. Look, as the sight of the Red Sea and the floating Egyptians, when they were drowned there, moved the Israelites to praise God; so when we consider the curse wherewith wicked men are overwhelmed, it is a great argument to quicken and stir us up to praise. Solomon would have us view the field of the sluggard. The brambles and briers that grow in the sluggard's field commend diligence; and so look upon the portion of wicked men—the snares, and brimstone, and horrible tempest, which is the portion of their cup: this commends our portion in Christ, and makes the promises more sweet.

Use 2. Direction how we are to use the threatening.

1. When you consider the threatening, let the punishment of loss be more terrible to you than the pain; I mean, let separation from God work more upon you, than your own misery and distress: 'Depart from me' is worse than 'eternal fire.' It is the greatest evil that can fall upon creatures to be separated for ever from the chiefest good. I press this, partly because nature will reflect upon its own pain, but grace counts the loss of God the chiefest misery. The wicked will think this no punishment to depart from God; they excommunicate, and cast God out of their company now—'Depart from us, for we desire not the knowledge of thy ways,' Job xxi. 14. And partly, because such considerations will be of great use; they that prize communion with God will be afraid to lose him by their sins; for they thus argue, this will work a divorce between me and my God. Look upon the privative part of the threatening rather than the positive part of it; 1 Cor. ix. 27, 'I keep under my body,' saith the apostle 'lest I be a castaway.' The main thing he feared was to be cast out of the favour of God, and lose the fellowship of God.

2. Consider the threatening, so as to weaken security, not to weaken faith. There is a great deal of difference between these two; we are not to weaken the certainty of faith, but the security of the flesh. It is good for christians to observe what is the issue and result of their fear, and of their reflections upon the threatenings, torment, or caution: 1 John iv. 18, 'Fear hath torment in it;' that is, slavish fear; but godly fear makes us more wary in our walking with God; it makes us more circumspect, but not less comfortable. Though there may be assurance to escape damnation, yet still there is care to avoid sin: this is the godly fear. Now to do that, you must consider God's ordination of punishment is with a supposition; that is, if I go on in a carnal course, then my end will be death, and I shall be undone for ever. It is with an 'if,' propounded to the children of God: Rom. viii. 13, 'If ye live after the flesh, ye shall die.' If it be possible that a man in Christ could live after the flesh, it is as possible and safe to conclude he should die for ever. So the apostle, Gal. vi. 8, 'If ye sow to the flesh, ye shall of the flesh reap corruption.' Where there is sin in the

seed, there will be a curse in the crop; not as if the children of God were actually to expect eternal death, but to look upon it as the proper demerit of sin, and so to depart from it.

3. The children of God should reflect upon the sad consequences of sin in the present life: 1 Cor. xi. 32, 'When we are judged, we are chastened of the Lord, that we should not be condemned with the world.' God hath still a bridle upon them. Though you are exempted from eternal death, yet your pilgrimage may be made very uncomfortable; you may feel the anguish of conscience, and be humbled by spiritual desertion, and lose and forfeit the sense of your joys and spiritual consolation; you may stand under a spiritual excommunication; that is, by being separated from the comfort of the covenant, and cast out of the actual fruition of God's favour, and be under much anguish of conscience, which is a spiritual part of discipline. A disobedient child may be whipped, though he be sure not to be disinherited; so God hath sore and bitter afflictions to lay upon you; he hath other evils besides damnation to bring on you.

4. The times when you should use this argument are these. When lusts are boisterous, it is good to oppose these stronger and more terrible motives of the terrors of the Lord; and when you are slack and remiss in the work of the Lord. When oxen do not labour, the husbandman useth the goad; when you begin to wax wanton and careless, it is good to use this spur—when we begin to grow deaf, slack, and cold in the work of God. So in the time of special temptation, when the fear of man is like to prove a snare, as Solomon saith, Prov. xxix. 25, say, I know the terrors of the Lord, and what a dangerous thing it is to please men, and to engage omnipotency against me. So after grievous offences, the children of God, when they foully sin, do not only lose their peace but their tenderness; therefore this will enforce them to run for their pardon.

Secondly, I come to the strength and force of Noah's faith, intimated in these words—' Of things not seen as yet—περὶ τῶν μηδέπω βλεπομένων—of things that by no means could be seen; not any way liable to the judgment of sense; by which the apostle means the tidings of the deluge and the manner of his own preservation in the ark, which were things strange, full of difficulty to be done, and likely to be entertained with the scoff and opposition of the world; yet he prepared an ark. To instance, either in the flood or ark. For the flood: never such a thing had been before, therefore it was more difficult to be believed, there being no precedent; for the world was but newly created, and it seemed unlikely to the men of that age that God would destroy it presently; besides, this judgment was to come after many years. By the grant of God himself they had the respite of a hundred and twenty years, and all others besides Noah were utterly secure; yet, though he had but the naked word of God, he believed. Then for his own gracious preservation, the means was by an ark, which was an improbable and incredible way of safety, as the flood was of the world's ruin; for the ark was made like a grave, or coffin, or sepulchre, wherein Noah for some months was to be buried, rather than preserved, without the comfort of light or fresh air; there was he with the cattle and all kinds of living creatures for many days. And besides, it was of that vast frame, that it was one hundred and twenty years a preparing, as appears by that of the apostle, 1 Peter iii. 20, 'The long-suffering of God waited all the while that the ark was a preparing.' Certainly a work of so great receipt must needs be of vast expense and charge, and take up a great deal of time to fit the matter, and to gather together all the species and kinds of living creatures. And it was a work that was like to meet with many mocks and scoffs in the world. Noah seemed to them, as one of our chronicles tells us, of one that out of a dread of a great flood built a house upon a high hill; so the wicked of that age, they looked upon Noah as a vain person, mocked and laughed at the design every day; he had a thousand discouragements, yet, being moved with fear, he prepared an ark. Now these things being so remote from sense, and only certain in God's word, it shows the great force and virtue of his faith, to be persuaded of the world's ruin, and his own preservation.

Doct. That it is the property of faith to be moved by such things as are not liable to sense.

The reasons are these—

1. Because when things are seen and known, there is no room for faith: Rom. viii. 24, 'Hope that is seen is not hope.' Hope there is put for the object—things hoped for; they are no more objects of hope when seen. Faith giveth over its work when we once come to fruition and view. When the sun is up, we feel the warm influences of it; we cannot be said so properly to believe it, as to feel it and know it. If we were in a dungeon we might believe one that tells us the sun shines, but when we see the glittering light it is otherwise. The elect, after the resurrection, cannot properly be said to believe the articles of faith, because faith and hope then ceaseth, and love only remains. Faith and sense are opposed, 2 Cor. v. 7, 'We walk by faith, not by sight.' Here things that are propounded to us, the glory of God in heaven and the reigning of the saints, they are not matters of sight and present sense and apprehension. In heaven it is quite contrary; there we have sight, but no faith; but here we walk by faith, and not by sight.

2. There is no trial in things that are seen, for all objects of sense force an impression upon us; we cannot choose but fear; when sense feels wrath, it is a judicial impression. There is none fears more than wicked men when wrath comes; they fear not wrath in the word, and wrath in the threatening, but wrath in the providence makes them to tremble: Isa. xxxiii. 14, 'The sinners in Sion are afraid; fearfulness surpriseth the hypocrite.' It is no exercise of faith, but a judicial impression. So the apostle saith—'The devils believe and tremble,' James ii. 19; because they are under their actual punishment, they cannot do otherwise. This is the difference between the godly and the wicked; the one trembles at the judgment, the other trembles at the threatenings—'He trembles at the word,' Isa. lxvi. 2. Wicked men do not consider the threatening, till, by all circumstances of providence, it is ready to be accomplished. The wicked tremble in hell, or at the hour of death; but the godly tremble in the church at the word of God. So did those in Noah's time, when they ran from the bottom of houses to the top, from thence to trees, from trees to mountains, but Noah trembled when God did but speak of these things. Feeling is left for the next life.

SERMON XXXVII.

By faith Noah, being warned of God of things not seen as yet.—
Heb. xi. 7.

THE use of the foregoing doctrine is—to check the security of the world, both in respect of particular and general judgments.

First, In particular judgments, the prophet saith, Hosea vii. 9, ' Ephraim hath gray hairs here and there upon him, and he knows it not.' Many times a nation is full of gray hairs. As gray hairs are the forerunners of death and the decay of nature, so many nations have gray hairs—sad intimations of ruin and destruction; and they do not tremble at it, especially if it be afar off, and if there be no visible preparation : if God be not upon his march, they do not tremble. When the world was given up to pleasure, when they were marrying and giving in marriage, who would believe that within a few years the rain and waters should cover the whole earth? Many would be ready to say, as that nobleman, 2 Kings vii. 2, ' If the Lord should make windows in heaven, could this be? ' Oh, consider all things are liable to change ; and when your mountain seems to stand strong, yet if there be such sins as are certain prognostics of ruin, there may be a change, notwithstanding the greatest flourish of outward prosperity ; for the gray hairs of a nation are not only the beginnings of misery and declensions of their glory, but their guilt, these are the saddest gray hairs : then you are liable to great ruin. See what the apostle speaks to the despisers of the gospel : Acts xiii. 41, ' Behold, ye despisers, and wonder, and perish : for I work a work in your days, a work which you shall in no wise believe, though a man declare it unto you.' The horrible devastation of Judea by the Chaldeans, who would believe it, that the city and temple should be so destroyed? and yet it came to pass. If a man should but tell you what God is about to do, you would think he were mad to mention such things,

Quest. You will say, you press us to believe, and all that you can do is but to bring conjectures ; you cannot give such infallible warning as Noah did.

I shall answer to this—

1. We may speak to you as the apostle did in Acts xiii, 40, ' Beware therefore, lest that come upon you which is spoken in the prophets.' Let me tell you, it is a ruled case—the despisers of the gospel shall surely meet with an unexpected judgment. The credit of every threatening stands upon two feet—the irresistibleness of God's power, and the immutableness of his counsel. Now we cannot say God will change his counsel, though he may his sentence; yet we may say, Take heed lest this be brought upon you : we know not future contingencies. God hath taken away that from a gospel ministry, because he hath given them a more excellent dispensation.

2. It is security and carnal confidence. If you neglect reformation, and depend merely upon present likelihoods, and say, It is impossible these things should be : Jer. iv. 14, ' O Jerusalem, wash thy heart from wickedness. How long shall vain thoughts lodge within thee? ' vain

thoughts, that is, reflections upon their present prosperity and great-ness.   You know there is much spoken of depending upon an arm of flesh and creature confidence.   Now when men neglect God's means, and trust to their own, this is a sure note of creature confidence in their present welfare and prosperity.   When we have no other shelter against judgments but prosperous armies, numerous ships and fortifica-tions, how soon may God blow upon these things?   Who would believe that which God did twice to the state of the Jews, both by the Chaldeans and Romans?   who would have believed thirty years ago what hath happened in Germany?   who would believe what befell the churches of Asia and Greece, that they should be overrun so?   If we should speak to you of England being unchurched, a man would think this were an idle dream that ever christianity should be banished from this island, that we should lose our church and our glory; and if yet we should look to the spiritual causes of such a judgment, there is nothing so probable as this.   God may in justice remove the old light, because we have set up so many new ones; and take away the candle-stick from us, because we are despisers of the gospel.

3. When prophets threaten, it is very likely it will come to pass, though we cannot absolutely determine future contingencies.   Certainly if a sparrow lights not to the ground without God, the messages of his servants, and the words that are uttered by them with reverence and fear, you cannot but acknowledge God in it: Hosea vi. 5, 'I have hewn them by my prophets, and I have slain them by the words of my mouth.'   Israel was a knotty piece of timber, and therefore God pursues them with blow after blow.   When a prophet falls a-hewing with blow after blow it is a sad intimation.   I do not justify every idle dictate and fond suggestion spoken out of passion and discontent; but when we make collection upon collection, when we show you the sin and the judgment out of scripture, it should not seem to you as an idle tale; and when we speak to you, we should not seem as Lot to his sons-in-law, 'as if he had mocked,' Gen. xix. 14.   All that you can pretend for your safety and security in such a case as this, is either your present strength or the mercy and free grace of God; but to pretend grace and mercy and neglect duty, is but to choke conscience. Mercy will never be exercised to the prejudice of God's truth and justice.

4. This is certain, it is better to believe the threatening than to feel the stripes and blows.   There can be no harm if we should take this occasion to humble ourselves before God.   It is true, in uncertain cases this is a good rule—hope the best; but yet it is good to prepare for the worst.   Carnal hope such as is lifted up against the threatening in the word is but a bad nurse to piety.   They that do not tremble at the word, but are left to be taught by sense, are taught in a sharp school of discipline; they are taught by briers and thorns.   It is better to learn by the word than by feeling blows and stripes: Prov. xiv. 16, 'A wise man feareth, and departeth from evil; but a fool rageth and is confident.'   Usually, when we speak of the evil of the times, men go away; and they fret and foam, and think we rail, and the word of God is to them but as a reproach; God leaves them to be taught by briers and thorns, by their own sorrow and fears.   So Prov. xxii. 3,

'A prudent man foreseeth the evil, and hideth himself'—here is the very description of Noah—'but the simple pass on, and are punished :' carnal men run desperately upon danger, and against warning.

Secondly, With respect to the general judgment, it reproves the security of the world.   We are apt to think it is but a well-devised fable to keep the world in awe.   Oh, consider, if Noah could believe the flood, we are much more bound to believe the general judgment—why ? Because we have the word of God for it, which is of more force than an oracle, and we have a pledge already ; and therefore the future destruction of the world by fire being more credible to us, God looks for a more active faith from us.

Quest. But you will say, Who doth not believe the day of judgment ?

I answer, Flatter not yourselves, for in the latter times men will be just as they were in the days of Noah ; there will be scoffers at the day of judgment ; and usually the best of us content ourselves with a loose and naked belief of things to come ; and therefore, that you may drive the privy atheism out of the heart, let me propound but two questions.—(1.) Are you affected with these things, as if you saw them ? (2.) Do you make a careful provision and preparation, as if this were a matter that you did believe,—'As Noah was moved with fear, and prepared an ark ? '

1. Are you affected with these things as if they were present ? So it should be ; for faith is the evidence of things not seen ; it substantiates our hopes, and makes them real to our souls ; therefore we should live as if we did see Christ coming in the clouds with power and great glory ; as if we heard the blast of the great trump, and the voice of the archangel, saying, Arise, and come to judgment.   God hath made a promise, 1 Cor. xi. 31, 'That if we judge ourselves, we shall not be judged of the Lord.'   Now, art thou affected with this promise, as if the judgment were set, and as if the books were opened ?   Consider, in the process of the great day, when all sinners stand trembling at the bar, and their faces gather blackness and paleness, if Christ should single thee out by name, and say to you, If thou judge thyself, thou shalt not be put to this severe trial ; with what thankfulness would we receive this offer ?   Now, an active faith should make this supposition. So again Christ saith, Luke xii. 8, 9, 'Whosoever shall confess me before men, I will confess him before the angels of God ; but he that denieth me before men, shall be denied before the angels of God.' When thy heart is tempted to carnal compliance, canst thou represent by a lively faith the day of judgment ? and say, Would I deny Christ before his face ? or by compliance betray the truth ?   Would I do this act if I heard Christ say, Father, these are mine, and these are not mine, when Christ is making a distinction between sheep and goats, and the two herds were standing before mine eyes ?   It is good to make suppositions and put cases concerning that great day.

Do you do as Noah did ? make serious preparation for things to come and yet unseen.   God doth not look to opinions, but to the disposition of your heart.   Actions have a voice before God.   We content ourselves with a naked and inactive belief, which, if it be searched to the bottom, will be found to be nothing but uncertain guess and con-

jecture. Do we do as Noah did, venture upon a work of such charge
and such difficulty? Though the flood was yet a great while to come,
he presently falls about it.

[1.] It was a work of great labour and trouble; and so is the work
of mortification, strictness, and the spiritual life; it is a work of labour
and trouble to weaken carnal desires, to subdue your affections to the
just temper of religion; yet, though it be harsh to nature, can you say,
Heaven will make amends for all? can you say, It is better to take
pains than suffer pains? can you say, If I digest the severities of religion, 'if I mortify the deeds of the flesh, I shall live?' Rom. viii. 13.
Can you reason as Noah did?

[2.] It was a work which he should have no use of a long time; so
can you tarry God's leisure and wait for the season of the promises,
and for the time of accomplishment? Always between the making of
the promise and the making good of the promise, there is a great deal
of time. The Israelites were long in the wilderness ere they came to
Canaan, and endured a tedious march; they might have gone over in
forty days, but God kept them in it forty years to exercise them. So
David was anointed king a long time before he reigned, 1 Sam. xvi. 13,
so long, that in the end he despaired of the kingdom; and therefore he
saith, 'I said in my haste, All men are liars,' Ps. cxvi. 11. So, can
you tarry God's leisure for the accomplishment of his promise, and
during the time of your pilgrimage wait, 'And be followers of them
who through faith and patience inherit the promise'? Heb. vi. 12. Seldom any go to heaven, but they have a long time to exercise their faith
and patience. Can you be content in your journey to Canaan to tarry
God's leisure, and wait for your deliverance?

[3.] It was a work that met with many scoffs in the world; they
looked upon Noah as an old doting man that envied their jollities and
pleasures. And truly, when you fear God and walk strictly, the world
will speak of you with great contempt—you will be set up to be as a
sign to be spoken against. You must expect this as your portion:
Gal. iv. 29, 'As then he that was born after the flesh persecuted him
that was born after the Spirit, so it is now.' So it was in the apostle's
time, and so it will be to the end of the world. There will be tongue
persecution at least; you must endure mocks for a good conscience, to
be counted hypocrites and foolish, and men that are prodigal of their
interests, and humorists and the like. I know not what secure presumptuous men may foster in themselves, and conceive the children of
God should have a dispensation. The carnal seed will always be
mocking. Now, can you endure all this and go on with your work of
strictness, and preciseness, and patience? They will howl for their
mocking when you shall be safe.

[4.] It was a work which put him upon great charges, to provide
the kinds of all living creatures, and to build an ark that might be of
so great receipt, to take in the beasts, and fodder for the beasts and
fowls of the air; so you should consider, At what expense have I been
for Christ? If I believe eternity and the everlasting recompenses,
what have I done for Christ? That which you lay out upon the flesh
and outward conveniences is mere prodigality; for you owe the flesh
nothing—'We are not debtors to the flesh,' but all that you have you

owe to Christ; and what have you done for him? God hath given you a promise, as a bill of exchange; now he takes it ill if you should protest against it. Jesus Christ will not own you at the last day: Luke xii. 33, ' Sell that you have (saith Christ) and give alms, and you shall have treasure in heaven.' This is Christ's bargain—whatever you lay out on earth, he will pay it in another country. Now, what have I ventured upon this promise? Christ saith, ' Sell that you have,' not to deny propriety of goods; but certainly it shows that rather than we should reserve our estate to purchase lands, and grow great in our families, we should rather lay them out to purchase an estate in heaven. Men are all for buying more rather than for selling that which they have; therefore Jesus Christ would bend the stick the other way; as he saith, John vi. 27, 'Labour not for the meat that perisheth;' not to deny honest labour, but to blunt the edge of our spirits, that we may labour more for better things. So, ' Sell that you have, and give alms;' rather than by hooking in an estate, you should be laying it out; you should look upon your estate as most safe in God's hands. Noah was at great charge and expense; no doubt wasted himself and his all; but what lost he by it? Noah and his sons had the possession of all the world when he came out of the ark. It is the best bargain that ever we made, when we lay out our estate upon religious uses. Thus may you try yourselves. It is the most foolish thing in the world altogether to look to the present. We that are not affected with things that are not seen, may learn of the creature. Solomon bids us go learn of the ant, Prov. vi. 6–8; so certainly if we did believe there was an after-reckoning, and that one day we must give an account, we would make more provision for our souls.

Thirdly, I go on to the fruits and consequences of Noah's faith— ' He was moved with fear'—εὐλαβηθεὶς—being wary, or piously fearing. The same word is used of Jesus Christ, Heb. v. 7. His holy and innocent fears are expressed by the same word—' He was heard in that he feared;' indeed, it is always used in a good sense in scripture. The word is sometimes used for caution and wariness, sometimes for reverence; in the latter sense often in scripture: as Acts ii. 5, ' Devout men in every nation.' In the original it is εὐλαβεῖς, reverend men; so Acts viii. 2, 'Devout men carried Stephen to his burial'—εὐλαβεῖς,— men touched with a reverence of God, and with a sense of religion; so was Noah moved with a godly reverence and godly caution. The note is this—

Doct. That godly fear is a fruit and effect of faith.

Faith, as it works upon the promises, begets love and hope; but as it works upon the threatening, so it begets fear. Love, fear, and hope, are not contrary, though they be different; they may stand together, and they all proceed from faith.

1. All graces are conjoined, though they seem contrary. See how they are conjoined in scripture. Ps. cxix. 119, 120, there is fear and love—' I love thy testimonies;' and then presently, ' My flesh trembleth because of thy judgments;' so Ps. cxii. 1, ' Blessed is the man that feareth the Lord, that delighteth greatly in his commandments.' Fear and delight are joined together: so Acts ix. 31, ' They walked in the fear of the Lord, and in the comforts of the Holy Ghost.' There

was something likely to entice them into a snare, and something likely to oppress them. That which was likely to draw and entice them out of the way was the relics of sin, the baits of the world, and the suggestions of Satan ; therefore they walked ' in the fear of the Lord.' That which was likely to oppress them was the burden of their own conscience, and outward crosses ready to overwhelm them ; therefore it is said, they walked in the ' comforts of the Holy Ghost.' There is need of a double remedy. They walked with ' fear' to keep them from sin ; and they walked in the ' comforts of the Holy Ghost' to keep them from sinking under affliction. On earth we still need this mixture ; in heaven there is all joy, no fear of punishment. But on earth there is a mixture of flesh and spirit, something to comfort us, and something to humble us ; there is no true piety without either. The object of these affections is often changed. The children of God can fear him for his goodness, and love him for his judgments : Hosea iii. 4, ' They shall fear the Lord and his goodness in the latter days ;' Ps. cxix. 62, ' At midnight I will arise to give thanks unto thee, because of thy righteous judgments.' Love would grow secure without fear, and fear would grow slavish without love ; therefore these graces are conjoined, that there may be a fit temper both of reverence and sweetness.

2. All these graces flow from faith ; for all affection is grounded upon persuasion. Who would fear the threatening that doth not believe it ? or fear to offend God that doth not love him, and that doth not acknowledge there is a God ? The fear of the people of Nineveh is excited by their faith : Jonah iii. 5, ' The people of Nineveh believed God, and proclaimed a fast, and put on sackcloth ;' and the word, which is the object of faith, is the object of fear. They that feared the word of the Lord housed their cattle, Exod. ix. 20 ; that is, they that believed the word.

But now the great question is, what is this godly fear ? There are three effects by which it may be discerned—caution, diligence, and reverence ; caution respects sin, diligence respects duty, dread and reverence respects God himself.

[1.] There is caution, or a cautelous prudence—a fear lest we should dash the foot of our faith against the several stumbling blocks that are in the world. Look, as those that carry precious liquor in a brittle vessel, are very cautelous ; especially if they walk in the dark or rough ways, they walk with care lest the vessel be broken—and the liquor spilt. The children of God know what a precious treasure they have about them, that they have a soul that cannot be valued ; and they know that the world is a rough passage, and here many stones of stumbling ; therefore they ' Work out their salvation with fear and trembling,' Phil. ii. 12. The main grace that keeps in and maintains the fire of religion in the soul is a cautelous fear ; they consider their own hearts, look for direction from the word, and call in the help of the Spirit : Heb. iv. 1, ' Let us therefore fear, lest a promise being left unto us of entering into his rest, any of us should seem to come short of it.' This doth not hinder the assurance of faith, but guard it.

[2.] There is diligence in fear, and that respecteth duty. Every good fear endeth in duty ; it ariseth from faith, and ends in duty ; it stirs up the soul to use all the means to prevent the danger. If Noah had not

believed, he had never feared ; if he had not feared, he had never prepared an ark.   The fear of the wicked ends in irresolution, perplexity,
and despair ; their terrors differ only in degree and duration from the
pains of hell—mere involuntary impressions, whose end is not duty, but
despair and torment ; but the fear of the godly sets them a-work.
Noah, being moved with fear, sets to building the ark.   It is said of
Jehoshaphat, 2 Chron. xx. 3, 'He feared, and set himself to seek the
Lord ;' so Paul, Acts ix. 6, 'He trembling and astonished said, Lord,
what wilt thou have me to do ?' As if he had said, Lord, I see my
danger, what is my work ?

[3.] There is in fear a reverence and a dread of God—his holiness,
his majesty, his power, his justice, and the like.   Now we may dread
God either as creatures or as sinners ; either as our maker, or as our
judge, or as both ; as our maker, so we dread God for himself ; as our
judge, so we dread him for our own sakes, because of sin.   These two
are distinct ; the one may be where the other is not.   As in heaven,
the saints and glorious angels fear God—fear being an essential respect
of the creature to God ; in heaven, it is a grace that never ceaseth.
Now they dread God as full of majesty and goodness, and as the great
creator of the world ; and in paradise there was this fear of reverence.
Adam did not fear God as a judge till he had sinned : Gen. iii. 10,
'I was afraid, therefore I hid myself :' this fear entered into the world
with sin.   Adam in innocency only reverenced him for his majesty,
goodness, and holiness, as the saints and angels do in heaven ; and
there may be fear where only God is feared as a judge.   The wicked
stand in fear of nothing but hell and wrath ; they fear not God for God,
but for themselves ; not because of the dignity of his majesty, but
because of their own danger.

Quest. If you ask me, then, what fear is lawful ?

I answer, It must be a mixed fear, partly because of his majesty and
holiness ; and partly, because of his justice while we are in the present
state, not wholly exempt from the strokes of God's justice ; and this
is the fear that is in the children of God, and is usually called by the
name of filial fear ; whereas the other in wicked men is called by the
name of servile and slavish fear.   The distinction is grounded on
scripture, and so called with allusion to the fear of children and servants ;
children fear their loving parents, and servants fear their hard and
cruel masters.   The grounds of this distinction are famously known—
the spirit of bondage and the spirit of adoption : Rom. viii. 15, 'Ye
have not received the spirit of bondage again to fear, but ye have
received the Spirit of adoption, whereby we cry, Abba, Father :' the
spirit of bondage is the root and ground of servile fear, and the spirit
of adoption is the ground of filial fear.   Now, though there may be
some servile fear in the children of God, yet it is more and more wrought
out the more we increase in the apprehension of God's love : 1 John
iv. 18, 'Perfect love casteth out fear.'   I take it there for the apprehension of God's love, not for our love to God.

Now I shall state the differences between these two kinds of fears,
servile and filial.

(1.) Filial fear is always coupled with love—for there is a harmony
between the graces—but servile fear with hatred.   Filial fear ariseth
from a humble sense of God's goodness, and thereby God is made

more amiable and lovely to the soul : Ps. cxxx. 4, ' There is forgiveness with thee that thou mayest be feared ; ' they are afraid to displease so good a God as they have found him to be in Christ : Hosea iii. 5, 'And they shall fear the Lord and his goodness.' Mark, it is not the Lord, and his wrath and his justice, but his goodness. Filial fear is rather because of his benefits past, than of his judgments to come ; but now servile fear ariseth merely from a sense of this wrath, and so causeth hatred of God. *Oderunt dum metuunt*,—they hate God while they fear him. Wicked men, it is true, stand in dread of God ; but they have hard thoughts of God, and they could wish there was no God, or that he were not such a God ; *aut Deum extinctum cupiunt aut exarmatum*—either they wish the destruction of his being or of his glory ; either that there were no God, or that he were a weak or powerless God ; not such a God, not so holy, just, and powerful. It is a pleasing thought to a carnal heart if there were no God to punish him. Such fear there is in the devils themselves : James ii. 19, ' They believe and tremble ; ' they abhor their own thoughts of God, and their bondage is increased with their knowledge. So do wicked men hate those characters of God engraven upon their consciences, they stand in dread of God, but it is a fear that is accompanied with hatred rather than love.

(2.) Filial fear is accompanied with a shyness of sin, but not with a shyness of God's presence. Adam, as soon as he had sinned, he bewrayed this slavish fear ; the more he feared, the more he ran away from God : Gen. iii. 10, ' I was afraid, because I was naked, and hid myself.' His guilt makes him run into the bushes. When men feel God's wrath they cannot endure the presence of his glory. Before man fell, there was nothing sweeter to him than familiarity with God ; but as soon as he sinned,—' I was afraid, and hid myself.' Now when fear makes us to fly from God, it must needs be culpable ; for the aim of all graces is to preserve a communion and a respect between God and the soul ; and therefore the proper use of fear is rather to fly from sin than to fly from God. In short, there is a fear that keepeth us from coming to God, and that is carnal ; and there is a fear that keepeth us from going away from God, which preserves the soul in a way of holy acquaintance and communion with God, and that is a holy fear : Jer. xxxii. 40, ' I will put my fear into their hearts, that they shall not depart from me.' Fear is the preserving grace, therefore it is mere bondage and horror that sets the soul at a distance from God ; yet this is in all wicked men ; they think they can never banish God far enough out of their thoughts ; they would, if they could, withdraw themselves from his government and get out of his sight ; they would fain run away from God ; they hate his presence in their consciences, because they carry their hell and their accuser always about them ; and it were happy for them they think if they should never more see God. But now a gracious fear makes the heart to cleave the closer to God. A child of God is troubled, because sin is apt to breed a strangeness ; and because they cannot more delight in his company, they are never near enough to God. A godly man is afraid of losing God, and a carnal man is afraid of finding him. The voice of slavish fear is—' Hide us from the face of him that sits upon the throne, and from the wrath of the Lamb,' Rev. vi. 16 ; but true fear is afraid lest God should hide himself — afraid lest God should shut up himself in a veil of displeasure. Observe that place : Hosea iii. 5, 'They shall seek the Lord their God, and David their king, and they shall fear the Lord and his goodness.' That filial fear which ariseth from the the goodness of God makes us to seek God and run after him. It is a blessed fear that drives us to seek the face of God, and bring us into his presence.

(3.) Servile fear only respecteth the loss and punishment, but true fear is mixed : it respecteth the punishment, but not only ; it respecteth both offence and punishment; only with this difference, they do not fear judgment so much as sin ; and in the punishment and judgment itself, to a gracious heart the loss is more horrible than the pain ; they are afraid lest there should be a divorce between them and God, lest they should grieve their good God, and cause him to depart from them. But now wicked men *non peccare metuunt sed ardere*—they are afraid to burn, but not afraid to sin. When it is merely for the punishment, then it is slavish fear. See how the apostle speaks of the habitual bondage that is in the heart of every wicked man : Heb. ii. 15, 'Through fear of death they are all their lifetime subject to bondage.' Now this kind of fear can never be gracious, partly because there is more of torment in it than there is of reverence ; and so it wants the chief and formal reason of fear, which is not the creature's danger, but God's excellency ; a carnal man fears hell more than God, which is an act of guilty and corrupt nature, not of religion. And partly, because it can never produce any genuine piety ; for if a wicked man should leave off sin out of this fear, it is not out of hatred to sin, but out of the fear of the punishment, as the bird is kept from the bait by the scarecrow. And so the sin is not hated, but forborne ; they love the sin and fear hell ; there is nothing restrained but the act ; servile fear restraineth the action, but the other mortifieth the affection. Godly men do not only forbear sin, but abhor sin, and hate it. A wicked man dares not sin, and a good man would not sin. Or suppose that out of this fear he should practise some duties (as a wicked man may out of the compunction of slavish fear), yet this is but forced from him ; and forced fruit is never so kindly as that which is naturally ripened. All the duties of a wicked man are rather a sin-offering, than a thank-offering ; not done out of any respect to God, or from reasons of religion, but to appease conscience. And therefore, upon the whole matter, we see that gracious fear must have another object besides the punishment; we may fear the punishment, but not only. A godly man doth not only fear hell, 'but fears an oath,' Eccles. ix. 2 ; that is, to be false to an oath. 'He fears the commandment,' Prov. xiii. 13. His greatest fear is lest he should cast off duty, and commit known sins.

(4.) Servile fear is involuntary. The wicked do not fear out of a voluntary act and exercise of faith, but a judicial impression. The fear that is in the godly ariseth naturally out of faith and tenderness of spirit; but in a wicked man, it is out of guilt of conscience ; there is bondage impressed and forced upon his heart, which, though it be not always felt, yet it is soon awakened—'All their lifetime they are subject to bondage,' Heb. ii. 15 ; and if God do but touch the conscience, then they are troubled. Belteshazzar seemed to have a brave spirit, and not to be daunted with the forces with which he was besieged ;

but God takes off the edge of his bravery with a few letters upon the wall—'Then his countenance was changed, and his thoughts troubled him; so that the joints of his loins were loosed, and his knees smote one against another,' Dan. v. 6. God arms wicked men's thoughts against them, and it is more than if he should bring the greatest terrors from without. At that time he was besieged with the Persian forces; but that one hand upon the wall works upon him more than all the forces with which he was beleaguered. So Felix of a sudden trembled, Acts xxiv. 25. A man would have thought the story should rather have said that Paul trembled; but mark, the prisoner makes the judge to tremble, but sore against his will, because he had the advantage of his conscience. Paul was discoursing there of temperance, righteousness, and judgment to come; now Felix was notoriously guilty of bribery and incontinency; Drusilla, though she was used as his wife, was but his minion; he took her from Azizus, king of the Emisenians; and when Paul rubs him up with judgment to come, trembling comes upon him, and he could not withstand it. And such trembling there is in wicked men in the midst of their revelling and bravery; guilty conscience recoils and boggles, and then they are afraid. This fear is involuntary, as will appear, partly because it is not constant, and comes but by fits and starts, and is a trouble to them: Prov. xxviii. 14, 'Happy is he that feareth always.' A child of God is under fear, not by fits and pauses, but he bears a constant respect to God, and seeth him that is invisible. A godly man looks upon it as a great blessing when he can work up his thoughts to a sight of God, that he may not sin in his presence. But now in wicked men it is not a fear begotten by the exercise of faith; but now and then enforced upon the soul by the evidence of a guilty conscience when it is awakened—a mere effect of the spirit of bondage. And it is plain this is involuntary, partly because wicked men are apt to take all advantages to enlarge themselves. Their desire is not to please God, but to dissolve the bonds of conscience, and to allay their fear; therefore they fly to the next carnal course. How often may we find that the Spirit is quenched, without a metaphor, by the excess of wine and the rays of conviction, when God darts them into the bosom, extinguished by mirth and company. As in Belteshazzar, there was a fit came upon him which sets him a-trembling, what doth he do? he sends to the star-gazers and astrologers, Dan. v. 7. Daniel was famous in the kingdom, and his skill well known in such cases; but anything serves, so we may come out of the stocks of conscience. Felix, when his conscience boggles, seeks to put it off when he cannot put it away, and foolishly dreams of a more convenient time.

(5.) Servile fear is a fear without any temperament of hope and comfort, and so it weakens the certainty of faith, rather than the security of the flesh. But now the gospel-fear is mixed with hope and joy: Ps. ii. 10, 'Serve the Lord with fear, and rejoice with trembling.' Because our affections are apt to degenerate, therefore God would have this mixture. Hope is apt to degenerate to presumptuous boldness, and joy to grow into a fond boasting; and therefore God hath required that we should allay the excess of one affection by the mixture of another, that so the spirit may be kept aweful, but not servile; and therefore in the children of God there is always such a mixture ; their fear it ends in reverence and caution, but not in torment ; for it is over-mastered by the apprehensions of God's love : 1 John iv. 18, ' There is no fear in love, but perfect love casteth out fear, because fear hath torment ; he that feareth is not made perfect in love.'   The fear of the godly makes them more circumspect, but not a jot less comfortable ; the more they fear, the more blessed, the more comfortable—' Blessed is he that feareth always.'   They are more wary and cautious in their walking with God, more serious in their special converses and confer-ences with God.   But now the issue of slavish fear is not love but tor-ment ; it is full of discomfort and dejection, and makes us anxious rather than cautious ; and therefore it is good to temperate your fear, that you may be comfortable in the use of holy duties, and your walk-ing with God.

Out of all you see that there is a godly fear, which is the fruit of faith.   There is a fear of reverence, proper to heaven ; a fear in the church, that is a fear of caution ; and a fear in hell, and that is despair, or a fearful looking for of the fiery indignation of the Lord.

SERMON XXXVIII.

Prepared an ark.—HEB. xi. 7.

IT follows in the text, ' Prepared an ark.'   As his fear was the fruit of his faith, so this was a fruit of his fear.   Faith by the affections hath an influence upon the practice and conversation.   I look upon this act of Noah in several regards.

1. As an act of great obedience.   Though it were a matter of high difficulty and charge, and likely to be entertained with scoffs in the world, yet Noah prepared an ark.   Observe that God must be obeyed, whatever it cost us.   Though duties cross interest and affections, and blast our repute in the world, yet God must be obeyed.   Noah was now put to trial, and so in all difficult cases we are put to trial.   Now, that we may not deny and retract our obedience, I shall show you upon what grounds we are to obey in difficult cases.   Partly, because we have entirely given up ourselves, and all that is ours, to God ; and when we have given a thing to another, he may do with it what he pleaseth. When thou art given up to God, thou art the Lord's, Rom. xiv. 7, 8. At first conversion there was a perfect resignation.   God had right in thee before, but thou then gavest up thyself by the consent of thine own will.   We did not then indent with God to say, Thus far I will obey, and no farther ; we reserved no part of our will, no interest, and no concernment of ours.   Now unless we will retract our own solemn vows, and our spiritual resignation, God must be obeyed.   Christ bids us at first to sit down and count the charges ; can you part with all for him ?   And partly, because we have no cause to repent of our bargain, whether we consult with our experiences or our obligations to

God. With our experiences, God is not a hard master; we never lost anything by God; we were gainers when we were the greatest losers. God puts his people to the question: Jer. ii. 5, 'What iniquity have your fathers found in me, that they are gone far from me?' Have I broken contract? Have I been worse than your expectation? So again: Micah vi. 3, 'O my people! what have I done unto you, and wherein have I wearied you? testify against me.' When Israel was grown weary of God, and began to stray and go off from God, saith God, What cause have I given you? Ignatius was an old and ancient servant of God, and saith he, These eighty-six years have I served God, and he never did me any harm. Certainly in those persecuting times that gracious soul met with a great deal of injury in the world, yet saith he, God never did me harm; he made it up again with consolation. And much more if we consult with our obligations to God. God doth not repent of the bargain made with Christ, and Christ doth not repent of the bargain made with God the Father; and why should we repent of our part of the covenant? God doth not repent of the bargain made with Christ: Ps. cx. 4, 'The Lord hath sworn, and will not repent, Thou art a priest for ever after the order of Melchizedek.' Though the world abuseth mercy, and puts many affronts upon grace, and abuseth the doctrine of the gospel, yet saith God, I have sworn, my word is past, Christ shall yet be a mediator. So Jesus Christ repented not; he did not only freely offer himself when the matter was propounded and broken to him at the first in the eternal treaty between God and him: Ps. xl. 7, 8, 'Lo, I come; I delight to do thy will, O my God,' but when he was about to engage in suffering, his love was hottest: John xiii. 1, 'Jesus therefore having loved his own, he loved them to the end.' The meaning is to the end of his own life, though it was exceeding difficult, for then came his torment and agonies for sinners. It is true indeed he said, 'Let this cup pass,' to show his natural abhorrency; yet he said, 'Not my will, but thy will be done,' to show his voluntary submission: Luke xxiv. 42, 'The cup which my Father gave me shall I not drink it,' John xviii. 11. When he was despitefully used by men, he did not repent of the bargain; so we should never repent of our solemn contract made with God.

2. I look upon this again as an act of obedience, as a means in order to his own safety; and then the note will be—Though a man be certain of safety, yet he must use the means. God had promised to save Noah and his household, he had made a covenant with him, Gen. vi. 18; but still Noah was to provide an ark; the covenant was upon this condition, that he should use those means. If Noah had made no ark, he must have taken his lot and share with the ungodly world. And as Noah had a promise of his own life and the life of his household, so Paul had a promise of the lives of all the men in the ship; yet, Acts xxvii. 31, 'Except these abide in the ship, ye cannot be saved;' he had told them before, ver. 22, 'Be of good cheer, there shall be no loss of any man's life among you, but of the ship,' yet 'except these abide,' &c.—not as if the accomplishment of the promise did depend upon second causes, and hang upon the endeavours of men, but only thus, he that hath appointed the end hath appointed the means, and we tempt God by putting that asunder which he hath joined together.

This being observed, it will be a check to libertinism; we cannot be saved if we live as we list. And assurance is no idle doctrine; though we be under a sure covenant with God, yet we are to mind our duty. Elijah, that had foretold rain, yet prays for it as earnestly as if the thing had been utterly uncertain and unlikely.

3. I observe again, that this means was instituted and appointed by God, not devised and invented by Noah. He might have been saved some other way; but he received a commandment concerning the matter, the proportion, the measure, and the fashion of the ark. And it is said, Gen. vi. 22, 'Thus did Noah; according to all that God commanded him, so did he.' The ark seemed an unlikely way to preserve him, being a dark receptacle, likely to be dashed in pieces against rocks; yet so did he as God commanded. The note is—we must use the means which God hath instituted in order to salvation, and that both with faith and obedience.

[1.] Use them in obedience. It is enough that God hath commanded them. All ordinances are simple in appearance, therefore the creature is apt to carp at them. In baptism there is but a little common water; yet baptism saves. As in the ark eight souls saved by water—'The like figure whereunto baptism saves,' &c., 1 Peter iii. 20, 21. So in the Lord's supper there is a little morsel of bread and a small draught of wine, yet they are high and mysterious instruments of our comfort and peace and grace. And so in the means that seem to be more rational, and to have some ministerial efficacy, as in the ordinance of the word: 1 Cor. i. 21, 'It pleased God by the foolishness of preaching to save them that believe.' The world thinks it a foolish way. Men will say, for substance, We know as much as they can teach us, and we can bring nothing sublime and new; and yet this way the Lord is pleased to work. Though there be no carnal allurements, yet mere obedience must keep up our respect to the institutions and ordinances of Jesus Christ.

[2.] We must use them in faith. It is a great part of the life of faith to live by faith in the use of ordinances; when we come to use them, and can refer ourselves to the mercy of God for a blessing, for edification, and strengthening in comfort and grace; nay though we want comfort a great while, yet when we will try again, because it is an ordinance that God hath appointed. There is more grace in waiting upon God, though there be more comfort in receiving. There is a command to keep up endeavours, and a promise to encourage expectation; and upon the bare command of God we must keep up our endeavours, though we have been discouraged by former experiences; as Peter: Luke v. 5, 'We have toiled all night, and caught nothing; yet at thy command we will let down the net;' Lord I have come again and again, and found no profit; yet I will come once more. Noah knew this was the instituted means, that he and his should be saved in the ark; and therefore he waited in the ark many months, ere the rain ceased and the flood was dried up.

4. I observe again that the only instituted means was the ark, which was a type of Christ, by whose resurrection, saith the apostle, we are saved: 1 Peter iii. 21, 'The like figure whereunto even baptism doth now save us, by the resurrection of Jesus Christ.' All God's dispensa-

tions to the fathers happened by way of type : 1 Cor. x. 11, 'All these things happened unto them—τύποι —as ensamples.' Observe, the faith of the fathers and the obedience of the fathers was conversant about a double object : spiritual good things promised to them, and in common to all believers—and then particular blessings which were proper to themselves, and were types of good things yet to come. So here was a temporal salvation in an ark, which was a figure of our spiritual deliverance by Christ. There is a great deal of similitude between Christ and the ark. The ark was the only means of salvation, and so is Jesus Christ : Acts iv. 12, 'Neither is there salvation in any other : for there is no other name under heaven given among men whereby we must be saved.' If they had builded towers, and gone up to the tops of mountains, though they were of a giant-like stature, they could not escape the flood that overwhelmed them. So all other things are but vain confidences ; though you are strict and severe in life, and practise many duties, yet out of Christ they signify nothing. So again, all without the ark perished in the waters. Many saw the ark ; but unless they entered into it, they were not safe. So, though you hear of Christ, and are of this opinion that there is a Christ, yet unless you be in Christ it will not avail you anything ; there is salvation in no other, and you must be in him before you can have any benefit by him. Therefore say as the apostle, 'Oh that I might be found in him,' Phil. iii. 9 ; that I may not only know Christ outwardly, but that there might be a real union between him and me. And look, as all that were gathered into the ark, so all that shall be saved shall be added and gathered to the church : Acts ii. 47, 'The Lord added to the church daily such as should be saved.' Those that were out of the ark, though many of them had large possessions and a great deal of money, yet that would not avail them. So 'riches profit not in the day of wrath,' Prov. xi. 4. When God comes to take us away in judgment, our estates which we idolise will be our greatest burden, and sit heavy upon our consciences ; they will be a trouble and no profit to us. Again, those that were once in the ark were sure and safe, and could not miscarry. So there is a sure salvation in Christ ; once in Christ, and salvation for ever ; all the floods of calamity can never overwhelm them, they will be your safety, and not your ruin. The flood mounted the ark higher, and made it safe from rocks. There is a notable expression of the apostle, 1 Peter iii. 20, 'They were saved by water,' the water that drowned others saved them, by hoisting up of the ark from the hills and mountains ; so all those conditions of life which to the wicked are a snare, shall be to you a blessing. When floods arise, this will be a great advantage ; afflictions and outward blessings are all faithful administrations.

Again, as Noah was buried alive in the ark for a good while, then had a joyful deliverance ; so we are 'buried with Christ in baptism,' Rom. vi. 4, mortified with affliction ; and we should live as if we were dead to the pomps of the world, and then the end will be glorious as it was to Noah. He came out and enjoyed the whole world ; so shall we when we are delivered from the prison of the body ; when our souls go forth as Noah out of the ark, we shall reign and triumph with Christ for evermore. Oh then, get into the ark, get an interest in

Christ. Noah prepared the ark himself; but the Lord hath prepared
an ark for us; all things are ready, there wants nothing but our faith.
The ark is built to our hands, and Christ is a complete saviour, fit to
shelter us and save us. Oh, let us enter into this ark!

To go on—'To the saving of his household.' It is meant of a
temporal salvation, though thereby the spiritual salvation was typified
and figured; for indeed some of Noah's house that were saved in the
ark, are represented in the scripture 'as accursed from the Lord:'
Gen. vi. 16, and vii. 1, 'Come thou and all thy house into the ark.'
There was Ham in the ark, as well as Shem and Japhet; wretched
Ham, in whose line the cursed offspring or malignant race was continued. Hence note—

Doct. Bad children of good parents are partakers of some temporal
blessings for their father's sake. Saving grace doth not descend from
parents to their children, yet many temporal blessings may for their
parents' sake. We read that Ishmael was blessed for Abraham's sake:
Gen. xvii. 20, 'I have heard thee for Ishmael; and behold I have
blessed him, and will make him fruitful, and multiply him exceedingly;
twelve princes he shall beget, and I will make him a great nation.'
Though he did not continue the blessed line, yet he had much of the
outward part of the covenant; he lived and had some common
privileges, the principal blessing was settled on Isaac. So when
Solomon had warped and turned aside from God, the Lord tells him,
1 Kings xi. 11, 12, 'I will rend the kingdom from thee, and will give
it to thy servant, nevertheless, in thy days I will not do it for David thy
father's sake, but I will rend it out of the hand of thy son.' There is
mercy to one child for his father's sake, and there is judgment to the
next child for his immediate parent's sake. See how various the dispensations of God are to children by reason of their parents; for that
is the reason given, because of his promise made to David—not for
Solomon's merit. The Lord doth not speak of Solomon's building the
temple, and those costly sacrifices that he offered; no, but for David's
sake. To instance in such a blessing as is parallel to the text of temporal deliverance, preservation, and safety: Gen. xix. 12, 'And the
men said unto Lot'—that is, the angels in men's appearance, 'Hast
thou here any besides? sons-in-law, and thy sons, and thy daughters,
bring them out of this place.' God would extend mercy for Lot's sake
to all his relations; not only to his sons and natural children, but to
his sons-in-law; nay, their relation at that time was exceeding loose,
for Lot's daughters were but espoused, for they are called virgins elsewhere. Yea, to express the largeness of his grace, God hath saved a
whole nation for their sakes, and therefore they are called 'the chariots
and horsemen of Israel,' 2 Kings ii. 12. And if ten righteous persons
had been found in Sodom, God would have spared all Sodom, Gen. xviii.
32, much more their kindred and their near relations.

To apply this—

Use 1. For encouragement to godly parents concerning their
children.

1. Consider the mercy of the covenant, how it overflows; it is not only
stinted to their persons, but runs over to their children; they are
beloved for our sake. Oh, fear the Lord not only for your own sakes,

but for your children's sake ! this will be the best way to provide for
your children ; not to heap up wealth and honour for them, but to
leave them the honour and wealth and privileges of the covenant.
It is true, the election shall obtain ; sanctification and regeneration
doth not descend from the parents to their children ; yet in outward
mercies they have their share, if they have nothing else. Though you
have nothing to leave them, yet leave them God's love, and that will
be enough. It is a usual observation, many parents go to hell in
getting an estate for them, and their' children go to hell afterward in
spending that estate. In Exod. xx. 5, 6, the commandment which
forbids idolatry and compliance with outward false worship, hath a
promise annexed concerning children. What should be the reason of
this ? Because parents are drawn to comply with things against their
conscience out of an aim to maintain their children and preserve the
interest of their families; therefore God hath made a special providence ; walk in the fear of the Lord, and the Lord will provide
for them; keep in God's ways and then you will leave them to
his blessings.

2. Instruct your children ; you have more encouragement to do so
than others, because they are born within the covenant, and by this
means you make way for the blessing: Gen. xviii. 19, ' I know
Abraham, that he will command his children and his household after
him, and they shall keep the way of the Lord.' Instruction makes
way for a blessing ; and so saith David to Solomon, 1 Kings ii. 3. 4,
' Keep the charge of the Lord thy God, and walk in his ways, . . .
that the Lord may continue his good word which he hath spoken concerning me, saying, If thy children take heed to their way to walk
before me in truth with all their heart and with all their soul, there
shall not fail thee a man on the throne of Israel.' Hereby you open
the dams and obstructions, that grace may have its free passage.

Use 2. If children are beloved for their parents' sake, then it serves
to shame and terrify them that are born of godly parents, yet are
not godly, but by their luxury and riot have forfeited all their blessings, their spiritual privileges in the covenant, and many times the
outward blessing too. Or if you have temporal blessings, they do but
harden you to greater torment, especially when you are so wicked to
mock and reproach yonr parents because of their strictness and holy
life. God looks for more from you than from others ; the natural
branches are more easily grafted into the good olive-tree. You are
natural branches of the covenant, and you might plead the promises
made to your parents with God ; you have had a greater sufficiency of
outward means ; the example of your parents, frequent instruction,
and many prayers have been laid out for you, and you have been more
acquainted with the ways of religion.

Use 3. It may press us to admire the grace of God to his children.
He cannot satisfy himself in doing good to you, but he must do good to
your children too. How should we entertain this with reverence !
When God told Abraham, I am thy God, and the God of thy seed,
' Abraham fell upon his face,' as humbly adoring the goodness of God,
Gen. xvii. 3 ; so David, when God spake concerning his house and his
children : 2 Sam. vii. 18, 19, ' What am I, O Lord, and what is my

house, that thou hast brought me hitherto?' And this was yet a small thing in thy sight, O Lord God; for thou hast spoken also of thy servant's house for a great while to come;' he stands wondering at this mercy of God.

Use 4. We learn hence that we are to save ourselves, and others committed to us. Noah prepared an ark 'for the saving of his household;' 2 Tim. iv. 16, 'In so doing, thou shalt save both thyself and them that bear thee.' It is good to instruct and teach our families: Gen xviii. 18, 'I know Abraham, that he will command his children and his household after him, that they shall keep the way of the Lord.' And this is to be done morning and evening: Deut. vi. 6, 7, 'And these words which I command thee this day shall be in thine heart: and thou shalt teach them diligently unto thy children, and shalt talk of them when thou sittest in thine house, and when thou walkest by the way, and when thou liest down, and when thou risest up.' All religion at first was in families, and to this we are bound by all the bonds of nature and religion.

I go on to another fruit and consequent of Noah's faith—'By which he condemned the world.' By the world is meant all mankind, except the family of Noah, But how did Noah condemn the world? It may be conceived in two ways: by his preaching, by his obedience. Let us see which will most suit this place.

1. By his preaching. That Noah was a preacher, it is clear from 2 Peter ii. 5, where he is called 'a preacher of righteousness.' All the while the ark was preparing he warned the wicked of their approaching danger, and admonished them to repent in time and turn to God, seeking the forgiveness of their sins through faith in the promised Messiah, or else they should perish: which is there meant by 'a preacher of righteousness.' Thus he might be said to condemn the world that admonisheth them by pronouncing the sentence of God upon the wicked world in case they did not repent. From hence I might observe—

Doct. That men receive their first sentence in the ministry of the word. There they are condemned first: John iii. 18, 'He that believeth not is condemned already;' that is, he that after warning and sufficient light stands out against the gospel, he can expect no other sentence from God. So John xx. 23, 'Whose soever sins ye remit, they are remitted: and whose soever sins ye retain, they are retained.' The sentence is first pronounced on earth, and then ratified in heaven. When we go to work according to the doctrine of faith and repentance, *clave non errante*, God will verify and make good that sentence. So Rom. ii. 16, 'In the day when God shall judge the secrets of men by Jesus Christ, according to my gospel;' according as it is declared in the gospel, so will the process of that day be. Mat. xii. 32, it is there said concerning the sin against the Holy Ghost, 'It shall never be forgiven in this world'—by the ministry of the word—'nor in the world to come'—by Christ at the last day, when the pardon of the elect shall be pronounced and ratified before all the world out of Christ's own mouth; therefore we have need to regard the present voice of the gospel. The church is the seminary of heaven. In the angel's song the word was, 'Peace upon earth,' Luke ii. 14. According as you make your peace with God upon earth, so it will be with you for ever. Those that obstinately stand out against the word, and put it away from them, they condemn themselves by their own fact; they pass a sentence upon their own souls, 'and judge themselves unworthy of everlasting life,' Acts xiii. 46. It is not we that condemn you, but you yourselves; you condemn yourselves interpretatively when you do such actions as will end in certain ruin; and the ministers of God condemn declaratively when they declare the mind of Christ; and Christ will do it authoritatively in the great and terrible day.

2. He condemned the world by his obedience. This sense is most proper: the words ' by which ' are to be referred to his preparing the ark, not to his faith, which is a more remote antecedent. A man is said to condemn another when he doth by his own actions and obedience declare what they should do, which they not doing are left inexcusable, and liable to the greater blame. So it is said, Mat. xii. 41, 42, ' The men of Nineveh shall rise in judgment against this generation, and condemn it: because they repented at the preaching of Jonas; and behold a greater than Jonas is here. The queen of the south shall rise up in judgment with this generation, and shall condemn it; for she came from the uttermost parts of the earth to hear the wisdom of Solomon, and behold a greater than Solomon is here.' The pains and diligence of others in a good course, unless it be imitated, serves but to aggravate men's sins to a greater judgment; and therefore it is said, the men of Nineveh and the queen of the south shall condemn that generation. So Noah condemned the world; that is, by his care, and pains, and cost, in preparing the ark; it was a means to aggravate their carelessness and security, and to leave them liable unto a greater judgment. Noah was a preacher of righteousness; but if he had spoken nothing, there had been sermon enough in his very building the ark to convince, condemn, and leave them without excuse. I shall prosecute this sense: the point is this—

Doct. That the carelessness and the security of the wicked is aggravated and condemned by the faith and obedience of God's servants. The pains which they take in their lives to escape wrath will be an argument by which your carelessness will be upbraided in the day of judgment. Indeed God condemned the world; but divine justice taketh notice of this argument whereby to make the process against sinners the more righteous, and by consequence the more dreadful.

To prove this point, the main reason is because we are responsible for every talent. Now the example of the godly is one of the talents. They that live among humble and mortified christians have more advantage than others have; they are entrusted with another talent for which they are to be responsible to God. That you may be sensible of it, I shall show how many advantages you have by the examples of the godly.

1. It is a means of grace appointed by God, and as all other means, it hath a ministerial, natural efficacy. The word is a means, and the word hath a ministerial efficacy. It is a rational way to deal by counsel, and the voice hath a natural force to work on the affections. So the conversation and example of the godly is a means God hath appointed, and it doth naturally provoke and draw us forth to imitation.

Saith the apostle, 1 Peter ii. 12, 'Having your conversation honest among the gentiles, that whereas they speak against you as evil-doers, they may by your good works, which they shall behold, glorify God in the day of visitation.' The first visit that God giveth the soul may be by their example. It is an ordinance of God that a man should seek to work upon his neighbours, by an innocent and comely carriage to draw them to God and religion. There is ἀγαθὴ ἔρις, an innocent emulation planted in our nature, by which we are moved, not only to imitate others, but to excel them ; therefore God would have us display the lustre of a godly conversation. So it is an ordinance of God that a woman should seek to gain an unbelieving husband : 1 Peter iii. 10, ' That if any obey not the word, they also may without the word be won by the conversation of the wives.' The wife, by lying in the bosom, and by the intimacy of converse, and as being void of suspicion of partiality, hath an excellent advantage to instil the knowledge of God and a care of religion, or at least to take off his prejudices by her holy conversation. For the apostle means there by ' winning,' not a formal conversion, but to gain them to a good liking and better opinion of the ways to God, that so they may wait upon the word, by way of preparation to receive further manifestations and discoveries of God. We are provoked by their endeavours ; example hath a natural force this way ; we love to do as others do, and to follow the track.

2. It confuteth atheism, and those prejudicate and hard thoughts which men have against religion. Godly men are God's witnesses to the world that there is a reality in religion ; they give a testimony to it by the strictness and mortifiedness of their lives. Certainly when men can abjure and renounce all the pleasantness of their lives, and all their dear contentments for the interest of religion, there is somewhat more in it than a mere notion and imagination, or a mere naked pretence. As the primitive christians, when they were so just, temperate, willing to suffer for the cause of God, the heathens cried out, It is impossible but that these men must be moved by some reasonable principle. Isa. xliii. 12, ' Ye are my witnesses, saith the Lord, that I am God.' Now miracles are ceased, God will leave the world no other confirmation of the truth of religion, but the efficacy of the word upon the conscience and the conversation of believers : John xvii. 10, ' I am glorified in them,' and ver. 17, 'Sanctify them by thy truth ; thy word is truth.' By their innocency, strictness, and sanctification, they discover the truth of the word unto the world ; which certainly should make christians very strict in their lives, for the honour and glory of the Lord Christ lies at stake. There is no such dangerous temptation to atheism as the scandalous lives of professors. They that pretend to special nearness to God, when they fall, it makes the world believe that christianity was a fancy ; as when one surprised a christian in a filthy act, he cried out, *Christiane ! ubi Deus tuus ?*—Christian, Christian ! where is thy God ? And as it confutes the privy atheism of the heart, so it confutes those devised scandals by which they would blot and stain the glory of religion. Worldly men cannot endure to be outshone ; and because they have no mind to be as good as others, they would fain make others to be as bad and as vile as themselves ; therefore they are full of hard thoughts and hard speeches against good men.

Now nothing convinceth the world so much as the godly life of professors. As the apostle speaks of the gravity of church-meetings : 1 Cor. xiv. 25, 'Falling down on his face, he will worship God, and report that God is in you of a truth.' When he shall see the christian assemblies managed with such awe and reverence, and all things disposed in a comely manner, it would be a means of conviction, and bring him to fall down on his face, and say, Surely God is here. So, if christians did not let fall the majesty of their conversation, the prejudices of the world would soon vanish, and those that live about you would be forced to say, Certainly God is with these men. Of all apologies, the real apology is the best : 1 Peter ii. 15, 'That with well-doing you may put to silence the ignorance of foolish men ; ' what we translate ' put to silence,' in the original, is φιμοῦν, that you may muzzle or bind up the mouth of a wicked man, that he cannot bark against religion. I like apologies well that are made to take off the prejudices of the world ; as those of Tertullian and Justin Martyr for christians, and others for reformed churches. But there is no apology like your own lives to put an end to all the reproaches of the world, for works are a visible evidence of our sincerity ; and so far the world seeth that the ways of God are to be approved and respected.

3. The examples of God's children are but the word exemplified, the rule drawn out into practice. The word is the means of conversion, wherever it is written, preached, or lived, and every christian is as it were a walking bible. As it was said of a learned man that he was μουϛεῖον περιαπτοῦν, a walking library ; so a child of God that walks in innocency and strictness of life is a walking and a living reproof ; therefore his life must needs convince and condemn the world. There are some whose special office it is to preach ; but every christian may live a sermon. You may be all preachers in this kind : 2 Cor. iii. 3, 'Forasmuch as you are declared to be the epistle of Jesus Christ.' Mark, Christ doth by his servants, as it were, declare and write his mind to the world ; they are a living rule. You that are believers are to make out the glory of Christ, the efficacy of his Spirit, and the strictness of his doctrine to the world ; you are to show forth—τὰς ἀρετας—' the virtues of him that hath called you,' 1 Peter ii. 9, to declare what manner of person Christ is, and what is his glory ; he sends you out as so many lively copies and stamps of his image. The gospel is called the image of God, and a christian is the image of God too. The gospel is the glass wherein we behold his glory : 2 Cor. iii. 18, ' We all as in a glass beholding the glory of the Lord,' &c ; it is the picture which Jesus Christ hath sent to his bride. As you know there is Cæsar's image upon his coin, and Cæsar's image upon his son, he is his living image ; so the scriptures are the image of God, where he hath displayed the excellency and perfection of his nature as we are capable to understand it ; but christians who are his sons and children are his living image that must discover his glory.

4. The example of the godly shows the strictness and severity of religion is possible ; so that by that means it condemns the world of their negligence. Men think the rules of the gospel, because they exceed the power and force of nature, are only calculated for angels.

But now when men that live in the flesh, that live such a kind of life as we do, yet live above the flesh, the world is left without excuse, and their negligence and carelessness is hereby condemned. 1 Peter iv. 4, 'They think it strange,' saith the apostle, 'that you run not with them to the same excess of riot.' Carnal men think that there is such a felicity in their kind of lives that they wonder others are not as greedy of it as they; but now they are condemned in their thoughts when they behold the strictness, the mortification, the self-denial that is in the lives of christians. You may do it, it is possible; for there are many about you that have done it; and if you do not, you are left without excuse: Heb. vi. 12, 'Be not slothful, but followers of them who through faith and patience inherit the promises.' When the apostle speaks of resisting of Satan, and maintaining the spiritual life against the assaults of the powers of darkness, he gives this as one reason: 1 Peter v. 9, 'Knowing that the same afflictions are accomplished in your brethren that are in the world.' Your brethren in the flesh—that have bodies as you have, that need the common supports of life as you do, that have not divested themselves of the interests and concernments of flesh and blood—they can resist a busy devil and a naughty world, and can wrestle with the corruptions of their own hearts: they that are of the same lump and nature that you are, they can do these things.

5. Because the examples of others make conscience work whenever you see it. Natural conscience doth homage to the image of God which is stamped upon his children. When they see their works and their strictness raised to such a height and proportion as nature cannot reach it, then they tremble; it makes their conscience to work: 1 Peter iii. 1, 2. 'They that obey not the word may without the word be won by the conversation of the wives, while they behold your chaste conversation, coupled with fear.' The word 'coupled' is not in the original, and the sense is perfect without it; it may be read thus, 'When they behold your chaste conversation with fear.' A wicked man cannot look upon a strict christian without trembling; when they behold the strictness and severity of their lives, it makes them to quake. It is said of Herod, Mark vi. 10, that 'he feared John;' not so much because he was a severe preacher, one that would rub truth upon his conscience; he did not only fear him as a prophet, but as a 'just man.' Innocency and strictness beget fear; they are objects reviving guilt, and make conscience return upon itself; when they see their holy and godly conversation, it makes them to think of their own carelessness and sin; it is like a blow upon a sore, which makes the heart ache. The presence of God is dreadful to sinners anywhere, be it in eminent providences or in ordinances; but in the lives of his children it begets secret fear and some nips of conscience: Deut. xxviii. 10, 'All the people of the earth shall see that thou art called by the name of the Lord, and they shall be afraid of thee;' when they behold the graciousness of conversation which the godly hold forth. That is the reason why wicked men are in prison when they are in good company; they are taken with a fit of trembling. How despicable soever the godly are in their eyes, yet there is one of their judges present that condemns them for the present, and will pass judgment upon them hereafter. Ignatius,

speaking of the bishop of the Trallians, saith, that he was of such severity of life, that I think the greatest atheist that is would even be afraid to look upon him. Mortification shines effectually into the conscience of a wicked man. The strictness of God's children darts itself into their breasts, and begets a veneration and reverence.

Use 1. To press christians to walk so that they may even preach in their conversations, that you may condemn the world, not by your censures,—that is not the christian way, it is forbidden in the gospel— but by your lives, especially ministers to second their doctrine with practice. It concerns all christians, especially when we have to do with them that are without. 'Walk wisely' saith the apostle 'toward them that are without,' Col. iv. 5. There needs a great deal of wisdom and care, whenever we are cast upon the company of wicked and carnal men. Of all things, be careful of your conversations before wicked men ; you are one of God's witnesses that must reprove and condemn them ; therefore be careful that thou dost not disparage thy testimony. That you may do so, take these directions and motives.

First, For the directions.

1. Be sure to show forth those graces which they approve in their consciences, though they are loth to practise them ; as strictness of life, which naturally strikes a veneration into the heart of a sinner: Mark vi. 20, 'Herod feared John, because he was a just man, and holy.' A loose christian that walks like the men of the multitude is a disgrace to his profession, and hardens carnal men in their wicked ways. Then diligence in the means of salvation. Certainly the world will see that there is somewhat in it when men are so busy and in earnest ; when they see the children of God, that are wise and discreet, so diligent in the means of godliness. It is somewhat answerable to that which is spoken of in the text : Noah's preparing an ark, and providing beasts to enter therein. So when you work out your salvation with fear and trembling, the world will think there is somewhat in it, or else you would not be so busy and careful. So for charity: James i. 27, 'Pure religion, and undefiled before God and the Father, is this, to visit the fatherless and the widow.' The world is mightily taken with these things: so that, Rom. v. 7, 'For a good man one would even dare to die.' A man that is only of a rigid and severe innocency, a sour man, it may be he may have little love in the world ; but he that is good and charitable, the world esteems him exceedingly. So also for suffering and constancy in the matters of religion. Venture somewhat upon your hopes, that the world may know they are worthy hopes. So for a contempt of the world ; it doth mightily affect a natural conscience, for they are transported with a greedy desire of earthly things ; therefore they wonder when they see christians deny their interests and overlook their concernments upon just and convenient reasons ; this hath a marvellous influence upon a natural conscience. I do the rather instance in this, because worldliness is a corruption that is incident to men that are serious, and of that kind of temper which is fit for religion. When you are full of cares, and covetous as the men of the world, you do exceedingly disparage and stain your profession, and you do not condemn the world.

2. What you do, do it in such a way as morality cannot reach it.

There are many corruptions which nature discovers, and we may avoid them upon such arguments as nature suggests. Now you are 'to show forth the virtues of Christ,' 1 Peter ii. 9, and the influences of the Spirit of Christ, and not 'walk only as men,' 1 Cor. iii. 3. When men only content themselves with the civil and orderly use of reason, they may be just and temperate; this is but to act as men. Your way should be above the rate of the world; you should be holy, and maintain an aweful reverent fear of God; this is such a way as the world cannot reach: Mat. vi. 46, 'If you love them that love you, what reward have ye? Do not even the publicans the same?' You should do somewhat above that which is enforced by the light of nature; as in giving, forgiving, and righteous dealing, a christian should be a point above others; so in loving enemies, in providing for the glory of God, and laying out himself for good uses. A christian should not be contented with the proportions of nature, but do somewhat to answer the self-denial of Christ, who when he was rich in the glory of the godhead, became poor for our sakes. There is a height becoming religion, above the size and pitch of morality; and this you should aim at.

3. Let all things come from the force of religion, and not from by-ends. There is nothing amiable but what is genuine and native. Forced actions lose their lustre and grace, and do not prevail with the world. It is said of the children of God, that they were altogether bent for the heavenly recompenses: Heb. xi. 16, 'They declared plainly that they sought a country.' You should declare plainly you have no designs but for heaven. Do all things for the love and fear of God; by-ends will never hold out. It is said of the hypocrite, Prov. xxv., 26, 'His wickedness shall be showed before the whole congregation.' Varnish will off; and whenever it happens, it will be much to the prejudice and disgrace of religion.

SERMON XXXIX.

By the which he condemned the world, and became heir of the righteousness which is by faith.—HEB. xi. 7.

Secondly, FOR the motives to press you to this: to live, so that you may condemn the world, that you may make them own their guilt and shame.

1. You may be a means to convert them. All are bound as much as they can to co-operate to the conversion of men. It is a debt of charity that we owe to the world, especially if we consider the relation we sustain as God's witnesses, as Christ's epistles. Now what an honour would this be to further the good of souls! What glory would it be to God, and honour to yourselves: Mat. v. 16, 'Let your light so shine before men, that they may see your good works, and glorify

your Father which is in heaven.' Oh, how sweet will this be when men shall come and bless God that ever they were acquainted with you, when they shall bless God for the lustre of your conversation, and for the light of holiness that shines forth in your lives! Ministers have a great deal of honour in that they are employed in the conversion of souls, when they are successful in the work; they will all have their crown and rejoicing in the day of Christ. Now God invites you that are private christians to the conversion of souls. It may be you formerly have done hurt by the carelessness of your lives. Nature is very susceptible of evil; we easily take sickness one from another, but not health; and therefore you should be the more earnest to lay the pious holy snares of a godly conversation, that you may be a means to win them to God.

2. If you do not convert them, you will leave them without excuse; you will have further cause to applaud the righteous counsels of God in the great day, when you shall sit with Christ upon the bench. The apostle saith, 1 Cor. vi. 2, that 'The saints shall judge the world;' then by sentence, now by conversation; then by applauding of the righteousness of God in their just execution. Now if you look to judge the world with Christ, begin it for the present, condemn the world in your conversation.

3. If you do not condemn them, you will justify them. A carnal profession justifies the world, and a godly christian condemns the world. Judah justified Sodom and Samaria: Ezek. xvi. 52, 'Be confounded, and bear thy shame, in that thou hast justified thy sisters.' You do justify their prejudices; you put an excuse into their mouths, as if religion were as bad as they make it. It will be sad for the account of hypocrites in the last day, when wicked men shall come forth as witnesses, and plead, Lord, we never thought these had been thy servants, because they were so proud, so self-seeking, so full of aspiring projects, so factious and turbulent. When wicked men are hardened by carnal professors, at the last day this will impress a shame upon them. A professor overtaken with sin may do more hurt than a thousand others; the Hams of the world will laugh to see a Noah drunk. The wickedness of some hypocrites crept in among the church hath always been a great means of hardening the world, and been a stone of stumbling to them; and by 'such the way of truth is evil spoken of,' 2 Peter ii. 2.

4. By condemning the world you will justify the ways of God; you will force wicked men whether they will or no, to say that the ways of God are holy and true, and to say these men are honest, and that which they profess is religion. It is the duty of every servant of God to justify his profession from the reproach and scandal of the world: Mat. xi. 19, 'Wisdom is justified of her children.' Justification implies condemnation and reproach. So Titus ii. 10, 'That you may adorn the doctrine of God your saviour.' Look, as men of great parts, and are carnal, when they take the wrong way, they put a varnish and ornament upon the devil's cause; so godly and strict christians, when they keep up the majesty of their conversation, they adorn their profession, and are an ornament and credit to Jesus Christ.

5. You will lose nothing by it; then God will not be ashamed of you as those, whose design was for heaven: Heb. xi. 16, 'God is not ashamed to be called their God.' God will think it to be no dishonour to himself that he hath such kind of servants; he will not be ashamed to be called your God, and Christ your Christ. But usually it may be said of most of us, *Dicimur christiani in opprobrium Christi;* we are called christians to the very disgrace of Jesus Christ, because of the folly and sinfulness of our lives.

Use 2. To wicked men, to press them to observe and improve the conversation of those godly and mortified christians with whom they do converse. Look to the frame of your hearts whenever you are cast into their company. How often hath thy heart smote thee when thou hast heard their gracious discourse, and seen their holy conversation? Observe, what hast thou done upon such occasions? Some wicked men, more touched with a sense of religion, when their consciences work, when they see the beauty and heavenliness of their lives, they seek to drive them out, and forget these things. Ah! consider, this will be a means not only to harden thee for the present, but to condemn thee; when men have had much remorse and smiting of conscience, if they do not observe it, they grow the more obdurate and hardened in sin, which will be a means of thy utter ruin. God hath a book of remembrance, and how many witnesses will there be brought against thee at that day? Not only ministers that have shaken off the dust of their feet against thee, but godly men who condemn thee by their lives. God will remember thee; those agonies and secret nips of conscience shall rise up in judgment against thee, to the confusion of thy face; thy rebellion is mightily aggravated and sealed up by it to destruction, when thou art condemned by the innocency of their lives. But now others, when they are smitten in conscience by observing the strictness and graciousness of God's children, they rage and rail, imagine scandalous thoughts against them; or else they hate and persecute them, as it is the old trick of the world to malign what they have no mind to imitate,—as 'Cain slew his brother because his works were righteous,' 1 John iii. 10. Few there are that confess the wickedness of their estate, that give glory to God when they are convinced. If thou canst not endure the lustre of godliness in a saint, how wilt thou endure the presence of Jesus Christ in that day? Noah condemned the world, and did not a judgment follow? When you are reproached in your conscience by the sight of their conversation, take notice of it that it may be a day of visitation to thy soul.

Use 3. For comfort against the reproaches of the world. They may condemn you in word, but you condemn them in life. When a man is running a race, no matter for the judgment of standers-by, or those that contend with us, all depends upon the master of the sports and the umpire of the race. So wicked men may scoff at you, standers-by may mock and slander your godly conversation; it is no matter, if God acquit you, and if you have praise with him. As a man that outruns another is said to cast his adversary; so you that outrun the wicked, and outshine them in godliness, you condemn them really, and the judge of the race will determine of your side. And therefore if the world reproach you, this is the revenge you should take upon them, to be the more strict, to give out the greater lustre of holiness, so you will be revenged upon wicked men in an innocent way; if you be more strict, this will stop their mouths.

Some things might be observed from that expression, 'the world,' viz.—

1. Observe, that we must obey God, and walk in innocency and strictness, though we be alone. As here most of the world were naught; there were but a few good, but eight persons, saved in the ark, and among them a Ham. Sometimes it is safer to go against the stream than with it.

2. Observe also, that multitudes cannot keep off the strokes of God's vengeance. God can dissolve all confederacies and combinations against himself: Prov. xi. 21, 'Though hand join in hand, the wicked shall not go unpunished.'

3. Observe also, compliance with the multitude doth not lessen the sin, but rather increase it. When we see men fall into the gulf, it is more foolish if we will follow after them.

I might clear a doubt which some move, whether all the world that were drowned in the flood were eternally lost? Certain we are the scripture rather doth carry it that they were all eternally lost, for they are called 'the world of the ungodly,' 2 Peter ii. 5, and the 'spirits that are now in prison, who sometimes were disobedient,' 1 Peter iii. 19, 20; and yet by probable conjectures some exception may be made, for it is probable that some might have time to call upon God for mercy, and some of them that perished came of the holy race, and possibly some might be moved with the approach of the judgment.

I come to the last words—'And became,' &c. To make way for the points, I shall first open the words—

'He became;' that is, he was then discovered to be so. Noah was righteous before, and had 'found grace in the eyes of God,' Gen. vi. 8; and verse 9, 'Noah was a just man, and perfect in his generation; and Noah walked with God.' Yet it is said after he built the ark, then 'he became;' that is, then he was discovered to be what he was. It is the fashion of scripture to say that things are done when they are clearly manifested and discovered. There is a parallel instance: James ii. 23, 'And the scripture was fulfilled which saith, Abraham believed God, and it was imputed unto him for righteousness;' then it was fulfilled when he offered up Isaac, yet the saying was used of Abraham long before he offered up his son: Gen. xv. 6, 'And he believed in the Lord, and he counted it to him for righteousness;' but the meaning is, then it appeared how truly it was said of him. God giving him again a solemn testimony: Gen. xxii. 12, 'Now I know that thou fearest God, seeing then thou hast not withheld thy son, thy only son, from me.' So it is here; Noah, after he had prepared an ark, 'became,' that is, then he was visibly declared to be, an heir of the covenant of grace; God dealing with Noah just as he dealt with Abraham, confirming his faith by a solemn testimony: Gen. vii. 1, 'God said to Noah, Come thou and all thy house into the ark; for thee have I seen righteous before me in this generation;' now I have found thou art righteous before me, that is, by a righteousness of faith;

for by the works of the law none can be righteous in his sight : Rom. iii. 20, 'By the deeds of the law there shall no flesh be justified in his sight.'   And to that testimony the apostle alludeth here.

'An heir.' The word 'heir' is sometimes put for 'possessor,' especially if we have a firm right, and if it be such a possession upon which there depends a further heritage.   So Jesus Christ, who is lord and possessor of all things, is said to be 'the heir of all things,' Heb. i. 2.   All firm and perpetual possession among the Hebrews is expressed by the term 'heritage ; ' so that to be an heir is nothing else but to obtain, to be a possessor, to be interested in this righteousness of faith. Though possibly the apostle might intend that he succeeded as immediate heir in the line of the church, or head of that race among whom the righteousness of faith is professed.

' Of the righteousness which is by faith.' By faith is meant faith in the Messiah ; and righteousness is here put for the righteousness of justification, or rather I conceive for the reward of righteousness—acceptance with God, possession of the whole world, and the enjoyment of the everlasting recompenses, all which are here called righteousness, because all these things are built and founded upon the righteousness of Christ which is possessed by faith ; of which righteousness Noah professed himself an heir.   And this is that righteousness he did press upon men in his age, inculcating and commending the same hopes to others. Therefore he is said to be 'a preacher of righteousness,' 2 Peter ii. 5, because he pressed them to return to God, and seek the forgiveness of their sins by faith in the Messiah.

The points are three—(I.) That there is a righteousness by faith ; (2.) This righteousness is an heritage ; (3.) That our title to this heritage is evidenced to be right and good by the special operations of faith.

Doct. 1. That there is a righteousness by faith.   This I have largely spoken of in ver. 4.   I shall only now observe two things—

1. That this righteousness is a righteousness opposed to the righteousness of the law, or exact obedience as fulfilled in our own persons. A clear place for that is Rom. iv. 13, where it is said of Abraham that ' the promise that he should be heir of the world was not to Abraham or to his seed through the law,'—mark the opposition,—' but through the righteousness of faith ; ' where there is a plain distinction and opposition of the law to the righteousness of faith.   The best of God's children are accepted out of grace, and justified by faith, not works. Noah was a just and perfect man in his generation ; he was the best alive in his time, and yet his claim was not of right but of grace ; ' he found grace' though he were 'a just man,' Gen. vi. 8, 9.   In the children of God there is a care of holiness and obedience ; but their reception into God's favour is not built upon their obedience, because that is imperfect and mixed with sin ; but upon the righteousness which is by faith.

2. It is a righteousness that is opposed to any act, virtue, and grace of our own.   When the apostle had spoken of his own personal excellences, he concludes all thus, Phil. iii. 9, 'That I may be found in him, not having mine own righteousness ; ' where Paul clearly shows that it is such a righteousness as we have by being found in Christ ;

such as doth not arise from any act of ours, but by virtue of our union with him. Our guilt is so great that when wrath makes inquisition for sinners, nothing will cover it but the righteousness of the Son of God: Rom. iii. 22, 'Even the righteousness of God, which is by faith of Jesus Christ unto all and upon all them that believe; so that there is no difference.' He saith it is the righteousness of God, either such as God hath appointed, or such as is merited by a person that is God; for indeed there is a righteousness of God, that essential righteousness which Christ hath with the Father, which is incommunicable either to man or angel, no more than God can communicate to the creature any other of his essential attributes, as omnipotency, eternity, &c; but it is the righteousness of Christ who is God-man, his cautionary or surety; righteousness, which he performed in our stead, which by virtue of our union to him is made ours; and the instrument on our part to receive it is faith, and therefore by consequence the objects of it are all believers without difference.

Doct. 2. That this righteousness is a heritage. So the apostle intimates when he saith he 'became an heir.' Now it is a heritage in several respects.

1. Because of the dignity and excellency of the blessing itself, with all the consequences of it. The blessing itself is a fair portion; it is a legacy left us by Jesus Christ. Look, as when Elijah went to heaven he left Elisha his cloak; so when Jesus Christ went to heaven he left us his garment, his own righteousness as a legacy to us, which is a covering that is not too short to make us accepted with God. The gospel is called the new testament; it is the will of Christ, and among other legacies he hath left us his righteousness. Look, as a father entails his land upon his children, so Jesus Christ hath left us what he had. As to the outward state, Christ had nothing to leave us, he was poor and despicable; but that which was eminent in Christ was his righteousness and obedience, and this he hath left to us as the pledge of his love. Christ's righteousness is an excellent privilege and heritage, a better heritage than all the world; he is a rich man indeed that hath it. All other things are but an additional supply, that is the main blessing: Mat. vi. 33, 'Seek first the kingdom of God, and the righteousness thereof, and all other things shall be added to you.' The great and main blessing that we should seek and look after in the world is an interest in the righteousness of Christ; other things are cast in as paper and packthread into the bargain. This is a jewel which cost Christ very dear to purchase it for us, and he is a rich man indeed that hath it. Look, as the wise merchant sold all to purchase the pearl of great price, Mat. xiii. 46; so if we suffer the loss of all, it will make us amends if we have this pearl of great price; all else is but dung and dross. Those in the world that have large revenues, that join house to house, and field to field, alas! they have but a spot of earth, in the map it is nothing; but he that hath Christ and his righteousness, he is the rich and great man, greater than the greatest monarch upon earth if he be carnal; and he may say with David, Ps. xvi. 6, 'I have a goodly heritage,' when he had made God his portion, and hath an interest in the righteousness of Christ.

2. It is called a heritage to note the largeness of our portion and

spiritual estate. Let us consider the consequences of this righteousness ; it is our title and claim to all other blessings that can be had.
The children of God have the largest patrimony that ever was—' All
things are yours,' saith the apostle, 1 Cor. iii. 21. Though God do
not give us the actual possession, yet we have a general right. And
all things are theirs by way of reduction in the final issue and event ;
all for the good of the heirs of promise, though all be not yours in the
way of actual possession and enjoyment ; that may be hurtful to us. But
to come to particulars, there cannot be two more magnificent words
spoken in the whole creation than heaven and earth, yet they are both
yours by virtue of this righteousness.

[1.] For the earth ; for most difficulty seems to be there. Many a
christian hath not a foot of land, yet it is true all things are his. It is
said of Abraham, Rom. iv. 13, ' For the promise that he should be the
heir of the world,' &c. And we have the blessing of Abraham, who
through the righteousness of faith was re-established in the right which
Adam had before the fall. Wherever God should cast his portion, he
might look upon it as his, as made over to him in Christ. Both the
comfortable and the sanctified enjoyment of the creature is a part of
our portion, we have it by virtue of this righteousness ; God hath
created all refreshments for believers that they might receive them
with thanksgiving: 1 Tim iv. 3, ' Commanding to abstain from meats,
which God had created to be received with thanksgiving of them which
believe and know the truth.' Believers only have a covenant right to
make use of the good creatures and outward supports and refreshments
of life. I cannot say that wicked men are usurpers of what they
possess, it is their portion : Ps. xvii. 14, ' The men of the world, which
have their portion in this life ;' yet they have not a covenant-title as
believers have ; they have not these things from a loving father, from
a God in covenant with them ; they do not work for good to their
souls. I say they are not usurpers before God ; they have a general
title and a creature right, but not a covenant right, till interested in
Christ; this they lost in Adam. The devils themselves have their
being by a creature right, so the young ravens have their food, so
wicked men have a creature right ; but all this is salted with a curse,
and proves a snare to them. But now, whatever a christian hath, he
hath it from his father from mercy, from a God in covenant with him,
so he is an heir of the world ; whatever of the world falls to his share,
he may look upon it as a blessing of the covenant, as that which will
not hinder but further his salvation. In Christ we have a new right
to the creature, and we have a sanctified use of it, Heb. i. 2. It is
said of Christ, that ' he is heir of all things ;' we can have no part of
the inheritance but by and through him, for Adam was disinherited,
and he lost his covenant right over the creature by his fall; but in
Christ the title is renewed. If all the world were yours, it would be
no blessing to you if you could not look upon it as a legacy from Christ,
as a thing that you hold by a covenant right, as that wherein you are
interested by the righteousness of faith.

[2.] As the world is theirs, so heaven is theirs too. You are an
heir-apparent to the kingdom of heaven : James ii. 5, ' Hearken, my
beloved brethren, hath not God chosen the poor of this world, rich in

faith, and heirs of the kingdom which he hath promised to them that love him?' He is an heir to a crown, and the fairest crown that ever was. A poor believer walks up and down in the world in a despicable appearance, like princes in disguise in a foreign country and strange land; they have a royal patrimony and a large estate, though their appearance be despicable; the world that looks upon them thinks them miserable, that all their hopes lie '*in terra incognita*,' in an invisible land, that shall never be found out. But it is not so far but the children of God may see it through the prospective of faith, which is the evidence of things not seen. Indeed the children of God are wont to do so, they go up often to the top of Pisgah, and view the promised land and with Abraham they walk through it, and do, as it were, hear God say, All this is made over to thee in Christ; and they live upon this reversion. The Lord would not weary us with expectation too much; therefore we have somewhat in hand, but the best of our portion is to come. We are all God's children, 'heirs and co-heirs with Christ,' Rom. viii. 17. Christ and we do, as it were, divide heaven betwixt us. We have a share in all his father's goods; we have one father, therefore hereafter we shall dwell in one house, and enjoy the same estate—'I go to prepare a place for you,' John xiv. 3; 'I will that they also may behold my glory,' John xvii. 24. Christ speaks as if he were not contented with his own heaven without our company.

3. It is called a heritage to show the nature of our tenure. You know of all tenures, inheritance is the most free, most sure, and the most honourable; and indeed in this way do we hold all the blessings of the covenant.

[1.] It is a free tenure. All that God seeks to magnify in the covenant is his glorious grace from first to last. In heaven we shall admire free grace: 2 Thes. i. 10, 'He shall come to be glorified in his saints, and admired in all them that believe.' Reward and wages are more servile terms, suited to a covenant made with servants; but heritage is for children. Therefore the apostle, speaking to godly servants, saith, Col. ii. 23–25, 'Servants, obey in all things your masters, according to the flesh; not with eye-service as men-pleasers, but in singleness of heart, fearing God . . . knowing that of the Lord ye shall receive the reward of the inheritance.' Mark how these are coupled : reward is suited to their outward relation, you will have wages; but then 'reward of inheritance,' that is suited to their inward and spiritual condition; as they are freemen and children of God, so they have an inheritance; and as servants they shall have a reward. When we come to heaven, it is a question which we shall admire most, grace or glory. It is a free manner of tenure, that so grace may be exalted. The heritage is bought before the heir be born many times. So this heritage was purchased before the children had done either good or evil. There was a covenant passed betwixt God and Christ, and that was a covenant of work and wages; Christ was to be a servant that we might be children.

[2.] It is honourable. Of all tenures, that of inheritance is best, better than holding of land by service. Now God hath put this honour upon us to make us co-heirs with his own Son : Rom. viii. 17, ' Heirs of God, and joint-heirs with Christ.' We do not hold as hired servants, but as children. Christ alone is the natural son; and we shall have Christ's own title, and are co-heirs by adoption: John i. 12, 'To as many as received him, to them gave he, ἐξουσίαν, power to be called the sons of God.' God needed us not; he had a son of his own that he delighted in before ever there was hill or mountain: Prov. viii. 30, 'Then was I with him as one brought up with him, and I was daily his delight.' It is the more to be admired by us because we were strangers and rebels, and could aspire to no other title than that— 'Make me as one of thy hired servants,' Luke xv. 19. Though we are very ambitious, yet conscience is so possessed with the sense of guilt that we can look for no more. But now he hath put this honour upon us that we shall have the title of children and hold by an inheritance.

[3.] It is a sure title, because it is built upon nature. A father may frown upon his son for his fault, but doth not easily disinherit him; but a servant, on his offence, is turned out-of-doors. When Adam held by the first covenant, he was but an honourable servant; therefore when he offended his master, he was turned out-of-doors. But now we have the title of children by Christ. Though God may chastise us, yet he will not disinherit us: Ps. lxxxix. 33, 34, 'My lovingkindness will I not utterly take from him, nor suffer my faithfulness to fail; my covenant will I not break, nor alter the thing that is gone out of my lips.' He hath reserved a liberty in the covenant, that he will chastise us: ver. 32, 'I will visit their transgressions with the rod,' &c., but he will never alter the purposes of his love and his counsel towards us. A child may be whipped, but not disinherited. God hath not only pawned his word to us, but given us earnest that he will not change his purpose; the inheritance is past over in court: 2 Cor. i. 22, 'Who hath sealed us, and given us the earnest of the Spirit in our hearts.' Those that make the purposes of God to be changeable, they cut the sinews of christian comfort; they make us to walk with God like dancers upon a rope, as if we were always ready to fall; but God hath given us earnest that he will never reverse the purposes of his grace. When we have once an interest in it, our right is indefeasible, and we cannot lose it. And mark, it is not only a sure title in regard of God, but also in regard of men; for as God will not take our heritage from us, so men cannot. We may lose goods, livings, lives, but we can never lose our heritage; this is sure in Christ, they cannot take away our better portion—'All things are yours,' even death among the rest, 1 Cor. iii. 22; that is a part of our heritage.

4. To show the condition of our present state, therefore it is called an heritage. Here we have little in hand like an heir that doth live in hope; so it is said: Titus iii. 7, 'That being justified by his grace, we should be made heirs according to the hope of eternal life.' We live altogether upon hope. Servants and mercenaries must have pay in hand, they covenant from quarter to quarter; so carnal men that are hired servants, they must have their reward, secular conveniences: Mat. vi. 2, Ἀπέχουσι τὸν μισθὸν αὐτῶν, 'They have their reward,' they give God a discharge. If he will give them honour, wealth, and riches in the world, they look for no more. They do not look after heaven; as a servant in the family doth not regard the heritage; he knows the master

reserves that for his son, but he must have his present wages. But we live in hope God will make amends for everything; not a frown or ill look of the world, but God will recompense it; as children are content with their present maintenance and education, they know when the heritage falls they shall have enough. Only there is this difference between the earthly and the heavenly heritage; in the spiritual heritage we possess in our father's lifetime. Men give their estates when they can possess them no longer; but Christ and we possess it together, we are glorified with him. In the outward heritage the father dies to give place to the son; but here the son must die that they may covenant with the father.

Doct. 3. That our title to this heritage is evidenced to be right and good by the operations of faith. Then ' he became heir of the righteousness which is by faith;' that is, in his own sense and feeling. God speaks to us by the Spirit, which witnesseth to us that we are heirs and children. Now this never will be till faith hath produced some good fruits; for without this conscience cannot witness, and the Spirit will not.

1. Conscience cannot witness. Habits lie out of sight till they are drawn out into action, then they come under the view of conscience. The seed lies hidden in the ground till it spring up into a stalk; the sap is an inward thing which you cannot see, it is only discovered by the blossom and fruit: so the inward habit of grace doth lie out of sight; it is discovered to the notice and view of conscience by the operations of it: 1 John iii. 19, 'Hereby we know that we are of the truth, and shall assure our hearts before him.' We may come and make good our claim when once faith appears in the fruits of holiness: 1 John ii. 3, 'Hereby we do know that we know him, if we keep his commandments.'

2. The Spirit will not witness without this. This is God's method. The testimony of the Spirit is always subsequent to the testimony of a renewed conscience: Rom. viii. 16, 'The Spirit itself beareth witness with our spirit, that we are the children of God.' It is God's method, first to pour in the oil of grace, then the oil of gladness; first to make Christ 'a king of righteousness,' and then 'king of peace,' Heb. vii. 2. And 'after that ye believed, ye were sealed with that Holy Spirit of promise,' Eph. i. 13. In the original there are three articles; ye are sealed ' by the Spirit,' ' by the Holy Spirit,' and ' by the Spirit of promise.' The apostle shows how the Spirit comes and seals up grace to the soul; as the 'Spirit of promise' upon gospel terms, ' after that ye believed;' and ' as the Holy Spirit,' having wrought holiness in the heart. We have a title as soon as we believe, but this title is not evidenced to us till faith be discovered to us in the fruits of holiness.

Use. To press you to examine yourselves. Are you, as Noah was, heir of the righteousness of faith? is this your condition? All depends upon that, and therefore I will propound two questions:—Have you the title of an heir? Have you the spirit of an heir.

1. Have you the title of an heir? Once clear up that, be a child, and thou shalt be sure of a child's part and portion. Now what can you say to this? Have you received the spirit of adoption? Faith is your title; and that faith must be evidenced by holiness. We are apt to mistake the work of faith, and cry up presumption for faith. Conscience will still be entering process against us, and citing us before the tribunal of God, if you cannot produce the fruits of holiness. How will you evidence

your faith ? St Paul saith, ' We are justified by faith,' Rom. iii. 28 ; St James, that ' we are justified by works, and not by faith only,' James ii. 24.   By faith we are justified from sin before God, and so we have peace with God ; and by works we are justified from hypocrisy in the court of conscience, so we have peace with ourselves.   This way must your title be made out to you.   Is there a care of duty and a diligent resistance of sin ?

2. Hast thou the spirit of an heir ?   What is the spirit of an heir ? Then—

[1.] Thy main care will be carried out to make the birthright sure. This will be the first and early design of the soul: Mat. vi. 33, ' Seek ye first the kingdom of God, and the righteousness thereof ; ' this is the great work you drive on in the world.   All the children of God cannot come to assurance, but they all labour after it ; and they make it their care to seek the kingdom of God, and make out their interest in him. A carnal man, if he can thrive and prosper in the way of his trade, he looks for no more, he gives God a discharge.   But now an heir cannot be content till his title to the heritage be sure.   Now can you live upon your reversion ; wait in hope, and be godly without secular encourage-ment ?   Servants must have wages, but an heir can live upon the reversion.

[2.] An heir will not easily part with his inheritance ; and therefore, have you honourable thoughts of your portion in Christ, and of the con-solation of the Spirit.   It is said of Esau, Heb. xii. 16, he was ' a pro-fane person, and for one morsel of meat sold his birthright.'   It is the highest profaneness in the world to have cheap thoughts of the consola-tions of the Holy Ghost : Job xv. 9, ' Are the consolations of God small with thee ? '   It is not profaneness only to be drunk, whore, and commit adultery ; but the greatest profaneness is to have cheap thoughts of spiritual privileges.   An heir values his birthright ; he is loath to sell the joy and comfort of his soul for carnal satisfactions and gratifications of the flesh.   Naboth would not part with his inheritance when the king comes to bargain with him : 1 Kings xxi. 3, ' The Lord forbid it me, that I should give the inheritance of my fathers unto thee.'   So if thou art an heir, thou wilt not part with thy portion in Christ for so vile a matter as thriving in the world.   Never part with the consolations of God for worldly pleasure.

[3.] An heir is much taken with his heritage, always looking for it when it will fall into his hands.   Therefore men that build their nests in the world as if they never looked for a better portion, which lavish out their strength upon the world, and never send any messengers, any spies into the land of promise, never send a believing thought into heaven, they have not the spirit of an heir : Rom. viii. 23, ' We ourselves, who have the first-fruits of the Spirit, groan within ourselves, waiting for the adoption, to wit, the redemption of our bodies.'   He that is a spiritual heir is always groaning, When shall I be with God and Christ, and he is feasting and entertaining his thoughts with suppositions of his future glory, and of the goodly heritage and portion that is made over to him in Christ ; he is waiting, groaning, and looking for it.   If thy heart be not taken up herewith, so as to favour things above, it is a sign thou hast not the spirit of an heir.

SERMON XL.

By faith Abraham, when he was called to go out into a place which he
should after receive for an inheritance, obeyed ; and he went out,
not knowing whither he went.—HEB. xi. 8.

THE scope of the apostle in this chapter is to prove that the doctrine
of faith is an ancient doctrine and that faith hath been always exercised
about things not seen, not liable to the judgment of sense and reason.
He had proved both points by instances of the fathers before the flood,
and now he comes to prove them by the examples of those that were
eminent for faith after the flood.   And in the first place he pitcheth
upon Abraham—a fit instance ; he was the father of the faithful, and
a person of whom the Hebrews boasted ; his life was nothing else but
a continual practice of faith, and therefore he insisteth upon Abraham
longer than upon any other of the patriarchs.   The first thing for which
Abraham is commended in scripture is his obedience to God, when he
called him out of his country ; now the apostle shows this was an effect
of faith.

In the words there are these circumstances—

1. The ground of Abraham's faith—*When he was called.*

2. The nature of that call—*To go out into a place which he should*
after receive for an inheritance. Wherein there is intimated a command
and a promise : a command to go out of his country into a certain place ;
then a promise that he should afterward receive it for an inheritance.

3. The effect and influence of his faith upon that call—*He obeyed,*
and went out.

4. The excellency and amplification of that obedience—*Not knowing*
whither he went.

[1.] For the ground of his faith—' Abraham, when he was called.'
Some read it πίστει ὁ καλουμενος Ἀβραὰμ, by faith he that was called
Abraham obeyed.   Abram's name was changed by special occasion.
Now some of the fathers would make the apostle in this place to
ascribe it to his faith.   But this exposition would offer manifest
violence to the words and scope of the apostle, we translate it better—
' By faith Abraham, when he was called,' for the apostle alludes to the
call of God, which is set down in the book of Genesis, chap. xii. 1,
' Now the Lord said to Abraham, Get thee out of thy country, and from
thy kindred, and from thy father's house, unto the land which I shall
show you.'   This was God's first call to Abraham, wherein he would
exercise and try his faith.   And this calling was not as the ordinary
way of calling is now, by the ministry of man, but by some extraordinary vision and oracle, which was God's ancient way ; and therefore it is said, Acts vii. 2, ' The God of glory appeared to our father
Abraham,' viz., in vision, and then gave him his call.

[2.] The second circumstance in the text is the nature of the call,
where there is a command to go out of his country, and a promise to
come into a place which he should after receive for an inheritance.

(1.) For the command—' To go out.'   In Genesis the words are
more emphatical—' Get thee out of thy country, from thy kindred,

and from thy father's house.' All which are cutting and killing words to flesh and blood ; to leave our dearest comforts, our nearest relations, or native soil. Go from thy country, saith God to him, a hard saying to flesh and blood. The soil in which we first drew breath seems to lay claim to a man's affections ; certainly by long custom it enchants us into a secret love, so that a homely cottage in our country seems sweeter than a palace in a strange land. It is very hard to part with things and places to which we are accustomed. What saith Austin, *Dulcia limina, atque amabilem larem, quem et parentum memoria, atque ipsius infantiœ rudimenta confirmant?* The sweet air where he was wont to converse with his father, friends, kinsfolk, must all these be left ? The smoke of our country seems more bright and comfortable than fire in a strange place ; yet God saith to Abraham, Go out of thy country. It is harder to Abraham than to another because of his blood and birth, and because he had great possessions there. Many may leave their country out of necessity and inconvenience when it is not well with them, or so well as they could wish at home ; but to rich Abraham it is said, Go out of thy country. And it followeth, 'From thy kindred, and from thy father's house.' Go thou, or go thyself. Though he should have no company with him, yet he was to go out of that idolatrous place. If we must needs leave our native soil, yet it were some comfort to have some of our friends and companions with us to solace our exile and erect a new home and country ; but Abraham was to forsake all his kindred. He did indeed labour all that he could with his kindred to make them sensible of the oracle and command of God, but he could not prevail. Some of them he got as far as Charran the borders of Canaan. For God's command did not exclude them in case they would follow him, but in case they refused ; then Abraham was to go alone. Lot went with him throughout, and Terah his father as far as Charran, and there died : Gen. xi, 31, 'And Terah took Abram his son, and Lot, the son of Haran, his son's son, and Sarah, his daughter-in-law, his son Abram's wife ; and they went forth with them from Ur of the Chaldees, to go into the land of Canaan ; and they came unto Haran, and dwelt there.' And though there be no mention of Abraham's brother, yet certainly he went as far as Charran too, as may be collected from other places of scripture. But this is not all, it follows, 'Unto a land which I shall show thee.' Abraham was not acquainted with the fixed place of his abode, he had no visible, certain hopes upon his removal. It is irksome to leave our country and father's house ; but if it were for better conveniences, it might be digested ; but who would change a certainty for an uncertainty, and leave that which was in hand for wide and unknown hopes? But thus it must be ; we must obey God, and not regard what flesh and blood can say to the contrary

[2.] For the promise—'Unto a land which he should afterward receive for an inheritance.' Abraham did not follow God for nought, he was no loser by God, there was an inheritance ; but however, faith for a great while was to conflict with much difficulty, before he should receive the inheritance. Consider how God tried Abraham's faith in his promise. It was long ere the place of his inheritance was fixed, ere God told him Canaan should be the land. The command and the promise were first made to him in Ur of the Chaldees in Mesopotamia,

before he dwelt in Charran, Acts vii. 2.   Well Abraham depends upon
this promise, goes towards Canaan from Charran.   And when he comes
into Canaan, he had not a foot of land : Acts vii. 5, ' He gave him no
inheritance, no, not so much as to set his foot on : yet he promised that
he would give it to him for a possession, and to his seed after him,
when as yet he had no child.'   The promise was to his posterity ; he
had not one foot himself till he purchased the cave of Machpelah to
bury his dead wife in.   Well, if his posterity might enjoy it, this was
a comfort ; but yet, for a great while he had no seed.   And when he
had seed, God told him his seed was to be four hundred years in Egypt
under miserable servitude and bondage, and then they should come
and inherit the land, Acts vii. 6.   And in the meantime the land was
possessed with mighty kings, giants, men of renown and honour, but
Abraham was a stranger there.   All this is said to show that faith is
contented with God's word ; it leaves God to the accomplishment of
the promise, and minds present obedience.   He went out, and that
was a great trial ; and what was his encouragement ? the promise that
he should receive it for an inheritance.

[3.] The third circumstance in the text, the effect and influence of
faith upon the call—' He obeyed, and went out ;' ἤκουσην καὶ ἐξῆλθε, he
' obeyed,' that signifies the consent of the mind ; and ' went out,' that
notes his practice and actual obedience ; he obeyed not only in word
but in deed ; there was a promise of obedience with actual performance.
It is easy to speak of these things, as the rebellious son said, Mat. xxi.
30, ' I go, sir, and went not.'

[4.] The fourth circumstance, the commendation of his obedience—
' Not knowing whither he went.'   God did not at first tell him of the
place, for the greater trial of his faith.   It is true, God had showed
him in the general how he should take his course and journey ; you
must not think he was ignorant whether he should go west or east,
towards Canaan or from it, but he did not know whether he went
towards the particular place where this inheritance lay, Gen. xi. 31.
As soon as Abraham received the call, he went towards Canaan.   He
knew not what kind of land the land of promise was, nor when it was
fixed—' The land that I shall show thee ;' but when he was in Canaan,
then God told him, This is the land I will give to thee ; so Gen. xii.
7, ' Unto thy seed will I give this land.'

I shall draw the words thus explained to some doctrinal issue and
conclusion.   The main point is faith's ready obedience to the call of
God.   Now there is a threefold call, and the text may be applied to
either of them.   There is a general call to the obedience of the gospel,
a particular call to some office and course of life wherein we may
glorify God, and a personal call to the exercise of that office.

1. There is *vocatio ad foedus*, a general call to the covenant of grace,
by which they are called by the ministry of the word, and the efficacy
of the Spirit, to the faith and obedience of the gospel.   It is called
general because it concerns all christians.

2. There is *vocatio ad munus*, a calling us to some office and course
of life wherein we may glorify God by exercising the gifts he hath
bestowed upon us, which is called a particular calling because it is not
common to all christians.

3. There is *vocatio ad exercitium muneris*, a personal call, by which

the particular circumstances are determined, and we are directed to the choice of the place and the people among whom we are to exercise this office and function to the glory of God. Of all these I shall treat in order, for to all these the circumstances of the text may be accommodated. Here was *vocatio ad fœdus;* when God appeared to Abraham it was not merely in a prophetical manner, and for some special intent ; but to call him to grace, for he was an idolater then, and that he might serve him by the obedience of faith. It is true, the reason was extraordinary, as all dispensations then were ; but this call was the means of his conversion, for by this means he was taken out from the idolatry and other corruptions of life, to which Chaldea was extremely given, and Abraham among the rest, so that he could not remain there without great danger. Then there was *vocatio ad munus,* to an office ; Abraham was called to a strange country, that God's blessing might appear in multiplying his seed, and he might be a means to glorify God in the sight of the Canaanites. Then there was *vocatio ad exercitium muneris,* a personal call to Canaan, the fixed place, that he might take possession of that country by faith and hope, and in that country typically of heaven, as in the next verse.

First, I shall apply the verse to the general call, and so many points are notable—

1. Observe, that faith, wherever it is, it bringeth forth true obedience—by faith Abraham, being called, obeyed God. Faith and obedience can never be severed; as the sun and the light, fire and heat. Therefore we read of the ' obedience of faith,' Rom. i. 5.. Obedience is faith's daughter. Faith hath not only to do with the grace of God, but with the duty of the creature. By apprehending grace, it works upon duty : Gal. v. 6, ' Faith works by love;' it fills the soul with the apprehensions of God's love, and then makes use of the sweetness of love to urge us to more work or obedience. All our obedience to God comes from love to God, and our love comes from the persuasion of God's love to us. The argument and discourse that is in a sanctified soul is set down, Gal. ii. 20, ' I live by the faith of the Son of God, who loved me and gave himself for me.' Wilt not thou do this for God, that loved thee ? for Jesus Christ, that gave himself for thee ? Faith, it works towards obedience by commanding the affections of love, of hope, of fear ; it makes use of love—'Faith works by love,' fills the soul with apprehensions of God's love; then what wilt thou not do for him ? Then it makes use of fear—' Noah, moved with fear, prepared an ark, for the saving of his household,' Heb. xi. 7. Sometimes it makes use of hope, as here, when Abraham hoped and expected these things of God, then ' he obeyed him, and went forth, not knowing whither he went.' There are no hopes equal to the reward it proposeth, no fears comparable to the terror it representeth, no motives so strong as it urgeth.

2. Observe, the ground of this obedience is God's call. Here are two instances together : Noah's faith wrought by fear, the ground of that was oracle—' Being warned of God ;' and Abraham's faith wrought by hope, the ground of it was God's call, ' By faith— Abraham, being called of God ; ' he had the express command and promise of God. Hence observe, till we have a call we cannot take

the honour of laying claim to the promises; for no man takes this honour but he that is called of God, and we shall have no warrant for obedience without a call. It is but will-worship without a call, and hope would be but a mere fancy. As those which stood idle in the market-place, when they were asked, Why do not you labour? they answered, None hath hired us: we were not called to work. Without a call the world would be but a general cell of monks, that leave kindred and father's house without any warrant.

3. Observe, this call consisteth of a command and a promise: 'Go thou,' there is the command—'and thou shalt receive the land for thy inheritance,' there is the promise. The command is the ground of duty, and the promise is the ground of hope and expectation. And still God dealeth with us in the same manner—'Believe, and thou shalt be saved;' with all the commands of God there is a promise annexed. Hence observe, it is God's mercy to propound encouragements when he might enforce. God will draw us with the cords of a man, and allure us into obedience by commands and promises. The brute-creatures are ruled by mere sovereignty, but God deals with men as men. We have election and choice; and therefore there is not only duty laid before us, but death and life. God said to Abraham, Go; it is a hard duty, but thou shalt not lose by it, for thou shalt have the land of Canaan for thy inheritance.

4. I observe again, this call is brought to men when they are in their worst estate; for mark, the call was made to Abraham when he was at Mesopotamia, Acts vii. 2, in Ur of the Chaldees; then God said to him, 'Leave thy country and thy father's house.' Therefore, when this call is mentioned, Gen. xii. 1, the phrase there is ' the Lord had said to Abraham;' God had spoken to him before he came from Charran. Now in Ur of the Chaldees they were idolaters: Josh. xxiv. 2, 3, 'Your fathers dwelt on the other side of the flood in old time, even Terah the father of Abraham, and the father of Nahor, and they served other gods. And I took your father Abraham from the other side of the flood,' &c. Then when he was serving idols, he and all his kindred, then God comes and enters into a treaty of grace with him. That is the reason the apostle makes Abraham to believe in God as ' justifying the ungodly,' Rom. iv. 5. Abraham before grace was, as we all are, ungodly, a worshipper of idols. Hence observe, when God comes to call us, he calls us out of mere grace. Consider this, that you may neither despair of mercy, nor yet ascribe grace to any merit or good dispositions of your own. Abraham, that was the father of the faithful, the chiefest of believers, when God came to take him to grace, he was as vile a sinner as any. The whole land was open to God, but God took Abraham your father. Was he better than others? No; he and his father served idols, the son could not be better than the father by whom he was educated; but God of his mercy singled him out from the rest. Paul, a persecutor, Abraham, an idolater, obtained mercy of God: 1 Tim. i. 13, 'Who was before a blasphemer, a persecutor, and injurious, but I obtained mercy.'

5. I observe again, that free grace makes a distinction between them of the same line and kindred; God called him alone, and blessed him—'Forsake thy country and thy father's house.' None of

Abraham's kindred, but only Lot were called; the rest were turned out: Isa. li. 2, 'Look unto Abraham your father, and unto Sarah that bare you; for I called him alone, and blessed him and increased him;' that is, though there were more besides him of his race and family. Thus God can make a difference between brother and brother, and between brother and sister; Jacob was loved, and not Esau; Abel was accepted, and not Cain. God can come into a town, and pick out two or three berries on the top of the uppermost branches—'One of a city, and two of a tribe,' Jer. iii. 14. God may leave the ninety-nine in the wilderness of the world to seek one sheep. Those that are in the same bed, in the same employment, feeding at the same meal, one shall be taken to grace, and the other shall be left to misery and judgment. He can put a distinction between husband and wife; free grace picks and chooses according to its own pleasure. Remember this, that thou mayest know who it was that made thee to differ, and admire not only the kindness, but the freedom of his grace: Rom. ix. 18, 'Therefore hath he mercy on whom he will have mercy.'

6. In this call I observe that God bids him to leave his country and his father's house; hence note—

Doct. When God calls us to grace, we are not only to leave sin, but to leave the world, and all things that are dear to us in the world.

As soon as God appeared to Abraham, he was to leave Chaldea, Charran, and all, for Canaan. Faith, where it is rightly planted, turns the heart not only from sin to God, but from the world to God, from the creature to the creator, from carnal things to those that are more excellent and heavenly. Not that we must leave our possessions and renounce our estates as soon as God calls to grace, without a special call, as that trial was: Mat. xix. 21, 'If thou wilt be perfect, go and sell that thou hast and give to the poor, and thou shalt have treasure in heaven, and come and follow me.' That was a special trial; but we must come out from the world in heart and affection: Ps. xlv. 10, 'Forget thy own people, and thy father's house.' We must not be wedded in our affection to the world, but contracted and wedded to Christ. Many, if they leave gross sins, they think they are safe; but in conversion there is a turning from the creature to God, as well as from sin to God: Mat. xix. 27, 'We have forsaken all and followed thee.' In vow and affection you must renounce the world, that you may keep your hearts loyal and chaste to Jesus Christ. You must sell all for the pearl of great price. And then take heed after conversion that you do not retract your vow, for your estate is no longer yours, but God's; you must part with your estate upon just and convenient reasons of religion; when it is not consistent with the conscience of our duty to God. Nabal was but a fool to say, 'Shall I take my bread and my wine,' &c. 1 Sam. xxv. 11, and the prodigal to say, I spend but my own. When thou art converted, it is not thine, but all is left and given to God, to be disposed of according to his will and pleasure; and when the keeping of an estate is not consistent with our duty to God, we must part with it. Sometimes Christ and the world will be together; but when they part, we must not forsake Christ to keep mammon company. When we cannot get an estate but we must quit our conscience, or keep an estate and a good conscience together; or when violence or death divorceth us from our comforts, our heart must not be overwhelmed with grief or trouble; let us remember by believing we forsook the world, and promised to cleave to God.

7. I observe again, that God shows him the worst even at his first calling. God might have given the call in one word, but it is amplified, Gen. xii. 1. Observe—

Doct. When we give up our names to Christ, the Lord would have us sit down and count the charges, that so we may meet trouble with the more resolution.

When a virgin was enamoured with that sour philosopher, he showed her his crooked back; thus Christ tells us the worst at first, what we must look for—trouble, hazard, inconveniences of the world. Can you deny yourselves in all this? Luke xiv 26, 'If any man come to me, and hate not his father, and mother, and wife, and children, and brothers, and sisters, yea, and his own life also, he cannot be my disciple.' It is a general case; and then he useth the similitude of building, that he must sit down and count the charges. When a man hath allotted so much for building, so long as he keeps within the bounds of his allotment he parteth with it freely; but when that is gone he parts with every penny after with grudging. It is good to make Christ large allowance at the first, that we may not grudge our bargain and contract.

8. It is said of Abraham, he obeyed and went out; he obeyed, that signifies the consent of his mind; and he went forth, that notes his actual obedience to that word: he not only promised, but performed. Observe—

Doct. It is the property of faith to subject all our wills and all our interests to God's pleasure.

Faith, when it takes, it gives; with one hand it takes Christ; with the other hand it resigns and gives up ourselves, our relations, and all our comforts to the will of Christ. There is a notable expression, and some understand it of Abraham's obedience, Isa. xli. 2, 'He called the righteous man from the east, called him to his foot.' When God called Abraham, he called him to his foot; and there Abraham would follow after God according to the pleasure of God. And so it is the property of faith to make us set foot by foot with God, to go after him wheresoever he goes. God's call must be readily executed, whatever comes on it.

9. He obeyed, and went forth; there was not only a consent of heart, but he readily performed. Observe—

Doct. We must not only give God good words, and make vows at our effectual calling, but we must be sensible of the vows of God.

Many are apt to speak good words, as Christ hath a parable of the formal professor: Mat. xxi. 28–30, 'A certain man had two sons, and he came to the first, and said, Son, go into the vineyard and work. And he saith, I will, and did not. And he came to the other, and he said, I will not; and after he repented, and went;' which is the better son? It is easier to talk of leaving friends, lands, and our father's house, and take upon ourselves a voluntary exile for a good conscience, than to do it. It is easy to talk of these things in the serene times of the gospel, but this is like him in the parable, 'I go, sir, and went not.' It is said of the children of God, Rev. xii. 11, that 'they loved not their lives to death;' that is, they did not only in prodigality and presumption give up their lives to God, but when it came to performance, when death was at hand, either they must die or renounce Christ, then they loved not their lives. So when God puts us to deny every near comfort, to quit country, parents, every dearest thing—when we cannot keep these things with a good conscience, then faith submits to it.

10. Consider, in the history there was some kind of halting, though it be said in the general that he obeyed, for he stayed at Charran about five years. When Terah went out of Ur, he was two hundred years old; when he died in Charran, he was two hundred and five years old. He stays there when he should have gone into Canaan, as may be gathered out of Gen. xi. 25, but there he stays till he had buried his father; and truly I do believe that then he was revived by some new call, and again admonished, when he was somewhat slack and negligent. Some deny a second call, but it is clear to me by what is said: Acts vii. 4, 'Then came he out of the land of the Chaldeans, and dwelt in Charran; and from thence, when his father was dead, he removed him into this land, wherein ye now dwell;' that is, by a new persuasion and excitation God awakened him again, and bid him to go into Canaan. And so, Gen. xii. 4, it is said that 'Abraham departed as the Lord had spoken to him.' Hence observe—

Doct. Faith may sometimes make a halt, and grow weary, but it rouseth itself up again.

So it is with us in our spiritual course; when we begin to look after God, we are apt to halt and linger, therefore we had need be roused again. A ship that is bound for such a harbour, yet by the violence of the storm may be driven back, but it makes way towards its port again; so by temptation we may be driven back for a time, but we must make way to our port and haven again. Oh, it is well if we can but make advantage of our falls, as a ball beaten down to the ground rebounds the higher.

11. I observe again, 'He obeyed.' That hath respect to the encouragement the promise gave, and yet how long was it ere the promise was accomplished. Hence observe—

Doct. True faith doth constantly adhere to God, though it presently finds not what it believes and expects from God.

Abraham left Ur, then Charran, and though he had not a foot in the land of Canaan, yet still he waits upon God. The famine drove him out of Canaan into Egypt, Gen. xii. 10; afterwards he had wars and conflicts with the kings of Canaan, they would not allow him a safe abode; he was burdened with envy, without children, yet still he waits for the accomplishment of the promise, and believes in hope against hope. Well then, we must trust God, though we have nothing of present feeling. Oh, it is an excellent thing when we can say as the people of God, Isa. xlv. 24, 'In the Lord my God I shall have righteousness and strength.' Well, I will wait upon God, though nothing comes to hand; though there be nothing in feeling, yet we must wait upon God. We read, Heb. iii. 6, of καύχημα τῆς ἐλπίδος, 'The rejoicing, or glorying of hope.' It is excellent when we can glory in our hopes, and in what we do expect. There is more of duty in waiting, though there is less of comfort; and when we have nothing in feeling and fruition, yet then to depend upon God; this is like an Abraham that built an altar, and offered a sacrifice of thanksgiving, Gen. xii. 8. Oh, that we could give thanks, and bless God for our hopes; and in the midst of difficulties, yet wait upon God for what we shall have.

12. I observe, 'He obeyed, not knowing whither he went.'

Doct. Upon a divine call we must obey, though we do not know what will come of it.

This is of excellent use to christians that are yet in the twilight of grace, between grace and nature; they do not know what will come of it, yet they venture upon Christ. The master calls; you are invited to grace, and you should make an essay. We owe God blind obedience. Blind men will follow their guides over hills and through dales fearing nothing; so should we follow God. Carnal reason will be full of objections, but in such cases we should not dispute but resolve; and let us cleave to Christ, and hang upon Christ, though we do not know what will come of it; as the lepers: 2 Kings vii. 4, 'If we say, We will enter into the city, then the famine is in the city, and we shall die there; and if we sit still here we die also. Now therefore come, and let us fall into the host of the Syrians; if they save us alive, we shall live; and if they kill us, we shall but die.' So also in discharging our duty; when we know not what success we shall have, still we must perform it; as the prophet in his public contests with an obstinate people gains acceptance with God, though not success with men: Isa. xlix. 4, 'I have laboured in vain, I have spent my strength for nought, and in vain; yet surely my judgment is with the Lord, and my work with my God.'

Secondly, I come now to apply the text to a particular calling, to some office, employment, and course of life wherein to glorify God. And here I shall inquire—

(1.) How we shall know that we are called to such an employment, now oracles are ceased, and God doth not so immediately speak to us as he did to Abraham. (2.) How must we behave ourselves in that calling; what is the obedience of faith. (3.) I shall handle some cases incident to this matter.

1. How we shall know that we are called of God. It is a matter necessary to be known, that we act in faith and obedience. A man cannot expect God's blessing but in God's way. And the general rule is, ἕπου Θεῷ, follow God. Now how shall we do to see God in our calling, that we may walk with him foot by foot? It is said, Isa. xli. 2, 'Who raised up the righteous man from the east, called him to his foot.' By way of answer to this necessary question, I shall lay down several propositions.

[1.] That every man must have a particular calling. Life was given us for somewhat; not merely to fill up the number of the world, or to grow in stature— so life was given to the plants, that they may grow bulky, and increase in stature; not merely to taste pleasures, that is the happiness of beasts, to enjoy pleasures without remorse. God gave men higher faculties of reason and conscience; reason to manage some work and business for the glory of God; and conscience, that he might review his work, and mind his soul. The rule is general, that all

Adam's sons are to eat their bread in the sweat of their brows : Gen. iii. 19, 'In the sweat of thy face shalt thou eat bread.' I know it doth not bind in the rigour of the letter ; the priests were not to sweat : Ezek. xliv. 18, 'They shall not gird themselves with anything that causeth sweat ;' yet in the intent it binds to some honest labour, the sweat of the body or of the brain. Adam's two sons were heirs-apparent of the world, and the one was employed in tillage and the other in pasturage. The world was never made for a hive for drones, and the word giveth no privilege to any to be idle. It is true, there is a difference between employments ; some live more by manual labours, others in more genteel employments, as the magistrate, the minister, and those that study for public good. Manual labour is not required of all, because it is not a thing that is required *propter se*, as simply good and necessary, but *propter aliud*, as for maintenance and support of life, to ease the church, to supply the uses of charity. When the ends of labour cannot otherwise be obtained, then handy labour is required. A minister is forbidden travail and labour, it being a means of distraction ; but he is to be laborious and diligent in his calling. A gentleman is to fit himself to do his country service, either in magistracy or ministry ; if need be in the ministry, it is not beneath them. The first-born were the priests, that is, the most noble, the most worthy, the most potent, ere God settled it in the tribe of Levi. Diligent they are to be in doing their country good one way or other, and to spend the more time in spiritual exercises, the less they need handy labour ; but when their whole life is spent in eating, drinking, sporting, sleeping, it is bestial. Idleness was one of Sodom's sins : Ezek. xvi. 49, 'Behold this was the iniquity of thy sister Sodom ; pride, fulness of bread, and abundance of idleness was in her and in her daughters.' It makes you lose your right to the creatures—'If any would not work, neither let him eat,' 2 Thes. iii. 10. Gentlemen are but robbers that live idly and without a calling ; though they are freed from servile and handy labour, yet they are not freed from work and business. If any man might be allowed to be idle, then one member would be lost in the body politic. Man is born a member of some society, family, city, world, and is to seek the good of it ; he is ζῶον πολιτικὸν. We see in the body natural there is no member, but it hath its function and use, whereby it becometh serviceable to the whole. All have not the same office, that would make a confusion ; but all have their use, either as an eye, or as a hand, or as a leg, and it must be employed. So in the politic body no member must be useless, they must have one function or another wherein to employ themselves, otherwise they are but unprofitable burdens of the earth. Again, every man is more or less intrusted with a gift, which he is to exercise and improve for the common good, and at the day of judgment he is to give up his accounts ; Mat. xxv. 19, 'After a long time the Lord of those servants cometh and reckoneth with them.' If he hath but one talent, it must not be hidden in a napkin. Well then, if every man hath a gift for which he is accountable to God, he must have a calling : 1 Cor. vii. 17, 'As God hath distributed to every man, as the Lord hath called every one, so let him walk,' and choose his state of life. Besides, a calling is necessary to prevent the mischiefs of idleness, and those inconveniences

that follow men not employed; standing pools are apt to putrify, but
running waters are sweetest. An idle man is a burden to himself, a
prey to Satan, a grief to the Spirit of God, and a mischief to others.
He is a burden to himself, for he knoweth not what to do with his
time. In the morning he cries, Would to God it were evening, and in
the evening, Would to God it were morning—the mind like a mill, when
it wanteth work, falleth upon itself. He is a prey to Satan; the devil
findeth the house 'empty, swept, and garnished,' Mat. xii. 44; the
devil findeth them at leisure, and then sets them a-work. When David
was idle on the terrace, he fell into a snare. Birds are not taken in
their flight, but when they pitch and rest. He is a grief to God's
Spirit: Eph. iv. 28, ' Let him that stole, steal no more; but rather let
him labour, working with his hands the thing which is good,' compared
with ver. 30, 'And grieve not the Holy Spirit of God.' Idle men
quench the vigour of natural gifts, and lose the ability of nature. He
is a mischief to others, 2 Thes. iii. 11—Μηδὲν ἐργαζομένους, ἀλλὰ
περιεργαζομένους—' Working not at all, but are busybodies.' They that
nothing will do too much; no work makes way for ill work. Censure do
and busy inquisition into other men's actions is the native fruit of idleness; and so they prove the fire-brands of contention and unneighbourly
quarrels. There must be a calling then to prevent these mischiefs.

[2.] That this calling must be good and agreeable to the word of
God, which is 'A lamp unto our feet, and a light unto our path,' Ps.
cxix. 105. It were not a perfect rule, if it did not direct us in all cases;
therefore in the choice of our course of life, we must consult with the
word, that we may not settle in a course of sin. Men may tolerate evil
callings, but God never appointed them, and therefore here we are not
called to them, but called off from them. Now if any calling be against
piety, temperance or justice, it is against the word,—for the word
'teacheth us to deny ungodliness and worldly lusts, and to live soberly,
righteously and godly in this present world,' Titus iii. 12. Against
piety, as to be an idolatrous priest, or to make shrines for idols, which
was Demetrius's calling in Ephesus; and Tertullian, in his book ' De
Idololatria ' showeth that this was the practice of many christians to
get their livings by making statues and images and other ornaments,
to sell to heathen idolaters. Against justice, as piracy, brokage, and
other oppressive courses. Against sobriety, as such callings as merely
tend to feed the luxury, pride, and vanity of men, as stage-plays and
the like, it were endless to instance in all. In the general, the calling
must be good and lawful, if we would see God in it.

[3.] This calling must not only be good, but we must see God in it.
Providence ruleth in everything that falleth out, even in the least
matters; especially hath the Lord a great hand in callings, and in
appointing to everyone his state and condition of life. In paradise,
God set Adam his work as a gardener to dress and prune the trees:
Gen. ii. 15, 'And the Lord God took the man, and put him into the
garden of Eden, to dress it, and to keep it;' and still he doth not only
give the ability and special inclination, but also disposeth of the
education of the parent, and passages of men's lives to bring them to
such a calling; Isa. liv. 16, ' Behold I have created the smith, that
bloweth the coals in the fire, and that bringeth forth an instrument for

his work.' Common trades and crafts are from the Lord. The heathens had a several god for every several trade, as the papists now have a tutelar saint; but they rob God of his honour, he giveth the faculty and the blessings; so it is said, Isa. xxviii. 24–29 *ad finem*, 'Doth the husbandman plough all day to sow? doth he open and break the clods of the ground?' &c. 'His God doth instruct him to discretion and doth teach him. For the fitches are not thrashed with a thrashing-instrument, neither is a cart-wheel turned about upon the cummin, &c. This also cometh forth from the Lord of hosts, who is wonderful in counsel and excellent in working.' God giveth the skill and appointeth the work. Your particular estate and condition of life doth not come by chance, or by the bare will and pleasure of man; but the ordination of God, without which a sparrow cannot fall to the ground: Prov. xx. 24, 'Man's goings are of the Lord; how can a man then understand his own way?'

[4.] In the higher callings of ministry and magistracy, our call from God must be more solemn, because in these callings God's glory and the good of human society are more concerned; and therefore such have need of a clear call that manage them. In ordinary callings there is required both fitness and inclination, or a fitness of gifts and inclination, which are the fruits of God's general providence. Fitness in every calling is a common gift of the Spirit; so it is said of Bezaleel, Exod. xxxi. 3, 'I have filled him with the Spirit of God in wisdom, and in understanding, and in knowledge, and in all manner of workmanship.' An inclination to such a calling is from God's general providence, depriving them of higher opportunities of advancement, and over-coming their hearts to make choice of such a work. Now the more weighty the business and affair of life is, the more is providence concerned in it: and therefore for magistracy and ministry much more doth God make them fit and willing. Fit: 2 Cor. iii. 6, 'Who hath made us able ministers of the new testament;' and willing: Mat. ix. 38, 'Pray ye therefore the Lord of the harvest, that he would send forth labourers into the harvest;' he thrusteth out labourers into the harvest. They are God's special gift, sought of God in prayer, and he giveth them commission. Again, there is an outward rail set about these callings, that men may enter in by the door, in an external lawful way, which is not so much required in other callings. Private callings are at the appointment of parents; public must be left to a solemn external call, lest all order be broken both in church and common-wealth; others serve only for the accommodation, but these are for the essence and foundation of human society.

[5.] The calling of magistrates must not be undertaken, whatever abilities and inclinations men have, till they have a fair invitation from those that have power to call them; and then it must not be refused. Men are God's instruments in this kind, and therefore we must not only have gifts from God but allowance from men; and therefore they sin that enter upon the magistrate's office by violence, or by money and bribery, and do not expect a call and the fair invitation of providence; as Absalom had an itch to be a judge and a ruler, but he got the office by rebellion. And again they sin, that when they have a fair call from God and men—from God by gifts, and from men by choice and allowance—refuse, out of a desire of ease and privacy, or for want of courage. But I will not meddle with this more now.

Ministers must expect both an internal and an external call—a call they must have, that they may not run till they are sent. Jesus Christ took not this honour upon him, till he was called by God. There is much of God to be observed in this calling, that we may expect a blessing, and digest the difficulties and inconveniences of it with patience: Acts xv. 7, 'God made choice among us, that the gentiles by my mouth should hear the word of the gospel and believe;' there was a choice of Peter among the rest of the apostles; so Acts. x. 41, 42, 'Not to all the people, but unto witnesses chosen before of God, even to us who did eat and drink with him after he rose from the dead. And he commanded us to preach unto the people,' &c. Well then, but when are we chosen? There is an internal call from God, and an external call from the church. The internal call from God, that is it chiefly which I am to speak of, though I shall touch on the other also. This is when a man is made fit and willing. Fit he must be; if the Spirit of God fitted Aholiab and Bezaleel for the material work of the temple, then much more is there a fitness required in the ministers of the gospel: 1 Tim. i. 12, 'I thank Christ Jesus our Lord, who hath enabled me, for that he counted me faithful, putting me into the ministry.' There must be some competent ability. If God ever puts us into the ministry, he first enableth us; and that is not all he must be willing: 1 Tim. iii. 1, 'If a man desire the office of a bishop, he desireth a good work.' There must be a strong inclination, that if God give a call, we will take up such a course of life. Well then, he hath not this inward call that is willing, but not fit, or fit, but not willing, much more he that is neither fit nor willing, but only is thrust upon such an office by the carnal importunities of friends; and he that hath both, hath the call of the Spirit. But now an internal call is not enough; there must be that which is external, as Peter was sent by an angel to Cornelius, and had an external call from Cornelius too, Acts x. So must we, having an inward call, wait for the outward call of the church, otherwise we cannot lawfully be admitted to the exercise of the calling. As in the old testament, the tribe of Levi was by God appointed to the service of the altar, yet none could exercise the ministry and calling of a Levite, till he was anointed and purified by the church: Exod. xxviii. 3, 'And thou shalt speak unto all that are wise-hearted, whom I have filled with the Spirit of wisdom, that they may make Aaron's garments to consecrate him, that he may minister unto me in the priest's office; so Num. iii. 3, 'These are the names of the sons of Aaron, the priests which were anointed, whom he consecrated to minister in the priest's office.' Thus the ministers of the gospel, though called by God, must have their external separation, and setting apart to that work by the church. The outward call belongs to the church, but it is to be done in order— election by the people, examination of life and doctrine with authoritative mission by the presbytery, confirmation by the magistrate: Acts vi. 3, 'Wherefore brethren look ye out among ye seven men, of honest report, full of the Holy Ghost and wisdom,.whom we may appoint over this business;' where election is referred to the body of the church and ordination to the elders: Acts xiv. 23, 'And when they had ordained them elders in every church, and had prayed with fasting, they commended them to the Lord, on whom they believed;' Acts xiii. 2, 3, 'The Holy Ghost said, Separate me Barnabas and Saul for the work whereunto I have called them. And when they had fasted and prayed, and laid their hands on them, they sent them away.' And the christian magistrate hath his share, to see that all things are done orderly; and then they are to have his confirmation.[1]

[7.] For ordinary callings then we are called by God; when God giveth ability and inclination, and openeth a fair passage in his providence, that is to be looked upon as a call. Inclination there must be, that we may be fit for our calling, and our calling fit for us; otherwise we are like a member out of joint, out of our place and way. If we be at our own disposal this must be observed; if not, parents and those that have the disposal of us, must observe it; they must consider the child's inclination, using prayer, calling in the advice of others. It is the weightiest affair of life; much is to be known by children's inclinations. The Athenians would set before their children, the trowel, the shovel, a sword, and a book, that they might choose their calling. As Nazianzen tells us, Athanasius acted the part of a bishop when a boy, which being observed by Alexander, bishop of Alexandria, he brought him up for the ministry. And Origen would be often asking his father, Leonides, concerning such and such places of scripture. Much of God's pleasure is seen in their inclinations, which if parents observe not, mischief follows—sometimes to the church, sometimes to the children themselves. And abilities and gifts must be observed both by the parent and by themselves when we come to maturity, and to choose our own way: Prov. xvi. 20, 'He that handleth a matter wisely shall find good.' And then providence is to be observed in the designment of education, and the advantages which God offereth for the choice of our course of life. Take all together, and it maketh a call for ordinary offices of life; otherwise, as great mischiefs arise, as if a man should walk with his hands and work with his feet.

SERMON XLI.

By faith Abraham, when he was called to go out into a place which he should after receive for an inheritance, obeyed and he went out, not knowing whither he went.—HEB. xi. 8.

2. How to behave ourselves in this calling, that we may, as Abraham did, manifest the obedience of faith.

[1.] Where you see God before you, you must cheerfully follow after. If you see God calling you to the ministry, magistracy, or any inferior course of life, therein doth he expect glory from you; and for that end did he give you gifts, an account of which you must render at the last

[1] See this more fully handled in the sermons on John xvii. 18.

day. We are apt to dispute with God, and to consult with our natural affections: Exod. iv. 13, 'Send I pray thee, by the hand of him, whom thou wilt send.' By gifts, by special instinct, by, the invitation of providence, by the call of the church and state, God hath declared his pleasure; and then sit down, count the charges, and put thy hand to the plough. Though it may be otherwise you might have a more quiet and a more splendid and plentiful course of life; yet this is the way God calleth you to; as here Abraham obeyed, and went forth.

[2.] Confine your endeavours within this calling, and keep within the bounds of it. If you do anything that is not within the compass of your calling, you can have no warrant that it pleaseth God. Christ would not intermeddle out of his calling: Luke xii. 14, 'Man, who made me a judge, or a divider over you?' Uzziah's putting his hand to the ark cost him dear. If troubles arise, we cannot suffer them comfortably; we are out of God's way. Mischiefs abroad come from invading callings, as tumults and confusions in nature, when elements are out of their places. Never do I look for peace and establishment till all things run in their own proper channels. *Pax est tranquillitas ordinis*, is a true description of external peace. Callings are not to be invaded by the magistrate, or the people. So Acts x, the angel appeareth to Cornelius; but he bids him send to Peter, to preach to him, and settle him in the faith. Why doth he not teach him himself? No; his commission was only to bring a message from God, not to preach the gospel. The magistrates that are as angels of God should not usurp spiritual administrations, but leave them to those that are called of God. When Saul would be doing the priest's office, God was angry with him, 1 Sam. xiii. 13, 14; Uzziah was smitten with leprosy for taking a censer to burn incense upon the altar of incense, 2 Chron. xvi. 18. The magistrates have enough to do about religion. Christ hath recommended his spouse to them, that they may give her house and harbour, and maintain and defend her. Let them do that; but it is a sacrilege and usurpation when they intermeddle in the minister's calling. Nor must it be usurped by the people. God hath chosen witnesses: Acts x. 40, 41, 'Him God raised up the third day, and showed him openly; not to all the people, but unto witnesses chosen before of God, even to us,' &c. Christ would not appear to the multitude. It is not everyone's work to preach, but of those that are chosen by God; for it is not a work of charity but a duty belonging to a particular calling. He that cannot say he is a chosen witness, why should he intermeddle? Let them increase their knowledge and instruct their families, taking all occasion of gaining neighbours; let them be much in examining their hearts and private meditations; they will have far more comfort, and show less of pride and usurpation.

[3.] Humbly wait upon God for his blessing in the use of means. Men must work, but cast their care upon God: Mat. vi. 31, 'Take no thought, saying, What shall we eat? or, What shall we drink? or, Wherewithal shall we be clothed?' God will not put the trouble of the event upon us—'Your heavenly Father knoweth that ye have need of these things,' ver. 32; 'Abraham obeyed, not knowing whither he went.' As in a pair of compasses, one foot is fixed in the centre, while another wandereth about in the circumference; so the work of faith is not to abate industry, but to fix the heart. Faith is not idle, but waiteth; this is the proper temper of a christian. Let us do our duty, and leave our care upon God. Anxiousness about the success and event is a sin, because then we take God's work out of his hands. Success is God's work, labour is ours. This life is called, ' The life of our hands;' God maintaineth it, but by our hands. Not to labour is to tempt providence; to cark is to distrust it. Miracles are not multiplied without necessity. When we neglect means, we discharge God of the obligation of his promise. If you starve for want of industry, you can blame none. God hath not undertaken that sin shall not be our ruin, but rather the contrary. But now by a quiet use of means you enter into God's protection, as the protection of the law is only for them that travel on the road: Ps. lv. 22, ' Cast thy burden upon the Lord, and he shall sustain thee: he shall never suffer the righteous to be moved.' Business is our work, but care is our burden, that must we cast on God. It is no more dishonour for God to bear our burden, than for Christ to bear our sins.

[4.] With patience digest the inconveniences of your calling. Affliction attendeth every state and condition of life; but we may go through them cheerfully—we are in our way, and in our place. You may meet with discouragements as a minister, or as a magistrate; yet go on whatever men do, God is a good pay-master, and your work is with the Lord. You may meet with discouragements as a servant, but it is thy calling, and therein God will be glorified. When troubles overtake us in our calling, we do not rush into them, but fall into them: James i. 2, ' My brethren, count it all joy, when ye fall into divers temptations.' It is matter of rejoicing when ye fall into divers trials, not when ye draw them upon yourselves, or thrust yourselves into them; some run into afflictions, and seek the cross, do not take it up when it stands in their way.

[5.] Bear up against opposition and difficulty with courage and boldness. Jonah smarted for declining the duty of his calling, because of danger. When you meet with unreasonable men—' The Lord is faithful, who shall stablish you, and keep you from evil,' 2 Thes. iii. 3. It is good to follow God wherever he leadeth. If to do any work, to undergo any danger, remember he is faithful; he is not wont to put an heavy burden upon weak shoulders: 1 Cor. x. 13, ' There hath no temptation taken you, but such as is common to man; but God is faithful, who will not suffer you to be tempted above that ye are able, but will with the temptation also make a way to escape, that ye may be able to bear it.'

3. There are some cases; as—

[1.] Suppose a man hath entered upon a calling, especially a higher calling upon carnal grounds, as profit and preferment; or by carnal means, as many enter into the ministry; and being taught better things, should they leave their office and employment?

Ans. If he findeth himself unfit for that calling into which he hath thrust himself out of an evil aim, or that he wants gifts for the exercise of it, he must lay it aside; for he cannot do faithful service to God in that calling, and he cumbereth the ground and occupieth the room of another; like that barren fig-tree, on which that sentence was passed:

Luke xiii. 7, ' Cut it down, why cumbereth it the ground ? ' But if there be hope, that he is able to discharge his duty in some measure, he must not desert his station ; he may afterwards by his repentance and faithfulness approve himself to God and the church ; at first, he wanted not gifts, but uprightness.

[2.] Whether a man may not change his calling ?

Ans (1.) Negatively. Not out of pride and disdain at the meanness of it. It is credit enough to do God's work ; if it be a servile calling to church or commonwealth, you do him service. There is no calling so mean but a humble heart may do God service in it ; you may adorn the gospel as long as you walk honestly. The apostle exhorts servants, Tit. ii. 10, ' Not purloining, but showing all good fidelity ; that they may adorn the doctrine of God our Saviour in all things.' Not out of covetousness ; Heb. xiii. 5, ' Let your conversation be without covetousness, and be content with such things as you have.' God will be sure to cross carnal desires. Not out of envy and ambition, because others have a better calling than we ; this breedeth mischief and confusion : 2 Sam. xv. 4, ' Absalom said moreover, Oh that I were made judge in the land, that every man which hath any suit or cause might come unto me, and I would do him justice ! ' Not out of distrust and impatience ; you will meet with like trials in every condition of life. He that cannot trust God in one calling, doth but trust himself in another. Not out of fond curiosity and levity of mind, out of inconstancy and itch of novelty ; they love to make experiments, though to their own loss and the public disturbance many times. It must not be done lightly and rashly, but upon weighty causes : 1 Cor. vii. 20, ' Let every man abide in the same calling wherein he was called.' Every one should be contented with his own place and station, Though the calling in itself be low, yet to him it is best, and most expedient for him ; otherwise you tax God's providence, who called you to such a function.

(2.) Positively. I confess it may be done ; for that place, 1 Cor. vii. 20, ' Let every man abide in the same calling wherein he is called ; ' the meaning is, the place wherein religion finds us is not to be changed merely upon receiving religion. It is true, a servant may become free ; Amos was an herdsman, yet was made a prophet ; Christ's disciples were fishermen. There are cases which may clear up the will of God to a man's conscience. Private necessity and public good may make a man change his calling. Private necessity, as when the former calling ceaseth to be useful, and to minister supply to us, as framing instruments of war in a time of peace, or when the course of trading is altered. Public good, as when a man may be more useful, if by mistake or the carnal affection of parents he have been diverted to another course of life.

[3.] Whether a man may offer himself to a calling, being sensible of his inward call, and after trial of strength of gifts, or should expect till he be invited by others ?

Ans. He may desire it ; therefore in a modest manner he may manifest his desire to whom it concerneth : 1 Tim. iii. 1, ' If a man desire the office of a bishop, he desireth a good work ; ' if a man be entrusted with fitting gifts, and set apart by God, he may offer himself to a lawful trial, without a presumption of his strength or a haughty ambition, but out of the conscience of an inward call, to employ his talent in the service of the Lord. Moses' tergiversation had like to cost him dear : Exod. iv. 14, 'And the anger of the Lord was kindled against Moses.'

Thirdly, I shall now apply the text to a personal calling, or a call to such a place, where we may exercise our talents and abilities for the glory of God, and the good of others.

This case is weighty, and necessary to be resolved—

1. Because the place falleth under a call, as well as the office itself. The apostles had not only a commission, but a passport ; upon every removal or resting they ever depend on the call of God. Paul was warned by oracle to tarry in Corinth : Acts xviii. 10, 'I have much people in this city ;' and by vision he was called into Macedonia : Acts xvi. 9, 'And a vision appeared to Paul in the night : there stood a man of Macedonia, and prayed him, saying, Come over into Macedonia, and help us.' Nay, when they purposed to go to one place, out of the judgment of reason, they were diverted to another by revelation : Acts xvi. 7, 'After they were come to Mysia, they assayed to go into Bithynia, but the Spirit suffered them not.' It is true, we cannot expect oracles, nor must we expect extraordinary dreams,—our removes are not of such consequence, and these are God's ancient ways ; yet our goings fall under a providence : Ps. xxxvii. 23, 'The steps of a good man are ordered by the Lord, and he delighteth in his way.' And it is not comfortable and safe to shift from place to place till we see God before us ; as the Israelites moved by the motion of the pillar of cloud by day and pillar of fire by night. And it is said, Acts xvii. 26, 'He hath determined the times beforehand, and the bounds of their habitation.' As their course of life, so also their place and dwelling are ordered by God.

2. We cannot else expect a blessing. There where God hath set us, there will he be with us, and bless us. This keepeth up our dependence upon him : Ezra viii. 21, 'Then I proclaimed a fast there, at the river Ahava, that we might afflict ourselves before our God, to seek of him a right way for us, and for our little ones, and for all our substance ;' and ver. 31, 'Then we departed from the river Ahava, on the twelfth day of the first month, to go to Jerusalem ; and the hand of our God was upon us, and he delivered us from the hand of the enemy, and of such as lay in wait by the way.' They went on cheerfully, and found God in the journey. Here he hath fixed me, and here will I expect his blessing.

3. It is necessary to still murmurings when we are reduced to straits. God trieth his people with difficulties and inconveniences ; though we have God's warrant for our way, we cannot expect an absolute freedom from them. Now if they light upon us in God's way, and the place where he hath called us, we may bear them with the more patience. As suppose poverty, troubles from ill neighbours, or sickness, if we have not asked God's leave and blessing, conscience will turn upon us, and sting us with remorse. But when we are persuaded that God hath called us, faith quiets the heart, and worketh a humble submission. The disciples were all sent to sea by Christ : Mat. xiv. 21, 'Jesus con-

strained his disciples to get into a ship;' there was a call, yet they were tossed with waves. Christ's warrant for the voyage did not exempt them from trouble and danger; yet we read of no fear till Christ appeared on the waves, then 'they thought him a spirit, and were sore afraid,' ver. 26. But Christ comforts them, and revealeth himself to them—'Be not afraid, it is I,' ver. 27. So usually it falleth out, this is a pattern of providence; there will be troubles, but in God's way we need fear no danger.

4. Because it is a piece of atheism not to acknowledge God in every accident and affair of life. God will have the dominion of his providence acknowledged: James iv. 13–15, 'Go to now, ye that say, To-day or to-morrow we will go into such a city, and continue there a year, and buy and sell, and get a gain, . . . for that ye ought to say, If the Lord will we shall live, and do this or that.' Such resolutions shut out God when conceived without prayer and inquiry of God. Do not first say, We will go to such a place, but, Lord, shall I? We are neither lords of lives nor of actions; it is a piece of religious manners to ask God's leave, and wait for his answer, if we expect his blessing: Judges i. 1, 'The children of Israel asked the Lord, saying, Who shall go up for us against the Canaanites first to fight against them.' Yea, profane Ahab: 1 Kings xxii. 6, 'Shall I go against Ramoth-gilead to battle, or shall I forbear?'

5. Because many cases are exceeding difficult, as when God calls us from a place of ease and safety to a place of hazard and danger; as when Christ called Peter to leave the ship, and come to him upon the waters, Mat. xiv. 29; so when God calls to forsake our dearest interests and relations. Now in such cases our call should be cleared up to us, lest we decline the duty of our calling, as Jonah did; God called him to go to Nineveh, and because it was a work of much danger and difficulty, he fleeth to Tarshish, to his great loss and hazard, for he was forced to take up his lodging for a while in the whale's belly. Or sometimes there is a more urgent call; God calleth one way, and our inclinations draw us another, and the question lieth between duty and interests, and yet interests want not excuses.

Well then, how shall we know the place when God hath called us to fix the place of our abode? The question concerneth either christians in general, or else more particularly ministers, whose service is more weighty, for in ordinary removes there is a greater latitude, or else gentlemen who travel to get knowledge and experience, or else merchants for traffic, whose affairs do often call them from country to country. Now something is to be spoken for their satisfaction, that they may see God therein.

First, For christians in general, and so there are two cases— (1.) Concerning the fixing of their abode; (2.) Concerning flying in times of persecution.

1. Concerning the fixing of their abode. What rules shall they observe to guide them in this weighty affair of life? Particulars are infinite, the general rules are these—

[1.] There is much in the designation of providence, there where God hath fixed our interests, birth, education, &c.: Acts xvii. 26, 'And hath made of one blood all nations of men for to dwell on all the face of the earth, and hath determined the times before appointed, and the bounds of their habitation.' There providence left us, and there without scruple we may expect to find God. I am sure there we have most opportunities to serve him, because of the privileges of our birth and interests; every man hath a right to the privileges of his native soil.

[2.] But we are not absolutely confined there, but that upon convenient reasons we may remove. 'The earth is the Lord's, and the fulness thereof.' God is not tied to places, nor we. As they laughed at his folly in Plutarch that said there was a better moon at Athens than there was at Corinth; certainly there is not a better God in one place than in another. God is the same in England, in France, in the Indies. And as God is not tied, so we are not tied: Ps. cxv. 16, 'The heaven, even the heavens are the Lord's; but the earth hath he given to the children of men.' The earth lieth freely open to all passengers. What partitions and restraints shall we fix but those that God hath fixed by providence and property? As long as we acknowledge providence in asking his leave, seeking his blessing, observing the way that he openeth to us, and as long as we do not invade property, and disturb the first occupants, we may remove.

[3.] This removal must not be out of levity and wantonness, but upon weighty cause. Some men are never fixed, but flit hither and thither, though still to their loss and inconvenience. A rolling stone never gathereth moss. This is to tempt God, as if his providence should be at our beck. It was the advice of a heathen, Where thou art well, keep thyself well, lest thinking to meet with better thou findest worse. Usually these rolling stones carry their curse with them, and when men will be trying conclusions; the last conclusion of all is want and inconvenience.

[4.] The weighty causes upon which we may remove are want of health, if the places we live in prove hard and barren, and we know not how to subsist, or want of ordinances, or a lawful calling from state and church, whereof we are members, as to be ambassadors, or messengers of the churches, or such like cases determinable by christian prudence. And so in conjugal relations: Ps. xlv. 10, 'Forsake thine own people, and thy father's house.' Only, where the remove is of greater hazard, the call must be more urgent: Mat. xiv. 22, 'And straightway Jesus' —ἠνάγκασεν—'constrained his disciples to get into a ship.'

[5.] Upon what cause soever we remove, we must consult with God for his leave: James iv. 1. 5, 'If the Lord will, we shall live, and do this or that;' for his blessing: Gen. xxiv. 12, 'O Lord God of my master Abraham, I pray thee send me good speed this day,' still consult with the oracle. It was the theology of the gentiles, *Dii magna curant, parva negligunt*—The gods regard great things, but neglect small things. This thought is in the heart of many christians, as if God did only care for the greater matters. The blind world sets up an idol called chance or fortune, and lives at peradventure: Prov. iii. 6, 'In all thy ways acknowledge him, and he shall direct thy paths.' The children of God dare not resolve upon any course till they have asked counsel of God; they run to the oracle or ephod. Jacob in his journey would not go to Laban, nor come from him without a warrant.

Jehoshaphat doth not send for the captains of the army, but the prophets of the Lord: 1 Kings xxii. 7, 'Is there not here a prophet of the
Lord, that we may inquire of him?' This is a great argument of the
fear of God. The heathens had their sybils, and oracles of Delphi
and Jupiter Ammon.

[6.] God's answer after prayer must be observed, otherwise we do but
mock God, and use it as a ceremony. Many ask God with an idol in
their hearts: Ezek. xiv. 3, 'Every man of the house of Israel that setteth up his idols in his heart, and putteth the stumbling-block of his
iniquity before his face, and cometh to the prophet; I the Lord will
answer him that cometh, according to the multitude of his idols.' Men
are resolved, and then pretend to consult God, as Jeremiah said to
Johanan and his company, Jer. xlii. 20, 'Ye dissembled in your hearts
when you sent me unto the Lord your God, saying, Pray for us unto
the Lord our God, and according unto all that the Lord our God shall
say, so declare unto us, and we will do it.' Observe then God's answer,
your comfort and happiness dependeth on it; as when God in the
course of his providence openeth a way, or by inward instinct directeth
us to such a course, or by powerful and persuading reasons poiseth the
judgment, usually by counsel in the heart: Ps. xvi. 7, 'My reins instruct me in the night season;' or such a fit accommodation of the circumstances and passages of providence, God inviteth and calleth forth
his people to follow him.

[7.] In doubtful cases we must not be swayed with interest but
conscience. All scruples must be determined by principles and reasons
of religion. It is carnal to measure all things by ease, peace, and
temporal welfare; we must consider where we can have the greatest
capacity of glorifying God; that is the general rule, even in civil affairs:
1 Cor. x. 31, 'Whether therefore ye eat or drink, or whatsoever ye do,
do all to the glory of God.' This is the great end of our lives. A
christian doth not altogether look how he may more gratify his own
concernments, but how he may be more useful, and serve the great end
for which he was sent into the world; as a traveller, when he cometh
to two ways, and knoweth not which to take, he doth not look which is
fairest or foulest, most smooth or plain, but which is most likely to suit
with the purpose of his journey. The plains of pleasure and profit
may be more grateful to the flesh, but they lie out of our road to heaven.
Means must be chosen with respect to the end; in all deliberate counsels
reasons of religion must bear sway. Usually we consult with flesh
and blood, and then the conflicts of lusts and knowledge breed scruples
and irresolutions; conscience saith one thing, and lust and interests
another, and so men are uncertain.

[8.] Whatever we do, we must go there where we have the ordinances,
and enjoy the communion of saints, otherwise we turn our backs upon
God, and that will not be our comfort: 1 Peter ii. 2, 'As newborn
babes desire the sincere milk of the word, that ye may grow thereby.'
True saints cannot be without ordinances. It was Lot's sin to choose
Sodom for the pleasantness of the situation: Ps. lxxxiv. 10, 'For a day
in thy courts is better than a thousand; I had rather be a doorkeeper in the house of my God, than to dwell in the tents of wickedness.'
It is observed of Cain, Gen. iv. 16, 'And Cain went out from the pre-

sence, of the Lord, and dwelt in the land of Nod, in the east of Eden.'
How did he go from the presence of the Lord, seeing God is everywhere ?
The meaning is, he went from that part and quarter of the world where
God had his church, the place of his special presence.   God's children
have left many conveniences to enjoy ordinances, as Moses left the
honours of Egypt for the company of the people of God.   It is a fault
in christians to turn their backs upon the church and go to a Sodom,
where they will be grieved to see and hear God dishonoured.

2. About flying in times of persecution.

[1.] In general, it is lawful in some cases.   We have a precept, at
least an allowance for it : Mat. x. 23, ' When they persecute you in this
city, flee ye to another '—viz., when our life shall serve more for God's
glory and the church's good, than our death can.   If God driveth us
out of our place, and provideth another, accept it with thankfulness.   I
prove this by example and reason.   By example—Christ fled into Egypt
when Herod sought his life : Mat. ii. 13, ' And when they were departed, behold the angel of the Lord appeareth to Joseph in a dream
saying, Arise, and take the young child and his mother, and flee into
Egypt, and be thou there until I bring thee word : for Herod will seek
the young child to destroy him.'   And Christ hid himself, and went
out of the temple, when the Jews threatened to stone him : John viii.
59, ' Then took they up stones to cast at him ; but Jesus hid himself,
and went out of the temple.' So the prophets and holy men in scripture
—Elijah fled to Beersheba when Jezabel sought his life : 1 Kings xix.
3, ' And when he saw that, he arose, and went for his life, and came to
Beersheba.'   Paul was let down by the wall in a basket to escape the
Jews : Acts ix. 25, ' Then the disciples took him by night and let
him down by a wall in a basket.'   We are bound to keep our lives
till God requireth them.   Life is a treasure he hath lent us, and we
must keep it till the owner demandeth it of us, and to lay it out for
his use ; as when a man delivereth money to you, you must answer for
it to him.   To draw danger on ourselves is to tempt God ; when means
of escape are offered, we must use them with thankfulness, and when
God in his providence openeth a fair door.   All this showeth that it is
not unlawful in itself.

[2.] Though it be lawful to fly in persecution, yet it is not lawful for
all.   Austin saith, *In graviori persecutione nec omnes fugere, neque
omnes man_re debent ;* all should not stay, nor should all fly, as not
those that are useful to the church : John x. 12, ' He that is an hireling and not the shepherd, whose own the sheep are not, seeth the wolf
coming, and leaveth the sheep, and fleeth ; and the wolf catcheth them,
and scattereth the sheep.'   This is not to avoid persecution, but to
run away from our duty.   He that should be an example of fortitude
and constancy should not first manifest fear.   Though in a personal
persecution, when pastors are most aimed at, they may fly, as in the
before-mentioned examples of Christ, Elijah and Paul, and the prophets
that were hid by Obadiah by fifty and fifty in a cave, 1 Kings xviii. 13.
Those that by a special instinct of the Spirit of God are called to suffer
and confront the adversaries of the truth must not decline it, ' Paul
went bound in spirit to Jerusalem,' Acts xx. 22 ; and when his sufferings were foretold, and the disciples besought him not to go to Jerusalem,

he answered : Acts xxi. 13, 'What mean you to weep, and to break my heart ? I am ready, not to be bound only, but to die at Jerusalem, for the name of the Lord Jesus.' God had picked him out for a champion, and he would not draw back. Or when all lawful means of escape are taken away from us, so that we cannot fly without dishonesty and disobedience, and scandal, we must go through it. God, that is Lord of thy life, requireth it of thee: Rom. xiv. 7-9, 'For no man liveth to himself, and no man dieth to himself ; for whether we live, we live unto the Lord, and whether we die, we die unto the Lord ; whether we live therefore or die, we are the Lord's.' For to this end Christ both died and rose and revived, that he might be lord both of dead and living.' By a base flying from suffering you retract your vows when God challengeth you upon them.

[3.] For a more particular determination general rules cannot be given, but it is left to every one's particular prudence and faithfulness, that we act so that we neither wound conscience nor dishonour God ; and we are not faithful unless we seek wisdom of God, what to do in this particular. It is most natural to us to fly, and think of starting holes ; but the best way is to fly to Christ, and make his name our strong tower. Otherwise we cannot fly from God ; the Jews brought a tempest with them whithersoever they went.

Secondly, More particularly concerning ministers, whose office is of public use and influence, what is to be observed in fixing their station and place of service ? Ministers are to be considered either as altogether free, or else as already related to some congregation and particular place.

1. If free already, the case is the more easy, these things make a call.

[1.] A fair invitation from those that have power to call ; providence is to be observed in stirring up the hearts of men. Besides authoritative mission, there is an election or call from the people, as Christ had his ordination from God and election from the church ; as Hosea i. 11, 'Then shall the children of Judah and the children of Israel be gathered together, and appoint themselves one head,' compared with Eph. i. 22, 'And give him to be the head over all things to the church.' It is notable that in Paul's vision the call is not managed by God, but by a man of Macedonia : Acts xvi. 9, 'And a vision appeared to Paul in the night : there stood a man of Macedonia, and prayed him, saying, Come over into Macedonia and help us.' Only if a people be not in a capacity to choose, then an authoritative mission is enough, and we must preach whether they will hear or whether they will forbear ; as Paul and Barnabas were sent from the elders of Antioch to go to the gentiles, Acts xiii.

[2.] When there is a universal concurrence of sweet providences removing all rubs and difficulties, there is a clear call of providence. Sometimes there is a call from a people, which a man cannot close with unless he should break through the hedge, and then a serpent will bite him. Sometimes there may be an inclination, and providence may hinder : Acts xvi. 7, 'They assayed to go into Bithynia, but the Spirit suffered them not.' God himself may cast some bar in his providence in our way. Or Satan may hinder : 1 Thes. ii. 18, 'Wherefore we would have come unto you (even I Paul) once and again, but Satan hindered us.' Satan hinders by stirring up opposition against the ministers of the gospel.   Or the greater necessities of other people may hinder us : Rom. xv. 22, 'For which cause' (speaking of his preaching the gospel where it had not been preached) 'I have been much hindered from coming to you.'   But then it is not every inclination of our own hearts which is sufficient, but an inclination spiritually raised by the instinct of the Holy Ghost, after prayer; not upon secular encouragements of plentiful revenues, or a fatter portion in the world.   It is upon my heart to live and die with you.

2. About removes from one place to another, take these rules.—

[1.] It is not simply unlawful.   Ministers are not so fixed, as that they cannot remove upon no accounts ; if so, raw and inexperienced persons might happen to supply the greatest places.   Churches are bound to spare to others out of their plenty ; as the elders at Antioch sent some of their company to preach to the gentiles, Acts xiii.   We are ministers of the catholic church rather than of any great congregation ; and where there is greatest necessity, or greatest aptness and proportion of gifts, there are our pains to be bestowed.   Greatest necessity and opportunity : the good shepherd runneth after the lost sheep, and leaveth the rest in the fold ; and where greatest measure of gifts.   God fitteth every light to every socket.

[2.] Whenever it is done, it must be with great advice and caution, and upon an urgent call, by which you may clearly gather that God hath called you to preach the gospel to them.   The call had need be urgent : whatever concurreth to an ordinary call must be double. It must be upon much seeking of God, clear evidence, consent of others, a spirit purged from secular interest, the consent of the church you leave gained, as much as may be, that they may deny themselves.

[3.] It is most comfortable when driven away by providence rather than our own choice, as by defect of maintenance—that is a negative or privative persecution, in which case we may fly to a another city ; or by violence of unreasonable men, that have not faith ; or upon contempt : Acts xix. 9, 'When divers were hardened and believed not, but spake evil of that way before the multitude, he departed from them ;' so Mat. xiv. 15, 'This is a desert place, and the time is now past ; send the multitude away.'   You are free of their blood if they will not hear.   Your rule is, Mat. x. 14, 'Whosoever shall not receive you nor hear your words, when you depart out of that house or city, shake off the dust of your feet.'

Thirdly, For gentlemen who travel to get knowledge and experience.

1. It must not be undertaken upon light grounds.   It is a great adventure, and it is a sin to tempt God to protect us by casting ourselves upon great hazards for so small a reason as for mere pleasure and curiosity, or pride and vain glory, to learn exotic fashions or the like.

2. It must not be to places idolatrous, and where true religion is under a restraint; you usually then put yourselves upon a snare. Abraham could not remain in Chaldea because of abominable idolatry and corruption, and you go into them voluntarily to learn of their ways.

3. If it be in places free from infection, where you may live with safety and a good conscience, to get more knowledge and experience, it is commendable ; as the Queen of Sheba came from far to hear the wisdom of Solomon, 1 Kings x. 1, for which she is commended by Christ, Mat. xii. 42.

Fourthly, For merchants, who remove for traffic, especially into places where the true religion is not professed, it may be suppressed with extremity of rigour.

1. It is lawful certainly to pass from country to country for traffic's sake and to maintain commerce, for there are divers commodities in divers places.

2. Conversation with heretics and infidels may be allowed, else we must go out of the world: 1 Cor. v. 9, 10, 'I wrote unto you in an epistle, not to company with fornicators, yet not altogether with the fornicators of the world, or with the covetous, or extortioners, or with idolaters, for then must ye needs go out of the world.' I speak of a civil commerce, which may be maintained with these cautions.

[1.] With all our traffic we must take all occasions to propagate religion in the truth and power of it especially when stirred up by impulse of spirit; Deut. xxxiii. 18, 19, 'And of Zebulun he said, Rejoice, Zebulun, in thy going out; and, Issachar, in thy tents. They shall call the people unto the mountain; there they shall offer sacrifices of righteousness, for they shall suck of the abundance of the seas and of treasures hid in the sand.'

[2.] Traffic must be managed by fit persons, not novices, and persons ungrounded in religion; it is very dangerous for such. This is as if you should turn a child loose among a company of poisons; an empty pitcher soon cracks by the fire.

[3.] There must be no fixed habitation; if you thus leave the ordinances and societies of saints for trade, religion is made to stoop to gain.

SERMON XLII.

By faith he sojourned in the land of promise, as in a strange country, dwelling in tabernacles with Isaac and Jacob, the heirs with him of the same promise: for he looked for a city which hath foundations, whose builder and maker is God.—Heb. xi. 9, 10.

The apostle is commending faith from the examples of the patriarchs; after the flood he beginneth with Abraham, the father of the faithful. In the former verse he speaks of the place whence he was called, in this of the place to which he was called; there he had commended him for his self-denial in obeying God's call, and here for his patience and constancy in waiting for the promise. From God's training up Abraham in a course of difficulties, we see it is no easy matter to go to heaven; there is a great deal of ado to unsettle a believer from the world, and there is a great deal of ado to fix the heart in the expectation of heaven. First there must be self-denial in coming out of the world, and divorcing ourselves from our bosom sins and dearest interests; and then there must be patience shown in waiting for God's mercy to eternal life, waiting his leisure as well as performing his will. Here is the time of our exercise, and we must expect it, since the father of the faithful was thus trained up ere he could inherit the promises.

In these two verses we have a second effect of Abraham's faith and the reason of it.

In the ninth verse we have the second effect of Abraham's faith— 'By faith he sojourned in the land of promise,' &c. There you may take notice of.

1. The act of obedience—*By faith he sojourned in the land of promise, as in a strange country.*

2. The symbol and rite by which this obedience was signified and expressed—*Dwelling in tabernacles.*

3. His fellows and followers in the same obedience—*With Isaac and Jacob, heirs with him of the same promise.* Of these in their order.

First, I begin with the act of obedience—'By faith he sojourned in the land of promise, as in a strange country.' The words may be taken in a double sense, as they imply his condition of life and his disposition of heart. Abraham was both a literal and a spiritual stranger in the land of promise.

1. Let us look upon the expression as implying his condition of life. Abraham was not in the condition of an inheritor, but of a sojourner in the land of Canaan; therefore it is called the land of his sojournings, or in which he was a stranger: Gen. xvii. 8, 'I will give unto thee, and to thy seed after thee, the land wherein thou art a stranger;' and so he confesseth to the children of Heth, Gen. xxiii. 4, 'I am a stranger and a sojourner with you.' This sojourning was an act of faith, because he was borne up by faith in the promise against all the troubles which he suffered. He had large lands and possessions in Ur of the Chaldees; but these he left, and when he came to Canaan, the land of promise, he might expect the fruit of his faith and labours; or else, having seen the land, to return with God's leave to the place from whence he came. But God had not yet done with the trial of his faith; from his father's house he was a voluntary and obedient exile; and in Canaan, where God brought him, he is still in the condition of a sojourner; the same faith that moved him to go he knew not whither, bindeth him there to wait God's leisure till he should enjoy the benefit of the promise, being contented in the meanwhile with what estate divine providence should allot.

I shall discuss but one question, and then come to the observations.

Quest. Why God would have Abraham tarry in Canaan? He might have shown him in the land, and then returned him to Ur of the Chaldees among his friends again. What are the reasons?

Ans. God's will is reason enough; but yet it seemed to be for these causes :—

1. Partly to avoid idolatry: Joshua xxiv. 2, 3, 'Your fathers dwelt on the other side of the flood in old time, even Terah the father of Abraham, and the father of Nahor: and they worshipped other gods. And I took your father Abraham from the other side of the flood, and led him throughout all the land of Canaan.' This was more dangerous among them of his own kindred, than among the Canaanites, and

more plausible, there being a greater acknowledgment of the true God, and so aptest to take.

2. For his trial and exercise, the father of the faithful was to be an example of self-denial, faith and patience.

3. To take livery and seizin of the land in behalf of his posterity, his faith was more stirred up by seeing it, and being constantly in it; by faith he could say, This is mine.

4. That he might be a means to bear forth the name of God among that people. The sins of the Amorites were not yet full. God sent them Abraham, as he sent Lot to Sodom.

5. To be a pattern of divine blessing and providence; for there he increased in riches wonderfully: Gen. xiii. 2, 'And Abraham was very rich in cattle, in silver, and in gold;' and so was an instance of the reward of obedience to the people of that land. He had not all in hope, but something in hand.

I come now to the notes; they may be taken from his condition, and from his submitting to that condition; for it was an act of his faith to sojourn in the land of promise, as in a strange land.

[1.] From his condition appointed by God upon special reasons.

(1.) Observe—From what inconsiderable beginnings the promise of God taketh place. Abraham cometh into Canaan as a poor sojourner; but yet to take seizin of the land, and there he is forced to borrow an habitation, and buy a burying-place. He borroweth an habitation, or place wherein to set his tent: Gen. xiv. 13, 'He dwelt in the plain of Mamre the Amorite.' He was as it were tenant and farmer to Mamre; the whole land was his by right and by the grant of God, but others had the possession. And he buyeth a place of burial: Gen. xxiii. 8, 9, 'Entreat for me to Ephron the son of Zohar, that he may give me the cave of Machpelah, which he hath, which is in the end of his field: for as much money as it is worth he shall give it me, for a possession of a burying-place among you.' Otherwise he had not land enough whereon to set his foot: Acts vii. 5, 'And he gave him none inheritance in it, no, not so much as to set his foot on.' A strange beginning for so great promises! The first thing he takes possession of was a place of burial for the dead; that was all the purchase he made; so that his infeoffment and entrance was rather a resignation and farewell, and he seemed to provide more for a departure than an abode. Thus wonderfully is God wont to work, and by unlikely means to bring about the greatest effects: dead bones keep possession for four hundred years. Hereby his power is known: Ps. cv. 11–13, 'Unto thee will I give the land of Canaan, the lot of your inheritance; when they were but a few men in number; yea, very few, and strangers in it. When they went from one nation to another, from one kingdom to another people.'

(2.) Observe, that God's promise is not always made good in kind. Abraham is called to a land which he should after receive for an inheritance; and instead of Canaan he hath heaven—a city founded not by the Amorites, but God. In performing temporal promises, God doth not always observe the letter, and give the particular blessing; but he giveth what is equivalent, or that which is better. This is the land that I will give thee; but yet 'he looked for a city that had foundations, whose builder and maker is God.' God's people have never cause to complain of his breach of promise; if he change their wages it is for the better ; a secret sense of his favour and possession of heaven is much better than to be king of all the world.   Jacob complains of Laban, Gen. xxxi 7, ' Your father hath deceived me, and changed my wages ten times,' but none have cause to complain so of God.   Temporal promises are not always fulfilled in the letter, because God is not absolutely bound ; but usually they have that which far exceedeth. If a man should promise another two hundred pounds, and give him an inheritance of so many hundreds or thousands by the year, here is no deceit.   God is often better than his word; but never cometh short.

(3.) Observe, that temporal blessings are usually made good to the posterity of the faithful.   Abraham was a stranger in the land of promise, and had not a foot of land there; but his posterity possessed it, and drove out the Canaanites.   Believers have enough in God; and however he dealeth with them, they can wait upon him ; but usually their posterity, if they have nothing else, enjoy many temporal blessings with respect to their father's faith.   A land of promise contents Abraham ; he leaveth the possession to his posterity.   Thus it often falleth out—the father is rich in faith, and the children, though carnal, are rich in this world ; they have the blessing of Ishmael, if not the blessing of Isaac.

(4.) Observe, that though God giveth a title, yet we must wait till providence giveth us fair possession.   Abraham had a title given him by God, but the Amorites had the possession, therefore ' he sojourned in the land of promise as in a strange land.'   Whatever our hopes are, faith maketh not haste.   If we may have right as an heir to his land, or a lord to an estate that is leased out, or an unjustly exiled man to his possessions, yet we must use no irregular means, not secretly with the death of those that enjoy it—that is murder, but we must be contented for awhile to be as mere strangers, as Abraham was in the land of promise.

(5.) Observe, that God doth not cast a people out of their possessions till their iniquities be full.   He had given the land of Canaan to Abraham, but he giveth him not the possession ; and the reason is rendered, Gen. xv. 16, ' For the iniquity of the Amorites is not yet full.' His posterity was not to possess it till four hundred years after the first grant.   Thus God gave the kingdom to David, but Saul possessed it a good while afterwards.   Great is the patience of God to sinners, and the sentence is not executed as soon as past.

(6.) Observe, that the accomplishment of promises is delayed till a fit time.   It was a land under promise; but yet to Abraham and his seed for awhile it was as a strange land.   When Abraham wandered up and down like a stranger, where was the heritage that was promised to him ?   He might say, Is this my land which others possess ?   but he lets God alone with his promise.   God is not slack, but we are hasty : Gal. iv. 4, ' When the fulness of time was come, God sent forth his Son, made of a woman, made under the law.'   Our times are always present, but God's time is not come.   The Lord tarried so long, till it was high time to take vengeance of the Amorites for their sins ; and till it was high time for the Israelites to shift dwellings, and the people were grown to such a number, that they might not come by way of miracle to take possession, but by conquest. When the oven is hot, then is the loaf set in ; so when all circumstances concur, then shall the promise be accomplished.

(7.) Observe, a man that is called to converse with idolaters must converse with them as sparingly as may be. While Canaan was full of idolaters, Abraham must be but a sojourner, and must dwell in tents to profess his religion. Thus we have considered Abraham's sojourning as appointed by God.

[2.] Let us consider it as an act of faith and obedience. 'By faith Abraham sojourned in the land of promise as in a strange country.' In his faith there are three things notable—his patience, his contentation, and his constancy.

(1.) His patience, not only in digesting the troubles of his present estate, but in waiting God's leisure. Observe, we must not be offended with delay, but must patiently wait for the accomplishment of God's promises. Abraham borrowed a place wherein to fix his tent ; Isaac is fain to struggle for a well ; and Jacob lived in a wandering and movable condition ; and yet they waited till God should make way for the possession of Canaan. What can we do in such a case ? can we live upon the reversion of a promise, especially of promises that are to be made good to posterity ? God is much glorified in our patient expectation, when we can think ourselves as well for that which shall come as if we were in actual and present possession. This is the property of faith : Heb. xi. 1, 'Faith is the substance of things hoped for, and the evidence of things not seen.' The word of God is enough to a believer, but carnal men are all for present possession ; they will trust God no further than they can see him.

(2.) His contentation. Observe, contentment with a small portion of earthly things is a great fruit of faith. By faith Abraham sojourned, though he had neither house nor home in the land of promise, but only a sepulchre ; this was enough. Faith doth not only beget a confidence, but also a composure of spirit, and submission to the Lord's will. A little thing will serve on earth, because we expect so much in heaven. Well then, do not always look to confidence, but to this contentation. Are carnal affections mortified ? can you submit to hardships ? Though in regard of temporals you find loss by trusting in God, yet is it enough that you have a promise of better things ? Then do you believe. Abraham was not covetous ; he looketh upon the spiritual rather than the earthly part of the promise ; he was not for fields and lands ; he saw that his Canaan must be heaven, and was content.

[3.] His constancy. You may observe in Abraham an unwearied constancy in obeying God and believing his promises, though all things seemed contrary. He sojourned where God would have him, and waited for what God would give him. Observe, that true faith adhereth to God, though it find not what it believeth, but is often disappointed, and seeth no probability of the thing promised. Abraham leaveth Ur of the Chaldees ; had not a foot of land in Canaan ; sojourneth among the Canaanites ; thence by a famine is driven into Egypt ; is often burdened with envy ; at length is told that the land belongeth to his seed ; yet he remaineth without issue for a long time, till he was a hundred years old ;

his seed threatened to suffer a long captivity, yet he hopeth against hope. Faith doth not look on the things promised, but on God; if it altogether looked on the things promised, it would soon fail and wax faint. Abraham's case was just like David's; the Canaanites were strong and mighty, and dwelt in cities, as wicked men, in David's time, when he was afflicted, 'prosper in the world, and increase in riches,' Ps. lxxiii. 12; but yet read verses 23–26, 'Nevertheless I am continually with thee; thou hast holden me by my right hand. Thou shalt guide me by thy counsel, and afterwards receive me to glory. Whom have I in heaven but thee? and there is none upon earth that I desire besides thee. My flesh and my heart faileth: but God is the strength my heart and my portion for ever.' They have God, and they have heaven, and thence ariseth this constancy of faith. Thus through all temptations must we be constant to the end. When difficulties arise, we think of returning into Egypt, still bear up.

Obj. But this is the property of strong faith.

Ans. No, but of all faith; strong faith overcometh temptations with less difficulty; but yet weak faith, if true, persevereth to the end through a thousand temptations. The disciples were ὀλιγόπιστοι, of little faith; yet saith Christ to them, Luke xxii. 28, 29, 'Ye are they which have continued with me in my temptations. And I appoint unto you a kingdom, as my Father hath appointed unto me.' Now though we have not such clear grounds to hope as Abraham, yet we have God's promises, and his word is as sure as an oracle. We trust in the same God, and look for the same heaven; therefore do not draw back, but continue with God, and own his cause in all trials.

Secondly, Let us look upon this expression of Abraham's sojourning in the land of promise as in a strange land; as it implieth the disposition of Abraham's heart, and not only the condition of his life. Canaan was assigned to Abraham, not only as a place of trial, but as a figure and pledge of heaven; therefore, because he expected a better country, and cities not built by the Amorites, but a city that hath foundations, built by God himself, therefore he is said to dwell there as in a strange country; he looked for another home, and therefore in Canaan he lived as a stranger. Thus the expression is taken elsewhere. When Abraham's seed was in a settled condition, and had taken possession of that land of which Abraham had only the promise, God tells them they were but strangers and sojourners: Lev. xxv. 23, 'The land shall not be sold for ever: for the land is mine; for ye are strangers and sojourners with me;' not only the wandering patriarchs, who flitted from place to place, but their posterity, even in the time of their greatest happiness and settled abode. David was a king; yet he saith, Ps. xxxix. 12, 'I am a stranger with thee, and a sojourner as all my fathers were.' Now, lest this should seem an expression suited to David's case, when he was chased like a flea, or hunted like a partridge upon the mountains, you shall see; when he was settled in his kingdom towards the end and close of his life; when he had gotten so many victories, and his people lived quietly in their own possessions; and they offered so many cartloads of gold and silver, yet then he confesseth, 1 Chron. xxix. 15, 'We are strangers before thee, and sojourners, as were all our fathers: our days on the earth are as a shadow, and there is none abiding.' The land never enjoyed greater peace, never flowed in greater wealth; the people never seemed to be more at home, everyone sitting and singing under his own vine and fig-tree, yet saith he, ' We are strangers before thee, and sojourners, as all our fathers were.' So we are taught in the gospel, 1 Peter. ii. 11, ' Dearly beloved, I beseech you, as strangers and pilgrims, abstain from fleshly lusts, which war against the soul.' They to whom Peter wrote were strangers in a literal sense : 1 Peter. i. 1, ' To the strangers scattered thoughout Pontus,' &c. But it is there taken in a spiritual sense, as appears by the exhortation. Out of all—

Observe, that the children of God there, where they have best right and most possessions, are but strangers and pilgrims. How settled soever their condition be, yet this is the temper of the saints upon earth, to count themselves but strangers. All men indeed are strangers and sojourners; but the saints do best discern it, and most freely acknowledge it. Wicked men have no firm dwelling upon earth, but that is against their intention ; their inward thoughts and desire is, that they may abide for ever ; they are strangers against their wills, their abode is uncertain in the world, and they cannot help it. And pray mark, there are two distinct words used in this case in Peter, ' as strangers and pilgrims '—ὡς παροίκους καὶ παρεπιδήμους ; and in the old testament ' strangers and sojourners.' A stranger is one that hath his abode in a foreign country ; that is not a native and denizen of the place, though he liveth there ; and in opposition to the natives he is called a stranger ; as if a Frenchman should live in England, he is a stranger. But a pilgrim and a sojourner is one that intendeth not to settle, but only passeth through a place, and is in motion travelling homeward. So the children of God, in relation to a country of their own in another place—namely, heaven, they are denizens there, but strangers in the world ; and they are sojourners and pilgrims in regard of their motion and journey towards their own country. Now, wicked men are only strangers in regard of their unsettled abode in the world but they are not pilgrims ; they have no inheritance to expect in heaven ; here is the place where they would abide for ever. Let God keep heaven to himself, so they might have the world ; they are sure to go out of the world, but they are not sure to go to heaven ; and so they are strangers, but not pilgrims. But briefly I shall show you— (1.) How christians are strangers and pilgrims ; (2.) The inferences of duty from hence ; (3.) How we may get our hearts into such a frame ;

1. The resemblance between the temper of the saints and the con-dition of a stranger and pilgrim. The allusion may be taken from an ordinary strangership and pilgrimage, or from the pilgrimage of Israel through the desert into Canaan.

[1.] From an ordinary pilgrimage.

(1.) A stranger is one that is absent from his country, and from his father's house. So are we ; heaven is our country ; God is there, and Christ is there. The apostle saith, 2 Cor. v. 6, ' Whilst we are at home in the body, we are absent from the Lord.' We are strangers there, where we are absent from God and Christ—*Ubi pater, ibi patria ;* our birth is from heaven, and thither we tend. Rivers run away from their springs, and never return more ; but it is not so with us ; our springs are in Christ, and our streams are to him ; the tendency is according to the principle. Our birth is from heaven, and thither are the motions and tendencies of renewed souls ; thence they came, and thither they tend.

(2.) A stranger in a foreign country is not known, nor valued according to his birth and breeding ; so the saints walk up and down in the world like princes in disguise—' The king's daughter is all glorious within,' Ps. xlv. 13. The world knoweth not our birth, nor our breeding, nor our hopes, nor our expectations.—' Our life is hid with Christ in God,' Col. iii, 3 ; and therefore we are often judged according to the flesh and outward appearance, but live unto God in the Spirit.

(3.) Strangers are liable to inconveniences ; so are godly men in the world—*Religio scit se peregrinam esse in terris*, saith Tertullian, it is like a strange plant brought from a foreign country, and doth not agree with the nature of the soil, it thriveth not in the world. Wicked men prosper here ; they are like thistles and nettles, that grow of their own accord ; the world is their native soil.

(4.) A stranger is patient, standeth not for ill-usage, and is contented with pilgrim's fare and lodging. We are now abroad, and must expect hardship—' In the world you shall have tribulation,' John xvi. 33. God permitteth inconveniences to arise to wean us from the world, and make us long for home.

(5.) A stranger is wary that he may not give offence and incur the hatred and displeasure of the natives. We had need to ' walk wisely towards them that are without,' Col. iv 5 ; we are in the land of our observers.

(6.) A stranger is thankful for the least favour ; so must we be thankfully contented with the things God hath bestowed on us. Anything in a strange country is much : 1 Chron. xxix. 13–15, ' We thank thee, and praise thy glorious name. But who am I, and what is my people, that we should be able to offer so willingly after this sort ? for all things come of thee, and of thine own have we given thee. For we are strangers before thee, and sojourners as were all our fathers.'

(7.) A stranger that hath a journey to go would pass over it as soon as he can ; and so we, who have a journey to heaven desire to be dissolved : Phil. i. 23, ' Having a desire to depart, and to be with Christ, which is far better.' It is the joy of their souls to think to be at home with Christ.

(8.) A stranger buyeth not such things as he cannot carry with him ; he doth not buy trees, house, household stuff, but jewels and pearls, and such things as are portable. So such things as we can carry with us to heaven should take up our time and care. Piety and godliness outlives the grave ; our wealth doth not follow us but our works follow us ; and therefore our great care should be to get the jewels of the covenant, the graces of God's Spirit, those things that will abide with us.

(9.) A stranger's heart is in his country ; so is a saint's : Phil. iii. 20, τὸ πολίτευμα ἡμῶν—' Our conversation is in heaven ; ' these are his thoughts, thither he is drawing home his trade ; so is a christian drawing his heart heavenward : heaven is his home, this life is but the way. But now when men lavish out their respects by wholesale upon the world, and can scarce retail a thought on heaven, they are not passengers but inhabitants; here they are at home.

(10.) A stranger is inquisitive after the way, fearing lest he should go amiss; so is a christian : Ps. cxix. 19, 'I am a stranger in the earth, hide not thy commandments from me.' We need direction in a strange place ; there are so many byways in the world that we may soon miscarry, and be led by our own lusts, or the suggestions of others, into such ways and practices as God doth not allow.

(11.) A stranger provides for his return, as a merchant that he may return richly laden. When you send a child for breeding beyond the seas, he taketh care that when he returns he may return as a man accomplished, so as to please his father. So we must appear before God in Sion ; what manner of persons ought we to be ? Let us return from our travel well provided.

[2.] It carryeth some resemblance with Israel's travelling in the wilderness, when they came out of Egypt to go into the land of Canaan. They were brought out of Egypt, and we are taken out of the power of darkness : Col. i. 13, ' Who hath delivered us from the power of darkness, and hath translated us into the kingdom of his dear Son.' They had the law given them in the wilderness, and God's word is our light during our pilgrimage : Ps. cxix. 105, ' Thy word is a lamp unto my feet and a light unto my path.' They were fed with manna from heaven, and we have Christ, who is hidden manna, the bread that came down from heaven : John vi. 31, 32, 'Our fathers did eat manna, in the wilderness, as it is written, He gave them bread from heaven to eat. Moses gave you not that bread from heaven, but my Father giveth you the true bread from heaven.' They were guided by the pillar of cloud and pillar of fire, which never forsook them till they came to Canaan, and we are under God's providence and fatherly care : Ps. lxxiii. 24, ' Thou shalt guide me with thy counsel, and afterwards receive me to glory.' In the wilderness they were troubled with fiery serpents as we are with fleshly lusts : 1 Peter ii. 11, ' Dearly beloved, I beseech you as strangers and pilgrims, abstain from fleshly lusts, that war against your souls.' Then Amalek rose up against them, and smote their rear, and we have our persecutors and oppressors in the world : 2 Tim. iii. 12, ' Yea and all that will live godly in Christ Jesus shall suffer persecution.' The clusters of grapes and excellent fruits of Canaan were brought to them in the wilderness, and we have the first-fruits of the Spirit : Rom. viii. 23, ' And not only they, but ourselves also, which have the first-fruits of the Spirit, even we ourselves groan within ourselves, waiting for the adoption, to wit, the redemption of our body.' We have the beginnings of heaven during our pilgrimage, grace, peace of conscience, and joy in the Holy Ghost ; these fruits are brought as a taste of the goodness of the land, and as a pledge of their interest in it. By the cluster of grapes God gave them livery and seizin of Canaan ; so by the first-fruits of the Spirit we have a taste and earnest of the heavenly state. Moses brought them to the borders of Canaan, but Joshua led them into the land, as Jesus leadeth us into heaven. Good works are the way, but not the cause of entrance.

2. What are the inferences of duty that may be drawn hence.

[1.] We learn to mortify fleshly lusts, because these weaken our desires of heaven, and hinder us in our journey. This is the apostle's inference: 1 Peter ii. 11, 'Dearly beloved, I beseech you as strangers and pilgrims, abstain from fleshly lusts, which war against the soul.' If we were not pilgrims bound for another world, it were more tolerable to gratify the senses, and to give contentment to every carnal desire; but we are in a journey, and therefore should mortify fleshly lusts. Brutish affections are all for the present, and weaken our desires of things to come; like the flesh-pots of Egypt, they make us forget heaven, and forget home. They distract the mind, and draw it another way, that it is cumbered with much serving; as it was said of Martha, Luke x. 40, 'Martha was cumbered about much serving.' The soul must have some oblectation and delight; love cannot remain idle. When the pipes leak, the course of the stream is diverted. And as they distract, so they load and clog the soul; we feel no more weight than a bird under her feathers, but indeed they are the soul's load: Heb. xii. 1, 'Let us lay aside every weight, and the sin which doth so easily beset us, and let us run with patience the race that is set before us.' Immoderate and carnal affections, like a weight, press the soul downward: 2 Tim. iii. 6, 'They lead captive silly women laden with sins, led away with divers lusts.' Fishes feel no weight, though they swim ever so low in the waters; heavy bodies are never heavy in their proper places. A man that hath set up his rest here doth not feel lust to be a weight and load to him; but to one that looketh towards heaven they are burdensome, as a clog to his soul, that depresseth him in all his heavenly flights and motions. And they do not only distract and clog, but they distemper the soul. The racers were dieted for the Isthmic games: 1 Cor. ix. 25, 'Every man that striveth for the mastery is temperate in all things.' So saith the apostle, 'I keep under my body, and bring it into subjection,' ver. 27. Lusts put us quite out of temper for a heavenly journey. Therefore as strangers and pilgrims you must mortify fleshly lusts by prayer, watchfulness, beating down the body, cutting off the provisions of the flesh, and the like means.

[2.] Do not embroil yourselves in the cares of this world. God is called a stranger and a wayfaring man when he seems not to administer to the wants and necessities of his people: Jer. xiv. 8, 'Why shouldst thou be as a stranger in the land, and as a wayfaring man that turneth aside to tarry for a night?' Do not entangle yourselves in worldly pursuits and practices; your abode is here but for a time, and you know not how soon you may be called hence: 1 Cor. vii. 29–31, 'The time is short: it remaineth that both they that have wives be as though they had none, and they that weep as though they wept not, and they that rejoice as though they rejoiced not, and they that buy as though they possessed not, and they that use this world as not abusing it; for the fashion of this world passeth away.' Use the world as if you used it not. You do not stay but lodge here, therefore use the things of the world as passengers do things in an inn; they use them as being willing and ready to leave them the next morning. Who would trouble himself to hang his room in an inn for a night? We are strangers, and our days are but as a shadow, and to-morrow we must

be gone ; and therefore, though we may follow our callings with cheerfulness and diligence, yet we should not make worldly gain our business.
You make the world your home when the heart is filled with sins and
the head with cares, and all to grow great, and shine in pomp and
pleasure.   A pilgrim doth not make purchases in a foreign country,
but he is contented with a *viaticum,* so much as will serve him in his
journey ; but when men join field to field as if they would shine alone,
it is a sign they make this their home.   Follow your callings, and be
content with God's allowance,—it is enough to make your journey
comfortable,—and let not these things take up your heart as if here
were your rest ; use them as an instrument of piety and charity, as a
help to a better life ; delight in them only as a help to the journey,
then they will not prove a hindrance.   We cannot get out of the world
when we please, we are tenants at will to God, but let us get the world
out of us ; and so shall we do if we use it as if we used it not, when
we do not make the world our end, our rest, our main work, but only
mind it in a subordination to a better life.   When we make it our end
by an irregular aim, our work by an intemperate use, our rest by an
immoderate delight, we are at home ; God may keep heaven to himself
for us.   God in mercy appoints us callings to busy our minds as a fit
diversion after worship ;—sins settle in us by idleness, as wheat grows
musty in the garner if it be not turned and stirred ;—and as a means
of our support and usefulness : Eph. iv. 28, ' Let him that stole steal
no more, but rather let him labour, working with his hands the thing
which is good, that he may have to give to him that needeth.'   But if
we labour in them with other ends, we seek not another country, even
heaven, and are contented with our pilgrimage.

   [3.]   Mind home more.   We should always be winding up our
affections, as those that keep clocks ; the weights run down of their
own accord, but we wind them up morning and evening : Ps. xxv. 1,
' Unto thee, O Lord, do I lift up my soul.'   Some there are who may
despise the profits of this world, but they are not heavenly ; they lose
something, but they find nothing in the room of it.   If we are pilgrims,
we should seek a city that is to come : Heb. xiii. 14, ' For here have
we no continuing city, but we seek one to come ; ' that is, in our desires,
thoughts, endeavours, and groans after it : Ps. cxx. 5, ' Wo is me that
I sojourn in Mesech, that I dwell in the tents of Kedar.'   Daily desires
and groans are the saint's harbingers, which are sent into heaven before
us ; and by this means we tell God that we would be at home.
Therefore you should be ever setting of your minds this way ; some
time should be redeemed for this purpose every day, that we may stir
up our affections and serious thoughts to converse with God.   We
have no help else against the snares of the world ; it is an infectious
air, and we had need take cordials and antidotes : 2 Peter i. 4, ' Whereby are given unto us exceeding great and precious promises, that by
these you might be partakers of the divine nature, having escaped the
corruption that is in the world through lust.'   This refresheth the
divine nature in us, and keepeth our hopes alive.   There are a great
many temptations in the world through lust, and it is needful, as well
as sweet and pleasant, to have our thoughts upon heaven.

   [4.]   Do not conform yourselves according to the fashions of the world : Rom. xii. 2, ' And be not conformed to this world, but be ye transformed by the renewing of your mind.' You are strangers here ; live not according to the customs and fashions of the world. If an Englishman were in America, where he saw none but rude savages that had not shame enough to cover their nakedness, would he conform himself to their fashions and guises ? We are in danger to miscarry by example, as well as by lust. It is the fashion of the world to be profane and unmortified, to be careless of God and heavenly things, to break the sabbath, to neglect private duties, and the exercise of religion in their families, to spend their whole time in eating and drinking, buying, selling, trading. You are of another country, Jerusalem that is above is the mother of us all; therefore you are to live by other laws, and in another fashion. Besides, in every age there is some wicked custom afoot, which, by being common, becomes less odious, and your course must be contrary to it. Dead fishes swim with the stream, and wicked men walk κατ' αἰῶνα, ' according to the course of this world,' Eph. ii. 2. Sin, when common, is less odious. But a stranger should by his habit and appearance declare his country, and that he is not ashamed to own it ; so do you declare that you are acted by higher principles and more glorious hopes than the men of the world are acted by. God hath chosen us out of the world, and we should discover the excellency of our principles and hopes by not conforming ourselves to the present world.

[5.] It teacheth us patience, to endure the inconveniences of this life without murmuring. Many that travel abroad are ill entreated, not respected according to their birth. But consider, we have but a little while to stay, and in the midst of all troubles remember home : Ps. xxvii. 13, ' I had fainted unless I had believed to see the goodness of the Lord in the land of the living.' Heaven is the true land of the living. There are commotions in the world, but heaven is a quiet place. If we are assaulted with troubles, it is to make us long for home, to better our hearts or hasten our glory. If the world did not vex the godly, it might possibly ensnare them, and entice their affections to love it and desire to abide in it. The world's hostility is the security of the saints : Gal. vi. 14, ' God forbid that I should glory, save in the cross of our Lord Jesus Christ, by whom the world is crucified unto me, and I unto the world.' The world never cared much for me, nor I much for the world. Their injuries turn to our gain, and mortification to make us look homeward.

[6.] It teacheth us submission to the hand of God for our godly departed friends. Let us not grieve for the departed in the Lord, they are but gone home. The apostle speaketh of some ' that were in Christ before him,' Rom. xvi. 7. They are in heaven before us, and we must wait our time ; after a wearisome journey they rest from their labours, and solace themselves in the bosom of Jesus Christ.

SERMON XLIII.

By faith he sojourned in the land of promise, as in a strange country,
dwelling in tabernacles with Isaac and Jacob, the heirs with him
of the same promise ; for he looked for a city which hath founda-
tions, whose builder and maker is God.—Heb. xi. 9, 10.

3. I now come to the means how to get our hearts into such a frame
as I have before discoursed on.

[1.] Let us enjoy as much of heaven as we can in our pilgrimage,
in the beginnings of grace, the first-fruits of the Spirit, and in the
ordinances.

(1.) In the first-fruits of the Spirit: grace is young glory, and joy
in the Holy Ghost is the suburbs of heaven. You enter upon your
country and inheritance by degrees; fulness of joy is for the life to
come, and joy in the Holy Ghost is the beginning of it. As the winds
carry the odours and sweet smells of Arabia into the neighbouring
provinces ; so the joys of heaven, those sweet smells and odours of the
upper paradise, are by the breathings and gales of the Spirit conveyed
into the hearts of believers. This is our advance-money, our taste in
the wilderness, our morning-glances of the daylight of glory. Union
with Christ is the beginning of heaven, it is heaven in the moulding
and framing.

(2.) In the ordinances. The time of our pilgrimage is a sad time.
How should we solace ourselves? Ps. cxix. 54, 'Thy statutes have
been my songs in the house of my pilgrimage,' our cordials to cheer
and strengthen us. The ordinances are types of heaven. Prayer
bringeth us to the throne of grace, and giveth us an entrance into God's
presence. In the word 'preached' is the presence of the blessed Trinity,
bringing down heaven itself to us, and the angels are attending on our
congregations: 1 Cor. xi. 10, 'For this cause ought the woman to have
power on her head, because of the angels.' The Lord's supper is a
pledge of that new wine we shall drink in our Father's kingdom. By
reading we talk with the saints departed, prophets and apostles, that
wrote what we read. Meditation bringeth us into the company of God,
and where we walk God walketh with us, and at home or abroad we
are still with God. The sabbath is a type of heaven: Heb. iv. 9,
'There remaineth therefore a rest for the people of God.' Here is a
ceasing from work, and there is a ceasing from sin and misery, and an
eternal rest and repose in the bosom of Christ. Psalms do fitly resemble hallelujahs, the word lectures of praise that shall be read over
the free grace of God and redemption by Christ to all eternity. The
congregation signifies the general assembly and congregation of saints
and angels above, Heb. xii. 23. So that a christian is even seated in
heaven when in and about the ordinances.

[2.] The enjoyment of any temporal blessing should stir us up to
the more serious consideration of heavenly blessings; there are better
things laid up in heaven. As the prodigal's husks put him in mind of
the bread that was in his father's house, and the cities of the Amorites
put Abraham in mind of the city that had foundations, whose builder

and maker is God; so should we be put in mind of heaven by those things we enjoy here. If a strange place affords us content and refreshment, will not our country much more? If the creature be sweet, heaven is better. Look through the glass to the sun, it is our medium, not our object. A spiritual use of the creature doth much raise our hearts. We help our souls by our bodies, and make the senses which were wont to be the inlets of sin to be instruments of heavenly-mindedness. Grace can work matter out of anything it seeth; a good man can distil precious liquor out of common matters; he can see another world in this world, and doth not only make a temporal use of the creatures, but a spiritual.

[3.] Go to God to circumcise the foreskin of the heart. There is a fleshliness that cleaves to us which maketh us altogether for a present good, the world is at hand. God can only cure this by infusing a divine nature: 2 Peter i. 4, ' That by these ye may be made partakers of a divine nature, having escaped the corruptions that are in the world through lust.' There must be a heavenly birth, or else a man taketh himself for this world's child, and will go no further.

[4.] Get a clearer and more sensible interest in Christ. He that is in Christ is in heaven already: Eph. ii. 6, ' And hath raised us up together, and made us sit together in heavenly places in Christ Jesus.' He is there in his head; a christian holdeth all *in capite*. When Christ was glorified, he seized on heaven in our right. We use to say of an old man, He hath one foot in the grave; so a believer that is in Christ hath more than a foot in heaven, his head is there, he is ascended with Christ. Nothing but faith can unriddle this mystery, how a believer should be on earth and yet in heaven; his head is there, and this draweth the heart after it; head and heart must be together. And therefore acquaint yourselves with Christ, clear up your interest in him, this will wean you from the world. The woman left her pitcher when she knew Christ, John iv. 28. There is your treasure, and your affections will carry you where Christ is: Col. iii. 1, ' If ye then be risen with Christ, seek those things which are above, where Christ sitteth at the right hand of God;' Phil. iii. 20, ' For our conversation is in heaven, whence we look for a saviour, the Lord Jesus Christ.'

[5.] Meditation is of great use; it bringeth a believer into the company of the blessed, and puts his head above the clouds, in the midst of the glory of the world to come. Meditation is but a more temperate ecstasy. As Paul by his rapture was in the third heavens, so are we by our thoughts; we get upon the top of Nebo or Pisgah, and take a view of the promised land. Great hopes are known by thoughts; thoughts are the spies of the soul. Where a thing is strongly expected, the thoughts are wont to spend themselves in creating images and suppositions of contentment we shall receive when we enjoy this thing. If a poor man be adopted into the succession of a crown, he would be feasting and entertaining himself with the happiness and pleasure of that estate. When a man minds only earthly things, earthly thoughts salute him first in the morning, busy him all day, lay him down in his bed, play in his fancy all night; the thoughts of God and his kingdom find no access. Glances only on heaven are an evidence of a carnal heart that is at home. The more heavenly a christian is, the more he is himself; as the more rational and considerate a man is, the more he is a man.

[6.] Prize the communion of saints, this is heaven begun. A godly man, when he was to die, said, I shall change my place, but not my company. They that expect to be there where God, and Christ, and the saints are, should delight more in converse with them here. In a foreign land a man is glad to meet with his own countrymen; we should be glad to meet with those that go with us to heaven. A christian will converse with such as he shall be with hereafter; it is of great use and quickening to him. Good discourse conveyeth warmth: Luke xxiv. 32, 'Did not our heart burn within us while he talked with us by the way, and while he opened to us the scriptures?' Saul in the company of the prophets became a prophet. Earthly men will gain benefit hereby; as a dead man will have some heat, being plied with warm clothes.

Use 1. Put in your name among them that profess themselves to be strangers and pilgrims: Heb. xi. 13, 'They confessed that they were strangers and pilgrims on the earth;' and that in your best estate, if it be in the land of promise, where you have most right, in the midst of peace, tranquillity, and worldly enjoyments, where you have most possessions. Consider what reason you have to count yourselves strangers and pilgrims, and what profit you will have by it.

1. What reason you have so to count yourselves. Consider how frail we are, how uncertain our comforts; how frail we are, this is not our rest. In our best estate we are but frail: Ps. xxxix. 5, 'Verily every man at his best estate is altogether vanity.' Every word is emphatical; there is an asseveration, 'verily;' a universal particle, 'every man,' and that 'at his best estate.' The sun in the zenith beginneth to decline. Paul's rapture was seconded with a messenger of Satan; after a sight of heaven he had a taste of hell. When worldly happiness is at the full, it beginneth to decline. And he is not only vain and weak, but vanity itself, and altogether vanity. No man hath a constant fixed abode in the world. And then the uncertainty of worldly things; we are mortal, and all our enjoyments have their mortality. The world is full of changes. Who would build a house where there were continual earthquakes? or set up his abode and dwelling-place upon the sea? or lay a foundation upon the ice, that is gone with the next heat and warmth? Especially God's children, who have least of the world. And then it is not our rest; if you had the world at will, you have higher things to look after; this is not your happiness. As that pilgrim said that was travelling to Jerusalem, But this is not the holy city: Micah ii. 10, 'Arise you, and depart, for this is not your rest.' It is the greatest judgment God can inflict upon thee, for thee to take up thy rest here, to be condemned to successes and worldly felicity; better never have a day of rest and ease in the world: Luke xvi. 25, 'Son, remember that thou in thy lifetime receivedst thy good things;' Ps. xvii. 14, 'From men of the world, which have their portion in this life;' Jer. xvii. 13, 'They that depart from me shall be written in the earth,'—it is a punishment laid on them that depart from God.

2. What profit you will have by it; it will keep you from lusts and

snares.   Birds when they soar aloft, need fear no snares; he that counts heaven his home, and the world a strange country, hath a great advantage of others, for he is delivered from the snares of the world. This disposition doth hurt to nothing but to carnal mirth; but it makes way for heavenly refreshings and sweet comforts.   Nay it is the best piece of good husbandry, for it is the best way to provide for the world: Mat. vi. 33, 'Seek ye first the kingdom of God, and his righteousness, and all these things shall be added unto you;' you drive on two cares at once.   None hold the world by a better tenure than those that are strangers.   Abraham dwelt in tents, and Lot dwelt in a city; and Lot in the pleasant valley found less rest than Abraham in his tent: his lingering in Sodom had cost him dear if God had not pulled him out.   It will make us end our days with comfort.   Death is an advantage to a spiritual stranger and pilgrim here; it is a going home after a tedious journey.   A man readily leaveth the place he abhorreth, and goeth to the place he loveth; so if once we could get our affections from the world, death would not be so dreadful.   Carnal affections make us unwilling to die; we are wedded to present things and that makes us loth to depart hence.

Use 2. Reproof to those that fix their rest here.   'It is good to be here,' saith Peter, but as applied to the world is a brutish speech; it is contrary to sense, experience, and reason.

1. Contrary to sense.   Let me confute you by your eyes.   Look to the frame of man's body, not only the constitution of his soul, but the frame of his body; we do not go grovelling on the earth as beasts, nor are we stuck into the ground as trees; man is of an upright stature, his head is to heaven and his feet to the earth, the seat of the senses is nearest heaven: Ps. viii. 6, 'Thou hast put all things under his feet.' But now when men spurn at heaven, when their heads and hearts are fixed on the earth, this is like a man standing upon his head.   Worldly men are like worms that come out of the earth, live on it, creep on it, and at length creep into it, and that is all.   Let me again confute thee by thine eyes.   Consider the frame of heaven; those aspectable heavens are the most glorious part of the creation, far more glorious than the lower world, and yet it is but the under part of the pavement of heaven.   What then is the heaven of heavens, if the lowest part of heaven be so beautiful.

2. Contrary to our experience, as men or as christians.

[1.] To our experience as men.   Why do you fix here?   The world thrusteth us from itself by miseries, and at last by death; then there is a violent ejection, here it entertaineth us as a stepmother; but we linger in it as Lot lingered, he was loth to go out of pleasant Sodom till the angels pulled him out: Gen. xix. 16, 'And while he lingered, the men laid hold upon his hand, and upon the hand of his wife, and upon the hand of his two daughters, the Lord being merciful unto him, and they brought him forth, and set him without the city.'   We are often frustrated by a just and merciful providence, and we should make use of our disappointments.   Providence doth often buffet us when it finds us busy where we should not; where we are more strangers, there we are most employed.   When we stick to the earth, God cometh to pull us off.

[2.] To our experience as christians. Afflictions serve to make a divorce between us and the world, but much more sins. Crosses are grievous to all, but sins to the godly; sin hindereth us of the free enjoyment of heaven, as crosses do of the comforts of the world. Sin is evil in itself, though we feel it not. Affliction is only evil to our feeling because it smarts; affliction is as wormwood, bitter; but sin is as poison, deadly; it separates us from God, which affliction does not. Sin is contrary to the new man, eclipseth the light of God's countenance, hindereth the enjoyment of God in Christ, which is a heaven upon earth, as desertion is the soul's hell. Many complain of crosses that complain not of sins; they look upon heaven as a reserve and place of retreat when beaten out of the world, which is neither a mark nor a work of grace. A beast will leave a place where it findeth neither meat nor rest. But this makes the children of God weary. Here is a condition of sinning and offending God which is most grievous to the godly. Paul groans on this account : Rom. vii. 24, 'O wretched man that I am! who shall deliver me from the body of this death?' If any had cause to complain of misery Paul had, being in perils and sufferings often; but that which he complains of is sin. What a grief is it to a christian to meet with a temptation at every turn, to find every sense a snare and every creature a bait; we can scarce open our eyes but we are in danger.

3. It is contrary to reason. We were not made for the world but the world for us. Whenever we enjoy the world, we see the error of our esteem; it cannot satisfy our desires, nor recompense our pains. Those that enjoy it least are safest; the world cannot make us better, it may make us worse; all the riches and honours of the world cannot endue thy person with any true good. That is good that makes us good, reason will judge so; now the whole world cannot make us better, but grace will. Beware then of fixing your rest here below, which is bewrayed by the complacency of your souls in worldly things, by your lothness to die, by seldom thoughts of heaven. Oh, this wretched disposition is contrary to sense, experience, and reason !

Secondly, We are now come to the ceremony and rite by which this obedience of Abraham was signified and expressed—'Dwelling in tents.' A tent is opposed to a house, or settled dwelling : 1 Chron. xvii. 5, ' For I have not dwelt in an house since the day that I brought up Israel unto this day, but have gone from tent to tent, and from one tabernacle to another.' The tabernacle was a figure of the church, and the temple of heaven. Houses were then in fashion ; Lot had his house in Sodom, Gen. xix. 2–4, and Abraham was rich and able to build ; it was not out of necessity but choice that he dwelt in tents. You may look upon it, partly, as an act of policy; partly, as an act of religion.

1. As an act of policy, that they might live in a strange country peaceably, free from the envy and grudge of the natives, who are not wont to brook the increase and greatness of strangers, but thenceforward seek to root them out. Thus the Rechabites, who were strangers in Israel, dwelt in tents : Jer. xxxv. 7, ' Neither shall ye build houses, nor sow seed, nor plant vineyard, nor have any ; but all your days ye shall dwell in tents, that ye may live many days in the land where ye

be strangers;' it was the advice of Jonadab their father to them. Such a thing befell Isaac, the grudge of the natives at the prosperity of his flocks: Gen. xxvi. 12–14, 'Then Isaac sowed in that land, and received in the same year an hundred-fold, and the Lord blessed him. And the man waxed great, and went forward, and grew until he became very great. For he had possession of flocks and possession of herds, and great store of servants. And the Philistines envied him.'

2. As an act of religion, to express their heavenly hopes, or to acknowledge the hopes and desires of a world to come in the midst of a profane age. Here they had no settled abode, as the tent was an ambulatory kind of dwelling, removed from place to place. As afterwards at the feast of tabernacles, for seven days the people remained in booths to put them in mind of heaven and their forefathers dwelling in tents: Lev. xxiii. 42, 43, 'Ye shall dwell in booths seven days; all that are Israelites born shall dwell in booths, that your generations may know that I made the children of Israel to dwell in booths when I brought them out of the land of Egypt.' Now what shall we learn out of this? I answer, Several lessons.

[1.] It teacheth us patience and contentation, if we have but a mean house and dwelling, or if we are forced to wander, or if we are burdened with the envy of a strange country.

(1.) If we have a mean house and dwelling. Abraham had none at all, but only a tent; yet there God appeared to him, and there he entertained angels, Gen. xviii. 1, 2. No place can be so mean as to exclude God; you may have as much communion with him in a thatched cottage as in a lofty palace, yea, many times more. The sun shineth as merrily on a hovel as on a magnificent structure; so doth God visit the poor, and shine upon them in Christ as well as the great and rich. Some of them, 'of whom the world was not worthy, wandered in deserts and in mountains, and in dens and caves of the earth,' Heb. xi. 38, places of mean retirement. John had his revelation in Patmos in an obscure cave; he had more visions of God in a cave than others could have in a palace.

(2.) If you are driven up and down, and have no certain dwelling-place, remember the patriarchs lived in tents, movable habitations, that were often shifted and changed. David had sweet experiences of God in the wilderness, when he was hunted up and down like a flea: Ps. lxiii. 3, 'Thy loving-kindness is better than life.' There, where others did converse with beasts, there did David converse with God; he was banished from his friends, from the temple, but still he had fellowship with God. So Ps. xc. 1, 'Lord, thou hast been our dwelling-place in all generations;' compare it with the title, and you shall see that psalm was penned by Moses when they were wandering in the wilderness. God's people, though they have no certain residence, yet they want not a dwelling-place; they find rest, and food, and protection, and room enough in God's own heart. A christian is everywhere at home but there where he is a stranger to God.

(3.) In case we are burdened with the envy of a strange country; so was Abraham, and so was Isaac. The patriarchs lived a wandering life, but still God was with them; and though they did what they could to avoid envy, yet still they met with it. This may be the case of persons exiled for religion and a good conscience; they may be driven abroad, and thrive abroad, and there meet with envy and opposition; as the Albigenses, wherever they had land they made it fruitful, which drew troubles upon them, and enforced their frequent removes. In such a case remember, if we have God's favour, no matter for man's envy.

[2.] It is caution to you that have stately houses, you have need look to yourselves that you do not forget heaven. God would have the patriarchs dwell in tents, ' that they might look for a city which hath foundations.' Let not your hearts be taken with earthly things. You have city houses and country houses, houses of profit, pomp, and pleasure; when you walk up and down in them, remember God, to do something for him that hath given you these comforts. And remember those that want such dwellings; Christ himself had not where to lay his head; many of his members, of whom the world is not worthy, have not any settled habitation, and make a hard shift for a short abode, they have no house but the wide world, no bed but the hard ground, and no other canopy than the heavens. And remember heaven—' We look for a house not made with hands, eternal in the heavens,' 2 Cor. v. 1; not of masons' and carvers' work, but of God's own handiwork. There are field meditations and house meditations. When you walk up and down in your stately houses, you should have these thoughts: Here I am for a while; I know not how soon God may destroy this cedar work by fire, by rough winds, or by the fury of men: Zeph. ii. 14, ' He shall uncover the cedar work.'

[3.] Here is instruction to us not to make a vain ostentation of riches and greatness, that draweth envy. This was one reason why God would have the patriarchs dwell in tents. When men hang out the ensigns of pride and vanity to public view in their costly apparel, pompous buildings, they do but court the envy and robbery of others. God will send the emptiers to empty them, Amos vi. 7. This note principally concerneth strangers that thrive in a foreign land; pomp and ostentation of riches have been fatal to them. I might bring several stories in England and France. The natives think the sap proper to them; when a foreign plant spreadeth in branches, it draweth envy and rage: Gen. xix. 9, ' This one fellow came in to sojourn, and he will needs be a judge.' And it concerneth persons of a mean original, advanced to offices, and places of trust and power. And it concerneth ministers, whose maintenance is dependant; they had need be sober in apparel, in household stuff, &c. People are apt to begrudge their portion, and therefore they should less put forth in the eye of the world than others; their thriving has always been an eyesore.

[4.] It exhorteth us to a profession of our hopes and expectations of another world, as the patriarchs did in the midst of the Canaanites; by dwelling in tents ' they declared plainly that they sought a country,' Heb. xi. 14. The rite bindeth not, but we should have a tent-disposition, and set the face of our conversations heavenward, renounce worldly conveniences, live as those that are not ashamed of their country, that we may draw others to be fellow-citizens with us: Phil. ii. 15, 16, ' That ye may be blameless and harmless, the sons of God, without rebuke in the midst of a crooked and perverse nation, among whom ye shine as lights in the world, holding forth the word of life.' A man should discover his hopes in his language, let it be the language of Canaan; in a mortified course of life, that all the world may see you are of another country. The world is in the dark; as the stars are the shining part of heaven, so the saints, if they live answerably to their condition, they are as stars, the glory of the world; as the stars guided the wise men to Christ, so that is their office to guide to Christ by their conversations. There are greater lights and lesser lights: ministers are as the greater lights to hold forth the word of God in doctrine, christians as the lesser lights to hold forth the word of life in practice. It is a prodigy to see the lights of heaven eclipsed; so to see blackness, darkness, and worldliness in your conversations would be as a prodigy. When your cares, griefs, desires, endeavours are carnal, you suffer an eclipse; you do not shine so brightly to the world, and make such an open profession as those should do that do spiritually live in tents.

[5.] The next duty we learn is moderation in houses and furniture. Abraham and the patriarchs dwelt in tents; we cannot be contented unless we have so many walks, galleries, turrets, pyramids; such setting up and pulling down, transposing and transplacing to make gay houses, and so much yearly spent in costly furniture, that we are much departed from the primitive simplicity. I know God hath given us a liberal allowance to make our pilgrimage comfortable, and that this allowance is straitened and enlarged according to our quality and degree in the world, and that in strength of buildings the safety and glory of a nation is much concerned, and that as nations are civilised, so their buildings are more fair and commodious; but yet there must be a restraint in pomp and excess. The scriptures often take notice of the vanity of sumptuous buildings and household stuff: Amos iii. 15, 'I will smite the winter house and summer house; the houses of ivory shall perish, and the great houses shall have an end.' It is made one of the causes of Israel's judgments: so Amos vi. 8, 'I abhor the excellency of Jacob, and hate his palaces,' and in many other places. Now the limits are, when they exceed our estate, and if not our estate, yet our degree and rank; when they divert our charity;—house-builders are not house-keepers; the walls are double clothed when the poor go naked, and that is spent upon polishing of stones which is due to the members of Christ;—and when men feed their luxury with oppression: Hab. ii. 11, 12, 'For the stone shall cry out of the wall, and the beam out of the timber shall answer it. Wo to him that buildeth a town with blood, and stablisheth a city by iniquity!' The stone shall cry, Lord, avenge us against the builder, we were laid in blood; and the beam shall answer, And we were purchased with rapine and public spoil.

[6.] The next thing we learn is self-denial, and enduring hardness for God's sake. Abraham dwelt in tents when God called him thereunto. God hath work for the patriarchs to do up and down the world, and therefore would not have their dwellings settled. So should we learn upon a call to give up all conveniences to God, and to be content with a mean condition; as for instance, when we can no longer keep them with a good conscience, when by particular impulse we are urged to such works as will forfeit our worldly conveniences, and the like.

[7.] It is a check to covetousness, when men seek to root here, and 'to join house to house, and field to field, till there be no place they may be placed alone in the midst of the earth,' Isa. v. 8.   This is quite contrary to Abraham, who left all and dwelt in tents; they are still purchasing, till they have engrossed all to themselves, and there be no room for any to dwell by them.

Thirdly, The next circumstance is his fellows and followers in this practice and profession, with Isaac and Jacob, 'the heirs with him of the same promise.'   The words will undergo a double sense, they imply imitation or cohabitation.

1. Imitation : they dwelt with them; it implieth likeness of practice ; they did it after Abraham's death.

2. Cohabitation : for Abraham was a hundred years old when Isaac was born, and Isaac at sixty years old begat Jacob and Esau ; so that Abraham lived with Isaac seventy-five years, and with Jacob fifteen years.   Compare Gen. xxi. 5, and xxv. 8, 26.   But Abraham and Isaac lived in distinct families when Jacob was born, therefore it is to be understood successively that Isaac dwelt in tents as well as Abraham : Gen. xxvi. 17, 'Isaac pitched his tent in the valley of Gerar ;' Gen. xxiv. 67, 'Isaac brought her into his mother Sarah's tent.'   And of Jacob it is said : Gen. xxv. 27, 'He was a plain man, dwelling in tents,' in opposition to Esau, who built cities.   Therefore Jacob's tents are used proverbially in scripture ; see Num. xxiv. 5, Jer. xxx. 18.

[1.] Observe, that saints are of the same spiritual dispositions.

(1.) Because acted by the same spirit : Acts iv. 32, 'And the multitude of them that believed were of one heart and of one soul.'   If it were possible that two bodies were acted by the same soul, they would weep together and rejoice together, and have the same gestures and motions.   These old believers were not only united to the same head, but acted by the same spirit ; Christ is the head of the church, and the Spirit is as it were the soul of the church.

(2.) They are governed by the same laws : Jer. xxxii. 39, 'I will give them one heart, and one way, that they may fear me for ever.' There are many ways to hell, and but one way to heaven.   They are all alike in regard of newness of heart, and there is but one rule of life and worship.   Men that will find out new ways to heaven put themselves into the highway to hell ; all the saints have trodden this path : Heb. vi. 12, 'Be followers of them who through faith and patience inherit the promises.'   They that seek to make the way to heaven more easy will find themselves at last mistaken.

(3.) They have all but one scope, to please God, and to glorify him upon earth.   Wicked men differ in their particular scope, though they agree in their hatred of the power of godliness ; like Samson's foxes that were tied by their tails, though their heads looked several ways ; it is but a faction and conspiracy.   But all the saints make this their scope.   Many times they differ in judgment, but agree in scope ; as two physicians that consult for the cure of a man that is dangerously sick may propose different courses, but both design the recovery of the sick man.

(4.) They are called to the same privileges, they are heirs of the same promise : 2 Peter i. 1, 'To them that have obtained like precious faith with us;' as a jewel held by a child and by a man is of the same worth. Jude 3, 'Beloved, when I gave diligence to write unto you of the common salvation.'

Use 1. It informeth us of the reason of differences in the children of God, partly, because they do not regard the spirit of communion, or mingle with those that have no share in it; partly, because of some partial error about the law and way they ought to walk in; partly, because through corruption they seek their own things, and forget they are called to the same privileges. In practicals, and in the power of godliness, they all agree, and in things necessary to salvation.

Use 2. It presseth us to search whether or no we have the same spirit by which all God's saints are acted, the same spirit of faith and of holiness, and of self-denial, and of heavenly-mindedness. Do we behave ourselves as heirs of the same promises? Ps. xxxix. 12, 'I am a stranger with thee, and a sojourner, as all my fathers were.'

[2.] Observe the fruit of godly education. Abraham dwelt in tents, and trained up Isaac in the same profession, and Isaac trained up Jacob. This is the way to continue religion in families, to bring up children 'in the nurture and admonition of the Lord,' Eph. vi. 4. God reckoneth upon it from those that are faithful; as he saith concerning Abraham, Gen. xviii. 19, 'For I know him, that he will command his children and his household after him, and they shall keep the way of the Lord.' Alas! many parents are negligent in this kind, whom in charity we may judge godly. We are careful to leave our children great estates, that they may be rich; but who is careful to leave them thus mortified, to train them up in the contempt of the world; nay, we rather strive to make them worldly. We do not teach them to dwell in tents; all that we care for is that they may not be given to prodigality and excess, that they may not waste what we have scraped up for them; but let them be as worldly as they will, we like that. Plutarch, taxing the abuse of parents that strive to leave their children rich and not virtuous, he saith, They do like those that are solicitous about the shoe, but care not for the foot. Oh, begin with them betimes! Jerome compareth youth to water spilt upon the table; it runneth after you that way which you draw your finger. Train them up to self-denial before their affections are stiffened by long use in the world. The best riches you can leave them is to teach them the art to despise riches, saith Chrysostom in one of his homilies on Timothy.

[3.] Observe the force of example, especially of parents. Abraham lived in tents, and so did Isaac and Jacob. You must not only educate your children, but give them an example; this works more than precepts. Nature is very catching at ill examples, therefore beware of them.

Ver. 10, *For he looked for a city which hath foundations, whose builder and maker is God.*

Here is the reason rendered of this effect of his faith, his thoughts did not run upon Canaan so much as heaven.

1. Observe, that serious thoughts and hopes of heaven make us to carry ourselves with a loose heart towards worldly comforts. This was the reason why Abraham was contented to be a stranger in Canaan.

1. I shall show you what is this looking.

2. The influence of it on our christian practice.

1. What is this looking for heaven. It is not a blind hope, such as is not advised, and is found in men that are ignorant and presumptuous, that regard not what they do;—the presumption of ignorant persons is a child of darkness. Not some glances upon heaven, such as are found in worldly and sensual persons; such are not operative, they come but now and then, and leave no warmth upon the soul; as fruit is not ripened that hath but a glance of the sun. But it is a serious hope, well built, such as ariseth from grace longing after its own perfection; therefore we are said, 'to be begotten again to a lively hope,' 1 Peter i. 3. Seed desireth growth, everything aimeth at perfection; as soon as grace is infused, there is a motion this way. And it is an earnest hope, such as is accompanied with longings and frequent thoughts: Rom. viii. 23, 'We ourselves groan within ourselves waiting for the adoption, to wit, the redemption of our body.' It is a lively hope, such as stirreth up rejoicing, as if the thing hoped for were already enjoyed: Rom. v. 2, 'We rejoice in hope of the glory of God;' as 'Abraham rejoiced to see Christ's day, and he saw it, and was glad,' John viii. 56. And yet it is a patient, contented hope: Rom. viii. 25, 'If we hope for that we see not, then do we with patience wait for it.'

2. The influence of it. It maketh us strangers in the world; partly, by purging the heart from vile and worldly affections: 1 John iii. 3, 'He that hath this hope in him, purifieth himself even as he is pure;' partly, by carrying us within the veil, by which the glory of the world is obscured: 2 Cor. iv. 18, 'We look not to the things that are seen, but to the things which are not seen; for the things which are seen are temporal, but the things which are not seen are eternal;' partly, by counterbalancing our afflictions with the future glory; it sets the joy before us in our sufferings, Heb. xii. 2, and so works a sweet and comfortable carriage in all states and conditions.

Use 1. It showeth us that they do not truly despise the world who despise it merely out of a slightness of disposition, and not out of the sense of glorious hopes; they do not despise the whole world; they are taken not with worldly pleasures, but they mind worldly profits; their corruptions run out another way: this is not to leave the world, but to make choice of it.

Use 2. It informeth us of the reason why the world hath such a power upon us; we do not awaken our hopes, and look for the city to come. We have a blind hope, that is ill built; we have a loose slight hope, that doth not stir up serious thoughts, earnest sighs, hearty groans, and lively tastes of heaven.

2. Observe, heaven is a city. It is so called in opposition to those solitary tents which Abraham and his family pitched in Canaan, and in allusion to those cities which the Canaanites then lived in. There are diverse resemblances betwixt heaven and a city. A city is a civil society that is under government; so is heaven a society of saints, there all believers meet: Heb. xii. 22, 23, 'Ye are come unto Mount Sion, and to the city of the living God, the heavenly Jerusalem, and to an innumerable company of angels, to the general assembly and church of the first-born which are written in heaven.' Sometimes it is com-

pared to a house where there are many mansions: John xiv. 2, 'In my Father's house are many mansions;' but lest that comparison should straiten our thoughts, it is compared to a city where there is a great deal of company, and Christ is the governor.   In cities they live in concord and amity; there is a sweet communion of saints in heaven, other manner of saints than we have here, without weakness and imperfection.   A city is a storehouse of good things, as of food and treasure; there is enough in heaven for our complete comfort.   A city hath liberties; there we are freed from Satan's tyranny, from the law's curse and condemning power, from all weakness, from all ill company, nothing that defiles shall enter there, from all temptations to sin— 'Glorious things are spoken of thee, O city of God,' Ps. lxxxvii. 3. All that are there speak one language, praising and glorifying God, though in the church here our language is divided.   The church is the suburbs of heaven, and we must first live in the suburbs before we come to live in the city: Eph. ii. 19, 'Now therefore ye are no more strangers and foreigners, but fellow-citizens with the saints, and of the household of God.'   The church is the seminary of heaven, where we first live and trade into heaven.   O you that are citizens! labour to be citizens of heaven: Heb. xiii. 14, 'For we have here no continuing city, but we seek one to come.'   And you that are countrymen! seek to get a right to the freedoms of this city; there is an excellent governor, Jesus Christ; excellent company, all the saints that ever have been from the beginning of the world to the end; there is a constant communion with God: Ps. xxvii. 4, 'One thing have I desired of the Lord, that will I seek after, that I may dwell in the house of the Lord,' &c.   This is the chiefest thing that above all other things we are to care for.

3. Observe, heaven is a city that hath foundations.   Tents are moving and ambulatory dwellings, they had no foundations; but this hath foundations, that is, it is a fixed and certain habitation, therefore called 'an abiding city,' Heb. xiii. 14.   We cannot have an abiding city in a perishing world.   Man must be suited to his happiness, and have a fit place wherein to enjoy it.

1. We are not suited and fitted to happiness while we are here; old bottles will not hold the new wine of glory.   Here we are not capable of the glorious presence of God; a mortal creature cannot endure the splendour of it.   We would have it here as Peter: Mat. xvii. 4, 'Lord, it is good for us to be here.'

2. The place wherein we live is not a fit place to enjoy it.   The world is not a fit place, because it is full of changes,— night and day, calm and tempest, summer and winter.   The earth is cursed for our sakes; we cannot have our blessings here; it is a fit place for our punishment and exercise, to be as a stage on which we act a part, or a scaffold on which we are executed, but it is not our city.   There is no country of so gentle a temperature as to preserve the inhabitants from all misery, sin, grief, sickness, and death.   Heaven then is the only place, it hath foundations, it is the fixed place of our rest and eternal abode.   There is hope of quiet, it is a sure blessed place of rest.   Here all things are fading—'Time and chance happeneth to all,' Eccles. ix. 11; but the safe commodious dwelling-place is there where we shall

be never molested more. The whole employment of our lives is to seek how to get thither; get a right and interest, and you are sure to enter at death. Christ hath purchased it by his merit, and hath taken possession of it for us.

4. Observe, God is the builder and maker of heaven. It is put in opposition to cities built by men. God made the earth as well as heaven; but the making of heaven is peculiarly ascribed to him because it is a rare piece of work. God hath spent most of his art on it; there he hath fixed his throne: Ps. ciii. 19, 'The Lord hath prepared his throne in the heavens.' There is most of his majesty seen, there he is fully enjoyed, and there is an everlasting manifestation of his glory. And he that is the maker of it is the disposer of it, please God, and he will give it thee.

5. Observe, that the fathers looked for an entry into this eternal rest after the ending of their pilgrimage. Here is a clear proof of it—'He looked for a city which had foundations, whose builder and maker is God.'

SERMON XLIV.

Through faith also Sara herself received strength to conceive seed, and was delivered of a child when she was past age, because she judged him faithful who had promised.—HEB. xi. 11.

THE apostle had spoken of the faith of Abraham, and thereupon taketh occasion to mention Sarah's faith. Therefore he saith, καὶ αὐτὴ Σάῤῥα, 'Through faith also Sara herself,' &c.

Observe, what a blessing it is when a husband and wife are both partners of faith, when both in the same yoke draw one way. Abraham is the father of the faithful, and Sara is recommended among believers as having a fellowship in the same promises, and in the same troubles and trials. So it is said of Zachary and Elizabeth: Luke i. 4, 'And they were both righteous before God, walking in all the commandments and ordinances of the Lord blameless.' It is a mighty encouragement when the constant companion of our lives is also a fellow in the same faith. The hint directeth us in matter of choice, she cannot be a meet help that goeth a contrary way in religion; when the sons of God went in to the daughters of men because they were fair, it brought a flood, Gen. vi. 2, 3. Such mixtures get a mongrel race. Religion decayeth in families by nothing so much as by want of care in matches.

But to come to the words, here is—(1.) The person believing; (2.) The commendation of her faith; (3.) The ground of it.

First, The person believing—καὶ αὐτὴ Σάῤῥα. Yea also Sarah herself, a woman,—and as to the point wherein her faith was exercised, a woman barren and stricken in age,—she through faith received strength to conceive seed.

Obs. A woman weak in sex may be strong in faith. This is a praise common both to men and women, they are 'heirs together of the same grace of life,' 1 Peter iii. 7. This should excite women to excel in grace and piety. Sarah hath her praise in the word as well as Abraham. The life of women is for the most part carried on in silence and privacy, yet there is an eminency proper to them. In public services men are most employed, yet women may glorify God in their hearts by faith; there are duties and promises that belong to their private station. As men can speak of Abraham, so women of Sarah. There is a stain upon their sex, that by them sin came first into the world; but then there is this honour put upon them, that by one woman's child salvation was brought into the world. Therefore let women strive, not to continue the stain, but the glory of their sex; not to be first in transgression, the most forward in a family to sin, but to get an interest in him who was made of a woman, and to approve themselves, not only to their husbands, but God; not merely to strive to get a jointure upon earth, but to be heirs with men of the same grace of life, to have an inheritance in heaven, especially if they have religious husbands.

But doth not the apostle contradict scripture in ascribing faith to Sarah? You shall see. In the original story, to which this place alludeth, Sarah is taxed for laughing, and when she was charged with it, denied it, Gen. xviii. 12–15. That laughing certainly was a sign of unbelief. It is true, Abraham laughed: Gen. xvii. 17, 18, 'Then Abraham fell upon his face and laughed, and said in his heart, Shall a child be born unto him that is a hundred years old? and shall Sarah that is ninety years old bear? And Abraham said unto God, O that Ishmael might live before thee!' Yet there was a difference between Abraham's laughing and Sarah's. Abraham laughed out of faith and holy joy, probably respecting the Messiah that should in process of time come out of his loins: John viii. 56, 'Your father Abraham rejoiced to see my day and he saw it, and was glad.' Yet there is a suspicion upon Abraham's laughter because of his reply—'Shall a child be born unto him that is a hundred years old? and shall Sarah that is ninety years old bear?' and because of his prayer for Ishmael,—'O that Ishmael might live before thee!' But the apostle acquits him: Rom. iv. 19, 20, 'Being, not weak in faith, he considered not his own body now dead when he was about an hundred years old, neither the deadness of Sarah's womb. He staggered not at the promise of God through unbelief, but was strong in faith, giving glory to God.' Abraham admireth, but staggereth not, and out of a natural affection he prayeth for Ishmael; God reproveth him not as he did Sarah. But now Sarah laughed out of unbelief, and denieth it when charged, because it is said, she laughed within herself, not openly and outwardly. Both laughed to justify the name of Isaac, but Sarah laughs out of distrust, out of the impossibility of the thing; this weakness is manifested to show the honour is not put upon her by her merits. But after the Lord had chidden her, and she began to see the promise came from God, she believed; and because the laughing came from mere weakness, not from scorn, God layeth no judgment on her, as he struck Zacharias dumb for his unbelief in the like case, Luke i. 20, and still an honourable mention is made of Sarah's carriage in this business, not only here, but also 1 Peter iii. 9, 'Even as Sarah obeyed Abraham, calling him lord.' Observe hence—

1. Many times the word doth not work presently : Sarah laugheth at first, but afterwards believeth.   Some that belong to the purposes of grace may stand out for a while against the ways of God till they are fully convinced; as Sarah laughed till she knew it to be a word not spoken in jest, but a promise made in earnest.   Little did Paul think that those whom he persecuted were so dear to Christ that he counted them himself—' Saul, Saul, why persecutest thou me ? ' Acts ix. 4. Therefore he says, 1 Tim. i. 13, ' I was before a blasphemer, a per-secutor, and injurious ; but I obtained mercy, because I did it ignorantly, in unbelief.' Many serious men, that walk according to the present light of conscience, may slight those ways which afterwards they find to be of God ; and therefore we should be gentle to one another and wait till God reveal the same thing.

2. Usually before the settling of faith there is a conflict—' Shall I have a child who am old : my lord being old also.' Reason opposeth against the promise. So it is usual, when we come to settle the heart in the belief of any promise. Look, as when the fire beginneth to be kindled we see smoke first before flame, so it is here before our comforts be established, we are full of doubts ; so that doubtings are an hopeful prognostic, it is a sign men mind their condition.

3. With great indulgence God hideth the defects of his children and taketh notice of their graces.   There is nothing spoken of Rahab's lie, ver. 31, of Job's impatience, James v. 11, and here Sarah's laughing is not remembered. Weak faith is accepted ; a spark shall not be lost, but blown up into a flame and greater increase. We give a beggar an alms though he receive it with a trembling palsy-hand ; and if he lets it fall, we let him stoop for it. Man overlooketh the good of others, and taketh notice of their ill, as flies pitch upon the sore place ; but God pardoneth the evil and remembereth the good. We upbraid men with the sins of childhood and of youth, committed before conversion ; as the papists did Beza with his lascivious poems that he wrote ere he had a taste of grace ; therefore he saith, *Hi homines invident mihi gratiam divinam ;* these men envy me the grace of God. The elder brother upbraided the younger brother with riotous living, when his father had received him to mercy : Luke xv. 30, 'As soon as this thy son was come, which hath devoured thy living with harlots, thou hast killed for him the fatted calf.' But how contrary is this to God ! If faith breaketh out at length, he accepteth it, and commendeth it in his word. Who would not serve such a gracious master, that winketh at our fail-ings and taketh in good part our weak services and our weak graces ? This for the person believing.

Secondly, The next circumstance in the text is the commendation of her faith from the matter, which was difficult—*She received strength to conceive seed, and was delivered of a child, when she was past age ;* where you may take notice of the fruit of her faith, and the amplification of it The fruit of her faith where we have the in-fluence of it, ' She received strength to conceive seed ;' and the effect of it, ' and was delivered of a child ;' The amplification of her faith, ' when she was past age.' I shall not stand opening the letter ; see what Beza, Gomarus, and Grotius say concerning the opening of that phrase, εἰς καταβολὴν σπέρματος. Let us observe somewhat—

1. From the influence of her faith —'She received strength to conceive seed.' Learn hence—

[1.] That though bringing forth of children be according to the course of nature, yet God hath a great hand in it. They that have children acknowledge them to be God's blessing, and that they are his gift: Ps. cxxvii. 3, 'Lo, children are an heritage of the Lord, and the fruit of the womb is his reward.' He can make the barren to bear: Ps. cxiii. 9, 'He maketh the barren woman to keep house, and to be a joyful mother of children. Praise ye the Lord.' It is notable that by God's special dispensation many precious women were a long time barren, as Sarah, Rachel, Hannah, Elizabeth, the mother of Samson. Partly to show that nature can do nothing without his power and blessing. Partly by these instances to facilitate the belief of the incarnation, as the lesser miracle maketh way for the belief of the greater; certainly that was the intent of Elizabeth bearing John just before Christ was born. If a dead womb can be fruitful, why may not a virgin conceive? It was not fit that another virgin should have this honour, therefore this was the nearest miracle in the same kind. Partly to exercise their faith and patience, and to make way for the greater increase of holiness. Partly that the birth might be more eminent, as Isaac, Samuel, Samson, John, &c. Well then, let them that go barren wait upon God by faith, and prayer, and patience; either God will give children, or one way or another this comfort will be made up to you. It is not always a punishment of sin; many times it is, as God punished Abimelech, till he rendered Sarah, by this, that every womb should be shut up: Gen. xx. 18, 'For the Lord had fast closed up all the wombs of the house of Abimelech, because of Sarah, Abraham's wife.' Michal's scoffing at David was punished with barrenness: 2 Sam. vi. 23, 'Therefore Michal the daughter of Saul had no child until the day of her death.' In Israel it was a great judgment: Hosea ix. 14, 'Give them, O Lord, what wilt thou give? give them a miscarrying womb, and dry breasts.' Little of eternity was known, therefore they strove to continue their memory on earth; that is the reason why men love their youngest children, and their grandchildren because they longest preserve their memory in the world. It was a blessing of the law-dispensation; it was a means to continue their faith; every one hoped to be the mother of the Messiah. Well, but now eternity is manifested, be contented, be fruitful in holiness, and your memory shall be provided for.

[2.] Let us improve it spiritually, God can make the church fruitful after a long barrenness: Isa. liv. 1, 'Sing, O barren, thou that didst not bear: break forth into singing, and cry aloud, thou that didst not travail with child, for more are the children of the desolate, than the children of the married wife, saith the Lord.' And Sarah is a type of the church. Let us be fruitful in our old age, let us receive strength to conceive that immortal seed which will bring forth a better issue, whose fruit is joy, peace, and everlasting life.

[3.] Faith hath a great stroke in making way for blessings—'By faith she received strength to conceive seed.' Means can do nothing 'without God, and God will do nothing without faith: Mat. xiii. 58, He did not many mighty works there, because of their unbelief.' It holdeth in all cases. The word of all instruments is most powerful, and yet is said, Heb. iv. 2, 'The word preached did not profit them, not being mixed with faith in them that heard it.' As a medicinal drink must have all the ingredients mixed with it, or else it worketh not, so if the word be not received in faith, a main ingredient is wanting ; this giveth strength to the means to work. By closing with the promise she received strength.

2. From the effect of this influence—' And was delivered of a child.' I observe hence—

[1.] Every promise received by faith will surely be seconded with performance. God's power is exercised when it is glorified, and they are sure to find him faithful that count him faithful : Luke i. 45. And blessed is she that believed, for there shall be a performance of those things which were told her from the Lord.' Therefore wait ; they that conceive by the promise at the appointed time shall see the birth, and it is a good forerunner of deliverance when we strongly exercise faith upon the promise that revealeth it.

[2.] Faith is the best midwife. By faith Sarah was delivered of a child. Women great with child are very solicitous about getting a good midwife ; the apostle commendeth one in this place, one that never miscarried in her work, and yet the saints have employed her for thousands of years. She expecteth not wages nor gifts ; faith doth most for them that are poor in spirit, and have nothing to give, that know not what to do without her. Other midwives come not willingly, but where there is some likelihood that they may go through with their business ; but faith doth best at a dead lift.

But to leave the metaphor, and to speak something by way of direction in this case, which certainly is of weighty concernment. The apostle saith, Gal. ii. 20, ' The life which I now live in the flesh I live by the faith of the Son of God, who loved me, and gave himself for me.' Faith is to be exercised, not only in acts of worship, but in acts of your callings, and the ordinary offices of life. We are to trade in faith, to eat in faith, to drink in faith, to sleep in faith, to study in faith, to preach in faith. Now usually in all other cases men are taught how to live by faith, but seldom is anything spoken in this weighty case. How to be delivered of a child by faith, as Sarah was, certainly the danger is great, and if in any extremity there is need of faith, much more where the life of the creature is so much concerned. Let me speak a few words to this matter.

(1.) We must be sensible what need we have to exercise faith in this case, that we may not run upon danger blindfold ; and if we escape then to think our deliverance a mere chance. Rachel died in this case, so did Phineas's wife, 1 Sam. iv. 19, 20, and it is a great hazard that you run ; therefore you must be sensible of it. God may take this advantage against you to cut you off ; you are in the very valley of the shadow of death ; deliverance, but that it is so ordinary, would be accounted miraculous. When you look upon it as a matter of course (and you need not trouble yourself about it but only to get the accustomed means), there is no room for faith to work ; when difficulty and danger is apprehended in the case, then faith comes : 2 Chron. xx. 12, 'O our God, wilt thou not judge them ? for we have no might against this great company that cometh against us, neither know we what to do, but our eyes are unto thee ;' 2 Cor. i. 9, ' We had the sentence of death in ourselves, that we should not trust in ourselves, but in God which raiseth the dead.'

(2.) Because the sorrows of travail are a monument of God's displeasure against sin, therefore this must put you the more earnestly to seek an interest in Christ, that you may have remedy against sin : Gen. iii. 16, 'Unto the woman he said, I will greatly multiply thy sorrow and thy conception ; in sorrow, thou shalt bring forth children.' Women's pains are more grievous than the females of any kind ; sin is the reason of it. Death waylays the child as soon as it is born ; the sentence is in force, and there is no remedy but in Jesus Christ the redeemer. Who durst venture upon the pains of travail without a sealed pardon ? The sweetness of the second Adam will be your comfort when you feel the bitterness of the first.

(3.) Muse upon God's promise : 1 Tim. ii. 15, 'Notwithstanding, she shall be saved in child-bearing if she continue in faith, and charity, and holiness, with sobriety.' The apostle speaketh there of the woman's being first in the transgression. There is the promise, and the . evidences of interest in the promise : ' She shall be saved in child-bearing ' that is the promise, which is made good temporally or eternally, as God seeth cause. Some render διὰ τῆς τεκνογονίας, by child-bearing, as if this was a way by which women go to heaven. But take it as we render it, ' in child-bearing,' it is a promise that serveth to awaken faith, that you may not be amazed with the danger, and if deliverance be obtained, you may look upon it as a blessing of the promise ; but generally it is to be understood as all temporal promises, with the exception of God's good pleasure.

(4) The faith you exercise must be glorifying his power, and casting yourselves upon his will. That expresseth that kind of faith which is proper to all temporal mercies, Lord, if thou wilt, thou canst save me ; which indeed is enough to ease the heart of a great deal of trouble and perplexing fear.

1st. To glorify his power. Consider to this end the experiences of the saints : Ps. lxxvii. 10, ' I said, This is my infirmity ; but I will remember the years of the right hand of the Most High ;' 2 Cor. i. 10, ' Who delivered us from so great a death, and doth deliver ; in whom we trust that he will yet deliver us.' For all that danger can do, he is able to deliver us. If you have not your own experiences, yet reflect upon the experiences of others ; how God hath assisted them in such-like cases. In every age there are monuments to which we may have recourse, as they said, Ps. lxxviii. 3, ' Which we have heard and known, and our fathers have told us.' So say, Lord, others have told us what thou hast done for them in such cases, supporting weak vessels in great dangers and extremities, why cannot God do the like ? yea, Lord, thou canst. Say it still ; do not consider your own frailty and fears, but God's power. In innocency there would be no pain at all, though it be caused by natural causes, yet God could have slacked it ; and now certainly after the fall, he can mitigate the sentence, especially to those that have an interest in Christ.

2dly. That you may cast yourselves without trouble and disquiet upon his love. Consider his providence extendeth to the beasts : Ps. xxix. 9, ' The voice of the Lord maketh the hinds to calve.' Doth God take

care for oxen, for hinds, for beasts, and will he not for the members
of Christ? Remember how soon the extremities of his people do
awaken him; he is a very present help in a time of trouble, he hath
put pity in a man towards a beast, and hath not the Lord bowels? If
a beast hath hard travail, how do we pity it! And will not God?
The work you are about is replenishing the world, multiplying the
church, things in which God delighteth; and therefore why should
you doubt of his assistance?

(5.) Urge all things with God in prayer; it is the work of faith to
plead, not only with ourselves, but with God. By this means we do
not work upon God, but draw forth principles of trust in the view of
conscience; we awaken ourselves; God need not to be informed, but
we need it. Therefore say, Lord, thou canst help me; Lord, thou art
gracious to the beasts, and thou hast made a promise to me. Especially
if you feel hope growing, urge it to God.

3. From the application of her faith—'When she was past age.'
There were two difficulties: she was naturally barren, Gen. xi. 30, and
she was now ninety years of age, and it ceased to be with her 'after the
manner of woman;' and therefore here lay the excellency of her
faith, that she could believe that she should be the mother of a mighty
nation. Barren I say she was by natural constitution, and now no better than dead, having so long outlived the natural time of bearing
children. Learn hence—

Obs. That no difficulty or hindrance should cause a disbelief of the
promise. The reasons are two: partly from God, that maketh the
promise; partly from faith, that receiveth the promise.

[1.] From God's nature. God is not tied to the order of second
causes, much less to the road of common probabilities; he will turn
nature upside down rather than not be as good as his word. He standeth
not upon his works so much as he doth upon his word, his word is over
all his works; therefore if God hath said it, it shall come to pass, though
heaven and earth be blended together in confusion. If God's hands
were tied, we might startle at a difficulty; but because nothing is hard
to providence, nothing is out of order to faith, therefore no difficulty
can stand in the way of faith and providence. We judge by our senses,
and that is the cause of the weakness of our faith: Zech. viii. 6, 'If it
be marvellous in the eyes of the remnant of this people in these days,
should it also be marvellous in mine eyes, saith the Lord of hosts?'

[2.] From the nature of faith, which is to guide the soul when reason
and sense faileth. Here in the world we are guided by three lights
—sense, reason, and faith, and all must keep their place: reason corrects
sense, and faith reason. A star to sense seems no bigger than a spangle,
yet reason telleth me that because it is seen at so vast a distance it must
needs be very big. So faith must believe against carnal reason and
present feeling; as Abraham: Rom. iv. 18, 'Who against hope believed
in hope;' that is contrary to all likelihood and probability.

Use. To press us to wait upon God in the greatest difficulties and
extremities. When faith hath a promise, impediments of accomplishment should increase it. *Periculum par animo Alexandri.* Here is
a fit occasion for my faith. What cannot God do? A woman past
age conceiveth! a thing quite contrary to natural course; so often God's

promises seem absurd and ridiculous to human reason.   Therefore wait
and hope in the most desperate cases.

But men plead when urged to faith, We have not such a clear promise
and oracle as Sarah had, when urged to self-denial, We have not such
a clear precept as Abraham had.   I answer—

1. General precepts and general promises are enough to try us.   God
doth not say, Get thee out of thy country; yet he says, Remove thy
lusts, and there we stick.   God doth not say, You shall have a numerous issue, or such a land for your inheritance; yet he hath promised
heaven, and that the gates of hell shall not prevail against his church.
Let us try our faith in these promises in a time of difficulty.

2. In all promises, though we have not and cannot have absolute
confidence of success, yet difficulty and danger should be no cause of
despair.   You have still cause to bear up your spirits upon the power
and care of God.   There may be other means to weaken our dependence, but the greatness of the danger and the unlikelihood of the blessing should never weaken it.   This is no matter of discouragement, for
we see that God can act contrary to the course of nature.   Now danger
of miscarrying and unlikelihood of success is the sole cause of distrust.
Men never fear but in case of danger: when things go happily on, they
are secure.   The questions of unbelief still run upon this, Can such or
such a thing be?   Ps. lxxviii. 19, 20, 'Can the Lord prepare a table in
the wilderness?   Behold he smote the rock that the waters gushed out,
and the streams overflowed.   Can he give bread also?   Can he provide
flesh for his people?'

3. There is a particular promise that answereth to the dead womb.
We are tried in that promise: John xi. 25, 26, 'I am the resurrection
and the life; he that believeth in me, though he were dead, yet shall he
live   And whosoever liveth and believeth in me shall never die.   Believest thou this?'   Sarah's dead womb was revived as soon as she believed; so sure shall we revive again; he that judgeth Christ faithful shall
see life spring from death.   But you will say, We know all this, and
believe this well enough, as she, John xi. 24, 'I know that he shall rise
again in the resurrection at the last day.'   But yet that is little probable, because present difficulties do so easily amaze us.   But to try you
a little in your faith and dependence upon this promise, if you hope
against hope, and can believe a resurrection out of the grave, this faith
will bewray itself in life and death.   That hope is worth nothing that
is good for nothing.

[1.] In life: we please ourselves in thinking that we believe the
resurrection of the dead, when there is no such matter.   He that
judgeth Christ faithful in the promise of eternal life, notwithstanding
death, esteemeth the faithful execution of his will dearer to him than
all the pleasures of this life.   Our thoughts are discovered in our actions,
and our hopes in the course of our lives: 2 Peter iii. 11, 'Seeing then
that all these things shall be dissolved, what manner of persons ought
ye to be in all holy conversation and godliness?'   Implying that they
that are not such manner of persons do not look for such things.   A
man that prostituteth his body to the service of lust, how can it be said
that he looketh for a glorious resurrection to eternal life.

[2.] In death: can we desire death, and check the terrors of it with the promise of eternal life? Death is your last enemy: can you triumph upon your sick-beds in these hopes, that these your enemies you shall see them no more for ever?

Thirdly, The next circumstance in the text is the ground of her faith—*Because she judged him faithful that had promised.* Hence observe:—

1. Wherever we put forth faith we must have a promise, otherwise it is but fancy, not faith. It is not a ground of expectation barely what God is able to do, but what God will do. As the two pillars of Solomon's house were called Jachin and Boaz, 1 Kings vii. 21; the one signifies 'Strength,' and the other, 'He will establish it.'

2. In closing with the promise, we should chiefly give God the honour of his faithfulness.

1. Because God valueth this most, he standeth much of his truth— 'Heaven and earth shall pass away before one jot or tittle of his word shall pass,' Mat. v. 18. The monuments of his power shall be defaced to make good his truth: Ps. cxxxviii. 2, 'Thou hast magnified thy word above all thy name.' All other attributes give way to this.

2. Because this giveth support and relief to the soul in waiting: Heb. x. 23, 'Let us hold fast the profession of our faith without wavering, for he is faithful that promised.' God hath promised no more than he is able to perform; his word never exceeded his power.

Use. Well then, meditate of this; silence discouragements when you have a clear promise. The course of nature saith, It cannot be; her own age saith, It cannot be; but still faith replies, God is faithful. In all your debates let this be the judgment and casting voice.

SERMON XLV.

These all died in faith, not having received the promises, but having seen them afar off, and were persuaded of them, and embraced them, and confessed that they were strangers and pilgrims on the earth.—HEB. xi. 13.

HAVING laid down the particular instances of the patriarchs, he speaketh of what they had in common, they went to the grave in hope, albeit the promises were not performed in their time.

Here you have the trial of their faith and the victory of their faith.

1. The trial of their faith—*They died, not having received the promises;* that is, they went to the grave ere the blessings God had promised were accomplished.

2 The victory of their faith, which is set forth—

[1.] By the several acts of the soul in and upon the promises, both elicite and imperate. There is an act of apprehension—*They saw them afar off;* an act of judgment or firm assent—*And were persuaded of them;* an act of affection—ἀσπασάμενοι, *And embraced them*—they hugged the promise; this will yield a Messiah.

[2.] By the effect and fruit of it in their lives and conversations—
And confessed that they were strangers and pilgrims in the earth.

Who are here spoken of? Some refer it to the numerous posterity
of Abraham mentioned in the former verse, who did not till the time
of Joshua enjoy the promised land of Canaan. But that cannot be,
because many of these were buried in the wilderness, and died murmuring, and in the displeasure of God. Therefore it is meant chiefly
of the patriarchs last recited—Abraham, Isaac, Jacob, and Sarah;
and you may take in the faithful that came of their race—Joseph, and
others that lived till the time of their going out of Egypt.

By promises are meant things promised. They must receive the
promise, or else there were no room for faith. Some take ἐπαγγελίας
for the spiritual promises; these they saw but in figure, or afar off.
Temporal promises they had of a numerous posterity, the calling of
the gentiles; an heir, Christ; an inheritance, Canaan; but this would
cross the apostle's scope. Understand it therefore of things promised.
But what were the things promised which they received not? *Ans.*
The possession of the land of Canaan, a kingdom, a city, a temple,
which was made good to their posterity, the coming of the Messias out
of their loins; these 'they saw afar off,' that is, by the eye of faith;
and were certainly 'persuaded' of the accomplishment of them, though
not in their time, and therefore 'embraced them,' shouted for joy, as
mariners when they see land at a distance. *Italiam læto socii clamore
salutant;* 'professed themselves strangers and pilgrims,' ἐπὶ τῆς γῆς
'in the earth,' sojourners in the land, as expecting a greater happiness
by the Messiah than they did yet enjoy. Yea, 'they died in faith'—
κατὰ πίστιν—'according to faith,' for ἐν πίστει; as Rom. viii., κατὰ σάρκα
for ἐν σάρκι. All these died by or according to faith. The meaning is,
they remained stable and firm to the end of their lives in this assurance,
notwithstanding the variety of conditions which they passed through.

From the first words, 'These all died in faith,' the points are two—

(1) It is not enough that we must live by faith, but we must also
die by faith. (2.) They that would die in faith must live in faith.

Doct. It is not enough that we must live by faith, but we must also
die by faith. So it is said of these patriarchs, 'All these died in faith.'
Faith is always of use on this side the grave; at death it doth us the
last office. In the other world there is no need of it; when we come
to enjoyment faith ceaseth.

The reasons of the doctrine are these—

1. Because faith is not sound unless we persevere therein to the end.
The patriarchs had many afflictions, they were tossed up and down,
yet they died in faith; that was their commendation: so unless we
hold out to the end, all is lost. The Nazarite under the law, if he did
defile himself before the days of his purification were accomplished,
was to begin all anew again: Num. vi. 12, 'The days which were
before shall be lost, because his separation was defiled.' So we lose
what we have wrought, if we do not remain stable till we come to
'receive the end of our faith, the salvation of our souls,' 1 Peter i. 9;
Ezek. xviii. 24, 'When the righteous turneth away from his righteousness and committeth iniquity, and doth according to all the abominations that the wicked man doth, shall he live? All his righteousness

that he hath done shall not be remembered.' All that is past is nothing unless we persevere to the end. Faith is not for a fit, we must hold on in it: Heb. iii. 6, 'Whose house are we, if we hold fast the confidence, and the rejoicing of the hope firm unto the end;' so ver. 14, 'We are made partakers of Christ if we hold the beginning of our confidence stedfast unto the end.' This was the commendation of these holy men, still their hearts were kept close to God, they died in faith: Prov. xvi. 31, 'The hoary head is a crown of glory, if it be found in the way of righteousness.' A Mnason, an old disciple, is a great honour. As Jacob wrestled with the angel till daylight: Gen. xxxii. 26, 'And he said, Let me go, for the day breaketh;' so we must constantly keep up the exercise of faith till the day break, and the shadows flee away. Elisha would not leave his master till he was taken from him into heaven; so faith will not leave us till we are taken to heaven. To be constant to the last is the crown and glory of faith; let the world know you have no cause to leave Christ. We read, Mat. xx., some were called into the vineyard sooner, some later; some were called early in the morning, some at the third, some at the sixth, some at the ninth, and some at the eleventh hour; but all tarried to the end of the day. So must we carry faith and religion with us to the grave; patient abiding is a sign of true faith. Many have outlived their religion and former profession.

2. Because the hour of death is a special season wherein faith cometh to be exercised, and the strength of it is tried. There is no notion doth so much express the nature of faith as this, the committing of the soul to God's keeping: 2 Tim. i. 12, 'I know whom I have believed, and I am persuaded that he is able to keep that which I have committed unto him against that day;' and 1 Peter iv. 18, 'Commit the keeping of your souls to him in well-doing, as unto a faithful creator.' The great work of faith is to put the soul into safe hands; it is our jewel, and it should be in safe hands; it is sensible of danger, and it is never safe till it is put into the hands of God through Christ, and therefore we must commit it to him. Now this never comes so much to the trial as at the hour of death; then to trust God with our souls, upon a confidence that he will keep them for us, that we may enjoy them in another world, this is a sensible discovery of faith, as appears by Christ's surrender when he was to die: Luke xxiii. 46, 'Father, into thy hands I commit my spirit;' and Stephen: Acts vii. 59, 'Lord Jesus, receive my spirit.' While we live we must put the soul into God's care; it is fit our jewel, our darling, should be in safe hands. But can you trust God with your souls when you are ready to die? And then is the time to put the promises in suit, and to express our confidence in them: Ps. xvi. 9, 'Therefore my heart is glad, and my glory rejoiceth; my flesh also shall rest in hope,' &c. The heart is filled with joy, and the tongue runneth over, when we can send our souls to God and our bodies to the grave in hope of a blessed resurrection. During life faith is most exercised in waiting for present supplies, but in death it is put to trial about future recompenses. While we have health and strength we do not mind the danger and hazard of the everlasting state; and that is the reason why we find it harder to trust God for present mercies, temporal supplies, strength

for duties and afflictions; but we are careless of things to come. But when we come to die faith is exercised about things to come; then it is put to the push to meet and grapple with the great and last enemy, death. Then we come to receive the great promise of our final estate; therefore to dismiss the body to the grave in hope, and recommend the soul to God, is a great trial of our faith.

3. There are great promises to be performed after our decease, and it is a great honour to God when we are ready to die, to go to the grave with assurance, and profess our confidence that God will make them good. There are two parts of this reason.

[1.] There are many promises to be accomplished when we are dead and gone, and they are either public or private.

(1.) Concerning the church there are many promises which we see not performed in our lifetime. This was the case of these patriarchs, they had a promise of Canaan that was now possessed by giants, of a numerous offspring, of a city, of a temple wherein God would be present, all unaccomplished. In every age of the church there is something to be waited for; and there are many public promises not accomplished in our days, as the prosperity of the church, the calling of the Jews, the second coming of Christ, the confusion of antichrist. Though we go to the grave, and see not these things, yet we should not doubt of them, for God hath been faithful hitherto: Rev. xiv. 8, 'Babylon is fallen, is fallen.' We should count it as done already, though we see it not performed in our days. God counts our purposes obedience; Abraham is said to offer Isaac because it was his vow and purpose to do it; and therefore we should count God's promises to be as good as performances. Go to the grave with this hope, we leave a God behind us, who is able to perform his promises whether we be or no. We hereby teach others to believe.

(2.) Concerning our families and relations that survive us, there are private promises. God cannot content himself with doing good to the person of a believer, but he hath promised also to do good to his posterity: 2 Sam. vii. 19, 'And this was yet a small matter in thy sight, O Lord God, for thou hast spoken also of thy servant's house for a great while to come.' God will act according to the highest laws of friendship; as David : 2 Sam. ix. 1, 'Is there any that is left of the house of Saul, that I may show him kindness for Jonathan's sake.' God hath not only spoken comfortably for our persons, but for our house, our families, our relations for a great while to come. Now when we can provide for them no longer, pray for them no longer, this is the last act that we can do, believe for them, go to the grave with confidence that God will be as good as his word, who hath promised to be a father to the fatherless and a husband to the widow. When you can leave them no inheritance, leave them a God in covenant, that is a good portion. God hath taken you off from being instrumental for their good, you can do no more for them; now believe that God will take the care upon himself : Gen. xvii. 7, 'I will establish my covenant between me and thee, and thy seed after thee in their generations, for an everlasting covenant, to be a God unto thee, and to thy seed after thee.' Our trust is not so pure in life, whilst we have opportunity to act for them, as in death, when we can leave them in the hands of

God; and leave them the promises for their portion, though you can leave them nothing else.

[2.] This is an honour to God, to profess our confidence in him when we are going to the grave. All faith bringeth glory to God: John iii. 33, 'He that hath received his testimony hath set to his seal that God is true;' but especially dying faith, because then we can do no more, and we leave all to the Lord, and because the speeches of dying men are wont to be observed as they are entering upon the confines of eternity, they are wiser and more serious than at other times, it is no time to dally or dissemble now, at the last gasp. Now speeches of living men are suspected of partiality to present interests, or are neglected as not having much weight in them : Gen. l. 16, ' Thy father did command before he died, saying, Thus shall you say unto Joseph,' &c. ; Josh. xxiii. 14, ' Behold this day I am going the way of all the earth.' When men return, as one expresseth it, ἐπὶ τὸ πρόγωνον θεῖον —to the divine original, they seem to be more possessed with the divine spirit than at other times; when they are dying, their speeches are more serious, grave, weighty, entertained with more consideration and readiness; therefore when we die, to profess our confidence in the faithfulness and truth of God, and go to the grave with this acknowledgment, this is a mighty honour to God.

4. There are most conflicts at death; sin is revived, and fears are revived. A man is never so serious as then; now we come to feel what we never felt before. Christ bids us come to him, as he did Peter on the waters, then if ever we have need of faith. And Satan is most busy now, as dying beasts bite shrewdly; Satan hath great wrath when he hath but a short time. This is the last enemy, and within a little time those Egyptians which ye shall now see, ye shall see them no more ; therefore now is a time to exercise faith. Besides, all carnal pleasures are then at an end, and have spent their force. Whilst we have plentiful accommodations wherewith to entertain the flesh, a little faith serveth the turn ; but death plucketh us from all these, and then we must bid good night to them, and unless we have other supports we are wholly shiftless and comfortless. Satan, that formerly tempted us, now troubleth us; and then we must immediately appear before God. Things near at hand do more affect us when we are entering upon the confines of eternity, and are to grapple with our last enemy. What shall we do ? Now faith is of use. Graces that are not of use in another world discover their highest and most consummate act in this world.

Use 1. Let us provide for this hour, that we may die in faith. We know not how near we may be unto death, or whose turn may be next; there is a providence goeth along with sermons, it may be some of us have more need of this discourse than we are aware; however, it is good to hear for the time to come. You come to sermons not only to learn to live, but to learn to die. You are often taught how to live in faith ; let me instruct you, and show you what it is to die in faith.

1. Profess your hearty and cheerful assent to the general articles of the christian faith, those articles which concern the end and the means. Those that concern the end, as the doctrines of the world to come, the immortality of the soul, and resurrection of the body, and life eternal. And those that concern the means, of making the promise sure on

God's part or our application. The means that concern the impetration, as the death, resurrection, and ascension of Christ. Christ's death is the ground of our triumph and victory: Heb. ii. 14, 'Forasmuch then as the children are partakers of flesh and blood, he also himself likewise took part of the same, that through death he might destroy him that had the power of death, that is the devil.' His resurrection is an act of conquest, he conquered death in its own territories. His ascension, he is gone to heaven to seize upon it in our name, from whence he sends his Spirit to fit us for it: Rom. v. 10, 'If when we were enemies we were reconciled to God by the death of his Son, much more being reconciled shall we be saved by his life.' The means that concern application are his justifying, sanctifying, assisting us in all conditions, especially in sickness: Ps. xli. 3, 'Thou wilt strengthen him upon the bed of languishing, thou wilt make all his bed in his sickness.' You must assent to this, these are ἐν πρώτοις, the first truths of christianity, and the foundation of our comfort and hope. The general belief of these things giveth life to the applicative acts of faith. Christ trieth our assent: John xi. 26, 'Whosoever liveth, and believeth in me shall never die; believest thou this?' 1 Tim. i. 15, 'This is a faithful saying, and worthy of all acceptation, that Christ Jesus came into the world to save sinners, of whom I am chief.'

2. Reduce these to practice.

[1.] Make application of reconciliation with God, and pardon of sins by Christ. Christ's blood shed made the atonement, and by his blood sprinkled we receive the atonement: Rom. v. 11, 'And not only so, but we also joy in God through our Lord Jesus Christ, by whom we have now received the atonement.' This is fit for a dying man: 1 Cor. xv. 55–57, 'O death! where is thy sting? O grave! where is thy victory? The sting of death is sin, and the strength of sin is the law; but thanks be to God, who giveth us the victory through our Lord Jesus Christ;' so the psalmist, Ps. xxxi. 5, 'Into thy hand I commit my spirit; thou hast redeemed me, O Lord God of truth.' Every one cannot thrust his soul upon Christ, but only those who are redeemed and reconciled by his blood. Redemption applied frees us from the power of the devil, and the tyranny of sin.

[2.] Resign up the soul to God with comfort; he calls for it, therefore resign it to him. The death of the godly is not a mere passion, but a lively and vehement action, by which they deliver up their souls to God; so Christ, Luke xxiii. 46, 'Father, into thy hands I commend my spirit;' so Stephen, Acts vii. 59, 'Lord Jesus, receive my spirit.' It is not lawful for us to procure our own death, or out of an impatiency of pain to hasten our end, nor cry out with Elijah in a pet: 1 Kings xix. 4, 'It is enough now, O Lord; take away my life, for I am not better than my fathers.' Yet on the other side we must not be merely passive, or die by force. Beasts when they die, are merely passive, and properly do suffer death. Wicked men struggle, and are loath to depart; their soul is not given up by them, but taken away from them: their death, though it be never so natural, yet it is a violent death; their souls are as it were snatched and torn away from them: Job xxvii. 9, 'What is the hope of the hypocrite, though he hath gained, when God taketh away his soul?' Luke xii. 20, 'Thou fool, this night thy soul shall be required of thee!' They do not commend their souls into the hands of God, but God requireth it of them. A wicked man would fain hold out a little longer, but God will not suffer him ; the Lord puts his bond in suit, he requireth their souls of them. The godly, though they cannot wholly lay aside their aversation from death, which is natural to every living thing, yet when they see the will of God, they hold out no longer, but overcome themselves and yield. Death is a sweet dismission of their soul, and a resignation of it into the hands of God. Resign up then the soul unto God upon these terms, you are going to a father, you are sent for home, death is not penal, as it is to the wicked ; to them it is the wages of sin, they are hailed before the judge, the body sent to the grave, and the soul to hell. There is a great deal of difference between death and death. Death hath many considerations ; as Christ endured it, so it was a ransom ; as wicked men suffer it, so it is wages; as godly men suffer it, so it is the gate of life, the messenger to bring them home to God,—the Lord will be no longer without your company, and therefore he sends for you. In what soft terms doth the scripture express the death of the saints; it is a dissolution, not a violent rending and tearing to pieces : Phil. i. 23, 'Having a desire to depart, and to be with Christ;' it is a departure, a setting sail for another world ; it is a sleep, the grave is a chamber and bed of rest : Isa. lvii. 2, 'He shall enter into peace, they shall rest in their beds;' it is a hastening to the great assembly that is above. Such soft terms the scripture useth concerning the death of the saints ; for death, though it is an enemy to nature, yet it is a friend to grace. And consider, you do not only give up your souls to God that gave them, but to Christ that redeemed them : Ps. xxxi. 5, 'Into thine hand I commit my spirit ; thou hast redeemed me, O Lord God of truth;' and you may be confident Christ will receive the soul which he hath purchased with his blood. Christ comes in a nearer way of enjoyment, that thou mayest receive the fruits of his own purchase. If thou belongest to God, thy heart was there long since, thou hast sent spies, thoughts and affections to take a view of that land, to see what it is, and they have brought a report of the goodness of the country in the promises, and now thou art going thither in person; therefore resign up thy soul to God, and say, I am going the way of all flesh, to yield up my soul to God, and death is ready to close mine eyes, Lord, I commit my soul to thee, I commend my spirit to thee ; I have trusted in thee and I do trust in thee ; thou hast made it, Christ redeemed it, and I hope the mark of thy Spirit will be found upon it. I do resign up my soul to thee.

[3.] Dismiss the body to the grave in hope of a joyful resurrection, sow it as good seed, that will spring up again. Say then, Go, flesh, rest in hope, take the covenant along with you to the grave: Ps. xvi. 9, 10, 'My flesh also shall rest in hope, for thou wilt not leave my soul in hell, neither wilt thou suffer thine holy one to see corruption.' Job could see life in death : Job xix. 25, 26, 'I know that my Redeemer liveth, and that he shall stand at the latter day on the earth. And though after my skin, worms destroy this body, yet in my flesh I shall see God.' This body must be turned into dust, but this dust shall be gathered together again ; this body must be eaten by worms, but the morsels of worms shall be parcels of the resurrection. Death is conquered by Christ ; it may kill, but it cannot hurt ; but the body shall be raised a glorious structure, conformed to Christ's glorious body. You are going to make experiment of that promise : John xi. 25, 26, ' He that believeth in me, though he were dead, yet shall he live ; and whosoever liveth and believeth in me shall never die.' Overlook all things that are between you and glory. It is a sweet close when the body and soul do part from one another in this manner ; when you can commend your spirits to God, and send the body to the grave to rest in hope ; when the body and soul are parting, that God and the soul may meet ; when conscience is a compurgator, and can say, I bear them witness that body and soul have spent their time together in the world well, in loving thee, and obeying thee. When body and soul thus take their leave one of another, it is a blessed parting ; as on the contrary it is a very sad parting, when conscience falleth a-raving, and the body and soul curse each other ; when the body complains of the soul as an ill guide, and the soul of the body as an unready instrument, and you curse the day of their first union, Oh, that I had been stifled in the womb, and never seen the light !

[4.] Meditate on the happiness into which you are entering. Stephen's eyes were opened—' And he looked up steadfastly into heaven, and saw the glory of God, and Jesus standing at the right hand of God,' Acts vii. 55. Whether in vision, or by ecstasy and the elevation of faith, I dispute not ; I only urge it for this, it is a good meditation, when at the point of death to think of God, and of the glory of his presence, and of Jesus Christ in heaven at his right hand ready to receive you. Your thoughts should be now taken up about the glorious things of another world ; think no more of heaven as at a distance, but as one going to take possession of it ; the angels are ready to conduct you to Christ, and Christ to present you to God, as a proof of the virtue of his death : Jude 24, ' Now unto him that is able to keep you from falling, and to present you faultless before the presence of his glory with exceeding great joy.' Death is ready to untie the soul from its chains, and to let it forth into liberty and glory ; look upon yourselves as ready to pass into the throng of spirits, to see Christ and all his blessed angels, and your everlasting companions. You are going to better company, to better employment, to a better place, where is your God, your head, the Lord Christ ready to receive you when you come thither. This is the time we longed for, looked for, prayed for ; now we are going to our preferment, and enter upon those glorious things that are represented to us in the gospel ; these things should take up your thoughts. It is not so with the wicked ; how horrid are the thoughts of death to him : he is going to suffer and feel that which he would never believe before ; death cometh to him as God's executioner, to rend the unwilling soul from the embraces of the body ; he sees an handwriting against him, great bills of uncancelled sins awakening and amazing the conscience, and breaking all his hope in pieces. How is the man perplexed ; what between the memory of past sins and the fear of future pains, the sense of an angry God and the presence of devils ready to carry him to accursed and damned spirits, and he has no comforter, no advocate to plead for him.

[5.] Commend your faith to others, this is to die in faith.   This is
the last time that you can do anything for God in the world, and
therefore this you should do, commend the faithfulness and goodness
of God, what a good master you have found him to be : John iii. 33,
' He that hath received his testimony hath set to his seal that God is true.'
Swans, some say, sing before their death ; so have God's servants commended their experiences of God's faithfulness to others ; as Moses :
Deut. xxxii. 4, ' He is a rock, his work is perfect ; for all his ways are
judgment : a God of truth, and without iniquity, just and right is he ; '
so Joshua, chap. xxiii. 14, ' Behold this day I am going the way of all
the earth ;   and ye know in all your hearts, and in all your souls, that
not one thing hath failed of all the good things, which the Lord your
God spake concerning you ;   all are come to pass unto you, and not
one thing hath failed thereof.'   He repeats it twice.   The words of
dying men are of most efficacy and authority, as being spoken out of
all their former experience, and with most simplicity, and without
self-seeking and sinister ends.   Therefore speak a good word of God,
let the world know what you have found God to be, I know him for a
true God, he is not behind-hand in one word.   So Jacob : Gen. xlviii.
15, 16, ' God, before whom my fathers Abraham and Isaac did walk,
the God which fed me all my life-long unto this day, the angel which
redeemed me from all evil.'   Carnal men do not honour their principles ;
they cannot speak of the worth of the world, and of the things they
have trusted to ; they fail them when they stand in most need of them,
and therefore they fall a-complaining of the world, how it hath abused
and deceived them.   But godly men can speak honourably of the God
they have trusted.   Stephen told them of his vision, though it increased
their rage against him : Acts vii. 56, ' He said, Behold I see the heavens
opened, and the Son of man standing at the right hand of God.'   He
would honour God that owned him, though it made them fall upon him
like madmen.   Thus you see what the duty of christians is when they
come to die, to die in faith and obedience, resigning their souls to God,
dismissing their bodies to the grave in hope, meditating on the great
things of eternity, honouring their principles, and speaking for God to
others.

Use 2. Can you thus die in faith ?   It is another thing to do it in
deed than what it is to do it in conceit.   They that stand on the shore
may easily speak to men in a storm, Sail thus and thus ; but when the
waves beat high, directions are not easily followed.   Can you then die
in faith ?   There is the great trial of faith.   A christian doth not only
make it his care to live in Christ, but to die in Christ : Rev. xiv. 13,
' Blessed are the dead which die in the Lord.'   It is a blessed thing
' to sleep in Jesus,' 1 Thes. iv. 14.   How is it with you ? are you provided for such an hour ?   There are two expressions I shall take notice
of on this occasion ; one is, 2 Cor. v. 3, ' If so be that being clothed,
we shall not be found naked ;' another is, 2 Peter iii. 14, ' Give diligence,
that you may be found of him in peace.'   O christians ! it is a sad
thing to be found naked ; you can never die with comfort, and appear
before God with confidence, if you are not clothed with Christ's righteousness.   A wicked man hath no garment to cover him ; but for the
righteous God puts one grace upon another, upon the righteousness of
Christ God puts on the sanctification of the Spirit, and upon the sancti-

fication of the Spirit he puts on the robes of glory. And it is a sad thing to die and not to be at peace with God, when death surpriseth us with our weapons of defiance in our hands. When a town is taken by storm, if there be pity shown to children and aged persons, yet they die without mercy that are taken with weapons in their hands; so when death comes and surprises us in our rebellion and war against him, the end will be full of horror. The scripture speaks of the wicked man, Jer. xvii. 11, 'At his end he shall be a fool.' A wicked man was ever a fool, because he neglects the best things for vile and contemptible pleasures; but at his latter end he shall be a fool; viz., in the conviction of his own conscience. A wicked man never comes to himself till he comes to die, and then his own heart will call him fool. O fool that thou wast, to neglect thy salvation, and run after trifles of no use and profit.

Obj. 1. But you will say many carnal men die quietly.

Ans. So much the worse, some die of a lethargy, as well as of a burning fever; as they live in carnal confidence, so they may die in carnal confidence, and this is a sad judgment; when their hearts like Nabal's are like a stone, it is an argument of the greater hardness and sottishness, they have not that calm and quiet that ariseth from an interest in Christ.

Obj. 2. Many good men may die with great conflicts, and to beholders have little expression of comfort and feeling of God's love.

Ans. God's children may have their conflicts, they may fear death, they are not as stones, their strength is not as brass, nor their sinews iron. Grace itself as well as nature requireth that we should be sensible of God's hand. Nature recoileth at what is destructive. Adam in innocency would have been affected if his body had been wronged; nay, and bodies of the best temper and complexion are most sensible, because they enjoy life at a higher and more valuable rate than others do. This is better than to die stupid; Christ himself had his agonies. Nay, many times corruption may interpose, and the best men, because of the remainders of sin in them, may have their agonies. God will show himself a free Spirit, not to come in at our hours; God will crown some in the very field and middle of the combat. But there is a great deal of difference between these conflicts that are in the godly and the horrors of the wicked: there is a mixture of faith pleading and disputing for God, and these conflicts arise, not out of a legal fear only, but from the height of hatred and displeasure against sin. Faith is usually discovered in the most glorious way at the last; if it be not glorified in triumphing, it is glorified in dependence, and casting ourselves upon the grace and mercy of God in Christ, notwithstanding all arguments to the contrary. Therefore how do matters stand between God and you? Are you thus fit to die in faith, to resign up your souls to God, and to glorify him in believing?

Use 3. To press you to get and keep faith to the end.

1. Get faith, it is an excellent grace, that standeth by us when all things else leave us. At death all comforts vanish; your wealth that you have gained will stand you in no stead: Job xxvii. 8, 'What is the hope of the hypocrite, though he hath gained, when God taketh away his soul?' When you look on your bodies, all is wasting: Ps.

lxxiii. 26, 'My heart and my flesh faileth;' this face, these arms, as Oblevian said, must now be meat for worms; when you look on your houses and habitations, these dwellings will know me no more; when you look on your children and friends mourning by you, you shall see them no more; but then faith will stand us in stead, it makes us to live with comfort, and to die with comfort. Faith is an excellent grace, that excelleth reason as much as reason excels sense; and what a difference is there between a toad and a man!

2. Keep faith to the end: Heb. iv. 1, 'Let us fear lest a promise being left us of entering into his rest, any of you should seem to come short of it.' We have more cause to persevere than they, we have clearer promises, a clearer sight of heaven, a clearer knowledge of Christ, greater advantages of grace than ever they had; and if they died in faith, and held out to the end, what a shame is it if we should give over!

Doct. 2. They that would die in faith must live in faith; as Abraham, Isaac, and Jacob, and such as confessed themselves strangers and pilgrims on the earth. Men would die well, however they live. Balaam wished, Num. xxiii. 10, 'Let me die the death of the righteous, and let my last end be like his.' There is a natural desire of happiness; men would die the death of the righteous though they are loth to live the life of the righteous. The snake, that was full of windings and circlings while it lived, yet when struck with a dagger it stretched itself out right. *At oportet sic vixisse.* It is not enough when you come to die to say, Oh that I were in such a man's case! We must live in faith if we would die in faith.

Reasons—

1. We had need make trial of that faith we must die by. *In bello non licet bis peccare.* Have you tried your faith? A man had need have experiences of the strength of his faith, and of the truth of God's word, that the word of the Lord is a tried word. Hath it been thy practice to make trial of promises all the days of thy life, that you may be able to say, I have had experience of God, and he hath never failed me? We try how to swim in shallow brooks before we venture to swim in the deep waters; so before we trust Christ with our eternal state we must try how we can trust him with temporals. There are daily cases wherein we make proof and trial of God: Ps. xxxvii. 5, 'Commit thy way unto the Lord; trust also in him, and he shall bring it to pass.' See how it succeedeth with you in present things, what establishment of heart you find by trusting in God during life: Prov. xvi. 3, 'Commit thy works unto the Lord, and thy thoughts shall be established.' We seek worldly things in good earnest, therefore we are troubled about them, and find it a great difficulty to rest on God for present supplies. There is some general inclination after happiness, but that is soon satisfied. How can you trust him with your souls, and with your everlasting concernments, if you cannot trust him for daily bread, and in present dangers? 1 Peter iv. 19, 'Commit the keeping of your souls to him in well-doing, as unto a faithful creator.' It will be hard work when you are put to it unless you are acquainted with God beforehand.

2. Then is a time to use faith, not to get it. It is no time to buy weapons when the battle is begun. The foolish virgins had their oil

to buy when the bridegroom was come, Mat. xxv. 10. We must lay up comforts against the hour of death; that is the great day of expense, wherein a man is to throw his last for everlasting life. Therefore did God give us so long a life to prepare for this hour. Now we are to make use of the articles of faith; not to learn to believe them, but to turn all into practice.

3. We need the strongest faith to grapple with our greatest and last enemy. Now faith is a grace that is wrought by degrees to strength and perfection: 1 Thes. iii. 10, 'That I may perfect that which is lacking in your faith;' Luke xvii. 5, 'Lord, increase our faith.' Now it is hard to encounter with the worst and last enemy at first. We had need to get promises ready, evidences ready, and experiences ready. Promises ready, upon which we dare venture our souls. Evidences ready: 2 Cor. i. 12, 'Our rejoicing is this, the testimony of our conscience, that in simplicity and godly sincerity, not with fleshly wisdom, but by the grace of God, we have had our conversation in the world;' 2 Tim. iv. 7, 8, 'I have fought a good fight, I have finished my course, I have kept the faith; henceforth there is laid up for me a crown of righteousness, which the Lord, the righteous judge, shall give me at that day; and not to me only, but also unto all them that love his appearing;' Isa. xxxviii. 3, 'Remember now, O Lord, I beseech thee, how I have walked before thee in truth, and with a perfect heart, and have done that which is good in thy sight.' Experience is ready, that all along you have found him a good God: Ps. xviii. 30, 'As for God, his way is perfect: the word of the Lord is tried: he is a buckler to all those that trust in him.' You have found him good to you in pardoning your sins on a penitent confession: 1 John i. 9, 'If we confess our sins, he is faithful and just to forgive us our sins, and to cleanse us from all unrighteousness.' In enabling you to duties of holiness: 1 Thes. v. 23, 24, 'And the very God of peace sanctify you wholly: and I pray God, your whole spirit, and soul, and body be preserved blameless unto the coming of our Lord Jesus Christ. Faithful is he that calleth you, who also will do it.' In bearing you through all your sufferings: 2 Thes. iii. 3, 'And the Lord is faithful, who shall stablish you, and keep you from evil.' You have found him a good God in all your cares, troubles, and sorrows; and will he fail you at last? There is nothing more easy than a slight inconsiderate trust; but you must make a business of believing; it is not a slight 'God have mercy upon us' that will serve the turn. Do you think to please the flesh, and hunt after the world as long as you can, and that Christ will take care of your souls? Do you think it is sufficient to say over a few devout words at last, as if you could do the work of an age in a breath?

Use 1. Reproof.

1. It reproves those that live as if they should never die, and then they die as if they should never live; they fill up the measure of their sins, and so do but provide matter for despair, and horror, and agonies on their deathbeds; for at their latter end they shall taste the fruit of their own doings. There is not such a quick passage as the world imagines—*a cœno ad cœlum*, from Delilah's lap to Abraham's bosom; there must be a sitting and preparing time to get up the heart to heaven.

2. It reproves such as please themselves with the hopes of a death-bed repentance. It is very hazardous whether we shall then have grace to repent; for it is just with God—*ut qui vivens oblitus est Dei, moriens obliviscatur*, he that hath forgotten God all his life, that he should not be remembered by God when he comes to die. It is very unseasonable, for then we need cordials, not work. Is it a time to have our oil to buy when we should use it? And it is suspicious. The scripture containeth an history of near about four thousand years, and there is but one instance of it—viz., of the good thief upon the cross; and there are special reasons for that. It was the first-fruits of Christ's merits, when the great oblation was actually made; the taste and handsel of his drawing power, John xii. 22; as princes will do extraordinary acts of grace on the day of their coronation. Never was such a season: Christ was now actually redeeming the world by his death, and he owneth Christ in the day of his highest abasement, when all others scorned him.

Use 2. Exhortation; it presseth us to live by faith. If you would have faith ready to die by, you must have faith ready to live by; otherwise, you will be either as a stone, or under horror, or at least in the dark—doubtful and anxious, and will not know what will become of you.

1. Disarm death beforehand by plucking out its sting, seeking reconciliation with God through Jesus Christ. The great business you have to do upon earth is to make and keep peace with God. Seek reconciliation with God through the merits of Jesus Christ, and keep up your friendship with him by following the guidance of the Spirit, and then you will pluck out the sting of death; otherwise sin will stare you in the face, and then death will be terrible.

2. Get your title to eternal life evidenced by holiness. Your right and title to eternal life is founded on the merits of Christ, who paid a price, and therefore heaven is called 'the purchased possession,' Eph. i. 14; but your evidence that you have to show for your interest in it is holiness—that is the first-fruits; and when we come to die, we come to have our fill. God qualifies all those whom he appoints to happiness, and prepares them for it; no unclean thing shall enter into heaven; swine, that wallow in the puddle and mire of the world, who would have profit and pleasure rather than grace, are not fit for this happiness. Your end should be to be safe in another world, to enjoy everlasting communion with God; and therefore the evidence of this is the weaning of your heart from the world, and getting it up to heaven, and making holiness the great business of your lives. This is your evidence, though the title comes by Christ.

SERMON XLVI.

These all died in faith, not having received the promises, but having seen them afar off, and were persuaded of them, and embraced them and confessed that they were strangers and pilgrims on the earth.—HEB. xi. 13.

THE next thing I shall observe in the text is the nature of faith, how it works in and upon the promises. Here are several properties of it : it eyes blessings promised, is firmly persuaded of them, and embraceth and huggeth them ; and all this was observable in these patriarchs, though they went to the grave without any experience of the fulfilling of them. Here I shall observe something from the general view of the text, and then from the several actings of faith.

First, From the whole, observe this doctrine—

Doct. Faith is contented with the promise, though it cannot have actual possession. It is enough to faith to see things at a distance, as these patriarchs did : it constantly adhereth to God, though it findeth not what it believeth ; yea, though it see no probability and reason for it. For this also was the case of these partriarchs. Canaan was promised to them, which was now possessed by the Canaanites ; and God hath told them of the calamity that should befal their posterity in Egypt, and yet that they should be a glorious nation, and have a temple and a city. These were very unlikely things, yet they went to the grave, and saw these blessings afar off, and embraced them. Usually God exerciseth his people in this kind ; so it was in the first believer—the Lord had made a promise of a blessed seed to Adam. Now for a great while there was no likelihood of the accomplishment of it—Abel was slain, Cain was a wicked man, and Adam was an hundred and thirty years old before Seth was born, Gen. v. 3, who was appointed instead of Abel, in whom God would continue the blessed line and race. And so it has been all along, there has been a time between the promise and the accomplishment ; therefore the apostle saith, Heb. vi. 12, 'Be ye followers of them, who though faith and patience inherit the promises.' Never any came to possess the things promised, but there was something to exercise their faith and patience ; there was some distance of time for the exercise of their faith, and the inconveniences of the present life to exercise their patience. But yet faith constantly adheres to God, notwithstanding all this. Now faith worketh thus partly because of the advantages it hath in the promises, and partly because of the work it putteth forth upon the heart of a believer.

1 Because of the advantage it hath in the promises ; for consider what the promises are in three things.

[1.] They are the eruption and overflowings of God's love. God's heart is so big with love to his people, that it cannot stay till the accomplishment of things ; but his love breaks out and overflows in the promise before the mercy be brought about : Isa. xlii. 9, 'Behold, the former things are come to pass, and new things do I declare ; before they spring forth I tell you of them.' God's purposes are a sealed fountain ; his promises are a fountain broken open. As when a river swells so high that the channel will not contain it, it breaks out and overflows; so the love of God is so great that the purposes of God, and the fountain of eternal grace towards a believer, swell and break out into actual promises, that we may know what he hath provided for us before they be accomplished. God might have done us good, and given us no promise of it; but love concealed would not be so much for our comfort. Now faith that hath such a testimony of God's love counts itself bound to be contented; for as God counts our purposes to be obedience, so should we count God's promises to be performance. When there is a purpose in the heart to do anything for God, God counts it as actually done. Abraham purposed to sacrifice his son, and it is said, Abraham offered Isaac, Heb. xi. 17. And God takes notice of David's purpose: 1 Kings viii. 18,' 'And the Lord said unto David my father, Whereas it was in thine heart to build an house unto my name, thou didst well that it was in thine heart.' Now as our purposes are the first issues of our love to God, so God's promises are the first issues of his love to us.

[2.] They are the rule and warrant of faith. The promises show how far God is to be trusted, because they show how far he is engaged. So far as the Lord hath promised, so far he hath made himself a debtor, and so hath given the creature a holdfast upon him, something for faith to lay hold upon. God's purposes are unchangeable, therefore the apostle speaks of the 'immutability of his counsel,' Heb. vi. 17; and his promises are his purposes declared, therefore here faith hath something to work upon, it can boldly challenge God upon his word. The word that is gone out of his mouth he will make good, as he hath said: Ps. lxxxix. 34, 'My covenant will I not break, nor alter the thing that is gone out of my lips.' The promises are a means whereby God tries our faith. God will try of what credit he is with men, whether we will depend upon his word or no, and besides they are a security put into our hands. We have now something to urge to God, and may challenge him by his promise: Ps. cxix. 49, 'Remember thy word unto thy servant, upon which thou hast caused me to hope.' They are as so many bonds wherein God is bound to us, and God loves to have his bonds put in suit. A usurer thinks himself rich, though it may be he hath little money in the house, because he hath bonds and good security; he that hath a thousand pounds in bonds and good security is in better case than he that hath only a hundred pounds in ready money. A christian though he hath little in his purse, yet he hath much in bonds; he is rich in promises, by which he hath a holdfast upon God, and therefore he is contented to wait.

[3.] They are a pawn of the thing promised, and must be held till performance come. God's truth and holiness lie at stake, and the Lord will set them free and recover his pawn again. God, when he leaves his promise in his people's hands, he leaves his glory, his truth, his holiness, and his justice there, and they are to remain as pledges with the creature till God sets them free again by performing his promise. This is the meaning of that solemn expression so often used—' As I live, saith the Lord.' He plights his essence; count me not a living God if I do not fulfil my word. So the saints plead with God, that he would free his attributes left in pawn by fulfilling his promises: Ps. cxv. 1. 'Not unto us, O Lord, not unto us, but unto thy name give glory, for thy mercy and for thy truth's sake.' As if they should say, Lord, we do not plead for ourselves, for our own profit, but for thy attributes; for thy mercy and truth. When mercies come according to the promise, God doth not only deliver us, but he delivereth his mercy and truth from calumny and reproach. Now upon all these advantages faith is as good as fruition; it is the 'substance of things hoped for, and the evidence of things not seen,' Heb. xi. 1; it maketh absent things present; it sets up a stage in the heart, and sees God acting over his counsels, and looks upon things to come as already accomplished or now a-doing. It doth not require the existence and presence of the thing we believe, but only the promise of it. Thus the patriarchs had Christ, and saw Christ, and embraced Christ—viz., in the figure and in the promise; therefore it is said, Heb. xiii. 8, 'Jesus Christ, the same yesterday, to-day, and for ever.' As our faith looketh backward, so did their faith look forward; and they are said to eat and to drink Christ: 1 Cor. x. 3, 4, 'And they did all eat the same spiritual meat: and did all drink the same spiritual drink; for they drank of that spiritual rock that followed them, and that rock was Christ.' They had the promise, and so a believer hath heaven in the promise : John viii. 36, 'He that believeth on the Son hath everlasting life;' Titus iii. 5, 'According to his mercy, he saved us by the washing of regeneration and renewing of the Holy Ghost.' As soon as we are regenerated we are saved. They have the love of God in the promise, they have an holdfast upon God by his promise, and they have the promise as a pawn till the performance, and they keep it by them; and this is as good as fruition to a believing soul.

2. Because of the work of faith upon the heart of a believer. There is not only a work of faith upon the promise, but a work of faith upon the heart of a believer.

[1.] It calms the affections and deadeneth the heart to present enjoyments. Carnal affections must have things present and pleasing to sense—'Demas hath forsaken us, having loved the present world,' 2 Tim. iv. 10; but faith causeth the soul to look within the veil, and acquaints us with better things than are to be seen in the world; and so the affections are altered : 2 Cor. iv. 18, 'While we look not to the things that are seen but to the things that are not seen; for the things that are seen are temporal, but the things that are not seen are eternal.' Faith carries the soul into heaven, above the clouds and mists that are here below, and causeth it to see the glory of the world to come; and when it looks to things not seen, things that lie within the veil and curtain of heaven, the soul is weaned from such things as are pleasing to sense. As a man that hath been looking on the sun, his eyes are so dazzled with the lustre of it, that he cannot for a while see anything else. Faith is ever accompanied with weanedness from the world, or else it could never do its office; it gets the heart up to heaven, and then all things are easy. Worldly cares and worldly fears arise from the affection of carnal sense, that is all for the present; but faith looketh to things that are to come, and so purifieth the heart from worldly affections; it acquainteth us with better things in Christ, and so spoileth the taste of other things.

[2.] It worketh patience and waiting the Lord's leisure. That is another effect upon the heart of a believer. Faith and patience are inseparable, and therefore they are often coupled together : Heb. vi. 12, 'Be followers of them, who through faith and patience inherit the promises ;' so Heb. x. 35, 36, ' Cast not away therefore your confidence, which hath great recompense of reward. For ye have need of patience, that after ye have done the will of God, ye might receive the promise.' Faith always worketh waiting, and quiet submission, balancing our sufferings with our hopes. It tarrieth the Lord's leisure ; the promise is sure, therefore faith is satisfied with the promise, and quietly hopeth for the performance of it ; and the promise is good, and will make amends for all ; and therefore faith is contented to wait, notwithstanding present inconveniences. There is longing and looking, yet tarrying and waiting ; the mercy is in sure hands, and when it comes it will make amends for all your waiting ; and if the blessing be deferred, there will be more glory to God and comfort to us when it cometh. It is but fit we should tarry the Lord's leisure. They are wicked heirs that desire the inheritance before it falleth, and wish the death of their parents ; and so they are carnal, that must have all things for the present and cannot wait, that would have blessings before they are ready for them. God is not slack, but we are hasty, and therefore the work of faith is to calm the affections and to subdue us to a quiet waiting upon the Lord, till he accomplish all his pleasure. As Naomi said to Ruth : Ruth iii. 18, ' Sit still, my daughter, until thou know how the matter will fall ; for the man will not be at rest until he have finished the thing this day.' So faith says to a believing soul, Be still ; he that hath begun will not rest till he hath brought this matter to pass.

Use 1. It presseth us to such a faith as will be contented, though it do not come to enjoyment—such a faith as can see that made up in the promise that is wanting in sense and actual feeling. In outward wants get such a faith ; it was the apostle's riddle : 2 Cor. vi. 10, 'As having nothing, and yet possessing all things ;' all things are in the promise, though nothing in actual possession. Now can you live upon a promise, and fetch life and encouragement and protection and maintenance from thence ? Ps. xc. 1, ' Lord, thou hast been our dwelling-place in all generations.' When was this said ? When they were wandering in the wilderness without house or home ; for it was a prayer of Moses, the man of God : they found a habitation in God, when they had none in the wilderness. If we want house, food, raiment, faith can see all this in the promise. The life of faith cometh nearest to the life of heaven. In heaven, God is all in all without the intervention of means ; when we can see all in the promise, it is some kind of anticipation of the life of heaven, because the promise shows us what we shall find in God. Can you fetch thence house, food, raiment, life, deliverance, a legacy and blessing for your children, when you die, and are in deep poverty ?

Again, in spiritual distresses, though you feel no comfort and quickening, yet you have his word. Men cast anchor in the dark, and a child takes his father by the hand in the dark ; can you stick to God in the dark ? Though you see nothing, yet can you cleave close to him, and wait and stay upon his name ? In the absence of the blessing there is room for faith ; can you take your father by the hand when you cannot see him? And when there is nothing appears to sense, can you stay upon the name of God? Christ may be out of sight, and yet you may not be out of mind. Sense makes lies of God: Ps. xxxi. 22, 'I said in my heart I am cut off from before thine eyes; nevertheless thou heardest the voice of my supplication when I cried unto thee.' When to sense and feeling all is gone, God may be very nigh, if we had but an eye of faith to see him. In the midst of the miseries of the present world canst thou comfort thyself with thy right in the promises of the world to come? Though thou hast not possession, thou hast the grant, and the deed is sealed; a man may buy lands that he never saw, if he be well informed about them. Thus heaven and earth differ; heaven is all performance, and here is very little performance; here we have the first-fruits and the earnest, enough to bind the bargain; thou hast the conveyances to show, and it is not *nudum pactum*, a naked bargain, there is earnest given in lieu of a greater sum; now can you wait?

Use 2 It informs us how much the happiness of a believer excels that of a worldling. A worldling hath much in hand, but he hath nothing in hope; he hath fair revenues and ample possessions, but he hath no promises; here they have their portion: Ps. xvii. 14, 'From men of the world, which have their portion in this life, and whose belly thou fillest with thy hid treasure; they are full of children, and leave the rest of their substance to their babes;' and when they come to die, there is an end of all; Luke xvi. 25, 'Son, remember, that thou in thy lifetime receivedst thy good things.' But now look upon a believer: Ps. cxix. 111, 'Thy testimonies have I taken as an heritage for ever.' His portion lies in God's promises, and God's promises concern the present life, as well as that which is to come: 1 Tim. iv. 8, 'Godliness is profitable for all things, having the promise of the life that now is, and of that which is to come.' For the present life all that he has comes with a blessing out of the womb of the promise, and as a fruit of the covenant; and a share he shall have as long as the Lord will use them and employ them; he will give them maintenance and protection as long as he expects service from them: and in the life to come he enters upon his heritage. Oh, it is a sad thing to have our portion here, and to look for no more; to have all in hand and nothing in hope. A christian is not to be valued by his enjoyments, but by his hopes. Do not look upon the children of God as miserable, because they do not shine in outward pomp and splendour, for they have meat and drink which the world knows not of—estate, lands and honours which lie in another world. It is better to be trained up in a way of faith, than to have our whole portion here. A worldly man hath his present payment, that is all he cares for; but a christian hath an ample portion—all the testimonies of God, and all his promises concerning this life and a better. And therefore he is a rich man, though stripped of all; his estate lieth in a country where there is no plundering, no sequestration, no alienation of inheritances. So that if he be stripped of all that the world can take hold of, he is a happier man than the greatest monarch of the world, that hath nothing but present things; because he is rich in bills and bonds, such as lie out of the reach of the world. Turn him where you will, yet still he is happy; turn him into prison, the promises bear him company, and revive and cheer him there ; turn him into the grave, still God goes along with him, and will revive and raise him up again ; his riches stand him in stead at death ; then is the time to put his bonds in suit.   When God comes to demand his soul, he gives it up cheerfully ; for then he comes to enjoyment, and to possess that which he expected ; the best is behind. So much for the general view of the text.

Secondly, More particularly, I shall speak to the several acts of faith, and they are three—

1. Apprehension—*They saw them afar off.*
2. Firm assent—*They were persuaded of them.*
3. Affection—*They embraced them.*

First, The first act of faith is apprehension of the blessings—' They saw them afar off.'   Hence I observe—

Doct. It is the property of faith to eye the blessings promised at a distance.

So Abraham : John viii. 56, ' Your father Abraham rejoiced to see my day, and he saw it, and was glad.'   Faith hath an eagle eye ; it is the perspective of the soul, by which it can see things at a distance. There were many ages between Abraham and Christ, and yet he saw Christ's day.   So Moses, Heb. xi. 26, ' He had respect,' ἐπίβλεπε he had an eye to the recompense of the reward.'   As the devil showed Christ the glory of the present world in a map or representation ;· so doth faith, which is the evidence of things not seen, represent to the soul the glory of the world to come ; there is a view of heaven and happiness.   Let me show you what there is in this view of faith.

1. It apprehends the blessing as a real thing, which without faith we can never do.   The promises are but as a golden dream to a carnal man ; they hear of these things as if they were in a dream, and do not look upon them as real objects : 2 Peter i. 9, ' He that lacketh these things is blind, and cannot see afar off '—τυφλὸς καὶ μυωπάζων,—the word signifies short-sighted.   Fancy and reason cannot out-look time, and see beyond death ; men have a guess and general traditional knowledge ; but there is no serious apprehension of the reality of these great blessings ; heaven doth not come in view to them, as it doth to a believer.   Carnal men may have a dream of such things as Elysian fields, and happy mansions in another world, but they have not an eye open to see God and Christ at his right hand ; as Stephen's eyes were opened : Acts vii. 55, ' He being full of the Holy Ghost, looked up steadfastly into heaven, and saw the glory of God, and Jesus standing at the right hand of God.'   There might be something of special dispensation there, but it is temperately done by faith.   The sight of faith differeth from that of fancy and reason, as the sight of the eye doth from report.   A man that hath seen a foreign country is more affected at the mention of it than he that knows it only by a map, or by the report of others.   Carnal men's hearts are only possessed with an empty notion of heaven ; but they do not see it as a real thing, worthy of their choice and pursuit.

2. It pondereth the worth of the blessings.   Faith is a considerate act, it takes a view of heaven ; as Abraham was to travel through the land of promise, and take a view of it, and Moses from Mount Pisgah

was to take a view of the land 'of Canaan.   As the prophets of old not only believed that Christ was to come in the flesh, but they diligently inquired into the salvation that was to come : 1 Peter i. 11, ' Of which salvation the prophets have inquired and searched diligently, who prophesied of the grace that should come unto you ; ' so doth faith employ the thoughts, and sends them out as spies into the other world to bring tidings of the state of the other country.   Faith languisheth for want of meditation ; for the promises are the food of faith, and meditation is, as it were, the chewing and the digesting of our food.   View them then often, let us be creating images and suppositions of our future happiness.   If a poor man were adopted into the succession of a crown, he would be pleasing himself with the thoughts of it ; so should we mind and ponder on the things that are above, thinking beforehand what a welcome there will be between us and Christ, when the angels shall bring us to Christ ; and in what a manner we shall be brought by Christ, and presented to the Father, as the fruits of his purchase ; what a pleasure it will be to see their fellow-saints with crowns of righteousness upon their heads.   Faith is a steady view.

3. There is actual expectation.   Faith, having a promise, looketh out after the blessing.   This the scripture expresseth by ἀποκαραδοκία, a lifting up the head ; as a man looks after the messenger he hath sent about some business, to see if he be coming back again : Rom. viii. 19, Ἀποκαραδοκία τῆς κτίσεως, &c., ' The earnest expectation of the creature waiteth for the manifestation of the sons of God.' So David, Ps v. 3, ' In the morning will I direct my prayer unto thee and will look up,' that is, to see if I can spy the blessing coming.   Faith not only looks up in prayer, but it looks out to see if anything be coming from God in a way of answer ; as Elijah when he had prayed earnestly for rain, sent his servant to look towards the sea, whether the rain was a-coming : Hab. ii. 1, ' I will stand upon my watch, and set me on the tower, and will watch to see what he will say unto me.'   He was resolved to wait for an answer of grace, withdrawing the mind from things visible, and elevating it to God, and looking above the mists and darkness of inferior accidents.   So faith, as from a watch-tower, looks and sees if it can spy the mercy afar off : 2 Peter iii. 12, ' Looking for and hastening to the coming of the day of God.'   Faith, or meditation on the certainty of the promise (for that is faith), doth thus erect the soul, and sets it in a posture of expectation, to behold if there be any tokens of God's coming, if they can hear the soundings of his feet, any approach of the mercy they look for.   As a man that hath bills or bonds due at such a day, waits for the time when they will come due ; so is faith watching when the time will expire, that he may come to the fruition of that he looks for.   So much for the first act of faith, apprehension.

Secondly. The second act of faith in and upon the promises in firm assent, πεισθέντες,—' They were persuaded of them.'   From hence I observe—

Doct. Faith is persuaded of the certainty of the blessings which it beholdeth in the promises.

That there is a firmness of assent and persuasion in faith, these scriptures evidence: Phil. i. 6, 'Being confident,' or firmly persuaded, 'of this very thing, that he which hath begun a good work in you will perform it until the day of Jesus Christ;' so Rom. viii. 38, πέπεισμαι, 'I am persuaded that neither death, nor life, nor angels, nor principalities, nor powers, nor things present, nor things to come; nor height, nor depth, nor any other creatures, shall be able to separate us from the love of God, which is in Christ Jesus our Lord;' 2 Tim. i. 12, 'I know whom I have believed, and I am persuaded that he is able to keep that which I have committed to him against that day.' Faith is not a moral conjecture, but a certain persuasion: and yet there may be many doubtings: Mat. xiv. 31, 'O thou of little faith, wherefore didst thou doubt?' which is an argument of the weakness, not of the nullity, of faith; but, however, doubts do not get the victory; but of this hereafter.

Now this persuasion of the certainty of the blessing promised stands upon two feet, God's truth in keeping promises, and his power to bring them to pass.

1. On God's truth. God is very tender of the honour of his truth: Ps. cxxxviii. 2, 'Thou hast magnified thy word above all thy name.' When we have the word of a man of credit we rest satisfied. Now we have not only God's word, but his bond. The great work of faith is to rest upon the promise. God would cease to be God if he were not a true God, and the chiefest honour that we can give him is to rest upon his faith: Heb. xi. 11, 'She judged him faithful who had promised.' Faith is a sealing to God's truth: John iii. 33, 'He that believeth his testimony, hath set to his seal that God is true;' whereas unbelief giveth God the lie, which is the worst reproach among men; 1 John v. 10, 'He that believeth not God hath made him a liar, because he believeth not the record that God gave of his Son.' Now God's truth should be the more credited,—

[1.] Because when we trust God upon his word, God is doubly engaged; for there are not only promises made to invite faith, that we may trust in him, but promises made to faith, because we trust in him: Isa. xxvi. 3, 'Thou wilt keep him in perfect peace whose mind is stayed on thee, because he trusteth in thee.' God counts himself bound in honour to fulfil that which we are firmly persuaded of, upon the ground of his word. God will not disappoint a trusting soul. When the soul dares upon the warrant of God's word to stay and rest upon him, God counts himself bound to satisfy such a soul. An ingenuous man would not disappoint one that reposeth his trust in him; much less will God, who is a God of faithfulness.

[2.] Because of the form of God's engaging his truth to us. It is not only in the form of a promise, which is *nudum pactum*, a naked bargain; but in the form of a covenant, which is the most solemn way of transaction and engagement between man and man; nay, and this covenant is ratified by an oath, which is the highest assurance among men: Heb. vi. 16, 'An oath for confirmation is to them an end of all strife.' Barbarous nations have been always very tender of an oath; take away the obligation of an oath, and you destroy all commerce among men. Herod made conscience of his oath when he promised half the kingdom, Mat. xiv. 9. Now the Lord interposeth an oath, and in every oath there is not only an invocation of God as a witness, but an implicit imprecation: God is called upon as a judge and avenger in case of falsehood. So in God's oath, he lays all his glory at stake, as in that oath,—'As I live, saith the Lord;' count me not a living God if this be not accomplished for you. So that not only is the word of God gone out of his mouth, but it is put into the form of a covenant, and that covenant is confirmed by the solemnity of an oath.

[3.] Because this covenant is ratified by the blood of Christ: 2 Cor. i. 20, 'All the promises of God in him are yea, and in him amen, unto the glory of God by us.' This gives us the more satisfaction, because the blood of Christ satisfies God's justice. All God's promises come from his mercy. Now that God's mercy might have a freer course, God represents himself as satisfied with the blood of Christ, which was a price to purchase our blessings. The covenant of grace is founded upon the covenant of redemption, which was made between God and Christ; so that God is not only engaged to us, but engaged to Christ; so some expound that text, Titus i. 2, 'In hope of eternal life, which God that cannot lie, promised before the world began;' and 2 Tim. i. 9, 'According to his own purpose and grace, which was given us in Christ Jesus before the world began.' It is clear that there was a covenant made between God and Christ: Isa. liii. 10, 'When thou shalt make his soul an offering for sin, he shall seek his seed; he shall prolong his days, and the pleasure of the Lord shall prosper in his hands.'

[4.] Because of the many experiences of his faithfulness, the saints have been witnesses of God's fidelity: Ps. xviii. 30, 'The word of the Lord is tried.' Never any had to do with God, but they have been witnesses of his truth. There is more than letters and syllables in the promises; there is comfort, support, life and peace in them: it had been cast in the fire, and come out again. His promises are tried promises; believers have not only been tried with troubles and dark afflictions, but the promises have been put to trial, and all the saints may come in as witnesses of God's faithfulness: Ps. xxii. 4, 5, 'Our fathers trusted in thee; they trusted, and thou didst deliver them, they cried unto thee and were delivered; they trusted in thee, and were not confounded.' Pray mark, how it is repeated,—'They trusted in thee; they trusted, and thou didst deliver them,' they were willing to make trial of God; they trusted, and trusted, and trusted, and still they kept up their trusting, notwithstanding they were exercised with troubles. When the first trust was ready to be broken off they continued the act of their trust, and waited upon God, and he did deliver them. All that have made trial of God will come in for witnesses. Did God disappoint Abraham, or David, or any of the patriarchs? and God is where he was. Hitherto in the story of our own lives we may come in as witnesses for God against our own unbelief, and may plead our own experience, that not one word hath failed of all that he hath promised. Now no wonder if faith that is thus founded on God's truth and faithfulness grows up to firm persuasion.

2. The other foot that faith stands upon is God's power: 2 Tim. i. 12, 'I know whom I have believed, and I am persuaded that he is able to keep that which I have committed unto him against that day.' This is the ground of our dependence on God, the Lord is able to make good his word to the full: so Rom. iv. 21, 'Being fully persuaded that

what he had promised he was able also to perform;' his sufficiency to make good his word was the ground of his faith. God hath made known his will in his promise; now all the doubt is about his power, and indeed unbelief stumbles there. How can this be? is the language of unbelief. But faith is persuaded of the absolute power of God, that God that made heaven and earth out of nothing can accomplish what he hath promised. And therefore it is notable, when the apostle in this chapter would lay down the strength of faith, first he begins with the creation: ver. 3, 'By faith we understand that the worlds were framed by the word of God.' This one article of faith helps us to believe all the rest, for if we believe the creation, then we may easily believe that he is able to accomplish all we trust in him for.

Thirdly, The third act of faith in and upon the promises is ἀσπασάμενοι, 'They embraced them,' or saluted them, and hugged them,—Oh, these are dear precious promises! This will yield Canaan, this will yield a Messiah, this heaven; as a man maketh much of bills, and bonds, and conveyances, and keeps them charily. Now in this act of faith I shall observe several things:—

1. I observe that faith is an act of the will, as well as of the understanding. There is in faith adherence as well as assent, and embracing as well as persuasion. Faith looketh upon the promises not only as true, but as good; they are 'yea and amen,' 2 Cor. i. 20. They are 'great and precious promises,' 2 Peter i. 4. Faith in scripture is not only expressed by sight but taste. The promises are as food to the renewed soul, and faith is a spiritual taste; it is a feeding upon the promises with delight. The trial of the soul is by affection; they that are all notion, and have no affection have no faith. Certainly if you did believe the promises that are so good, and so true, you would be more affected with them, you would entertain the promises with respect and delight, though you do not receive present satisfaction; for where faith is, there is love and delight in the things believed. We think we are persuaded, but where is our love and comfort? for this necessarily follows, they saw them afar off, and were persuaded of them, and embraced them.

2. I observe the order and method here laid down by the Holy Ghost, for these things follow one another in a very natural order, sight makes way for persuasion, and persuasion for delight. Sailors at sea, when they see land afar off, shout and make towards it with joy; so when the soul sees that blessing at a distance, it stirs up actual rejoicing in God, because of his word. There would be no embracing if there were no sight; the eye affecteth the heart, and according to the strength of conviction and persuasion, so is the strength of affection to the blessings promised. Therefore if you would have more lively affections to the promises, you must oftener think of them and be more firmly persuaded of them. Think of them oftener, the oftener the soul is in heaven the more joy, a man cannot take comfort in that whereupon he doth not often meditate. The mind must engage the heart, and serious thoughts must make way for these embracings. God's method is first to enter upon our judgments and consideration, and then to ravish the heart, the great things of the covenant do enter upon the mind, and then they affect and ravish the heart. And be more firmly persuaded of the promises; if men were persuaded of them, they would

not be so coldly affected as they are.   We that are so dead-hearted to
heavenly things, surely we do not judge them real.   It may be we do not
actually call them in question, but we have not a firm persuasion of the
truth of them ; if we had, we would more 'rejoice in hope of the
glory of God,' Rom. v. 2.   For we should find the scripture always
maketh delight a fruit of faith : 1 Peter i. 8, 'In whom, though now ye
see him not, yet believing, ye rejoice with joy unspeakable and full of
glory.'   Rejoicing is wrought in us by believing, and being persuaded
of the reality, and worth of things that are come.   So Rom. xv. 13,
'Now the God of hope fill you with all joy and peace in believing.'
This is the natural order : faith is wrought in the soul, then these
affections, and embracings, and rejoicings in God are stirred up.

3. The affection that is exercised in this embracing is joy.   There
are other affections, I know, that are exercised, as hope and love, but
chiefly our joy, as appears by that parallel place, John viii. 56, 'Your
father Abraham rejoiced to see my day, and he saw it, and was glad.'
John Baptist did not only leap in the womb, because of Christ's day,
when it was ready at hand, but Abraham, that lived at so great a
distance.   Joy is the affection proper to enjoyment, but faith behaveth
itself as if it were already come to possession.   This joy ariseth from
the certainty of the promise, and the excellency of it, and our interest
in it ; they rejoice because such great and precious promises are made
over to them in Christ, being assured they shall be made good to them
in due time : so did the patriarchs, and so doth every believer.

4. This joy is manifested two ways, partly by the lively act of it in
meditation, partly by the solid effects of it in our conversation.

[1.] By the lively act of it in meditation, it doth our hearts good to
think of it.   Thus they hugged the promises, O sweet promises !   A
man cannot think of a little pelf, or any petty interest in the world
without comfort, when he knows he has a right to do it ; and can a
man think of the promises, and not be affected with them ?   Carnal
men may think and think again, they have no spiritual appetite, and
therefore they feel no savour, their joy is intercepted and prepossesed
with vanity and carnal delights, and therefore the promises to them
are as a dry chip, or withered flowers.   Swine do not value pearls ; but
now to believers their hearts leap within them to think of the promises,
and what God hath provided for them in Christ : Luke vi. 23, 'Rejoice
ye in that day, and leap for joy ; for behold your reward is great in
heaven.'   Whatever our condition be in the world, this maketh us full
of comfort ; there is an actual rejoicing, a hugging our happiness, as if
we were in the midst of the glory of the world to come.   A carnal man
feeleth contentment, sudden rapt motions of joy every time he doth
actually think of his bags, riches, and honours ; and shall not a
christian find contentment, when he thinks of the heavenly glory ?
What ? an heir of God, and co-heir with Christ, and be no more
affected ?   1 Sam. xviii. 23, 'Seemeth it to you a light thing to be a
king's son-in-law ?'   We should 'rejoice in hope of the glory of God,'
Rom. v. 2.   In meditation faith and hope is acted.

[2.] By the solid effects of it in our conversation.   It is not a joy
for a pang or fit, the practical joy is the best sign.   The solid effects of
it are these, cheerfulness in duties, comfort and support in afflictions,
and weanedness from worldly pleasures.

(1.) Cheerfulness in duties. When we go cheerfully about our work, because we have heaven in our eye, it is a sign we have embraced the blessings made known to us in the promises : 1 Cor. xv. 58, ' Be ye stedfast, immovable, always abounding in the work of the Lord, forasmuch as you know that your labour is not in vain in the Lord.' It will quicken us to obedience. A christian is persuaded that whatever he does will turn to a good account, and therefore he cheerfully holds on his course in holiness. You know a horse goes cheerfully, when he goes homeward ; so a christian that is hastening to God, and every day draws nearer his home, goes cheerfully on in his work. So far as you are backward in God's work, so far is your delight in the promises weakened. Therefore a christian is cheerful, and holdeth on his journey to heaven with delight, because he looketh upon grace as a bud of glory, and upon duty as the way to heaven.

(2.) Comfort and support in afflictions. There is not only an extramission of acts of faith, but an intromission of comfort and strength to support the heart. As the heart acteth towards the promise, so doth the promise work upon the heart. David professeth his experience in this kind, Ps. cxix. 50, ' This is my comfort in my affliction, for thy word hath quickened me.' True faith draweth life, comfort and quickening out of the word of promise ; so ver. 81, ' My soul fainteth for thy salvation, but I hope in thy word.' Faith looking to the word gathereth strength and hope. This is no disparagement to the Spirit of God, for faith is the instrument, the word the means, and the Spirit the author of all this grace which we receive. This is God's established order, the Spirit by the word, through our faith conveyeth strength and support to us. God doth not cast in comfort and quickening into the soul whilst we are idle ; it is by his grace, but upon the acting of our faith : Ps. cxix. 92, ' Unless thy law had been my delight, I should then have perished in mine afflictions.' The worth of the word and the excellency of faith would not have been known unless God had cast into afflictions ; then is the time to make trial of the virtue of the word, the excellency of faith, and the comforts of another world.

(3.) This joy is manifested by a weanedness from worldly pleasures. There cannot be such an affectation of worldly greatness, because by embracing the promises the affections are diverted and prepossessed. The affections are the most active faculties of the soul, and they cannot remain idle ; as water in the pipe must needs run, so must our affections have some vent and oblectation. Now when the promises have taken up our delight, when we have chosen them for our heritage, then the relish of other things is marred and spoiled : Ps. cxix. 3, ' Thy testimonies have I taken as an heritage for ever, for they are the rejoicing of my heart.' Our choice is a tie upon our hearts. Till we are acquainted with better things we take up with the world, but when we are once acquainted with the sweetness of the promises, we look no further ; when a man hath embraced the promises, and taken them for his portion, and resolved to adhere and stick to them, that ties up his heart from other things. Garlic and onions may be pleasing to him that hath tasted no better food, but who can relish aloes that hath tasted honey ? so when the heart is acquainted with better things, with the delights of another world, with the sweetness of God in Christ, it is withdrawn from outward comforts and carnal pleasures. As the woman of Samaria left her water-pot when she was acquainted with Christ: John iv. 28, 'The woman then left her water-pot, and went her way into the city,' &c. And Zaccheus, when he came to Christ, then saith he, 'Lord, the half of my goods I give to the poor; and if I have taken anything from any man by any false accusation, I restore him fourfold,' Luke xix. 8.

SERMON XLVII.

These all died in faith, not having received the promises, but having seen them afar off and were persuaded of them, and embraced them, and confessed that they were strangers and pilgrims on the earth.—HEB. xi. 13.

Use 1. Of information in two things.

1. If these be the actings of faith, it shows what need there is of the power of the Spirit of God in the whole business of faith, to accomplish all these things. It is the apostle's expression, 2 Thes. i 11, 'Wherefore we pray always for you, that our God would count you worthy of this calling, and fulfil the good pleasure of his goodness, and the work of faith with power.' It will never be done without power from above. We can neither see, nor be persuaded of, nor embrace these things, except the grace of God come in upon the heart mightily to enable it. We cannot see afar off, nature is short sighted; so the apostle prays, Eph. i. 17, 18, 'That the God of our Lord Jesus Christ, the father of glory, may give unto you the spirit of wisdom and revelation in the knowledge of him. The eyes of your understandings being enlightened, that ye may know what is the hope of his calling, and what the riches of the glory of his inheritance in the saints.' A man cannot look into the other world without the light of the Spirit. All things must be seen with a proper light,—spiritual things with a spiritual light. Now till God open our eyes we can never look through the curtain of the clouds and see the riches of the glory of our inheritance in Christ. A fond conjecture there may be of happiness to come, but no certain, steady sight. Then for persuasion; nothing is so natural to guilty creatures as doubts and jealousies. Man's heart is prone to unbelief above all things, and therefore the heart cannot be persuaded without the Spirit: 1 Cor. ii. 10, 11, 'But God hath revealed them to us by the Spirit; for the Spirit searcheth all things, yea the deep things of God. For what man knoweth the things of a man, save the spirit of man which is in him? even so the things of God knoweth no man save the Spirit of God.' It is God must persuade the heart to believe, embrace, and take hold of the covenant: Gen. ix. 27, 'God shall persuade Japhet, and he shall dwell in the tents of Shem.' And then for embracing, God hath reserved this power in his own hands to bring our hearts and the promise together. Joy is a fruit of the Spirit as well as an effect of faith.

2. It informeth us of the difference between faith and other things, as between faith and presumption. Presumption hath no bottom to

work upon, but only some general persuasion that God will be merciful and gracious ; but faith hath the word of God, though it hath nothing else. Presumption is a rash bastard confidence, it never looketh to the grounds of it; but faith, though it may be without things promised, yet it cannot be without the promise ; it must have some solid grounds to work upon, and not fallible conjectures : 2 Tim. i. 12, 'I know whom I have believed, and I am persuaded that he is able to keep that which I have committed to him.' It proceeds from know-ledge and clear grounds, and is not a trust that is taken hand over head. Again we learn hence the difference between faith and sense ; sense must have something in hand, but it is enough to faith to have a promise. Sense cannot see, nor be persuaded of, nor embrace things till they are present; faith, though it receive not the blessings, yet it sees them afar off, and is contented with a ground of hope. Again, we learn the difference hence between faith and reason ; reason looketh to outward probabilities, it observeth the clouds ; but faith is contented with God's word, how improbable soever things be. Reason sees things in their causes; but faith sees things in the promises, and rests upon the authority of God's word. Reason sees more than sense, but faith sees much more than reason, let the case be never so desperate, and things never so far off ; to sense a star is but as a spark or spangle, but reason considereth the distance, and knows them to be vast and great bodies. Faith corrects reason, and though there be no causes, no probabilities, no appearances, faith can see things to come. Again, we see the dif-ference between faith and conjecture ; conjecture is but a blind guess, it may be so, or it may not be so ; but faith is a certain persuasion, it shall be so, as the Lord hath spoken. Again, it shows the difference between faith and opinion, which is somewhat more than conjecture ; a man verily thinks it is so, but there is *formido oppositi*, a fear of the contrary ; but faith falls embracing and hugging the mercy, is per-suaded of it, and rejoiceth and triumpheth as if the blessing were already enjoyed.

Use 2. Of examination. Have you such a faith? What kind of actings have you towards the promises ? Do you see the blessings pro-mised afar off ? are you persuaded of them ? do you embrace them ? Are you contented with the word of promise though you have not the blessings promised ?

1. Are you careful to get an interest in the promises, to thrust in for a share in them, that you may see your own name in God's bond ? Negligence is a sure sign of unbelief ; if you hear of so great salvation, and are careless and negligent, and do not put in for a share, it is a sign you do not believe that which God hath promised. Not only actual doubting, but carelessness gives God the lie ; when you hear of precious promises, but regard them not, you do not count them true. You know what David says : Ps. cxix. 111, 'Thy testimonies have I taken as an heritage for ever, for they are the rejoicing of my heart.' Now have you chosen these for your portion, and made it the scope of your lives not to grow great in the world, but to have an interest in the promises ? I do not say he is no believer that cannot say, I have an interest in the promises, but I dare say that he is no believer that doth not take the promises for his heritage, and doth not part with all

things that he may get an interest in them. When a good bargain is offered upon easy terms, if men do not regard it, it is a sign they do not believe it. Here is the best bargain that ever can be offered to you, eternal salvation and the enjoyment of God and Christ; if you do not put in for a share, it is a sign of unbelief.

2. Do you prize and esteem them? 2 Peter i. 4, 'To us are given exceeding great and precious promises;' so they are in the account of every believer, not small things, but great and of great consequence to us. Do I believe these things, and am I no more affected with them? If a great man that may be changeable in point of will, and defective in point of power, promises great matters to us, how do we build upon it, and are pleased with his promise! When the great God hath promised great things of such high concernment, it is an ill sign not to be moved and taken with these things. David doth often profess his respect to the word: Ps. cxix. 14, 'I have rejoiced in the way of thy testimonies as much as in all riches.' Faith sees more comfort in the promises than in the dearest things we have in the world; gold and silver are nothing to them. Is there such an esteem of the promises? That you may not deceive yourselves, know this esteem of the promises is accompanied with a disesteem of earthly things. When a man embraceth a thing, all other things fall out of his hands; when the hands are full of the world, you cannot hug the promises. It will take you off from worldly admiration; the world will seem less if the promises seem great and precious, for the promises do not establish the love of the world, but the love of heaven: Prov. viii. 10, 'Receive my instruction, and not silver, and knowledge rather than choice gold.' It is not said, 'and not *above* silver,' but 'and not silver;' the soul by faith is diverted, and hath less esteem of these things. If you are as earthly-minded as ever, you have no faith.

3. Do you often call them to mind and comfort yourselves in the remembrance of them? He that is a stranger to the promises doth not believe them. A man looketh upon his bills, and bonds, and evidences, and views them often, and consults with them, they are all he hath to show for his estate; so a believer consults with the promises, they are the obligation he hath upon God: Ps. cxix. 24, 'Thy testimonies are my delight and my counsellors,' or the men of my counsel. Every strait drives him to the promises, there to consult with the mind and will of God; as David went to the sanctuary, Ps. lxxiii. 17. A man cannot have any satisfaction of his doubts, any allay of his fears, but by calling to mind the promises. In short, wants bring a man to the promises, the promises to Christ, and Christ to God. Wants bring a man to the promises; for there is a plaster for every sore; and the promises to Christ, for in him they are all yea and amen; and Christ to God, as the fountain of all blessings. Saith David, Ps. cxix. 92, 'Unless thy law had been my delight, I should then have perished in mine affliction.' Do you thus call to mind the promises, and reckon upon them in all straits and afflictions, and find real support from them: Heb. x. 34, 'Ye took joyfully the spoiling of your goods, knowing in yourselves that you have in heaven a better and an enduring substance,' that is, acting your thoughts upon it. It is good to see whence our supports come, and how we are borne up in all cases, it is by knowing and thinking upon what God hath promised.

4. Do they put you upon thanksgivings in the midst of wants, straits, and miseries? Faith is a bird that can sing in winter, and a believer can rejoice in his hopes when he hath little in hand. The patriarchs built altars, and offered sacrifices of praise, whenever God renewed the promises to them. Faith triumphs before the victory; though you have not the blessing, can you praise God for the promise? Ps. xiii. 5, 'But I have trusted in thy mercy; my heart shall rejoice in thy salvation.' You are assured mercy shall come, though never so unlikely and never so far off. Is thy heart thus carried out to triumph in God when you have but his bare word, to hug the promises with delight, to praise God not only for his blessings, but for his word, and to rejoice and give thanks before the mercy come? So Ps. lvi. 10, 'In God will I praise his word, in the Lord will I praise his word.' Can you praise him not only for his acts of mercy, but for his promises of mercy? Though there be nothing of performance, yet there is ground not only of hope but of praise that we have his word; and David redoubleth it, as a thing of undoubted experience.

5. Do the promises stir up any longing and looking for the blessings promised? There will be looking, there will be not only more frequent meditation, but a more earnest expectation. Faith will thrust out the head, and look if it can see God a-coming, there will be a constant observation how the word is made good; for faith is required not only for our comfort, but that we may be witnesses of God's faithfulness, that we may see how he makes good his promises: Joshua xxiii. 14, 'Not one thing hath failed of all the good things which the Lord your God spoke concerning you; all are come to pass unto you, and not one thing hath failed thereof.' And then for longing, when shall it once be? The nearer we come to enjoy Christ, the more impatient should we grow: 2 Peter iii. 12, 'Looking for and hastening unto the coming of the day of God.' Faith is earnest, but it doth not give over looking out for the mercy expected.

6. What influence have the promises of God upon your prayers? Can you come into God's presence with more confidence because you have the word of God on your side, and cast yourselves upon his word in the midst of doubts and fears, and in the face of discouragements? Can you put promises in suit? Ps. cxix. 25, 'My soul cleaveth unto the dust; quicken thou me according to thy word.' Can you throw in to God his hand-writing, and put him in remembrance of his promises? Lord, whose are these? As Tamar, when Judah was about to condemn her, said, Gen. xxxviii. 25, 'Discern, I pray thee, whose are these, the signet, and bracelets, and staff.' Prayer is faith acted; there we come to exercise that trust that we have had in the promises: James i. 7, 'But let him ask in faith, nothing doubting;' there we show how we can bear up ourselves upon the word, and put a humble challenge upon the Lord; we come to put his bond in suit. Now can you thus draw near to God, seeking the full performance of his word? as David: Ps. cxix. 49, 'Remember thy word unto thy servant, upon which thou hast caused me to hope.' David there pleads two things; God's promise, and his hope. The grant of a promise and the gift of faith; thou hast caused me to hope, therefore make good thy promise. By two things God becomes a debtor, *Deus promittendo se fecit debit orem, et Deus donando debet*—God makes himself a debtor by pro

mising, and by giving grace. He will not disappoint faith, otherwise he would stir up such an excellent grace in vain.

7. What influence have the promises upon your practice and conversation? By that you may judge whether you have this faith: 2. Peter iii. 11, 12, 'What manner of persons ought ye to be in all holy conversation and godliness; looking for and hastening to the coming of the day of God.' The course of our lives doth discover the certainty of our hopes; they that are not such manner of persons do not look for such things. Can a man look for the resurrection of the body, and only use his body as a strainer for meats and drinks, and a channel for lust to run in? Can a man look to be one of the virgins that shall follow the Lamb, that defiles his soul with every base lust? Can a man look to see God, and suffer his eyes to run after vanity? to be with Christ hereafter, and walk in disobedience to his commands for the present? And as the quality of our hopes will be hereby discovered, so will the strength of our hopes also: James i. 8, 'A double-minded man is unstable in all his ways.' He that is full of doubts will be off and on in point of obedience; he will be unstable in his way because unstable in his faith. You may know the rate and measure of your faith by your conversation: he that is firmly persuaded, and hath his heart fixed in the promises, will be more constant in the course of his obedience; his religion will not be by fits and starts, now and then a good pang, and then off again. For the promises are the great motives of obedience, we work as we are persuaded of them; but when we are up and down, at least it argues an interruption of faith. A wavering trust and a fickle carriage go together.

8. Do they engage you to any self-denial? Do you part with anything upon your hopes? as these patriarchs left their country, and lived as sojourners in a strange land, for they looked for a better country, that is a heavenly. Whoever hopes for anything from God must leave something for God; one time or another God will put him upon trial. Now what do you quit for God? Do you live upon your hopes, or upon your riches, honours, and pleasures? God doth not count that you trust his promises unless you venture something on them. Every grace makes a venture,—charity: Eccles. xi. 1, 'Cast thy bread upon the waters, for thou shalt find it after many days.' So saith the Lord, Mal. iii. 10, 'Prove me if I will not open the windows of heaven, and pour you out a blessing.' God would not have a proof of our fidelity, nor we a proof of his faithfulness, if we did not sometimes make ventures. Zeal makes adventures in a way of conscientious obedience; and mortification, it ventures upon the promises—he that loseth his life shall save it; he that parts with worldly conveniences for the interests of conscience shall have treasure in heaven. Now at what expense have you been, and what adventures have you made in a way of self-denial and obedience upon the promises? By these things you may know whether you have such a faith as these patriarchs.

Use 3. To press you to get such a faith as will wait for future blessings with such patience and contentation as if they were already enjoyed. The arguments I shall urge are these—

1. We have more cause than the patriarchs, for we live nearer to the accomplishment of God's promises. Every age downward hath great

advantages of believing. The first patriarchs were so far from the things typified that they had the types; Abraham, Isaac, and Jacob did not enjoy Canaan, the type of heaven; nor did they see the temple, the type of Christ; nor the rites of the Levitical administration, which were the type of his sufferings; nor the numerous posterity, which was a type of the calling of the gentiles. The next age had more advantages; they had the types, but not the things typified; they were grown into a numerous multitude and a nation; they had the temple, and legal administrations and sacrifices: but Christ was not come in the flesh; the calling of the gentiles was not brought about; they had not such discoveries of heaven, and of the glory God had prepared for them that love him; the entrance into the holy place was not yet set open; they were legalised, not evangelised. Afterward when Christ was come in the flesh, the first christians were not so near salvation; heaven was still at a distance; there was τὸ κατέχον, something that hindered the discovery of antichrist. They were to look for the discovery of antichrist, we for the ruin of antichrist; they for the taking away what letted, that antichrist might be discovered, viz., the Roman Empire, we for the consuming of antichrist by the Spirit of Christ's mouth, and the brightness of his coming. There is but a little time between us and the day of judgment, it is the last times we now live in. All things are clearer to us than to the patriarchs; that which was prophecy to them is history to us, and history is clearer than prophecy, because it is more sensible; our light is clearer, our means and helps are greater. What a shame is it that our faith should be so weak! that they should have eagle's eyes to see things at a distance, and we should be such owls and bats. We have the experience of all former ages, and we draw nearer and nearer still to our great hopes; surely then our condemnation will be greater if we should not believe and wait for the blessings promised with such patience and contentation as they did. It is said, Zech. xii. 8, 'He that is feeble at that day shall be as the house of David.' God expects much from you, that you should be as Abraham and David, for you have greater helps, higher advantages, and clearer discoveries of the will of God.

2. Unless your faith work thus, to keep heaven in sight, it will be of no use and profit to you. Looking to present things is the ground of all miscarriages, you will not be able to bear afflictions if you have not such a faith as to be contented with the promises till performance come: Heb. xii. 11, 'No chastening for the present seemeth to be joyous, but grievous.' When you feel nothing but the smart rod, you will certainly miscarry. Nor will you be able to withstand temptations, but present profits and present pleasures will withdraw your hearts from God: 2 Tim. iv. 10, 'Demas' (a glorious professor, one of the seven deacons) 'hath forsaken us, having loved this present world.' Nor will you be able to wait for the future glory; the children of God have been always ready to confess their miscarriages when they have been in haste, when they have been all for the present: Ps. cxvi. 11, 'I said in my haste, All men are liars;' he speaks of Samuel and the prophets who had promised him the kingdom, and yet he was chased like a flea, and hunted like a partridge upon the mountains; and Ps. xxxi. 22, 'I said in my haste, I am cut off from before thine eyes.' Passion will

break out into irregular thoughts and words. If you have not this faith, you will never be able to hold out till the crown come. This bore up Paul, that he looked beyond the present life: Rom. viii. 18, ' I reckon that the sufferings of this present time are not worthy to be compared to the glory which shall be revealed in us.' Without this faith you cannot abound in charity, nor do anything for God in that kind, for the reward comes after many days: Eccles. xi. 1, 'Cast thy bread upon the waters, for after many days thou shalt find it.' You cannot mortify lusts, that is irksome and tedious to present sense: 1 Cor. ix. 27, ' I keep under my body, and bring it in subjection;' he had a crown in his eye, he alludes to those in the Isthmic games, that dieted themselves to run; now saith he, ' They do it to obtain a corruptible crown, but we an incorruptible,' ver. 25. How will you neglect the honours, pleasures, and profits of the present world, when you are put to a sore trial? you will surely faint if you have not such a faith as is here described.

3. It is the glory of faith to see things to come, and delight in them as if they were present. It cometh near to the vision of God, to that manner of sight that God hath of things. We say of God that he seeth all things that may be in his own all-sufficiency, and all things that shall be in his own degree, and it is all one to him, as if they were actually existing. This is somewhat like to the vision that God had of the world before it was: Prov. viii. 31, ' Rejoicing in the habitable parts of the earth,' before hill or mountain were created. So doth faith see all things in the all-sufficiency and truth of God long before they come to pass, as if they were already in being, and were already brought to pass. The sight of faith is a glorious sight, like God's before things appear.

4. As it is for the honour of faith, so it is for the honour of God. He gave out a promise for this end and purpose to exercise our faith, and try how far we would trust him, for else he might have kept us in the dark; and therefore such a kind of trust gives God the glory of his power, mercy, and truth—' Abraham was strong in faith, giving glory to God,' Rom. iv. 20. Faith is called ' a justifying God,' Luke vii. 29. Faith not only justifies a believer, but it justifies God. To justify is a relative word, and implies to clear another from accusations brought against him. Now faith clears God from the calumnies and slander of the world and our own hearts. God is not honoured by anything so much as faith; it is not your dead service, pompous worship, cere- monious duties, that honour God; but it is faith that gives him the glory of his mercy, faithfulness, and all-sufficiency. So much for the arguments.

Now for the means, what shall we do to have such a faith as is here described? Here is something supposed, and something to be done.

[1.] There is something supposed, and that is, that you get an interest in the promises, otherwise your faith is but a fancy and delusion: Job. viii. 13, ' The hypocrite's hope shall perish.' There must be an accept- ing of the general covenant before we can make use of the particular promises; if you have not an interest, you do but embrace a cloud, and not the promises. Did you ever choose God to be your God, and give up yourselves to be his? then may you come and sue out the promises, and look for the blessings promised : Ps. cxix. 34, 'I am thine, save me,' ' I am thine,' that is, bound to thee in covenant ; so Ps. xxiii. 1, ' The Lord is my shepherd, I shall not want.' There must be a good ground and foundation laid. Now is God yours ? have you chosen him ? then may you draw a conclusion, and comfort yourselves ; though as to sense you want all things, yet you lack nothing, for the Lord is your shepherd. When Christ prayed for his disciples, he pleads this argument : John xvii. 6, 'Thine they were, and thou gavest them me.' Then may we expect salvation temporal and eternal when we can say, Lord! I am thine. A covenant supposeth both parties engaged ; it doth not leave one party bound and the other at large. Can you say then, Lord, I would not be mine own, but thine ? Then you may plead God's promises.

[2.] There is something required to be done by us ; something on the heart, and something on the promises.

First. There is something required to be done upon the heart : the eye must be kept clear and the affections tender ; they saw the promises afar off, and were persuaded of them, and embraced them.

1. Keep the eye clear, the world is a very blinding thing : 2 Cor. iv. 4, ' In whom the god of this world hath blinded the minds of them which believe not.' Satan hath that title of ' the god of this world ' because the world is the means that he useth to blind men withal ; the profits of the world are as dust cast into the eyes. So 2 Peter i. 9, ' He that lacketh these things is blind, and cannot see afar off ;' these things, that is, temperance and sobriety in the pursuit and use of outward comforts. Brutish and carnal affections send up the fumes and steams of lust, and then the eye is clouded, and you cannot have a clear sight of heaven, and of the blessings to come. A carnal man may discourse of heaven, but he hath not such a lively affective sight of it.

2. Keep the heart tender. An hard heart, that is settled in the guilt and love of sin, cannot rejoice in the hope of glory, nor hug the blessings promised, nor behave itself as if it were already come to enjoyment. Take heed of benumbing the affections, of soaking and steeping the soul in carnal pleasures ; these take away the heart, that is the tenderness of the heart. Carnal profits darken the eye, and carnal pleasures bring a brawn upon the heart, that we have no affections for Christ and things above. They that were given to uncleanness were past feeling : Eph. iv. 19, ' Who being past feeling, have given themselves over unto lasciviousness, to work all uncleanness with greediness.' There will be no hugging ncr embracing the promises as long as we allow a carnal liberty in fleshly pleasures, for they will bring a deadness on the heart.

Secondly. Something must be done as to the promises.

1. You must understand the nature of them, and the tenure of them.

[1.] The nature of them ; it is good to know our portion. Abraham walked through the land of promise ; so it is good now and then to survey the land of promise, to see what God hath made over to us in Christ. In every bargain we look to the conditions, and what advantage we shall have. God's covenant-notion is God all-sufficient ; there is nothing wanting in the covenant ; the plaster is as broad as the sore.

In the covenant you may find protection, maintenance, peace, strength, deliverance, comfort, meat, drink, everlasting happiness. Look, as the psalmist bids us, Ps. xlviii. 12, 13, ‘Walk about Sion, and go round about her ; tell the towers thereof, mark ye well her bulwarks, consider her palaces,’ there is nothing wanting necessary for use or ornament ; so go to the covenant, there is every blessing for body, soul, goods, and good name ; every blessing is adopted and taken into the covenant : I Cor. iii. 23, ‘All things are yours, for you are Christ’s, and Christ is God’s.’ Ordinances, providences, things present, things to come, life, death, afflictions, mercies, all things are yours. There is no scantiness in the covenant, but an overflow of mercy : Ps. xxiii. 5, ‘ My cup runneth over.’ There are privative mercies and positive mercies : Ps. lxxxiv. 11, ‘ The Lord God is a sun and a shield. The Lord will give grace and glory ; no good thing will he withhold from them that walk uprightly.’ He will give all kind of mercies for your persons, for your relations. For your persons : man is made up of a body and soul, and there are promises for both. For the body : not only for hereafter, that God will raise it up to be a glorious body like to Christ’s body ; but for the present, to give it health, strength, supply, meat, and drink, and clothing. Then for the soul there are promises of pardon, life, light, grace, quickening, all things that are necessary for the soul. It is good to fetch every mercy out of the covenant both for soul and body, our bread and clothing, for ‘ man doth not live by bread alone, but by every word that proceedeth out of the mouth of God,’ Mark iv. 4. For your relations, and those that you care for in the world, your posterity, the grace of the covenant runneth over. God cannot satisfy himself in doing good to our persons, but he will do good to our children : Deut. v. 29, ‘ That it may be well with them, and with their children for ever.’ God takes notice of the children of his old friends, when they are dead and gone. So for the church of God, those that mind the affairs of Sion have promises to bear them up, as promises for the conversion of the world, that nations shall come in to Christ, and the like. It is good to have store of promises by us ; collect them in your reading and hearing ; happy is the man that hath his quiver full of them.

[2.] Know the tenure of them as well as the nature. God hath promised nothing absolutely but eternal life, and necessary grace to bring us thither ; all other things are promised with a limitation, as the Lord shall see them good for us ; and there the work of faith is to calm the heart to submit to God’s pleasure, and refer all to him. A man that is ignorant of the tenure of the covenant cannot fix his faith aright. Now the promises are either temporal, spiritual, or eternal.

(1.) For promises of temporal mercies.

1st. They are to be understood with limitation of convenience. God knows what is best and fit for us, therefore we must trust his choosing. Agur prays, Prov. xxx. 8, ‘ Give me neither poverty nor riches ; feed me with food convenient for me.’ A garment too short will not cover our nakedness, and a garment too long will be a dirty rag to trip up our heels. God is bound in covenant only to do that is convenient for us, and that we must leave to God to judge ; the sheep must not choose the pastures, but the shepherd. If a man were left to carve out his own portion, he would be his own greatest enemy ; a sick man would make his palate his physician ; children think green fruit the best diet.   Many things suit with our appetite that do not suit with God's wisdom.   What strange creatures should we be if we were at our own finding!

2dly.   In these temporal promises God will either give us the thing specified (and then it comes sweetly when it comes from a promise), or he will give us that which is equivalent.   Our Saviour says, Mat. xix. 29, 'Every one that hath forsaken houses, or brethren, or sisters, or father, or mother, or wife, or children, or lands, for my name's sake, shall receive an hundred-fold.'   Julian was wont to mock the christians with that promise, that they should have a hundred fathers and a hundred mothers, &c.   The meaning is, they shall have an equivalent, and what they lose in this world shall be abundantly made up to them.

3dly.   All temporal mercies are promised with an exception of the cross and persecution, when it is for God's glory, or for the honour of the truth, or for the correction of our sins.   When David had sinned, David must be punished : 2 Sam. xii. 13, 14, 'The Lord hath put away thy sin ; thou shalt not die.   Howbeit, because by this deed thou hast given great occasion to the enemies of the Lord to blaspheme, the child also that is born unto thee shall surely die.'   God hath reserved this liberty in the covenant to visit our transgressions with rods, though he will not take away his love : Ps. lxxxix. 31–33, 'If they break my statutes, and keep not my commandments, then will I visit their transgression with the rod, and their iniquity with stripes ; nevertheless, my loving-kindness will I not utterly take from him, nor suffer my faithfulness to fail.'   In all these temporal promises we must expect what God sees convenient and best for us, and may conduce to his glory, and that shall be made up to us another way.

(2.) For spiritual promises, understand the tenure of them.   God hath promised to give necessary grace to all such as have an interest in Christ, but for the perfection of grace that God hath not promised in this life, and for the measures and degrees of grace, and the actual motions and assistances of his Spirit, here he works according to his own pleasure.   Perfection we cannot have in this life.

(3.) For eternal promises, they are always sure and safe, and these things chiefly faith should keep in its eye.   Though we are miserable creatures, accompanied with weakness and infirmities, yet we shall have a happy state hereafter in another world.

2. Acquaint yourselves with the promises, make them the men of your counsel : Ps. cxix. 24, 'Thy testimonies also are my delight and my counsellors.'   We cannot think too often of them: Ps. cxix. 97, 'Oh how love I thy law ; it is my meditation all the day.'   If they have gained upon heart and affections, your thoughts will be more taken up with them, that you may not have them to seek in an hour of trial.   It is good to make them familiar to us.

3. Work them into the heart.   The promises are given us, not only that we may plead them with God in prayer, but that we may plead with ourselves.   As Paul, when he had laid down the privileges of believers: Rom. viii. 31, 'What shall we say to these things ?' so we should reflect upon ourselves if we have such great privileges, and such great hopes, Why do we not live more holily, and go about our duty more cheerfully ?   Soul ! what dost thou say to these things ?   So

David : Ps. xlii. 11, 'Why art thou cast down, O my soul ? and why art thou disquieted within me ? ' If God, Christ, and heaven be thine, and all the blessings of the covenant thine, why art thou so dejected ?

4. Make use of them in all your straits. Our wants lead us to the promises, which are as many and as particular as our wants ; the promises bring us to Christ, in whom they are all yea and amen, and shall be accomplished and fulfilled to us, as we are united to him, found in him, and one with him ; and Christ brings us to God as the fountain of grace, and there we turn them into prayers, put the bond in suit, plead with God, and show him his handwriting. Suit the promise to your exigence, and then go to God in the name of Christ with confidence. Our addresses to God take their rise from our wants : James i. 5, 'If any man lack wisdom, let him ask it of God.'

5. Observe how they are made good. You will have a double advantage hereby, for you will have a more clear ground for faith and thankfulness. It will show you what mercies come as blessings. It is not enough to observe nakedly how a mercy comes to us, but whether it comes by virtue of a promise, pleaded, trusted in, and believed by us. And it will strengthen our thankfulness ; they are blessings that come out of the womb of the covenant : Ps. cxxviii. 8, 'The Lord shall bless thee out of Zion.' It is observable in the text that the blessing is called 'the promise ;' it is not a blessing, nor so sweet to us, except it come by virtue of a promise. And by this means God's truth is more confirmed, which still keepeth the heart thankful and believing : Ps. ix. 10, 'They that know thy name will put their trust in thee, for thou, Lord, hast not forsaken them that seek thee.' You can give no instance to the contrary : it increaseth our trust for the future to observe what he hath done in time past ; what he hath spoken with his mouth he hath fulfilled with his hand. By this means your own faith will be confirmed, and you will invite others to trust in God ; we have had experience of the truth of his promises, and we shall be witnesses of his faithfulness to others.

SERMON XLVIII.

These all died in faith, not having received the promises, but having seen them afar off, and were persuaded of them, and embraced them, and confessed that they were strangers and pilgrims on the earth.—Heb. xi. 13.

I observed in the whole verse the trial of faith and the victory of faith. The trial of faith—'These all died in faith, not having received the promises;' that is, they went to the grave ere the blessings God had promised were accomplished. The victory of faith is set forth—

1. By a threefold act of faith in and upon the promises—'They saw them afar off, and were persuaded of them, and embraced them.'

2. By the effect and fruit of it in their lives and conversations—

' And confessed that they were strangers and pilgrims in the earth.'
This I come now to speak to.

'*Strangers and pilgrims.*' The notion of strangers and pilgrims I
opened to you in the 9th. verse. But how were these holy men
strangers and pilgrims? Men may be strangers and pilgrims two
ways: either in regard of condition, or in regard of disposition and
affection.'

1. In regard of condition, so all men are strangers. For that is our
home where we live longest. Now all men live longest in another
world; there they are for ever, and here but for a while. And as all
men are strangers, so they are pilgrims; they are hastening homewards as they yield to the decays of nature; and draw nearer to their
long home every day. Every man, both good and bad, is on a journey,
travelling homewards; all the difference is in the way that they take.
There are some that take the broad way that leadeth to destruction,
that as they grow in years they increase in sins, and so are going down
to destruction, and hastening to the chambers of eternal death; they
are strangers and pilgrims, going out of this world into a worse. But
others take the narrow way, and they are entering upon their everlasting happiness by degrees; here is not their home, they are going
to God and Christ.

2. In regard of affection and disposition; so these latter sort, the
children of God, are only strangers and pilgrims. The voice of wicked
men is, 'It is good to be here;' let God do with heaven what he
pleaseth, they are contented with their present portion; they would
not give their portion in this world for a portion in paradise. But
the children of God are strangers in affection; they count themselves so and they confess themselves so, for that is implied in their
confession, that it is not only their inward thoughts, but their outward
profession before all the world.

But how do they count themselves so?

[1.] By considering the shortness of their present abode, which
wicked men do not. There is no truth more obvious and common,
and yet none less thought of by wicked and carnal men, than the frailty
of our present condition. Wicked men have no firm dwelling upon
earth, but that is against their intention, their inward thought and
desire is that they may abide here for ever: Ps. xlix. 11, 'Their
inward thought is that their houses shall abide for ever, and their
dwelling-place to all generations.' They are strangers against their
wills; their abode is uncertain in this world, and they cannot help it,
and they govern their lives as if they should abide here for ever, and
were never come to a reckoning. David begs of God in Ps. xc. ver.
12, ' So teach us to number our days that we may apply our hearts
unto wisdom.' It is a lesson we learn by grace to know the shortness
and frailty of our present life; therefore they that have grace in their
hearts, and are taught of God, count themselves strangers in this sense
because they are sensible, and reckon upon it, that here they shall
abide but for a while.

[2.] By being unsatisfied with their present comforts. The children
of God would not abide here for ever if God would give them leave.
It is good to be here, saith a worldling; here is not our rest, saith a

child of God: Micah ii. 10, 'Arise ye, and depart, for this is not your rest.' They cannot sit down contented; if the Lord should give them the world for ever without the enjoyment of himself, this cannot satisfy them; they are strangers in disposition and affection, they desire and groan to be elsewhere. It is a grief to a wicked man to think of a departure, and to be taken off from present things, from sucking the dugs of worldly consolation.

[3.] Because they have another inheritance to expect, they have a home to go to. He that hath no home is nowhere a stranger, wherever he is. Wicked men are only strangers in regard of their unsettled abode in this world; they have a long home, but they have no inheritance to expect; they are sure to go out of the world, but they are not sure to go to heaven, and so they are strangers, but not pilgrims. But the children of God have a home which they expect, something beyond the present life, therefore they are strangers and pilgrims; they know and are sensible that these things are but short in continuance, and they cannot satisfy; that there are better things to be had, a better portion in another world, which will satisfy: Ps xvii. 15, 'I shall be satisfied when I awake with thy likeness.' They must live here a while, and then go down into the grave and sleep for a while; but when they awake, then they shall have enough.

Three points I shall observe from the words.

Doct. 1. That true believers confess themselves to be strangers and pilgrims in the world.

They count heaven their home, and the world a strange country. Faith makes them to count themselves strangers and pilgrims in the present world. I showed you in the other verse how christians are pilgrims in the world. Here I shall show two things—(1.) The reasons why believers account themselves so; (2.) The influence that faith hath upon this work.

First, The reasons why believers account themselves so. Partly as they look upon heaven, and partly as they look upon the world.

1. In respect of heaven, they count that their home, and that for these reasons—(1.) Because thence they are born; (2.) There lies their inheritance; (3.) There are all their kindred; (4.) There they abide longest.'

2. In respect of the world. As they consider what heaven is, so they consider what the world is, and therefore they cannot count it their home. The world is Satan's walk, the devil's circuit, where their father's enemy reigns: Job ii. 2, 'And the Lord said unto Satan, From whence comest thou? And Satan answered the Lord, and said, From going to and fro in the earth, and from walking up and down in it.' It is a place that is defiled with sin: Isa. xxiv. 5, 'The earth is defiled under the inhabitants thereof, because they have transgressed the laws, changed the ordinance, broken the everlasting covenant.' It is a hard thing to walk up and down and keep ourselves unspotted in such a place as the world is. The earth is given to the children of men: Ps. cxv. 16, 'The heaven, even the heavens, are the Lord's; but the earth hath he given to the children of men.' It is the slaughter-house and shambles of the saints: Rev. xviii. 24, 'In her was found the blood of

---

[1] See Sermons on Ps. cxix.

prophets and of saints, and of all that were slain upon the earth.' It is a receptacle not only for God's enemies and reprobate men, but for the very beasts, a place that beareth the marks of man's sin, therefore surely they cannot count it their home. They find ill entertainment in the world ; God in his providence orders it so that the world should be the more unkind to the saints that they might look after a better place. If the world did not vex them as it doth, possibly it might ensnare them, so that the world's hostility becomes their security ; as Paul found the world crucified to him, and therefore he was crucified to the world : Gal. vi. 14, ' The world is crucified to me, and I unto the world.' The injuries they receive here turn to their gain and mortification. God's children usually have the worst of it here in the world, and therefore they account themselves but strangers and pilgrims in the world.

Secondly, The influence that faith hath upon this work.

1. Faith shows the truth and worth of things to come. It presents another home, and a better home.

[1.] Faith presents another home : Heb. xi. 1, ' Faith is the evidence of things not seen.' We can see nothing but clouds, stars, and earth round about us ; faith looks into the invisible world where God is, and Christ at his right hand, and saints and angels round about him. Reason hath but a dark guess at these things ; faith openeth a light into the unknown world, where is our father's house, where is our elder brother, and the best of our kindred : Eph. i. 18, ' The eyes of your understandings being opened, that we may know what is the hope of his calling, and what the riches of the glory of his inheritance in the saints.' Unless our eyes are opened we cannot look into these things ; faith gives a knowledge of what is above the clouds, there it seeth him that is invisible.

[2.] Faith shows a better home. Faith values all things according to the presence of God ; it values all states and conditions as we enjoy God in them. Here in the world there is but little enjoyment of God : 2 Cor. v. 6, ' Whilst we are at home in the body we are absent from the Lord.' A christian is nowhere a stranger but where he is without God. Faith sees God in the world, but it sees that there is another manner of enjoyment of God without sin, and without sorrow, where there is no absence of God, and no clouding of his presence. A gracious heart is everywhere at home but where it wants God ; we could not be so much strangers here if we were not in a great part strangers to the comforts of his presence. If we could have our whole portion here, we should look no further ; we have, it may be, enough to support us, but not to satisfy us, but there we shall have all at full : Ps. xvii. 15, ' As for me, I will behold thy face in righteousness ; I shall be satisfied when I awake with thy likeness.' For the present we may behold God's face while we are engaged in acts of grace, and in the duties and exercises of religion, this is for our support ; but when awake, when we are got into the other world, we shall be satisfied. Here there are many clouds upon the face of God, and we provoke him to withdraw from us ; there we shall see him without a cloud in his face. Here we are weary even of gracious enjoyments ; there we shall enjoy him without satiety and weariness.

2. Faith gives us a right and title to what it sees : John i. 12, ' But as many as received him, to them gave he power to become the sons of God, even to them that believe on his name.' Faith is not only a spy to show us the land of promise, but it giveth us an interest in it ; a man cannot count anything his own till his interest be cleared ; madman call all their own that they see. Now faith gives us a joint-interest with Christ. A believer hath the whole privileges of the sons of God ; not only support and maintenance here, as an heir is maintained by his father in a foreign country, but he hath an interest in the inheritance : Rom. viii. 17, ' If children, then heirs, heirs of God and joint-heirs with Jesus Christ.' Faith does not only see that heaven is, and that it is better than earth, but that it is ours, and expects it as an inheritance. So James ii. 5, ' Hath not God chosen the poor of this world, rich in faith, and heirs of the kingdom which he hath promised to them that love him?' A believer may be a poor man in the world, but he is a prince in disguise.

3. In regard of the fruit of it; ' Faith works by love,' Gal. v. 6. Now true love carries the soul thither where the thing beloved is. Love is the poise of the soul, as everything tends to its centre. What is inclination in the creatures, instinct in the beasts, that is love in man. *Amor meus pondus meum.*

Use 1. For trial of your faith, dost thou behave thyself as a stranger and pilgrim? You may know it by these marks.

1. There will be a greater weanedness from the comforts of this life. Men that are altogether for present enjoyments, that labour, strive, contend and gape for earthly things, surely they do not look after heaven as their home. A christian is a stranger at home in his own family, where he hath many comforts about him : 1 Cor. vii. 31, ' And they that use the world, as not abusing it,' using all comforts as expecting a greater happiness, using them as a type, and as a motive, and as an help. As a type, that may put you in mind of a better and greater happiness. The enjoyment of temporal blessings should stir us up to a more serious consideration of heavenly things, as the prodigal's husks, when he was abroad, put him in mind of the bread in his father's house ; so if there be such comfort and sweetness in the world, the place of our trial, what is there in heaven, our father's house ? If the company of our relations be so pleasing and acceptable to us, what is it to be in our father's house for ever in the company of God and Christ ? As Fulgentius said when they showed him the beauty and splendour of Rome, If an earthly city be so glorious, what is the heavenly ? The cities of the Amorites put Abraham in mind of the city that had foundations: Heb. xi. 9, 10, ' By faith he sojourned in the land of promise as in a strange land, for he looked for a city which had foundations, whose builder and maker is God.' These are but the comforts of a strange place. You abuse the world when you forget home, use these things as typing out better ; if the creature be sweet, heaven is better. Use them as a motive to quicken you to glorify God, ' who hath given you all things richly to enjoy,' 1 Tim. vi. 17. The moon is never eclipsed but when at full. It is naught to kick with the heel, when we wax fat to be the worse for kindness. And then use them as a help, not a hindrance, as instruments of piety and charity, as a *viaticum* in our journey, and helps to a better life.

2. You will be taken off from worldly admiration.   This is a thing we are very prone to, to say, 'Happy is the people that is in such a case;' but if you are strangers and pilgrims, you will say, ' Happy is the people whose God is the Lord,' Ps. cxiv. 15.   If the heart were above, the world would not seem such a glorious thing.   The stars are great and vast bodies of light, but they seem to be but little spangles, because we here upon earth are at a great distance from them ; so if the heart were taken up with heaven, worldly admiration would cease, the honours, pleasures, and profits of the world would not tickle and affect us so much as they do.

3. You would not desire long life if you had the disposition of strangers and pilgrims.   A traveller would pass over his journey as soon as he can and hasten home.   A heathen could say, *Ex hac vita discedo tanquam ex hospitio, non tanquam ex domo,* &c.; I go out of this world as out of an inn, not as out of a dwelling-house ; this world is the place of our abode for a time, not of our constant habitation. They are sots that lie guzzling in an inn, and delight to be there, when they should hasten home ; so to desire long life because of carnal enjoyments is brutish.   To desire to stay here to do God service is gracious ; but to set up our rest here, and not to look after our home, this shows that we do not count ourselves to be strangers and pilgrims.

4. You will be making provision for another world, and laying up in store a good foundation against the time to come, that you may lay hold of eternal life, 1 Tim. vi. 19.

5. You will be hastening homewards more and more, by growing in holiness.   Every degree of holiness is a step towards heaven : Ps. lxxxiv. 7, 'They go from strength to strength, every one of them in Zion appeareth before God.'   It is an allusion to those that went up to the temple to worship, whither the males were to go three times in a year ; in the Hebrew it is from troop to troop, they strove how to overtake one another.   So he that is in the heavenly journey is growing in grace, and increasing every day more and more, till he comes to appear before God in the glorious temple that is above.   So the apostle, Phil. iii. 11, 12, ' If by any means I might attain unto the resurrection of the dead, not as though I had already attained, either were already perfect.'   And if they step out of the way they cannot rest till they get into their path again ; as a mariner at sea, that is driven back with winds, yet strives to make to his port again ; so is a christian every day getting homewards, getting some advantage over his corruptions, and perfecting holiness in the fear of God.

6. You will be often thinking of home.   Christ says, ' Where the treasure is, there will the heart be also,' Mat. vi. 21.   A believer to whom heaven is his home, will be longing, Oh! when shall I come to my country, to my elder brother, my kindred, Abraham, Isaac, and Jacob?   Oh, wo is me that I dwell in Mesech! here I am travelling, when shall I be at home ?   Do you send your desires and thoughts as harbingers to prepare a place for you ?   When the soul thus longs for the sight of God and Christ, we do as it were tell God we long to be at home.   As Paul, 2 Tim. iv. 8, ' Henceforth there is laid up for me a crown of righteousness.'   He was reckoning what a happy time it would be when the crown of righteousness should be set upon his head,

when he shall get home to his father's house, and enjoy his inheritance and the happiness God hath provided for him. By these marks you may inquire whether you have this faith, to count yourselves strangers and pilgrims here. [1]

Use 2. To stir us up to be strangers and pilgrims, put in your names among them that profess themselves to be so. Here—(1.) I shall offer you some motives to quicken you ; (2.) I will give you some directions.

1. To quicken you to this work consider these things.

[1.] It is the greatest judgment that can be inflicted upon you, to suffer you to take up your rest here, to be condemned to worldly happiness, and to look for no more. That is a sad doom : Luke xvi. 25, 'Son, remember that thou in thy lifetime receivedst thy good things.' That that is their choice, is their judgment : Ps. xvii. 14, 'From men of the world, who have their portion in this life, whose belly thou fillest with hid treasures ;' if you look for no other wages, you shall have no other. It is a punishment laid on them that depart from God, and leave the fountain of living waters for the puddles of this world : Jer. xvii. 13, 'All that forsake thee shall be ashamed, and they that depart from me shall be written in the earth, because they have forsaken the Lord, the fountain of living waters.' This is their judgment, to be written in the earth, that is, they shall be men great and famous, taken notice and accounted of here, but this is their portion. It were better for them to be followed with afflictions, to be driven to beg their bread, than to be written in the earth in a way of judgment ; better never have a day of rest and ease in the world, but still to be tossed to and fro in trouble, than to be condemned to worldly felicity. God's children many times, by a just and merciful providence, have least of the world, because they have their portion elsewhere ; the world entertains them as a stepmother, that they may look after their own mother Jerusalem, that is above. But when God suffers men to be great and prosperous in the world, and to enjoy worldly comforts to the full, and this is all they are like to have, it is the heaviest judgment that can befall them. Therefore what reason have you to put in your names among them that profess themselves strangers and pilgrims, though you are in your best estate, and live in the midst of peace and tranquillity, and worldly delights flow in with great abundance, yet remember, I am but a stranger and pilgrim here.

[2.] If you had the world at will, you have no reason to take up your rest here, because the happiness of this world is short, unsatisfactory, and not perfective. It is short, we are mortal, and all things about us have their mortality, and many times these things are more fading than we are. Many a man outlives his happiness, as the stalk may remain when the flower is gone ; but if not, we are mortal, and must flit into the other world, whether we will or no. The world thrusteth us from itself by miseries, and at last by death ; then there is a violent ejection ; we hang upon it though we are thrust from it, as Lot was loth to go out of pleasant Sodom till the angel pulled him out, Gen. xix. 15. When we stick in the earth, God comes to pluck us up. Why should we set our hearts on this world, and like foolish birds build a nest, when to-morrow we must be gone ? And it is not satis-

[1] See sermon on Ps. cxix.

factory, our souls were made for God, and cannot be satisfied without God. When we enjoy most still we want something; as Noah's dove could not find a place for the sole of her foot, till she came back to the ark. One thing or other is still wanting, how little do we find of what we expected; when we come to enjoy the world, we see the error of our esteem. If we would make use of our own disappointments, certainly it would wean us more from worldly comforts; especially if we would but consider how unsatisfactory they are in death: what will all this world then profit us? Job xxvii. 8, 'What is the hope of the hypocrite, though he hath gained, when God taketh away his soul?' And then they are not perfective, they can add no value to the soul. Who would dig for iron with mattocks of gold? The soul is better than all the world; we were not made for the world but the world for us. The world may make us worse, but it cannot make us better; and it is a very hard matter to keep ourselves from being worse by the world. All the riches, honours, and profits of the world cannot endue thy person with any true good. That is good which maketh us good, so doth grace whereby there is a conformity between us and the chiefest good: James i. 27, 'Pure religion and undefiled before God and the Father is this, to visit the fatherless and widows in their affliction, and to keep himself unspotted from the world.' It is the hardest matter to use the world and not to be defiled by it, and therefore let us seek out another home.

[3.] You have higher and better things revealed to you. If we had no other things to look for, then we might take up our abode here, and satisfy ourselves, and take our fill of what the world yields; but there are higher things, and they are revealed to us. Let thine eye convince thy soul; look upon the aspectable heavens, they are the most glorious part of the creation; and if the under part of the pavement is so glorious, what is the inner court, the holy of holies! And these are revealed to us as hereafter to be 'revealed in us,' Rom. viii. 18, and that both in body and soul. Now they are revealed to you as kept for you in heaven; if we had no other things to look for, it were good to be here; and they are not only revealed to our ears, but we have received our advance-money; a pawn, a pledge, an earnest, and first-fruits, all to make us say, 'Arise and let us depart, for this is not our rest,' Micah ii. 10.

[4.] These higher things are not only revealed to you, but you are fitted for them. We read not only of heavens being prepared for the saints, but of the saints being prepared for heaven. There is a divine nature given to us, and the new nature can never be satisfied, where we may sin and grieve God. Afflictions are contrary to our old nature and make the world a troublesome place; so sin is contrary to our new nature, for the new man seeketh a perfect state.

[5.] Consider Christ's choice: John xvii. 16, 'They are not of the world, even as I am not of the world.' Christ passed through the world to sanctify our place of service, but he left the world as a place not fit for him; if we would choose as Christ chose, we should be strangers here. Christ's judgment is better than ours; if the world had been worth anything, he would have chosen that kind of life. But he that was Lord of all, and had the fairest title to all that was in the world, yet behaved himself as a stranger, and had neither house nor home: Ps. lxix. 8, ' I am become a stranger unto my brethren, and an alien unto my mother's children.' The world frowned upon Christ as one that was not fit for their turn.

[6.] Consider, nature teacheth us this lesson, to look upward for our home. Look to the frame of man's body, not only to the constitution of his soul, but to the frame of his body; we do not go grovelling on the ground as beasts, nor are we stuck into the earth as trees. God hath given man an upright stature; his head, which is the seat of the senses, is placed next to heaven, to teach us that man should look up thither; and his feet are on the earth: Ps. viii. 6, ' Thou hast put all things under his feet.' A worldly man is like a man standing upon his head, spurning at heaven with his heels, and his head and heart fixed to the earth; or like worms that come out of the earth, they are bred there and creep on the ground, and then creep into it; so they are dwellers upon the earth, as the antichristian state is always called.

[7.] Consider the profit of being strangers and pilgrims on the earth.[1]

2. To direct you how you should do so.

[1.] As to the pleasures of the world, avoid fleshly lusts. Brutish affections are all for a present good; these weaken our desires of heaven, they cloud the eye, and deaden the heart, as the flesh-pots of Egypt made Israel to despise Canaan. Carnal lusts are a great hindrance. Men diet themselves for a race: 2 Cor. ix. 25, ' Every man that striveth for the mastery is temperate in all things ;' and ver. 27, ' I keep down my body, and bring it into subjection.'

[2.] As to the profits of the world take these directions—

(1.) Take heed of a resolution to be rich, of fixing this as your end and scope, making gain the business of your lives: 1 Tim. vi. 9, ' They that will be rich fall into temptation and a snare.' He doth not say he that is rich, for a godly man may through the blessing of God increase in this world's goods; but he that will be rich, the devil has you upon the hip when you make that your business and scope.

(2.) Grasp not at too much in the way of your calling; take heed of enlarging worldly desires: Isa. v. 8, 'Woe unto them that join house to house, and field to field, till there be no place, that they may be placed alone in the midst of the earth.' When men fill the head with cares, and the heart with sins, when they grasp at too much, and jostle out better things, then they offend. Some business is necessary to drain the spirits; whilst we are in the body, we cannot wholly mind spiritual employments; in great condescension God hath appointed diligence in our callings as a part of our work. Our journey to heaven lies not only through duties of religion, but through the duties of our callings; moderate labour is a help, not a hindrance; but then take heed that you be not immoderate to waste the vigour of your spirits, and jostle out better things.

(3.) If gain come in but slowly, be content with God's allowance. A little will serve the turn for a *viaticum* for our journey to help us to heaven: 1 Tim. vi. 7, 8, 'For we brought nothing into the world, and it is certain we can carry nothing out; and having food and raiment, let us be therewith content;' it is enough for our passage, we are

---

[1] See sermon on verse 9.

travelling to heaven, and when we come there the soul shall be filled
up as full as it can hold.   When we came into the world we were contented with a cradle, and when we go out we must be contented with a
grave; and whilst we are here, worldly goods serve only for a more
plentiful life.   David sums up worldly felicity: Ps. xvii. 14, 'Whose
belly thou fillest with thy hid treasure; they are full of children, and
leave the rest of their substance to their babes.'   They that have the
greatest portion in this life may have more variety of God's creatures
upon their tables and backs, and what they do not thus spend, the rest
of their substance they leave to their children.   Now a more plentiful
estate is but fuller of snares; and for our posterity, our children are
under a providence as well as we; they have but a journey to go, and
a little will serve their turn as well as ours, and when we die we leave
a God behind us to provide for them.   It is carnal confidence,—nay,
worse, it is ｡blasphemy and idolatry,—to think we can better provide
for them than God.   And therefore be contented with God's allowance,
such as comes in with moderate labour in your callings.

(4.) If God give abundance, take heed of carnal complacency: Ps.
lxii. 10, 'If riches increase, set not your heart upon them;' when you
rejoice in them, and grow proud of them, as if there were any real
addition to your worth, it is a sign you have them for your whole portion.   Remember you are to use them as God's stewards; if God give
you abundance, you must give an account of it how you lay it out.   If
you think you are lords and not stewards, you are at home.   The
abundance that God hath given you is but a larger trust: Luke xvi.
9, 'Make to yourselves friends of the mammon of unrighteousness, that
when ye fail, they may receive you into everlasting habitations.'   The
more you have, the greater advantages you have of doing good; and
when you die, you will be welcomed to heaven with the applauses and
suffrages of the poor saints.

[3.] Meditate often on the promises, they are our cordials in our
journey: Ps. cxix. 54, 'Thy statutes have been my songs in the house
of my pilgrimage.'   They are cordials to cheer us and strengthen us
in our way; and it is good to feed and strengthen the soul.   And they
are our antidotes against the infection of the world: 2 Peter i. 4,
'Whereby are given unto us exceeding great and precious promises,
that by these ye might be partakers of the divine nature, having
escaped the corruption that is in the world through lust.'   The world
is an infectious air, but the promises preserve us against the corruptions that are in the world through lust; and they refresh the divine
nature, and keep our hopes alive.

[4.] Enjoy as much of heaven as you can on the earth.
[5.] Go to God to circumcise the foreskin of your heart.
[6.] Get a clearer and more sensible interest in Christ.
[7.] Meditate on the happiness you shall have at home.
[8.] Prize the communion of saints.[1]

'They confessed.'   Abraham told the people of the land of Canaan,
Gen. xxiii. 4, 'I am a stranger and a sojourner with you;' Jacob told
Pharaoh: Gen. xlvii. 9, 'The days of the years of my pilgrimage are an
hundred and thirty years.   Few and evil have the days of the years of

---

[1] See these directions handled on Verse 9.

my life been, and have not attained unto the days of the years of the life of my fathers in the days of their pilgrimage.' It seems it was their general and open profession wherever they came; before idolaters they declared what they were and whither their hopes tended, though it laid them open to the scorn and hatred of those among whom they lived. So David: Ps. xxxix. 12, 'I am a stranger with thee, and a sojourner, as all my fathers were.' From hence we observe—

Doct. 2. That the making an open confession of the truth is a necessary duty: Rom. x. 9, 10, 'If thou shalt confess with thy mouth the Lord Jesus, and shalt believe in thine heart that God raised him from the dead, thou shalt be saved. For with the heart man believeth unto righteousness, and with the mouth confession is made unto salvation.' It is not enough that our hearts be right with God, but there must be a confession with the mouth.

Quest. But are we bound always to make this confession? Is it not said, Rom. xiv. 22, 'Hast thou faith? have it to thyself before God.'

Ans. 1. Profession of the main things of godliness is always necessary in those that have given up their names to Christ: Mark xvi. 16, 'He that believeth and is baptized shall be saved.' Now baptism is to be attended with an open profession of our faith: so Rom. x. 9, 'If thou shalt confess with thy mouth the Lord Jesus, and believe with thy heart that God raised him from the dead,' &c., which is the foundation of the christian faith, and the great article then in question. It is for the glory of God that his servants should own him, and for the profit of others.

2. When we are called thereunto, then we must witness a good confession. But when are we called thereunto? I answer, We are called by God and by men. (1.) By God: partly by his providence, and partly by a special impulse. Partly by his providence; when a good cause is like to be deserted for want of followers, then God seems by the voice of his providence to say, Who is on my side? Who? When the non-profession of the truth is equivalent with the denial of it. This was Daniel's case: Dan. vi. 10, 'Now when Daniel knew that the writing was signed, he went into his house, and his windows being open in his chamber toward Jerusalem, he kneeled upon his knees three times a day, and prayed and gave thanks before his God, as he did aforetime.' You will think he might have omitted the opening of his windows; but to have shut his windows would have been implicitly to have yielded to the unjust decree not to call on the God of Israel. Partly by the impulse of the spirit, for that doth determine the circumstances of a known duty; as Paul at Athens: Acts xvii. 16, 'His spirit was stirred in him when he saw the city wholly given to idolatry;' and Acts xviii. 5, 'Paul was pressed in spirit, and testified to the Jews that Jesus was Christ.' (2.) We are called thereunto by men, when they desire an account of our faith for their instruction: 1 Peter iii. 15, 'Sanctify the Lord God in your hearts, and be ready always to give an answer to every man that asketh a reason of the hope that is in you with meekness and fear.'

3. In many cases we must have faith to ourselves, and we are not bound to make possession of it; as for instance, when the cause we maintain may receive detriment by an unseasonable agitation, for every

thing hath its season ; or when others may receive detriment, and we are like to give offence to our weaker brethren : Rom. xiv. 1, ' Him that is weak in the faith receive ye, but not to doubtful disputations.' Our liberty in indifferent things is not to be urged to the prejudice of our brethren.   Again we are not to make a profession till we have matured and ripened our persuasion ; rash men that profess suddenly whatever they conceive to be right put themselves upon a double inconvenience, either of continuing in the defence of an error when their opinion is declared, or lie under the scandal of changeableness if they submit to the truth, which doth much weaken their testimony.

Doct. 3. Christians should more plainly discover that their journey lies heavenward.

Here I shall show you why they should do so, and how they should do it.

1. Why they should do so.   And that for these reasons—

[1.] It is for the glory of God that we should profess our hopes, that the world may know that we have wages that we expect in another world.   God would be ashamed to be called our God if we did not seek a country : Heb. iii. 6, ' Whose house are we if we hold fast the confidence, and the rejoicing of the hope, firm unto the end.'   We should not only comfort ourselves in our hopes but boast of them, and glory in our hopes that we have such a good master ; we may boast of our wages.

[2.] It is for the comfort and quickening of others.   A man is glad to meet with his own countrymen in a foreign land ; so when others see you ready to go with them to heaven, it is a great comfort and support to them, especially when we are talking and discoursing of heaven ' : 1 Thes. iv. 18, ' Wherefore comfort one another with these words.'   Good discourse conveys a warmth ; Saul in the company of prophets prophesieth.

[3.] It is for the reproof of the world, for the more explicit our profession is, the more are wicked men condemned ; the blind careless world is awed by these means.   Noah by building the ark, ' condemned the world,' Heb. xi. 7.   So when they see you so busy for heaven, it is a real reproof of their carelessness and wickedness.

2. How we should make this discovery.

[1.] By often speaking to one another : Mat. xxvi. 73, ' Surely thou art one of them, for thy speech bewrayeth thee.'   So the speech of God's people bewrays them.   Christ is often speaking of heaven, and of his Father's house.   The primitive christians were impeached of treason because they were often speaking of the happiness of that kingdom which they expected : John iii. 31, ' He that is of the earth is earthly, and speaketh of the earth.'   Worldly men will be talking of worldly things ; so they that are for heaven will be confessing and declaring that they seek a country, and they will be speaking to one another of these things.

[2.] By practice and conversation ; hereby you should make your confession more explicit.   Show what you are by your lives : Phil. iii. 20, ' For our conversation is in heaven, from whence also we look for the saviour, the Lord Jesus Christ.'   A christian's heart is not only above, but his life is above.   But how should we show forth this heavenly conversation ?   I answer—

(1.) By a contempt of worldly things. A self-denying christian showeth whither his journey lieth; they dare not take all advantages of growing great; they do not make it their business to be high in the world: Heb. xiii. 5, ' Let your conversation be without covetousness, and be content with such things as you have.' Covetousness is a sin in the heart, but many times it is seen in the life, and when it breaketh out, men shame their profession.

(2.) By our garb and behaviour; thus should you make a distinction between yourselves and the men of the world : Rom. xii. 2, ' Be not conformed to this world.' A christian is a man of another garb, he doth not put himself into the world's dress. He lives a distinct life from the world, and doth not do as the most do, so as the world wonders at them as we do at a foreigner that goes in a distinct garb and habit: 2 Peter iv. 4, ' Wherein they think it strange that you run not with them to the same excess of riot.'

(3.) By special holiness and strictness, that your lives and conversations should carry an express conformity and likeness to your hopes. 1 Thes. ii. 12, ' That ye would walk worthy of God, who hath called you unto his kingdom and glory.' You should discover what manner of hopes you have by the holiness, raisedness, and heavenliness of your lives and conversations.

Use 1. This may reprove those that are Nicodemites, christians too much in the dark. In times of persecution fear takes off from an open profession, but in times of profaneness shame is an hindrance; men are ashamed to own Christ, *coguntur esse viles, ne mali habeantur.* Men are ashamed of strict carriage and good discourse, they had rather be wicked than base and vile in the esteem of the world. No, rather say, If this be to be vile, I will be more vile; as David, 2 Sam. vi. 23, ' I will be yet more vile than thus'; and Paul, Rom. i. 16, ' I am not ashamed of the gospel of Christ.' If you are ashamed of Christ, he will be ashamed of you : Luke ix. 26, ' Whosoever shall be ashamed of me, and of my words, of him shall the Son of man be ashamed when he shall come in his own glory, and in the Father's, and of his holy angels.' Who would endure a servant that will be ashamed to own his master ? We should not be ashamed to be forward in godliness and religion, it is a sign we esteem as basely as the world doth of godliness. It argues a mighty depravation when our shame is there, where our confidence and our glorying should be ; you condemn hereby your profession, and justify the reproaches and slanders that wicked men cast on it. Christ despised the shame: Heb. xii. 2, ' Who for the joy that was set before him endured the cross, and despised the shame.' It argueth too great a desire of the love and praise of men : John xii. 42, 43, ' Nevertheless among the chief rulers also many believed on him; but because of the Pharisees they did not confess him, lest they should be put out of the synagogue ; for they loved the praise of men more than the praise of God.' Wicked men declare their sin openly: Isa. iii. 9, ' The show of their countenance doth witness against them, and they declare their sin as Sodom, they hide it not.' God is not ashamed of us though we be vile, base, and despicable: Heb. xi. 16, ' God is not ashamed to be called their God ;' and shall we be ashamed of God, and of his recompenses ? If dogs bark at you, they will do so at strangers, it is their kind.

Use 2. It condemns the backwardness of God's children, that they do no more talk of their hopes, and the glory of their kingdom, and of the world to come, that they may go hand in hand, and comfort and quicken one another in God's ways.

SERMON XLIX.

For they that say such things declare plainly that they seek a country.—
And truly, if they had been mindful of that country from whence
they came out, they might have had opportunity to have returned.
But now they desire a better country, that is, an heavenly : where-
fore God is not ashamed to be called their God, for he hath pre-
*pared for them a city.—*HEB. xi. 14–16.

IN these verses the apostle proves that the patriarchs had an eye to heaven, from their constant profession ; wherever they came, they were telling the world that they were strangers and pilgrims. He frames his argument thus : those that are strangers and pilgrims seek another country. This was not the country whence they came, for they might have returned thither when they would, but they look for another country, that is, an heavenly.

I shall go over these verses with brief hints.

First, From their language he concludes the disposition of their hearts. From whence we may observe this—

Doct. That a man should speak nothing, but what he really thinks.

A lie is naught everywhere, but especially in matters of religion ; and therefore I shall show—(1.) How naught it is in any case ; (2.) How exceeding naught it is to act a false profession of mortification and strictness in the ways of God when there is no such matter ; for that is the case in hand.

1. A lie is naught everywhere.

[1.] It is the right of our neighbour that we should speak the truth to him ; for speech is a kind of traffic and commerce, a commodity by which men trade one with another, and therefore in justice the commodity should be right. When you defraud your neighbour of his right, you are guilty of theft, as it is theft to give him counterfeit gold and silver for true gold and silver ; and so if you give him false words for true, you rob him of his right. As men, we are bound to speak the truth every one to his neighbour : Eph. iv. 25, ' Wherefore putting away lying, speak every man truth with his neighbour, for we are a members one of another.' When you speak that which is false, it is a violation of commerce ; for where there is no truth there is no trust, and where there is no trust there is no commerce, truth being the bond and foundation of human society.

[2.] A lie is the perversion of the order of nature. It is the office of the tongue to be the interpreter of the mind ; now if the interpreter of another man should take upon him to speak contrary to what he commands, this were a manifest wrong and disorder. So when the tongue speaks otherwise than the mind thinks, it is a great disturbance and deordination.

[3.] We resemble the devil in nothing so much as in falsehood and lies : John viii. 44, 'Ye are of your father the devil, and the lusts of your father ye will do ; he was a murderer from the beginning, and abode not in the truth. When he speaketh a lie, he speaketh of his own ; for he is a liar, and the father of it.' And on the contrary, truth is no small part of the image of God ; for he is called the God of truth, as Satan is the father of lies ; and truth is made to be one special effect of regeneration : Eph. iv. 24, 25, 'That you put on the new man, which after God is created in righteousness and true holiness. Wherefore putting away lying, speak every one truth with his neighbour.' The main thing that is wrought in regeneration is to make the heart perfect, upright ; and true regeneration doth not introduce a total perfection into the soul, but it introduces uprightness ; he that is born again is not without sin, but he is without guile : Col. iii. 9, 'Lie not one to another, seeing that ye have put off the old man with his deeds.' The old man is nothing but a bundle of deceits and crookedness ; the new man consists in truth and uprightness.

[4.] This is of consideration also, that God never dispensed with this precept. He hath upon special occasions dispensed with other commandments, and made a particular exception from a general law, but he never dispensed with the ninth commandment. God dispensed with the eighth commandment in the theft of the Israelites when they borrowed the jewels of the Egyptians ; he dispensed with the seventh commandment in the polygamy of the patriarchs ; he dispensed with the sixth commandment in the case of Abraham, when he bid him to offer Isaac ; he dispensed with the second commandment in Hezekiah's passover ; when they were not purified according to the preparation of the sanctuary, yet God allowed them to eat the passover : 2 Chron. xxx. 18, 'For a multitude of the people, even many of Ephraim and Manasseh, Issachar and Zebulun, had not cleansed themselves ; yet did they eat the passover, otherwise than it was written ;' but God never dispensed with the ninth commandment upon any pretence whatsoever ; a man must not lie for God : Job xiii. 7, 'Will you speak wickedly for God, and talk deceitfully for him ?' Because this commandment hath more in it of the justice and truth and immutable perfection of God than others.

[5.] By the light of nature, nothing is more odious than a lie. We love a just and true man, that is without guile, we acknowledge it a moral perfection ; but a lie among men is accounted the greatest disgrace. And nothing stirs up revenge and wrath more than the imputation and charge of a lie ; because it comes from slavish fear, and tendeth to deceit, both which argue baseness of spirit, and are contrary to the gallantry of a man, and to that moral equity which nature discovereth. Therefore nature disproves and taxeth it as an odious crime.

2. Especially a lie is odious in matters of religion, to pretend that we are not ; as to profess ourselves strangers and pilgrims when it is no such matter, this is very bad. Because it is in a weighty matter ; and the more weighty the matter is in which we lie and speak falsely,

the more heinous the lie ; for in a more weighty matter God is more appealed to, he is more challenged as a witness, and especially in the profession of religion, more than he is in acts of commerce between man and man.   Religion should check and restrain a lie, and therefore when religion itself is made a lie, it is a great evil.   It is an interpretative blasphemy : Rev. ii. 9, 'I know the blasphemy of them that say they are Jews and are not, but are the synagogue of Satan.'   To profess that we are the people of God when we are not is blasphemy. Why ? because it is an implicit denial of God's omnisciency, as if he could not see, and did not regard us ; for you do in effect say, If we can but carry it fair before men, we need care for no more ; there is no God to see us.

Use 1. Let us beware of all lying, especially of dissimulation of respect to God or men.   Let our words consent with our mind, and our mind with the thing itself.   To move you hereto, consider, a lie is most odious to God, it is reckoned among the things that are an abomination to him : Prov. vi. 16, 17, 'These six things doth the Lord hate, yea, seven are an abomination to him, a proud look, a lying tongue,' &c. A christian that loves God dares not yield to that which God so expressly hates ; he doth, as it were, hear God speak in his ears, Jer. xliv. 4, 'Oh, do not this abominable thing that I hate !'   And then it is a sin that shall not escape unpunished : Prov. xix. 5, 'A false witness shall not be unpunished ; and he that speaketh lies shall not escape.' God that is the judge of truth, that is appealed to as the great witness of all that is done in the world, he will reveal it to your shame.   Nay, God expects it from all you that fear his name ; he reckoneth upon it that you should be far from this evil : Isa. lxiii. 8, 'For he said, Surely they are my people, children that will not lie.'   Disappointment is the worst vexation.   When the Lord standeth upon his honour in your carriage, Well, I can trust them, they are a people that will not lie ; if you disappoint him, you do, as much as in you lies, make God a liar.[1]

Obj. But you will say, What needs all this ?   Speak to children to warn them of lying, or to heathens or profane persons that make no conscience of the truth.

Ans. Lying is a more general and common sin than we imagine, it is natural to us : Ps. lviii. 3, 'The wicked are estranged from the womb, they go astray as soon as they be born, speaking lies.' We suck in the deceitful old man with our milk ; nay, we brought him into the world with us.   There was a lie in our hearts long before there was a lie in our mouths.   And consider how little nature is subdued even in the best ; David prays, Ps. cxix. 29, 'Remove from me the way of lying, and grant me thy law graciously.' You shall find him tripping herein in his dissembling before Achish and the like.   Is there not a lying to God in public and private worship ?   In public worship, it was the complaint God took up against his people, Hosea xi. 12, 'Ephraim compasseth me about with lies, and the house of Israel with deceit.'   How often do we show love with our mouths, when our hearts are at a distance from God ; as it was said of the Israelites, their hearts were in Egypt, when their bodies were in the wilderness : Acts vii. 39, 'In their hearts they turned back again into Egypt ;' so here, we prattle

---

[1] See this subject handled at large, Ps. cxix. 29.

words without sense and spiritual affection; and what is this but to compass God with lies, when the heart is gone after and taken up with vanity? And then in private worship; how often in confession of sins do we lie to God! not that we can speak worse of ourselves than we do deserve, but we do not believe that is true which we confess; for if we did but confess half so much to a man who is but our fellow-creature, and hath but a drop of indignation against sin, how should we be ashamed! Thus we often compass God with lies in confession. And then in prayer we pray, but as if we would not be heard. Conscience enlightened tells us what we should pray for, but the carnal heart retracts our prayers; as Austin, when he prayed against his lusts, Lord, give me strength against my carnal affections, *sed noli modo*, do not yet, Lord; he was loth to have his requests granted. We pray out of course, and that is but a lie. As children shoot away their arrows, and never look after them; so we throw away our prayers, and never mind what comes of them. If a man make a supplication to the king, he would be hearkening what answer the king gave; so if we prayed in earnest, we would be looking after our prayers. And then we give thanks without meltings of heart. Custom and natural light tells us something must be done in this kind, but how hard a matter is it 'to draw nigh to God with a true heart!' Heb. x. 22. Though we cannot draw nigh to God with a sinless heart, yet we should with a sincere heart, and come without guile into his presence. Lies in worship are worst of all; a lie in commerce between man and man is bad; a lie about worship, to pretend what we are not, is worse; but a lie in worship, this is to dare and mock God to his face, and God will not be mocked. Again, would we not be accounted better than we are? Where is the man that would be thought as ill as he hath cause to think of himself? We storm if others should but speak half so much of us as we speak of ourselves to God. Again, doth not rash suspicion make us speak worse of others than they deserve? Do not we take up reports of others without search, and out of envy blaze them abroad? In much talk do not unworthy expressions drop from us that cannot be justified? Are there not many rash promises that we make to God which it may be may suit with present sense, but all things are not considered: Ps. lxxviii. 36, 37, ' Nevertheless they did flatter him with their mouth, and they lied unto him with their tongues; for their heart was not right with him, neither were they steadfast in his covenant.' All these things show that we had need to pray with David, Ps cxix. 29, ' Remove from me the way of lying.' Surely, though you should set aside gross lying in a way of testimony, and with an intent to deceive, yet you see there are many ways wherein we may be guilty of lying; indeed seldom are our speeches the image of our minds, and so we are guilty of this sin which is so odious to God, so contrary to the new nature, and such a blemish to the profession that we have taken upon ourselves.

Secondly, The next thing we learn hence is the use of consequences. That doctrine, that is not expressed in plain words of scripture, yet is deduced thence by just consequences, is a scripture doctrine. Our Lord proves the resurrection by a consequence: Mat. xxii. 31, 32, ' But as touching the resurrection of the dead, have ye not read that which was spoken unto you by God, saying, I am the God of

Abraham, and the God of Isaac, and the God of Jacob ?   God is not the God of the dead, but of the living.'

Use 1. We learn that in all controversies and the decision of cases genuine deductions are not an obscure proof. The apostle saith of these patriarchs, they ' declare plainly that they seek a country.' The Arians reject the consubstantiality of Christ and the trinity because they are not scripture words.   The Donatists called Augustine not the christian, but dialecticum, the logician, because he argued from consequences in disputing with them.   And so nowadays in the controversy about infant baptism, they require plain scripture for it ; we prove it by consequence, that they are in covenant, and therefore they have a right to the seal of the covenant ; they are disciples, members of the church, and therefore have a right to the privileges of the church. And so for the sabbath ; we must not instruct God how to set down his mind. The Jews say, If Christ had been the true Messiah, he would have come in such a way as all his own countrymen might have known him ; so will men say, Had this been the mind of God, it would have been more plainly and expressly revealed in scripture ; thus will foolish men give laws to God. If a doctrine can be deduced from scripture, it is as much as if it were in express words of scripture.

Use 2. We learn hence that in reading of the scriptures we are to mark not only what is spoken, but what may be thence inferred. It is notable that Jesus Christ taxeth the Sadducees as ignorant of the scriptures, because they were ignorant of the consequences of scripture : Mat. xxii. 29, ' Ye do err, not knowing the scriptures nor the power of God.' Though they knew the letter of the scripture, yet they did not know the consequence and import of it. A christian is bound, and must aim at it more and more, to know all the doctrines revealed in the scripture, and all the consequences of them. You have reason given you to meditate, to argue and debate matters, otherwise how can we resolve cases and try spirits ? 1 John iv. 1, ' Beloved, believe not every spirit, but try the spirits, whether they are of God.' We are to draw inferences of faith and practice from what we read in the scriptures, by comparing scriptures with scriptures.

Thirdly, Let us come to the apostle's argument, 'they seek a country ; ' it must be that whence they came, or else an heavenly country. But it was not the country from whence they came, therefore it must be an heavenly country. Mark, the apostle knew but two places of residence for the saints in the old testament, either in this life on earth, or in the life to come in heaven. From this distribution, it must be in earth or heaven. Learn this point—

Doct. That there are but two places of residence for the saints, either the place of exercise, that is here upon earth, or the place of their reward or recompense, and that is in heaven.

From the beginning of the world to this day so it has been, there is no third place.   The papists, besides heaven, hell, and purgatory, have two vaults ; they have their *limbus patrum*, some obscure cabins for the faithful that died before Christ came in the flesh, where they are kept as in a dark prison, out of heaven, yet without torments, as they are without blessedness : and they have their *limbus infantum* for those that died without baptism.   Others imagine there are *beatœ sedes, et secreta animarum receptacula,* blessed seats, and secret receptacles and places for souls, besides the heaven of heavens, where the just remain till the day of judgment. But all this is without scripture. Here the patriarchs expected an heavenly country; that their souls should immediately go to God, and their bodies should be raised in due time. But let us come to the proof and making out of this argument; he proves the first, that Mesopotamia, or Ur of the Chaldees, the place from whence they came, was not their country, 'for, saith he, verse 15, 'Truly if they had been mindful of that country whence they came out, they might have had opportunity to have returned.' From whence we may observe two things—

Doct. 1. That God's children do not contemn the world out of necessity, but out of choice.

They might have returned if they had a mind; they were not necessitated to stay here, but it was their wise choice to follow and obey God. Many do despise riches and greatness in the world because they cannot attain to it; as the fox in the fable did the grapes that he could not reach, or as ignorant persons despise learning, because they cannot attain to it. Some may speak contemptibly of these things out of envy. Many do not affect great things because they do not lie within their grasp and reach; it is not every man that can rationally aspire to be a ruler. So many think they could prefer a naked Christ before all the world, because they have not an offer and a temptation; therefore the trial of your hearts is when the temptation cometh: Ps. lxii. 10, 'If riches increase, set not your heart upon them.' Can you then contemn them, and think meanly of them? Are they as low and base things in your esteem as when you were in your deep poverty? How are you to the temptations that are incident to your rank and station? Every one is apt to seek great things for himself as far as his grasp reacheth. A thousand pounds to some kind of persons may not be so great a matter as an hundred pounds to others. Men think that because they do not aim at such vast and great worldly profits as others have, therefore they are not worldly; but the reason is because these great things are not within their grasp and reach. The devil doth not come to all, as he did to Christ, to offer him all the kingdoms of the earth; some will accept of less with thanks. The devil suiteth his temptations to men's conditions, and the opportunities that are put into their hands, and all the trial is, how you behave yourselves as to these temptations that you meet withal. In all this I do not deny, but that outward providence is an help, and there is much of the care of God seen in removing the temptation, as well as in abating the affection; as Paul took notice of God's providence: Gal. vi. 14, ' The world is crucified unto me, and I unto the world.' He observed not only the deadness of his own heart to the world, but the world's frowning upon him, and its uselessness to him. We are to take notice of the love of providence, as well as of the power of grace. It is a mercy to be acknowledged that we have not the temptations or the opportunities to depart from God that others have. But then the people of God are apt to reflect upon their own carnal disposition, and to say, Surely I have a heart as bad as others, and should have been as bad as others; if God did not shut me up, and keep me low, my heart would be high, carnal and proud as well as others. To apply this—

Use 1. Do not reckon the absence of a temptation to be grace. Grace is seen in the conflict, when you have an opportunity to start from him, and yet your hearts keep close to God; the opportunity is present, but grace forbids. Joseph had not only a temptation, but an opportunity, but grace resisted it: Gen. xxxix. 9, 'How can I do this great wickedness, and sin against God?' These patriarchs might have had an opportunity to return; nothing kept them back, but the command of God. *Esse bonum facile est, ubi quod vetat esse, remotum est*—It is easy to be good when we cannot be otherwise, or when all temptations to the contrary are out of the way. All the seeming good that is in many, they owe it to the want of a temptation, and to the want of an opportunity of doing otherwise. Some have not the wit to be heretics, nor an estate to be luxurious, or the like.

Use 2. It showeth us the evil of those that can break through the restraints of providence; when their way is hedged up with thorns, yet they will find a path. As the Lord complains, Isa. xxvi. 10, 'In the land of uprightness they will deal unjustly;' they will stumble when stumbling-blocks are removed out of the way; they be proud in deep poverty, wicked in godly families, sin, when the awe of parents should restrain them. They have not an opportunity and an occasion to sin, but they make one, and draw iniquity with cart-ropes. Where the channel is cut, the water followeth easily; so where there is an opportunity the heart runs out to sin; this is sinful; but when men overthrow the banks and cut down the dam, that corrupt nature might find an issue or course, it is exceeding sinful.

Use 3. It presseth us to a voluntary mortification, in the fulness of all things to be strangers and pilgrims; not upon necessity, but upon reasons of conscience, as it was with these here in the text. David professeth himself to be a stranger and a pilgrim, not only when he was hunted like a partridge upon the mountains, but when he was in his palace, and in his best estate. We are not to renounce our comforts, and throw away God's blessings; but we are to renounce our carnal affections. We cannot get out of the world when we please, but we must get the world out of us. It is a great trial of grace to refuse the opportunity; it is the most difficult lesson to learn how to abound, more difficult than to learn how to want, and to be abased; to have comforts, and yet to have the heart weaned from comforts; not to be necessarily mortified, but to be voluntarily mortified and by choice. We use to say, Such an one would do well to be a lord or a lady, when we see him proud, and masterful, and dainty in fare and apparel. Oh it is a harder matter than we are aware of, when we have an opportunity to be evil, worldly and carnal, not to be evil, worldly and carnal, but in the fulness of all things to be as if we had nothing; to possess all things as if we possessed not, as the apostle speaks and directs, 1 Cor. vii. 30, 31, 'That they that rejoice be as though they rejoiced not; and they that buy as though they possessed not; and they that use the world as not abusing it.'

Again, I observe the constancy of these patriarchs; they kept constant to their purpose, and were unmindful of their country from whence they came. They were hated, maligned by the inhabitants of the land, burdened by the envy of the natives; they could not dig a well, but they were fain to strive for it; but though they had these hard conditions, yet they were not mindful of that country from whence they came, because God had called them out of it. This affords a second doctrine.

Doct. 2. When we have renounced the world and sin, we must take heed of an hankering mind after these things again.

Drawing back is very hateful to God: Heb. x. 38, ' If any man draw back, my soul shall have no pleasure in him.' This is a dog's nature, to lick up his vomit; it is a swine's trick, to return to wallowing in the mire : 2 Peter ii. 22, ' It is happened unto them according to the true proverb, The dog is turned to his own vomit, and the sow that was washed to her wallowing in the mire.' Christ tells us, Luke ix. 62, ' No man having put his hand to the plough, and looking back, is fit for the kingdom of God.' We shall never be fit for Christ, or any good and excellent use, unless we be unmindful of what we have left for Christ, and hold on our course. The crab that goes backward, was an unclean creature under the law.

Use. This note is useful in public reformations and private conversation.

1. In public reformations. Israel was ready to return to Egypt when they were sensible of the difficulties and inconveniences of the wilderness. So because reformation is clogged with many inconveniences, sottish people wish for their old times of mass and matins, and hanker after the flesh-pots of Egypt. But these patriarchs were of another temper, they were unmindful to return, though they had inconveniences where they were, and an opportunity to go back. So those carnal Jews : Jer. xliv. 17, 18, ' We will certainly do whatsoever thing goeth out of our own mouth, to burn incense unto the queen of heaven, and to pour out drink-offerings unto her, for then had we plenty of victuals, and were well, and saw no evil. But since we left off to burn incense unto the queen of heaven, and to pour out drink-offerings unto her, we have wanted all things, and have been consumed by the sword and by the famine.' Times of reformation are usually thus encumbered. Oh ! but let us not return thither from whence we came.

2. In private conversation ; when we renounce the devil, the world, and the flesh, we should not retract our vows. One said, he would launch out no farther into the deeps of religion than he might get to shore again. Oh, take heed of such a spirit ! when you are embarked with Christ, take heed of looking back ; forget your father's house, and the flesh-pots of Egypt. To this end count the charges when you give up your names to Christ. When a man is to build, he makes a good allowance ; and as long as he keeps within his allowance, he never grudges it ; but when that is exceeded, it grieves him to disburse more. Oh, make the Lord a good allowance, that you may not go back, but follow him fully ! This is the first part of the apostle's argument, the negative part of it, ' They were unmindful of that country from whence they came, though they had opportunity to return.'

But now as to the positive part of the proof—' But now they desire a better country, that is, an heavenly.'

Doct. It is not enough to despise this world, but we must have our hearts carried forth after better things ; we must believe and desire a better country.

Many out of a slight temper may renounce the world, their corruptions do not lie that way, they have not a genius fit for scraping and heaping up wealth. Others are of a prodigal humour, and may abhor baseness and forbid sparing, but they are not heavenly; they despise but a piece of the world, not the whole world; they are taken with worldly pleasures, though they regard not worldly profits; their hearts are not carried forth to better things.

You may clearly discern whether the temper of your hearts be right with God by these two marks—Do you renounce the world? and do you look after better things?

1. Do you renounce the world for God's sake? But you will say, Do you persuade us to voluntary poverty? possibly some may be full of fears and doubts concerning their estate, because they prosper in the world, when they consider the condition of the patriarchs who left all at the call of God. How are we therefore to renounce the world? I answer, We must not renounce the good things of this life but upon God's call, for otherwise we should cast away the blessings of the covenant. Temporal blessings are adopted and taken into the covenant as well as spiritual mercies: 1 Tim. iv. 8, 'Godliness is profitable unto all things, having promise of the life that now is, and of that which is to come.' To run into voluntary poverty were to despise God's bounty. But what then is that renouncing of the world that is required of every christian? It lies in four things.

[1.] We must be contented with that portion of worldly things which comes to us in a fair way of providence, without carking, and caring, and turmoiling ourselves about the things of the present life; we must be satisfied with our Father's allowance and blessing: Heb. xiii. 5, 'Be content with such things as you have.' But when men are greedy after worldly things, this is to seek the world. Whatever comes to us in a way of obedience and dependence upon God, we must be contented with as our portion.

[2.] We must avoid the corruption that is in the world. Take heed you be not corrupted by the world; use it as if you used it not; let not your hearts be entangled with the world: 1 Cor. vii. 31, 'And they that use the world as not abusing it.' Though you must not throw away God's common blessings out of your houses, yet let them not engross the heart. If we do not get out of the world, we must get the world out of us, that it may not encroach upon God's rights: Ps. lxii. 10, 'If riches increase, set not your heart on them.'

[3.] We must get a sanctified use of the things of the world. Then we have such a sanctified use of them, when they make us love God more, and not less. That which comes from love causeth love; when the blessings of this world are given us from God in love to us, they work up the heart to love God again, and then have we a sanctified use of them.

[4.] We must be willing to quit them upon God's call, or upon the just reasons of religion. This is to renounce the world as these patriarchs did. But when doth God call us? Partly, when otherwise we cannot keep a good conscience; when we cannot hold the world, and maintain the conscience of our duty to God; as Joseph left his coat to keep a good conscience, Gen. xxxix. 15. Partly, when God offers us occasions of charity : 1 Tim. vi. 17, 18, ' Charge them that are rich in this world, . . . that they do good, that they be rich in good works, ready to distribute, willing to communicate,' that is, to those that are in need, when God offers us opportunity.

2. Do you look after better things ?   But how shall we discover that ?   Observe here, by what words these patriarchs' respect to their heavenly country is described : they looked for a country, they desired a country, they sought a country, and they declared plainly that they sought a country.   Now all these things do discover a heavenly mind and heart.

[1.] They look for a country ; so verse 10, it is said of Abraham, ' He looked for a city which hath foundations, whose builder and maker is God.' It noteth an actual expectation of blessedness to come, such as stirreth up serious and frequent thoughts of it ; not a glance only, such as is forced upon us, or cometh into the mind by chance, but a constant serious expectation, an entertaining of the soul with the thoughts of a blessedness to come.   If you look for a city as they did, you will be entertaining and solacing your souls with the hopes of it.

[2.] They desire a country ; they are groaning and longing, Oh, when shall it once be that I shall come to my country ? here I am but a stranger, wandering up and down, when shall I come home to my father's house, to my elder brother, to the rest of the family, and to my heavenly inheritance ?   When the children of Israel had tasted of the grapes of Canaan, how did they long for the soil where they grew ! a man cannot have the first-fruits of the Spirit, but he will be waiting and groaning for the adoption : Rom. viii. 23, ' We ourselves, which have the first-fruits of the Spirit, even we ourselves groan within ourselves, waiting for the adoption, to wit, the redemption of our body.' A man that hath had a taste of heaven in the joys of the Spirit, his heart is always groaning, Oh, when shall I come to the full of my inheritance ? they are always waiting for the happy time when their inheritance shall fall into their hands.

[3] They seek a country : Heb. xiii. 14, ' We have no continuing city, but we seek one to come.'   It implies that it must be our great aim, and that the business of our lives must be to get to heaven, to be at home at our Father's house, to be there where God and Christ are. It must be the great aim and scope of our lives, next to the glory of God, and the great work and business of our lives.   Provision and supports for the present life are but our by-work ; but to be fitting and preparing ourselves to get home, this is the great business and employment of a christian in this life.   More particularly, our great work is to be getting dispositions for heaven and evidences for heaven.   To be getting dispositions for heaven, to be meet to live above : Col. i. 12, ' Giving thanks to the Father, who hath made us meet to be partakers of the inheritance of the saints in light.'   Before God calls us hence, and translates us to heaven, he first makes us meet for it.   As Esther, when she was chosen to be bride to Ahasuerus, she was to accomplish the months of her purification, to purify herself with odours and sweet oils, Esther ii. 12. So the time of our lives is as the months of our purification, and our great business is to get a fit frame of heart, to live above among the glorified spirits.   As Christ's business in

heaven is to prepare heaven for us, so our business on earth is to prepare and fit ourselves for heaven, to be providing and trimming our
lamps against the bridegroom comes. So, to get evidences for heaven
as well as dispositions—to get it certified and ratified to our souls every
day more and more, this is a christian's employment—'To be laying
up a good foundation against the time to come, that we may lay hold
of eternal life,' 1 Tim. vi. 18 ; to get his evidences more cleared up
every day, that we may take hold of eternal life, that is, that we may
seize upon it as a man doth upon his own right and portion.

[4.] They declare plainly that they seek a country. There was not
only a verbal, but a real confession ; for by dwelling in tents they did
more openly acknowledge their desires of another country. They did
not go up and down, and tell men that they were strangers and pilgrims;
but by dwelling in these poor movable habitations, when the Canaanites
dwelt in cities, and built houses, hereby they declared to all that lived
about them, that they looked for another country. So, christians, your
business is to declare plainly that your journey lies towards heaven ;
you should discover your hopes more in your lives than you do, by
walking suitably and answerably thereunto, and as those that are not
ashamed of their country, that so you may draw in others to be companions with you in your journey to heaven. When all your cares,
griefs, desires and endeavours are for civil and carnal things, you
declare plainly that you savour of the world; but when the heart is
taken up with better things, and the face of your conversation lies
another way, then you declare plainly your journey is for heaven. And
this is it which is meant everywhere by walking worthy of God and
worthy of our vocation, that is, answerably and suitably to, and becoming your great hopes, and that kingdom and glory to which God hath
called you. A christian should not live unsuitably to his hopes, but
should discover them in his life, that all that see him may know that his
heart and his hopes are above, and that God hath called him to his
kingdom and glory : 1 Thes. ii. 12, ' That you would walk worthy of
God, who hath called you unto his kingdom and glory.' This will
discover whether you have a heavenly mind, yea or no.

SERMON L.

*Wherefore God is not ashamed to be called their God, for he hath
prepared for them a city.*—HEB. xi. 16.

WHAT is the meaning of this—' God is not ashamed to be called their
God ? ' This shame might be supposed to arise from the unworthiness
of these patriarchs, or from the slenderness of their reward.

1. From the contemptibleness and unworthiness of these patriarchs ;
and so the sense would be that God is not ashamed to abase himself to,
put honour upon his servants that honour him. Abraham, and Isaac
and Jacob were persons of contemptible appearance, a few poor wan-

dering men, of small power and possessions, in comparison of the Amorites, who were lords of the soil and country where they were; and yet the great God of heaven and earth was not ashamed to take his title from them, and to be known in the world as the God of Abraham, the God of Isaac, and the God of Jacob. Or else—

2. From the slenderness of their present condition and reward which he had given them. If Canaan had been all the reward which they had, and if God had no better thing to give them, he would have been ashamed to be called their God; if we had had no other recompense, but what he gave to Abraham, Isaac, and Jacob in this life, it were a poor business. But now when they sought a heavenly country, God can own the title with honour, that he is the God of Abraham, and the God of Isaac, and the God of Jacob. It is allurement enough to draw in the world to him, that they shall have the blessing of Abraham, and shall have such a country as Abraham has, and that they shall sit down with Abraham, Isaac, and Jacob in the heavenly kingdom. Hence it is that Christ proveth the resurrection from this title: Mat. xxii. 32, 'I am the God of Abraham, and the God of Isaac, and the God of Jacob.' The argument standeth on three feet.

[1.] To be a God to any is to be a benefactor, and to do them good. The tenor of the covenant on God's part is expressed by this, I will be their God; the tenor of the covenant on our part is expressed by this, They shall be my people. Now God cannot be called the God of any, but he must do them good.

[2.] To be a God to any is to be an eternal benefactor, not only in this life, but after this life was ended, that he had benefits for them in the other world. For it was after the death of the patriarchs that God assumed this title: Exod. iii. 6, 'I am the God of thy father, the God of Abraham, the God of Isaac, and the God of Jacob.' This argues that there shall be an eternal communication of glory to them.

[3.] This covenant was made with the whole man; not only with their souls, but with their bodies. As whole God in the covenant is made over to Abraham, so God will be a God to the whole of Abraham; and therefore he bore circumcision, which was the mark of the covenant, on his body. Now if Abraham, Isaac, and Jacob had perished in their death, it had been a dishonourable thing for God to be called their God; and therefore as the soul hath a blessed immortality, so the body shall have a glorious resurrection.

By opening this place our text will receive some light. If the patriarchs had nothing to look for but what they had in this world, it had been a dishonourable thing for God to be called their God and their benefactor; but now he hath prepared for them a city. It is called a city with allusion to the walled towns of the Canaanites, they were not great lords as the Amorites, nor possessors of towns and cities, but they had a city above.

Obs. 1. Those that renounce the world for God's sake shall be no losers.

These patriarchs left their country, and wandered up and down at God's command; they had no settled abode, but God had prepared for them a city. Levi had no portion among his brethren, but God was his portion: James ii. 5, 'Hearken, my beloved brethren, hath not God chosen the poor of this world, rich in faith, and heirs of the kingdom which he hath promised to them that love him?'

Obs. 2. Heaven is fitly set forth under the notion of a city.

Heaven is expressed by several metaphorical names in scripture. Sometimes it is called paradise, or a garden of delight: 2 Cor. xii. 4, 'How that he was caught up into paradise, and heard unspeakable words;' and that you might not think he meant an earthly paradise, he calls it 'the third heaven,' ver. 2. Sometimes it is called a house: John xiv. 2, 'In my Father's house are many mansions.' Sometimes it is called a kingdom: James ii. 5, 'Heirs of the kingdom which he hath promised to them that love him.' And here it is called a city. All these notions do help one another. For the pleasantness of it, it is called a garden or paradise; but because in a garden there is not a fixed abode, therefore it is called a house. But a house may be too strait for the great number of the inhabitants, and therefore it is called a city; but a city hath not that splendour in it that a court hath, therefore it is called a kingdom. So that for the pleasantness it is called paradise; to note our abode and rest, a house; for the amplitude of it, a city; for the splendour of it, a kingdom. Take it again: in a kingdom there are many that never knew one another's names, nor saw one another's faces, therefore it is called a city, to show that in heaven all the saints are neighbours, and know one another; but then to note our constant and more entire familiarity, it is called a house; and to note the pleasantness of it, it is called a garden: or paradise. And it is notable that all these names are given to the church; it is called a garden of spices: Cant. v. 1, 'I am come into my garden, my sister, my spouse;' the house of God: 1 Tim. iii. 15, 'That thou mayest know how thou oughtest to behave thyself in the house of God, which is the church of the living God;' the city of God: Ps. lxxxvii. 3, 'Glorious things are spoken of thee, O city of God'; and Eph. ii. 19, 'Believers are said to be fellow-citizens of the saints, and of the household of God.' And it is called the kingdom of heaven in many places, because here we are trained up for the kingdom that is above; the church is the seminary of heaven; here are the suburbs of the great city, where all the elect of God do meet to live and dwell for evermore.

The notion that I am to prosecute is a city. There are diverse resemblances between heaven and a city. In a city there is a multitude of inhabitants; so Christ's people, take them all together, are a multitude which none can number. In a city there are plenty of all things; so in heaven there is no lack, for there God is all in all.[1]

But it differs from other cities in the world in this, that there are no wars, no tumults, no confusions, as there may be here below. When the nations are represented as in a tumult, it is said, God sitteth in the heavens, in a quiet posture: Ps. ii. 4, 'He that sitteth in the heavens shall laugh, the Lord shall have them in derision.' All is quiet in heaven, when all the world is in a hurry, striving against Christ. This is a city where there is no death; in an earthly city, if a man be absent ten or twenty years, there is a new face of men and things, for all things below are obnoxious to change; but this heavenly city always

---

[1] See the resemblances between heaven and a city, Ver. 10.

hath the same face.   There is no abiding city in a perishing world :
Heb. xii. 14, 'For here have we no continuing city, but we seek one
to come.'   There are no vicissitudes of night or day, calm or tempest,
summer or winter, but all things are in an eternal spring of beauty and
flourishing, where the inhabitants are preserved from all sin, misery,
sickness, and grief.   It is a city where there is no use of carpenters and
masons, but 'whose builder and maker is God,' ver. 10.

Use. O ye that are citizens! put in for an interest in this great city ;
that you may go to a better city when you are called away from this ;
that you may go to the citizens above, and enjoy the freedom of that
happy place.   You who are countrymen, take heed you be not shut out
of this city of God.

Obs. 3. This city is a city prepared.   But how is it prepared ?

1. It is prepared for us by God the Father in his decree : Mat. xxv.
34, 'Come, ye blessed of my Father, inherit the kingdom prepared for
you from the foundation of the world ;' so 1 Cor. ii. 9, 'Eye hath not
seen, nor ear heard, neither have entered into the heart of man the
things which God hath prepared for them that love him ;' that is,
intended for the heirs of promise.   God hath designed the persons, the
particular portion, and degree of glory which the saints shall enjoy, long
before the world was.

2. It is prepared for us by Christ ; for we hold heaven not only by
gift, but by purchase.   Christ hath been at great cost to prepare heaven,
and furnish this city for us ; he came from heaven to prepare it for us ;
he laid the foundation of it in his own merit, from whence our title
groweth, and therefore it is called 'the purchased possession,' Eph. i.
14.   Christ opened the door for us, that was before shut.   And as he
came from heaven to prepare the way, so he is gone to heaven to set
all things to rights, from whence he will come, and fetch home his
bride with triumph : John xiv. 23, 'I go to prepare a place for you.
And if I go and prepare a place for you, I will come again, and receive
you to myself, that where I am, there ye may be also.'   He is gone to
heaven as our legal head, to seize upon it in our right, and to possess
it in our name ; and there he maketh intercession for us, that our sins
may be no impediment to us.   And as our mystical head, or author of
grace, so he sendeth abroad the Spirit.

3. It is prepared by the Spirit.   This concerneth the inhabitants.
Heaven is not only prepared for us, but we are said to be prepared for
heaven : Rom. ix. 23, 'And that he might make known the riches of
his glory on the vessels of mercy, which he hath afore prepared unto
glory.'   So as heaven is said to be kept for us, we are kept for it : 1
Peter i. 4, 5, 'To an inheritance incorruptible and undefiled, and that
fadeth not away, reserved in heaven for us, who are kept by the power
of God through faith unto salvation.'   Christians ! God is ready, if we
are ready ; there it stoppeth : old bottles will not hold the new wine
of glory.   We should soon be translated if once we were fit.   As corn
is gathered into the garner as soon as it is ripe, so if we were ripe for
heaven, our translation would not be long deferred.

But I shall come to the main point.

Obs. 4. The top of all happiness is to have God for our God.
That was the ground of the patriarch's blessedness, that 'God is not

ashamed to be called their God;' Ps. cxliv. 15, 'Happy is that people that is in such a case; yea, happy is that people whose God is the Lord.' The judgment of the flesh is, Happy are those who have no complaining in their streets, no want in their families; but the judgment of the flesh is corrected and retracted by the judgment of faith —'Yea, rather, happy is the people whose God is the Lord.' So doth grace determine that this is the top of our happiness, to have God for our God. Here I shall inquire into three things—(1.) What it is to have God for our God. (2.) Who are they that have God for their God. (3.) How it may be improved.

First. What it is to have God for our God? I will be a God to thee, is more than to say, I will be thy friend, I will be thy father, I will be thy benefactor. There is a greater weight and emphasis in this expression than if he should say, I will give thee heaven and everlasting life. 'Do this and live,' was the covenant made with Adam; in the covenant of grace it is, 'I will be thy God,' and I will infallibly work whatever shall conduce to thy salvation. Here are three questions to be answered. (1.) Who is engaged? (2.) To what he is engaged. (3.) How he will perform this engagement.

1. Who is engaged? *Ans.* The infinite God, *quantus, quantus est,* as great and glorious as he is; he is our portion. God loves to speak magnificently in the covenant; therefore he doth not only say, I will give heaven, grace, and glory to thee, but I will be a God to thee: Gen. xvii. 7, 'I will establish my covenant between me and thee, and thy seed after thee in their generations, for an everlasting covenant, to be a God unto thee and to thy seed after thee.' Whatever he is, or hath, or can do, that is thine. We do not believe it, but we have God's word for it often in scripture—'I will be thy God.' All things in God are thine, the essence of God, and the subsistences in the godhead.

[1.] The essence of God is thine; he will do all things answerably to an infinite power and goodness; as glorious, as infinite, as mighty, as excellent as he is, it is wholly made over to us. His mercy, wisdom, love, power, justice, all this is thine; his mercy is thine, to pardon thee; his wisdom is thine, to provide for thee; his love is thine, to bestow grace and glory, and all good things on thee; his power is thine, to secure all to thee, and preserve thee to salvation; his justice is thine, to fulfil all his promises to thee. Whole God is made over to us in covenant, and will be given to us as far as the proportion of the creature will stretch to receive him. If we be imperfective, the fault is in ourselves; there is no fault in our portion; it is able to perfect us in the way, if we were capable of perfection in it.

[2.] The subsistences in the godhead are ours. God the Father is ours to love us and to elect us—'The Father himself loveth you,' John xvi. 27. God the Son is ours to redeem us, to be born for us, to die for us, to rise again for us, to ascend up into heaven for us, and to sit at God's right hand for us: Isa. ix. 6, 'For unto us a child is born, unto us a son is given;' Cant. ii. 16, 'I am my beloved's, and my beloved is mine.' And God the Holy Ghost is ours to dwell in us and work in us, and to conduct and guide us to glory: 1 Cor. iii. 16, 'Know ye not that ye are the temple of God, and that the Spirit of God dwelleth in you?' So that whatever Father, Son, and Holy Ghost is or can do for your salvation, it is yours, and made over to you in covenant. Look, as when there was a covenant made between Jehoshaphat and the king of Israel, Jehoshaphat promised Ahab whatever he had and could do : 1 Kings xxii. 21, ' I am as thou art, my people as thy people, my horses as thy horses ; ' so in this covenant, whatever God can do is ours ; his power is ours ; whatever God doth is for our good ; his providence is ours. ' I will be thy God,' that is, I will do all that a God can do for thy everlasting happiness.

2. To what he is engaged ? *Ans.* To give us a better thing than the world can afford , to give us all spiritual and eternal blessings, and other things in order thereunto. This is the first and fundamental promise, ' I will be thy God ; ' it implieth pardon, grace, glory, the conduct of providence, or the subserviency of all the accidents and emergencies of the present life for our spiritual good, all these are included in the covenant. In the covenant of works there is no such promise, for there God did not infallibly bind himself to conduct them to glory, as he doth in the covenant of grace. The tenor of the covenant of works was, ' Do this and live, sin and die.' God made not this promise to Adam so explicity, ' I will be thy God.' When God saith, ' I will be thy God,' he means he will give us such blessings as are proper for a God to give, which none other can give ; as to pardon and justify, and God is the supreme judge, his sentence is decisive ; to sanctify, which is beyond the power of a creature ; to bless providences, God is the disposer of all human affairs—' Of him, and through him, and to him are all things,' Rom. xi. 36 ; to glorify ; and it is in his power alone to bestow heaven. These things God hath bound himself to : he will justify, which is an act of the highest judicature ; he will sanctify, which is an act of divine power, or an act of the supreme cause ; he will bless providences, which is an act of the sovereign Lord ; and he will glorify us, which is an act of the chiefest good.

3. How God will perform this engagement ? *Ans.* He will do all things answerable to the infinite power, greatness, and goodness of a God. As it was said of Arauna : 2 Sam. xxiv. 23, ' All these did Arauna, as a king, give unto the king.' Arauna was of the blood royal of the Jebusites, and he gave like a man of such extraction, with a royal mind. So in this promise, ' I will be thy God,' God hath promised that he will not only act for us, but act as a God ; he will act by a firm covenant ; we have an interest in all that he can do for our salvation ; he will pardon as a God : Hosea xi. 9, ' I will not execute the fierceness of mine anger ; I will not return to destroy Ephraim, for I am God, and not man, the Holy One in the midst of thee.' Alas ! our thoughts are limited, our patience is soon tired ; we soon grow weary of forgiving if we forgive seven times : What ! must we forgive seven times a day ? but now he will pardon as a God, as one that hath infinite mercy, love, and patience. And he will sanctify as a God ; he will create a clean heart ; and the divine power is set a-work to give us all things necessary to life and godliness : 2 Peter i. 3, ' According as his divine power hath given unto us all things that pertain unto life and godliness.' And he will as a God supply our wants ; he will not only give us water out of the fountain, but out of the rock, when

he seeth it good for us. And he will glorify as a God; the apostle speaks of ' a far more exceeding and eternal weight of glory,' 2 Cor. iv. 17. As God is an infinite God, so he will give an infinite reward; and as he is an eternal God, so he will give an eternal reward; for in heaven God doth act like himself. Thus he will do all things in a divine manner, all things that are a help and not a hindrance to bring us to our everlasting state.

Secondly. Who are the persons and the people whose God is the Lord ? *Ans.* In regard of superiority and supremacy, God is the God of all the earth : Ps. xxiv. 1, ' The earth is the Lord's, and the fulness thereof; the world, and they that dwell therein.' Nay, in regard of common bounty, he is the God of all the earth, as he gives life, breath, protection, and maintenance to all creatures. But then there is a peculiar people, and so it is said more especially, the visible church is God's portion and heritage : Deut. xxxii. 9, ' For the Lord's portion is his people ; Jacob is the lot of his inheritance ;' 1 Chron. xvii. 24, ' The Lord of Hosts is the God of Israel, even a God to Israel.' Mark how distinctly the scripture speaks; he is not only the God of Israel, in regard of supremacy, and superiority; but he is a God to Israel, in regard of his bounty, goodness, and communicative grace. But within the bounds of the church there are a peculiar people. There may be a great deal of bran in the visible church, for the visible church is too coarse a boulter to get these people severed; therefore God useth a finer searce : Zech. xiii. 8, ' Two parts therein shall be cut off and die, but the third shall be left therein.' There are ἐκλεκτῶν ἐκλεκτότερον, the elect out of the elect, God's own peculiar people, who have a special interest in him, and not only a public interest, as the church hath in him. Now these people may be known (1.) By the manner of their coming into this relation ; (2.) By their manner of living in this relation.

1. By their manner of coming into this relation ; something God doth, and something they do, and so they are brought into this relation.

[1.] Something God doth to bring them into this relation. God calls them by an effectual calling : Heb. v. 4, ' No man taketh this honour to himself, but he that is called of God, as was Aaron.' By effectual calling God's election is put into act, and by his Spirit he taketh actual possession of the hearts of those who belong to the election of grace. And it is necessary that God should begin with us : God must choose us before we can choose him ; he takes possession of our hearts by his Spirit before we can take possession of him as our God : Zech. xiii. 8, 9, ' Two third parts therein shall be cut off and die, and the third shall be left therein.' He will cut off some out of the church, and some in the church—' And I will bring the third part through the fire, and will refine them as silver is refined, and will try them as gold is tried. They shall call on my name, and I will hear them ; I will say, It is my people, and they shall say, The Lord is my God.' First the Lord chooseth us for a people, and then he frames our hearts to choose him for the Lord our God : so Hosea ii. 23, ' I will say to them which were not my people, Thou art my people ; and they shall say, Thou art our God.' God begins : he makes the first motion. The saints do not only choose God because of his alluring worth, but from his attractive virtue and power, whereby he breaks in upon their hearts to draw them strongly and powerfully, yet freely and and willingly, to himself. He turns out the devil, and brings them to the obedience of the gospel.

[2.] Something we must do. When God hath taken possession of the heart, we choose him for our all-sufficient portion, and resign, surrender, and give up ourselves to him.

(1.) We choose him for our all-sufficient portion and chiefest good: Ps. lxxiii. 25, ' Whom have I in heaven but thee ? and there is none upon earth that I desire besides thee.' The blind world choose the gifts of God, and the meanest of his gifts, the honours, riches, pleasures of this world ; but the saints choose God himself, in the sense of his love, and by the power of his grace. In the sense of his love ; they know God as he knoweth them, and so love and choose him as he does them. And by the power of his grace. Turning from the creator to the creature was our first parent's sin, and corrupt nature goes on in that averseness. They that are strangers from the womb can never return to God that made them till they have another heart put into them ; they run away from God, and are for temporal good things : Ps. iv. 6, ' Who will show us any good ? ' there is the worldling's blind choice. They are wandering and groping about for good ; but the children of God cry out, ' Lord, lift thou up the light of thy countenance upon us.' This is their choice : they choose God for their portion, his favour for their happiness, and their souls are satisfied in him. Naturally all men are Gadarenes, who preferred their swine before Christ ; they prefer their lusts, pleasures, profits, carnal satisfactions, pleasing of their senses, gratifying their corrupt desires, before the favour of God and the enjoyment of God. But now grace altereth the temper of the heart, that the saints choose God for their portion, and his testimonies for their heritage.

(2.) We resign and surrender ourselves to God. When the saints choose God for their portion, they give up themselves to God again. Look, as in the covenant that was made between the prophet and his wife : Hosea iii. 3, ' Thou shalt not be for another man, so will I also be for thee,' so in the covenant that is between the Lord and us ; he is for us, and we are to be for him ; we take him for our portion, and give up ourselves to him again as his people. All that is God's is ours, his grace, mercy, love, justice, truth, wisdom, all is made over to us ; and all that is ours must be God's, our life, strength, reputation, time, parts, estate, interests, relations, our all is his : 2 Chron. xxx. 8, ' Yield yourselves unto the Lord,' or give the hand unto the Lord. God and we do as it were strike hands, and there is a bargain made between us ; all that God is and can do, so far as we can receive it, is made over to us ; and then all that we are and can do is altogether for God. We eat and drink to him, and trade to him, and set ourselves apart to live and act for God. There is a mutual taking and giving : Cant. vi. 3, ' I am my beloved's, and my beloved is mine.' Thus they may be known by the manner of their coming into this relation.

2. By their manner of living and walking in this relation. They glorify him as God. It was the fault of the gentiles that ' when they knew God, they glorified him not as God,' Rom. i. 21. But the people

of God glorify him as God by subjection and dependence; in respect of his superiority and supremacy, so they profess subjection to God; and in respect of sufficiency and ability, so they profess dependence upon God.

[1.] By subjection to him. When God gave the law, he said, 'I am the Lord thy God,' Exod. xx. 2. Many would depend upon God when they would not obey him; they will lean upon the Lord, and say, 'Is not the Lord among us?' Micah iii. 11. But they are God's people that walk in obedience to him. God is our God whether we will or no, in point of supremacy; he hath a right to rule and govern us, and a power to punish and destroy us; but we own him as a God by a full, and free, and voluntary subjection and obedience to his laws. When the people of Israel entered into covenant with the Lord, you find: Exod. xxiv. 7, 'He took the book of the covenant, and read in the audience of the people, and they said, All that the Lord hath said will we do, and be obedient.' And you may observe that Moses sprinkled half the blood upon the altar and half the blood upon the people, vers. 6, 8. The covenant bindeth mutually. God doth come under an obligation to us: there is half the blood sprinkled upon the altar, and we come under an obligation to be subject to God; there was half the blood sprinkled upon the people. Subjection is a necessary respect from the creature to the creator: God never made any creatures but he put them under some law. The angels are under a law, and they must yield him homage, love, and service. The whole frame of nature is under a law and decree that they cannot pass; so are we under a law to God; but we would tread out the corn, and will not endure the yoke. But as we take God for our God, so we must yield him homage, love, and service.

[2.] By dependence. Trust is the creature's best respects, and proper to God. There is a moderate love that we have to other things, but if we trust in them, we rob God of his proper due; and this is idolatry, for we make that our God which we depend upon, and have recourse to in straits and extremities, as the 'mariners called every man upon his god,' Jonah i. 5. Love is an acknowledgment of God's goodness, but trust acknowledgeth many of his attributes at once, his power, his love, his truth, his justice, and so glorifieth God as God. In the covenant God requireth obedience, but chiefly dependence, because we depend upon him for strength to yield that obedience. We do not only depend upon him for blessings to be performed on his part, but likewise for strength to perform the duties that are required on our part. The great intent of the covenant of grace is that we may be nothing in ourselves, and look for all from God; and therefore those people whose God is the Lord, as they choose God, and give up themselves to him, so they live in subjection to him and dependence on him.

Thirdly. How is it to be improved?

1. To contentment and complacency in our portion. Surely we have cause to be contented. To our happiness there needeth no more than God. Can we find any want in him? Ps. xvi. 5, 6, 'The Lord is the portion of mine inheritance, and of my cup; thou maintainest my lot. The lines are fallen to me in a pleasant place; yea, I have a

goodly heritage.' He that hath God for his portion hath enough. All other portions have a want annexed to them, but this alone sufficeth: Rev. xxi. 7, ' He that overcometh shall inherit all things, and I will be his God, and he shall be my son ; ' therefore he shall inherit all things, because God is his God. *Possidet possidentem omnia,* he possesseth him that possesseth all things. God is sufficient to his own happiness, much more to ours : God is enough for himself, and that which will satisfy God will much more satisfy a creature ; as that which will fill an ocean will fill a small vessel. You disparage the all-sufficiency of God when you have God for your portion, and yet are perplexed with base, earthly desires as others are, as if he that fills all things could not fill up thy heart. This is the misery of a worldly man's portion, that while he hath what he desires still there is a want, and still his sore runneth. Here is all that we can need or desire if we had eyes to see it.

2. Improve it for comfort in deep distresses. When all is gone, yet if we have a covenant-interest in God left, that is enough to support the heart. David was plundered at Ziglag, and lost all he had, yet David ' encouraged himself in the Lord his God,' 1 Sam. xxx. 6.

Sometimes a poor christian hath no friends in the world, but God is his friend ; though all be gone, yet God is not gone ; God is alive still, and God is mine still; as one said, *Deus meus, et omnia mea* —God is mine, and all things are mine. So Hab. iii. 17, 18, ' Although the fig-tree shall not blossom, neither shall fruit be in the vine ; the labour of the olive shall fail, and the fields shall yield no meat; the flock shall be cut off from the fold, and there shall be no herd in the stalls ; yet I will rejoice in the Lord, I will joy in the God of my salvation.' If the oil in the cruse and the meal in the barrel be spent—if the creatures have spent all their allowance, yet God is not spent. This is the life of heaven, to live immediately upon God, for in heaven God is all in all. It is an anticipation of heaven when we can see all things in God—house, home, life, food, maintenance, and protection; as they in the wilderness, when they wanted houses: Ps. xc. 1, ' Lord, thou hast been our dwelling-place in all generations.' This expoundeth Paul's riddle: 2 Cor. vi. 10, ' As having nothing, and yet possessing all things; ' as having nothing in our own hands, but all things in God's. If God bear the purse for us we cannot be poor. Surely they do not know what it is to have God for their God who are wholly dejected with worldly losses, as if there were no God in heaven, as if there were no covenant, no such engagement of God to us. Who would complain of the loss of a candle when he hath the sun ? To live altogether upon outward supplies is the mere life of sense; but when we have no friend in the world, no help in the creature, none to stead us or stand by us, then are we put to prove the virtue of our portion. God takes away the creature that we may have an experience of the goodness of our interest in him, what it is to have God for our God.

3. It must be improved to dependence upon God for the future supplies of the present life, till our work be done, and we come to heaven: Ps. xxiii. 1, ' The Lord is my shepherd, I shall not want.' We have a God who hath the command of all things. If God carry the purse in his own hands, we are never in the worse condition ; he is our father,

and·will give us what is necessary for us. He is worse than an infidel that will not provide for his own. If we are God's, he will provide for us; and therefore when we are in any doubt, conflicting with unbelief, we may plead with God, and say, 'I am thine, save me,' Ps. cxix. 94. And you may plead with yourselves, and say, 'Why art thou cast down, O my soul? and why art thou disquieted within me? Hope in God; for I shall yet praise him, who is the health of my countenance, and my God,' Ps. xliii. 5. Thus may christians improve their interest, as an encouragement to trust.

4. We must improve it especially to a hope and expectation of a better happiness than the world yields—to give us hope in life and in death, that we may expect all those things which God hath promised. We must shoot the gulf before we can pass into the land of promise, where God will indeed show himself to be our God; and therefore when death begins to hasten upon us, let us remember that he is our God, and that he hath better things to give us, else he would be ashamed to be called our God. The world is not a fit place wherein to give us our portion; it is a fit place for dogs to have their portion, but not for children. Now our interest must keep up our hopes. Surely our God hath some better thing than the world yields to bestow upon us; as the patriarchs went to their graves professing their hopes of a better state: Ps. lxxiii. 26, 'My flesh and my heart faileth, but God is the strength of my heart, and my portion for ever.' When the decays of nature creep upon you apace, say, I have an interest in God, and I look for an eternal portion; when my flesh begins to fail, and consume, and waste away—when the heart and life is even spent, and the lamp is ready to go out, yet thou art my God, and my portion for ever. As Olevian comforted himself, My hearing is gone, and my smelling is gone, and my sight is a-going, and my speech and feeling is almost gone; but the lovingkindness of God shall never depart from me. When worldly men see the vanity of their portion, and begin to discover how the world hath cheated them, then you see the happiness of yours. The error of their choice is best seen at death: when their portion is gone, then yours remaineth; their good things are past, yours are to come: Jer. xvii. 11, 'As the partridge sitteth on eggs, and hatcheth them not; so he that getteth riches, and not by right, shall leave them in the midst of his days, and at his end shall be a fool.'

Application.

Use 1. Information; It informs us of two things.

1. Of the great love of God, that he would be our God, and take us for his people. The apostle saith, Heb. vi. 13, 'Because he could swear by no greater, he sware by himself.' So when God had no greater thing to give us, he gave us himself. There is nothing more infinite and glorious than himself, and he hath bestowed himself on us. If we had all things else, and should want God, it would not perfect us. Oh, the greatness of his love, that he would take us to be his, and that he would be ours! Christ shed his blood for us to this end. These are the two great things that set forth the love of God; the covenant, and the death of Christ; the death of Christ, by which he got a new title to us; and the covenant, by which we have an interest in him.

2. Of the happiness of the children of God above wicked men. Wicked men may have Ishmael's blessing and Esau's portion ; they may have the world to be theirs, but they have not God to be theirs, as the saints have. You think it is a great matter when a carnal man can say, This house is mine, this estate is mine, this lordship is mine, this kingdom is mine ; but a christian can say more, This God is mine, this Christ is mine, this Holy Spirit is mine. Alas ! riches, honours, and worldly greatness are poor things to God, made ours by a covenant interest ; these things may suit better with our present humours, but they can never yield us solid contentment.

Use 2. Caution. Take heed of those things that may withdraw God from us. Sin in the general makes God stand at a distance from us : Isa. lix. 2, ' Your iniquities have separated between you and your God.' It robbeth us even of God himself ; and in robbing a man of God, it robbeth him of all other things ; for in God we have all ; his favour is life ; better never have been born than to live out of the favour of God : Ps. lxiii. 3, ' Thy lovingkindness is better than life. He is house and home to us : Ps. xc. 1, ' Lord, thou hast been our dwelling-place in all generations.' He is wealth, and honour, and pleasure to us, his face maketh heaven—' In thy presence there is fulness of joy,' Ps. xvi. 11. Let us then walk more watchfully ; especially let us take heed of making bold with God to please men. Doth your happiness depend upon them or upon God ? Upon having their favour or God's favour ? Carnal compliance is a very provoking sin, and most contrary to the duties of the covenant.

Use 3. Exhortation. It exhorteth us (1.) To take God for our portion ; (2.) To make it sure that God is our portion.

1. To take God for our portion. We are known by the choice of our portion. There is nothing distinguisheth man and man so much as this—what do we choose for our happiness and portion ? A worldly man is not dainty in his choice, anything contents him, that which comes next to hand, which yields a present satisfaction. But a godly man cannot be so contented ; he is more dainty in his choice ; he must have a portion to satisfy the desires of that divine nature that is infused into him—a portion that must endure for ever ; he must have his soul contented, his conscience as well as his affections ; he must have something that will stead him when he comes to die, otherwise he cannot be contented. Let me urge two or three arguments.

[1.] There is none so fit as God to be our portion ; he is the best and greatest, and he is the most durable and lasting portion.

(1.) He is the best portion ; there is none greater than he, none better than he. It is never well with us till we subscribe Christ's conclusion : Mat. xix. 17, ' There is none good but one, that is God.' God is good of himself, the fountain of good ; other things, whatever good they have is of him, and it is infinitely greater and better in him than in them ; and that small good that other things have is not to hold us on them, but to lead us to God who is originally good, infinitely good, and communicatively good. He is good of himself, which nothing else is—good in himself, yea, goodness itself. The heart is never in a good frame till we see that none is good but God—no good above him, besides him, or beyond him ; unless it cometh from him, it is not good. Oh! be not of a Gadarene spirit, to prefer a seeming good before a real, the stream before the fountain, the shadow before the substance.

(2.) He is the most durable portion. The good things of this life are perishing ; our life is short and they serve for this life only ; they do not go down with us to the grave; it were well if they did continue to the grave. We are mortals, and they are more mortal— 'Riches make themselves wings ; they fly away as an eagle towards heaven,' Prov. xxiii. 5. There are many wings by which an estate flies away ; there is the winds, the sea, the fire, the bad debtor, the displeasure of the magistrate, and the fury of the times. Experience hath taught us, that these things are not mere speculations, but real things. Many a man's estate hath died before himself, and then he hath lived like a neglected stalk when the flower is gone. But now God endures for ever ; he was before the world was, and he will be when the world shall be no more. God will stand us in stead in death and after death.

(3.) He is most able to give us contentment, for he is sufficient to himself. Conscience cannot take contentment in the world, though the heart may be besotted with the world. The conscience is a sore place, and all the world cannot give us a plaster for it. Worldly things, the more we enjoy them, the more we see the vanity of them ; but the more we enjoy God, the more we see the worth of God, and the more will the heart be ravished with him. You see what a sufficient durable good God is ; but 'what hope hath the hypocrite, though he hath gained, when God taketh away his soul?' Job. xxvii. 8. The error of wicked men will be seen in death ; when their portion is taken away from them, their grief will surpass the joy they took in it. What do wicked men think of their portion in hell when their good things are past? Are they more angry with it, or with themselves for choosing it? the folly of their choice is a part of their torment: Luke xvi. 25, 'Son, remember that thou in thy life-time receivedst thy good things.' All their happiness in the world doth but yield matter for the worm to gnaw upon, that worm of conscience that shall never die. What would they give for one day of God's patience ! But there they bewail themselves for choosing so unfit a portion for their souls. But then a godly man hath his portion at the full, whereas he hath but the beginnings here. There was a great deal of difference between Dives and Lazarus in this world, and there is much more in the other world.

[2.] As God is only fit, so there is none more willing to be taken for our portion. The Lord is not only goodness itself, but a communicative goodness ; he communicates himself to us in Christ : Isa. lv. 2, 'Wherefore do ye spend your money for that which is not bread ? and your labour for that which satisfieth not? Hearken diligently unto me, and eat ye that which is good, and let your soul delight itself in fatness.' Before we come to take God for our portion, we taste his common goodness ; he beginneth with us with common bounty. Many hunt after the world, and miss it ; but who ever failed that resolved to take God for his portion ? He complains that men would not take him for their God : Ps. lxxxi. 11, 'My people would not hearken to my voice, and Israel would none of me.' He offereth himself to the world, but the world refuseth him.

[3.] In having God for our portion we have all things else, so far as it conduceth to our happiness. We have the worldly man's portion, and that upon better terms. When God gave Solomon liberty to ask what he would, he asked not riches and honours, but wisdom, and he had other things too: 1 Kings iii. 13, 'I have also given thee that which thou hast not asked, both riches and honour, so that there shall not be any among the kings like unto thee all thy days.' It is acceptable to God, when we pass by other things and choose himself; and when we choose him, we have other things with a blessing: Mat. vi. 33, 'Seek ye first the kingdom of God, and the righteousness thereof, and all these things shall be added to you.' God doth not promise outward things so as to make against our spiritual good; he promiseth them with himself and with his Christ, not against himself and against Christ. You would not have them to hinder you from your main portion, but so far as they are blessings you shall have them.

2. It presseth us to make it sure that God is our portion. This is our greatest business in the world, yet we take least pains to get it, and evidence it. *Tolle meum et tolle Deum.* If we cannot say that God is ours, it will be our torment, as it is the devil's, to think of God. Let us not be quiet till we can say, God is my God. Many say God is their God, but they are not his; he doth not own them for his people; therefore we must have some evidences, something to show for it: John i. 12, 'To as many as received him, to them gave he power,' ἐξουσίαν, this privilege, 'to be called the sons of God.' We must have a grant and evidence to show for it, that God is our God. And if we have God for our portion, and do not know it, it is a great weakening of our comfort.

Quest. But how shall we know whether God be our God?

1. Did you ever enter into contract and covenant with him? Upon what terms and considerations did you enter into covenant with God? None but God has a right by conquest; God has a right and title to us every way; but when he comes to convert a sinner, he has another title; then he has a title by conquest. Was your spirit ever subdued to yield to him? Do you remember when you were bond-slaves of Satan, that God broke in upon you with a mighty and powerful work of grace, subduing your heart, and causing you to yield, to give the hand to him, to come and lie at his feet, and lay down the weapons of defiance? Didst thou ever come as a guilty creature, willing to take laws from God, and cry, Lord, what wouldst thou have me to do? Though it be God's condescension to capitulate with us, yet we do not capitulate with him as equals, but as a subdued creature. who is taken captive and ready to be destroyed every moment, and is therefore willing to yield and cry quarter.

2. How do you behave yourselves in the covenant? Do you love God as the chiefest good? Do you seek his glory as the utmost end? Do you obey him as the highest Lord? Do you depend on him as your only paymaster? For this is to give God the glory of a God.

[1.] Do you love him as the chiefest good? After marriage there is embracing; so when we enter into contract with God, we love God. Every one will say, They love God it were pity they should live else; but what dost thou do for him? Dost thou do more for him than any else? What is it you desire in the world? his favour, or outward things? What is your care to get and keep most? What are those things about which you find joy and grief most exercised? These are the signs of love; if the enjoyment of God's favour be the greatest joy and contentment of your souls, and if the offending of God, and grieving of his Spirit, and the loss of the light of his countenance for that, be the greatest grief of your heart, then you love God as the chiefest good.

[2.] Do you seek his glory as the utmost end? God would have us in all things we do, to aim at his glory: 1 Cor. x. 31, 'Whether therefore ye eat or drink, or whatever ye do, do all to the glory of God.' We are set apart for this end and purpose; and therefore, is your living, a living to God?

[3.] Do you obey God as the highest lord and law-giver? Obedience is necessary; God will be glorified in his sovereignty, and that is a great evidence of your interest in him.

[4.] Do you depend upon him as your paymaster and benefactor? When you do all things as looking for your reward from God, it is a great evidence: Rom. ii. 29, 'He is a Jew which is one inwardly, whose praise is not of men, but of God.' Is your heart taken up with the praise of God, the approbation of God, and the rewards of God?

But if all this will not help you to judge your hearts, there are but two things will give you comfort, and that is your own choice, and your own resignation. Your choice—Do you choose God for your portion? though you cannot say, God hath chosen you, and that he is yours, yet will you choose him? Are you resolved you will not be satisfied without him? Will you not be put off with anything besides God? And then, do you resign up yourselves to him? Do you say, Lord! I will be thine, I will not be mine own? As that nation that came to the Romans, and they refused to help them, they came with this plea, If you will not look upon us as your allies, look upon us as your vassals and subjects, as we resolve to be; so do you by an importunate faith thus fasten yourselves upon God, and say, Lord! if thou wilt not honour me, love me, bless me as thine; I am resolved to be thine, and if I perish, one must perish that desires to be thine. When you thus force yourselves as it were upon the Lord, that is all that is left for the relief of your souls, and to evidence your happy state.

SERMON LI.

By faith Abraham, when he was tried, offered up Isaac; and he that had received the promises offered up his only-begotten son, of whom it was said, That in Isaac shall thy seed be called: accounting that God was able to raise him up, even from the dead; from whence also he received him in a figure—HEB. xi. 17–19.

THIS chapter is the chronicle of faith, or a record of the heroical acts which that grace had produced in all ages; or, if you will, the history of the most eminent believers, that ever have been in the world. When he had spoken of the patriarchs in common, he cometh to speak of them in particular, and beginneth with Abraham, who in this glorious constellation shineth forth as a star of the first magnitude, and therefore is fitly styled the father of the faithful.   And among all the acts of Abraham's faith nothing was more eminent than the offering of his son Isaac, that I have chosen to propound to your imitation ; and the rather because Abraham was tried, not only for a proof of his own sincerity, but for a rare example to all future generations.

In these verses you have three circumstances.

1. An occasion for the exercise of Abraham's faith—*When he was tried.*

2. The greatness of the trial—*He offered up Isaac, and he that had received the promises offered up his only-begotten son : of whom it was said, That in Isaac shall thy seed be called.*

3. The work of faith, or his behaviour under this trial—*Accounting that God was able to raise him up, even from the dead ; from whence also he received him in a figure.*

[1.] The occasion — ' When he was tried.' πειραζόμενος — when he was tempted, and that by God: Gen. xxii. 1, ' God did tempt Abraham,' &c.   But now God tempts no man : James i. 13, ' Let no man say, when he is tempted, I am tempted of God ; for God cannot be tempted with evil, neither tempteth he any man ; ' that is, by inward suggestion and solicitation, but only by presenting the outward occasion, or by some extraordinary command.   By presenting an outward occasion : Exod. xvi. 2, ' I will rain bread from heaven for you, and the people shall go out, and gather a certain rate every day, that I may prove them, whether they will walk in my law or no.'   Or else, by an extraordinary command, as God here tried Abraham, or as Christ tried the young man : Mat. xix. 21, ' Go and sell that thou hast, and give to the poor.'   There is no injustice in these extraordinary commands ; the lawgiver may make what exception to his own laws he pleaseth.   We are bound to the law, but the lawgiver himself is not bound.   But why should God try Abraham ?   Austin saith, *Non ut ipse hominem inveniat, sed ut homo se inveniat*—Not that he might know Abraham, but that Abraham might know himself.   God knows already what we are ; but he tries us that we may be manifest to ourselves, and to others for their example.   It is true, he saith, Gen. xxii. 12, ' Now I know that thou fearest God, seeing thou hast not withheld thy son, thy only son from me.'   But that is *humanitus dictum ;* God speaketh as a man that knoweth not till after trial, as if he should say, Now there is a sufficient proof of thy sincerity, I have caused it to be known, and will accept of it as a good and sufficient proof.

[2.] The greatness of the trial, or the occasion amplified from the person offering, the person offered, and the work itself ; and in all these respects it will appear that the trial was very great.

(1.) The person offering, Abraham, who is looked upon here as a father, and as one that had received the promises—ὁ τὰς ἐπαγγελίας ἀναδεξάμενος—which noteth not only the revelation of the promises concerning a numerous issue, and the Messiah to come of his loins, but his entertaining of them, and cordial assent to them ; he received them not only as a private believer, but as a feoffee in trust for the use of the church. In the first ages of the world, God had some eminent persons who received a revelation of God's will in the name of all the rest. This was Abraham's case; he is here considered as a father, a loving father, and as one that hath received the promises as a public person, and father of the faithful—the person whom God had chosen in whom to deposit the promises.

(2.) The person offered—Isaac, not bullocks, or goats, or rams, or lambs, but Isaac—a son, and a son whom he loved: Gen. xxii. 2, 'Take now thy son, thine only son Isaac, whom thou lovest, and get thee into the land of Moriah, and offer him there for a burnt-offering upon one of the mountains, which I shall tell thee of.' He was the son of Sarah, his legitimate wife, the heir of the lawful bed. Ishmael was cast out of doors, and Isaac's posterity was only to be reckoned to Abraham, as the blessed seed, among whom God would have his church. He was given to Abraham, after he had long gone childless, and when Sarah's womb was dead, and therefore he had never hopes of more children. But all this was nothing to what follows—'Of whom it was said, That in Isaac shall thy seed be called;' a child upon whom the accomplishment of the promises depended. Nature and grace concurred to incline Abraham's heart to favour Isaac. Nature; for love is descending, and the children of age are most loved: Abraham's age, when almost expired, was wonderfully renewed in the birth of Isaac, and an only son in whom he might hope to survive. Grace concurred also, the promises pitched on him; there was no possibility in nature, or promise above nature, that he should have any more children by Sarah; and Isaac himself was without children, and there was a plain affirmation, that the people which should be accounted his seed should spring from Isaac; not only natural affection, but faith was against it—to kill Isaac was to cut off all his hopes. There is sometimes a quarrel between lust and lust, but here between grace and grace, between faith and obedience; Isaac being lost, all hopes of the promise seemed to be lost, which was confirmed to him by God's own mouth—the same mouth that gave him the promise, gave him the command to slay the son of the promise. Abraham was now to put all the promises to slaughter; to cut off Isaac was in effect to cut off all hope of eternal life by Christ, who was to descend of him. Christ was included in in Isaac, and in Christ all the hopes of the church. If the conflict had only been with natural affection, it had been no such great matter; but the command and promise seemed to clash; if he had disobeyed the command, he had not been faithful Abraham; and if he had disbelieved the promise, still he had not been faithful Abraham.

[3.] The act itself. All this was to be done by his own hand—an aged father to kill his own son! the father of the faithful to sacrifice the son of the promise! A jewel lately given was now demanded again. If God had told Abraham that his son must die, it had been grievous, but that he must offer him, here was the trial.

3. Let us now look upon Abraham's behaviour under this great trial. Here is no disputing; he never questioned the oracle; it is God's will, and I must obey; he will provide for his promise well enough. 'In the mount of the Lord it shall be seen,' Gen. xxii. 14. Here is no delay, Gen. xxii 3, 'And Abraham rose early in the morning, and

saddled his ass, and took two of his young men with him, and Isaac his son, and clave the wood for the burnt-offering, and rose up, and went unto the place of which God had told him.' Here is no shifting, though he carried the matter closely, concealing it from Isaac, and his servants. 'By faith he offered Isaac;' faith is the root and principle of the action. 'He offered,' but Abraham did not offer him; God interposed and prevented him. Yet God counts it done: James ii. 21, 'Was not Abraham our father justified by works, when he had offered Isaac his son upon the altar?' And God said, Gen. xxii. 12, 'Now I know that thou fearest God, seeing thou hast not withheld thy son, thine only son, from me.' Partly because of his purpose, and partly because it was not a naked purpose; all things were ready, if God had not interposed—his son bound, and laid upon the altar.

Doct. 1. It is the property of faith to carry us through the greatest trials, with a ready, and cheerful, and acceptable obedience, and submission to the will of God.

To draw forth the marrow of the text, I shall branch this doctrine into some lesser propositions.

First I observe,—Ere we come to heaven, we all have our trials. It is the common lot of the saints to be tried. God's trials, which he suffereth to befall us, are in scripture compared unto two things—to the winnowing of wheat, and to the refining of gold. To the winnowing of wheat: Luke xxii. 31, 'And the Lord said, Simon, Simon, Satan hath desired to have you, that he may sift you as wheat.' The devil may shake and toss us as the wheat is tossed from sieve to sieve, but all to purge away our chaff. Then it is compared to the refining of gold: 1 Peter i. 7, 'That the trial of your faith, being much more precious than of gold that perisheth, when it is tried with fire, might be found unto praise, and honour, and glory, at the appearing of Jesus Christ.' Gold is melted, and loseth nothing of its substance but its dross; so it is for our improving and bettering, that God permits us to be tossed and shaken by Satan and bitter afflictions. There is need of trials, or else God would not make use of this dispensation: 1 Peter i. 6, 'Though now for a season, if need be, ye are in heaviness through manifold temptations.' All of us take our turn and share. God trieth some of his people to discover their weakness to themselves, and he trieth others to manifest the grace that is in them.

1. God will have the weakness of his own servants tried, that they may not conceit they have more grace than they have; and that the evil which before lay hid, may be discovered and cured. Thus God tried Hezekiah: 2 Chron. xxxii. 31, 'God left him to try him, that he might know all that was in his heart.' And Christ tried Philip: John vi. 6, 'This he said to prove him, for he himself knew what he would do.'

2. He will have their grace tried; and that for our comfort and for his own glory.

[1.] For our comfort. We have not ordinarily so clear a proof of the reality of grace, as under sore trials: Rom. v. 4, 'Tribulation worketh patience, and patience experience,' δοκιμήν, trial, and δοκιμὴ, experience, or trial, hope: then is any grace most seen. By knocking upon the vessel we see whether it be full or empty, cracked or sound, so by these knocks of providence we are discovered. Stars that lie hid in the day shine in the night. The rose is not so sweet on the tree as in the still. A sore tempest discovereth the goodness of the ship and the skill of the pilot, so in the night of afflictions the splendour of grace is best seen. When we are set over the fire, our fragrancy is discovered, and a christian's skill in a tempest is obedience.

[2.] It is for God's glory, that our ready self-denial and submission, and dependence on his wisdom, should be known, as the centurion said of his servants: Mat. viii. 9, 'I say to this man, Go, and he goeth; and to another, Come, and he cometh, and to my servant, Do this, and he doeth it.' There was an exact discipline in the Roman camps; so the Lord is honoured when his servants are tried, and they discover what a spirit of God and glory resteth upon them: 1 Peter iv. 14, 'If ye be reproached for the name of Christ, happy are ye, for the Spirit of glory and of God resteth upon you; on their part he is evil spoken of, but on your part he is glorified.' God will have the world know that he hath a people who are at his beck, as he is said, Isa. xli. 2, 'To raise up the righteous man from the east, and call him to his foot.' Abraham went to and fro at God's command, as God did appoint him. The Lord hath a people that love him better than their lives, than their choicest comforts, and will endure any misery rather than deny any part of their duty. At the last day, by trial our faith will be found to praise and honour: 1 Peter i. 7, 'That the trial of your faith, being much more precious than of gold that perisheth, though it be tried with fire, might be found unto praise, and honour, and glory, at the appearing of Jesus Christ;' then it will be found to be such a faith as Christ will accept and reward. Now these trials are manifold: 1 Peter i. 6, 'Ye are in heaviness through manifold temptations;' and diverse: James i. 2, 'Count it all joy when ye fall into diverse temptations;' because diverse things are to be tried. As,—

(1.) Our sincerity. We have but notions about the comforts of christianity till we are cast into great afflictions. The word of God cometh to us in word only, but then we prove our belief and sense of it. A gilded potsherd may shine till it cometh to scouring, then the varnish is worn off. When all things are prosperous, and our interest leads us to the profession of religion, the truth of grace is not so much discovered; but in deep troubles it is seen: 2 Cor. vi. 4, 'But in all things approving ourselves the ministers of God, in much patience, in afflictions, in necessities, in distresses.' When God searcheth men, and trieth men to the purpose, hirelings become changelings. The stony ground seemed fruitful till the sun did arise with a burning heat, Mat. xiii. 20, 21, and then it withered away; and all that comfort and joy which they formerly had by the word is lost. The blade on the stony ground made as fair a show for awhile as any of the rest, but it had no rooting.

(2.) Faith is tried: 1 Peter i. 7, 'That the trial of your faith, being much more precious than of gold that perisheth, though it be tried with fire, might be found unto praise, and honour, and glory, at the appearing of Jesus Christ.' So Abraham was here tried; so the woman of Canaan was tried, Mat. xv. 25–28. While all things are quiet and comfortable, we live by sense rather than by faith. As the worth of a soldier is not known in times of peace, and when he is out of action. *Ad fortiter faciendum opus est aliquâ rerum difficultate ;* when we are put to some difficulty and strait, then is faith seen ; but we dobut brave it, and word it at other times.

(3.) Our patience, humility, and submission to God are tried. When his mighty hand is upon us, then it is seen whether we are content to be what God would have us to be. The devil accused Job for an hypocrite, and would fain have him put upon this kind of trial : Job i. 9–11, 'Doth Job serve God for nought? Hast thou not made an hedge about him, and about his house, and about all that he hath on every side ? Thou hast blessed the work of his hands, and his substance is increased in the land. But put forth thine hand now, and touch all that he hath, and he will curse thee to thy face.' It is no wonder to see us without murmuring, when our houses are filled with good things ; or cheerful, while we have increase and plenty—what have we to complain of? But then is the trial, if we can suppress murmuring and discontents when God's hand is against us.

(4.) Our ready obedience in the most difficult points of duty. So Abraham was tried here ; and so Moses was tried when God sent him to Pharaoh, Exod. iii. 10.

(5.) Our contempt of earthly things. This is never so much seen as in a patient submission to the loss of them : Heb. x. 24, 'They took joyfully the spoiling of their goods, knowing in themselves that they have in heaven a better, and a more enduring substance.' When a man can take losses not only patiently, but joyfully, as reckoning upon a happiness elsewhere, it is a notable proof how little we set by outward things. God's children know not how to judge of their mortification when they abound in plenty, and all things flow in upon them according to their heart's desire.

(6.) Our dependence and trust in God : Hab. iii. 18, 'Yet will I rejoice in the Lord, I will joy in the God of my salvation ;' Ps. cxii. 7, ' He shall not be afraid of evil tidings ; his heart is fixed, trusting in the Lord.'

Use. Seeing we must have our trials, let us look for them, and prepare for them ; and when they come, see that we discover nothing but what will become obedience and submission to God.

1. Let us look for them, partly that we may not be perplexed at God's dispensation when it cometh : 1 Peter iv. 12, ' Beloved ! think it not strange concerning the fiery trial, which is to try you, as though some strange thing happened unto you'—$\mu\dot{\eta}$ $\xi\epsilon\nu\dot{\iota}\zeta\epsilon\sigma\theta\epsilon$. We are amazed and perplexed, as men that meet with some new and strange thing, when God cometh to try us in our sweetest earthly comforts, and to blast that which is dearest to us—as credit, liberty, life. We should make these things familiar to us before they come. But, alas ! we are secure when trials are nearest us, as the disciples were astonished when God was about to smite the shepherd and scatter the sheep, Mat. xxvi. 31. We are ready to dream of much worldly ease and comfort : Acts i. 6, 'Lord ! wilt thou at this time restore again the kingdom to Israel ?' We get a little breathing time from trouble, and promise ourselves perpetual exemption : Ps. xxx. 6, 'In my prosperity I said, I shall never be moved ;' so loth are we to forecast for trials, or to put ourselves

out of our fool's paradise. We promise ourselves too much when we dream of nothing but pleasure and contentment, as if we would go to heaven without exercise, without warrings within and fightings without. God hath but one Son without sin, but he has none without a cross. We must all be tried before we get to heaven. Partly, that we may try how we can bear them in imagination. It is good to suppose the worst; it hurts not. See the suppositions of faith, Ps. xxiii. 4, 'Yea, though I walk through the valley and shadow of death, I will fear no evil.' He compares himself to a sheep. Suppose I should be like a poor sheep wandering in the night when beasts of prey come out, ready to be devoured every moment. Presumption is a coward, and a runaway; it cannot endure to think of evil, or to look the enemy in the face; but faith meets it in the open field, provides for it when evil is not present; it makes suppositions: Hab. iii. 17, 'Suppose the fig-tree should not blossom,' &c. Suffer fear to prophesy, that faith may be the better prepared. Suppose the Lord should turn the tables, and bring on such a sad condition—nothing to help me, no friends to stand by me, all my children and near relations taken from me, all the supports and comforts of the present life should fail me,—what then? Thus faith supposeth evils that are feared, and then they are more comfortable. Before we take up a burden we poise it, and are wont to make an essay of our strength, that we may fit our back and shoulders to it; so it is good to poise our burdens before God lays them upon our backs. What if God put me upon such a trial? And as we should look for it; so—

2. Prepare for it: let us get soundness of grace, and strength of grace.

[1.] Get soundness of grace into your hearts. A hireling, when he comes to trial, will be changeable: guile of spirit will never hold out. Many have made a fair profession, but when put to trial, they have fallen foully. God loves to unmask hypocrites, to take off their disguise: Prov. xxvi. 26, 'The wicked shall be showed before the congregation;' and therefore it is good to prepare for them, to get soundness of grace, that you may be able to bear them. They that have no root cannot endure scorching weather. When the tree is soundly shaken, rotten apples fall to the ground; so in great trials guile of spirit will fail. And then—

[2.] Get strength of grace. Why? we cannot set bounds to trouble; we know not what God may do, and we must prepare for the worst. A little grace and a strong temptation will not do well together; therefore take heed, be not overlaid, and overcome. We are to look after not only truth, but growth of grace; to grow more holy, heavenly, humble; but above all, to increase in faith every day—'I have prayed that your faith fail not,' Luke xxii. 52. Chaff is lost in tossing from side to side, but full-eared corn remains behind. This is our Saviour's direction to the apostles: Mat. xxvi. 41, 'Watch and pray, that ye enter not into temptation.' They had not received as yet the promise of the Spirit; they were weak, they had not such soundness of grace as was fit for trial; therefore 'watch and pray,' that is, look for trial and pray for grace, for the full measures of the Spirit, that you may not be overcome. As, you know, the steward, Luke xvi. 3, was preparing— What if I should be turned out of my stewardship? how shall I live

then ?   So it is good to see how you shall live in a dear year when
creatures fail, when the Lord turns the tables, when the course of his
providence alters.   Have I a God to trust to ? have I grace to bear
me out?

3. When you are upon your trial, see that you discover nothing but
what will become obedience and submission to God—no impatience, no
murmuring, no worldliness, no distrust of God.   God taketh much
notice of your behaviour then, and your sincerity is put to the test.
What doth the trial bring forth ?   Hab. ii. 21, ' Behold his soul which
is lifted up is not upright in him ; but the just shall live by his faith.'
If it bring forth pride, swelling against God's sovereignty, censures of
his providence, distrust of his fatherly love, it is a sad case ; but if it
produce a lively exercise of faith, oh what a confirmation will this be
to you!   So that it is of great importance to your peace to see how
you carry yourselves.   When the vessel is pierced, it discovereth the
liquor that is within, whether it be thick, or dreggy, or musty.   Now
God cometh to pierce us, to give vent to that which is within us.

Doct. 2. Observe,—the greater the faith, the greater the trial.

Abraham is put to offer his only son.   Look, as Jacob drove, as the
little ones were able to endure, Gen. xxxiii. 14 ; such is· the conduct
of providence : God proportions our trials as he hath given in strength
of grace : 2 Cor. x. 13, ' There hath no temptation taken you, but such
as is common to man ; for God is faithful, who will not suffer you to be
tempted above that you are able.'   God doth not love to put an angel's
work upon a man, nor a man's work upon children, nor the work of
strong faith upon a weak believer ; but still, according to our particular
strength, he proportions our work.   We count him a cruel man that
overdrives or overlades his beast ; and will the gracious and wise God
seek to crush you ?   His trials are not that he may destroy, but that he
may prove.   But then, on the other side, strong faith must look for
strong trials ; and after God hath richly furnished us with comfort and
the graces of the Spirit, God will put us upon expense.   When he
hath laid in much there will be a time of laying out.   Satan's rage is
against the best : Heb. x. 32, ' After ye were illuminated, ye endured
a great fight of afflictions.'   When the castle is victualled, then he
suffers the devil to lay siege ; when God hath provided us with a stock
of grace and of the comforts of the Holy Spirit, he calls us to a time of
trial.   As Paul, after his rapture, had his buffetings : 2 Cor. xii. 7,
' Lest I should be exalted above measure through the abundance of the
revelations, there was given to me a thorn in the flesh, the messenger
of Satan to buffet me, lest I should be exalted above measure.'   It is
notable, in the story of Christ's own life, when he received a voice from
heaven, Mat. iii. 17, ' This is my beloved Son, in whom I am well
pleased.'   Then he was led by the Spirit into the wilderness, to be
tempted of the devil,' Mat. iv. 1 ; and Luke iv. 1, ' Jesus, being full of
the Holy Ghost, returned from Jordan, and was led by the Spirit into
the wilderness.'   So when we have the highest assurances of God's
love, and are feasted with the comforts of his Spirit, we must look for
trials and exercise.

Use. Let not the weakest despond and be discouraged, and let not
the best be secure.   Let not the weakest despond : there is a propor-

tion between your graces and afflictions; when God hath fitted you, he will call you out to battle, and not before.   Let not the best be secure; Satan's rage is most against you, Satan labours mightily to regain his hold—' He hath desired to sift thee as wheat,' Luke xxii. 31.   He is very jealous of his kingdom, and he loves to foil God's champions.   He had a special spite against Job, and therefore he moved the Lord against him.   *Hos quærit dejicere quos videt stare,* saith Cyprian.   The devil doth not look after those that are tottering and falling of their own accord; but when he sees God's champions, for his cause, honour, and truth, his spite is against them.

SERMON LII.

*By faith Abraham, when he was tried, offered up Isaac: and he that had received the promises, offered up his only begotten son, of whom it was said, That in Isaac shall thy seed be called: accounting that God was able to raise him up, even from the dead; from whence also he received him in a figure.—*HEB. *xi. 17–19.*

Obs. GOD hath a hand in all our trials.   ' It came to pass, after those things, God tempted Abraham,' Gen. xxii. 1.   He tempts no man by way of solicitation to sin, but for trial of our integrity and obedience. How doth God tempt?   He doth not tempt now by extraordinary command as before in the time of the old testament.   When the people of God were confined within a narrow corner of the world, then God tried them by extraordinary command; then they were not called to martyrdom, nor to suffer exquisite torment for the name of God, to put faith and patience to trial; then they were not scattered among wolves, as they now are.

In the new testament we are often put to the trial, whether we will love our lives unto the death.

But what hand hath God in temptation now?

1. Sometimes he withdraws his grace that he may try us: 2 Chron. xxxii. 31, ' God left Hezekiah to try him, and that he might know all that was in his heart.'   God tries some to discover their graces, and he tries some by withdrawing grace, that he may discover their own personal weakness, without his concurrence, as well as the strength of his own grace.   When we grow proud and secure, God takes away the staff and stay, and then the poor creature falls to the ground; or, as the nurse withdraws her hand and lets the child take a knock, so God leaves us that he may prove and try us, and show what is in our heart.

2. Sometimes he permits us to be tempted by Satan or evil men. By Satan; thus we pray, ' Lead us not into temptation;' that is, give us not up to the devil's tempting.   And Christ tells Peter, Luke xxii. 32, ' I have prayed that thy faith fail not.'   He doth not say, I have prayed that temptation come not, but that thy faith fail not.   When

the Lord suffers Satan to toss and winnow his children, it is but to try them, that so their graces may be discovered, and they may be acquainted with themselves. Sometimes by evil men; so Deut. xiii. 3, ' The Lord your God proveth you, to know whether you love the Lord your God with all your heart, and all your soul.' When doth the Lord prove them ?—when a dreamer of dreams, when lying and seducing spirits are gone abroad, that is a time when God tries his people. He suffers those winds to blow, that so solid grain may be distinguished from the chaff. We are then tried what we are, when seducing spirits go abroad, and plausible errors are broached and vented in the world.

3. Sometimes doth the Lord try us by the course of his providence; and there both by afflictions and mercies. By afflictions: Deut. viii. 2, ' And thou shalt remember all the way which the Lord thy God led thee these forty years in the wilderness, to humble thee, and to prove thee, to know what was in thy heart, whether thou wouldest keep his commandments or no.' This was the end of that tedious and long walk in the wilderness. Why did the Lord keep them forty years in a howling wilderness, walking about, forward and backward, when they might have reached Canaan in forty days ?—to humble, and prove, and try them. So the Lord suffers affliction to seize upon you; he takes away your nearest and dearest comforts, and relations, to see what you will discover; whether murmuring or supplication, rebellion or trust. Afflictions broach the vessel, and according to the liquor that is in it so it runs; yet the broaching of the vessel doth not cause it to run musty, or dreggy; that is from within. By affliction, God discovers whether grace or corruption will be discovered. And sometimes by the violence of evil men, he suffers rough winds to discover the solid grain from the chaff: Luke ii. 37, ' A sword shall pass through thy own soul also, that the thoughts of many hearts may be revealed.' It is spoken of the Virgin Mary, when she saw Christ upon the cross, it was as if a sword passed through her heart. And as the Lord tries his people by affliction, so by the blessings of his providence, God gives a full condition to try you. Our trial doth not lie in miseries only, but in abundance; to see whether we will love him when he gives us abundance of all things; whether we will forget him, or cleave close to him, and own him the more. As you try a servant by leaving loose money about the house; so God tries his people by the comforts of this world, therefore doth the Lord give Israel dainties; that is, a great proportion, a certain rate every day, that he might prove them whether they will suffer their hearts to be carried out after the world, or whether they will love him : Exod. xvi. 4, ' Behold I will rain bread from heaven for you, and the people shall go out, and gather a certain rate every day, that I may prove them, whether they will walk in my law or no.'

4. God hath a great hand in correcting, limiting, and ordering the temptation. God sets bounds to the tempter, and orders the kind of the temptation. When Satan moved the Lord against Job, God gives him leave—Go, touch his substance, but not his person by any means. And when his commission is enlarged to inflict botches upon his skin, yet take heed of his life. Thus far shall the trial go, and no farther, even as the Lord will. When we are in Satan's hands, Satan is in God's hand. It was said of the conspiracy against Julius Cæsar, all

that was noble in it belonged to Brutus, but all the malice and cruelty in the design was imputed to Cassius ; so all that is good and tends to good, that is from the Lord, as the moderation and sanctification of temptation, the gracious use his people make of it ; all this is from God, but the evil and malignity comes from the devil.   It is said in Mat. 4. 1, ' The Spirit led him into the wilderness to be tempted of the devil.' The devil had not only a hand in Christ's temptations, but the Spirit.

Use. Well then, acknowledge God in all your afflictions ; he hath a great hand in them.   We suffer a spaniel to hunt a duck, not to devour or destroy it ; so the Lord suffers the devil to toss us and try us, but he hath a hand over him that he shall not devour and tear us in pieces ; therefore acknowledge God in all.   Christ hath directed our address to him—' Lead us not into temptation, but deliver us from evil ; ' wherein we desire, first that God would keep the temptation off, if he see fit ; for who would desire poison to try the strength of an antidote ?   Therefore we first desire that the Lord would keep off the trial ; if not, then we beg of him that he would moderate temptation, that he would give us strength, that we may not be foiled by it.   We have deserved to be led into temptation, and left there to be foiled and overwhelmed ; and therefore we deprecate this judgment.

Obs. We are never tried to purpose till we are tried in our Isaac.

This was Abraham's trial—' Offer now thy son, thine only son, whom thou lovest,' Gen. xxii. 2 ; so we are tried in our Isaac.   What is that ? in things that are nearest and dearest to us.   It was an easy matter that Solomon offered so many thousand beasts—' Twenty thousand oxen, and a hundred and twenty thousand sheep,' 1 Kings viii. 62 ; but here was a greater offering.   But when are we put to such a trial, to offer up our Isaac ?

Ans. In three cases—In case of submission ; in case of self-denial ; in case of mortification.

1. In the case of submission to the strokes of providence, when near relations are taken away from us—a husband, a wife, a beloved and an only child.   God knows how to strike us in the right vein ; there will be the greatest trial where our love is set, when God deprives us of those things which we most affect.   As, suppose the providence of God is not past, and God is ready to take them from you, and you are afraid ; here your trial is in a willing resignation ; give up your Isaac to the will of the Lord, as Abraham did when God called him.   There cannot be such a concurrence of so many endearing circumstances in any relation of yours as there was in Abraham's Isaac, a son of his love, a son of his old age, a son that was conceived by virtue of the promise, a son in whom the promise was pitched.   To take away Isaac was to take away Christ and eternal life, that was included in Isaac ; for Christ was to come of Isaac.   I will but use this argument to press you to resign up your comforts into the hands of God.   When you are willing and ready to part with your comforts at God's call, it is the only way to keep them.   Abraham offered his Isaac, and was no loser by it ; he kept him.   This is the way, and the only way to preserve them, to resign them to the will of the Lord.   But if the providence be already past, the stroke of God hath lighted upon your relations and your family, and your comforts are taken from you, then your trial is in a

patient submission, as before in a willing resignation : if you submit to
the will of God, this is to offer up your Isaac.   And here you have an
advantage of Abraham too.   Your relations do not fall under the
weight of your arm, and by your own hands, as Isaac was to be offered
by his own father ; for Abraham knew nothing to the contrary, but that
he was to be his executioner, and yet he submitted.   In all such cases
remember it is a trial, and men upon trial are wont to do their best.
When God comes to pierce and broach you, will you discover nothing
but murmuring, worldly sorrow, vile affections, impatience, unsubjec-
tion to the will of God ?   When God had tried Abraham, he said, Gen.
xxii. 12, ' Now I know that thou fearest God, seeing thou hast not
withheld thy son, thy only son, from me.'   What ! shall the Lord say
I tried Abraham and found him faithful ; but now I know your stubbornness, disobedience, taxing my providence, quarrelling at my justice ?
God comes to make a sensible proof of us.

2. In case of self-denial, forsaking our choicest interests for a good
conscience.   To this purpose doth the apostle bring this instance, to
persuade them to martyrdom, to take the spoiling of their goods cheerfully, without murmuring and repining.   Can anything be nearer and
dearer to us than Isaac was to Abraham ?   Life and all must go if God
call for it.   If anything be nearer and dearer to us than other, God
must have it : Luke xiv. 26, ' If any man come to me, and hate not
father, and mother, and wife, and children, and brethren, and sisters,
yea, and his own life,' &c.   Either you must hate God, or hate the
creature ; there is no medium.   Whatever we are unwilling to quit
for God's sake, we love it more than God and Christ.   There he num-
bers up all relations—father, mother, brother, sister, wife, children.
Why ? because at all times christians are not called to lay down their
lives ; but we must venture the displeasure of near relations, father,
mother, &c., upon conscience of our duty to God, and when reasons of
religion call us thereto.   God came now to prove whom Abraham loved
most, whether he loved his God or his Isaac best.   Abraham loved
Isaac well, but God better.   So many times God puts us to a sensible
trial,—which we love best, whether our worldly interests or the Lord
himself.   When a servant followeth two men that walk together, you
cannot tell to whom he belongeth ; but when they part, then you see
whose servant he is.   God stands on the one side, interest on the other ;
either you must turn to your interests, or turn to God.   The Lord may
put us to such a trial, as usually he doth his children one time or other.
Now consider in such cases Abraham's self-denial.   Here was the slay-
ing of an innocent person, and this his son—son on whom the promises
were pitched, for they were to be fulfilled in him.   The more difficult
any piece of obedience is, the more excellent ; and the more self-denial,
the more difficult ; and the more we are to deny reason itself, as well
as our natural affection, the more self-denial.   All these circumstances
concurred here : Abraham was to overcome his natural affection.
What was dearer to him than Isaac ?   And therefore we must not only
part with mean things, but such as we prize above anything in the
world.   When God requireth we should forsake father, and mother,
and all our dearest relations, we must not grudge at it.   Nay, our lives
should not be dear to us : Acts xx. 24, ' Neither count I my life dear

unto myself, so that I might finish my course with joy,' &c. Nay, Abraham was to deny his reason : he might doubt whether the revelation were from God, or a delusion of Satan, or whether he were absolutely obliged ; no, but he simply resigneth up himself to God's wisdom and will. We are apt to distinguish and wriggle ourselves out of a sense of our duty ; but here was no such matter, no disputing, no debating, but a ready compliance. Nay, consider the Lord's love to us in Christ ; for in all this Abraham was a lively type of God's love to us in Christ, who gave his Isaac for us, his only-begotten and dearly-beloved Son, better than all the world, who was made a burnt-offering for us, and was slain indeed. We can never deny ourselves so far as to answer what God hath done for us.

3. Because this is not every day's trial, this sensible self-denial ; therefore we are tried in our Isaac in mortification, in renouncing our bosom lust. This is a daily trial, and this is a sure trial, for lusts stick closer to us than interests. It is easier to part with rams and rivers of oil than to part with one sin ; they are as a joint and member of the body, therefore called members, Col. iii. 5 ; and the ' right hand,' and the ' right eye,' Mat. v. 29, 30. Now in mortifying those corruptions which are so contrary to the spiritual life, and yet so rooted in our nature, here we are tried, whether we will give up our Isaac. Some corruptions stick closer to us than others, and in renouncing those, the sincerity of our love is tried : Ps. xviii. 23, ' I was upright before him, and I kept myself from mine iniquity.' What lust did you ever leave for God ? Can you ever remember the plucking out the right eye and the cutting off the right hand ? or the withstanding your natural inclinations ? or the renouncing your lusts and corruptions for the Lord's sake ? Can you remember his love prevailed with you to part with that which was so near and dear to the soul, that was so close as a joint to the body ?

Use. Do not measure your uprightness by a lower trial, that doth but demolish the outworks of sin, and weaken some petty interest It is no warrant to a captain to give up the town, as soon as the great guns come, or when the enemy hath taken the outworks. If you give up at the first assault, it is a very bad sign. As Julian the Apostate once said, If you cannot endure our scoffs, how will you endure the darts of the Persians ? Jer. xii. 5, ' If thou hast run with the footmen, and they have wearied thee, then how canst thou contend with horses ? ' So if you cannot endure a frown, a little hazard of your interest, a little brow-beating from those that are in power and place, how will you be able ' to resist to blood ' ? Heb. xii. 4. So to quit a lesser sin, and it may be a sin that will bring inconvenience upon you, that is no trial ; it is no trial to submit to a lesser stroke of providence—it may be you were not affected with it—but to part with your Isaac, there is the trial ; when God takes away your nearest comforts and relations, then to keep your hearts upright, this is a trial to purpose.

2. Again, it shames us that we stick at a trifle ; a little ease and sloth, and every slight temptation, causeth us to make bold with God, or to neglect the worship of God, or disobey the command of God ; and every lesser excuse is enough to cause you to omit duty. When you stick at anything in the ways of the Lord, because it is irksome to flesh

and blood, and seems tedious, will you reason with yourselves—How can I look for Abraham's blessing when I am so far from Abraham's temper? he was willing to offer up Isaac. If you had Abraham's trial, if you were to conflict with natural affections and reason, if you were to reconcile the command and promise, what should you do? But a small thing, a little difficulty and inconvenience, is enough to turn us out of the way, and discourages us.

Obs. Faith maketh us go through such trials with honour to God, and acceptation with him.

Here I shall show the influence of faith, what power and operation it hath upon the heart to carry on the soul in such trials.

1. Faith teacheth us how to value and esteem invisible and spiritual things : it judgeth of all things aright. Faith is a spiritual prudence ; it is opposed not only to ignorance, but also to folly. So much unbelief as we have, so much folly we have ; and so much faith as we have, so much the wiser are we in spiritual things—' O fools, and slow of heart to believe ! ' Luke xxiv. 25. But now faith is a spiritual wisdom ; it teacheth us how to value the favour of God and the comforts of the other world, and the smiles of his countenance ; it shows us that all outward things are nothing in comparison of inward comfort. Reason will teach us how to value the interests and concernments of the present life, and the worth of riches and honour ; and sense will teach us the worth of pleasures ; but now it is faith that teacheth us how to value the favour of God, even above life itself : Ps. lxiii. 3, ' Thy loving-kindness is better than life.' Therefore because faith makes us wise in this kind, it makes us part with things never so near and dear to us, because they are base and vile in respect of the favour of God. It is faith makes us judge that the greatest suffering is better than the least sin, because the least sin makes us hazard the favour of God : Heb. xi. 26, ' Esteeming the reproach of Christ greater riches than the treasures of Egypt.' The greatest suffering may occasion a greater sense of his favour, and that brings us nearer to God. The worst and most afflictive part of christianity with the lowest enjoyment of God is better than the highest enjoyment of all things that are in the world. Faith shows us that the wrath of man is nothing to the wrath of God : Heb. xi. 27, ' By faith he forsook Egypt, not fearing the wrath of the king ; for he endured, as seeing him that is invisible.'

2. Faith solves all doubts and riddles, whenever we are in a puzzle ; for Abraham was divided—What ! shall I offer Isaac, and put the promises to slaughter, or must I disobey God on the other side ? Now faith doth silence this riddle—' He accounted that God was able to raise him from the dead.' Faith by a resolute dependence saith, Let Isaac go, God will provide for the promise well enough. Faith believes the accomplishment of the promise, whatever reason and sense say to the contrary ; and if the command of killing his son contradict the whole gospel of the promised seed, yet, because both comes from God, faith leaveth it to God to solve his own riddle ; it cuts the knot asunder by a resolute dependence upon the power of God. I must kill Isaac, and yet God's power is sufficient to make good his promise. Faith reconciles the greatest contradictions, and so settles doubtful thoughts : Job xiii. 15, ' Though he slay me, yet will I trust in him ;' though he

make breach upon breach, yet faith can reconcile the hand of God, though most heavy, with the heart of God ; it can reconcile death with life ; nothing with all things ; anger with favour.   And so for the commands of God.   Unsanctified reason is an unfit judge of divine commands ; but with faith God's authority prevails, whatever our private reason may allege to the contrary.   Men take their measures amiss when they make human reason the supreme judge of all things in religion ; no, faith is an absolute submission to the authority of God : 2 Cor. x. 5, ' Casting down imaginations, and every high thing that exalteth itself against the knowledge of God, and bringing into captivity every thought to the obedience of Christ.'   If anything appear to be a divine revelation, as the doctrine of the trinity, and the resurrection, human reason must not be heard against it ; neither must we question the truth of any divine promise for the improbability and difficulty of the fulfilling of it.

3. Faith looketh for the restitution of our comforts again, in kind or in value, when they seem to be most lost.   Faith knows it is a saving bargain to lose things for God's sake.   The way to save is to lose ; he can and will, beyond comparison, recompense whatever is lost for him : Mark x. 29, 30, ' Whoever forsakes father, or mother, or wife, or children, or lands, for my sake, shall have an hundredfold,' &c. ; that is, shall have his parents, relations, and comforts in kind ; or else he shall have it abundantly made up to him.   Carnal sense knows not what to make of these promises, and therefore Julian the Apostate scoffed at this promise, as if it were a very great absurdity, that Christ should say, He that loseth father, or mother, shall receive an hundredfold.   What !   Shall they have a hundred fathers and a hundred mothers ?—No ; but we shall have them in value.   Abraham knew he should receive Isaac here one way or other, though he could not see which way—' He received him in a figure,' as is said in the next verse. The king of Israel, when the Lord bade him to dismiss the army that he had hired, was mightily troubled ; saith he, 2 Chron. xxv. 9, ' What shall we do for the hundred talents which I have given to the army of Israel ?   And the man of God answered, The Lord is able to give thee much more than this.'   All trouble ariseth from this, when sense cannot tell how our comforts shall be made up.   What recompense shall we have for those things we part with for God's sake ? for when a thing appears not, we think it quite gone.   Faith saith, God is able to give thee more than this.   When a man is made a beggar for God's sake ; when he is exposed to the frowns of the world, to poverty and contempt, for God's sake, sense says, How shall we live ? how shall our family and children be provided for ?   God is able to give thee more ; these things shall be supplied, the comforts we lose shall be made up again ; for a man can be no loser by God.

4. Faith is a grace that looks to things, and then the harshest trials seem nothing.   Sense looks to things present ; then it is bitter, harsh, and troublesome to deny ourselves upon the justest reasons of religion ; but faith looks to things to come, and then afflictions are light : 2 Cor. iv. 17, 18, ' For our light affliction, which is but for a moment, worketh for us a far more exceeding, and eternal weight of glory.   While we look not to the things that are seen, but to the things that are not seen ;

for the things that are seen are temporal, but the things that are not seen are eternal.' Give me a man that hath a sight of eternity, and then turn him loose to the frowns of the world—to the favours of the world, to temptations and trials, they are nothing, he goes through them merrily, because his heart is taken up with higher and better things. When he hath the perspective of faith, and looks into the other world, and hath had a ravishing affective sight of the glorious inheritance, he can easily part with the world when God calls for it. There is nothing great to him that knows the greatness of eternity; it is nothing to be judged of man's judgment, to be exposed to man's wrath; they are acquainted with eternity, and the things of another world. Faith looks within the veil, and so hath a mighty influence on the support of the soul in times of trial.

5. Faith worketh by love, and then nothing is too near and dear to him, so God may be glorified. Faith doth not only look forward, but backward; not only forward to things to come, but backward to things past. It reports to the soul the great things God hath done for us in Christ; he hath given us his Son, who is infinitely worth all that we can give to him. It apprehends the love of God in Christ, and thus argues, When God hath given me himself, and his Christ, his only son, to die for me, shall I stick at anything? If God give Christ, shall Abraham stick at Isaac? If the blessed seed to come, shall his only seed be spared? God hath told Abraham, Gen xv. 1, 'I am thy shield, and thy exceeding great reward;' and Gen. xxii. 18, 'In thy seed all the nations of the earth shall be blessed.' And, therefore, will the Lord have my Isaac? I love him well, but I love my God better; Isaac shall be offered. The very comforts we part with, we had them from God, and he demandeth what he lent. Thus faith goes to work, urging the soul with the love of God, that we may out of thankfulness to God, part with those comforts which he requireth of us.

6. Faith committeth events to God, and so we are eased of many tossings of mind or unquiet agitations, that otherwise would obstruct us: Prov. xvi. 3, 'Commit thy works unto the Lord, and thy thoughts shall be established.' So Abraham here committed the event to God, not determining this or that, but was satisfied in God's all-sufficiency, ver. 19, 'Accounting that God was able to raise him up from the dead.' He was not certain that God would do it that way, but he was certain God was able to do it. This is the nature of faith, not to determine the event and to prescribe to God, but to refer it to him, and to wait for the promised deliverance, though we cannot imagine the manner how it shall be brought about.

Use. Well then, if we miscarry in trials, it is for want of faith; and if we would not miscarry, set faith a-work. We do not consult with faith, but with sense and carnal reason; and then no wonder we miscarry. If we did but set faith a-work to solve our doubts and riddles, and to see the restitution of our comforts, we should not easily be nonplussed. Let faith judge of spiritual things, and not reason. If we let reason judge of spiritual things, then the consolations of God will seem small. But let faith tell you how able God is; let it look forward and backward, and this will bring the soul through the temptation.

I observe one point more. It is said 'By faith Abraham offered.'

How did he offer? Abraham is said to have offered him, though he did not consummate and complete the obligation; in his heart he had parted with him, and given him wholly to God, and he began really to do what he had resolved upon. As to the consummation, there was no impediment on his part; but the Lord interposed and hindered the execution of his purpose, and therefore it is said, Abraham offered; and God tells him, 'Thou hast not spared thy son.' Isaac was rescued and spared; yet because it was his vow and his serious purpose so to do, and all things were ready, therefore God counted it as if he had offered up his son.

Hence observe, if faith be hindered in the accomplishment, the vow and purpose is accepted with God.

Many times we are put upon services that we cannot bring to a perfect issue; now the purpose God takes notice of. David was troubled that he should dwell in a house of cedar, and the ark of God dwell within curtains, and that God had not a house, therefore he purposes to build a house for God. Now, saith God, 1 Kings viii. 18, 'Since it was in thine heart to build a house for my name, thou didst well that it was in thine heart;' and 2 Cor. viii. 12, 'If there be first a willing mind, it is accepted according to that a man hath, and not according to that he hath not.' When all things are ready on our part, and there wants but a providence for our effecting what we intended, God takes notice of the ready mind. Many intend to do such a thing, but God's providence permitteth it not. These obstacles which happen, without our fault, do not hinder the acceptance of our purpose. So God took notice of David's purpose: Ps. xxxii. 5, 'I said, I will confess my transgressions unto the Lord, and thou forgavest the iniquity of my sin.' Though it were but a purpose, God gave in the comfort of a pardon. This may answer their doubts, who are wont to say, Abraham was called to this great trial, to show his love and obedience. When are we called thus? Christians, every one of us, one way or other, are called to trial. There are martyrs in vow and preparation of mind, though not in actual accomplishment, because not called to suffering. There must be a solemn purpose to give up all to Christ, when we come to Christ. All that are saved are martyrs, either actually or habitually; actually, if the honour of your profession and conscience of your duty to God require it; or else, habitually, in the purpose and preparation of your minds.

Use. I would apply it thus—If God takes purposes for performances, and accounts things done when really purposed, let us take God's promises for performances; if God saith, it shall be done, account it as if it were done—'Babylon is fallen, is fallen,' Rev. xiv. 8.

SERMON LIII.

*Accounting that God was able to raise him up, even from the dead ;
from whence also he received him in a figure.*—HEB. xi. 19.

HERE we have—

1. The working of his faith under this trial—*Accounting that God
was able to raise him up, even from the dead.*

2. The fruit and success of it—*from whence also he received him in
a figure.*

First, See the manner how his faith wrought — λογιζομενος,
'Accounting,' or reasoning. When we have any notable work to do,
we are full of thoughts and full of reasonings. The soul of man being
an understanding essence, it will not be settled without sound reason.
Now in all these debates it is excellent when reason serves faith, when
that which was wont to be an enemy is made a servant and handmaid
to faith. Nothing is so great an enemy to faith as reason, and the
perverse disputings of our own mind ; but when reason is made a
handmaid, it is an excellent advantage. Abraham reasoned, 'God was
able to raise him up.' What shall we learn from this reasoning of
Abraham ?

Obs. 1. In difficult cases we must take the duty part to ourselves,
and refer the event and success to the power of God.

We must do our work ; let God see to the fulfilling of his promises,
and let us see to the discharge of our duty. Abraham offered Isaac,
he reckoned 'God was able to raise him up ;' let him see to that : 2 Sam.
x. 12, 'Be of good courage, and let us play the men for our people,
and for the cities of our God ; and the Lord do that which seemeth
him good.' This is the right way ; let us mind that which is our work,
and leave to God that which is his work. To be troubled about events,
carking about the success of things, is to take God's work out of his
hands, and neglect our own. In every work there is a duty and a
the burden. What shall we do ? that is the question which concerns
duty ; but what shall become of us ? that is the question which concerns
burden. The duty belongs to us, and the burden, that must be turned
off upon God : Ps. lv. 22, 'Cast thy burden upon the Lord, he shall
sustain thee.' If a man were to go a journey, would he take a burden
upon him ? Look, as God laid your sins upon Christ, so he will have
your burdens to be cast upon himself—' Cast your care upon the Lord,
for he careth for you,' 1 Peter v. 7. It is no more dishonour to God
to bear our burdens than for Christ to bear our sins. I shall urge two
arguments.

1. It will ease the soul of a great deal of trouble. In all doubtful
events carking and trouble ariseth from encroaching upon God, from
minding more work than what is our own. For instance, in duties of
your calling, in dangers, when God calls you to go through them, as
women with child, or in the main duties of religion, mind what is your
duty, and refer the success and event to God : Phil. iv. 5, 'Be careful
for nothing.' What! must we be careless, senseless ? I answer, No,
not careless of the work, nor senseless of the danger ; but we must do

the work, and refer all to God as to the success; we must be mindful of the danger, and then commend it to God by prayer. We would not be so uncomfortable as we are if we would learn this, if we would not cark after the event what we shall eat, what we shall drink, or wherewithal we shall be clothed, and what will become of us, but turn that upon God. In any danger, when a call is evident, What would God have me to do? is our question, not, What will become of me?

2. It would keep us upright. When men will be meddling with more than belongs to them, they will turn aside to crooked ways. It is fear of success, and distrust of the event, makes us to act unworthily. When we are troubled about the event, we shall either neglect duty or take such a course as is more likely to carnal reason. If Abraham had taken care of the promise, Isaac had never been offered; but Abraham takes care of the command; the promise was God's part, and God's work in the covenant. Always the cause of miscarrying is stepping out of our bounds, and taking of God's work out of his hands.

Obs. 2. To encourage us to cast our burden upon God, we should consider his fidelity and his ability, or his truth and his power.

One is implied, the other expressed. Truth is implied, in that he looked for Isaac to be restored to him again because of the promise; and the ground of his expectation is expressed to be God's almighty power—'God is able,' &c. Sometimes we find truth and mercy joined together as the grounds of hope; we find this seven times in Ps. lxxxix. All three are grounds of trust—mercy and power, and truth engaged by a promise. So Bernard, *Tria considero quibus tota spes mea consistit, caritatem adoptionis, veritatem promissionis, et potestatem redditionis.* —There are three things that do support my hope; there is the readiness of grace, the truth of the promise, and the power of performance; this is a triple cord, that is not easily broken. But I will not wander. Here we are to consider two attributes, truth and power, which, as Aaron and Hur held up the hands of Moses, so do these support our faith, and hold up our hearts in waiting upon God. Abraham's faith and Sarah's faith do well together. If you mark in scripture, Sarah is commended for the acknowledging of God's truth: Heb. xi. 11, 'She judged him faithful who had promised.' And then Abraham's faith is pitched upon God's power: Rom. iv. 21, 'Being fully persuaded that what he had promised he was able to perform.' So here in the text, he knew 'God was able to raise him up from the dead.' Before he had a son, he expected him from God's power; and when he hath a son, he offers him up upon the confidence of God's power. He made no question of his truth, but having a large heart, being more sensible of the difficulties, he magnified God's power. And that which supported Abraham should support us; that God can do whatever he pleaseth, there is his power; and that God will do whatever he hath promised, there is his truth,—here are the two grounds which uphold our heart.

1. For God's truth, a word of that. Meditate upon the truth of God, if you would be supported in believing. Abraham had such high thoughts of it that he was confident that God would disturb the whole course of nature rather than not make good his word—that he should have his Isaac given him from the dead, that he would raise up an

Isaac out of the ashes of the sacrifice, rather than the promise should not be performed : he would pitch upon anything rather than to count God unfaithful. God will dissolve and alter the whole frame of the world rather than lose his truth ; he stands much upon the honour of his faithfulness. Say then to your souls, Surely it cannot be but God must be true ; that which God hath promised must come to pass. That which supported Abraham will also support us, if we had hearts to make use of it. God stands more upon the honour of his truth than upon aught else : Ps. cxxxviii. 2, 'Thou hast magnified thy word above all thy name.' The word of God is a monument of God's truth, as the works of God and the course of nature are the monuments of his wisdom and power. Now the monuments of his wisdom and power shall be defaced rather than the monuments of his truth—'Heaven and earth shall pass away, but not one jot or tittle of my word shall pass away,' Mat. v. 18. There is not a waste word in the covenant that shall fall to the ground : Ps. xii. 7, 'The words of the Lord are pure words, as silver tried in a furnace of earth purified seven times.' There is no dross in the promises, but all pure ; none of them shall fall to the ground. His power is beyond his declared will ; he can do no more than he hath done, or will do, but it doth not come short of it ; he hath not promised more than he is able to perform ; and his truth engageth his power : Heb. x. 23, 'He is able that hath promised.'

2. For the power of God. And here I shall show—

(1.) That God's power is the great encouragement to faith. (2.) How hard a matter it is to believe God's power. (3) How sinful it is not to believe it. (4.) To direct you what to do in this case.

[1.] God's power is the great encouragement of faith. From first to last we are still directed to depend and cast ourselves upon the power of God. In our first coming to God, waiting upon him for the work of conversion, what will support a poor soul that is troubled with the power of its corruption ? God is able. When Christ told his disciples, Mat. xix. 23, 'That a rich man shall hardly enter into the kingdom of God,' the disciples wondered : ver. 25, 'Who then can be saved ?' But Christ answers, ver. 26, 'With men this is impossible, but with God all things are possible.' The heart of man is not too hard for God, for then he would have a creature more mighty than himself. He is able to overpower the corruption of a man's heart : Eph. i. 19, 20, 'What is the exceeding greatness of his power to us-ward who believe, according to the working of his mighty power which he wrought in Christ when he raised him from the dead ;' and Rom. iv. 17, 'God, who quickeneth the dead, and calleth those things which be not, as though they were.' But then, when once we are gotten in with God, what is it that supports us, and keeps us up, and carries us through the whole business of salvation ? The power of God : 2 Tim. i. 12, 'I know whom I have believed ; and that he is able to keep that which I have committed to him.' How come the children of God to put their souls into God's hands?—'I know he is able ;' 1 Peter i. 5, 'Who are kept by the power of God through faith unto salvation ; and Jude 24, 'Unto him that is able to keep you from falling.' This supports the soul in the midst of all assaults and temptations that we meet with in the present life—'God is able to keep us.' And then for abilities of grace and present supplies: Phil. iv. 13, 'I can do all things through Christ that strengtheneth me;' Eph. vi. 10, 'My brethren, be strong in the Lord, and in the power of his might.' It is the power of God that carrieth us through: 2 Peter i. 3, 'The divine power giveth us all things pertaining to life and godliness.' So also for things to come. The resurrection is a very riddle to nature, that life should spring out of death, that the way to go upward is to go downward to the grave, that our dust shall be severed from common dust, and every flesh shall have his own body—riddles to nature. But that which doth facilitate, and makes the belief of it easy, is the mighty power of God: Phil. iii. 21, 'Who shall change our vile body, that it may be fashioned like to his glorious body, according to the working whereby he is able to subdue all things to himself.' This is that which supports the soul in an expectation of the blessed resurrection. Therefore the Sadducees that denied the resurrection, Christ tells them, Mat. xxii. 29, 'Ye err, not knowing the scriptures, nor the power of God.' The scriptures show what shall be, and the power of God what may be. So for all public promises, for the calling of the Jews; when a man considers how obstinate and hardened they are in their prejudices against Christ, who would think the Jews should ever be called? Nay, when we consider still how that people are scattered up and down in the world, we know not what is become of the ten tribes, the remnant of them; yet it is said, 'God is able to graft them in again.' So for the avenging of antichrist; when we consider how antichrist is supported with the interests, and power, and force of princes, and how the nations wonder after the whore, we cry out, How shall these things be accomplished? Rev. xviii. 8, 'Her plagues shall come in one day, death, and mourning, and famine, and she shall be utterly burnt with fire; for strong is the Lord God who judgeth her.' Still we are referred to the power of God; so that the life and vigour of faith is very much concerned in the belief of God's power. And he that believes the first article of the creed, 'God, the Father Almighty,'—will easily believe all the rest. It is put in the front to show how all those things shall be accomplished —'The forgiveness of sins, the resurrection of the body, and life ever-sting.'

[2.] Let me show you how difficult it is to believe his power. Do but consider what our foolish thoughts do most of all dash themselves against, clearly at the power of God, for men never doubt but in case of danger and difficulty. When things go on happily, then they are secure; but as soon as dangers and difficulties arise, they are full of fears, suspicions, and distrust. What should be the reason, but only doubting of God's power? Observe the instances of scripture, and you shall find the greatest stumblings of unbelief have always been at God's power; as in Sarah: Gen xviii. 12, 'After I am old, shall I have pleasure, my lord being old also?' she urgeth the difficulty; so Moses: Num. xi. 21, 22, 'There are six hundred thousand footmen, and thou hast said, I will give them flesh, that they may eat for a whole month together. Shall the flocks and the herds be slain for them to suffice them? or shall the fish of the sea be gathered together for them to suffice them?' so Ps. lxxviii. 19, 'Can the Lord prepare a table in the wilderness?' It is not will the Lord, but can the Lord do it? There we dash our unbelieving thought. So 2 Kings vii. 2, 'If the Lord should make windows in heaven, might this thing be?' So the virgin Mary, when the message was brought to her by the angel, that she should conceive Christ in her womb, and her substance should be assumed and sanctified, and concur to the making up of the person of Christ, she replies, Luke i. 34, 'How can this be?' Men deceive themselves when they think they doubt of the will of God; their main hesitancy, and sticking, is at the power of God. So when Christ came to raise Lazarus, saith Martha. John xi. 39, 'He stinketh by this time, for he hath been dead four days;' as if it were past the power of God to raise him up. And thus we do, we can easily believe the power of God in the theory. A man may draw out a fluent discourse of the omnipotency of God, and yet not be able to confute his own unbelief. To make a practical improvement of the power of God in time of distress and danger, that is no easy matter, And it ariseth, partly, from the imperfection of our understanding. A young child does not know his father's strength. We are poor weak creatures, and cannot conceive fully of the perfections of God; we know not what the power of God can do for us. And partly, because we are inured to principles of sense, and regard the ordinary working of second causes; therefore if there be any rub in God's way, we stumble presently. And partly, because there is such a deep and strong sense of present danger and difficulty that all actual thoughts of God's power are shut out when we are put upon temptation, and the soul hath not liberty to think of it; therefore it is we dash here most against God's power.

[3.] I come to show that this is a great sin, God takes it ill to be circumscribed and limited in his power. It is his complaint, Ps. lxxviii. 41, 'They limited the Holy One of Israel.' The great sin of Israel in the wilderness was circumscribing and confining God to the course and circle of second causes. So he that doubted, 2 Kings vii. 2, 'If the Lord should make windows in heaven, might this thing be?' And you know what exemplary judgment God laid upon him, God let him live to see it, and then he was trodden to death—God let him live to see his unbelief confuted, but he had no benefit by it. Now why is it such a heinous sin to question God's power? Partly, because this is to deny him to be God; if God were not omnipotent, he could not be a help to his friends nor a terror to his enemies. And partly, to deny him his power is to pull him out of the throne, because we have so much to prove and evidence the omnipotency of God that therefore it is the more heinous sin to deny it. It is a thing plainly displayed in the creation: Rom. i. 20, 'The invisible things of him from the creation of the world are clearly seen, being understood by the things that are made, even his eternal power and godhead.' His goodness is wrapt up in the covenant; his love is displayed in the church; but his power is displayed before all the world. The heathens see the invisible things of his goodness and power. We cannot be certain of his will in many things, but there is enough to inform us of the power of God.

[4.] To direct you how to make use of God's power so as to find support in it. I answer—

(1.) In mercies absolutely promised we may reason from his power to his will. If God be able, surely it will be accomplished : Rom. xi. 23, ' They shall be grafted in, for God is able to graft them in again.' It is the apostle's own argument. In the temple there were two pillars, Jachin and Boaz, 1 Kings vii. 21 ; the one signifies ' strength and might,' and the other ' God will establish it.' So Dan. iii. 17, the three children having particular instinct and revelation, therefore they say, ' Our God is able to deliver us, and he will deliver us.' So John x. 28, 29, ' They shall never perish, neither shall any man pluck them out of my hand. My Father which gave them me is greater than all, and no man is able to pluck them out of my Father's hand.' Christ reasons from his power ; he would have us secure our souls upon the omnipotency of God ; he must pluck God out of his throne, before he can hinder the salvation of his people.

(2.) In mercies conditionally promised, there we are to magnify his power, and refer the matter to his will : as Mat. viii. 2, ' Lord, if thou wilt, thou canst make me clean.' Give him the glory of his power, and refer your case to his will ; God will do what is for the best.

(3.) In all cases take this rule : whatever be your discouragements to weaken faith, difficulty or unlikelihood should be none, because of the almighty power of God in whom we trust. Usually the great cause of discouragement is danger and difficulty, now that is dishonourable to God ; we should conceive of him by his power : Job xlii. 2, ' I know that thou canst do everything ;' so Dan. iii. 17, 18, ' Our God is able, and he wilt deliver us ; but if not, we will not serve thy gods' ; we will not be discouraged with the difficulty of the case. This will strike all discouragements down, when we have right apprehensions of God's power.

Use. If this be the great attribute that will support our faith, the power of God, then it presseth you to meditate often upon the power of God. The life of faith and confidence lies in it. How shall we do to improve the power of God in meditation ?

1. Consider how much God's power can outwork our thoughts. God were not infinite if he could be comprehended ; surely he hath more power than we are able to apprehend, therefore we can never be competent judges of it. Look, as we cannot empty the ocean with a nut-shell, so neither can we fathom the depth of God with the plummet of our thoughts. We no more know God than a worm knows a man. There is a greater distance between God and a man than between a worm and a man ; both are finite creatures, but God is infinite, and therefore we cannot fathom God, and so we are unmeet judges of his power. When our thoughts are able to reach no farther, yet God can outreach our thoughts : Zech. viii. 6, ' If it be marvellous in your eyes, should it also be marvellous in mine eyes ? saith the Lord of Hosts.' The Lord was angry there because they confined him to the model of their own thoughts—because they would measure infiniteness by their own last— because we cannot see how a thing should be done, shall we conclude that therefore God cannot do it ? God can outgo our thoughts : Eph. iii. 20, ' Unto him that is able to do exceeding abundantly above all that we ask or think, according to the power that worketh in us.'

2. Consider the special instances of God's power.

[1.] In creation. O christian ! remember the creating power of God.

David saith, Ps. cxxiv. 8, 'Our help is in the name of the Lord who made heaven and earth.' As if the psalmist had said, As long as I see heaven and earth I will never distrust. I hope in that God which made all these things out of nothing; and therefore as long as I see those two great standing monuments of his power before me, heaven and earth, I will never be discouraged. So the apostle: 1 Peter iv. 19, 'Commit the keeping of your souls to him in well-doing, as unto a faithful creator.' O christian! remember when you trust God you trust an almighty creator, who is able to help, let your case be never so desperate. God could create when he had nothing to work upon, which made one wonder, What is become of the tools wherewith he made the world? Where is the trowel wherewith he arched the heaven? and the spade wherewith he digged the sea? What had God to work upon, or work withal when he made the world? He made it out of nothing. Now you commit your souls to the same faithful creator. Then,—

[2.] Consider the providence of God, that will help you; partly, because providence is nothing else but a continued creation. The same power that made all things upholds all things; and this is a great relief to the soul, for it shows us that God is the same still: Isa. xl. 28, 'Hast thou not known, hast thou not heard, that the everlasting God, the Lord, the creator of the ends of the earth doth, not faint, neither is weary?' There is no wrinkle upon the brow of eternity. He that made all things by his word holds all things by his own almighty grasp; and if he loosen his hand, and take away the influence and supportation of his providence, all things would return to nothing again. And partly, because providence gives us new instances of God's power in sustaining and governing all the world, providing for all creatures. You trust in him that fills the mouth of every living thing, and that keeps a table for all the world: Ps. cxlv. 16, 'Thou openest thine hand, and satisfiest the desire of every living thing.' How many mouths doth God feed only with opening his hand? The whole creation hangs upon him, as vessels do upon a nail in a sure place.

[3.] Then consider not only God's general providence, but your own particular experiences. Experience is a most affective and near thing; and things wherein we are concerned ourselves leave a more sensible impression upon the soul: Rom. v. 4, 'Experience worketh hope.' When we have had a particular trial of God's power, we can the more readily trust him. I verily believe Abraham's experience was a mighty confirmation to his faith. For mark—it is said, 'He accounted God was able to raise him from the dead; from whence also he had received him in a figure.' God had given Isaac, as it were, from the dead at the first: ver. 12, 'Therefore sprang there of one, and him as good as dead, as many as the stars of the sky for multitude, and as the sands on the sea-shore innumerable;' so Rom. iv. 19, 'He considered not his own body now dead, when he was about an hundred years old, nor yet the deadness of Sarah's womb.' I say this made him more capable of this reasoning and arguing, because he had experience God had given him Isaac from a dead body and a dead womb; therefore he concluded God was able to raise him from the dead. So for our particular trials; when we have had experience of the power of God, it is a mighty confirmation of our faith.   The apostle saith, 2 Cor. i. 9, 10, ' We have had the sentence of death in ourselves, that we should not trust in ourselves, but in God, which raised the dead.   Who delivered us from so great a death, and doth deliver ; in whom we trust that he will yet deliver us.'   If you have had great deliverances and experiences of the power of God, this is a mighty confirmation in believing.   And then consider the spiritual experiences, and not only experiences in general ; partly because these are the highest instances of God's power.   God showed a great deal of power in making the world, but he shows more power in renewing the heart of man ; for as there was nothing to work upon in making the world, so nothing to resist ; but when he comes to form you anew, and create you in Christ Jesus to good works, there was a great deal of resistance ; that God which hath overpowered thy spirit-ual corruptions hath herein showed us his power.   And partly, because this is an engaging instance, that they may wait upon God for the future effects of his power, *Deus donando debet.*   I urge this the rather because the apostle urgeth us to consider of it : Eph. i. 19, 'And what is the exceeding greatness of his power to us-ward that believe.'   He doth not refer us to the power of God, by which the world was made, but that which works in them that believe.   Again, Eph. iii. 20, ' Who is able to do exceeding abundantly above what we ask or think, accord-ing to the power that worketh in us.'   He doth not speak of his mighty power which made the world, or that wrought then in the church in working of miracles ; no, but the mighty power that worketh in our hearts, and thence gathers that God is able to do far above what we can ask or think.

Obs. 3. God's power reacheth to the grave, and beyond the grave, even to give life to the dead.

God can not only preserve the creatures while they are in life and being, but when life is lost he can restore it again.   It is an easier matter to make a vessel out of clay, than when it is dashed into pieces to re-store and set it up in form again.   So here God did not only make us at first out of nothing, but when we are broken into pieces again, he can raise us from the dead.   Abraham had no experience of the resurrec-tion as we have, yet Abraham concluded thus, Oh, let it shame us ! The apostle argues, Acts xxvi. 8, ' Why should it be thought a thing incredible with you that God should raise the dead ? '   Abraham believed the resurrection at that distance : Christ was not then risen, there were none ever quickened from the dead, yet he believed God was able to raise Isaac out of his ashes ; but we have more reason to believe it.   There is no more reason to disbelieve the resurrection than the creation.   It is as easy for God to raise us up as it was for God to make us at first ; it is as easy for God to do one as the other.

Obj. You will say, What needs all this ado ? surely we believe the resurrection.

Ans. I doubt you do not as much as you should.   For—

1. If you did believe the resurrection, why are you so easily amazed at lesser difficulties ? John xi. 24, 25, Christ confutes Martha ; Martha said, ' I know that he shall rise again in the resurrection at the last day.   Jesus said unto her, I am the resurrection and the life ; he that believeth in me, though he were dead yet shall he live ; believest thou

this?' Canst thou believe the general resurrection, and canst thou not believe this, that I can raise him up now? Christians, in every difficult case your faith in the resurrection of the dead is tried when you come to depend upon God in extreme danger. So much is intimated by Paul: 2 Cor. i. 9, 'We had the sentence of death in ourselves, that we should not trust in ourselves, but in God which raiseth the dead.' God tries whether you can trust him that raiseth the dead, when the dead are gone and lost as to outward appearance and probability. If you cannot depend upon God, and magnify his power, and refer yourselves to his will in difficult cases, how can you say you believe the resurrection?

2. If you have such a faith, this will bewray itself in life and death. That hope is worth nothing that is good for nothing. As—

[1.] This faith will discover itself in life. If we believe the resurrection, we will count the faithful fulfilling of Christ's will better than all the pleasures of the world; that faith will have such an influence upon your life. Faith is discovered in action in the course of your conversation. · They that are not such manner of persons do not look for such things, 2 Peter iii. 11. Doth he look for the resurrection that useth his body only as a strainer for meats and drinks? that prostitutes his body to base lusts? that doth not employ himself with labour and diligence in the work God hath given him to do?

[2.] You will know the strength of this faith in death. Can we see life at the back of it? Can we desire death, and check the fears of it? Can we triumph over the last enemy, and be constant in Christ's cause to the latter end? and die cheerfully upon this ground, because we look for a joyful resurrection? A man goes to bed willingly and cheerfully, because he knows he shall rise again the next morning, and be renewed in his strength. Confidence in the resurrection would make us go to the grave as cheerfully as we go to our beds; it would make us die more comfortably, and sleep more quietly in the bosom of the Lord.

From whence also he received him in a figure.

Secondly, the success of his faith is the next thing to be spoken to. There is a great deal of ado about the meaning of that place. Some look backward and refer it to the time past, as if the meaning were, he looked God should raise him from the dead, because from thence he received him in a figure, that is, he had him from the dead before, from a dead womb and a dead body; but I think that is not so proper. Some look forwards, and refer it to the time to come, either to Christ or the resurrection. To Christ: Isaac was a type or figure of Christ's dying and rising. Or to the resurrection: his being freed from his present danger was an image of the resurrection from the dead, but it is not *for* a figure or a type, but *in* a figure; and therefore I think it is nothing but thus—he was even as good as dead, dead in his father's purpose and in his own thoughts; and from thence he received him again; which also was a kind of image of the resurrection from the dead; he that was just offered, and bound to the altar, seemed as it were to rise again.

Here I might observe several things.

Obs. 1. That in extremity God will be seen.

All was as good as dead, and yet he receives him again, when the knife was just at his throat: Gen. xxii. 10, 'And Abraham stretched forth his hand, and took the knife to slay his son.' When he had lifted up his hand, just as the knife was at his throat, then the Lord speaks to him and saith, Offer not Isaac. So Paul, 2 Cor. i. 9, when he had the sentence of death, was ready to be torn in pieces, then God useth such a dispensation. When Christ was brought to the very brow of the hill, and they thought to throw him down, then he escaped, Luke iv. 29. 30. And when there was but a hair's breadth between the Jews and ruin in Esther's time, then posts were sent to stop execution. Thus the Lord casts his people into great extremities to try their trust. When the case is desperate, and in human sense we are gone, then God appears: Ps. cxviii. 18, 'The Lord hath chastened me sore, but he hath not given me over unto death.'

Obs. 2. The success of believing. Believe and have; he counted God would raise him from the dead, and then he received him again. God's power, when glorified by an actual faith, will turn to a good account. When we trust God, we lose nothing by it. Trust among men is engaging. If another man trust you, in ingenuity you will not disappoint and fail him. Sure, then, God will not fail a trusting soul: John xi. 40, 'Said I not unto thee, that if thou wouldst believe thou shouldst see the glory of God?' We shall not see the power of God, nor the beauty of his providence, if we do not trust him. It is said in the Gospel, 'Christ could do no mighty works, because of their unbelief,' Mark xiii. 58, compared with Mark vi. 5. He could not, because he would not. Where his power is not glorified, there it shall not be exercised: 2 Chron. xvi. 8, 'Because thou didst rely on the Lord, therefore he hath delivered them into thine hand.' God is mightily pleased and honoured by it; and a waiting and trusting soul shall never be disappointed. Abraham counted God was able, and then he hath his Isaac again.

Obs. 3. Faith doth succeed always, though not in the way that we imagine and fore-conceive.

Abraham looked for Isaac out of the ashes of the sacrifice, but God gave him in another manner. The Lord doth not love that we should always see his way and work; for he will not only glorify his power in the eyes of them that believe, but he will glorify his wisdom, and will accomplish deliverance in a way they thought not of: Isa. xlv. 15, 'Verily thou art a God that hidest thyself, O God of Israel, the Saviour.' God loves to be a saviour under a veil; to hide himself, that we shall not see the way of his working; so Isa. xlviii. 7, 'They are created now, and not from the beginning, even before the day when thou heardest them not; lest thou shouldst say, Behold I knew them.' God will not have a creature look to the end of his work; and therefore let us not limit the Holy One of Israel, nor confine him to our means, but leave God to his own way and work. God will do that he hath promised, though we cannot imagine how. There are hidden depths of God's dispensations; he often carries himself very closely and covertly.

Obs. 4. Though things do not succeed in a way we forecast and imagine, yet they shall succeed in a better way.

It was better to have Isaac saved in this manner than to have him slain, and burnt to ashes, and then restored again. So God's way still is the best way, our way is not so good a way as God will find out for us; therefore do not confine him to a model of your own framing, but leave God to his own way.

Obs. 5. We receive our comforts anew and our relations anew from God every time when they are rescued out of imminent danger.

It is said he received him. How? Abraham twice received him; first in his birth by the grant of God—he was born when Abraham was aged; and now Isaac hath a new life, he received him again. Therefore when God gives in a relation to you out of a hazardous case, as wife, children, or husband, after a dangerous sickness, receive them as new pledges of God's love, take them as mercies newly bestowed. They seem to have a new life that are preserved in an imminent danger.

Use. If we would do as Abraham did, we must—

1. Acknowledge the supremacy and sovereignty of God, that he hath an absolute power over his creatures to do with them as he pleaseth, either as to life or death. This relieved Abraham as to the lawfulness of the fact, and this will be a great help to us in all our submission to God: 1 Chron. xxix. 11, 12, 'Thine, O Lord, is the greatness, and the power, and the glory, and the victory, and the majesty; for all that is in the heaven, and in the earth is thine; thine is the kingdom, O Lord, and thou art exalted, as head above all. Both riches and honour come of thee and thou reignest over all, and in thine hand is power and might, and in thine hand it is to make great, and to give strength unto all.' He hath power to command us and ours, and what he commandeth we must yield unto. All cometh of him, and we hold all from him and for him. All is at his dispose, he hath power to take away from us, will we, nill we, only he dealeth with us as rational creatures, leaveth us to our choice. Willingly to yield to him is an act of grace, but to be discontented with his dealings showeth we would withhold from him what we could.

2. That the Lord's wisdom is infinite, and he can solve those difficulties which are mere riddles to us; and therefore all thoughts of ours are be to captivated to his will, for he hath ways and means to bring about his purposes, which come not within our ken and perceivance. Alas! how easily will reason be nonplussed in what concerneth either our obedience or our faith. Christ's words to Peter are of use here: John xiii. 7, 'What I do thou knowest not now, but thou shalt know hereafter.' There are many things which we know not the reason of; but wait a little while, and obey the voice of God, and all things shall be clear and evident. He is wise in heart, and 'wonderful in counsel, and excellent in working,' Isa. xxviii. 29; and therefore we owe him blind obedience. He that can bring all things out of nothing, light out of darkness, meat out of the eater, one contrary out of another, deserveth to be waited upon with a constant reliance. We cannot dive into the depth of his counsel, but must yield an implicit obedience to his will, and go on with our duty, referring events to him; we must absolutely yield to his will because it is his will, and wait his leisure, till we know the reason of it.

3. That that which we give to God out of true faith and love shall be

received again one way or other. Isaac was dead in Abraham's purpose, yet Isaac lived, and was received in a figure. That which is spent in charity is lost to us in all visible appearance, yet it is lent to the Lord, and he will pay it again : Prov. xix. 17, 'He that hath pity on the poor lendeth unto the Lord ; and that which he hath given, will he pay him again ;' and Eccles. xi. 1, 'Cast thy bread upon the waters, for thou shalt find it after many days ;' all is thought to be cast away as if were thrown into the sea, but it will be repaid with advantage. So what is lost for God's sake shall be found again : Mat. xvi. 25, 'Whosoever will lose his life for my sake shall find it.'

4. When we have had experience of what God can do in former difficulties, we should the less stick at latter. This was Abraham's case, he had received Isaac, as from the dead : Rom. iv. 19, 'He considered not his own body, now dead, when he was about an hundred years old, neither yet the deadness of Sarah's womb ;' Heb. xi. 12, 'Therefore sprang there, even of one, and him as good as dead, so many as the stars of the sky in multitude.' Isaac's conception, generation, and birth, were above the power of nature ; his generation was a kind of resurrection, or very like it ; when he begat him he was as dead ; and Sarah's womb, as to any generative power, was dead too ; therefore it is added, ver. 19, 'Accounting that God was able to raise him up even from the dead : from whence he had received him in a figure.' So to us in like manner : Mat. xvi. 8, 9, 'O ye of little faith, why reason ye among yourselves because ye have brought no bread ? Do ye not yet understand, neither remember the five loaves of the five thousand, and how many baskets ye took up ?' They had experience that Christ could give bread at pleasure ; to be anxious about worldly things after he had shown that he can feed many with a little food, showed a weak faith.

SERMON LIV.

By faith Isaac blessed Jacob and Esau concerning things to come.—HEB. xi. 20.

THE apostle, after he had spoken of Abraham, proceeds to speak of Isaac. That which was notable in his story is the blessing of Jacob and Esau, wherein he showed much faith, though some weakness. His faith is here described—

1. By the act whereabout it was conversant—*He blessed.*
2. The persons so blessed—*Jacob and Esau.*
3. The matter of the blessing—*Concerning things to come,* where the strength of his faith is intimated, that though these blessings were not for a long time to be accomplished, yet that he could pronounce them so confidently in God's name. To open these circumstances.

[1.] The act whereabout his faith was conversant—'He blessed.' There is a blessing by way of prayer, and a blessing by way of prophecy.

By way of prayer, as ordinary parents bless their children, praying for blessings for them. Or else by way of prophecy, foretelling what should befall them in time to come. Of this kind is Isaac's blessing; to which also Noah's is exactly parallel, his blessing Shem and Japheth afterward, and his cursing Ham: Gen. ix. 25-27, 'Cursed be Canaan, a servant of servants shall he be unto his brethren. And he said, Blessed be the Lord God of Shem, and Canaan shall be his servant. God shall enlarge Japheth, and he shall dwell in the tents of Shem, and Canaan shall be his servant.' There is much in the ordinary blessing of parents. Micah, you know, was afraid of his mother's curse, Judges xvii. 2. The Lord, to keep up a reverence and a respect to parents, takes notice of their blessings and curses; if they be uttered with a right spirit, they are not spoken in vain; they are not as water spilt upon the ground. But there was more in the blessing of the patriarchs, for therein they were in a peculiar manner directed by God, and their blessing was a kind of solemn enfeoffment, a disposing or conferring a right to the parties blessed.

[2.] The persons blessed—'Jacob and Esau.' Jacob is put first, as having obtained the precedency, though the younger son, by the peculiar direction of God in this matter.

[3.] The matter of the blessing—'Concerning things to come,' that is, the great things which should happen to his posterity. Which things were revealed to him, partly, by a general promise: Gen. xxvi. 24, 'I will bless thee, and multiply thy seed for my servant Abraham's sake;' partly, by a peculiar instinct at the time of blessing, wherein, according to the extraordinary dispensations of those times, the Lord had a special hand and direction. You see the scope and drift of the words. I shall take this method in the handling of them—(1.) I shall give brief observations upon the passages of this story of blessing Jacob and Esau so far as they relate to the text. (2.) Wherein the virtue and strength of Isaac's faith was manifested. (3.) What is to be learned out of the whole for our comfort and instruction.

First, For the observations upon the passages of the story, which is here alluded unto. You have the story in Genesis xxvii. In reading of it, you may observe these things—

1. I observe (and so the text intimates) that both were blessed; 'He blessed Jacob and Esau.' Esaus have their portion as well as Jacobs. Partly, as they are creatures: God will have all his creatures to taste somewhat of his goodness. Look, as Abraham gave the heritage to Isaac, but yet he gave gifts to the sons of the concubines, Gen. xxv. 5, 6. Or as Jehoshaphat gave to his 'sons silver and gold, precious things, and fenced cities in Judah; but the kingdom he gave to Jehoram,' 2 Chron. ii. 1-3. So though the Lord hath given himself to his people, and given them a portion among the sanctified, yet he will give gifts also to his creatures, they shall all taste of his goodness: Ps. xvii. 14, 'The men of this world have their portion in this life, whose belly thou fillest with thy hid treasures.' All God's creatures, as they are his creatures, taste of his common bounty; he provides for the young ravens, they have their food from him; much more men, that are made after his image. Partly he doth it, not only as they are his creatures, but many times as they descend from parents in covenant

with him. And thus you know Isaac had his blessing, and Ishmael had his blessing, both for Abraham's sake. As Isaac had the great blessings of the covenant, so Ishmael had temporal benefits. The children of the covenant, they that are born of parents in covenant with God, though they have not the blessing of Isaac, yet they have the blessing of Ishmael, many temporal mercies for their father's sake. And so here, Jacob had the blessing of Abraham, he had the special blessing; and Esau, because born of Isaac, he had a blessing too; they carry away the temporal part of the covenant with them. And partly, because many times they make some common profession of the name of God. God will be behind hand with no creature; so far as they are good, they shall see good. A wicked man hath his reward, he is no loser by what he doth for God. Ahab's humiliation, you know, had a courteous message, a reprieve of the judgment, 'It shall not come in thy days,' 1 Kings xxi. 29. And Esau, for his general profession, at least because he was in Isaac's family, therefore God makes provision for him, he hath his portion—'The dew of heaven from above, and the fatness of the earth,' Gen. xxvii. 39. As far as they work, they have their reward.

Use. Well then, learn from hence, that we can draw no argument of love or hatred from outward things. Many ungodly men may prosper in this world; they cannot say therefore that God loves them. Prisoners have an allowance till the time of their execution, so have carnal men; God in the bounty of his providence gives them a great many comforts and mercies in the present life. And many times their allowance is very plentiful; partly, to wean the godly from placing their happiness in these enjoyments. When men of God's hand, Ps. xvii. 14, that is, men of violence, have their bellies filled with hid treasure, this is a hint to the children of God that this is not the happiness they should expect. They that are not favourites of God are suffered to grow great and wealthy, to have riches and honours heaped upon them. God may give a large store of carnal comforts to wicked men, that we may say, Ps. cvi. 4, ' Remember me, O Lord, with the favour that thou bearest unto thy people;' that we may reason thus, What! shall we be contented with wicked men's mercies, that have not one drachm of grace, no interest in God's favour and peculiar love? Partly for the increase of their judgment, that conscience may gnaw more in the place of torments. The happiness that wicked men enjoy in this world is but matter for the worm that never dies to feed upon. When they are cast out among the devils and damned spirits, their consciences will tell them how good the Lord was to them while they lived in the world. and that it is by their own fault that they are come into that place of torment.

2. I observe again, that Jacob, the younger, had the precedency and principal blessing, and therefore he is named first. There are two parts of this observation—(1.) The younger brother is preferred; (2.) The quality of his blessing, that it was choice and principal blessing.

[1.] The younger brother was preferred. It is a course the Lord often took, even from the beginning of the world, to take the younger and leave the elder to perish in their own ways. Abel, the younger, was preferred before Cain; the Lord accepted him to be a priest.

For that was the contest between them, when they made their offerings to the Lord, they were then appearing before the Lord ; as Moses bid Korah and his accomplices take censers, and see whom the Lord would own ; so Cain and Abel were appearing to see whom he would own as priest and prince of the family, that should continue the line of the church, and be accepted ; and there Abel, the younger, is preferred before Cain, the elder. And afterwards Abraham, the younger, is taken to be God's favourite. And next there is Jacob's blessing, and by the direction of God he preferred Ephraim, the younger, before Manasseh, the elder son of Joseph. So Shem was preferred before Japheth ; the Spirit of God takes notice of this, he is called ' the brother of Japheth, the elder,' Gen. x. 21. And afterwards David, who was the youngest, the ruddy youth, is chosen to be the man after God's own heart. What doth the Lord signify by such a dispensation as this ? Some think that which is natural is first, and then that which is spiritual. Others, the preferment of the gentile, the younger brother in grace, before the Jew, the elder ; and that many times it falls out, they that are first shall be last, and they which are last shall be first. But rather, hereby the Lord would manifest the freedom of his counsels. In election God hath no respect to age ; and the order of nature and grace is not the same : Mal. i. 2, ' Was not Esau Jacob's brother ? ' Were they not in all points like ? or if there was any preferment, it was on Esau's side ; was he not the elder brother ? ' Yet Jacob have I loved.' God would still write, as with a sunbeam in the course of his providence, the liberty of his counsel, and that he will have mercy on whom he will have mercy ; a dispensation which we must admire and adore God for the wisdom of it, but not murmur against him. But then—

[2.] For the other part of the observation, namely, the quality of his blessing. If we look into the letter of the words, when Isaac comes to bless Jacob, you will find nothing but what is of a temporal concernment, and little differing from the blessing of Esau : Gen. xxvii. 28, therefore saith he, ' God give thee of the dew of heaven and the fatness of the earth, and plenty of corn and wine ; ' this was Isaac's blessing. Now compare it with ver. 38, 39, when Esau came to him, ' Hast thou but one blessing, O my father ? And Isaac his father answered and said unto him, Behold, thy dwelling shall be the fatness of the earth and of the dew of heaven from above.' When you compare these two blessings together there is little difference, only that Jacob should have the pre-eminence above Esau ; therefore where lies the peculiarity of this blessing ?

I answer, If there had been nothing spiritual in the promise, it would have been no comfort to Jacob at all, for the temporal blessings here mentioned did not concern his person, for he was to be tossed up and down, and pass through many hazards and uncertainties of his life—' Few and evil have the days of the years of my life been,' as he gives an account to Pharaoh, Gen. xlvii. 9. And the bowing down of the nations concerned his posterity. And if this had been all his portion, it had been no such matter of envy to Esau, for Esau hated him, and had a purpose to kill him, Gen. xxii. 41, because he had got away ' the blessing,' the chief blessing, the peculiar blessing. Isaac's eyes were grown dim, hastening to the grave, and now he was about to dispose of the great promises (for the blessing of the patriarchs was a kind of enfeoffment or investing of them in the right of the great promises; he was now to put Jacob into the possession of the great promises), that was his intent; and the very words Isaac useth do imply something spiritual. When he speaks of submission to his posterity, he chiefly intends the dominion and sovereignty of the Messiah—'Let the people serve thee, and nations bow down to thee,' ver. 29; that is, to the top branch that shall come and proceed from thee; and the bowing down of his brethren to him literally implies he should be the top branch of the family, and he should have the priestly dignity. And whereas it is added at the end of his blessing—'Cursed be he that curseth thee, and blessed be he that blesseth thee;' it is part of God's blessing to Abraham, Gen. xii. 3. And therefore we must understand Jacob's blessing according to the latitude of the blessing which was bestowed upon Abraham: Gen. xii. 3, 'In thee shall all the families of the earth be blessed.' That is, in him that shall proceed from thee in the Messiah. Therefore this is clearly intended, and is that which is in the bowels of it, that the Messiah should come from Jacob; and all that would not acknowledge him, a curse should be upon them. Nay, when the blessing is repeated by Isaac, for he blessed Jacob twice, first by mistake, afterward solemnly and purposely: Gen. xxviii. 4, 'God give the blessing of Abraham to thee, and to thy seed with thee, that thou mayest inherit the land wherein thou art a stranger.' What was that blessing of Abraham? To be the head of the blessed line of which the Messiah should come, to be the priest that should continue the worship of God and teach the laws of God, and to be in covenant with God—these were the great blessings. And there is added the possession of Canaan, where the Lord meant to record his name, and to continue and preserve his people. Well then, we see what was Jacob's blessing. Besides much temporal felicity, there are three special things I shall take notice of that were Jacob's privileges, and that appertain to Jacob's blessing: there was the being the father of the Messiah, the continuance of the priesthood, and so of the church, in his family, and the entering into covenant with God. Esau was rejected, and Jacob taken into covenant with God, and so the blessing of Abraham came upon him—'I will be thy God, and the God of thy seed.'

(1.) To be the father of the Messiah, to have relation to Christ, that is a great blessing. We have a relation to him now, not in blood, but in grace; that way is the kindred now reckoned, it is a spiritual kindred, when we are members of his body, and partake of his Spirit, and do his will: Mat. xii. 50, 'Whoever will do the will of my Father which is in heaven, the same is my brother, and sister, and mother.' This is the top happiness, to have relation to Christ. As that was Jacob's peculiar blessing, to be the father of the Messiah; so our blessing lies in this, that we are children of the Messiah, begotten to be to him for a seed. Look, as those were rejected whose genealogy could not be cleared, Ezra ii. 62; so if you cannot make out your kindred and relation to Christ, you are those that will be put by and rejected of the Lord.

(2.) Herein lay also Jacob's blessing, to be in the church, and to have the church continued in his line. It is a great happiness to be in the church, much more to have it continued in our race, to have a people born of us that shall worship God, and call upon the name of God. To be in the church, that is a very great blessing. Esau was left to run at large upon the mountains; but Jacob was to possess the land where God would record his name. Theodosius said, It is a greater privilege to be a member of a church than emperor of the world. The church is the ark of Noah, which is only preserved in the midst of floods and deep waters. The church is the land of Goshen, which only enjoys the benefit of light when there is nothing but darkness round about elsewhere. It is the fleece of Gideon, which is wet with the dews of heaven, and moistened with the influences of grace when all the ground round about us is dry. It is the house of Rahab, which alone escaped out of the ruins of Jericho. And then it is a great blessing to have the church continued in our line. It is very notable that Moses, when he doth come to Shem, he mentions him with this commendation: Gen. x. 21, 'These were born of Shem, the father of all the children of Eber;' that is, the father of the Hebrews which worship God and acknowledge God. This is his prerogative above all his brethren, above Japheth, and above Ham, his brethren, that he was the father of the children of Eber. Eber was not his immediate son, but one that was to come of his loins, of whom the people of God were to come. Shem was the father of many mighty nations: the father of the Syrians, Lydians, Persians, Armenians, the Elamites, all these came of Shem; but because these were ignorant of the true God, and did not worship the true God, therefore he doth not take his title from them, but is called 'the father of the children of Eber.' This was his great prerogative, that Abraham came from him, and all Israel, the people whom God had chosen to himself, among whom he would record his name, and in the midst of whom he would be worshipped while all the rest of the world lay in darkness. One would have thought Moses when he commended Shem would have commended him otherwise, and have taken notice of his long life. This is that Shem that lived 600 years, the last of the long-lived patriarchs; or this is that Shem that saw both worlds, before the flood and after; this was one of the heirs of Noah; this was one of the three great princes of the world; this was one that obtained Asia for his inheritance, the paradise of the earth; a land that was rich in jewels, gold, silver, spices of all kinds, fell to his lot and share. One would have thought Moses would have reckoned the mighty kings and princes which had descended from his loins, the great nations—Assyrians, Persians, &c. Nations that were famous for power, art, greatness of their empire and monarchy, all these came of Shem. No; Moses puts by all this; here is his commendation, Shem 'the father of the children of Eber,' of a contemptible nation, that was shut within the precincts of a little spot of land; but 'to whom pertaineth the adoption, and the glory, and the covenants, and the giving of the law, and the promises,' Rom. ix. 4. This was the honour of Shem. Oh, then, how should we strive to continue religion in our families, that so we may be the fathers of the children of the covenant, the fathers of the race of those that owned and acknowledged God. This is a great honour, and God expects it from you: Gen. xviii. 19, 'I know Abraham, that

he will command his children and his household, and they shall keep
the way of the Lord, to do judgment and justice.' This is that which
God expects from you, that you should teach them the worship of the
Lord, and charge them to worship the true God, that when you are
dead and gone, there may be some of your line and race to call upon
God.

(3.) Another privilege of Jacob above Esau was this, that he was
taken into covenant with God—' The blessing of Abraham shall come
upon thee.' What is that ? 'I will be thy God, and the God of thy
seed,' Gen. xvii. 7. Oh, this is the great happiness of a people, to have
God for our God. This I have opened at large, ver. 16. So it is very
notable, when Noah comes to pronounce blessings and curses upon
his children in the spirit of prophecy : Gen. ix. 26, ' Blessed be the
Lord God of Shem—' there lay Shem's happiness—' and Canaan shall
be his servant.' When he comes to curse Ham he curses him in his
person ; but when he comes to speak of the blessings of Shem, he doth
not bless him so much in person as in the God that was made over to
him in covenant. That was happiness enough for Shem, to have God
for his God ; as he had Ham for his servant, so he had God for his
master. This was the great promise which was so often repeated and
made to the patriarchs, Gen. xvii. 7. There it was made to Abraham
—' I will be a God to thee, and to thy seed after thee.' Then it is
repeated to Isaac : Gen. xxvi. 24, ' I am the God of Abraham thy
father ; fear not, for I am with thee, and will bless thee ;' and then to
Jacob : Gen. xxviii. 13, ' I am the Lord God of Abraham thy father,
and the God of Isaac ; the land whereon thou liest, to thee will I give
it, and to thy seed : ' and in this Heb. xi. 9, Abraham, Isaac, and Jacob,
are called 'heirs of the promise.' What was the great privilege that
Isaac had above Ishmael ? or Jacob above Esau ? They had God for
their God, and were in covenant with God. And afterward the same
promise is made to all Israel : Exod. xx. 2, ' I am the Lord thy God,
which brought thee out of the land of Egypt, out of the house of
bondage.' Hence that dialogue between God and the church : Hosea ii.
23, ' I will say, Thou art my people, and they shall say, Thou art my
God.' To be a God to any is to supply them with all good things
necessary for the temporal or spiritual life, to give them all things pertaining to this life, and to a better. To this life for temporal blessings :
Gen. xxviii. 20, 21, ' If God will be with me, and keep me in the way
that I shall go, and will give me bread to eat and raiment to put on,
so that I come again to my father's house in peace, then the Lord shall
be my God.' You must not understand this place as if Jacob did
capitulate, and indent with God upon these terms. If he should not
give me raiment to put on, and food to eat, I will not own him to be
God ; but the meaning is, Then I shall know him to be a God to
me ;—for to be a God to any is to be a storehouse of all kind of good
things that they stand in need of ;—then I shall acknowledge him to
be the only author of my life and estate.

And then for spiritual blessings. Illumination, and bending the
heart to obedience : Jer. xxxi. 33, ' I will put my law into their inward
parts, and write it in their hearts ; and I will be their God, and they
shall be my people.' So the spirit of regeneration is begged upon

this ground : Ps. cxiii. 40, ' Teach me to do thy will, for thou art my God. Thy spirit is good, lead me into the land of uprightness.' As if it were implied in the relation ; if God undertake to be a God to us, it is to give us his Spirit, to write his law in the heart, and bend our mind to the obedience of his will. And then for the happiness of the other world, the resurrection of the body : Mat. xxii. 32, ' I am the God of Abraham, the God of Isaac, and the God of Jacob. God is not the God of the dead, but of the living.' And the fulness of joy and comfort in the everlasting state : Rev. xxi. 2, 3, ' They shall be his people, and he will be their God. And God shall wipe away all tears from their eyes,' &c. All this is implied in God's being a God to us, that he will give us all blessings, temporal, spiritual, and eternal.

Use. Well then, do not admire Esau's portion, but Jacob's, and put in for a share of it, Ps. cxliv. 15. If you mark, there is a dialogue there between the flesh and the spirit. The flesh and carnal nature is taken with pomp, and bravery, and outward comforts ; there the flesh speaks, admiring worldly excellences, where there is no complaining in the streets, &c.—' Oh, happy are the people that are in such a case.' Then the spirit speaks, and corrects the voice of the flesh—' Yea rather, happy is the people whose God is the Lord.' However I be dealt withal as to Esau's portion, let me have Jacob's portion, and be a member of Christ, in covenant with God.

3. I observe from the story : this difference of blessings between them was founded in an eternal decree and purpose of God, that was declared while the children were as yet struggling in the womb : Gen. xxv. 23, ' The Lord said, Two nations are in thy womb, and two manner of people shall be separated from thy bowels ; and the one people shall be stronger than the other people, and the elder shall serve the younger.' Here was a decree of God manifested before the children were born ; the younger should have the pre-eminence, and go away with the chiefest blessing ; and hence the apostle concludes election to be of mere grace, without any reason in the creature : Rom. ix. 11–13, ' For the children being not yet born, neither having done any good or evil, that the purpose of God according to election might stand, not of works, but of him that calleth, it was said, The elder shall serve the younger. As it is written, Jacob have I loved, but Esau have I hated.' The apostle accommodates it to the purpose of election and reprobation. Here is a notable instance of God's distinguishing grace, two brothers, two twins, and if any should have the preference the elder might seem to be the man ; but God's thoughts are not as man's thoughts, when they were both alike in themselves, ' they had done neither good nor evil,' the Lord would show that his pleasure is the highest cause of difference between man and man. Why is the gospel hid from the wise and prudent ? Why is it manifested to babes ? Christ would give no other reason but this, ' Even so, O Father, for so it seemed good in thy sight,' Mat. xi 26. ' It is not of him that willeth, nor of him that runneth, but of God that showeth mercy.' All the good we have comes from the grace of God.

4. I observe again : as the difference of the blessings was founded on an eternal decree, so the decree is accomplished to Jacob, notwithstanding Isaac's reluctation and unwillingness, and that by Isaac's

mistake and Jacob's sin.   Mark, the decree was accomplished notwithstanding the reluctancy and unwillingness of Isaac ; Isaac's heart was much set upon Esau, being the eldest son, and he was the person that prepared him savoury meat : Gen. xxv. 18, ' And Isaac loved Esau, because he did eat of his venison ; ' and therefore he would fain have put Esau into this privilege, and have settled the blessing upon him, that he might have the great privileges of primogeniture.   But God's counsel stands, notwithstanding all lets and hindrances.   Isaac had sent him off a message to try his obedience, and then intended to give him the blessing, Gen. xxvii. 3, 4 ; but God settles it upon the head of Jacob, and thus you see the counsel of the Lord stands ; notwithstanding all lets and hindrances, God keeps on his course and pace.   The Lord is compared to fire, in the prophet, that passeth through briars and thorns.   Briars and thorns, do not quench the fire, but feed the flame and yield fuel to the fire which find its way through them.   So briars and thorns, things that seem to be contrary, they do not hinder God's purposes, but rather make way for them.   Joseph is sold that he might be worshipped ; cast into the pit, or else he had never been set upon the throne.   There is no let to the almighty ; Isaac either forgetting the promise, or through carnal affection seeking to misplace the blessing, this makes way for Jacob's receiving it.   And then it was accomplished, notwithstanding Isaac's mistake and Jacob's lie ; he took Jacob for Esau when he felt his hands, and smelt his priestly perfumed garments which he received together with the birthright, which he bought of Esau.   By the mistake of Isaac the blessing was settled upon the head of Jacob ; but that which is casualty and mistake with us, is providence with God.   Isaac stumbles upon the right object, and so unawares fulfils God's decrees.   Thus the Lord overrules all things ; things that we call chance do execute and bring his purpose to pass.   So many have come to an ordinance and found a blessing ; there is a special purpose of God in it.   And Jacob gets it by a lie ; so that you see that not only those things which we call mistakes, but also sins fall under the government of God's providence : Jacob sinned in seeking the blessing this way, and yet by that means it is accomplished and brought to pass.   It is true, it was to Jacob's cost, for God afterwards paid him in his own coin ; he that supplanted was supplanted ; he that, being the younger son, came to his father, and said, I am thy first-born, he had Leah, the elder daughter, brought to him instead of Rachel, the younger.   But though God's purpose may be brought to pass this way, yet the instruments that accomplish God's will are not without sin, because they act according to their own inclination ; as the artificer makes the mill, but the water runs of its own accord.   Though the Lord makes use of the evil of our actions, yet because we follow our own inclination, which is corrupt, therefore we are guilty.

5. Again, I observe : as to the rejection of Esau, it is notable, for the clearing of God's justice, Esau was not rejected from the principal blessing till he had first rejected it himself.   Whatever God had purposed within his own heart, Esau was not actually rejected till he had rejected the blessing.   The primogeniture was not only assigned by God to Jacob, but despised by Esau, Gen. xxv. 34, he sold it for

a mess of pottage. The birthright had the priesthood and promises annexed to it, and having sold the birthright, he had no right to the blessing. Therefore he is called 'a profane person,' because he sold his birthright; and he goes and seeks affinity with idolators, and marries into the stock of the cursed Canaanites, and therefore he is called a fornicator: Heb. xii. 16, 'Lest there be any fornicator, or profane person, as Esau, who for one morsel of meat sold his birthright.' He degenerates and falls off from God, therefore no wonder God cut him off; that he grew wild, though he were a branch of a good stock. He having sold the birthright, had no right to the privileges of it, therefore he is justly deprived of them. Thus wicked men fit themselves for destruction, whatever God's counsels are in himself. The vessels of mercy are not only determined, but prepared and fitted by God for glory: but he endures with much long-suffering vessels of wrath, till they fit themselves for destruction; so they are compassed about with a fire of their own kindling.

6. I observe again: Jacob receives this blessing in the perfumed garment which belonged to the first-born, and particularly the garment wherein Esau as priest ministered, and which was sold to him with the birthright. The first-born, who was to perform the priest's office, was herein a type of Christ, who is *primogenitus et unigenitus,* the first-born and only-begotten son of God. We put on Christ, and the garment of his righteousness, and so we are blessed of the Lord.

7. I observe again: the blessing being pronounced, Isaac would not retract it when he was sensible of the mistake: Gen. xxvii. 33, 'I have blessed him, and he shall be blessed.' And though Esau sought it with tears, and would fain have the thing reversed again, yet he could not have it. 'The gifts and calling of God,' and his special blessings, 'are without repentance,' Rom. xi. 29. 'He found no place for repentance,' Heb. xii. 17; that is, for changing the mind of Isaac. The Lord doth not change his mind, but continues the blessings where they are settled.

Secondly, Wherein lay the strength of Isaac's faith? For it is said, 'By faith Isaac blessed Jacob and Esau concerning things to come.'

1. In that he doth with confidence pronounce a blessing concerning things to come, and doth dispose of Canaan as if he had the peaceable possession of it, and could dispose of it at pleasure. He that will consider Isaac's case with an eye of sense would wonder at his confidence, that he that had not a foot of land in Canaan, and had no right to anything there but a burying-place, and that was now exiled by a famine, and lived a sojourner in the land of Gerar, that he should pronounce those magnificent words and speeches: Gen. xxvii. 29, 'Let people serve thee, and let nations bow down to thee, and be thou lord over thy brethren.' To a man that looks upon the outward case of Isaac, all this would seem to be ridiculous pageantry. Could he confer dominions that was scarce free himself, but tossed up and down? Yet by faith he speaks as confidently of future blessings, as if he saw them fulfilled. So should we be as certain of the blessings to come that God hath promised, as if they were present, though we see no likelihood of them. The word of God should be assurance enough, though

we have nothing of sense to bear us up. Do but observe two things before these blessings could be accomplished—(1.) The promise was to suffer a long delay; (2.) As to sense, it was often contradicted; yet ' by faith he blessed them.'

[1.] The promise was delayed for a long time. Esau had his blessing sooner than Jacob; a fat soil, and power and force to maintain his lot, Gen. xxxvi. Esau multiplied into many and great families, he presently grew great and mighty; there came dukes and captains from him: ver. 15, ' duke Teman, duke Omar, duke Zepho,' &c.; whereas Jacob was but a servant in the house of Laban till he was a hundred years old, labouring for his living; and it was three hundred years ere a people proceeded from him that were numerous and powerful, as the stars of heaven, as the Lord had said. Nay it was not fully accomplished till David's time; Saul began when he smote the Amalekites, 1 Sam. xv. 3, and David says, Ps. lx. 8, ' Over Edom will I cast out my shoe.' So Ishmael grows presently great; twelve princes came of him, Gen. xxv. 16; whereas Isaac continued in a private and low estate. Thus will God try the faith of his people in things to come, when it is a long time ere the blessing be obtained that is promised to them.

[2.] This promise and this blessing seemed to be contradicted as to sense. Jacob's blessing runs thus, ' Be lord over thy brethren, and let thy mother's sons bow down to thee,' Gen. xxvii. 29, and yet Jacob was fain to bow and cringe to Esau, Gen. xxxiii. 3. The promise seems to be contradicted by the providence of God. So Gen. ix. 26, ' Blessed be the Lord God of Shem, and Canaan shall be his servant.' Ay, but before Ham was Shem's servant, that is, the servant of the posterity of Shem, viz., before the Canaanite was subdued by the Israelites, they were subject to Ham's posterity, Ham bore rule over Shem; for the father of the Egyptians was the son of Ham, and they were in vile subjection in Egypt, and ran many hazards. For a great while the promise seemed to be contradicted, and quite lost, yet they could speak of them as confidently as if they were at hand. Well then, go you and do likewise, get a patient faith, get an obstinate faith.

(1.) Get a patient faith that will tarry the Lord's leisure though he delays his coming. The good things which faith expects are things to come; you shall have them in due time. Would you have the meat before it be roasted? and mercies before they are ready for you? Get a waiting faith, to depend upon the Lord in the midst of all delays. When your portion is fitted and prepared for you, then you shall have it.

(2.) Get an obstinate faith that will depend upon God in the face of contradictions; when the Lord seems to march against us, to believe his heart is with us. When Ham domineers, then to believe God is making way for his subjection to Shem; and when Esau lords it, then to think God will bring him down, and he shall stoop to Jacob. As he in the story which held the boat with his right hand, and that being cut off, he takes hold with his left hand, and when that is cut off he fastens on it with his teeth; so when one help is cut off, and then another, yet faith doth fasten upon God as long as it hath his word to fasten on; when God makes breach after breach, then to depend upon him. And as the blind man that was rebuked, yet he cried the more; so to follow after God the more you are rebuked, this is a faith indeed.

Herein was Isaac's faith seen in a confident believing of things to come, though he passed through many hazards, and his present condition were mean, and those that were rejected grew great and prince-like in the world.

2. His faith was seen herein, that as soon as he seeth God's hand, against his own natural affection he yields and submits to the Lord. He would fain have settled the blessing upon Esau's head, but God's providence ordered it otherwise, and he would not retract the blessing —'Jacob is blessed, and he shall be blessed;' nay he confirms it again: Gen. xxviii. 3, 4, 'The Lord give the blessing of Abraham to thee, and to thy seed after thee.' Wherein he doth knowingly and purposely, and more explicitly, give the blessing to him, though before he did it by mistake. It is a good work of faith to make the soul to yield to God's will against our own inclinations, or the persuasions of our own reason, and the bent of our heart. Faith knoweth that God is so great, powerful, and glorious, that his will must be obeyed.

Thirdly, I shall give you some lessons from hence, from Isaac's blessing Jacob and Esau.

1. We are to seek blessings for our children. Though we cannot bless as prophets, yet we should bless as parents. What must we do to leave them a blessing? Found a covenant interest for them in your own persons, this is a way to leave a blessing behind you. All God's blessings run sweetly in the channel of the covenant, therefore do not cut off the right of your children: Gen. xvii. 7, 'I will be a God to thee, and to thy seed.' First to thee, and then to thy seed. And then lay up prayers for them, as Job, who offered sacrifice for his children day by day, according to their number. By head and poll he seeks to God for a blessing: Prov. xxxi. 2, Bathsheba calls Solomon the son of her vows. With her prayers she mingled vows, so make your children the children of your vows; as it was said to Austin's mother, *Filius tot precum et lachrymarum perire non potest*—a child of so many prayers and tears cannot miscarry. And then lay up promises for them. Believe for them too. The faith of a parent doth good to the child; hereby you remove obstructions, and mercies run out more freely to them. Though the parent's faith be not a principal cause, yet it is an occasional means to stave off destruction from, and to further the salvation of his children: Heb. xi. 23, 'By faith Moses, when he was born, was hid three months of his parents.' The faith of Moses' parents preserved him in the water when a babe; the sprinkling of the door-posts preserved the first-born, it was a fruit of the parents' faith. Noah's house was saved by faith, Heb. xi. 7. Faith doth not only look for personal mercies, but for family mercies; you have God's word for your children as Isaac had, he left his children the blessings of God's word. Therefore believe for them. And then 'bring them up in the nurture and admonition of the Lord,' Eph. vi. 4. Let them know God from our mouths, that they may have the awe of God upon them. Acquaint your children with, and urge God's mind to them, as they are capable of instruction. You are not worthy of the name of

fathers till you do this. You dispersed the old Adam; now if you had conveyed the stone, or some hereditary disease to them, surely you would seek a remedy for them, or direct them to one if you could tell them of one. Oh! begin with them betimes. Timothy 'from a child had known the holy scriptures,' 2 Tim. iii. 15.

2. Observe again: faith believeth God's truth, however revealed, ordinarily or extraordinarily. Those that had extraordinary revelation, yet they had a need of faith. It is not said by the light of prophecy, Isaac blessed Jacob and Esau, but by faith. Though much of God's will was made known to him by an extraordinary way of revelation, yet he needs faith still. And you that have the promises of God's word have as much to depend upon as they that had oracles from heaven, and as good ground to trust him. They are commended for the strength of their faith in depending upon God, and you have the word of God to show for it; promises to bear you up, to support you, and carry you forth; that is ground enough for faith.

3. You may learn how the Lord connives at the infirmities of his children where the heart is sound. Isaac blessed Jacob by error, yet he blessed him by faith. Isaac purposed to bless Esau with the special blessing, either forgetting the promises (for some divines excuse him so), or misinterpreting the promise—'The elder shall serve the younger,' thinking it concerned only his posterity, not the person of Esau, God, no further enlightening his mind, that his counsel and wisdom might the more be seen; or out of inadvertency, not regarding the promise. But his heart was upright, and as soon as he seeth God in it, he persisteth not in his error; he will not reverse the blessing, though Esau sought it with tears. And now the Lord winks at his infirmity, and saith, 'By faith Isaac blessed Jacob and Esau.' Where we do not sin voluntarily and wilfully, but only out of error, incogitancy, or weakness, and the heart is upright with God, the Lord will pardon our infirmities, he will put a finger upon the scar. Here is nothing said of Isaac's infirmity or weakness, but only his faith is mentioned.

Use. Take heed of losing this privilege of having the covenant blessings continued in your line. To this end—

1. Take heed of cutting off yourselves from the communion of the church. All along, as the branches of the covenant began to grow wild, God still cut them off. Cain came of Adam in covenant with God, but Cain was cut off because of his contempt of the privilege, and disobedience: Gen. iv. 16, 'He went out from the presence of the Lord.' What is the meaning of that? Surely there is no going from the face of the Lord in one sense, from his all-seeing eye: Ps. cxxxix. 7, 'Whither shall I go from thy Spirit? or whither shall I flee from thy presence?' But he went out from the communion of the church; God having rejected him, and therefore the posterity of Cain are called sons and daughters of men; but the posterity of Seth, in whom the line of the church was continued, are called the sons of God: Gen. vi. 2, 'The sons of God saw the daughters of men, and took them wives of all which they chose;' that is, those that were of Seth's line, which was the church line, matched into the stock of cursed Cain, who was cursed because he was cut off for his disobedience and contempt of God, therefore they are called 'the daughters of men.' Again, Ishmael was

born of Abraham, but now Ishmael was cut off for malignity and enmity at the power of godliness; for mocking and scoffing at Isaac, which the apostle interprets to be a persecution of those that are born after the Spirit: Gal. iv. 29, 'As then, he that was born after the Spirit persecuted him that was born after the flesh,' meaning Ishmael and Isaac, 'so it is now;' therefore he was cut off. Again, Esau in the text, he is cut off. Why? For profaneness, Heb. xii. 15, 16; therefore he lost his covenant privilege, because of his profaneness in slighting of it. And afterwards the Jews, they were cut off; though they were the natural branches, they grew upon a covenant root, yet they were 'cut off because of unbelief,' Rom. xi. 20. God bore with them after the shedding of the blood of Christ; though they murdered the Lord of life, yet they continued, and their covenant privileges continued to them; but when once they contemned the everlasting doctrine of the gospel that was brought to them, and first offered to them, but they rejected it, then they were cast out of the covenant state. Therefore take heed lest for any of these things the Lord should break you off from this great privilege of a covenant state.

2. Do not cut off your children by a contempt or neglect of baptism. Parents are guilty of more sin than they are aware of in depriving their children of this privilege; it is a wrong to God, a wrong to their children, a wrong to the church, a wrong to themselves, and it gratifies none but the devil. It is a great wrong to God, for we veil the glory of his preventing grace. It is the grace of God that he began to us in this external way; he chose us to be a portion to himself, and took us to be a seed to himself, before we knew or sought after him; and we rob him of his portion. God challengeth an interest in the children that were born of covenanted parents: Ezek. xvi. 20, 21, 'Moreover, thou hast taken thy sons and thy daughters whom thou hast born to me, and these thou hast sacrificed. Is this of thy whoredoms a small matter, that thou hast slain my children?' God takes our children to be his children, he hath an interest in them. As he is a God to us and our seed, so we and our seed are to be his people. And then it is a wrong to your children; partly, in that you begrudge God's bounty to them. God hath bestowed a privilege upon them, and you rob them of this privilege. And partly, in not engaging them in their infancy, but leaving them at large. The people of God have many times blessed God that they came under this obligation by baptism in infancy, before they had liberty to choose their own way. Sure it will be brought as an aggravation at the day of judgment against all those that have not walked answerable to their baptismal vow. Then you rob the church of a great part of their members, of the children of the kingdom, Mat. viii. 12, of the most innocent part of the church, those that dishonour God least; but chiefly in this respect you do as much as in you lies seek to cut off the succession of churches, and their continuance. It is a mighty comfort to the people of God that they see a stock of little ones that are in covenant with God: Ps. cii. 28, 'The children of thy servants shall continue, and their seed shall be established before thee.' And then you wrong yourselves. God hath put this honour upon his saints, that 'their children are holy,' 1 Cor. vii. 14. Whatever his secret counsel be (for there God will take a liberty),

they are under the visible, ordinary administration of the covenant of
grace, which is entailed upon them.   You know Abraham fell upon
his face when God came to tender him this privilege: Gen. xvii. 3, 7,
' I will be thy God, and the God of thy seed.'   The people of God have
thankfully taken hold of such a privilege and mercy as this is.   And
so David: 2 Sam. vii. 19, ' And this was yet a small thing in thy sight,
O Lord God, for thou hast spoken also of thy servant's house for a
great while to come.'   And you gratify none but the devil, who ever
hath had a spite at the holy seed.   As Amalek smote Israel in the
rear, where there were little ones, so the devil would fain crush Christ's
kingdom in the egg.   At first, when God accepted Abel's sacrifice, and
fire came down from heaven, then Abel was chosen to be the holy seed,
and the devil stirs up Cain to murder him, that in Abel he might destroy all the race of the church. After, when they were multiplied, still
he seeks either to corrupt them when they are grown, or cause their
parents to cut them off from God, and to dedicate them to Moloch.

3. Strive to keep up religion in your families by the education of
your children.   It is an excellent thing to see religion preserved, to run
downward from father to son, and have those born of our loins that
may worship and serve the Lord.   I remember it is spoken of Abraham,
Heb. xi. 9, that ' he dwelt in tents with Isaac and Jacob, the heirs with
him of the same promise.'   This is sweet, when father, and son, and
grandson are all heirs of the same promise.   Pliny reports, it was
counted a great honour and height of felicity, that in one family of the
Fabii there were three presidents of the senate one after another, and
in one house of Curio's were three excellent orators one after another;
but what honour is this when there is a constant succession of the power
of godliness from father to son, and from son to grandchild!   In the
third descent you count men gentlemen of a new and opulent family.
Here is Jacob the grandson of Abraham.   This is true nobility, to
have a holy kindred; there is no gentility like to this.   It is a high
honour to be father of such a race.   Whereas otherwise *omnis sanguis
concolor*, all blood is of a colour.   Take care then that this succession
be not cut off.   Great persons are careful to entail their lands and
estates upon their children, but for religion they are not careful for
them.   It is much better to be heir of our father's faith and religion
than to be heir of our father's lands and demesnes.   It is a high honour when we can say, My God, my father's God, and my grandfather's
God, 2 Tim. i. 5.   My father, my grandfather, and my great grandfather feared the Lord: Prov. xxvii. 10, ' Thine own friend and thy
father's friend forsake not.'   When we can look upon the God of our
progenitors, surely then we must not forsake our father's God.   Therefore let not your blood be stained in this kind, but teach your children,
that this honour may be kept up in your line and family.   None stain
their blood so much as they that forsake the faith.   Treasons and mis-
demeanours are a stain to noble ancestors; so is also apostasy, and loss
of church privileges.

SERMON LV.

*By faith Jacob, when he was a-dying, blessed both the sons of Joseph;
and worshipped, leaning upon the top of his staff.*—Heb. xi. 21.

We are come to the third patriarch, which is Jacob; his faith is set
forth—

1. By the time—*When he was a-dying.*
2. By the actions wherein his faith was exercised; they were two—
The blessing the sons of Joseph, and—*The worshipping on the top of
his staff;* for I look upon both these actions as distinct.

First, For the time—' Jacob, when he was a-dying,' in a weak body
he shows a strong faith. He could hardly turn in his bed, yet in the
failing of all his strength he discovereth his respect to God and his
faith in the promises; he would be worshipping, and commending the
promises and the covenant. We may learn hence—

Doct. That faith is a grace that steads us, and honoureth God both
in life and death.

I have spoken of the exercise of faith at death in the 13th verse,
and therefore shall but touch of it now.

1. Faith steadeth us at death. True grace doth best at last. Carnal wisdom doth best for a while; none seem to live such lives as carnal men for a while; but when death comes, there is the great trial—
'What hope hath the hypocrite, though he hath gained, when God
takes away his soul?' Job xxvii. 8. Wicked men are forced to die,
whether they will or no,—God takes away their souls. They would
fain keep them. That is the meanest part of wisdom, to provide for
our being in the world; but to die well, to go out of the world comfortably, that is true wisdom. Carnal wisdom will stead you well
enough for the present life, though many times it is blasted and frustrated. Therefore Job speaks by way of supposition—' Though he
hath gained.' Usually he doth well enough; but when God comes to
take away his soul, we see a failure in all these things. Natural courage will bear us out in lesser brunts. Security and ignorance will help
us to die sottishly; but to die comfortably, to die worshipping and
glorifying God for the promises, that is the privilege and work of faith.

2. Faith honours God, not only in life, but in death; for it doth not
only yield comfort to ourselves, but enables us to confirm others. A
carnal man cannot speak well of the world when he comes to die; oh,
he dares not commend his worldly life to others! But a godly man
can speak well of God, and commend the covenant and promise to
others: Gen. xlviii. 15, 16, ' The God which fed me all my life long
to this day, the angel which redeemed me from all evil, bless the lads.'
As if he had said, I have had much experience of the angel of the
covenant, who hath been with me, and kept me in all my ways. I do
not commend you to Pharaoh, nor desire him to be kind to you, nor
advance you as he hath done your father; no, but the angel of the
covenant bless you; no blessing like that.

Use 1. Well then, get such a faith as this is. Nothing will hold
out in death but this. The world fails; riches have done their office,

and their work is at an end when death comes, for they are only supplies for the present life. And courage fails ; for then we have not to do with men, but with God, and ' Can your heart endure or your hands be strong in the day that I shall deal with you ? ' Ezek. xxii. 14. Security fails : that is the devil's policy while we live, to keep us secure ; but when we come to die, he hath another engine to destroy us, and that is despair. And presumption or false faith, that fails, for now men begin to be serious ; as they come nearer to eternity, they grow wiser, and then a false faith will not serve the turn, that will not keep up that confidence it kept up before. Therefore nothing will stead you but true faith in such an hour. If christians did oftener think of death, they would not be contented with such a slight provision for eternity as they usually make. Oh ! could I die comfortably, would I venture my eternal condition in this estate ?

Use 2. Act faith after this manner when you come to die, that it may yield comfort to you and glory to God. Comfort to you : a christian is not to be passive in his death, to die as a beast. Think of the covenant which yieldeth comfort for soul, and for body, and for children. Jacob worshipped when Joseph had sworn to bury his bones in Canaan with his father, their society in the grave was a type of their communion in heaven ; then he worshipped upon the top of his rod, I am going to God and Christ, to Abraham and Isaac, to dwell with them in the presence of God ; this was his comfort. Get such a faith, I say, that you may have comfort for your bodies, and souls, and children ; for here Jacob blesseth his children, and comforts himself that he should go to the state of the blessed ; for that was figured in carrying the bones thither. So also such a faith will honour and glorify God. This is the last time you can do anything for God. Now it is a great honour to God when you can give him a good testimony as the fruit of all your experience, as Joshua doth : Joshua xxiii. 14, ' I am going the way of all the earth : and ye know in all your hearts and in all your souls that not one thing hath failed of all the good things which the Lord your God spake concerning you ; all are come to pass unto you, and not one thing hath failed thereof.' So Jacob here commends the God of the covenant, the angel of the covenant, and the blessings of the covenant, and gives it out as the result of all his experiences.

Secondly, Let us come to the actions about which his faith was conversant it is said—

First, ' He blessed both the sons of Joseph.' In the original it is ἔκαστον τῶν υἱῶν, every one of the sons of Joseph, though we read but of two, therefore it is well translated, ' both.' Here I shall show (1.) The reasons of the blessing ; (2.) The manner ; (3.) How it was done by faith.

1. For the reasons ; why were Joseph's children blessed rather than others ? Why doth the apostle only mention them ?

[1.] Because they were born in Egypt, in a foreign land, out of Jacob's family, and now they were to be incorporated and taken into the body of the holy seed, the people of God. For mark, when Jacob blesseth them, what doth he say ?' Gen. xlviii. 16, ' Let my name be named on them, and the name of my fathers, Abraham and Isaac ; and let them grow into a multitude in the midst of the earth.' He doth not say, The Lord make you great in Egypt; the Lord preserve you in your honour and happiness, for they had powerful alliance and great respect in the country. No, but the name of Abraham and Isaac be on them; that is, be you reckoned among the people of God. As for those other nations that were not taken into the church, the name of Abraham was not named among them; the name of the patriarchs was quickly extinguished in Ishmael's and Esau's family. But let the name of Abraham and Isaac be upon them; that is, keep there, join yourselves there. He seeks by this blessing to withdraw them from Egypt, and from their kindred there, that they might have a name among the rest of the tribes, and remain annexed to the church, and take the common share and lot with the people of God.

[2.] Because of Jacob's special affection to Joseph, and God's special providence in and about Joseph. He makes Joseph's two sons to be two distinct tribes; as he did not the sons of his other children, but they were called after the name of their father, the children of Reuben, and the children of Simeon, no notice of their sons, but Manasseh and Ephraim are made distinct tribes. Now the reason of this is, Joseph had the privilege of the first-born, and the first-born was to have a double portion. Now that Joseph might have a double portion, Ephraim and Manasseh had both a share in the land of Canaan. That it was the right of the first-born to have a double portion appeareth by Deut. xxi. 17, 'He shall acknowledge the son of the hated for the first-born by giving him a double portion of all that he hath, for he is the beginning of his strength, the right of the first-born is his.' Reuben was the first-born, but he forfeited his right, and then it was vested in Joseph : 1 Chron. v. 1, 2, 'Reuben was the first-born, but forasmuch as he defiled his father's bed, his birthright was given unto the sons of Joseph, the son of Israel, and the genealogy is not to be reckoned after the birth-right. For Judah prevailed above his brethren, and of him came the first ruler, but the birth-right was Joseph's.' And indeed of right it belonged to him, if Laban had not deceived Jacob by substituting Leah in Rachel's place, and Joseph was her first-born, and now by the providence of God the primogeniture is restored to him. Indeed when Israel was branched into twelve tribes, the right of the first-born was thus divided; the priesthood, that was one right of primogeniture, was bestowed upon Levi ; the sovereignty, another right of primogeniture, was bestowed upon Judah ; there was David's throne, from whom the Messiah came ; and then the third right was the double portion ; that is clearly settled upon Joseph ; therefore his two sons are made two distinct tribes.

2. In what manner was this blessing bestowed? Here again the younger, by the special providence of God, was preferred before the elder : Gen. xlviii. 14, 'And Israel stretched forth his right hand, and laid it upon Ephraim's head, who was the younger, and his left hand upon Manasseh's head.' Jacob, though blind, guided his hands wittingly it was not a thing of chance, but there was much of the providence of God. In the Hebrew it is, He made his hand understand, God was with him, to take this son and leave that; to settle the supremacy upon Ephraim, and the children that sprang out of him ; for in the light of prophecy he foresaw the kingdom should be in the race of

Ephraim, Num. i. 32; compared with ver. 34; there it is said, first, 'The children of Joseph, to wit, by Ephraim were forty thousand and five hundred;' afterwards, 'The children of Manasseh were thirty and two thousand and two hundred.' So when the tribes were sealed, Rev. vii. the tribe of Manasseh is mentioned, ver. 6, and the tribe of Ephraim is called the tribe of Joseph, ver. 8. Ephraim had the pre-eminence, and had Joseph's right devolved upon him.

3. Wherein lay the faith; for it is said, 'By faith he blessed the two sons of Joseph.' Partly, in embracing the revelation that was made to him by God in prophecy. Partly, in pronouncing the blessing according to the tenor of that revelation; for as the cordial assent is an act of faith, so confession with the mouth is a fruit of faith. Partly, in looking through the present difficulties to things to come. Isaac blesseth in Gerar, Joseph in Egypt, where he died an exile, yet he beholdeth things to come, as if present. Partly, in a contempt of the world, in minding them of Canaan, and of the covenant, when they had great honours, renown, and power in Egypt. Joseph was governor in Egypt, yet he comes to settle such a blessing as notwithstanding which they should be exiled and banished, and oppressed with the rest of their brethren, that he might withdraw them from the honours of Egypt. The great end of the blessing was to keep themselves joined to the body of the church whatever befell them.

Obs. 1. It is no small privilege to be taken into visible covenant with God, or to be joined with the body of the church.

Jacob doth not desire the continuance of their present greatness in Egypt, but puts them in mind of the covenant and of the name of Abraham. Joseph would have left to his children nobility of blood, a rich patrimony in Egypt, but he brings them to his father Jacob to receive his blessing. And what is that? An infeoffment into the visible privileges of the covenant. The blessings of Egypt are nothing in comparison to the blessings of Sion. Now it is no small privilege to be joined to the body of the church, because there we may have communion with God, and with the people of God. There we know God most, and there we enjoy God most. There we know God most, Ps. xxvii. 4, 'One thing have I desired of the Lord, that will I seek after, that I may dwell in the house of the Lord all the days of my life, to behold the beauty of the Lord,' &c. Mark, in the house of the Lord, that is, in the church; for the temple was a figure of the spiritual church, there we behold the beauty of the Lord. By the light of nature we may know God; but it is by track or footprint, or some obscure shadow; but in his house we see his glory, his wisdom, his grace, his beauty. The great end why we are brought to heaven is to behold the beauty of the Lord, to see him face to face. Now this is begun in the church, we come more immediately to look upon his wisdom, glory, and goodness in Christ, and the riches of the covenant of grace. And there we have most enjoyment of God. There are common blessings God gives to the world, but then there are blessings come out of Sion, therefore it is said: Ps. cxxviii. 5, 'The Lord shall bless thee out of Sion;' and Ps. cxxxiv. 3, 'The Lord that made heaven and earth bless thee out of Sion;' Ps. cxxxiii. 3, 'There,'—that is, out of Sion,—'the Lord commanded the blessing, even life for evermore.' To have a blessing merely from a creator, as he is the maker of heaven and earth, that is no such enjoyment of God; but in Sion there he will communicate himself to his people; there is the light of his countenance, pardon of sin, sanctification of common mercies, and the graces of his Spirit. Ever since the creation there are some places where God will be enjoyed. The angels had a proper place to enjoy God in heaven; therefore the apostle takes notice that they 'kept not their first estate, but left their own habitation,' Jude 6. Mark, it is ἴδιον οἰκητήριον, their proper place, where they were to enjoy God; therefore they lost their original state of happiness and glory, because they left their own habitation. Paradise was the place Adam was to enjoy God in; when he was driven out of his place, then he loses his communion with God. We enjoy God in the church, there he will be found of us; therefore it is good to keep our place; God will communicate himself to his people there. There also we have communion with the saints and children of God, and are helps one to another, and that is a great happiness. Our communion with the saints is a privilege, as well as our communion with God. The fire is kept in when the coals lie together; so the converse of the people of God together keeps in the fire of religion. Wine is best preserved in the hogshead. Our fellow-members are appointed to be means of our mutual edification and spiritual supply: Eph. iv. 16, ' By that which every joint supplieth.'

Use. This showeth what we should chiefly respect and seek, both for ourselves and for our children. For ourselves, that we may have a nail in the holy place, an interest in the church, that the blessings of Abraham may come upon us. You should esteem more of God's covenant, and of being members of the church, than of all the honours of the world besides. So for our posterity, parents should not strive so much to make their children great as good; to see them joined to the body of Christ's church, that is the best blessing you can leave them. It is not your work merely to prefer them to such an office or such an estate, to make them free of such a city or corporation, but to look that these spiritual privileges may be continued in those that come from your loins. For a man truly spiritual will desire spiritual privileges, not only for himself, but for others, that there they may be where God is enjoyed; that they may edify one another in love and faith, and forward one another in spiritual worship.

Obs. 2. In conferring this blessing there is a difference here again; Ephraim, the younger, is preferred before Manasseh, the elder, the regality is entailed upon him. Learn thence, there is a difference not only between the blessings of the wicked and the godly, but between the blessings of the godly and the godly. In the former verse you have Jacob and Esau represented with their different blessings; Esau hath his common portion, and Jacob his covenant blessing; there is a godly and a wicked man. But here Ephraim and Manasseh, two branches of the covenant, and they have different blessings; Ephraim is preferred, that he might have the pre-eminence, and that Joseph's portion may be entailed upon him. And still God keeps the same course, the Lord doth not deal alike with his children, neither in temporals nor spirituals. There is ἐκλέκτων ἐκλεκτότεροι, the elect of the elect, the flower of God's people, that have more choice privileges than others. In the little body of Christ's own disciples there were some were treated more familiarly than others. Peter, James, and John, were taken to see the transfiguration of Christ, Mat. xvii. 1, and afterward to see the passion of Christ, Mat. xxvi. 37. There are some to whom God will manifest himself more familiarly, give them larger supplies of comfort, and a more plentiful allowance in the course of his providence. As in the sphere of reprobation there is a great deal of difference between God's dispensations—all are not passed by alike, some have more means, better tempers, advantages of education, though the Lord hath not given them special grace; so also in the sphere of election there is a great deal of difference—some have more advantages to glorify God than others, more comfortable and sweeter incomes of the Spirit of God, higher opportunities of service, greater supplies of grace, more abilities of parts, and the like. There is a difference in grace, all have not a like measure, there are stars of the first magnitude; the same fountain filleth several cisterns, but all have not a like measure. There is a difference in comfort,—some are kept mournful, and others walk more comfortably; some travel the upper, and some the lower way to heaven. There is a difference in gifts: 1 Cor. xii. 8, 'To one is given by the Spirit the word of wisdom, to another the word of knowledge by the same Spirit,' &c. There is a difference in estate and outward supply; levelling is not God's way, 'The poor you have always with you,' Mat. xxvi. 11. God will be glorified in every relation,—by some as servants, by others as masters of families, for in all things God will be free, and we must submit. The talents were not equally distributed,—one had five, another three, another one. Therefore let us not murmur, we have all more than we can well improve. If these things happened according to chance or to man's designation, we might murmur; but there is a wise providence in it. God is the disposer of honours, and dignities, and estates: 1 Sam. ii. 7, 'The Lord maketh poor and maketh rich; he bringeth low and lifteth up.' And so he disposeth of comforts; we must tarry till the master of the feast bids us sit higher. Do not limit him, and begrudge the Lord the freedom of his counsels. Thou art there where God hath set thee, and if thou canst not improve this relation to the glory of God, thou wilt never improve an higher. The tree that cannot thrive in the valleys, will never thrive on the bleak mountains and tops of barren hills. We are not to choose what part we will act in the world; God is the great master of the scenes. Say then, I have that which the Lord sees fit for me; this should be the temper of a christian, to say, I have a covenant portion, though I do not come up to the height of what others enjoy. God will never maintain all his servants at the same rate, but some shall have more, some less, according to his own wise distribution.

Obs. 3. The prophetical blessing is again ascribed to faith.

The light of faith and the light of prophecy differ in some things, yet they agree in many. They differ in the extraordinariness of the revelation; the light of prophecy depends upon an extraordinary revelation, but faith hath the ordinary word of God. Peculiar instinct and vision makes way for the light of prophecy, but we have the common ground of the word of God. They had oracles, we 'a sure word of prophecy,' 2 Peter i. 19. In prophecy there is an immediate illumination ; there is not discourse and argument so much as there is in faith. In prophecy the particular event is more expressly foretold, the Lord binds his hands as it were by prophecy ; but we must refer ourselves to the general tenor of the covenant, that 'all things shall work together for good,' Rom. viii. 28. And they agree in this in having the same general ground, divine revelation ; we have the word of God to show, as well as they ; and as to the particular event, an actual trust is not disappointed, and sometimes in those that enjoy communion with God there may be particular instincts for special mercies. Thus much for the first action, wherein he showed the strength of his faith in the weakness of his body—'Jacob, when he was dying, blessed both the sons of Joseph.'

Secondly, For the other action—' He worshipped leaning upon the top of his staff.' Here you have (1.) The action—' He worshipped ;' (2.) The gesture 'Leaning upon the top of his staff.'

1. The action—'He worshipped.' This worship was not a civil worship performed to Joseph, but religious worship to the Lord. The indefinite expression shows that it must be taken in a more noble sense ; that is, he worshipped God. Now what kind of worship was this? He was about to resign his soul, and therefore there is thanksgiving contained in it for mercies already received, and prayer for mercies to come.

[1.] There is thanksgiving in it. So the Targum, *Laudes Dei cecinii super spondam suam.* Joseph had sworn and promised to bury him in the land of Canaan, to lay him with his fathers ; the society of the grave was a pledge of the communion of saints in heaven, then he sings the praises of God upon his bed's head, and glorifies God in the midst of his weak estate. I find the like passage concerning David when he heard the shouting and the acclamations of the people when the kingdom was settled upon Solomon, it is said, 1 Kings i. 47, ' The king bowed himself upon the bed.' So Jacob, having obtained his desires, and passed through the pikes, and all the dangers of the present life, falls a-praising and glorifying of God. As men are, so are their thoughts and carriage at death : Jacob is worshipping, blessing, and praising God for past experiences, for present assurance, and for future hopes ; so we should go out of the world praising and glorifying God both for what is past, and present, and to come, that we shall have a society with Abraham, Isaac, and Jacob for ever.

[2.] It may imply his prayer to God likewise, that those blessings might be accomplished.

2. The gesture—' Leaning on the top of his staff.' It is said, Gen. xlvii. 31, ' Israel bowed himself upon the bed's-head.' Some reconcile these places thus ; that to give the greater honour to God, he rose out of his bed, and sat upon his bed, leaning upon his staff ; for it is said, after these blessings were finished, he gathered up his feet into the bed and died. The most genuine reconciling of the place is this, to acknowledge a condescension of the Holy Ghost, in making use of a corrupt translation that was then in use. The Septuagint, they read as the apostle doth

here, προσκύνησεν ἐπὶ τὸ ἄκρον τῆς ῥάβδου αὐτοῦ, 'That he worshipped upon the top of his staff.' When the Hebrew bible was without pricks or vowels, there might be a mistake of the word מִטָה, *lectus*, a bed, for מַטֶּה, *baculus*, a staff or rod. But possibly it might be both, he might lean upon his bed, and upon the top of his staff at the same time. And the apostle would not contend in a thing indifferent, nor bring any other exposition than what was now in their hands, for he writes to the Hebrews; and the Jews living among the Grecians had accustomed themselves to the Septuagint. The apostles were not so scrupulous but that they did accommodate themselves to the weak in things not weighty, to show what condescension we should use in like cases to the infirmities of others. But what is the meaning of this posture and gesture? Many fond superstitions are drawn from hence, as all matters of external gesture and ceremony are apt to be abused; superstition presently gets in, and improves them to vile uses. Some plead from hence for bowing to the east, and bowing to the cross, which they suppose figured in Jacob's hands laid cross upon Joseph's sons; others to some supposed image upon the top of his staff. But this gesture was used, partly, to show his reverence and humility in the worship of God. Though he was now grown weak and impotent with age and sickness, and could hardly get out of his bed, yet he was loth to use an irreverent gesture. Having special business with God, he raiseth up himself leaning upon his bed, and praises the Lord; he doth, as well as he can, put himself into the posture of such as worshipped with a bended knee, an expression of reverence and humility. And partly, this gesture was a public profession of his dependence and reliance upon God's promises. I find there are two interpretations made of this gesture. Some (as Grotius and others) make it to be an emblem of faith, as trust is often compared to leaning. Trust in the creatures is compared to leaning upon a reed or staff in 2 Kings xviii. 21, 'Behold thou trustest upon the staff of this bruised reed, even upon Egypt, on which if a man lean, it shall go into his hand.' So they make it to be an emblem or public profession of his faith, and that, I think, it is in general. Another more suitably and more probably conceives Jacob's leaning upon his staff was, not only to sustain his feeble body, but that he might use this gesture as a profession of his pilgrimage—and faith in the heavenly country. The patriarchs were wont upon all occasions to declare they were pilgrims; now a staff was an emblem of their pilgrimage: Gen. xxxii. 10, 'With my staff I passed over this Jordan;' Exod. xii. 11, they were to eat the passover 'with their staff in their hands;' and Mark vi. 8, the disciples were commanded 'to take nothing for their journey but a staff,' &c. So Jacob, to declare his hopes were in another and a better country, that here he was but a sojourner and pilgrim, he leaned on his staff. But I will rather content myself with the general observation, that it is the gesture by which he did publicly express and declare his humility and thankfulness to God for the great mercies bestowed on him, and his faith in God.

Obs. 1. That our addresses to God must be reverent, both as to the frame of the soul and as to the gesture of the body.

Poor impotent Jacob desires to put himself into the posture of sup-
plicants. As to the frame of the soul, our addresses to God must be
reverent. Reverence is a special qualification in worship. A child of
God cannot be always affectionate, for affection depends much upon
the vigorous motion of bodily spirits and other accidental causes, therefore a child of God cannot always pray with like affection; but a child
of God should be always reverent and serious. Without this it is no
worship ; we forget with whom we have to do. To come otherwise is
a lessening of the greatness and majesty of God. As those which
offered a corrupt thing, the Lord confutes them with this: Mal. i. 13,
' I am a great king, saith the Lord of Hosts, and my name is dreadful
among the heathen.' They that come in a carnal, formal manner to
the Lord, they do not consider they have to do with a great king, and
with the God of all the world, Superficial dealing in God's service
argues we have mean thoughts of God, and are enemies to his greatness: we go about to persuade the world that God is not so great and
terrible. The first reason, ' I am a great king,' implies it is a lessening
of his majesty ; and the second reason, 'My name is dreadful among
the heathen,' implies that familiarity and acquaintance should not
lessen and weaken our dread of God. The very heathens have an awe
of divine powers ; those that pray now and then upon some eminent
judgment of God or affrightment of conscience, are full of dread. But
though we should be familiar with God, we should not forget that his
name is dreadful ; it is custom and formal worship, unless those that
pray constantly are possessed with an awe of God. Heathens: that
have but a little light to see into the nature of God, yet they see enough
to fear that which they suppose to be God. Therefore christians that
know more of God, should come with a dread of his presence, and with
a heart awed with a sense of God's glory. Our familiarity and constant
converse should abate nothing of our godly fear and reverence, for they
that know the least of God know enough to reverence him, though not
to put confidence in him : ' My name is known among the heathen.'
And as there should be reverence in the frame of the soul, so also in
the gestures of the body ; for God that made both body and soul, will
be served by both ; and Christ that redeemed both, will be served by both
—' Glorify God in your bodies, and in your spirits, which are God's,' 1
Cor. vi. 20. Not that I would here stand upon gestures, you are not
bound absolutely to this or that; and the examples of saints recorded
in scripture are various and different, whether standing, kneeling, or
falling upon the face, to show that in such things christians are left to
their own liberty ; but at least we may collect this much in the general
that there is a necessity laid upon us that the gesture should be reverent and serious, and when we are not hindered by any just cause, we
must choose such gestures, as do most of all savour of humility and
reverence in worship of the great God, and such as doth argue that we
are not backward. Sitting, and lying along at prayer, does not savour
so much of reverence, humility and zeal as we should show. As to
the particular gesture God would give no law, for according to the
affection of the heart, such will be the motion and posture of the body ;
and the received custom of the nation doth most show what is decent ;

and the use and practice of the church is to be regarded, that we may give the least offence; that unless we are hindered by invincible impotency and weakness of body, we should be careful of our very gestures.

Obs. 2. That where faith gives a willing mind, bodily infirmities shall be no let and hindrance from duty.

Faith makes us to do our best, to do all that we can to glorify God; and then duty is most acceptable where most self-denial is shown; when we recover it out of the hands of a temptation, from our lazy, self-loving heart, duty is sweet then. Timothy was a weak man, he had his infirmities, 1 Tim. v. 23; yet he did not cease from his work in the gospel, or neglect his charge. Now I shall show how faith works upon such an occasion: faith looks backward, forward, round about us, and every way it engageth and encourageth the soul against bodily distempers, to be doing something that may bring glory to God, and may conduce to the worship of his majesty. Faith looks backward: and thus faith represents Jesus Christ as dying upon the cross, what pains Christ endured in his own body,—his face spit upon, his hands and feet nailed to the cross, his head crowned with thorns, and shall we stand upon the body? Christ exposed his body to the utmost suffering; pain was poured in upon him by the conduit of every sense; and if Christ stood not upon his body, but neglected his refreshment to do good to souls, shall we stand upon our bodies? Thus faith looks backward upon the love of Christ, and urgeth the soul to do what we are able, notwithstanding bodily infirmities; as old Jacob raised up himself in his bed when he was hardly able to move, leaning upon his staff, worshipping of God. Then faith looks round about us, and shows how far lust prevaileth with men; and shall not the love of God prevail with us? Carnal men in pursuance of their fleshly lusts can weary and waste the body; and shall we stand upon every lesser excuse? Shall others beat their brains, tire and waste their spirits, go to bed late, rise early, and all to accomplish their worldly projects, and to satisfy their vile lusts and will; and will you not do something for God, and deny your ease and pleasure for God? We are willing to put ourselves on self-denial for everything but for God's sake. Sin is a tyrant, it wastes and weakens men; yet still it hath obedience paid to it. Men make their bodies drudges to their lusts and vile affections; and in all sports and pleasures what pains will men take! Pain seems to be the very sauce of pleasure; and shall we begrudge a little pains taken in prayer, a little struggling and wrestling with God in private and secret prayer? So faith looks forward to things to come when this earthly tabernacle shall be dissolved, 2 Cor. v. 1, and the body crumbled to dust and ashes. It is better to be worn out with labour than eaten out with rust and consumed with idleness. Faith looks upward, and there beholds the blessed recompenses for the body; the great things God hath provided not only for your souls (that is indeed the heaven of heaven, and the chiefest part of our happiness), but for your bodies. The body that hath a share in labours shall have also a share in the happiness: Phil. iii. 21, 'Who shall change our vile bodies,' &c. Though you waste and spend your bodies in the service

of the Lord, yet they will be repaired again.   Oh, how glorious was
Christ's body !   It may be discerned in part in his transfiguration,
there were such beamings forth of light from the body of Christ that
the disciples could not bear it.   Such kind of bodies for clarity, brightness, and strength shall the saints have ; this massy clog of flesh and
blood which is such a hindrance to us, it shall then be made like to
Christ's glorious body.   There will be nothing lost by Christ ; he that
could heal Malchus's ear, can restore what is lost, wasted, spent and
worn out in constant duty.   He will make up all again.   Then faith
looks downward ; there are hell's torments which are provided, not
only for the soul, but for the body.   Then faith judgeth, it is better to
take pains than to endure pains ; it is better to be bound with cords of
duty than with chains of darkness ; these pains are nothing to what
the wicked shall endure in hell.   Though I do not believe there is
corporal fire in hell, yet clearly there are pains that shall immediately
be inflicted upon the body ; not only pains in the body resulting from
the sympathy it hath with the soul, but upon the body itself : Mat. x.
28, ' Fear him which is able to destroy both body and soul in hell.'
And there is a place of torment, but what it is we cannot tell.   Now
faith represents this, the terrors that are to come, and shall we stand
for a little pains for God.

Use. It shames us for our laziness and love of ease.   Love of ease
and pleasure is the bane of christianity ; away with those nice christians
that are so sparing and tender of their bodies !   Oh, let not the body
betray the soul !   If you would gratify one part above another gratify
the soul, for that is the better part ; and in gratifying the soul, you
gratify the body in the issue.   If out of love to duty you should
neglect the body a little, the body will lose nothing by it at last.
Christians, whenever ease and laziness creep upon you, remember it
is good to interest the body in some self-denial, that it may the better
look for its share.   Jacob was willing to rouse up himself, to put himself into a posture of suppliant, to give a good example to his children.
Consider, duty is never sweeter than when there is some difficulty, and
when it is recovered out of the hands of indisposition.   Shall we serve
God with that which cost us nothing ?   Though it put us to pain, and
be some intrenchment to our ease, it will be sweeter at length.   Contempt of ease and pleasure is the greatest pleasure in the end.   That
is worth nothing that cost nothing, and excuses are a sign of an unwilling heart.   Where the spirit is willing, though the flesh is weak, a
christian will be doing what he can, he will not sit out.   And consider,
the body is Christ's as well as the soul : 1 Cor. vi. 20, ' Ye are bought
with a price ; therefore glorify God with your bodies and with your
spirits, which are God's.'   When duty proves grievous and burdensome,
consider, your bodies are not your own, they are bought by Christ, and
let it not be grievous and burdensome to you to give Christ his own.
He expects the body should be put to some pains.   To conclude, when
we are lazy, and ease is apt to creep upon us, then set faith a-work,
looking backward, forward, upward, downward.   Let it argue and
plead for God from what is past, and what is to come.   Let faith be
expecting, waiting, looking up, there will a time come when the body

will not be a clog, but will be a spiritual body, that is, more fit for spiritual employments and spiritual enjoyments, that it shall never be weary of.   There is no weariness in heaven, both soul and body shall ever remain fresh, to rejoice in and praise the Lord; there is no indisposition, no weakness there.   Then let it argue, If God hath provided such things for us, what! shall I be backward?   And if it be difficult, here is an occasion to show my love.

SERMON LVI.

By faith Joseph, when he died, made mention of the departing of the children of Israel, and gave commandment concerning his bones.— HEB. xi. 22.

HERE we have (1.) The person; (2.) The times; (3.) The effects of his faith.

First. The person mentioned for his faith—*Joseph.*

1. Let us consider him as Jacob's son, for still the line of believers is continued.   The three former are called heirs of the same promise. Now the next in rank is Joseph, who was eminent for faith; the rest had their privileges, but the scripture taketh notice of this most notably.   It is an advantage to be born of godly parents; Timothy is said to be 'the son of a Jewess woman that believed,' Acts xvi. 1. Though the piety of the parents doth not hinder but that children are born in sin, and so are under the curse; yet they have a treble benefit.

[1.] The children of such, without any scruple, are to be accounted children of the covenant, and belonging to the church, till they do actually declare the contrary: Rom. xi. 16, 'For if the first-fruit be holy, the lump is also holy; and if the root be holy, so are the branches.' They are a covenant stock; the apostle useth two comparisons, of the first-fruits, and of the root: 1 Cor. vii. 14, 'Else were your children unclean, but now are they holy.'

[2.] That in their infancy they are seasoned with good education, and the sprouts of sin are cut off betimes, before they come to be hardened and strengthened by custom.   Though education cannot kill sin, yet it hindereth the growth of sin; the vessel is seasoned betimes. Letters graven in the bark of a tree grow with a tree; a little scratch will come to be a deep dent or gap; this is hindered.   And this is to be supposed of all godly parents: Gen. xviii. 19, 'I know Abraham that he will command his children, and his household after him, and they shall keep the way of the Lord.'   You hinder the impressions of sin at least, if God's blessing give not more.

[3.] There God usually chooseth and bestoweth his special grace, though he be not absolutely tied. The grace of the covenant runneth most kindly in the channel of the covenant; these are the natural branches: Rom. xi. 24, 'How much more shall those that be the natural branches be grafted into their own olive-tree?' The apostle thence evinceth the Jews conversion.

And this was Joseph's case; when he was young in his tender years, he was seasoned with good education; and though he was sold into Egypt, and a long time lived among idolaters; yet the grace of God findeth him out, and followeth him, because of his father's covenant. He seemed to be cast off and lost, yet still God looketh on him as a branch of the covenant—'By faith Joseph, when he died,' &c.

Use 1. Well then, you see how hurtful the wickedness of those that have children is, they hurt not only their own souls, but as much as in them lieth they destroy their children too, and so are not only *patres*, but *peremptores*, as Bernard called them; they murder their own posterity.

Use 2. And hence is the wickedness aggravated of those that are born of godly parents, that were seasoned with good education, yet have broken out; none sin as they do, they sin against preventing grace, against privileges and warnings. If there be a hotter place in hell, they shall have it.

Use 3. It is some plea to say, I am thy servant, and the son of thine handmaid. God delighteth to be owned as our father's friend: Ps. cxvi. 15, 'O Lord, truly I am thy servant; I am thy servant, and the son of thine handmaid.' As David showed kindness to Mephibosheth for Jonathan's sake, 2 Sam. ix. 11.

2. Let us look upon Joseph as a great courtier in Egypt, as a man that had run through various conditions, but was now well settled, counted a father in the country. But all that wealth, delight, and honour, which he enjoyed there, could not induce a forgetfulness or neglect of the promise, nor entice his heart to be set on Egypt; it was another country to Joseph. It was better with him there than at home, yet he telleth them of their departure; and to show his affection to the land of promise, he would not have a bone left there. Note, That honour and riches do not hurt faith in themselves, where there is a gracious heart to manage them. In themselves they are God's gifts, and must be improved to his glory.

[1.] I shall show that the rich are not excluded from the exercise of faith: Ps. xxii. 26, 'The meek shall eat and be satisfied;' and ver. 29, 'All they that be fat upon earth shall eat and worship.' The rich and the poor have the same ransom: 1 Tim. vi. 17, 'Charge them that are rich in the world that they be not high-minded, nor trust in uncertain riches, but in the living God, who giveth us richly all things to enjoy.' God will choose men of all conditions; not all poor, lest religion should be trodden underfoot; not all rich, lest it should seem to be supported by a secular arm, and lest there be a disparagement of the blessings of his providence. *Dantur bonis, ne putentur mala,* &c.—They are given to good men, lest they be thought not to be good things, and to wicked men, lest they be esteemed to be the chiefest good.

[2.] There is as much faith seen, yea more, in moderating the affections in a full estate, as in depending upon God for supplies ; to learn to abound is a hard lesson, to see the love of God in all, and to keep from settling here : Ps. lxii. 10, ' If riches increase, set not your heart upon them.' To be thankful and to be useful. The poor have not such temptations as the rich. Diseases that arise from plenty are most usual, though diseases that arise from want are most dangerous ; so that a full estate hath most temptations. Joseph's brethren had their temptations, yet they had not such temptations as Joseph had. Men that have nothing are as it were driven to it, beaten to dependence upon God ; but here there is more of choice, when they are full and well. If Joseph had liked the pomp of Egypt, he might have had enough there.

Use. Well then, it maketh for the comfort and caution of rich men.

1. For their comfort. There are some of your order, though not many : 1 Cor. i. 26, ' Not many mighty, not many noble, are called.' Joseph, a courtier in Egypt ; and the eunuch in Acts viii. 27, was treasurer of queen Candace. Usually the poor receive the gospel, in the first times of the gospel especially, lest it should seem to be supported by human force and power, but not always. God hath taken in great ones, there is room for your faith.

2. For their caution. Be of Joseph's temper, let Egypt be nothing to Canaan. This is the true greatness of mind, in counting the highest things which you enjoy as nothing in comparison of heaven. There are none bound to look after better things so much as you ; for you have tasted more of God's bounty, you have more occasion to make trial of the world's vanity and nothingness, you are in a condition wherein many miscarry ; as in a dangerous way we are more careful of our steps. Say then, All this is nothing to heaven ; let me go there where my home, my country, my estate, my treasure, my inheritance is.

Secondly, The time when his faith was exercised—*When he died,* τελευτῶν, at his ending ; it alludeth to his speech : Gen. l. 24, ' I die ; and God will surely visit you, and bring you out of this land.' He saw that death was at hand, and he meeteth it with a confident spirit. It is one of the blessings which God bestoweth upon his children, that when they are about to go out of the world he begetteth a knowledge of it, or maketh it sensible to them that their end draweth nigh, that they may dispose of their affairs, and compose their spirits for their dissolution. ' When he was dying ; ' all of them are said before to die in faith, and therefore is this circumstance so often repeated. Observe how willing the children of God were to renew their own faith, and to encourage, and strengthen others a little before their death. We brought you the examples of Abraham, Isaac and Jacob, and here is Joseph's instance, he comforts himself and his brethren with the memorial of the promise. I showed you their grounds, because this was the last act of love, and then their words were received with most reverence. Now I shall only press you that you may go and do likewise, to be providing for such a time. All our lifetime we should be preparing for our dying speech and valediction, that we may not go out in a snuff, but may take our leave from the world with honour to God and comfort to ourselves.   Christians, is your dying speech ready? Consider, there is no dissembling then, you must be able to speak it in truth of heart, and it had need be pressing, and serious, and stirring, for you shall never speak for God more in the world.   I say, Is it ready?   Can you call to mind promises?   Can you yield up your souls to God?   Are you furnished with experiences to confirm others? A christian is not to die like a beast, to be only passive, merely to yield to the necessity of nature, and there is an end.   It is a harder matter to die well than you are aware.   Can you take your soul in your hand, and yield it up to God in a confidence of the promises?   Oh! let us all provide, we are all hastening this way; some of you are young, and you hold life but by an uncertain tenure.   When swine come into a garden, they crop off the buds as well as the grown flowers; death maketh no distinction.   Some of you are old, you are as good as dead already: Heb. xi. 12, 'Therefore sprang there of one, and him as good as dead,' &c.   A little provision will not serve the turn; many of God's eminent servants have been even foiled in this last combat; you had need gather up many experiences, you had need be acquainted with the promises, that you may have them ready.   In the text it is said, 'He made mention,' or remembered, ἐμνημόνευσε; if we would make use of the promises in a dying time, we should keep them in sight and mind that they may be ever ready.   It is the last enemy you are to grapple with, you had need of armour of proof.   It is an enemy that will come well provided with weapons ready drawn, and if we are not wholly armed, we shall go by the worst; nay, we shall put weapons into the enemy's hand by our sins and fears.   If you have not the breast-plate of faith and the helmet of salvation, what will you do? Alas! you never met with such an enemy in your lives as this last enemy; you have lived forty or fifty years, and have rubbed out well enough, but this is another manner of enemy.

Thirdly, The effects of this faith, or if you will, the effect, and the sign, and visible symbol of it.

First, The first effect of his faith is—*He made mention of the departure of the children of Israel:* Gen. l. 24, 'I die, and God will surely visit you, and bring you out of this land into the land which he sware to Abraham, Isaac, and Jacob.'   'In visiting he will visit you.' Now this he mentioneth, not only to testify his own faith and hope, but also to confirm his brethren that they might hope well though he should die; and to draw them out of Egypt as much as he could.   Now the strength of his faith was shown in this, that this deliverance and departure out of Egypt was a great while yet to come, to come to pass a great many years afterwards; and in the meantime they were to be after his death under a hard and cruel oppression in Egypt; for in all this he alludeth to the promise: Gen. xv. 13, 14, 'Know of a surety that thy seed shall be a stranger in a land that is not theirs, and shall serve them, and they shall afflict them four hundred years.   And also that nation whom they shall serve will I judge, and afterwards shall they come out with great substance.'   There is a great deal of faith

shown in the public deliverance of God's people.   Here I shall
show—

1. Why faith is to be herein exercised.

[1.] So far as a christian is interested to act and look after blessings,
so far is he bound to believe.   Now a christian is not only to seek his
own things, but the common welfare of the saints: Phil. ii. 21, 'All
seek their own, not the things of Jesus Christ.'   If men do so, though,
it is against humanity, for man is ζῶον πολίτικον, a sociable creature.
The heathens were sensible of a duty they owed to their country; yet
if men do so, let not christians.   It is a self-excommunication to be
selfish and senseless, to have such narrow lines of communication as
our own private sphere, and the interests and concernments of our own
families; you cast yourselves out of the body.   It is not enough to look
to your own estate, to your own souls; but that it is also well with the
body, and to help on the common good; and therefore he is bound so far
to believe. For all action is supported by faith; men would soon stick else
in duties of public relation which mostly expose to danger and hazard.

[2.] So far as God hath promised, so far we are bound to believe.
Now God hath made promises, not only to our persons, but to the church
in general; to particular persons, and to Sion: not only for our preservation, but for the preservation of the church as a church, to believers
considered in a collective body, that 'the gates of hell shall not prevail against it,' Mat. xvi. 18.

2. How we must believe promises.

[1.] That they will be accomplished, though long delayed.   Faith
looketh over that length of time that is between the promise and the
accomplishment.   For a long time they were to lie under Egyptian
thraldom, yet surely God will visit you: Hab. ii. 3, 'For the vision is
yet for an appointed time, but at the end it shall speak, and not lie:
though it tarry, wait for it; because it will surely come, it will not
tarry.'   It is the weariness of the flesh that thinketh that God tarrieth
—'He is a present help in trouble,' Ps. xlvi. 1.   And if it were seasonable,
you should have it next hour, if there were not more of the beauty of
providence to be seen, and more profit to redound to the church—'He
that believeth shall not make haste,' Isa. xxviii. 16.   Hold out then,
God's delays are not to deny our prayers and frustrate our hopes, but
to quicken us to call upon him, and to fit us for the mercy we look for.

[2.] Though the case of the children of God be very afflicted, yet
faith is to wait.   In Egypt they were in sore bondage.   Faith is to outwork all difficulties—'Though he slay me, yet will I trust in him,' Job
xiii. 15; and Ps. xxiii. 4, 'Yea, though I walk through the valley of
the shadow of death I will fear no evil; for thou art with me, and thy
rod and thy staff they comfort me.'   When we are ploughed enough,
then God will cut their cords asunder; he may suffer the ploughers to
make long furrows, yet Christ will have his crop.   *Quando duplicantur
lateres, tum venit Mose*—When the tale of bricks was doubled, then
Moses came and delivered them.

3. Propositions to help us.

[1.] It is not for the profit of the church always to enjoy serenity.
As to the fruitfulness of the earth and the health of men, it is not pro-

fitable that the face of heaven should always be serene and glittering ; we have need of rains, and winds, and tempests, and foul weather as well as fair.   The welfare of the church needs to be interrupted some-times.   If the church and the members of it were merely spirit, with-out any flesh and corruption, they might enjoy a continual peace ; but we need troubles and persecutions to keep us in order, lest the worser part prevail : Isa. liv. 11, ' O thou afflicted, tossed with tempests, and not comforted ! ' Where we would have no chaff, we use much fanning.

[2.] The church may be much afflicted, but in the issue the church shall have the best; it shall not be utterly destroyed.   Christ cannot be a king without subjects : Mat. xvi. 18, 'The gates of hell shall not prevail against it ; ' and Ps. cxxix. 1, 2, 'Many a time have they afflicted me from my youth, may Israel now say ; many a time have they afflicted me from my youth, yet they have not prevailed against me.'   Ever since there was a church, there was a delivering God ; the whole history of the bible is a tragi-comedy.   Hence Mordecai's confi-dence: Esther iv. 14, ' For if thou altogether holdest thy peace, then shall there enlargement and deliverance arise to the Jews from another place.'   The Jews were then the only visible people of God, and Esther the only visible deliverer ; but if she held her peace, yet deliverance would come. *Premi potest veritas, non opprimi*—Truth may be pressed, but it shall not be oppressed.   Now what God ever hath been, he is still the same, the same God is above still.   We have as good promises as they.   The Jews watched Christ's sepulchre, yet Christ rose again. The enemy hath designed in all ages to destroy the people of God, but God hath defeated their designs and rendered their opposition ineffectual.

[3.] God many times deferreth help to the last : Acts xii. 6–8, Peter was the next day to be executed, and the night before God brought him out ; till the very last point of time did the Lord defer help.   This is the Lord's fashion : Gen. xxii. 14, ' In the mount of the Lord it shall be seen.'   Isaac was just ready to be offered up ; and then the Lord called to Abraham out of heaven, and staid his hand.   When the Israelites were shut up, Exod. xiv. 13, ' Moses said to the people, Fear ye not, stand still, and see the salvation of the Lord, which he will show to you to-day, for the Egyptians whom ye have seen to-day, ye shall see them again no more for ever.'   2 Kings vi. 25, in the siege of Samaria there was a great famine, that ' an ass's head was sold for fourscore pieces of silver, and the fourth part of a cab of dove's dung for five pieces of silver.'   And the wicked king said, ver. 33, ' This evil is from the Lord ; why should I wait any longer ? '   Yet God of a sudden gave an incredible plenty to them, chap. vii.   So Ps. lxix. 1-3, ' Save me, O God, for the waters are come in unto my soul. I sink in deep mire, where there is no standing ; I am come into deep waters, where the floods overflow me.   I am weary of my crying, my throat is dried, mine eyes fail, while I wait for my God.'   David was nigh to perishing, like a drowning man, but he cried unto God ' in an acceptable time,' vers. 13-15, and God delivered him, and kept his head above the waters, that he was not drowned.   As the disciples in the storm were in great danger: Mat. viii. 24, 'Behold there arose a great tempest in the sea, insomuch that the ship was covered with the waves.' And the disciples came to Christ, ver. 25, 'Lord, save us, we perish!' And then 'he arose and rebuked the winds and the sea, and there was a great calm,' ver. 26. The devil thought he had gotten a great advantage there; the apostles were to preach the gospel, and Christ and his apostles were all embarked in one bottom. So it was with Peter: Mat. xiv. 30, 'When he saw the wind boisterous, he was afraid, and, beginning to sink, he cried, saying, Lord, save me!' He began to sink, his faith would hold out no longer, and the sea would bear him no longer. And so also God loveth to delude the expectations of his enemies, when they come to the top of their desires they miss their aim: Isa. xxix. 7, 8, 'And the multitude of all the nations that fight against Ariel, even all that fight against her and her munition, and all that distress her, shall be as a dream of the night vision. It shall be as when a hungry man dreameth, and behold he eateth; but he awaketh and his soul is empty: or as when a thirsty man dreameth, and behold he drinketh; but he awaketh, and behold he is faint, and his soul hath appetite; so shall all the multitude of the nations be that fight against Mount Sion.' Sennacherib feedeth himself with the surprisal of Jerusalem, Isa. xxxvi. Now God suffers this that grace may have the fuller exercise, and that his glory may be the more seen. Help is not denied though it be delayed. Therefore wait for the salvation of God.

[4.] God is punctual at his time, neither sooner nor later; he will come to make good his truth: Exod. xii. 40, 41, 'Now the sojourning of the children of Israel who dwelt in Egypt was four hundred and thirty years. And it came to pass at the end of the four hundred and thirty years, even the self-same day it came to pass, that all the hosts of the Lord went out from the land of Egypt.' Mark the words—'Even the self-same day it came to pass;' God will keep exact touch; God brought them out of Egypt, but he deferred it till the last day; his bond was almost forfeited, yet he paid it before sunset. God is most exact in performing his promises; though they are very ancient, he keepeth touch even to a day. So Ezek. xxiv. 2, 'Son of man, write thee the name of the day, even of this same day, the king of Babylon set himself against Jerusalem, the same day.' So there is a time for the calling of the Jews, the fall of antichrist, and other promises that are to be fulfilled and when. So of Joseph it is said, 'Until the time that the word came, the word of the Lord tried him,' Ps. cv. 19. It may be the troubles of the church do not end when we would wish, but they have a set time determined and appointed by God, and then there shall be an end of them; there is a secret word of his decree which will in time be manifested; as when we are sufficiently humbled, then it is fit that means should work for our deliverance. God deferreth till the last hour be running: Job vii. 1, 'Is there not an appointed time for man upon earth? are not his days as the days of an hireling?' Doth not a hireling keep exact reckoning? Will he serve beyond his time? If he covenanted for three years, will he serve four? Mercy is not always ready at our call; God hath his own seasons for afflicting, trying, and delivering his people: Hab. ii. 3, 'The vision is for an appointed

time, but at the end it shall speak, and not lie ; though it tarry, wait
for it, because it will surely come, it will not tarry.' The vision is silent
for a while ; there is delay, there is misery and oppression, and so it
seemeth to lie ; ay, but it doth but seem to tarry.

[5.] The church in the latter times hath an advantage of the former,
as their hopes draw nearer. Their troubles, though they did redound to the good of the church in the end, yet they made way for the
revelation of antichrist, 2 Thes. ii. 9, the inundations of these barbarous nations, the Goths, and Vandals, and Lombards, to weaken
the Roman empire. But now, though we cannot be confident at particular occurrences, yet one or other tend to the destruction of antichrist. God taketh his aim afar off. The providences of latter times
are like great eclipses, which have not their operations presently, yet
it is good to observe their general aim and tendencies.

[6.] God many times worketh contrary to outward likelihoods.
When the bricks were doubled, who would look for deliverance ? As
the Hebrew tongue must be read backward, or as the sun going back
ten degrees in Ahaz, dial was a sign of Hezekiah's recovery ; so is providence to be read backward. Joseph was made a slave that he might
be made a favourite ; who would have thought that the dungeon had
been the way to the court ? that error is a means to clear truth ? and
bondage maketh way for liberty ? Persecution and oppression are like
an iron in the fire, which, heated too hot, burneth their fingers that
hold it. Christ loveth to befool his enemies in the height of their wisdom : Exod. i. 10, ' Come on, let us deal wisely with them, lest they
multiply, and it come to pass that when there falleth out any war, they
join also with our enemies, and fight against us, and so get them up
out of our land.' When the project is laid finely, the wise are taken
in their own craftiness. All looketh towards ruin and destruction, but
nothing is out of order to providence ; the wise God can make use of
the most cross accidents, he is never out of his way. Nothing is out
of order to faith and providence.

All afflictions continued upon the people of God work for the glory
of God and their good.

(1.) For the glory of God ; that is dear to his children. The malice
and wickedness of the enemies is compared to ploughing : Ps. cxxix.
3, ' The ploughers have ploughed upon my back, they made long their
furrows.' We have fallow ground that must be broken and ploughed
up ; and when they have ploughed enough, he cuts their cords asunder.
It is for our benefit and God's glory ; they plough, but the harvest is
Christ's, the crop belongeth to the owner of the field. We must distinguish between God's aims and the enemy's aims. The water keepeth
its course, but the wise husbandman maketh it drive the mill : Isa. x.
7, ' Howbeit he meaneth it not so, neither doth his heart think so, but
it is in his heart to destroy and cut off nations not a few ;' and Ps.
lxxvi. 10, ' Surely the wrath of man shall praise thee, the remainder
of wrath shalt thou restrain.' God will restrain wrath when the work
is done ; when the mill hath nothing to grind, we shut the sluices, but
that which breaketh out turneth to God's praise.

(2.) For our good temporal, spiritual, and eternal.[1]

---

[1] *Vide* the Life of Faith as to afflictions.

[7.] If we should miscarry in this work, God cannot want instruments. If we should miscarry sinfully by negligence and silence : Esther iv. 14, ' If thou altogether holdest thy peace at this time, then shall there enlargement and deliverance arise to the Jews from another place.' Her petitioning was the only likely way of preserving the people of God. Or if we miscarry by death ; if Moses die, there will be a Joshua. God knoweth how to help when we are at an utter loss : Micah v. 7, ' And the remnant of Jacob shall be in the midst of many people as a dew from the Lord, as the showers upon the grass, that tarrieth not for man, nor waiteth for the sons of men.' The herbs of the garden have a visible means of supply by the water-pot, which dependeth upon man's providence and industry ; but dews and showers do not fall at the pleasure of man, and the grass in the wilderness groweth by the mere providence of God.

[8.] They that act for the church shall be no losers ; their endeavours shall not be lost, however they speed in the world : Isa. xlix. 4, ' Then I said, I have laboured in vain, I have spent my strength for nought, and in vain ; yet surely my judgment is with the Lord, and my work is with my God.' God doth not take notice of success, but affection : 2 Chron. vi. 8, ' Forasmuch as it was in thine heart to build a house for my name, thou didst well that it was in thy heart.' Actions intended for God's glory, if they fail of their aim, they shall not fail of their reward ; as fountains run, though none drink of them.

Use is to reprove us,

1. That we dono more regard the public welfare of God's people. A man is known by his affection to Sion ; dying Joseph comforts himself, not only with his own happiness, but the happiness of God's people after his death. Every true member of the church hath life in Christ, and this life giveth feeling, and that feeling stirreth up the affections of joy or sorrow. It is a part of our care that it may be well, not only with our souls, but with the church : Ps. cxxxvii. 6, ' If I do not remember thee, let my tongue cleave to the roof of my mouth ; if I prefer not Jerusalem above my chief joy.' They could as well forget themselves as forget Sion, here was their chief happiness. Their own private calamities have not been so grievous as the public ; it was ill with every member when in Babylon, but it was ill with Sion as well as ill with them, and the church sorrow is the chiefest. As Phinehas's wife complained : 1 Sam. iv. 22, ' The glory is departed from Israel, for the ark of God is taken.' It is not, My father is dead, my husband is dead ; but the ark of God is taken, the glory is departed from Israel. When it is well with them and ill with the church, they cannot but mourn, as Daniel and Nehemiah, and those in Ps. cxxxvii. 6. Possibly their own private condition may be tolerable. When it is well with the church, though ill with them, it is a comfort, their private griefs are swallowed up in the public joy. Paul in prison rejoiceth in the progress of the gospel, though with his particular loss, Phil. i. 15–18. But when it is well with them and the church too, it doubleth their contentment : Ps. cxxviii. 5, 6, ' The Lord shall bless thee out of Zion, and thou shalt see the good of Jerusalem all thy days ; yea, thou shalt see thy children's children, and peace upon Israel.' To have public and private mercies together is very sweet, that we have

no occasion to be out of tune, but can join in comfort with the people of God. Yea, when they are entering upon their great happiness, church promises are a comfort, as well as private particular promises. Jesus Christ thought of his in the world when he was going to his Father : John, xiii. 1, ' When Jesus knew that his hour was come that he should depart out of the world unto his Father, having loved his own which were in the world, he loved them unto the end.' He was landing at the haven, but he had left friends at sea, conflicting with winds and waves.

2. It reproveth us that we do no more put forth faith upon these occasions. We are not only to pray down, but believe down troubles and oppositions: Heb. xi. 34, ' By faith they turned to flight the armies of the aliens.' You will think that this is easy, a little confidence will serve the turn ; so it is to those that do not mind the affairs of Sion ; but to them that long, pray, and wait, that prefer the affairs of the church above their chief joy, it is a hard thing. It is hard to settle the heart upon the promises for church deliverances, else what mean so many fears and despondencies which God's people complain of? Men are not deeply enough engaged in the church's quarrel, and therefore do not mind the church's deliverance. However these bewray that they cannot believe, by their murmurings when God's interest and theirs is not combined, and by their apostasy ; it is ' an evil heart of unbelief that maketh them depart from God,' Heb. iii. 12.

Secondly, Another effect of faith we have in the next clause of the text—*And gave commandment concerning his bones.* This is a circumstance often taken notice of in scripture: Gen. l. 25, ' And Joseph took an oath of the children of Israel, saying, God will surely visit you, and ye shall carry up my bones from hence ;' so Exod. xiii. 19, ' And Moses took the bones of Joseph with him ;' after a hundred and fifty years they did it ; and Joshua xxiv. 32, ' And the bones of Joseph, which the children of Israel brought up out of Egypt, they buried in Shechem.' The same desire Jacob made before he died: Gen. xlvii. 30, ' I will lie with my fathers, and thou shalt carry me out of Egypt, and bury me in their burying-place.' This request was not out of superstition, or with respect to any contentment or pleasure which departed saints take in the disposal of their bodies, nor as if there were a more easy resurrection in that soil rather than another, it is all one in Egypt or in Canaan ; nor as if they hoped to be some of those that should rise out of their graves at the resurrection of Christ, Mat. xxvii. 52, 53 ; nor that they might be partakers of the prayers and sacrifices there offered, as Bellarmine thinks, besides the impiousness of the conceit that prayers can avail the dead, and that to the blessings obtained by prayer local nearness is necessary,—at this time there were none, nor two hundred years afterwards. No, there were special reasons for this desire.

1. To show their belief in the promise ; though they could not go thither in person, they would have their bones carried thither to take possession, which was a visible symbol or public testimony of their faith that they doubted not of the promised possession.

2. It was an excitement to posterity not to settle their minds in

Egypt, lest being overcome by the wealth and pleasures of the country, they should forget the land of promise. It was as a trumpet to awaken them.

3. It was a public memorial, by which upon all occasions they might call to mind the truth of the promise when it came to pass. We see now, it is true, what Joseph spake concerning his bones; as they called to mind that parabolical speech of Christ's destroying the temple and building it in three days: John ii. 22, 'When therefore he was risen from the dead, his disciples remembered that he had said this unto them, and they believed the scripture and the word which Jesus had said.' They now believed that he spake of the temple of his body.

4. It was a pledge of their communion with the saints; living and dying they would have no communion with idolaters, they would not lie in the same grave with them.

5. Canaan was a symbol of their eternal inheritance; so to show their heavenliness, they desired to be in Canaan, living and dead, that is, in the land of promise, where Christ conversed, lived, died, rose again. That they did not merely look upon the temporal enjoyment of Canaan is clear, for Joseph was better in Egypt; but they looked upon heaven, and the great promises and blessings of the covenant figured thereby, they looked for the translation of their souls to heaven, and a future resurrection of all the blessed hereafter. In short, Joseph would have all know that he did not die an Egyptian, but in expectation of the enjoyment of a heavenly life with all the patriarchs, of which this country was a figure. Hence the phrase is often used of ' being gathered to their fathers,' which did not only imply their lying in one common sepulchre, but their going to them in heaven, the true Canaan, and place of rest and establishment.

What shall we learn hence?

[1.] Papists would gather the veneration of relics from the translation of Joseph's bones, but fondly, for this was a thing which the Israelites would never have done if not bound thereunto by oath. These bones were carried into the land of promise to be kept, not for show and worship, but for burial.

[2.] Superstitious persons would gather hence a necessity of burying in holy or consecrated places, but fondly, for there were special reasons why these holy men desired to be buried in Canaan. Now there is no promise made to one place rather than another, it maketh nothing *ad animæ levamentum*, to the good of souls.

And the custom of burying in places of worship, as it is very unhealthy and unseemly, so it is very modern. The Jews buried without the city, and Abraham in the cave beside Mamre. Deborah was buried under an oak, Gen. xxxv. 8; Rachel, in the way, ver. 19; and Joseph, in the field of Shechem, Joshua xxiv. 32.

But what is to be learned hence?

(1.) Joseph maketh mention, not only of a departure out of Egypt, but of an introduction into Canaan. The blessings of the covenant are privative and positive; we are not only delivered from hell, but we have an entrance and admission into heaven: John iii. 16, 'That who-

soever believeth in him should not perish, but have everlasting life.'
If we had only been delivered from the power of darkness, it is more
than we could expect, as the prodigal son said, 'Make me as one of thy
hired servants,' Luke xv. 19. But to be preferred to the privileges of
the gospel, that is higher, and more glorious. Well then, let your
obedience be privative and positive ; do not only depart from evil, but
abound in the work of the Lord. Many are not vicious, but they do
not look after communion with God.

(2.) Joseph was a great man in Egypt, yet his heart was elsewhere,
he had no mind to the country where he was so well at ease. So though
we live in Egypt, let our hearts be in Canaan ; if we cannot get out of
the world, let us get the world out of us : John xvii. 16, 'They are not
of the world, even as I am not of the world.' There was their abode;
but their hearts were not there. Oh, it is an excellent frame of spirit
when we can enjoy much in the world, as Joseph lived in great dignity ;
and yet not be of a worldly spirit, and in the fulness of all worldly
things to mind better things.

(3.) There is a communion between the saints departed in the Lord.
Bury me with my fathers, saith Jacob ; and Joseph lying in the same
grave is a pledge of their communion in heaven. They are called, 'a
family,' Eph. iii. 15 ; and a society or company—'The spirits of just
men made perfect,' Heb. xii. 23. There is a double evil of death, it
separates the body and the soul, and it separateth from our relations,
fathers and children, and friends one from another. Now there is
comfort against both ; the soul is separated from the body and joined
to the Lord, loosed from hence, that we may be with Christ. And
then as to company, we go to better company in heaven, we go to those
that long for us, and look for us every day, to ' the spirits of just men
made perfect.' Let us delight in the communion of saints for the
present, that when we change our place, yet we may not change our
company, unless it be for the better ; that we may be with our fathers.
Wicked men are tormented in their society.

(4.) Living and dying we should make profession of our faith.
Joseph, when he died, would be known to be an Israelite, and not an
Egyptian.

(5.) We may gather hence that it is fit the saints, where it may be
had, should have decent burial. It is made a work, not only of honesty,
but piety : Acts viii. 2, 'Devout men carried Stephen to his burial;'
so 2 Sam. ii. 5, 6, 'Blessed be ye of the Lord, who have showed this
kindness unto your lord, even to Saul, and have buried him. And now
the Lord show kindness unto you.' And it is mentioned as great
impiety in the enemies : Ps. lxxix. 2, 3, 'The dead bodies of thy
servants they have given to be meat for the fowls of heaven, the flesh
of the saints unto the beasts of the earth. Their blood have they shed
like water round about Jerusalem, and there was none to bury them.'
And it is a curse : Ps. lxiii. 10, 'They shall fall by the sword, they
shall be a portion for foxes.' So that it is agreeable to the word of
God that there should be such burials.

1st. It is agreeable to the sentence pronounced against sinners : Gen.
iii. 19, 'Dust thou art, and to dust shalt thou return.' We bury the

dead to show that we are not forgetful what we were by nature ; it is a confession of the curse due to sin.

2*dly*, It is agreeable to our hope of the resurrection. We do not cast away their bones and remains, but lay them up ; not as we do the carcases of beasts, but as we sow wheat in the ground, that it may rise again with increase. They do but 'rest in their beds,' Isa. lvii. 2. They are but κοιμητήρια, sleeping-places.

3*dly*, It is agreeable to the honour God hath put upon the bodies of his saints. They are parts of Christ's purchase, 1 Cor. vi. 20. And Christ hath a charge to lose nothing, John vi. 39, ' But to raise them up at the last day.' And they are temples of the Holy Ghost, dedicated to him in covenant, and members of Christ.

4*thly*, It is agreeable to the love we bear to them. Joseph of Arimathea showed his love to Christ in burying him ; and the men of Jabesh Gilead showed their love to Saul. It is the last office we can do them, to lay them up safe.

5*thly*, Well then, funerals are lawful, if lawfully used. Not superstitiously by confining God to places, or as if it did good to patter words over the dead, or to bury in consecrated places—' the earth is the Lord's, and the fulness thereof.' God knoweth where to fetch our substance again, wherever our remains are cast. Not pompously, this is to sin after death, to continue the monuments of our pride when we can sin no longer. Not in a dead carnal manner ; too often it falleth out that the dead bury their dead, the dead in heart bury the dead in body. There are funeral and grave thoughts. It is a monument of the fruit of sin ; the full power of it remaineth over the wicked, and the grave to them is a prison. We should have humbling thoughts, that dust we are, and to dust we shall return ; and we should have believing thoughts, we have our friends in the grave ; but God doth not leave them, he taketh care of the bones of the saints. The grave is now opened with difficulty, but afterwards with ease, and all that are in it shall come forth. The dust of bodies is now mingled together, but God will soon sever them, and give to every man his own body. And we should have mortifying thoughts, we are all hastening this way ; as a candle, as soon as it is lighted, decreaseth. Our bodies will soon be loathsome carcases. They that are dear before, within a little while will become loathsome and intolerable : Gen. xxiii. 4, ' Give me a possession of a burying-place with you, that I may bury my dead out of my sight.' Their best friends would fain be rid of them. How soon is the glory of flesh stained, and turned into a stink and rottenness !

6*thly*, There is faith shown in disposing of our bones. So did Joseph, so should we look upon the grave as sanctified by Christ; the waters of baptism he sanctified in his own person. And so for the grave, Christ hath been there ; to him it was not a prison, but a bed : Isa. liii. 9, ' He made his grave with the wicked, and with the rich in his death.' Now the jaws of it are broken, that you cannot be holden of it. These bones shall be clothed with skin and flesh. Christ is the guardian of the grave : John vi. 39, ' Of all that he hath given me I shall lose nothing, but raise it up again at the last day.' He hath a charge given him, and he must give an account of it—'The sea gave up the dead that were in it, and death and hell (or the grave) delivered up the dead which were in them,' Rev. xx. 13. We should not be afraid to go down to the grave now we hear of such a glorious resurrection from it. This is the way for the body to go to heaven.

<hr />

SERMON LVII.

By faith Moses, when he was born, was hid three months of his parents, because they saw he was a proper child; and they not afraid of the king's commandment.—HEB. xi. 23.

THE apostle goeth on with the story of the church; and having done with the patriarchs, he goeth on to their posterity. Egypt had been kind to Israel, but now oppressed them, and the posture of things is changed. Pharaoh, a domineering commander that knew not Joseph, now bore sway, Exod. i. 8. He made a bloody law that the male children of the Hebrews should be destroyed, Exod. i. 10. Now the text showeth what Moses' parents did with respect to this bloody edict—' By faith Moses, when he was born, was hid three months of his parents,' &c.

The faith of Moses' parents is described—

1. By the action wherein it was shown—*Moses, when he was born, was hid three months of his parents.*

2. The considerations on which it was done.

[1.] In the action there is—

(1.) The action itself—'He was hid.'

(2.) The duration—'Three months.'

[2.] In the considerations are two things; the one external, the other internal.

(1.) The occasion, or external impulsive cause—*Because they saw he was a proper child.*

(2.) The internal moving cause—*They not afraid of the king's commandment.*

But three things I shall consider in the words—(1.) What is commended; (2.) Who is commended; (3.) The commendation itself.

First, What is commended—'By faith.' What great matter of faith was here? Brute creatures are careful to preserve their young ones; their endeavour to save him might seem to be a work of natural affection, but the Holy Ghost ascribeth it to faith. Natural affections sanctified are subservient and useful to faith; grace doth not abolish nature, but perfect it. We are to obey God against our natural affection; as by faith Abraham offered his son Isaac; nature was against it. And we are to obey God with natural affection: by faith Moses was hid of his parents; there nature was for it. Many times God's interests and ours are twisted together, and then nature is allowed to work, but grace must bear sway; sometimes they are severed, and then we must leave nature to keep company with God.

Use 1. It informeth us, that to strengthen faith we may and must take in the help of nature; it is God's allowance, that we may be carried out more cheerfully in the work of God: Philem. 16, 'Dear to thee, both in the flesh and in the Lord.' When a dictate of grace and the inclination of nature concur, and nature and grace run in one channel, the stream is the more violent. This is seen in labouring for the conversion of a child, in seeking the life of a near relation, or in laying to heart their sufferings.

2. That their wickedness is very great that sin against nature. Some men will be held in with no restraints, neither with the bonds of nature nor grace, nor both together. The more unnatural a sin is, the more aggravated; yet it is usual that most sins have an inconvenience to nature annexed to them. Envy and anger troubleth our own flesh, and eats like a cannibal; lust sucketh the bones; love of pleasure, of corn, wine, and oil, wastes the purse. We have reasons in nature to be against carking, and many other sins.

3. In all these mixed actions look to your principles, what beareth sway and worketh most—faith or natural affection. God alloweth nature to work, and accepts it as a gracious action if faith beareth sway. There are many common actions which a man would do by nature, but then he doth them in another manner, as in and to the Lord, out of love to God, and fear of God, and respect of God's glory, and so the nature of the action is changed; as meek deportment in our relations is for our own quiet, but it is to be done in obedience to God, and out of the fear of God, and so second table duties are acts of faith, fear, and love to God.

Quest. But wherein lay the faith of this action?

Ans. Chiefly in overcoming fear, in trusting God's protection for the preservation of the child; and possibly there might be something of a public regard and consideration, in believing the future deliverance of the church and people of God out of Egypt. Josephus saith that it was revealed to Amram in a dream that he should have a son, who in time should free the children of Israel from the bondage of Egypt; but that is uncertain. But this might be gathered out of that general promise: Gen. xv. 14, 'That nation whom they shall serve will I judge, and afterwards they shall come out with great substance.'

Here are three propositions—

[1.] Whether the tyrant would or no, God's people should be preserved.

[2.] Out of the male children a deliverer should arise.

[3.] In all probability this child might be he; by special instinct, seeing the beauty of the child, they might conceive hopes of him. Faith spieth light at a little hole. The patriarchs had dark presignifications of the Messiah, yet they saw his day: John viii. 56, 'Your father Abraham rejoiced to see my day, and he saw it, and was glad.' They regard the word; every dust of it is precious: Ps. xii. 6, 'The words of the Lord are pure words, as silver tried in a furnace of earth, purified seven times.' Not a dust of them shall fall to the ground; they make much of what others pass over carelessly, they pry into it— 'Of which salvation the prophets inquired and searched diligently,' 1 Peter i. 10. They have a deeper insight than others—'The secret of the Lord is with them that fear him,' Ps. xxv. 14. None have such a quick, eagle eye, as they that have most communion with God, they pierce deeper into a promise than others do.

Use. It reproveth us that are so slow of heart to believe what is more clear and open. We must have line upon line; such is our dulness in believing and apprehending spiritual things. The disciples at first understood not Christ's sayings till they received the Spirit. Let us make much use of the word, and wait for more of the Spirit. A dull servant must be told his work over and over again.

Secondly, Who are commended—ὑπὸ τῶν πατέρων αὐτοῦ, ' By his parents.' Moses ascribeth it to his mother: Exod. ii. 2, 'And when she saw that he was a goodly child, she hid him three months;' Stephen, to his father, ' He was nourished up in his father's house three months,' Acts vii. 20. The apostle here ascribeth it to both. So the Septuagint—ἐσκέπασεν αὐτὸν μῆνας τρεῖς; but Moses ascribeth it to his mother, either because she was the author of this counsel, or took the care of managing the business upon herself. I would observe here the concurrence that should be between husband and wife in promoting that which is good: the father did it, the mother did it, both joined together. When there is strife, it is like the jostling of two persons in a boat, which may overset it. Husband and wife should go hand in hand to the throne of grace, and join together in every good thing; they should agree together in the worship of God, and promoting the good of their children. When the will of the wife and the will of the husband fall in, like the tenon and the mortise, the building goes on; but when one draws one way, and another the other way, like untamed heifers in the yoke, all cometh to ruin. The prophet observes with what a ready diligence idolatry is promoted in a family when all set their hands to it: Jer. vii. 18, ' The children gather wood, the fathers kindle the fire, and the women knead their dough, to make cakes to the queen of heaven.' They all hang in a string.

Thirdly, The commendation itself; and there we have the action, and the considerations on which it was done.

1. The action, where—

[1.] The time—'When he was born.'

[2.] The action itself—' He was hid.'

[3.] The duration—' Three months.'

[1.] The time—' Moses, when he was born;' that is, as soon as he was born, for then he was in danger. So Rev. xii. 4, ' The dragon stood before the woman that was ready to be delivered, for to devour the child as soon as it was born.' The early buds are soon nipt. Jesus Christ was sought to be destroyed by Herod as soon as he was born. So it hath been with all the people of God: Ps. cxxix. 1, 'Many a time have they afflicted me from my youth, may Israel now say.' Satan is a murderer from the beginning; and it is no wonder, for in destroying of Abel he thought to have cut off all the church at once. It is no wonder to see Satan so busy; as soon as a man beginneth to look towards God, some frown him out, some flatter him out of his religion : Heb. x. 32, 'After ye were illuminated, ye endured a great fight of afflictions.' At first conversion they meet wirh scoffs, frowns, and mocks, because they are called to give a proof of their faith and love to Christ. But rather observe here the wisdom and power of God in preserving his church, which Satan seeketh to crush in the egg. I do the rather note it because this was Pharaoh's design at this time, but God's counsel standeth : he made Egypt and Pharaoh's court nourish their own destroyer. Herod kills all the children at Bethlehem, and some say, to make sure work, his own also. Thus can God outwork the counsels of men, and overshoot the devil in his own bow.

[2.] The action itself was hid. Though faith overcometh fear, yet we may use lawful means to overcome the danger ; she hid the child. They do ill that needlessly thrust themselves upon danger : unless we are especially called to bear witness, wary carriage is required. God counts it faith : faith is far from compliance or obeying carnal commands, yet it is cautious and wary. Moses was called to kill the Egyptian, yet he looketh about to see if anybody saw him. Faith doth not tempt God ; though it rests upon his providence, yet it useth means. Christ, though he certainly knew his Father's will to save him, yet he withdrew himself from the enraged multitude, Mark xii. 15.

Use 1. Learn hence, that it is no want of faith to avoid danger by lawful means.

2. It is no neglect of trust to use means where we are sure of the event : Acts xxvii. 31, 'Except these abide in the ship you cannot be saved.' Christ never supplied himself by a miracle where ordinary means might be had.

[3.] The duration—'Three months.'

(1) They hid him three months, and no longer. But why so ? Either because, as some think, at every three months' end they made a stricter search ; or possibly some neighbouring Egyptian had spied out the matter ; or the cries of the child being stronger every day might bewray them. But now their weakness beginneth.

Observe, that God takes notice of their faith as long as it lasted.

It was an act of weakness at three months' end to expose the child ; yet God winketh at that ; and it is said, By faith he is hidden. As often you have it in this chapter, the faith, and not the failings of good people are recorded,—' By faith Isaac blessed Jacob,' &c. ; ' By faith Rahab the harlot perished not with them that believed not ;' her faith is mentioned, but not her lie.

Use. It should encourage us to serve God, who will graciously accept of what is good in us, and pardon our failings. Man overlooks all the good ; if there be any evil in an action, we are sure to look upon that. As flies pitch upon the sore place, or as a kite flies to the carrion, passing by the pleasant gardens, so men pitch upon the worst. But it is otherwise with the Lord ; he taketh notice of what is good and sincere. This should not encourage us in our failings but in our duties.

(2.) When the three months were ended, they made careful provision for him. You have the story in Exod. ii. If he had been kept at home, they saw a certain danger; there was some weakness not to trust God. But she doth not drown him in the river, but maketh an ark of bulrushes, well prepared, and set his sister to watch him; and it is likely she chose the place where Thermutis, the king's daughter, was wont to resort. Faith may trip, but it doth not fail totally. It trippeth sometimes; as Abraham dwelt in Haran for a while; and Peter cometh to Christ upon the waters, but there he is ready to sink, Mat. xiv. 30; Moses smote the rock twice. The Israelites ever and anon were returning to Egypt. Lot said, 'I cannot escape to the mountains, lest some evil take me, and I die,' Gen. xix. 19. A sincere faith may tire a little, and grow weary; but up it gets again, it doth not wholly fail. Such kind of infirmities are consistent with faith, where there is not a total disobedience.

2. I come now to the considerations on which it was done.

[1.] The external impulsive cause—'Because they saw he was a proper child,' ἀστεῖον, comely, and fair, Acts vii. 20. At what time Moses was born he was exceeding fair— ἀστεῖος θεῷ, fair to God; as to all things that did excel in their kind they were wont to add the name of God to them, as the Hill of God, for an exceeding high hill.

But what reason was this? Moses' beauty, take it in a vulgar consideration, did more stir up στοργὴν, natural affection; but here in a special sense they saw something divine in him to stir up their faith. Beauty is not always a sure sign of excellency—*fronti nulla fides*, there is no trust to the brow; but they saw special lineaments of majesty, and of a heroical disposition in his countenance, which, being accompanied with some secret instinct, moved them to think that God had designed him to some eminent work, probably to the deliverance of his people. Otherwise, beauty is not always a sign of excellency: 1 Sam. xvi. 7, 'Look not upon his countenance, nor the height of his stature, because I have refused him; for the Lord seeth not as man seeth, for man looketh on the outward appearance, but the Lord looketh on the heart.'

Use 1. God hath means to preserve his children in danger when he hath use for them. Moses' extraordinary beauty did excite and move the natural love of his parents, and gain the heart of Thermutis. Some of God's servants have been preserved for their eminent wit and parts; others for their skill in rare artifices, when their fellows have been slain round about them, Dan. ii. 24. I observe this to show you the wisdom of providence, and how this is one means of his children's preservation.

2. Where God will make special use of instruments, he giveth them answerable endowments, both of body and mind. Moses, in his very childhood, had a majesty and invincible grace in his countenance. There are some upon whom God hath set a mark for special work and service; this is a kind of presage what he will do with them in time to come. This hint is of use to parents, to observe their children's disposition; and where there are special endowments, to dispose of them to public work. Much of the duty of parents is seen in providing meet callings for their children, that the man may suit the calling, and the calling the man. Otherwise mischief ariseth; many public gifts are smothered, and lie hid in a private employment; or else mis-

chief ariseth by invasion of callings, and there is never any quietness while that lasteth ; as when elements are out of their place, or a member of the body is out of joint; it is as if a man should go about to walk on his hands, or write with his foot. This must be done with much seeking of God, observing their dispositions, and inclinations, and natural gifts ; and if it were made a matter of public care, so much the better. Nazianzen, in his epistles, showeth that this was the practice of the Athenian magistrates, to make public trial of the ingenuity and disposition of children. For want of this there hath been much obtruding of unworthy men into public ministries and offices, dull men, who have been more fit for the plough; and others have been hindered by poverty and want of supply who gave great hopes of eminency in better employments than they were set to.

3. That beauty is a gift of God, but not to be rested in, nor to be abused to feed pride. It is a gift of God; we might have been deformed by nature, and the crookedness of the soul have been stamped upon the body. It is a good portion which a body brings to a virtuous soul ; beauty is a beam of the majesty of God, it hath a natural magic in it. Absalom gained much by his beauty. There is the greatest cognation and sympathy between the soul and the body. As some forerunning beams foretell day, so beauty is a good presage, but it is not to be rested in. Beauty was a mark of special service in Moses, but not in Elijah. Sometimes the stuff doth not answer the show. It is often joined with folly and filthiness, and other vices. Paul was a little old man. In itself it is one of God's lower blessings, but it is but skin-deep: Prov. xxxi. 30, 'Favour is deceitful, and beauty is vain.' It is soon withered with sickness and old age. Well then, let them that excel in gifts of the body look to excel also in gifts of the mind, and then it is a mark of honour ; if you abuse it, you lay your crowns in the dust.

[2.] The internal moving cause—'And they not afraid of the king's commandment,' that bloody law of destroying their children,—τὸ διάταγμα τοῦ βασιλέως, the constitution of the king.

Here are three points—

(1.) Princes must not be obeyed in things contrary to the word of God. Here was διάταγμα, a commandment of the king, and yet it was disobeyed. We have both doctrine and example for it. Doctrine: Eph. vi. 1, ' Children, obey your parents in the Lord.' We must not obey magistrates simply and absolutely ; that is proper to God, whose will cannot be controlled. Therefore if their edicts be against the law of God, they bind not, for then they would be honoured above God. And examples : Acts iv. 19, ' Whether it be right in the sight of God to hearken unto you more than unto God, judge ye ;' he leaveth it with them ; and Acts v. 29, ' Then Peter and the other apostles answered and said, We ought to obey God rather than men.' When they forbid what God hath commanded, or command what God hath forbidden, it is a part of religious manners to break with the magistrate rather than God : so Dan. iii. 16–18, ' Shadrach, Meshach, and Abednego, answered and said unto the king, O Nebuchadnezzar, we are not careful to answer thee in this matter ; our God whom we serve is able to deliver us from the burning fiery furnace, and he will deliver us out of thine hands, O king ; but if not, be it known unto thee, O king, that we will not serve thy gods, nor worship the golden image which thou hast set up.' For, (1.) The magistrate hath not his power from himself, 'he is the minister of God for good,' Rom. xiii. 4. Now the power of the minister or servant is not of force against the master, when he either forbiddeth what God hath commanded, or commandeth what God hath forbidden. (2.) He is under authority As the centurion that came to Christ said, I am a man of authority, and have others subject to me, Mat. viii. 9 ; so there is a higher than the highest, whose will alone must be observed.

Use. It informeth us that it is no excuse though magistrates enjoin or connive at things evil. In human laws the husband shall not answer for the wife, nor the children for the parents ; and therefore in all these cases say as Christ said to his earthly parents, Luke ii.49, 'Wist ye not that I must be about my Father's business ?' It is no stubbornness, but a well-tempered zeal. You are wont to produce your commission, but that will not bear you out before God.

(2.) The commands of kings and princes have been a usual trial of God's children, as Nebuchadnezzar's command was to fall down and worship the golden image. Magistrates have not always been the best friends to Christ. God loves to put his people upon such trials. They that are not faithful to their God will never be faithful to their princes. But it is usual with men to make bold with God to please men. This is very natural to us, to hearken to men rather than God, and either out of fear or favour of men to do things unlawful. It is worse to do it out of favour of men than out of fear ; for the temptation of favour is not so great, nor the danger of not obeying so imminent. What is done out of fear is done with reluctancy : a compliance for the favour of men discovers more of the consent of our wills, and willingness is a great aggravation of sin : Hos. v. 11, 'Ephraim is oppressed and broken in judgment, because he walked willingly after the commandment.' That is a most heinous sin when men consent of their own inclination, or the simple command of men, without any terrors, doth draw them to be at the beck of carnal potentates, and they are carried hither and thither at the pleasure of them that have power over them.

Use. This should draw us off from men. To this end consider—

1*st*, We are bound to God more than to men. We have protection from men under God ; but we have life, and being, and breath, and all things from God. Men can only protect us at God's pleasure. How soon is a prince pulled out of his throne ! Or if they could protect against men, yet not against God. There is no wall to be made against heaven ; all is open above. Therefore if protection draweth allegiance, I owe most to him from whom I have most protection. The greatest potentate is but an instrument of providence, and therefore my greatest obligation is to the Lord.

2*dly*, None can reward our obedience as God can—'Will the son of Jesse give you fields and vineyards ?' 1 Sam. xxii. 7. Have they such life and glory to bestow as God hath ? They have power to take off a civil forfeiture, but they cannot continue life for a moment ; much less can they give eternal life and glory. Herod promised to the half of his kingdom to his minion. They can give you offices and places of power and trust, but they cannot give you a crown that shall never fade. As stage-players can set up a king for an hour, the world is but a play of a little longer continuance; and at last, as chessmen are all thrown into the bag together, so in the grave there is no distinction; skulls wear no wreaths and marks of honour. They cannot give a glorious body, or a better soul. But there is full contentment to be had in God, who hath other manner of rewards than men can bestow.

3*dly*, None can punish our disobedience so as God can: Mat. x. 28, 'Fear not them which kill the body, but are not able to kill the soul; but rather fear him which is able to destroy both body and soul in hell.' Man's power reacheth only to the body; they may burn, and rack, and torture the body, but the soul lieth out of their power. If God now lay his finger on the conscience, all the engines of torture in the world cannot beget such a terror as there is in a wounded conscience. And what, then, will it be hereafter, when God sets himself a-work to torment you; when omnipotency falleth upon a worm; when God sets the body on the soul, and the soul on the body, and makes the body to accuse the soul as an evil instrument, and the soul the body as an evil guide, how dreadful is this punishment!

4*thly*, We live longer with God than we do with men; therefore if a man would study to please, he should rather please God than men. God is eternal, man is but mortal: Isa. li. 12, 'Who art thou, that thou shouldst be afraid of a man that shall die?' &c.; Isa. ii. 22, 'Cease from man, whose breath is in his nostrils; for wherein is he to be accounted of?' 1 Kings i. 21, 'When my lord the king shall sleep with his fathers, I and my son Solomon shall be accounted offenders;' Ps. cxlvi. 4, 'His breath goeth forth, he returneth to his earth; in that very day his thoughts perish.' A man may outlive his friends and outlive his happiness. Nay, we ourselves must perish; and when we come to die, then we shall say, Oh! if I had been as careful to please God as to please my prince, it would have been better with me than now it is. But when men are dead and gone, God liveth for ever.

5*thly*, God can make others our friends: Prov. xvi. 7, 'When a man's ways please the Lord, he maketh even his enemies to be at peace with him.' Zealous resistance sooner gaineth friends than carnal compliance. Who would offend a king to please one of his slaves? The respects of others are in God's hands, and he can give us favour in the eyes of others, as the captive children found favour in the eyes of the king of Babylon. If God be our friend, we need not fear; we do not fear the sword if we do not fear him that weareth it. Man is frail, and can do nothing without God; he is the creator and sovereign cause of all things.

6*thly*, They that please men shall have enough of it: Hos. v. 12, 'Ephraim is oppressed and broken in judgment, because he willingly walked after the commandment.' They were as willing to obey as he to command, and therefore they shall have yoke upon yoke. When we study to please men they often prove sad scourges to us.

(3.) In such cases carnal fear doth betray us, and faith carries us through: Isa. viii. 12, 13, 'Say ye not, A confederacy, to all them to whom the people shall say, A confederacy, neither fear ye their fear, nor be afraid ; sanctify the Lord of Hosts himself, and let him be your fear, and let him be your dread.'   Faith vanquisheth carnal fear, as it setteth the fear of God a-work.   The Egyptian midwives' saving the children is made to be an act of the fear of God : Exod. i. 17, ' But the Egyptian midwives feared God, and did not as the king of Egypt commanded them, but saved the men-children alive.'   Faith represents a higher king and greater terrors ; it sets authority against authority, law against law, terror against terror.   It fetcheth in invisible supplies : Heb. xi. 27, ' By faith he forsook Egypt, not fearing the wrath of the king ; for he endured, as seeing him who is invisible.'

Use. When you are apt to miscarry by carnal fear, set faith a-work. When tyrants set forth unjust edicts, when you fear the loss of parents' favour for God's sake, let faith represent to you the favour of God, and the wrath of God.   What is the favour of men to the favour of God ? and the wrath of potentates to the wrath of God ?

SERMON LVIII.

By faith Moses, when he was come to years, refused to be called the son of Pharaoh's daughter.—HEB. xi. 24.

IN this chapter you have a short chronicle of the worthies of God ; and in this constellation Moses shines forth as a star of the first magnitude.   The apostle had spoken first of that faith by which he was saved by his parents ; and now he comes to speak of that faith by which he saved himself ; and here is one instance of it—' By faith Moses, when he was come to years, refused to be called the son of Pharaoh's daughter.' He is commended here for his principle and his carriage.

1. For his principle—*By faith.*
2. For his carriage—*When he was come to years,* &c.

His carriage is set forth.

[1.] By the season—*When he was come to years.*
[2.] By the act of self-denial—*He refused to be called.*
[3.] By the greatness of the temptation—*The son of Pharaoh's daughter.*

I shall give you—

(1.) The explication of the words.
(2.) The vindication of the act.
(3.) The commendation of it.

1. For the explication of the words.

[1.] His principle—' By faith.'   His faith was fixed ; partly upon the eternal recompenses : he had never left the delights of the court, if he had not looked for greater blessings.   And partly on the particular promises made to God's people, for he believed that the seed of Abraham should be blessed ; though now they were very miserable and oppressed with hard servitude and bondage, yet he knew the promises of God to Abraham, and this faith urged him hereunto.

[2.] Here is his carriage.   Where observe—

(1.) The season of it—'When he was come to years;' μέγας γενόμενος' when he was grown great.   The same is observed, Exod. ii. 11, 'When Moses was grown, he went out to his brethren, and he was then forty years old;' and Acts vii. 23, 'When he was full forty years old, it came into his heart to visit his brethren the children of Israel.'   He had visited his brethren before, for his original was not unknown to him; but now he comes to visit them—that is, to take share and lot with them, to visit them as their guide, that he might lead them out of Egypt; and·this he did when he was full forty years of age.   Some say, when he was a child, he cast the crown that was put upon his head to the ground.   Josephus reports of him that he trampled upon it, which was looked upon by the Egyptians as an ill omen.   But if that be fabulous, the Holy Ghost takes no notice of his childish actions, but what he did 'when he came to years.'   Now this circumstance is put down to show that Moses was of discretion to judge; it was not out of childish ignorance, he knew what he did, for he had forty years experience of this course of life.   And partly to excuse the errors of his childhood; those errors are not reckoned upon, if afterwards amended; as Paul said, 'When I was a child I spake as a child, I understood as a child, I thought as a child,' 1 Cor. xiii. 11.   Partly to show that as soon as he was ripe for business he did delay no longer, when he was of full age and strength.   And partly to show that he grew in the gifts and graces of the Spirit, as well as in years; as Christ 'increased in wisdom and stature,' Luke ii. 42.   Moses, when he was come of years, was another manner of person than Moses a child.

(2.) The act of self-denial—ἠρνήσατο λέγεσθαι, 'He refused to be called.'   He would not so much as be called so, a pert and open profession: and this not by compulsion; he was not cast out or disowned, but he refused.   He might have held the honour of this adoption still, if it had so liked him; but he would rather be called an Hebrew than Pharaoh's grandchild.   This was the language of his heart, not so much of his words.   We do not read he made a formal renunciation of his kindred; but indeed he left the court, and joined himself to God's people.

(3.) Here is the greatness of the temptation; what would he not be called?—'The son of Pharaoh's daughter.'   Pharaoh bore full sway at that time in Egypt; and the condition of the worst Egyptian was better than of the best Israelite; yet even then he would not be called the son of Pharaoh's daughter; he would not yield to an honour so high, so great.   His daughter was Thermutis, Josephus tells us; that Pharaoh had no other child, and she no other heir; so probably he might have succeeded in the throne; and that when he was gone to the Israelites, that Pharaoh should say, I intended to make this child partaker of the kingdom.   If this be uncertain, there is enough in what the Holy Ghost sets down.to make it a glorious instance of faith.   Thus I have opened the words.

2.   For the vindication of the act.   You will say, Why would Moses do this?   Or what great business was there in this?   Joseph had faith as well as Moses, and he did not leave the court, but lived there till he died.   I answer, Their conditions were not alike, nor their occasions

alike. God raised up Joseph to feed his people in Egypt, therefore his
abode in the court was necessary under kings that favoured them ; but
Moses was called, not to feed his people in Egypt, but to lead them out of
Egypt ; and the king of Egypt was now become their enemy, and kept
them under bitter bondage. To remain in an idolatrous court of a pagan
prince is one thing; but to remain in a persecuting court, where he
must be accessary to their persecutions, is another thing.   However,
this is notable too, that Joseph, though he retained his honour to his
death, yet he was willing that his family should take his lot with the
people of God.

Obj. But Moses' act might seem ingratitude or folly. It was not ingratitude to his foster-mother ; it was not any silly discontent, or unworthy incivility to her, who had compassion on him, to save him when
he was ready to perish, and had manifested singular love to him, and
special care of him in his education and advancement. But it was a
free and noble act of his divine and sanctified soul, whereby he being
illuminated from heaven, did by faith see the baseness, uncertainty,
and danger of a great estate, of honour, wealth, and power ; and upon
this account alone he was willing to part with them for better delights
and greater good, and that he might be faithful to God and his people.
All relations must give way to the conscience of our duty to God.
God's right is the first, and our greatest relation is to him ; therefore,
Luke xiv. 26, ' If any man come to me, and hate not his father and
mother, and wife and children, and brethren and sisters, yea, and his own
life also, he cannot be my disciple.'   God hath done more for us than
any other hath done, therefore our obligation is the greater.   Our
Lord Christ when they taxed him for want of respect to his earthly
parents, said, Luke ii. 19, ' Wist ye not, that I must be about my
Father's business ? ' There is a higher authority, and a higher relation
which must take place, and all other relations must give way to it.

But then would not this seem folly, for to do as Moses did, who had
an opportunity of saving himself and his own stake, or of soliciting the
good of the people of Israel at the court of Pharaoh ? I answer, An
opportunity to do good is to be valued ; yet when it cannot be lawfully
enjoyed, we must prefer God's command even before not only our
safety, but those seeming opportunities we have of doing good to
others, and expect a supply from his providence ; for God is not tied
to means. Now this was the case here. Moses would continue no
longer there without sin; for it is said, ver. 25, ' Choosing rather to
suffer affliction with the people of God, than to enjoy the pleasures of
sin.' The contentments of that estate he now had was called ' the
pleasures of sin ;' either because those delights began to be snares, to
besot his mind, and so keep him from a sense of his brethren's afflictions ; or by the contagion of example he might be ready to be entangled in them ; or God would no longer dispense with his living
without ordinances, or out of the communion of his people ; or from
the impulse that was upon his heart, which was very great, he being
now fit for business, and to tarry longer were to delay his obedience to
the divine calling ; or else, as the court was then constituted, Moses
could no longer live there without being used as an instrument to
oppress his own countrymen. Whether this or that were the reason.

the Holy Ghost calleth the advantages of his former life 'the pleasures of sin;' and then it was high time for him to remove.

3. Having explained the words, and also vindicated this act from exception, let me now restore it to its true glory, commendation, and honour. Certainly this was a very great instance of self-denial, and highly conduceable to check the affectation of natural greatness.

[1.] The more advisedly a good work is done, the more commendable. He knew what he did; it was not a rash and childish act, for he was grown up, μεγὰς γενόμενος. For a child to prefer an apple before a pearl, it is according to his childish judgment; but the Holy Ghost says he was come to years. An advised obedience is acceptable to God, not headstrong resolutions; therefore when he was grown, when he had maturity of judgment, and could weigh things in his mind, then 'he refused to be called the son of Pharaoh's daughter.'

[2.] The greater the temptation, the more self-denial. To bear a frown is nothing, to bear a scoff is nothing, to be kept low and bare is nothing; but here is a principality despised, that he might join himself to a contemptible oppressed people. And here all temptations came abreast, and assault him at once; there was a complication of them, honours, pleasures, and treasures. Here are honours, 'to be called the son of Pharaoh's daughter.' In the next verse we read of pleasures, which are called 'the pleasures of sin,' for the reasons before-mentioned; and then for treasures, ver. 26, 'He esteemed the reproach of Christ greater riches than the treasures of Egypt.' Now these things, honours, treasures, and pleasures, usually besot or corrupt the judgment, so that we cannot see what is good in theory, cannot discern true good from false; they obstruct our resolution, withdraw our minds, and charm us that we cannot follow God's call, nor obey him in the things he hath given us to do. But Moses had all these at once; the honour of being called the son of Pharaoh's daughter, a great office that brought him in great plenty—the treasures of Egypt were in a great measure at his dispose—and here were the pleasures of sin. How hard is it for us to part with a small estate! We find it a hard matter to suffer a little disgrace, and to leave a petty interest for Christ's sake. As Mat. xix. 27, the apostles spoke to Christ, 'We have left all, and followed thee.' What did they forsake? A great all! a net, a fisher-boat; but yet they speak magnificently of it; but Moses refused the honours, pleasures, and treasures of Egypt.

[3.] The more thorough the self-denial the better. He left the court of Pharaoh, and all his honours there, and openly professed himself to be a Hebrew. There was not only an inward dislike of the Egyptian idolatry and practices, and an inward approbation of the worship of God, that was kept up among his people, and of spiritual privileges; but here was an open profession, 'He refused to be called,' &c.

[4.] The purer the principle, the better the action. It was not discontent, or any sullen and vexing humour that put him upon this resolution, but faith. The principle much varies the action: Prov. xvi. 2, it is said, 'God weighs the spirits.' God doth not look to the bulk and matter of the action only but to the spirit, with what heart, upon what principle, with what aim it is done. Now, here was a pure spirit. Possibly others may have done somewhat like. We read in ecclesiastical story of Dioclesian, a bitter persecutor, that left his empire, but it was out of discontent. He had set himself against Christ, and his discontent chiefly rose from this—he was resolved to root out the christians, but they grew upon his hand; and though the persecution was very bitter and grievous at that time, yet he could not root them out, and therefore through very discontent at the disappointment he left his empire. But Moses did all this *pio animo*, upon a holy and gracious consideration; it was from the influence of his faith, because he was convinced of the good estate of God's people, though afflicted; he could see glory and happiness at the end, therefore it is said, ' By faith he refused,' &c. Affectation of privacy and quiet, or natural stoutness, or a politic retreat, differ from self-denial.

The doctrine I shall insist upon is this—

Doct. That faith is a grace that will teach a man openly to renounce all worldly honours, and advancements, and preferments, with the advantages annexed thereto, when God calls us from them, or we cannot enjoy them with a good conscience.

For here is honour, ' to be called the son of Pharaoh's daughter; ' here are the appendages of that honour, ' the pleasures of sin, and the treasures of Egypt; ' and these are not only disesteemed, but actually quitted and forsaken; and all this upon God's call, and upon reasons of conscience; and the main turning circumstance, and that which inclined him so to do, was his faith. Here I shall show you—

1. How far the honours and glories of the world are to be renounced and forsaken.

2. What influence faith hath to induce us to do this.

First, How far honours and worldly advantages are to be renounced and forsaken. There are two rocks that we must avoid; on the one side the rock of Popish and superstitious mortification, or a sluggish retreat from business, to live an idle life, sequestered from other christians, as we find in their monkery; on the other side carnal compliance, or an affectation of worldly greatness.

1. It is not simply evil to enjoy worldly honour; good men have lived sometimes in bad courts—Obadiah in Ahab's court, Joseph in Pharaoh's; and we read, Phil. iv. 22, of saints that were in Nero's household, under the very noise, and in the sight of that grievous persecutor and monster of mankind; Mordecai in Ahasuerus' court, and Daniel in Nebuchadnezzar's. And Acts xiii. 1, we read of Manaen, a prophet or teacher, who had been brought up with Herod the Tetrarch; in that wicked court he was godly; and so we read, Acts viii. 22, ' There was a man of Ethiopia, an eunuch of great authority, under Candace, queen of the Ethiopians, who was a pagan, and had the charge of all her treasures; ' and we read of an Ebedmelech in Zedekiah's court. God, to show the freedom of his mercy, and the power of his truth, and that christianity is no enemy to civil relations, and that his people may have occasion more eminently to show forth his grace, and to express their self-denial, that they have something of value to esteem as nothing for Christ; God, I say, doth so order it that even in the courts of pagan princes have been found those who have been very sincere with God; therefore these honours are not unlawful, nor to be renounced but upon just and convenient reasons.

2. Though honours must not be renounced, yet when we enjoy them, they are to be entertained with a holy jealousy and watchfulness. And though honours be not simply renounced, yet we must consider how we come by them ; if we be advanced by the fair providence of God, and God sets us there, we may enjoy them with a good conscience, and may the better venture upon the ordinary temptations that attend them. He that ventures upon slippery places had need have a good warrant, and that his calling be clear. David refused not a crown when God put it upon his head ; yet he says, Ps. cxxxiii. 1, 'Lord, my heart is not haughty, nor mine eyes lofty ; neither do I exercise myself in great matters, or in things too high for me.' He did not aspire after great things, nor seek to wrest the kingdom out of the hands of Saul ; but though he had God's promise that he should enjoy it at length—and though he was incited by the bitter persecutions of Saul, yet he contains himself within the bounds of his duty and calling. But ambition is restless, it hurries on men, and is like a whirlwind that tears down all that is in our way, and breaks down whatever may seem to oppose our greatness ; a good conscience, and all, must go to the ground that they may rise. Moses would not keep that when there was sin attending it, which came in fairly and by God's providence. Therefore if it be got by ill means, if men renounce, deny, dissemble truth, stretch conscience to the humours of men, and all that they may be great, and enjoy something here in the world that is honourable and glorious, then we must abandon it. Nay, though it be not so, yet ambition and affectation of worldly greatness is not only seen when means are apparently evil, but when men make much ado to get honours, and their hearts are set upon them, and they do not tarry for a fair invitation of God's providence, but put themselves forward ; this is exercising ourselves in great things, and in matters too high for us ; therefore it is said, Prov. xxv. 27, 'For men to search their own glory is not glory ;' that is, to be so earnest and so greedy upon such a thing. If men were worthy of honour, their worth would be attractive ; as a violet shrouded by its leaves is found out by its smell. Where the matter is combustible, we need not blow the fire so hard ; but when men are so vehement and earnest to thrust themselves into slippery places, this is that which must be checked by such an instance as Moses. Again, though we come by it by never so holy means, by a fair course of God's providence, yet it must be entertained with a holy jealousy and watchfulness, that the heart may not be puffed up, but still kept humble, as a spire that is least in the top : Prov. xvi. 19, 'Better it is to be of an humble spirit with the lowly, than to divide the spoil with the proud.' Better to be left out of the account and tale with men, than to be called to divide the spoil, and to be puffed up. But this is not all, negatively, that our hearts be not corrupted by it ; therefore, positively, see it be improved for God. Whatever honour, greatness, and outward advantage you enjoy, reckon that you must some way or other be a gainer by it, and this must be improved for God's glory. Has God that honour that he expecteth ? What a shame is it that you should enjoy so much, and God should have so little glory ! When David was advanced to a crown, he was thinking what to do for God, 2 Sam. vii. 2, 'I dwell in an house of cedar, but the ark of God dwelleth within curtains.' God

hath provided for me, he hath advanced me to great empire and sovereignty, but what have I done for God?' So Neh. i. 11, he says there,
'The Lord prosper thy servant this day, and grant him mercy in the
sight of this man (for I was the king's cup-bearer).' That parenthesis
hath great significancy,—'I was the king's cup-bearer.' When the Lord
ordered it so that one of the captivity was advanced to such a high
ministry and service about that great king, he was considering, What
do I for that God? and how ought I to improve it for the glory of
God? So must a christian consider with himself, How have I entered
upon this honour? how have I carried myself? It is a slippery place,
and therefore we had need be the more watchful.

3. Honours must be actually renounced when they are sinful in
themselves, or cannot be kept and enjoyed without sin.

[1.] When they are sinful in themselves; as an office that is unlawful, a calling that is superstitious, idolatrous, and antichristian, whatever honour, pleasure, and treasure is annexed to it. Thus Paul was
employed as an officer by the high priests to vex the saints. Better be
low and despicable than high and not in God's way. Rev. xvii. 4, the
whore of Babylon is said to propine her abominations in a golden cup.
Preferment is usually the bait of that carnal and political religion that
lords it over God's heritage. Popery is a pseudo-christianity, a christianity calculated for this world, and not for the next; and there all
goes by greatness, honour, and preferment; it is nothing but a faction
and combination of men; they have debauched the law of Christ to
serve a carnal turn and worldly purpose; and therefore all that honour
which depends upon that, though it hath pleasure and profit annexed
to it, this must certainly be denied. Or,

[2.] When honour cannot be enjoyed with a good conscience, or kept
without sin. One that was brought up in a great court said, 'I had
rather be Christ's exile than a companion of a great king.' Manaen
would rather be a poor teacher at Antioch than a glorious courtier at
Jerusalem. A great man—yet he did not disdain to take upon him the
ministry, which is usually held so mean a calling. So it is said of
Galeacius Caracciolus, that he left his honours in the world, and became an elder at Geneva. Therefore if the thing be sinful, or cannot
be kept but by sin, it ought to be renounced. This sin may be either
of omission or of commission.

(1.) Of omission, we ought to be 'valiant for the truth,' Jer. ix. 3.
Still Christ's interest must be preferred. But now, when to keep our
places we must smother our sense of religion, and cannot explicitly
declare ourselves to be for God, then it is sinful, for then you prefer
it before Christ. We read of Terentius, an orthodox christian, a captain under Valens, an Arian emperor, when he returned from Armenia
with a great victory, the emperor bade him ask what he would, and he
should have it; he only presented his supplication for liberty for a
church of the orthodox. The emperor tore it in pieces, and bade him
ask another thing. 'No;' said he, 'I will ask nothing for myself
where I am denied for my God.' This is that temper which possesses
christians where their hearts are sincere with God: Luke ix. 26, 'For
whosoever shall be ashamed of me, and of my words, of him shall the
Son of man be ashamed when he shall come in his own glory, and in

his Father's, and of the holy angels.' Look, as he that will not own his poor parents, though he do not renounce or formally deny them, is blameworthy; so he that will not own Christ, though he do not formally deny religion, he that stifles his profession altogether in his bosom (I speak when God calls him to confession), and is forced to smother it for his honour's sake, he is not sincere.

(2.) When the sin is a sin of commission; that either they must renounce Christ or their honour in the world; when both come in competition, that they must part with the one or the other. This is a grievous thing, for a man to part with his religion for a little honour and greatness in the world. Thus Pilate, against his conscience, condemned Christ, when they touched him to the quick, and told him, You are no friend to Cæsar unless you condemn him. This is, in short, the case: certainly honour is lawful, and may be improved for God; but we must consider how we come by it; and when we have it, we must possess it with a holy jealousy. But when it cannot be kept without sin—that is, without smothering our profession, or without actual renouncing the truth, then the case is clear.

Secondly, To show the influence that faith has hereupon—

1. It looks for better things that are to come, and so we can the better part with these things. It does exercise the mind about greater things, such as Christ's coming to judgment, and eternal glory and blessedness.

[1.] Faith makes the soul to reflect upon the day of Christ's coming; it is very notable that this is one great principle of, and a great help to, self-denial, to reflect upon the great day, when all things shall be reviewed, and when it shall be clearly discerned what is glorious and what is base. Our Lord tells his disciples, Mat. xvi. 24–27, 'If any man will come after me, let him deny himself.' What is that? It is to abridge ourselves of those conveniences that are grateful to the flesh. Now there are three things that we highly prize—life, wealth, and honour; and Christ accordingly propounds three maxims of self-denial to suit this treble interest. Life, which makes us capable of the enjoyment of all other good things; and as to this, our Lord tells us, ver. 25, 'Whosoever will save his life shall lose it, and whosoever will lose his life for my sake, shall find it.' Then for wealth he tells us, ver. 26, 'For what is a man profited, if he shall gain the whole world, and lose his own soul?' Then for honour, ver. 27, 'For the Son of man shall come in the glory of his Father with his angels.' Why does he mention the glory of the Father? You are dazzled with outward splendour, you stand upon honour and acceptation with men; but the Son of man shall come in the glory of his Father, 'and then he will reward every man according to his works;' those that have confessed him before men, he will confess them before his Father in heaven. Oh, what honour will it then be to be one of Christ's train, when he comes in the glory of his Father, and all his mighty angels! it will be greater honour than to have lived in the courts of princes. Christ, in the fulness of his glory, will acknowledge and own such before God and the world, and he shall then be admired in such, 2 Thes. i. 10. When David was crowned in Hebron, those six hundred despicable men which followed him were made captains of hundreds, and captains of thousands. So those that are not ashamed to make profession of his name, when he comes in the glory of his Father, then they will have honour and glory enough. Now this is that which faith pitches upon, and so defeats the present temptation.

[2.] Faith pitches upon the eternal fruition of God in heaven. God hath greater things for us than we can quit for his sake. What is worldly honour in comparison of that glory, honour, and immortality which Christ hath provided for us? Worldly honour is a poor thing, it must be left on this side the grave; and when you are laid in the dust, you will be no more in remembrance than others that have been before you, as to men. Here we are going to the grave, only some are going the higher and some the lower walk, but there they all meet: Job iii. 19, 'The small and the great are there.' Within a little while small and great, master and servant, must meet in the grave, and the world will think as meanly of you as you have done of others. Within a little while the honourable and base will lie under the ground which all trample upon, but there will be an everlasting distinction between holy and unholy, between clean and unclean, between a believer and an unbeliever, between the carnal and the sanctified. It will not be a pin to choose within a little while, what part we have acted in the world, whether we have been rich or poor, high or low; but much will lie upon this, whether we have kept a good conscience, whether we have been sincere with God, for they shall have 'a far more exceeding and eternal weight of glory,' 2 Cor. iv. 17. Well then, faith pitcheth upon this eternal glory, and compares it with this poor, vanishing happiness which men enjoy here, that shine in the greatest glory. The most shining glory will be soon burnt out into a snuff; and if it be not extinguished by a churly blast, it will at length consume of itself. Now these things are very great in themselves, the glory wherein Christ shall come, and the glory he will put upon his followers; and if we could apprehend them by faith, they would mightily work upon us; for though they be afar off, faith makes things exist in our mind, as if we were possessed of them, and saw the Lord Christ in his glory, distributing glory to his followers. Therefore in the first verse, 'Faith is the substance of things hoped for, and the evidence of things not seen.' The great reason why the glory of the world prevails with us is because it is present, and matter of sense. Now to counterbalance the temptation, faith looks upon these glorious things as sure and near, and so it works upon us. You must take in both, for though a thing be never so great and sure, yet if it be at a distance, it will not work. As a star in the heavens, though it be a vast globe of light that is bigger than this earth, yet it seems to us but a little spangle because of the distance. It is so with the mind as with the eye; an evil at a distance doth not work: Amos vi. 3, 'Ye put far away the evil day, and cause the seat of violence to draw near.' And a good thing at a distance doth not shine with such glory into the soul. But faith shows it is a thing will soon come about; it will not be long ere all this pageantry of the world will be over and taken down, and the Lord Jesus will come in all his glory, to distribute honours and rewards to those that have been faithful to him.

2. Faith gives us right thoughts of things present. It shows us the nothingness of worldly greatness, and the greatness of present spiritual privileges.

[1.] The nothingness of worldly greatness and honours. It is but a vain appearance, a mere pageant, a nothing, a fancy: Acts xxv. 23, 'Agrippa and Bernice appeared with great pomp,' μετὰ πολλῆς φαντασίας, with great fancy. It is but a vain show, more in appearance than in reality: Ps. xxxix. 5, 6, 'Every man at his best estate is altogether vanity. Surely every man walketh in a vain show;' Prov. xxvi. 5, 'Wilt thou set thine eyes upon that which is not?' They are but poor, gilded nothings. Nature and sense do judge amiss. As faith makes Christ and heaven another thing, so it makes the world another thing: Prov. xxiii. 4, 'Labour not to be rich; cease from thine own wisdom.' How doth the Holy Ghost put these things together! If a man be guided by his natural understanding, and by carnal and present sense, all his business will be to be great, honourable, and rich; but if he hath a spiritual light, and doth cease from his own understanding, if he looks upon these things by an eye of faith, then he sees these poor empty things nothing in comparison of those better things which are offered to us by Christ: Ps. cxix. 96, 'I have seen an end of all perfection;'—it was not only his observation but experience; a man that hath an eye of faith may look to the end of worldly greatness and see through and through it;—'but thy commandment is exceeding broad;' that is the benefit we have by obeying the commandment of God, we cannot see through and through it. So that faith helps us to look upon present things, and to discern what a poor, gilded nothing, what a fashion, what a vain appearance all worldly things are!

[2.] On the other side, it shows us the worth of spiritual privileges, that peace of conscience is better than worldly happiness; that communion with God and his people, though they be an afflicted people, is better than the pleasures of the court; that it is better to be a member of God's church than to have a being in the courts of princes; that adoption is better than to be an heir to the greatest kingdom,—to be a son of God is much more than to be the son of Pharaoh's daughter. Faith rectifies our judgments about things spiritual. Carnal men cannot value these things, because they have no spiritual discerning, neither of the truth, nor of the worth of these things: 1 Cor. ii. 14, 'For the natural man perceiveth not the things of the Spirit of God, for they are foolishness unto him, neither can he know them, because they are spiritually discerned.' Mark, the world cannot well be understood without faith, nor spiritual things without faith. They which constantly attend upon God, and depend upon him, have much more a sweeter life than those that wait upon princes with great observance and expectation: Ps. cxviii. 9, 'It is better to trust in the Lord than to put confidence in princes.' A servant of the Lord is better provided for than the greatest favourites and minions of princes.

SERMON LIX.

By faith Moses, when he was come to years, refused to be called the son of Pharaoh's daughter.—HEB. xi. 24.

FAITH apprehends two things, that the servant of the Lord hath a sweeter taste, and that he is upon surer terms ; and therefore to faith all the honours of the world are but a child's game, or a man's dream, to the true privilege and real glory that we have by being the servants of God.

1. The service of the Lord is a sweeter work. It is much better to serve the Lord than to humour the highest princes of the earth. The life of the greatest courtier in the world is an unprofitable drudgery in comparison of the life of the poorest saint, who daily is taken up with attendance upon God, and is by faith a courtier and family-servant of the King of kings, the infinite Sovereign of heaven and earth. What a happy life doth he lead whose heart is employed in loving of God, and in praising of God, and in serving of God! This man while he remains on the earth hath his conversation in heaven, and converseth with God in the spirit, and waits upon God.

2. They are upon surer terms, because of the uncertainty of princes' love and life. Of their love, they depend upon God that never changes: Mal. iii. 6, ' I am the Lord, I change not;' they have a surer interest in the love of God than the highest favourites have in their prince's love. They are beloved of God that are faithful and upright with him, and careful to serve him. They have access to him upon every just occasion, they have daily supplies, renewed testimonies of the favour of God ; they live here upon his grace, and expect shortly to live with him in glory. Then for life: Ps. cxlvi. 3, 4, 'Put not your trust in princes, nor in the son of man, in whom there is no help ; his breath goeth forth, he returneth to his earth ; in that very day all his thoughts perish.' Mark, the drift of that place is to show that princes are not able to do so much for their servants as God is able to do for his servants. They seem to be able to promote us to great dignity and honour here in the world ; but they neither can deliver you nor themselves from death. Mark, ' He returneth to his earth.' A prince is earth in his constitution, dust is his composition, and he will be dust again in his dissolution—' Then shall the dust return to the earth as it was,' Eccles. xii. 7. So does the dust of the prince ; their whole being every moment depends upon the will of God. What then ? When he returneth to his earth, as all mortals shall, then ' in that very day all his thoughts perish ;' his thoughts, that is, his designs, purposes, promises, are frustrated, and come to nothing : it may be he hath a great good-will to his servants, but when he dies all will come to nothing. The speech of Bathsheba is to be regarded, 1 Kings i. 21, ' When my lord the king shall have slept with his fathers, I and my son Solomon shall be counted offenders.' Then they that have been most faithful to their prince, and most assured of his favour, it may be, shall be offenders in the eyes of the successor for their fidelity to their former prince. Now faith sees all this, and

shows how much more sure a child of God is of God's love ; he hath a greater interest in his love, and hath a dependence upon a God that is unchangeable, that will never fail. Now faith seeing all this, it mightily prevails upon the heart.

3. Faith sees that nothing is lost that is quitted for God's sake. The gospel way to lose is to save, and the way to save is to lose. Moses refused to be called the son of Pharaoh's daughter; but he lost no honour by it, for he grew 'mighty in words and in deeds,' Acts vii. 22. It may be his name was lost in the Egyptian annals and records among their potentates, or buried in deep silence, or branded with ignominy. Oh, but what a mighty name hath he in all the world to all ages ! And therefore there is nothing lost, no, not many times as to this world, to be sure not in the next. A man, when he is to part with anything for God, he doth it huckingly, and is apt to say as the disciples to Christ, ' Behold we have forsaken all, and followed thee ; what shall we have therefore ? ' Mat. xix. 27. Christ answers fully, ver. 28, 29, ' Ye which have followed me in the regeneration, when the Son of man shall sit in the throne of his glory, ye also shall sit upon twelve thrones, judging the twelve tribes of Israel. And every one that hath forsaken houses, or brethren, or sisters, or father, or mother, or wife, or children, or lands for my name's sake, shall receive a hundredfold,'—either in kind or in value,— ' and shall inherit eternal life.' It is notable to take notice of that passage in 2 Chron. xxv. 9, ' Amaziah said to the man of God, But what shall we do for the hundred talents which I have given to the army of Israel ? And the man of God answered, The Lord is able to give thee much more than this.' It is better to obey God with the greatest inconveniences, than to sin against God with the greatest advantages ; for he is able to give us more than this. You remember the story of Theodoret, in his third book, chap. xxv. He speaks of Valentinian that had accompanied Julian the apostate to the temple of the heathens ; and when the priest came to sprinkle water upon those that came to worship, he, by office being a captain, called to attend the emperor to the heathen temple, seeing the water upon him, cried out, I am defiled, and threw away his belt, for I am a christian, and so protested against the impious rites there used. Within a little while, as the reward of his obedience and faithful dealing, the Lord advanced him to the empire ; therefore there is nothing lost for God. Now faith goes upon this, to take off the heart from anything that cannot be kept without sin. And though faith doth not determine he will do so, yet usually he gives a hundredfold.

4. Faith resigns to God what we first received from him, when we can keep it no longer with fidelity to him. It is the ground of submission, Job i. 21, ' The Lord hath given, and the Lord hath taken.' And so it is a great principle of self-denial,—of submission when God takes, of self-denial when we yield it up to God, and he doth not take but what he first gave. An honest debtor will not deny the sum when it is called for again, but says, Here it is ; so when God doth by his providence call, he will interest us in the act ; we must give it up, and say, I had it in God's way, and upon God's call I will give it to him again.

5. Jesus Christ hath denied greater things for us. Now faith goes

upon this, Shall I not deny myself for Christ? For a time he did lay aside his glory, because it was God's will he should sacrifice himself upon the cross: 2 Cor. viii. 9, 'You know the grace of our Lord Jesus Christ, that though he was rich, yet for our sakes he became poor, that we through his poverty might be rich.' How was he rich? In the fulness of the glory of the godhead, and yet he did by an unspeakable dispensation abscond his glory, and leave it for a while, that he might sacrifice himself upon the cross. Shall it be irksome to you to leave a little glory and honour here in the world for Christ? The Son of God left his glory; therefore he prays, John xvii. 5, 'And now, O Father, glorify thou me with thine own self, with that glory which I had with thee before the world was.' He had it before the world was, but now it was obscured, it was hidden, as a candle in a dark lanthorn, by the veil of his flesh; but now he prays that it might be restored. If the sun of righteousness went back so many degrees, shall it be grievous to us to go back a few degrees? Faith doth not work altogether out of spiritual interest, and with respect to the great honour and immortality God will put upon us hereafter, but out of love; it not only looks forward, but backward, it shows us how infinitely we are engaged to Christ, who made himself of no reputation for us; and shall I not be willing to deny a little honour in the world? By all these considerations and reasonings, faith, through the blessing of God, doth convey such a noble and excellent spirit into the hearts of believers, so that they are carried above themselves, that they are willing to quit all the glory of the world for a good conscience, and that they may still keep their peace with God, and may be faithful with him.

Use 1. You will say, What is all this to us? What use shall private christians make of it, that are not exercised with these temptations? What shall we be the better for this sermon? What glory have I to renounce or to deny for God?

Ans. 1. There is nothing done by Moses but what is required of all christians. See a few scriptures: Luke xiv. 26, 'If any man will come to me, and hate not his father, and mother, and wife, and children, and brethren, and sisters, yea and his own life also, he cannot be my disciple.' Christians, what do you think? Is this an evangelical council that belongs to perfect christians, or a necessary precept that belongs to all christians? Or do you think this was only calculated for the first christians? You cannot have such unworthy thoughts, that those which have the same privileges, the same spirit, the same advantages, that they should never be put to the same self-denial; surely it holds in all ages: ver. 33, 'Whosoever of you he be that forsaketh not all that he hath, he cannot be my disciple.' And that we may not think this only belongs to the first ages, as if they were to suffer for us, and we fail in a full stream of worldly happiness, never to hazard our interest, or lose anything for God, you shall see, Mat. xiii. 45, 46, 'The kingdom of God is like unto a merchant seeking goodly pearls, who when he had found one pearl of great price, he went and sold all that he had, and bought it.' We must renounce all we have in the world, while we are seeking the blessed heavenly kingdom; we must part with and forsake all things,

even the most delicious, glorious things, though we affect them never
so much. How must we forsake them? Always in preparation of
mind, and a thorough, unbounded resolution, otherwise we are not
sincere with Christ; when we cannot have these things without sin,
when we cannot keep them with fidelity to God's service, all shall
go. Then actually when God calls hereunto; we must forego the
enjoyment of them, when they are inconsistent with, or prejudicial
to our spiritual and eternal happiness. Christians, do not flatter yourselves, it is not enough to forsake sin itself, but such things as you may
justly love and lawfully enjoy; otherwise our resignation and dedication of ourselves to Christ is not true; when God puts you upon the
trial, it must be verified and made good. Oh! think of the case of the
young man: he would fain enjoy the things of the kingdom of God—
Mark x. 17, 'What shall I do that I may inherit eternal life?'—but
he stuck at Christ's terms, 'and went away sad,' ver. 22. We would
all fain have the kingdom of eternal glory and ·blessedness in the
other world; but we cannot make the way to the kingdom wider or
narrower than it is. Therefore if you do not like Christ's terms, that
is, to resign all in your purpose and resignation of mind, and actually
forsake all when called thereunto, you shall not enter into the kingdom of God.

2. It teacheth us the nature and influence of faith. We mistake
it if we think it only to be a strong confidence. It is so indeed; but
there are other things also. It is such an appreciative esteem of
Christ and his benefits, that all other things are lessened in our opinion,
estimation, and affection. The nature of faith is set forth by the
apostle when he saith, Phil. iii. 7–10, 'What things were gain
to me, those I counted loss for Christ; yea, doubtless, and I count all
things but loss for the excellency of the knowledge of Christ Jesus my
Lord, for whom I have suffered the loss of all things, and do count
them but dung that I may win Christ; and be found in him, not
having mine own righteousness which is of the law, but that which
is through the faith of Christ, the righteousness which is of God by
faith; that I may know him, and the power of his resurrection, and
the fellowship of his sufferings, being made comformable unto his
death.' And therefore true faith makes us dead to the world, and
all the interests and honours thereof: and is to be known not so
much by our confidence, as by our mortification and weanedness;
when we carry all our comforts in our hands, as ready to part with
them, if the Lord called us to leave them. It is faith alone, and God
by faith can only bring us to this resolution: Mat. xix. 26, 'With
man it is impossible, but with God all things are possible;' he is able
to work this temper of soul. Here in the text it was not the spirit of
the world, but this mighty faith whereby Moses refused to be called
the son of Pharaoh's daughter. Most men would rather refuse to be
called the sons of God, and count it a greater honour to be advanced
in prince's courts than to be adopted into God's family. A man void
of faith, which is true heavenly wisdom, is strongly inclined to the
glory, honour, wealth, and delights of this world, and prefers them
before heaven and the eternal felicity thereof. But faith is tried by
great weanedness from the world, and carrying your comforts in your

hands, as ready to part with them at God's call. There may be a degree of resolution in some more strong than others, in some a greater deadness to the world, and a greater sense of the world to come than in others, but all must have it in some measure and degree, and be willing thus to part with all for God's sake.

3. It is of great use to shame us, that we have no more profited in the gospel. Mark why I give you this note. Moses was of this disposition and temper, though he lived in the court of a heathen prince; and should not we be of this disposition and temper who live in the bosom of the church, where we have the benefit of being trained up in the institutions of Christ, and have the example of self-denying christians? Moses had no such example in Pharaoh's court; what instructions he had I cannot tell, it is not mentioned; possibly he had some concealed converse with his parents or brethren, the people of Israel, who might inform him of some divine and saving truths which might produce this faith; but it was much that in the midst of these temptations those truths did so prevail with him. But, however, God supplied the lack of means by extraordinary grace. Certainly then we should be ashamed that are born and bred up in the church, and live where the light of the gospel doth continually shine upon us, and at the door of whose hearts God is continually knocking, and who have so many helps and means to improve the principle of faith to a more complete self-denial. We should grow more dead to all things that are of a worldly nature.

4. It is useful to wean us from the world. It is good for the children of God to wean themselves from the world by all kinds of instances. Present things seem so glorious, and taste so sweet to the flesh, that they strangely infatuate and captivate our minds, and seem to promise us rare contentment and happiness, that we have much ado to check this worldly expectation. Therefore men seek after these things, and pursue them earnestly and eagerly, hoping and expecting much good from them; and if once they possess and enjoy them, they are loth to quit them, preferring them before heaven and happiness. Yea, the flesh within us is so greedy of the bait, that though we see the hook, yet we are ready to swallow it. Therefore it concerns us mightily to take all occasions to wean us from the world. Now the instances and examples of God's children are one means, when the Lord hath enabled them, even those that have not those advantages of instruction we have. It is a mighty thing that may be urged against temptation. Moses here, the man of God, refused to be called the son of Pharaoh's daughter; thou art not called to deny so much of the world as he; he lived in the court that was the centre of all pleasure, and he was a great man there, the son of Pharaoh's only daughter. Think of this instance, that it may deaden your desires. The more excellent God's children are, the more they are contemning the world, and still calling off their hearts from it. Abraham left his father's house; Moses left Pharaoh's court. Surely these are not the good things we should look after. They are 'the smallest matters,' 1 Cor. vi. 2. There is a better portion reserved for us.

5. This is very necessary, to teach us to value our spiritual privileges by Christ. We have not high thoughts enough of these privi-

leges. Do you know the worth of them? Moses, that had experience of the pleasures, treasures, and honours of Egypt, left all that he might attain them. No earthly thing is to be compared with the fruition of the favour and fellowship of God, yea, and the service of God. Moses left all for that which God hath bestowed or will bestow upon his people—'Esteeming the reproach of Christ greater riches than the treasures of Egypt.' Oh, therefore, value your own mercies! The most painful condition of life joined with any measure of communion with God is better than the most quiet, easy, plentiful condition without it: Ps. lxxxiv. 10, 'A day in thy courts is better than a thousand; I had rather be a doorkeeper in the house of my God, than to dwell in the tents of wickedness.' Better be in any mean service and ministration about God than enjoy all honours. And now will you repine and grudge if God hath given you his favour, though he keeps you low and bare? If wicked men grow fat with common mercies, why should we wax lean from day to day if God hath vouchsafed us better things? Ps. xvii. 14, 15, 'They have their portion in this life, whose belly thou fillest with thy hid treasure; they are full of children, and leave the rest of their substance to their babes. As for me, I will behold thy face in righteousness; I shall be satisfied when I awake with thy likeness.' Worldly men have a sweet portion, they ransack all the storehouses of nature, all delicacies are brought to their table, they are well fed and well clothed, they have lands, and heritages, and mansions, which they leave to their children. Oh, but God hath given you communion with himself—'This should put more gladness into your heart than in the time that their corn and wine increased,' Ps. iv. 7. We have no reason to envy wicked men their life of ease, pomp, and honour, for God hath better things for you, which all wise men would quit all other things for.

6. It gives a check to daily temptations, for if we cannot deny a little ease of the flesh, alas! how shall we deny pleasures, treasures, honours, and be so upright and faithful with God as Moses was? We should be ashamed to hear of such things, we that give up at the first assault, and are borne down with every petty temptation, and even 'sell our birthright for one morsel of meat,' Heb. xii. 16; when every slothful suggestion can take us off from God; when we cannot overcome, though but a little profit and respect, that we may manifest our integrity, and show our faithfulness to God when we are disallowed and discountenanced.

7. It should teach us patience, if God should retrench us in our worldly conveniences, if he should lessen us by his providence, if he should make us go back some degrees in the state wherein we have lived before. Shall we not yield to God's power, and submit to that which we must bear, whether we will or no? God did not snatch them from Moses, but he left them by choice: and shall we murmur in such cases? But if God sees these comforts too good for us, and therefore takes them away, shall we be merely passive? No, we should be active, show our willingness to part with them by a quiet submission. And such kind of instances help us.

8. It is of use to us: and now I come to the main thing I am upon, to check ambition and affectation of worldly greatness, and the scrambling for honours and great places, either gain, power, or government

in the world which doth possess the hearts of men. Moses was in the possession of these things, and did quit them; and shall we hunt after that which he quitted for God? And here are sundry considerations and motives.

[1.] The true value of life is by service to God. It is not who lives most plentifully, but who lives most serviceably to God's glory; therefore honour and greatness should not be the game in chase, but service. All our care in the world should be to serve God in our generation, to be an instrument to do his pleasure: Acts xiii. 36, 'David, after he had served his generation according to the will of God, fell asleep.' Every one hath his office and use, from the king to the peasant. We murmur if creatures made to serve us should fail in their seasons; and therefore since we were born for this, and sent into the world for this end, to serve God in our seasons, these for this age of the world, and those for that, therefore this should be our aim. We live to ourselves when our honour, and great, and commodious subsistence is more regarded than our work and service, for then self is put in the room and place of God.

[2.] Our service is determined by the call of God's providence. He is the great master of the scenes, that assigns to every man his calling and state of life, and appoints him what part he is to act; therefore if we do not submit to his will, we take his work out of his hands. We must not be our own carvers, and prescribe to God at what rate we will be maintained, and what work we will do. God is our potter, he will make one vessel to honour, and another to dishonour; he appoints to every one his calling and work, and doth dispose of every one's condition in the world: Prov. xxix. 26, 'Many seek the ruler's favour;' every one would have the ruler's countenance and respect. But, alas! our affectation meets with shameful disappointment; for 'every man's judgment cometh from the Lord;' he rules all things according to his own pleasure. Servants that have no relation to you may covenant and make their bargain whether they will be employed in the chamber or in the kitchen. But we are at God's absolute dispose. If the master will use us as vessels of honour or dishonour, we must be contented. God appoints a man to his calling, not only in fitting him and giving him abilities,—therefore the apostle dateth his calling from the womb: Gal. i. 15, 'But when it pleased God, who separated me from my mother's womb,' when men's parts and temper are framed,—but in giving us occasion to exercise those abilities and gifts. If God hath a mind to use thee, he knoweth when and how without thy care and trouble. We must not fit the garland to our own heads: he that exalteth himself, God sets himself against him to pull him down. In all such cases we must tarry till the master of the feast sets us higher. What a man should use for God, he must take it out of God's hands: John xvii. 4, 'I have glorified thee on the earth; I have finished the work which thou gavest me to do;' that is, the work to which I was fitted by God, inclined by God, and disposed by God in the course of his providence. There is indeed a question, How far a man may offer himself to places of gain or government, either in church or commonwealth? *Ans.* A man may desire the employment of his gifts in a suitable way: 1 Tim. iii. 1, 'If a man desire the office of a bishop, he desireth a good work.' Out of conscience of his internal call, he may lie at the pool modestly till some put him in, and offer himself to such work as God hath called him unto, and upon a fair call he must not draw back. But yet we should wait and tarry God's leisure, without thrusting and obtruding ourselves. If thy worth be not known, bear it patiently; Jesus Christ lay hid for a long time, and was not known. It was John's testimony concerning Christ, John i. 26, 'There standeth one among you, whom ye know not.' So Joseph, that notable man for business, lay obscurely in prison, and was kept as a slave a long time; and Daniel a long time was nourished among the captive children before his worth and eminency was taken notice of; and David did follow the ewes great with young before the Lord called him out to feed his people, and there was an opportunity to discover his spirit and valour; Moses is a shepherd with his father-in-law, ere he was captain of the people. In the meantime we must not use ill means, nor much trouble ourselves in the use of lawful means. We must not use ill means. Ambition is like a whirl-wind to tear all things in our way; it treads down all that stands in their way; truth, gospel, good conscience, all must go down, so they may rise. Moses would not keep honour upon base terms, and will you get it? When a man is in possession, the temptation is the greater; but you never had it, and therefore yours is the greater sin, if for favour and preferment you should deny or dissemble the truth, or stretch conscience to the size of the times to humour men. If we had it, and enjoyed it in the highest manner we are capable of, yet it must be left; but to break through all restraints of honour and conscience to get it, this is sinful. Nor must we much trouble ourselves in the use of lawful means: Prov. xxv. 27, 'For men to seek their own glory is not glory.' Ambition is a mark of indignity; if you were worthy of honour, your worth would attract it, as a violet is found out by its smell. Where the matter is combustible, we need not blow the fire so hard. By eager sucking honour, you disparage yourselves. There is no temper so base as the ambitious; how do they bend, cringe, stoop, fawn, flatter, and all to raise themselves!—' Having men's persons in admiration because of advantage,' Jude 16. Absalom kisseth the people; such carking, caring, and fawning argueth little worth. It disparageth God, as if he did not care for you, and did not know where to employ and set you. And then you tax his providence when with such carking and solicitude you are hunting after great places. And in the end God will make you know that all is at his dispose: Prov. xxix. 26, ' Many seek the ruler's favour, but every man's judgment cometh of the Lord;' what God hath determined concerning his course of life. Men's hearts are in God's hands; worldly potentates are not masters of their own respects, but meet often with a shameful disappointment.

[3.] God may be as well served and glorified in a lower calling as in a higher, if you perform the duties of your present station. The apostle speaks of poor servants, 'that they may adorn the doctrine of God their Saviour in all things,' Titus ii. 10. They have their work and sphere of activity, though it be a lower one; and if they are conscionable in it, and do the duty of their place out of fear and reverence to God, it is a mighty honour to God. The gnat proclaims God as really as the sun, though the sun more notably. Some shine in a more glorious orb and sphere, but all have their opportunities of service. We must give an account of our talents ; he that had but one talent was to employ it : John xvii. 4, ' I have finished the work that thou hast given me to do.' Do what God calls for in the place he hath set you, and trouble not yourself in aspiring thoughts and endeavours to be great ; the discharge of your duty will be your comfort and peace.

[4.] Many times in a private life there are many advantages of enjoying God, which we cannot have in more power. Though we are not to refuse power, but improve it if called thereto, yet this should satisfy you ; a private condition hath greater advantages of enjoying more communion with God—being often in the meditations of God, in prayers to and praises of him. In a private life you have many pleasant opportunities of retirement for communion with God. Those that live upon mountains have very tempestuous habitations ; so men that live in a clatter of worldly business have not such advantages of enjoying the Lord, they are continually exposed to the storms of the envy and jealousy of others, where it is hard to please men, or to please God, or to please ourselves. It is hard to please men, because of the uncertainty of their humours ; and there we have the greatest hindrances of pleasing God, our hearts being taken up with these things. Ay, and few find that pleasure they expect from it themselves ; therefore who would covet and aspire for that condition wherein there are so few advantages either to please God, himself, or men.

[5.] Consider, as their advantages are less, so their snares are more ; the higher their station, the more dangerous. He had need have a steady head that walks upon a precipice ; the snares of worldly greatness are many. Trees planted on the tops of mountains are more exposed to bleak winds ; and when we are full, we are apt to forget God : Jer. v. 5, ' I will get me unto the great men ; but these have altogether broken the yoke.' Rank pastures breed weeds ; little fishes escape, when the great ones are held in the net ; the moon is eclipsed when it in the full ; so that unless we be in love with our temptation, we should not thus earnestly desire greatness in the world. When the sons of Zebedee desired to be set, one at Christ's right hand, and the other at his left, says Christ, Mat. xx. 22, ' Ye know not what you ask ;' so when you seek honour, you know not what you seek, for your snares, sins, and burdens, are greater. Your snares are greater, for there are more temptations ; and your sins are greater, because of the eminency of your station ; for the higher your station is, every sin you commit is the greater ; when others are lost in a crowd, you are taken notice of. And your burden is the greater ; the more talents, the greater account you have to make ; more duty is required of you than of others ; you have talents enough already to answer for. He that cannot bear a lesser burden, how shall he bear a greater ?

[6.] Self-seekers are many times the greatest self-losers, for God will cross them ; God will appear against them, for he loves to resist the proud. The shadow follows them that run from it ; and usually they that seek their own interest least do most convince the world of their real worth, which, where it is, will speak for itself. Therefore those that torture themselves with restless, aspiring thoughts, do not attain their end many times : Ps. cxxvii. 2, ' It is vain for you to rise up early, to sit up late, to eat the bread of sorrow;' that is, it is in vain for you, Absalom, to think to rise by a tedious observance of the people, and for you, Adonijah, to torture yourself with restless, ambitious thoughts and pursuits; you toil yourselves to no purpose, 'for God will give his beloved sleep.' Solomon was called Jedidiah, the beloved of the Lord (that is the private sense); God will give the crown to whom he intends it; and so men lose all their travail and pains, it comes to nothing but ruin. Climbing proves very dangerous to men if they have not a good holdfast, as putting up too much sail overturns the ship many times.

[7.] The true ambition is the spiritual ambition; to seek the true glory, the things of heaven and Christ. There we cannot be too earnest, we must take no nay; as Luther said, *Valde protestatus sum me non sic à Deo satiari*—I protested that I would not be put off with these things. It is no crime or treason to offer violence to the kingdom of heaven, Mat. xi. 12. This is ambition becoming a christian, to affect the crown of glory, to follow God, and not be put off by him. This will make us despise other things. Remember these are the great things, and that others are but small things in regard of these. Compare two places together, 2 Peter i. 4, with 1 Cor. vi. 2. In the latter place he calls the things of the world 'the smallest matters,' and the promises 'exceeding great and precious promises.' These are the greatest things; to have the favour of God, and to have hopes of the glory of God; these are the things that we should most busy our thoughts about.

[8.] That true greatness lies not in honour, but in real worth and grace. A dwarf is but a dwarf though he stand upon a mountain : he may have the advantage-ground, but he is never a whit the taller. A horse is not the better for his trappings, but for his strength and swiftness. A man exalted is not any whit the greater, nothing is added to him. And the Lord to put a scorn upon these outward things gives them sometimes to the basest of men. In troubled waters the mud cometh on the top; as it was told Anastatius, he was exalted, not because he was worthy of the government of the city, but they were not worthy of a better governor. All these considerations should help to free the soul of this cursed weed that is apt to grow and vent itself in our hearts, this affectation of worldly greatness.

Use 2. Exhortation to the high, and those that are in honour, to be of Moses' spirit, actually to quit these things upon trial, but at present in the preparation of your mind. Two things I would press you to—weanedness and resolution.

1. To weanedness. To this end—

[1.] Consider the short continuance of worldly greatness. It is a part acted upon the stage of this world for a while. Others have been in the places you enjoy, and they are dead and gone, and there is no remembrance of them. You are going to the grave only the higher walk : Job iii. 19, 'The small and the great are there, and the servant is free from his master.' Within a little while, and the world will think as meanly of you as you do of them that are gone before you. There will ever be a distinction between holy and unholy, between clean and unclean, between the believer and the unbeliever,

between the carnal and the regenerate ; but there will be no distinction
between the rich and the poor, between the honourable and the base.
Within a little while there will not be a pin to choose between them ;
the most shining glory will be quickly burned to a snuff, though no
churlish blast should extinguish it.

[2.] The true value of life is by our service to God. That is the
best life wherein we are most serviceable to God, and most helped on
to heaven.

[3.] Many times the greater you are in earth, the lesser you shall
be in heaven : Lazarus was poor in this world, and Dives was rich ; but
one went to heaven, and the other was sent to hell : Mat. xi. 5, ' The
poor have the gospel preached to them.'

2. To a resolution—

[1.] To use what you have for the present for God. You must
not throw them away. Consider what advantage hath God for thy
advancement. It is not enough to see that they do us no hurt, but
you must ' honour the Lord with your substance, and with the first-
fruits of all thine increase,' Prov. iii. 9. We should have nothing
but God should be honoured by it. Nehemiah was the king's cup-
bearer, and his interest was improved for the good of God's people,
Neh. i. 11.

[2.] To carry these things in your hands, that when God calleth
for them you may be ready to leave them. God giveth you these
things that you may have something of value to esteem as nothing
for Christ. David carried his life in his hand, as a thing ready to
be gone from him : Ps. cxix. 109, ' My soul is continually in my hand.'
So should you sit loose to worldly things, expecting God's call to part
with them.

[3.] Wisely to discern the interest of Christ, that your honour may
not be incompatible with it : Ps. ii. 10, ' Be wise now therefore, O ye
kings ; be instructed, ye judges of the earth.' Of all men they should
be most inquisitive, that they do not stand in Christ's way, and get
all the instruction they can of their duty.

Use 3. Examination ; examine your faith and self-denial. The
one discovereth the other.

1. Examine your faith by your self-denial. Have you gone back
any degrees for Christ ? What have you refused for him ? But
because every one is not put upon such actual eminent trial, inquire, doth faith take off your hearts from the things of the
world ? Your weanedness from the world will be an evidence of your
faith ; when you have low thoughts of the world, of the honours, and
pleasures, and treasures of it. It may be we may speak contemptibly
of the world, but this is not enough ; look to the settled disposition
of your souls. Two things you may know it by ; what is your first
care, and choice delight ?

[1.] What is your first care ? Mat. vi. 33, ' Seek ye first the
kingdom of God, and the righteousness thereof, and all these things
shall be added to you.' It a sign of a worldly spirit when the only
thought is to get increase, the only business is to hunt after honour,
this is the prey and game in chase. Every man hath a first thing,
which is his τὸ ἔργον, his work and business. When men are never at

rest till they have gotten this honour, and then that preferment, and are still gaping after more, it is a sign the heart is not purged from worldly lusts and vile affections.

[2.] What is your choice delight? Is it in the Lord Jesus Christ, to be a fellow-heir with him, who is your elder brother? Is it to enjoy communion with God? What is it that you muse upon? See the musings of a worldly great man, Dan. iv. 30, 'Is not this great Babylon that I have built for the house of the kingdom, by the might of my power, and for the honour of my majesty?' But the musings of a godly man we have, Ps. lxxxiv. 10, 'For a day in thy court is better than a thousand; I had rather be a doorkeeper in the house of my God, than to dwell in the tents of wickedness.' It is a delightful thing to them to think of a covenant interest in God, and of liberty of access to him by Christ: Ps. iv. 6, 7, 'There be many that say, Who will show us any good? Lord, lift thou up the light of thy countenance upon us. Thou hast put gladness in my heart, more than in the time that their corn and their wine increased.' What is it that puts gladness into your hearts? Is it to have worldly things increased? or that God is reconciled to you, and that you have hopes of enjoying him in glory?

2. Examine your self-denial by your faith. Some have not an opportunity to show it, and some men's lusts are turned another way, as swine care not for pearls, but for swill; sometimes men deny themselves out of humour and discontent; or their self-denial is but a politic retreat, or an affectation of privacy and quiet, or from a natural stoutness of spirit. But if you would be satisfied about the sincerity of your self-denial inquire—

[1.] How is it gotten? Is it the fruit of much humiliation, and brokenness of heart, and seeking God, and great strugglings with him? As Esther ventureth all upon her seeking of God: Esther iv. 16, 'Go, gather together all the Jews that are present in Shushan, and fast ye for me, and neither eat nor drink three days night or day: I also and my maidens will fast likewise; and so will I go in unto the king, which is not according to the law; and if I perish, I perish.'

[2.] What are your motives? Do religious reasons bear sway? How do you reason with yourselves? What draweth you to self-denial? Is it upon divine grounds and arguments, such as love to God, and our great hopes? Faith makes use of the sword of the Spirit, not the motives and reasonings of flesh and blood.

[3.] What is the fruit of it? doth it makes us more humble, both to God and men? To God: Acts v. 41, 'They departed from the presence of the council, rejoicing that they were counted worthy to suffer shame for his name;' not boasting and glorying, but wondering that unworthy creatures should be so honoured. And then it will make it meek towards men, as Stephen prayed for his persecutors: Acts vii. 60, 'Lord, lay not this sin to their charge;' not return railing for railing, or reviling for reviling, or seeking revenge for the wrong they do us, but pitying and praying for them. By these things you may try the truth of your self-denial.

SERMON LX.

Choosing rather to suffer affliction with the people of God, than to enjoy the pleasures of sin for a season.—HEB. xi. 25.

THE apostle is amplifying Moses' self-denial. In the former verse we heard what Moses had refused—'he refused to be called the son of Pharaoh's daughter;' and here we learn for what he refused it, even for the afflicted state of God's people, together with the reasons of his choice. In this choice of Moses you may observe the wisdom, the justice, and the piety of it. The wisdom of it. It was a wise choice; why? Because it was πρόσκαιρος ἀπόλαυσις, a temporary enjoyment that he quitted; what we render 'to enjoy the pleasures of sin for a season,' is in the original, πρόσκαιρον ἔχειν ἁμαρτίας ἀπόλαυσιν—for the temporal enjoyment of sin. There was his wisdom; sin could yield him but a temporary enjoyment. Then the justice of it. It was just and fit it should be so. Why? because it was the pleasures of sin; they were not only unstable, but sinful; he could not without sin enjoy them. Then the piety of it, in casting the scales upon religious reasons. Choice is *actualis prælatio unius rei præ altera.* You must suppose a balance erected; in the one part of the balance there are afflictions, banishment, hard service, bitter afflictions; so the word signifies συγκακουχεῖσθαι τῷ λαῷ, choosing to be evilly-handled, evilly-entreated; but it is with the people of God where God is enjoyed and glorified, and whom God hath undertaken to protect and deliver. Here is bitter afflictions, and nothing to allay them but the company of God's people. Then in the other scale there are the pleasures of sin for a season. Now godliness prevails and casts the scale—' He chooseth rather to suffer affliction with the people of God,' &c. The only difficulty that needs to be opened is 'the pleasure of sin that is but for a season;' the temporal enjoyment or delight of sin; so it is in the original. Wherein lay the sin of Moses' former condition? *Ans.* In living out of the communion of God's people, and the public worship of God, forbearing profession after conviction. For now he was come to years of discretion, it would have been a sin to embody himself with the Egyptians, to disown the true religion, and neglect fellowship and communion with God's people. Or else it may be now he was in danger to be tainted with the vices of the court; there were such pleasures there that might draw off his heart from God, to forsake God and his service. Or it may be he could no longer retain his honours unless he had a hand in promoting those cruel edicts for the prosecution of his own countrymen, a thing evil in itself, and against the light of his conscience. Or, which I rather prefer above all the rest, he could no longer enjoy this estate and obey God's call. He had a special impulse and call from God to be the deliverer of his people; now he could not manifest his obedience to this call unless he forsook the court and the pleasures there.

From these words many things might be observed. The main point is this, that it is the property of a gracious heart to choose the greatest affliction before the least sin. When once it came to sin, Moses could abide in the court no longer. It was Moses' judgment he was not overseen, for he is commended for it by the Spirit of God. We may learn also from hence other things, as that it is the usual lot and portion of God's people to be afflicted—'He chose rather to suffer affliction.' We see here also the value of the communion of saints, what a great privilege it is ; he chose rather to suffer affliction 'with the people of God.' Again, learn hence the snare of pleasures, or worldly delights, how they draw off the heart from God ; and the transitoriness of these delights, it is but an enjoyment for a season. All these were so many ingredients in Moses' faith. Delights are a snare ; they are apt to draw our heart from God : and they are very transitory ; they are but for a season. But I shall speak only to the main point.

Doct. That it is the property of a gracious heart to choose the greatest affliction before the least sin.

Before I prove it, let me illustrate it a little. Take the emphasis of the point along with you. Put sin in one balance, the least sin, and conceive of it as having great advantages. The least sin is a transgression of God's law ; the greatest affliction that is, is but a diminution of our happiness, or a breach upon our interest or outward welfare. The least sin is a violation of God's law : Mat. v. 19, 'Whosoever shall break one of these least commandments, and shall teach men so, he shall be called the least in the kingdom of heaven.' The least part of the law is of weighty and momentous consideration. The least sin is a sin, and it deserves hell : Rom. vi. 23, 'The wages of sin is death.' The apostle doth not say the wages of a great sin is death, but of sin ; that is, of every sin. The less the sin is, the more imprudence to break with God, and to offend God, and to hazard our own happiness for a thing of no value. Conceive, again, of this little sin as having great pleasures and honours annexed to it. So it was here in the case of Moses' tarrying at court. But whatever advantages sin hath, let it have all that it can have, though every man is not put upon such temptations, but let it have honours, riches, all kind of advantages annexed thereto, the greatest pleasure a court life can yield ; yet, Luke vi. 20–26, Christ pronounceth a woe against them that had worldly advantages in a sinful state. Though men had never such fulness, plenty, honour, and esteem in the world, yet still they are in a miserable condition, make the best of it that can be made, riches, honours, pleasure, applause ; and though we could ruffle it out in a bravery and fulness of outward comfort every day, yet all this will not make us happy. If wicked men should join all their forces together, take what every man doth enjoy severally, and what they all jointly possess, yet a little and a good conscience is better—'A little that a righteous man hath is better than the riches of many wicked,' Ps. xxxvii. 10 ; Prov. xvi. 8, 'Better is a little with righteousness, than great revenues without right ;' Prov. xv. 16, 17, 'Better is a little with the fear of the Lord, than great treasure and trouble therewith. Better is a dinner of herbs where love is, than a stalled ox and hatred therewith.' A dinner with herbs, poor, mean fare, coarse apparel, and hard life, yet with a good conscience this is a great deal better than all the conveniences of the world. But descend a step lower. If there were nothing to be enjoyed, take the greatest affliction ; if a man were wholly left destitute, and had nothing but labour and sorrow, and fell from the highest condition to the most afflicted state, as the Israelites now were under great tyranny and slavery ; though we are loth to descend and go backward, yet still it is a greater misery to be in a sinful state than in an afflicted state. Moses is far more happy among the people of God, that were now oppressed and held in hard slavery, than when he was in the court. So he judgeth, and so we should, if we would judge aright. All honours must be renounced for the most afflicted state that can fall upon the people of God. In managing and proving this point—

1. I shall show the reasons why the greatest affliction is better than the least sin.

2. Why the people of God make such a choice as this is.

First, For the reasons why the greatest affliction is better than the least sin.

1. In suffering the offence is done to us, but in sinning the offence is done to God; and what are we to God? It is nothing to offend and weary men; but to offend God, and weary God, that is the highest aggravation: Isa. vii. 13, ' It is a small thing to weary men, but will ye weary my God also ? ' All injuries receive a value from the person against whom they are committed. Now sin is an injury to God, and affliction is only an infringement of our outward happiness. We are not masters of our own interests ; to affect a dominion over ourselves is a usurpation upon God's right. Now to break the law of God is to lift up ourselves against God, and to jostle him out of the throne. Better that all creatures should perish, than God should suffer any wrong; better that we and ours be wholly destroyed, rather than there should be an offence done to God. Therefore, because sin is an offence to God, a gracious soul would rather endure the greatest affliction han meddle with the least sin.

2. Sin separates us from God, but suffering and affliction doth not, and therefore the greatest affliction is to be chosen before the least sin. Certainly that is an evil which separates us from the chiefest good ; now God is the chiefest good, and sin separates us from God: Isa. lix. 2, ' Your iniquities have separated between you and your God.' But affliction doth not separate us from God, but is a means to make us draw nigh to God. Many there are who have been chosen in the fire ; and so the time of affliction is to them the time of loves,—a time to bring God and man acquainted, that they are brought nearer to God than ever they were before ; and therefore surely sin in a gracious eye is worse than affliction. Let a man be never so poor, blind, and lame, and roughcast with sores, let him be never so outwardly loathsome, yet the Lord loves him, and takes pleasure in him if he be in a state of grace; he is near and dear to God, and God kisses him with the kisses of his mouth. Nothing makes us loathsome to God but sin. God is at a distance from us, and we are at a distance from God; he cannot look upon us without loathing, and we cannot think of him without horror, and dare not come into his presence.

3. Sin is evil in itself, whether we feel it or no ; but affliction is only evil in our sense and feeling: Heb. xii. 11, ' Now no chastening for the present seemeth to be joyous, but grievous.' Though it smart, it is a wholesome thing to the children of God ; it is smarting only to our sense. Sense is a lying thing. A bitter medicine is wholesome; in itself it is a medicine against sin ; it is no pain to a benumbed

joint to be scourged. But now sin is evil whether we feel it or no ; nay, it is worse when we feel it not. To be 'past feeling' is a heavy judgment, Eph. iv. 19. Sin ceaseth not to be evil, whether we feel it or no:

[4.] Affliction brings inconvenience upon the body only, and the concernments of the body ; but sin brings inconvenience upon the soul. There are soul-afflictions indeed, but they come from God, and they are to be reckoned amongst the fruits of sin ; but affliction concerns the body, and as long as the soul is whole, all is whole. Afflictions themselves cannot reach the soul, they hurt only the body— 'The spirit of a man will sustain his infirmities,' Prov. xviii. 14 ;—if the body be weak, as long as the heart is whole, a man can endure it ;—'but a wounded spirit,' when conscience is filled with the terrors of the Lord, 'who can bear?' Persecutions they cannot reach the inward man. Blindness, lameness, tortures bring an inconvenience only to the body, they cannot reach the soul. But now sin brings an inconvenience upon the soul. The body, that is but the sheath ; as, Dan. vii. 15, 'Daniel was grieved in my spirit in the midst of my body ;' we render, it in the middle of my body ; in the margin it is, in the middle of my sheath. It was the saying of a philosopher You may batter the case to pieces, but you cannot reach my jewel. Persecution may come at the body, but they cannot hurt the soul, nor infringe our comforts in the Lord.

5. An afflicted state may consist with the love of God, but a sinful state cannot. Afflictions come from the love of God—'Whom the Lord loves he chastens,' Heb. xii. 6 ; and their design is love ; God's aim is to give his people a greater proof of his love. But now sins are permitted to befall to thee in hatred ; it is a sign of God's dreadful displeasure when he gives us up to sin, it is to hasten our own ruin and everlasting destruction : Prov. xxiii. 27, 'A whore is a deep ditch ; he that is abhorred of the Lord shall fall therein.'

6. Affliction may be good, but sin is never good, the nature of it cannot be altered: Rom. viii. 28, 'All things shall work together for good to them that love God ;' so Ps. cxix. 71, 'It is good for me that I have been afflicted.' It is a medicine to the godly. But we cannot say, It is good for me that I have sinned against thee ; but 'Woe unto us, for we have sinned,' Lam. v. 16. A man may rejoice in his troubles because they may be good, and tend to good, but he cannot rejoice in his sins. New creatures have approved of afflictions, but they never approved of their sins ; the children of God have ever groaned bitterly under their sins ; as Paul : Rom. vii. 24, 'O wretched man that I am ! who shall deliver me from this body of death ?' If any man had cause to complain of affliction, Paul had ; he was in perils often, in hunger, thirst, and nakedness ; he was whipped, imprisoned, &c. But Paul doth not cry out, When shall I get rid of my affliction? but, Oh ! when shall I get rid of this body of death? His lust troubled him more than his scourging ; and his captivity to the law of sin was worse to him than a prison.

7. There is nothing that debaseth a man more than sin. It degradeth him from the dignity of his nature, which afflictions do not. 1 Cor. x. 13, the apostle speaking of affliction saith, 'No temptation hath taken us but what is common to man ;' but he that sins, he is

as 'a beast that perisheth,' Ps. xlix. 20 ; and Ps. lxxiii. 22, 'I was as a beast before thee.' It was not so bad for Daniel to be put into the lion's den, nor such a judgment for Nebuchadnezzar to have the heart of a beast, and be turned out among beasts. Here was no degrading of his nature ; and therefore to be wicked is more than to be afflicted. Natural evils are less than moral : there is a violence offered to a principle of reason by sin, the nature of man is altered by it ; our outward interest is only infringed by affliction.

8. Afflictions come from God, but sins from the devil. Afflictions are God's penal dispensations, the act of his justice ; but sin is the devil's work ; therefore it is said, Christ came 'to destroy,' or to dissolve, 'the works of the devil,' that is, the sins of men ; and they are called his lusts : John viii. 44, 'Ye are of your father, the devil, and the lusts of your father ye will do.' Affliction comes from the Lord, it springs not out of the dust : Amos iii. 6, 'Shall there be evil in the city, and the Lord hath not done it ? ' This comes from a holy and just God ; and the other from our naughty heart, and from the temptations of Satan. One are the acts of God's justice, and so they are good ; the other are the acts of a sinful creature.

9. Affliction is sent to prevent sin ; but sin must not be committed to prevent affliction. The use and intent of God in affliction is to purge away sin : Isa. xxvii. 9, ' By this shall the iniquity of Jacob be purged, and this is all the fruit to take away his sin.' The Lord thrasheth us that our husk may go off.

10. The evil of suffering is but for a moment : 2 Cor. iv. 17, ' Our light affliction, which is but for a moment,' &c. ; but the evil of sin is for ever. Affliction, like pain, dries up of its own accord ; within a little while *nubecula est, cito transitura*, it is like a cloud or storm that is soon blown over. The evil of suffering is but for the present : Isa. liv. 8, ' In a little wrath have I hid my face from thee for a moment ;' Ps. xxx. 5, ' Weeping may endure for a night, but joy cometh in the morning.' If it should continue throughout our lives, it is but a little moment in comparison of eternity : Gen. xlvii. 9, ' Few and evil have the days of the years of my life been.' If they are evil, it is a great comfort they are but few, and do not last long. Men will endure a little pain, to have their flesh torn and cut, to be rid of a lasting torment. *Hic ure, hic seca, Domine, modo parcas in eternum ;* Lord, burn me here, cut me here, that I may not be punished for ever. 1 Cor. xi. 32, ' We are chastened of the Lord, that we should not be condemned with the world.' Better endure a little affliction than lie under the evil of sin for ever. The evil of sin is for ever, the delight passeth, but sin remaineth ; though the act be over, yet the guilt and punishment still remains for ever in the conscience. We read of ' a worm that doth never die, and of fire that never is quenched,' Mark ix. 44. The fuel abides for ever, and the breath of the Lord that kindles it. At the best, affliction is but during our abode in the world ; and therefore it cannot be so great an evil as the least sin, that in itself renders us obnoxious to the wrath of God.

11. We lose nothing so much by suffering as we do by sin. In sufferings and persecutions we lose the favour of men, but by sins we lose the favour of God ; and that is a sad purchase to buy the favour

of men with the offence of God, to lose heaven, to undergo the wrath of God. Look what difference there is between man and God, between this life and eternity; so much difference is there between the evil of an afflicted state, and the evil of a sinful state. Shall I hazard the love of an infinite God for the pleasure of a finite comfort? Shall I hazard eternity for a moment?

12. To suffer is not in our choice, we shall not be responsible for that; but to sin, that is in our choice whether we will or no. Afflictions are laid upon us, we are not active but passive only so far as in bearing them we submit to the will of God, but the Lord lays affliction upon us; but we never sin but by our own consent. Afflictions are inflicted, sins are committed, and they will be required of us because they are our own voluntary acts.

13. Sin is the cause of affliction, therefore it is worse. There is more in the cause than in the effect. Sin is worse than hell, because it made hell; and if there were no sin, there would be no hell. And you know the speech of him, *Si hic inferni horrorem, illic peccati pudorem,* &c.; if here I should set the horror of hell, and there the filthiness of sin, I would rather be damned than endure the filthiness of sin. We are not put to the choice; however, it is a clear argument that because sin is the cause of affliction, therefore it is worse, for afflictions are but a part of the curse that was introduced by sin.

14. An afflicted man may die cheerfully, but a sinner cannot. Every man when he comes to die would choose this side: Num. xxiii. 10, 'Let me die the death of the righteous, and let my latter end be like his.' But the sinner 'at his end shall be a fool,' Acts xvii. 11; when they come to die, they discern their own folly.

15. Sin is contrary to the new nature, to the noblest being; but affliction is only contrary to the old nature. It is the flesh that complains of affliction, but the spirit of sin. Paul was buffeted, scourged, and in prison often, yet Paul never groans for his affliction, but groans mightily for his sins. If any had cause to complain of affliction Paul had,—in perils often, in nakedness, in watchings, in fastings, 2 Cor. xi. 25–27. But he complains not of them, but of sin: Rom. vii. 24, 'O wretched man! who shall deliver me from the body of this death?' Sin is the greatest offence to the noblest being on this side heaven, to the new nature infused into the soul.

16. When you deliberately choose sin, it will within a little while bring greater affliction; it will bring the curse of God along with it on all you have: Deut. xxviii. 17, 18, 'Cursed shall be thy basket and thy store,' &c. He is not cursed in the want of an estate, but in his basket and store, and in his increase; and the more estate he has, the greater is his curse. And therefore you have not your choice, for you have both sin and affliction too. So much for the first question.

Secondly, Why the people of God make such a choice as this is. They cannot be gracious unless they do so.

1. The great work of grace is to choose God for our God. This is the first article of the covenant, 'Thou shalt have no other gods but me.' What is it to choose God for our God? To give him the preeminence and uppermost place in the heart; to glorify him as God. God hath not the glory of a god unless we honour him thus. As a

prince hath not the honour of a prince if he be respected only as a common man; so if God have not the uppermost place in the heart, we do not glorify him as God.   Now God cannot have the uppermost place till his favour be valued above all things, and we stand in dread of breaking with God above all things; we have not till then consented to the articles of the covenant.   As long as we can break with God to preserve any worldly interest of ours, we prefer that interest before God; as when a man can be content to offend God rather than displease his parents: Mat. x. 37, ' He that loveth father or mother more than me is not worthy of me; and he that loveth son or daughter more than me is not worthy of me.'   So when to advance and prefer our children we displease God : 1 Sam. ii. 29, ' Thou honourest thy sons above me.'   Eli was the high priest and the magistrate, and he should put his sons by the priesthood when they were scandalous; but for the advancement and honour of his family, he continues them.   So when out of love to carnal pleasures we break with God, we love pleasure more than God : 2 Tim. iii. 4, 'Lovers of pleasures more than lovers of God ; ' when we can break a law to salve an interest, when willingly and with full consent we sin against God ; therefore it is impossible you can be gracious.

2. We can do nothing in the spiritual life till we take up such a resolution, and really be of such a disposition of heart.   We are often put to such a choice ; it is not a rare case, but such as falls out in every day's experience, whether we will choose sin or some inconvenience. Many times duty and danger come together, and they are offered to our choice ; if we discharge our conscience, it will be dangerous; but if not, there will be sin.   Sin and pleasure often come together, and the trial is whether you will renounce pleasure or satisfy your lust. Here I shall content myself, gratify my lust and interest, and there I shall offend my God.   Therefore Christ draws up the indenture, Mat. xvi. 24, 'If any man will come after me, let him deny himself and take up his cross, and follow me.'   It is in vain to put our hands to the plough, except we are resolved to go on whatever we meet with. There is sin, and pleasure, and profit; here is duty and affliction, poverty, meanness, and a low estate.   This often falls out; now which do you choose?

3. Such a disposition of heart is a necessary fruit of grace, for when God works grace, surely this will be wrought.   These three things are necessary to this: a clear understanding, a tender heart, and a zealous respect and love to God.   There cannot be grace but it must be so, and all these concur to this resolution.   Grace gives a clear understanding, that we may know the will of God and like it; and it gives a tender heart, to smite when we decline from it; and it gives a zealous love and a respect to God, so that we dare not offend him.   It gives a clear understanding, to judge in such cases; faith opens the eye of the soul ; it is a spiritual prudence, it is good at choosing, for it sees what is good and evil, and how much we are concerned in the choice.   Others may have higher speculations, but the good understanding is the fruit of grace: Ps. cxi. 10, ' A good understanding have all they that do his commandments.'   So the gracious man is the only wise man.   Faith is opposed to ignorance as well as folly.   Vint-

ners have more wine in their cellars than housekeepers, but it is for sale, not for use. Then grace gives a tender heart, therefore they dare not offend God, though to get never so much by it. Broken bones are very tender. So when the heart is broken and made tender by grace, it will startle at small sins. David's heart smote him for cutting off the lap of Saul's garment. And grace gives a zealous respect to God that will interpose when we are tempted to sin : Gen. xxxix. 9, 'How can I do this great wickedness, and sin against God?' A godly man will rather wrong himself a thousand times over, and hazard all his interest, than wrong the Lord. An honest man would not wrong a friend. God must not be offended whatever it cost; how can I break with my gracious God? Love is shown by a care to please and a fear to offend; when this is in the heart, it comes to this result and issue, that there is such a tender disposition in their souls that they will rather choose great inconveniences in the world than to sin in the least manner.

Use 1. First, it shows how evil they are that cannot deny themselves, even when their very sin proves an affliction to them, and an inconvenience. The children of God can choose affliction rather than sin, though they had comfort and profit by it. Now you have no profit and comfort by it, but your very sin is your affliction, and yet your hearts run out to it. Alas! to many it is meat and drink to commit sin; and though it be with loss to themselves, not only with loss of heaven, and exposing them to the wrath of God, but with temporal inconveniences; though they hazard life, health, credit, profit, trading by it. Thus will a sinner break through all restraints; not only when an angel stands in the way, but when afflictions stand in the way, still they break through, and are martyrs to their own lusts. Many times some are maimed by their uncleanness, others brought to rags by their drunkenness, riot, and voluptuousness. How often do you see sin's martyrs walk up and down the streets! It is comfortable for God's martyrs to be afflicted for a good conscience; but to bear the marks of sin, to be maimed by lust, to be brought to rags by riot, and voluptuous living, and negligence; this shows men's hearts are set upon their sins.

Use 2. Have we such a temper of soul as this is, as to choose the greatest affliction rather than the least sin? We may say so and judge so out of the temptation, but how is it upon the trial, when there is a worldly convenience, and a spiritual inconvenience? what do we when we are put upon the choice? A man is known by his choice. Many men are of a Gadarene spirit, they can part with Christ rather than their swine; part with peace of conscience and favour of God, and all their communion with God, rather than not give satisfaction to their lusts. They are of Esau's spirit, can sell the birthright for a mess of pottage, Heb. xii. 15. But now a child of God riseth up in indignation against such offers as these. Look, as when there was an offer made in Jotham's parable to the trees of the field to reign, saith the vine, 'Shall I leave my sweetness?' and the olive-tree, 'Shall I leave my fatness,' to rule over the trees? So doth the heart of a child of God rise up in indignation upon such a trial, Shall I hazard peace of conscience, the favour of God, and all communion with God, for a little temporal profit and temporal conveniences?

Therefore how is it upon the trial? Were you ever acquainted with self-denial in this case? or do you decline duty to avoid a danger? or do evil to get a little profit, and so yield upon that occasion? Are not you discouraged in the ways of God, or from the ways of God, because of inconveniences you have cheapened? but you will not go through with the price, you will not buy. Are you not turned out of the way because of reproach, and shame, and hatred of friends? and have you not often withdrawn from God, when the devil makes a proffer to you? Can you venture upon duty in the face of danger, and say, 'If I perish, I perish,' as Esther? How is it upon a trial? And if this be not sensible enough to give you farther light into your own heart, then let me ask you concerning some concomitant dispositions that will go along with this disposition.

(1.) If you be of such a temper as to choose the greatest affliction rather than the least sin, then it will be seen by this which is your greatest grief, sin or misery? what troubles you most, that you suffer loss in the world, or that you have displeased God? what pains and grieves you most, sin or affliction? Surely godly sorrow should come behind no sorrow: Zech. xii. 10, 'They shall look up to him whom they have pierced, and they shall mourn for him as one mourneth for his only son, and shall be in bitterness for him, as one is in bitterness for his first-born.' Therefore how is it with you? Many are complaining of poverty, of the toothache, the headache, and never complain of sin, and of the body of death. What puts you upon most bitter complaints? To be carnal is worse than to be miserable. To wallow in ease and pleasure is a more cursed estate than to suffer nakedness, cold, hunger, and thirst. I confess that sensitive sorrow is more violent in the expressions of it; as sorrow for the loss of a child or any outward comfort may be more violent in outward expressions, because nature and grace run in one channel; as the flood was mightily increased when the windows of heaven were opened from above, and the fountains of the great deep were broken up from below. A worldly loss may cause a more lively stirring of grief; but for a cordial hatred, real resistance, and deep trouble of heart, that will be more about sin and corruptions than about worldly losses. Look, as in another affection we laugh more at a trifle than we do when we receive solid benefit, the act of joy is more lively; so here, grief may be more sensibly stirred upon an outward loss; but serious and deep trouble of heart will be about corruption. Drawing of a tooth is more painful, and extorts greater roaring from us, than the decays of a consumption that are dangerous and deadly; yet this afflicts more inwardly, and begets a more deep, constant, lasting grief; so the children of God, above all evils they will bewail the evil of sin. If you be of such a temper to choose the greatest affliction rather than the least sin, you will be troubled more for sin than for affliction, and grieve because you can mourn no more for sin.

2. When you are afflicted, what do you desire most, to have affliction sanctified or removed? You will find it by your behaviour in such an estate: if you murmur under the affliction, and would fain have it gone, and be rid of the troublesome physic, but care not whether the affliction hath its due effect upon thee yea or no, then

surely you hate the affliction more than the sin.   Job was censured for this: Job xxxvi. 21, 'Take heed, regard not iniquity, for this hast thou chosen rather than affliction.'   When men are troubled more with what is painful and a damage to their interest, and smart to sense and feeling, than they are for what is offensive and contrary to God, and do not look to the working out of sin by their afflictions, they hate the affliction more than the sin.   The saints do not conceive prayers out of interest, but out of the new nature.   To be freed from the trouble and affliction is a common mercy, but to have the affliction sanctified is a special mercy; therefore they that have gracious hearts aim at this, to have it sanctified and improved.   Carnal men may be without affliction, but they cannot have the experience of grace. Therefore mere deliverance from affliction is no sign of special love; a child of God cannot be content with that, he would not only be delivered from the grave, but 'be loved from the grave,' as Hezekiah saith, Isa. xxxviii. 17.   Paul at first was all to have the thorn in the flesh gone.   The expression seems to import that it was some torture of the stone or gout, or racking pain in the body, and he would have it removed; but God tells him, 'My grace is sufficient for thee, for my strength is made perfect in weakness.'   What then?   'Most gladly therefore will I rather glory in my infirmities, that the power of Christ may rest upon me,' 2 Cor. xii. 7-9.   His heart seems to be contented with the experiences of grace, and he was glad of this trouble which had occasioned such sweet experience of God.   So 2 Tim. iv. 17, 18, 'I was delivered out of the mouth of the lion,' he hath delivered me, and taken me out of affliction.   'And the Lord shall deliver me from every evil work, and he will preserve me to his heavenly kingdom.' Paul pitcheth chiefly upon that, he is more solicitous in trouble to be freed from sin than from trouble.   Salvation is God's great work in us, to be kept safe to the heavenly kingdom, and to be fitted for heaven, and therefore our greatest design should be for that; so the main care be cared for, we need not care what becomes of us here.   In general, it is a mark of grace if we can with patience bear the evil of punishment that we may escape the evil of sin, which of all evils is the worst.

3. What is your care? to be great or good?   Which way doth your ambition run?   To excel in grace, or to grow great in the world? What would you ask of God if you were put to Solomon's choice? Wisdom or riches?   Or, in your daily prayers, what do you beg of God every day?   Lord, for outward things do with me what thou wilt, but keep me from sin, let me be anything rather than a sinful creature? As David, in Ps. cxli. 4, 'Incline not my heart to any evil thing, to practise wicked works with them that work iniquity, and let me not eat of their dainties.'   As if he should say, Ah, Lord! for dainties I do not desire to taste of them at such a rate, but keep me from sin.   Do you refer yourselves to God for other things, but are constant and earnest every morning to be kept from sin?   Good you would be, but you are content to be high or low, as God shall cast you.   No matter how mean you be, so you may enjoy his favour, peace of conscience, and live under the guidance of his Spirit.

4. What do you most watch against, strive against, and pray against? Sin or trouble?   A man is not to bring trouble upon himself; no, he

is to keep it off by lawful means. But what is your main care? that you may avoid trouble or sin? Is this your business, that you may not dishonour God in any condition? It is no matter what becomes of you else, so you may be obedient, you refer that to God.

5. How do you make use of Christ? to save you from trouble, sorrow, sickness, or from sin? The great thing Christ came to save us from was sin: Mat. i. 21, 'Thou shalt call his name Jesus, for he shall save his people from their sins.' Now how would you make use of him? to save you only from the evil after sin, or the evil of sin? A true broken heart is not only troubled for the guilt of sin, but for the power of it. They would not only be saved from hell and the horrors of a wounded conscience, but would be freed from the tyranny of sin; they would have sin subdued as well as pardoned, and not only be eased from the smart of it. Therefore the prophet admires God upon this account, both for the pardoning and subduing of sin: Micah vii. 18, 19, 'Who is a God like unto thee that pardoneth iniquity? . . . He will subdue our iniquities, and thou wilt cast all their sins into the depth of the sea.' They would fain be acquainted with mortification as well as pardon. A loose desire of happiness is but natural: John vi. 34, 'Lord, evermore give us this bread!' All would be happy.

6. What makes you most to desire heaven? afflictions or sins? A beast will forsake the place where it can find neither meat nor rest. And therefore to desire heaven only because it keeps off affliction and trouble, that may be but a natural act. Men usually make heaven a reserve and a retreat; when they are beaten out of the world, they then fly to heaven. But now when we are troubled, we are here in this world conflicting with and complaining of sin, while others are glorifying God above, freed from all sin; we groan for heaven not out of a burden of afflictions, but out of the longings of the new nature, we have had a taste of some beginnings of grace, and would fain have it perfected; this discovers a right temper of spirit: Rom. vii. 23, 'We which have the first-fruits of the Spirit groan within ourselves, waiting for the adoption—to wit, the redemption of our bodies;' when the corruptions we have here make us groan for heaven: Rom. vii. 24, 'O wretched man that I am! who shall deliver me from this body of death?'

SERMON LXI.

Esteeming the reproach of Christ greater riches than the treasures in Egypt: for he had respect unto the recompense of the reward.
—HEB. xi. 26.

IN the constellation of worthies represented in this chapter, Moses shineth forth as a star of the first magnitude, and his faith is commended to us for vanquishing all sorts of temptations. We are assaulted both on the right hand and on the left with the delights of sense and the terrors of sense; *per blanda et aspera*, by rough encounters, and by the softer

and more insinuating sort of temptations.   But terrors could not break
the constancy of his resolution for God, nor delights pervert him, and
detain him from God and his service.   Not terrors.   The account of
his withstanding left-hand temptations you have, ver. 27, ' By faith he
forsook Egypt, not fearing the wrath of the king.'   The wrath of
Pharaoh could not affright him from his duty.   Nor could delights
pervert him.   Now the right-hand temptations, which are of the
most pleasing sort, were not of one kind.   Moses' trial was a complicated trial ; all things that might gain upon the heart of man were
presented to him.   That which is wont to entice men from God is
either honours, pleasures, or riches.   Any of these singly is enough to
prevail with a heart disposed or biassed by a carnal inclination.   But
Moses was of another temper, he despised all these at once ; though
Satan thought to detain and withhold him from God by a threefold
cord, yet it was too weak to hold him.   Solomon tells us, Eccles. iv. 12,
' A threefold cord is not easily broken.'   Yet still by faith he broke
through ; this threefold cord was too weak to hold him from his duty.
We are told, in 1 John ii. 16, ' All that is in the world is either the
lusts of the flesh, the lusts of the eyes, or the pride of life.'   A world
of temptation was let loose upon Moses at once.   If honour would move
him, he was adopted and taken to be the son of Pharaoh's daughter ;
but he would not nibble at that bait, ver. 24.   If pleasure would have
moved him, he might have enjoyed the height and cream of it in
Pharaoh's court ; whereas, in the course he took he could expect
nothing but afflictions and tedious labours ; but yet this would not do
either—' He chose rather to suffer affliction with the people of God,
than to enjoy the pleasures of sin for a season,' ver. 25.   The third
worldly interest was riches, and how he overcame this temptation is in
this 26th ver.—' Esteeming the reproach of Christ greater riches than
the treasures of Egypt.'

In which words observe—

1. The effect of his faith—*He esteemed the reproach of Christ
greater riches than the treasures of Egypt.*

2. The ground of it—*For he had respect unto the recompense of reward.*

First, Let us begin with the effect and fruit of his faith ; that is set
down comparatively.   Where take notice (1.) Of the things compared ;
(2.) The esteem and preference of the one above the other.

1. The things compared are ' the reproach of Christ, and the treasures of Egypt.'   The latter needs no explication, for Egypt was known
to be a fruitful and an opulent kingdom, and Moses might have had a
large share of the riches of it in Pharaoh's court, being adopted to be
his daughter's son ; these are the treasures of Egypt.   Only the other
branch, ' the reproach of Christ,' needs a little opening.   How could
Moses delight in the reproach of Christ, who was not now in being, I
mean as to the flesh ?   Let me open that a little.   The word ' reproach ' is not taken here for reproach in word, but in deed ; not for
reviling, but for oppression, poverty, bondage, persecutions ; the people
believing in the Messiah were most reproachfully afflicted and
oppressed in Egypt, that is the meaning of the word reproach.   But
how was this ' the reproach of Christ ? '   It must be so called either—

[1.] Because it was such another thing as the reproach of Christ, or somewhat like the shameful suffering which he afterwards endured; or else—

[2.] Because it was a type of Christ's reproach; or—

[3.] Because Christ was the occasion of it, and it was endured for his sake; or else—

[4.] It must be for this reason, because Christ had relation to that people, and communion with them as their head; for he was always head of the church, whether of Jews or Gentiles. Now let us see which of these reasons is to be preferred.

1. The first cannot be said that it is called the reproach of Christ, because it was like the shameful death Christ endured. It is not the manner of scripture to express things by the name of everything they are like unto; then why not the reproach of David, Isaiah, or some other of the prophets, or the reproach of Paul himself, as well as the reproach of Christ, if there were no more special reason for it but only the likeness? The indignities they suffered in Egypt were as like the sufferings of Paul or Isaiah, as the sufferings of Christ.

2. Nor is it as if this reproach were a type of Christ's sufferings; for the type is not called by the name of the antitype; that cannot well be. The brazen serpent is not called Christ, nor manna Christ, nor Samson Christ, nor David Christ. Indeed the antitype may be called by the name of the type; Christ may be called the brazen serpent, and David, and the propitiation, and the sacrifice, to show the accommodation of those things to him. The antitype, the substance, may take the name of the type; but it is no way convenient to imagine that the type should have the name of the antitype and substance.

3. Neither was it for Christ's sake, or for their faith in the Messiah, that the Egyptians thus disgracefully oppressed the Israelites; for neither did the Israelites incur those afflictions for Christ's sake, nor did the Egyptians inflict them upon that account. There was no thought of any such matter on the one side nor on the other. That that moved them to oppress Israel was their envy at their increasing multitude, as you may see, Exod. i. 9, 10. And therefore they cannot be called the reproaches of Christ, as if they were endured for his sake.

4. Well then, nothing remains but the last reason, that they are the reproaches of Christ, because Christ then had communion with that people, though he were not yet born according to the flesh. And so the phrase teacheth us a double truth.

1. That Christ had a being before he was born of the virgin. He tells us so, John viii. 58, 'Before Abraham was I am.' And we read of tempting of Christ in the wilderness: 1 Cor. x. 9, 'Neither let us tempt Christ, as some of them also tempted him.' Christ was perpetual head of the Church, and in his own person did lead his people, and was present in the midst of them under the notion of the angel of the covenant: Exod. xxiii. 20-22, 'Behold I send an angel before thee, to keep thee in the way, and to bring thee into the place which I have prepared: beware of him, and obey his voice; provoke him not, for he will not pardon your transgressions, for my name is in him. For mine angel shall go before thee, and bring thee in unto the Amorites,' &c.

This angel can be no other than Christ; it is his office to keep us in the way, and to bring us into the place which God hath prepared for us; it is he that must be obeyed by the people of God; it is he that must pardon our transgressions; upon him is God's name, for he will not give his glory to another, nor communicate his name to any other that is not of the same substance with himself. Well then, whatever this people suffered, it was the reproach of Christ, who had taken them into his protection. As their tempting of God was a tempting of Christ, who led them in the wilderness, so their sufferings was the reproach of Christ.

2. It informs us also of this truth, that there is a communion between Christ and his people. The reproach that lighteth upon the members reflecteth upon the head: Isa. lxiii. 9, 'In all their afflictions he was afflicted, and the angel of his presence saved them.' Look to the context, and you shall see he plainly alludes to the angel of the covenant that he spake of before. So Zech. ii. 8, 'He that toucheth you toucheth the apple of his eye;' what is done to them, is done to him, either by way of injury or courtesy. So Mat. xxv. 34, 'Inasmuch as ye have done it unto one of the least of these my brethren, ye have done it unto me;' and Acts ix. 4, 'Saul, Saul, why persecutest thou me?' And to come closer to the notion of the text: 2 Cor. i. 5, 'As the sufferings of Christ abound in us, so our consolation also aboundeth by Christ.' All that we endure are called the sufferings of Christ. Nay, nearer yet, it is called Christ's reproach: Heb. xiii. 13, 'Let us go forth therefore unto him without the camp, bearing his reproach.' Well, the meaning is this—Moses yielded to be contemned with the people of God, out of faith in the Messiah to come. All the Israelites were an abomination to the Egyptians, Gen. xlvi. 34, and they handled them ignominiously; yet Moses counted them the people of God, and the people of Christ, and therefore he chose to profess himself to be one of them, and he esteemed the reproach of Christ above all the treasures of Egypt. Thus I have opened the things that are compared.

2. The preference of the one above the other—'He esteemed the reproach of Christ greater riches than the treasures of Egypt;' that is a far more desirable thing than all the wealth and power of that country. Mark, it is not said only he was willing to bear his share in their reproach; no, but he esteemed it, and esteemed it as riches and treasures; that is more emphatical.

Secondly, His ground for all this, what was that which induced him so to esteem this ignominious people of God before his honour in the court?—'For he had respect unto the recompense of reward.' There observe the thing, and his respect to it.

1. The thing itself, and what it was that did cast the balance. A blessed eternity that he had in his eye, called 'the recompense of reward,' that was that he looked to. By the reward we must understand the great and final reward of eternal glory, which is given by God, and received and enjoyed by us as a compensation for all our sufferings.

2. His regard of it—'He had respect unto the recompense.' The word is ἀπέβλεπε. Look, as ἐπέβλεπε is to look towards a thing; so ἀπέβλεπε is to look off from one thing to another; it signifies a removal of the eye from one object to behold another. Apply this now

to the eye of the mind, and the sense is, he turned his mind and heart from the treasures, honours, and pleasures of Egypt, and fixed them upon the rewards of godliness, or the honours, riches, and pleasures of heaven. The word seems to be best explained by the apostle, 2 Cor. iv. 18, 'While we look not at the things which are seen, but at the things which are not seen;' there is the taking off the eye from things temporal, and fixing it on things that are eternal; shutting the eye of sense, and opening that of faith. If we did look oftener from that which is present to that which is to come, we should be much wiser than we are. In short, he knew his reproach would be recompensed with exceeding great glory and happiness, which God hath promised to all afflicted believers. Therefore turning off his eye from what was before him to that which was to come, the temptation took no hold of him.

Doct. We are not right christians till we have such an esteem of Christ, that the worst things which can befall us in his service should be more to us than the best things of the world.

This was done by Moses, as the text shows; and this was done also by the apostle Paul: Phil. iii. 8, 'Yea doubtless, and I count all things but loss for the excellency of the knowledge of Christ Jesus my Lord: for whom I have suffered the loss of all things, and do count them but dung that I may win Christ.' Paul might have made his market with the Pharisees, by whom he was highly esteemed, and intrusted with a commission to persecute the church of God; but when once the light of the gospel shined into his heart, then all his Jewish honours and prerogatives were loss and dross in comparison of his gain by Christ; and when he had leisure to review what he had done, he repented not of his bargain—'I have counted,' yea, and 'I do account' these things loss for Christ. All things compared with Christ, or set in opposition to Christ, were base and vile in his eyes; so base that a word bad enough could not be found to express his indignation and contempt of them, therefore he calls it σκίβυλα, we express it dung; it is a thing fit to be thrown to the dogs, that they might not be a snare to him.

Here, that you may be possessed of the true spirit of christianity—

1. I shall a little open the nature of our esteem of Christ.

2. I shall show why Christ must be thus esteemed, that the worst things that can happen in our case should be more to us than the best things of the world.

First, How Christ must be esteemed; not only speculatively, but practically.

1. Speculatively. A man may be easily persuaded that God is the chiefest good, that his favour is our only happiness, and the fruition of him our ultimate blessedness, that there is no enjoyment of him but by Christ, and that upon this account Christ should be dear and precious to us. A man may be easily persuaded of all this, but all that see the truth do not presently embrace it, and carry themselves accordingly. We often approve in our judgments those things which we do not follow in our practice: Rom. ii. 18, 'Thou knowest his will, and approvest the things that are excellent;' and yet they had no mind to embrace them, for he tells us there, they had but μόρφωσιν τῆς

γνώσεως, a cold form of knowledge. A man is not constituted good by his opinions, but by his affections. The opinions of many carnal men are right, but their affections incline them to other things; and therefore this is not enough to have a speculative esteem or a bare approbation.

2. Practically.

[1.] God must be owned as our felicity, not only by the esteem of our judgments, but the choice of our wills, and a thorough resolution to seek him above all as our only hope and happiness. Therefore it is not enough to think that surely this is a truth that the favour of God is better than life, that all the world cannot countervail the loss of it; but we must resolve so to live that we may seek after the favour of God in Christ whatever it cost us, and determine with ourselves, and bind it upon our hearts: Ps. lxxiii. 28, 'It is good for me to draw near to God.' This must be my care and my business, or I am undone for ever. We must choose the better part as well as approve of it. Mary is commended for that: Luke x. 42, 'Mary hath chosen that good part, which shall not be taken away from her.'

[2.] Not only must this esteem be seen in our resolution, or in the choice of our wills, but in our practice, and the constant and uniform business of our lives and actions; we must show that we prefer Christ above other things. Our esteem must be verified and made good in two cases: in actual trials, and in the constant course of our lives.

(1.) In actual trials, when we are put to the proof of it, which we esteem most. We must be prepared to lose all for Christ; that is common to all christians, to be martyrs in preparation of heart; but when we are actually called thereunto, we must not shift and wriggle, and distinguish ourselves out of our duty, but plainly let go all rather than be unfaithful to Christ. Paul, in that place quoted but now, Phil. iii. 8, he doth not only say, ἡγοῦμαι πάντα ζημίαν, 'I count all but loss,' but τὰ πάντα ἐζημιώθην, 'I have suffered the loss of all things.' He proves the sincerity of his purpose and esteem by his actual self-denial. He had lost the favour of his friends, his honour in his country, and all things which might be dear to him in the flesh, that he might become a christian. He did not only account all things nothing worth, and to be despised for Christ, and profess that he should take it contentedly if he were stripped of all for his sake—such expressions might seem only brags when temptation is at a distance; no, but he really suffered the loss of all, and was hungry, naked, scourged, imprisoned, and went often in danger of life, and at length actually laid it down; he quitted his honour and credit with his countrymen, and great acquaintance among the Pharisees, who before had a high esteem of him. So Moses here actually refused the pleasures, honours, and profits of the world—the honours which so many greedily catch at, and the pleasures which secretly enchant the hearts of men, and entice them from God, and cause them to neglect God and forget their souls; and the treasures of the earth, which worldly men so much affect, were no other but trash and dung to him, compared with the reproach of Christ. Thus must all do when God comes to try us; not only make liberal offers to God, when we hope he will not take us at our word, or because there is no visible danger, or probability that our resignation will cost us anything, as men will make a liberal offer to a friend to do him a courtesy when they think he will not take it; no, but we must carry all our temporal felicity in our hands, as ready to give it up whenever God demands it; when the Lord in his providence calls us to disgraceful sufferings, we must willingly undergo them.

2. In the whole drift and tenor of our lives we must act as those that live by this principle. Our chief endeavour must be to get and keep in with Christ: Matt. vi. 33, ' Seek ye first the kingdom of God, and the righteousness thereof.' The strength of our souls, and the vigour of our endeavours must run in this channel. A dull approbation of that which is good will serve no man—no, not in the most prosperous times of religion; but more or less he must manifest his esteem of Christ and contempt of the world by some act of self-denial, for none can be true to his duty but he will meet with trouble in the flesh. Some of his interests must be sacrificed for Christ's sake, either his reputation, and ease, and peace with the world, or the opposition and scorn of dear friends and relations, and the scorn of our old acquaintance; at least his religion, if it be serious, will put him upon some expense and cost, if not upon uncompliance with the vain fashions of the world, yet upon duties unpleasing to the flesh, and which bring their own charge with them. And it may be we shall be laughed at for these things, but the reproach of Christ is greater riches than the treasures of Egypt. This must be our constant dominating principle that must govern and regulate our lives, that everything relating to Christ recommends itself to us, how unpleasing soever it be to ourselves or others.

Secondly, Why we ought to have such an esteem of Christ. I shall give the reasons in these considerations.

1. Christians can never be safe till they do esteem what they choose. The reason is, because there are many competitors for our hearts. Now, as estimation is the ground of our choice, so it is also the strength of it, and therefore we can never be faithful to Christ till he be valued above all that cometh in competition with him, or is set in opposition against him. As the actual estimation of our judgment swayed our choice at first, so the habitual estimation preserves it, that those things which rival Christ in our hearts may have no entertainment there to his wrong and prejudice. At first we renounced all secular advantages that we might have Christ and his benefits, and if we continue of the same mind we are safe: Heb. iii. 6, ' Whose house are we, if we hold fast the confidence and the rejoicing of the hope firm unto the end.' Oh, we were exceedingly glad, and blessed ourselves in the hopes we have by Christ, when first we were acquainted with him! Are you of the same mind still? 1 Peter i. 7, ' To you that believe he is precious.' They know his worth and value, and believe it, and count it of infinite advantage to themselves, and they cannot be drawn from him: Ps. lxxiii. 25, ' Whom have I in heaven but thee? and there is none on earth I desire besides thee.' But when once you begin to lose your esteem of Christ, and he is not so dear as before, you are backsliders in heart, and shall soon prove so in practice. Our love is gone, and a

man is held better by his heart than his head, by his love than by his
opinions. If any worldly thing is nearer and dearer to us than Christ,
the heart is tainted, and you are prepared for a revolt from him.

2. He that will not err in esteeming, choosing, and cleaving to
Christ, needs three things; a clear understanding, an unbiassed will,
and a serious consideration of matters propounded to our choice and
esteem.

[1.] A clear understanding; for if the mind be blind, how is it able
to judge between things that differ? John iv. 10, 'If thou knewest
the gift of God,' &c.; if Christ were rightly known he would be more
prized, and they would see such an excellency in him as cannot be
countervailed. I remember it is said, John vi. 40, 'He that seeth the
Son, and believeth on him,' &c.; all believing comes from seeing the
Son. If we did but see the Son, and had a true knowledge of his
worth and excellency, we would venture all for his sake, and would
entirely trust ourselves in his hands. So Paul, 2 Tim. i. 12, 'I know
whom I have believed, and I am persuaded that he is able to keep that
which I have committed unto him against that day.'

2. An unbiassed will. For the bias of the will will easily prevail
against the light of the understanding. We need not only a mind to
know God, but a heart to know God and Christ: Jer. xxiv. 7, 'And
I will give them a heart to know me.' That is, to acknowledge, to
esteem, to choose me for their God, and for their portion and happiness. This is a work of the heart, and depends upon a right disposition of the heart rather than the mind. The right disposition of the
will is God's great covenant gift.

3. A serious consideration of the object propounded to choice; for
otherwise, through inadvertency, the poorest paltry vanities may be
preferred before the most excellent things in the world. Men do not
consider, they do not weigh things: Eccles. v. 1, 'They consider not that
they do evil.' They consider not 'there is a lie in their right hand,'
Isa. xliv. 19, 20. Therefore, to make a right choice, we should beg of
God to be free from a blind, injudicious mind, from a depraved heart,
and from a slight and frothy spirit, that we may judge, resolve, and
choose what is best for our souls, and weigh all things in a true and
impartial balance.

3. That there can be no due or right consideration without a comparison, and giving everything its due weight. For so the apostle
represents Moses; on the one side he considers what he was to quit—
'the treasures of Egypt;' on the other side, what he was to incur and
run the hazard of—'the reproach of Christ,' disgraceful sufferings;
and to flesh and blood reproach is more than pain. Therefore he
compared these things together. The treasures of Egypt were great,
but of a finite value, and there is an infinite recompense of reward
which God had set before him. The reproach of Christ was bitter,
but it was the way to glory. Man has a power thus to compare things,
and traverse them in his mind: Isa. xlvi. 8, 'Remember this, and
show yourselves men; bring it again to mind, O ye transgressors.'
Consider well of it, and do not rush on like brute beasts. Everything
must be brought to the balance of the sanctuary; we have no way else

to clear our mistakes, and prevent the delusions of the flesh, than by serious comparing of things and things.

4. Because the comparison lies between things present and things to come, faith must guide us, that sense may not mislead us; for all this is made the fruit of his faith. Moses looks off from the world to the recompense of reward. The treasures of Egypt were before his eyes, but he removes his mind to another object, the joys and glory of heaven. Things of sense are known easily, and known by all, but things of faith are only known by them who are enlightened by the Holy Spirit. Present things are comfortable to our sense, but they are nothing to what faith propounds; and therefore we must look upon these things through the spectacles of faith. Earthly treasures, compared with the treasures of heaven, will appear no more than trash and dung, if we had but this enlightened mind to apprehend the worth and certainty of these heavenly things. Therefore, all your care must be that these things may be clearly seen and much eyed, that the Spirit may first open the eyes of our minds, and then keep them open, Eph. i. 18. That we often think of the hope of Christ's calling, for this is that which strikes all temptations of sense dead. Three things are here.

[1.] We must be persuaded that all disgraceful sufferings for Christ shall have their recompense: Mat. v. 12, 'Rejoice and be exceeding glad, for great is your reward in heaven.' There is a reward, and a reward due by covenant, to all such as are faithful to God, and shall in time be given to them; but not of merit, but of grace; our sufferings do not merit the reward, but qualify us for the enjoyment of it, and give us a title by virtue of God's promise, upon the account of Christ. Surely God is so good that we can be no losers by him; he will not suffer anything to be done or suffered for his sake without a recompense.

[2.] As there is a reward, so it is so great that all the treasures of the world cannot purchase it, nor parallel it, and therefore it is a folly to part with it for trifles. There is a double μισθαποδοσία, a double recompense, *poenæ et præmii*, the recompense of punishment, and the recompense of reward. Both may be considered; wealth and greatness, with the neglect of God and his children, and interest in the world, is punished with the flames of hell; but affliction and reproach for Christ is rewarded with heaven and bliss. The recompense of punishment is to be made use of when the temptation hath invaded us; when the heart begins to run into the snare, then we must make use of that part of the Spirit's discipline. Ay, but at other times, when we are not in such great danger of miscarrying, here we must think of the recompense of reward, of the great blessings Christ hath provided, the heavenly bliss he hath provided for his people. Now, there is no comparison between the things that are of this world and this blessedness: Rom. viii. 18, 'I reckon that the sufferings of this present time are not worthy to be compared with the glory that shall be revealed in us;' 2 Cor. iv. 17, 'This light affliction, that is but for a moment, worketh for us a far more exceeding and eternal weight of glory.'

[3.] That the intention of the mind should be much taken up about it. A glance does little affect; the greatest truths work not if we do not think of them. Moses, he had respect, ἀπέβλεπε, he took off his eye from these things, and fixed it seriously on those things; so a christian must measure all things by his scope: 2 Cor. iv. 18, 'While we look not to the things which are seen, but to the things which are not seen,' &c. Nothing draws our esteem, and fixes our choice so much as a serious respect to eternal things. Well then, these heavenly things must be respected, that they may cast the balance of our choice. If we certainly believe, and earnestly look for this recompense of reward, we shall better resolve for God against all present temptations; for the heart in heaven is the christian's preservation; if it be much there, all temptations lose their force.

Obj. There lies one little scruple against this. But is not this mercenary, and want of love to God, to be swayed by the reward? I answer, No. Hypocrisy and unsoundness lies not in aiming at a reward in general, but in subordinating religion to a temporary reward, as they 'followed Christ for the loaves,' John vi. 26. But as to the eternal reward, God's glory and our eternal happiness are so linked together, that the belief and expectation of the reward doth no way abate of our love to God in Christ; no, rather, it is an act of love, for because we love him, we desire to enjoy him at any rate, to see him and be like to him; and this enjoyment is nothing but the exercise of a more perfect reception of his benefits, or the fruits of his love to us.

5. The comparison is rightly stated when the world's best and Christ's worst are brought into competition or consideration; as here 'the reproach of Christ' and 'the treasures of Egypt;' even that which you abhor in a christian's case, that which you account his misery. And the worst of Christ is better than a worldly man's condition, and better than all that for which they lose their souls. If the reproach of Christ be better than all the treasures that are so highly esteemed in the world; if to be scorned for Christ is better than to have the world at will, this strikes temptations to the heart. And as Moses, so Paul doth thus, Phil. iii. 10, compared with ver. 8, 'I count all things but loss and dung for the excellency of the knowledge of Christ Jesus my Lord,' &c. 'That I might know him, and the power of his resurrection, and the fellowship of his sufferings, being made conformable unto his death.' What is the fellowship of his sufferings and conformity to his death? The meaning is, that I may be disgracefully handled for Christ, as Christ was for me and my salvation. I count this to be such excellency as all else is but dung and dross. To clear this to you there are five ways of comparison which a christian should use.

[1.] Comparing temporal good things and eternal good things, the good and the good, as the portion of a carnal man, and the happiness of a child of God. This way of comparison is used in Ps. xvii. 14, 15. The men of this world they have their portion, and what good doth it do them? Their bellies are well filled, their backs well clothed, they have heritages which they leave to their children after them, that they may live a life of pomp and ease in the world. Now when the christian is set upon his duty, to enjoy communion with God, it will check the temptation—'But as for me, I shall behold thy face in righteousness. When I awake, that is, out of the sleep of death, I shall be satisfied with thy likeness.' That vision will make way for fruition, and that fruition for an exact likeness to God. Or, suppose when sensual delights are compared with those pleasures that we have at God's right hand for evermore; the poor dreggy pleasures, which enchant men's souls, and lull them asleep, are compared with those chaste satisfactions and holy delights that we shall have for ever with God: Ps. xvi. 11, 'In thy presence is fulness of joy; at thy right hand there are pleasures for evermore.' So when vainglory is compared with eternal glory: John v. 44, 'How can you believe, that receive honour one of another, and seek not the honour that cometh from God only?' Is not God's glory better than a little vainglory? And so compare temporal deliverance with our final escape: Heb. xi. 35, 'Not accepting deliverance, that they might obtain a better resurrection.' They refused deliverance upon man's terms. They were stretched out like a drum, but these bodies shall rise again.

[2.] Another way of comparison is when temporal evil things are compared with eternal evil things; as suppose killing the body with the casting of body and soul into hell fire, Luke xii. 4, 5. We read in the story concerning Biblis, a woman that revolted from the faith for fear of burning, when she saw the fire kindled upon her fellow-martyr, the historian tells us, that she thought of the eternal fire, and then repented of her apostasy, and was burnt together with her fellow. So if we compare a prison with hell, or compare the wrath of man with the wrath of God, or compare shame and scorn in the world now with the confusion of face that shall be at the last day.

[3.] Compare temporal good with eternal evil. As suppose men do pretty well with their worldly portion; ay, but what will become of them for ever? Job xxvii. 8, 'What is the hope of the hypocrite, though he hath gained, when God taketh away his soul?' Put the supposition, every hypocrite doth not make a thriving bargain in the world; ay, but what if he hath gained, what will it avail him when he hath forfeited his soul into the hands of God's justice? He is loth to let it go, but God comes and takes it away: Mat. xvi. 26, 'What shall it profit a man, if he shall gain the whole world, and lose his own soul? or what shall a man give in exchange for his soul?' The merry life of worldlings, if it be compared with endless torment, alas! it will be no temptation to us; or if we compare the pleasure of sin for a season with the pains and torments of the soul which are for ever; when we see the hook in the bait, we shall not be so willing to catch at it.

[4.] There is another way of comparison in scripture; compare temporal bad things with eternal good things. This is the case here in the text, 'the reproach of Christ,' and 'the recompense of reward.' And so in many other places: Heb. x. 34, 'Ye took joyfully the spoiling of your goods, knowing in yourselves that ye have in heaven a better and an enduring substance.' They were brought before tribunals and exposed to outrage; now he compares their loss with their gain; their goods were spoiled by envious neighbours, but they had an enduring substance: 2 Cor. iv. 17, 'For this light affliction, that is but for a moment, worketh for us a far more exceeding and eternal weight of glory.' There is the temporal evil compared with the eternal good. Afflictions here are *breves et leves*, short and light afflictions, but there is an eternity of blessedness and a weight of glory.

[5.] Another way of comparison is by comparing the evils of chris-tianity in the present state, and the happiness of worldly men in the present state. This is the full case in the text, ' He counted the re-proach of Christ greater riches than the treasures of Egypt.' Take them with their adjuncts and concomitants ; take the world's best now, and a christian's worst now. The world's best, it is but a sorry por-tion, it lies in treasures, pleasures, and honours. Now all these Moses might have enjoyed, which were vast and magnificent to a carnal heart, but it was accompanied with sin ; it was πρόσκαιρος ἀπόλαυσις ἁμαρτίας, the pleasures of sin for a season ; for though it be spoken but of one thing, of pleasures, yet it must be referred to every one of the temptations, to honours and treasures as well as to pleasures ; here is a worlding's best. Now, where a man lives in sin, he can never have any solid pleasure in what he enjoys, for no complacency can be sincere where God is angry, and the soul is in danger of his wrath every moment ; it is ill dancing about the brink of hell ; here is all the pleasures, treasures, honours of worldly men. But on the other side, take a christian's worst, ' the reproach of Christ,' take it as it is now abstracted from ' the recompense of reward.'

(1.) It hath a relation to Christ. Now everything is sweetened and made honourable to us by its relation to Christ. It is sweetened by our love to him. If we love Christ, his work will be sweet to us ; and it is made honourable because Christ is ' the Lord of glory,' James ii. 1, he is the proper fountain of honour. If there were no more in it but its relation to Christ, it were honourable. When the apostles were whipped, and scourged, and disgraced for Christ's sake, they looked upon it as their honour: Acts v. 41, ' They departed from the presence of the council, rejoicing that they were counted worthy to suffer shame for his name.' Disgrace for Christ's sake is an honour. Thuanus tells us of a French nobleman that was condemned to die with other protestants, and because of the dignity of his birth he was not bound as they were, and that he called to the executioner, *Cur non et me quoque torque donas ?* &c. ; give me my chain and rope too, and make me a knight of this excellent order. I bring it for this, to show that those which love Christ, and are possessed of Christ, every-thing that relates to Christ is honourable to them ; so that if the godly might have their choice, they had rather be miserable with the people of God, than happy with his enemies.

(2.) Take the other concomitant that goes along with ' the reproach of Christ,' viz., the strong supports and consolations of the Holy Spirit: 2 Cor. xii. 10, ' I will take pleasure in infirmities, in reproaches, in necessities, in persecutions, in distresses for Christ's sake ; for when I am weak, then am I strong.' Nay, I will rejoice in the worst of Christ, because of the mighty supports of the Spirit ; there is a more liberal allowance of the supports and comforts of the Holy Ghost given to God's afflicted people than to others, or given to them then more than at other times ; they have rich consolation in their afflic-tions. The Lord proportions comfort to their troubles, that as the affliction doth abound, so doth the comfort: 2 Cor. i. 5, ' For as the sufferings of Christ abound in us, so our consolation also aboundeth by Christ.' God's wrestlers, when called to conflict, he anoints them with this holy oil of the Spirit : 1 Peter iv. 14, 'If ye be reproached for the name of Christ, happy are ye, for the Spirit of glory and of God resteth upon you.' Though eternity, and the great reward, puts all out of question, yet this is not to be overlooked.

Use. To persuade us to get this temper of soul, to prefer Christ's worst before the world's best.

First argument. It is absolutely necessary ; you cannot be christians without it, for it immediately flows from the three· essential or fundamental graces which constitute the new creature, which are faith, hope, and love.

1. Faith, which believes the promises of the new covenant, and consents to seek after the benefits offered in them, how dear soever they cost us, and takes this blessedness for its whole felicity, Mat. xiii. 45, 46, and Heb. x. 39. There is in faith assent and consent. The assent that is in faith calls for it, for if we believe the great things God hath promised, it necessarily lessens all other things in our opinion and estimation of them, and affection to them. Faith is like a perspective, that greatens things at a distance, and lessens things near at hand ; so faith greatens heavenly things, and lessens worldly things ; so that riches and honours, and all worldly things, seem vile and base so far as they divert us from better things. Some value we should have for natural comforts in our pilgrimage, they are the gift of God, but take heed lest they be a snare ; we cannot be thankful for them if we have not some esteem for them, nor humbled at afflictions, when God takes them away ; but they are lessened so as they are base in comparison of those other things. Then the consent of faith much more inferreth it. The consent of faith is nothing but a subscription to Christ's terms, selling all for the pearl of price : Mat. xiii. 45, ' He sold all that he had, and bought it.' This is the disposition of a disciple of Christ, to part with all rather than his happiness : Heb. x. 39, ' He believes to the saving of the soul.' Mark, believing is all for saving the soul ; sense is all for saving the flesh. The word signifies saving the soul with the loss of other things ; we must purchase the salvation of our souls at the dearest rate that may be. Now if we be believers, we have this disposition.

2. Our love shows it, for our love to Christ must be transcendent and superlative, not a bare love, but a love above our love to other things : Mat. x. 32, ' He that loveth father or mother more than me, is not worthy of me ; and he that loveth son or daughter more than me, is not worthy of me.' He that loves every base thing, the dirt in the streets, more than you, cannot be said to love you. So to pretend love to Christ, if we do not love him above all other things, is not rightly to love him : Luke xiv. 26, ' If any man come to me, and hate not his father, and mother, and wife, and children, and brethren, and sisters, yea, and his own life also, he cannot be my disciple.' He can in some sense trample upon the comfort that results from all his natural relations, and he that hates them not in that sense cannot be my disciple. I rather speak upon this point because love to God is the heart of the new creature, as self-love is the heart of original sin ; that inclines us to love, prize, and esteem the things of God ; inordinate self-love makes us love the flesh more than our souls. Now if

you have the true love of Christ, you will hate all other things in comparison of him and faithfulness to him. Our love to Christ is but a transcript of his love to us, for unless our religion make a due impression upon us, we were never acquainted with the power of it. Now Christ was satisfied to be anything for our sakes, and he was made sin, he was made a curse for us; he pleased not himself that he might promote the glory of God and our salvation; when he thought of all the shame and bitter agonies our redemption would cost him, he was satisfied: Isa. liii. 11, 'He shall see of the travail of his soul, and shall be satisfied.' When he had from all eternity leisure enough to cast up his accounts, what it would cost him to save souls, to redeem sinners, yet he earnestly longed for it: Luke xii. 50, 'I have a baptism to be baptized with, and how am I straitened till it be accomplished!' Now how can we manifest our love and thankfulness to him for these disgraceful sufferings and bitter agonies, by which he procured the pardon of our sins and eternal life, if we cannot deny our pleasures, and the contentments of the flesh in the way of our duty?

3. The next necessary grace is hope, which is a certain and desirous expectation of the promised blessedness. Therefore our hearts should so fix upon this blessedness, that we may not be diverted from it, either by the comfortable or troublesome things we meet with in the world. Either these things are greater than those we expect, or they are not: if they are greater, why do we so desiringly expect other things as our happiness? Let us sit down with these things; if they be not, surely in reason we should be at some cost for our supreme happiness; if you take the joys of heaven for your whole portion, all your worldly prosperity must give way to it. Can you desirously expect this as your treasure, when you will not venture anything for it? Therefore if we had hopes of living with God, this would set us a-work for heaven, whatever we endured, and whatever it cost us here in the way. But when there is a secret reserve to save the world or spare the flesh, your hopes are not placed in heaven; the expectation is neither certain nor desirous. Not certain enough, for you find the calamity or trouble in the flesh certain, but you are not persuaded that the felicity you expect is so certain, and therefore it is so irksome to let go your hold of present things for what is future, and in your opinion uncertain. Nor is it desirous enough, for if you had such an earnest desire of glory to come, you would look after your bodily welfare no farther than would stand with your great hopes. And so, though you have some sentiments of future happiness, you are not very earnest to enjoy it, for you would not have it cost too dear a rate. No; if you did trust in the living God, you would both labour, and suffer reproach: 1 Tim. iv. 10, 'For therefore we both labour and suffer reproach, because we trust in the living God.' Divine hope sets men at work for heaven, and their souls, and Jesus Christ; but carnal hope for the devil, the world, and the flesh; to reconcile both is lost labour.

Second argument. We cannot manifest our fidelity to Christ unless we be of this disposition; much of his service is painful, and cross to the inclinations of the flesh, and the world dislikes many of his ways so that our fidelity to Christ will lay us open to the disgrace and reproach of the world.   Now then, unless we mean to be false and partial hypocrites, and to cull out the easy, cheap, and safe part of christianity, and neglect the rest, we must not only submit to and be content with what befalls us in his ways, but be glad and rejoice that we have occasion of evidencing our sincerity: Mat: v. 11, 12, 'Blessed are ye, when men shall revile you, and persecute you, and say all manner of evil against you falsely for my sake.   Rejoice, and be exceeding glad; for great is your reward in heaven.'   We lie more fair for the promise when it is thus with us; for it is said that the very reproach and affliction helpeth it on: 2 Cor. iv. 17, 'For this light affliction, that is but for a moment, worketh for us a far more exceeding and eternal weight of glory;' as it mortifieth us to the false happiness, and increaseth the evidence of our right to the true happiness: 2 Tim. ii. 11, 12, 'It is a faithful saying, for if we be dead with him, we shall also live with him.   If we suffer, we shall also reign with him.'

Third argument.   This is of good use to us, to abate our eagerness after worldly prosperity, which is a weight at our heels, and the great impediment of our obedience: 1 John v. 4, 'This is the victory whereby we overcome the world, even our faith.'   When we are not only indifferent to worldly things, but count that we have felicity enough if we may approve ourselves to Christ in the meanest condition.

Well then, from the whole learn—

1. Whatever is a means to our great end should be made lovely to us upon that account, if it conduceth to the great recompense of reward.

2. That whatever relateth to Christ should be prized by us, the cross as well as the crown, and our painful sufferings as well as our felicity.

SERMON LXII.

Through faith he kept the passover, and the sprinkling of blood, lest he that destroyed the first-born should touch them.—Heb. xi. 28.

In this chapter you have a catalogue of God's worthies.   Now in this great constellation of saints Moses shines forth as a star of the first magnitude, for the eminency and efficacy of his faith: and the rather is he propounded to these Hebrews, lest they should judaise, and return again from the faith of Christ to the ceremonies of the law. Moses' faith is commended for three things—

1. For the self-denial which his faith produced; he had all kinds of temptations, honours, pleasures, treasures, the three great idols of the world.   We shrink at one single temptation, and Moses went through all, though these temptations were all great in their kind. It is irksome to us to deny any of our petty interests, or to go back two or three degrees in the esteem of others, or in pomp of living;

but Moses despiseth the greatest enjoyments for communion with God and his people in an afflicted estate.

2. His faith is commended for his courage and resolution, when he carried the people of God out of Egypt after the tenth plague, whether Pharaoh would or no ; he feared not the wrath of the king, nor the force of Egypt, that made a hot pursuit after him, for he looked up to him that was invisible ; that is, assured himself of a divine protection against all those discouragements. Certainly sound believers we can never be till we overcome the terrors of the world as well as the delights of sense.

3. The third instance and fruit of his faith is his piety and religion in observing the rite of the passover according to the command of God ; that you have in the text—'Through faith he kept the pass-over,' &c.

In the words take notice—

1. Of his principle—*By faith.*

2. The act of obedience—*He kept the passover, and the sprinkling of the blood.*

3. The end and benefit to be obtained thereby—*Lest he that destroyed the first-born should touch them.*

This verse is but an abridgment of the 12th of Exodus ; you cannot have a better comment upon it than that chapter ; yet a particular explication of the terms will not be amiss. Take we notice then—

1. Of his principle—'By faith ;' that is, either his belief of the promise of the delivering of the first-born of Israel from the destroying angel, that when the destroyer came to kill the first-born of Egypt, the first-born of Israel should be safe ; or else his faith in the Messiah.

2. His obedience, seen in a double act, keeping the passover and sprinkling the blood.

[1.] Keeping the passover ; πεποίηκε τὸ πάσχα—he made the passover. The word may relate either—(1.) To the primary institution of this ordinance, and so the old English translation reads it, 'By faith Moses ordained the passover,' for *mado* is often put for *ordained* : Mark iii. 14, 'Christ ordained twelve, ἐποίησε δώδεκα ;' it is the same word, he made twelve ; and Acts ii. 36, 'Αὐτὸν ὁ Θεὸς ἐποίησε, God hath made that same Jesus whom ye have crucified both Lord and Christ ;' that is, ordained him to be so and so. By faith Moses ordained it ; that is, as a prime instrument Moses delivered it as an ordinance of God to the people. (2.) It may relate to the observation and celebration of the passover ; thus we read it, and I think better, in our new translation, 'By faith Moses kept the pass-over.' So Mat. xxvi. 18, 'I will make the passover at thy house with my disciples ;' ποιήσω, we translate it *keep* the passover, which I bring to show that it is a phrase usual in this matter. Moses' act is mentioned because the people kept it by his injunction and decree. It is just such an expression as is used of the next succeeding magistrate to Moses : Joshua v. 2, 'Make thee sharp knives, and circumcise again the children of Israel the second time ;' certainly not with his own hands, but he enjoined it and commanded it that it should be

so done : and so 'he kept the passover ;' that is, he observed it in
his own person, and caused all the people to observe it, being faithful
in declaring God's ordinance to them.

[2.] The second act of his obedience is, his sprinkling the blood.
In the first passover this was enjoined, that when the paschal lamb
was killed, the blood should be sprinkled upon the lintels and posts of
the door, Exod. xii. 11–13, as a sign to the destroyer, and an assurance
to the household, that he which slew the first-born in every house of
the Egyptians, should pass over the houses of the Israelites, and
destroy none of them. This right was only used the first time of
celebrating the passover, because it was a sign of that particular
deliverance, that then only was given ; afterward there was not the like
occasion, and it had not only that present signification, but also it pre-
signified, that Christ our paschal lamb is sacrificed for us, 1 Cor.
v. 7. This blood must be sprinkled, not upon the threshold (for so
apostates are said to tread under foot the blood of the Son of God),
but upon the lintels of the door. His blood must be sprinkled upon
the door of our hearts, whose blood applied by the Spirit, and sprinkled
by faith upon our hearts, assures us of our deliverance from the
destroying wrath of God, and the punishments of hell, and encourageth
us to pass on safely towards our heavenly Canaan, the place of our
eternal rest. When this blood is sprinkled upon our hearts, not lightly
set by, but highly prized and esteemed by us, it is a mark of preservation,—we are freed from the destroying wrath of God that shall light
upon the wicked, and all that tribulation and anguish that shall be
their portion for ever ; and being sprinkled thereby from an evil
conscience, we may cheerfully go on to serve the living God.

3. Here is the end and benefit to be obtained thereby, ' Lest he that
destroyed the first-born should touch them ;' that is, the avenging
angel that destroyed the first-born of man and beast among the
Egyptians, lest he should come nigh to do them harm. Now, as Moses
celebrated the passover in assurance that the destroying angel should
not touch the people of Israel, so may every believer be certified, if he
will take God's prescribed course, that the grace promised and sealed
in the sacrament shall be bestowed upon him.

Therefore by Moses' example we are encouraged, (1.) To obedience
in the right use of God's signs ; (2.) To confidence that God's ends
shall be obtained in the use of those instituted signs, and that the
ordinances shall be effectual unto the ends for which God hath appointed them. Therefore waiving all other points, I shall insist upon
this one alone.

Doct. That rightly to celebrate the sacrament of the Lord's supper,
there is great need of the vigorous and lively work and exercise of
faith.

Here I shall prove—

1. In general, that whosoever would have commerce with God must
have some faith.

2. That this faith, as it is necessary to religion in general, so especially to all acts of worship.

3. That among all other acts of worship, faith is most necessary in
the use of sacraments.

First, In general, whoever would have any commerce with God must have some faith. He must believe steadfastly those two primitive and supreme truths, God's being and bounty, his essence and his providence; that there is a God, and that it is not in vain to serve God. This general faith there must be: Heb. xi. 6, 'He that cometh to God must believe that he is, and that he is a rewarder of them that diligently seek him.' For if there be no God, why should we trouble ourselves about religion? And if there be no providence, it is all one whether we forbear or observe those rites which concern his worship and service, or whether we go about them with any life and seriousness; if we only comply with the common error and fashion of the times we live in, we are safe. Therefore certainly this general faith must be at the bottom of all religion; we must be soundly persuaded of these truths that there is a God, and that he is a rewarder, and bind them upon our hearts, that they may excite us to diligence and seriousness in the practice of those duties which they enforce. And therefore I would counsel every christian that is conscious to himself of too much deadness and formality, when he is about to come to God, to excite himself with these two short thoughts—that God is, and that he will not be sought in vain. Remember that God, into whose presence thou art coming, takes notice of thy duties, and will reward thee accordingly. Secret atheism will either tempt us to neglect all religion, and cast off all care of the duties thereof, or else to go about it only in a compliance with a popular and vulgar error that is set afoot in every age or place where our lot casts us. Or if natural conscience convinces us that there is a God, and that he must be worshipped (as certainly if we hearken to the dictates of it, it will easily do so), yet if we are not persuaded that he is good to mankind, and that he will reward those that worship him sincerely and according to his will, all that we do in religion will be but perfunctory, and looked upon as a heavy task, and bondage or slavery in which we have no delight. So that this general faith is necessary; you should say, Verily, I go not before an idol, but before the living God; and they that thus seek him shall praise him: Ps. xxii. 26, 'They shall praise the Lord that seek him;' something shall be given that shall excite their hearts to praise him.

Secondly, As this faith is necessary to religion in general, and all that respect we show to God, so all the duties of worship must be gone about in faith and obedience, otherwise they are not acceptable to God, for God accepts of nothing but what he hath appointed and instituted. Now God's institution, which is the rule of commerce between him and the creature, consists partly, in a word of command requiring such service at our hands, and partly, in a word of promise, and therefore the institution can never be rightly observed and complied with unless we act in obedience to his command, and with a confidence that God will perform his promise. As, for instance, take any duties of worship—prayer: Ps. l. 15, 'Call upon me in the day of trouble, and I will deliver thee.' There is an institution of prayer as a part of gospel worship, and a promise of hearing us; therefore now I must make conscience of praying, and that whatever my unbelieving heart saith to the contrary, with confidence that God will hear me, that my prayers shall not be in vain, but enter into my bosom. So for hearing the word of God: Isa. lv. 3, 'Hear, and your soul shall live.' There is the command, 'hear,' and the promise, 'your souls shall live.' Make conscience of attending upon the word, and this shall be a means to beget and increase the life of grace in your souls. Therefore now when I go to hear, I should say, Lord, thou hast commanded it, and thou hast promised a blessing; with respect to thy command I come with obedience, with respect to thy promise I come with confidence. So in the institution of the passover they were to slay the paschal lamb, and sprinkle the blood upon the door-posts; there is the command, and there is a promise, that the angel shall not touch them, Exod xii. Therefore I must obey and depend upon his promise: though there will be a great destruction and slaughter this night, yet I know it shall not touch anything in my house. So Acts ii. 38, 'Repent, and be baptized every one of you in the name of Jesus Christ for the remission of sins, and ye shall receive the gift of the Holy Ghost.' Fulfil the qualification, then take baptism for an assurance that your sins shall be forgiven, and that that life shall be begun by the Spirit that shall never be lost, but be perfected in heaven; be willing to break off your sins and return to God; then submit to baptism, and your sins shall be forgiven. So for the Lord's supper: Mat. xxvi. 26, 'Take, eat; this is my body;' and vers. 27, 28, 'Drink ye all of it: for this is my blood of the new testament, which was shed for many for the remission of sins;' that is to say, this bread thus given and taken shall prove to you my body; that is, it shall solemnly put you into possession of me, and all the benefits I have purchased for you in the body of my flesh. Thus the institutions everywhere run in a way of command and promise; a command requiring something to be religiously and conscientiously done on our part, and a promise that God for his part will not be wanting, but will give us the grace annexed thereunto. God might have enforced duty out of mere sovereignty, and appointed his worship as a task only, and for a testimony of our homage, and obedience, and dutifulness to him who is our creator and preserver. But all the ordinances are means to the obtaining some notable spiritual effect, which God hath assured us of by promise. Well then, if we act suitably to God's institutions, and go about any part of worship in the right manner, we must act in faith and obedience, out of conscience of God's command, and in confidence of his promise. And faith hath an influence upon both, upon our obedience and confidence. Upon our obedience, for it doth urge our conscience with the authority of God: Ps. cxix. 66, 'I have believed thy commandments.' And it sways and inclines our hearts by a sense of our gratitude to God; it so apprehends God's respects to us, that it makes us ready and willing to take all occasions to testify our due respects to God again; as Moses was very faithful in observing all that which God had expressly enjoined him; their faith had an influence upon his obedience, and then it hath an influence upon our confidence, for Moses was firmly persuaded in his heart that this would be a means, that the destroyer which slew the first-born in every house of the Egyptians, would pass over the houses of the Israelites, and destroy none of them. Well then, let us go and do likewise; by complying with God's institutions we may expect the blessings he hath promised;

for Christ saith, ' Do this,' and bids me take and eat, and I am to believe it shall be 'the body of Christ' to me, and that I shall be possessed of all the benefits obtained by it.

Thirdly, There are special reasons why the work and exercise of faith is required in the use of these sacramental signs. I have hitherto showed you the necessity and use of faith to all acts of religion in the general, now I shall show it more particularly as to sacraments. There is faith in prayer, and faith in the word, but especially in the use of the sacraments; and here they have a fourfold use.

1. To interpret the signs according to the use and end for which they were appointed, and to discern the mysteries represented thereby, namely, that God doth as effectually give Christ to the soul as he doth give bread and wine to the body; or, to use the apostle's phrase, to help us 'to discern the Lord's body,' that the eye may affect the heart: 1 Cor. xi. 25, 'He that eateth and drinketh unworthily, eateth and drinketh damnation to himself, not discerning the Lord's body.' Now the Lord's body may be discerned either speculatively or practically. It is not meant speculatively, so as to be able to discourse of it, and to say, what is the meaning of the bread, and what is the signification of the wine. No, no, that is but a speculative discerning, a common knowledge and the fruit of historical faith or tradition that is current among us; the apostle means a spiritual practical discerning, such as stirreth up suitable reverence, as if we had seen him on the cross: Gal. iii. 1, 'Before whose eyes Jesus Christ hath been evidently set forth crucified among you.' It is such a discerning as stirs up suitable affections, a holy joy, and a delightful converse with him. It is such a discerning as is not opposite to ignorance, but to irreverence and slightness; when a man doth not consider what he is about, he hath no true sight and sense of Christ in the duty. Many a man is able to unfold the mystery, that hath no spiritual discerning; and therefore it is such a sight and sense of the mysteries, as doth impress a dread and an awe upon the soul, and a holy rejoicing and delighting in God; for we do not come to Christ as a condemning lawgiver, which gave the laws upon Mount Sinai in a terrible manner, but we come to a feast, and we must come with a heart prepared for such a feast. He that bears no more respect to the sacrament than to an ordinary meal, or to common food, he doth not discern the Lord's body. But he that comes to it as to an institution of Christ, which represents Christ's death as a price given for our life and pardon, and accordingly comes with diligent preparation and serious thoughts, and feeds not upon the elements, but on Christ, he doth discern, or difference, or sanctify the Lord's body, and set it apart from all other things. The sight of faith is a lively thing, and begets such thoughts as stir up spiritual affections in our hearts; that is to say, a more lively sense of the wonderful love of God and our Redeemer, a more thorough hatred of sin, a more fixed resolution for our duty, and obedience, and service, and revives and cheers us in a more delightful praising of God and our Redeemer. These are the things which should accompany that discerning; now that we may discern it so, there needs faith.

2. Faith is necessary, that we may not be offended at the mean and

despicable appearance in the sacraments. Here are excellent mysteries, veiled under the simplicity of a few outward rites that make no fair show in the flesh. Now a carnal heart is soon prejudiced. When Naaman, the Syrian, was bidden to wash in Jordan seven times, and his own fancied course was not observed, his vain conceit was, that the prophet would have struck his hand upon the leprosy, and have made some solemn prayers to his God; or that he would have used some rites, and ceremonies, and charms about him; but the prophet only bids him go and wash in Jordan, and be clean; he said, 1 Kings v. 12, ' Are not Abana and Pharpar, rivers of Damascus, better than all the waters of Israel? May I not wash in them and be clean?' Are they not as clear and pleasant streams as Jordan? What is it to wash in Jordan? Why, God had instituted it. Tertullian saith in his book ' De Baptismo,' *Nihil adeo offendit hominum mentes, ac simplicitas divinorum operum,* &c.; There is nothing doth so much offend the minds of men as the simplicity of God's ordinances, as (he instances) in baptism. What! wash in water, and that this should be a renouncing the devil, and growing dead to the world, and a recovery into a state of freedom and liberty from sin, and a becoming new creatures! and is all this done by a little washing of water? This was it which offended the gentiles. Here Moses believed the promise, though the outward rite was mean; what were a few drops of blood upon the door-posts to keep off the wrath of God? What a sorry charm or talisman is this to drive away a destroying angel? Still in such ordinances despicable rites are consecrated to signify the highest mysteries. Washing in water, what will that do to purge the soul from sin? Eating a piece of bread, and taking a sip or small draught of wine, mean ceremonies in show, weak, but very mysterious, and very powerful in their use to save the soul. To see life in a bit of bread, and ravishing comforts in a draught of wine, requires a very lively and active faith; and so we shall judge if we be serious and attentive to reconcile the appearance with the institution, and the elements with the blessings; that we may look upon this mean feast as the livery and seisin of Christ, and heaven, and grace, and glory. Surely sense will never teach us this; faith alone must do it, that is the evidence of things unseen.

3. The nature of these signs is to excite and confirm faith. There are three uses of signs—to represent, to put in remembrance, and to confirm; and so signs are either significative, commemorative, or confirming and assuring.

[1.] There are significative signs or ceremonies, to represent spiritual things. As the patriarchs dwelling in tents or booths declared plainly that they sought a country, Heb. xi. 9, compared with ver. 16. They did not look upon the world as their fixed habitation, but they sought for a home and country elsewhere, and here they were but strangers and pilgrims.

[2.] Some signs are commonitive, or commemorative, set up for a memorial of some things that were done; as Jacob and Laban did set up a heap of stones as a witness and a memorial of the covenant made between them, Gen. xxxi. 46–48. And great potentates in the world will have their royal jests or deeds not only recorded in chronicles and histories, but usually, where they have obtained great victories, they set up public and visible monuments of their victory and triumph, to keep up the remembrance of them.

[3.] There are confirming and assuring signs; as Hezekiah, 2 Kings xx. 8, 'What shall be the sign that the Lord will heal me, and that I shall go up into the house of the Lord the third day?' When the prophet came to him with a promise of recovery when he was sick, he begged an assuring sign that he might be confident he should escape that sickness.

Now, since there are several sorts of signs, unto which of these shall we refer the sacraments?

Ans. That must be determined by God's institution; for mark, the sacraments are not natural signs, as smoke is a sign of fire, but instituted signs; bread doth not naturally signify the body of Christ, or wine the blood of Christ, but only by institution. Now, in all instituted signs we must look to the author and the end—to the author by whom, and the end for which they are appointed. Instituted signs in religion can have no author but God, therefore no creature can institute a sacrament, because they cannot give the grace that is signified thereby, nor bind God to give that grace by a sign of their own devising. But now to what end hath God instituted these signs? whether to signify or to admonish, or to certify and assure? I answer, In some sense for all these ends, but chiefly the latter. In regard of our understandings they are notifying or significative signs; they are glasses wherein spiritual things are represented to us, and set forth as if they were done before our eyes; as water in baptism signifieth the washing away of sin. Then with respect to our memories, they are commonitive signs, as trophies to renew the remembrance of some things past and done, as the glorious mystery of our redemption by Christ—'Do this in remembrance of me.' The sacrament is, as it were, Christ's trophy and visible monument. Christ would have his royal deeds to be recorded, not in chronicles, but in our minds. But with respect to our wills, and so to our trust and devoting ourselves to God, which are acts of the will, they are confirming signs; they are seals and pledges of that grace which God will give us in and by Christ; and so God appointed them. Accordingly it is said, Rom. iv. 11, 'Abraham received the sign of circumcision, a seal of the righteousness of the faith which he had, being yet uncircumcised.' God hath spoken of great things in the covenant of grace. Now he, knowing how apt we are to be wrought upon by visible and sensible things, he will give us some sign to assure us, and confirm us in waiting upon him, that he will do those great things for us. God is content in mercy and goodness to comply with man's infirmity; he knows the hand of our faith is too short to reach to heaven, therefore he will stoop down to us in certain visible signs, and hereby assure our hearts that he will be as good to us as he hath promised—that as sure as the water in baptism is applied to us, so surely will God give us the grace signified thereby. So in the Lord's supper. And therefore faith is required, that we may humbly embrace God's offer of love, and may encourage ourselves to a patient continuance in well-doing upon these hopes. The sacraments are not only instituted to represent Christ and his benefits, or to put us in remembrance of Christ and his benefits, but to confirm us in our hopes of deliverance from that destruction wherein the whole world is involved by the law, and that he will indeed save us from the wrath to come. The Israelites sprinkled the door-posts because they hoped for the passing over of the destroying angel; and we are to use these rites that we may encourage ourselves in well-doing by the hopes of the blessings of the covenant: Luke xxii. 20, 'This cup is the new testament in my blood;' that is, it is a pledge and seal of it, that visible sign that God hath given us for our assurance, that we may trust God that he will make good his part of the covenant, and also give us grace that we may accomplish our part. He hath given us a binding and assuring sign that we shall have Christ and all his benefits if there be not a bar and let on our part; if we faithfully take him for our God, and give ourselves up to be his people, he will maintain us, and carry us on to eternal salvation. So that here is the exercise of faith, because it is a sealing ordinance. Whatever those extraordinary signs were that God gave to his people of old, that is baptism and the Lord's supper to us. As when God promised Abraham the land of Canaan, Gen. xv. 8, 'He said, Lord God, whereby shall I know that I shall inherit it?' And God confirmed the promise to him by a sign and a vision, in the following part of the chapter. So when God sent Moses upon a difficult business, he gave him signs that he might believe; as his turning his rod into a serpent, Exod. iv. 3, 4; making his hand leprous, ver. 6; turning water into blood, that he and the children of Israel might believe in the Lord God of their fathers. So Judges vi. 37, Gideon would have a sign that he might believe that God would save Israel by his hand. God knoweth man's backwardness to believe and proneness to distrust, and hath an earnest desire that we should partake of the benefit of the promises, and therefore he hath given us a sign. It is true, not a miraculous sign; that needeth not after so long owning of the gospel; a miracle is a sign for infidels: 1 Cor. xiv. 22, 'Wherefore tongues are for a sign, not to them that believe, but to them that believe not;' but as binding and as assuring a sign. Therefore we must use it in faith, and with confidence that God will be as good as his word.

4. There is this peculiar to sacraments above other duties, that they imply a closer application. In the word Christ is evidently set forth and propounded to all in general; the word speaks to all promiscuously, 'He that believeth shall be saved,' Mark xvi. 16; but the sacraments apply it to every one in particular. By the word none are excluded from accepting the grace offered to them upon God's terms; but by the sacrament every one is expressly bound and particularly admonished of his duty. It is one thing when no man is excluded, another thing when I am particularly called, bound, and admonished to my duty, and called, as it were, by name. The object revealed in the word is like the brazen serpent, which without difference was exposed to the eyes of all, that whosoever looked upon it might recover his health; but the same object offered in the sacrament is like the blood sprinkled upon the door-posts, that every man may be assured in particular that his family should be saved. The reason of this difference between the word and the sacrament is because in the word the promises are

propounded and offered in order to consent, as matters are debated to and fro till the parties are agreed ; but the sacraments are not of use till both sides have consented and agreed to the conditions of the covenant. The word conduceth to the making of the covenant, but the sacraments suppose it already made and agreed ; therefore the word universally propounds that which in the seals is particularly applied, in which there is a special advantage, for those things do not excite us so much that are spoken indifferently to all, as those that are particularly applied to ourselves ; these stir up a more accurate care and endeavour that we may answer the duty taken upon us. In the promises of the word the conditions are propounded, that if you will be my people, take me for your benefactor, redeemer, and sanctifier, and will live in faith and obedience to me, I will be your God to pardon your sin, to guide and conduct you safe to eternal life ; this is propounded in the word. But the sacraments suppose that my consent is actually given ; and that I have undertaken to do the duty, that we have chosen God to be our God, and given up ourselves to be his people, and then God cometh and saith, Take this as an undoubted pledge that I will be thine, that I will love and bless thee, and thou shalt have whatever I have promised—then he cometh to give us livery and seisin, or to put us into the actual possession of Christ, and all his benefits by the rites of bread and wine. So that these seals do not only bind the covenant, but confirm our interest in the blessings thereof, and convey a right to us : 1 Cor. x. 16, ' The cup of blessing which we bless, is it not the communion of the blood of Christ ? The bread which we break, is it not the communion of the body of Christ ? ' They give us a right if the bar be not on our side, if the consent be sincere, otherwise the covenant is void. If you have not given a sincere consent to take the privileges of the covenant for your happiness, and the duties of the covenant for your work, how can you expect it ? for God is bound to none but those that accept and thankfully give up themselves to the terms of the covenant. Now this is in part true of both the sacraments, but especially of the Lord's supper. Baptism supposes faith in grown persons, but infants are baptized unto faith and unto repentance : Mat. iii. 11, ' I indeed baptize you with water, εἰς μετά-νοιαν, unto repentance,' that the party baptized may be obliged to mind the work of repentance, and be encouraged to look up to God for grace to perform it when he comes to years of discretion. But for the Lord's supper, there we are expressly required to examine ourselves : 1 Cor. xi. 28, ' But let a man examine himself, and so let him eat of that bread, and drink of that cup.' We must examine ourselves, that we may make out our title and interest, so that God may not seal to a blank ; we must examine whether we be in the faith. We do not come that faith may be forgotten, but we must bring it along with us, that it may be strengthened and confirmed. Here we are to eat and drink, and turn things into our own substance; and so we make particular application, and appropriate and apply to ourselves what Christ hath done and suffered for us. Now consider what a horrible usurpation it is to challenge privileges that do not belong to thee. Here God cometh to say to us, All this is thine, that we may cry out with Thomas, ' My Lord, and my God,' John xx. 28.

Application. The use is to instruct us what to do in and about the supper of the Lord—

1. What to do before we come.
2. What to do in the supper of our Lord.
3. What to do after the supper.

First, What to do before the supper.

1. Before we come to remember Christ, we must first consider ourselves, and reflect upon our own state. Have I such a constitution of heart towards God as he requires, knowing what his spiritual laws are, and what temptations are incident to a christian? Can I in the strength of God resolve to take the duties required in the covenant as my work, and the privileges offered in it as my happiness? and how doth my heart agree or disagree with the nature of this institution? 1 Cor. xi. 28, 'Let a man examine himself, and so let him eat of that bread and drink of that cup.' The great thing that is required of me is discerning the Lord's body, that I may come with that hope, joy, delight, reverence, and all those affections that are necessary. But in vain do we discern the Lord's body, unless we have all things that are necessary to the participation of this body, and are prepared to receive what God offers. What will it profit us to know that Christ hath precious benefits to bestow, unless we have a right to them, or mean to take the way wherein we should receive them? When we press people to examine, they ask us what we must examine ourselves about? Why, examine whether you have received the covenant of God, whether you are in the faith: 2 Cor. xiii. 5, 'Examine yourselves, whether ye be in the faith.' It concerns us to have faith, and it is an advantage to know that we have it, that we may celebrate the sacrament in a right manner, and may have no prejudice to hinder our feasting and holy rejoicing in God; for we must rejoice in God, 'as those that have received the atonement,' when we are actually interested in that salvation Christ hath purchased for us, Rom. v. 11. Without faith we shall want an eye, we cannot discern the Lord's body, nor have a true sense and use of these spiritual mysteries; and without faith we shall want a hand thankfully to take what God offers, even Christ and all his benefits; and without faith we shall want a mouth to feed upon Christ, that we may suck and draw life and strength from him. Without faith the whole duty will prove an empty ceremony, scarce a reasonable service, much less spiritual nourishment to our souls. Oh, then, see that you believe, and that you know that you do believe; without the one this ordinance will be a nullity as to any profit to your souls; and without the other you will lose much of your sweet converse with God. To know what Christ hath done, and suffered, and merited, is to know the ground of our rejoicing; but there is still something wanting to make it full peace and joy to us, till we can in some measure see faith wrought in us, and so see our right in him. Therefore do not stupidly and in a blindfold manner rush upon such a duty. How can you, then, without great presumption and usurpation, apply and take home unto yourselves Christ crucified, and all the benefits of his death? Draw near then, christians; stand not aloof from Christ. Then do we draw nigh with most rejoicing and thankfulness, when we 'draw nigh with a true

neart, and full assurance of faith, having our hearts sprinkled from an evil conscience, and our bodies washed with pure water,' Heb. x. 22 ; ' with a true heart,' unfeignedly purposing to perform the duties of the gospel ; ' in full assurance of faith,' that is, absolutely depending upon the promises of God, and expecting the privileges of the gospel ; ' having our hearts sprinkled from an evil conscience, and our bodies washed with pure water ; ' when you have applied the blood of sprinkling, you may confidently look up to God.

Obj. But you will say, Is the assurance of our sincerity, and of our interest in Christ always necessary ; and will you persuade none to come to the Lord's table but those that are assured of their own sincerity ? then what shall poor souls do that are in a dark and doubtful estate ?

Ans. I am far from saying this. It is the thing, and not the certainty of the thing, that is necessary ; that which is necessary is sincere and saving faith, but it is not absolutely necessary that we should know it. I would have you come believing, and as much as you can, get it clear ; why should it be a doubt with you concerning your own sincerity? Though it be comfortable to know our sincerity, yet it is not absolutely necessary, for Christ may welcome a doubting believer, but he takes more pleasure in those that draw nigh in the full assurance of their own interest. And certainly he expects it at our hands, because he hath condescended to our infirmities, and hath added seals to the covenant for our greater confirmation, and that the heirs of promise might have ' strong consolation,' Heb. vi. 18. We suffer for want of bringing the traverses and doubts of our souls to a certain issue by our laziness. Therefore we should aim at assurance, and not lose such a benefit through our negligence and want of looking after it ; but it is not absolutely necessary ; and therefore though we have our doubts, I would advise none wholly to abstain from God's ordinance, which was appointed for a help to a weak faith, and a relief to doubting christians. Here there is represented the blood of Christ shed for the remission of sins, Mat. xxvi. 28. Here we have a sign and seal of the righteousness of faith, Rom. iv. 11. Here God reacheth out his hand to us from heaven, and doth singularly apply his benefits to our souls : here we have Christ offering himself to us by name, and exciting our souls to lay hold of his benefits. You consent to the duties of the covenant, only you are afraid it is not deep and strong enough ; but usually mists and clouds are dispersed in the sacrament. Look, as Jesus was known to his disciples in the breaking of bread, Luke xxiv. 30, 31 ; so all jealousies and misunderstandings between God and his people are removed, and our being in Christ is more evidenced, which was before dark, doubtful, and litigious. Therefore examine yourselves and come.

2. For the manner in which you ought to come.

[1.] Come judging and condemning yourselves, and humbled under the sense of your own vileness and unworthiness, that Jesus Christ may be more sweet to you. Though you do not know yourselves to be the children of God, yet you must know yourselves to be sinners, condemned by the law, and needing a saviour to reconcile and justify you, that you may humbly cast yourselves at the feet of grace, begging mercy to such a poor vile sinner as you are.   All do not go to heaven by the hilly country, some go a lower, darker, and it may be the safer way; though they cannot look upon Christ as their saviour and redeemer, yet they can look upon him as one whom they have pierced, Zech. xii. 10.   And so they acknowledge the merit of sin, though they cannot apply the comfort of salvation; though they cannot say with Paul in one place, viz., Gal. ii. 20, 'Who loved me, and gave himself for me;' yet they can say with Paul in another place, viz., 1 Tim. i. 15, 'This is a faithful saying, and worthy of all acceptation, that Christ Jesus came into the world to save sinners, of whom I am chief.'   Surely I am sinner enough for Christ to save, and so creep in at the back-door of the promise, by a darker kind of assurance, or a humbling application,   Certainly he that knows and is affected with his unworthiness and necessities is not unwelcome to the Lord: 1 Cor. xi. 31, 'If we would judge ourselves, we should not be judged;' and the publican that cried, 'Lord, be merciful to me a sinner, went away justified,' Luke xviii. 13, 14.   If we cannot come with the joy of faith, let us come with the more brokenness of heart; and we must come with an earnest desire after a saviour, if cannot come with a holy delight in him.

[2.] They must come with hunger and thirst after sacramental benefits, the comforts and saving graces of the Spirit.   God invites such, whatever discouragements they have upon them: Isa. lv. 1, 'Ho, every one that thirsteth, come ye to the waters; and he that hath no money, come ye, buy and eat; yea come, buy wine and milk, without money, and without price.'   If ye cannot come with delight, come with an appetite: John vii. 37, 'Jesus stood and cried, saying, If any man thirst, let him come unto me and drink;' and he hath promised such shall be satisfied: Mark v. 6, 'Blessed are they that hunger and thirst after righteousness, for they shall be filled.'   Surely Christ would not flatter you with a vain hope, for he calls such as thou art. Though he doth not speak to thee by name, yet he speaketh to thee by qualification.   Therefore you must plead as David: Ps. lxiii. 1, 'My soul thirsteth for thee; my flesh longeth for thee.'   He that is duly affected with the want of Christ, and unfeignedly desires to be found in Christ, and to depart from iniquity, such a one is not altogether a stranger to Christ and the work to his Spirit.

[3.] They are to bewail their unbelief, and to make what application of Christ they can: when they cannot apply Christ to themselves, they must apply themselves to Christ; they must go to Christ with that faith they have, and say as the father of the child, Mark ix. 24, 'Lord, I believe; help thou my unbelief.'   And they must run to Christ for refuge: Heb. vi. 18, 'Who have fled for refuge, to lay hold upon the hope set before us.'   Though there be not assurance, yet there must be some application—Here I come to take my portion; the bread is broken and distributed, the wine poured out and distributed, Take, eat, every one of you.   Therefore I am not to be a looker-on in this feast, but an actor; I must not be an idle observer only, but a guest; my hand must be in Christ's dish, and as I am able, I must lay hold upon him, and take out my share of the common salvation. In short, there must be an adherence to Christ, though there be not assurance.   Because thou seest not thy own qualification, excite thy soul to wait upon the Lord, and to trust in him for these benefits. It would be, I confess, a very great satisfaction to the soul to believe that God loves us, and that he is reconciled to us, and doth take us for his children.   Come then, and see what he hath done for you; was he not in Christ reconciling the world unto himself?   Pray, what is here represented to you but the death of Christ for the expiation of sin?   And can you use such a duty without seeing or feeling the love of God?   What is set forth before our eye but a God incarnate, a Christ crucified, a covenant sealed in his blood?   A God incarnate, and come near to us for our converse and delight; a Christ crucified, that he might pay our debts, and that we might come now and put our hands into the holes of his wounded side, and be healed; and a covenant sealed, that it may be the charter of our hopes.   Therefore act that faith you have upon these things, and see what God will do for you.

[4.] Renew thy consecration, and consent to surrender and give up thyself to the tuition and service of Christ; for the more we mind our duty, the more ready is God to prepare our comfort for us.   The covenant is mutual indeed: Cant. vi. 3, ' I am my beloved's, and my beloved is mine;' though I cannot say he is mine, yet I am resolved to be his.   You are to resign and consecrate yourselves to him by the sense of his great mercies, Rom. xii. 1.   We first consent that we will be his before we can know that he is ours.   Now if we cannot claim by one part of the covenant, it is some confidence when we can say, I am thine, wholly thine, only thine, everlastingly thine: Ps. cxix. 94, ' I am thine, save me.'   David did not say, Thou art mine, but he could say, I am thine; and thereupon he pleads with God. Though we cannot say, I am thine by God's acceptance, that he hath taken us for his own; yet I am thine by my own resignation, I have given up myself to thee, to serve and please thee.   As the men of Campania, who came as neighbours and allies to Rome in great distress, to seek for help from them against the Grecians, but when the Romans refused to help them, they went and gave up their whole country in vassalage to the Romans, and used this plea, *Si nostra tueri non vultis, at vestra defendatis; quicquid passuri sumus, dedititii vestri patientur*—If you will not help us as your allies, help us as your subjects, for we are resolved to be subjects to the Romans; what we suffer, your tributaries shall suffer.   It is some holdfast upon God when you have chosen him for your God, and given up yourselves to his use and service.   We must with a holy art fasten ourselves upon God: Lord! if I perish, one that is resolved to be thine shall perish.   When you thus devotedly and strongly give up yourselves to his use and service, though you cannot with such boldness and the joy of faith make out your own claim, yet you may rely upon him.

Secondly, What we are to do in the supper of the Lord.   Oh, look that you excite and stir up faith!   It is not enough to have it, but it must be exercised; ay, and that in a lively and vigorous manner: Cant. i. 12, ' When the king sitteth at his table, my spikenard sendeth forth the smell thereof.'   Here faith is to be acted and put forth. There is a twofold faith to be exercised; a faith that respects the whole duty, and a faith that is more specially terminated on the person of Christ.

1. A faith that respects the whole duty and transaction, and that is nothing but an expectation of the blessings of God's ordinances, or the comforts annexed by promise to his institution. And certainly they act customarily that do not look to the end of the service, but like a horse and mule, go on in a track and course of duties and observances without considering why and wherefore: Mat. xi. 7, 'What went ye out into the wilderness for to see?' Man is to work for an end, to design somewhat in every serious business, but especially in the duties of worship, which are the most serious and important actions of our lives. Now God that hath appointed the work hath appointed the ends to be promoted by it. The work falls under the command of God, and the ends and benefits are put into the promise. The command is the reason of the duty, and the promise is our great encouragement. Now, you must use this ordinance as an ordinance under the blessing of an institution. Christ, when he instituted it, instituted it with prayer; he prayed over it to bless it for our use, and therefore we must use it in faith, in the face of all discouragements, and continue waiting, though the success be not presently visible; it is God's ordinance, and I will wait: Isa. xl. 3, 'For they that wait upon the Lord shall renew their strength;' and though, it may be, presently it doth not appear, yet I will use God's means: Isa. xlv. 24, 'Surely shall one say, In the Lord have I righteousness and strength.' Christ will be master of his own mercies, and keeps the dispensations of grace in his own hands, and gives them out when he pleaseth, not at our beck and command, as if it were a due debt. We are bound, but God is free; not bound to our time, and to the measure that we expect, only this is the way, and it is good to be waiting in God's way.

2. There is a faith that is conversant about the person of Christ. The duty was ordained by Christ, and it is well observed when it leadeth you to Christ. Here Christ makes a new offer of himself, 'Take, eat, this is my body.' Now certainly we are to take and accept an offered Saviour, with his benefits. Christ makes here an offer of himself as our lord and saviour to bring us into grace and favour with God, and to wash us from our sins in his blood, and to dwell in us by his Spirit as a fountain of living waters, or of everlasting refreshing to us, and to call us from deserved wrath to undeserved mercy and happiness. Accordingly we are to take and eat, to eat his flesh, and drink his blood, 'to receive of his fulness, and that grace for grace,' John i. 16. We are to receive him into our hearts, to trust in his merits, to rejoice in his love, to give up ourselves in a perpetual covenant that shall not be forgotten: Ps. l. 5, 'Gather my saints together unto me, those that have made a covenant with me by sacrifice.' So ought you to sue out your pardon, to renew your charter of grace, for the confirmation of your hopes. Look upon the blood of Christ as the price of reconciliation; set open the doors of your hearts, that he may live in your heart, and by his Spirit keep up an everlasting refreshing day there.

Thirdly, What we are to do after the Lord's supper. Examine what exercise and increase of faith there hath been—Have I acted faith in this duty? how shall I know it? If you have in the acting of faith been waiting upon God for the blessings of the institution, the effects will show it. The effects are these—

1. It will stir up joy and thankfulness; you will find it will increase both. Look, as the eunuch after his baptism, it is said, Acts viii. 39, 'He went on his way rejoicing.' As men are pleased when they have a lease of a good bargain sealed to them that yields them a great benefit; so the people of God, when they have renewed pledges of God's love, and a real sense of their interest in such inestimable benefits by Christ as the pardon of their sins, the gift of the Spirit, and hopes of glory, they are excited and stirred up to praise the Lord, and they are ready to cry with David, Ps. ciii. 1–3, 'Bless the Lord, O my soul; and all that is within me, bless his holy name. Bless the Lord, O my soul, and forget not all his benefits, who pardoneth all thy iniquities, and healeth all thy diseases.' When there is somewhat that urges the soul to bless God, it is a sign we have acted faith, and have been persuaded and encouraged to wait for such special benefits that we are to receive by Christ.

2. It will produce a longing to meet with God another time, that we may be thus kindly refreshed, and have another good meal from God, and be feasted in his house: Ps. lxiii. 2, 'To see thy power and thy glory, so as I have seen it in the sanctuary.' Look, as one circle begets another in the water, and a little water cast into the pump when the springs are low brings up more; so our experience kindles affection, and makes us long for more: 1 Peter ii. 3, 'If so be that you have tasted that the Lord is gracious.' When you find benefit by one duty, it will be an encouragement to come again. You have tasted that the Lord is gracious, and therefore you come for new quickening and refreshing.

3. There will be resolution to serve the Lord the more faithfully, and walk with him in all the ways of holiness; you have been with God, and you go aside and say, Ps. cxvi. 12–14, 'What shall I render to the Lord for all his benefits towards me? I will take the cup of salvation, and call upon the name of the Lord. I will pay my vows unto the Lord now in the presence of all his people;' and Ps. lxxxv. 8, 'I will hear what God the Lord will speak, for he will speak peace unto his people, and to his saints; but let them not turn again to folly.' When it is so, when there is more care of holy walking with God, then certainly there hath been some acting of faith and grace in this duty, and we have met with Jesus in it.

4. For the present the heart should be more warm and serious, and all those things omitted, for a time at least, which rather savour of the flesh than of the spirit, which, though they do not directly belong to the flesh, yet they border on it. And those things will be omitted which do not well agree with the lively sense and fervour of godliness, which should be stirred up in us in an action so important. To leap presently into a vain, worldly frame, and to fall to worldly discourse, shows that we have not been serious in it, and that we have not had such a lively sense of sin, and that we have not been so deeply affected with the wonders of God's redeeming grace as we should have been. Certainly, however it be with us at other times, and whatever liberty

we take, yet after the participation of the Lord's supper, men ought to study much purity and heavenliness of mind, and raisedness of heart towards God. And the rather I press it, because the devil loves to affront the worshippers of the Lord Jesus Christ, and to tempt them after some solemn duty to some unbecoming practice and behaviour. The devil entered into Judas after the sop: John xiii. 2, 'And supper being ended, the devil having now put it into the heart of Judas Iscariot, Simon's son, to betray him,' &c. Satan never gets greater advantage on wicked men than after a careless use of such precious ordinances. But now for the people of God there will be a favour abiding upon their hearts a good while afterward.

SERMONS UPON HEBREWS XI.

SERMON LXIII.

By faith they passed through the Red Sea as by dry land ; which the Egyptians assaying to do were drowned.—Heb. xi. 29.

This chapter is a chronicle and history of the mighty acts done by faith. The instance which I shall now produce is that of the believing Israelites, who all together, with Moses, their leader, passed through the divided waters of the Red Sea; but the Egyptians, pursuing and trying to follow them, were overwhelmed and destroyed.

In the text you have two things—the preservation and safety of Israel, and the destruction of the Egyptians. The one illustrates the other; the one was the fruit of faith, and the other of presumption and unbelief. In the first, take notice of the act. (1.) *They passed through the Red Sea ;* (2.) The success,—*As by dry land.* And suitably in the other part there is—(1.) The attempt,—*Which the Egyptians assaying to do ;* and (2.) The issue,—*They were drowned.*

To understand which passages, we must remember the story recorded by Moses, Exod. xiv. The sum is this: When Pharaoh at last had consented to let the Israelites go, he soon repented of his grant; and understanding by spies how they were entangled in the jaws and straits of Pihahiroth, this occasion invited him to make pursuit after them. What should the poor Israelites do? Fight they durst not, being a multitude of undisciplined people of all ages and sexes, and pursued by a regular and potent army of enemies. Fly they could not, having the sea before them, the Egyptians behind them, the steep and unpassable hills on either side of them. This was the case, and in human reason nothing but destruction could be expected. But Moses, by special order from God, commandeth Israel to march forward, and expect the salvation promised. And when Moses gave the signal by his rod, the sea miraculously retreated, standing up like heaps of congealed ice on each side while they passed through. This is done, and they go on safely; the sea flanked them on both sides; the rear was secured by the cloudy and fiery pillar interposing between them and Pharaoh's army till such time as all were out of danger, and safely arrived at the further shore; and so neither man nor child was hurt. The Egyptians follow the chase, as malice is perverse and blind, and those whom God designeth to destruction take the ready course to bring it upon their own heads; for at the signal again of Moses stretching forth his rod, the returning waters swallowed them all up in a moment. This was a strange and glorious work of God's almighty power and unspeakable mercy, and the fruit of their faith; and it teaches us both to believe and how to believe in God—to believe, since with respect to faith God produceth such wonders; and how to believe with an unlimited confidence in the greatest straits, for nothing is too hard for God to do.

But you will say the age of such miracles is long since past, and these are antiquated dispensations, now no more in use, nor reasonably to be looked for; and, therefore, what is this to us?

I answer—Their passage through the Red Sea may be considered three ways:—

1. Historically.

2. Sacramentally.

3. Applicatively, with respect to the use for which the apostle produceth this instance.

First, Historically, as a notable pattern of providence; and so it represents to us two things—

1. Unspeakable comfort to all believers in the midst of their extremities. God can disentangle and help them out, for he is with them in all their dangers. See how he promises his presence to his people: Isa. xliii. 2, 'When thou passest through the waters, I will be with thee; and through the rivers, they shall not overflow thee; when thou walkest through the fire, thou shalt not be burnt, neither shall the flames kindle upon thee.' For the waters, Israel is an instance; both in the Red Sea and in the river of Jordan, God preserved them: for the fire, the three children is an instance; when they were cast into the fiery furnace, they walked in it unsinged and untouched, nothing burned but their bands, Dan. iii. 27. Where God calls his people to be, there he will be with them; and therefore we must be content to follow God through fire and water. Surely he can secure his people in the greatest dangers and difficulties, and find a way of deliverance for them in the most desperate cases. As David, when Saul was eagerly hunting after him, Saul on this side of the mountain and David on that, yet God brought him off. There is no danger so great but God can deliver out of it; and many times God's deliverance is nearest when our danger is greatest. Only, those that look for such deliverances must be upright, for to such the Lord shows himself strong: 2 Chron. xvi. 9, 'For the eyes of the Lord run to and fro throughout the whole earth, to show himself strong in the behalf of them whose heart is perfect before him.'

2. It speaks terror to the wicked, and such as maliciously pursue the people of God, as the Egyptians did here. They were engaged in an evil design, they had neither command nor promise from God; yea, they went against God's command, for they acted out of malice, pride, cruelty, and desire of revenge, and so justly perished. So that here is a dreadful glass wherein to see the judgments of God against the enemies and pursuers of his people: Prov. xi. 8, 'The righteous is delivered out of trouble, and the wicked cometh in his stead.' Pharaoh

would either kill them or drive them into the sea, and there all his chariots were overwhelmed. Daniel was cast into the lions' den, but the lions did not devour him, but devoured his accusers, Dan. vi. 22–24. That which was a preservation to God's people was the destruction of the Egyptians; passing through the Red Sea is the means of their safety, but of the others' ruin. Which should check the pride and daring attempts of wicked men, who pursue their evil designs to their own destruction; being blinded with malice and hatred, they neither remember things past, nor consider things present, nor foresee things to come, but are led by a fanatical spirit, which is furious and driving, till it hurries them to their own destruction. Thus, if we consider it historically, it is a notable passage to encourage us to trust in the Lord.

Secondly, Sacramentally. The apostle tells us, 1 Cor. x. 2, 'That they were all baptized unto Moses in the cloud and in the sea;' that is, in the cloud that hid them from the Egyptians, and in their passage through the Red Sea. This passage had the same signification that baptism hath. How were they baptized in the sea?

1. They were baptized unto Moses in the sea; that is, Moses' ministry was confirmed by that miracle, and so they were bound to take Moses for their leader and lawgiver; as the miraculous dispensations by Christ assure us that he was sent by God as our lawgiver, whom we should hear and obey.

2. It is called a baptism, because it signified the difference that God puts between his people and their enemies, or the deliverance of his people from the common destruction of mankind was sealed to them by this passing through the sea, for here God shows that he would put a difference between his people and others. For which respect baptism is said to be ἀντίτυπος, an answerable figure to the ark of Noah; so Peter urgeth it, 1 Peter iii. 20, 21, 'While the ark was a preparing, wherein few, that is, eight souls, were saved by water. The like figure whereunto even baptism doth also now save us.' They that were in the ark were exempted from the deluge. So they that are baptized into Christ, that enter into covenant with God by Christ, they are exempted from the deluge of wrath which overwhelms the rest of the world. So that though we have not extraordinary ways of preservation, as the people of God had of old, yet we have special privileges by Christ which answer to it, and a deliverance of a far better nature.

3. They were baptized in the cloud and sea, because by submitting to God's command they gave up themselves to God's direction and the conduct of his providence by this initiating act, that he should lead them through the wilderness unto Canaan, and the land of promise; as we pass through the waters of baptism, that we may give up ourselves to be led through this world, which answers to the wilderness, to heaven, to Canaan, the land of promise, to be commanded and governed by him till he brings us to our rest.

Thirdly, Applicatively, with respect to the use for which the apostle brings these instances; and it is to confirm believers in the faith of Christ, though they were sorely pushed at, and endured great sufferings for Christ's sake. These examples of faith, which the apostle produces, serve for a double use—either to show the nature of that faith by which the just do live, or else to commend the excellency of that faith, that we may get it, and exercise it, and be eminent in it; and so these instances of faith are of use in all ages, when the miraculous dispensations are ceased.

But now this instance that we have in hand serves not only for one of these ends, but for both uses—to show the true nature of faith, and also to commend the excellency of it.   Therefore—

1. I shall show what is the nature of faith, which we may learn from this instance.

[1.] Faith inclined them to obey God's command, and upon obedience to expect the mercy promised: Go through the Red Sea and you shall be saved.   Now this is the common nature of all faith: Ps. cxix. 66, 'Lord, I have hoped for thy salvation, and done thy commandments.' This is the great business of faith, as the Israelites were to obey God, and to wait for his salvation out of this imminent danger.

[2.] For the command, faith gives courage to obey God in the most difficult cases.   If we be bidden to go into the Red Sea, we must not forbear; for none of God's commands must be disputed, how contrary soever they be to flesh and blood.   If God will command Abraham to take his only son, and offer him for a burnt-offering, he must not stick at it: Gen. xxii. 2, 'Take now thy son, thine only son, Isaac, whom thou lovest, and get thee into the land of Moriah, and offer him there for a burnt-offering.'   If God commands us to sell all, that we may have treasure in heaven, we must not murmur as the young man did: Mark x. 22, 'He went away sorrowful, for he had great possessions.' We must give up our lives and all our comforts into the hands of Christ, and nothing must be abated; whatever God commands we must do, though it be never so difficult.

[3.] For the promise, the Red Sea was as a grave to them in visible appearance, and for a considerable time they walked every moment in the valley of the shadow of death.   But this is the nature of faith, it teaches us to depend upon God's promises in the greatest extremities. Going down to the Red Sea is as our going down to the grave, yet the promise of eternal life is sure to us, and the belief of it is required of all christians: John xi. 26, 'Whosoever liveth, and believeth in me, shall never die;' that is, never wholly die; 'believest thou this?'   Faith can find a way to salvation through the great deep, and a passage to life through death and the grave; it can see a heaven when we are in the midst of the Red Sea.   This passage through the Red Sea had a respect to baptism, and we are said 'to be buried with Christ in baptism,' Col. ii. 12.   Now, among other senses implied in the phrase, one great sense is our willingness to die, out of a confidence to enjoy life in heaven, though they are killed all the day long.

2. This instance doth very much commend to us the excellency of this grace of faith, which was so necessary to believers in that age, when they were exposed to such great sufferings.   Now, how it is manifested from this instance.

[1.] God's promise produces its miraculous effect through faith, and not otherwise.   God could do it, whether the Israelites did believe, yea or nay; but their faith must concur: 'Through faith they passed through the Red Sea.'   The apostle doth not mention the mercy, or the power of God, but their faith. It is true the supreme original cause is the goodness and power of God, but the means is faith. So 1 Peter i. 5, 'Ye are kept by the power of God through faith unto salvation.' When we rest upon his word, who is faithful and able to save to the uttermost, then the power of God is exercised for us: Mark ix. 23, 'If thou canst believe, all things are possible to him that believeth;' that is, then thou art capable of having the glorious power of God exercised on thy behalf, beyond the ability of nature. On the contrary, nothing but unbelief puts an impediment in God's way: Mark vi. 5, 6, 'He could do no mighty works there,' &c., and 'he marvelled at their unbelief;' there was no occasion or opportunity, for where faith is wanting, how can the power of God be owned and seen? Now, since the promise of God produces its glorious effect by the means of faith, so that our faith must concur, this doth mightily commend faith.

[2.] Here is another circumstance which commends faith likewise: this faith was weak at first, and mingled with unbelief; for first they murmured, as you may see: Exod. xiv. 11, 12, 'And they said to Moses, Because there were no graves in Egypt, hast thou taken us away to die in the wilderness? Wherefore hast thou dealt thus with us, to carry us forth out of Egypt? Is not this the word that we did tell thee in Egypt, saying, Let us alone that we may serve the Egyptians? For it had been better for us to serve the Egyptians, than that we should die in the wilderness;' words of impatience and distrust, and very near to a plain revolt from God; and yet at length these murmurers, through faith they passed through the Red Sea, as if it had been firm land. There was a great mixture of unbelief, but where faith prevails, it is accepted with God. Though first they murmured, yet afterwards they believed. Now, when after such great faults God takes it so kindly, we will believe the promise, we should address ourselves to believe in him.

[3.] There is yet another circumstance in this instance; all of them were not true believers, but the faith of some made others partakers of the benefits. The ungodly receive many temporal benefits by the faith of others: Acts xxvii. 24, 'God hath given thee all them that sail with thee;' while yet many of them were infidels. The faith of some may save a community; 'through faith,' that is, the faith of Moses, and some of the eminent godly Israelites. We must not think all this multitude had faith; but it was so pleasing to God, that for their sakes the community passed safe, and did arrive at the opposite shore. Now this showeth how much God esteemeth the faith of his children.

[4.] It is commended to us again by the distinction God makes between believers and unbelievers; the one pass through the sea as on dry land, and the other sink as lead, and are drowned. We see our privileges in their destruction. Salvation is not a common favour: John iii. 36, 'He that believeth on the Son hath everlasting life; and he that believeth not the Son, shall not see life, but the wrath of God abideth on him.' There is salvation for believers, and nothing but destruction for unbelievers. Presumption ruins, as faith saves. Oh! who would not then be of the number of those that believe in Christ to salvation, since God makes such a distinction between them and others?

Having laid this foundation, the doctrine is this—

Doct. That they who, upon the belief of God's promises, do resolve to run all hazards with Christ in the performance of their duty to him, are only capable of salvation by him.

This is the end why the apostle produces this instance, to encourage the New Testament believers to constancy in the many sufferings they were exposed to for owning Christ; and to continue faithful to Christ, and depend upon the promises still, though they were butchered and slaughtered everyday. To evidence this, take these five considerations—

First, That true faith receives the promise of God, with the terms and conditions which it requireth. This proposition, I suppose, will not be questioned. If the Israelites in the text hoped to see the salvation of God, they must do what God directed them to do. And of all others the like is required; if they will believe, and expect any benefit from God, certainly they must do what God hath required in order to that benefit. All that can reasonably be supposed to invalidate the truth of this proposition is this: either that the gospel is no benefit, but a due debt from God, which we may expect from his natural goodness, and so that God hath not power to give it upon condition; or that he will give it without condition. One of these must be supposed. Now, if all these be false, then the proposition stands firmly.

1. The first supposition, that the gospel is no benefit, but a due debt from God, which we may expect from his natural goodness, do we whatever we will to the contrary, is an absurd conceit; for the privileges of the gospel are always represented as a benefit. 1 Tim. vi. 2, the apostle shows that christian masters should not be despised by their christian servants, ' but rather do them service, because they are faithful and beloved partakers of the benefit; ' that is, of the privileges of the gospel: it is always represented as a benefit. And it is such a benefit as is called grace, and this oppositely to debt: Rom. iv. 4, ' Now to him which worketh is the reward reckoned, not of grace, but of debt; ' for God is not bound by any merit to give this grace to any. Well, then, if it be God's free gift, then he hath a power to impose conditions; it is at the liberty of the donor to give it upon what terms he pleases, for who but the Almighty can prescribe conditions and laws of commerce betwixt him and his creatures? It belongs to every donor and free benefactor to make his own terms, and to dispose of his own gifts and donations according to his will. If it be a right which belongs to every ordinary person who is an owner to do with his own as pleaseth him, Mat. xx. 15, much more the great God may determine of his own gifts, and how a right to them may be conveyed to us. Well, then, thus far we go on clearly that the privileges of the gospel are a grace, and a grace to be disposed of by him according to the pleasure of his own will. But then—

2. I add further; either God will give them without any conditions, or he will give those benefits upon certain terms and conditions which he liketh to impose upon the creature. Now, to grant as much as may be granted, there are certain benefits indeed which God gives without asking our consent, or imposing any condition upon us on our part;

as the giving of a redeemer to take our nature and fulfil the law, and satisfy his provoked justice on our behalf, and to merit grace sufficient for our deliverance from sin, and death, and hell, and the devil ; this he did without our knowledge and consent, for he considered us as creatures in misery, and in more inextricable straits than the Israelites were when they were shut up between mountains and entangled in the land, as Pharaoh saith.   But having laid this foundation, God having given a redeemer, then he doth enact and propound a covenant, without asking our consent, or treating with us in the making of it, that we may bring it down, and model it according to our humour. No ; the matter is not left free for us to debate ; the covenant is formed to our hands, and we are thankfully to accept of it, and submit to it, not to mould it to our turn ; for we must take it as we find it ; and so the saints are described, Isa. lvi. 4, 'Those that choose the things that please me, and take hold of my covenant.'   The question now is, Whether there be any terms or no terms in this covenant? Surely there are ; for these blessings are not given to all, as experience manifests, for some die in their sins. How shall poor creatures make out their interest, unless God hath declared upon what conditions we shall be possessed of these privileges ?   Well, now, if God hath once declared the conditions, if we would have the benefit, we must consent to them ; as the Israelites, if they would be safe, they must take God's direction, and pass through the Red Sea, though it seem to threaten apparent death.   If we would have justification and adoption into God's family, we must believe in Christ : John i. 12, 'For to as many as received him, to them gave he power to become the sons of God, even to them which believe on his name.'   If we would look for everlasting life, 'we must by a patient continuing in well-doing seek for honour, and glory, and immortality,' Rom. ii. 7.   To expect a benefit without terms is to lay the foundation of a great building upon a shadow, and to deceive ourselves with a covenant of our own making, or to presume of that which was never given to us by God.   Indeed, whence we have the grace to perform the condition, whether from God or ourselves, that is another question ; but a condition there is ; we are only proving the way and order of being instated into the benefits promised, and the necessity that true faith should submit to it.   It is true we have the first grace from God ; the conversion of the heart is from God as a free lord ; it is his resolved gift to the elect. But we are speaking now, not of what God does as a free lord, but of a condition stated by our proper and rightful sovereign—the giving of the grace whereby we fulfil the condition that belongs wholly to his free dominion ; but appointing the condition, that belongs not wholly to his free dominion, but his being the supreme ruler and governor of the world.   Now we must take the promise with the terms and conditions annexed.

Secondly, That the conditions which God requireth are, partly a belief of the promise, and partly obedience to the command annexed ; as the Israelites were to believe that God would carry them safe and sound to the next shore through the Red Sea as upon firm land ; and therefore, believing this, they were, upon the authority of God's word, to resolve to go down into the great deep, and try what God would do for them. Their faith was seen in trusting him with the event, without any anxiety and trouble of mind ; and their obedience was seen in taking the course and way they were prescribed by God, even through the deep water ; though it was so unlikely a way for their preservation, yet they ventured themselves. So we, that believe in Christ for eternal life, must first believe God's promise, that he will bring us to that blissful estate through the way appointed ; and so we must resolve to take this way, and follow God whithersoever he leads us by his word and Spirit, that we may obtain this happiness. It is a great point, and a part of faith, to believe the promise ; there is very much in that; for though we all desire to be happy, yet this happiness being promised by an invisible God, and lying in an invisible world, it is not easily assented unto ; it is not received with that trust and strength of faith by us while we dwell in flesh, and have a corrupt nature within us, which is importunate to be pleased with present things or carnal vanities, which are nigh at hand, and therefore ready to be enjoyed. Therefore it is a great work of the Lord's grace 'to open our eyes, that we may know what is the hope of his calling, and what the riches of the glory of his inheritance in the saints,' Eph. i. 18 ; to look to things unseen, which are eternal, and to overlook those that are seen, that are temporal : 2 Cor. iv. 18, ' While we look not at the things which are seen, which are but temporal, but at the things which are not seen, which are eternal.' This is a mighty act of faith. Most men mind earthly things, cannot take heaven for their whole happiness, or the word of God for their great security, for that is only done by a soul that sincerely believes : Ps. cxix. 111, ' Thy testimonies I have taken as an heritage forever, they are the rejoicing of my soul.' The next part is to resolve to seek this happiness in God's way, to follow it close whatever it cost us, to hold on in our journey, be our way safe or dangerous, rough or pleasant : Phil. iii. 11, ' If by any means I might attain unto the resurrection of the dead.' A christian must come to this ; whatever way it is that God leads me into by his word and Spirit, so I may attain happiness at last, I will hold on my course. And so it may fall out that we must ' hate our own lives, and forsake all we have,' Luke xiv. 26, 33 ; not as casting it away needlessly and unprofitably, but venturing it for God's sake, running the hazard of life, and leaving all we have, rather than miss of eternal life, and being unfaithful to Christ.

Thirdly, These being the conditions, the belief of the promise, and thorough obedience to submit to the appointed way; lest we deceive ourselves with a notion, God loves to try us, to see if we have received the promise sincerely, whether we thoroughly believe his word, and are fully obedient to his commands: James i. 12, ' Blessed is the man that endureth temptation, for when he is tried he shall receive the crown of life, which the Lord hath promised to them that love him.' The Lord loves a tried obedience, because it is most for his honour when his people are tried, and they are faithful to him; and it is most for our comfort to make our sincerity evident to us. Sometimes the difficulties lie against our assent to the truth of the promise ; at other times, against our resolution to follow God's way, cleaving to him and Christ, and not looking back.

1. Against the strength of our assent, whether we can believe such unlikely things as God hath promised (for so it seems to carnal reason), as that he can carry his people through the deep waters, and they shall not overflow them.   Certainly many doubts arise in our minds concerning unseen things, which we cannot enjoy till we shoot the gulf of death.   Now Abraham, the father of the faithful, was so called because he could assent so strongly to the promises, and give glory to God 'by believing in hope against hope :' Rom. iv. 18–20, ' And being not weak in faith, he considered not his own body, now dead, when he was about an hundred years old, neither yet the deadness of Sarah's womb ; he staggered not at the promise of God through unbelief, but was strong in faith, giving glory to God.'   Faith can expect a deliverance when it seems impossible to reason.   When Abraham was childless, and had been so for many years, yet he expects an issue that for number shall be as the sand upon the sea-shore.   If there be not some difficulty in the thing to be believed, it is not an object of faith ; for things present within the view of sense, and things easy and next at hand, are, as it were, already enjoyed.   It is no trial of your faith to look for probable things ; but if you can believe when the case is never so difficult, if you can depend and rest yourselves upon the word of God, that you shall be carried through the sea and not be drowned, because you have God's word for it, this is faith.   Many difficulties may be objected against such things as God hath revealed in his word ; yet it is enough to a believer that God hath revealed them.   Our inquiry, when we come to look into the things we are to believe, should not be, How can these things be ? No ; but, Are these things revealed by God, yea or nay ?   How can these things be ? is the voice of unbelief, at the least, of a weak and staggering faith.   Nicodemus said, ' How can these things be ? ' John iii. 9. We are to receive supernatural truths as men take pills, not chew, but swallow them, take them upon the credit of the revealer ; if the testifier be God himself, his word should be more to us than the greatest evidence in the world.

2. Sometimes the difficulties lie against our resolution to take God's way.   A total resignation of ourselves to the will of God is required of all that will be saved.   Now by dangers we are tried whether we will keep this resolution.   Strength of assent excludes speculative doubts and errors ; strength of resolution fortifies us against worldly temptations, both on the right hand and on the left.   On the right hand temptations do arise from worldly profit, pleasure, and glory ; on the left hand temptations do arise from fears of danger and terrors of sense.   Now, when these come with full power upon the soul, they are ready to shake the most confirmed resolution ; but a christian is to maintain the vigor of his faith, and cherish such a confidence in God's promises as may check all fear, and cause him, when God calls him thereunto, to venture on the greatest dangers rather than quit his duty: Ps. xxiii. 4, ' Yea, though I walk through the valley of the shadow of death, I will fear no evil.'   It was a comfortless journey in the midst of waves for so many men, women, and children to hold it ; yet a believer that ventures upon God's command fears nothing : Dan. iii. 17, 18, ' If it be so, our God, whom we serve, is able to deliver us from the burning fiery furnace, and he will deliver us out of thine hand, O king !

But if not, be it known unto thee, O king, that we will not serve thy gods, nor worship the golden image which thou hast set up.' Thus are we to show our undaunted confidence of God's protection and deliverance.

Fourthly, Because we are fickle creatures, God will have us, by the solemn profession of such a faith, visibly to enter into his covenant. As God meant to season Israel for after trials, therefore they were baptized in the cloud and in the sea, as was said before, that they might the better submit to his conduct throughout the wilderness, before he brought them into the land of promise ; so all those that are willing to take Christ and his cross, Christ and his yoke, the Lord will not leave them under the tie of a bare purpose and resolution, but will have it solemnised in the baptismal covenant, wherein we profess a belief of God's promises, and vow to run all hazards with Christ in our warfare against the devil, the world, and the flesh. We cannot forsake the devil, but he will make as hard pursuit after us as Pharaoh did after Israel, to bring us back again into bondage ; he doth violently assault new converts. We cannot renounce the world, and the vain courses thereof, but it will hate us, and be exasperated against us. The world only loveth its own, and those that are of a worldly strain, and will not part company with them ; they hate others, speak evil of them, and do evil to them. The flesh will entice us to some unfaithfulness to Christ, and compliance with the world, and disobedience to God, and it will be troublesome to resist its motions. Therefore God will have us solemnly roll ourselves in this calendar, and as soon as we are baptized we put on our armour : Rom. vi. 13, 'Wherefore yield ye your members instruments, ὅπλα, weapons of righteousness;' and Rom. xiii. 12, 'Let us cast off the works of darkness, and put on the armour of light.' Then we are solemnly listed in Christ's service. He was baptized as the captain of our salvation, and we as his soldiers: and when we are baptized soldiers we are to arm ourselves with this resolution, through many tribulations to enter into the kingdom of God. Christ's first work is to lead us into the waters, that we may be seasoned for other encounters, or that fight of afflictions and troubles we are likely to meet withal before we get to heaven : Heb. x. 32, 'After ye were illuminated, ye endured a great fight of affliction.' Baptism was heretofore called an enlightening, because there was wonderful grace given in the use of that ordinance in the primitive times. Now, when we are enlightened, we presently enter upon our warfare, and we must look for a fight.

Fifthly, Having thus solemnly entered into covenant with God, certainly we are bound to make it good, if we would have benefit by it. For it is not enough to make covenant, but all the promises run to him that keepeth covenant. Salvation is promised not to the undertaker, but the conqueror : Rev. ii. 7, 'To him that overcometh will I give to eat of the tree of life, which is in the midst of the paradise of God;' and ver. 11, 'He that overcometh shall not be hurt of the second death ;' and ver. 17, 'To him that overcometh will I give to eat of the hidden manna, and I will give him a white stone, and in the stone a new name written, which no man knoweth, saving he that receiveth it;' and ver. 26, 'He that overcometh, and keepeth my works unto the end, to him will I give power over the nations;' and chap.

iii. 5, 'He that overcometh, the same shall be clothed in white raiment, and I will not blot out his name out of the book of life, but I will confess his name before my father and before his angels.' Therefore it is not enough to undertake, but we must perform; it is not enough to renounce, but we must overcome, not only forsake the devil, but resist him: James iv. 7, 'Resist the devil, and he will flee from you;' Peter v. 9, 'Whom resist, steadfast in the faith.' We must not only renounce the flesh, but we must mortify and subdue it by the Spirit: Gal. v. 24, 'They that are Christ's have crucified the flesh, with the affections and lusts thereof;' Rom. viii. 13, 'If ye, through the Spirit, mortify the deeds of the body, ye shall live.' We must not only renounce the world, but overcome it: 1 John v. 4, 'Whosoever is born of God overcometh the world, and this is the victory whereby we overcome the world, even our faith;' and we must be crucified to it: Gal. vi. 14, 'The world is crucified to me, and I unto the world,' and so persevere in our duty to God.

Use 1. To inform us of the nature of true faith, so to believe the promises as to be ready to do what God commandeth, to obtain the benefit of them. It concerneth us very much to understand the nature of faith, for we live by it: Gal. ii. 20, 'I live by the faith of the Son of God;' and can we live by it and not know what it is? What is it then? It is such a trusting ourselves in the hands of Christ, upon a confidence of his promises, that we are willing to do anything and suffer anything rather than commit the least sin, and be unfaithful to him. Or a resolution to go on with our duty, trusting ourselves entirely in his hands, whatever dangers befall us. This is called a committing of our souls to him in well-doing: 1 Peter iv. 19, 'Wherefore let them that suffer according to the will of God commit the keeping of their souls to him in well-doing, as unto a faithful creator.' And the apostle saith, 2 Tim. i. 12, 'I know whom I have believed, and I am persuaded that he is able to keep that which I have committed to him against that day.' The Israelites, when they went into the Red Sea, did entirely commit and put themselves into God's hands. It is a notable faith when we can so readily believe God, and hold on our duty with quietness, whatever evils do befall us, or whatever dangers threaten us: Ps. xxxvii. 34, 'Wait on the Lord, and keep his way, and he shall cause thee to inherit the land.' Obey God's directions, and see how God will make good his word.

Use 2. Reproof. It condemneth several sorts of persons—

1. Those that are always urging difficulties against their duty, and pretend danger when there is no cause: Prov. xxii. 13, 'The slothful man saith, There is a lion without; I shall be slain in the streets.' And again, Prov. xxvi. 13, 'The slothful man saith, There is a lion in the way, a lion is in the streets.' In those countries lions were frequent, and their range was in the night, when they went forth to seek for their prey: Ps. civ. 20, 21, 'Thou makest darkness, and it is night, wherein all the beasts of the forest do creep forth. The young lions roar after their prey, and seek their meat from God.' Now the slothful man's pretence was, that if he should go forth too early to his labour, he should meet a lion in the very streets. Now it is used proverbially of those that urge any slight danger against their

duty; because sometimes the lions came into the cities and inhabited places, therefore he durst not go out of his house. There are some that will not venture a frown or a scorn for Christ, and dare not own religion, when there is no probable cause for fear; and so are frighted out of their necessary duty, not only by real dangers, but by imaginary fears: the shadow of any trouble quite discourageth them.

2. Those that attempt anything without a lawful call. The Israelites had a good call; they had a command from God to enter into the Red Sea, and they had a promise of God's protection. He that will undergo dangers, let him see how his matters stand with God, and what ground he hath both for his undertaking and for his confidence and courage.

[1.] For his undertaking. For these Israelites, who at God's bidding could enter the Red Sea, yet presuming against God's warrant to go up against the Canaanites, were beaten: Num. xiv. 44, 45, 'But they presumed to go up unto the hill top: nevertheless the ark of the covenant of the Lord and Moses departed not out of the camp. Then the Amalekites came down, and the Canaanites which dwelt in that hill, and smote them, and discomfited them, even unto Hormah.' The case was this, they had murmured at the report of the spies, and when they had smarted for that by a sore plague, they would all of a sudden go up and fight the Canaanites to expiate the suspicion of their cowardice. The ark removed not, but at the removal of the cloud, Num. v. 17, 21; and Moses would abide by the ark. But God showed his dislike of the action, because they went without the Lord, and the signs of his grace.

[2.] What ground there is for their courage and confidence; for in particular events we have no assurance but from God's especial promise. Indeed, in all lawful undertakings we have the promise of God concerning eternal life to bear us up, and we may be confident of this: Luke xii. 32, 'Fear not, little flock; for it is your father's good pleasure to give you the kingdom.' But for other things we must refer them to God. For eternal salvation we may be sure, but for other things nothing but a particular promise can be the strong pillar of our confidence.

Quest. But if we have no express promise, may we not bear up ourselves against difficulties and improbabilities by believing in God?

Ans. If believing be meant only of a confidence in God's power, not determining the certainty of the event, we may. Many times we are cast upon God's providence; all human refuge and helps fail, there is no possibility of escape; but then God forbiddeth despair: 2 Cor. i. 9, 10, 'But we had received the sentence of death in ourselves, that we should not trust in ourselves, but in God, which raiseth the dead. Who delivered us from so great a death, and doth deliver, in whom we trust that he will yet deliver us.' It was when the furious multitude at Ephesus was let loose upon him. But the truer trust is showed in a ready adherence to his call and to our duty: Ps. xliv. 18, 19, 'Our heart is not turned back, neither have our steps declined from thy way, though thou hast sore broken us in the place of dragons, and covered us with the shadow of death.'

3. It condemneth them who pretend to faith, and yet do not make a total resignation of themselves to God.

[1.] Some reserve their interests. Now you have not saving faith till you can sell all for the pearl of price: Mat. xiii. 45, 46, 'The kingdom of heaven is like to a merchantman seeking goodly pearls; who, when he had found one pearl of great price, he went and sold all that he had, and bought it.' One cometh boldly to Christ: Mat. viii. 19, 'Lord, I will follow thee whithersoever thou goest;' but when he heard, ver. 20, 'The foxes have holes, and the birds of the air have nests, but the Son of man hath not where to lay his head,' we hear no more of him. The young man came to Christ to know 'what good thing he should do to have eternal life,' Mat. xix. 16; but when Christ said to him, 'Sell all thou hast, and give to the poor, and thou shalt have treasure in heaven, and come and follow me,' ver. 21; when the young man heard that saying, he went away sorrowful, for he had great possessions, ver. 22. Therefore faith being so necessary to salvation, cheat not yourselves with the image of it.

[2.] Some reserve their lusts; but true faith is inconsistent with the predominancy of any lust or sin; for a christian wholly giveth up himself to the will of God. Therefore he that continueth in his sins, not resolving in his heart to forsake them and to renounce all righteousness in himself, and wholly and solely to rely upon the mercy of God and merit of Christ, betaking himself to a new course of life, mistakes God's promise, and his faith will end in shame and confusion: Isa. lv. 7, 'Let the wicked forsake his way, and the unrighteous man his thoughts, and let him return unto the Lord, and he will have mercy on him, and to our God, for he will abundantly pardon.'

Use 3. Of exhortation. To exhort you to such an entire resignation of yourselves to the will of God, and dependence upon his promises, that you may be prepared to go on with your duty, whatever hazards you incur by it.

To press you to this, consider how obedience and dependence do mutually befriend each other. It may be made good by these two considerations—(1.) None can hope for salvation but he that keeps God's way; (2.) None can keep God's way but he that hopes for salvation. They each depend upon one another.

1. None can hope for salvation but he that would keep God's way, because God hath by a wise ordination conjoined ends and means. He hath not simply promised blessedness, but requires a qualification and a performance of duty in the persons to whom the promise is made: Ps. i. 1, 2, 'Blessed is the man that walketh not in the counsel of the ungodly, nor standeth in the way of sinners, nor sitteth in the seat of the scornful: but his delight is in the law of the Lord, and in his law doth he meditate day and night.' And Ps. cxix. 1, 2, 'Blessed are the undefiled in the way, who walk in the law of the Lord: blessed are they that keep his testimonies, and that seek him with the whole heart.' There is blessedness; ay, but we must keep the way of the Lord, and that punctually, and be undefiled in that way. To look upon one side of the covenant, as upon the promises only, is a groundless presumption; so that whosoever live in any sin against conscience, they may take notice how fearful their estate is

for the present, how needful it is to begin a good course before they can have any good hope towards God.

Besides, there is no such course to damp our hope and weaken our confidence as sin. Surely we cannot trust him whom we offend freely and without restraint. Sin will breed shame and fear, as pain will follow upon the prick of a needle; and where it is allowed, you will soon find the effects of it. On the contrary, faith and love go together; faith that hopes in his promises, and love that seeketh to please God. Sin, that now weakens the faith we have in the commandment, will in time weaken the faith we have in the promises. It may be for the present our confidence in God's mercy and promises is not directly assaulted; we bear on with a little slight hope till the hour of death, or the time of some extraordinary trial; but when the evil day comes, the consciousness of any one sin which we have indulged, allowed, and lived in, will be of like force to withdraw our assent from God's mercies, as the delight and pleasure of sin is now to tempt us to transgress his commandments: 'For the sting of death is sin, and the strength of sin is the law,' 1 Cor. xv. 56. When we feel the stings of sin, then we shall doubt of the mercies of God. And that is the reason why dying persons, when they are serious, have so many troubled thoughts within them. And take the experience of the godly, they find this still; when they have been acquainted with a spiritual life, their hope increases by their diligence in a holy life. And the scripture tells us so: Heb. vi. 11, 'And we desire that every one of you do show the same diligence to the full assurance of hope unto the end.' The more diligent we are in a holy life, the more hope and the more confidence we shall have in God's mercy and in the merits of Christ; for then our qualification is more clear. So far as a man neglects his duty and abates in his qualification, so far does his assurance abate; it must needs be so. Therefore, mark, none can hope for salvation but he that will keep God's way, and that is resolved to be at God's direction.

2. None can keep God's way but those that hope for his salvation; for without this we can never have a heart or head to do anything for God. It is a notable passage of Bernard, *Peccator nihil expectat, indeque peccator est, quod bonis præsentibus non solum detentus, sed etiam contentus*—A sinner hopes for nothing, and therefore he is a sinner, because he is not only withheld by present things, but satisfied with them. They that look for no great matters from God in another world, no wonder they are so negligent and careless of their duty; they can never be diligent in his service, or faithful and true to him. Besides, the difficulties and dangers which attend us, if we will be sincerely obedient, are so many and great, that if we begin with God, we shall not go on with him unless we surely depend on the blessedness he offereth to us: Heb. x. 39, 'We are not of them that draw back to perdition, but of them that believe to the saving of the soul;' that is, who purchase the salvation of the soul with the loss of other things, as the word signifies. Well, then, let these always be coupled: if we would keep the commandments of God, we must hope for the salvation of God; and if we would hope for the salvation of God, we must keep the commandments of God. This is most acceptable to God, most comfortable to you, and most honourable to religion. It is

most acceptable to God: Ps. cxlvii. 11, 'The Lord taketh pleasure in them that fear him, in those that hope in his mercy.' Oh! when these two are coupled, the fear to offend him and dependence upon his grace in Christ, the Lord takes pleasure in them. And it will be most comfortable to you: Acts ix. 31, 'They walked in the fear of the Lord, and in the comforts of the Holy Ghost.' And it is most honourable to religion, for this is the religion of Christ's making; religion is then in its true constitution and frame: Mat. xi. 29, 'Take my yoke upon you, and learn of me, for I am meek and lowly of heart, and ye shall find rest for your souls.' When we reflect upon the proper ground of comfort, the mercy of God, the covenant of grace, and the merits of the Redeemer, and keep up a due care of obedience, this is christian religion. And it is an honourable thing in the world; and this will show that you are sincere and upright; and that after a while that you have gone on walking in his fear, and in the comforts of the Holy Ghost, you shall enjoy his blessed presence in heaven.

SERMON LXIV.

By faith the walls of Jericho fell down, after they were compassed about seven days.—HEB. xi. 30.

IN the last verse we have represented the faith of Israel under the conduct of Moses, now we shall represent their faith under the conduct of Joshua. There we saw what was done in their passage out of Egypt, here we shall see what is done in their entrance into Canaan. 'By faith the walls of Jericho fell down,' &c. Here is—

1. The grace exercised—*Faith.*

2. The event that followed—*The walls of Jericho fell down.*

3. The manner how it was accomplished—*After they were compassed about seven days.* Where—(1.) The means, 'They were compassed about;' (2.) The time, 'Seven days.'

1. The grace exercised—Faith. The great skill of christians is to find out the new testament pre-signified in the old, and the old testament fulfilled in the new; both agree to tell us the way of living by faith in Christ. Joshua was a type of Christ, as his name shows, which in the new testament is always written *Jesus:* as Acts vii. 45, 'They were brought in with Jesus into the possession of the gentiles,' and Heb. iv. 8, 'If Jesus had given them rest;' that is, Joshua. Now this also was the name of our Lord: Mat. i. 21, 'Thou shalt call his name Jesus (which signifies a saviour), for he shall save his people from their sins.' Joshua was a great captain; and Christ is the 'captain of our salvation,' Heb. ii. 10. Joshua was to overcome strongholds, and whatever let the people's possessing the land of promise; so doth Christ demolish all strongholds, the devil and the grave, death and hell, that he may introduce us into the heavenly Canaan, the land of our eternal rest. Joshua overcame by God's appointed means, by

the priests marching before, and the ark of the covenant following, and then the people: Joshua vi. 8, 'And it came to pass when Joshua had spoken unto the people, that the seven priests, bearing the seven trumpets of rams' horns, passed on before the Lord, and blew with the trumpets, and the ark of the covenant of the Lord followed them,' &c. So doth Christ overcome by the gospel; the ark of the covenant is our strength: Ps. cv. 4, 'Seek the Lord and his strength, seek his face evermore.' The priests blowing with trumpets of rams' horns is a figure of the power of the ministry; for so the apostle explains this: 2 Cor x. 4, 5, 'For the weapons of our warfare are not carnal, but mighty through God to the pulling down of strongholds, casting down imaginations, and every high thing that exalteth itself against the knowledge of God, and bringing into captivity every thought to the obedience of Christ.' As they by the blast of their trumpets were to throw down this strong city, the way to be partakers of this benefit is faith; they walked about with the ark of the covenant, and the priests blowing their trumpets, submitting to God's direction; they expected the event; and so the prayer of faith will do very much to the demolishing of the strongholds of Satan as we go to the promised land.

2. The event that followed—the walls of Jericho falling down; their hope was not frustrated. If we will believe God's promises, and execute his commands, we need no shifts, or artifices, or secular policy, or means of our own, to work deliverance for us. To evidence the greatness of the success, we must know—

[1.] That Jericho was a strong and well-fenced city, one of those which frighted the spies who were sent to view the land: Num. xiii. 20, 'The cities are walled, and very great.' And see how the people aggravate the report of the spies: Deut. i. 28, 'The cities are great, and walled up to heaven; and, moreover, we have seen the sons of the Anakim there.' Every rumour increases in the spreading. This city, amongst others, to men's eyes seemed impregnable, so much we gather from Joshua, chap. vi. 1, 'Now Jericho was straitly shut up, because of the children of Israel; none went out, and none came in.' In the Hebrew (and so it is noted in the margin), the city 'did shut up itself;' that is, it was strongly fortified in itself, both by its situation and by art, and was shut up by the obstinacy of the inhabitants.

[2.] It was a frontier town, the first that kept them from entering far into Canaan, being the first city of Canaan on the west side of Jordan, by which the people entered into the land; and until this rub and impediment was taken out of the way, they could not safely make any further passage. Now, if they should miscarry in their first attempt, it would, in the eyes of the Canaanites, bring a disreputation upon their arms and contradict the report of the mighty wonders that were wrought for them; and in the eyes of the Israelites it would be a great discouragement to their faith. Therefore, in this first attempt, God would open a safe and ready way and passage to his people, and by this victory give them a pledge of further mercy. And therefore, upon their faith and obedience to God, the walls fell flat to the ground, Joshua vi. 20, for nothing can stand before the power of God and the faith of his people. Now this gave great courage to Israel to see that God owned them in it; but it was a great terror to the Canaanites; for in fighting against his people, they were to fight with God.

3. The manner, how it was accomplished—'After it was compassed about seven days:' where take notice of the means and time.

[1.] The means is intimated in the word, 'They were compassed about.' To understand which, we must have recourse to the story. They had a special command from God to walk about Jericho, and had a promise that it should fall down flat, Joshua vi. 4, 5. Now their faith was manifested by obedience to his command and dependence upon his promise. The means may be considered negatively or positively; what they did not, and what they did.

(1.) Negatively, what they did not. (1.) They make no trenches to keep themselves safe. (2.) They stand not in battle array to repel the excursions of their enemies, but march on one after another in the order prescribed: Joshua vi. 9, 'The armed men went before the priests that blew the trumpets; and the rear-ward came after the ark, the priests going on and blowing with the trumpets.' (3.) They lay no formal siege to assault the city; set no engines of battery against the walls. (4.) The people raised no cry to create terror: Joshua vi. 10, 'And Joshua had commanded the people, saying, Ye shall not shout, nor make any noise with your voice, neither shall any word come out of your mouth, until the day I bid you shout, then shall ye shout.' It was meet that no noise should be heard, but that God's voice should be attended upon with silence and quietness on the people's part, that it might visibly appear their enemies were not overcome by the power of men, but of God. So that, by this negative view, we see the victory was not to be accomplished by force of arms, effusion of blood, or any other means which carnal reason or common sense would suggest; for God, without blow or bloodshed, can bring mighty things to pass.

(2.) Positively, what means they used: nothing but a procession of the ark, and armed men, and seven priests with seven trumpets of rams' horns sounding to them. Silver trumpets were not used, though in a general case they were prescribed: Num. x. 9, 'And if you go to war in your land against the enemy that oppresseth you, then ye shall blow an alarm with the trumpets, and ye shall be remembered before the Lord your God, and ye shall be saved from your enemies.' And an instance of the success of it we have in the Jews' war against apostate Israel, when they say, 2 Chron. xiii. 12, 'And, behold, God himself is with us for our captain, and his priests with sounding trumpets to cry alarm against you: O children of Israel, fight ye not against the Lord God of your fathers, for you shall not prosper.' This promise annexed to the signs was fulfilled, and was a type and pledge of God's blessing when his ministers stir up his people against Satan, sin, and antichrist, wherein the Lord will be with them and bless their labours. This was to be ordinarily done by silver trumpets, but in this case God would try them by more despicable means, by trumpets made with rams' horns. And then the ark followed the priests, which was a special evidence of God's presence among them; for when the ark was lifted up, the priests were to cry, 'Rise up, Lord, and let thine enemies be scattered, and let them that hate thee flee before thee,' Num. x. 35. A type of Christ's ascension and conquering the enemies of our salvation;

as ye shall see the same words are used, Ps. lxviii. 1, ' Let God arise, and let his enemies be scattered ; let them also that hate him flee before him.' And that psalm is a prophecy of Christ's ascension, as appears by the 18th and 19th verses, compared with Eph. iv. 8–10. As the ark was among the Israelites, so is Christ among his people ; and what ground the church had because of that pledge of God's presence to expect deliverance, we have the same ground, yea, a more sure ground of confidence in Christ. Whenever he begins to stir and show himself, woe be to those that oppose his kingdom and interest in the world ; he hath the same care, power, and faithfulness towards his people that ever he had at first. When he ascended up to heaven, he went thither conquering and triumphing, and still can subdue and conquer a rebellious world to himself. Well, in this order they went round about the city for six days together ; and the event succeeded : this was to prove their faith the more, and to try their obedience and patience.

[2.] We come to the time—' After they had compassed about the city seven days.' They were every day to make this procession once ; and the event appeared not till the last and seventh day. No reason can be given why it must be the seventh day but God's will ; only a septenary is a sacred number. On the seventh day, when the signal fore-appointed was given, the people gave a shout, and the event succeeded ; the walls fell down.

Now, from the means thus positively considered, I might observe two things—

(1.) That the means seemed ridiculous in the eye of reason ; for what could seven priests blowing of seven rams' horns be to overturn such great and strong walls ? But God's command and promise will do great matters, for he can bring his ends to pass by means that have not any natural aptitude and fitness thereunto. And the apostle saith, 2 Cor. x. 4, ' The weapons of our warfare are not carnal, but mighty through God to the pulling down of strongholds.' And faith must use such means as God hath appointed, though they seem weak.

(2.) Though these means seem ineffectual at first, yet we must tarry God's leisure ; they will succeed in time, and they shall do what God intendeth to do by them. The walls of Jericho shall not fall down till the seventh day God hath his set time to bring his people out of Egyptian bondage, and he kept touch to a day, though he seemed almost to break his word, for it was night before they went forth : Exod. xii. 41, ' And it came to pass, at the end of the four hundred and thirty years, even the selfsame day it came to pass, that all the hosts of the Lord went out from the land of Egypt.' And so in many other cases. Our times are always present with us out of impatiency of the flesh, when it may be God's time is not yet come. But they that would faithfully promote the interests of Christ's kingdom must tarry God's leisure.

Doct. That it is the property of faith to adhere faithfully to the interest of Christ's kingdom, quietly waiting for his salvation.

The business of the apostle in this chapter is to confirm the minds of the believers in adhering to christianity against the temptations of that age, which were of two sorts—(1.) The slender appearance of the growth and progress of that religion; the church of God being but as a grain of mustard-seed cast into the ground, and coming up at first but with a few slender stalks and branches, which promised no great increase. (2.) The other temptation was the manifold oppositions they met with; their profession exposing them to great troubles, therefore they were quite discouraged, some began to forsake the assemblies of the faithful, and to be weary of persecuted christianity. Now, to cure them of this disease, he shows them what faith hath done in all ages, and what great things have been accomplished by weak means, whilst God's people had a heart to depend upon him; and among the rest, he produces this instance of the taking and demolishing of Jericho by the blowing of rams' horns. If this instance were useful for them, it is so for us; for all ages have their discouragements, and feeble minds soon faint and give out upon the least opposition. Therefore let us see what we shall learn from thence. I shall lay down seven propositions—

First, That Christ's purpose after his ascension was to destroy the kingdom of darkness. This is evident: Ps. cx. 1, 'The Lord said unto my Lord, Sit thou on my right hand until I make thine enemies thy footstool.' Christ upon the throne hath enemies here in the world, but in due time they shall be his footstool. He shall gain upon opposition, and against opposition, and by opposition; and they shall be so far from overturning his throne, that his enemies shall be a step or footstool to get into it. The same is emblematically set forth, Rev. vi. 2, 'And I saw, and behold a white horse: and he that sat on him had a bow; and a crown was given unto him: and he went forth conquering, and to conquer.' This is a notable representation of the rise and progress of Christ's kingdom; he comes forth upon a white horse, and his furniture is a crown and a bow. His crown notes his dignity, and his bow the armour and weapons whereby he promotes his authority: Ps. xlv. 3, 4, 'Gird thy sword upon thy thigh, O most Mighty, with thy glory and thy majesty. And in thy majesty ride prosperously, because of truth, and meekness, and righteousness; and thy right hand shall teach thee terrible things.' Christ is furnished to subdue and conquer, and bring as many as he pleases into a subjection to his kingdom; for it is added, ver. 5, 'Thine arrows are sharp in the heart of the king's enemies; whereby the people fall under thee.' He hath weapons to wound the consciences of sinners, and pierce deep into their hearts. Having a grant of a kingdom over the nations, his design is to conquer and carry all before him, and he will do it.

Secondly, This kingdom of darkness is the state which is opposite to Christ's kingdom as mediator. The devils are said to be 'rulers of the darkness of this world,' Eph. vi. 12; and their power is called the power of darkness, as opposite to the kingdom of Christ, 'Who hath delivered us from the power of darkness,' Col. i. 13. The gospel kingdom is a kingdom of light, life, and love, where we have the clearest knowledge of God that begets life in us, and love to God and his people. Now opposite to light is ignorance and error; opposite to life is a religion that consists of shows and dead ceremonies; and opposite to love is uncharitableness, malice, hatred, especially of the power of godliness. Now, where these eminently prevail, there is an opposite kingdom set up against the kingdom of Christ, and this is done by two sorts of people—(1.) By all those that continue in the old apostasy and defection of mankind from God; as all men in their natural state, and eminently by the gentiles and idolatrous heathen world, who live in ignorance of the true God, and are dead in trespasses and sins, and where envy, pride, malice, and ambition reign, instead of the spirit of goodness and love which the gospel would produce. Now these men oppose the light that shines to them: John iii. 19, 'This is the condemnation, that light is come into the world, and men loved darkness rather than light, because their deeds were evil.' (2.) It may be and is done by a second falling away from Christ, which is foretold: 2 Thes. ii. 3, 'That day shall not come, except there come a falling away first, and that man of sin be revealed, the son of perdition;' that is, the day of judgment will not come till there be a falling away first. Now this falling off from Christ's kingdom is there where, in opposition to light, error is taught and ignorance is counted the mother of devotion, and people are restrained from the means of knowledge, as if the height of christian faith and obedience did consist in believing what men would impose upon them by their bare authority. And where, instead of life, men place their whole religion in some superficial rites and ceremonies, and some trifling acts of seeming devotion and exterior mortification; this is a kingdom opposite to that lively religion which Christ hath established. And instead of love to God and souls, all things are sacrificed to men's private ambition; and conscience is forced by the highest penalties and persecutions to submit to the corruptions of the christian faith and worship. And wherever this prevails, there is a manifest perversion of the interest of Christ's kingdom. Now this is the Jericho, the block in the way of God's people in their passage to the heavenly rest. Now both these apostasies, the general apostasy from God, and the special apostasy from Christ, are defended by the authority and power of the world, and upheld by the interests of several nations which own and practise these things; and God's people, in opposing them, are put to great difficulties. Therefore we are told that God's witnesses are slain in the city: 'And their dead bodies shall lie in the street of the great city which spiritually is called Sodom and Egypt, where also our Lord was crucified,' Rev. xi. 8; that is, the city which answers to Sodom for impurity, to Egypt for idolatry, and to Jerusalem for persecution of the saints; for that is the city wherein our Lord was crucified; he would not say Zion, because that is the name of the church. And till the wall of the city fall down (as it is prophesied there the tenth part of the wall shall fall down), there is an impediment and block in the way of christianity.

Thirdly, To demolish this corrupt estate we are all to be active in our several places; for we are employed as soldiers under the captain of our salvation. Our great business in the world is to promote the kingdom of light, life, and love; to be sure we enter into it ourselves, and to bring as many as we can along with us. (1.) That we enter into it ourselves, for much of the kingdom of God is within us: Luke xvii. 21, 'For behold the kingdom of God is within you.' And we must all become light in the Lord: Eph. v. 8, 'Ye were sometimes darkness, but now are ye light in the Lord.' And we that were dead in trespasses and sins must be quickened in Christ: Eph. ii. 1, 'You hath he quickened, who were dead in trespasses and sins.' And then the love of God must bear rule in our hearts, and fill us with all meekness, purity, charity, goodness, holiness, and heavenly-mindedness; we must see we be not of the opposite party of Christ. Now Christ hath much to do with every individual person before he can settle his kingdom in their hearts. There is a mighty combat between Christ and Satan for the rescue of every sinner that is recovered to God. The strong man seeks to keep his castle till a stronger than he comes to dispossess him: Luke xi. 21, 'When the strong man armed keeps the house, his goods are in peace.' Satan is the strong man armed, and the heart of every unconverted sinner is his garrison, which he keeps shut up against Christ by prejudices, carnal interests, worldly inclinations, and sensual allurements; and this strong man must be cast out, and his fort stormed and demolished, before a sinner can be gained, and brought to change masters, and leave his obstinate impenitency. Christ draws one way, the sinner another; for many times we seem ready to repent, but then we are drawn off again, loath to quit our carnal pleasures and company, and we would sit down and be quiet in our sins, but Christ will not let us alone, till at last we leave the fort to him. (2.) When Christ's government is set up in the heart, where Satan reigned before, then we must most earnestly seek to promote his interest in the world, and that others be fellows with us in the same grace. Naturally 'all seek their own things, and not the things of Jesus Christ,' Phil. ii. 21. But when we are the Lord's, and really made partakers of his grace, every one in his place must be a priest to God, we must blow the trumpet; by our desires, prayers, endeavours, and holy example, we must seek to promote Christ's kingdom, and draw others into the divine life. For this is one great effect of the love of God planted in our hearts, to convert others when we are converted ourselves: Luke xxii. 32, 'When thou art converted, strengthen thy brethren.' We are to invite them to have communion with us, as we have with the Father and the Son: 1 John i. 3, 'That which we have seen and heard declare we unto you, that ye also may have fellowship with us; and truly our fellowship is with the Father, and with his Son Jesus Christ.' Grace is and will be diffusive of itself; as fire turns all near it into fire, so every one in his capacity will endeavour to bring home others to God.

Fourthly, To do this we have means in the eye of sense very weak, whatever they are in the eye of faith. Our means are to appearance weak; like those in the text, they carried about the ark of the covenant, and made a blast with rams' horns. The preaching of the gospel, the prayers of the church, the faith and holy conversation of believers, and the patience of the saints, these are the means—by these and such like is the kingdom of sin, Satan, and antichrist demolished, and Christ's kingdom is set up in the world. These means are proper to the Mediator's dispensation, whose kingdom 'comes not with observation,' Luke xvii. 10. But his kingdom is not carried on in a way of external pomp, but by internal power and virtue. The word preached is one means, as the apostle tells us that by the preaching of the cross he was the great solicitor to proselyte, gain, and recover the world:

1 Cor. i. 18, ' The preaching of the cross is to them that perish foolishness, but unto us which are saved it is the power of God.' Use this means, and see what it will do. So the prayers of the church; for Christ taught us to pray, 'Thy kingdom come.' Acts iv. 24, 'And when they heard that, they lift up their voice with one accord;' ver. 31, 'And when they had prayed, the place was shaken, where they were assembled together, and they were all filled with the Holy Ghost, and they spake the word of God with boldness.' So also the holy conversation of believers: Mat. v. 16, ' Let your light so shine before men, that they may see your good works, and glorify your Father that is in heaven;' 1 Peter ii. 12, 'Having your conversation honest among the gentiles; that whereas they spake against you as evil-doers, they may, by your good works which they shall behold, glorify God in the day of visitation;' 1 Peter iii. 1, 'If any obey not the word, they may without the word be won by the conversation of their wives.' This overcomes prejudice, and endeareth and reconciles religion, and represents the goodness of it to the consciences of men. Another means is by meek and humble sufferings: Rev. xii. 11, ' And they overcame him by the blood of the Lamb, and by the word of their testimony : and they loved not their lives unto the death.' These were the means by which they got the victory over the pagan world. Thus is the opposition made by the kingdom of darkness against the kingdom of Christ borne down and demolished, and these strongholds brought to nought.

Fifthly, Though the means be weak, yet our faith must be strong ; for there are mighty props to bear us up,—viz., the decree and designation of God, seconded with his mighty power, the death and resurrection of the Lord Jesus, and the promise and power of the Holy Ghost.

1. The decree and designation of God, seconded with his mighty power. The decree of God: Ps. ii. 6, 'Yet have I set my king upon my holy hill of Sion ;' that is, appointed Christ to rule over the nations ; and they that set themselves against God's decree, they do but imagine a vain thing, ver. 1. Now this is a mighty encouragement to all those that seek in their place to remove the corruptions whereby Christ's interest is obstructed and interrupted in the world, that they act with God, and seek to advance that which his decree hath established and his heart is set upon. The other branch is, that this purpose of God is backed with his almighty power, which can easily remove all impediments ; and when he will take to himself and put forth his great power, opposition gives way of itself. So the scripture speaks: Ps. cxiv. 3, ' The sea saw it, and fled ; Jordan was driven back.' He alludes to the drying up of the sea and the water of Jordan to give his people passage ; and when God puts forth his power, no opposition can hinder nor impediment stand in the way. Acts xii. 7, Peter's chains fell off from his hands when the angel bid him arise, and the iron gate opened on its own accord ; so here the walls of Jericho fell down. We expect not miracles, yet still there are acts of wonderful power for the preserving and advancing of Christ's interest in the world, and when the season is come, opposition shall give way of itself.

2. You have the merit and intercession of Christ, the merit of his humiliation here upon earth, and the power of his intercession in

heaven. His merit on earth, for one end for which the blood of Christ was shed was to promote the interest of his kingdom, and to fetch men off from their inveterate prejudices and superstitions; and therefore the apostle saith, 1 Peter i. 18, 19, 'You are redeemed not with corruptible things, as silver and gold, from your vain conversation received by tradition from your fathers, but with the precious blood of the Son of God,' &c. How shall we bring men off from their opposition which is confirmed in them, and hath been the religion of their fathers and grandfathers for many generations? Oh! see what the blood of Christ can do; it hath a mighty virtue in it to take off this opposition. And so his intercession in heaven: Ps. cx. 1, 'The Lord said unto my Lord, Sit thou on my right hand, until I make thine enemies thy footstool.' Christ is at the right hand of God, and there he is to sit till all opposition be destroyed, which is a mighty encouragement to all that are factors and agents for his kingdom here below. He is at God's right hand, pleading for them before God the Father: John xvii. 10, 'All mine are thine, and thine are mine, and I am glorified in them.' They are those that take his part in the world; and he is their advocate and intercessor at God's right hand, to prosper their endeavours, to pardon their failings, to remove impediments that lie in their way,—there he is pleading with God.

3. The mighty and all-conquering spirit that proceedeth both from the Father and the Son. Of this Spirit of God I shall say two things— (1.) That he is invincible and almighty, and therefore his operations are suitable to the agent. Oh! what mighty things hath this Spirit done as to the demolishing strongholds! Heretofore by this Spirit the apostles and messengers of Christ wrought miracles, cured diseases, cast out devils, conveyed gifts by laying on of hands, silenced oracles, and so everywhere destroyed the kingdom and power of Satan, and convinced the world of the truth of this despised religion. And still his mighty force is seen in enlightening and convincing men's minds of the truth of the christian religion, and furnishing his people with gifts, and converting others, and changing them from sinners to saints: 1 Cor. vi. 11, 'Such were some of you, but ye are washed, but ye are sanctified, but ye are justified in the name of the Lord Jesus, and by the Spirit of our God.' (2.) This Spirit is promised to be with us in the faithful dispensing of Christ's ordinances: Mat. xxviii. 20, 'Lo, I will be with you always to the end of the world.' In the whole flux and course of the gospel kingdom he is with us. Now Christ is with us by his Spirit; for when he departed, the Comforter came to supply his absence: therefore, if he be with us, it is by his Spirit. Therefore, upon all these grounds, how mean and despicable soever the means appear, let us believe the Lord our God, who hath set his King on his holy hill, established him by his decree, which is backed by a mighty power, and the Lord Jesus represents his merit, and we have the presence and promise of a mighty conquering Spirit: 2 Chron. xx. 20, 'Believe in the Lord your God, so shall ye be established; believe his prophets, so shall ye prosper.'

Sixthly, If our whole dependence be upon God, we must be sure to keep God's direction, and use only regular and holy means, such as he hath prescribed as our duty to observe. Here the Israelites every day were to make the procession about the city, and the seventh day seven times, and all in silence; unless it were with blowing the rams' horns, they were not to raise a shout till the signal was given. We cannot expect success in what is not of faith. By carnal and unlawful means we forfeit God's protection, and lose his blessing, for he is not bound to maintain us in our sin. Our dependence supposes obedience; if we trust in God we must be true to him: Ps. xxxvii. 34, 'Wait on the Lord, and keep his way;' 1 Peter iv. 19, 'Commit the keeping of your souls to him in well-doing.'

Seventhly, Keeping to God's direction, you must wait his leisure, or tarry for the time and season which God hath appointed. Six days the wall stands fast, not a stone stirred, and for a good part of the seventh, but upon the evening of the seventh day all comes tumbling down: Hab. ii. 3, 'The vision is yet for an appointed time, but at the end it shall speak, and not lie; though it tarry, wait for it; because it will surely come, it will not tarry.' Every dispensation of God hath its prefixed period; as the mercy, so the timing of the mercy is merely in God's hand. It is not always ready at our beck and call, but we must wait God's time, who hath his seasons of afflicting and trial as well as of delivering. We must not miscarry through weakness or haste, either give over as discouraged, or break out into any unlawful action to help ourselves: Isa. xxviii. 16, 'He that believeth will not make haste.' It is in vain to hope, but while we are waiting and acting in our place and calling. For the promoting of God's kingdom in the world we must tarry God's leisure. We can neither prevent nor put off God's time.

Use 1. The use is to encourage all those who wish well to the propagation of Christ's kingdom, and are troubled at the stumbling-blocks that are in the way. Consider what may be done, and what hath been done, and both will encourage you to wait upon God.

1. Consider what may be done.

[1.] Christ is the governor of the world; all power is put into his hands, to be employed for the good of his people: John v. 22, 'The Father hath committed all judgment to the Son.' He hath the government of angels, devils, men, and of all events in the world. Things are not left to their own arbitrament and uncertain contingency, but they are administered by our wise and powerful Redeemer. It is not Satan which governs the world, but Christ; therefore all that are of Christ's confederacy are of the surer side, for they are with the governor of the world, and then what may not be done?

[2.] He is the head of the church as well as governor of the world: Eph. v. 22, 'And hath put all things under his feet, and gave him to be head over all things to the church.' He is more concerned than we can be. The church is not ours, but his; and he is fitter to be trusted with the concernments of it than we, and more tender of its welfare than we are or can be; therefore by the prayer of faith let us recommend his own affairs to him.

[3.] Christ's manner of governing should not be disliked by those that have faith, though sense despise it. His manner is not to subdue the world by the visible force of a strong hand, as an earthly conqueror, but by his word and Spirit, and the secret conduct of his providence: Zech. iv. 6, 'Not by might, nor by power, but by my Spirit, saith the Lord of hosts.' The world dotes upon might and power, because that is the next visible means; but God will do his business another way. A little key will open a door sooner than an iron bar. His holy and invisible means will do it better than all those ways which carnal wisdom suggests.

[4.] Considering the groundwork laid in his death and intercession, surely these means should not be contemptible. (1.) His word is a powerful instrument: Ps. cx. 3, 'The Lord shall send the rod of thy strength out of Zion; rule thou in the midst of thy enemies.' The word of the Lord is the rod of his strength; and it is called the 'arm of the Lord,' Isa. liii. 1, and 'the power of God unto salvation,' Rom. i. 16. A mighty word it is, and doth mighty things in the hearts of God's people and in the world. Satan's kingdom is demolished, and so is antichrist destroyed by his word: 2 Thes. ii. 8, 'Then shall the wicked be revealed, whom the Lord shall consume with the spirit of his mouth.' (2.) Then for the other branch, what can stand before the all-conquering Spirit of Christ? You see it in that servant of God, Stephen: Acts vi. 10, 'They could not resist the wisdom and spirit by which he spake.' There is a spirit dispensed by the gospel that can turn a lion into a lamb: Isa. xi. 6, 'The wolf shall dwell with the lamb, and the leopard shall lie down with the kid;' bring us to love what we hate; 'to delight in the law of God,' Rom. vii. 22. Whereas before, our carnal mind was 'enmity against God,' Rom. viii. 7, that can change us, that bore the image of Satan and the earthly one, into the image and likeness of God: 2 Cor. iii. 18, 'We all with open face beholding as in a glass the glory of the Lord, are changed into the same image from glory to glory, even as by the Spirit of the Lord.' He can turn a 'thorn into a fir-tree, and the briar into a myrtle-tree,' Isa. lv. 13. All these expressions the scripture useth to set forth the mighty things and changes which the Spirit of God can make. Thus consider what may be done.

2. Let us consider what is past, and how the gospel was planted at first. When the Lord Jesus first came to set up the kingdom of light, life, and love, what did he do? The gospel was planted at first not by force or human power, but only by the heavenly divine power of the Lord's grace. It was not the power of the long sword, but the demonstration of the Spirit, which converted the world. The apostles, when they were sent abroad, had no temporal interests to lean to, no worldly powers that were friendly to back them; yet the gospel prevailed and got up in the world. These things were remarkable in the first spreading of the gospel—

[1.] The doctrine itself is contrary to corrupt nature; it doth not court the senses nor woo the flesh by the offers of pleasure, or profit, or splendour of life; but teaches us to deny all these things, and to expect persecutions, and to be contented with spiritual comforts, and the recompenses of the other world: Mat. xvi. 24, 'If any man will come after me, let him deny himself, and take up his cross, and follow me.' Christ did not allure his followers, as Mahomet, with fair promises of security and carnal pleasure, but tells us of mortification and the cross. It teaches us to row against the stream of flesh and blood

and to bear out sail against all the blasts and furious winds of opposition. The stream runs smoothly when wind and tide go together,
where a carnal doctrine is set afoot among carnal men. But in Christ's
doctrine there is nothing lovely to move a carnal eye; this doctrine
taught the proud world humility; the uncharitable world, love to all
men, even to their enemies; the unchaste world, that a lustful glance
is adultery; the revengeful world, to turn the other cheek to the
smiter; the covetous world, to be liberal, not to cark and take thought
for worldly things, but to lay up our treasure in heaven; the dissolute
world, to walk circumspectly in all godliness and honesty. This was
the doctrine that prevailed.

[2.] Who were the persons and instruments that were made use of
to promote this doctrine? They were contemptible persons, a few
fishermen, destitute of all worldly props and aids, of no power, and
wealth, and authority, and other such advantages as are apt to beget
a repute in the world; yet they preached, and converted many nations,
though they had no public interest to countenance them, though they
were not backed with the power of princes or the countenance of
worldly potentates. We are told, Prov. xxix. 26, 'Many seek the
ruler's favour.' But the gospel had a firm footing in the world long
ere there was a prince to countenance it, and many to persecute it.
And as the instruments were poor, so the first professors of the christian religion were generally poor also: James ii. 5, 'God hath chosen
the poor of this world, rich in faith;' and 1 Cor. i. 26, 'Not many wise
men after the flesh, not many mighty, not many noble are called.'
And therefore it is much, being so destitute of worldly succour and
support, that the gospel should be able to hold up its head in the
world; but it did.

[3.] The powers of the world, as they were not friendly to it, so
they were set against it. Bonds, sufferings, and afflictions did abide
for them everywhere that professed this way; yea, fires were kindled,
horrible tortures invented; but no fire was hot enough to consume the
gospel. When Satan made his hottest onset against it by his bands
of persecutors, even in the midst of persecution did the church increase
her strength and glory; and the martyrs' blood was the church's seed.
No rage of man was strong enough to bear down Christ, no sword sharp
enough to wound his truth to the death; never did war, pestilence, or
famine sweep away so many as the first persecutions did; the poor
christians were murdered, slaughtered, butchered everywhere, yet still
they multiplied and increased, as the Israelites did in Egypt under
their cruel bondage, or as a tree lopped sends forth more sprouts.

[4.] Not only the powers of the world were irritated by Satan, but
he raised up the most learned philosophers to dispute against the
gospel, and bend the force of their learning against it; yet it prevailed
above all the power of their carnal wit. It was the purpose and
design of God that the gospel should be sent forth, and set up in such
a place and age, where and when there were the most learned enemies
in all the world, that so all their learning might be nonplussed, and
the gospel triumph over it. Never were there so many learned men
as about the time of Christ and his apostles; and if ever reason and
learning could have disgraced truth, it would have been then. They

pleaded with words, but Christ with mighty works; they used sophisms and lies to get into men's souls, and he shined into men's souls with an insuperable light; their weapons were weak and carnal, but his strong and spiritual; all was carried on in a plain way, without the pomp of words and secular arts, lest the cross of Christ should be of non-effect, and that the faith of the world might not stand in high-flown notions or the wisdom of men, but in the power of God, 1 Cor. ii. 4, 5. Those simple plain men were to deal with men of excellent parts and learning, some of which received the gospel, and suffered for it. Thus, as Aaron's rod devoured the magicians' serpents, so the gospel was too hard for the wisdom of the world, and in the mouths of babes did Christ show forth his praise, Ps. viii. 2.

[5.] Do but consider the wonderful success of the gospel; it did diffuse and spread itself like leaven in the mass and lump throughout all the parts of the known world, and that within the space of thirty or forty years, or thereabout. Saith Tertullian, *Hesterni sumus*, &c.—We are but of yesterday, and yet how are we increased! Look upon christians, and you shall find them in all places, in cities, villages, isles, castles, free towns, councils, armies, senates, markets; everywhere but where their religion forbids them to be, in the idols' temples. Such a wonderful increase and success the gospel had in such a short time, as the apostle tells the Colossians, chap. i. 6, 'The gospel is come unto you, as it is in all the world, and bringeth forth fruit, as it doth also in you.'

[6.] There is this circumstance notable in it too; there were Jerichos to be demolished, the world was leavened with prejudices, and possessed with many false religions, wherein they and their fathers had been bred up and lived a long time. Christ did not seize upon the world, as a waste is seized upon by the next comer. No; the ark of God was to be set up in the temple that was already occupied and possessed by Dagon. Before Christ could be seated in the government of the nations, and settle his law, first Satan was to be dispossessed; the wolf was to be hunted out, that the flock might remain in peace. Superstitions received by a long tradition and prescription of time were to be removed. Men keep to the religion of their ancestors with much reverence and respect. People are loath to change their gods, though their worship be never so vain and foolish, the gods to whom they have prayed in their adversities, and whom they have blessed in their prosperities; to break their images that they have worshipped, and to destroy their temples and altars for which they had such veneration and reverence, this seemeth hard and severe. How dear idols are to their worshippers, and how people are habituated to those superstitions, appears by Rachel's stealing away her father's idols, Gen. xxxi. 34. Though she was one of them which built God's Israel, yet she had a hankering mind after her father's idols. Therefore these things stick by us, and no humours are so obstinately stiff as those which are found in religious custom. The Jews accused Stephen of saying, Acts vi. 14, 'That this Jesus of Nazareth shall destroy this place, and shall change the customs which Moses delivered us;' and Paul, Acts xvi. 31, 'That he did teach customs which are not lawful for us to receive, nor to observe, being Romans.' Certainly it is a very hard thing to bring men out of an old religion to a new one; yet, when the trumpet of the gospel sounded, down went all the altars, images, and superstitions of the gentiles, and the religion of Jesus took place.

[7.] I have but one consideration more, and that is, when Satan had raised up heretics in the church, to rend the body and divide it, as worms that breed in the body and devour it, that so by the church he might destroy the church, yet Christ confounded them, and a little time did break each sect in pieces, so that those which were the great scourge and vexation of one age were scarce known to the next but by their names and some obscure report. The church of Ephesus had Nicolaitans among them; but they hated their doctrine, and within a little while it came to nothing: Rev. ii. 6, ' But this thou hast, that thou hatest the deeds of the Nicolaitans, which I also hate.' And the church of Pergamus had those which held the doctrine of Balaam, yet there were ' those that held fast Christ's name, and did not deny the faith,' ver. 1; and so this heresy vanished and departed. So for others, where the light of the gospel did quickly disperse those fogs as soon as they arose. When any mists arose which did darken the kingdom of light, they were presently scattered and confounded. Well, then, here is encouragement for our zeal and fidelity to Christ, to support us in difficult cases whatever obstructions are made. Let us trust Christ's means, wait upon him with faith and patience, and in due time he will do his work.

Use 2. Let none of us build Jericho again. Joshua imposed a solemn curse on those that built the wall of Jericho, because thereby they would obliterate the memory of divine power and justice: Joshua vi. 26, ' And Joshua adjured them at that time, saying, Cursed be the man before the Lord that raiseth up and buildeth this city Jericho; he shall lay the foundation thereof in his first-born, and in his youngest son shall he set up the gates thereof.' Which curse we find fulfilled: 1 Kings xvi. 34, ' In his days did Hiel the Bethelite build Jericho; he laid the foundation thereof in Abiram his first-born, and set up the gates thereof in his youngest son Segub, according to the word of the Lord, which he spake by Joshua the son of Nun.' Cursed are they that revive old superstitions.

SERMON LXV.

By faith the harlot Rahab perished not with them that believed not, when she had received the spies with peace.—HEB. xi. 31.

IN this verse observe—

1. The person spoken of—Rahab, an harlot and a stranger, bred up among idolators.

2. The effect of her faith—*She received the spies with peace.*

3. The benefit—*She perished not with them that believed not.* Let us open these things.

1. The quality of the person, Rahab the harlot; she was a gentile before, and in that gentile estate an hostess (for the word signifies both an harlot and an hostess), and most probably an harlot, for so she is spoken of in scripture, and so defiled both in body and mind with idolatry and adultery.

2. Here is the effect of her faith—'She received the spies with peace;' that is, with good-will, and entertained them safely. Harbouring God's persecuted servants is reckoned an effect of faith in scripture. The story is in the 2d chapter of Joshua, where take notice—

[1.] Of the coming of the spies to her house, which might be done on their part ignorantly, not knowing it to be a brothel-house; or by divine providence guiding them thither where he had a soul to convert; or they might choose it to avoid suspicion, and that they might have the greater liberty to espy all things, she living near the walls; but God makes use of it to another purpose, to be an occasion of saving her and her family.

[2.] The discovery of the spies by that watchful and jealous people; for it was told the king of Jericho that some of the children of Israel were come to spy out the land, chap. ii. 2, and he sends to her to bring them forth, so that she not only entertains them kindly, but conceals them, hazarding her life for their safety; as we are also 'to lay down our lives for the brethren,' 1 John iii. 16. She was willing to expose her life to danger to save her guests, rather than gain the favour of the king of the country by betraying them. Here we learn that the weakest faith is tried, and does expose us to some self-denial. For this young and raw convert is put upon this: the spies came to her house, and she in good-will conceals them, when the king sends to know what was become of them.

[3.] The course she took to hide them; partly by an honest means, covering them with stalks of flax in the upper part of the house; and partly by an officious lie, as if they were gone in the dark before the shutting in of the gate. Her lie was an infirmity, pardoned by God, and not to be exaggerated by men; as here the apostle mentions her faith, but not a word of her lie. There was some weakness in the action, but for the main of it, it was a duty expressing great confidence in God; and the Holy Ghost puts the finger upon the star, and, contrary to the guise of the malignant world, who overlook the good and reflect only upon the evil of an action, he takes notice of the good, but passeth by the evil.

[4.] Before the spies were gone from her, she makes a confession of her faith to them: Joshua ii. 9–11, 'I know that the Lord hath given you the land, and that your terror is fallen upon us, and that all the inhabitants of the land faint because of you: for we have heard how the Lord dried up the water of the Red Sea for you, when you came out of Egypt; and what you did unto the two kings of the Amorites that were on the other side Jordan, Sihon and Og, whom ye utterly destroyed. And as soon as we had heard these things, our hearts did melt, neither did there remain any more courage in any man, because of you; for the Lord your God he is God in heaven above, and in earth beneath.' Here is her profession of faith, which is very notable in this new convert. In it observe—

(1.) The ground of it, the rumours of the great things which God had done for his people. It is said, Rom. x. 14, 'How shall they believe in him of whom they have not heard?' This woman had heard of God, and the mighty wonders he had done for Israel, and this was the ground of her faith.

(2.) The efficient cause. God thereby touched her heart, and gave her some saving knowledge of himself. The Canaanites had heard, as well as she, of those mighty works of God, yet they believed not, but grew obstinate, and perished in their resolution to resist the Israelites, and therefore were exterminated. They heard to some degree of fear, 'for their hearts melted within them;' but they heard not to any degree of faith, for they submitted not, but prepared to resist the purpose of God, and his design of giving his people the land. Thus it was by the secret power of God's Spirit.

(3.) The fulness of her profession. It is well observed by Origen, *Illa, quæ aliquando erat meretrix, cum Spiritu Sancto repleta est, et de præteritis confitetur, de præsentibus vero credit, prophetat et prænuntiat de futuris*—The woman that was sometimes an harlot, when she was wrought upon by the Holy Ghost, she believeth what is past, she acknowledgeth what is present, she foretelleth what is to come. So that here is a full confession. For what is past, she acknowledgeth the truth of the miracles which God had wrought, to show his love and care over his people. For what is present, she believes God to be the true God. For what is to come, she believes confidently that God would give the land into their hand; though the people of the city think themselves safe within their city and walls, and think to carry it by mere strength, and fear not, and are not sensible either of their sins or dangers, yet she was confident of the future success of God's people, and destruction of her country. The consideration of God's mighty wonders, blessed by the Spirit of God, bringing such a confession from her.

(4.) She is careful to save the house she came of, and therefore takes an oath of the spies to save her and her father's house: Joshua ii. 12, 'Now therefore, I pray you, swear unto me by the Lord, since I have showed you kindness, that ye will also show kindness unto my father's house, and give me a true token.' And accordingly the bargain is made, if she did not betray them, that she was to hand out the line by which they were let down upon the wall. This shows that all believers have their assurance from a covenant, and that this covenant is confirmed by certain signs, which faith makes use of as the means of preservation. For she was to hang out the scarlet line by which she and all her house might be kept in safety. So much for the effect of her faith; she received the spies with peace.

3. Let us come to the benefit—'She perished not with them that believed not;' that is, when the incredulous and idolatrous people were destroyed, she and all her family were preserved; as God can, and often doth, save his people in the midst of general calamities. You shall see, when the city was taken, Joshua keeps faith with her: Joshua vi. 22, 23, 'Joshua said unto the two men that had spied out

the country, Go into the harlot's house, and bring out thence the woman, and all that she hath, as you sware unto her. And the young men that were spies went in, and brought out Rahab, and her father and mother, and her brethren, and all that she had; and they brought out all her kindred, and left them without the camp of Israel;' and when they had fired the city, ver. 25, ' Joshua saved Rahab the harlot alive, and her father's household, and all that she had; and she dwelleth in Israel even unto this day; because she hid the messengers which Joshua had sent to spy out Jericho.' Thus I have opened the words. The notes from this instance the apostle gives are three—

[1.] From the quality of the person, observe that God shows wonderful mercy to penitent sinners, if they return to him, and believe in him.

[2.] From her faith, observe that true faith, wherever it is, will show itself by some eminent and notable effects.

[3.] From the benefit, observe that the rewards of true faith are excellent and glorious.

Doct. 1. That God is ready to show wonderful mercy to penitent sinners, if they return to him, and believe in him, how great soever their sins have been before. Rahab the harlot is an instance. She had been a gentile, and lived an unclean life, yet when she owned the true God she is pardoned, and placed in the catalogue of God's worthies who are eminent for faith. There are many such instances given us in scripture; not to lessen the nature of their sins, but to amplify God's grace. In John iv. we have an instance of the woman of Samaria; she was a vile woman; for (ver. 18) Christ tells her, ' Thou hast had five husbands, and he whom thou now hast is not thy husband;' yet afterwards she was a notable means of promoting the faith of Christ. Former sins will not hinder their acceptance with God who seriously come to seek grace. The same also may be observed in another woman ' which washed Christ's feet with tears, and wiped them with the hairs of her head,' Luke vii. 38. The woman was a heathen, and one that had lived in a sinful course, but she then relented, and lets fall drops of tears plentifully upon Christ's feet, which tears were the effects of sorrow and love; and because she wept much and loved much, it argued a great expression of gratitude from her, because of the great mercy showed to her in the pardon of her sins: ver. 47, ' Her sins, which are many, are forgiven, for she loved much.' The throne of grace is open for all sinners; it admits of no exception of persons. ' Turn and live,' is the great tenor of the gospel: Ezek. xviii. 33, ' I have no pleasure in the death of him that dieth, saith the Lord God; wherefore turn yourselves, and live ye;' Ezek. xxxiii. 11, ' As I live, saith the Lord, I have no pleasure in the death of the wicked; but that the wicked turn from his way and live: turn ye, turn ye, from your evil ways; for why will ye die, O house of Israel?' And publicans and harlots, though infamous amongst men, yet they are not excluded, but accepted with God if they turn from their evil course. Nay, many times they enter into the kingdom of God before self-justiciaries: Mat. xxi. 31, ' The publicans and the harlots go into the kingdom of God before you.' For there is nothing that lies so cross to the spirit of the gospel as self-righteousness. Now, when people pride and please themselves in an external righteousness, there is more hope of a publican than of them. Christ invites and calls such, and we must not keep them off: Mat. ix. 13, 'I came not to call the righteous, but sinners to repentance.' But we must remember two cautions—

1. That they must break off the course of their sins. For our commission is this (and we cannot speak comfortably to you upon any other terms), 'Turn and live.' We call them not to confidence while they live in their sins, but to repentance, that they may break off the course of their sins. To tell them of trusting in God's mercy while they remain in their wickedness is a vile flattery, and the worst sort of flattery; but to invite them to repentance is charity. See Isa. lv. 7, 'Let the wicked forsake his way, and the unrighteous man his thoughts, and let him return unto the Lord, and he will have mercy upon him, and to our God, for he will abundantly pardon;' and Dan. iv. 27, 'Break off thy sins by righteousness, and thy iniquities by showing mercy to the poor.' He speaks this to a cruel oppressing king, Nebuchadnezzar, who had troubled all the world by his ambition, that he would let go his captives, and behave himself more righteously, restore the prey unjustly taken for the enlarging his empire and territory. And so I may say to all sinners; if their faith be unfeigned, if their repentence be serious and sincere, there are hopes of mercy for them, not otherwise.

2. There is another caution, and that is, to be as eminent in their repentance as they have been in their sins; so was Rahab, so was that gentile woman that came to wash Christ's feet, so was the woman of Samaria. The apostle requires it as an equitable proposal to all converts: Rom. vi. 19, 'I speak after the manner of men, because of the infirmity of your flesh;' that is, which men will judge to be equal; that which, if you have but reason and conscience within you, you cannot but judge reasonable. I know how bad you are, and you cannot yield God such entire obedience as he doth require and as he doth deserve, and I have regard to the infirmity of your flesh; but 'as ye have yielded your members servants to uncleanness and to iniquity; even so now yield your members servants to righteousness unto holiness;' be as eminent in your sanctification as formerly you have been in serving your base lusts and vile affections; serve God as well as you have served the devil; and as you have been guilty of such foul sins as render you infamous among men, so serve God now exemplarily. It is equitable you should be as eminent in holiness as you have been in sins and wickedness.

The grounds of this, why the Lord shows wonderful mercy to penitent sinners, whatever their sins have been before, are—

[1.] The infiniteness of God's mercy, that can pardon all, even our greatest sins. We sin as men, but he pardons as a God: Hosea xi. 9, 'I am God, and not man; therefore Ephraim is not destroyed.' It was well Ephraim had to do not with revengeful men, but with a pardoning God. God acts like himself in the exercise of his mercy. Sure an emperor's revenue can pay a beggar's debt. Surely so great and infinite mercy can pardon and absolve our obligation to punishment. Alas for us men! it is tedious to think of forgiving seven times a day, to forgive when still a man is perverse and multiplying his offences; but to forgive seventy times seven, it breaks the back of all our patience; but God will pardon like himself, after many and many offences.

[2.] The infiniteness of Christ's merit. Surely his blood can wash and cleanse out all these stains. An ocean can cleanse one nasty sink, be it ever so foul. 'The blood of Christ his Son cleanseth us from all sin,' 1 John i. 7.

[3.] The covenant of grace exempts no sin but the sin against the Holy Ghost: Mat. xii. 31, 'All manner of sin and blasphemy shall be forgiven unto men, but the blasphemy against the Holy Ghost shall not be forgiven unto men.' There is no sin but this one which hath not been forgiven, or may not be forgiven, in one person or another; therefore, though they have fallen very foully, yet we should not despair of them.

[4.] The power of the Holy Ghost can change and sanctify the vilest heart, and can turn a dunghill into a bed of spices; for nothing is too hard for the hand and power of God. He that made all things out of nothing, he can make a graceless heart to become gracious; for what is too hard for the Almighty? When the Lord speaks, all things are possible to God. He can make sometimes 'the last to be first,' Mat. xix. 39. He can make those that set out last for heaven to do more than an early professor; indeed, they must be more earnestly diligent. When Celsus objected against Origen that christianity was a sanctuary for flagitious persons, because of the large terms of the gospel, he made this answer—'The gospel,' saith he, 'is not merely a sanctuary to receive them, but it is an hospital to cure them.' There is a mighty Spirit that can turn them from those sins, and change their hearts; they come to it as to an hospital to cure them of their foul diseases, which no other physician can do but Christ.

Use. To check despair for ourselves or others.

First, For ourselves. There is a twofold despair—a raging and a sottish despair. Raging despair is when we are filled with terror, and are afraid of the wrath of God, that we think we shall never be forgiven, having daily offended him. Sottish despair is when we think of sin, and go on to please our lusts.

1. This point serves to cure the raging despair. This is spoken of in Cain: Gen. iv. 13, 'My punishment is greater than I can bear;' and Judas, who said, Mat. xxvii. 4, 5, 'I have sinned in that I have betrayed innocent blood; and he cast down the thirty pieces in the temple, and departed, and went and hanged himself.' To cure this raging despair, consider, if you have but a mind to return from your great and infamous sins, the Lord is more ready to receive and pardon you than you can be to return. While the prodigal was yet a great way off, 'the father ran to meet him,' Luke xv. 20. And when David had fallen foully, and his conscience was full of trouble, Ps. xxxii. 5, 'I said I will confess mine iniquities unto the Lord, and thou forgavest the iniquity of my sin.' When he did but conceive the purpose, the Lord renewed the pardon. Oh! do not stand aloof from a pardoning God; you have a sure and sufficient remedy before you in Christ Jesus, and in the covenant of grace. The Lord saves none as innocent, but

he excepts none as penitent: Therefore to say, My sin is greater than can be forgiven, is to please the devil and cross God's design in the work of redemption. Is your disease so great that the physician of souls cannot cure it?

2. There is a sottish despair, when men are not much troubled for their sins, but think they shall never be converted, and be brought to love this strict, holy, and heavenly life, and so resolve to go on and make the best they can of a carnal course, and drive off all remorse of conscience. This is spoken of, Jer. xviii. 12, 'And they said, There is no hope, but we will walk after our own devices, and we will every one do the imagination of his evil heart;' and Jer. ii. 25, 'Thou sayest, There is no hope: No, for I have loved strangers, and after them will I go.' They think there is no possibility of their ever being reduced or reclaimed to a holy and heavenly life, and so past cure, past care; and are resolved to live as they list: The case is desperate, say they, and I am at a point; and thus they are resolved to continue, and go on in their evil course. These are obstinate in their infidelity and impenitency, and therefore they are worse than the former. Despairing fears are not so bad as these desperate resolutions, because they do not only doubt of God's mercy, but question his sovereignty, and refuse subjection to him, and despair of sanctification rather than pardon, and draw wilful rebellious conclusions from it. Oh! do not cherish such a thought, nor yield to such despondency. God can turn and pardon you; and though with men it is impossible, yet not with God.

Secondly, This is of use to check our despair for others; for when you find some of your relations, after many warnings, to relapse into gross sins, certainly we are bound to do all we can to reclaim them from them. Give not over praying and warning; you ought still to represent to them the danger of such courses, but cut them not off from all hopes, for God can reclaim the most odious sinners; and show them that there may yet be hope of mercy for them, and that no past sins can hinder our conversion to God if the Lord pleases; and that they ought to put themselves into a posture to seek his grace; though still you are always to represent the danger of those desperate courses wherein they are engaged.

Doct. 2. From her act—'By faith the harlot Rahab perished not,' &c. Observe, that true faith, where it is weakest, will show itself by some eminent and notable effect. We, in the latter age, to excuse ourselves from duty, have involved all things into controversy; therefore it is good to look to the ancient faith. How did the holy ones of God live heretofore? Here is an instance of an ancient faith, and the lowest of the kind; it is a firm belief of such things as God hath revealed to us, so as to make us fruitful and faithful in obedience to him. And I would have you observe, that in all this catalogue and chronicle of the faithful and eminent believers, no instance is propounded to us of an idle and barren faith, and always the apostle shows what was done by faith; for surely the working faith is only the true faith: Gal. v. 6, 'Faith which worketh by love.' Rahab's faith was no dead faith, but manifested by works; therefore the apostle James saith, chap. ii. 21, 'Was not Abraham our father justified by works, when he had offered

Isaac his son upon the altar?' and ver. 25, 'Likewise also was not Rahab the harlot justified by works, when she had received the messengers, and had sent them out another way?' In this raw and young convert faith was not without its effect.

To make this more evident, let us consider the temper of her faith, since it is so good to live by the ancient faith.

1. The ground of her faith was the fame and the report of God's wondrous works which he had done for his people. She had heard of the true God, as much as was necessary to acknowledge his power against his enemies and his grace towards his people, and this was sufficient as a means to beget saving faith in her soul. And if so, then we have greater grounds of faith than she had; for we have heard of the stupendous wonders of our redemption by Christ. Now, where more is given, the more we must account for: Luke xii. 48, 'For unto whomsoever much is given, of him shall be much required; and to whom men have committed much, of him they will ask the more.' The more light God bestows, the greater improvement he expects. We have not only general rumours to build upon, as she had, but the sure word, where these things are more certainly and clearly discovered to us; and therefore God expects a better tempered faith from us.

2. She makes a confession of that faith which was wrought in her heart; for to the spies she acknowledges God to be the only true God, both in heaven above and the earth beneath; and she acknowledges the Israelites to be his peculiar people, whom he had owned and loved, and that she could not be saved but as gathered to that people under the head, Messiah; and in heart and affection she was already become 'one of God's servants, and this she professed to the spies. And the same is required of us: Rom. ix. 10, 'If thou confess with thy mouth the Lord Jesus Christ, and shalt believe in thy heart that God hath raised him from the dead, thou shalt be saved; for with the heart man believeth unto righteousness, and with the mouth confession is made unto salvation.' Let us own the true God in Jesus Christ, and love him, and own and love his people. When once we are brought to this, to run hazard and take our lot with them, then we are in the right posture.

3. This faith and confession was evinced by some effect; for she entertained the spies, which was all she was capable of doing at present, and she entertains them as some of the people of God, as members of the true church, or as of the number of them who worshipped that God whom she believed to be the true God. And truly much faith is shown in harbouring the saints and being kind to God's people. Many shall be tried at the last day by this: Mat. xxv. 35, 'I was an hungered, and ye gave me meat; I was thirsty, and ye gave me drink; I was a stranger, and ye took me in,' &c. Everything is accepted with God according to the principle from whence it flows. Now, what might it have been, for anything in the nature of the act, but her trade, an entertaining and being kind to her guest, for she kept a house of public entertainment? or what might it have been but a bare act of civility? Yet, because of her faith in God, and love to his people, it is counted an act of love and obedience, not civility, but religion. So our Lord hath told us, Mat. x. 41, 'He that receiveth a prophet in the name of

a prophet, shall receive a prophet's reward; and he that receiveth a righteous man in the name of a righteous man, shall receive a righteous man's reward: and whosoever shall give to drink to one of these little ones a cup of cold water in the name of a disciple, verily I say unto you, he shall in no wise lose his reward.' It is accepted of God if it be in Christ's name; and if we give because we believe they are Christ's disciples, who is our Lord and Saviour, it is respected as done to himself, and shall be accounted as a fruit of faith. But now those that love a gospel without charges, and whose faith shows itself by talk and high-flown and curious notions of religion, rather than by any solid fruit, their faith is but an imaginary delusion, a shadow of faith, not any true grace. Faith that is true is a plain thing—to believe in one God, and that this God hath a people with whom I must travel to heaven; they are to be my everlasting companions. If I am true to this God, and kind to his people, the thing is put to a plain issue.

4. This effect was accompanied with much self-denial, which was seen in two things—(1.) In preferring the will of God before the safety of her country, and cherishing those guests who were strangers before the gratifying and pleasing her own citizens. We are bound to love, and we are bound also to seek the welfare of our country; but we are bound to love God more than our country. Therefore we owe fidelity to him first, and then to the place we live in, and we are to promote their welfare so far as is consistent with our fidelity to our supreme Lord. (2.) The other instance of her self-denial was her venturing her life rather than betraying those messengers of Joshua, that were the worshippers of the true God. It was an action that might have been of dangerous consequence to her; but, to manifest her fidelity to God, she overlooks the threatenings and cruelty of her citizens, the promiscuous events of war, and the burning of the city in which she and her parents lived; and so in the effect, by her faith, she renounced all to serve the true God. It is not every act will manifest true faith, but acts of self-denying obedience, in which we do deny ourselves for God, check our natural love, and thwart our lusts and hazard any interests. When God calls us to it, can we part with our conveniences of life, all that is near and dear to us in the world, upon the proper and sole encouragement of faith? This is a mighty evidence of faith.

5. I observe there was a mixture of infirmity in this act, an officious lie, which cannot be excused, though God in mercy pardoned it. This is not for our imitation, yet it is for our instruction; and it shows us this, that faith in the beginning hath many weaknesses. Those that have faith do not altogether act out of faith, but there is somewhat of the flesh mingled with that of the spirit. But this is passed by out of God's indulgence; he accepteth us notwithstanding our sins before faith, and notwithstanding our weaknesses in believing. Before faith she was a harlot; in believing she makes a lie. God doth reward the good of our actions and pardon the evil of them, not to encourage us in sinning, but to raise our love to him who forgives us so great a debt, and receives us graciously, and pardons our manifold weaknesses.

But why is this the true believing? The reasons are—

[1.] From the nature of faith, which is such an apprehension of the love of God, and of the blessedness that he offers to us, as makes us willing to do whatever we can for him, and that in some eminent way of self-denial. Faith works both by love and hope, as it looks backward and forward. As it looks backward, the love of Christ is so great and condescending that it moves us to gratitude; as it looks forward, the blessedness hoped for is so glorious that it draws off our hearts from all other things, and lessens our esteem of them, that this gratitude may more self-denyingly be expressed by parting with them, yea, by the loss of all that is near and dear to us, to show our fidelity to Christ. They are nothing in comparison of our love to Christ: Phil. iii. 8, ' I count all things but loss for the excellency of the knowledge of Christ Jesus my Lord, for whom I have suffered the loss of all things, and do count them but dung, that I may win Christ.' Here are the two considerations which faith works upon—what Christ hath done for us, and what he will yet do for us. And if we consider these two things, faith may well afford self-denying obedience, and forsake all easily for Christ's sake. This great love of Christ overcomes all our natural self-love to our interest and worldly comforts, that we may own Christ, and be faithful to him.

[2.] The gospel requires such a kind of faith, and therefore we must exercise it. All that will enter into life should hate father and mother, &c., so far as they may stand in competition with Christ: Luke xiv. 25, ' If any man come to me, and hate not his father and mother, and wife and children, and brethren and sisters, yea, and his own life also, he cannot be my disciple;' and ver. 33, ' Whosoever he be of you that forsaketh not all that he hath, he cannot be my disciple.' He that had found the pearl of great price sold all to buy it, Mat. xiii. 45, 46. He did not only cheapen it, but he did go through with the bargain. Let all go that is inconsistent with your trust and love.

[3.] This is that faith which honours God and Christ in the world, and assures us of salvation: 2 Thes. i. 11, 12, ' We pray that God would fulfil the work of faith with power, that the name of our Lord Jesus Christ may be glorified in you, and ye in him.' Would you honour Christ, and have Christ glorified in you, then you must mind the work of faith. He speaks not of the illicit, but imperative acts of faith. Self-denying obedience is the imperative act of faith: then the name of the Lord Jesus Christ is glorified in you, then you are glorified in him, and then you have the assurance of salvation. A faith that rests in the heart only, and is discovered by no self-denying act, brings Christ no glory in the world, and will bring us little comfort and peace; but faith which shows itself in acts of love to God and his people, and that with self-denial, is more evident, and doth much honour God in the eyes of the world. When we are willing to do and suffer so much for him, this brings us comfort, and doth show this faith is real, that we are true to God, whom we own and acknowledge.

Use. The use is to press you to see whether you live by this ancient faith.

1. It is not a bare assent to the report of God's love in Christ. Many may think it true that Christ died and rose again, that yet feel no force of it upon their souls. Surely a dead opinion is not that lively faith that enableth the people of God to do such great things for him. The devil knows there is a God and Christ,—will you put your salvation

upon this? No; 'Faith without works is dead,' James ii. 20. If you
do not feel the force of it upon your hearts, to make you deny yourselves, and give up all your interest for God, and run all hazards for
him and his people, you do not truly believe.

2. It is not a bare confession, nor a loose owning the name of
Christ. Rahab made a confession, but rests not there. So, many
own him as the God of the country, and cry up his name, but neglect
his office; as the Jews made much ado with the names of Abraham
and Moses, but they were of a quite different spirit; they did neither
do the works of Abraham: John viii. 39, ' If ye were Abraham's
children, ye would do the works of Abraham;' nor hearken to the
words of Moses: John v. 46, 'Had ye believed Moses, ye would have
believed me.' So you believe there is a Christ, and own him; but if
you be christians, you would do works becoming christians.

3. It is not a confidence in God's mercy; that is not enough, if we
will do nothing for him. For faith is such a trusting in God, through
Christ, for eternal life, that we are willing to forsake all rather than
be unfaithful to him; and we care not what we lose, and what hazard
we run, so that we may have a portion among God's people, and obtain the heavenly inheritance. When the apostle distinguisheth the
true believers from the false, what saith he? Heb. x. 39, ' We are not
of them that draw back to perdition, but of them that believe to the
saving of the soul.' There are some that believe, yet will save the
flesh; but others that will save the soul, though their interests in the
flesh be hazarded. Now, the apostle shows there that there are some
will purchase the saving of their soul with the loss of other things.
God tries us in some necessary part of confession, which may expose
us to loss, shame, and hazard in the world; now, if we will not spare
the flesh, but save the soul, this is to cleave to him.

4. Nothing then remains to justify our faith but such an acknowledging of the true God as causes us to confess his name and to prefer his interest before our own, and so to be willing to endure anything
for his sake, and be ready upon this faith to show all self-denying acts
of obedience; to part with what we have for the relief of others and
the advancement of religion, when we cannot keep it without betraying religion. Alas! that religion which costs nothing is worth nothing; it is idle, empty, and foolish; that, when you come to die, will
bring terror, and never yield solid peace.

Doct. 3. There is one thing more in the text, and that is the benefit which affords us this point, that the rewards of faith are excellent
and glorious. Rahab is an instance of this also, for when she by faith
entertained the spies in peace, ' she perished not with them that believed not;' that is, she was not destroyed with the Canaanites. Let
us a little see her privileges.

1. From a child of the devil, she is made a daughter of God, and
adopted into God's family. And so, if you be sincere in the faith of
the gospel, you shall be also; the Lord will take you for his children,
that were the children of wrath before: John i. 12, ' To as many as
received him, to them gave he power to become the sons of God, even
to them that believe on his name.'

2. From a citizen of Jericho she is reckoned among the people of

Israel, and incorporated into the body of God's church: Joshua vi. 25, 'She dwelleth in Israel even unto this day.' So, if we have the sincere faith, we are not only of the visible church of professing christians, but are reckoned among the elect, and have our names written in heaven; that is a matter of great joy: Luke x. 20, 'Rejoice in that your names are written in heaven;' for this is a 'better name than of sons and daughters,' Isa. lvi. 5,—a name that shall continue to all eternity.

3. We find, when there was a destruction of all the rest, she was not destroyed with the Canaanites, but God by his servant Joshua took great care for her preservation. So believers are saved from everlasting destruction: John iii. 16, 'Whosoever believeth in him shall not perish, but have everlasting life.' They are not involved in the wrath and destruction which shall light upon the unbelieving and impenitent world. This is the portion of all those that fly to the true God, and to the communion of the true church. If it be sure that the unbelieving world shall perish (as sure it is, as sure as God is true), then it is a great mercy we shall not perish with them. Certain it is that all that come not out of the apostasy shall perish forever. But we that are willing to return to our duty to God, to trust God, and trust his promises, and take his way, blessedness will be our portion.

4. Another privilege which Rahab had was, that she was honourably married to a prince in Israel, and one of the ancestors of Christ, namely, to Salmon, father of Boaz: Mat. i. 5, 'And Salmon begat Boaz of Rachab.' Laying all ends together, we certainly find it is the same Rahab, that Salmon married her, who was one of the spies, a head and prince of Israel. Thus God can heap honour upon those that trust in him: her name is mentioned in the genealogy of our Lord and Saviour Jesus Christ. Now they that sincerely believe have a better marriage, they are married to Christ himself: Rom. vii. 4, 'Wherefore, my brethren, ye also are become dead to the law, by the body of Christ, that ye should be married to another, even to him who is raised from the dead, that we should bring forth fruit unto God.' They are taken into a nearer relation to him, our covenanting with him being a kind of marriage. If we believe as Rahab did, we shall have the reward Rahab had. But how can we reconcile the two apostles? Paul ascribes it here to her faith, but James to her works: James ii. 25, 'Was not Rahab the harlot justified by works, when she had received the messengers, and sent them out another way?' Here is no contradiction; the apostles fairly agree together, for they speak not of the same faith. Paul speaks of the lively, James of the dead faith; Paul speaks of the faith working by love, and so she was justified by faith, but James speaks of an empty naked profession of faith without works; so that a man is not justified by an empty faith without works. A dead faith little profits us, but a living faith makes us obedient to God, and ready to every good work; that justifies us, and qualifies us for this blessed and glorious reward.

But let us see the general case. What are the privileges and the rewards of faith? (for hitherto we have only considered them with respect to Rahab). It justifies, sanctifies, glorifies.

[1.] It justifies: Rom. v. 1, 'Being justified by faith, we have peace with God.' O sinners! do you know what it is to be condemned by the law of God? for sinners impleaded, and that justly, in the court of God's justice, and to be condemned to everlasting wrath? If you did, then you would see that it is a mighty privilege to be justified, to be accepted with God, and freed from the deserved condemnation, or that dreadful punishment which sin hath made our due. Now, this generally in scripture is ascribed to faith.

[2.] It sanctifies, or is the Spirit's great instrument in sanctification. For, Acts xv. 9, it is said, 'Purifying their hearts by faith.' It is faith that promotes purity and sanctity. It is the first stone in the spiritual building: 2 Peter i. 5, 'Add to your faith virtue,' &c. Faith is made the bottom of all, as that which gives life and strength to all the rest; without which virtue would be nothing but a little dead and cold morality, however it is cried up in our age, if not enlivened by the love of God in Christ, and hopes of eternal glory, as it is when it proceeds from faith. Christ prays, John xvii. 17, 'Sanctify them through thy truth.' We are sanctified by the truth of the gospel. But now what makes the gospel operative but faith? 1 Thes. ii. 13, 'Ye received it, not as the word of men, but as it is in truth, the word of God, which effectually worketh also in you that believe.'

[3.] It glorifies; because they that believe eternal life so as to seek after it, and that whatever it cost them, they shall have it. You may always observe, in all God's dispensations of grace and favour, he would do nothing for men till they believe; he could not, or rather would not, do it for them. We find it true of God's dispensation to the old church, and in the life of Christ upon earth—Can you believe? Mark ix. 23, 'If thou canst believe, all things are possible to him that believeth.' So it is true of eternal life. But then this belief is supposed to be operative, and that we are resolved to take the way God hath appointed. As soon as we believe, we have a right and title: John v. 24, 'He that heareth my words, and believeth on him that sent me, hath everlasting life, and shall not come into condemnation, but is passed from death to life.' And when we verify our faith by taking God's way, though others neglect it, then our right is confirmed: Mat. xix. 28, 'Ye that have followed me in the regeneration, when the Son of man shall sit on the throne of his glory, ye also shall sit upon twelve thrones, judging the twelve tribes of Israel.' Take regeneration either for a new state of the church (as some few do), when all things are new in the church, and old things are passed away, you shall be elders in the church (so some expound it); but I think properly and principally it is taken for the regeneration at the last day, when we shall have new bodies and new souls; then we shall have all that our hearts can wish. When our service is over, we shall receive the end of our faith: 1 Peter i. 9, 'Receiving the end of our faith, the salvation of our souls.'

Use. Let this commend faith to us, which is the great grace; we must still exercise it in this world. Where we know God by hearing, faith is of use to us; when we know him by vision and sight, the use of it ceases, but the fruit remaineth, for sight is the fruit of faith: John xx. 31, 'These things are written, that ye might believe that

Jesus is the Christ the Son of God, and that believing ye might have life through his name.' You shall have life in his name if you will believe in the Lord Jesus Christ. All that I shall press you to is a faith like Rahab's. Rahab heard the rumours of God's gracious works for Israel, and of his judgments upon their enemies, and upon this she owns the true God, and runs hazards for his people.

1. You have heard that God hath sent his Son into the world to save sinners; believe it, and believe it strongly; here is the grand truth you must live by.

2. This God hath given a law of grace, that we may be partakers of these benefits. Possibly the spies might inform Rahab of God's giving a law upon Mount Sinai; for it is not likely she would join herself so suddenly to Israel, if she knew not what laws they should live by. If that be uncertain, we are sure the Lord hath given a law of grace from Mount Zion, or the new covenant, wherein God hath showed us how we shall attain eternal life. Now heartily consent to stand to this covenant.

3. Upon this faith be sure to demonstrate by some real effects that it hath prevailed in your heart. For if you believe God's great promises, what do you venture upon them? Surely we do not believe great things if we do nothing to obtain them. I ever look upon this as a truth, that there is much more of unbelief in neglect than there is in humbling trouble or despairing fears. For the troubled person believes indeed the covenant of God, but he cannot make out his title, therefore he lies under despairing fears. The neglecter showeth that he accounts these things a fable, else he would more look after them, and exercise himself self-denyingly in godliness: 2 Peter i. 5, 10, 16, compared together; ver. 5, 'Giving all diligence, add to your faith virtue,' &c.; ver. 10, ' Give diligence to make your calling and election sure;' ver. 16, ' For we have not followed cunningly-devised fables, &c. They that do not give diligence to grow in grace, they that do not give diligence by all self-denying acts to make their calling and election sure, they count the gospel a fable, and neglecting their duty, they show themselves to be unbelievers.

4. That which you do, let it be some self-denying act for God and his people. I join both together, because if a man love the one he will love the other, and the Lord's interest is only upheld by his people here in the world; his interest liveth and dieth with his people. And therefore, when we are willing to deny ourselves that we may own God's people, and join with them in all their sincere endeavours to advance the kingdom of Christ, then we shall know we believe in God, and that we have this true faith God requireth of us.